Psychology
From Science to Practice

Robert A. Baron
Rensselaer Polytechnic Institute

Michael J. Kalsher
Rensselaer Polytechnic Institute

Boston • New York • San Francisco
Mexico City • Montreal • Toronto • London • Madrid • Munich • Paris
Hong Kong • Singapore • Tokyo • Cape Town • Sydney

Executive Editor: Karon Bowers
Editorial Assistant: Lara Torsky
Senior Marketing Manager: Wendy Gordon
Editorial-Production Administrator: Annette Joseph
Editorial-Production Service: Colophon
Text Designer: Roy Neuhaus
Photo Editor: Katharine S. Cook
Electronic Composition: Omegatype Typography
Composition/Prepress Buyer: Linda Cox
Manufacturing Buyer: Megan Cochran
Cover Administrator: Linda Knowles
Cover Designer: Susan Paradise

For related titles and support materials, visit our online catalog at www.ablongman.com.

Between the time website information is gathered and then published, it is not unusual for some sites to have closed. Also, the transcription of URLs can result in typographical errors. The publisher would appreciate notification where these errors occur so that they may be corrected in subsequent editions.

Library of Congress Cataloging-in-Publication Data

Baron, Robert A.
    Psychology : from science to practice / Robert A. Baron, Michael J. Kalsher.
        p. cm.
    ISBN 0-205-42201-2 (alk. paper)
    1. Psychology—Textbooks. I. Kalsher, Michael J. II. Title.

    BF121.B325 2004
    150—dc22

                                        2004051591

Printed in the United States of America

10 9 8 7 6 5 4 3 2 1   VHP   09 08 07 06 05 04

Photo Credits: opposite p. 1: Ryan McVay/Getty Images, Inc.–PhotoDisc; p. 3, l: Kwame Zikomo/SuperStock, Inc.; p. 3, c: Rob Gage/Getty Images, Inc.–Taxi; p. 3, r: EyeWire Collection/Getty Images, Inc.–Photodisc; p. 4: Science Photo Library/Photo Researchers, Inc.; p. 6: Goldberg Diego/Corbis/Sygma; p. 10, l: Rommel Pecson/The Image Works; p. 10, r: Dan Lamont/CORBIS-NY; p. 11: Ryan McVay/Getty Images, Inc.–PhotoDisc; p. 13: Michael Newman/PhotoEdit; p. 16: Robert A. Baron; p. 18: Toru Yamanaka/Getty Images, Inc.–Liaison; p. 24: Dex Images/CORBIS-NY; p. 28: Andy Belcher/ImageState/International Stock Photography Ltd.; p. 30, l: Spencer Grant/PhotoEdit; p. 30, c: Steve Rubin/The Image Works

Credits continue on page 579, which constitutes a continuation of the copyright page.

To the people who bring love, joy, and happiness into my life:

Rebecca, Randy, Paul, Jessica, Ted, Richard, and Ruth

R.A.B.

To Erin, for her love and inspiration; and to Ryan—the "old soul"
who keeps me young

M.J.K.

Brief Contents

Contents

1

Psychology: What It Is . . . and What It Offers   1

2

Biological Bases of Behavior   29

3
Sensation and Perception: Making Contact with the World around Us   59

4
States of Consciousness   97

5

Learning: How We're Changed by Experience 127

6

Memory: Of Things Remembered . . . and Forgotten 163

7

Cognition and Intelligence 191

8 Human Development   235

9 Motivation and Emotion   281

10

Personality: Uniqueness and Consistency in the Behavior of Individuals   313

11

Health, Stress, and Coping   345

12

Mental Disorders:
Their Nature, Causes,
and Treatment   379

13

Social Thought and Social Behavior 429

14

Industrial/Organizational Psychology: Understanding Human Behavior at Work 463

Preface

IN SEARCH OF THE IDEAL BALANCE: THOUGHTS ON PSYCHOLOGY'S DUAL NATURE—AND HOW TO REFLECT IT

In an important sense, psychology has a distinctly dual nature. On the one hand, it is a member of the family of natural sciences; in their efforts to understand all aspects of human behavior and human thought, psychologists consistently rely on the same methods of research as those employed in other scientific fields— methods such as systematic observation and experimentation. On the other hand, psychology is also an extraordinarily *practical* field: It seeks to *use* the knowledge and information it acquires to solve important problems of everyday life and to enhance human welfare in many different ways. We believe strongly that any useful introductory psychology text should reflect *both* of these aspects of modern psychology. The key question, though, is *where*, precisely, should the balance between them be struck? Should a text emphasize the scientific side of the field and focus largely on cutting-edge research and theory? Or should it concentrate mainly on the practical value of psychology—ways in which the vast body of knowledge it has already acquired can be used? Together, we have taught courses in psychology for more than fifty-five years, and this experience leads us to agree with the poet Kahlil Gibran, who once remarked, *"knowledge that acts is worth infinitely more than . . . knowledge that is idle."* In other words, we feel that a text that emphasizes the practical, useful aspects of psychology—while at the same time fully representing its scientific nature—might well be ideal for many students and in many educational settings.

This reasoning, in turn, led us to formulate three specific goals for this book— goals we have worked vigorously to achieve:

GOAL I

Write a text that makes it clear to students how they can actually *use* the findings and knowledge of psychology in their own lives and careers.

How did we attempt to meet this goal? Primarily, by keeping it clearly in mind as we wrote each chapter. The result is that we consider the *practical meaning* and *uses* of psychology throughout the book—in every chapter and in many discussions within chapters. In addition, we have also included several special features designed to call this theme to students' attention:

SPECIAL SECTIONS WITHIN EACH CHAPTER ENTITLED

■ Psychology Goes to Work and ■ Psychology Lends a Hand

PSYCHOLOGY GOES TO WORK

Are You Suited to Becoming an Entrepreneur? A Quick Self-Assessment

Do you ever dream of becoming an entrepreneur—of starting your own business, and then—perhaps—making large donations to your favorite charities, to education, or to scientific research? If so, you are in good company, because the role of entrepreneur has recently taken on an aura of glamour. Famous entrepreneurs like Bill Gates and Michael Dell are in the news frequently, and reports of the size of their personal fortunes lead many people to think, "Why not *me*?" In fact, though, most new companies fail—more than 60 percent within the first three years (Baron & Shane, 2004). Many factors play a role in such failures, but an important one is this: Many people who decide to become entrepreneurs are simply not suited for this role. Research on this topic (much of it conducted by psychologists) indicates that to be a successful entrepreneur, people need a number of different characteristics. Here is a list of the most important ones. Consider them carefully and then ask yourself, "Do I have these characteristics?" If so, you are a good candidate to start your own business (or become a franchisee). If not, you might well be better off considering some other career.

- **High self-efficacy.** As noted, entrepreneurs—especially successful ones—are higher in self-efficacy than other people. In other words, to succeed in this role, you must believe that you can accomplish whatever you set out to accomplish. If you are lacking in such confidence, becoming an entrepreneur is probably not for you.
- **Tolerance for uncertainty and ambiguity.** Starting a new business means jumping off into the unknown. You must develop new products or services, find markets for them, deal with new competitors—who often seem to arise out of nowhere—and many other uncertainties. So, if you are very uncomfortable in such situations, becoming an entrepreneur is probably not your cup of tea.
- **High energy, good health, and high tolerance for stress.** Most entrepreneurs report that

they work 80 or 100 hours a week, and frequently face highly stressful situations. Do you have the energy, health, and stress tolerance for this kind of life? If so, get started! If not, think again.
- **An ability to learn what you need "on the fly."** Most entrepreneurs do not know everything they need to know to run their businesses successfully; they learn it "on the fly" as they proceed. Are you willing to do this? Or would you feel uncomfortable in that kind of situation? If so, you are probably not well suited to become an entrepreneur.
- **Excellent social skills.** Are you good with people? Can you be persuasive? Make a good first impression? As an entrepreneur, you will have to convince investors to back your company with hard cash, persuade customers to try your product, and convince talented people to give up secure jobs to work with you. Research findings (e.g., Baron & Markman, 2003) indicate that to succeed in these tasks, you need good social skills. So, if you don't have them, either start now to acquire them or give up the idea of becoming an entrepreneur.
- **Can you share control?** One problem that destroys many new companies is an inability of the founding entrepreneurs to share control and power with others: They want to do it all themselves. That doesn't work, because as a new company grows, it is impossible for any one person to do everything. Are you the kind of person who can let others take responsibility? If not, you are probably not suited to becoming an entrepreneur.

Consider all these points carefully, because becoming an entrepreneur is a major decision: It can consume all your time, money, and energy. If you possess the characteristics discussed here, this may be the right career move for you. If not, think again, because the costs of failure can be very high.

---

p s y c h o l o g y l e n d s a h a n d

How to Study Psychology—or Any Other Subject—Effectively

Among the topics that psychologists know most about are learning, memory, and motivation. (We examine these in Chapters 5, 6, and 9.) Fortunately, all of these topics are directly relevant to one activity you must perform as a student: studying. You must be motivated to study, must learn new materials, and must remember them accurately after they have been mastered. Knowledge gained by psychologists can be very useful to you in accomplishing these tasks. Drawing on what psychology knows, here are some useful tips to help you get the most out of the time you spend studying.

- **Begin with an overview.** Research on memory indicates that it is easier to retain information if it can be placed within a cognitive framework. So when you begin to study, try to see "the big picture." Examine the outline at the start of each chapter and thumb through the pages once or twice. That way, you'll know what to expect and will form an initial framework for organizing the information that follows.
- **Eliminate (or at least minimize) distractions.** To enter information into your memory accurately, you must devote careful attention to it. This means that you should reduce all distractions; try to study in a quiet place, turn off the television or radio, put those magazines out of sight, and unhook your phone. The result? You will learn more in less time. *Don't do all your studying at once.* All-nighters are very inefficient. Research findings indicate that it is easier to learn and remember new information when learning is spaced out over time rather than when it is crammed into a single long session. So, try to spread your study sessions out in the final analysis, this will give you a much greater return for your effort (see Figure 1.13).
- **Set specific, challenging, but attainable goals.** One of the key findings of industrial/organizational psychology is that setting certain kinds of goals can increase both motivation and performance on many different tasks. This principle can be of great help to you in studying, and it's relatively easy to apply. First, set a concrete goal for each session—for example, "I'll read twenty pages and review my class notes." Merely telling yourself, "I'll work until I'm tired," is less effective because it fails to give you something concrete to shoot for. Second, try to set challenging goals, but ones you can attain. Challenging goals will encourage you to "stretch"—to do a little bit more. But impossible ones are simply discouraging. Because you are the world's greatest expert on your own limits and your own work habits, you are the best judge of what would be a challenging but attainable goal for you. Set such goals when you begin, and the results may surprise you.
- **Reward yourself for progress.** As you'll see in Chapter 5, people often perform various activities to attain external rewards, ones delivered to them by others. But in many cases, we can provide our own rewards. We can pat ourselves on the back for reaching goals we've set for or other accomplishments; this "pat on the back" can take many different forms: eating a favorite dessert, watching a favorite TV program, or visiting

FIGURE 1.13
All-Nighters: Not the Best Strategy for Studying
Psychological research indicates that we learn more efficiently—and remember more of what we learn—when we spread our work sessions out over time. For this reason, as well as several others, all-nighters are the not best or most efficient way to study.

friends. Again, you are the world's greatest expert on what you enjoy, so you can readily choose rewards that are appropriate. Whatever you choose, though, be sure to reward yourself for reaching your goals.
- **Engage in active, not passive studying.** As you probably know, it is possible to sit in front of a book or a set of notes for hours without accomplishing much—except daydreaming! In order to learn new information and retain it, you must do mental work—that's an inescapable fact of life. You must think about the material you are reading, ask yourself questions about it, relate this new information to things you already know, and so on. The Key Questions sections in each chapter are designed to help you do this, but in the final analysis, it's up to you. To the extent you really try to answer these questions and engage in other forms of active learning, you will absorb more information, and more efficiently.

We know: Following these guidelines sounds like a lot of . . . work! But once you master them, the whole process will get easier. You will learn and remember more, get better grades, and improve the value of your own education—and do it more efficiently than ever before. So, in this case, a little extra effort is well justified.

These special sections are designed to help students understand how they can actually use the findings and principles of psychology in their own lives and careers. **Psychology Lends a Hand** sections focus on ways in which students can use psychology to gain increased self-insight, to get along better with others, and to handle a wide range of life situations—everything from resisting sales pressure more successfully to being a better spouse or parent. **Psychology Goes to Work** sections illustrate how students can use psychology to have better and more successful careers. Here are a few examples of both types of sections:

Psychology Lends a Hand: Reducing High-Risk Behavior among Young Males (Chapter 2)

Psychology Goes to Work: The Harmful Effects of Noise: Let's Turn Down the Sound (Chapter 3)

Psychology Goes to Work: Drug Testing at Work—What Are Your Rights? (Chapter 4)

Psychology Goes To Work: Using Memory Principles to Boost the Fairness, Accuracy, and Favorableness of Your Own Performance Appraisals (Chapter 6)

Psychology Lends a Hand: On Becoming More Creative—Some Useful Tips (Chapter 7)

Psychology Lends a Hand: Combating Childhood Obesity (Chapter 8)

Psychology Lends a Hand: Becoming a Very Happy Person (Chapter 9)

Psychology Goes to Work: Job Stress—What Can You Do to Control It? (Chapter 11)

Psychology Lends a Hand: Preventing Suicide—How You Can Help (Chapter 12)

Psychology Goes to Work: How to Make a Good First Impression in Job Interviews (Chapter 13)

Psychology Lends a Hand: How to Give Feedback to Team Members (Chapter 14)

SPECIAL EXERCISES AT THE END
OF EACH CHAPTER ENTITLED

PSYCHOLOGY: UNDERSTANDING ITS FINDINGS

and

MAKING PSYCHOLOGY PART OF YOUR LIFE

These exercises give students direct practice in applying the findings of psychology to their own lives. **Psychology: Understanding Its Findings** exercises focus on giving students practice in thinking about and understanding the major ideas and concepts contained in the chapter they have just read. The exercises in **Making Psychology Part of Your Life,** in contrast, show students how they can apply these ideas and concepts to their own lives. Here are a few examples:

Psychology: Understanding Its Findings: Do People Inherit Their Personalities?

Psychology: Understanding Its Findings: Can Hypnosis Solve Your Personal Problems?

Making Psychology Part of Your Life: Choosing Your Career: Finding a Good Match for Your Personal Characteristics

Making Psychology Part of Your Life: Seeking Help at Work: Employee Assistance Programs

Psychology: Understanding Its Findings: How Feelings Affect Our Judgment: A Personal Demonstration

Making Psychology Part of Your Life: Managing Stress—Some Useful Tactics

---

278   CHAPTER 8   Human Development   www.mypsychlab.com

PSYCHOLOGY: UNDERSTANDING ITS FINDINGS

Can You Reason with a Three-Year-Old?

While the view that young children are just "miniature adults" is no longer widely accepted, many parents act as though they believe it: They often try to "reason" with their children about why the children should (or should not!) engage in certain actions, and often try to explain highly abstract ideas or principles to them (e.g., fairness, justice, loyalty). According to Piaget's theory of cognitive development and modern findings about children's cognitive abilities, why do these efforts often fail? At what age *can* children begin to reason like adults and understand abstract principles and ideas? And until they can, what techniques should parents use to influence their children's behavior?

MAKING PSYCHOLOGY PART OF YOUR LIFE

Choosing Your Career: Finding a Good Match for Your Personal Characteristics

As we noted earlier, research on choosing a career indicates that people are happiest—and most successful—when the careers they choose provide a close match to their personal characteristics and preferences. What are your characteristics and what careers would fit them best? These are complex answers that can't be answered fully in a brief exercise, but to get you started in the right direction, follow these steps:

1. **Rate your own standing on the following clusters of traits:** (Use a 5-point scale, in which 1 = very low; 2 = low; 3 = average; 4 = high; 5 = very high.)
   a. Practical, stable
   b. Analytic, introverted, reserved, precise
   c. Creative, impulsive, emotional
   d. Sociable, outgoing, need affection
   e. Confident, energetic, assertive
   f. Dependable, disciplined, orderly

2. Now, to increase the accuracy of your assessments, have three friends who know you well rate you on the same dimensions.
3. Next, consider the pattern of your traits: On which are you highest? Next highest? Lowest?
4. A major theory of career choice—Holland's *theory of vocational choice* (Gottfredson & Holland, 1990)—suggests that persons high on each of the clusters of previously mentioned traits can be described by the terms shown in the following table, enjoy certain kinds of environments or activities, and would most prefer the jobs listed in the table below.

The jobs shown are only examples. Can you think of others that would provide you with a good match to your personal traits?

Cluster Label	Preferred Environments or Activities	Preferred Jobs
Realistic	Working with hands, machines, tools	Auto mechanic, mechanical engineer
Investigative	Discovering, collecting, analyzing, and problem solving	Systems analyst, dentist, scientist
Artistic	Creating new products or ideas	Novelist, advertising copywriter
Social	Serving or helping others, working in teams	Social worker, counselor, nurse
Enterprising	Leading others, achieving goals	Manager, politician stockbroker
Conventional	Performing systemic manipulation of data or information	Accountant, banker, actuary

---

GOAL 2

Prepare a book that also presents psychology as a *science*.

Writing a book that emphasizes the applied side of the field would be inappropriate if it did not at the same time call attention to the *scientific nature* of psychology. Thus, we have definitely *not* short-changed presentation of the scientific nature of psychology in any way. In fact, all chapters incorporate the most current findings and include research published in 2003 and 2004. Thus, *cutting-edge research* is definitely included, and this emphasizes the fact that psychology is scientific in orientation; in fact, it is this scientific orientation that makes psychology so valuable and useful. We include discussions of recent research in every chapter, clearly demonstrating to students that psychology is scientific in nature. (Examples of the recent, cutting-edge topics and research are presented in the next section.)

GOAL 3

Write a book that presents the major findings of psychology without overwhelming students with too much detail.

We believe that many students—and instructors—would prefer a shorter book, but one that covers all the bases. That's precisely what we have sought to accomplish. As a result, this text is briefer than many others but still covers *all* major topics. In fact, we believe that it actually offers *broader* coverage of the field than many considerably longer texts. The text includes fourteen chapters—the number of weeks in the semester in most colleges and universities—and each chapter presents a major area of the field. Here are some examples of topics covered in this text that are often *not* included in many others:

Brain Plasticity and Behavior (Chapter 2)

Loneliness and Sleep Efficiency (Chapter 4)

Memory and Diversity: Own-Race Bias in Remembering Faces (Chapter 6)

Sources of Bias in Memory for Emotions (Chapter 6)

Infant Timekeeping (Chapter 8)

The Curse of Knowledge (Chapter 8)

Positive Emotions as a Factor in Personal Happiness (Chapter 9)

The Emotion of Forgiveness versus the Emotion of Revenge (Chapter 9)

The "Big Five" Dimensions and Becoming an Entrepreneur (Chapter 10)

The Role of Personality in Happiness and in Human Aggression (Chapter 10)

The "Color-Blind" Therapist (Chapter 12)

Computer and Internet-Based Therapies (Chapter 12)

Changing Female Preferences for Male Faces over the Menstrual Cycle (Chapter 13)

The Low-Ball Technique and Other Means for Gaining Compliance (Chapter 13)

The Role of Cultural Factors in Conceptions of Love (Chapter 13)

Many Aspects of Industrial/Organizational Psychology (Chapter 14)

Additional Strengths

In addition to the features just noted—ones closely linked to our major goals—we have also tried to build a number of other benefits into this text. Here are some of the major ones:

CHAPTER

6

Memory: Of Things Remembered . . . and Forgotten

*S*everal years ago, I (Robert Baron) was having a conversation with my father, and I asked him, "What ever happened to great-grandfather's uniform?" (My great-grandfather had been an officer in a European Army before he came to the United States, and I had vivid memories of his uniform.) My father looked puzzled for a moment and then said, "Grandfather threw it away in the 1930s—when I was in high school, so I don't think you could ever have seen it." "You must be mistaken, Dad," I replied. "I remember it very well. It was black and had gold braid on the right shoulder." My father agreed that I was correct but repeated his belief that I could never have seen it, because it was gone long before I was born. I was sure he was mistaken, because I could visualize the uniform perfectly, hanging there in my grandfather's closet. I remembered how it felt and how it smelled (of mothballs), and wanting to play with the medals. To this day, I have never solved this mystery: Did I ever see my great-grandfather's uniform? Or was my memory playing tricks on me?

Inclusion of Many Pedagogical Aids: Each chapter starts with an outline and is followed by an introduction that is as interesting and attention-grabbing as we could make it. Some of these introductions focus on events and experiences in our own lives, while others use different approaches. All are designed to accomplish two goals: (1) seize students' attention and (2) provide a brief overview of what, precisely, will be covered in the chapter.

In addition, all key terms are printed in **boldface type** like this, and are defined in the text and in marginal entries—as well as in a glossary at the end of the book. Each major section of a chapter is followed by **Key Questions,** which ask students to think about the major points just presented. Answers to these are provided at the end of the text in a **Summary and Review of Key Questions** section. Another important feature is that all *graphs* and *charts* have been specially created for this book. Thus, they are all easy for students to read and understand, and all have special labels that call attention to the major points being illustrated. Overall, then, we feel that our book is very convenient for students to use and is, in this respect, unusually user-friendly.

Coverage of Industrial/Organizational Psychology: I/O psychology is an important branch of the field, and one that truly illustrates how psychology can be

---

Psychology and the Scientific Method | **11**

account of multiculturalism and diversity in all of their professional activities. What does this mean? In essence, that psychologists should be aware of and sensitive to the fact that individuals' cultural, ethnic, and racial heritages often play a key role in their self-identity, and that this, in turn, can exert important effects on their behavior. This is in sharp contrast to the point of view that prevailed in the past, which suggested that cultural, ethnic, and gender differences are relatively unimportant. In contrast to that earlier and now discredited perspective, psychologists currently believe that such differences are *very* important and must be taken carefully into account in our efforts to understand human behavior. As a result, psychology now adopts a **multicultural perspective**—one that carefully and clearly recognizes the potential importance of gender, age, ethnicity, sexual orientation, disability, socioeconomic status, religious orientation, and many other social and cultural dimensions.

This perspective has led to major changes in the way psychologists teach, interact with clients, and conduct research (see Figure 1.7). For example, recent studies conducted by psychologists have focused on ethnic and cultural differences in everything from memory for faces of persons belonging to one's own race or another race (Meissner & Brigham, 2001), through cultural differences in binge drinking (Luczak, 2001) and ethnic differences in optimism and pessimism (Chang & Asakawa, 2003). In short, modern psychology has increasingly adopted a truly multicultural perspective, and this theme—and everything related to it—will be reflected throughout this book.

FIGURE 1.7
A Multicultural Perspective: A Guiding Theme of Modern Psychology
The United States and many other countries have become much more ethnically and culturally diverse in recent decades. As a result, psychologists build awareness of such diversity into everything they do—teaching, research, counseling, and therapy.

KEY QUESTIONS

- What is the definition of psychology as it exists today?
- What ideas in philosophy and several branches of science (biology, physiology, computer science, physics) have contributed to the form and scope of modern psychology?
- What are the three "grand issues" about behavior addressed by psychology?
- What are the major perspectives adopted by psychologists and how do they differ?
- What is evolutionary psychology and how does it contribute to our understanding of human behavior?
- What do the authors mean when they speak of the "exportation" of psychology?
- What is the multicultural perspective, and what role does it play in the activities of modern psychologists?

PSYCHOLOGY AND THE SCIENTIFIC METHOD

Remember the group of people we described earlier in this chapter as "doubters"—people who believe that psychology is nothing more than common sense? Here's where we respond in detail to their doubts. In essence, our answer is simple: Psychology is far more than common sense because the knowledge it provides rests firmly on the *scientific method*. Let's take a closer look at this method to see why it makes the knowledge gathered by psychologists much more valid and useful than common sense.

Multicultural Perspective
A perspective that clearly recognizes the potential importance of gender, age, ethnicity, sexual orientation, disability, socioeconomic status, religious orientation, and many other social and cultural dimensions.

put to practical use. Moreover, interest in I/O psychology has increased greatly in recent years among both students and faculty. To reflect these important trends, we have included a chapter that reviews many of the major findings and applications of I/O psychology. This chapter covers such high-interest, central topics as work motivation, appraising performance, leadership, and team building.

Coverage of Diversity Issues Is Integrated into the Text, Not Added On: We feel that diversity and multicultural perspectives are key themes of modern psychology. To reflect this, we introduce discussions of diversity and related topics at many points in the text—places where such discussions are especially relevant and where interesting, new findings are available. A few examples:

Discrimination and Cardiovascular Activity (Chapter 2)

Ethnic and Group Differences in Binge Drinking (Chapter 4)

Memory for Faces: Effects of Race and Ethnicity (Chapter 6)

Person Perception and the Menstrual Cycle (Chapter 9)

Race and Self-Esteem (Chapter 10)

Gender and Responses to Stress (Chapter 11)

Diversity and Psychotherapy (Chapter 12)

A Full Range of Ancillary Materials

We firmly believe that no text is complete—or useful!—without a full range of excellent ancillary materials. Thus, this text is accompanied by a complete teaching and learning package. The key parts of this package are described below:

Instructor's Supplements

▪ Instructor's Manual and Test Bank

Debra Hollister—Valencia Community College, Instructor's Manual
Lynn McCutcheon—DeVry University, Orlando, Test Bank
Lauren Miller—Florida State University, Test Bank
Paul Wellman—Texas A&M University, Test Bank

This Instructor's Manual/Test Bank is an excellent tool for classroom preparation and management. Each chapter of the Instructor's Manual includes an At-a-Glance Grid with detailed pedagogical information linking to other available supplements; a detailed chapter outline; teaching objectives covering major concepts within the chapter; a list of key terms; lecture material; lecture extensions and in-depth activities; a comprehensive list of psychology and popular videos and media; and an updated list of Web links. In addition, this manual includes a preface and a sample syllabus, and the appendix includes a comprehensive list of student handouts. A Test Bank includes challenging questions that target key concepts. Each chapter includes over one hundred questions including multiple choice, true/false, short answer, and essay, each with an answer justification, page reference, a difficulty rating, and type designation.

▪ TestGen 5.5—Computerized Test Bank (Available for Windows and Macintosh)

TestGen 5.5 is an integrated suite of testing and assessment tools for Windows and Macintosh. You can use TestGen to create professional-looking exams in just minutes by building tests from the existing database of questions, editing questions, or adding your own. TestGen also allows you to prepare printed, network, and online tests.

PowerPoint Presentation

Paul Wellman—Texas A&M University

This interactive tool for use in the classroom includes key points covered in the textbook, images from the textbook, and demonstrations.

Transparencies for Introduction to Psychology

Approximately two hundred full-color overheads are provided to enhance classroom lecture and discussion, including images from Allyn and Bacon's major Introduction to Psychology texts.

Insights into Psychology, Volumes I and II

These interactive videos include two to three video clips per topic, with sixteen topics total. Clips cover such topics as animal research, parapsychology, health and stress, Alzheimer's news, bilingual education, genetics and IQ, and much more. Critical thinking questions accompany each clip. In addition, the video guide provides further critical thinking questions and Internet resources for more information. Also available on DVD.

Allyn and Bacon Digital Media Archive for Psychology, 4.0

This is a comprehensive source for images, including charts, graphs, tables, and figures, with audio clips and related Web links, all from Allyn and Bacon's major Introduction to Psychology texts. Animation and video clips include classic psychology experiments footage from Stanley Milgram's *Invitation to Social Psychology*, a silent film, biology animations, and more—with coverage of such topics as eating disorders, aggression, therapy, intelligence, and sensation and perception. This is a powerful tool for customized classroom presentation.

CourseCompass

Powered by Blackboard, this course management system uses a powerful suite of tools so instructors can create an online presence for any course.

Student Supplements

MyPsychLab

MyPsychLab is a state of the art, interactive and instructive course management solution for introductory psychology. Designed to be used as a supplement to a traditional lecture course, MyPsychLab combines multimedia, tutorials, audio, video, simulations, animations, and controlled assessments, along with an electronic copy of the textbook, to engage students. Go to **www.mypsychlab.com** for more information.

Research Navigator Guide: Psychology, with access to Research Navigator™

Allyn & Bacon's Research Navigator is the easiest way for students to start a research assignment or research paper. Complete with extensive help on the research process and three exclusive databases of credible and reliable source material, including EBSCO's ContentSelect Academic Journal Database, *New York Times* Search by Subject Archive, and "Best of the Web" Link Library, Research Navigator helps students quickly and efficiently make the most of their research time. The booklet contains a practical and to-the-point discussion of search engines; detailed information on evaluating on-line sources and citation guidelines for Web resources;

Web activities for psychology; Web links for psychology; and a complete guide to Research Navigator.

Mind Matters II CD-ROM

A unique tool that combines major concepts with interactivity. This CD-ROM contains a wide range of learning opportunities, including activities with immediate feedback, video clips of historic experiments and current research, animations, simulations, and an interactive glossary of key terms. See sample modules at **www.ablongman.com/mindmatters.**

Psych Tutor

This service provides free tutoring via phone, fax, e-mail, and Internet during Tutor Center hours to students who purchase a new Allyn and Bacon text (ordered with the Tutor Center access code). Qualified college psychology instructors tutor on all material covered in the text (access code required). Visit the site at **www.aw.com/ tutorcenter/psych.**

Some Concluding Thoughts

We can honestly say that we have spared no effort in our attempts to reach the goals outlined here. As a result, we feel that we have produced a book that emphasizes the practical, useful side of psychology while simultaneously highlighting its scientific nature. In other words, we have prepared a book that, we hope, approaches the "ideal balance" mentioned in the title of this Preface.

Although we feel that we have made progress toward this goal, we also realize that *all* human endeavors and efforts are flawed and that, despite our best efforts, there is certainly room for improvement. For that reason, we earnestly invite your candid input. We will listen carefully to it and will do our best to incorporate your comments and suggestions into future versions of this book. So please e-mail us at the addresses below. To echo the theme with which we began—and the words of Kahlil Gibran—we will use the information (knowledge) you provide as the basis for *action*—for concrete steps designed to improve this book. Our sincere thanks, in advance, for your help.

Robert A. Baron
baronr@rpi.edu

Michael J. Kalsher
kalshm@rpi.edu

Acknowledgments

SOME WORDS OF THANKS

Each time we write a book, we gain a stronger appreciation of the following fact: We really couldn't do it without the help of many talented, dedicated people. While we can't possibly thank all of them here, we do wish to express our appreciation to those whose help has been most valuable.

First, our sincere thanks to Rebecca A. Henry for contributing the chapter on industrial/organizational psychology. Rebecca is an I/O psychologist by training, and her expertise is obvious in this chapter, which truly covers all the bases and provides an outstanding overview of her field.

Second, we wish to thank the following colleagues, who responded to our survey regarding our goals for this book. Their input was invaluable to us in many ways.

Joel Alexander, Western Oregon University

Cheryl Armstrong-Ross, Fitchburg State College

Julie Barbadillo, DeVry University, Seattle, Federal Way

Joseph Barda, Robert Morris College

Barb Bates, DeVry University, Westminster

Eric Belky, Ball State University

Dr. Irwin Bernstein, University of Georgia

Judy Bowie, DeVry University, Chicago

Birgit Bryant, Le Moyne College

Dr. Tom Caldwell, Middle Georgia College

Dr. Jim Calhoun, University of Georgia

Dr. Bernardo Carducci, Indiana University–Southeast Campus

Yung May Chen, Rutgers State University

Maria Clapham, Drake University

James Collins, DeVry University, Tinley Park

James Collins, Middle Georgia College

Jacqueline Conyers, DeVry University, Philadelphia, Fort Washington

Joan Cook, County College of Morris

Dr. Steven Cox, DeVry University, Seattle, Federal Way

Don Crews, Southwest Georgia Technical College

Paul D'Agostino, Gettysburg College

Grace Davis, Marshall University

Joe DeBoni, DeVry University, DuPage

Michael De Vries, Trinity Christian College

Vicki Dretchen, Volunteer State Community College

Joy Easton, DeVry University, Orlando

Ken Elliott, University of Maine at Augusta

Rebecca Fincher-Keiffer, Gettysburg College

Dr. Joseph Fitzgerald, Wayne State University

E. Scott Geller, Virginia Polytech

Greg Greguras, Louisiana State University

Christina Halawa, DeVry University, Tinley Park

Dave Hansen, University of Nebraska–Lincoln

John Harris, Towson University

Myra Harville, Holmes Community College

Kris Horn, DeVry University, Phoenix

Brian Kaufman, University of Maine–Farmington

Dr. Jada Kearns, Valencia Community College–East

George Keiser, Bismarck State College

Dr. C. Kilbourn, Northern Arizona University

Stanley Klein, University of California, Santa Barbara

Dr. Richard Kushner, University of New Hampshire

Dr. Lori Lange, University of North Florida

Kenneth Laughery, Rice University

Lawrence Lewandowski, Syracuse University

Kristen Link, SUNY at Oswego

Laura Madson, New Mexico State University

Kathy McCormick, Ocean County College

Lynn McCutcheon, DeVry University, Orlando

Todd McElroy, Wake Forest University

Steven Mewaldt, Marshall University

Joel Morgovsky, Brookdale Community College

Kathleen Nolan, DeVry University, DuPage

Dr. Jelena Ozegovic, Robert Morris College

Gary Piggrem, DeVry University, Columbus

Chrislyn Randell, Metropolitan State College of Denver

David Renjilian, Marywood University

Gabriel Repassy, Bentley College

Chuck Robertson, North Georgia College

Beth Rene Roepnack, DeVry University, Alpharetta

Maris Rose, DeVry University, Chicago

Melanie Roudkovski, University of West Alabama

Leonard Santarseiro, Southern Connecticut State University

Lynn Schuchman, DeVry University, Kansas City

William Scott, Oklahoma State University

Susan Shepard, Middle Georgia College

Carol Smart, University of Dubuque

Michael Sonntag, Lander University

Mark Stackpole, DeVry University, Fremont

Pat Stewart, Northern Virginia Community College

Dr. Eric Stone, Wake Forest University

Rebecca Stultz, University of Akron–Wayne College

Kelsey Tyler, DeVry University, Seattle, Federal Way

Jess F. Veasey, Community College of Southern Nevada–Cheyenne

Nancy Walker, Cape Cod Community College

Dr. Charlie Wall, University of Maine at Augusta

Ron West, DeVry University, Chicago

Theresa White, Le Moyne College

Dr. Diane Wille, Indiana University–Southeast Campus

Stella Young, Gateway Tech College

Mollie Zahorik, Robert Morris College

Anthony Zoccolillo, DeVry University, North Brunswick

Third, our sincere appreciation to the colleagues who read and commented on the manuscript. We found their comments extremely helpful and thank them for taking the time from their busy lives and schedules to share their expertise with us:

Melinda Blackman, California State University, Fullerton

Lorry Cology, Owens Community College

Christian Fossa-Andersen, DeVry University, Southern Florida Campus

Debra Hollister, Valencia Community College

Jan Pascal, DeVry University, Kansas City

Carolyn Paul, DeVry University, Pomona

Paula Popovich, Ohio University

Lindsay Reid, DeVry University, Crystal City

Susan Siaw, California State Polytechnic University, Pomona

Joshua S. Spitalnick, University of Georgia

Keith Syrja, Owens Community College

Sheree Watson, University of Southern Mississippi

Adelia Williams, DeVry University, Arlington, Virginia

Michael Zickar, Bowling Green State University

Fourth, we offer our personal thanks to Karon Bowers, our editor at Allyn & Bacon. She has been immensely helpful throughout the project. It has been a true pleasure to work with her.

Fifth, our thanks to Kristina Smead for very careful and constructive copyediting. Her comments were insightful and thought-provoking, thus providing valuable help in improving and clarifying our words.

Sixth, our thanks to all of those others who contributed to various aspects of the production process: to Katharine Cook for photo research, to Erin Liedel for her work on the photos and supplements, to Roy Neuhaus for design work, and to Linda Knowles and Susan Paradise for the cover design.

Finally, our sincere thanks to Debra Hollister for outstanding work on the Instructor's Resource Manual; to Lynn McCutcheon, Lauren Miller, and Paul Wellman for their work on the Test Bank; to Paul Wellman for his work on the PowerPoint; and to Christian Fossa-Andersen for his work on the Curriculum Guide. To all of these truly outstanding people, and to many others, too, our warmest personal regards and thanks.

Robert A. Baron

Michael J. Kalsher

About the Authors

Robert A. Baron is Professor of Psychology and the Wellington Professor of Management at Rensselaer Polytechnic Institute. He received his Ph.D. from the University of Iowa in 1968. Professor Baron has held faculty appointments at Purdue University, the University of Minnesota, the University of Texas, the University of South Carolina, and Princeton University. In 1982 he was a Visiting Fellow at Oxford University. From 1979 to 1981 he served as a Program Director at the National Science Foundation (Washington, D.C.). He has been a Fellow of the American Psychological Association and is also a Fellow of the American Psychological Society. In 2001, he was appointed and Invited Senior Research Fellow by the French government, and held this post at the Université des Sciences Sociales at Toulouse, France.

Professor Baron has published more than one hundred articles in professional journals and thirty-five chapters in edited volumes. He is the author or co-author of forty-two books, including *Social Psychology* (10th ed.) and *Behavior in Organizations* (8th ed.). Professor Baron holds three U.S. patents based on his research, and served as President of his own company (Innovative Environmental Products, Inc.) from 1992 to 2000. Professor Baron's current research focuses mainly on the social and cognitive factors that influence entrepreneurs' success.

Michael J. Kalsher is Associate Professor of Psychology and Cognitive Science at Rensselaer Polytechnic Institute. Kalsher served as Chair of the Department of Cognitive Science at Rensselaer from 1997 through 2002. He received his Ph.D. in 1988 from Virginia Tech. Professor Kalsher is a member of both the American Psychological Society and the American Psychological Association. He is also a member of the Human Factors and Ergonomics Society for which he currently serves as the Chair of the Arnold M. Small Safety Lecture series. Professor Kalsher has published more than fifty articles in professional journals, a number of chapters in edited books, and has given more than one hundred presentations at professional meetings.

Kalsher's company (Kalsher and Associates, L.L.C.) specializes in applying the principles of psychology to enhance human performance and workplace safety, including providing litigation support (e.g., as an expert witness) in product liability cases. Professor Kalsher's current research interests focus on human factors issues, including development and evaluation of warnings and instructions, allocation of blame for consumer product injuries, and the use of emerging technologies to enhance communications in noisy environments (e.g., tanks, helicopters).

Rebecca A. Henry is currently Visiting Associate Professor at Rensselaer Polytechnic Institute. She received her Ph.D. in 1989 from the University of Illinois and was on the faculty in the Department of Psychological Sciences at Purdue University for 14 years. She has published articles in several journals, including *Psychological Bulletin, Journal of Applied Psychology,* and *Organizational Behavior and Human Decision Processes (OBHDP).* Professor Henry supervised over a dozen doctoral and master's students and served as the Director of Undergraduate Studies in the Department of Psychological Sciences at Purdue. While at Purdue, she taught several undergraduate- and graduate-level courses and was honored as the Department's undergraduate teaching award nominee several times.

Professor Henry's research has spanned several topic areas in industrial/organizational psychology, including group decision making, organizational citizenship, and ability testing. She currently serves on the editorial boards of *Psychology and Marketing* and *OBHDP.*

Psychology: What It Is . . . and What It Offers

*I*t never fails. We are at a party talking to someone we've just met and they ask, "What's your field?" When we answer, "Psychology," they usually react in one of three ways. Some people—we think of them as supporters—express great enthusiasm about psychology. Usually, we get into a spirited discussion with them about one or more aspects of human behavior—anything from weight loss to eyewitness testimony or workplace violence. A second group, which we describe as volunteer patients, reacts quite differently. They view meeting us as an opportunity for free counseling. They tell us about their personal problems, ask us to interpret their dreams, and sometimes request the name of a good hypnotist!

We describe the third group as doubters, and such persons let us know right away that, in their opinion, psychology is just "common sense" and is definitely not in the same league as chemistry, physics, or other fields of science. Others grudgingly admit that psychology might be scientific in nature (barely!) but express the view that it is not really useful: In their opinion, it is just so much fun and games—mainly for psychologists.

What do these experiences tell us? Primarily, two things. First, because the first group (supporters) is by far the largest, it is clear that most people are deeply interested in psychology. They view it as a source of fascinating information about themselves and other persons, and a source of valuable help with their personal problems. Second, these experiences remind us that not everyone shares these views. On the contrary, the group we label *doubters* has serious reservations about the value, scientific nature, and usefulness of psychology.

In a sense, this book is dedicated to all three groups. For those who already believe that psychology is interesting and valuable, it will offer a vast array of intriguing and potentially useful information about human behavior. For the skeptics, it will provide a solid basis for changing their minds—for coming to see psychology as the fascinating and eminently *useful* field that it is.

But this book is designed to do more than this. It also seeks to provide you with a *new perspective* on human behavior. We have long believed that psychology offers far more than a collection of interesting facts; it also provides a new way of thinking about your own feelings, thoughts, and actions, and those of other persons. After reading this book, we believe, *you will never think about yourself, other people, and your relations with them in quite the same way as before.* And we also predict that this new perspective will enrich your life in many different ways.

Before turning to the specific content of psychology—what it has discovered about human behavior, and how it can be useful to *you*—it is important to provide you with a framework for interpreting this information. Why? Because a basic finding of cognitive psychology (one important branch of the field) is that new information is easier to understand, retain, and use when a mental framework for holding it exists. In view of this fact, we'll use the rest of this introductory chapter for providing such a framework, and this will involve several tasks.

First, we'll define psychology, say a few words about its origins, and describe some of the major issues with which it grapples (e.g., to what extent our behavior is shaped by experience versus built-in, inherited tendencies). Second, we'll comment on the scientific nature of psychology, describing the *scientific method,* how psychologists use it, and how you, too, can put it to good use. Third, we'll describe basic *research methods* used by psychologists in their efforts to increase our knowledge of human behavior. Because the vast majority of the information and findings reported in this book was acquired through the use of these methods, it is important that you understand them. After presenting that information, we'll consider another important issue: Why should you be here studying psychology? In other words, what's in it for you? In our view, quite a lot; we believe—passionately!—that psychology is tremendously useful, and that the title of this book is accurate: Knowing about psychology will be very helpful to you in your life and in your career. Finally, we'll provide you with an overview of the special features of this book—features designed to make it easier to read, understand, and use. Now, without further delay, let's turn to the questions of what modern psychology is and where it came from.

THE FIELD OF PSYCHOLOGY: WHAT IT IS AND HOW IT ORIGINATED

Suppose you stopped fifty people on the street and asked them to define the field of psychology; what would they say? Probably, many different things: "The field that studies the unconscious," "A branch of medicine that analyzes people," or even "Hypnotism, ESP, and stuff like that." If you posed this question to fifty psychologists, however, you'd obtain much greater agreement: They would largely agree that **psychology** is best defined as *the science of behavior and cognitive processes.*

Psychology
The science of behavior and cognitive processes.

FIGURE 1.1
Psychology: The Science of Behavior and Cognitive Processes
Modern psychology is concerned with all aspects of human behavior and human cognition—everything we do, feel, think, or experience.

Both parts of this definition deserve further comment. First, note that psychologists view their field as basically *scientific* in nature. Second, this definition suggests that psychologists view their field as being very broad in scope. Indeed, they perceive it as being concerned with virtually everything we do, feel, think, or experience (see Figure 1.1).

By the term *behavior,* in other words, they mean any observable action or reaction by living organisms—everything from overt actions (anything we say and do) through subtle changes in the electrical activity occurring deep inside our brains. If it can be observed and measured, then it fits within the boundaries of psychology. Similarly, by *cognitive processes,* psychologists mean every aspect of our mental lives—our thoughts, memories, dreams, fantasies, reasoning, and so on—all aspects of the human *mind.*

Psychology was not always defined in this broad and inclusive way. In fact, during its formative years, major battles were fought among early psychologists who disagreed about such issues. One particularly divisive issue was whether psychology should focus only on overt, observable behavior (the *behaviorists*) or should the focus be expanded to include systematic investigation of mental processes. One group, in fact, thought that psychology should focus *only* on consciousness (they were known as *structuralists*).

As the field took shape and matured, however, the definition offered above—the science of behavior and cognitive processes—became the standard one and is currently accepted by virtually all psychologists throughout the world.

The Origins of Modern Psychology: Multiple Roots

Have you ever seen the television program *Connections*? In it, the brilliant historian James Burke explains how seemingly unrelated and unconnected events and ideas can combine to produce major advances in technology—and in human welfare. For instance, he notes that the telephone did not suddenly emerge as an independent idea. On the contrary, its inventor, Alexander Graham Bell, simply combined unrelated technical advances in several fields (e.g., the production and measurement of sound; the nature and use of electricity) to develop the *idea* of the telephone—and the telephone itself (see Figure 1.2 on page 4).

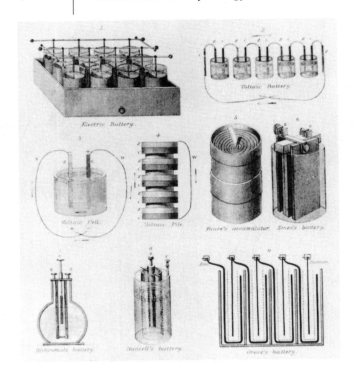

FIGURE 1.2
Nothing Is Entirely "New"
Did Alexander Graham Bell invent the telephone? In one sense, he did: He produced the first working model. But the idea for such a device was based on advances in many other fields. What Graham did was what other inventors do: He "connected the dots" into a new pattern—and changed the world!

In other words, new ideas often emerge out of existing ones, which, when combined, produce something that really *is* new and different. This same process applies to the emergence of modern psychology. The idea of a scientific field that would study human behavior developed, logically, out of advances in several other fields, which paved the way for its occurrence. One basis for the idea of a science of human behavior came from *philosophy* (and more specifically, from the *philosophy of science*), which suggested that the methods of science can be applied to virtually anything in the natural world—including human behavior. Another important foundation was provided by the fields of biology and physiology, whose findings shed important new light on the nature and function of the nervous system, on how our senses operate, and on the relationship between physical stimuli (light, noise, heat) and how we perceive them.

Additional foundation stones of modern psychology, especially in recent decades, involved advances in engineering and computer science, which provided psychologists with tools for presenting stimuli to research participants in a very precise manner, and for measuring the speed with which they responded to these stimuli. This, in turn, provided key techniques for investigating memory, thinking, and many other forms of mental activity. Finally, physics and medicine combined to provide the means for studying activity occurring in people's brains as they think, reason, and make decisions. Together, these diverse factors contributed to the emergence and progress of modern psychology—a field that includes within its boundaries every aspect of human behavior and human thought you can possibly imagine (see Figure 1.3).

PSYCHOLOGY: GRAND ISSUES, KEY PERSPECTIVES

More than ten years ago, one of us (Robert Baron) went to the thirtieth reunion of his high school class. He hadn't been to any previous reunions, so he knew he was in for an interesting time. Would he be able to recognize his former classmates? Would they be able to recognize him? The results were mixed. Everyone had changed physically, of course, but amazingly, Prof. Baron could still recognize many people. And even those who had changed so much that he couldn't recognize their faces still showed many of the traits he remembered from thirty years earlier. This experience calls attention to one of what might be termed psychology's *grand issues*—large-scale questions or themes that crosscut the field. This question has to do with *stability versus change*: To what extent do we remain stable over time, and to what extent do we change? We'll meet this issue over and over again in this book as we address changes over time in cognitive abilities, physical functioning, personality, and other aspects of behavior.

A second and closely related theme centers around the following question: To what extent are various aspects of our behavior shaped by inherited tendencies, and to what extent are they learned? This is usually known as the *nature–nurture* question, and we'll meet it repeatedly in future chapters. Does aggression stem primarily from innate tendencies, or is it the result of experiences that "trigger" it in a given situation? Do we find certain persons attractive because we have built-in tendencies to find certain characteristics (e.g., smooth, clear skin) attractive, or because we learn, through experience, what is considered beautiful in our own

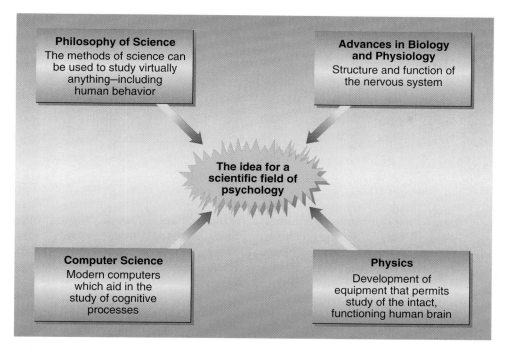

FIGURE 1.3
Modern Psychology: Some of Its Many Roots
Modern psychology derives from many different sources; some of them (but by no means all of them) are shown here.

culture? As you'll soon see, the answer to such questions is *not* one suggesting that either experience or heredity dominates; rather, many aspects of behavior seem to represent the result of complex interactions between these factors. In any case, the nature–nurture question has recently come to the fore in psychology because of the development of a new field that focuses on the potential role of *evolution* in human behavior—*evolutionary psychology*. This field is so intriguing and has stirred so much interest among psychologists that we'll discuss it in more detail in a later section of this chapter.

Now for the third major theme. Answer quickly: Would you eat a chocolate shaped exactly like a cockroach—hairy legs, long antennae, and all? If you feel some reluctance, you are like many people. But now ask yourself *why* you would be reluctant to do so. The chocolate has no relationship to a real insect, so why should the fact that it is shaped like one stop you from eating it? The answer, in most general terms, is this: In many cases, we are *not* completely rational. We know very well what the logical response or reaction would be in a given situation, but our reason is overridden by other factors—our emotions, our gut-level feelings, and so on. This is one illustration of a third major theme you'll find throughout this book: *rationality versus irrationality*. Need more examples? Then consider these: Have you ever underestimated the amount of time it would take you to complete a task? Have you ever lashed out at another person not because of something he or she did or said, but simply because you were in a rotten mood? If so, then you already have direct experience with the less than completely rational side of human nature. Psychologists are fascinated by these and other illustrations of the fact that we are not always perfectly logical, because they often offer insights into how the mind works. We'll return to this theme again and again as we examine such issues as decision making, eyewitness testimony, and how we form first impressions of other persons.

FIGURE 1.4
Contrasting Perspectives of Modern Psychology
Psychologists observing this scene could adopt any of several different perspectives in their efforts to understand it—behavioral, cognitive, biological, evolutionary, psychodynamic, and cultural. Each perspective would add to our understanding of these events.

Be on the lookout for these three grand issues—they are central questions that have captured the attention of psychologists for decades and that have played an important role in shaping the questions asked by psychologists in their research.

Key Perspectives in Psychology: The Many Facets of Behavior

Imagine the following scene: A young woman wearing a beautiful silk costume embroidered with threads of gold, walks into the middle of a large arena, watched by a huge crowd. Suddenly, a large bull enters. The woman waves a red cape at the bull, and it charges directly at her. She steps gracefully out of the way at the last minute, and the crowd cheers with enthusiasm. Again and again the woman waves the cape and the bull charges. After many narrow but stylish escapes from the bull's horns, she kills the animal with one skilled and merciful stroke of a sword. The crowd goes wild with admiration (see Figure 1.4).

How would a psychologist interpret this intriguing situation? The answer is, from many different perspectives—perspectives that cut across the three "grand issues" noted above (change versus stability, nature versus nurture, rationality versus irrationality). One, known as the *behavioral* perspective, would emphasize the overt actions occurring—the bullfighter's skilled performance, the bull's charges, the reactions of the crowd. Another, the *cognitive* perspective, would focus on cognitive factors in this situation, such as the bullfighter's thoughts as the scene unfolds. What is going through her mind? What strategies does she plan? What does she think about killing the bull?

A third perspective would emphasize the *biological* factors that play a role in this situation. What are the emotions of the bullfighter as she faces the charging bull? What are the emotions of the crowd? What systems in her brain allow her to time her escapes so closely that she is literally inches from death? Closely related to this approach would be the *evolutionary* perspective. This perspective would focus on such questions as whether the bull's tendency to charge moving red objects is part of its inherited behavioral tendencies, and if so, what functions does this tendency serve? The evolutionary perspective might ask whether choosing such a dangerous occupation reflects inherited tendencies for the bullfighter as well—perhaps a genetically determined desire for high levels of excitement, or a genetically determined desire for status, which gives high-status persons a wider choice among possible mates.

Yet another perspective that could be adopted by a psychologist observing this incident would focus on factors relating to hidden forces within the bullfighter's personality. This *psychodynamic* approach might focus on what aspects of the bullfighter's personality, and what motives—conscious or unconscious—played a role in her choice of this unusual and dangerous occupation.

Finally, a psychologist observing this situation could seek to understand it in terms of social or cultural factors. What is it about the young woman's culture that makes bullfighting so popular—and turns successful bullfighters into heroes? And why is it that in some countries the bull is killed at the end of the fight, while in others it is spared and returned to pasture? Interest in the effects of cultural and ethnic factors has recently become a major theme of modern psychology; in fact, this growing *multicultural perspective* is so important that we will consider it in detail in the later section Growing Commitment to a Multicultural Perspective (American Psychological Association, 2003). For now, the main point to remember is this: Human behavior is extraordinarily complex and is influenced by many different factors. Thus, any aspect of behavior can be examined from many different perspectives. All these add to our understanding of behavior, so all will be represented throughout this book. (Table 1.1 summarizes these contrasting points of view or approaches.)

TABLE 1.1	Major Perspectives in Modern Psychology

As shown here, psychology studies behavior from many different perspectives.

Perspective	Description
Behavioral	Focuses on overt behavior
Cognitive	Focuses on cognitive processes such as memory, thought, reasoning
Biological	Focuses on the biological processes that underlie behavior
Evolutionary	Focuses on the possible role of evolved psychological mechanisms (inherited tendencies shaped by evolution) in human behavior
Developmental	Focuses on changes in behavior and cognitive processes over the life span
Psychodynamic	Focuses on the role of hidden, often unconscious processes (e.g., unconscious motives)
Cultural/multicultural	Focuses on the role of social and cultural factors and especially on differences between cultural, ethnic, gender, sexual preference, and racial groups

PSYCHOLOGY IN THE TWENTY-FIRST CENTURY: EXPANDING HORIZONS

Psychology is a tremendously diverse field. As shown in Table 1.2 on page 8, psychologists specialize in many different aspects of behavior. As a result, there is always a lot going on and the field develops and changes in many ways at once. Among recent trends, however, three seem so important that they are worthy of special note. One is psychology's growing attention to the possible role of *evolution* in human behavior. The second is what we describe as the increasing "exportation" of psychology—a growing trend for other fields to use the principles and findings of psychology to help solve a wide range of practical problems. The third is psychology's adoption of a truly *multicultural perspective*.

Evolutionary Psychology: A New Perspective on "Human Nature"

Is there such a thing as "human nature"—a set of qualities or behaviors that define us as a unique species? Until about ten years ago, most psychologists would have expressed skepticism on this point. While they would certainly have agreed that our biological nature is, in part, inherited, many would have pointed to learning and the effects of experience rather than genes or evolution as the main sources of our behavior. In recent years, however, the pendulum of scientific opinion has swung in the opposite direction, and today, most psychologists believe that genetic factors do play some role in many aspects of our behavior—everything from mate selection and mating strategies (e.g., why males express greater jealousy than females over sexual infidelity by their partners) through creativity and our desires for status and prestige (e.g., Pinker, 1997; Figure 1.5 on page 9).

One major reason for this shift in opinion is the development and rapid growth of the new field of **evolutionary psychology** (Buss, 1999). This new branch of

Evolutionary Psychology
A new branch of psychology, suggesting that as a result of evolution, human beings possess a number of *evolved psychological mechanisms* that help (or once helped) us deal with important problems relating to survival.

TABLE 1.2   Major Subfields of Psychology

Psychologists specialize in studying many different aspects of behavior. The approximate percentage of all psychologists in each specialty is shown in this table; other subfields not listed separately make up the missing few percent.

Subfield	Description	Percentage
Clinical psychology	Studies diagnosis, causes, and treatment of mental disorders	43
Counseling psychology	Assists individuals in dealing with many personal problems that do not involve psychological disorders	10
Developmental psychology	Studies how people change physically, cognitively, and socially over the entire life span	5
Educational psychology	Studies all aspects of the educational process	6
Experimental psychology	Studies all basic psychological processes, including perception, learning, and motivation	14*
Cognitive psychology	Investigates all aspects of cognition—memory, thinking, reasoning, language, decision making, and so on	(Included under experimental)
Industrial/ organizational psychology	Studies all aspects of behavior in work settings	4
Psychobiology and evolutionary psychology	Investigates biological bases of behavior and the role of evolution in human behavior	1
Social psychology	Studies all aspects of social behavior and social thought—how we think about and interact with others	6

*Figure includes cognitive psychology.

psychology suggests that our species, like all others, has been subject to the process of biological evolution throughout its history, and that as a result of this process, we now possess a large number of *evolved psychological mechanisms* that help (or once helped) us to deal with important problems relating to survival. The theory of evolution, in its modern form, is quite complex, but basically, it suggests that the members of any given species (including our own) show variation along many different dimensions, and many of these variations can be passed on from one generation to the next. Over time, variations that help organisms survive and become parents of the next generation tend to become more common. This kind of change in the characteristics of a species over time is the concrete outcome of evolution.

Evolutionary psychology suggests that human beings, like all other species on the planet, have always faced basic problems relating to survival: obtaining food, finding shelter, avoiding predators and other dangers, and combating disease. Over time, natural selection assured that variations which helped our ancestors survive and reproduce became increasingly common. Together, these inherited tendencies constitute our human nature and often play an important role in shaping our behavior. Does this mean that our behavior is genetically determined and cannot be changed? Absolutely not! Rather, it suggests that, as human beings, we come equipped with a set of mechanisms that interact with the environment; it is this interaction that determines whether, to what extent, and in what form they are actually expressed. For instance, one evolved mechanism we possess is the ability to form calluses (hard patches of skin) on our hands and feet. Do we develop them? Only if we handle hard objects or walk on hard surfaces. If we spend our days turning the pages of books or walking on soft carpets, calluses never appear. Similarly, evolved psychological mechanisms only provide the *potential* for certain behaviors of tendencies to occur; whether they do or do not depends on external factors or experience. As for our ability to change, consider this: Once we know that walking on hard surfaces will lead to the development of calluses on our feet, we can take steps to prevent them—for instance, wearing shoes with soft rubber soles or avoiding hard surfaces. So, yes, evolutionary psychology suggests that our behavior is influenced by inherited mechanisms or tendencies, but, no, it does *not* imply that it is totally determined solely by these mechanisms—far from it!

One more point that is sometimes misunderstood. The existence of evolved psychological mechanisms does *not* in any way imply that our genes "force" us to act in certain ways, that we can't resist these impulses or change, or that our sole motivation in life is to reproduce. Rather, evolutionary psychology merely suggests that as human beings we come equipped with many mechanisms designed to help us survive in a complex and challenging world. These mechanisms are real, but they interact with the external environment and our experience and leave tremendous room for individuality and change. Please note that evolutionary psychology is only one of many different perspectives in psychology, and we in no way wish to endorse it or emphasize it here. We describe it in some detail mainly because it has received a great deal of recent attention.

"Do you know who you're talking to, Buster? You're talking to the guy with the biggest desk, biggest chair, longest drapes, and highest ceiling in the business!"

FIGURE 1.5
Genetic Factors: They May Play a Role in Many Forms of Human Behavior
Currently, most psychologists believe that genetic factors play some role in many forms of human behavior—even in the desire for status or prestige shown by the character in this cartoon.
Source: © The New Yorker Collection 1981 Dana Fradon from cartoonbank.com. All Rights Reserved.

The Exportation of Psychology: From Science to Practice

Most people realize that several branches of psychology are *applied*—not only do they seek to acquire basic knowledge about human behavior, they also attempt to put it to practical use. For instance, *clinical psychologists* help individuals deal with emotional and psychological problems, whereas *industrial/organizational psychologists* focus on solving many practical problems relating to work (e.g., increasing motivation, evaluating employees' performance both fairly and accurately). So, right from its very beginnings, psychology has had a practical as well as a scientific side. In recent years, however, application of psychology's knowledge about human behavior has expanded far beyond psychology itself. Many fields have found answers to some of their most important questions in the findings and principles of psychology and have begun to draw on this knowledge to an increasing degree. In other words, as psychology has matured and become an ever richer source of knowledge about human behavior, persons in other fields have recognized this fact and put it to good use. Please don't misunderstand: We are not referring here to people who are *not* trained psychologists but who try to use psychology anyway—for example, to design psychological tests, conduct therapy, or advise businesses about how to handle their employees. Rather, we are referring

FIGURE 1.6
Studying the Psychology of Entrepreneurs: An Example of the "Exportation" of Psychology
Recently, a growing number of psychologists have turned the principles and findings of their field to the task of studying entrepreneurs. This research may yield important social benefits because entrepreneurs do not only create wealth for themselves, but also create good jobs for many thousands of people. (*Left*) Bill Gates; (*Right*) Jeff Bezos.

to much more legitimate uses of psychological knowledge, often with the help and guidance of trained psychologists who serve as "exporters" of the findings of their field. To mention just a couple of examples, in recent years, psychologists have helped anesthesiologists—doctors who specialize in putting patients to sleep safely during operations—design equipment that greatly reduces the chance that patients will receive too much anesthetic and so be greatly harmed. Similarly, a growing number of psychologists have been working with colleagues in the field of business to help understand entrepreneurship—for instance, why some people but not others choose to become entrepreneurs, why some people but not others recognize opportunities for new products or services (e.g., Baron, 2004; Baron & Markman, 2003). Because entrepreneurs create jobs and wealth not just for themselves but also for many other persons, obtaining answers to these questions is very important and can mean a better life for millions of people (see Figure 1.6).

This is just one example of what we mean by the exportation of psychology; many others exist, too, and we will highlight them throughout the text. The main point is simply this: In the twenty-first century, recognition of the practical as well as scientific value of psychology has increased greatly, with beneficial effects that few people would have predicted just two or three decades in the past.

Growing Commitment to a Multicultural Perspective

There can be no doubt that the United States is undergoing a major social and cultural transformation. The census of 2000 indicates that 67 percent of the population identifies itself as white (of European heritage), while fully 33 percent identifies itself as belonging to some other group (13 percent African American, 4.5 percent American Indian, 13 percent Hispanic, 4.5 percent Asian/Pacific Islander, and 7 percent some other group). This represents a tremendous change from the 1960s, when approximately 90 percent of the population was of European descent. Indeed, in several states (e.g., California, New Mexico, Texas, Arizona), persons of European heritage are no longer a clear majority. In response to these tremendous shifts, psychologists have increasingly recognized the importance of taking cultural factors and differences into careful account in everything they do—teaching, research, counseling, and therapy. Indeed, in 2003, the American Psychological Association issued new guidelines that strongly encouraged psychologists to take account of multiculturalism and diversity in all of their professional activities. What does this mean? In essence, that psychologists should be aware of and sensitive to the fact that individuals' cultural, ethnic, and racial heritages often play a key role in their self-identity, and that this, in turn, can exert important effects on their behavior. This is in sharp contrast to the point of view that prevailed in the past, which suggested that cultural, ethnic, and gender differences are relatively unimportant. In contrast to that earlier and now discredited perspective, psychologists currently believe that such differences are *very* important and must be taken carefully into account in our efforts to understand human behavior. As a result, psychology now adopts a **multicultural perspective**—one that carefully and clearly recognizes the potential importance of gender, age, ethnicity, sexual orientation, disability, socioeconomic status, religious orientation, and many other social and cultural dimensions.

FIGURE 1.7
A Multicultural Perspective: A Guiding Theme of Modern Psychology
The United States and many other countries have become much more ethnically and culturally diverse in recent decades. As a result, psychologists build awareness of such diversity into everything they do—teaching, research, counseling, and therapy.

This perspective has led to major changes in the way psychologists teach, interact with clients, and conduct research (see Figure 1.7). For example, recent studies conducted by psychologists have focused on ethnic and cultural differences in everything from memory for faces of persons belonging to one's own race or another race (Meissner & Brigham, 2001), through cultural differences in binge drinking (Luczak, 2001) and ethnic differences in optimism and pessimism (Chang & Asakawa, 2003). In short, modern psychology has increasingly adopted a truly multicultural perspective, and this theme—and everything related to it—will be reflected throughout this book.

KEY QUESTIONS

- What is the definition of psychology as it exists today?
- What ideas in philosophy and several branches of science (biology, physiology, computer science, physics) have contributed to the form and scope of modern psychology?
- What are the three "grand issues" about behavior addressed by psychology?
- What are the major perspectives adopted by psychologists and how do they differ?
- What is evolutionary psychology and how does it contribute to our understanding of human behavior?
- What do the authors mean when they speak of the "exportation" of psychology?
- What is the multicultural perspective, and what role does it play in the activities of modern psychologists?

PSYCHOLOGY AND THE SCIENTIFIC METHOD

Remember the group of people we described earlier in this chapter as "doubters"—people who believe that psychology is nothing more than common sense? Here's where we respond in detail to their doubts. In essence, our answer is simple: Psychology is far more than common sense because the knowledge it provides rests firmly on the *scientific method*. Let's take a closer look at this method to see why it makes the knowledge gathered by psychologists much more valid and useful than common sense.

Multicultural Perspective
A perspective that clearly recognizes the potential importance of gender, age, ethnicity, sexual orientation, disability, socioeconomic status, religious orientation, and many other social and cultural dimensions.

The Scientific Method: Its Basic Nature

To many people, the term *science* conjures up images of people in white coats working around complex equipment in impressive laboratories. On the basis of such images, they then conclude that the word *science* applies only to fields such as chemistry, physics, or biology. Actually, this term simply refers to a special approach for acquiring knowledge—an approach involving the use of several key values or standards. Viewed in this light, the phrase *scientific method* means using these methods and adopting these values in efforts to study virtually any topic, including human behavior and human cognition. It is adoption of the scientific method that makes psychology a science—and that makes the information it acquires so valuable.

Because the actual procedures used by psychologists in applying the scientific method are described in a later section, we focus here on essential values and standards—the basic "rules of the game" by which all scientists, psychologists included, must play. Among the most important are these:

Accuracy: A commitment to gathering and evaluating information about the world in as careful, precise, and error-free a manner as possible.
Objectivity: A commitment to obtaining and evaluating such information in a manner as free from bias as humanly possible.
Skepticism: A commitment to accepting findings as accurate only after they have been verified over and over again, preferably by many different scientists.
Open-mindedness: A commitment to changing one's views—even views that are strongly held—in the face of evidence that these views are inaccurate.

Psychology, as a field, is deeply committed to these values. It is primarily for this reason that psychology can be described as a branch of science. In other words, because psychology accepts and follows the requirements of the scientific method, it can indeed be described as scientific in nature.

Advantages of the Scientific Method: Why Common Sense Often Leads Us Astray

Earlier we noted that knowledge gathered by means of the scientific method is superior in several ways to conclusions based on common sense. Here, we explain why this is so. Two factors are most important in this respect. First, knowledge about behavior based on common sense is often inconsistent and contradictory. Consider the following statement: "Absence makes the heart grow fonder." Do you agree? Is it true that when people are separated, they miss each other and so experience even stronger feelings of attraction? Perhaps, but what about this statement: "Out of sight, out of mind." It suggests exactly the opposite. Or how about this pair of statements: "Birds of a feather flock together" (people who are similar like each other) and "Opposites attract." We could continue, but by now you probably see the point: Common sense is often an unreliable guide to human behavior.

This is not the only reason we must be wary of common sense, however; another relates to the fact that unlike Mr. Spock of "Star Trek" fame, we are *not* perfect information-processing machines. On the contrary, echoing the "rationality versus irrationality" theme mentioned earlier, our thinking is subject to many forms of error that can lead us badly astray (e.g., Bernstein et al., 2004). While these errors often save us mental effort and are generally helpful to us, they suggest the need for caution in relying on intuition or common sense when trying to understand human behavior. What are these errors like? We'll examine them in detail in later chapters (e.g., 6, 7, 16), but let's take a brief look at some of the most important ones here.

▪ The Confirmation Bias: The Tendency to Verify Our Own Views

If you are like most people, you prefer to have your views confirmed rather than refuted. Consider what this means when we attempt to use informal observation as a source of knowledge about human behavior. Because we prefer to have our views confirmed, we tend to notice and remember mainly information that lends support to these views—information that confirms what we already believe. This tendency, known as the **confirmation bias,** is very strong (e.g., Johnson & Eagly, 1989), and when it operates, it places us in a kind of closed system where only evidence that confirms our existing beliefs is noticed, remembered, or accepted. Clearly, this is one tendency that can lead to error in our efforts to understand others and ourselves.

The Availability Heuristic: Emphasizing What Comes to Mind First or More Readily

Quick: Are there more words in English that start with the letter *k* (e.g., *king*) or more words in which *k* is the third letter (e.g., *awkward*)? If you answered, "More words that begin with *k*," you are like most people. Actually, though, this answer is wrong—more words have the letter *k* in the third position. What's responsible for this type of error? A mental shortcut known as the **availability heuristic.** This shortcut, which is designed to save us mental effort, suggests that the easier it is to bring something to mind, or the more information we can think of about it, the greater its impact on subsequent decisions or judgments. In general, this tendency makes sense—when we can bring information about something to mind easily, it often *is* important. But the availability heuristic can also lead us into error.

FIGURE 1.8
Sunk Costs in Action
Often, once we have made a decision, we have a strong tendency to stick with it, even if it is producing negative outcomes. This is known as *sunk costs* (or *escalation of commitment*) and may be one reason why many persons stay in relationships that are obviously very bad for them.

Why? Because sometimes what we can bring to mind most readily isn't especially important; it's just highly memorable because it is dramatic or unusual (e.g., Rothman & Hardin, 1997). For instance, because airplane crashes are more dramatic and easier to remember than automobile accidents, many people believe that the chances of being killed in a plane are higher than those of being killed while driving—a conclusion that is totally false. Judgments based on common sense or intuition are often strongly influenced by the availability heuristic, so they are often untrustworthy for this reason.

Getting Trapped in Bad Decisions: The Dangers of "Sunk Costs"

When one of us (Robert Baron) was a young assistant professor, he owned a car that almost drove him to financial ruin. It was a powder-blue Toyota, and although Toyotas are famous for being reliable, this one was nothing but trouble. First it was engine problems; then the brakes; next the clutch. Finally, to add insult to injury, it began to rust—to the point that the doors had more metal patch than metal in them! When the problems first started, it made sense to repair them. After a while, though, it became clear that this car was a true lemon. The rational thing to do was simple: Get rid of it. But Prof. Baron didn't do that; instead, he continued to pour more and more money into the car. Why? Partly because of a cognitive "trap" known as *sunk costs.* This refers to the fact that once we make a decision, we find it very hard to reverse it, even if it becomes increasingly clear that it was a bad one. The same mental trap occurs when people buy a stock and then fail to sell it as it continues to go down in value, or when they stay in terrible relationships that cause them nothing but increasing pain (see Figure 1.8). Why do we get trapped in this way? Partly because it is so hard to admit we made a mistake, and partly because we hope to make up for our past losses (the stock *will* go up; the car *will* become more reliable; the relationships *will* get better; see Figure 1.8). The result? We throw good money, effort, or love after bad, right to the bitter end. Rational? Hardly!

Confirmation Bias
The tendency to notice and remember primarily information that lends support to our views.

Availability Heuristic
A mental shortcut suggesting that the easier it is to bring something to mind, the more frequent or important it is.

We could continue, because there are many other aspects of our thinking that can lead us astray. The main point, though, is clear: Because our thinking is subject to such potential sources of bias, we really can't rely on informal observation or common sense as a basis for drawing valid conclusions about human behavior. We are on much firmer ground if we employ the scientific method, which is specifically designed to reduce such potential sources of error. By adopting the scientific method, therefore, psychologists vastly increase the probability that their efforts to attain valid information about human behavior will succeed. It is this commitment to the scientific method, more than anything else, that sets psychology apart from other efforts to understand human behavior, and makes its findings so valuable from the perspective of enhancing human welfare.

KEY QUESTIONS

- Why can psychology be viewed as a branch of science?
- What values are central to the scientific method?
- Why is common sense such an uncertain guide to human behavior?
- What are confirmation bias, the availability heuristic, and sunk costs, and what roles do they play in our efforts to understand human behavior?

The Scientific Method in Everyday Life: The Benefits of Critical Thinking

Recently, I (Robert Baron) encountered the following headline in my local newspaper: **Men Listen With Half a Brain.** The article accompanying it went on to suggest that when listening to others, men mostly use the left side of their brains—the side specialized for understanding language (we discuss this topic in detail in Chapter 2), while women listen with both the left and the right sides (the right side is often viewed as better for understanding emotions). The conclusion? Women who believe that men never listen to them are at least partly right! The study was based on brain scans from ten men and ten women, taken while they wore headphones and listened to taped excerpts from a best-selling book.

What do you think? Are these gender differences real? And if so, do they really help explain why women often become exasperated with men for not listening to them? Situations like this, in which we are asked to evaluate information about human behavior—or any other topic, for that matter—call for a kind of thinking that is based, to a large extent, on the scientific method: **critical thinking.** Such thinking closely examines all claims and assumptions, carefully evaluates existing evidence, and cautiously assesses all conclusions. In short, critical thinking mirrors the key values of the scientific method and represents efforts to apply these values in everyday life. In actual practice, critical thinking involves the following guidelines:

Never jump to conclusions; gather as much information as you can before making up your mind about any issue.

Keep an open mind; don't let your existing views blind you to new information or conclusions.

Always ask "How?" as in "How was the evidence obtained?"

Be skeptical; always wonder about *why* someone is making an argument, offering a conclusion, or trying to persuade you.

Never be stampeded into accepting some view because others accept it.

Be aware of the fact that your own emotions can strongly influence your thinking, and try to hold such effects to a minimum.

Applying these guidelines to the article described above, you might ask such questions as these: "Do we have enough evidence to reach firm conclusions? Ten

Critical Thinking
Thinking that avoids blindly accepting conclusions or arguments and, instead, closely examines all assumptions, evidence, and conclusions.

people of each gender is not very many." "Could it be that the women found the book more interesting than the men, and *that's* why they they listened with both sides of their brain?" "In fact, what information was presented in the excerpts the men and women heard? If the information was more interesting to women, no wonder they listened more carefully!"

In short, critical thinking involves considering issues, ideas, or claims in the way that scientists—including psychologists—do. Now, can you remember our earlier claim that you would learn much more than a mere collection of interesting facts from your first exposure to psychology? At this point, we can be more specific: The "extra" we had in mind was practice in *critical thinking*. Throughout this text, you'll see how psychologists think carefully and systematically about complex aspects of human behavior. As a result, we believe you will sharpen your ability to think critically—carefully, cautiously, and systematically—about human behavior, your own and that of others. The habit of thinking in this way will be one of the key benefits you'll take away with you from this book and your first course in psychology.

KEY QUESTIONS

- What is critical thinking?
- What role does it play in psychology?
- How can you use it in everyday life?

RESEARCH METHODS IN PSYCHOLOGY: HOW PSYCHOLOGISTS ANSWER QUESTIONS ABOUT BEHAVIOR

Now that we've explained what modern psychology is and described the scientific method and its relation to critical thinking, it's time to turn to another key issue: How do psychologists actually perform the task of adding to our knowledge about human behavior? Primarily, you'll soon see, through the use of three basic procedures:

1. Observation
2. Correlation
3. Experimentation

Observation: Describing the World around Us

One basic technique for studying behavior, or any other aspects of the world around us, involves carefully observing it as it occurs. Such observation is not the kind of informal activity that all of us practice from childhood on. Rather, in science, it is **systematic observation** accompanied by *careful, accurate measurement.* One way in which psychologists use systematic observation is in *case studies*—an approach in which one or perhaps a few persons are studied carefully, often over long periods of time. Several famous psychologists have used this method. For instance, Sigmund Freud, one of the most famous psychologists of all time (although, in fact, he was trained as a medical doctor), used a small number of cases as the basis for his famous theories of personality and mental illness. (We discuss these in Chapter 12.)

Is the **case method** really useful? In the hands of talented researchers, it does seem potentially useful. Moreover, when the behavior involved is unusual, the case method can sometimes be quite revealing, as we'll see in our discussion of mental disorders in Chapter 12. However, this method suffers from several important drawbacks. First, because all human beings are unique, it is difficult to draw conclusions that can be generalized to all other persons. Second, because researchers using

Systematic Observation
A basic method of science in which the natural world, or various events or processes in it, are observed and measured in a very careful manner.

Case Method
A method of research in which detailed information about individuals is used to develop general principles about behavior.

FIGURE 1.9
**The Survey Method
in Action**
The survey method can be used
to measure people's views on
almost any topic—from politics
to the use of cell phones.

the case method often have repeated contact with the persons they study, there is the real risk that they will become emotionally involved with these persons and so lose their scientific objectivity, at least to a degree. Because of such drawbacks, the case method is not widely used by psychologists today, although it *is* widely used in several fields, such as management, which studies individual companies instead of individual persons.

Another form of systematic observation—and one that is used much more frequently by modern psychologists—is the **survey method.** Instead of focusing in detail on a small number of persons, researchers using this method obtain a very limited sample of behavior from large numbers of individuals, usually through their responses to questionnaires (surveys). Surveys are used for many purposes: to measure attitudes toward specific issues, voting preferences, and consumer reactions to new products, to mention just a few. Surveys can also be repeated over long periods of time to track changes in public opinion or other aspects of behavior. For instance, surveys of *job satisfaction*—individuals; attitudes toward their jobs—have continued for more than forty years. Similarly, changing patterns of sexual behavior have been tracked by the Kinsey Institute since the 1940s.

The survey method offers several advantages. Information can be gathered quickly and efficiently from many thousands of persons. In fact, surveys using the Internet have recently gathered data from hundreds of thousands of respondents (Gosling et al., 2004). Further, because surveys can be constructed quickly, public opinion on new issues can be obtained almost as soon as they arise. For instance, suppose you wanted to find out how people feel about the use of cell phones in public places such as restaurants and theaters. Information on this topic could be gathered quickly—and accurately—by means of the survey method (see Figure 1.9). To be useful as a research tool, however, surveys must meet certain requirements. First, if the goal is to predict some event (e.g., the outcome of an election), great care must be devoted to the issue of **sampling**—how the persons who will participate in the survey are selected. Unless these persons are representative of the larger population about which predictions will be made, serious errors can result.

Another issue deserving careful attention is the way in which the surveys are worded. Even changing a single word in a question can sometimes shift the meaning and strongly influence the results. For example, recently, the governor of the state where we live reduced the number of state employees in the capital by 450. How did people react to these reductions? In one poll they were asked to indicate how they felt about the governor's "slashing" of the workforce, while in another, they were asked to indicate how they felt about the governor's "pruning" of the workforce. You can guess the results: The poll that used the word *slashing* indicated that the public was strongly against this action, while the one that used the word *pruning* produced the opposite result.

In sum, the survey method can be a useful approach for studying some aspects of human behavior, but the results obtained are accurate only to the extent that issues relating to sampling and wording are carefully addressed.

Survey Method
A research method in which large numbers of people answer questions about aspects of their views or their behavior.

Sampling
With respect to the survey method, sampling refers to the methods used to select persons who respond to the survey.

Correlation: The Search for Relationships

At various times, you have probably noticed that some events appear to be related to each other: As one changes, the other appears to change, too. For instance, you have probably observed that as people grow older, they often seem to gain weight; that when interest rates drop, the stock market rises; and that the older people are, the more conservative they tend to be in their political views. When such relationships between events exist, they are said to be *correlated* with each other (or that a *correlation* between them exists). This means that as one changes, the other tends to change, too. Psychologists and other scientists refer to aspects of the natural world that can take different values as *variables,* so from now on, that's the term we'll use here.

From the point of view of science, the existence of a correlation between two variables can be very useful. This is because when a correlation exists, it is possible to predict one variable from information about one or more other variables. The ability to make such *predictions* is one important goal of science, and psychologists often attempt to make predictions about human behavior. To the extent predictions can be made accurately, important benefits follow. For instance, consider how useful it would be if we could predict from current information such future outcomes as a person's success in school or in various occupations, effectiveness as a parent, length of life, or likelihood of developing a serious mental disorder.

The occurrence of correlations between variables allows us to make such predictions. In fact, the stronger such correlations are, the more accurate the predictions that can be made. These facts constitute the basis for an important method of research—the **correlational method.** In this approach, psychologists or other scientists attempt to determine whether and to what extent variables are related to each other. This involves making careful observations of each variable and then performing statistical analyses to determine whether and to what extent the variables are correlated—to what extent changes in one are related to changes in the other. Correlations range from –1.00 to +1.00, and the more they depart from zero, the stronger the correlation. For instance, a correlation of –.82 is stronger than one of +.23. Positive correlations indicate that as one variable increases, the other increases, too. For instance, the greater the number of hours students study for their psychology tests, the higher their grades tend to be. Negative correlations indicate that as one variable increases, the other decreases. For example, the less satisfied people are with their jobs, the more likely they are to search for other jobs and to leave their current ones. In other words, as job satisfaction decreases, quitting increases. Now, let's examine a concrete example of how psychologists actually use the correlational method.

◼ The Correlational Method of Research: An Example

Suppose that a psychologist wanted to determine whether breathing pure oxygen for brief periods of time causes the persons who do so to feel more alert and happier, and helps them to perform better on many tasks. (Claims for such effects have recently been featured in the popular press; see Figure 1.10 on page 18.) How could research on this topic be conducted by the correlational method?

Many possibilities exist, but one approach would involve a means of measuring both variables: the amount of pure oxygen breathed by people and their subsequent performance on various tasks. Oxygen use could be measured in terms of the amount of oxygen people consume during their visits to "oxygen bars" (where breaths of oxygen are available in measured amounts). Performance on various tasks could be assessed by asking the participants to perform them right after they finish receiving their dose of oxygen. These two sets of numbers would then be analyzed by statistical procedures (statistics are a form of mathematics) to determine whether they are correlated. If a positive correlation were obtained, this would offer support for the hypothesis and suggest that breathing pure oxygen does enhance task performance.

So far, so good. But watch out, for we are approaching a real danger zone—one in which many people seem to forget about the principles of critical thinking described earlier. On the basis of the finding that as the amount of pure oxygen

Correlational Method (of research)
A research method in which researchers attempt to determine whether and to what extent different variables are related to each other.

FIGURE 1.10
**Breathing Pure Oxygen:
A Boost to Mood—and Task
Performance?**
Recently, a large number of "oxygen bars," where people can breathe pure oxygen from special tanks, have opened. Customers claim that the oxygen makes them feel more alert and energetic, and that it boosts their work performance. Only careful research using appropriate methods can provide scientific evidence about the accuracy of such beliefs.

breathed increases, performance, too, rises, many people would jump to the following conclusion: Breathing pure oxygen *causes* improvements in performance. This seems to make sense; after all, the greater people's use of oxygen, the higher they rate their job performance. But, in fact, such conclusions would *not* be justified, because correlational research does not, by itself, provide strong or direct evidence about cause-and-effect relationships. Indeed, this is one of the major drawbacks of such research. In this case, we have found that as oxygen use increases, performance rises, but *we do not know whether these effects result from breathing pure oxygen or from some other variable that is related to both breathing oxygen and task performance.*

For instance, it is quite possible that breathing oxygen gives people a break from the stress of their daily lives, and it is this—not the oxygen itself—that improves their performance. Similarly, it could be the case that the more often people visit oxygen bars, or the more oxygen they choose to inhale, the stronger are their beliefs that oxygen is beneficial. And it could be these beliefs, not oxygen itself, that is the cause of any improvements in performance. In other words, people who breathe oxygen show improved performance because they expect this to happen, and so perhaps work harder at the tasks. In short, although the correlational method of research can be very valuable—and is sometimes, for reasons we'll soon describe, the only method psychologists can use to study a specific topic or question—it cannot establish cause-and-effect relationships. This research would tell us only that breathing oxygen is positively related to performing better on various tasks; it would *not* necessarily indicate that it is the oxygen that produces these effects. For this reason, psychologists often use another research method, to which we'll now turn.

KEY QUESTIONS

- What is naturalistic observation?
- What is the correlational method of research and how do psychologists use it?
- Why are even strong correlations between variables *not* evidence that changes in one cause changes in the other?

The Experimental Method: Knowledge through Systematic Intervention

**Experimentation
(the experimental
method of research)**
A research method in which researchers systematically alter one or more variables in order to determine whether such changes influence some aspect of behavior.

The method we just discussed is known as **experimentation** or the **experimental method,** and it involves a strategy centering around intervention—making changes in the natural world to see what effects, if any, these changes produce. Specifically, the scientist systematically changes one variable, and the effects of these changes on one or more other variables are carefully measured. If changes in one variable produce changes in one or more other variables (and if additional conditions we'll consider later are also met), it is then possible to conclude with reasonable certainty that there is indeed a causal relationship between these variables—that changes in one variable do indeed *cause* changes in the other. Because the experimental method is so valuable in answering this kind of question, it is frequently the method of choice in psychology, just as it is in many other fields. But bear in mind that there is no single "best" method of research; rather, psychologists choose the method that is most appropriate for studying a given topic and one that is consistent with practical and ethical constraints we'll soon consider.

Experimentation: Its Basic Nature

In its most basic form, the experimental method in psychology involves two key steps: (1) The presence or strength of some variable believed to affect behavior is systematically altered, and (2) the effects of such alterations (if any) are carefully measured. The logic behind these steps is this: If the variable that is systematically changed actually influences some aspect of behavior, then individuals exposed to different levels or amounts of it should differ in their behavior. For instance, exposure to a low amount of the variable should result in one level of behavior, while exposure to a higher amount should result in a different level, and so on.

The factor systematically varied by the researcher is termed the **independent variable,** while the aspect of behavior is termed the **dependent variable.** In a simple experiment, then, different groups of participants are exposed to contrasting levels of the independent variable (such as low, moderate, high). The researcher then carefully measures their behavior to determine whether it does in fact differ depending on the level of the independent variable to which research participants are exposed.

To illustrate the basic nature of experimentation in psychological research, let's return to the possible effects of oxygen on task performance. One way in which a psychologist could study this topic through the experimental method is as follows. First, the psychologist would recruit persons who want to improve their job performance. These persons would make appointments to come to the psychologists' office or laboratory, and once there, they would be treated in one of two contrasting ways. One group (those in the experimental condition) would breathe a carefully controlled amount of real oxygen, while the other group (those in the *control* condition) would breathe normal air. Breathing of oxygen and air would be done through an identical apparatus, so participants could not tell what they have actually breathed. Following this, participants in both groups would perform one or more tasks. The psychologist would then compare the performance on these tasks shown by the two groups. If the group that breathed the pure oxygen did better, this would provide evidence that oxygen does indeed enhance task performance; if the two groups showed the same level of performance, this would suggest that breathing pure oxygen does not enhance performance.

Experimentation: Two Requirements for Its Success

Earlier, we noted that in order to provide clear information on cause-and-effect relationships, experiments must meet two basic requirements. The first of these involves what is termed **random assignment of participants to experimental conditions.** This means that all participants in an experiment must have an equal chance of being exposed to each level of the independent variable. The reason for this rule is simple: If participants are *not* randomly assigned to each condition, it may later be impossible to tell whether differences in their behavior stem from differences they brought with them to the study, from the impact of the independent variable, or both. Imagine that in the study on oxygen, all the persons who receive pure oxygen are strong believers in its benefits, while all those who breathe air are skeptical of such effects. Now, assume that those receiving the oxygen show higher performance. Is this due to the effects of the oxygen, their belief in its benefits, or both factors? We can't tell. If, in contrast, the believers and the skeptics had been randomly assigned to each condition, a difference between the conditions would be revealing: It would suggest that oxygen really does have some real, measurable effects.

The second condition essential for successful experimentation is this: To as great a degree as possible, all factors *other* than the independent variable that might also affect participants' behavior must be held constant. To see why this is so,

Independent Variable
The variable that is systematically changed in an experiment.

Dependent Variable
The variable that is measured in an experiment.

Random Assignment of Participants to Experimental Conditions
Assuring that all research participants have an equal chance of being exposed to each level of the independent variable (i.e., of being assigned to each experimental condition).

consider what would happen in the study on oxygen if those who breathe pure oxygen are treated in a kind and encouraging manner by the experimenter, while those who breathe air are treated in an unfriendly and discouraging fashion. Again, those who breathe real oxygen show higher performance. Why? Again, we can't tell, because the independent variable (exposure to oxygen or normal air) is *confounded* with another variable: the way in which the experimenter treats the participants. Kind, friendly treatment might well enhance performance, while rude, harsh treatment might reduce it. The conclusion should be clear: To the extent variables other than the independent variable are permitted to change in an experiment, the value of the study may be greatly reduced or even totally eliminated (see Figure 1.11).

When these two conditions are met, however, experimentation is highly effective and is, in fact, the crown jewel among psychology's research methods. Why, then, isn't it the only method used by psychologists? One reason is that the other methods offer several important advantages—for example, the vast amount of information that can be collected quickly through the survey method, and the high generalizability provided by naturalistic observation. Another is that, in many cases, practical and ethical constraints prevent psychologists from using experimentation. For instance, suppose that 5 percent of all people asked to breathe pure oxygen for more than a few minutes suffer harmful health effects. Could the psychologist conduct the experiment? No, because it would be on *very* shaky ethical grounds: There would be a risk of doing real harm to some participants. In short, although experimentation is a powerful tool and one often preferred by psychologists, it cannot be used to investigate all questions about behavior. Please see

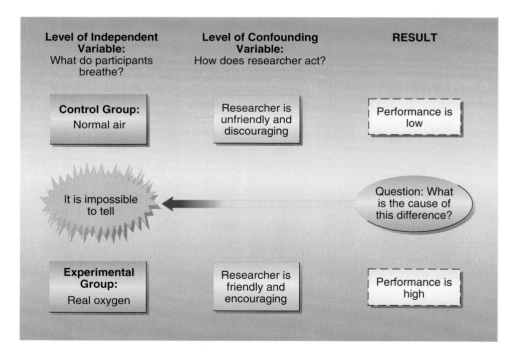

FIGURE 1.11
Confounding of Variables: A Fatal Flaw in Experimentation
In the experiment illustrated here, breathing oxygen—the independent variable—is confounded with another variable—contrasting treatment by the researcher. This person is friendly and encouraging to those who breathe oxygen but unfriendly and discouraging to those who breathe normal air. As a result of this confounding, it is impossible to tell whether any differences between the behavior of participants in these two conditions stem from the independent variable, the confounding variable, or both.

TABLE 1.3 Various Research Methods: Advantages and Disadvantages

As shown here, psychologists use several different research methods. Each offers a mixture of advantages and disadvantages.

Method	Description	Advantages	Disadvantages
Systematic observation	Systematic study of behavior in natural settings	Behavior is observed in the settings where it normally occurs	Cannot be used to establish cause-and-effect relationships; often costly and difficult to perform
Case method	Detailed study of a small number of persons	Detailed information is gathered; individuals can be studied for long periods of time	Generalizability of results is uncertain; objectivity of researcher may be compromised
Surveys	Large numbers of persons are asked questions about their attitudes or views	Large amount of information can be acquired quickly; accurate predictions of large-scale trends can sometimes be made	Generalizability may be questionable unless persons surveyed are a representative sample of a larger population
Correlational research	Researchers measure two or more variables to determine if they are related in any way	Large amount of information can be gathered quickly; can be used in field as well as laboratory settings	Difficult to establish cause-and-effect relationships
Experimentation	The presence or strength of one or more variables is varied	Cause-and-effect relationships can be established; precise control can be exerted over other, potentially confounding variables	Results can be subject to several sources of bias (e.g., experimenter effects); generalizability can be doubtful if behavior is observed under highly artificial conditions

Table 1.3 for an overview of the advantages and disadvantages of all the research methods described in this section.

KEY POINTS

- What is the basic nature of experimentation?
- Why is random assignment of participants to conditions required in experiments?
- What is confounding of variables in an experiment?

PSYCHOLOGY: WHAT'S IN IT FOR YOU?

Why are you taking this course? When we ask our own students this question, they give us many different answers, including some that are quite routine: "It's required," or "I thought it might be interesting." But others provide answers suggesting that they expect a lot from their first exposure to psychology. Some talk about gaining *self-insight:* "I want to understand myself better, and I think psychology can help." Others add that this enhanced insight, in turn, will make them happier, better-adjusted persons. Another group of students mentions what we term *enhanced life skills*—an improved ability to get along with other people (family, friends, romantic partners) and to deal with a wide range of everyday life situations (everything from raising children to resisting sales pressure). And a third group talks about their *careers:* They believe that psychology can help them attain success.

Are these reasonable goals? Will your first course in psychology, and this book, help you to gain self-insight and acquire useful life and career-related skills? We believe—passionately!—that it will. Psychology, in an important sense, has a

"Mind if I put on the game?"

FIGURE 1.12
Enhanced Life and Career Skills: A Potential Benefit of Exposure to Psychology
Will the man shown here have a good relationship with his new wife? It seems unlikely. He seems to be severely lacking in basic social skills—and in insight into the effects of his own behavior. Perhaps he, unlike you, never took any psychology courses!
Source: © The New Yorker Collection 1986 Robert Mankoff from cartoonbank.com. All Rights Reserved.

dual nature: It is scientific in nature and obtains its knowledge and findings through the scientific method. At the same time, though, it is strongly oriented toward application. As a result, it offers knowledge, principles, and information you can put to practical use in your own life *once you know and understand them.* And that is a major theme of this text: (1) We want to help you to understand the key findings and principles of modern psychology, so we will work hard to present these in as accurate, understandable, and up-to-date a manner as we can; and (2) we want to help you *apply* this knowledge to your own lives—to acquire enhanced self-insight and specific, beneficial life and career skills (see Figure 1.12).

In every chapter and every discussion, therefore, we will first summarize the key findings and principles obtained through systematic research and then explain what these findings mean to you and how, potentially, you can use them. Most texts do this to some extent, but we plan to carry such efforts further by emphasizing the fact that *every* branch of psychology and virtually every line of research can contribute to the quality and richness of your life. Here are a few examples of what we mean—ways in which psychology can help answer practical questions relating to your own life.

Learning (Chapter 4): How can you enhance your self-control (e.g., your ability to hold your temper in check)?

Memory (Chapter 6): What are the best techniques for improving your memory?

Human Development (Chapter 8): What steps can you take to make sure that you age slowly—and gracefully?

Motivation and Emotion (Chapter 9): How can you avoid the "obesity epidemic" and control your own weight? How you can use self-set goals to enhance your motivation—and performance?

Personality (Chapter 10): How can you tell whether you are suited for the job or career you want?

Social Psychology (Chapter 13): What are the best means for persuading others or exerting influence over them? What are the most effective ways of handling conflict at work and at home?

Industrial/Organizational Psychology (Chapter 14): If you have to give other persons negative feedback on their work, what is the best way to do it?

In short, after reading this text, we hope that you will not only have acquired a broad acquaintance with the major findings and principles of psychology, but also have begun the task of using this knowledge in your own life. In this sense, we agree strongly with the poet Kahlil Gibran (1960), who once said, "A little knowledge that acts is worth infinitely more than much knowledge that is idle."

KEY QUESTIONS

- What three things can you gain from psychology?
- Can you gain these from only some branches of psychology or from all of them?

USING THIS BOOK: AN OVERVIEW OF ITS SPECIAL FEATURES

Although it is many years since we were students, we both remember the following fact very well: Not all textbooks are equally useful or equally easy to read. For this reason, we have taken many steps to make this book one of the good ones—a book you will find convenient and easy to use, and one that is, we hope, interesting to read. Here is an overview of the steps we have taken to reach this goal.

Each chapter begins with an **outline** and ends with a **summary.** Within the text itself, key terms are printed in **dark type like this** and are defined. These terms are also defined in a running marginal glossary and in a glossary at the end of the book. In addition, throughout each chapter, we call your attention to important points in special **Key Questions** sections. If you can answer these questions, that's a good sign that you understand the central points in each section. (They are answered for you at the end of the chapter.) As you'll soon notice, all figures are clear and simple, and most contain special labels and notes designed to help you understand them.

Two special sections focus on our key theme of helping you to both understand the key findings of psychology and use them in your own lives. These sections are headed **Psychology Lends a Hand** and **Psychology Goes to Work,** and both occur at the end of major sections of the text. The first type (see p. 24 for an example) focuses on explaining how you can use the findings of psychology to deal with a wide range of important life situations (e.g., using basic principles of learning to train your pet; how to tell when another person is lying or being truthful). The second type (Psychology Goes to Work) focuses on applying the findings of psychology to work settings and to your career (e.g., how to interview effectively; coping with the problems of dual careers). Together, these sections will get you started on the road toward that new perspective we mentioned at the start of this chapter— the perspective of modern psychology.

Finally, each chapter is followed by two brief exercises; one is designed to give you practice in understanding key points and information in the chapter (**Psychology: Understanding Its Findings**), while the other (**Making Psychology Part of Your Life**) is designed to give you practice in applying this information to your life and your career.

We hope that, together, these features will help to make reading this book a stimulating and enjoyable experience. In any case, we are confident about one thing: In the pages that follow, you will discover something we first learned several decades in the past: Psychology is indeed fascinating, enjoyable, and . . . useful!

p s y c h o l o g y   l e n d s   a   h a n d

How to Study Psychology—or Any Other Subject—Effectively

Among the topics that psychologists know most about are learning, memory, and motivation. (We examine these in Chapters 5, 6, and 9.) Fortunately, all of these topics are directly relevant to one activity you must perform as a student: studying. You must be motivated to study, must learn new materials, and must remember them accurately after they have been mastered. Knowledge gained by psychologists can be very useful to you in accomplishing these tasks. Drawing on what psychology knows, here are some useful tips to help you get the most out of the time you spend studying.

- **Begin with an overview.** Research on memory indicates that it is easier to retain information if it can be placed within a cognitive framework. So when you begin to study, try to see "the big picture." Examine the outline at the start of each chapter and thumb through the pages once or twice. That way, you'll know what to expect and will form an initial framework for organizing the information that follows.

- **Eliminate (or at least minimize) distractions.** To enter information into your memory accurately, you must devote careful attention to it. This means that you should reduce all distractions; try to study in a quiet place, turn off the television or radio, put those magazines out of sight, and unhook your phone. The result? You will learn more in less time. *Don't do all your studying at once.* All-nighters are very inefficient. Research findings indicate that it is easier to learn and remember new information when learning is spaced out over time rather than when it is crammed into a single long session. So, try to spread your study sessions out; in the final analysis, this will give you a much greater return for your effort (see Figure 1.13).

- **Set specific, challenging, but attainable goals.** One of the key findings of industrial/organizational psychology is that setting certain kinds of goals can increase both motivation and performance on many different tasks. This principle can be of great help to you in studying, and it's relatively easy to apply. First, set a concrete goal for each session—for example, "I'll read twenty pages and review my class notes." Merely telling yourself, "I'll work until I'm tired," is less effective because it fails to give you something concrete to shoot for. Second, try to set challenging goals, but ones you can attain. Challenging goals will encourage you to "stretch"—to do a little bit more. But impossible ones are simply discouraging. Because you are the world's greatest expert on your own limits and your own work habits, you are the best judge of what would be a challenging but attainable goal for *you.* Set such goals when you begin, and the results may surprise you.

- **Reward yourself for progress.** As you'll see in Chapter 5, people often perform various activities to attain external rewards, ones delivered to them by others. But in many cases, we can provide our own rewards. We can pat ourselves on the back for reaching goals we've set or for other accomplishments; this "pat on the back" can take many different forms: eating a favorite dessert, watching a favorite TV program, or visiting

FIGURE 1.13
All-Nighters: Not the Best Strategy for Studying
Psychological research indicates that we learn more efficiently—and remember more of what we learn—when we spread our work sessions out over time. For this reason, as well as several others, all-nighters are the not the best or most efficient way to study.

friends. Again, you are the world's greatest expert on what you enjoy, so you can readily choose rewards that are appropriate. Whatever you choose, though, be sure to reward yourself for reaching your goals.

- **Engage in active, not passive studying.** As you probably know, it is possible to sit in front of a book or a set of notes for hours without accomplishing much—except daydreaming! In order to learn new information and retain it, you must do mental work—that's an inescapable fact of life. You must think about the material you are reading, ask yourself questions about it, relate this new information to things you already know, and so on. The **Key Questions** sections in each chapter are designed to help you do this, but in the final analysis, it's up to you. To the extent you really try to answer these questions and engage in other forms of active learning, you will absorb more information, and more efficiently.

We know: Following these guidelines sounds like a lot of . . . work! But once you master them, the whole process will get easier. You will learn and remember more, get better grades, and improve the value of your own education—and do it more efficiently than ever before. So, in this case, a little extra effort is well justified.

SUMMARY AND REVIEW OF KEY QUESTIONS

The Field of Psychology: What It Is and How It Originated

- **What is the definition of psychology as it exists today?**
  Psychology is the science of behavior and cognitive processes.

- **What ideas in philosophy and several branches of science (biology, physiology, computer science, physics) have contributed to the form and scope of modern psychology?**
  Philosophy supplied the idea that virtually any aspect of the natural world can be studied by the methods of science. Biology and physiology provided new insights into the function of the nervous system and brain. Computer science provided means for studying cognitive processes, and physics offered equipment for scanning the human brain as it performs many complex functions.

Psychology: Grand Issues, Key Perspectives

- **What are the three "grand issues" about behavior addressed by psychology?**
  The three issues are stability versus change, nature versus nurture, and rationality versus irrationality.

- **What are the major perspectives adopted by psychologists and how do they differ?**
  Major perspectives in psychology include the behavioral, cognitive, biological, psychodynamic, social, and evolutionary approaches. These perspectives focus on different aspects of behavior but are complementary rather than competitive in nature.

Psychology in the Twenty-first Century: Expanding Horizons

- **What is evolutionary psychology and how does it contribute to our understanding of human behavior?**
  This is a new branch of psychology that suggests that human beings have been subject to the process of biological evolution and, as a result, possess many *evolved psychological mechanisms* that influence our behavior.

- **What do the authors mean when they speak of "the exportation" of psychology?**
  They are referring to a growing tendency for other fields to use the findings and principles of psychology to solve a wide range of practical problems.

- **What is the multicultural perspective, and what role does it play in the activities of modern psychologists?**
  This refers to increased sensitivity to and recognition of the importance of cultural, ethnic, racial, and other differences. Psychologists now include this perspective in all their activities—teaching, research, and counseling or therapy.

Psychology and the Scientific Method

- **Why can psychology be viewed as a branch of science?**
  Psychology can be viewed as a branch of science because psychologists adopt the scientific method in their efforts to study human behavior.

- **What values are central to the scientific method?**
  Values central to the scientific method include accuracy, objectivity, skepticism, and open-mindedness.

- **Why is common sense such an uncertain guide to human behavior?**
  Common sense often suggests inconsistent and contradictory conclusions about behavior, and it is influenced by several important forms of bias.

- **What are confirmation bias, the availability heuristic, and sunk costs, and what roles do they play in our efforts to understand human behavior?**
  These are cognitive errors we make in thinking about the world around us. They often lead us to false conclusions about human behavior.

- **What is critical thinking?**
  Such thinking closely examines all claims and assumptions, carefully evaluates existing evidence, and cautiously assesses all conclusions.

- **What role does it play in psychology?**
  Critical thinking is a basic aspect of the scientific method and is an integral part of efforts by psychologists to understand behavior.

- **How can you use it in everyday life?**
  You can use critical thinking to assess claims about human behavior made in newspaper and magazine articles, on television shows, and in many other contexts.

Research Methods in Psychology: How Psychologists Answer Questions about Behavior

- **What is naturalistic observation?**
  This involves carefully observing behavior in the settings where it normally occurs.

- **What is the correlational method of research and how do psychologists use it?**
  This is a basic method of research in which two or more variables are carefully observed to see if changes in one are related to changes in the other. Psychologists use it to make predictions about one variable from observations of another variable.

- **Why are even strong correlations between variables *not* evidence that changes in one cause changes in the other?**
  Even strong correlations don't necessarily indicate causality, because changes in both variables may stem from the influence of some other variable.

- **What is the basic nature of experimentation?**
  In experimentation, researchers produce systematic changes in one variable (the independent variable) to observe whether these changes affect another variable (the dependent variable).

- **Why is random assignment of participants to conditions required in experiments?**
  Because if participants are *not* randomly assigned to each condition, it may later be impossible to tell whether

differences in their behavior stem from differences they brought with them to the study, from the impact of the independent variable, or from both.

- **What is confounding of variables in an experiment?** Confounding occurs when one or more variables other than the independent variable are permitted to vary during an experiment.

Psychology: What's In It for You?

- **What three things can you gain from psychology?** You can acquire enhanced self-insight and skills useful in many life situations in your career.

- **Can you gain these only from some branches of psychology or from all of them?** All branches of psychology offer knowledge that is useful.

PSYCHOLOGY: UNDERSTANDING ITS FINDINGS

Designing an Experiment

Earlier in this chapter we noted that experimentation is the research method preferred by psychologists—when it can be used. As a result, much of the information presented in this book is based on this method. Try the following exercise to gain some first-hand experience with the joys—and challenges!—of designing an experiment. Here's the hypothesis: *One effective way to get people to say "yes" to a request is to flatter them first, then make the request.* Now, design an experiment to test this hypothesis. To do this, follow these steps:

1. Define the independent and dependent variables and indicate how you will measure them.

2. Decide how you will change the independent variable systematically in order to determine whether it produces effects on the dependent variable.
3. Describe the various conditions of your study (e.g., no flattery, a small amount of flattery, a lot of flattery).
4. Who will be the participants? Why will they participate? How long will the study take?

Suppose the results offered support for your hypothesis: What would this mean? Could the information be put to practical use?

MAKING PSYCHOLOGY PART OF YOUR LIFE

Interpreting the Results of Surveys: "To Believe or Not to Believe," That Is the Question

Surveys are reported frequently in newspapers, on the evening news, and in magazines. Should you accept their results as accurate? This is a complex question but one you should consider carefully in the light of information presented in this chapter. Here's an example of what we mean:

Suppose that one day you came across an article in a newspaper describing the results of a recent survey. The survey indicated that among married or co-habiting couples, the more often the man in the couple said "Yes, dear" to the woman (i.e., agreed with her or gave the woman her way), the happier the couples were. How would you go about interpreting these results—deciding whether to believe them or not?

In other words, now that you know something about the "basics" of psychological research, what questions would you ask yourself about these results? (Hint: One might be, "Who were the participants?" Another might be, "Are they a representative sample of all couples?")

Make a list of the questions you would ask and then try to decide which are crucial to your accepting the results of the study as valid. This is precisely the kind of procedure you should use *whenever* you learn about the findings of a survey. Merely accepting them as accurate because they appear in a newspaper or magazine can be misleading—and dangerous. As we note in this chapter, only to the extent surveys meet specific requirements can the results be viewed as accurate and informative.

KEY TERMS

2

Biological Bases of Behavior

*C*onsider, for a moment, the many experiences you have during a single day. When you wake up, you may feel tired and down, but after you have a cup of coffee, you feel much more alert. On the way to work or school, you think about an important deadline that is approaching and experience a sinking feeling in the pit of your stomach. When you start your daily routine in class or at work, you greet many people you know, including one you find very attractive and would very much like to know better; in fact, when this person walks into the room, your heart literally skips a beat. As lunch hour approaches, you begin to feel hungry, and when you visit a nearby restaurant and smell the pizza, these feelings are intensified and you think, "How delicious!" Later that day, you catch sight of a stranger who reminds you of an old friend; as a result, you spend several minutes reminiscing about the past. This makes you feel happy, and when you leave for home, you are feeling very cheerful—when suddenly, another driver cuts you off in traffic, almost causing you to have an accident. Waves of fear and anger sweep over you, and you roll down your window to shout at the other driver.

When you get home, you are still upset, so you pour yourself a glass of wine.

Soon, you feel more relaxed, but when you turn on the evening news, the

events it shows are so depressing that you turn it off and begin to think

about dinner. Later that night, you have several vivid dreams, including one

about that person you find so attractive. As a result, you wake up with a

smile the next morning. And so it goes each day—experiences, emotions, and

thoughts following one another in continuous succession. Truly, as one

famous author (Ernest Hemingway) put it, life really is "a moveable feast."

But now for the key question: Which of these experiences and events are related to biological processes occurring inside your body? The answer is simple: Every one of them. In fact, almost all psychologists currently agree that *everything we think, feel, or do has a basis in biological processes and events*—primarily, in activities occurring in our brains and other portions of the nervous system (see Figure 2.1). Are you reading and understanding these words? If so, it is the result of activity in your brain. Do you feel sleepy? If so, it is the result of activity in your brain and other biological events. Can you remember what your psychology professor looks like? What it felt like to have your first kiss? The sound of your first-grade teacher's voice? Again, your ability to do so is the result of activity in several areas of your brain.

Given this basic fact, it seems only fitting to begin our study of psychology by considering the biological processes that underlie all aspects of our behavior. But please note: Our goal is certainly *not* to make you an expert in these events. This is a course in *psychology,* not biology, and we promise not to forget it. But as you'll soon see, we really can't obtain full answers to many questions about behavior without attention to biological factors—especially activity in our brains.

This is not the only reason why psychologists are interested in the biological events and foundations of behavior, however. In addition, they realize that understanding these roots may often suggest effective treatments for behavioral problems. As we'll see in Chapter 12, much progress has been made in understanding

FIGURE 2.1
All Aspects of Behavior Have Biological Roots
In an ultimate sense, everything we do, feel, think, or experience is related to biological processes occurring in our bodies—and especially in our brains and nervous systems.

the biological causes of mental disorders—depression, schizophrenia, and anxiety disorders, to name just a few. Such knowledge, in turn, has led to the development of effective drugs for treating these disorders (we examine these in detail in Chapter 12). Similarly, growing understanding of the biological mechanisms that play a role in drug addiction is now pointing the way toward more effective treatment of this serious problem.

There's still one more reason for beginning with this chapter, and it has to do with scientific progress. Modern technology has provided impressive new tools for studying the living brain—for seeing where activity is centered as people solve problems, listen to music, reason, or memorize new information (e.g., Mason & Just, 2004). These new tools, which are described in a later section, have done for psychologists what the microscope did for biology and medicine and what the telescope did for astronomy: They have provided researchers with new ways of examining events and processes that were previously hidden from view. The result has been nothing short of a revolution in our understanding of how the brain works and the role it plays in the complex forms of behavior that make us human. So, get ready for some amazing surprises: We are truly on the verge of obtaining a much fuller understanding of the mysteries of the human mind than ever before.

To provide you with an overview of these exciting new discoveries, we'll first examine the structure and function of *neurons,* the building blocks of the nervous system. Next, we'll turn to the structure and function of the *nervous system,* devoting special attention to the *brain,* the marvelous organ that is ultimately responsible for consciousness—and for the fact that you are now reading and understanding these words. After this, we'll put psychology rather than biology center stage by examining important links between the brain and behavior—what we currently know about the neural bases of speech and other *higher mental processes*—reasoning, problem solving, and so on. As we'll soon see, the modern tools we mentioned earlier have provided new insights into all of these topics. Finally, we'll examine the role of *genetic factors* in human behavior, and the possible role of evolution in our behavior—a topic investigated by the field of *evolutionary psychology.* To start at the beginning, let's turn now to *neurons*—the building blocks of which, ultimately, our consciousness is composed.

NEURONS: BUILDING BLOCKS OF THE NERVOUS SYSTEM

You are driving down a winding country road when suddenly your friend, who is sitting in the seat next to you, shouts, "Watch out for the deer!" Immediately, you experience strong anxiety, step on the brake, and look around in every direction. The process seems automatic, but think about it a moment: How did information from your ears get "inside" and trigger your emotions and behavior? The answer involves the activity of neurons—cells within our bodies that are specialized for the tasks of receiving, moving, and processing information.

Neurons: Their Basic Structure

Neurons are tremendously varied in appearance, but most consist of three basic parts: (1) a *cell body,* (2) an *axon,* and (3) one or more *dendrites.* **Dendrites** carry information toward the cell body, whereas **axons** carry information away from it. Thus, in a sense, neurons are one-way channels of communication. Information usually moves from dendrites or the cell body toward the axon and then outward along this structure. A simplified diagram of a neuron and actual neurons are shown, magnified, in Figure 2.2 on page 32. Scientists estimate that the human brain may contain more than 100 billion neurons.

Neurons
Cells specialized for communicating information; the basic building blocks of the nervous system.

Dendrite
The part of the neuron that conducts action potentials toward the cell body.

Axon
The part of the neuron that conducts action potentials away from the cell body.

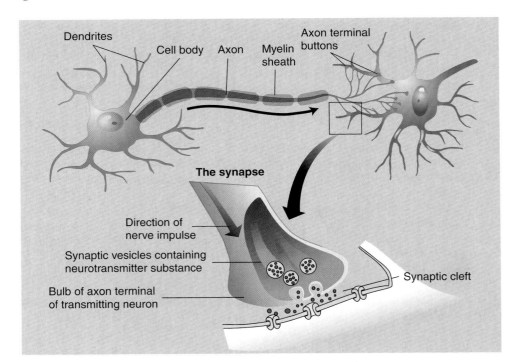

FIGURE 2.2
Neurons: Their Basic Structure
Neurons vary in form, but all possess the basic structures shown here: a cell body, an axon (with axon terminals), and one or more dendrites.

Axon Terminals
Structures at the end of axons that contain transmitter substances.

Synapse
A region where the axon of one neuron closely approaches other neurons or the cell membrane of other types of cells, such as muscle cells.

Action Potential
A rapid shift in the electrical charge across the cell membrane of neurons. This disturbance along the membrane communicates information within neurons.

Synaptic Vesicles
Structures in the axon terminals that contain various neurotransmitters.

Neurotransmitters (transmitter substances)
Chemicals, released by neurons, that carry information across the synapse.

In many neurons, the axon is covered by a sheath of fatty material known as *myelin.* The myelin sheath (fatty wrapping) is interrupted by small gaps (places where it is absent). Both the sheath and the gaps in it play an important role in the neuron's ability to transmit information, a process we'll consider in detail shortly. Near its end, the axon divides into several small branches. These, in turn, end in round structures known as **axon terminals** that closely approach but do not actually touch other cells (other neurons, muscle cells, or gland cells). The region at which the axon terminals of a neuron closely approach other cells is known as the **synapse.** The manner in which neurons communicate with other cells across this tiny space is described next.

Neurons: Their Basic Function

We just noted that neurons closely approach but do not actually touch other neurons. How, then, does one neuron communicate across this gap? Generally, like this. When a neuron responds to some stimulus either from inside or outside the nervous system, it generates a tiny electrical reaction known as the **action potential,** which then travels along the axon to the axon terminals. Within the axon terminals are many structures known as **synaptic vesicles.** Arrival of the action potential causes these vesicles to approach the cell membrane, where they empty their contents into the synapse (please refer to Figure 2.3). The chemicals thus released—known as **neurotransmitters**—travel across the tiny synaptic gap until they reach specialized receptor sites in the membrane of the other cell.

These receptors are complex protein molecules into whose structure neurotransmitter substances fit like chemical keys into a lock. Specific neurotransmitters can deliver signals only at certain locations on cell membranes, thereby introducing precision into the nervous system's complex communication system. Upon binding to their receptors, neurotransmitters either produce their effects directly or function indirectly through the interaction of the neurotransmitter and its receptor with other substances.

Neurotransmitters produce one of two effects. If their effects are *excitatory* in nature, they make it more likely for the neuron they contact to fire. If, instead, their effects are *inhibitory,* they make it less it less likely that the neuron will fire. What

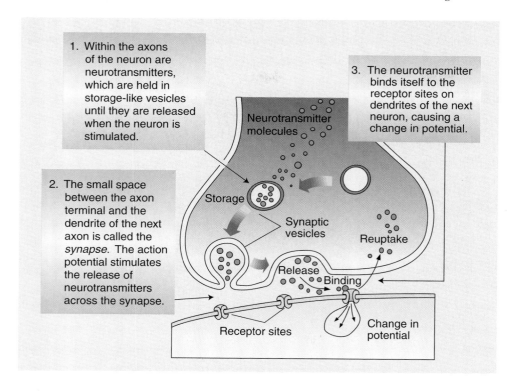

1. Within the axons of the neuron are neurotransmitters, which are held in storage-like vesicles until they are released when the neuron is stimulated.

2. The small space between the axon terminal and the dendrite of the next axon is called the *synapse*. The action potential stimulates the release of neurotransmitters across the synapse.

3. The neurotransmitter binds itself to the receptor sites on dendrites of the next neuron, causing a change in potential.

Neurotransmitter molecules

Storage

Synaptic vesicles

Reuptake

Release

Binding

Receptor sites

Change in potential

FIGURE 2.3
Synaptic Transmission
The axon terminals found on the ends of axons contain many *synaptic vesicles.* When an action potential reaches the axon terminal, these vesicles move toward the cell membrane. Once there, the vesicles fuse with the membrane and release their contents (*neurotransmitters*) into the synapse.

happens to neurotransmitters *after* they cross the synapse from one neuron to another? Either they are taken back for reuse in the axon terminals of the neuron that released them, a process known as *reuptake,* or they are broken down by various enzymes present at the synapse—in a sense, chemically deactivated.

It is important to note that our comments so far greatly simplify things by describing a situation in which one neuron contacts another across a single synapse. In fact, this is rarely, if ever, the case. Most neurons actually form synapses with many others—ten thousand or more in some cases! Thus, at any given moment, most neurons are receiving a complex pattern of excitatory and inhibitory influences from many neighbors. Whether a neuron conducts an action potential or not, then, depends on the total pattern of this input—for example, whether excitatory or inhibitory input predominates. Further, the effects of excitatory and inhibitory input can be cumulative over time, in part because such effects do not dissipate instantaneously. Thus, if a neuron that has recently been stimulated, but not sufficiently to produce an action potential, is stimulated again soon afterward, the two sources of excitation may combine so that an action potential is generated.

In one sense, then, neurons serve as tiny *decision-making* mechanisms, firing only when the pattern of information reaching them is just right. The fact that individual neurons affect and are, in turn, affected by many others strongly suggests that it is the total pattern or network of activity in the nervous system that is crucial. As we will see in later discussions, it is this intricate web of neural excitation that generates the richness and complexity of our conscious experience.

Neurotransmitters: Chemical Keys to the Nervous System

The fact that transmitter substances produce either excitatory or inhibitory effects might seem to suggest that there are only two types. In fact, there are many different neurotransmitters, and many more chemical substances, that can mimic the effects of neurotransmitters—for instance, many drugs produce their effects in this way. Several known neurotransmitters and their functions are summarized in Table 2.1 on page 34. Although the specific role of many transmitter substances is still

TABLE 2.1 Neurotransmitters: An Overview

Neurons communicate with each other across the synapse through neurotransmitters. Several of these are listed and described here.

Neurotransmitter	Location	Effects
Acetylcholine	Found throughout the central nervous system, in the autonomic nervous system, and at all neuromuscular junctions.	Involved in muscle action, learning, and memory.
Norepinephrine	Found in neurons in the autonomic nervous system.	Primarily involved in control of alertness and wakefulness.
Dopamine	Produced by neurons located in a region of the brain called the substantia nigra.	Involved in movement, attention, and learning. Degeneration of dopamine-producing neurons has been linked to Parkinson's disease. Too much dopamine has been linked to schizophrenia.
Serotonin	Found in neurons in the brain and spinal cord.	Plays a role in the regulation of mood and in the control of eating, sleep, and arousal. Has also been implicated in the regulation of pain and in dreaming.
GABA (gamma-aminobutyric acid)	Found throughout the brain and spinal cord.	GABA is the major inhibitory neurotransmitter in the brain. Abnormal levels of GABA have been implicated in sleep and eating disorders.

under study, we are now fairly certain about the functions of a few. Perhaps the one about which we know most is *acetylcholine*. It is the neurotransmitter at every junction between motor neurons (neurons concerned with muscular movements) and muscle cells. Anything that interferes with the action of acetylcholine can produce paralysis. South American hunters have long used this fact to their advantage by dipping their arrow tips in *curare,* a poisonous substance that occupies acetylcholine receptors. As a result, paralysis is produced, and the unlucky animal dies quickly through suffocation. Some evidence suggests that the memory loss experienced by persons suffering from *Alzheimer's disease* results from a degeneration of cells that produce acetylcholine. Examinations of the brains of persons who have died of this disease show unusually low levels of this substance (Coyle, Price, & DeLong, 1983).

Drugs and Neurotransmitters

Have you ever taken a painkiller? A drug to help you sleep? One to make you more alert (we almost all do that; see Figure 2.4)? If so, you may have wondered how these drugs produce their effects. The answer is that, in many cases, they do so by altering the process of synaptic transmission. Drugs that change our feelings or behavior are similar enough in chemical structure to natural neurotransmitters to occupy the receptor sites normally occupied by the neurotransmitters themselves (e.g., Kalivas & Samson, 1992). In this respect, drugs can produce two basic effects: They can mimic the effects of the neurotransmitter, in which case they are described as being **agonists,** or they can inhibit the effects normally produced by the neurotransmitter, in which case they are described as being **antagonists.** Many painkillers (analgesics) occupy receptor sites normally stimulated by endorphins; thus, they block pain and produce a temporary "high." Addicting drugs such as opium, heroin, and crack also occupy these sites and produce more intensely pleasurable sensations than endorphins. This seems to play a key role in their addicting properties.

Agonist
A chemical substance that facilitates the action of a neurotransmitter at a receptor site.

Antagonist
A chemical substance that inhibits the impact of a neurotransmitter at a receptor site.

"Nowadays, Hal is ninety-nine per cent caffeine-free."

FIGURE 2.4
Drugs: Many Produce Their Effects by Affecting Synaptic Transmission
Almost everyone uses drugs to change their own behavior at one time or another. And as suggested by this cartoon, we can quickly become dependent on them!

Source: © The New Yorker Collection 1993 Mort Gerberg from cartoonbank.com. All Rights Reserved.

KEY QUESTIONS

- What do neurons do and what are their basic parts?
- What are action potentials? How do neurons communicate with one another?
- What are the effects of neurotransmitters?
- How do drugs produce their effects? What are agonists? Antagonists?

THE NERVOUS SYSTEM: ITS BASIC STRUCTURE AND FUNCTIONS

If neurons are building blocks, then the **nervous system** is the structure they erect. The nervous system is actually a complex network of neurons that regulates our bodily functions and permits us to react to the external world in countless ways, so it deserves very careful attention. But remember: This is *not* a course in biology, so the main reason for focusing on the nervous system is to understand its role in all aspects of our behavior.

The Nervous System: Its Major Divisions

Although the nervous system functions as an integrated whole, it is often viewed as having two major portions—the **central nervous system** and the **peripheral nervous system.** These and other divisions of the nervous system are presented in Figure 2.5 on page 36.

The Central Nervous System

The central nervous system (CNS) consists of the brain and the spinal cord. Because we'll soon describe the structure of the brain in detail, we won't examine it here. The spinal cord runs through the middle of a column of hollow bones known as vertebrae. You can feel them by moving your hand up and down the middle of your back.

The spinal cord has two major functions. First, it carries sensory information from receptors throughout the body to the brain and conducts information from the brain to muscles and glands. Second, it plays a key role in various **reflexes.** These are seemingly automatic actions evoked rapidly by particular stimuli. Withdrawing

Nervous System
The complex structure that regulates bodily processes and is responsible, ultimately, for all aspects of conscious experience.

Central Nervous System
The brain and the spinal cord.

Peripheral Nervous System
That portion of the nervous system that connects internal organs and glands, as well as voluntary and involuntary muscles, to the central nervous system.

Reflexes
Seemingly automatic actions evoked rapidly by specific stimuli.

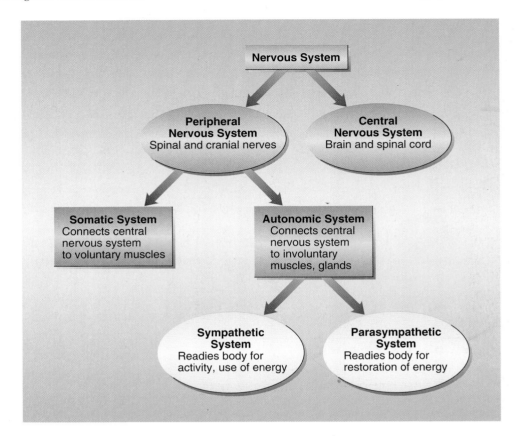

FIGURE 2.5
Major Divisions of the Nervous System
As shown here, the nervous system consists of several major parts.

Somatic Nervous System
The portion of the nervous system that connects the brain and spinal cord to voluntary muscles.

Autonomic Nervous System
Part of the peripheral nervous system that connects internal organs, glands, and involuntary muscles to the central nervous system.

Sympathetic Nervous System
The portion of the autonomic nervous system that readies the body for expenditure of energy.

Parasympathetic Nervous System
A portion of the autonomic nervous system that readies the body for restoration of energy.

your hand from a hot object or blinking your eyes in response to a rapidly approaching object are common examples of reflex actions. Spinal reflexes offer an obvious advantage: They permit us to react to potential dangers much more rapidly than we could if the information first had to travel all the way to the brain.

The Peripheral Nervous System

The peripheral nervous system consists primarily of nerves, bundles of axons from many neurons, that connect the central nervous system with sense organs and with muscles and glands throughout the body. Most of these nerves are attached to the spinal cord; these spinal nerves serve all of the body below the neck. Other nerves known as *cranial nerves* extend from the brain. They carry sensory information from receptors in the eyes and ears and other sense organs; they also carry information from the central nervous system to muscles in the head and neck.

As you can see in Figure 2.5, the peripheral nervous system has two subdivisions: the **somatic** and **autonomic nervous systems.** The somatic nervous system connects the central nervous system to voluntary muscles throughout the body. When you engage in almost any voluntary action, such as ordering a pizza or reading the rest of this chapter, portions of your somatic nervous system are involved. In contrast, the autonomic nervous system connects the central nervous system to internal organs and glands and to muscles over which we have little or no voluntary control—for instance, the muscles in our digestive system.

We can't stop dividing things here, because the autonomic nervous system, too, consists of two distinct parts. The first is known as the **sympathetic nervous system.** In general, this system prepares the body for using energy, as in vigorous physical actions. Thus, stimulation of this division increases heartbeat, raises blood pressure, releases sugar into the blood for energy, and increases the flow of blood to muscles used in physical activities. The second portion of the autonomic system, known as the **parasympathetic nervous system,** operates in the opposite manner.

It stimulates processes that conserve the body's energy. Activation of this system slows heartbeat, lowers blood pressure, and diverts blood away from skeletal muscles (e.g., muscles in the arms and legs) and to the digestive system. Figure 2.6 on page 38 summarizes many of the functions of the sympathetic and parasympathetic divisions of the autonomic nervous system.

Before concluding, we should emphasize that while the autonomic nervous system plays an important role in the regulation of bodily processes, it does so mainly by transmitting information to and from the central nervous system. Thus, it is the central nervous system that ultimately runs the show.

KEY QUESTIONS

- What structures compose the central nervous system? What is the function of the spinal cord?
- What two systems make up the peripheral nervous system?
- What are the roles of these two systems?
- What are the functions of the sympathetic and parasympathetic nervous systems?

The Endocrine System: Chemical Regulators of Bodily Processes

Although the nervous system is our primary system for moving and processing information—for responding to the world around us and to our own internal states—another exists as well. This is the **endocrine system,** which consists of a number of *glands* that release chemicals called **hormones** directly into the bloodstream. These hormones exert profound effects on a wide range of processes related to basic bodily functions. Of special interest to psychologists are *neurohormones*—hormones that interact with and affect the nervous system. Neurohormones, like neurotransmitters, influence neural activity. However, because they are released into the circulatory system rather than into synapses, they exert their effects more slowly, at a greater distance, and often for longer periods of time than neurotransmitters.

One major part of the endocrine system is the **pituitary gland.** It is sometimes described as the *master gland* of the body, for the hormones it releases control and regulate the actions of other endocrine glands. This gland is also closely connected to important regions of the brain that play a role in emotion—areas we'll discuss in the next section. Another important part of the endocrine system is the *adrenal glands,* which sit on top of the kidneys. In response to messages from the autonomic nervous system, the adrenal glands release *epinephrine* and *norepinephrine* (also known as *adrenaline* and *noradrenaline*). These hormones help the body to handle emergencies—increasing heart rate, blood pressure, and sugar in the blood.

KEY QUESTIONS

- What is the endocrine system?
- What are some of its major parts?

THE BRAIN: WHERE CONSCIOUSNESS DWELLS

There can be no doubt about it: Modern computers are impressive and getting better. At present, though, none comes even close to matching the amazing abilities packed within the roughly three pounds of tissue that make up the human brain. Computers can "crunch numbers" at amazing speeds, but they cannot do many things we take for granted: recognize thousands of different faces, speak one and perhaps several languages fluently, add just the right amount of salt or pepper to

Endocrine System
A system for communication within our bodies; it consists of several glands that secrete hormones directly into the bloodstream.

Hormones
Substances secreted by endocrine glands that regulate a wide range of bodily processes.

Pituitary Gland
An endocrine gland that releases hormones to regulate other glands and several basic biological processes.

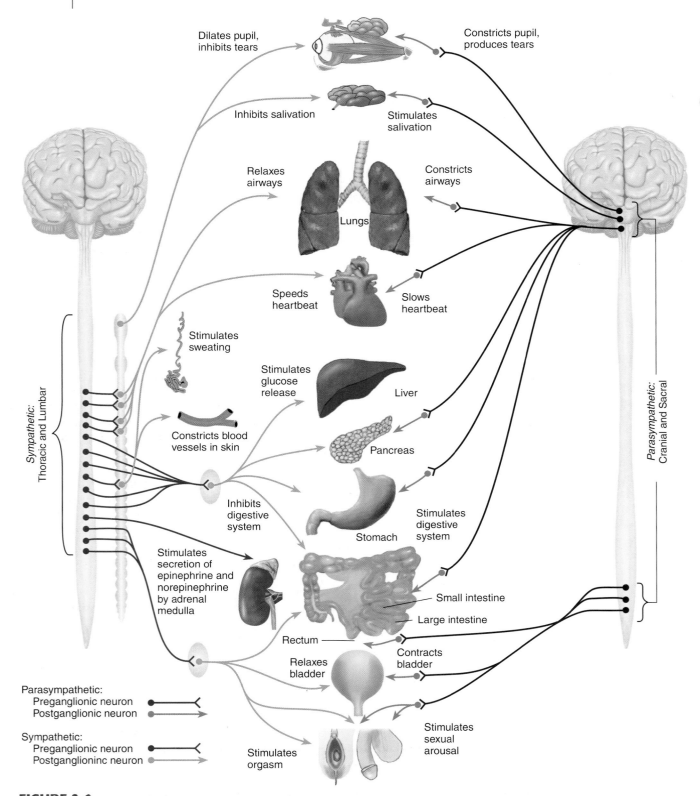

Dilates pupil, inhibits tears

Constricts pupil, produces tears

Inhibits salivation

Stimulates salivation

Relaxes airways

Constricts airways

Lungs

Speeds heartbeat

Slows heartbeat

Stimulates sweating

Stimulates glucose release

Liver

Constricts blood vessels in skin

Pancreas

Inhibits digestive system

Stimulates digestive system

Stomach

Stimulates secretion of epinephrine and norepinephrine by adrenal medulla

Small intestine

Large intestine

Rectum

Contracts bladder

Relaxes bladder

Stimulates sexual arousal

Stimulates orgasm

Sympathetic: Thoracic and Lumbar

Parasympathetic: Cranial and Sacral

Parasympathetic:
  Preganglionic neuron
  Postganglionic neuron

Sympathetic:
  Preganglionic neuron
  Postganglioninc neuron

FIGURE 2.6

The Autonomic Nervous System: An Overview

The autonomic nervous system consists of two major parts, the sympathetic and parasympathetic nervous systems. Some of the functions of each are shown here.

Source: From Neil R. Carlson, *Foundations of Physiological Psychology*, 4/e © 1999. Published by Allyn and Bacon, Boston, MA. Copyright © 1999 by Pearson Education. Reprinted by permission of the publisher.

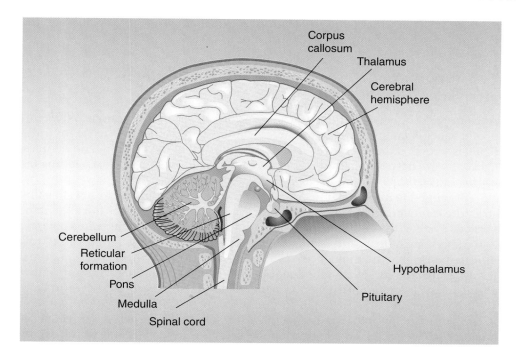

FIGURE 2.7
Basic Structure of the Human Brain
In this simplified drawing, the brain has been split down the middle, the way you would cut an apple in half through its core, to reveal its inner structure.

a dish we are cooking. Nor can they experience the emotions we label "love," "hate," and "sorrow." So, clearly, the human brain is truly a marvel.

Although the brain is complex, it can be divided into three major parts that are concerned with (1) basic bodily functions and survival; (2) motivation and emotion; and (3) our higher mental processes, including language, planning, problem solving, and reasoning.

The Brain Stem: Survival Basics

Let's begin with the basics: the structures in the brain that regulate the bodily processes we share with many other life forms on earth. These structures are located in the *brain stem,* the portion of the brain that begins just above the spinal cord and continues into the center of this complex organ (refer to Figure 2.7).

Two of these structures, the **medulla** and the **pons,** are located just above the point where the spinal cord enters the brain. Major sensory and motor nerves pass through these structures on their way to higher brain centers or down to effectors (muscles or glands) in other parts of the body. In addition, both the medulla and the pons contain a central core consisting of a dense network of interconnected neurons. This is the **reticular activating system,** and it has long been viewed as a part of the brain that plays a key role in sleep and arousal—a topic we'll discuss in greater detail in Chapter 4. The medulla contains several *nuclei*—collections of neuron cell bodies—that control vital functions such as breathing, heart rate, and blood pressure, as well as coughing and sneezing.

Behind the medulla and pons is the **cerebellum** (refer again to Figure 2.7), which is primarily concerned with the regulation of motor activities, serving to orchestrate muscular activities so that they occur in a synchronized fashion. Damage to the cerebellum results in jerky, poorly coordinated muscle functioning. If such damage is severe, it may be impossible for a person to stand, let alone walk or run. In addition, the cerebellum may also play a role in certain cognitive processes, such as learning (e.g., Daum et al., 1993).

Above the medulla and pons, near the end of the brain stem, is a structure known as the **midbrain.** It contains an extension of the reticular activating system as well as primitive centers concerned with vision and hearing. The midbrain also

Medulla
A structure in the brain concerned with the regulation of vital bodily functions, such as breathing and heartbeat.

Pons
A portion of the brain through which sensory and motor information pass and that contains structures relating to sleep, arousal, and the regulation of muscle tone and cardiac reflexes.

Reticular Activating System
A structure within the brain concerned with sleep, arousal, and the regulation of muscle tone and cardiac reflexes.

Cerebellum
A part of the brain concerned with the regulation of basic motor activities.

Midbrain
A part of the brain containing primitive centers for vision and hearing. It also plays a role in the regulation of visual reflexes.

contains structures that play a role in the pain-relieving effects of opiates and the control of motor movements by sensory input.

The Hypothalamus, Thalamus, and Limbic System: Motivation and Emotion

Ancient philosophers identified the heart as the center of our emotions. While this poetic belief is still reflected on many valentine cards, modern science indicates that it is wrong. If there is indeed a center for our appetites, emotions, and motives, it actually lies deep within the brain in several interrelated structures, including the *hypothalamus, thalamus,* and the *limbic system.*

Although the **hypothalamus** is less than one cubic centimeter in size, this tiny structure exerts profound effects on our behavior. First, it regulates the autonomic nervous system, thus influencing reactions ranging from sweating and salivating to the shedding of tears and changes in blood pressure. Second, it plays a key role in *homeostasis*—the maintenance of the body's internal environment at optimal levels. Third, the hypothalamus seems to play a role in the regulation of eating and drinking, signaling us when to begin eating or drinking and when to stop. We'll consider this role in detail in our discussion of motivation and emotion (Chapter 9). The hypothalamus also plays a role in other forms of motivated behavior, such as mating and aggression. It exerts this influence, at least in part, by regulating the release of hormones from one of the endocrine glands (the *pituitary gland*).

Above the hypothalamus, quite close to the center of the brain, is another important structure, the **thalamus.** This structure consists of two football-shaped parts, one on each side of the brain. This has sometimes been called the great relay station of the brain, and with good reason. The thalamus receives input from all of our senses except olfaction (smell), performs some preliminary analyses, and then transmits the information to other parts of the brain.

Finally, we should consider a set of structures that together are known as the **limbic system.** The structures that make up the limbic system play an important role in emotion and in motivated behavior, such as feeding, fleeing from danger, fighting, and sex. The largest of these structures, the **hippocampus,** plays a key role in the formation of memories (e.g., Eichenbaum & Bunsey, 1995; Gluck & Myers, 1995), a topic we'll consider in Chapter 6. The **amygdala,** also part of the limbic system, is involved in aspects of emotional control, so that damage to this structure can produce striking differences in behavior; for example, a typically docile cat may become uncontrollably violent.

The Cerebral Cortex: The Core of Complex Thought

Now, at last, we come to the part of the brain that seems to be responsible for our ability to reason, plan, remember, and imagine—the **cerebral cortex.** This outer surface of the brain is only about one-eighth of an inch thick, but it contains billions of neurons, each one connected to thousands of others. The cortex is divided into two nearly symmetrical halves known as the *cerebral hemispheres.* Thus, many of the structures described subsequently appear in both the left and right cerebral hemispheres. As we'll soon see, however, this similarity in structure is not entirely matched by similarity in function. The two hemispheres appear to be somewhat specialized in the functions they perform.

In humans, the cerebral hemispheres are folded into many ridges and grooves, which greatly increase their surface area. In other organisms, there are fewer folds or no folds at all. The result is that the human cortex covers much more area than does the cortex in other species. Each hemisphere is usually described, on the basis of the largest of these grooves or fissures, as being divided into four regions or lobes: frontal, parietal, occipital, and temporal.

Hypothalamus
A small structure deep within the brain that plays a key role in the regulation of the autonomic nervous system and of several forms of motivated behavior, such as eating and aggression.

Thalamus
A structure deep within the brain that receives sensory input from other portions of the nervous system and then transmits this information to the cerebral hemispheres and other parts of the brain.

Limbic System
Several structures deep within the brain that play a role in emotional reactions and behavior.

Hippocampus
A structure of the limbic system that plays a role in the formation of certain types of memories.

Amygdala
A limbic system structure involved in aspects of emotional control and formation of emotional memories.

Cerebral Cortex
The outer covering of the cerebral hemispheres.

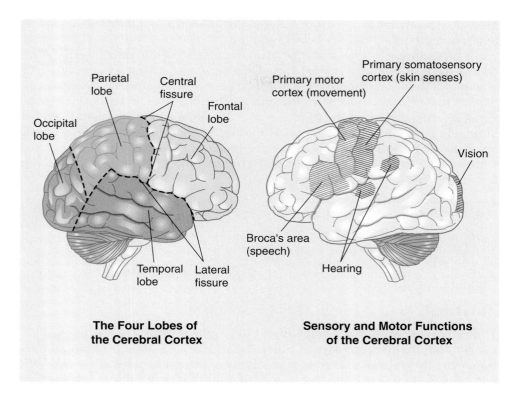

**The Four Lobes of
the Cerebral Cortex**

**Sensory and Motor Functions
of the Cerebral Cortex**

**FIGURE 2.8
Major Regions of the
Cerebral Cortex**
The cerebral cortex is divided
into four major lobes (*left
drawing*). Specific areas in these
lobes are concerned with sensory
and motor functions and with
our higher mental processes
(*right drawing*).

Occupying the area of the brain nearest the face, the **frontal lobe** is bounded by the deep *central fissure.* Lying along this fissure, just within the frontal lobe, is the *motor cortex,* an area concerned with the control of body movements (see Figure 2.8). Damage to this area does not produce total paralysis. Instead, it often results in a loss of control over fine movements, especially of the fingers.

Across the central fissure from the frontal lobe is the **parietal lobe.** This area contains the *somatosensory cortex,* to which information from the skin senses—touch, temperature, pressure, and so on—is carried. (Refer to Figure 2.8.) Damage to this area produces a variety of effects, depending in part on whether injury occurs to the left or right cerebral hemisphere. If damage involves the left hemisphere, individuals may lose the ability to read or write, or they may have difficulty knowing where parts of their own bodies are located. In contrast, if damage occurs in the right hemisphere, individuals may seem unaware of the left side of their bodies. For example, a man may forget to shave the left side of his face.

The **occipital lobe** is located near the back of the head. Its primary functions are visual, and it contains a sensory area that receives input from the eyes. Damage to this area often produces a "hole" in the person's field of vision: Objects in a particular location can't be seen, but the rest of the visual field may remain unaffected. As with other brain structures, injury to the occipital lobe may produce contrasting effects, depending on which cerebral hemisphere is affected. Damage to the occipital lobe in the right hemisphere produces loss of vision in the left visual field, whereas damage to the occipital lobe in the left hemisphere produces loss of vision in the right visual field.

Finally, the **temporal lobe** is located along the side of each hemisphere (see Figure 2.8). The location makes sense, for this lobe plays a key role in hearing and contains a sensory area that receives input from the ears. Damage to the temporal lobe, too, can result in intriguing symptoms. When such injuries occur in the left hemisphere, people may lose the ability to understand spoken words. When damage is restricted to the right hemisphere, they may be able to recognize speech but

Frontal Lobe
The portion of the cerebral cortex that lies in front of the central fissure.

Parietal Lobe
A portion of the cerebral cortex, lying behind the central fissure, that plays a major role in the skin senses: touch, temperature, and pressure.

Occipital Lobe
A portion of the cerebral cortex involved in vision.

Temporal Lobe
The lobe of the cerebral cortex that is involved in hearing.

may lose the ability to recognize other kinds of sound—for example, melodies, tones, or rhythms.

It is interesting to note that when added together, areas of the cortex that either control motor movements (motor cortex) or receive sensory input (sensory cortex) account for only 20 to 25 percent of the total area. The remainder is known as the *association cortex* and, as its name suggests, is assumed to play a critical role in integrating the activities in the various sensory systems and in translating sensory input into programs for motor output. In addition, the association cortex seems to be involved in complex cognitive activities such as thinking, reasoning, remembering, language, recognizing faces, and a host of other functions. We'll return to several of these in the next major section.

KEY QUESTIONS

- What structures compose the brain stem? What are their functions?
- What are the functions of the hypothalamus and thalamus?
- What is the role of the cerebral cortex?

Two Minds in One Body? Our Divided Brains

The two hemispheres of the brain appear to be mirror images of one another. Yet, a large body of evidence suggests that, in fact, they are specialized to perform somewhat different functions. In general terms, the left hemisphere is the *verbal* hemisphere—it is specialized for speech and other verbal tasks. In contrast, the right hemisphere specializes in the control of certain motor movements, in synthesis (putting isolated elements together), and in the comprehension and communication of *emotion*. Two kinds of evidence point to these conclusions: (1) studies of persons whose cerebral hemispheres have been isolated from each other either through accident or (more typically) surgery performed for medical reasons, and (2) studies of the rest of us—persons in whom the two cerebral hemispheres are connected in the normal way.

▪ Research with Split-brain Persons

Under normal conditions, the two hemispheres of the brain communicate with each other through the **corpus callosum,** a wide band of nerve fibers that passes between them (Hoptman & Davidson, 1994). Sometimes, though, it is necessary to cut this link for medical reasons—for example, to prevent the spread of epileptic seizures from one hemisphere to the other. Such operations largely eliminate communication between the two hemispheres, so they provide a unique opportunity to study the effects that result. Careful study of individuals who have undergone such operations provides intriguing evidence for the view that the two hemispheres of the brain are indeed specialized for performing different tasks (Gazzaniga, 1984, 1985; Sperry, 1968).

Consider, for instance, the following demonstration. A man whose corpus callosum has been cut is seated before a screen and told to stare, with his eyes as motionless as possible, at a central point on the screen. Then the word *tenant* is flashed across the screen so that the letters *ten* appear to the left of the central point and the letters *ant* appear to the right. What does the man report seeing? Before you guess, consider the following fact: Because of the way our visual system is constructed, stimuli presented to the *left* visual field of each eye stimulate only the *right* hemisphere of the brain; items on the *right* side of the visual field of each eye stimulate only the *left* hemisphere (refer to Figure 2.9).

Now, what do you think our split-brain person reports? If you said, "Ant," you are correct. This would be expected, because only the left hemisphere, which controls speech, can answer verbally. However, when asked to *point* to the word he saw with his left hand (which is controlled by the right hemisphere), the man reacts

Corpus Callosum
A band of nerve fibers connecting the two hemispheres of the brain.

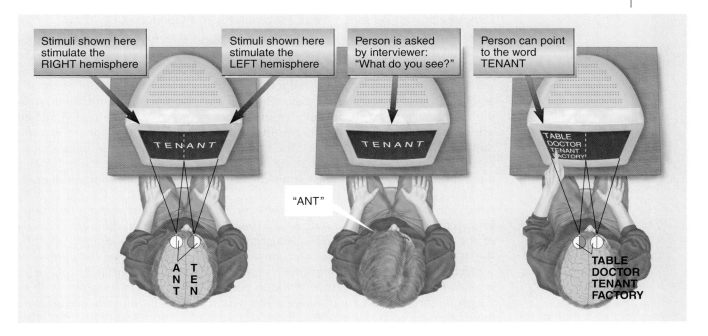

FIGURE 2.9
Some Intriguing Effects of Severing the Corpus Callosum
A man whose corpus callosum has been cut stares at a central point on a screen (*left drawing*). The word *tenant* is flashed across the screen so that the letters *ten* appear to the left of the central point and the letters *ant* appear to the right. Because of the way our visual system is constructed, stimuli presented to the *left* visual field of each eye stimulate only the *right* hemisphere of the brain; items on the *right* side of the visual field of each eye stimulate only the *left* hemisphere. When asked, "What do you see?" (*middle drawing*), the man answers, "Ant." But when asked to *point* to the word he saw with his left hand (*right drawing*), he points to the *ten* in the word *tenant*. These findings provide evidence for lateralization of function in the two cerebral hemispheres.

differently: He points with his left hand to the word *ten* (part of the word *tenant*). So the right hemisphere has indeed seen and recognized this stimulus; it can't describe it in words, but it *can* point to it. While the left hemisphere is better at verbal tasks, the right hemisphere is superior in other respects—in copying drawings, recognizing faces, and expressing emotion. For instance, look at the photos in Figure 2.10. Which one shows the emotion of disgust most clearly? Most people choose the photo on the right (photo C). It is constructed from mirror images of the left side of the face—the side controlled by the right cerebral hemisphere. In other words, two photos showing only the left side of the face have been combined to form this composite photo. It seems to show disgust very strongly. In contrast, the photo on the left is constructed from mirror images of the right side of the face—the side controlled by the left hemisphere. It appears to show much less intense emotion. (The person as he actually appears is shown in the middle photo, photo B.)

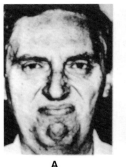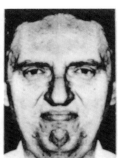

    A   **B**   **C**

FIGURE 2.10
Evidence for Superiority of the Right Hemisphere in the Expression of Emotions
Which photo shows the most intense emotion? Most people choose the one on the right (photo C), which is constructed from mirror images of the *left* side of the face—the side controlled by the right cerebral hemisphere. In contrast, the photo in the middle (photo B) is constructed from mirror images of the *right* side of the face—the side controlled by the left hemisphere. It seems to show much less intense emotion. Photo A shows the person as he really appears.
Source: Sackheim & Gur, 1978.

▪ Research with Persons Whose Hemispheres Are Connected

Additional evidence for specialization of function in the two hemispheres is provided by research on persons whose corpus callosum is intact—the great majority of us. For instance, consider the following kind of research, conducted with persons who are about to undergo brain surgery. First, they are asked to describe traumatic emotional events (e.g., a near-fatal traffic accident). Not surprisingly, they do so in vivid terms. Then, as preparation for surgery, they receive a drug injected into an artery that leads to the right hemisphere; as a result, this hemisphere is anesthetized. When asked to describe the same events again, they do so in much less intense terms. This provides evidence for the view that the right hemisphere plays a key role in the experience and expression of emotions (e.g., Ross, Homan, & Buck, 1994).

Additional evidence for this view is provided by studies using a technique known as *PET scans;* such scans reveal the levels of activity in different portions of the brain occurring as individuals perform various tasks—the more active the area, the more vivid the color. Research with this technique indicates that when individuals speak or work with numbers, activity in the left hemisphere increases. In contrast, when they work on perceptual tasks—for instance, tasks in which they compare various shapes—activity increases in the right hemisphere (e.g., Springer & Deutsch, 1985). Interestingly, additional research suggests that while individuals are making up their minds about some issue, activity is higher in the left than in the right hemisphere (Cacioppo, Petty, & Quintanar, 1982). However, once logical thought is over and a decision has been made, heightened activity occurs in the right hemisphere, which seems to play a larger role in global, nonanalytic thought—for instance, overall reactions of the "I like it" or "I don't like it" type.

In sum, a large body of evidence suggests that, in a sense, we *do* seem to possess two minds in one brain: The two cerebral hemispheres are specialized for performing somewhat different tasks. Why does such specialization exist? From an evolutionary perspective, the answer might be, "Because it is beneficial and increases our chances of survival." For instance, because the right hemisphere specializes in responding to emotion-provoking events (e.g., dangers in the world around us), it can respond very quickly—more quickly than if the two hemispheres were identical in function.

Now that we've examined the structure of the brain and the functions of its major parts, we are just about ready to explore its complex role in many forms of behavior. Before discussing this topic, however, we'll pause to briefly examine the methods used by psychologists to study brain–behavior links.

How Psychologists Study the Nervous System and the Brain

While many procedures for studying the nervous system exist, most fit under three major categories: observing the effects of *damage* to various parts of the brain; *recording neural activity,* and techniques for studying the *intact, living brain.*

▪ Observing the Effects of Damage

The world, unfortunately, can be a dangerous place. Many people sustain damage to their brains in automobile or industrial accidents; many others develop illnesses that damage their brains directly, or that lead to medical procedures (e.g., surgery) that produce such effects. While these events are tragic for the persons who experience them, they provide psychologists with an invaluable research opportunity. By observing the symptoms or deficits shown by such persons, it is sometimes possible to determine which portions of their brains are involved in various forms of behavior. For instance, consider a person who shows the following, baffling set of symptoms. If one object is held in front of her, she can name it. If two objects are held in front of her, however, she can name one of them but not the other. In addition, she can recognize that one wooden block is larger than another, but when asked to pick one up, she fails to adjust the distance between her fingers and thumb according to the size of the object. What is responsible for these strange symptoms? By studying a number of persons who show them, psychologists have determined that they involve damage to an area of the brain on the border between the parietal and occipital lobes (e.g., Broussaud et al., 1996; Goodale et al., 1994). In many instances, then, studying persons who have experienced damage to areas of their brains can provide valuable information.

Where people are concerned, psychologists must wait for naturally occurring damage or medical procedures to see what effects result from harm to the brain. With laboratory animals, in contrast, it is possible to produce such damage in order to study the effects that occur. Although this may sound cruel, it is, of course, done under highly humane conditions and produces no pain in the subjects (the brain has no pain receptors). Moreover, such research is performed only when the information to be acquired can contribute to human welfare (e.g., to develop new treatments that are best for reducing chronic pain).

Recording a Neural Activity

A second method for studying the brain concerns recording the electrical activity that occurs within it. This can involve recording the activity of individual neurons (with tiny *microelectrodes* implanted into the brain) or of brain regions (with larger *macroelectrodes*). In both cases, changes in patterns of activity that occur in response to specific stimuli, or during various activities, are recorded. (Changes in response to specific stimuli or events are referred to as *event-related brain potentials,* or ERPs for short). The results can often help identify the specific functions of different regions of the brain. With humans, electrodes cannot generally be implanted in the brain, so recordings are made from the outside of the scalp (the *electroencephalogram*).

Images of the Intact, Functioning Brain

In recent years, advances in technology have provided an array of valuable new techniques for studying the brain as it actually functions. Many of these exist, but here we'll briefly describe two of the most important. The first of these is **magnetic resonance imaging,** or **MRI.** This technique is based on the fact that hydrogen atoms, found in all living tissue, emit measurable waves of energy when exposed to a strong magnetic field. In MRI, these waves are used as a basis for constructing extremely clear images of the brain. A recent development is *functional MRI,* in which images can be scanned much more quickly than in the past.

A second important technique is **positron emission tomography,** or **PET.** PET scans peer into the functioning brain by measuring blood flow in various neural areas, or by gauging the rate at which glucose, the brain's fuel, is metabolized. Individuals undergoing PET scans are injected with small amounts of harmless radioactive isotopes attached to either water or glucose molecules. Blood flow (containing the radioactive water molecules) is greatest in the most active areas of the brain. Similarly, glucose is absorbed by brain cells in proportion to their level of activity, with the most active cells taking in the greatest amount of glucose. As a result, PET scans allow scientists to map activity in various parts of a person's brain as she or he reads, listens to music, or engages in a mental activity such as solving math problems. For instance, look at the PET scans in Figure 2.11 on page 46. The top row shows brain activity while a person is in a relaxed state; the lower scans show the same person's brain while he is clenching and unclenching his fist. Scans can be made while people perform almost any activity you can imagine, or in order to compare persons having various mental disorders with persons who do not show such disorders. As you can guess, PET scans provide psychologists with an extremely valuable tool.

Magnetic Resonance Imaging (MRI)
A method for studying the intact brain in which images are obtained by exposing the brain to a strong magnetic field.

Positron Emission Tomography (PET)
An imaging technique that detects the activity of the brain by measuring glucose utilization or blood flow.

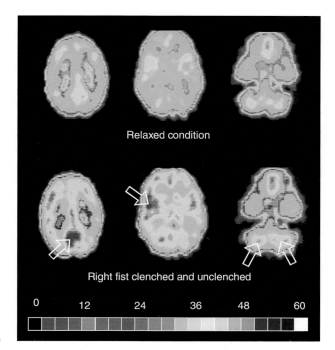

FIGURE 2.11
PET Scans: An Example
PET scans reveal the amount of activity occurring in different parts of the brain as individuals perform various tasks. The scans in the top row were made while the individual was at rest. The ones in the bottom row were made as he clenched his right fist and then unclenched it. Clearly, this motor action was associated with increased activity in many parts of the brain. (The brighter the color, the more activity, as shown in the color chart below the photos.)
Source: Courtesy of Brookhaven National Laboratory.

Now that we've described the basic methods used by psychologists to study the brain, let's see what recent research using such methods has revealed. These methods have definitely lived up to their promise, and have added tremendously to our knowledge of the intricate—and intimate—links between the brain and behavior.

KEY QUESTIONS

- Who are "split-brain" persons? What evidence do they provide for specialization of function in the two cerebral hemispheres?
- What evidence from persons with intact brains supports such specialization?
- What methods are used by psychologists to study the brain and its role in behavior?

THE BRAIN AND HUMAN BEHAVIOR: WHERE BIOLOGY AND CONSCIOUSNESS MEET

Armed with the new techniques and procedures described previously, psychologists and other scientists have begun to understand how the brain functions to produce human consciousness—our perceptions of the world around us, our thoughts, memories, and emotions. As you can probably guess, the findings of this research are complex, but they also tell a fascinating story.

How the Brain Functions: A Modern View

Do modern computers provide a good model of how the brain works? As we'll see in Chapter 6, such a model has been useful in the study of memory because our brains and computers do seem similar in certain respects. Both can receive information, enter it into storage (memory), and retrieve it at a later time. But, in fact, computers and the human brain are different in a fundamental way. Computers are *serial* devices: They work on information one step at a time. In contrast, our brains appear to process information in a *parallel* fashion; this means that many *modules*—collections of interconnected neurons—process information in different ways simultaneously. These modules may be scattered at widely different locations in the brain. Moreover, each may work on a different aspect of a task. The more complex the task, the greater the number of modules that are called into operation. The result is that even very complex tasks can be handled very quickly, because different aspects of them are performed at the same time. In contrast, a computer proceeds in a serial manner, working on one step at a time, and this can result in slower performance, especially for complex tasks.

As a concrete illustration of this difference, let's consider visual perception. We could readily program modern computers to differentiate between simple shapes such as triangles and squares. How would the computer do this? If we started with a drawing of, for instance, a triangle, this could be scanned by an input device (e.g., a scanner). The computer would then use this information to calculate the location of each line in the drawing, the angles between them, and so on. This information would then be compared with definitions of *triangle* and *square* previously entered into the computer's memory (or the program), and the computer would classify each figure as "triangle" or "square," depending on how closely it matched these definitions. So far, so good. But what if we wanted the computer to recognize human faces? The program for *this* task would be truly immense, and step-by-step serial processing might take a long time because each new face would be compared with all the ones stored in the computer's memory. In contrast, because our brains employ parallel processing, we can handle this task with ease. So the fact that our brains act as parallel processors is a big advantage. (Figure 2.12 illustrates the difference between these two kinds of processing.)

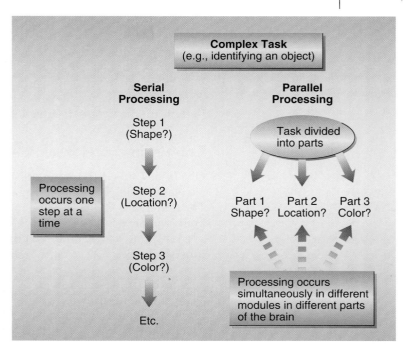

FIGURE 2.12
Parallel versus Serial Processing
In serial processing, tasks are performed one step at a time, in sequence. In parallel processing, in contrast, tasks are divided into subtasks, and all of these are performed simultaneously. Growing evidence suggests that our brains function through parallel processing, in which separate *modules* (collections of interconnected neurons) work on various parts of a task simultaneously.

Plasticity of the Human Brain: How the Brain Is Shaped by Experience

Now that we've described how the brain functions, it's important to consider another basic fact about it: its *plasticity*. Psychologists use this term to refer to the fact that the brain is actually altered by experience. So, for example, if you learn a new skill, such as how to play a musical instrument, changes occur in the structure of your brain—changes that can, potentially, be observed and measured. Similarly, our capacity to retain information in memory, too, is related to structural changes in the brain. Many factors, aside from experience, are capable of producing such changes, including various drugs, hormones, illness, and stress (Kolb, Gibb, & Robinson, 2003). What kinds of changes are produced by these and other aspects of our life experience? Changes in the number of neurons in various parts of our brain, and changes in the length of dendrites and dendritic "spines," areas where neurons form synapses with many other neurons. For instance, when animals are placed in complex, stimulating environments, either as juveniles, in adulthood, or even in old age, they experience structural changes in their brains. The precise nature of these changes, though, may vary with their ages—thus illustrating how complex the interplay between our brains and the external world actually is (e.g., Kolb, Gibb, & Gorny, 2003).

Plasticity of the brain also extends to what happens after injuries. If the areas damaged are not too extensive or crucial, functions lost can be recovered, as other neurons and other regions of the brain "take over" the tasks performed by the damaged areas. For instance, after suffering serious strokes that damage motor areas of their brains, many patients can no longer work. After undergoing months of physical therapy, however, they may regain this ability as other, nearby regions "learn" to perform the necessary functions.

The Brain and Human Speech

One of us (Robert Baron) once had a fascinating experience while visiting France. He was walking behind a young couple and their child, a little girl of perhaps three. The father was French and the mother was British, and the little girl's command of both languages was amazing. She switched back and forth between them without even a slight pause; and even more impressive, it soon became clear that every time she spoke, *she chose the language that allowed her to say what she meant with the fewest words!* Feats like this indicate that our capacities to produce and understand speech are truly remarkable. And, fortunately, these amazing abilities aren't nearly as mysterious as they once were. In recent decades, psychologists and other scientists have gained a much clearer picture of the regions of our brains that play a key role in speech. We say "regions" because, in fact, several areas are important, and it is the integrated functioning of all of them that allows us to produce and understand speech.

Let's start with speech production. Here, a region in the frontal lobe near the primary motor cortex, known as **Broca's area,** is crucial. Damage to this area disrupts the ability to speak, producing a condition known as *Broca's aphasia.* People with Broca's aphasia produce slow, laborious speech that does not follow normal rules of grammar. For instance, on being asked to describe a picture of a girl giving flowers to her teacher, one patient said, "Girl . . . wants to . . . flowers . . . flowers and wants to . . . The woman wants to . . . The girls wants to . . . the flowers and the women" (Saffran, Schwartz, & Marin, 1980). In addition, persons with Broca's aphasia can't seem to find the word they want, and even if they do, have difficulty pronouncing these words. What do all these symptoms mean? One interpretation is that this portion of the brain, and the regions immediately around it, contain memories of the sequences of muscular movements in the mouth and tongue that produce words. When it is damaged, therefore, the ability to produce coherent speech is impaired.

The task of speech comprehension—understanding what others say—seems to be focused largely in another region of the brain located in the temporal lobe. Damage to this region—known as **Wernicke's area**—produces three major symptoms: inability to recognize spoken words (i.e., to tell one from another), inability to understand the meaning of these words, and inability to convert thoughts into words. Together, these symptoms are known as *Wernicke's aphasia.* Careful study of these symptoms has revealed that, in fact, they stem from somewhat different kinds of damage to the brain. For instance, if Wernicke's area alone is damaged, *pure word deafness* occurs—individuals can't understand what is said to them and they can't repeat words they hear; that's the first major symptom listed above. They aren't deaf, however; they can recognize the emotion expressed by the tone of others' speech (e.g., that they are angry or sad), and can hear other sounds, such as doorbells or the barking of a dog. Further, they can understand what other people say by reading their lips. Other kinds of damage produce the other symptoms mentioned (e.g., inability to convert thoughts into words).

Putting these and related findings together, the following model of human speech has emerged. The meanings of words involve our memories for them—what they represent (objects, actions), and such memories are stored in sensory association areas outside Broca's and Wernicke's areas. *Comprehension* of speech

Broca's Area
A region in the prefrontal cortex that plays a role in the production of speech.

Wernicke's Area
An area in the temporal lobe that plays a role in the comprehension of speech.

involves a flow of information from Wernicke's area to the posterior language area and then to sensory association areas and back again. In contrast, speech *production* involves the flow of information from sensory association areas to the posterior language area and then to Broca's area. This is probably an oversimplification of a highly complex process, but it is consistent with current knowledge about the role of the brain in speech. Figure 2.13 summarizes this emerging and model.

The Brain and Higher Mental Processes

Try this simple problem: Maria has longer hair than Takesha. Takesha has longer hair than Brianna. Does Maria have longer hair than Brianna? The answer is obvious, but how do you obtain it so effortlessly? The basic theme of this chapter ("Everything psychological is ultimately biological") suggests that reasoning, problem solving, planning, and all of our *higher mental processes* must involve events occurring in our brains. But what parts of our brains? And what kind of events? These are among the questions currently being investigated by psychologists in their efforts to understand the role of the brain in all aspects of human behavior (e.g., Johnson et al., 2004; Robin & Holyoak, 1995). As an example of this research, let's consider recent findings concerning the neural foundations of one important kind of reasoning.

Relational Reasoning

Relational reasoning, one important kind, is illustrated by the hair-length example. In essence, reasoning depends on the ability to manipulate mental representations of relations between objects and events in our minds: You don't have to see Maria, Takesha, and Brianna to know that Maria's hair is longer—you can tell just from reasoning about them. But here's the crucial point: While you can tell that Maria's hair is longer than Takesha's directly from the sentence "Maria's hair is longer than Takesha's," there is no statement comparing Maria and Brianna, so here, you must mentally integrate available information to attain the correct solution. This ability, many experts believe, may underlie several of our higher mental processes. For instance, consider planning. To formulate effective plans, we must be able to arrange many goals and subgoals according to their importance, and this, again, involves being able to mentally manipulate information so that we can see, for instance, that goal C is more important than goal D, which, in turn, is more important than goal F (e.g., Delis et al., 1992).

Now for the key question: Does any part of the brain play a special role in such reasoning? A growing body of evidence suggests that the *prefrontal cortex*—part of the association areas of the brain—is a likely candidate (e.g., Graham & Hodges, 1997; Waltz et al., 1999).

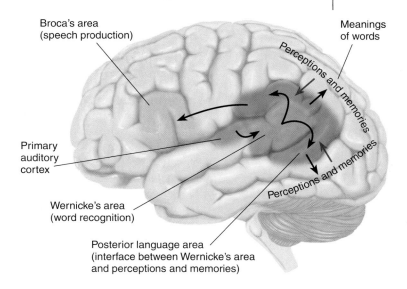

Broca's area (speech production)

Meanings of words

Perceptions and memories

Primary auditory cortex

Wernicke's area (word recognition)

Posterior language area (interface between Wernicke's area and perceptions and memories)

Perceptions and memories

FIGURE 2.13
The Neural Basis of Human Speech: One Model
Existing research suggests that *comprehension* of speech involves the flow of information from Wernicke's area to the posterior language area and then to sensory association areas and back again. (The meanings of words may be stored in sensory association areas.) Speech *production* involves the flow of information from sensory association areas to the posterior language area and then to Broca's area.

Source: From Neil R. Carlson, *Foundations of Physiological Psychology*, 4/e © 1999. Published by Allyn and Bacon, Boston, MA. Copyright © 1999 by Pearson Education. Reprinted by permission of the publisher.

KEY QUESTIONS

- What is the modern view of how the brain functions?
- What is brain plasticity and why is it important?
- What evidence suggests that processing of visual information occurs in a parallel fashion?
- What is the modern view of speech production and speech comprehension?
- What portions of the brain are involved in relational reasoning?

HEREDITY AND BEHAVIOR: GENETICS AND EVOLUTIONARY PSYCHOLOGY

When my (Robert Baron's) daughter Jessica was very young and we went places together, people would often say things like this to us: "I can tell whose little girl *you* are!" or "My, don't you look like your daddy!" (You can judge for yourself in the photo in Figure 2.14.) The fact that we do often resemble people to whom we are closely related illustrates the powerful impact of **heredity**—biologically determined characteristics—on our physical appearance and traits. But what about behavior? Does heredity affect the ways in which we behave and think, too? A growing body of evidence suggests that it does, although the relationship between heredity and complex forms of behavior is very complex. Let's take a look, first, at the basic processes through which we inherit the predisposition or potential for a wide range of characteristics from our parents. After that, we'll consider some of the evidence for the impact of heredity on complex and important forms of behavior.

Genetics: Some Basic Principles

Every cell of your body contains a set of biological blueprints that enable it to perform its essential functions. This information is contained in **chromosomes,** structures found in the nuclei of all cells. Chromosomes are composed of a substance known as DNA, short for deoxyribonucleic acid. DNA, in turn, is made up of several simpler components arranged in the form of a double helix—something like the twisting water slides found by the sides of large swimming pools. Chromosomes contain thousands of **genes**—segments of DNA that serve as basic units of heredity. Our genes, working in complex combinations and together with forces in the environment, ultimately determine many aspects of our biological makeup.

Most cells in the human body contain forty-six chromosomes, existing in pairs. When such cells divide, the chromosome pairs split; then, after the cells have separated, each chromosome replicates itself so that the full number is restored. This kind of cell division is known as **mitosis.** In contrast, sperm and ova—the male and female sex cells, or gametes—contain only twenty-three chromosomes. Thus, when they join to form a fertilized ovum from which a new human being will develop, the full number (forty-six) is attained. For each of us, then, half of our genetic material comes from our mother and half from our father. In general, the members of each pair of chromosomes look very similar—with one exception. One chromosome pair is directly linked to biological sex: females possess two chromosomes that are "full-size" and contain one thousand or more genes (X chromosomes). Males, in contrast, possess an X chromosome and a much shorter Y chromosome, which contains fewer than one hundred genes. Because there is only one Y chromosome, it cannot divide like other chromosomes during mitosis. Rather, it bends in half and reproduces in this manner (Wade, 2003).

These basic mechanisms explain why persons who are related resemble one another more than persons

FIGURE 2.14
The Role of Heredity in Physical Appearance
Do this father (Robert Baron) and his daughter (Jessica) look alike? At the time the photo was taken, many people said that they did. Do you agree? If so, this is a clear illustration of the role of genetic factors in physical characteristics such as facial appearance.

who are unrelated, and also why the closer the familial tie between individuals, the more similar they tend to be physically. The closer such links, the greater the proportion of chromosomes and genes family members share. And because genes determine many aspects of physical appearance, similarity increases with closeness of relationship. Thus, siblings (children of the same parents) tend to be more alike than cousins (the children of siblings). In the case of identical twins, or *monozygotic* twins, a single fertilized egg splits in two and forms two embryos; in contrast, non-identical or *fraternal* twins grow from two eggs fertilized by two different sperm. Because identical twins share all of their genes, they are usually remarkably similar in appearance. They are surprisingly similar in other respects as well, including—amazingly!—their religious beliefs, their television viewing preferences, and even their grief responses (e.g., Segal & Bouchard, 1993).

While genes may strongly affect our physical characteristics, their relationship to psychological characteristics and to behavior is often highly complex. Genes do not *control* behavior or other aspects of life directly. Rather, they exert their influence indirectly, through their impact on chemical reactions in the brain or other organs. Moreover, as we'll soon see, these reactions may be strongly influenced by environmental conditions. In short, our genes equip us with predispositions to develop or show certain patterns of behavior or traits, but the environments in which we live play a major role in determining whether, and to what extent, such tendencies become reality. To make matters even more complex, most human traits are determined by more than one gene. In fact, hundreds of genes acting in concert with environmental forces may be involved in shaping complex physical or cognitive abilities (Lerner, 1993; McClearn et al., 1991). So, while there is increasing evidence for the role of genetic factors in many aspects of human behavior, heredity is only part of the total story.

Disentangling Genetic and Environmental Effects: Research Strategies

If both heredity and environment influence human behavior, the next question is obvious: How do we separate these factors in order to determine the relative contribution of each to any particular aspect of behavior? This question relates, of course, to the *nature–nurture controversy* described in Chapter 1, and psychologists use a number of different methods to address it. Two of these, however, have proven to be most useful: *twin studies* and *adoption studies.*

Twin studies are helpful in disentangling the relative roles of genetic and environmental factors in a given form of behavior because of the fact mentioned earlier: Identical twins share the same genes, while fraternal twins do not. Under normal conditions, however, both kinds of twins are raised in environments that, if not identical, are at least very similar. After all, pairs of twins are normally raised in the same homes, attend the same schools, and so on. Thus, if a given aspect of behavior is strongly influenced by genetic factors, we'd expect identical twins to resemble each other more closely in this respect than fraternal twins. If an aspect of behavior is *not* influenced by genetic factors, however, we would not anticipate such differences. As we'll see in Chapter 14, psychologists have used this approach to investigate the role of genetic factors in many forms of mental disorder and have found that, indeed, genetic factors *do* play a role in several of these (e.g., phobias, autistic disorders, depression, schizophrenia; e.g., Merkelbach et al., 1996).

A major problem with such twin studies, however, is obvious: The environments in which they are raised are often *not* identical. This is especially true for fraternal twins who may differ in sex, and so are treated quite differently by parents and other persons. For this reason, twin studies, while revealing, cannot provide conclusive evidence on the relative role of genetic and environmental factors. Actually, *no* single type of study can provide such evidence, but a second research approach—*adoption studies*—does seem to come closer to this goal. Such research focuses on identical

Heredity
Biologically determined characteristics passed from parents to their offspring.

Chromosomes
Threadlike structures containing genetic material, found in nearly every cell of the body.

Genes
Biological "blueprints" that shape development and all basic bodily processes.

Mitosis
Cell division in which chromosome pairs split and then replicate themselves so that the full number is restored in each of the cells produced by division.

FIGURE 2.15
Identical Twins: More Than Mere Look-Alikes
Growing evidence suggests that identical twins are highly similar with respect to many aspects of behavior—not just in the way they look. Moreover, this is so even if they are separated very early in life and raised in different environments. These findings suggest that genetic factors play a role in a much wider range of human behavior than was once believed.

twins who, because they are adopted into different homes, are separated very soon after birth. Because the twins have identical genes, differences between them with respect to various aspects of behavior can reasonably be attributed to environmental factors. We'll describe research using this approach at several points in this book, and as we'll see in those discussions, adoption studies involving identical twins provide compelling evidence for the role of genetic factors in many aspects of human behavior. Even when they are raised in sharply contrasting environments, identical twins show remarkable degrees of similarity in everything from various aspects of their personalities, to attitudes and values, hobbies, career choices, and even job satisfaction (see Figure 2.15; Lykken et al., 1992; Hershberger, Lichtenstein, & Knox, 1994).

Using such methods, psychologists have been able to arrive at estimates of what is known as **heritability** for various traits. This term refers to the extent to which variations among individuals with respect to a given aspect of behavior or a given trait are due to genetic factors. So, if it is found that heritability for a given trait is 0.50, this suggests that 50 percent of the differences between individuals in this trait is due to genetic factors. For instance, suppose it were found that the heritability of intelligence is 0.50 (it actually is). This means that 50 percent of the variation in intelligence among individuals in the population for which heritability has been estimated is due to genetic factors. It does *not* mean that half of each person's intelligence is determined by genetic factors and half by environmental factors. So, heritability estimates should be treated with caution. Still, they do provide a rough index of the extent to which genetic factors influence any aspect of behavior, and so are of considerable interest.

We just mentioned that intelligence (at least the kind measured by IQ) has a heritability index of 0.50. This might lead you to conclude that scientists should be able to identify specific genes that contribute to a high IQ. In fact, though, efforts to do this have run into major obstacles. While it appears that some genes (probably many) are related to intelligence, each makes a very small contribution. Thus, it is primarily the complex interplay between these genes, and between genes and the environment, that determines intelligence. For instance, a very small difference in intelligence produced by genetic factors may be magnified, over time, by differences in experience. A child who starts out with slightly above-average intelligence may spend more time reading and thus may receive more praise from teachers than a child who starts out with average intelligence. These experiences may serve to magnify the first child's initially small advantage in intelligence. Similarly, children raised in environments that stimulate and challenge them intellectually may develop higher IQs as a result of these experiences (Begley, 2003). So, clearly, single genes do *not* determine anything as complex as intelligence. Rather, such multifaceted traits are shaped by intricate interplay between genetic and environmental forces. (We'll describe these in detail in Chapter 7).

Heritability
The extent to which variations among individuals, with respect to a given aspect of behavior or a given trait, are due to genetic factors.

Evolutionary Psychology: Genes in Action

Do you recall our discussion of the new field of **evolutionary psychology** in Chapter 1? To refresh your memory: This field suggests that our species, like all others on the planet, has been subject to the process of biological evolution throughout its history. As a result, we now possess a large number of *evolved psychological mechanisms* that help (or once helped) us to deal with important problems relating to survival. These have evolved because organisms vary greatly in many different ways, and some of these variations can be passed from one generation to the next through genes. Because some of these variations give individuals who possess them an advantage in terms of reproduction, natural selection ensures that, over time, these variations become more common in the species. But watch out: Just because a characteristic or behavioral tendency exists among members of a species (including our own) does *not* in any way guarantee that it is useful (adaptive). On the contrary, it may simply exist because it is linked, genetically, to something else that *is* useful (de Waal, 2002). For instance, consider the structure of the human back: Because it is not well suited for our upright posture, many people suffer serious back problems (slipped disks, neck pain). Why, then, do we continue to have the back structure we do? Perhaps because the advantages conferred by an upright posture are so great that they outweigh these problems. This illustrates the fact that just because something exists in a species does *not* guarantee that it is useful or adaptive; it may, in fact, be the "by-product" of something else that *is* adaptive.

We examined some examples of evolutionary psychology in Chapter 1, so here we'll simply note that this perspective has been used to shed light on a wide range of behaviors: everything from *dominance motivation*—why people often desire to attain positions of high status in their societies (e.g., Ellis, 1995)—through the tendency to help others—to show *prosocial behavior* (Buss, 1999). In fact, recent studies suggest that even our preference for fair treatment may reflect a genetic component. Consider research by Brosnan and de Waal (2003), conducted with monkeys. Pairs of monkeys working in full view of each other were first rewarded with tokens that they could then trade for slices of cucumber. After the monkeys had learned to do this, conditions were changed so that one was rewarded with grapes while the other continued to receive cucumbers. Because monkeys strongly prefer grapes to cucumbers, the key question was this: Would the underrewarded monkeys (the ones still receiving cucumber) object? In fact, they did; many refused to exchange their tokens for this inadequate reward, and some even threw the cucumber away after receiving it! One interpretation of these findings is that the desire for fairness is "built into" our primate nature (although, of course, other explanations exist, as well; for instance, perhaps the monkeys had already learned to value fairness through their past experience). We'll return to the role of perceived fairness in work settings in Chapter 14.

In sum, evolutionary psychology provides a unique and intriguing perspective on the question of *how* our genes can, over time, shape our behavior. Whether the explanations it provides will turn out to be valid, however, can be determined only by further, careful research. (If a tendency to behave in some way is an evolved psychological mechanism, does this mean it cannot be changed? Absolutely not! For an example of how behaviors that may partly reflect genetic factors may be altered, please see the **Psychology Lends a Hand** section.)

Evolutionary Psychology
A new field of psychology, suggesting that as a result of evolution, human beings now possess a large number of *evolved psychological mechanisms* that help (or once helped) us deal with important problems relating to survival.

KEY QUESTIONS

- How do psychologists seek to separate the role of genetic and environmental factors in many forms of behavior?
- What is heritability?
- Why is it true that the existence of a trait or behavior among members of a species does not guarantee that the trait or behavior is useful or adaptive?
- How can behaviors that stem, at least in part, from genetic factors be changed?

p s y c h o l o g y   l e n d s   a   h a n d

Reducing High-Risk Behavior among Young Males

Statistics indicate that young males under the age of twenty-five are several times more likely to be involved in fatal automobile accidents than any other group. Why? Evolutionary psychology suggests that the tendency to engage in reckless driving and other forms of dangerous behavior may be an evolved psychological mechanism: Performing such actions may help young males attract potential mates by demonstrating that they (the young males in question) are so strong and fit that they can engage in risky actions without getting hurt (Nell, 2002). If this tendency is indeed part of our genetic inheritance (an interesting but as yet unverified possibility), how can it be reduced? Psychology suggests several effective steps that *you* can use to discourage risky behavior on the part of people whose health and well-being are important to you (Nell, 2001).

One approach would be to convince young males who engage in such behaviors that many females do *not* find these actions sexy or attractive; on the contrary, they are frightened by them. Because high-risk behaviors would then be counterproductive from the point of view of obtaining attractive mates, males might be less likely to engage in them. So, if you want to discourage such behavior on the part of someone you know, this might well be a useful approach: Get several attractive women to let this person know

that they are not impressed by high-risk actions and, in fact, think less of men who engage in them.

Another technique would involve finding out what it is that young males *do* fear; while they are not, apparently, afraid of death or injury (partly because they feel they are invulnerable), they may be afraid of disfiguring injuries; after all, this would cause them to be less attractive to females. Carrying this even further, they are almost certainly afraid of injuries to sensitive parts of their bodies—injuries that would prevent them from engaging in sexual relations. So, if you want to discourage a friend, relative, or lover from engaging in high-risk behaviors, showing them examples of these kinds of consequences might well do the trick.

The main point of this discussion is simply this: Just because a tendency or behavior stems, in part, from genetic factors in no way means that it cannot be modified. Remember: The nervous system and brain show a high degree of plasticity. As a result, new experiences and information can modify the underlying structures that shape our behaviors. So, while biology *is* important, it is *not* destiny where human beings are concerned: Change is always possible, and adaptability may, in fact, be the most useful evolved psychological mechanism we possess!

SUMMARY AND REVIEW OF KEY QUESTIONS

Neurons: Building Blocks of the Nervous System

- **What do neurons do and what are their basic parts?**
  Neurons are cells specialized for receiving, processing, and moving information. They are made up of a cell body, an axon, and one or more dendrites.

- **What are action potentials? How do neurons communicate with one another?**
  Action potentials are rapid changes in the electrical properties of the cell membranes of neurons. They constitute a mechanism by which information travels through the nervous system. Graded potentials occur in response to a physical stimulus or stimulation by another neuron; they weaken quickly and their strength is directly proportional to the intensity of the physical stimulus that produced them. Neurons communicate across tiny gaps (synapses) that separate them by means of neurotransmitters.

- **What are the effects of neurotransmitters?**
  Neurotransmitters produce one of two effects: Excitatory effects make it more likely that a cell will fire; inhibitory effects make it less likely that the cell will fire.

- **How do drugs produce their effects? What are agonists? Antagonists?**
  Many drugs produce their effects by influencing synaptic transmission. Agonists are drugs that mimic the impact of neurotransmitters at specific receptors; drugs that inhibit their impact are termed *antagonists*.

The Nervous System: Its Basic Structure and Functions

- **What structures compose the central nervous system? What is the function of the spinal cord?**
  The central nervous system includes the brain and the spinal cord. The spinal cord carries sensory information from receptors of the body to the brain and carries infor-

mation from the brain to muscles and glands. It also plays an important role in reflexes.

- **What two systems make up the peripheral nervous system?**
  The peripheral nervous system consists of the somatic and autonomic nervous systems.

- **What are the roles of these two systems?**
  The somatic nervous system connects the brain and spinal cord to voluntary muscles throughout the body; the autonomic nervous system connects the central nervous system to internal organs and glands and to muscles over which we have little voluntary control.

- **What are the functions of the sympathetic and parasympathetic nervous systems?**
  The sympathetic nervous system prepares the body for using energy, whereas the parasympathetic nervous system activates processes that conserve the body's energy.

- **What is the endocrine system?**
  A communication system that operates by releasing hormones into the bloodstream.

- **What are some of its major parts?**
  The endocrine system includes the pituitary and adrenal glands, plus several others.

The Brain: Where Consciousness Dwells

- **What structures compose the brain stem? What are their functions?**
  The brain stem—including the medulla, pons, and cerebellum—is concerned primarily with the regulation of basic bodily functions. The cerebellum, however, may be involved in higher cognitive processes, such as learning.

- **What are the functions of the hypothalamus and thalamus?**
  The hypothalamus is a brain structure involved in the regulation of motivated behavior and emotion. The thalamus serves as a relay station, directing incoming messages to appropriate brain regions.

- **What is the role of the cerebral cortex?**
  The cerebral cortex is the hub for such higher mental processes as thinking, planning, reasoning, and memory.

- **Who are "split-brain" persons? What evidence do they provide for specialization of function in the two cerebral hemispheres?**
  These are persons whose cerebral hemispheres have been isolated from each other through surgery. Evidence they provide suggests that the left hemisphere is specialized for verbal tasks while the right hemisphere is specialized for perceptual tasks and expression and recognition of emotions.

- **What evidence from persons with intact brains supports such specialization?**
  PET scans of normal persons reveal that when they speak or work with numbers, activity in the left hemisphere increases. When they work on perceptual tasks, activity increases in the right hemisphere.

- **What methods are used by psychologists to study the brain and its role in behavior?**
  These methods involve examining the effects of damage to various portions of the brain or nervous system, recording and stimulating neural activity, and obtaining images of the intact, living brain.

The Brain and Human Behavior: Where Biology and Consciousness Meet

- **What is the modern view of how the brain functions?**
  The brain processes information in parallel, in many modules.

- **What is brain plasticity and why is it important?**
  Plasticity refers to the fact that the structure and functioning of the brain are influenced by experience. Plasticity is important because it is these changes that permit us to learn, remember information, and adapt to an ever-changing world in many different ways.

- **What evidence suggests that processing of visual information occurs in a parallel fashion?**
  Evidence indicates that visual information about object identification is processed separately from information about where an object is or how we can react to it.

- **What is the modern view of speech production and speech comprehension?**
  Speech *production* involves the flow of information from sensory association areas to the posterior language area and then to Broca's area. *Comprehension* of speech involves a flow of information from Wernicke's area to the posterior language area and then to sensory association areas and back again.

- **What portions of the brain are involved in relational reasoning?**
  Such reasoning seems to occur primarily in the prefontal cortex.

Heredity and Behavior: Genetics and Evolutionary Psychology

- **How do psychologists seek to separate the roles of genetic and environmental factors in many forms of behavior?**
  They do this primarily with twin studies and adoption studies.

- **What is heritability?**
  The extent to which variations among individuals with respect to a given aspect of behavior or a given trait are due to genetic factors.

- **Why is it true that the existence of a trait or behavior among members of a species does not guarantee that the trait or behavior is useful or adaptive?**
  Presence of a trait or behavior does not guarantee that it is useful or adaptive because the trait or behavior may simply be a "by-product" of something else that *is* useful.

PSYCHOLOGY: UNDERSTANDING ITS FINDINGS

Do People Inherit Their Personalities?

Have you ever heard someone say, "She's real out-going, just like her father," or "He's very organized, just like his mother"? Statements like this suggest that genetic factors play a role in personality. Do you think this is true? Suppose you were interested in obtaining evidence on this intriguing issue, how would you go about it? In other words, what kind of research would you conduct to find out whether at least

some aspects of personality can be inherited? Here are some steps to help you get started:

1. State the hypothesis you want to test.
2. Identify the aspects of personality you want to measure.
3. Formulate a list of environmental variables that might affect these aspects of personality.
4. Identify methods you could use to separate the effects of these factors from the effects of genetic factors.

MAKING PSYCHOLOGY PART OF YOUR LIFE

Observing Your Own Evolved Psychological Mechanisms

Evolved psychological mechanisms are inherited patterns of behavior or behavior tendencies that help the members of a given species survive and reproduce. Many people find it difficult to accept that many aspects of their behavior—everything from their choice of a mate through their desire for status—may stem, at least in part, from genetic factors. How do you feel about this possibility? Before making up your mind, try the following exercise.

1. Think about two key areas of life: love (seeking romantic partners) and food (what you like to eat). For each, make a list of your preferences (i.e., what you are seeking in romantic partners; foods you like to eat).
2. Now for each item on your list, consider the following question: Could this preference stem from genetic factors? In other words, could having this preference be beneficial in terms of survival and reproduction?
3. Examine the pattern of your answers; do you find many aspects of your behavior and preferences that could, indeed, reflect evolved psychological mechanisms?

KEY TERMS

Action Potential, p. 32
Agonist, p. 34
Amygdala, p. 40
Antagonist, p. 34
Autonomic Nervous System, p. 36
Axon, p. 31
Axon Terminals, p. 32
Broca's Area, p. 48
Central Nervous System, p. 35
Cerebellum, p. 39
Cerebral Cortex, p. 40
Chromosomes, p. 51
Corpus Callosum, p. 42
Dendrite, p. 31
Endocrine System, p. 37
Evolutionary Psychology, p. 53
Frontal Lobe, p. 41

Genes, p. 51
Heredity, p. 51
Heritability, p. 52
Hippocampus, p. 40
Hormones, p. 37
Hypothalamus, p. 40
Limbic System, p. 40
Magnetic Resonance Imaging
    (MRI), p. 45
Medulla, p. 39
Midbrain, p. 39
Mitosis, p. 51
Nervous System, p. 35
Neurons, p. 31
Neurotransmitters (transmitter sub-
    stances), p. 32
Occipital Lobe, p. 41

Parasympathetic Nervous System,
    p. 36
Parietal Lobe, p. 41
Peripheral Nervous System, p. 35
Pituitary Gland, p. 37
Pons, p. 39
Positron Emission Tomography
    (PET), p. 45
Reflexes, p. 35
Reticular Activating System, p. 39
Somatic Nervous System, p. 36
Sympathetic Nervous System, p. 36
Synapse, p. 32
Synaptic Vesicles, p. 32
Temporal Lobe, p. 41
Thalamus, p. 40
Wernicke's Area, p. 48

Sensation and Perception: Making Contact with the World around Us

*T*his past summer, my eight-year-old son (Ryan Kalsher) was selected to play on his little league's all-star team. In many respects, he clearly deserved this honor. He has terrific vision, good hand–eye coordination, and he is well rounded as a baseball player. During one particular game in the all-star series, the coach decided to put him in left field, a position he had not played before. Soon after Ryan had taken the field, an opposing player got up to bat and hit a towering shot to—you guessed it—left field! The coach (and nearly everyone else at the game) immediately began shouting, "Heads up, Ryan!" to alert my son to the event. I anxiously watched as my son sized up the situation. Just as it seemed he had it under control, and had positioned himself where he anticipated the ball would come down, I saw the helpless look on his face as he watched the ball fly well over his head. It landed fully twenty feet behind him and then continued rolling toward the left field fence. Although Ryan quickly retrieved the ball, thereby preventing a home run, he had clearly misperceived the flight of the ball.

FIGURE 3.1
Experiencing the World around Us: The Role of Sensory Processes
Our ability to interact successfully with the world around us, such as making correct judgments about the predicted path of moving objects, is the result of complex processes occurring within the nervous system.

Sensation
Input about the physical world provided by our sensory receptors.

Perception
The process through which we select, organize, and interpret input from our sensory receptors.

Sensory Receptors
Cells of the body specialized for the task of *transduction*—converting physical energy (light, sound) into neural impulses.

Transduction
The translation of a physical energy into electrical signals by specialized receptor cells.

Why do we start with this example? Because we believe it helps to illustrate the fact that the world around us is complicated, even for relatively simple events, such as the baseball incident just described (please refer to Figure 3.1). Moreover, the processes that help us make sense out of the sights, sounds, smells, tastes, and feelings that constantly bombard us are not as simple or direct as common sense might suggest. Careful psychological research conducted over the past one hundred years has shown that we do not understand the external world in a simple, automatic way. Rather, we actively construct our interpretation of sensory information through several complex processes.

To clarify how we make sense of the world around us, psychologists distinguish between two key concepts: *sensation* and *perception*. The study of **sensation** is concerned with the initial contact between organisms and their physical environment. It focuses on describing the relationship between various forms of sensory stimulation (including electromagnetic, sound waves, pressure) and how these inputs are registered by our sense organs (the eyes, ears, nose, tongue, and skin). In contrast, the study of **perception** is concerned with identifying the processes through which we interpret and organize this information to produce our conscious experience of objects and relationships among objects. It is important to remember that perception is not simply a passive process of decoding incoming sensory information. If this were the case, we would lose the richness of our everyday stream of conscious experiences.

The complementary processes of sensation and perception play a role in virtually every topic we will consider in later chapters. For these reasons, we will devote careful attention to them here. We'll begin by exploring in detail how the receptors for each sensory system transform raw physical energy into an electrochemical code. As we'll soon note, our sensory receptors are exquisitely designed to detect various aspects of the world around us. We'll also consider the possibility of subliminal perception—perception without any underlying sensation. Next, we'll turn our attention to the active process of perception. Here, we'll focus on how the brain integrates and interprets the constant flow of information it receives from our senses. Finally, we'll conclude by examining evidence concerning the possibility of extrasensory perception or *psi*.

SENSATION: THE RAW MATERIALS OF UNDERSTANDING

The sight of a breathtaking sunset, the pleasant fragrance of a summer rose, the smooth texture of a baby's skin, the sharp "crack" of a starter's pistol at the beginning of a race: Exactly how are we able to experience these events? As you may recall from Chapter 2, all of these sensory experiences are based on complex processes occurring within the nervous system. This highlights an intriguing paradox. Although we are continually bombarded by various forms of physical energy, including light, heat, sound, and smells, our brain cannot directly detect the presence of these forces. Instead, it can only respond to intricate patterns of action potentials conducted by *neurons*, special cells within our bodies that receive, move, and process sensory information. Thus, a critical question is how the many forms of physical energy impacting our sensory systems are converted into signals our nervous system can understand.

Highly specialized cells known as **sensory receptors**, located in our eyes, ears, nose, tongue, and elsewhere, are responsible for accomplishing this coding task. Thus, sights, sounds, and smells that we experience are actually the products of **transduction**, a process in which the physical properties of stimuli are converted into neural signals that are then transmitted to our brain via specialized sensory nerves. To illustrate how our nervous system makes sense out of the surging sea of physical energies in our environment, we'll begin by focusing on two critical concepts: *thresholds* and *sensory adaptation.*

Sensory Thresholds: How Much Stimulation Is Enough?

Although our receptors are remarkably efficient, they do not register all the information available in the environment at any given moment. We are able to smell and taste certain chemicals but not others; we hear sound waves only at certain frequencies; and our ability to detect light energy is restricted to a relatively narrow band of wavelengths. The range of physical stimuli that we and other species can detect, however, is uniquely designed to maximize survival potential. Because human survival is tied to our unique capacity for spoken language, it is not surprising that our auditory system is best at detecting sound frequencies that closely match the frequencies of human speech (Goldstein, 2002).

For more than a century, psychologists have investigated the sensory capabilities of the various sense organs. An important goal of this area of research, termed **psychophysics,** has been to establish the relationship between physical properties of stimuli, such as brightness and loudness, and people's psychological experience of them. A casual observer might assume such a relationship to be a direct one. In other words, given a stimulus of sufficient intensity, we should always be able to detect its presence. This suggests that at levels above a certain intensity, a person would always report detecting the stimulus. In practice, this pattern of results almost never occurs. Why? One reason is that our sensitivity to stimuli changes from moment to moment. Bodily functions change constantly in order to maintain the body's internal environment at optimal levels, a state termed *homeostasis.* It is not surprising that as a result of these changes, the sensitivity of our sensory organs to external stimuli also varies. For this reason, psychologists have coined the term **absolute threshold** to describe our sensory threshold and define it as the smallest magnitude of a stimulus that can be reliably discriminated from no stimulus at all 50 percent of the time.

■ Sensory Thresholds: Some Complications

Our discussions to this point seem to indicate that sensory thresholds are not really "fixed," but instead change in response to a number of factors, including fatigue, lapses in attention, and moment-to-moment fluctuations that occur within our nervous system. Additional research suggests that *motivational factors,* or the rewards or costs associated with detecting various stimuli, may also play an important role.

According to **signal detection theory,** complex decision mechanisms are involved whenever we try to determine if we have or have not detected a specific stimulus (Erev, 1998; Swets, 1992). An important point to remember is that stimuli (signals) are usually embedded in the context of other competing stimuli, or background "noise." Obviously, the challenge is to distinguish signal from noise. Two concepts—*sensitivity* and *bias*—help to explain how these signals are either detected or missed. *Sensitivity* refers to a person's ability to distinguish between a faint stimulus (the signal) and the background (the noise). *Bias* refers to a person's willingness to report noticing the stimulus—in other words, how strong the stimulus needs to be before the person says he or she detected it. To illustrate the relationship between these two concepts, consider the following example (refer to Figure 3.2 on page 62). Imagine that you are a radiologist and while scanning a patient's X-ray you think you detect a faint spot on the film, but you're not quite sure. What should you do? If you conclude that the spot is an abnormality, you must order more scans or tests—an expensive and time-consuming alternative. If further testing reveals an abnormality, such as cancer, you may have saved the patient's life. If no abnormality is detected, though, you'll be blamed for wasting resources

Psychophysics
A set of procedures psychologists have developed to investigate the relationship between physical properties of stimuli and people's psychological experience of them.

Absolute Threshold
The smallest amount of a stimulus that we can detect 50 percent of the time.

Signal Detection Theory
A theory suggesting that there are no absolute thresholds for sensations. Rather, detection of stimuli depends on their physical energy and on internal factors, such as the relative costs and benefits associated with detecting their presence.

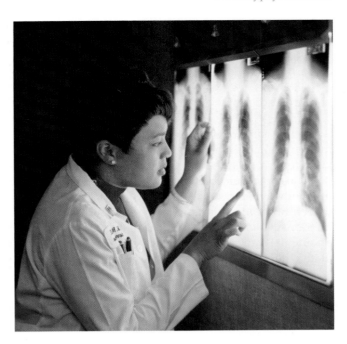

FIGURE 3.2
Signal Detection Theory: Separating Sensitivity from Motivational Factors
Signal detection theory seeks to explain why people detect signals in some situations but miss them in others. It does so by attempting to separate sensitivity from motivational factors.

and unnecessarily upsetting the patient. Alternatively, if you decide the spot is *not* an abnormality, then there's no reason to order more tests. If the patient remains healthy, then you've done the right thing. However, if the spot really is cancerous tissue, the results could be fatal. As you can see, deciding whether we have detected a given stimulus is not always easy and involves much more than a simple determination of the relationship between amount of physical energy present in a stimulus and the resulting psychological sensations. Your decision is also likely to be influenced by the rewards and costs associated with each choice alternative.

Difference Thresholds: Are Two Stimuli the Same or Different?

A good cook tastes a dish, then adds salt to it, then tastes it again to judge the change. This illustrates another basic question relating to our sensory capacities: How much change in a stimulus is required before a shift can be noticed? Psychologists refer to the amount of change in a stimulus required for a person to detect it as the **difference threshold.** Obviously, the smaller the change we can detect, the greater our sensitivity. In other words, the difference threshold is the amount of change in a physical stimulus necessary to produce a **just noticeable difference (jnd)** in sensation. As it turns out, our ability to detect differences in stimulus intensity depends on the magnitude of the initial stimulus; we easily detect even small changes in weak stimuli, but we require much larger changes before we notice differences in strong stimuli. For example, if you are listening to music at a low sound intensity, even small adjustments to the volume are noticeable. But if you crank up the volume, much larger changes are required before a difference is apparent. We are also more sensitive to changes in some types of stimuli than to changes in others. For example, we are able to notice very small shifts in temperature (less than one degree Fahrenheit) and in the pitch of sounds, but we are somewhat less sensitive to changes in loudness or in smells (Galanter, 1962).

Stimuli Below Threshold: Can They Have an Effect?

The possibility of **subliminal perception** has been a source of controversy for many years. Subliminal perception first captured the public's attention in the 1950s when a marketing executive announced he had embedded subliminal messages like "Eat popcorn" and "Drink Coke" into a then-popular movie. Supposedly, the embedded messages were flashed on the screen in front of movie audiences so briefly (a

Difference Threshold
The amount by which two stimuli must differ in order to be just noticeably different.

Just Noticeable Difference (jnd)
The amount of change in a physical stimulus necessary for an individual to notice a difference in the intensity of a stimulus.

Subliminal Perception
The presumed influence on the behavior of a stimulus that is below the threshold for conscious experience.

fraction of a second) that audience members were not aware of them (Brean, 1958). Although the executive later confessed to the hoax (no messages were actually presented), many people remained convinced that subliminal messages can be powerful sources of persuasion.

An important question raised by this, and other subsequent incidents, is whether we can sense or be affected by stimuli that remain outside our conscious awareness. The most direct answer to this question has come from studies that have used *visual priming,* in which participants are "primed" with brief exposures (often less than one-tenth of a second) to words or simple pictures. The duration of the exposure is long enough to be detected by the nervous system, but too brief for people to be consciously aware of its presence. Participants are usually unable to name the visual primes, but their reactions to stimuli presented subsequently (e.g., words or pictures) do seem to be affected.

Studies have shown that subliminally presented visual stimuli can have small but measurable effects on many aspects of our cognition and emotion, including our liking for ambiguous stimuli and words (e.g., Greenwald, Draine, & Abrams, 1996; Murphy & Zajonc, 1993), our attraction to members of the opposite sex (Bargh et al., 1995), and even our attitudes toward people (Kawakami, Dovidio, & Dijksterhuis, 2003). Repeated exposure to the same subliminal stimuli tends to strengthen their effects, and the positive effect resulting from such exposure can become associated with other unrelated stimuli (Monahan, Murphy, & Zajonc, 2000). Thus, a person who has just seen a good movie may leave the theater not only with positive feelings toward the movie, but also in a better mood that may, in turn, affect how she reacts to other people and events beyond that particular setting.

Some researchers speculate that subliminal perception may have evolved as a tool to help humans and other animals avoid predators. This intriguing idea is based on evidence showing that people are slightly better at detecting *negative* than positive stimuli when both are presented subliminally. Applied to prey animals, such as deer and rabbits, this makes sense, because being even a few milliseconds late in detecting a would-be predator could prove fatal, while being a little late in detecting possible food sources would not be so bad.

Research by Dijksterhuis and Aarts (2003) may help illustrate these findings. These researchers subliminally presented a list of words to a group of participants. Half the words had positive connotations (e.g., baby, happiness, smile), whereas the other half had negative connotations (e.g., fear, bomb, cancer). After each word was "flashed" to them, participants were asked to indicate whether it was positive or negative and to categorize the word in terms of its meaning by guessing which of two words was its synonym. The results showed that participants were slightly more accurate in detecting the negative words than the positive words (please refer to Figure 3.3). By contrast, there was no difference in participants' accuracy in categorizing the (positive and negative) words, arguably a higher-level process that would not be crucial to success in the preceding predator example.

These findings provide further evidence that the priming stimuli used in studies of subliminal perception—despite their brief duration—are registered at some level within the nervous system. However, several cautions are warranted. First, we should emphasize that speculation concerning the possible evolutionary role of subliminal perception is just that. Additional research is needed to confirm or refute this possibility. Second, the effects of visual priming are generally small, and most laboratory studies show that the effects of priming are short-lived. Finally—and perhaps most importantly—no evidence currently supports the possibility that

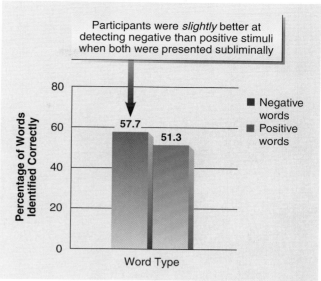

FIGURE 3.3
Subliminal Perception and Visual Priming
Although nearly all participants indicated that they had not seen anything at all, but had merely guessed throughout the experiment, they were slightly more accurate in detecting the negative words than the positive words when both were presented subliminally. Thus, despite their brief duration, these stimuli were registered at some level within the nervous system.

Source: Based on data from Dijksterhuis & Aarts, 2003.

FIGURE 3.4
Sensory Adaptation
At first, icy water feels freezing, but later it feels refreshing due to sensory adaptation.

subliminal messages are a powerful means of persuasion, as was implied earlier in this section.

Unfortunately, these facts have not slowed the explosion of self-help materials that offer to help people lose weight, stop smoking, get smarter, or improve their sex lives. Their manufacturers continue to insist that the effectiveness of these products is due to the presence of subliminal messages. Are these claims true? Systematic evidence seems to cast doubt on this possibility. Instead, any improvements people experience are more likely the result of other factors, such as motivation and expectations (Greenwald, 1991; Urban, 1992).

Sensory Adaptation: "It Feels Great Once You Get Used to It!"

I have vivid memories of summer camping trips I took as a young boy with my friends. On particularly hot afternoons we would cool off with a dip into an icy mountain lake or stream. Although the initial shock of the icy water was overpowering, as illustrated in Figure 3.4, it eventually felt refreshing. This experience illustrates the process of **sensory adaptation,** the fact that our sensitivity to an unchanging stimulus tends to decrease over time. When we first encounter a stimulus, such as icy water, our temperature receptors fire vigorously. Soon, however, they fire less vigorously, and through the process of sensory adaptation, the water then feels just right.

Sensory adaptation has some practical advantages. If it did not occur, we would constantly be distracted by the stream of sensations we experience each day. We would not adapt to our clothing rubbing our skin, to the feel of our tongue in our mouth, or to bodily processes such as eye blinks and swallowing. However, sensory adaptation is not always beneficial and can even be dangerous. After about a minute, for example, our sensitivity to most odors drops by nearly 70 percent. This drop in sensitivity is useful in everyday situations in which we encounter unpleasant but harmless odors, such pet odors or your roommate's smelly sneakers. On the other hand, sensory adaptation can be maladaptive by reducing our sensitivity to odors that signal danger, such as the smell of a gas leak in a home heated by natural gas. In general, though, the process of sensory adaptation allows us to focus on important changes in the world around us, and that ability to focus on and respond to stimulus change is usually what is most important for survival.

Now that we've considered some basic aspects of sensation, let's examine in detail each of the major senses: vision, audition, touch, smell, taste, and the kinesthetic and vestibular senses.

KEY QUESTIONS

- What is the primary function of our sensory receptors?
- What does the term *absolute threshold* refer to?
- Why is signal detection theory important?
- What is a difference threshold?
- Can subliminal messages affect our behavior?
- What is the role of sensory adaptation in sensation?

VISION

Sensory Adaptation
Reduced sensitivity to unchanging stimuli over time.

Light, in the form of energy from the sun, is part of the fuel that drives the engine of life on earth. Thus, it is not surprising that we possess exquisitely adapted organs for detecting this stimulus: our eyes. Indeed, for most of us, sight is the most

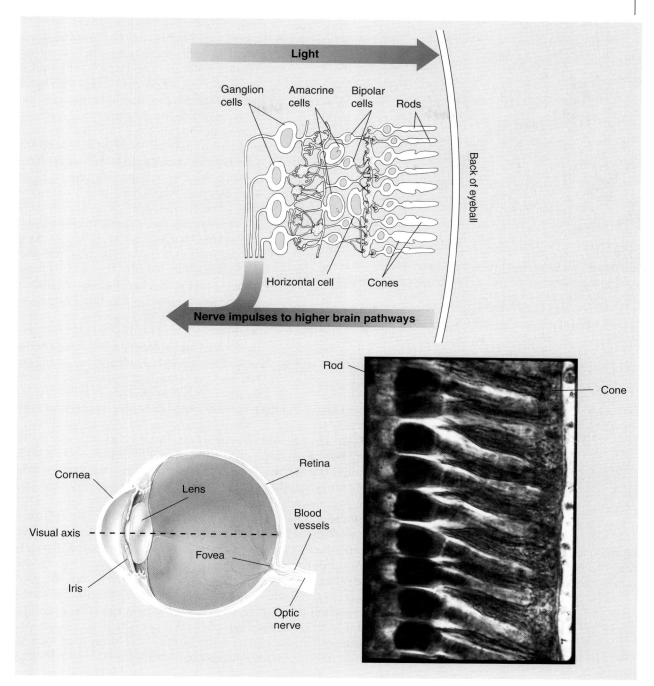

FIGURE 3.5
The Human Eye
Light filters through layers of retinal cells before striking receptors (rods and cones) located at the back of the eye and pointed away from the incoming light. The rods and cones stimulate bipolar cells, which, in turn, stimulate the ganglion cells. The axons of these cells form the fibers of the optic nerve.

important way of gathering information about the world. Figure 3.5 shows a simplified diagram of the human eye.

The Eye: Its Basic Structure

How is light energy converted into signals our brain can understand? The answer lies in the basic structure of the eye. It is in the eye that light energy is converted into a

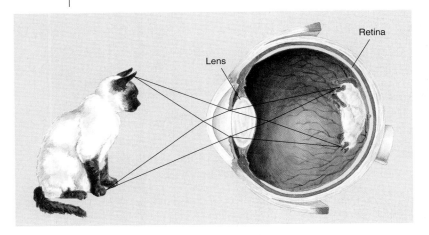

FIGURE 3.6
The Upside Down and Reversed Image Projected onto the Retina
The lens bends light rays entering the eye so that the image projected onto the retina is upside down and reversed: Light rays from the top of an object are projected onto receptors at the bottom of the retina, and light rays from the left side of an object are projected onto receptors on the right side of the retina. Our brain rearranges this information and enables us to see the object correctly.

neural code understandable to our nervous system. Light rays first pass through a transparent protective structure called the **cornea** and then enter the eye through the **pupil,** a round opening whose size varies with lighting conditions: The less light present, the wider the pupil opening (refer to Figure 3.5). These adjustments are executed by the colored part of the eye, termed the **iris,** which is actually a circular muscle that contracts or expands to let in varying amounts of light. After entering through the pupil, light rays pass through the **lens,** a clear structure whose shape adjusts to permit us to focus on objects at varying distances. When we look at a distant object, the lens becomes thinner and flatter; when we look at a nearby object, the lens becomes thicker and rounder. As we age, the lens tends to lose its flexibility, causing older people to have trouble seeing nearby objects and reading. Light rays leaving the lens are projected on the **retina** at the back of the eyeball. As illustrated in Figure 3.6, the lens bends light rays in such a way that the image projected onto the retina is actually upside down and reversed; but the brain reverses this image, letting us see objects and people correctly.

The retina is a postage stamp–sized structure that contains two types of light-sensitive receptor cells: about 5 million **cones** and about 120 million **rods** (Goldstein, 2002). Cones, located primarily in the center of the retina in an area called the **fovea,** function best in bright light and play a key role both in color vision and in our ability to notice fine detail. In contrast, rods are found only outside the fovea and function best under lower levels of illumination, so rods help us to see in a darkened room or at night. At increasing distances from the fovea, the density of cones decreases and the density of rods increases. Once stimulated, the rods and cones transmit neural information to other neurons called *bipolar cells.* These cells, in turn, stimulate other neurons, called *ganglion cells.* Axons from the ganglion cells converge to form the **optic nerve** and carry visual information to the brain. Interestingly, no receptors are present where this nerve exits the eye, so there is a **blind spot** at this point in our visual field. We usually remain unaware of our blind spot because the brain automatically "fills in" the blind spot with an extrapolation of the surrounding image. Please refer to Figure 3.7 to check out your own blind spot.

Cornea
The curved, transparent layer through which light rays enter the eye.

Pupil
An opening in the eye, just behind the cornea, through which light rays enter the eye.

Iris
The colored part of the eye that adjusts the amount of light that enters by constricting or dilating the pupil.

Lens
A curved structure behind the pupil that bends light rays, focusing them on the retina.

Retina
The surface at the back of the eye containing the rods and cones.

Cones
Sensory receptors in the eye that play a crucial role in sensations of color.

FIGURE 3.7
The Blind Spot
You can demonstrate the existence of your own blind spot. First, close your right eye and align the cross with your left eye. While looking at the cross with your left eye, move the book slowly toward you (or your eye toward the page). When your eye is six to twelve inches from the book, the circle should disappear. This is the point at which the image of the circle is falling on the blind spot.

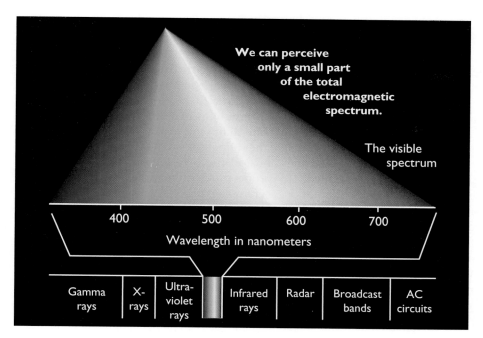

FIGURE 3.8
The Electromagnetic Spectrum
Visible light, the part of the electromagnetic spectrum we can detect, occupies only a narrow band in the entire spectrum.

Light: The Physical Stimulus for Vision

At this point we will consider some important facts about light, the physical stimulus for vision. First, the light that is visible to us is only a small portion of the electromagnetic spectrum. This spectrum ranges from radio waves at the slow or long-wave end to cosmic rays at the fast or short-wave end (refer to Figure 3.8).

Second, certain physical properties of light contribute to our psychological experiences of vision. **Wavelength,** the distance between successive peaks and valleys of light energy, determines what we experience as **hue** or color. As shown in Figure 3.8, as wavelength increases from about 400 to 700 nanometers (a nanometer is one-billionth of a meter), our sensations shift from violet through blue (shorter wavelengths), green, yellow, orange (medium wavelengths), and finally red (longer wavelengths). The intensity of light, the amount of energy it contains, is experienced as **brightness.** The extent to which light contains only one wavelength, rather than many, determines our experience of **saturation;** the fewer the number of wavelengths mixed together, the more saturated or "pure" a color appears. For example, the deep red of an apple is highly saturated, whereas the pale pink of an apple blossom is low in saturation.

Basic Functions of the Visual System: Acuity, Dark Adaptation, and Eye Movements

The human visual system is remarkably sensitive and can detect even tiny amounts of light. However, another important aspect of vision is **acuity,** the ability to resolve fine details, as on the familiar chart at an eye doctor's office. If you wear eyeglasses or contact lenses designed to improve your visual acuity, chances are that your visual deficit stems from a slight abnormality in the shape of your eye or the cornea. If your eyeball is too long or the cornea is too stiffly curved, you suffer from **nearsightedness,** in which you see near objects clearly, but distant objects appear

Rods
One of the two types of sensory receptors for vision found in the eye.

Fovea
The area in the center of the retina in which cones are highly concentrated.

Optic Nerve
A bundle of nerve fibers that exit the back of the eye and carry visual information to the brain.

Blind Spot
The point in the back of the retina through which the optic nerve exits the eye. This exit point contains no rods or cones and is therefore insensitive to light.

Wavelength
The peak-to-peak distance in a sound or light wave.

Hue
The color that we experience due to the dominant wavelength of a light.

Brightness
The physical intensity of light.

Saturation
The degree of concentration of the hue of light. We experience saturation as the purity of a light.

Acuity
The visual ability to see fine details.

Nearsightedness
A condition in which the visual image entering our eye is focused slightly in front of our retina rather than directly on it. Therefore, near objects can be seen clearly, while distant objects appear fuzzy or blurred.

blurry. This occurs because the image entering your eye is focused slightly in front of the retina rather than directly on it. Similarly, in **farsightedness,** your eyeball is too short or the cornea too flat, and the lens focuses the image behind the retina. Fortunately, recent advances in laser surgery have made it possible to correct certain visual acuity problems by changing the shape of the cornea.

Another aspect of visual sensitivity is **dark adaptation,** the increase in sensitivity that occurs when we move from bright light to a dim environment, such as a darkened movie theater. Initially, we find it difficult to see. Why? When we're exposed to bright light, a pigment inside the retinal cells is bleached. When we move from bright light to dark, the cones and rods become temporarily nonfunctional until the pigment is regenerated. This occurs much more rapidly for cones than for rods, so, in essence, dark adaptation is a two-step process. During the first few moments, the cones are more sensitive. Thus, we rely on them to see until the rods catch up and then surpass the cones in terms of light sensitivity. The cones reach their maximum sensitivity in about five to ten minutes. The rods overtake the cones in sensitivity in about seven to ten minutes, but take about thirty minutes to complete this process (Goldstein, 2002). When completely dark-adapted, the eye is about 100,000 times more sensitive than the light-adapted eye.

Eye movements also play a role in visual acuity. To appreciate the importance of the ability to move your eyes, just imagine how inefficient it would be to read a book or play your favorite sport if your eyes were stuck in one position. In order to change the direction of your gaze, you would have to move your entire head. Eye movements are of two basic types: *version movements,* in which the eyes move together in the same direction, and *vergence movements,* in which the lines of sight for the two eyes converge or diverge. As we'll discover later in this chapter, vergence movements are crucial to our ability to perceive distance and depth.

Color Vision

A world without color would be sadly limited, for color—vivid reds, glowing yellows, restful greens—is a crucial part of our visual experience. For many people, though, some degree of color deficiency is a fact of life. Nearly 8 percent of males and 0.4 percent of females are less sensitive than the rest of us either to red and green or to yellow and blue (Nathans, 1989). And a few individuals are totally color blind, experiencing the world only in varying shades of white, black, and gray.

There are two leading theories to explain our rich sense of color. The first, **trichromatic theory,** suggests that we have three different types of cones in our retina, each of which is maximally sensitive, though not exclusively so, to a particular range of light wavelength—a range roughly corresponding to blue (400–500 nanometers), green (475–600 nanometers), or red (490–650 nanometers). Careful study of the human retina suggests that we do possess three types of receptors, although as Figure 3.9 shows, there is a great deal of overlap in each receptor type's sensitivity range (DeValois & DeValois, 1975; Rushton, 1975). According to trichromatic theory, the ability to perceive colors results from the joint action of the three receptor types. Thus, light of a particular wavelength produces differential stimulation of each receptor type, and it is the overall pattern of stimulation that produces our rich sense of color. This differential sensitivity may be due to genes that direct different cones to produce pigments sensitive to blue, green, or red (Mollon, 1993; Nathans, Thomas, & Hogness, 1986).

Trichromatic theory, however, fails to account for certain aspects of color vision, such as the occurrence of **negative afterimages**—sensations of complementary colors that occur after staring at a stimulus of a given color. For example, after staring at a red object, if you shift your gaze to a neutral background, sensations of green may follow. Similarly, after staring at a yellow stimulus, sensations of blue may occur.

The **opponent-process theory** addresses these aspects more effectively by accounting for what happens after the cones in the retina transmit their information to

---

Farsightedness

A condition in which the visual image entering our eye is focused behind rather than directly on the retina. Therefore, close objects appear out of focus, while distant objects are in clear focus.

Dark Adaptation

The process through which our visual system increases its sensitivity to light under low levels of illumination.

Trichromatic Theory

A theory of color perception suggesting that we have three types of cones, each primarily receptive to different wavelengths of light.

Negative Afterimage

A sensation of complementary color that occurs after staring at a stimulus of a given hue.

Opponent-Process Theory

A theory that describes the processing of sensory information related to color at levels above the retina. The theory suggests that we possess six different types of neurons, each of which is either stimulated or inhibited by red, green, blue, yellow, black, and white.

other cells of the retina (e.g., the *bipolar* and *ganglion cells*) and to a structure in the thalamus termed the *lateral geniculate nucleus* (Goldstein, 2002). This theory suggests that we possess specialized cells in these structures that play a role in sensations of color (DeValois & DeValois, 1993). Two of these cells, for example, handle red and green: One is stimulated by red light and inhibited by green light, whereas the other is stimulated by green light and inhibited by red. This is where the phrase *opponent process* originates. Two additional types of cells handle yellow and blue: One is stimulated by yellow and inhibited by blue, while the other shows the opposite pattern. The remaining two types handle black and white—again, in an opponent process manner. Opponent-process theory can help explain the occurrence of negative afterimages (Jameson & Hurvich, 1989). The idea is that when stimulation of one cell in an opponent pair is terminated, the other is automatically activated. Thus, if the original stimulus viewed was yellow, the afterimage seen would be blue. Each opponent pair is stimulated in different patterns by the three types of cones. It is the overall pattern of such stimulation that yields our complex and eloquent sensation of color.

Although these theories competed for many years, we now know that both are necessary to explain our impressive ability to respond to color. Trichromatic theory explains how color coding occurs in the cones of the retina, whereas opponent-process theory accounts for processing in higher-order nerve cells. We'll now turn to a discussion of how visual information is processed by the brain.

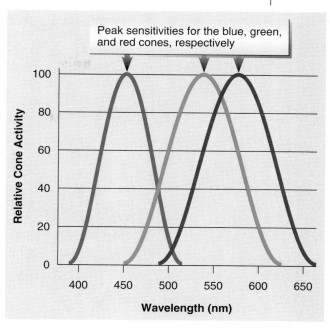

FIGURE 3.9

Three Types of Receptors Contribute to Our Perception of Color

Color vision appears to be mediated by three types of cones, each maximally sensitive, but not exclusively so, to wavelengths corresponding to blue, green, and red.

Source: From "Retinal mechanisms of color vision" by E. F. MacNichol, pp. 119, 133 from VISION RESEARCH. Copyright © 1964. Reprinted with permission from Elsevier.

Vision and the Brain: Processing Visual Information

Our rich sense of vision does not result from the output of single neurons, but instead from the overall pattern of our sensory receptors. In other words, there is more to vision than meets the eye. But how, then, do the simple action potentials of individual neurons contribute to our overall conscious experience? To help answer this question, let's consider how the brain "invents" our visual world.

The visual world we perceive results from a complex division of labor that only *begins* in the retina. In other words, it is only light that enters our eyes—we really see with our brains. Research seems to indicate that the brain processes information hierarchically (Lappin & Craft, 2000). Groups of neurons analyze various properties of visual information and send their results to other groups of neurons for further analysis. At successive stages in this process, increasingly complex visual information is analyzed and compiled—eventually producing the coherent and flowing scenes that constitute our perception of the world around us (Zeki, 1992).

Our understanding of the initial stages of this process was greatly advanced by the Nobel Prize–winning series of studies conducted by Hubel and Wiesel (1979). These researchers conducted studies on **feature detectors**—neurons at various levels in the visual cortex. Their work revealed the existence of three types of feature detectors. One group of neurons—known as **simple cells**—responds primarily to bars or lines presented in certain orientations (horizontal, vertical, and so on). A second group—**complex cells**—responds maximally to moving stimuli such as a vertical bar moving from left to right, or to a tilted bar moving from right to left. Finally, **hypercomplex cells** respond to even more complex features of the visual world, such as length, width, and even aspects of shape, like corners and angles. Since then,

Feature Detectors
Neurons at various levels within the visual system that respond primarily to stimuli possessing certain features in the visual cortex.

Simple Cells
Cells within the visual system that respond to specific shapes presented in certain orientations (e.g., horizontal, vertical).

Complex Cells
Neurons in the visual cortex that respond to stimuli that move in a particular direction and that have a particular orientation.

Hypercomplex Cells
Neurons in the visual cortex that respond to complex aspects of visual stimuli, such as width, length, and shape.

researchers have identified additional specialized neurons. Some respond to specific shapes, whereas others respond only to shapes combined with a color or a texture. For example, Tanaka and colleagues (1991, 1993) identified a type of cell that responds to (a model of) an apple, but stops responding if the apple's stem is removed.

Important clues about the specialized nature of visual processing in the brain have come from studies of people with brain damage. Damage to the temporal lobe, for example, can cause **prosopagnosia,** a condition in which people lose the ability to recognize familiar persons (even themselves!) by their faces but still retain relatively normal vision in other respects (Schweinberger, Klos, & Sommer, 1995). Studies using brain-imaging techniques have shown that pictures of faces activate neurons in a structure within the temporal lobe of the brain called the *fusiform face area* (FFA) (e.g., Bentin et al., 2002; Kanwisher, McDermott, & Chun, 1997). Studies like this further highlight the specialized nature of the visual system.

Some evidence suggests the nervous system may have evolved such structures to enhance an animal's ability to survive. Neurons in the visual cortex of newborn monkeys, for example, signal information about the direction in which objects are moving and the relative depths of objects—qualities key to a monkey's survival (Chino et al., 1997). This evidence suggests that such specialization may be "built in." However, other research seems to indicate that experience, or learning, is also important (Smith, 2003). Gauthier and her colleagues (1999) attempted to determine whether practice in recognizing non-face objects increases the activity of neurons in the FFA. The researchers first determined the level of activity in the FFA that occurred in response to faces and to computer-generated objects called "greebles." As predicted, neurons in the FFA responded strongly to the faces, but weakly to the greebles (please refer to Figure 3.10). Participants then received intensive training to help them become experts in recognizing each of the many different greebles and their names. After the training, neurons in the FFA responded about as well to greebles as to faces. Apparently, neurons in this area possess a plasticity that allows them to respond not just to faces, but also to other stimuli—ones that are seen often and are behaviorally important (e.g., Kolb, Gibb, & Robinson, 2003).

Taken together, these findings highlight the fact that "seeing" the world is a complex process—one that requires precise integration across many levels of our visual system. They also highlight the practical usefulness of such findings; for example, they help to explain why we are more apt to remember a person's face than their name. They also help to explain how people and other animals are able to "tune in" to relevant danger signals in their respective environments.

Prosopagnosia

A rare condition in which brain damage impairs a person's ability to recognize faces.

FIGURE 3.10
The Specialized Nature of Visual Processing

Participants were trained to recognize each of the "greebles" by name. Before the training, neurons in the fusiform gyrus (FG) responded strongly in response to faces but weakly to the "greebles." Following training, the FG neurons responded about as well to the Greebles as to faces.

Source: Based on data from Gauthier et al., 1999.

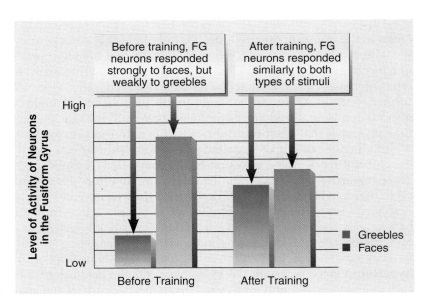

HEARING

The melody of a baby's laughter, the roar of a jet plane, the rustling of leaves on a crisp autumn day—clearly, we live in a world full of sound. And, as with vision, human beings are well equipped to receive many sounds in their environment. A simplified diagram of the human ear is shown in Figure 3.11; please refer to it as you proceed through the discussion.

The Ear: Its Basic Structure

Try asking a friend, "When did you get your pinna pierced?" The response will probably be a blank stare. **Pinna** is the technical term for the visible part of our hearing organ, the *ear*. However, this is only a small part of the entire ear. Inside the ear is an intricate system of membranes, small bones, and receptor cells that

Pinna
The external portion of our ear.

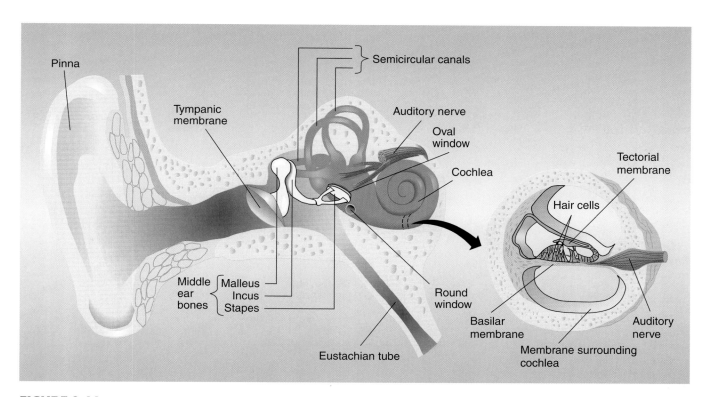

FIGURE 3.11
The Human Ear
A simplified diagram of the human ear. Sound waves (alternating compressions and expansions in the air) enter through the external auditory canal and produce slight movements in the eardrum. This, in turn, produces movements in the fluid within the cochlea. As this fluid moves, tiny hair cells shift their position, thus generating the nerve impulses we perceive as sound.

transform sound waves into neural information for the brain. The *eardrum,* a thin piece of tissue just inside the ear, moves ever so slightly in response to sound waves striking it. When it moves, the eardrum causes three tiny bones within the *middle ear* to vibrate. The third of these bones is attached to a second membrane, the *oval window,* which covers a fluid-filled, spiral-shaped structure known as the **cochlea.** Vibration of the oval window causes movements of the fluid in the cochlea. Finally, the movement of fluid bends tiny *hair cells,* the true sensory receptors of sound. The neural messages they create are then transmitted to the brain via the *auditory nerve.*

Sound: The Physical Stimulus for Hearing

In discussing light, we noted that relationships exist between certain of its physical properties, such as wavelength and intensity, and psychological aspects of vision, like hue and brightness. Similar relationships exist for sound, at least with respect to two of its psychological qualities: *loudness* and *pitch.*

Sound waves consist of alternating compressions of the air, or, more precisely, of the molecules that compose air. The greater the *amplitude* (magnitude) of these waves, the greater their loudness to us; see Figure 3.12. The rate at which air is expanded and contracted constitutes the *frequency* of a sound wave, and the greater the frequency, the higher the **pitch.** Frequency is measured in terms of cycles per second, or hertz (Hz), and humans can generally hear sounds ranging from about 20 Hz to about 20,000 Hz, but are most sensitive to sounds between 2,000 and 4,000 Hz, the range of frequencies that is most important for understanding speech (Goldstein, 2002). Older adults progressively lose sensitivity, particularly for higher

Cochlea
A portion of the inner ear containing the sensory receptors for sound.

Pitch
The characteristic of a sound that is described as high or low. Pitch is mediated by the frequency of a sound.

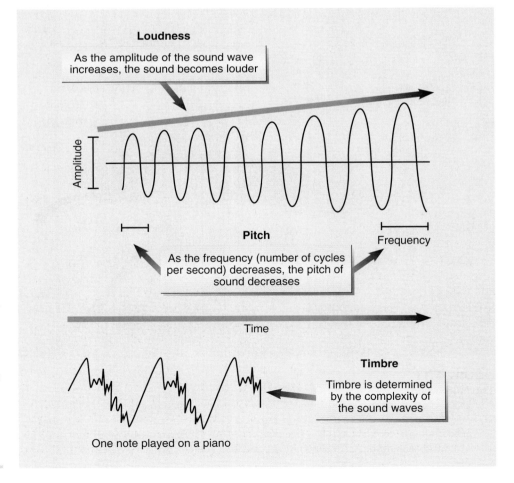

FIGURE 3.12
Physical Characteristics of Sound
Our perception of sounds is determined by three characteristics. *Loudness* depends on the amplitude, or height, of the sound waves; as amplitude increases, the sound appears louder. *Pitch* is determined by the frequency of the sound waves—the number of sound waves that pass a given point per second. *Timbre* refers to the quality of the sound we perceive and is the characteristic that helps us to distinguish the sound of a flute from the sound of a saxophone.

sound frequencies. This form of hearing loss, termed *presbycusis,* affects men more severely than women. This may be due, at least in part, to long-term exposure to workplace noise or other loud noises.

A third psychological aspect of sound—its **timbre**—refers to a sound's quality. This quality depends on the mixture of frequencies and amplitudes that make up the sound. For example, a piece of chalk squeaking across a blackboard may have the same pitch and amplitude as a note played on a clarinet, but it will certainly have a different quality. In general, the timbre of a sound is related to its complexity—how many different frequencies it contains. However, other physical aspects of the source of the sound may be involved as well, so the relationship is not simple.

Pitch Perception

When we tune a guitar or sing in harmony with other people, we demonstrate our ability to detect differences in pitch. Most of us can easily tell when two sounds have the same pitch and when they are different. Some lucky individuals have **perfect pitch**—the ability to name or produce a note of particular pitch in the absence of a reference note. Interestingly, the prevalence of perfect pitch is greater among people in countries where tone languages are spoken (Deutsch, 2002). In tone languages, such as Mandarin Chinese, the same word takes on different meanings depending on the way it is spoken. So, for example, among Mandarin speakers, the same word—say, *ma*—can mean either "mother" or "hemp," depending on the particular pitch, or combination of pitches, used to pronounce it. Cultural differences such as this seem to indicate that learning, or experience, plays a role in pitch perception.

Sensory mechanisms that work at a more basic level are also involved. We'll discuss these next. **Place theory** (also called the *traveling wave theory*) suggests that sounds of different frequencies cause different places along the *basilar membrane* (the floor of the cochlea) to vibrate. These vibrations, in turn, stimulate the hair cells—the sensory receptors for sound. Actual observations have shown that sound does produce pressure waves and that these waves peak, or produce maximal displacement, at various distances along the basilar membrane, depending on the frequency of the sound (Narayan et al., 1998; von Békésy, 1960). High-frequency sounds cause maximum displacement at the narrow end of the basilar membrane near the oval window, whereas lower frequencies cause maximal displacement toward the wider, farther end of the basilar membrane. Unfortunately, place theory does not explain our ability to discriminate very low frequency sounds whose frequencies differ by as little as 1 or 2 Hz, because displacement on the basilar membrane is nearly identical for these sounds.

A second explanation, termed **frequency theory,** suggests that sounds of different pitch cause different rates of neural firing. Thus, high-pitched sounds produce high rates of activity in the auditory nerve, whereas low-pitched sounds produce lower rates. Frequency theory seems to be accurate up to sounds of about 1,000 Hz—the maximum rate of firing for individual neurons. Above that level, the theory must be modified to include the *volley principle*—the assumption that sound receptors for other neurons begin to fire in volleys. For example, a sound with a frequency of 5,000 Hz might generate a pattern of activity in which each of five groups of neurons fires 1,000 times in rapid succession—that is, in volleys.

Because our daily activities regularly expose us to sounds of many frequencies, both theories are needed to explain our ability to respond to this wide range of stimuli. Frequency theory explains how low-frequency sounds are registered, whereas place theory explains how high-frequency sounds are registered. In the middle ranges between 500 and 4,000 Hz, the range that we use for most daily activities, both theories apply.

Timbre
The quality of a sound resulting from the complexity of a sound wave that, for example, helps us distinguish between the sound of a trumpet and that of a saxophone.

Perfect Pitch
The ability to name or produce a note of particular pitch in the absence of a reference note.

Place Theory
A theory suggesting that sounds of different frequency stimulate different areas of the basilar membrane, the portion of the cochlea containing sensory receptors for sound.

Frequency Theory
A theory of pitch perception suggesting that sounds of different frequencies (heard as differences in pitch) induce different rates of neural activity in the hair cells of the inner ear.

Sound Localization

You are walking down a busy street when suddenly a familiar voice calls your name. You instantly turn in the direction of this sound and spot one of your friends. How do you know where to turn? Research on **localization**—the ability of the auditory system to locate the source of a given sound—suggests that several factors play a role.

The first is the fact that we have two ears, placed on opposite sides of our head. As a result, our head creates a *sound shadow,* a barrier that reduces the intensity of sound on the shadowed side. Thus, a sound behind us and to our left will be slightly louder in our left ear. The shadow effect is strongest for high-frequency sounds, which have difficulty bending around the head (Phillips & Brugge, 1985). The placement of our ears also produces a slight difference in the time it takes for a sound to reach each ear. Although this difference is truly minute—often less than one millisecond—it provides an important clue to sound localization.

What happens when sound comes from directly in front or directly in back of us? In this instance, we often have difficulty determining the location of the

Localization
The ability of our auditory system to determine the direction of a sound source.

PSYCHOLOGY GOES TO WORK

The Harmful Effects of Noise: Let's Turn Down the Sound!

The National Institute of Occupational Safety and Health (NIOSH) estimates that more than 30 million U.S. workers are regularly exposed to hazardous noise. Not surprisingly, high levels of ambient noise are one of the most prevalent environmental stressors in the workplace. Here are some facts that can help you avoid hearing loss, both at work and at home.

How Much Noise Is Too Much?

As shown in Figure 3.13, long-term exposure to even moderate noise levels—ones louder than 85 decibels (dB)—can produce stress-related disorders and permanent hearing loss. A *decibel* is a unit that measures the intensity of sound. A normal conversation is about 60 dB; noisy restaurants and office environments clock in at about 90 dB. However, one-time exposure to extremely loud noises, such as the sound of a gun at close range (165 dB), can produce permanent damage.

Personal Sound Systems: The Facts

One of the biggest offenders when it comes to hearing loss is personal sound systems—especially those with headphones. These devices produce sounds as loud as 105 to 120 dB if turned up to maximum levels. Many people listen to their portable headsets at dangerous levels across a wide variety of activities, including while at work, riding the subway, exercising, or walking to and from work. Workplace guidelines help to protect a worker's hearing, but the same protection is not available for the use of personal stereo systems with headphones. So, the next time you get the urge to pump up the volume of your portable headset while exercising or at work, don't give in to temptation—keep the sound at safe levels.

Steps to Protect Your Hearing While Listening to Personal Stereo Systems

Look for a personal stereo system with an "automatic volume limiter," which limits the output of the system to safe levels. Some manufacturers

sound source, because the sound reaches our ears at the same time. Head movements can help resolve a problem like this. By turning your head, you create a slight difference in the time it takes for the sound to reach each of your ears—and now you can determine the location of the sound and take appropriate action (Moore, 1982).

In summary, our auditory system is ideally constructed to take full advantage of a variety of subtle cues. When you consider how rapidly we process and respond to such information, the whole system seems nothing short of marvelous in its efficiency. However, as with anything in life, too much of a good thing can often be harmful! This also holds true for sound. Currently, approximately 30 million Americans are affected by hearing loss; and 50 million have *tinnitus*, an early indicator of hearing loss (Dangerous Decibels, 2004). The use of modern conveniences, such as stereo headsets, electric blow dryers, and leaf blowers are partly to blame. So, too, is living near or working in a noisy environment. For additional information on the harmful effects of sound in the workplace, please refer to the following **Psychology Goes to Work** section.

psychology goes to work (continued)

include an automatic volume limiter that limits the output to 85 dB.

- Set your system at a comfortable level in a quiet room. Do not turn it up when you are in a noisy setting to "block out" the noise. This will only add to the noise and increase the risks of hearing loss.
- Limit the amount of time you use the personal stereo system with headphones.
- Follow this simple rule of thumb: If you cannot hear other people talking when you are wearing headphones or if other people have to shout to you to be heard at three feet away while the headphones are on, the decibel level could be damaging to your hearing.
- If you notice any ringing in your ears or that speech sounds are muffled after wearing a personal stereo system, discontinue its use and have your hearing checked by a qualified audiologist.

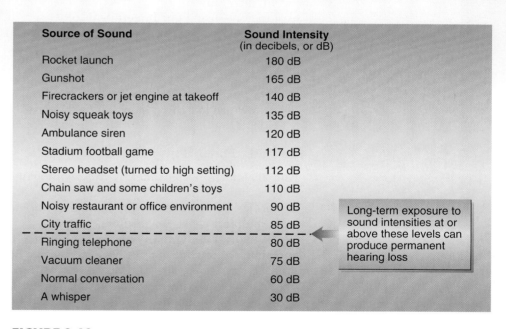

Source of Sound	Sound Intensity (in decibels, or dB)
Rocket launch	180 dB
Gunshot	165 dB
Firecrackers or jet engine at takeoff	140 dB
Noisy squeak toys	135 dB
Ambulance siren	120 dB
Stadium football game	117 dB
Stereo headset (turned to high setting)	112 dB
Chain saw and some children's toys	110 dB
Noisy restaurant or office environment	90 dB
City traffic	85 dB
Ringing telephone	80 dB
Vacuum cleaner	75 dB
Normal conversation	60 dB
A whisper	30 dB

Long-term exposure to sound intensities at or above these levels can produce permanent hearing loss

FIGURE 3.13
Decibels in Everyday Life
Examples of sound intensities (in decibels) that are a part of modern daily life. It is important to note that long-term exposure to relatively moderate sound intensities (85 db and above) can contribute to permanent hearing loss.

KEY QUESTIONS
- What is the physical stimulus for hearing?
- How do psychologists explain pitch perception?
- How do we localize sound?

TOUCH AND OTHER SKIN SENSES

The skin is our largest sensory organ and produces the most varied experiences: everything from the pleasure of a soothing massage to the pain of an injury. Actually, there are several skin senses, including touch (or pressure), warmth, cold, and pain. Microscopic examination has revealed several different receptor types that differ in terms of the type of stimulation to which they respond best. Because each receptor is specialized to respond to different types of stimulation, stimulating the skin usually activates a number of types of receptors, some more strongly than others, depending on the stimulus. Therefore, our overall perception of particular objects is determined by the total pattern of nerve impulses reaching the brain (Goldstein, 2002).

Have you ever wondered why certain areas on your body are more sensitive than others? As it turns out, the receptors in skin are not evenly distributed; the touch receptors in areas highly sensitive to touch, such as the face and fingertips, are much more densely packed than receptors in less sensitive areas, such as the legs. Additionally, areas of the skin with greater sensitivity also have greater representation in higher levels of the brain.

In most instances we discover the texture of an object through active exploration—using our fingertips or other sensitive areas of our body. Psychologists distinguish between *passive touch,* in which an object comes in contact with the skin, and *active touch,* in which we place our hand or other body part in contact with an object. We are considerably more accurate at identifying objects through active than through passive touch, in part because of feedback we receive from the movement of our fingers and hands when exploring an object (Matlin & Foley, 1997). Let's now turn to a discussion of how the sense of touch helps us experience pain.

Pain: Its Nature and Control

Pain plays an important adaptive role; without it, we would be unaware that something is amiss with our body or that we have suffered some type of injury. Sources of pain, such as intense pressure, extreme temperature, or burning chemicals, stimulate receptors called **nociceptors.**

Actually, two types of pain seem to exist. One can best be described as quick and sharp—the kind of pain we experience when we receive a cut. The other is dull and throbbing—the pain we experience from a sore muscle or an injured back. The first type of pain seems to be transmitted through large myelinated sensory nerve fibers (Campbell & LaMotte, 1983). You may recall from Chapter 2 that impulses travel faster along myelinated fibers, and so it makes sense that sharp sensations of pain are carried via these fiber types. In contrast, dull pain is carried by smaller unmyelinated nerve fibers, which conduct neural impulses more slowly. Both fiber types synapse with neurons in the spinal cord that carry pain messages to the thalamus and other parts of the brain (Willis, 1985).

Pain Perception: The Role of Physiological Mechanisms

The discovery of the two pain systems described above led to the formulation of an influential view of pain known as the **gate-control theory** (Melzack & Wall, 1965; 1988). Gate-control theory suggests that there are neural mechanisms in the

Nociceptor
A sensory receptor that responds to stimuli that are damaging.

Gate-Control Theory
A theory of pain suggesting that the spinal cord contains a mechanism that can block transmission of pain to the brain.

spinal cord that sometimes close, thus preventing pain messages from reaching the brain. Apparently, pain messages carried by the large fibers cause this "gate" to close, while messages carried by the smaller fibers—the ones related to dull, throbbing pain—cannot. This may explain why sharp pain is relatively brief, whereas an ache persists. The gate-control theory also helps to explain why vigorously stimulating one area to reduce pain in another sometimes works. Presumably, countermeasures such as rubbing the skin near an injury, applying ice packs or hot water bottles, and even acupuncture stimulate activity in the large nerve fibers, closing the spinal "gate" and reducing sensations of pain.

Gate-control theory has been revised to account for the importance of several brain mechanisms in the perception of pain (e.g., Fields & Basbaum, 1999; Weissberg, 1999). For example, our current emotional state may interact with the onset of a painful stimulus to alter the intensity of pain we experience. The brain, in other words, may affect pain perception by transmitting messages that either close the spinal "gate" or keep it open. The result: When we are anxious, pain is intensified; and when we are calm and relaxed, as illustrated in the cartoon in Figure 3.14, pain may be reduced.

Pain Perception: The Role of Cognitive Processes

A large body of evidence shows that pain may exert its unpleasant effects by interrupting ongoing thought and behavior and redirecting our attention to the pain (Eccleston & Crombez, 1999). The extent to which we experience pain results from a dynamic interplay between characteristics of the pain (e.g., its intensity, novelty, predictability) and the context in which we experience pain. Cognition, or thought, plays a critical mediator role, determining the extent to which we focus on pain relative to these factors and the degree of threat that they pose to us. This cognitive activity may help explain why procedures that redirect our attention are effective countermeasures for pain. Hypnosis, for example, has been shown to be effective in reducing the effects of pain, apparently by activating a supervisory attention-control system in the brain that shifts the focus of our attention away from the pain (Crawford, Knebel, & Vendemia, 1998). (Please refer to Chapter 4 for additional information on hypnosis.)

A group of therapies, collectively termed *cognitive–behavioral procedures*, have also been shown to be effective in counteracting the effects of pain (Morley, Eccleston, & Williams, 1999; Novy et al., 1995). These procedures are based on the fact that our thoughts, feelings, and beliefs—as well as our overt responses— before, during, and after painful episodes can dramatically influence our perceptions of pain (Stroud et al., 2000; Turk & Okifuji, 2002). Hypnosis appears to enhance the effectiveness of these procedures (Milling, Levine, & Meunier, 2003).

To appreciate the important role of cognitive processes in pain perception, let's consider a study by Montgomery and Kirsch (1996). Participants in their study were led to believe they would be helping to test a new topical anesthetic for its pain-reducing effect. The fictitious pain reliever (placebo) was actually a harmless but medicinal-smelling mixture dispensed from a bottle labeled "Trivaricane: Approved for research purposes only." The researchers applied the mixture to either the left *or* right index finger of each participant. After waiting a brief period of time to allow the "medication" to take effect, the researchers delivered equal

By recounting family vacations, Dr. Ingersoll was able to perform extractions without the use of anesthetics.

FIGURE 3.14

Brain Mechanisms and Pain Perception: Closing the Gate on Pain

Our current emotional state may interact with the onset of a painful stimulus to alter the intensity of pain we experience. When we are calm, or relaxed, as illustrated in this humorous example, the pain we experience may be reduced.

Source: CLOSE TO HOME © (2000) John McPherson. Reprinted with permission of UNIVERSAL PRESS SYNDICATE. All rights reserved.

intensities of a painful stimulus (pressure) to both the left *and* right fingers. As predicted, the placebo was effective in reducing the participants' perceptions of pain; ratings of pain intensity and unpleasantness were significantly lower for "treated" fingers than for "untreated" fingers. These results illustrate the important role cognitive processes play in determining the extent to which we experience pain. They also form the basis for designing procedures to help people learn to tolerate pain. This is particularly important for people who are allergic to pain medications, or in instances of chronic pain, in which the long-term use of such substances could become addicting.

Pain Perception and Culture

Although we commonly view pain as something automatic and universal, large cultural differences in the interpretation and expression of pain do exist. But what is the basis for these differences? At first glance, it is tempting to conclude that cultural differences in pain threshold—physical differences—are the cause. However, no consistent evidence supports this view (Zatzick & Dimsdale, 1990). Instead, observed cultural differences in the capacity to withstand pain seem to be perceptual in nature and to reflect the effects of social learning (Morse & Morse, 1988; Sargent, 1984). To illustrate this point, consider a study by Clark and Clark (1980). These researchers gave electric shocks to a group of Western participants and to a group from Nepal (a country in Southeast Asia, between India and China). Participants were asked to indicate the intensities at which they experienced *faint* and *extreme* pain, respectively. Both groups began to detect the shocks at about the same intensity, but the Nepalese participants required much higher intensities before they said they experienced either faint or extreme pain. Similar findings have been observed in many other studies and in different cultures. In sum, the evidence suggests that pain may be universal—at least in some respects—and that differences in pain perception result from the powerful effects of social learning, not from physical differences among various groups of people.

KEY QUESTIONS

- What is the physical stimulus for touch?
- Where does the sensation of pain originate?
- What role do cognitive processes play in the perception of pain?
- What role does culture play in pain perception?

SMELL AND TASTE: THE CHEMICAL SENSES

Although smell and taste are separate senses, we'll consider them together for two reasons. First, both respond to substances in solution—that is, substances that have been dissolved in a fluid or gas, usually water or air. That is why they are often referred to as the *chemical senses*. Second, in everyday life, smell and taste are interrelated.

Smell and Taste: How They Operate

The stimulus for the sensation of smell consists of molecules of various substances (odorants) contained in the air. Such molecules enter the nasal passages, where they dissolve in moist nasal tissues. This brings them in contact with receptor cells contained in the *olfactory mucosa* (see Figure 3.15). Human beings possess about 10 million of these receptors. Dogs, in contrast, possess about 1 billion receptors (Goldstein, 2002). Nevertheless, our ability to detect smells is impressive. In a "scratch-and-sniff" smell survey, for example, six different odors were embedded separately onto panels about 1.75 by 1.25 inches in size. Less than one ounce of each odor was needed to place the smells onto 11 million copies of the survey (Gibbons, 1986; Gilbert & Wysocki, 1987). Yet, despite the tiny amounts deposited on each survey, people were easily able to detect the smells.

Our olfactory senses are restricted, however, in terms of the *range* of stimuli to which they are sensitive. Just as the visual system can detect only a small portion of the total electromagnetic spectrum, the olfactory receptors can detect only certain odorants. Each molecule of an odorant has a particular size and weight; humans seem to be able to smell odorants with weights ranging from 15 to about 300 (Carlson, 1998). This explains why we can smell alcohol but not table sugar. The molecules that comprise alcohol fall within this range (46), whereas the ones that comprise table sugar do not (342). Several theories have been proposed for how smell messages are interpreted by the brain. *Stereochemical theory* suggests that substances differ in smell because they have different molecular shapes (Amoore, 1970, 1982). Unfortunately, support for this theory has been mixed. Nearly identical molecules can have extremely different fragrances, whereas substances with very different chemical structures can produce very similar odors (Engen, 1982; Wright, 1982). Other theories have focused on isolating "primary odors," similar to the basic hues in color vision. But these efforts have been unsuccessful because there is often disagreement in people's perceptions of even the most basic smells.

One additional intriguing possibility is that the brain's ability to recognize odors may be based on the overall pattern of activity produced by the olfactory receptors (Sicard & Holley, 1984). According to this view, humans possess many different types of olfactory receptors, each one of which is stimulated to varying degrees by particular substances. This may, in turn, result in different patterns of output that the brain recognizes as specific odors (Cowart & Rawson, 2001). How the brain accomplishes this task is not yet known.

We'll now turn to a discussion of the other chemical sense—*taste*. The sensory receptors for taste are located inside small bumps on the tongue known as *papillae*. Within each papilla is a cluster of *taste buds* (Figure 3.16 on page 80). Each taste bud contains several receptor cells. Human beings possess about 10,000 taste buds. In contrast, chickens have only 24, while catfish would win any "tastebud counting contest"—they possess more than 175,000 scattered over the surface of their bodies. In a sense, they can "taste" with their entire skin (Pfaffmann, 1978).

For decades, scientists have agreed that we have four basic food tastes: sweet, salty, sour, and bitter. Recent research, however, seems to indicate there could be several more. Scientists now agree on a fifth sense, *umami*, which is evoked by the amino acid glutamate, a substance found in meats, meat broths, and monosodium glutamate (MSG). Glutamate contributes significantly to the "savory" taste of many natural foods, including fish and cheese (Damak et al., 2003; Nelson et al., 2002). Emerging evidence also hints at the possibility of a sixth basic taste: *fattiness*. Until recently, it was generally accepted that the fat in food doesn't have any taste, but instead provides textural cues or is detected through the smell it imparts to foods. However, newer research shows that when these factors are controlled, people and other animals can still detect fat. Studies of rats have shown that fats cause electrical changes in taste cells, evidence that there is a "fat" detection system at work. Preliminary research with humans has revealed similar findings (e.g., Mattes, 2001).

Interestingly, findings like these may help to explain why people do not seem to find fat-free food alternatives as satisfying as their full-fat counterparts. They

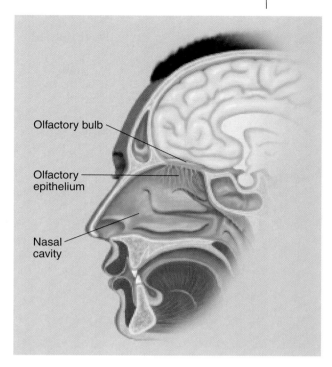

FIGURE 3.15
The Receptors for Smell
Receptors for our sense of smell are located in the olfactory epithelium, at the top of the nasal cavity. Molecules of odorous substances are dissolved in moisture present in the nasal passages. This brings them into contact with *receptor cells*, whose neural activity gives rise to sensations of smell.

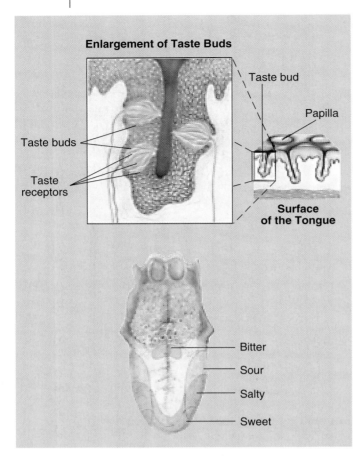

Enlargement of Taste Buds

Taste bud

Papilla

Taste buds

Taste receptors

Surface of the Tongue

Bitter

Sour

Salty

Sweet

FIGURE 3.16
Sensory Receptors for Taste
Taste buds are located inside small bumps on the surface of the tongue known as papillae. Within each taste bud are a number of individual receptor cells.

also give rise to the following important question: Given the fact there are only a relatively small number of basic tastes, why do people generally believe they can distinguish many more flavors than the ones just described? The answer lies in the fact that we are aware not only of the taste of the food but also of its smell, its texture, its temperature, the pressure it exerts on our tongue and mouth, and many other sensations. When these factors are removed from the picture, only the basic tastes remain (see Figure 3.16).

Smell and Taste: Some Interesting Findings

Perhaps because they are more difficult to study, smell and taste have received far less attention from researchers than vision and hearing. However, this does not imply that these senses are not important. Indeed, individuals who have lost their sense of smell (a state known as anosmia) often become deeply depressed; some even commit suicide (Douek, 1988).

Despite the relative lack of research effort, many interesting facts have been uncovered about smell and taste. For example, it appears that we are not very good at identifying different odors (Engen, 1986). When asked to identify thirteen common fragrances (such as grape, smoke, mint, pine, and soap), individuals were successful only 32 percent of the time. Even when brand-name products or common odors are used, accuracy is still less than 50 percent. Some research suggests that we lack a well-developed representational system for describing olfactory experiences (Engen, 1987). In other words, we may recognize a smell without being able to name the odor in question—sometimes called the "tip-of-the-nose" phenomenon (Lawless & Engen, 1977; Richardson & Zucco, 1989).

Actually, although our ability to identify specific odors is limited, our memory of them is impressive (Schab, 1991). Once exposed to a specific odor, we can recognize it months or even years later (Engen & Ross, 1973; Rabin & Cain, 1984). This may be due, in part, to the fact that our memory for odors is often coded as part of memories of more complex and significant life events (Richardson & Zucco, 1989).

Knowledge about the chemical senses—especially smell—can also have important practical implications, a fact that has not escaped manufacturers of scented products. Commercial success has led to numerous claims regarding the potential benefits of fragrance. For example, practitioners in a field called *aromatherapy* claim that they can successfully treat a wide range of psychological problems and physical ailments by means of specific fragrances (Tisserand, 1977). Aromatherapists claim, for example, that fragrances such as lemon, peppermint, and basil lead to increased alertness and energy, whereas lavender and cedar promote relaxation and reduced tension after high-stress work periods (Iwahashi, 1992). Can fragrance influence human behavior in measurable ways? A growing body of evidence indicates the answer is "yes." But whether specific fragrances produce contrasting effects is still uncertain. Although some findings support this claim, others do not. A study by Diego and his colleagues (1998) provides some supporting evidence. Participants in this study were exposed to either lavender, supposedly a "relaxing" odor, or rosemary, presumably an "alerting" odor. Results showed that participants exposed to the rosemary fragrance were indeed more alert following the exposure, as gauged by self-report measures and changes in their EEG patterns.

And although both fragrances led to *faster* performance on a math computation task, only participants exposed to the lavender fragrance showed improved *accuracy.*

Findings from other research, however, seriously question the claim that specific odors produce specific effects (e.g., Baron, 1997; Baron & Bronfen, 1994; Baron & Thomley, 1994). Research conducted by Robert Baron and his colleagues suggests that any fragrance people find pleasant enhances their mood slightly, and that these positive feelings then influence their cognition and behavior. The specific fragrance doesn't seem to matter as long as it is one people find pleasant.

Nevertheless, even these more limited effects may have practical applications. For example, Baron and Kalsher (1998) showed that participants' performance on a simulated driving task was significantly enhanced by the presence of a pleasant ambient lemon fragrance, suggesting that the use of fragrance may be an inexpensive but effective tool for maintaining alertness in persons engaged in potentially dangerous activities, such as driving. So, no, pleasant fragrances don't seem to have the powerful and highly specific effects aromatherapists claim; but yes, they do seem to influence behavior in interesting and potentially important ways.

K E Y   Q U E S T I O N S

- What is the physical stimulus for smell and where are the sensory receptors located?
- Where are the sensory receptors for taste located?
- What are the practical benefits of using pleasant ambient fragrances?

KINESTHESIA AND VESTIBULAR SENSE

One night while driving, you notice flashing lights on the roadside ahead. Because traffic has slowed to a crawl, you get a close look at the situation as you pass by. A state trooper is in the process of administering a sobriety test to the driver of the car he has pulled over. The driver's head is tilted back at an angle, and he is trying to touch each of his fingers to his nose but is having great difficulty doing so. This example illustrates the importance of our *kinesthetic* and our *vestibular senses*—two important but often ignored aspects of our sensory system.

Kinesthesia is the sense that gives us information about the location of our body parts with respect to each other and allows us to perform movements—from simple ones like touching our nose with our fingertips to more complex movements required for gymnastics, dancing, or driving an automobile. Kinesthetic information comes from receptors in joints, ligaments, and muscle fibers (Matlin & Foley, 1997). We also receive important kinesthetic information from our other senses, especially vision and touch. To demonstrate how your kinesthetic sense system draws on other senses, try the following experiment: Close your eyes for a moment and hold your arms down at your sides. Now, without looking, touch your nose with each of your index fingers—one at a time. Can you do it? Most people can, but only after missing their nose a time or two. Now, try it again with your eyes open. Is it easier this way? In most instances it is, because of the added information we receive from our visual sense.

Whereas kinesthesia keeps our brain informed about the location of our body parts with respect to each other, the **vestibular sense** gives us information about body position, movement, and acceleration—factors critical for maintaining our sense of balance (Schiffman, 1990).

The sensory organs for the vestibular sense are located in the inner ear (see Figure 3.17 on page 82). Two fluid-filled *vestibular sacs* provide information about the body's position in relation to the earth by tracking changes in linear movement. When our body accelerates (or decelerates) along a straight line, as when we are in a bus that is starting and stopping, or when we tilt our head or body to one side,

Kinesthesia
The sense that gives us information about the location of our body parts with respect to each other and allows us to perform movement.

Vestibular Sense
Our sense of balance.

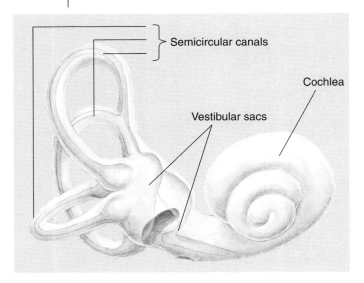

FIGURE 3.17
The Structures Underlying Our Sense of Balance
Shown here are the organs of the inner ear that comprise the vestibular sense. Structures in the two *vestibular sacs* provide information about the positions of the head and body with respect to gravity by tracking changes in linear movement, whereas those in the *semicircular canals* provide information about *rotational acceleration* around three principal axes.

hair cells bend in proportion to the rate of change in our motion. This differential bending of hair cells causes attached nerve fibers to discharge neural signals that are sent to the brain.

Three fluid-filled *semicircular canals,* also in the inner ear, provide information about rotational acceleration of the head or body along the three principle axes. Whenever we turn or rotate our head, the fluid in these canals begins to move and causes a bending of hair cells. Because these structures are arranged at right angles to each other, bending is greatest in the semicircular canal corresponding to the axis along which the rotation occurs. Note that the vestibular system is designed to detect *changes* in motion rather than constant motion. For example, it helps us to detect the change in acceleration that accompanies take-off in an airplane, but not the constant velocity that follows. We also receive vestibular information from our other senses, especially vision—a fact that can produce "queasy" consequences if the information from these senses are in conflict (Jefferson, 1993).

KEY QUESTIONS

- What information does the kinesthetic sense provide to the brain?
- What information does the vestibular sense provide to the brain?

PERCEPTION: PUTTING IT ALL TOGETHER

Up to this point, we have focused on the sensory processes that convert raw physical stimulation into usable neural codes: vision, hearing, touch, taste, smell, and the kinesthetic and vestibular senses. But you may now be wondering how this array of action potentials contributes to the richness of conscious experience. Stop for a moment and look around you. Do you see a meaningless swirl of colors, brightnesses, and shapes? Probably not. Now, turn on the radio and tune it to any station. Do you hear an incomprehensible babble of sounds? Certainly not—unless, of course, you've tuned to a foreign-language or heavy metal station. In both cases, you "see" and "hear" more than the raw sensations that stimulate the receptors in your eyes, ears, and other sense organs; you see recognizable objects and hear understandable words or music. In other words, transmission of sensory information from sensory receptors to the brain is only part of the picture. Equally important is the process of perception—the way in which we *select, organize,* and *interpret* sensory input to achieve a grasp of our surroundings. The remainder of this chapter concerns some basic principles that influence perception.

Perception: The Focus of Our Attention

Based on the preceding discussion, you may realize that your attention, or mental focus, captures only a small portion of the visual and auditory stimuli available at a given moment, while ignoring other aspects. But what about information from our other senses? By shifting the focus of our attention, we may suddenly notice smells, tastes, and tactile sensations that were outside our awareness only moments ago. For example, if you're absorbed in a good book or watching a suspenseful movie, you may be unaware of the sound of someone knocking at the door, at least temporarily.

One thing is certain—we cannot process all of the available sensory information in our environment. Thus, we *selectively attend* to certain aspects of our environment while relegating others to the background (Johnston & Dark, 1986). **Selective attention** has obvious advantages, because it allows us to maximize information gained from the object of our focus while reducing sensory interference from other irrelevant sources. We are, however, faced with many everyday situations in which we must cope with multiple conflicting inputs. Think back to the last time you were at a crowded party with many conversations going on at once. Were you able to shut out all voices except for the voice of the person you were talking to? Probably not. Our attention often shifts to other aspects of our environment, such as a juicy bit of conversation or a mention of our own name (Moray, 1959). This is often referred to as the **cocktail party phenomenon** and illustrates one way in which we deal with the demands of divided attention.

Although we control the focus of our attention, at least to some extent, certain characteristics of stimuli can cause our attention to shift suddenly. Features such as contrast, novelty, stimulus intensity, color, and sudden change tend to attract our attention. Psychologists often refer to this phenomenon as *pop-out*. As you might expect, the ability to shift the focus of our attention to detect such changes plays a crucial survival role in aspects of our everyday life by alerting us to immediate natural dangers in our environment.

As we've seen throughout this section, attention plays an important role in our ability to safely navigate the world around us. However, many aspects of modern living have begun to test the limits of our attentional capabilities. Perhaps the most widespread of these is the use of cell phones while driving. For a discussion on the dangers of using these devices while driving, please see the **Psychology Lends a Hand** section on page 84.

Perception: Some Organizing Principles

Look at the illustrations in Figure 3.19 on page 85. Instead of random smatterings of black and white, you can probably discern a familiar figure in each. But how does our brain allow us to interpret this confusion as a dog and a horseback rider? The process by which we structure the input from our sensory receptors is called *perceptual organization*. Aspects of perceptual organization were first studied systematically in the early 1900s by **Gestalt psychologists**—German psychologists intrigued by certain innate tendencies of the human mind to impose order and structure on the physical world and to perceive sensory patterns as well-organized wholes rather than as separate isolated parts (*Gestalt* means "whole" in German). These scientists outlined several principles that influence the way we organize basic sensory input into whole patterns (gestalts). Some of these are described below.

Figure and Ground: What Stands Out?

By looking carefully at Figure 3.20 on page 85, you can experience a principle of perceptual organization known as the **figure–ground relationship.** What this means, simply, is that we tend to divide the world around us into two parts: *figure*, which has a definite shape and a location in space; and *ground*, which has no shape, seems to continue behind the figure, and has no definite location. The figure–ground relationship helps clarify the distinction between sensation and perception. While the pattern of sensory input generated in our receptors remains constant, our perceptions shift between the two figure–ground patterns in Figure 3.20; thus, we may see either the skull or the woman looking in the mirror, but not both. Note that the principles of perceptual organization apply to the other senses, too. For instance, consider how the figure–ground relationship applies to audition: During a complicated lecture, you become absorbed in whispered gossip between two students sitting next to you; the professor's voice becomes background noise. Suddenly you hear your name and realize the professor has asked you a question; her voice has now become the sole focus of your attention, while the conversation becomes background noise.

Selective Attention
The process of focusing on a particular quality, object, or event for relatively detailed analysis.

Cocktail Party Phenomenon
The effect of not being aware of other people's conversations until something of personal importance, such as hearing one's name, is mentioned and then suddenly hearing it.

Gestalt Psychologists
German psychologists intrigued by our tendency to perceive sensory patterns as well-organized wholes rather than as separate isolated parts.

Figure–Ground Relationship
Our tendency to divide the perceptual world into two distinct parts—discrete figures and the background against which they stand out.

psychology lends a hand

Exceeding the Limits of Our Attention: The Dangers of Using Cellular Phones While Driving

The use of cellular phones in this country, and throughout the world, has skyrocketed. More than 100 million people in the United States alone currently own cell phones (Cellular Telecommunications Industry Association, 2001). So what's the problem? A lot of people use their cell phones while driving—nearly 85 percent in one survey (Goodman et al., 1999). Unfortunately, this practice can be dangerous. Redelmeier and Tibshirani (1997) reviewed the cell phone records of several hundred people involved in motor vehicle accidents and found that a significant portion of them had been talking on their cell phones just prior to the accident.

One interpretation of these findings is that the use of cell phones distracts people, similar to the effects you might expect from doing other activities while driving, such as putting on makeup, eating or drinking foods, or listening to music. However, research suggests that the particular type of attention demanded by active listening or conversing is what makes it so dangerous (Spence & Read, 2003). To test this possibility, Strayer and Johnston (2001) asked some of their participants to perform a simulated driving task, and others to perform the driving task while either talking on a cell phone or listening to the radio. To separate the effects of attention from manual manipulation of the phone itself, half of the participants used a handheld cell phone, while the other half used a hands-free phone. As shown in Figure 3.18, driving performance was worse among participants who talked on the cell phone compared to those who listened to the radio while driving. The use of a hands-free cell phone did not alleviate the negative effects of using a cell phone while driving. Moreover, these effects were even stronger for more complicated versions of the driving task.

To avoid the possibility of injuring yourself, or someone else, while driving, please consider the following driving safety tips:

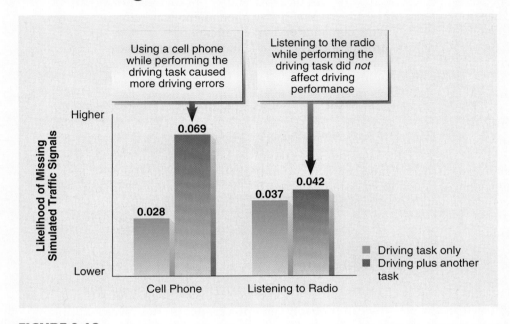

FIGURE 3.18

The Dangers of Talking on Cell Phones While Driving: Attention Appears to Be the Key

As shown here, performance on the simulated driving task was worse among participants who talked on the cell phone compared to those who listened to the radio while driving. The use of a hands-free cell phone did not alleviate the negative effects of talking on the cell phone while driving.

Source: Based on data from Strayer & Johnston, 2001.

- **Don't use your cell phone while driving.** Talking on a cell phone—even a hands-free one—while driving is dangerous, because of the type of attention it demands. If you must use your cell phone, pull off the road into a safe place before dialing *or* answering your cell phone.

- **Avoid other competing activities.** Talking on a cell phone is not the only problem; eating, drinking, and applying makeup are also dangerous activities because they divert attention away from driving.

- **Drive defensively.** As the information in this section shows, a significant portion of drivers now use cell phones while driving—even in states in which it is against the law. This could affect their driving. So, plan ahead for the unexpected. Always be prepared to react to the other driver.

FIGURE 3.19
Perceptual Organization
Look carefully at each of these figures. What do you see? Our perceptual processes often allow us to perceive shapes and forms from incomplete and fragmented stimuli.

Grouping: Which Stimuli Go Together?

The Gestaltists also called attention to a number of principles known as the **laws of grouping**—basic ways in which we group items together perceptually. Research suggests that these principles play a key role in visual perception; they help explain how small elements become perceptually grouped to form larger objects and how a scene is segmented into relevant regions to help us recognize individual objects (Sekuler & Bennett, 2001). Several of these laws are illustrated in Figure 3.21 on page 86. As you can see from this figure, they do offer a good description of our perceptual tendencies.

Laws of Grouping
Simple principles describing how we tend to group discrete stimuli together in the perceptual world.

Still, some observers have questioned whether these principles are innate—as the Gestaltists contended—or the product of learning and experience. Proponents of this latter view have suggested these principles may apply only to people who have had experience with geometrical concepts. To illustrate this, let's consider a classic study by Luria (1976). Luria presented stimuli like those depicted in Figure 3.22 on page 86 to several groups of participants that included uneducated people from remote villages and students in a teacher's school. Lucia reasoned that if Gestalt principles were innate, then all participants—regardless of level of education—should perceive the objects in similar ways. The results showed that the students tended to identify the shapes by category (e.g., circle, triangle, square), regardless of the "completeness" of the stimuli or the presence of other features (e.g., color)—a tendency that may have emerged from their experience with two-dimensional drawings of three-dimensional objects. In contrast, the participants with no formal education tended to name the shapes according to familiar objects they resembled. Apparently, in their eyes, a circle resembled a plate or the moon—not the abstract categories named by the students. This type of evidence seems to indicate that the Gestalt principles may not be universal, but instead depend on the effects of learning and experience (e.g., Matsumoto, 2000; Quinn et al., 2002). In any case, principles of perceptual organization are readily visible in the natural world, and they are effective in helping us organize our perceptual world.

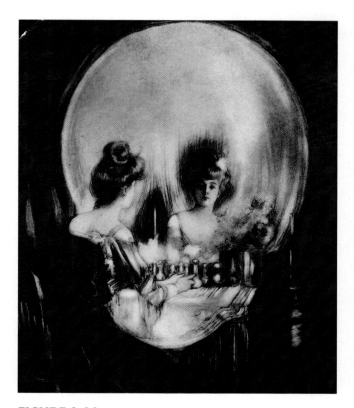

FIGURE 3.20
A Demonstration of Figure–Ground
What do you see when you look at this drawing? Probably, a woman looking into a mirror or a skull. Because this is an ambiguous figure, your perceptions may switch back and forth between these two possibilities.

Laws of Similarity
Tendency to perceive similar items as a group

Laws of Proximity
Tendency to perceive items located together as a group

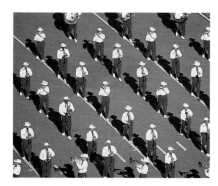

Laws of Common Region
Tendency to perceive objects as a group if they occupy the same place within a plane

Law of Good Continuation
Tendency to perceive stimuli as part of a continuous pattern

Law of Closure
Tendency to perceive objects as whole entities, despite the fact that some parts may be missing or obstructed from view

Laws of Simplicity
Tendency to perceive complex patterns in terms of simpler shapes

FIGURE 3.21
Laws of Perceptual Grouping
We seem to possess strong tendencies to group stimuli together in certain ways. Several of these *laws of grouping* are illustrated here.

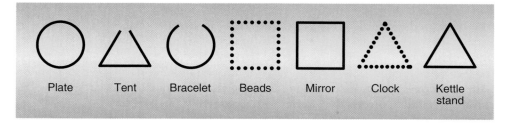

Plate   Tent   Bracelet   Beads   Mirror   Clock   Kettle stand

FIGURE 3.22
Gestalt Principles: Innate Principles or a Product of Learning?
People with formal education tend to refer to these shapes as circles, squares, triangles, and other geometric forms. In contrast, people from cultures without formal education perceive them in terms of their resemblance to familiar objects in their environment.
Source: Based on data from Luria, 1976.

Constancies and Illusions: When Perception Succeeds—and Fails

Perception, we have seen, is more than the sum of all the sensory input supplied by our eyes, ears, and other receptors. It is the active selection, organization, and interpretation of such input. It yields final products that differ from raw, unprocessed sensations in important ways. Up to now, this discussion has focused on the benefits of this process. But perception, like any other powerful process, can be a double-edged sword. On the one hand, perception helps us adapt to a complex and ever changing environment. On the other hand, perception sometimes leads us into error. To see how, let's consider *constancies* and *illusions*.

◼ Perceptual Constancies: Stability in the Face of Change

Try this simple demonstration. Hold your right hand in front of you at arm's length. Next, move it toward and away from your face several times. Does it seem to change in size? Probably not. The purpose of this demonstration is to illustrate the principles of perceptual **constancies**—our tendency to perceive aspects of the world as unchanging despite changes in the sensory input we receive from them. The principle of **size constancy** relates to the fact that the perceived size of an object remains the same when the distance is varied, even though the size of the image it casts on the retina changes greatly. Under normal circumstances, such constancy is impressive. Consider, for example, seeing a friend we are meeting for lunch walking toward us, though still several blocks away. Distant objects—including cars, trees, and people—cast tiny images on our retina. Yet, we perceive them as being of normal size. Two factors seem to account for this tendency: size–distance invariance and relative size.

The principle of *size–distance invariance* suggests that when estimating the size of an object, we take into account both the size of the image it casts on our retina and the apparent distance of the object. From these data we almost instantly calculate the object's size. Only when the cues that normally reveal an object's distance are missing do we run into difficulties in estimating the object's size (as we'll see in our discussion of illusions that follows). We also notice the **relative size** of an object compared to objects of known size. This mechanism is especially useful for estimating the size of unfamiliar things.

But size is not the only perceptual feature of the physical world that does not correspond directly with the information transmitted by our sensory receptors. The principle of **shape constancy** refers to the fact that the perceived shape of an object does not alter as the image it casts on the retina changes. For example, all of us know that coins are round; yet we rarely see them that way. Flip a coin into the air: Although you continue to perceive the coin as being round, the image that actually falls onto your retina constantly shifts from a circle to various forms of an ellipse.

The principle of **brightness constancy** refers to the fact that we perceive objects as constant in brightness and color, even when viewed under different lighting conditions. Thus, we will perceive a sweater as dark green whether indoors or outdoors in bright sunlight. Brightness constancy apparently prevails because objects and their surroundings are usually lighted by the same illumination source, so changes in lighting conditions occur simultaneously for both the object and its immediate surroundings. As long as the changes in lighting remain constant for both the object and its surroundings, the neural message reaching the brain is unchanged. Brightness constancy breaks down, however, when changes in lighting are not equivalent for both the object and its surroundings (Sekuler & Blake, 1990).

Although most research on perceptual constancies has focused on size, shape, and brightness, constancy pervades nearly every area of perception, including our other senses. For example, imagine listening to background music while riding on an elevator. When one of your favorite "oldies" begins, but recorded by a different group, you can't believe what they've done to "your song." Nonetheless, you are still able to recognize it, despite differences in its loudness, tone, and pitch.

Constancies
Our tendency to perceive physical objects as unchanging despite shifts in the pattern of sensations these objects induce.

Size Constancy
The tendency to perceive a physical object as having a constant size, even when the image it casts on the retina changes.

Relative Size
A visual cue based on a comparison of an object of unknown size to one of known size.

Shape Constancy
The tendency to perceive a physical object as having a constant shape, even when the image it casts on the retina changes.

Brightness Constancy
The tendency to perceive objects as having a constant brightness when they are viewed under different conditions of illumination.

Whatever their basis, perceptual constancies are highly useful. Without them, we would spend a great deal of time and effort reidentifying sensory information in our environments each time we experienced the information from a new perspective. Thus, the gap between our sensations and the perceptions provided by the constancies is clearly beneficial.

Illusions: When Perception Fails

We've seen that perception organizes sensory information into a coherent picture of the world around us. Perception can also, however, provide false interpretations of sensory information. Such cases are known as **illusions,** a term used by psychologists to refer to incorrect perceptions. Actually, there are two types of illusions: those due to physical processes (e.g., mirages) and those due to cognitive processes. Our focus will be on the latter type of illusion—those involving cognitive processes.

Countless illusions related to cognitive processes exist, but most fall into two categories: illusions of *size* and illusions of *shape* or *area* (Coren et al., 1976). Natural examples of two well-known size illusions are presented in Figure 3.23, and as you can see, their effects are powerful. But, why do illusions occur? Some evidence suggests that illusions generally have multiple causes (Schiffman, 1990). One explanation is provided by the *theory of misapplied constancy.* It suggests that when looking at illusions, we interpret certain cues as suggesting that some parts are farther away than others. Our powerful tendency toward size constancy then comes into play, with the result that we perceptually distort the length of various lines (refer to Figure 3.23). Learning also plays an important role in illusions, as shown in the examples of the *Müller–Lyer illusion* in Figure 3.24. Past experience tells us that the corner shown in the figure on the right is usually farther away than the corner in the figure on the left. Therefore, although the size of the retinal image cast by the vertical lines in both figures is identical, we interpret the vertical line as longer in the figure on the right. Moreover, learning seems to affect the extent to which our perception is influenced by illusions: Many visual illusions decline in magnitude following extended exposure, although they do not disappear entirely (Greist-Bousquet, Watson, & Schiffman, 1990).

Another type of illusion is that of *shape* or *area.* A powerful example of this type of illusion is provided by the *Ames room.* Originally created by ophthalmologist Adelbert Ames, characteristics of the Ames room leads us to perceive people as being very different in size (refer to the photo in Figure 3.25). The reason for this misperception of size lies in the unusual shape of the room. When an observer looks into an Ames room, the room *appears* normal and rectangular, but its true shape is cleverly distorted (refer to the diagram at the right side of Figure 3.25). The floor, ceiling, some walls, and the far windows are actually trapezoidal surfaces.

Illusions
Instances in which perception yields false interpretations of physical reality.

FIGURE 3.23
Powerful Illusions of Size
Natural examples of two powerful illusions of size. The horizontal–vertical illusion stems from our tendency to perceive objects higher in our visual field as more distant. This illusion helps explain why the St. Louis Gateway (*left*) falsely appears taller than it is wide; its height and width are actually equal. In the Ponzo illusion (*right*), the line in the distance appears larger, although both lines are actually the same size.

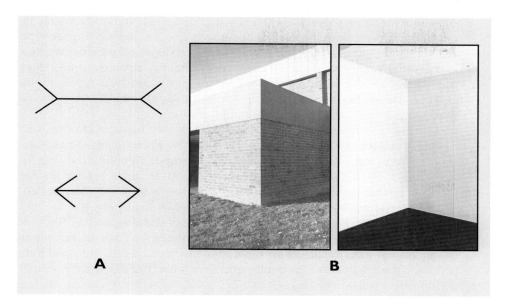

FIGURE 3.24
The Müller–Lyer Illusion

In the Müller–Lyer illusion, lines of equal length (A) appear unequal. The line with the wings pointing outward looks longer than the line with the wings pointing inward. Now carefully examine the vertical line in each of the photographs (B). Which line is longer? Most people perceive the vertical line in the photo on the right as longer, although careful measurement shows they are exactly the same length.

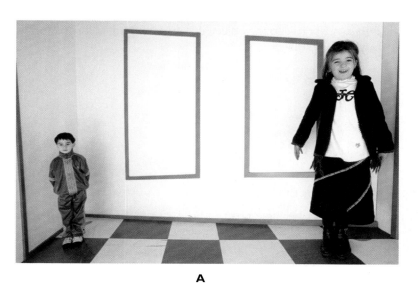

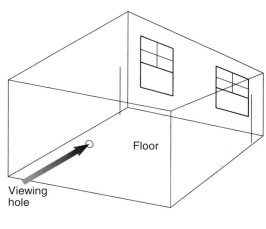

FIGURE 3.25
The Ames Room

(A) An observer looking into this Ames room might conclude that the person on the right is much taller than the person on the left even though they are about the same height. (B) From an observer's perspective, the Ames room appears normal and rectangular. However, the trapezoidal shape of the windows, floor, and some walls and sloping ceiling and floors provide misleading cues. Because these cues lead observers to believe the two people are the same distance away, they perceive the person on the right to be much larger than the person on the left.

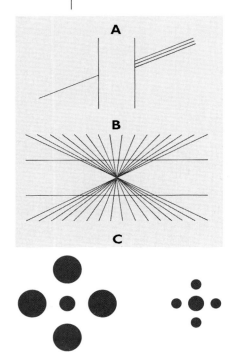

FIGURE 3.26
Illusions of Area or Shape
Illusions of shape or area, too, can be quite powerful. In drawing A, known as the Poggendorf illusion, which of the three lines on the right continues the line on the left? Check your answer with a ruler. In drawing B, known as the Hering–Helmholtz illusion, are the horizontal lines straight or bent in the middle? Again, check for yourself. Finally, in the third, are the sizes of the center circles the same or different? When you check, you'll see why sometimes you can't believe what you think you see!

Although the floor appears level, it is actually at an incline (the far left corner is much lower than the near right corner). The two corners appear to be the same size and distance away, but the left corner is actually twice as far away from the observer as the right corner. What's happening in the Ames room? Because we think we are looking into a normal rectangular room, and because the two people appear to be at the same distance, we perceive the person on the left to be much smaller.

Like illusions of size or area, shape illusions (see Figure 3.26) can exert powerful influences on our perception—sometimes producing some unsettling consequences. Consider a real-world example involving the *Poggendorf illusion.* In this illusion, a line disappears at an angle behind a solid figure, reappearing at the other side—at what seems to be the incorrect position. As reported by Coren and Girgus (1978), two airplanes were about to arrive in New York City in 1965, and because of the Poggendorf illusion, they perceived that they were on a collision course. Each of the pilots changed their path to correct for what they perceived as an error, and thus collided. The result was four deaths and forty-nine injuries—all because of an illusion.

One final point: Illusions are not limited to visual processes. Indeed, there are numerous examples of illusions for our other sensory modalities, including touch and audition (Shepard, 1964). One well-known illusion that you can demonstrate for yourself is that of touch temperature. First, place one hand in a container of hot water and the other hand in cold water. Then, place *both* hands in a container of lukewarm water. Most people experience a dramatic difference in perceived temperature between the two hands; the hand initially placed in hot water feels the lukewarm water as cool, whereas the hand initially placed in cold water feels it as hot. How do we explain this illusion? When we touch an object, the temperature of the area of our skin in contact with it shifts toward that of the object's surface. So, when we perceive an object to be warm or cool, our experience stems partly from the temperature difference between the object and our skin, not solely from the actual temperature of the object.

KEY QUESTIONS

• Why is selective attention important?
• What role do the Gestalt principles play in perceptual processes?
• What are perceptual constancies?
• What are illusions?

Some Key Perceptual Processes: Pattern and Distance

Perception is a practical process because it provides organisms with information essential to survival in their normal habitat. The specific nature of this information varies greatly with different species. Nonetheless, it is probably safe to say that virtually all living creatures need information concerning (1) what's out there and (2) how far away it is. Humans are no exception to this general rule, and we possess impressive perceptual skills in both areas.

Pattern Recognition: What's Out There?

The fact that you are able to read the words on this page depends on your ability to recognize small black marks as letters and collections of such marks as words. How do we accomplish this task? Research on this issue suggests the following two possibilities, termed the *bottom-up* and *top-down theories* of pattern recognition.

As their names imply, these adopt somewhat opposite perspectives on the basic question of how we recognize patterns of visual stimuli. The **bottom-up**

Bottom-Up Approach
Suggests that our ability to recognize specific patterns, such as letters of the alphabet or objects, is based on simpler capacities to recognize and correctly combine lower-level features of objects, such as lines, edges, corners, and angles.

approach to pattern recognition suggests that our ability to recognize specific patterns, such as letters of the alphabet or objects, is based on simpler capacities to recognize and correctly combine lower-level features of objects, such as lines, edges, corners, and angles. One theory, termed *recognition-by-components*, proposes that objects are represented in terms of a set of simple geometric components called *geons* (Biederman, 1987). According to this view, common objects are readily recognized, given only two to three geons in the proper alignment. Another view, termed *feature integration theory*, proposes that object perception occurs according to a sequence of stages (e.g., Triesman, 1998). A third, termed the *computational approach*, treats the visual system as if it were a computer that has been programmed to assemble basic features within the visual scene (Marr, 1982). Although each of these approaches differs in many respects, they all converge on the idea that pattern recognition is constructed from simpler perceptual abilities through a discrete series of steps.

In contrast, the **top-down approach** emphasizes the fact that our knowledge and expectancies play a critical role in shaping our perceptions. We often proceed in accordance with what our past experience tells us to expect, and therefore we don't always analyze every feature of most stimuli we encounter. Although top-down processing can be extremely efficient (think about the speed with which you can read this page), it can also lead us astray. Nearly everyone has had the experience of rushing over to another person who appears to be an old friend, only to realize he or she is actually a stranger. In such cases, our tendency to process information quickly from the top down can indeed produce errors.

Which of these views is correct? Current evidence seems to indicate that perception often involves both bottom-up and top-down processing working together. To illustrate this point, consider the plight of pharmacists who must interpret the messy handwriting evident in many doctors' prescriptions. To decipher a prescription, a pharmacist might begin with bottom-up processing, which is based on an analysis of the lines and squiggles that compose the writing. However, top-down processing also comes into play as he uses his knowledge of the names of drugs—and perhaps his experience with this particular doctor's writing—to solve the problem.

▪ Distance Perception: How Far Away Is It?

Our impressive ability to judge depth and distance occurs because we make use of many different cues in forming such judgments. These cues can be divided into two categories, *monocular* and *binocular*, depending on whether they can be seen with only one eye or require the use of both eyes. (Please refer to Figure 3.27 on page 92.)

Monocular cues to depth or distance, include the following:

1. *Size cues.* The larger the image of an object on the retina, the larger it is judged to be; in addition, if an object is larger than the other objects, it is often perceived as closer.
2. *Linear perspective.* Parallel lines appear to converge in the distance; the greater this effect, the farther away an object appears to be.
3. *Texture gradient.* The texture of a surface appears smoother as distance increases.
4. *Atmospheric perspective.* The farther away objects are, the less distinctly they are seen—smog, dust, and haze get in the way.
5. *Overlap* (or interposition). If one object obscures another in the visual field, it is seen as being closer than the one it obscures.
6. *Height cues* (aerial perspective). Below the horizon, objects lower down in our field of vision are perceived as closer; above the horizon, objects higher up are seen as closer.
7. *Motion parallax.* When we travel in a vehicle, objects far away appear to move in the same direction as the observer, whereas close objects move in the opposite direction. Objects at different distances appear to move at different velocities.

Top-Down Approach
Approach to pattern recognition that starts with the analysis of high-level information, such as our knowledge, expectancies, and the context in which a stimulus is seen.

Monocular Cues
Cues to depth or distance provided by one eye.

FIGURE 3.27
Monocular Cues to Depth Perception
As illustrated, artists make effective use of a variety of monocular cues to convey a sense of depth in their paintings.

Binocular Cues
Cues to depth or distance resulting from the fact that we have two eyes.

Extrasensory Perception (ESP)
Perception without a basis in sensory input.

Psi
Unusual processes of information or energy transfer that are currently unexplained in terms of known physical or biological mechanisms. Included under the heading of psi are such supposed abilities as telepathy (reading others' thoughts) and clairvoyance (perceiving distant objects).

We also rely heavily on **binocular cues**—depth information based on the coordinated efforts of both eyes. Binocular cues for depth perception stem from two primary sources:

1. *Convergence.* In order to see close objects, our eyes turn inward, toward one another; the greater this movement, the closer such objects appear to be.
2. *Retinal disparity* (binocular parallax). Our two eyes observe objects from slightly different positions in space; the difference between these two images is interpreted by our brain to provide another cue to depth.

The list of monocular and binocular cues provided here is by no means exhaustive. By using the wealth of information provided by these and other cues (Schiffman, 1990), we can usually perceive depth and distance with great accuracy.

KEY QUESTIONS
- What are the bottom-up and top-down approaches to pattern recognition?
- How are we able to judge depth and distance?

PSI: PERCEPTION WITHOUT SENSATION?

Have you ever wondered if we have a "sixth sense"? In other words, can we gain information about the external world without use of our basic senses? Many persons believe we can and accept the existence of **extrasensory perception**—literally, perception without a basis in sensation. The first and most basic question we can ask about ESP is, "Does it really exist?" This question has been recast by Bem and Honorton (1994) in terms of a hypothetical process known as **psi**. These researchers define *psi* as unusual processes of information or energy transfer that are currently unexplained in terms of known physical or biological mechanisms.

Psi: What Is It?

Parapsychologists, those who study psi and other *paranormal events,* or events outside our normal experience or knowledge, suggest there are actually several distinct forms of psi (or ESP). One form of psi is *precognition,* the ability to foretell future events. Fortunetellers and psychics often make their livings from the supposed ability to make such predictions. *Clairvoyance,* the ability to perceive objects or events that do not directly stimulate your sensory organs, is another form of psi. While playing cards, if you somehow "know" which one will be dealt next, you are experiencing clairvoyance. *Telepathy,* a skill used by mind readers, involves the direct transmission of thought from one person to the next. Another phenomenon often associated with psi is *psychokinesis,* the ability to affect the physical world purely through thought. People who bend spoons or move objects with their mind or perform feats of levitation (making objects rise into the air) claim to have powers of psychokinesis.

Psi: Does It Really Exist?

The idea of a mysterious sixth sense is intriguing, and many people are passionately convinced of its existence (Bowles & Hynds, 1978). But does it really exist? Most psychologists are skeptical about the existence of psi for several reasons. The first reason for doubting its existence is the repeated failure to replicate instances of psi; that is, certain procedures yield evidence for psi at one time but not at others. Indeed, one survey failed to uncover a single instance of paranormal phenomena that could be reliably produced after ruling out alternative explanations such as fraud, methodological flaws, and normal sensory functioning (Hoppe, 1988). Moreover, it appears that the more controlled studies of psi are, the less evidence for psi they have provided (Blackmore, 1986).

Second, present-day scientific understanding states that all aspects of our behavior must ultimately stem from biochemical events, yet it is not clear what physical mechanism could account for psi. In fact, the existence of such a mechanism would require restructuring our view of the physical world.

Third, much of the support for psi has been obtained by persons already deeply convinced of its existence. As you might expect, scientists are not immune to being influenced in their observations by their own beliefs. Thus, while studies suggesting that psi exists may represent a small sample of all research conducted on this topic, perhaps only the few experiments yielding positive results find their way into print; perhaps the many "failures" are simply not reported.

In short, no reliable evidence supports the existence of psi or ESP. So, the next time you read about or see people on television who claim they can read minds, tell the future, or bend objects with their minds—don't be fooled! Instead, think about other more tangible ways they might have accomplished these feats.

KEY QUESTION

- How do most psychologists view the possibility of extrasensory perception or psi?

Parapsychologists
Individuals who study ESP and other paranormal events.

SUMMARY AND REVIEW OF KEY QUESTIONS

Sensation: The Raw Materials of Understanding

- **What is the primary function of our sensory receptors?**
Sensory receptors transduce raw physical energy into neural impulses, which are then interpreted by our central nervous system.

- **What does the term *absolute threshold* refer to?**
The absolute threshold is the smallest magnitude of a stimulus that can be detected 50 percent of the time.

- **Why is signal detection theory important?**
Signal detection theory helps to separate sensitivity from motivational factors.

- **What is a difference threshold?**
Difference threshold refers to the amount of change in a stimulus required for a person to detect it.

- **Can subliminal messages affect our behavior?**
Research using visual priming suggests that stimuli that stimulate the sensory receptors, but remain outside conscious awareness, produce measurable effects on cognition and behavior. However, research fails to support the use of subliminal messages as tools of persuasion.

- **What is the role of sensory adaptation in sensation?**
Sensory adaptation serves a useful function by allowing us to focus on important changes in our environment.

Vision

- **What are the basic structures of the eye and what is the physical stimulus for vision?**
Light rays first pass through the cornea and then enter the eye through the pupil. Adjustments to lighting conditions are executed by the iris. The lens is a clear structure whose shape adjusts to permit us to focus on objects at varying distances. Light rays leaving the lens are projected onto the retina at the back of the eyeball. The physical stimulus for vision is electromagnetic wavelengths that stimulate the rods and cones in the retina.

- **What are the basic functions of the visual system?**
The basic functions of the visual system include acuity, dark adaptation, and eye movements. Acuity refers to the ability to see fine details. Dark adaptation refers to the increase in sensitivity that occurs when we move from bright light to a dim environment. Various types of eye movements are crucial to our ability to track moving objects and to perceive distance and depth.

- **How do psychologists explain color perception?**
Our rich sense of color stems from mechanisms at several levels of our nervous system. Two leading theories that explain how we perceive color are trichromatic theory and opponent-process theory.

- **Why is visual perception a hierarchical process?**
Visual perception is a hierarchical process because increasingly complex visual information is analyzed and compiled at successive stages, eventually yielding a coherent and flowing visual world.

- **What are the basic building blocks of visual perception?**
The basic building blocks of visual perception begin with feature detectors—neurons in the visual cortex that respond when particular types of stimuli, with characteristic features, are detected.

Hearing

- **What is the physical stimulus for hearing?**
The physical stimulus for hearing is sound waves that stimulate tiny hair cells in the cochlea.

- **How do psychologists explain pitch perception?**
Place theory and frequency theory help explain how we perceive pitch.

- **How do we localize sound?**
The sound shadow created by our head causes sound to reach one ear slightly faster than the other. This small time difference helps us localize the source of sound.

Touch and Other Skin Senses

- **What is the physical stimulus for touch?**
The physical stimulus for touch is a stretching of or pressure against receptors in the skin.

- **Where does the sensation of pain originate?**
Sensations of pain originate in receptors called nociceptors.

- **What role do cognitive processes play in the perception of pain?**
Our thoughts, feelings, and beliefs appear to play an important mediator role, determining the extent to which we focus on pain.

- **What role does culture play in pain perception?**
Observed cultural differences in the capacity to withstand pain seem to be perceptual in nature and reflect the effects of social learning.

Smell and Taste: The Chemical Senses

- **What is the physical stimulus for smell and where are the sensory receptors located?**
The physical stimuli for sensations of smell are molecules that stimulate receptors in the nose.

- **Where are the sensory receptors for taste located?**
The sensory receptors for taste are located in papillae on the tongue.

- **What are the practical benefits of using pleasant ambient fragrances?**
The use of pleasant fragrances can increase alertness among persons engaged in potentially dangerous activities, such as driving.

Kinesthesia and Vestibular Sense

- **What information does our kinesthetic sense provide to the brain?**
Kinesthesia informs the brain about the location of body parts with respect to each other.

- **What information does the vestibular sense provide to the brain?**
The vestibular sense provides information about body position, movement, and acceleration.

Perception: Putting It All Together

- **Why is selective attention important?**
Selective attention reduces the interference from irrelevant sensory sources.

- **What role do the Gestalt principles play in perceptual process?**
The Gestalt principles of perceptual organization help us to structure the input from our sensory receptors.

- **What are perceptual constancies?**
Perceptual constancies are principles describing our ability to perceive aspects of the world as unchanging despite variations in the information reaching our sensory receptors, such as information about size, shape, or brightness.

- **What are illusions?**
Illusion is a term used by psychologists to refer to errors in interpreting sensory information.

- **What are the bottom-up and top-down approaches to pattern recognition?**
The bottom-up approach suggests that pattern recognition stems from our ability to recognize and combine basic visual features. In contrast, the top-down approach emphasizes the role that knowledge, expectations, and the context in which stimulation occurs play in shaping our perceptions.

- **How are we able to judge depth and distance?**
Judgments of depth and distance result from both binocular and monocular cues.

PSI: Perception without Sensation?

- **How do most psychologists view the possibility of extrasensory perception or psi?**
Most psychologists remain highly skeptical about its existence and await the results of further careful research.

PSYCHOLOGY: UNDERSTANDING ITS FINDINGS

Putting Fragrance to Work

Research by the authors (Baron and Kalsher) showed that a pleasant ambient fragrance (a lemon scent) exerted an alerting effect on participants performing a simulated driving task. Other research by Professor Baron indicates that fragrance can improve our mood; the specific fragrance doesn't seem to matter as long as it is one people find pleasant. Try the following exercise to put scent to work for you.

Most of us have at least one time during the day when we feel less alert. Mine happens to occur at about 4:00 p.m.; yours may be different. To identify your alertness "peaks" and "valleys," use the following scale to record your level of alertness at several points during the day. You can also use it to rate your mood. Next, find a fragrance that you like and introduce it into your living space at a time when your alertness level is relatively low. Does the fragrance increase your alertness? Does it improve your mood? If so, by how much? Did your alertness or mood change more in response to a particular scent than to another? Keep a diary for a week or two to track the effects of one or more fragrances on your alertness. Your friends may want to try this, too.

Alertness:

Low   1   2   3   4   5   6   7   High

Mood:

Bad   1   2   3   4   5   6   7   Good

MAKING PSYCHOLOGY PART OF YOUR LIFE

Managing Your Pain: Some Useful Tips

As a long-time sports enthusiast, I (Michael Kalsher) am very familiar with the predictable muscular aches and pains that occasionally result from overdoing it. When I run too far or overdo it while weight lifting, I can usually count on muscle soreness—or worse—the following day. Although these and other types of minor injuries definitely have a physical component, the degree to which we experience pain can be influenced by many factors, including how we think about the pain. Although you should do everything to avoid getting injured (e.g., stretching before you run or work out), here are a few things that you can do to lessen the impact of the minor aches and pains that accompany exercise.

1. Use *counterirritants*. As we learned in this chapter, there are neural mechanisms in the spinal cord that sometimes close, thereby preventing pain messages from reaching the brain. Counterirritants can help close the gate and are particularly useful to relieve the sharp pain that occurs when we stub our toes or close a door on our fingers. To use this technique, vigorously rub the surrounding area right after the injury occurs.

2. Use deep massage or apply ice packs or heat to help soothe the more generalized pain that results from sore, achy muscles should you overdo it during a run or workout.

3. Use *cognitive–behavioral techniques* to change the way you think about the pain.
   - Dwelling on negative thoughts usually intensifies your perceptions of pain. Try substituting negative thoughts with positive ones.
   - Distraction is another effective technique. Try focusing your attention away from the pain by getting involved with another activity that attracts your interest.
   - Induce an emotional state incompatible with pain—for example, laughter. Expose yourself as quickly as possible to something—or someone—you find humorous. If no one is around, think of something that makes you laugh.

4. **Caution!** Remember that pain serves a useful purpose that should definitely not be ignored. Indeed, use pain as a guide to hasten your recovery.

KEY TERMS

4

States of Consciousness

*H*ave you ever sat in class and followed the professor with your eyes as she or he moved around the room while, in fact, your thoughts were a thousand miles away, on something totally unrelated to the lecture? Are there certain times of the day when you feel most alert, and other times when focusing on any task requiring a lot of attention or energy is much more difficult? And when you go to sleep at night, do you dream? If you do, what do you dream about? Do your dreams seem related to events in your life, or are they total journeys into fantasy? And do you ever use drugs to change your mood—to calm your nerves, help you sleep, or just to feel better? If you ever have these experiences—and virtually all of us do—you already know that each day, you pass through many different **states of consciousness**—varying levels of awareness of ourselves, our behavior, and the world around us (see Figure 4.1 on page 98). It's on those changes, and the contrasting states of consciousness they involve, that this chapter focuses.

FIGURE 4.1
Changing States of Consciousness: A Part of Daily Life
During the course of each day, we experience several different states of consciousness.

$\mathbf{P}$sychologists have been studying states of consciousness for several decades, and have uncovered many fascinating—and useful—facts about them. To provide you with an overview of these findings, we'll focus on the following topics. First, we'll examine *biological rhythms*—naturally occurring, cyclical changes in many basic bodily processes and mental states that occur over the course of a day or longer periods of time. While this topic is also related to personal health and could be discussed in Chapter 11, some of the changes produced by biological rhythms involve shifts in consciousness, so it makes sense to consider them here. Next, we'll consider some aspects of *waking consciousness*—changes in consciousness that occur while we are awake. After examining these changes, we'll turn to what is, perhaps, the most profound shift in consciousness we experience on a daily basis: *sleep.* Here, we'll consider the nature of dreams and what functions, if any, they may serve. Our next topic will be *hypnosis,* what it is (and isn't) and the effects it produces. Hypnosis is a controversial topic in psychology, but careful research by psychologists has helped us to understand it—and to remove some of the mystery that surrounds it—so considering it here seems useful in several ways. Finally, we'll examine the *consciousness-altering drugs* and how they produce their effects.

BIOLOGICAL RHYTHMS: TIDES OF LIFE— AND CONSCIOUS EXPERIENCE

States of Consciousness
Varying degrees of awareness of ourselves and the external world.

Biological Rhythms
Cyclic changes in bodily processes.

Circadian Rhythms
Cyclic changes in bodily processes occurring within a single day.

Are you a morning person or an evening person? When do you feel most alert and energetic? Whatever your answer, it's clear that most of us experience regular shifts in these respects each day. Psychologists and other scientists refer to such changes as **biological rhythms**—regular fluctuations in our bodily processes and in consciousness over time. Many of these fluctuations occur over the course of a single day and are therefore known as **circadian rhythms** (from the Latin words for "around" and "day"). Other fluctuations occupy shorter periods of time (for instance, many people become hungry every two or three hours). And still others occur over longer periods, such as the mating seasons shown by many animals—they only mate at certain times of the year—and the female menstrual cycle, which is roughly 28 days. Because circadian rhythms have been the focus of most research, however, we'll focus primarily on these.

Circadian Rhythms: Their Basic Nature

Most people are aware of fluctuations in their alertness, energy, and moods over the course of a day, and research findings indicate that such shifts are closely related to changes in underlying bodily processes (e.g., Moore-Ede, Sulzman, & Fuller, 1982). Daily cycles occur in the production of various hormones, core body temperature, blood pressure, and several other processes. For many persons, these functions are highest in the late afternoon and evening and lowest in the early hours of the morning. However, large individual differences in this respect exist, so the pattern varies greatly for different persons. In addition, circadian rhythms seem to shift with age; as people grow older, their peaks often tend to occur earlier in the day.

As you might expect, these cyclic fluctuations in basic bodily functions—and our subjective feelings of alertness—are related to task performance. In general, people do their best work when body temperature and other internal processes are at or near their personal peaks. However, this link appears to be somewhat stronger for physical tasks than for mental ones, especially tasks that require considerable cognitive effort (Daniel & Potasova, 1989).

If bodily processes, mental alertness, and performance on many tasks change regularly over the course of the day, it seems reasonable to suggest that we possess some internal biological mechanism for regulating such changes. In other words, we must possess one or more *biological clocks* that time various circadian rhythms. While there is not as yet total agreement on the number or nature of these internal clocks, existing evidence points to the conclusion that one structure—the **suprachiasmatic nucleus (SCN)** located in the hypothalamus—plays a key role in this respect (Lewy, Sack, & Singer, 1992; Moore & Card, 1985).

We should note, by the way, that the SCN is not a totally "sealed" clock, unresponsive to the outside world. On the contrary, it responds to light, which serves as a *zeitgeber* (German for "time giver"). Morning light resets our internal biological clock, synchronizing it with the outside world. Why is this necessary? Because left to its own devices, our biological clock (and that of many other species) seems to operate on a 25-hour cycle; thus, if it were not reset each day, our internal biological rhythms would get further and further out of synch with the world around us. We know this from research studies in which volunteers have lived in caves where no sunlight could penetrate. Under these conditions, most persons seem to shift toward a "day" of about 25 hours (Moore-Ede, Sulzman, & Fuller, 1982).

Individual Differences in Circadian Rhythms: Are You a Morning Person or a Night Person?

Before reading further, please answer the questions in Table 4.1 on page 100. How did you score? If you answered "Day" to eight or more questions, the chances are good that you are a **morning person.** If instead, you answered "Night" to eight or more questions, you are probably an **evening (night) person.** Morning people feel most alert and active early in the day, while night people experience peaks in alertness and energy in the afternoon or evening. Such differences are more than purely subjective. Studies comparing morning and evening persons indicate that the two groups differ in several important ways. Morning people have a higher overall level of adrenaline than night people; thus, they seem to operate at a higher overall level of activation (e.g., Akerstedt & Froberg, 1976). Similarly, morning people experience peaks in body temperature earlier in the day than do night people (Wallace, B., 1993).

That these differences in alertness and bodily states translate into important effects on behavior is indicated by research demonstrating that students who are morning persons earn higher grades in early-morning classes, while those who are evening persons receive higher grades in classes offered later in the day (e.g.,

Suprachiasmatic Nucleus (SCN)
A portion of the hypothalamus that seems to play an important role in the regulation of circadian rhythms.

Morning Persons
Individuals who experience peak levels of energy and physiological activation relatively early in the day.

Evening (Night) Persons
Individuals who experience peak levels of energy and physiological activation relatively late in the day.

TABLE 4.1	Are You a Morning Person or a Night Person?		

If you answer "Day" to eight or more of these questions, you are probably a morning person. If you answer "Night" to eight or more, you are probably a night person.

Answer each of the following items by circling either "Day" or "Night."

1.	I feel most alert during the	Day	Night
2.	I have most energy during the	Day	Night
3.	I prefer to take classes during the	Day	Night
4.	I prefer to study during the	Day	Night
5.	I get my best ideas during the	Day	Night
6.	When I graduate, I plan to find a job during the	Day	Night
7.	I am most productive during the	Day	Night
8.	I feel most intelligent during the	Day	Night
9.	I enjoy leisure-time activities most during the	Day	Night
10.	I prefer to work during the	Day	Night

Source: Based on items from Wallace, 1993.

Guthrie, Ash, & Bandapudi, 1995). So, if you are a morning person, try to take your classes at that time, but if you are an evening person, it's better to sign up for afternoon or evening classes. If you follow this strategy, the result may be a higher grade point index.

Disturbances in Circadian Rhythms: Jet Lag and Shift Work

Under normal conditions, the existence of circadian rhythms poses no special problems; we simply adjust our activities to these daily fluctuations in energy and alertness. For instance I (Robert Baron) have a "down" period around 2:00 P.M. every day, so I try to schedule less-demanding tasks for that time of day. There are two situations, however, in which external conditions cause our circadian rhythms to get badly out of phase with events in our lives: rapid travel across several time zones and shift work.

When we fly across several time zones, we may experience considerable difficulty in adjusting our internal clock to the new location—an effect known as *jet lag*. Persons suffering from jet lag feel tired, dull, and generally miserable. Research on circadian rhythms indicates that, in general, it is easier to reset our biological clocks by delaying them than by advancing them. In other words, we experience less disruption when we fly to a time zone where it is *earlier* than the one in which we normally live, than when we fly to one where it is *later*. So, for instance, if you live in New York and fly to Seattle, where it is three hours earlier, you simply stay up a few extra hours, and then go to sleep. In contrast, if you live in Seattle and fly to New York, where it is three hours later, you may experience greater disruption and take longer to adjust your internal clock.

Why is this so? One explanation is suggested by the fact that light acts as a *zeitgeber*, resetting our biological clocks (see Figure 4.2). If you travel from New York to, say, Paris, and start out in the evening (most flights depart at that time), you fly into darkness and then, just when you are really tired and about to fall asleep, dawn occurs, and the cabin is filled with brilliant sunlight. Your SCN responds, and resets your biological clock to morning. But in fact, you haven't had a night's sleep, and aren't really prepared for a new day. As a result, you feel awful and it may take you several days to get back to normal. If you fly to the West, however, you leave

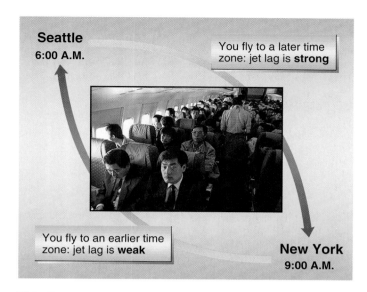

Seattle
6:00 A.M.

You fly to a later time zone: jet lag is **strong**

You fly to an earlier time zone: jet lag is **weak**

New York
9:00 A.M.

FIGURE 4.2
Zeitgebers and Jet Lag: When Dawn Comes Too Early!
Passengers flying across several time zones to the east (e.g., from New York to Paris or London) often start their journey in the evening. Just when their biological clocks are signaling "time to sleep," the plane flies into a new dawn. The bright light acts as a *zeitgeber*, resetting their biological clocks and contributing to their fatigue.

FIGURE 4.3
Shift Work: Often, It Disturbs Biological Rhythms
Tens of millions of employees work at night all around the world. This often disturbs their biological rhythms and can contribute to both reduced performance and the occurrence of accidents.

in daylight and arrive in daylight, and so don't experience the same unsettling effects. You "gain" several hours, and just stay up a little longer than usual—although after you fall asleep, you may wake up very early because your biological clock is indicating that it is much later in the day than it is in your new location.

A second cause of difficulties with respect to circadian rhythms occurs in *shift work*, which requires individuals to work at times when they would normally be sleeping (for instance, midnight to 8:00 A.M.). This is an important issue, because about 20 percent of all employees in the United States and several other countries work at night (usually from 11:00 P.M. or 12:00 P.M. until 7:00 A.M. or 8:00 A.M.; Fierman, 1995). To make matters worse, shift workers often face a schedule in which they work on one shift for a fairly short period (say, a week), get two days off, and then work on another shift. The results are, for many people, quite unsettling, and the reason is clear: Such individuals have to reset their biological clocks over and over again, and this process is draining, both physically and psychologically (e.g., Czeisler, Moore-Ede, & Coleman, 1982). These effects, in turn, have been linked to poorer job performance, increased industrial and traffic accidents (see Figure 4.3), and adverse effects on health (Lidell, 1982; Meijmann, van der Meer, & van Dormolen, 1993). So clearly, when biological clocks clash with work schedules, the results can be very serious. How can you minimize the discomfort and other adverse effects of jet lag and shift work? For the advice offered by psychology, please see the **Psychology Lends a Hand** section on the next page.

KEY QUESTIONS

- What are biological rhythms? What are circadian rhythms?
- How do morning persons and night persons differ?
- What effects do jet lag and shift work have on circadian rhythms?
- What steps can you take to counter the effects of jet lag and shift work?

psychology lends a hand

Dealing with Disruptions to Our Circadian Rhythms

The fatigue, reduced alertness, and inability to concentrate that often occur when our circadian rhythms are disrupted can have adverse effects on our health, cause accidents, and greatly reduce performance on many tasks. In short, they are *serious*. What can we do about these problems? While there are no simple, no-fail techniques, psychological research points to the following steps:

To Reduce the Effects of Jet Lag

1. **Prepare for the trip.** Get as much sleep as possible during the days before the trip so that you don't start out fatigued.
2. **Drink plenty of water.** The air on jet planes is very dry, and this causes you to become dehydrated unless you drink more than normal. Being dehydrated, in turn, seems to magnify the discomfort produced by jet lag. So drink plenty of water. (Alcohol, by the way, causes even more dehydration, so try to avoid it.)
3. **Try to sleep on the plane.** We know—this is easier to say than do. But if you can block out light and noise (e.g., by wearing a mask to cover your eyes and "noise-canceling" earphones; see Figure 4.4), you stand a better chance of sleeping—and that will be a big help.
4. **Try to sleep when you arrive** (west-to-east travel), **or to stay up a little longer** (east-to-west travel). These actions will help you reset your biological clock, and that can be a "plus."
5. **Avoid alcohol and other drugs.** While a glass of wine or a tranquilizer may help you to feel relaxed, these drugs often interfere with normal circadian rhythms, and this can intensify the negative effects produced by jet lag. So if at all possible, don't give in to the temptation to try them.

To Reduce the Effects of Shift Work

1. **Stay on one shift as long as possible.** Although it may not be under your control, if your job permits, stay on a single shift. Changing to another shift, especially after you have adjusted to the first, can magnify the problems.
2. **Try to stay on the same schedule, even on the weekend.** Many people who work unusual hours (e.g., they start very early in the day, or work from midnight until morning) try to get back on a fully normal schedule during the weekend. The result? When Monday comes around, they are truly wiped out! So, avoid the temptation to sleep late on Saturday and Sunday; if you stay a little closer to your regular schedule over the weekend, you will find it much easier to return to it when the work week starts.
3. **Try exposure to very bright light** (if you have to work at night). Exposure to very bright light when you begin to feel sleepy can help reset your circadian rhythm so that it more closely matches the requirements of your job (e.g., Houpt, Boulus, & Moore-Ede, 1996).

Although none of these procedures will totally solve the problem of disrupted circadian rhythms, research conducted by psychologists suggests that they can help, so give them a try—they may well prove useful.

FIGURE 4.4
One Way to Avoid or Reduce Jet Lag
Recently, noise-canceling earphones have become available. They are highly effective at blocking outside noise, thus helping people sleep in noisy environments. Use of these earphones on long flights may help reduce jet lag.

WAKING STATES OF CONSCIOUSNESS

Have you ever had the experience of reading a page in a book and then realizing that while you had scanned the words, you could not remember anything about them? In contrast, have you ever noticed that you can have a conversation with another person while doing something totally routine, such as combing your hair or tying your shoelaces? Such experiences suggest that even during our normal waking activities we often shift between various states of consciousness; one moment you are paying careful attention to a lecture or the words in a book, and the next you are lost in a vivid daydream. Let's take a closer look at these everyday shifts in consciousness.

Controlled and Automatic Processing: Two Modes of Thought

Often, we perform two tasks at the same time—for example, brushing our teeth while our thoughts wander far and wide, or talking to another person as we drive a car. How can we do this? The answer involves the fact that there are two contrasting ways of controlling ongoing activities—different levels of attention to, or conscious control over, our own behavior (e.g., Folk & Remington, 1996; Logan, 1985, 1988).

The first level uses very little of our *information-processing capacity,* and seems to occur in an automatic manner with very little conscious awareness on our part. For this reason, psychologists refer to it as **automatic processing,** and it *does* seem to be automatic. For this reason, several different activities, each under automatic control, can occur at the same time (e.g., Shiffrin & Schneider, 1977; Shiffrin & Dumais, 1981). Every time you drive while listening to the radio, you demonstrate such automatic processing: Both activities can occur simultaneously because both involve automatic processing.

In contrast, **controlled processing** involves more effortful and conscious control of thought and behavior. While it is occurring, you direct careful attention to the task at hand and concentrate on it. Processing of this type consumes significant cognitive resources; as a result, only one task requiring controlled processing can usually be performed at a time.

Research on the nature of automatic and controlled processing suggests that these two states of consciousness differ in several respects. First, behaviors that have come under the control of automatic processing are performed more quickly and with less effort than ones that require controlled processing (Logan, 1988). In addition, acts that have come under automatic processing can be initiated without conscious intention; they are triggered in a seemingly automatic manner by specific stimuli or events (e.g., Norman & Shallice, 1985). In fact, it may be difficult to inhibit such actions once they are initiated. If you ever played "Simple Simon" as a child, you are well aware of this fact. After following many commands beginning "Simple Simon says . . . ," you probably also responded to the similar command "Do this" Why? Because your imitation of the leader's actions was under automatic control, and you obeyed even when you should have refrained from doing so.

Another example of this kind of automatic processing is provided by our ability to respond to others' facial expressions in an automatic manner—even if we can't recognize them overtly (Ohman, 2002). For instance, if individuals are exposed to faces showing angry, neutral, or happy expressions, and the exposure time is so brief that they cannot recognize these expressions (they can't report which ones they have seen), they still show reactions in their own facial muscles that mimic these expressions. For instance, when they see happy faces, electrical activity occurs in muscles that pull the corner of their mouths upward, as in a smile. And when they see angry faces, activity occurs in muscles that play a role in frowning

Automatic Processing
Processing of information with minimal conscious awareness.

Controlled Processing
Processing of information involving relatively high levels of conscious awareness.

(Dimberg, Thunberg, & Elmehed, 2000). Findings such as these indicate that important aspects of our behavior do in fact reflect automatic processing.

Is either of these types of processing superior? Not really. Automatic processing is rapid and efficient, but can be relatively inflexible—precisely because it is so automatic. Controlled processing is slower, but is more flexible and open to change. In sum, both play an important role in our efforts to deal with information from the external world. One final point: Automatic and controlled processing are not hard-and-fast categories, but rather ends of a continuous dimension. On any given task, individuals may operate in a relatively controlled or a relatively automatic manner. In general, we match the level of our processing to the demands of the situation and so are almost totally unaware of such shifts. It is only when the demands on us change suddenly (e.g., a near-miss in traffic) that we become aware of the fact that our behavior is "on automatic" when, in fact, we should be paying more careful attention to what is happening around us!

We should briefly mention that recent research suggests that automatic processing may play a role in racial and ethnic prejudice. Apparently, many persons have negative stereotypes of various groups (ones based on race, ethnicity, religion, and so on), but they are not aware of these views (e.g., Kawakami & Dovidio, 2001). Yet, they can be activated in an automatic manner by various events (e.g., some stimulus linked to members of that group—for instance, a symbol of their religion, or mention of a food associated with their culture). And once activated, these stereotypes can, although they are not conscious, result in subtle forms of bias against the groups in question (O'Sullivan, 2003; Towles-Schwen & Fazio, 2001). In short, beliefs we don't recognize, that are triggered or primed automatically, and of which we are not aware can have important effects on our behavior.

Self-Awareness: Some Effects of Thinking about Ourselves

Right now, you are (we hope!) thinking about the words on this page. But pause and think about how you feel: Are you comfortable? Getting hungry? Tired? And if there is a mirror nearby, look into it; are you happy with your appearance, or is there something you'd like to change? As soon as you turn your attention on yourself, you enter a state of consciousness psychologists term **self-awareness.** Entering this particular state of consciousness has many interesting effects, so we'll examine a few of them here.

▪ Why Do We Become Self-Aware and What Happens When We Do?

The first question about self-awareness that arises is straightforward: "Why do we enter this state?" One answer is that self-awareness is triggered by external events. Passing a mirror is one, speaking to or performing in front of an audience is another, and having our picture taken is yet another. In these situations, we are induced to think about ourselves (see Figure 4.5). Once we do, an interesting process is initiated. According to one theory of self-awareness, *control theory,* when we focus our attention on ourselves, we compare our current state (our feelings, thoughts, and performance) to internal standards—how we would *like* to feel, think, and perform (Carver & Scheier, 1981). If the gap between reality and these standards is small, everything is fine. If the gap is large, however, we have two choices: (1) We can "shape up," changing our thoughts or actions so that they fit more closely with these standards and goals; or (2) we can "ship out"—withdraw from self-awareness in some way. Such withdrawal can range from simple distraction (we stop thinking about ourselves and how we are falling short of our own internal standards) to more dangerous actions such as drinking alcohol, engaging in binge eating, or—in the extreme—ending our own existence through suicide (Baumeister, 1990).

What determines whether we try to change or try to escape from unpleasant self-awareness? Research findings suggest that a key factor is our beliefs concerning whether we *can* change successfully or not. If we believe that the chances are

Self-Awareness
A state of consciousness in which we focus our attention inward, upon ourselves.

FIGURE 4.5
Becoming Self-Aware
In situations like these, we focus our attention inward on ourselves, and so become *self-aware*. Such self-awareness, in turn, produces important effects on our behavior and thought.

good that we can, we concentrate on meeting our internal standards and goals. If we believe that we are unlikely to succeed in doing so, then we may seek escape (e.g., Gibbons, 1990). In sum, self-awareness can have stronger and more far-reaching effects on behavior than you might at first guess.

A Failure in Self-Awareness: Why We Are Often Unaware of Our Own Incompetence

Quick: How good a driver are you? Better than average? Average? Worse than average? How about your ability to think logically? Better than average? Average? Worse than average? If you are like most people, you probably answered "Better than average" to both questions. In fact, most people think they are better than average on almost every imaginable task. Obviously, this can't be true—we can't all be better than average on everything! What this implies is that we often overestimate our own competence or overlook our incompetence. Even worse, it appears that the poorer our actual performance, the more we tend to overestimate it. For instance, in one recent study (Dunning et al., 2003), college students were asked to estimate how well they had done on an exam immediately after completing it. As you can see from Figure 4.6 on page 106, most overestimated their scores, and the poorer they actually did, the greater this tendency. Why does this occur? Apparently because the skills needed to do well on various tasks are similar to the ones needed to evaluate our own competence accurately. In other words, if you are not very competent on a given task, you lack not only the ability to perform it well, but also the ability to estimate how well you can do it!

This tendency to overlook our own incompetence can produce serious effects. For instance, consider a doctor who does not recognize the limits of his or her knowledge, and fails to send a patient to see a specialist. Or consider an accountant who overestimates his knowledge of current tax laws, and so gives very bad advice to a client. Situations like this call attention to the fact that our self-awareness is not always accurate. The moral of this point is clear: Although we often *think* we know ourselves very well, we often don't—and that, in turn, can get us into serious difficulties!

KEY QUESTIONS

- What is the difference between automatic processing and controlled processing?
- What is *self-awareness* and why do we sometimes enter this state of consciousness?
- Why do we tend to overestimate our performance on many tasks (i.e., overlook our incompetence)?

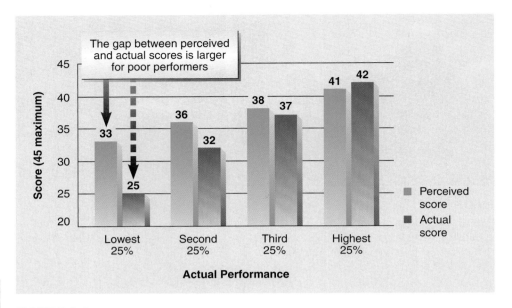

FIGURE 4.6
Failure to Recognize Our Own Incompetencies
As shown here, most students estimated their scores on an exam as being higher than they actually were. Such effects were strongest for students who actually did poorly on the exam, indicating that they were worst at evaluating their own performances.
Source: Based on data from Dunning et al., 2003.

Sleep
A process in which important physiological changes (e.g., shifts in brain activity, slowing of basic bodily functions) are accompanied by major shifts in consciousness.

Electroencephalogram (EEG)
A record of electrical activity within the brain. EEGs play an important role in the scientific study of sleep.

Electromyogram (EMG)
A record of electrical activity in various muscles.

Alpha Waves
Rapid, low-amplitude brain waves that occur when individuals are awake but relaxed.

Delta Activity
High amplitude, slow brain waves (3.5 Hz or less) that occur during several stages of sleep, but especially during stage 4.

REM Sleep
A state of sleep in which brain activity resembling waking restfulness is accompanied by deep muscle relaxation and movements of the eyes. Most dreams occur during periods of REM sleep.

SLEEP: THE PAUSE THAT REFRESHES?

What single activity occupies more of your time than any other? Though you may be tempted to say "studying" or "working," think again. The correct answer is probably **sleep**—a process in which important physiological changes and slowing basic bodily functions are accompanied by major shifts in consciousness. In fact, most people spend fully one-third of their entire lives asleep (Dement, 1975; Webb, 1975). What is the nature of sleep? What functions does it serve? And what are dreams? These are key questions on which we'll focus. To get started, let's first consider the question of how psychologists study sleep.

The Basic Nature of Sleep

Everyone would agree that when we sleep, we are in a different state of consciousness than when we are awake. But what is sleep really like? To find out, psychologists carefully monitor changes in the electrical activity occurring in people's brains and muscles as they fall asleep. Recordings of electrical activity of the brain are known as the **electroencephalogram** (or EEG for short), while those for muscles are known as **electromyogram** (or EMG for short). Research using these methods indicates that as people fall asleep, they move through four distinct stages during which faster activity in the brain is gradually replaced by slower activity (**alpha waves** replace faster *beta waves*). Then, as we fall more deeply asleep, activity slows still further, and **delta activity** appears. This may represent a synchronization of neurons in the brain, so that an increasingly large number of neurons fire together, in unison (see Figure 4.7). Such sleep is known as *slow-wave sleep*.

About ninety minutes after we begin to fall asleep, something quite dramatic often happens: We enter a very different phase of sleep known as **REM (rapid eye**

movement) sleep. During this phase, the electrical activity of the brain quickly comes to resemble that shown when people are awake. Slow delta waves disappear, and fast, low-voltage activity returns. Sleepers' eyes begin to move about rapidly beneath their closed eyelids, and there is an almost total suppression of activity in body muscles (as measured by the EMG).

These shifts in brain activity and bodily processes are accompanied, in many cases, by one of the most dramatic aspects of sleep: *dreams.* Individuals awakened during REM sleep often report dreaming. In some cases, eye movements during such sleep seem to be related to the content of dreams (Dement, 1975). It is as if dreamers are following the action in their dreams with their eyes, but this relationship has not been clearly established.

Periods of REM sleep continue to alternate with the other stages of sleep throughout the night. The duration is variable, but the REM periods tend to increase in length toward morning. Thus, while the first REM period may last only five to ten minutes, the final ones—from which many people awake—may last thirty minutes or more (Hartmann, 1973; Kelly, 1981).

In sum, the picture of sleep that has emerged from scientific research is of a gradual movement through deeper and deeper stages of sleep, punctuated, irregularly, by periods of a much more active phase—REM sleep—during which we dream and show brain activity that is more like when we are awake than when we are deeply asleep.

Sleep: What Functions Does It Serve?

Any activity that fills as much of our lives as sleep must serve important functions, but what, precisely, are these? Several possibilities exist, and they may differ for slow-wave (stages 3 and 4) sleep and REM sleep.

■ Possible Function of Slow-Wave Sleep

Here, the most obvious possibility is that this kind of sleep serves mainly a restorative function, allowing us—and especially the brain—to rest and recover from the wear and tear of the day's activities. Several findings provide evidence for this suggestion. First, if sleep allows our brains to rest, then we would expect to see more delta (slow-wave) activity in portions of the brain that have experienced intense activity during the day. The findings of several studies suggest that this is so (e.g., Kattler, Djik, & Borbely, 1994). For instance, PET scans of the brain (which reveal the level of activity in various areas) indicate that portions of the brain that are most active during the day are indeed the ones showing most delta activity during the night.

Similarly, vigorous physical exercise seems to increase slow-wave, "resting" sleep, but only if such exercise raises the brain's temperature (Horne, 1988). Because higher temperatures in the brain raise its metabolism, this, too, fits with the general suggestion that slow-wave sleep may be, at least in part, a mechanism for allowing our brains to rest after intense periods of activity. Incidentally, the fact that our need for sleep seems to increase after the brain's temperature has been raised suggests one reason why a hot bath may indeed be one effective technique for bringing on a good night's sleep.

A second possible function of slow-wave sleep emphasizes the relationship of sleep to circadian rhythms. According to this view, sleep is merely the neural mechanism that evolved to encourage various species, including our own, to remain inactive

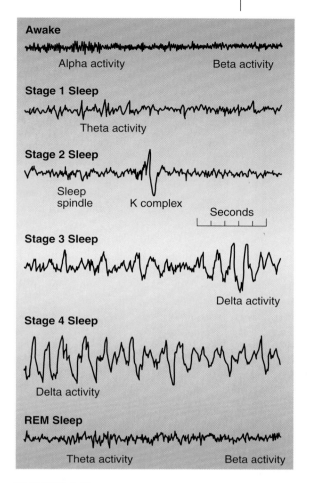

FIGURE 4.7
States of Sleep
As shown here, there are four distinct stages of sleep, each characterized by changes in the electrical activity of our brains. In addition, another stage of sleep—REM sleep—is markedly different, and during this stage, activity in our brains closely resembles, in some respects, the activity that occurs when we are awake.

during those times of day when they do not usually engage in activities related to their survival. As one well-known sleep researcher (Webb, 1975) has put it, sleep is nature's way of keeping us quiet at night—a dangerous time for our ancestors, and for us, because we are not equipped with sensory capacities suited for nighttime activity.

■ Possible Functions of REM Sleep

Turning to REM sleep, some findings are consistent with the view that such sleep plays a crucial role in learning and in allowing us to consolidate memories of the preceding day or, perhaps, to eliminate unnecessary memories and other "mental clutter" from our brains (e.g., Crick & Mitchison, 1995). If REM sleep performs functions related to learning, then two predictions follow: (1) Animals who undergo training of some kind but are then deprived of the opportunity to engage in REM sleep will show poorer performance than animals not deprived of such sleep; and (2) after intense learning, animals will show more REM sleep than at other times. Studies offer support for both predictions. For example, in one investigation, Block, Hennevin, and Leconte (1977) trained rats to run through a complex maze. As training on this task continued, the rats ran faster *and* spent an increasing proportion of their sleep in REM sleep. So, REM sleep does appear to play a role in learning.

KEY QUESTIONS

- How do psychologists study sleep?
- What are the major stages of sleep?
- What happens during REM sleep?
- What are the possible functions of slow-wave and REM sleep?

Effects of Sleep Deprivation

Another way of discovering the functions of sleep is to see what happens when we are deprived of it. Everyone has had the experience of feeling completely miserable after a sleepless night, so it seems reasonable to focus on sleep deprivation as a possible source of information about the functions of sleep. So what *are* the effects of sleep deprivation? Among humans, even prolonged deprivation of sleep does not seem to produce large or clear-cut effects on behavior for many persons. For example, in one famous demonstration, seventeen-year-old Randy Gardner stayed awake for 264 hours and 12 minutes—eleven entire days! His motivation for doing so was simple: He wanted to earn a place in the *Guinness Book of Records,* and he did. Although Randy had some difficulty staying awake this long, he remained generally alert and active throughout the entire period. After completing his ordeal, he slept 14 hours on the first day, 10 hours on the second, and less than 9 on the third. Interestingly, his sleep on these nights showed an elevated proportion of slow-wave (stages 3 and 4) sleep and REM sleep but did not show a rise in the early stages (1 and 2). So, it was as if his brain focused on making up the deprivation in slow-wave and REM sleep but could get along fine without compensating for the losses in stages 1 and 2. Randy suffered no lasting physical or psychological harm from his long sleepless period, but please don't consider trying to beat Randy's record: There are potential risks in long-term sleep deprivation, including an increased chance of serious accidents and harm to personal health.

That long-term deprivation of sleep *can* be harmful to human beings, however, is suggested by several recent findings. First, growing evidence suggests that sleep deprivation is associated with physiological changes (e.g., lowered glucose tolerance, elevated activity in the sympathetic nervous system) that mark increased wear and tear on our bodies (e.g., Spiegel, Leproult, & Van Cauter, 1999). These findings suggest that sleep serves a restorative function. Second, Cacioppo and his colleagues (Cacioppo et al., 2003) have found that lonely people—individuals who have few if any friends and few social ties of any kind—show poorer quality sleep than persons who are not lonely. While the total time lonely and non-lonely people sleep is about the same, lonely people show lower *sleep efficiency:* They are asleep a smaller percentage of the time they are in bed and spend more time awake after initial sleep onset (see Figure 4.8). These findings suggest the possibility that one reason lonely people show poorer health is that they experience poorer sleep.

Finally, a disorder known as **fatal familial insomnia** (e.g., Gallassi et al., 1996), suggests that sleep may truly be essential. In this disorder, individuals experience increasingly severe disturbances in sleep until, finally, slow-wave sleep totally disappears and only brief periods of REM sleep occur. The disease is fatal, but whether this is due to the sleep disturbances themselves or whether the sleep disturbances are simply a sign of other neurological problems, remains uncertain.

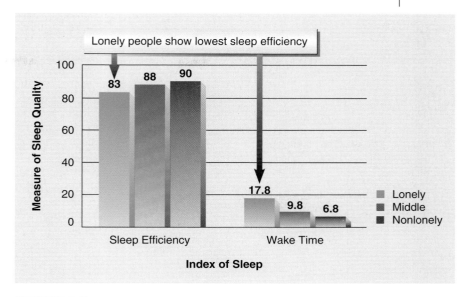

FIGURE 4.8
Loneliness and Sleep Quality
Lonely individuals show lower sleep quality than persons who are not lonely. As a result, they may be sleep deprived. This, in turn, may contribute to their relatively poor health.
Source: Based on data from Cacioppo et al., 2003.

Sleep Disorders: No Rest for Some of the Weary

Do you ever have trouble falling or staying asleep? If so, you are in good company: Almost 40 percent of adults report that they sometimes have these problems, known, together, as **insomnia** (Bixler et al., 1979). Further, such problems seem to increase with age and are somewhat more common among women than men. Although many people report insomnia, it is not clear that the incidence of this problem is as high as these self-reports might suggest. When the sleep habits of people who claim to be suffering from insomnia are carefully studied, it turns out that many of them sleep as long as people who do not complain of insomnia (Empson, 1984). This does not mean that such persons are "faking"; rather, it is possible that although they attain an amount of sleep that falls within normal limits (6.5 hours or more per night), this is not enough to meet their individual needs. Further, the quality of their sleep may be disturbed in ways not yet measured in research. Still, such arguments aside, it does appear that many people who believe that their sleep is somewhat inadequate may actually be getting a normal amount. So, what can *you* do when you have trouble sleeping? Please see the **Psychology Lends a Hand** section on the next page for some suggestions.

While insomnia is the most common sleep disorder, it is not the only one. Several other disorders exist; some are related to REM sleep and some to slow-wave sleep. Let's consider some in each category.

Disorders Associated with REM Sleep

Perhaps the most dramatic disturbance of REM sleep is **narcolepsy,** a disorder in which sleep occurs at inappropriate—and often unexpected—times. Persons suffering from narcolepsy often have *sleep attacks* in which they experience an irresistible urge to sleep in the midst of waking activities. They sleep for from two to five minutes and then awake, refreshed. I once had a colleague who had sleep attacks in class. He would stop lecturing, put his head down on the desk, and—

Fatal Familial Insomnia
A genetic disorder in which individuals experience increasing disturbances in sleep; the disorder is, as its name suggests, fatal.

Insomnias
Disorders involving the inability to fall asleep or maintain sleep once it is attained.

Narcolepsy
A sleep disorder in which individuals are overcome by uncontrollable periods of sleep during waking hours.

psychology lends a hand

How to Get a Good Night's Sleep

Insomnia is a real problem for many persons, at least occasionally. Although nothing can guarantee you a good night's sleep every day, research findings indicate that the following steps may be helpful:

- **Read something pleasant or relaxing just before going to sleep.** Do *not* choose a scary or violent mystery or one with lots of sexual content. The idea is to read something that will distract you while making you feel calm, so choose carefully.
- **Arrange your schedule so you go to sleep at the same time each night.** If you do this, your circadian rhythms will be working for you rather than against you. Remember: If you change your sleep cycle greatly on the weekend, it may be hard to readjust when Monday rolls around.
- **Avoid doing non-sleep-related activities in bed.** Above all, don't work there or do things that tend to make you alert or that are associated with activities you do during the day.
- **Take a warm bath or have a massage before going to sleep.** As noted earlier, when brain temperature rises, we tend to become drowsy, so a warm bath can be very helpful.
- **Avoid coffee or tea late in the day.** These are stimulants, and may keep you awake.
- **Exercise every day, but not just before going to sleep.** We often get our best night's sleep when we are physically tired. For this reason, exercise can be helpful, but not close to the time you go to bed. (If you exercise close to your normal bedtime, you may be too activated to fall asleep.)

- **Don't smoke.** Nicotine is a stimulant and it may prevent you from sleeping.
- **Don't nap during the day.** If you nap during the day, you may already have had a good portion of the sleep and rest you need.
- **Don't worry about not being able to fall asleep.** Almost everyone experiences difficulty falling asleep sometimes, so don't be overly concerned unless the problem persists for more than a few days. Believe it or not, one major cause of insomnia is worrying about the inability to fall asleep. So read or do something to distract yourself, and sleep will generally come quickly and effortlessly.
- **If, despite these measures, you find yourself tossing and turning, get up and read, work, or watch television until you feel drowsy.** You really can't force yourself to sleep, especially if you are upset or worried. So again, being calm is a key step.

One more point: Sleeping pills—prescription as well as non-prescription—are not usually an effective, long-term answer. They may induce sleep at first, but tolerance to them develops quickly so that larger and larger doses are needed, and the result is *drug dependency insomnia*—insomnia caused by the side effects of ever-larger doses of sleeping medicines. Further, some drugs used for this purpose interfere with REM sleep, which can lead to other sleep disturbances. So drugs should be a last-resort approach that you use only when everything else fails; and they should be used only under a doctor's supervision.

---

much to the amusement of his students who made many jokes about "putting himself under"—sleep.

Another symptom of narcolepsy is **cataplexy,** in which the individual falls down suddenly and without warning. Often, such persons will remain fully conscious, but their muscles are paralyzed, as during REM sleep. And sometimes they experience vivid dreams while in this state: In other words, they are dreaming while awake!

■ Disorders Associated with Slow-Wave Sleep

Perhaps the most dramatic disorder associated with slow-wave sleep is **somnambulism**—walking in one's sleep. This is less rare than you might guess; almost 25 percent of children experience at least one sleepwalking episode (see Figure 4.9; Empson, 1984). A second, related disorder is **night terrors.** Here, individuals, especially children, awaken from deep sleep with signs of intense arousal and powerful feelings of fear. Yet, they have no memory of any dream relating to these feelings. Night terrors seem to occur mainly during stage 4 sleep. In contrast, *nightmares*, which most of us have experienced at some time, occur during REM sleep and can often be vividly recalled. Both somnambulism and night terrors are linked to disturbances in the functioning of the autonomic system, which plays a key role in regulating brain activity during sleep.

Cataplexy
A symptom of narcolepsy (a sleep disorder) in which individuals fall down suddenly, like a sack of flour.

Somnambulism
A sleep disorder in which individuals actually get up and move about while still asleep.

Night Terrors
Extremely frightening dream-like experiences that occur during non-REM sleep.

Another disturbing type of sleep disorder is **apnea.** Persons suffering from sleep apnea actually stop breathing when they are asleep. This causes them to wake up, and because the process can be repeated hundreds of times each night, apnea can seriously affect the health of persons suffering from it.

The causes of sleep disorders are as varied as the complex neural and chemical systems that regulate sleep itself; thus, discussing them here would lead us into many complex topics well beyond the scope of this book. Suffice it to say that sleep disorders have their roots in the mechanisms and brain structures that regulate arousal, slow-wave sleep, and REM sleep.

Dreams: "Now Playing in Your Private, Inner Theater . . ."

What is the most dramatic aspect of sleep? For many persons, the answer is obvious: **dreams**—jumbled, vivid, sometimes enticing and sometimes disturbing images that fill our sleeping minds. What are these experiences? Why do they occur? Here are the answers provided by psychological research.

1. *Does everybody dream?* The answer seems to be *yes*. While not all people remember dreaming, EEG recordings indicate that everyone experiences REM sleep.
2. *How long do dreams last?* Dreams run on "real time": The longer they seem to last, the longer they really are (Dement & Kleitman, 1957).
3. *Can external events become part of dreams?* Yes, at least to a degree. For example, Dement and Wolpert (1958) sprayed water on sleepers who were in the REM stage of sleep. When they woke them up, more than half reported water in their dreams.
4. *When people cannot remember their dreams, does this mean that they are purposely forgetting them, perhaps because they find the content disturbing?* Probably not. Research on why people can or cannot remember their dreams indicates that this is primarily a function of what they do when they wake up. If they lie quietly in bed, actively trying to remember the dream, they have a good chance of recalling it. If, instead, they jump out of bed and start the day's activities, the chances of remembering the dream are reduced. While we can't totally rule out the possibility that some people actively try to forget their dreams, there is little evidence for its occurrence.
5. *Do dreams foretell the future?* There is no scientific evidence for this belief.
6. *Do dreams express unconscious wishes?* Again, there is no convincing scientific evidence for this view.

Now that we've considered some basic facts about dreams, let's turn to several views concerning their nature and function.

▪ Dreams: The Psychodynamic View

One view of dreams is that they are a mechanism for expressing unconscious wishes or impulses. Such beliefs can be traced largely to Freud, who popularized the view that dreams reveal the unconscious—thoughts, impulses, and wishes that lie outside the realm of conscious experience. In dreams, Freud believed, we give expression to impulses and desires we find unacceptable during our waking hours. Freud based this view on careful analysis of his patient's dreams and reported that he often gained important insights into the causes of their problems from their dreams. In fact, however, these views are *not* supported by convincing scientific evidence. There is no clear or convincing scientific evidence that dreams offer a unique means for exploring the unconscious. So this view is *not* accepted by most psychologists.

▪ Dreams: The Physiological View

If dreams aren't reflections of hidden wishes or impulses, what are they? Another answer is provided by what is sometimes known as the *physiological view* of dreams

FIGURE 4.9
Sleepwalking: One Disorder of Slow-Wave Sleep
About 25 percent of children show one or more episodes of *somnambulism*, walking in their sleep. I remember having such experiences myself as a child; I'd suddenly awaken to find that, without being aware of this fact, I had gotten out of bed and walked into another room. These episodes stopped by the time I was about ten years old.

Apnea
A sleep disorder in which sleepers stop breathing several times each night, and thus wake up.

Dreams
Cognitive events, often vivid but disconnected, that occur during sleep. Most dreams take place during REM sleep.

BLONDIE

FIGURE 4.10
Dreams: Sometimes, They *Do* Reflect Aspects of Our Memories for Events in Our Daily Lives
As shown here, dreams sometimes do reflect what is happening in our current lives.
Source: Reprinted with permission of King Features Syndicate.

(Hobson, 1988). According to this perspective, dreams are simply our subjective experience of what is, in essence, random neural activity in the brain. Such activity occurs while we sleep simply because a minimal amount of stimulation is necessary for normal functioning of the brain and nervous system, and our dim awareness of it is the basis for dreams (Foulkes, 1985; Hobson, 1988).

A logical extension of this view suggests that the activity of which we try to make sense is not actually random; rather, it occurs primarily in the two systems of the brain that are most active when we are awake—the visual system and the motor system. As this view suggests, dreams are usually silent, but are filled with visual images; and although many contain images of movement, few persons report experiencing smells, tactile (touch) sensations, or tastes in their dreams (Carlson, 1999).

Dreams: The Cognitive View

Another and closely related explanation of dreams suggests that they represent our cognitive systems' efforts to interpret activity in our brains while we are sleep. This perspective (Antbrobus,1991), suggests that two facts about REM sleep are crucial to understanding the nature of dreams: (1) During REM sleep, areas of the brain in the cerebral cortex that play a role in waking perception, thought, and regulation of motor processes are highly active; (2) yet, at the same time, there is massive inhibition of input from sensory systems and muscles (these are suppressed during REM sleep). As a result, the cortical structures or systems that normally regulate perception and thought have only their own activity as input, and this forms the basis for the imagery and ideas in dreams.

Does this mean that dreams are meaningless? Not at all. Because they represent interpretations of neural activity by our own brains, they reflect aspects of our memories and waking experience (Wegner, Wenzlaff, & Kozak, 2004; see Figure 4.10). Convincing evidence for this connection between dreams and important events in our lives is provided by the fact that persons attempting to make important changes in their own behavior—for example, to quit smoking or drinking—report having **dreams of absent-minded transgression**—DAMIT dreams for short (e.g., Gill, 1985). In such dreams, people suddenly notice that they have absent-mindedly slipped into the habit they wish to break—they are smoking or drinking without having planned to do so. This realization leads to feelings of panic or guilt in the

Dreams of Absent-Minded Transgression
Dreams in which persons attempting to give up the use of tobacco, alcohol, or other drugs see themselves slipping into the use of these substances in an absent-minded or careless manner.

dream. In many cases, the dreamers awake at that point feeling quite disturbed. Interestingly, having such dreams is positively related to success in breaking the habits in question (e.g., in giving up smoking; Hajek & Belcher, 1991). So, this kind of dream, at least, does seem to be related to important events in our daily lives.

KEY QUESTIONS

- What are the effects of sleep deprivation?
- What steps can you take to help get a good night's sleep every night?
- What are important disorders of REM sleep? Of slow-wave sleep?
- How do the psychodynamic, physiological, and cognitive views of dreams differ?

HYPNOSIS: ALTERED STATE OF CONSCIOUSNESS . . . OR SOCIAL ROLE PLAYING?

Have you ever seen a professional hypnotist at work? If so, you may have been *very* impressed by the strange effects this person seemed to produce. For instance, the hypnotist may have placed several seemingly normal women and men into a deep trance and then, while they were in this state, given them instructions about how they should behave when they woke up. And sure enough, they seemed to obey the hypnotists' instructions when this performer snapped his fingers and awakened the willing "victims." For instance, if told to bark like a dog each time the hypnotist uttered the words "Good boy," that's what they did. Or if told to imagine they were a ballerina when the hypnotist snapped her fingers, they would begin acting like one when the hypnotist gave this signal.

But is **hypnosis**—a special type of interaction between two persons in which one (the hypnotist) induces changes in the behavior, feelings, or cognitions of the other (the subject) through suggestions—actually real? Or is it merely a clever hoax? Psychologists have studied these questions from many angles, so let's see what their research indicates.

Hypnosis: How It's Done and Who Is Susceptible to It

Let's start with two basic questions: (1) How is hypnotism performed? (2) Is everyone susceptible to it? With respect to the first, standard techniques for inducing hypnosis usually involve *suggestions* by the hypnotist that the people being hypnotized feel relaxed, are getting sleepy, and are unable to keep their eyes open. Speaking continuously in a calm voice, the hypnotist suggests to the subjects that they are gradually sinking deeper and deeper into a relaxed state—not sleep, but a state in which they will be highly susceptible to suggestions from the hypnotist, suggestions concerning the way they feel, their thoughts, and their behavior. Another technique involves having the subjects concentrate on a small object, often one that sparkles and can be rotated by the hypnotist (Figure 4.11 on page 114). The result of such procedures, it appears, is that some people (emphasize the word *some*) enter what appears to be an altered state of consciousness that is definitely not sleep—EEG recordings from hypnotized persons resemble those of normal waking, not any of the sleep stages described earlier (Wallace & Fisher, 1987).

Now for the second question: Can everyone be hypnotized? The answer seems clear. Large individual differences in hypnotizability (or *hypnotic suggestibility*) exist. About 15 percent of adults are highly susceptible (as measured by their response to a graded series of suggestions by the hypnotist); 10 percent are highly resistant; the rest are somewhere in between. What makes people highly susceptible to hypnotic suggestions? Research finds that four characteristics are important: *expectancy*—the extent to which individuals believe that they will respond to hypnotic suggestions; *attitudes* toward hypnosis—the more positive these are, the

Hypnosis
An interaction between two persons in which one (the hypnotist) induces changes in the behavior, feelings, or cognitions of the other (the subject) through suggestions. Hypnosis involves expectations on the part of subjects and their attempts to conform to social roles (e.g., the role of the hypnotized person).

FIGURE 4.11
Hypnosis: How It Is Performed
Hypnotists sometimes ask the persons they are hypnotizing to concentrate on a small object that the hypnotist rotates or moves in some other way.

more they will respond to suggestions; *fantasy proneness*—highly hypnotizable individuals often have vivid fantasies; and *absorption*—the tendency to become deeply involved in sensory and imaginative experiences. The greater the extent to which individuals possess these characteristics, the greater their susceptibility to hypnosis.

Hypnosis: Contrasting Views about Its Nature

Now, let's turn to a more complex question, one we mentioned earlier: Is hypnosis real? Does it produce actual changes in consciousness? Systematic research on hypnosis has led to the formulation of several contrasting views concerning this issue.

The Social-Cognitive or Role-Playing View

The first approach, the **social-cognitive or role-playing view,** suggests that, in fact, there is nothing strange or mysterious about hypnosis. On the contrary, the effects it produces are simply a reflection of a special type of relationship between the hypnotist and the subject. According to this perspective, persons undergoing hypnosis have seen many movies and read stories about hypnosis, have clear ideas about what it involves, and what, supposedly, will happen to them when hypnotized. These views lead them to play a special *social role*—that of *hypnotic subject*. This role implies that they will be "in the hypnotist's power," unable to resist this person's suggestions. When they are then exposed to hypnotic inductions from the hypnotist—instructions to behave in certain ways or to experience specific feelings—they tend to obey, because this is what the social role they are enacting indicates *should* happen (e.g., Lynn, Rhue, & Weekes, 1990; Spanos, 1991).

It's important to note that this view does *not* imply that persons undergoing hypnosis are consciously faking. On the contrary, they sincerely believe that they are experiencing an altered state of consciousness and that they have no choice but to act and feel as the hypnotist suggests (Kinnunen, Zamansky, & Block, 1994). But these behaviors and experiences are due mainly to their beliefs about hypnosis and the role of hypnotic subject rather than to the special skills of the hypnotist or their entry into an altered state of consciousness.

The Neodissociation and Dissociated Control Views

Two additional views suggest that hypnosis does indeed produce an altered state of consciousness. The first of these—the **neodissociation theory**—contends that hypnosis induces a split or dissociation between two basic aspects of consciousness: an *executive or central control function,* through which we regulate our own behavior, and a *monitoring function,* through which we observe it. According to Hilgard (1986, 1993), the most influential supporter of this view, these two aspects of consciousness are normally linked. Hypnosis, however, breaks this bond and erects a cognitive barrier—referred to as *hypnotic amnesia*—that prevents some experiences during hypnosis from entering into normal consciousness. The result is that persons who are hypnotized are indeed in a special altered state of consciousness in which one part of their mind accepts and responds to suggestions from the hypnotist, while the other part—which Hilgard terms "the hidden observer"—observes the procedures without participating in them. Because of this split in consciousness, these two

Social-Cognitive or Role-Playing View
A view suggesting that effects produced by hypnosis are the result of hypnotized persons' expectations about hypnosis and their social role as "hypnotized subject."

Neodissociation Theory (of hypnosis)
A theory suggesting that hypnotized individuals enter an altered state of consciousness in which consciousness is divided.

cognitive mechanisms are no longer in direct contact with each other. So, for example, if hypnotized persons are told to put their arms into icy water but instructed by the hypnotist that they will experience no pain, they will obey and will indeed report no discomfort. However, if asked to describe their feelings in writing, they may indicate that they *did* experience feelings of intense cold (Hilgard, 1979). In other words, they have the experience of pain, but it is not available to their conscious thought as it would be normally, when they are not hypnotized.

More recently, Bowers and his associates (e.g., Bowers, 1992; Woody & Bowers, 1994) have modified this view by proposing the **theory of dissociated control.** According to this theory, hypnotism does not necessarily involve a division of consciousness. Rather, it simply weakens control by the central function over other cognitive and behavioral subsystems. Thus, these subsystems can be invoked directly by the hypnotist's suggestions in an automatic manner that is *not* mediated by normal cognitive mechanisms.

Which of these views is more accurate—the social-cognitive view or the theories emphasizing dissociation? Existing evidence offers a mixed and complex picture (e.g., Reed et al., 1996; Kirsch & Lynn, 1998; Noble & McConkey, 1995). Overall, though, it seems fair to say that clear support for the two views that emphasize dissociation (the neodissociation and dissociated control theories) is lacking (Green & Lynn, 1995; Kirsch & Lynn, 1998).

In contrast, evidence for the social-cognitive view seems more convincing (e.g., Kirsch & Lynn, 1998; Spanos, 1991). Most of the unusual or bizarre effects observed under hypnosis can readily be explained in terms of hypnotized persons' beliefs in the effects of hypnotism and their efforts—not necessarily conscious—to behave in accordance with these expectations. In addition—and this, perhaps, is the key argument—the effects of hypnotic suggestion can often be produced in the absence of hypnosis! Here's what we mean: In a typical study on the effects of hypnosis, a hypnotic-induction ritual is first performed and then people are given various suggestions—they are told that they will not be able to move certain muscles (they will experience paralysis), that they will not be able to remember certain kinds of information (they will experience amnesia), or that they will perceive stimuli that aren't really there (hallucinations). If these effects are observed in their behavior, it is concluded that hypnosis has worked. In fact, though, the same kind of effects can often be produced *without the hypnotic ritual* (e.g., Braffman & Kirsch, 1999). In other words, "hypnotic effects" can occur even though no one has been hypnotized! Why? Because some people are simply highly suggestible—they have an astonishing capacity to alter their experience or behavior in profound ways. They are *not* faking; they really do experience the paralysis, amnesia, or hallucinations they are asked to experience; but they do so in the absence of hypnosis. Such findings indicate that hypnotic suggestibility is simply nonhypnotic suggestibility augmented by the hypnotic context—by individuals' beliefs in hypnosis and the effects it will produce (see Figure 4.12 on page 116).

So where does all this leave us? With the conclusion that hypnosis is neither real nor fake. On the one hand, it *can* produce dramatic effects—changes in people's behavior or perception that are often quite astounding. And some of these effects have important beneficial uses. For instance, growing evidence suggests that hypnotic suggestion can be helpful in the treatment of acute pain (e.g., pain produced by serious burns) and chronic pain (e.g., chronic headaches; Patterson & Jensen, 2003). Indeed, overall, existing evidence indicates that hypnosis is more effective in treating acute pain than other forms of treatment (e.g., relaxation training, distraction, emotional support). So, in a sense, hypnosis *is* real.

On the other hand, hypnotic suggestibility may *not* be unique or special in any way. Rather, it is just a relatively modest enhancement of nonhypnotic suggestibility—the ability, possessed by some persons, to alter their own experiences and behavior in amazing ways. All hypnosis does is to provide a context in which such abilities are slightly amplified (Kirsch & Braffman, 2001). So be on guard: A scientific

Dissociated Control, Theory of
A theory of hypnosis suggesting that hypnotism weakens control by the central function over other cognitive and behavioral subsystems, thus permitting these subsystems to be invoked directly by the hypnotist's suggestions.

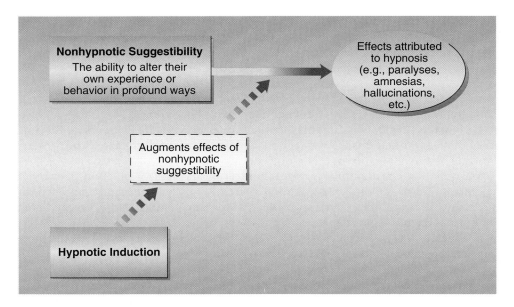

FIGURE 4.12
Hypnosis: An Extension of Nonhypnotic Suggestibility
Growing evidence suggests that the effects produced by hypnosis are mainly the result of nonhypnotic suggestibility—the ability of some persons to alter their own experiences or behavior in amazing ways. Hypnosis merely augments this tendency.

approach to this intriguing topic suggests that it is not nearly as mysterious or mystifying as many people believe. On the contrary, it can be readily understood in the context of cognitive processes that have nothing to do with trances or magical powers possessed by hypnotists.

KEY QUESTIONS

- What is hypnosis? How are volunteers hypnotized?
- How do the social-cognitive, neodissociation, and dissociative control views of hypnosis differ?
- What do most psychologists conclude with respect to the question of whether hypnosis is real?

CONSCIOUSNESS-ALTERING DRUGS: WHAT THEY ARE AND WHAT THEY DO

Have you ever taken aspirin for a headache? Do you drink coffee or soft drinks to boost your alertness? If so, you are in good company: each day, hundreds of millions of persons all around the world use drugs to change the way they feel—to alter their moods or states of consciousness. Much of this use of consciousness-altering drugs is completely legal—soft drinks and coffee are freely available everywhere, and many other drugs are consumed under a doctor's supervision. Often, though, people use drugs that are illegal, or use legal ones to excess. The effects of doing so can be both dramatic and tragic, so in this final section, we'll consider several issues relating to the use of consciousness-altering drugs.

Drugs
Compounds that change the functioning of biological systems.

Consciousness-Altering Drugs: Some Basic Concepts

Let's begin with some basic issues. First, what are **drugs?** One widely accepted definition states that they are compounds that, because of their chemical structure, change the functioning of biological systems (Grilly, 1989; Levinthal, 1999). *Consciousness-altering drugs,* therefore, are drugs that produce changes in consciousness (Wallace & Fisher, 1987).

Suppose you conducted a careful inventory of all the drugs in your medicine cabinet. How many would you find? Unless you are very unusual, quite a few. Many of these drugs are probably perfectly legal and can be obtained in any pharmacy without a prescription (e.g., aspirin). Others are prescribed by a physician. Using drugs in both categories is generally both safe and appropriate. The term **drug abuse,** therefore, applies only to instances in which people take drugs purely to change their moods, and in which they experience impaired behavior or social functioning as a result of doing so (Wallace & Fisher, 1987).

Unfortunately, when people consume consciousness-altering drugs on a regular basis, they often develop *dependence*—they come to need the drug and cannot function without it. Two types of dependence exist. One, **physiological dependence** occurs when the need for the drug is based on biological factors, such as changes in metabolism. This type of dependence is what is usually meant by the term *drug addiction*. However, people can also develop **psychological dependence,** in which they experience strong desires to continue using the drug even though, physiologically, their bodies do not need it. As we'll soon see, several psychological mechanisms probably contribute to such dependence.

Continued use of a drug over a prolonged period of time often leads to drug **tolerance**—a physiological reaction in which the body requires larger and larger doses in order to experience the same effects. For example, I (Robert Baron) once had a friend who drank more than twenty cups of coffee each day. He didn't start out this way; rather, he gradually increased the amount of coffee he consumed over the years until he reached this very high level. In some cases, one drug increases tolerance for another; this is known as **cross-tolerance.**

Why do people use consciousness-altering drugs? For several different reasons. First, many consciousness-altering drugs have *rewarding properties*—taking them makes the users feel good or reduces negative feelings and sensations. Second, many persons, especially teenagers, use consciousness-altering drugs because it is the "cool" thing to do. Their friends use these drugs, and they believe that if they do, too, this will enhance their social "image" (e.g., Sharp & Getz, 1996). Third, people sometimes use consciousness-altering drugs because doing so has become automatic (in the sense of automatic versus controlled processing). Using a specific drug may be an automatic response to internal cues such as feeling tired or depressed. Similarly, drug use may become an automatic reaction to external cues—for example, being in an environment in which they have enjoyed this drug in the past, such as a bar (Tiffany, 1990). In sum, the use of consciousness-altering drugs stems from many factors, which is one reason why combating drug abuse is such a difficult task.

KEY QUESTIONS

- What are drugs? What is drug abuse?
- What are physiological and psychological dependencies on drugs?
- Why do people use consciousness-altering drugs?

Consciousness-Altering Drugs: An Overview

While many different drugs affect consciousness, most seem to fit under one of four major headings: *depressants, stimulants, opiates,* or *psychedelics* and *hallucinogens.*

Depressants

Drugs that reduce both behavioral output and activity in the central nervous system are called **depressants.** Perhaps the most important of these is *alcohol,* probably the

Drug Abuse
Instances in which individuals take drugs purely to change their moods, and in which they experienced impaired behavior or social functioning as a result of doing so.

Physiological Dependence
Strong urges to continue using a drug based on organic factors such as changes in metabolism.

Psychological Dependence
Strong desires to continue using a drug, even though it is not physiologically addicting.

Drug Tolerance
See Tolerance.

Tolerance
Habituation to a drug so that larger and larger doses are required to produce effects of the same magnitude.

Cross-Tolerance
Increased tolerance for one drug that develops as a result of taking another drug.

Depressants
Drugs that reduce activity in the nervous system and therefore slow many bodily and cognitive processes. Depressants include alcohol and barbiturates.

FIGURE 4.13
Excessive Use of Alcohol Often Equals Uninhibited Behavior
When individuals consume large amounts of alcohol, their behavior often becomes uninhibited—or downright wild!

most widely consumed drug in the world. Small doses seem, subjectively, to be stimulating—they induce feelings of excitement and activation. Larger doses, however, act as a depressant. They dull the senses so that feelings of pain, cold, and other forms of discomfort become less intense. Large doses of alcohol interfere with coordination and normal functioning of our senses, often with tragic results for motorists. Alcohol also lowers social inhibitions, so that after consuming large quantities of this drug, people become less restrained in their words and actions, and more likely to engage in dangerous forms of behavior, such as aggression (see Figure 4.13; e.g., Pihl, Lau, & Assaad, 1997). Alcohol seems to produce its pleasurable effects by stimulating special receptors in the brain. Its depressant effects may stem from the fact that it interferes with the capacity of neurons to conduct nerve impulses, perhaps by affecting the cell membrane directly.

Growing evidence suggests that alcohol abuse may have a strong genetic component. Two major patterns of alcohol abuse exist. One group of abusers drinks consistently at high levels (steady drinkers); people in this group usually have a history of antisocial acts—fighting, lying, and so on. In contrast, another group of abusers can resist drinking alcohol for long periods of time, but when they do drink, they cannot control themselves and go on binges. The first of these patterns of alcohol abuse seems to be influenced strongly by heredity, while the second pattern of alcohol abuse—binge drinking—seems to be influenced by both heredity and environment. Binge drinking seems to be related to variations in what is known as the aldehyde dehydrogenase (ALDH2) gene. Not everyone has this gene, but people who do are less likely to engage in binge drinking than are those who do not.

Interestingly, the frequency of binge drinking also varies across different ethnic groups. For instance, in one revealing study (Luczak et al., 2001), binge drinking rates in three groups—Chinese, Korean, and White (European heritage) college students—were compared. In addition, information was obtained on whether participants in the study possessed the ALDH2 gene. Results indicated that binge drinking was more common among Whites, less common among Koreans, and least common among Chinese students. In addition, for the Chinese and Korean students, possessing the ALDH2 gene was an added protective factor against binge drinking.

Barbiturates, which are contained in sleeping pills and relaxants, constitute a second type of depressant. First manufactured in the late nineteenth century, these drugs depress activity in the central nervous system and reduce activation and mental alertness. How these effects are produced is not certain, but some evidence suggests that barbiturates may reduce the release of excitatory neurotransmitters by neurons in many different locations. Initially, high doses of barbiturates can produce feelings of relaxation and euphoria—a kind of drunkenness without alcohol. Barbiturates often then produce confusion, slurred speech, memory lapses, and reduced ability to concentrate. Wide swings of emotion, from euphoria to depression, are also common. Extremely large doses can be fatal, because they result in paralysis of centers of the brain that regulate breathing.

Because some barbiturates induce sleep, people often try to use them to treat sleep disorders such as insomnia. However, these drugs do not seem to produce

Barbiturates
Drugs that act as *depressants*, reducing activity in the nervous system and in behavior output.

Stimulants
Drugs that increase activity in the nervous system (e.g., amphetamines, caffeine, nicotine).

Amphetamines
Drugs that act as *stimulants*, increasing feelings of energy and activation.

normal sleep. They suppress REM sleep, and this sleep stage may rebound sharply after individuals stop taking the drugs.

Stimulants

Drugs that produce the opposite effects of depressants—feelings of energy and activation—are known as **stimulants.** Included in this category are **amphetamines** and **cocaine.** Both of these stimulants inhibit the reuptake of the neurotransmitters dopamine and norepinephrine. As a result, neurons that would otherwise stop firing continue to respond. Such drugs raise blood pressure, heart rate, and respiration—signs of activation produced by the sympathetic nervous system. In addition, stimulants yield short periods of pleasurable sensations, twenty to forty minutes during which users feel extremely powerful and energetic. As the drug wears off, however, users often experience an emotional "crash" involving anxiety, depression, and fatigue.

Was cocaine ever really present in Coca-Cola? Despite advertising claims about Coke's energizing effects (see Figure 4.14), the answer is *no* (Levinthal, 1999). Since 1903, when "Coke" was first made, the Stepan Company in New Jersey has had the task of removing cocaine from high-grade coca leaves. The remainder, known as "decocanized flavor essence" was then sent to the Coca-Cola Company to flavor the world-famous drink. Many soft drinks do contain caffeine, however, often in doses as high as that found in coffee or tea. So you *can* get a lift from Coke or Pepsi, but not because they contain cocaine.

Cocaine is usually consumed by *snorting*, a process in which it is inhaled into each nostril. There it is absorbed through the lining of the nose directly into the bloodstream. Cocaine can also be swallowed, usually in liquid form, but this produces weaker effects. When cocaine is heated and treated chemically, a form known as **crack** is produced. This can be smoked, and when it is, the drug affects the brain almost instantly. This produces a high during which individuals experience powerful feelings of energy, confidence, and excitement. Although cocaine is not usually considered to be addicting, it often produces strong psychological dependence. And crack appears to have much stronger effects of this type. In order to obtain crack, heavy users turn to prostitution, theft, and anything else they can think of that will provide enough money for the next dose.

Other stimulants in common use include caffeine (found in coffee, tea, and many soft drinks) and *nicotine* (found in tobacco). Many experts view nicotine as highly addicting, and it is difficult to argue with this view when more than 50 percent of persons who have been operated on for lung cancer continue to smoke after their surgery (Carlson, 1999)!

Opiates

Another group of drugs in widespread use is the **opiates.** These drugs include opium, morphine, heroin, and related synthetic drugs. Opium is derived from the opium poppy. (Do you remember the scene in *The Wizard of Oz* in which Dorothy and the Cowardly Lion fall asleep in a field of beautiful poppies?) Morphine is produced from opium, while heroin is derived from morphine. Opiates produce

FIGURE 4.14
Coca-Cola: Did It Ever Contain Cocaine?
Ads like this one suggest that Coca-Cola can greatly enhance energy and alertness, but despite this claim, Coca-Cola never actually contained cocaine, a powerful stimulant.

Cocaine
A powerful stimulant that produces pleasurable sensations of increased energy and self-confidence.

Crack
A derivative of cocaine that can be smoked. It acts as a powerful stimulant.

Opiates
Drugs that induce a dreamy, relaxed state and, in some persons, intense feelings of pleasure. Opiates exert their effects by stimulating special receptor sites within the brain.

lethargy and a pronounced slowing of almost all bodily functions. These drugs also alter consciousness, producing a dreamlike state and, for some people, intensely pleasurable sensations. While opiates have legitimate uses—for instance in treating chronic, intense pain (e.g., in cancer patients)—they can pose serious risks. Heroin and other opiates are extremely addicting and withdrawal from them often produces agony for their users. Growing evidence indicates that the brain produces substances (opioid peptides or endorphins) closely related to the opiates in chemical structure and also contains special receptors for them (Phillips & Fibiger, 1989). This suggests one possible explanation for the pain experienced by opiate users during withdrawal. Regular use of opiates soon overloads endorphin receptors within the brain. As a result, the brain ceases production of these substances. When the drugs are withdrawn, endorphin levels remain depressed. Thus, an important internal mechanism for regulating pain is disrupted (Reid, 1990). To make matters worse, tolerance for opiates such as heroin increases rapidly with use, so physiological addiction can occur very quickly. To reiterate: Although opiates have legitimate medical uses, when used outside of this context they can be highly dangerous.

Psychedelics and Hallucinogens

Perhaps the drugs with the most profound effects on consciousness are the **psychedelics,** drugs that alter sensory perception and so may be considered mind-expanding, and **hallucinogens,** drugs that generate sensory perceptions for which there are no external stimuli. The most widely used psychedelic drug is *marijuana*. Use of this drug dates back to ancient times; indeed, it is described in a Chinese guide to medicines from the year 2737 B.C. Marijuana was widely use in the United States and elsewhere for medical purposes as late as the 1920s. It could be found in almost any drugstore and purchased without a prescription. It was often prescribed by physicians for headaches, cramps, and even ulcers. Starting in the 1930s, however, the tide of public opinion shifted, and by 1937, marijuana was outlawed completely in the United States. When smoked or eaten (e.g., in cookies) marijuana produces moderate physiological effects: increased heart rate (up to 160 beats per minute), changes in blood pressure (the direction seems to depend on whether the individual is sitting, standing, or lying down), and dilation of blood vessels in the eye, thus producing bloodshot eyes. Short-term psychological effects include heightened senses of sight and sound and a rush of ideas, which leads some individuals to conclude that marijuana increases their creativity. Unfortunately, marijuana also interferes with the ability to carry out tasks involving attention and memory, and reduces the ability to judge distances. This latter effect can lead to serious accidents when users of the drug drive a car or operate machinery. Other effects reported by some, but not all, users include reduced inhibitions, feelings of relaxation or drowsiness, and increased sexual pleasure. Most of these effects seem to vary strongly with expectations—what marijuana users believe will happen to them. In the United States, many people believe that marijuana will make them sexually aroused, and they report such effects. In India, in contrast, marijuana is believed to be a sexual depressant, and this is what users report. So, as we have noted throughout this text, cultural factors often exert powerful effects on behavior. This is why modern psychology adopts a fully multicultural perspective (American Psychological Association, 2003).

Because marijuana is still illegal in many nations, it is produced by unreliable sources who frequently blend it with other substances; the result is that users never know exactly what they are getting, and this can be dangerous.

More dramatic effects are produced by *hallucinogens*—drugs that produce vivid hallucinations and other perceptual shifts. Of these drugs, the most famous is **LSD** (lysergic acid diethylamide), or *acid*. After taking LSD, many persons report pro-

Psychedelics
See Hallucinogens.

Hallucinogens
Drugs that profoundly alter consciousness (e.g., marijuana, LSD).

LSD
A powerful hallucinogen that produces profound shifts in perception; many of these shifts are frightening in nature.

FIGURE 4.15
The War against Drugs: Can It Be Won?
Efforts to reduce or even totally eliminate the sale of illegal drugs have continued for many years but, to date, have not succeeded in achieving these goals.

found changes in perceptions of the external world. Objects and people seem to change color and shape, walls may sway and move, and many sensations seem to be more intense than normal. There may also be a strange blending of sensory experiences such that colors produce feelings of warmth or cold, while music yields visual sensations. Such effects may sound exciting, but many others produced by LSD are quite negative. Objects, people, and even one's own body may seem distorted or threatening. Users may experience deep sorrow or develop intense fear of close friends and relatives. The effects of the drug are unpredictable, so users have no way of predicting how it will affect them.

Finally, we should mention **designer drugs**—drugs that are designed to resemble already existing illegal drugs. Perhaps the most famous of these is *MDMA*, or *ecstasy*. Users of MDMA report that it increases their awareness of their own emotions, changes in visual perception, and feelings of closeness to others (which is why it is sometimes called the "hug drug"). Prolonged use may lead to confusion, fatigue, nausea, and depression. MDMA is often used at rave parties and has now been used by up to 40 percent of all teenagers.

Drug Use and Abuse: A Concluding Comment

Efforts to reduce or eliminate the use of illegal consciousness-altering drugs have continued for many decades, and, in general, results have been mixed (see Figure 4.15). Drug use continues, with three key results: (1) The drugs sold to millions of people cannot be checked by the government for purity; (2) The prices of such drugs are very high; and (3) The profits from their sale enriches organized crime. Does this mean we should adopt a new policy, one that, perhaps, makes some of these drugs legal (and therefore places them under supervision of the government)? This is a complex question and we have no simple answers, but it is one with which many societies will have to grapple in the future because, clearly, it will not simply go away. (Use of drugs in work settings raises additional, complex issues. For discussion of these, please see the **Psychology Goes to Work** section on the next page.)

KEY QUESTIONS

• What are the effects of depressants?
• What are the effects of stimulants? Opiates? Psychedelics? Hallucinogens?

Designer Drugs
Drugs designed to resemble illegal drugs that already exist.

PSYCHOLOGY GOES TO WORK

Drug Testing at Work—What Are Your Rights?

In 1991, the driver of a New York City subway train fell asleep at the controls because he had consumed a large amount of alcohol. The result: 5 passengers were killed and 200 injured. Incidents like these suggest that the use of drugs at work can have devastating effects. Faced with these possibilities, many large companies have adopted *random drug testing,* in which a random sample of employees is tested each day to determine whether they are using illegal drugs.

Court rulings on the legality of such testing vary from state to state in the United States, but, in general, employers can adopt random testing if they have a legitimate reason for doing so (e.g., to protect the public or other employees). So, if you are selected for such testing, what should you do? Probably, you should agree unless you have a special reason for objecting—for instance, you are taking drugs prescribed by your doctor, drugs that may show up in the tests. The weight of law is generally on the employer's side be-

cause of legislation such as the *Drug-Free Work-place Act,* which requires employers to assure that their work environments are drug-free. But you should agree to be tested only if you know that the drug-testing procedures are fair. This means that (1) every employee has an equal chance of being tested (e.g., names are selected randomly by a computer program); (2) tests are done by at least two different laboratories, as a check on accuracy; and (3) blood or urine samples are sealed and stored properly until collected for testing.

If you have doubts about any of these points, *object strongly.* The law protects you from unfair or sloppy testing, which may be done to obtain grounds for firing certain employees rather than to protect the health and safety of all employees. Your best protection? Don't even think about using drugs while at work, and avoid illegal drugs anywhere, at any time. The health and career you protect will be your own!

SUMMARY AND REVIEW OF KEY QUESTIONS

Biological Rhythms: Tides of Life— and Conscious Experience

- **What are biological rhythms? What are circadian rhythms?**
  Biological rhythms are regular fluctuations in our bodily processes. Circadian rhythms are biological rhythms that occur within a single day.

- **How do morning persons and night persons differ?**
  Morning persons feel most alert and energetic early in the day. Night persons feel most alert and energetic late in the day.

- **What effects do jet lag and shift work have on circadian rhythms?**
  Both jet lag and shift work produce disturbances in circadian rhythms, thus affecting our performance on many tasks and our health.

- **What steps can be taken to counter the effects of jet lag and shift work?**
  For jet lag, sleep as much as possible before the trip; drink lots of water; try to sleep on the plane; try to sleep when you arrive, or stay up a little longer; and avoid alcohol. For shift work, stay on one shift as long as possible, try to keep the same hours on weekends, and try exposure to bright light.

Waking States of Consciousness

- **What is the difference between automatic processing and controlled processing?**
  In automatic processing, we perform activities without directing conscious attention to them. In controlled processing, we direct conscious attention to various activities.

- **What is *self-awareness* and why do we sometimes enter this state of consciousness?**
  Self-awareness is a state of consciousness in which we turn our attention inward, toward ourselves. We enter this state because of situational factors (e.g., we pass a mirror), our affective states, or because we possess a predisposition to enter this state.

- **Why do we tend to overestimate our performance on many tasks (i.e., overlook our incompetence)?**
  We tend to overestimate our performance on many tasks because the skills needed to do well on these tasks are very similar to the ones we need to estimate our performance accurately.

Sleep: The Pause That Refreshes?

- **How do psychologists study sleep?**
  Sleep is often studied by examining changes in the EEG and EMG.

- **What are the major stages of sleep?**
  There appear to be four major stages of sleep and a very different stage known as REM sleep.

- **What happens during REM sleep?**
  During REM sleep, the EEG shows a pattern similar to that of waking, but the activity of body muscles is almost totally suppressed. Most dreams occur during REM sleep.

- **What are the possible functions of slow-wave and REM sleep?**
  Slow-wave sleep provides an opportunity for the brain to rest. REM sleep may play a key role in learning and in the consolidation of memories.

- **What are the effects of sleep deprivation?**
  Long-term sleep deprivation can adversely affect the health of both human and animals.

- **What steps can you take to help get a good night's sleep every night?**
  Read something pleasant or relaxing just before going to sleep. Arrange your schedule so you go to sleep at the same time each night. Take a warm bath or have a massage before going to sleep. Avoid coffee or tea late in the day. Exercise every day, but not just before going to sleep. Don't smoke. Don't nap during the day.

- **What are important disorders of REM sleep? Slow-wave sleep?**
  Disorders of REM sleep include narcolepsy, cataplexy, and atonia. Disorders of slow-wave sleep include insomnia, somnambulism, night terrors, and apnea.

- **How do the psychodynamic, physiological, and cognitive views explain dreams?**
  The psychodynamic view suggests that dreams reflect suppressed thoughts, wishes, and impulses. The physiological view suggests that dreams reflect the brain's interpretation of random neural activity that occurs while we sleep. The cognitive view holds that dreams result from the fact that many systems of the brain are active during sleep while input from muscles and sensory systems is inhibited.

Hypnosis: Altered State of Consciousness . . . or Social Role Playing?

- **What is hypnosis?**
  Hypnosis involves a special type of interaction between two persons in which one (the hypnotist) employs suggestions to induce changes in the behavior, feelings, or cognitions of the other (the subject).

- **How do the social-cognitive, neodissociation, and dissociative control views of hypnosis differ?**
  The social-cognitive view suggests that the effects of hypnosis stem from the hypnotized person's expectations and their efforts to play the role of hypnotized subject. The neodissociation view suggests that the effects of hypnotism stem from a split in consciousness between the executive cognitive function and a monitoring function. Dissociative control theory suggests that hypnotism weakens control by the central function over other cognitive and behavioral subsystems.

- **What do most psychologists conclude with respect to the question of whether hypnosis is real?**
  On the basis of scientific evidence, most psychologists have concluded that the effects produced by hypnosis are real, but that they stem primarily from the ability possessed by some persons to produce dramatic alterations in their own experience or behavior—nonhypnotic suggestibility—rather than from special properties of hypnosis itself.

Consciousness-Altering Drugs: What They Are and What They Do

- **What are drugs? What is drug abuse?**
  Drugs are substances that, because of their chemical structures, change the functioning of biological systems. Drug abuse involves instances in which people take drugs purely to change their moods, and in which drugs produce impaired behavior or social functioning.

- **What are physiological and psychological dependencies on drugs?**
  Physiological dependence involves strong urges to continue using a drug based on organic factors, such as changes in metabolism. Psychological dependence involves strong desires to continue using a drug even though it is not physiologically addicting.

- **Why do people use consciousness-altering drugs?**
  People use consciousness-altering drugs for several reasons: The drugs make them feel good or eliminate negative feelings, they experience social pressure to use the drugs, and using them has become automatic behavior.

- **What are the effects of depressants?**
  Depressants (e.g., alcohol) reduce both behavioral output and neural activity.

- **What are the effects of stimulants? Opiates? Psychedelics? Hallucinogens?**
  Stimulants produce feelings of energy and activation. Opiates produce lethargy and pronounced slowing of many bodily functions, but also induce intense feelings of pleasure in some persons. Psychedelics such as marijuana alter sensory perception, while hallucinogens such as LSD produce vivid hallucinations and other bizarre perceptual effects.

PSYCHOLOGY: UNDERSTANDING ITS FINDINGS

Can Hypnosis Solve Your Personal Problems?

Have you ever seen an ad for a hypnotist who claims to be able to help people lose weight, stop smoking, or get over their shyness? We see them every so often in our local newspaper. What do you think? Taking account of the information in this chapter on hypnotism, do you think it can produce such beneficial changes? If so, why? If not, why?

Now, whatever your own opinion, ask this question of several of your friends—especially ones who have *not* read this chapter. What do *they* think? We predict that they will have more faith in the effectiveness of hypnotism than you do. To make this study more useful, ask them to answer the following questions:

1. Do you think hypnotism is real—that once hypnotized, people will do whatever the hypnotist tells them to do?

   Definitely No   Definitely Yes
     1   2   3   4   5

2. Do you think that hypnotism can help people to lose weight?

   Definitely No   Definitely Yes
     1   2   3   4   5

3. Do you think hypnotism can help people to stop smoking?

   Definitely No   Definitely Yes
     1   2   3   4   5

4. Do you think hypnotism can help people get over being shy?

   Definitely No   Definitely Yes
     1   2   3   4   5

Add up the responses of your friends to see how they feel, in general, about the usefulness of hypnotism.

MAKING PSYCHOLOGY PART OF YOUR LIFE

How Aware Are You of Your Own Incompetencies?

Earlier in this chapter, we noted that many people tend to overestimate their own competence at various tasks—in other words, they are not fully aware of how well they actually perform them. How aware do you think *you* are in this respect? Do you know what you are good at and what you are not so good at doing? To find out, complete the following exercise.

Rate your own performance of each of these tasks:

1. **Driving**

   Much Worse   Much Better
   Than Average   Than Average
     1   2   3   4   5

2. **Getting along well with other people**

   Much Worse   Much Better
   Than Average   Than Average
     1   2   3   4   5

3. **Thinking logically**

   Much Worse   Much Better
   Than Average   Than Average
     1   2   3   4   5

4. **Serving as a leader**

   Much Worse   Much Better
   Than Average   Than Average
     1   2   3   4   5

5. **Getting things done on time**

   Much Worse   Much Better
   Than Average   Than Average
     1   2   3   4   5

Now, have at least three of your friends rate you on each dimension. Finally, compare their ratings with yours. Any difference between their ratings and your own will give you added insight into just how accurately you perceive your own competencies.

KEY TERMS

Alpha Waves, p. 106
Amphetamines, p. 118
Apnea, p. 111
Automatic Processing, p. 103
Barbiturates, p. 118
Biological Rhythms, p. 98
Cataplexy, p. 110
Circadian Rhythms, p. 98
Cocaine, p. 119
Controlled Processing, p. 103
Crack, p. 119
Cross-Tolerance, p. 117
Delta Activity, p. 106
Depressants, p. 117
Designer Drugs, p. 121
Dissociated Control, Theory of, p. 115
Dreams, p. 111

Dreams of Absent-Minded
    Transgression, p. 112
Drug Abuse, p. 116
Drugs, p. 116
Drug Tolerance, p. 117
Electroencephalogram (EEG), p. 106
Electromyogram (EMG), p. 106
Evening (Night) Persons, p. 99
Fatal Familial Insomnia, p. 109
Hallucinogens, p. 120
Hypnosis, p. 113
Insomnias, p. 109
LSD, p. 120
Morning Persons, p. 99
Narcolepsy, p. 109
Neodissociation Theory (of hypnosis),
    p. 114

Night Terrors, p. 110
Opiates, p. 119
Physiological Dependence, p. 117
Psychedelics, p. 120
Psychological Dependence, p. 117
REM Sleep, p. 106
Self-Awareness, p. 104
Sleep, p. 106
Social-Cognitive or Role-Playing
    View, p. 114
Somnambulism, p. 110
States of Consciousness, p. 98
Stimulants, p. 118
Suprachiasmatic Nucleus (SCN), p. 99
Tolerance, p. 117

5

Learning: How We're Changed by Experience

*O*n a recent trip to another country, I (Michael Kalsher) was relieved to learn that the signage at the airport and at my hotel presented information in both the native language of that country (Korean) and in English. All the flight attendants and most of the hotel staff spoke English, too. Unfortunately, this luxury didn't extend to other parts of the city, particularly to the local restaurants. One evening, a friend and I decided to try out a restaurant well known for its barbecue (a style in which a portion of the meal is cooked on a grill embedded in the customer's table). Upon arriving at the restaurant, we were anxious to get started with the meal. Although none of the restaurant staff could speak English, we were able to order because the menu contained pictures next to each of the dishes listed. Thus, we pointed and the wait staff seemed to readily understand what we wanted. The first course proceeded without a hitch. The server grilled slices of meat and vegetables at the table and demonstrated how we were to eat the food; she placed some of the meat and veggies onto a large leaf of lettuce and then wrapped it up, much like a taco. Then she dipped it into a bowl of sauce, *handed it to me, and motioned for me to eat it. Relieved, I began to settle in to enjoy the rest of the meal. But then, something rather unsettling happened. Another dish the server had brought us consisted of rice and a dipping sauce, each in separate bowls. Just as I was about to eat a spoonful of rice that I had dipped into the sauce, the woman began to speak loudly and waved her arms in a way that clearly said I should stop. However, it was less clear why my actions were wrong and what I needed to do instead. After several unsuccessful attempts to clue me in through gestures, the woman—frustrated at this point—took the spoon from me and showed me that the appropriate way of eating the dish was to first take a spoonful of rice, and only then, a separate spoonful of the sauce. To avoid the possibility of another misstep, I consumed the rest of the dish in this way—and looked to other customers in the restaurant for additional clues. Fortunately, the rest of the meal went smoothly and it ended up a very positive experience.*

As illustrated by this example, the learning process is important to all organisms, including people, because it helps us acquire important skills and adapt to changing conditions in the world around us. In this chapter, we'll examine several basic principles that help to explain how many forms of behavior are affected by experience. Psychologists refer to these effects on behavior as learning. Specifically, they define **learning** as any relatively permanent change in behavior, or behavior potential, produced by experience. Several aspects of this definition are noteworthy. First, the term *learning* does not apply to temporary changes in behavior such as those stemming from fatigue, drugs, or illness. Second, it does not refer to changes resulting from maturation—the fact that you change in many ways as you grow and develop. Third, learning can result from *vicarious* as well as from direct experiences; in other words, you can be affected by observing events and behavior in your environment as well as by participating in them (Bandura, 1986). It is important to note that the effects of learning are not always apparent, emphasizing the need to differentiate learning from performance. This highlights the importance of including changes in "behavior potential" in the definition of learning. Finally, the changes produced by learning are not always positive in nature. As you well know, people are as likely to acquire bad habits as good ones.

There can be no doubt that learning is a key process in human behavior. Indeed, it appears to play an important role in virtually every activity we perform. Although the effects of learning are diverse, many psychologists believe that learning occurs in several basic forms: *classical conditioning, operant*

Learning
Any relatively permanent change in behavior (or behavior potential) resulting from experience.

conditioning, and *observational learning.* We'll begin with *classical conditioning,* a form of learning in which two stimulus events become associated in such a way that the occurrence of one event reliably predicts the occurrence of the other. Classical conditioning is the basis for many learned fears and also helps explain how we acquire aversions to certain foods or beverages. Next, we'll turn to *operant conditioning,* a form of learning in which organisms acquire associations between behaviors and the stimuli that precede (antecedents) or follow (consequences) them. Here, we'll see how psychologists have applied basic operant principles to promote certain positive behaviors, such as recycling and safe driving, and to discourage inappropriate or dangerous ones. Finally, we'll explore *observational learning,* a form of learning in which organisms learn by observing the behaviors—and the consequences of the behaviors—of others around them.

CLASSICAL CONDITIONING: LEARNING THAT SOME STIMULI SIGNAL OTHERS

Imagine the following situation. You're visiting friends. It's 7:00 A.M. and you are drifting somewhere between sleep and waking. In the next room you hear a soft click. Then, almost immediately, you are practically knocked out of bed by a loud noise. You are about to rush out of the room to find out what's happened, when you figure it out: Your friends have switched on the bathroom fan, and, being old, it is extremely noisy. You try to go back to sleep, but your heart is pounding so hard that you decide to get up. Because you are staying with your friends for two weeks, the same events are repeated each morning. Would there be any change in your behavior during this period? The chances are good there would be. Gradually, you might begin to respond not just to the sound of the fan, but to the soft click as well. The reason is simple: Because it is always followed by the noisy fan, the click comes to serve as a signal for the onset of this loud, irritating sound. In other words, hearing the click, you expect the fan noise to follow, and you react accordingly—you are startled and you experience increased arousal (see Figure 5.1).

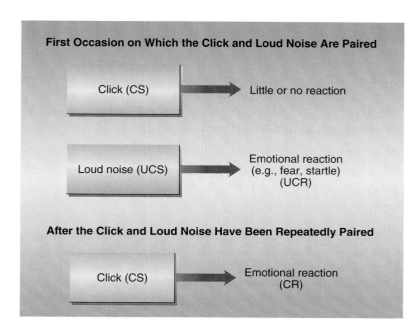

First Occasion on Which the Click and Loud Noise Are Paired

Click (CS) → Little or no reaction

Loud noise (UCS) → Emotional reaction (e.g., fear, startle) (UCR)

After the Click and Loud Noise Have Been Repeatedly Paired

Click (CS) → Emotional reaction (CR)

FIGURE 5.1
Classical Conditioning: A Simple Example
At first, a soft click would have little effect on your behavior (*top diagram*). After the click has been paired with a loud noise on several occasions, you might begin to react to the click alone (*lower diagram*). This reaction would be the result of classical conditioning. CS, conditioned stimulus; UCS, unconditioned stimulus; UCR, unconditioned response; CR, conditioned response.

This simple incident provides an everyday example of **classical conditioning,** the first type of learning that we will consider. In classical conditioning, a physical event—termed a **stimulus**—that initially does not elicit a particular response gradually acquires the capacity to do so as a result of repeated pairing with a stimulus that *can* elicit the response. Learning of this type is quite common and seems to play a role in such varied reactions as strong fears, taste aversions, some aspects of sexual behavior, and even racial or ethnic prejudice (Baron & Byrne, 2002). Classical conditioning became the subject of careful study in the early twentieth century, when Ivan Pavlov, a Nobel Prize–winning physiologist from Russia, identified it as an important behavioral process (Pavlov, 1928).

Pavlov's Early Work on Classical Conditioning: Does This Ring a Bell?

Pavlov did not actually set out to investigate classical conditioning. Rather, his research focused on the process of digestion in dogs. During his investigations he noticed a curious fact: The dogs in his studies often began to salivate when they saw or smelled food but *before* they actually tasted it. Some even salivated at the sight of the pan where their food was kept or at the sight or sound of the person who usually brought it. This suggested to Pavlov that these stimuli had somehow become signals for the food itself: The dogs had learned that when the signals were present, food would soon follow.

Pavlov quickly recognized the potential importance of this observation and shifted the focus of his research accordingly. The procedures that he now developed were relatively simple. On *conditioning trials,* a neutral stimulus that had previously been shown to have no effect on salivation—a bell, for example—was presented. This was immediately followed by a second stimulus known to produce a strong effect on salivation: dried meat powder placed directly into the dog's mouth. The meat powder was termed the **unconditioned stimulus (UCS),** because its ability to produce salivation was automatic and did not depend on the dog's having learned the response. Similarly, the response of salivation to the meat powder was termed an **unconditioned response (UCR);** it too did not depend on previous learning. The bell was termed a **conditioned stimulus (CS),** because its ability to produce salivation depended on its being paired with the meat powder. Finally, salivation in response to the bell was termed a **conditioned response (CR).**

The basic question was whether the sound of the bell would gradually come to elicit salivation in the dogs as a result of its repeated pairing with the meat powder. In other words, would the bell elicit a CR when it was presented alone? The answer was clearly yes. After the bell had been paired repeatedly with the meat powder, the dogs salivated upon hearing it—even when the bell was not followed by the meat powder.

Classical Conditioning: Some Basic Principles

Let's turn now to the principles that govern the occurrence of classical conditioning.

■ Acquisition: The Course of Classical Conditioning

In most instances, classical conditioning is a gradual process in which a conditioned stimulus gradually acquires the capacity to elicit a CR as a result of repeated pairing with a UCS. This process—termed **acquisition**—proceeds quite rapidly at first, increasing as the number of pairings between CS and UCS increases (please refer to Figure 5.2). However, there is a limit to this effect; after a number of pairings of CS and UCS, acquisition slows down and finally levels off.

Although psychologists initially believed that conditioning was determined primarily by the number of CS-UCS pairings, we now know that this process is

---

Classical Conditioning
A basic form of learning in which one stimulus comes to serve as a signal for the occurrence of a second stimulus. During classical conditioning, organisms acquire information about the relations between various stimuli, not simple associations between them.

Stimulus
A physical event capable of affecting behavior.

Unconditioned Stimulus (UCS)
In classical conditioning, a stimulus that can evoke an unconditioned response the first time it is presented.

Unconditioned Response (UCR)
In classical conditioning, the response evoked by an unconditioned stimulus.

Conditioned Stimulus (CS)
In classical conditioning, the stimulus that is repeatedly paired with an unconditioned stimulus.

Conditioned Response (CR)
In classical conditioning, the response to the conditioned stimulus.

Acquisition
The process by which a conditioned stimulus acquires the ability to elicit a conditioned response through repeated pairings of an unconditioned stimulus with a conditioned stimulus.

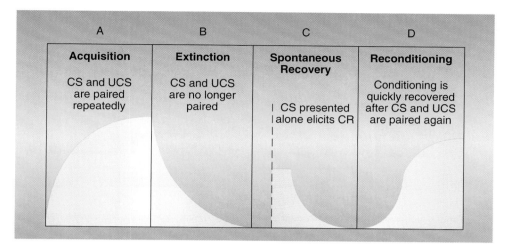

FIGURE 5.2
Acquisition and Extinction of a Conditioned Response
During *acquisition*, the strength of the conditioned response rises rapidly up to a point and then levels off (*panel A*). The process of *extinction* begins once the conditioned stimulus is no longer paired with the unconditioned stimulus (*panel B*). As shown in panels C and D, extinction can be disrupted through the processes of *spontaneous recovery* and/or *reconditioning*. Finally, although not shown in the figure, if no subsequent conditioned stimulus–unconditioned stimulus pairings occur, the conditioned response will decrease once again.

affected by other factors. As shown in Figure 5.3 on page 132, one such factor is *temporal arrangement* of the CS-UCS pairings. Temporal means time-related: the extent to which a CS precedes or follows the presentation of a UCS. The first two temporal arrangements shown, **delay conditioning** and **trace conditioning,** are examples of what is termed *forward conditioning,* because the presentation of the CS (light) always precedes the presentation of the UCS (shock). They differ, however, in that the CS and the UCS overlap to some degree in *delay* conditioning but not in *trace* conditioning. Two other temporal arrangements are **simultaneous conditioning,** in which the conditioned and unconditioned stimuli begin and end at the same time; and **backward conditioning,** in which the UCS precedes the CS.

Delay conditioning is generally the most effective method for establishing a CR. This is because in delay conditioning, the CS helps predict forthcoming presentations of the UCS (Lieberman, 1990). To illustrate this point, consider the following example: You are taking a shower when suddenly the water turns icy cold. Your response—a startle reaction to the cold water—is a UCR. Now imagine that just before the water turns cold, the plumbing makes a slight grinding sound. Because this sound occurs just before and overlaps with the onset of the icy water, delay conditioning can occur. If this situation is repeated several times, you may acquire a startle reaction to the slight grinding sound; it serves as a CS. In contrast, suppose you do not hear the sound until after the water turns cold, as in backward conditioning, or until the precise instant at which it turns cold, as in simultaneous conditioning. In these cases, you would probably not acquire a startle reaction to the grinding sound, because it provides no information useful in predicting the occurrence of the icy water.

Several additional factors also appear to affect conditioning. In general, conditioning is faster when the *intensity* of either the CS or UCS increases (Kamin, 1965). In other words, conditioning is more likely when conditioned stimuli stand out, relative to other background stimuli. Second, conditioning also depends on the time interval between presentations of the two stimuli. Extremely short intervals— less than 0.2 second—rarely produce conditioning. In animal research, the optimal

Delay Conditioning
A form of forward conditioning in which the onset of the unconditioned stimulus (UCS) begins while the conditioned stimulus (CS) is still present.

Trace Conditioning
A form of forward conditioning in which the onset of the conditioned stimulus (CS) precedes the onset of the unconditioned stimulus (UCS) and the presentation of the CS and UCS does not overlap.

Simultaneous Conditioning
A form of conditioning in which the conditioned stimulus (CS) and the unconditioned stimulus (UCS) begin and end at the same time.

Backward Conditioning
A type of conditioning in which the presentation of the unconditioned stimulus (UCS) precedes the presentation of the conditioned stimulus (CS).

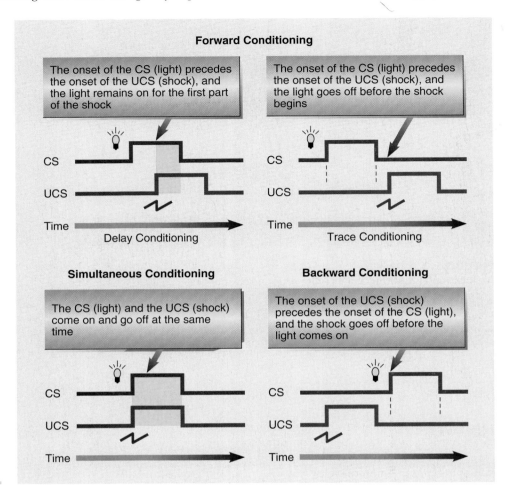

FIGURE 5.3
Temporal Arrangement of the CS and UCS Affects the Acquisition of a Conditioned Response
Four CS-UCS temporal arrangements commonly used in classical conditioning procedures are shown. *Temporal* refers to timing: the extent to which a conditioned stimulus precedes or follows the presentation of an unconditioned stimulus. *Delay conditioning* generally produces the most rapid rate of learning. *Simultaneous* and *backward conditioning* are usually the least effective procedures.

CS-UCS interval seems to be between 0.2 and 2 seconds; longer intervals make it difficult for animals to recognize the CS as a signal for some future event (Gordon, 1989). Finally, *familiarity* can greatly affect conditioning. In contrast to the laboratory, in which stimuli selected for study are often novel, many of the potential conditioning stimuli found in the environment are familiar to us. Thus, our day-to-day experiences often teach us that certain stimuli, such as the background noise usually present in an office setting or the odors ordinarily present in our homes, do not predict anything unusual (Baker & Mackintosh, 1977).

■ Extinction: Once Conditioning Is Acquired, How Do We Get Rid of It?

Suppose that you and your coworkers have been working night and day to prepare a proposal crucial to the survival of the marketing firm for which you work, and things are not going well. Over the past week the president of the company has chewed you out at least a dozen times. Now, whenever you hear his approaching footsteps, your heart starts racing and your mouth gets dry, even though he has not yet reached your office. Fortunately, the company's directors are impressed by the proposal, and your boss is no longer angry when he enters your office. Will you continue to react strongly to his footsteps? Probably not. Gradually, his footsteps will cease to elicit the original CR from you. The eventual decline and disappearance of a CR in the absence of an *un*conditioned stimulus is known as **extinction.**

The course of extinction, however, is not always smooth (please refer to Figure 5.2). Let's consider the behavior of one of Pavlov's dogs to see why this is true. After many presentations of a bell (CS) in the absence of meat powder (UCS), the dog no longer salivates in response to the bell. In other words, extinction has oc-

Extinction
The process through which a conditioned stimulus gradually loses the ability to evoke conditioned responses when it is no longer followed by the unconditioned stimulus.

curred. But if the CS (the bell) and the UCS (the meat powder) are again paired after the CR of salivation has been extinguished, salivation will return very quickly—a process termed **reconditioning.**

Or suppose that after extinction, the experiment is interrupted: Pavlov is caught up in another project that keeps him away from his laboratory and the dog for several weeks. Now will the sound of the bell, the CS, elicit salivation? The answer is yes, but the reaction will be in a weakened form. The reappearance of the reaction after a time interval is referred to as **spontaneous recovery.** If extinction is then allowed to continue—that is, if the sound of the bell is presented many times in the absence of meat powder—salivation to the sound of the bell will disappear relatively quickly compared to extinction of the initial CR.

FIGURE 5.4
Stimulus Generalization Can Sometimes Be Dangerous
Young children may become trusting of *all* adults through the process of stimulus generalization. Unfortunately, this process can lead to unfortunate consequences if it extends to certain strangers.

■ Generalization and Discrimination: Responding to Similarities and Differences

Suppose that because of several painful experiences, a child has acquired a strong conditioned fear of hornets: Whenever she sees one or hears one buzzing, she shows strong emotional reactions and heads for the hills. Will she also experience similar reactions to other flying insects, such as flies? She almost certainly will, because of **stimulus generalization,** the tendency of stimuli similar to a CS to elicit similar CRs. The more closely new stimuli resemble the original CS—in this instance, hornets—the stronger the response will be. As you can readily see, stimulus generalization often serves a useful function. In this example, it may indeed save the girl from additional stings. The red lights that we encounter at certain intersections while driving also illustrate the important function served by stimulus generalization: Even though these signals often vary in brightness, shape, or location, we learn to stop in response to all of them, and it's a good thing we do.

Although stimulus generalization can serve an important adaptive function, it is not always beneficial and in some cases can be dangerous. For example, because of many pleasant experiences with parents and other adult relatives, a young child may become trusting of all adults through stimulus generalization. Unfortunately, this process will not be beneficial if it extends to certain strangers. You can understand why stimulus generalization can be maladaptive—even deadly (please refer to Figure 5.4). Fortunately, most of us avoid such potential problems through **stimulus discrimination**—a process of learning to respond to certain stimuli but not to others. A few years ago a friend was severely bitten by a dog. Until that incident she had no fear of dogs. Because she was so frightened by the attack, I was concerned that the incident would generalize to other breeds of dogs—perhaps even to her own dog. Fortunately, because of stimulus discrimination, this didn't happen; she becomes fearful only when she encounters the breed of dog that bit her.

Reconditioning
The rapid recovery of a conditioned response (CR) to a CS-UCS pairing following extinction.

Spontaneous Recovery
Following extinction, reinstatement of conditioned stimulus-unconditioned stimulus pairings will produce a conditioned response.

Stimulus Generalization
The tendency of stimuli similar to a conditioned stimulus to evoke conditioned responses.

Stimulus Discrimination
The process by which organisms learn to respond to certain stimuli but not to others.

KEY QUESTIONS

- What is learning?
- What is classical conditioning?
- Upon what factors does acquisition of a classically conditioned response depend?
- What is extinction?
- What is the difference between stimulus generalization and stimulus discrimination?

Classical Conditioning: The Neural Basis of Learning

Now that we've discussed the basic principles of classical conditioning, let's turn to another question that has puzzled scientists for many years: What is the neural basis of this and other kinds of learning? Psychologists have started to unravel this mystery, at least for some forms of learned behavior (Brembs, 2003; Daum & Schugens, 1996; Schoenbaum et al., 2003; Woodruff-Pak, 1999).

Research with animals, for example, has resulted in nearly complete identification of the neural circuitry that underlies eyeblink classical conditioning (Steinmetz, 1996; Thompson et al., 1997). To establish eyeblink classical conditioning, scientists repeatedly pair the presentation of a stimulus that does not ordinarily cause us to blink, say a tone or a light (a CS), with one that does, say a puff of air to the eye (a UCS). People and other animals quickly learn to blink in response to the light or tone (a CR). The site essential to the acquisition and performance of this type of CR is the cerebellum. When the cerebellum of animals is surgically destroyed, previously learned associations can be severely disrupted, and the ability to learn new associations eliminated altogether (Thompson & Krupa, 1994). Other brain structures known to be involved in eyeblink conditioning include the hippocampus, amygdala, and brain-stem areas that project to or receive information from the cerebellum (Steinmetz, 1996).

Studies of humans who have sustained damage to the cerebellum or related structures reveal a similar pattern of results. These persons blink normally (UCR) in response to a puff of air to the eye (UCS), indicating that their motor functions and ability to respond to external stimulation remains intact. However, efforts to establish a CR to, say, a light or a tone, are usually unsuccessful (Daum & Shugens, 1996; Topka et al., 1993).

Because the neural circuitry underlying eyeblink classical conditioning is so well known, behavioral researchers have begun to use this procedure to investigate a variety of basic processes in humans (e.g., Ivkovich et al., 1999; Clark & Squire, 1999), including the biological correlates of certain mental disorders. For example, we know that the symptoms experienced by people with *obsessive–compulsive disorder* arise from learned associations that are maladaptive and particularly resistant to extinction. Obsessive–compulsive disorder is characterized by intrusive, unwanted, and uncontrollable thoughts, images, compulsions, or urges that are often accompanied by repetitive behaviors or mental acts that the person feels driven to perform (see Chapter 12 for additional information). Interestingly, eyeblink classical conditioning appears to proceed much more quickly in individuals who exhibit these tendencies than in those who do not, suggesting that some people may be biologically predisposed to establish associations between feelings of fear and anxiety and otherwise neutral objects (Tracey et al., 1999). Clearly, these findings will play an important role in designing more effective treatments for obsessive–compulsive disorder or, conversely, in learning how to prevent the development of the maladaptive associations that characterize this disorder altogether.

More recent research with humans has identified the parts of the brain involved in the acquisition, storage, and expression of learned fears, which, in turn, may help psychologists develop more effective ways to treat them (e.g., Cheng et al., 2003; LeDoux, 2000). Although scientists are just beginning to understand the complex relationship between brain functions and behavior in humans, it is clear that our knowledge of the neural basis of learning is expanding at a rapid pace, and that it has important practical applications—for instance, in developing better treatments for various forms of psychological disorders.

Classical Conditioning: Exceptions to the Rules

When psychologists began the systematic study of learning at the turn of the twentieth century, they saw their task as that of establishing general principles of

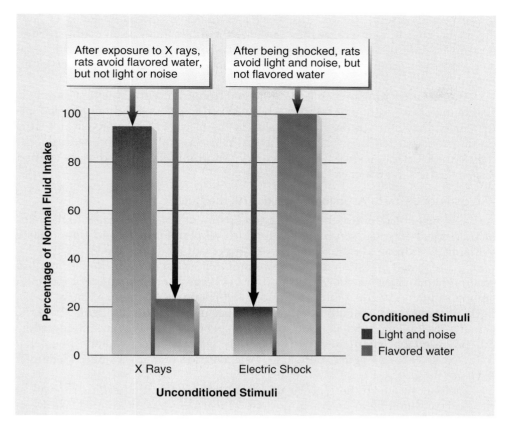

After exposure to X rays, rats avoid flavored water, but not light or noise

After being shocked, rats avoid light and noise, but not flavored water

FIGURE 5.5
Biological Constraints and Characteristics of the CS and UCS Affect the Acquisition of a Conditioned Response
Rats quickly acquired an aversion to a flavored water when it was followed by X rays that made them ill, but they did *not* readily acquire an aversion to the flavored water when it was followed by an electric shock. In contrast, rats learned to avoid a light–noise combination when it was paired with shock but *not* when it was followed by X rays. These findings indicate that classical conditioning cannot be established with equal ease for all stimuli and for all organisms.
Source: Based on data from Garcia & Koelling, 1966.

learning—principles that applied equally well to all organisms and to all stimuli. Beginning in the 1960s, however, some puzzling findings seemed to indicate that not all organisms learn all responses or all associations between stimuli with equal ease.

The most dramatic evidence pointing to such conclusions was reported by Garcia and his colleagues (Braverman & Bronstein, 1985; Garcia, Hankins, & Rusiniak, 1974). In perhaps the most famous of these studies, Garcia and Koelling (1966) allowed two groups of rats to sip saccharin-flavored water from a device that emitted a bright flashing light and a loud clicking noise (conditioned stimuli) whenever the rats licked the water. While both groups were drinking, one group of rats was exposed to X rays that later made them sick (a UCS); the other group received painful shocks to their feet (also a UCS). Traditional principles of classical conditioning suggest that *both* groups of rats should have learned to avoid all three stimuli—the flavored water, the bright light, and the clicking noise. After all, for both groups, these stimuli were followed by a strong UCS (either X rays or a painful shock). But this was not what Garcia and Koelling found. Rats exposed to the painful shock learned to avoid the light and noise but not the flavored water; rats that were made to feel ill learned to avoid the flavored water but not the light or noise (see Figure 5.5). In short, it seems that rats—and other organisms—are predisposed to associate nausea and dizziness with something they've consumed (the flavored water) and to associate pain with something they've seen or heard (the bright light and clicking noise). Similar findings from many different studies suggest that acquisition of a CR does *not* occur with equal ease for different stimuli.

Further research has also shown that in regard to conditioning, important differences exist among species. Because of these **biological constraints on learning,** types of conditioning readily accomplished by some species are only slowly acquired by others. And often, the types of conditioning most readily accomplished by one species are the very ones it needs to survive in its normal habitat (Shettleworth, 1993). For example, rats eat a varied diet and are most active at night. Thus,

Biological Constraints on Learning
Refers to the fact that all forms of conditioning are not equally easy to establish with all organisms.

it is especially useful for them to be able to associate specific tastes with later illness, because in many cases they can't see the foods they eat. In contrast, birds depend heavily upon vision for finding food. For a bird it is more useful to be able to form associations between visual cues and later illness (Wilcoxon, Dragoin, & Kral, 1971).

Another intriguing outcome that emerged from Garcia and Koelling's study is also noteworthy: Although the rats who received the X rays did not get sick immediately, they still acquired an aversion to the taste of the flavored water. This finding contradicted the widely held belief that classical conditioning can occur only if the UCS follows the CS within a very short interval. We'll discuss learned taste aversions in greater detail next.

Conditioned Taste Aversions: Breaking All the Rules?

As we've just noted, one of the clearest demonstrations of an exception to the rules of traditional classical conditioning involves what is termed **conditioned taste aversion.** Conditioned taste aversions are important for survival because they inhibit the repeated ingestion of dangerous and toxic substances in animals' natural environments. Surveys show that food or beverage aversions are very common among humans (Logue, Ophir, & Strauss, 1981; Logue, Logue, & Strauss, 1983). Such aversions are unusually strong and can occur despite our thoughts about the actual cause of our illness. For example, many people report that even though they are convinced that a particular food or beverage was not the cause of the illness that followed, they continue to experience a taste aversion to that substance (Seligman & Hager, 1972).

The way in which these powerful associations are formed differs from most classical conditioning in several important respects. First, a conditioned taste aversion can usually be established with a single CS-UCS pairing, termed *one-trial learning,* in contrast to the many pairings involved in most Pavlovian conditioning. Second, conditioned taste aversions have been reported when the CS was presented hours before the occurrence of the UCS. In contrast, most instances of conditioning require a CS-UCS interval of not more than a few seconds. Finally, conditioned taste aversions are extremely resistant to extinction; in fact, they may last a lifetime.

Conditioned taste aversions create serious problems for some people. For example, radiation and chemotherapy used to treat cancer often cause nausea or vomiting as a side effect (Burish & Carey, 1986). Thus, cancer patients may acquire taste aversions to food ingested before therapy sessions. Research shows that even thinking about the sight or smell of these foods can produce anticipatory nausea and vomiting in some patients.

Fortunately, patients receiving chemotherapy can reduce the likelihood of developing a conditioned taste aversion. First, they should arrange their meal schedules to decrease the chances of establishing an association between ingestion of the food and illness; the interval between their meals and chemotherapy should be as long as possible. Second, patients should eat familiar food, avoiding new or unusual foods before therapy. Because familiar foods have already been associated with feeling good, it is less likely that cancer patients will acquire an aversion to them. Finally, because the strength of a CR is related to the intensity of the CS, patients should eat bland foods and avoid strongly flavored ones; foods with strong odors, such as chocolate and coffee, may frequently become the targets for aversions (Bernstein, 1999).

Conditioned Taste Aversion
A type of conditioning in which the UCS (usually internal cues associated with nausea or vomiting) occurs several hours after the CS (often a novel food), leading to a strong CS-UCS association in a single trial.

KEY QUESTIONS
- Where in the brain does classical conditioning take place?
- Is classical conditioning equally easy to establish with all stimuli for all organisms?
- How do we acquire conditioned taste aversions?

Classical Conditioning: A Cognitive Perspective

Many psychologists believe that classical conditioning involves more than just formation of a simple association between stimuli. We now know, for example, that regular pairing of a CS with a UCS provides subjects with valuable *predictive* information; it indicates that whenever a CS is presented, a UCS will shortly follow. Thus, as conditioning proceeds, subjects acquire the *expectation* that a CS will be followed by a UCS.

The idea that cognitive processes involving expectation play a role in classical conditioning is supported by several types of evidence (Rescorla & Wagner, 1972). First, conditioning fails to occur when unconditioned and conditioned stimuli are paired in a random manner. With random pairings, subjects cannot acquire any firm expectation that a UCS will indeed follow presentation of a CS. Therefore, for conditioning to occur, the CS-UCS pairing must be consistent.

Second, the cognitive thesis is supported by a phenomenon known as *blocking*—the fact that conditioning to one stimulus may be prevented by previous conditioning to another stimulus. For example, suppose that a dog is initially conditioned to a tone. After repeated pairings with presentation of meat powder, the tone becomes a CS, capable of causing the dog to salivate. Then a second stimulus, a light, is added to the situation. It too occurs just before the presentation of food. If classical conditioning occurs in an automatic manner, simply as a result of repeated pairings of a CS with a UCS, then the light, too, should become a CS: It should elicit salivation when presented alone. In fact, this does not happen. Why? Again, an explanation in terms of expectancies is helpful. Because the meat powder is already predicted by the tone, the light provides no new information. Therefore, it is of little predictive value to the subjects and fails to become a CS.

The idea that cognitive processes play a role in classical conditioning is also supported by studies of mental imagery (Dadds et al., 1997). Research suggests that the cognitive processes underlying the generation, manipulation, and scanning of mental images closely mirror the processes involved in perceiving actual physical stimuli (Kosslyn, 1994). Studies using brain imaging techniques indicate that areas of the brain known to be involved in visual processing are also active during visual imagery tasks (Farah, 1988).

Mental images of physical stimuli also appear to elicit reactions that closely resemble the ones elicited by their physical counterparts (please refer to Figure 5.6). For example, asking people to *imagine* drinking a sour solution causes them to

FIGURE 5.6
Cognitive Processes and Classical Conditioning
As illustrated by this example, mental images of certain stimuli can sometimes elicit reactions that closely resemble the ones elicited by their physical counterparts, evidence of the powerful role of cognitive processes in conditioning.
Source: Reprinted with permission of King Features Syndicate.

salivate as if they were actually drinking it; in contrast, asking people to drink a glass of water does not (Barber, Chauncey, & Winer, 1964).

Taken together, these findings suggest that classical conditioning involves much more than the formation of simple associations between specific stimuli. In short, both memory and active comparison processes play a role in what might at first seem to be an automatic function.

Classical Conditioning: Turning Principles into Action

Before concluding, we should call attention to the fact that knowledge of the basic principles of classical conditioning has been put to many practical uses to help people. One of the earliest applications of classical conditioning was in the treatment of learned fears, or *phobias,* an issue we'll discuss in Chapter 12. These principles have also been applied to other important problems, and we'll consider these next.

Classical Conditioning and Drug Overdose

Knowledge of conditioning processes has helped to explain some instances of drug overdose. For example, it is well known that certain drugs become less effective over time. But why does this occur? One possibility is that when a person uses drugs in a particular context repeatedly, the stimuli in that environment become conditioned stimuli and so elicit a CR (Siegel, 1984; Siegel & Ramos, 2002). For certain addictive drugs, this CR can be just the opposite of the UCR. Such learned responses have been termed *conditional compensatory responses,* or CCRs (Siegel et al., 1982, 2000).

This suggests that environmental cues associated with the environment in which drugs are consumed serve as conditioned stimuli and prepare drug users' bodies partially to counteract the effects of the drug. Drug users who have nearly died following drug use commonly report something unusual about the environment in which they took the drug (Siegel, 1984). Often these environmental differences are quite subtle, a fact that emphasizes the powerful effects produced by conditioning. These results have important implications for drug treatment, because the environments to which former drug users return often contain cues that may produce drug-related CRs, such as withdrawal symptoms and drug cravings (Ehrman et al., 1992). Researchers have compared relapse rates among treated drug users who have either returned to environments rich in drug-associated cues or relocated to an environment very different from that in which they used drugs. The relocated patients generally show far less relapse (Siegel & Ramos, 2002).

Classical Conditioning and the Immune System

Research also indicates that it is possible to alter the immune system through classical conditioning (Ader et al., 1993; Husband et al., 1993). In one study, Alvarez-Borda and her colleagues (1995) used classical conditioning to enhance specific immune functions in rats. On conditioning day, one group of rats was allowed to drink a distinctive beverage—saccharin-flavored water (the CS)—before receiving an injection of a substance (the UCS) known to raise the level of certain antibodies in their systems. A second group of rats received only water before receiving the same injection. As predicted, both groups showed an enhanced immune response (UCR) to the injection. Then, after the effects of the injection had faded (more than a month later), the researchers tested to see if conditioning had taken place. Half of the rats that had been exposed to saccharin-flavored water during conditioning were again exposed to saccharin-flavored water, while the other half received only water. The group that had received only water during conditioning also received water during the test trial. The researchers' predictions were supported: Reexposure to the saccharin-flavored water (the CS) resulted in a significant elevation of antibodies in these rats, despite the fact that no further injections (the UCS) were given. In contrast, there was no enhanced immune response in the other groups;

measurements indicated that antibody levels in these rats were not significantly different from levels assessed prior to conditioning.

Research suggests that conditioning can be also effective in enhancing aspects of the immune systems of humans, too (Miller & Cohen, 2001). Together, these results show that conditioning can exert powerful effects on the immune system—in the absence of the original substance that produced it. As you may have guessed already, the implications of these results are enormous. Indeed, they offer tremendous hope to people whose health is compromised due to depressed immune systems—for example, persons who are HIV-positive or have AIDS.

KEY QUESTIONS

- How do modern views of classical conditioning differ from earlier perspectives?
- What is blocking?
- How can classical conditioning principles solve problems of everyday life?

OPERANT CONDITIONING: LEARNING BASED ON CONSEQUENCES

When a local politician started his campaign for state office, his speeches contained many remarks about the need for higher spending. He would note, with considerable passion, that the state's schools were in serious trouble, its roads and bridges were falling apart, and that the salaries paid to its employees were below the national average. The crowds he addressed, however, weren't favorably impressed by these views. Whenever he mentioned raising taxes, many persons would shake their heads, boo, or get up to leave. Now, several months later, his speeches have an entirely different flavor. He rarely if ever mentions the need for higher spending. Instead, he emphasizes efficiency—getting full value from every tax dollar spent. And when he makes such remarks, people smile, applaud, and cheer.

What happened here? Why did this politician change the nature of his speeches? The answer should be obvious: As many politicians do, he changed his remarks in response to the consequences they produced (see Figure 5.7).

FIGURE 5.7
Operant Conditioning: Learning Based on Consequences
Operant conditioning is a form of learning in which behavior is maintained, or changed, through consequences. The views politicians express are often shaped by the reactions of those who listen—or by the results of polls.

Statements that yielded hisses and boos from voters decreased in frequency, while those that yielded applause and cheers increased. In other words, he learned to perform behaviors that produced positive outcomes and to avoid behaviors that yielded negative ones. This process is known as *operant conditioning* and it is the second major form of learning we will consider.

The Nature of Operant Conditioning: Consequential Operations

In situations involving **operant conditioning,** the probability that a given response will occur changes depending on the consequences that follow it. Psychologists generally agree that these probabilities are determined through four basic procedures, two of which strengthen or increase the rate of behavior and two of which weaken or decrease the rate of behavior. Procedures that *strengthen* behavior are termed *reinforcement,* whereas those that *suppress* behavior are termed *punishment.*

▪ Reinforcement

There are actually two types of **reinforcement:** positive reinforcement and negative reinforcement. *Positive reinforcement* involves the impact of **positive reinforcers**— stimulus events or consequences that strengthen responses that precede them. In other words, if a consequence of some action increases the probability that the action will occur again in the future, that consequence is functioning as a positive reinforcer. Some positive reinforcers seem to exert these effects because they are related to basic biological needs. Such *primary reinforcers* include food when we are hungry, water when we are thirsty, and sexual pleasure. In contrast, other events acquire their capacity to act as positive reinforcers through association with primary reinforcers. Such *conditioned* reinforcers include money, status, grades, trophies, and praise from others.

Preferred activities can also be used to reinforce *less*-preferred activities, a principle referred to as the **Premack principle.** If you recall hearing "You must clean your room before you can watch TV" or "You must eat your vegetables before you get dessert" when you were growing up, then you're already familiar with this principle. As you can guess, the Premack principle is a powerful tool for changing behavior.

Please note that a stimulus event that functions as a positive reinforcer at one time or in one context may have a different effect at another time or in another place. For example, food may serve as a positive reinforcer when you are hungry, but not when you are ill or just after you finish a large meal. Also, at least where people are concerned, many individual differences exist. Clearly, a stimulus that functions as a positive reinforcer for one person may fail to operate in a similar manner for another person. We will return to this important point later on in this chapter.

Negative reinforcement involves the impact of **negative reinforcers**—stimuli that strengthen responses that permit an organism to avoid or escape from their presence. Thus, when we perform an action that allows us to *escape* from a negative reinforcer that is already present or to *avoid* the threatened application of one altogether, our tendency to perform this action in the future increases. Some negative reinforcers, such as intense heat, extreme cold, or electric shock, exert their effects the first time they are encountered, whereas others acquire their impact through repeated association.

There are many examples of negative reinforcement in our everyday lives. To illustrate this, imagine the following scene. On a particularly cold and dark winter morning, you're sleeping soundly in a warm, comfortable bed. Suddenly, the alarm clock across the room begins to wail. Getting out of your cozy bed is the last thing you want to do, but you find the noise intolerable. What do you do? If you get up to turn off the alarm—or, on subsequent mornings, get up early to avoid hearing the sound of the alarm altogether—your behavior has been *negatively* reinforced. In other words, your tendency to perform actions that allow you to escape from or

---

Operant Conditioning
A process through which organisms learn to repeat behaviors that yield positive outcomes or that permit them to avoid or escape from negative outcomes.

Reinforcement
A procedure by which the application or removal of a stimulus increases the strength of a specific behavior.

Positive Reinforcers
Stimuli that strengthen responses that precede them.

Premack Principle
The principle that a more preferred activity can be used to reinforce a less preferred activity.

Negative Reinforcers
Stimuli that strengthen responses that permit the organism to avoid or escape from their presence.

avoid the sound of the alarm clock has increased. Another everyday example of negative reinforcement occurs when parents give in to their children's tantrums—especially in public places, such as restaurants and shopping malls. Over time, the parent's tendency to give in may increase, because doing so stops the screaming. In short, the parent's behavior has been negatively reinforced.

To repeat, then, *both positive and negative reinforcement are procedures that strengthen or increase behavior.* Positive reinforcers are stimulus events that strengthen responses that precede them, whereas negative reinforcers are stimulus events that strengthen responses that lead to their termination or avoidance.

Punishment

In contrast to reinforcement, **punishment** refers to procedures that weaken or decrease the rate of behavior. As with reinforcement, there are two types of punishment: positive punishment and negative punishment. In *positive punishment,* behaviors are followed by stimulus events termed *punishers.* In such instances, we learn not to perform these actions, because aversive consequences—punishers—will follow. And this highlights a point about which there is often much confusion. Contrary to what common sense seems to suggest, punishment is *not* the same as negative reinforcement. Here is an example to illustrate the difference. Imagine that you are driving home in a hurry, exceeding the speed limit. A sick sensation creeps into your stomach as you become aware of flashing lights and a siren. A state trooper has detected you speeding (please refer to Figure 5.8). Your eyes bug out when you see how much the ticket will cost you; and after paying that fine, you now obey the posted speed limit. This is an example of the impact of *punishment*—an unpleasant outcome follows your speeding, so the chances that you will speed in the future *decrease.* Now imagine that a year later you are again caught speeding. Apparently the punishment suppressed your speeding behavior only temporarily. Because you are a past offender, the judge handling your case gives you an interesting choice: either attend a month-long series of driver education classes or lose your driver's license. To avoid losing your license, you attend every class. This is an example of *negative reinforcement:* You attend the driver education classes to *avoid* an aversive event—the loss of your license.

In *negative punishment,* the rate of a behavior is weakened or decreased because it is linked to the loss of potential reinforcement (Catania, 1992; Millenson & Leslie, 1979). For example, parents frequently attempt to decrease the frequency of certain behaviors of their teenagers (e.g., hitting younger siblings or talking back to their parents) by temporarily denying them access to reinforcers, such as driving the family car on weekend dates. Negative punishment is also commonly referred to as "time-out," a procedure you may have experienced as a youngster growing up. Thus, both positive and negative punishment are procedures that weaken or decrease behavior. For more information on the use of some of the procedures described in this section, please refer to the following **Psychology Lends a Hand** section.

FIGURE 5.8
Operant Conditioning: The Effects of Punishment
Punishment refers to procedures that weaken or decrease the rate of behavior. In this instance, the ticket the driver has received for speeding may decrease the likelihood she will do so in the future. In such instances, we learn not to perform certain actions, because aversive consequences—punishers—will follow.

KEY QUESTIONS

- What is operant conditioning?
- What are examples of primary reinforcers? Of conditioned reinforcers?
- Which operant techniques strengthen behavior? Weaken behavior?
- How do negative reinforcement and punishment differ?

Punishment
A procedure by which the application or removal of a stimulus decreases the strength of a behavior.

psychology lends a hand

Spare the Rod, Spoil the Child?: The Wisdom of Using Punishment with Children

One of the most controversial issues concerning the use of punishment centers on whether parents should use corporal punishment with their children; in other words, whether parents should, or should not, spank them for their misbehavior. A large body of research spanning more than fifty years seems to cast doubt on both the appropriateness and effectiveness of corporal punishment as a disciplinary tool (Gershoff, 2002). Why? There are actually several reasons that we'll explore in the following sections.

Problems Associated with the Use of Punishment

Although corporal punishment can be effective at temporarily suppressing problem behaviors or getting children to comply with their parent's requests, there can also be significant negative side effects associated with its use.

One problem is that, over time, milder forms of punishment can escalate into physical abuse (e.g., Wolfe, 1987; Zigler & Hall, 1989). Why does this happen? Earlier in this chapter we learned that when behavior is rewarded it tends to be repeated. If a parent punishes misbehavior with a spanking and the behavior stops, the parent's use of corporal punishment is negatively reinforced by the termination of the child's misbehavior; the child's cessation of the misbehavior is negatively reinforced by the termination of the parent's punishment. In such a scenario, we would predict that both parental punishment (perhaps at increasing levels of severity) and their child's compliance to it will continue.

A second problem is that some children might become angry after experiencing physical punishment, particularly if they believe

they were punished unfairly or inappropriately (Izard, 1991). A child's anger at being spanked can erode bonds of trust and closeness and lead them to withdraw or avoid their parents. In some instances, they may even retaliate against the parents. Such acts of aggression may become particularly dangerous as children get older—and stronger.

A third potential problem with the use of physical punishment is that it models aggression. As we'll learn a bit later in this chapter, modeling and imitation are thought to be key learning mechanisms by which children become aggressive. Because children see aggression modeled, in the form of corporal punishment, and rewarded, in the form of their own compliance with it, they learn that aggression is an effective way to manipulate other people's behavior.

The Use of Punishment as a Disciplinary Tool

Psychologists and other professionals are still divided on the question of whether the potential benefits of using corporal punishment outweigh the risks. Those opposed to its use argue that corporal punishment is not only ineffective, but also harmful (e.g., American Academy of Pediatrics, 1998; Straus, Sugarman, & Giles-Sims, 1997; Straus & Stewart, 1999).

Proponents of corporal punishment suggest that it can be used effectively in some circumstances—for example, if a child's behavior is aggressive or is a threat to his or her own or others' safety (e.g., Baumrind, 1996; Larzelere, 1998). They defend their position by pointing to research documenting the conditions under which punishment is effective (e.g., Domjan, 2000). To be effective,

Operant Conditioning: Some Basic Principles

In classical conditioning, organisms learn associations between stimuli: Certain stimulus events predict the occurrence of others that naturally trigger a specific response. In addition, the responses performed are generally *involuntary*. In other words, they are *elicited*—pulled out of the organism—by a specific UCS in an automatic manner; for example, salivation to the taste of food, blinking the eyes in response to a puff of air.

In operant conditioning, in contrast, organisms learn associations between particular *behaviors* and the consequences that follow them. Additionally, the responses involved in operant conditioning are more voluntary and are *emitted* by organisms in a given environment. To understand the nature of this form of conditioning, then, we must address two basic questions: (1) Why are certain behaviors emitted in the first place? (2) Once they occur, what factors determine the frequency with which they are repeated?

punishment must be immediate, consistent (applied after every offense), sufficiently intense (at least for the first offense), and delivered without warning.

Unfortunately, these conditions are usually difficult to meet. To illustrate this last point, consider a situation in which a child throws a tantrum in a shopping mall because his parents refuse to purchase a toy that he wants them to buy. Are they likely to follow each of the conditions outlined above? Probably not, in part because of the public attention they might draw from their actions. Parents may instead choose to give in to the child's tantrums by buying the toy, threatening him with a later punishment (e.g., "Just wait until we get home!"), or leaving the store altogether. Should they choose to punish the child on the spot, there is a chance they may be overly harsh, particularly if they are angry at the time.

Please note that these results do not mean that all children who experience corporal punishment turn out to be aggressive or suffer other lasting adverse effects. Research by Baumrind (1996) seems to indicate that the consequences of spanking vary depending on the quality of the parent–child relationship. Children who have a warm relationship with their parents, have not experienced any violence in the home, and are only spanked as a last resort tend not to suffer any long-term consequences. Additional evidence indicates that although a large majority of Americans are spanked as children (Straus & Stewart, 1999), most people do not suffer any long-term effects from it.

What Can Parents Do to Address Problem Behaviors?

So, given the potential drawbacks of using punishment, what can parents do to get their children to behave appropriately? Fortu-

nately, there are a number of effective alternatives to corporal punishment. One procedure that works particularly well with young children is *time-out* (from reinforcement). As the name implies, *time-out* means removing a child from toys or activities that she likes whenever she misbehaves. In practice, this typically means placing the child in a chair in a quiet corner for a few minutes (under supervision, of course!), then giving the child the opportunity to behave appropriately once time-out has ended. With older children, corrective action may take the form of removing privileges for a prescribed period of time, contingent upon the cessation of the misbehavior or the appearance of desired behavior (e.g., doing their homework).

You might have noticed that the procedures just described are examples of negative punishment (see the earlier section on punishment). Procedures involving *positive* reinforcement are also effective. Please remember, however, that all people—including children—have different likes and dislikes, so it is important to select rewards that are appropriate and appealing. One technique for handling this issue with young children involves a system in which they earn tokens (secondary reinforcers) for instances of good behavior. Over time, they can accumulate and then trade these in for valued activities (e.g., miniature golf, going to the movies) or toys. Older children often receive a weekly allowance, which, again, can be made contingent upon meeting their responsibilities (e.g., completion of their homework and chores)—and, of course, good behavior. Regardless of age, children generally appreciate receiving praise (that is genuine) for their good deeds, so it is important that parents regularly acknowledge and encourage desirable behaviors. By consistently reinforcing appropriate behavior, so goes the argument, it is less likely that problem behaviors will occur.

Shaping and Chaining: Getting Behavior Started and Then Putting It All Together

Many of the behaviors that we perform each day require little conscious effort on our part. But what about new forms of behavior with which we are unfamiliar? How are these behaviors initially established? The answer involves a procedure known as shaping.

In essence, **shaping** is based on the principle that a little can eventually go a long way. Subjects receive a reward for each small step toward a final goal—the target response—rather than only for the final response. At first, actions even remotely resembling the target behavior—termed *successive approximations*—are followed by a reward. Gradually, closer and closer approximations of the final target behavior are required before the reward is given. Shaping, then, helps organisms acquire, or construct, new and more complex forms of behavior from simpler behavior.

Shaping
A technique in which closer and closer approximations to desired behavior are required for the delivery of positive reinforcement.

FIGURE 5.9

A Simple Demonstration of Shaping and Chaining

The dual processes of shaping and chaining help to explain the development of complex behavior. Please note that *complex*, however, is a relative term—relative to the abilities and limitations of each organism.

What about even more complex sequences of behavior, such as the routines performed by certain animals? (Please refer to Figure 5.9.) These behaviors can be cultivated by a procedure called **chaining,** in which trainers establish a sequence, or chain, of responses, the last of which leads to a reward. Trainers usually begin chaining by first shaping the final response. When this response is well established, the trainer shapes responses earlier in the chain, then reinforces them by giving the animal the opportunity to perform responses later in the chain, the last of which produces the reinforcer. Shaping and chaining obviously have important implications for human behavior. For example, when working with a beginning student, a skilled dance teacher or ski instructor may use shaping techniques to establish basic skills, such as performing a basic step or standing on the skis without falling down, by praising simple accomplishments. As training progresses, however, the student may receive praise only when he or she successfully completes an entire sequence or chain of actions, such as skiing down a small slope.

Shaping and chaining techniques can produce dramatic effects. In one study, researchers investigated whether shaping could help cocaine users kick their drug habit (Preston et al., 2001). For eight weeks, cocaine users in a methadone maintenance program were given the opportunity to earn vouchers that were exchangeable for goods and services that were consistent with a drug-free lifestyle (e.g., movie passes, exercise equipment). Half of the participants (the abstinence group) were rewarded for cocaine-free urine samples only, whereas the other half (the shaping group) were rewarded for each urine specimen with a 25 percent or more decrease in cocaine metabolite during the first three weeks and then only for cocaine-free urine specimens during the last five weeks. The results showed that during the last five weeks, cocaine use was lower among participants in the shaping group, suggesting that shaping was useful in helping them to curb their drug use.

The Role of Reward Delay in Impulsiveness and Procrastination

Operant conditioning usually proceeds faster as the *magnitude* of the reward that follows each response increases. But the effectiveness of rewards can be dramatically affected by *reward delay*—the amount of time that elapses before the reward is delivered. In general, longer delays produce poorer levels of performance. A study by Capaldi (1978), for example, examined how reward delay affected running behavior in two groups of rats. Although both groups received the same amount and quality of food on each trial, one group received the reward immediately and the other group received it after a ten-second delay. As you might guess, subjects in the immediate-reward group performed better than subjects in the delayed-reward group.

The effects of reward delay are also evident in humans. For example, children will often choose smaller, immediate rewards over rewards of greater value that they must wait to receive, a tendency sometimes referred to as *impulsiveness* (Green, Fry, & Myerson, 1994; Logue, 1988). Please note, however, that adults, too, frequently engage in impulsive behavior, even when the long-term consequences for their impulsiveness are deadly. Smokers and heavy drinkers, for instance, choose the immediate pleasures they derive from smoking or consuming alcoholic beverages over the potentially negative consequences they may suffer later on, such as cancer (Rachlin, 1995; Steele & Josephs, 1990).

The processes underlying impulsive behavior just discussed also seem to describe another type of behavior with which you may be familiar: *procrastination*—the tendency to put off until tomorrow what we should do today. The decision

Chaining

A procedure that establishes a sequence of responses that lead to a reward following the terminal or final response in the chain.

facing procrastinators is whether to perform a smaller, less effortful task now or a larger, more effortful task later on. Although the most efficient decision in terms of time and effort is obvious—do the less effortful task now—research shows that people, and animals, often choose the more delayed alternative, even when it leads to more work (e.g., Mazur, 1996). Some recent findings suggest that procrastination can even exert negative effects on our health, including higher levels of stress and illness.

To illustrate this last point, let's consider a semester-long study of college students by Tice and Baumeister (1997). At the start of the term, the researchers told the students they would be required to write a term paper and were given a completion deadline. Procrastinators were identified by their scores on standardized measures designed to assess this tendency. The researchers also obtained several measures of stress, health, and performance at several points during the semester. As expected, students who were late in handing in the required paper scored much higher on the procrastination scales than students who handed their papers in on time. Moreover, procrastinators did not benefit from the extra time available to them to absorb course-related information, as they received significantly lower grades on the paper and exams than nonprocrastinators.

The results also revealed intriguing differences between procrastinators and nonprocrastinators in terms of their reported levels of stress and illness. As shown in Figure 5.10, procrastinators reported significantly fewer symptoms of illness at the beginning of the term than nonprocrastinators. However, this relationship was reversed at the end of the term, when procrastinators reported significantly more stress and symptoms of illness than nonprocrastinators. These results seem to suggest that procrastination can be explained, at least in part, by people's tendency to follow the path of least resistance. In other words, we tend to procrastinate because of the short-term benefits that it provides to us. Unfortunately, as this study illustrates, these benefits are later outweighed by the negative effects that procrastinating exerts on many aspects of our performance and health.

Schedules of Reinforcement: Different Rules for Delivery of Payoffs

Through experience, you may already realize that under natural conditions reinforcement is often an uncertain event. Sometimes a given response yields a reward

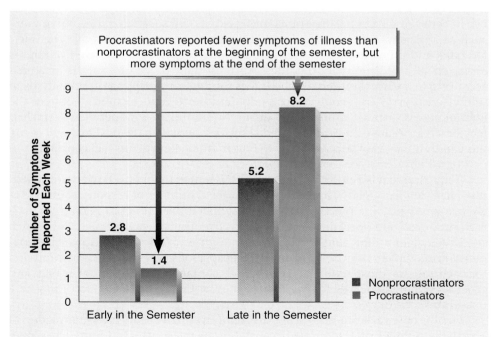

FIGURE 5.10
The Potential Negative Effects of Procrastination
The short-term benefits of procrastinating appear to be offset by the negative effects it exerts on our performance and health later on. Procrastinators reported fewer symptoms of illness at the beginning of the semester, compared to nonprocrastinators. Late in the semester, when procrastinators were faced with impending deadlines, this relationship switched.
Source: Based on data from Tice & Baumeister, 1997.

Schedules of Reinforcement
Rules determining when and how reinforcements will be delivered.

Continuous Reinforcement Schedule
A schedule of reinforcement in which every occurrence of a particular behavior is reinforced.

Fixed-Interval Schedule
A schedule of reinforcement in which a specific interval of time must elapse before a response will yield reinforcement.

Variable-Interval Schedule
A schedule of reinforcement in which a variable amount of time must elapse before a response will yield reinforcement.

Fixed-Ratio Schedule
A schedule of reinforcement in which reinforcement occurs only after a fixed number of responses have been emitted.

Variable-Ratio Schedule
A schedule of reinforcement in which reinforcement is delivered after a variable number of responses have been performed.

every time it occurs, but sometimes it does not. For example, smiling at someone you don't know may produce a return smile and additional positive outcomes. On other occasions it may be followed by a suspicious frown or other rejection. Similarly, putting a coin in a soda machine usually produces a soft drink. Sometimes, though, you merely lose the money.

In these cases, the occurrence or nonoccurrence of reinforcement seems to be random or unpredictable. In many other instances, though, it is governed by rules. For example, paychecks are given out on certain days of the month; free pizzas or car washes are provided to customers who have purchased a specific amount of products or services. Do such rules—known as **schedules of reinforcement**—affect behavior? Several decades of research suggest that they do. Many different types of schedules of reinforcement exist (Ferster & Skinner, 1957; Honig & Staddon, 1977). We'll concentrate on several of the most important ones here.

The simplest is called the **continuous reinforcement schedule** (CRF), in which every occurrence of a particular behavior is reinforced. For example, if a rat receives a food pellet each time it presses a lever, or a small child receives twenty-five cents each time he ties his shoes correctly, both are on a continuous reinforcement schedule. As you might imagine, continuous reinforcement is useful for establishing or strengthening new behaviors.

Other types of schedules, however, termed *partial* or *intermittent reinforcement*, are often more powerful in maintaining behavior. In the first of these, known as a **fixed-interval schedule,** the occurrence of reinforcement depends on the passage of time; the first response made after a specific period has elapsed brings the reward. When placed on schedules of this type, people generally show a pattern in which they respond at low rates immediately after delivery of reinforcement, but then gradually respond more and more as the time when the next reward can be obtained approaches. A good example of behavior on a fixed-interval schedule is provided by students' studying habits. After a big exam, little if any studying takes place. As the time for the next test approaches, the rate of studying increases dramatically.

Reinforcement is also controlled mainly by the passage of time in a **variable-interval schedule.** Here, though, the period that must elapse before a response will again yield reinforcement varies around some average value. An example of behavior on a variable-interval schedule of reinforcement is provided by employees whose supervisor checks their work at irregular intervals. Because the employees never know when such checks will occur, they must perform in a consistent manner in order to obtain positive outcomes, such as praise, or avoid negative ones, such as criticism. This is precisely what happens on variable-interval schedules: Humans and other animals respond at a steady rate without the kind of pauses observed on fixed-interval schedules. An important procedure that is arranged according to a variable-interval schedule is random drug testing of individuals in safety-sensitive jobs—people whose impaired performance could endanger the lives of others, such as airline pilots, air-traffic controllers, or operators at nuclear reactor sites. Because they cannot predict the day on which the next test will occur, these individuals may be more likely to refrain from using drugs that can either impair or unfairly enhance their work performance.

Reinforcement is determined in a very different manner on a **fixed-ratio schedule.** Here, reinforcement occurs only after a fixed number of responses. Individuals who are paid on a piecework basis, in which a fixed amount is paid for each item produced, are operating according to a fixed-ratio schedule. Generally, such schedules yield a high rate of response, though with a tendency toward a brief pause immediately after reinforcement. Salespersons who receive a commission for each sale, or those who collect beverage containers, office paper waste, and other recyclable materials for the money they bring are behaving according to a fixed-ratio schedule.

Finally, on a **variable-ratio schedule,** reinforcement occurs after completion of a variable number of responses. Because organisms confronted with a variable-ratio schedule cannot predict how many responses are required before reinforcement will occur, they usually respond at high and steady rates. The effect of such schedules on human behavior is readily apparent in gambling casinos, where high rates of responding occur in front of slot machines and other games of chance.

Variable-ratio schedules also result in behaviors that are highly resistant to *extinction*—ones that persist even when reinforcement is no longer available. This phenomenon is known as the *partial reinforcement effect* and seems to occur for the following reason. Under a variable-ratio schedule, many responses are not followed by reinforcement. Many golfers are well acquainted with the partial reinforcement effect; for each great shot they hit, they hit many more poor ones, yet they continue to play the game. Suppose that a golfer fails to hit even one good shot over the course of an entire season—will she continue to play? The chances are good that she will. When reinforcement is infrequent and intermittent in its delivery, people or other organisms may continue to respond because it is difficult for them to recognize that reinforcement is no longer available (Mowrer & Jones, 1945).

As summarized in Figure 5.11 and evident throughout the preceding discussion, different schedules of reinforcement produce distinct patterns of responding. Each schedule helps describe how the delivery of consequences affects our behavior.

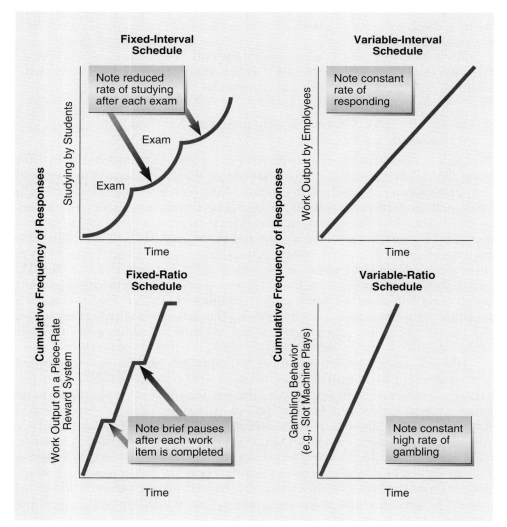

FIGURE 5.11
Schedules of Reinforcement: A Summary of Their Effects
Rates of responding vary under different schedules of reinforcement. Note that the steeper the line in each diagram, the higher the rate at which responses are performed.

Concurrent Schedules of Reinforcement and the Matching Law

Many psychologists readily admit that the schedules of reinforcement just described do not fully account for the complex forms of human behavior observed in everyday life (e.g., Hanisch, 1995; Pierce & Epling, 1994). Each day people are faced with alternatives and must choose one to the exclusion of others. For example, on a given evening, students must choose between doing homework and other behaviors they could do instead, such as going out with friends, talking on the telephone, doing their laundry, or watching TV. This describes a **concurrent schedule of reinforcement:** a situation in which a person's behavior is free to alternate between two or more responses, each having its own schedule of reinforcement (Catania, 1992).

To illustrate, let's consider a typical animal experiment involving a concurrent schedule of reinforcement in which a rat is free to press lever A or lever B at any time, or to press neither. Now suppose the consequences of pressing each lever (e.g., food reward) are arranged according to distinct variable-interval schedules of reinforcement. How will the rat distribute its lever presses? The rate of responding on each lever will tend to match the rate of reinforcement each lever produces. In other words, the rat will distribute its behavior between alternatives in such a way that maximizes the reinforcement it receives for its efforts. This phenomenon has been termed the *matching law* (Herrnstein, 1961).

The matching law also helps to explain why particular events are reinforcing at certain times and in certain contexts but not others (Herrnstein, 1970). For instance, on a particular Friday night, cleaning your room might not seem so bad if nothing else is going on. In contrast, the same chore may be unappealing if there is something better to do.

Please note that consequences are not the only determinants of behavior. As we'll see in the next section, stimuli that precede behavior and signal the availability of certain consequences are also important.

Stimulus Control of Behavior: Signals about the Usefulness (or Uselessness) of Responses

People and other animals readily learn to pay attention to cues in the environment that reliably signal certain consequences for their actions. Children may learn, for example, that when their father whistles, it is an indication he is in a good mood and therefore more likely to respond favorably to requests for money or permission to do something fun with their friends. Aspects of the father's mood, such as whistling or singing, are actually signals: He is likely to give in to requests when he is in a good mood (e.g., when he is whistling), but unlikely to do so when he is in a bad mood or not feeling well. Over time, you learn to make requests only in the presence of these signals—termed **discriminative stimuli.** In short, their behavior has come under **stimulus control** of the sound of his whistling (or related cues): They are obeying the signal as to whether they should ask for something they want now or wait until he is in a better mood (Skinner, 1938).

Stimulus control has important practical applications, too. For example, one type of graphic discriminative stimulus, the *Mr. Yuk* sticker, has been used to prevent accidental poisonings among small children who can't yet read warning labels or understand the dangers of many household products (please refer to Figure 5.12). How do Mr. Yuk stickers work? Initially parents place the stickers on all poisonous products in their home and explain to their children that Mr. Yuk means "No, don't touch." Then, each time a child attempts to handle a product containing the sticker, he or she receives a scolding. Soon Mr. Yuk comes to signal unpleasant consequences, and children quickly learn to avoid products with Mr. Yuk stickers. Clearly, stimulus control has important implications for solving a variety of problems in everyday life.

FIGURE 5.12
Using Stimulus Control to Prevent Accidental Poisonings
Stimulus control can help solve important problems of everyday life—in this case, preventing accidental poisonings among very small children.
Source: Mr. Yuk is a registered trademark of Children's Hospital of Pittsburgh and is reprinted with permission.

Concurrent Schedule of Reinforcement
A reinforcement schedule in which two or more schedules are available.

Discriminative Stimulus
Signals the availability of reinforcement if a specific response is made.

Stimulus Control
When a behavior occurs consistently in the presence of a discriminative stimulus.

KEY QUESTIONS

- What are shaping and chaining?
- How does reward delay affect operant conditioning? What are the effects of procrastination?
- What are schedules of reinforcement?
- When is the use of continuous reinforcement desirable?
- What are concurrent schedules of reinforcement and the matching law?
- What is a discriminative stimulus?

Operant Conditioning: A Cognitive Perspective

Do cognitive processes play a role in operant conditioning as they do in classical conditioning? This continues to be a point on which psychologists disagree. Operant psychologists have contended that there is no need to introduce cognition, or mental processes, into the picture: If we understand the nature of the reinforcers available in a situation and the schedules on which they are delivered, we can accurately predict behavior. But many other psychologists believe that no account of operant conditioning can be complete without attention to cognitive factors (e.g., Colwill, 1993). Several types of evidence support this conclusion.

Learned Helplessness: Throwing in the Towel When Nothing Seems to Work

Perhaps the most dramatic evidence is the existence of a phenomenon known as **learned helplessness:** the lasting effects produced by exposure to situations in which nothing an organism does works—no response yields reinforcement or provides escape from negative events. After such experiences, both people and animals seem literally to give up. And here is the unsettling part: If the situation changes so that some responses will work, they never discover this fact. Rather, they remain in a seemingly passive state and simply don't try (Seligman, 1975; Tennen & Eller, 1977). Although it is not yet clear why learned helplessness occurs, it seems impossible to explain it entirely in terms of contingent relations between individual responses and the consequences they produce.

Research on learned helplessness seems to suggest that its onset stems partly from our perceptions of control; when we begin to believe that we have no control over our environment or our lives, we stop trying to improve our situations (Dweck & Licht, 1980). For example, many children growing up in urban slums perceive they have little control over their environment and even less hope of escaping it. As a result of learned helplessness, they may simply resign themselves to a lifetime of disenfranchisement, deprivation, and exclusion. Please note, however, that not all people respond in this way. Indeed, a large number of studies show that even people whose early lives were ravaged by traumatic experiences, such as the early death of a parent, divorce, war, or extreme poverty, often grow up optimistic and resilient (e.g., Haggerty et al., 1994; Seabrook, 1995; Stewart et al., 1997). This suggests that other factors must also be involved.

Researchers have begun to speculate that genetic factors may also play a role in learned helplessness. One such factor that has gained attention is a genetically inherited impairment in the ability to experience pleasure termed **hypohedonia** (Meehl, 1975). According to Hamburg (1998), this tendency may cause children who inherit it to interpret the feedback they receive for their actions quite differently from children who do not. Apparently, these individuals experience the rewarding consequences they receive from their actions as if they were on an extinction schedule. This peculiar tendency to misinterpret rewarding feedback may lead to perceptions of lack of control and helplessness.

In Hamburg's theory, when normal children make mistakes while practicing a skill, such as playing soccer, it is typical for them to experience frustration, anger, and disappointment. However, when they eventually perform the skill correctly, it usually results in feelings of satisfaction and pride. Over time, the steady accumulation

Learned Helplessness
Feelings of helplessness that develop after exposure to situations in which no effort succeeds in affecting outcomes.

Hypohedonia
A genetically inherited impairment in the ability to experience pleasure.

of positive experiences leads them to believe, for example, that they are good at soccer, that it is not as difficult as they initially thought, and that they will likely want to continue to play soccer. When children with inherited hypohedonia make the same mistakes, they are likely to experience similar negative feelings but to feel them more intensely. And unfortunately, when they eventually perform the skill successfully, they may not experience the same positive feelings enjoyed by their unaffected peers. They may instead experience a carryover of the frustration, anger, and disappointment elicited by previous mistakes. Over time, the steady accumulation of negative feelings may lead them to believe that they are not good at soccer, that soccer is hard, and that they will continue to perform poorly in the future. They may also generalize these expectations to other task domains. According to Hamburg, there is a strong likelihood that these children will eventually experience learned helplessness, particularly if they are faced with difficult circumstances later in life.

Please note that Hamburg's theory has not yet been validated by empirical research and therefore requires further study. However, it does help to explain why some people tend to give up in the face of adversity, while others remain resilient.

Evidence That It's All Relative: The Contrast Effect

Some evidence suggests that our behavior is influenced not only by the level of rewards we receive, but also by our evaluation of rewards relative to our experiences with previous rewards. Studies have shown that shifts in the amount of reward we receive can dramatically influence performance, a temporary behavior shift termed the *contrast effect* (e.g., Crespi, 1942; Flaherty & Largen, 1975; Shanab & Spencer, 1978). When laboratory animals are shifted from a small reward to a larger reward, there is an increase in their performance to a level greater than that of subjects consistently receiving the larger reward. This increase is known as a *positive contrast effect.* Conversely, when subjects are shifted from a large reward to a smaller reward, their performance decreases to a level lower than that of subjects receiving only the smaller reward—a *negative contrast effect.* But positive and negative contrast effects are transient. Thus, the elevated or depressed performances slowly give way to performance levels similar to those of control animals that receive only one level of reward.

The existence of contrast effects indicates that level of reward alone cannot always explain our behavior and that experience with a previous level of reward—and consequent expectancies—can dramatically affect our performance. Contrast effects also help explain certain instances of our everyday behavior. For example, following an unexpected raise in salary or a promotion, a person is initially elated, and his or her performance skyrockets—at least for a while. Then, after the novelty wears off, performance falls to levels equal to that of others already being rewarded at the same level.

Tolman's Cognitive Map: A Classic Study in the History of Psychology

Finally, evidence suggests that cognitive processes play an important role in learning among animals, as well. In a classic study by Tolman and Honzik (1930), rats were trained to run through a complicated maze. One group, the reward group, received a food reward in the goal box at the end of the maze on each of its daily trials. A second group, the no-reward group, never received a reward. The third group, the no-reward/reward group, did not receive a food reward until the eleventh day of training. As illustrated in Figure 5.13, rats in the reward group showed a steady improvement in performance, decreasing the number of errors they made in reaching the goal box. Rats in the no-reward group showed only a slight improvement in performance. Rats in the no-reward/reward group showed performance similar to those in the no-reward group—for the first ten days. However, their performance improved dramatically immediately after the introduction of the food reward. In fact, their performance was as good as that of rats who had been rewarded for their performance all along.

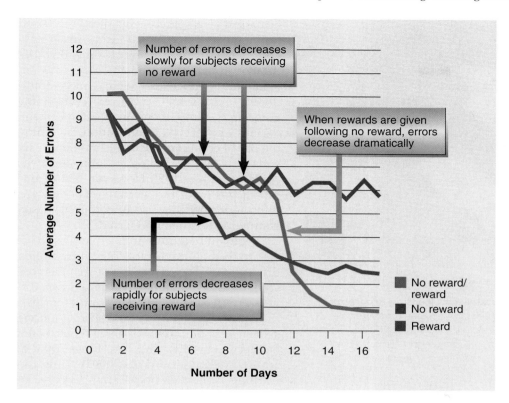

FIGURE 5.13
The Role of Cognitive Processes in Learning
Performance for rats in the no-reward/reward group improved dramatically immediately after the introduction of the food reward. Because the improvement was so dramatic, these data suggest that the animals "learned" something during previous trials—even though they received no reward for their efforts. Tolman used this as evidence for the importance of cognitive processes in learning, suggesting that the rats may have formed a "cognitive map."
Source: Based on data from Tolman & Honzik, 1930.

How do we account for these results? An explanation based on reinforcement alone is not sufficient; the performance of the third group was too sudden. Obviously, the rats had learned something in the previous trials. Tolman and others point to these data, and to the results of other studies (e.g., Colwill & Rescorla, 1985, 1988), as evidence for the importance of cognitive processes in learning. In fact, Tolman theorized that the rats may have formed what he termed a *cognitive map*—a mental representation of the maze. Although the existence of such maps has not yet been clearly established, a growing body of evidence supports the view that animals do, in fact, form mental representations of their environment (Capaldi, Alpetekin, & Birmingham, 1997; Capaldi & Birmingham, 1998).

Applying Operant Conditioning: Solving Problems of Everyday Life

Because positive and negative reinforcement exert powerful effects on behavior, procedures based on operant conditioning have been applied in many practical settings—so many that it would be impossible to describe them all here. An overview of some of these uses will suffice, though.

First, principles of operant conditioning have been applied to the field of education. One of the most impressive operant-based teaching techniques involves the use of computers in the classroom—often termed *computer-assisted instruction,* or *CAI.* Research indicates that intelligent software can be programmed to successfully monitor, assess, diagnose, and remediate each student's performance on a variety of tasks (Salas & Cannon-Bowers, 2001). The success of CAI as a learning tool can be traced, at least in part, to the fact that it provides students with immediate and consistent feedback regarding their performance. CAI has been extended to enhance lecture-based distance education in which the instructor and learners are located at different sites throughout the world, but brought together through high-speed communication technologies. Other emerging technologies, such as

FIGURE 5.14
Operant Conditioning in Action: Graduated Licensing Programs
Learning principles are an important ingredient in graduated driver licensing (or GDL) programs. In GDL programs, teen drivers are given provisional licenses that allow them to drive unsupervised, but subject to certain restrictions. Advancement to full licensure is made contingent upon compliance with these restrictions and evidence of safe driving.

desktop video conferencing and Web-based training also offer the ability to reach anybody, anywhere, at nearly any time. But does the use of technology in the classroom enhance its effectiveness beyond more traditional instructional practices? When the criterion is comprehension or achievement, various approaches to education, including the use of computer-based technologies, fare equally well (e.g., Boling & Robinson, 1999; Andrews et al., 1999). However, if students' satisfaction with the learning experience is important, then the use of computer-based instruction is usually preferred.

Operant conditioning principles have also played an important role in promoting driver safety. For example, research has consistently shown that newly licensed teen drivers are overrepresented in traffic crashes. In fact, the per-mile fatal crash rate among sixteen-year-old drivers is three times that of eighteen-year-olds and ten times that of adults (McKnight & Peck, 2002). How can learning principles help? Traffic safety experts have used learning principles to develop graduated driver licensing (or GDL) programs (Waller, 2002; Williams, 2002). In GDL programs, teen drivers are given provisional licenses that allow them to drive unsupervised, but subject to requirements that reduce their exposure to risky situations, such as late-night driving and transporting other teens (please refer to Figure 5.14). Advancement to full licensure is made contingent upon compliance with the program's requirements and evidence of safe driving (e.g., no traffic violations and the consistent use of their safety belt while driving). Evaluation research has shown a reduction in teen crashes in states where GDL has been implemented (Shope & Molnar, 2002).

Finally, principles of operant conditioning have been applied in interventions for solving socially significant issues in our communities, such as crime, energy conservation and recycling, health care issues, consumer affairs, and safety promotion (Geller, 1996; Hickman & Geller, 2003; Greene et al., 1987).

Some efforts to increase recycling behavior, for example, have focused on manipulating the consequences consumers receive for recycling (Oskamp et al., 1994). In one study, Geller and his colleagues (1975) showed that paper recycling on a college campus increased as a function of a recycling contest between dormitories and delivery of raffle tickets to individuals who participated. In another study, Jacobs and Bailey (1982) increased participation in recycling programs in a residential community through the use of a lottery and monetary rewards. Other researchers have shown that merely arranging features of the environment to make recycling easier also seems to work. For example, scheduling recycling pickups to coincide with garbage collection days, providing free recycling bins, and arranging the placement of collection bins to make recycling more convenient all tend to increase recycling (e.g., Kalsher et al., 1993; Reid et al., 1979).

Operant conditioning principles have also formed the basis of interventions designed to increase people's use of safety belts (e.g., Geller, 1996). Some studies have tried to accomplish this goal through the use of rewards, whereas others have focused on the use of punishment—typically in the form of a traffic ticket and a fine for nonuse. Both approaches tend to increase safety belt use, although the effectiveness of programs involving punishment tends to vary with the intensity and consistency of enforcement. For example, in one example of the punishment approach, the New York State Police launched a high-intensity enforcement program during the spring of 1999 in Elmira, New York, termed the "Buckle Up Now!" program (Williams et al., 2000). Following the introduction of the program, safety belt use increased from 69 percent to 90 percent, illustrating the powerful effects of operant conditioning principles. In short, these principles can be useful in helping to solve many important problems of everyday life. For information on how operant conditioning principles can be used to help enhance your study habits, please refer to the following **Psychology Lends a Hand** feature.

KEY QUESTIONS

- What evidence supports the involvement of cognitive factors in operant conditioning?
- Why is knowledge of operant conditioning important?

psychology lends a hand

On Becoming a Better Student: Using Learning Principles to Improve Your Study Habits

Over the years, I've noted that many students report that the job of "student" is a difficult one. Why? The reasons they offer are varied, but the most common answer seems to suggest their difficulties stem, at least in part, from poor study habits. Many of the learning principles in this chapter can be useful in helping to enhance study skills—we've included a few of these here. Following these tips may lead to better academic performance and an enhanced learning experience.

1. Shaping—one step at a time. Your current study habits did not develop overnight. It is therefore reasonable to expect that developing new ones will also take time. Trying to do too much at first can punish your efforts and quickly lead to failure. To avoid this pitfall, start slowly. You may want to begin, for example, by establishing a fixed time each day for studying. Over time, you can slowly increase the amount of time you spend studying.

2. Use contingent rewards to maintain your study behavior. As the information in this chapter suggests, many forms of behavior (including studying) are governed by their consequences. But remember, where people are concerned, many individual differences exist. A stimulus that functions as a reinforcer for one person may fail to operate in a similar manner for another person, or at a different time. So, choose rewards that are meaningful to you and make access to these rewards contingent upon successful completion of your study goals. It is also important to select rewards that are consistent with these goals (e.g., taking time out to exercise or seeing a movie with friends), not ones that could serve to undermine your study efforts (e.g., consum-

ing alcohol; staying out too late on a school night). Over time, you may find that the positive feedback you receive from your instructors may also help to maintain your motivation to study.

3. Don't procrastinate. As you probably know, many people follow the path of least resistance and this holds true for studying. Doing a little bit of studying on a regular basis will more than offset the pain—and perhaps poor performance—that will come your way should you choose to put off studying or doing your homework until the last minute.

4. Arrange your environment wisely. Research on concurrent schedules of reinforcement and the matching law has helped to clarify why particular events are reinforcing at certain times and in certain contexts but not others. Applied to studying, this suggests that sitting down to study on a particular night may not seem so bad if nothing else is going on. So, plan ahead and avoid scheduling your study sessions during periods that compete with other more desirable activities (e.g., a social event or favorite television program). Or better yet, make your participation in these activities contingent upon completion of your homework or studying, a practical application of another principle we discussed earlier, the Premack principle.

5. Ask for help. Many students get into trouble because they don't ask their instructors for help. If you are having difficulty understanding an assignment or the material in a particular class, make an appointment with the course instructor and ask for help. You'll be surprised at how quickly doing so can get you back on track!

OBSERVATIONAL LEARNING: LEARNING FROM THE BEHAVIOR AND OUTCOMES OF OTHERS

In the opening story of this chapter, I recounted my experience in learning proper etiquette in a restaurant in a foreign country. You, too, have probably encountered numerous situations in which you have acquired new information, forms of behavior, or even abstract rules and concepts from watching the actions of other people and the consequences they experience. Such **observational learning** is a third major way we learn, and it is a common part of everyday life (Bandura, 1977, 1986). Indeed, a large body of evidence suggests it can play a role in nearly every aspect of behavior.

More formal evidence for the existence of observational learning has been provided by hundreds of studies, many of them performed with children. Perhaps the most famous of these studies are the well-known "Bobo doll" experiments conducted by Bandura and his colleagues (e.g., Bandura, Ross, & Ross, 1963). In these studies one group of nursery-school children saw an adult engage in aggressive actions against a large inflated Bobo doll. The adult who was serving as a model knocked the doll down, sat on it, insulted it verbally, and repeatedly punched it in the nose. Another group of children was exposed to a model who behaved in a quiet, nonaggressive manner. Later, both groups of youngsters were placed in a room with several toys, including a Bobo doll. Careful observation of their behavior revealed that those who had seen the aggressive adult model often imitated this person's behavior: They too punched the toy, sat on it, and even uttered verbal comments similar to those of the model. In contrast, children in the control group rarely if ever demonstrated such actions. While you may not find these results surprising, they may be significant in relation to the enduring controversy over whether children acquire new ways of aggressing through exposure to violent television programs and movies. We'll return to this issue shortly. For the moment, let's consider the nature of observational learning itself.

Observational Learning: Some Basic Principles

Given that observational learning exists, what factors and conditions determine whether, and to what extent, we acquire behaviors, information, or concepts from others? The following four factors appear to be the most important (Bandura, 1986).

First, in order to learn through observation, you must direct your *attention* to appropriate *models*—that is, to other persons performing an activity. And, as you might expect, you don't choose such models at random but focus most attention on people who are attractive to you; on people who possess signs of knowing what they're doing, such as status or success; and on people whose behavior seems relevant to your own needs and goals (Baron, 1970).

Second, you must be able to *remember* what the persons have said or done. Only if you can retain some representation of their actions in memory can you perform similar actions at later times or acquire useful information from them.

Third, you need to be able to convert these memory representations into appropriate actions. This aspect of observational learning is termed *production processes*. Production processes depend on (1) your own physical abilities—if you can't perform the behavior in question, having a clear representation of it in memory is of little use; and (2) your capacity to monitor your own performance and adjust it until it matches that of the model.

Finally, *motivation* plays a role. We often acquire information through observational learning but do not put it into immediate use in our own behavior. That is why we define learning as a relatively permanent change in behavior, or *behavior*

Observational Learning
The acquisition of new forms of behavior, information, or concepts through exposure to others and the consequences they experience.

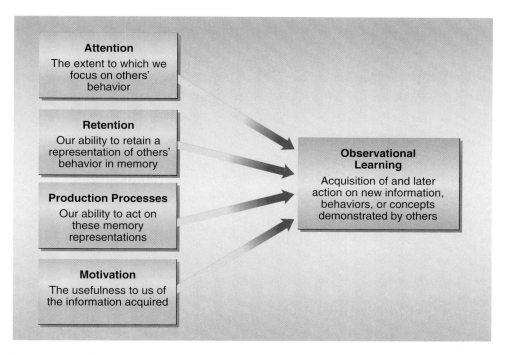

FIGURE 5.15
Key Factors in Observational Learning
Observational learning is affected by several factors or subprocesses. The most important of these are summarized here.

potential, produced by experience. You may have no need for the information, as when you watch someone tie a bow tie but have no plans to wear one yourself. Or the observed behaviors may involve high risk of punishment or be repugnant to you personally, as when you observe an ingenious way of cheating during an exam but don't want to try it yourself. Only if the information or behaviors acquired are useful will observers put them to actual use. Figure 5.15 summarizes factors affecting observational learning.

As you can see, observational learning is a complex process—far more complex than mere imitation—and plays an important role in many aspects of behavior. This point is perhaps most forcefully illustrated by the controversy that has persisted in psychology, and in society as a whole, since the early 1960s: whether children, and perhaps even adults, are made more aggressive by long-term exposure to violence on television shows or in movies.

Observational Learning and Aggression

The *National Television Violence Study* (1996, 1997) analyzed nearly 4,500 hours of programming on cable and broadcast television and found that approximately 60 percent of these programs contained some form of violence. But does merely watching violence on television lead people to commit similar acts?

A large body of research indicates that aggression may indeed be learned through observation (Baron & Richardson, 1994; Centerwall, 1989; Snyder, 1991; Wood, Wong, & Chachere, 1991). Apparently, when children and adults are exposed to new ways of aggressing against others—techniques they have not previously seen—they may add these new behaviors to their repertoires (please refer to Figure 5.16 on page 156). Later, when angry, irritated, or frustrated, they may put such behaviors to actual use in assaults against others. Research also

FIGURE 5.16
Observational Learning and Aggression
Experts continue to worry that exposure to violence on television and in movies may encourage children to perform violent acts. Research on this topic suggests that the negative effects of exposure to violence may be most pronounced for individuals who are highly aggressive by nature.

suggests that the negative effects of exposure to violence may be most pronounced for individuals who are highly aggressive by nature. Bushman (1995), for example, showed that participants who scored higher on a measure of aggressive tendencies were more likely to choose a violent film to watch, more likely to *feel* angry after watching it, and more likely to commit aggressive acts after viewing videotaped violence than their less aggressive counterparts.

Of course, exposure to media violence, whether on the evening news or in movies or television programs, has other effects as well. It may convey messages that violence is an acceptable means of handling interpersonal difficulties, particularly if children identify with the violent characters; after all, if heroes and heroines can do it, why not viewers (Huesmann et al., 2003)? It may elicit additional aggressive ideas and thoughts, convincing viewers, for example, that violence is even more common than it actually is (Berkowitz, 1984). And it may also lessen emotional reactions to aggression and the harm it produces, so that such outcomes seem less upsetting or objectionable (Thomas, 1982). When these effects are coupled with new behaviors and skills acquired through observational learning, the overall impact may contribute to an increased tendency among many persons to engage in acts of aggression (Eron, 1987; Eron et al., 1996).

It is important to note that not all findings support such conclusions (Freedman, 1986; Widom, 1989) and that the effects of exposure to media violence, when they occur, seem to be modest in scope. In addition, some evidence suggests that those concerned about the effects of televised violence may be getting help from companies who sponsor these shows. For example, in one study, the presence of violence actually *decreased* viewers' memories of brand names and commercial messages (Bushman, 1998). Thus, sponsoring violent programs on television might not be a profitable venture for advertisers, which may help to reduce the proliferation of these types of shows.

However, given the fact that many children spend a significant amount of time watching television, playing violent video games, and more recently, surfing the Web, the potential influence of such experiences on behavior seems worthy of careful attention.

Observational Learning and Culture

As we've already noted, observational learning plays an important role in many aspects of behavior. Much of our understanding of the world around us—including our language and customs—comes to us by observing the behaviors of others around us. Psychologists have applied principles of observational learning to help companies throughout the world prepare their employees for the business environment of the new millennium—an environment that will require a broad range of skills and the ability to interact effectively with persons from other cultures (Adler & Bartholomew, 1992; Feldman & Tompson, 1993). Dramatic differences in language, customs, and lifestyle often lead to unintended misunderstandings between persons from different cultural backgrounds. Behaviors that are acceptable in one country may be quite offensive to persons from another country.

To soften the effects of culture shock, experts in the area of cross-cultural training have advocated an experiential approach based on behavioral modeling (Black & Mendenhall, 1990). Trainees first watch films in which models exhibit the correct behaviors in a problem situation. Then, they participate in a situation role play exercise to test their knowledge. Finally, they receive constructive feedback regarding their performance.

Some evidence suggests that this approach can be quite effective. In one study, Harrison (1992) compared the effectiveness of several approaches to cross-cultural training: One group of participants received culture-relevant information only; another received behavioral modeling training only; a third received both components; and a fourth, the control group, received no training. The results showed that participants who received both forms of training—information and behavioral modeling—performed best on measures of culture-specific knowledge and on a behavioral measure.

These findings illustrate the important role that observational learning plays in alleviating the effects of culture shock. It initially enables us to perform behaviors appropriate to our own cultures, but later helps us to adapt to the demands of a rapidly changing world.

Observational Learning: Some Practical Applications

As you can see from the previous discussions, the effects of observational learning on our behavior can indeed be powerful—and not always for the good. For example, observational learning may contribute to the development of unhealthy behaviors, including smoking, especially among adolescents (Hahn et al., 1990). Because acceptance by peers is so important to persons in this age group, it is possible that observing peers who smoke contributes to their own decisions to start smoking (Hawkins, Catalano, & Miller, 1992). Some evidence seems to indicate this is true (e.g., Aloise-Young, Graham, & Hansen, 1994).

Fortunately, there is also a large body of evidence showing that peer influence can also be used to promote more productive behaviors (please refer to Figure 5.17 on page 158). In one interesting study, Werts and her colleagues (1996) examined whether mildly retarded children enrolled in a regular classroom could acquire skills by having their nondisabled peers model the skills for them. The to-be-learned

FIGURE 5.17
Modeling Appropriate Behaviors Can Make a Difference
People, particularly young persons, can often be influenced in positive ways when they have appropriate role models to emulate.

skills included spelling their name, using a calculator to perform simple arithmetic, and sharpening a pencil. The results revealed that the disabled children learned the skills in a relatively short period of time (less than a month). It is noteworthy that the time the peers spent modeling the behaviors averaged about five minutes per day, suggesting that observational learning can be an efficient tool in the learning process. To summarize, then, observational learning plays an important role in many aspects of behavior.

KEY QUESTIONS

- What is observational learning?
- What factors determine the extent to which we acquire new information through observational learning?
- In what forms of behavior does observational learning play a role?
- In what ways can observational learning be used to solve problems of everyday life?

SUMMARY AND REVIEW OF KEY QUESTIONS

Classical Conditioning: Learning That Some Stimuli Signal Others

- **What is learning?**
  Learning is any relatively permanent change in behavior (or behavior potential) produced by experience.

- **What is classical conditioning?**
  Classical conditioning is a form of learning in which neutral stimuli (stimuli initially unable to elicit a particular response) come to elicit that response through their association with stimuli that are naturally able to do so.

- **Upon what factors does acquisition of a classically conditioned response depend?**
  Acquisition is dependent upon the temporal arrangement of the CS-UCS pairings, the intensity of the CS and UCS

relative to other background stimuli, and the familiarity of potentially conditioned stimuli present.

- **What is extinction?**
  Extinction is the process through which a conditioned stimulus gradually ceases to elicit a conditioned response when it is no longer paired with an unconditioned stimulus. However, this ability can be quickly regained through reconditioning.

- **What is the difference between stimulus generalization and stimulus discrimination?**
  Stimulus generalization allows us to apply our learning to other situations; stimulus discrimination allows us to differentiate among similar but different stimuli.

- **Where in the brain does classical conditioning take place?**
  Research shows that the cerebellum, a structure in the brain involved in balance and coordination, plays a key role in the formation of simple forms of classically conditioned responses. Other brain structures known to be involved include the hippocampus, amygdala, and brainstem areas that project to or receive information from these structures.

- **Is classical conditioning equally easy to establish with all stimuli for all organisms?**
  Because of biological constraints that exist among different species, types of conditioning readily accomplished by some species are only slowly acquired—or not acquired at all—by others.

- **How do we acquire conditioned taste aversions?**
  Conditioned taste aversions are usually established when a food or beverage (conditioned stimulus) is paired with a stimulus that naturally leads to feelings of illness (unconditioned stimulus). Conditioned taste aversions can be established after a single CS-UCS pairing.

- **How do modern views of classical conditioning differ from earlier perspectives?**
  Modern views of classical conditioning emphasize the important role of cognitive processes. Research shows that conditioning is a complex process in which organisms form mental representations of the relationships among a variety of factors.

- **What is blocking?**
  In blocking, conditioning to one stimulus is prevented by previous conditioning to another stimulus.

- **How can classical conditioning principles solve problems of everyday life?**
  Basic principles of classical conditioning have been used to solve a variety of everyday problems, including phobias (learned fears) and unexplained instances of drug overdose. They can also be used to enhance aspects of the immune system.

Operant Conditioning: Learning Based on Consequences

- **What is operant conditioning?**
  In operant conditioning, organisms learn the relationships between certain behaviors and the consequences they produce.

- **What are examples of primary reinforcers? Of conditioned reinforcers?**
  Primary reinforcers include food, water, and sexual pleasure; conditioned reinforcers include money, status, and praise.

- **Which operant techniques strengthen behavior? Weaken behavior?**
  Both positive and negative reinforcement strengthen or increase behavior. In contrast, positive and negative punishment are procedures that suppress or weaken behavior.

- **How do negative reinforcement and punishment differ?**
  Both negative reinforcement and punishment involve aversive events. They differ, however, in terms of their effects on behavior: Negative reinforcement is a procedure in which behaviors that allow an organism to escape from an aversive event, or to avoid it altogether, are *strengthened*. Punishment is a procedure in which an aversive event *weakens* the behavior it follows.

- **What are shaping and chaining?**
  Shaping is useful for establishing new responses by initially reinforcing behaviors that resemble the desired behavior, termed *successful approximations*. Chaining is a procedure used to establish a complex sequence or chain of behaviors.

- **How does reward delay affect operant conditioning? What are the effects of procrastination?**
  When asked to choose between a smaller-but-sooner and a larger-but-later reward, people often choose the former option, a tendency termed *impulsiveness*. People exhibit a similar tendency when faced with a choice between performing a smaller, less effortful task now and performing a larger, more effortful task later on: They *procrastinate*, choosing the more delayed alternative, even when it leads to more work, lower performance, and illness.

- **What are schedules of reinforcement?**
  Schedules of reinforcement are rules that determine the occasion on which a response will be reinforced. Schedules of reinforcement can be time based or event based, fixed or variable. Each schedule of reinforcement produces a characteristic pattern of responding.

- **When is the use of continuous reinforcement desirable?**
  A continuous reinforcement schedule is desirable for establishing new behaviors; partial or intermittent schedules of reinforcement are more powerful in maintaining behavior.

- **What are concurrent schedules of reinforcement and the matching law?**
  In a concurrent schedule, an organism's behavior is free to alternate between two or more responses, each of which has its own schedule of reinforcement. The matching law suggests that an organism distributes its behavior among response alternatives such that it maximizes the reinforcement it receives from each alternative.

- **What is a discriminative stimulus?**
  Discriminative stimuli signal the availability of specific consequences if a certain response is made. When a behavior occurs consistently in the presence of a discriminative stimulus, it is said to be under stimulus control.

- **What evidence supports the involvement of cognitive factors in operant conditioning?**
  Studies of learned helplessness and the presence of a genetically inherited impairment in the ability to experience pleasure, contrast effects, and memory of reward events support the conclusion that cognitive factors play an important role in operant conditioning.

- **Why is knowledge of operant conditioning important?**
  Procedures based on operant conditioning principles can be applied to address many problems of everyday life—for example, in improving classroom instructional technology, in promoting driver safety, and in the development of interventions to solve community-based problems, such as crime, health care, and safety.

Observational Learning: Learning from the Behavior and Outcomes of Others

- **What is observational learning?**
  Observational learning is the acquisition of new information, concepts, or forms of behavior through exposure to others and the consequences they experience.

- **What factors determine the extent to which we acquire new information through observational learning?**
  For observational learning to be effective, we must pay attention to those modeling the behavior, remember the modeled speech or action, possess the ability to act on this memory, and have the motivation to do so.

- **In what forms of behavior does observational learning play a role?**
  Observational learning plays an important role in many types of behavior, including aggression.

- **In what ways can observational learning be used to solve problems of everyday life?**
  Observational learning can play an important role in work settings; for example, in training workers to interact more effectively with people from different cultural backgrounds. It can also play a role in the development of both appropriate and inappropriate forms of behavior.

PSYCHOLOGY: UNDERSTANDING ITS FINDINGS

Using Learning Principles in Everyday Life

Throughout this chapter, we have discussed several basic principles of learning and shown their usefulness for solving a variety of important problems of everyday life. You may recall from our discussions that one of these procedures—punishment—while useful in certain specific situations, can often have a host of negative side effects. Do the following exercises to see how alternatives to punishment can be useful in your own life.

1. Think of situations in which you may have inadvertently used punishment (e.g., saying something negative to a friend to get them to stop an annoying behavior) or have been on the receiving end of someone else who has used this technique with you. Now, try to think of other procedures we've discussed that might have been more effective alternatives. (Hint: you may want to consider procedures for rewarding behaviors that are incompatible with the undesirable behavior—a procedure that psychologists refer to as *differential reinforcement of other behavior*, or *DRO*). Now, try these procedures the next time the occasion arises. Were they effective?

2. Are there certain goals that you would like to accomplish? For example, developing better study habits or learning to budget your money more effectively? Write each goal on a piece of paper and then think of how the learning principles we've discussed could be used to reach your goals. (Hint: Do you think the shaping, stimulus, control, and schedules of reinforcement might be useful concepts?). Be sure to track your progress!

MAKING PSYCHOLOGY PART OF YOUR LIFE

Getting in Shape: Using Principles of Learning to Get Fit . . . and Stay Fit

Although it is well known that keeping fit is important to good health, a report from the U.S. Surgeon General suggests that staying in shape may help offset some less healthy behaviors, such as smoking, drinking alcohol, or overeating. Apparently, people who overindulge but exercise regularly may be less at risk for premature death than people who appear fit but are couch potatoes. If you need to get back into shape or lose a pound (or twenty), why not make learning principles a part of your fitness system?

First, it is important to *set realistic goals* (see Chapter 10 for additional information on goal setting). Don't try to lose all twenty pounds in one week, or try to run ten miles the first time out. Why not? If you recall our discussion of reinforce-ment and punishment, you'll recognize that doing so will actually punish your efforts, making it even more difficult to stay with your program. If you've tried and failed to stick with a diet or exercise program in the past because of this, you can probably appreciate what we're saying.

Second, set yourself up for small wins by taking advantage of the principle of *shaping*—rewarding yourself initially with modest rewards for successive approximations to your ultimate exercise and weight-reduction goals. Then, slowly increase the amount of exercise that you do or the amount of weight that you lose, building on each of your previous successes.

Third, take care in your selection of rewards—choose ones that are desirable but consistent with your goals. For example, if you are trying to lose weight, reward yourself with a movie or clothes with a smaller waist size, not with a hot fudge sundae!

Fourth, be sure to specify the amount and intensity of the exercise you will do or the amount of weight you intend to lose—and write it down. Some people find that it is helpful to chart their progress in order to receive accurate and immediate feedback regarding their progress—feedback that will serve to reinforce or punish their behavior. Also, by placing the chart in a prominent place for yourself, your spouse, or other family members to see, you can work to receive the positive attention that will come your way as a result of making progress. Negative reinforcement may also help keep you on track with your fitness system. By posting your progress publicly you can work to *avoid* the negative feelings that may occur should you be tempted to take a day off.

Fifth, stimulus control can play an important role in setting the occasion for healthy responses. Avoid being in places at times when you may be tempted to consume unhealthy food or beverages; instead, go to places (e.g., a health club) and associate with people who are likely to occasion healthy responses.

Finally, take advantage of the principles of observational learning by identifying people with traits and skills that you admire. By observing and then emulating their behaviors, you may become more efficient in reaching your goals. So, make psychology a part of your fitness system—to get fit and stay fit!

KEY TERMS

6

Memory: Of Things Remembered . . . and Forgotten

Several years ago, I (Robert Baron) was having a conversation with my father, and I asked him, "What ever happened to great-grandfather's uniform?" (My great-grandfather had been an officer in a European Army before he came to the United States, and I had vivid memories of his uniform.) My father looked puzzled for a moment and then said, "Grandfather threw it away in the 1930s—when I was in high school, so I don't think you could ever have seen it." "You must be mistaken, Dad," I replied. "I remember it very well. It was black and had gold braid on the right shoulder." My father agreed that I was correct but repeated his belief that I could never have seen it, because it was gone long before I was born. I was sure he was mistaken, because I could visualize the uniform perfectly, hanging there in my grandfather's closet. I remembered how it felt and how it smelled (of mothballs), and wanting to play with the medals. To this day, I have never solved this mystery: Did I ever see my great-grandfather's uniform? Or was my memory playing tricks on me?

As this incident suggests, **memory** is indeed a tricky thing: We forget information we would like to remember, only to have it pop into our minds at a later time—perhaps when we don't need it so much! We remember experiences we would prefer to forget; and sometimes we "remember" events that could never possibly have happened to us. So memory is certainly not a perfect system for retaining information. Yet, life without it would be impossible. If we did not possess memory, we would be unable to remember the past, could not retain new information, solve problems, or plan for the future. Psychologists have long recognized the importance of memory. Indeed, it was the focus of some of the earliest research in the field, performed by Hermann Ebbinghaus (1885) one hundred and twenty years ago. What have we learned from these decades of scientific effort? A great deal. In fact, it is probably safe to say that we know more about memory than any other aspect of cognition. To provide you with an overview of this intriguing knowledge, we'll proceed as follows. First, we'll consider the picture of human memory that has emerged from psychological research—a picture suggesting that we possess several different kinds of memory rather than one. Next, we'll explore the nature and operation of each of these aspects of memory—working memory, memory for facts, memory for skills, and memory for events in our own lives. Please note that animals, too, have memories; in fact, chimpanzees can remember how many bananas are placed in two opaque containers and then choose the one with more bananas (Beran & Beran, 2004). After this, we'll examine *forgetting*—how information is lost from memory—and how, sometimes, information is distorted or changed over time so that, in a sense, it becomes less accurate. Next, we'll consider the role of memory in *everyday life*—for instance, how we remember to do things we plan to do—and memory for emotional events. Finally, we'll briefly consider memory *impairments* and what these tell us about the biological basis of memory.

HUMAN MEMORY: AN INFORMATION-PROCESSING APPROACH

Because we can't observe memory directly (even with modern brain scans), psychologists have found it useful to construct *models* of it—representations of how it functions and the systems it must include in order to produce the kind of effects that it does, for instance, long-term storage of vast amounts of information, and shorter-term storage of small amounts of information, such as a phone number you dial but then promptly forget (e.g., Anderson, 1993; Baadley & Hitsch, 1994; Raajimakers & Shiffrin, 1981). Many different models have been proposed, but one that has proven to be very useful is known as the **information-processing approach** (Atkinson & Shiffrin, 1968).

This model takes note of the fact that there are certain similarities between computer memory and human memory. For instance, both computer memory and human memory must perform three basic tasks: (1) **encoding**—converting information into a form that can be entered into memory, (2) **storage**—somehow retaining information over varying periods of time; and (3) **retrieval**—locating and accessing specific information when it is needed at later times (see Figure 6.1).

For computers, encoding involves complex programs that convert what you type on the computer keyboard into codes the program can process. For humans, encoding involves converting information brought from our senses into neural information that can be processed in our brains. Storage presents a more complex picture. Computers generally contain two kinds of systems for storing information: *random-access memory*—what's open on your desktop at any given moment—and a larger and more permanent memory in which information is stored for longer periods of time (a hard drive). The information-processing model of memory suggests that, in contrast, human memory involves *three* distinct systems for storing

Memory
Our cognitive system(s) for storing and retrieving information.

Information-Processing Approach
An approach to human memory that emphasizes the encoding, storage, and later retrieval of information.

Encoding
The process through which information is converted into a form that can be entered into memory.

Storage
The process through which information is retained in memory.

Retrieval
The process through which information stored in memory is located.

Sensory Memory
A memory system that retains representations of sensory input for brief periods of time.

Short-Term Memory
See Working Memory.

Long-Term Memory
A memory system for the retention of large amounts of information over long periods of time.

information. One of these, known as **sensory memory,** provides temporary storage of information brought to us by our senses. If you've ever watched someone wave a flashlight in a dark room and perceived trails of light behind it, you are familiar with the operation of sensory memory. A second type of memory is known as **short-term memory.** Short-term memory holds relatively small amounts of information for brief periods of time, usually thirty seconds or less. This is the type of memory system you use when you look up a phone number and dial it. Our third memory system, **long-term memory,** allows us to retain vast amounts of information for very long periods of time. It is this type of memory system that permits you to remember events that happened a few hours ago, yesterday, last month, or many years in the past. And it is long-term memory that allows you to remember factual information such as the capital of your state, the name of the president, and the information in this book.

With respect to retrieval, both computers and human memory must be able to find information that has previously been stored. Computer memory requires that you precisely specify the location of the information for it to be found. In contrast, you can often find information in your own memory, even on the basis of partial information ("I know his name . . . it rhymes with "home" . . . oh yeah, *Broam!*"). Also, when information is lost from computer memory, it is often lost permanently, or at least becomes very difficult to restore. In contrast, information we cannot retrieve from our own memories is often still present and sometimes pops into mind at a later time, when we are not actively trying to find it.

How does information move from one memory system to another? Although there's not complete agreement about this important point, much evidence suggests that information in sensory memory enters short-term memory when it becomes the focus of our attention, that is, when we notice it or concentrate on it. In contrast, information in short-term memory enters long-term storage through *elaborative rehearsal*—when we think about its meaning and relate it to other information already in long-term memory. Unless we engage in such cognitive effort, information in short-term memory too quickly fades away and is lost. (See Figure 6.1 for a summary of the information-processing model.)

In sum, the key points to remember are these: The *information-processing perspective* suggests that (1) memory involves encoding, storage, and retrieval of information; and (2) we possess several different kinds or types of memory. Though this model has proven very useful, we should note that it is certainly not the only one psychologists have found useful. In recent years, other views—especially, ones that emphasize the kind of *parallel processing* of information in our brains that we described in Chapter 2—have received growing attention. These models (e.g., Lindsay & Reed, 1995) suggest that because our brains process information in many locations at once, memories, too, must be represented in this manner and must involve activity in many different *modules* or *neural units* in the brain. Full description of these complex models is beyond the scope of this discussion, but we do want to note that a new picture of human memory that closely reflects our growing understanding of how our brains function to produce consciousness is emerging and is certain to become more influential in the years ahead.

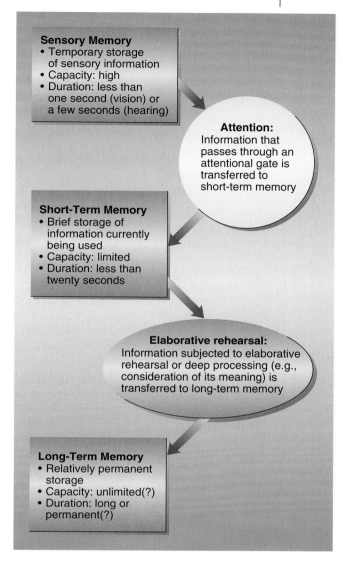

Sensory Memory
- Temporary storage of sensory information
- Capacity: high
- Duration: less than one second (vision) or a few seconds (hearing)

Attention: Information that passes through an attentional gate is transferred to short-term memory

Short-Term Memory
- Brief storage of information currently being used
- Capacity: limited
- Duration: less than twenty seconds

Elaborative rehearsal: Information subjected to elaborative rehearsal or deep processing (e.g., consideration of its meaning) is transferred to long-term memory

Long-Term Memory
- Relatively permanent storage
- Capacity: unlimited(?)
- Duration: long or permanent(?)

FIGURE 6.1
Human Memory: The Information-Processing View

One view of memory (the information-processing perspective) suggests that we possess three basic memory systems: sensory memory, short-term memory, and long-term memory. Each of these systems must deal with the tasks of encoding information, storing it, and retrieving it when needed.

Source: Based on suggestions by Atkinson & Shiffrin, 1968.

KEY QUESTIONS
- According to the information-processing model, what key tasks are carried out by memory?
- What are sensory memory, short-term memory, and long-term memory?

OUR DIFFERENT MEMORY SYSTEMS

As you already know from your own experience, your memory holds many kinds of information. Some of it is factual and relates either to (1) *general information* you can remember (e.g., "Hawaii is located in the Pacific Ocean," and "George Washington was the first President of the United States") or (2) events and experiences in your own life that you can recall (e.g., "I really liked my first grade teacher," "I saw my friend Joe this morning for the first time in more than two months"). But your memory holds much more than factual information. Can you play a musical instrument? Ride a bicycle? If so, you realize that you also have another, distinctly different type of information stored in memory—information that allows you to perform such activities. And here's the interesting point: Although you can verbally state that your friend is moving or that Hawaii is in the middle of the ocean, you really can't describe the information that allows you to play the piano or guitar, to ride your bicycle without hands (don't do it!), or type without thinking of individual keys (see Figure 6.2). And what about information in memory that tells you when to do something, for instance, take your medicine, leave for school or work, and so on? This is yet another kind of information stored in memory until it is needed. So memory actually holds several kinds of information. We'll now examine the memory systems that allow us to store these different kinds of information.

Working Memory: The Workbench of Consciousness

Working Memory

A memory system in which information we are processing at the moment is held; formerly called *short-term memory*. Recent findings suggest that it involves more complex levels and forms of processing than was previously believed.

Have you ever had the following kind of experience? You obtain some useful piece of information—a telephone number, a personal identification code, a word in a foreign language—and can use it right after you see or hear it. But then, a few minutes later, it is totally gone and you can't remember it no matter how hard you try. What's going on here? What happened to that wonderful system we term *memory*? The answer involves the operation of what psychologists term **working memory.** Initially, this term and *short-term memory* were used interchangeably, but now memory experts generally distinguish between them. Short-term memory, as we saw earlier, refers to the temporary storage of information. In contrast, the term *work-*

FIGURE 6.2
Memory for Different Kinds of Information
We store many kinds of information in memory—factual information about the world around us and information that permits us to perform many kinds of skilled actions. Although we can readily describe the first type of information, we usually find it difficult to put the second type into words.

ing memory involves both storage capacity *and* a mechanism of attention that regulates the contents of this system (Engle, 2001). In a sense, working memory is the "workbench" of consciousness—the "place" where information we are using *right now* is held and processed. Let's take a look, first, at short-term memory, and then at how working memory operates.

Short-Term Memory: How Much Can It Hold?

Initial research on short-term memory focused on the following question: How much can it hold? Research findings suggested a clear answer: As a storage system, short-term memory can hold only about seven (plus or minus two) discrete items. Beyond that point, the system was overloaded, and if new information entered, existing information was lost (e.g., Miller, 1956). However, each of these "items" can contain several separate bits of information—bits that are somehow related and can be grouped together into meaningful units. When this is the case, each piece of information is described as a *chunk,* and the total amount of information held in chunks can be quite large. For example, consider the following list of letters: IBFIMBWBMATWIAC. After hearing or reading it once, how many could you remember? Probably no more than about seven. But imagine that, instead, the letters were presented as follows: FBI, IBM, BMW, TWA, CIA. Could you remember more now? In all likelihood you could, because now you could combine them into meaningful chunks—acronyms for famous organizations. Because of the process of *chunking,* short-term memory can hold a larger amount of information than you might guess, even though it can retain only seven to nine separate items at once.

Working Memory: Short-Term Storage with a Very Important Plus

If all short-term memory could do is store small amounts of information for limited periods of time, it would not be very interesting. But in fact, this aspect of our memory is much more than simply a temporary holding place for incoming information. On the contrary, active processing of information occurs in it as well—processing that may well determine how effectively we can perform very complex tasks such as reasoning (Engle et al., 1999). This is why psychologists now distinguish between short-term memory and working memory; the later term suggests that something *active* is happening, and, in fact, it is. Not only does working memory store information, it also involves a mechanism of attention that permits us to determine *what* information is retained in short-term storage and what information is ignored or actively blocked from entry. In fact, one influential model of working memory (Baddeley, 1992) suggests that working memory involves three different parts: (1) temporary storage of information (short-term memory), (2) a mechanism that permits rehearsal of this information so that is maintained and perhaps moves into long-term storage, and (3) a mechanism of attention that permits some information to enter while ignoring other information (see Figure 6.3 on page 168).

The third of these components—the attentional mechanism—has important implications not just for memory, but for our ability to perform a wide range of complex cognitive tasks. To understand why, first consider the fact that *working memory capacity* (or span) is not the same as *short-term memory capacity.* Short-term memory capacity refers to the amount of information people can retain for brief periods of time. Working-memory capacity, in contrast, refers to the ability to use attention to maintain or suppress information—in essence, to pay attention to what it is important to remember. For instance, one measure of working memory capacity is obtained in the following manner. Individuals read sentences out loud, with each sentence being followed by an unrelated word. After the last sentence–word combination, they try to recall the list of unrelated words. The more they can recall, the higher their working memory capacity.

Now, here's the truly interesting part: the higher individuals' working memory capacity (as measured by tasks such as this one), the better their performance on complex cognitive tasks such as following directions, understanding complex

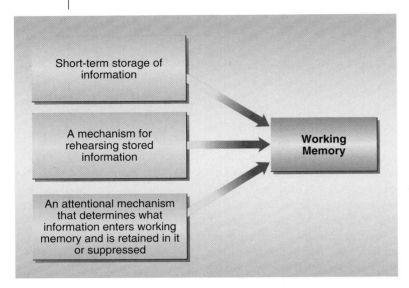

FIGURE 6.3
A Model of Working Memory

One modern model of working memory suggests that it involves the three distinct components shown here.

Source: Based on suggestions by Baddeley, 1992.

written passages, writing, reasoning, and even writing computer programs (Engle, 2001). In other words, the ability to focus one's attention on what's important is related to an important aspect of general intelligence—fluid intelligence, the ability to think and reason.

Is working memory capacity really related to being able to focus our attention? Research findings indicate that it is. For instance, consider a task in which individuals read the names of various colors (e.g., red, green) printed in ink that is either the same color as the word (red ink for the word *red*) or a different color (green ink for the word *red*). Their task is to name the color of the ink. If the word and ink color are different, many errors occur: People say the word rather than name the color of the ink. Performance on this task should involve the ability to focus attention on what's important—in this case, the color of the ink—while ignoring the words themselves. In one recent study (Kane & Engle, 2001), the proportion of words in which the ink and word were different was varied (0 percent, 50 percent, 75 percent). If working memory capacity reflects an efficient attentional mechanism, then persons with high working memory capacity should do better on this task, especially when 75 percent of the color names are printed in a different color (e.g., the word *blue* in yellow). As you can see from Figure 6.4, that's exactly what happened.

Where does all this leave us? With a view of working memory as much more than a temporary "holding area" for information. In fact, it is our system for paying attention to what's most important with respect to a given task or situation. And this ability, it appears, is closely linked to our capacity to perform many complex cognitive tasks.

KEY QUESTIONS

- What is the difference between short-term memory and working memory?
- What are the three major components of working memory?

FIGURE 6.4
Working Memory Capacity: A Measure of the Ability to Focus Attention

Individuals with a high working memory span perform better on a task that requires them to focus their attention on one aspect of words—the color in which they are printed—while ignoring the words themselves. This suggests that working memory capacity (span) is closely related to the ability to focus attention on what is most important in a given situation.

Source: Based on data from Kane & Engle, 2001.

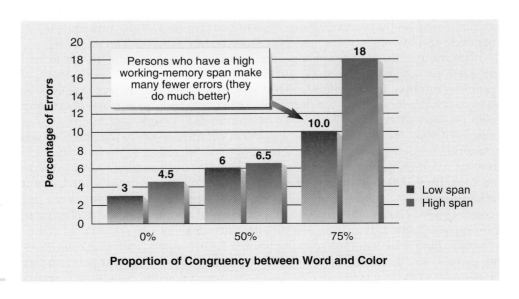

Memory for Factual Information: Episodic and Semantic Memory

Now that we have examined the nature of working memory, we'll turn to several aspects of long-term memory—our memory systems for retaining large amounts of information for long periods of time. We'll begin with the systems that permit us to retain factual information. As noted earlier, such information can relate to general knowledge about the world, which is stored in **semantic memory,** or to events that happen to us personally, which are stored in **episodic memory.** Let's take a closer look at both kinds of memory.

Episodic Memory: Some Factors that Affect It

As a student, you have lots of first-hand experience with the functioning of episodic memory. Often, you must memorize definitions, terms, or formulas. Such information is stored in episodic memory because we know that we learned it at a specific time, in a specific place (e.g., a course in college). What can you do to improve such memory? Research on semantic memory suggests that many factors influence it, but among these, the most important are the *amount and spacing of practice.* The first finding seems fairly obvious; the more often we practice information, the more of it we can retain. However, the major gains occur at first, and then further improvements in memory slow down. For this reason, spacing (or distribution) of practice is important, too. Therefore, spreading out your efforts to memorize information over time is helpful. For instance, two sessions of thirty minutes are often better, in terms of retaining information, than one session of sixty minutes.

Another factor that has a powerful effect on retention is the kind of processing we perform. When we study a list of words, we can simply read them or, alternatively, we can think about them in various ways. As you probably know from your own studying, it is possible to read the same pages in a text over and over again without remembering much of the information they contain. However, if you actively try to understand the material and think about it (e.g., its meaning, its relationship to other information), you stand a better chance of remembering it when the exam booklets are handed out.

Two psychologists, Craik and Lockhart (1972), took careful account of this fact in an influential view of memory known as the **levels of processing view.** They suggested that the more deeply information is processed, the more likely it is to be retained. What are these levels of processing like? *Shallow processing* involves little mental effort and might consist of repeating a word or making a simple sensory judgment about it—for example, do two words or letters look alike? A deeper level of processing might involve more complex comparisons—for example, do two words rhyme? A much deeper level of processing would include attention to meaning—for instance, do two words have the same meaning? Does a word make sense when used in a specific sentence?

Considerable evidence suggests that the deeper the level of processing that takes place when we encounter new information, the more likely it is to enter long-term memory. (e.g., Craik and Tulving, 1975). However, important questions still exist with respect to this model. For example, it is difficult to specify, in advance, just what constitutes a deep versus a shallow level of processing.

Another, and very important, factor that influences episodic memory involves what are known as **retrieval cues**—stimuli that are associated with information stored in memory and so can help bring it to mind at times when it cannot be recalled spontaneously. Many studies suggest that such cues can often help us remember; indeed, the more retrieval cues we have, the better our ability to remember information entered into episodic memory (e.g., Tulving & Watkins, 1973)—and they don't have to be as obvious as the ones shown in Figure 6.5 on page 170 to work! Perhaps the most intriguing research on this topic involves what

Semantic Memory
A memory system that stores general, abstract knowledge about the world—information we cannot remember acquiring at a specific time and place.

Episodic Memory
Memory for factual information that we acquired at a specific time.

Levels of Processing View
A view of memory suggesting that the greater the effort expended in processing information, the more readily it will be recalled at later times.

Retrieval Cues
Stimuli associated with information stored in memory that can aid in its retrieval.

FIGURE 6.5
Retrieval Cues: Usually—but Not Always—Helpful!

Retrieval cues, stimuli associated with information stored in memory, are often helpful in bringing such information to mind. They don't have to be this obvious to work!

Source: Reprinted with permission of King Features Syndicate.

is known as **context-dependent memory**—the fact that material learned in one environment or context is easier to remember in a similar context or environment than it is in a very different one. Many illustrations of this effect exist, but one of the most intriguing—and unusual—is a study conducted by Godden and Baddeley (1975).

In this experiment, participants were experienced deep-sea divers. They learned a list of words either on the beach or beneath fifteen feet of water. Then, they tried to recall the words either in the same environment in which they had learned them or in the other setting. Results offered clear support for the impact of context—in this case, physical setting. Words learned on land were recalled much better in this location than underwater, and vice versa. Interestingly, additional findings suggest that it is not necessary to be in the location or context where information was first entered into long-term memory; merely imagining this setting may be sufficient (Smith, 1979). In other words, we seem capable of generating our own context-related retrieval cues. So, if you study for an exam in your room, and then take the exam in a very different setting, it may be helpful to imagine yourself back in your room when you try to remember specific information. Doing so may provide you with additional, self-generated retrieval cues.

External cues are not the only ones that can serve as aids to memory, however; a growing body of evidence indicates that our own internal states can sometimes play this role, too. The most general term for this kind of effect is **state-dependent retrieval,** which refers to the fact that it is often easier to recall information stored in long-term memory when our internal state is similar to that which existed when the information was first entered into memory. For example, suppose that while studying for an exam, you drink lots of coffee. Thus, the effects of caffeine are present while you memorize the information in question. On the day of the test, should you also drink lots of coffee? The answer appears to be "yes," and not just for the boost in alertness the caffeine may provide. In addition, being in the same physical state may provide you with retrieval cues that may help boost your performance (Eich, 1985). The basic principle that underlies all these effects is sometimes described as the **encoding specificity principle:** Retrieval of information is successful to the extent that the retrieval cues match the cues the learner used during the study phase. The more these are similar, the more memory is facilitated.

Semantic Memory: How Information Is Organized in Memory

Now let's turn to semantic memory—memory for information we don't remember acquiring at a specific time or in a specific place. (For instance, can you remember when you first learned that drivers in the United States drive on the right?) Because each of us already possesses a very large amount of information in semantic memory, psychologists have focused primarily on how such information is organized, rather than on how it is entered into memory in the first place. One important basis of such organization is in terms of **concepts**—mental categories for objects or events that are similar to one another in certain ways. For instance, the words

---

Context-Dependent Memory
Refers to the fact that information entered into memory in one context or setting is easier to recall in that context than in others.

State-Dependent Retrieval
Occurs when aspects of our physical states serve as retrieval cues for information stored in long-term memory.

Encoding Specificity Principle
Retrieval of information is successful to the extent that the retrieval cues match the cues the learner used during the study phase.

Concepts
Mental categories for objects or events that are similar to one another in certain ways.

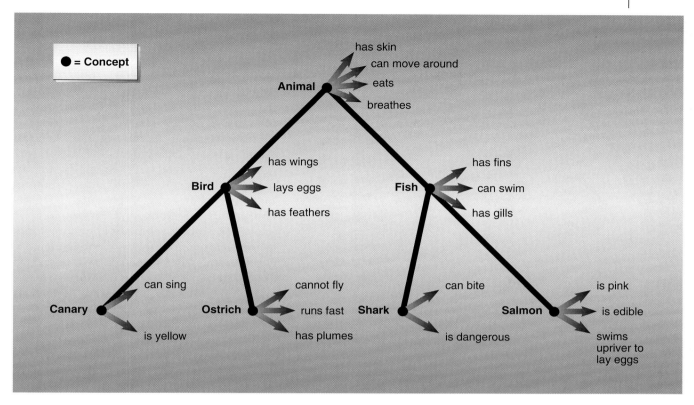

FIGURE 6.6
Semantic Networks

Semantic memory contains many concepts; these seem to exist in networks reflecting the relationships between them. One such network is shown here.

bicycle, airplane, automobile, and *elevator* are included in the concept for *vehicles* or *means of transportation.* The words *shoes, shirts, jeans,* and *jackets* are included in the concept of *clothing.*

Concepts in semantic memory seem to exist in networks reflecting the relationships between them—semantic networks. One such network is shown in Figure 6.6. As you can readily see, this illustration shows a hierarchy of concepts: *animals* includes both *birds* and *fish,* and *birds,* in turn, includes ostriches and canaries. Similarly, *fish* includes *sharks* and *salmon.* However, unless the person whose semantic memory is represented here is confused, it does *not* contain *porpoises,* because they are mammals, not fish.

Because both episodic memory and semantic memory hold factual information, how do we know that they are really separate memory systems? Because research evidence indicates that they are distinct. For example, in some medical patients, disease or operations that have damaged certain parts of the brain leave semantic memory intact while diminishing episodic memory, or vice versa (Schachter, 1996). In addition, other research using PET scans or recordings from individual brain cells indicate that different brain regions are active when individuals attempt to recall general information (from semantic memory) versus information they acquired in a specific context and that related to experiences in their own lives (from episodic memory; e.g., Kounious, 1996). So, there do seem to be grounds for the distinction between semantic memory and episodic memory.

K E Y   Q U E S T I O N S

- What are episodic memory and semantic memory?
- What is the levels of processing view?
- What are retrieval cues and what role do they play in memory?
- What are concepts and what role do they play in semantic memory?

FIGURE 6.7
Procedural Memory in Action
Skilled athletes can't readily describe how they excel in their sports—the knowledge they possess is stored in procedural memory, and so can't be readily expressed in words. That such knowledge exists, however, is indicated by their highly outstanding performances.

Procedural Memory
A memory system that retains information we cannot readily express verbally—for example, information necessary to perform various skilled motor activities, such as riding a bicycle. Also called *implicit memory.*

Implicit Memory
A memory system that stores information we cannot readily put into words and of which we may not be consciously aware. *See also* Procedural Memory.

Explicit Memory
Memory for information we are consciously aware of and can readily put into words.

Memory for Skills: Procedural Memory

Can you ride a bicycle? Most people can. But now, can you state, in words, how you perform this activity? Probably, you would find that hard to do. And the same principle applies to many other skills we have acquired—for instance, can a champion golfer like Tiger Woods explain how he hits the ball so far? Again, not very readily. Situations like this indicate that we often have information in memory that we can't readily put into words. Our ability to store such information is known as **procedural memory** or sometimes as **implicit memory** (both semantic memory and episodic memory, in contrast, described as being aspects of **explicit memory**—we can intentionally recall such information and can readily put it into words). Both terms are informative: We often know how to perform some action but can't describe this knowledge to others (e.g., can Mark McGwire tell us how he hits so many home runs?); what we can't put into words is, in one sense, implicit (see Figure 6.7).

Evidence for the existence of procedural memory is provided by the way in which many skills are acquired. Initially, as we learn a skill, we think about what we are doing and can describe our actions and what we are learning. As we master the skill, however, this declarative (explicit) knowledge is replaced by procedural knowledge, and we gradually become less and less able to describe precisely how we perform the actions in question (Anderson, 1993). (Recall our discussion of automatic processing in Chapter 4; procedural memory plays a role in such behavior.)

What about memory itself? Can it be viewed as a skill that can be improved? Absolutely. We'll examine some techniques for improving memory in the **Psychology Lends a Hand** section on page 187 but, for now, we should note that memory does indeed improve with practice. For instance, consider this incident: Just before a concert, a musician in the orchestra came to the great conductor Arturo Toscanini and told him that one of the keys on his instrument was broken. Toscanini thought for a moment and then said, "It is alright—that note does not occur in tonight's concert." In a flash, he had somehow examined all of the notes to be played and concluded that the broken key wouldn't matter! Could Toscanini explain how he did this? He was certainly demonstrating a very highly developed memory!

KEY QUESTION
• What is procedural memory?

FORGETTING: SOME CONTRASTING VIEWS

When are we most aware of memory? Typically, when it fails—when we are unable to remember information that we need at a particular moment. Often, it seems to let us down just when we need it most, for instance, during an exam! Why does this occur? Why is information entered into long-term memory sometimes lost, at least in part, with the passage of time? Many explanations have been offered, so here we'll focus on the ones that have received the most attention.

The earliest view of forgetting was that information entered into long-term memory fades or decays with the passage of time. While this seems to fit with our subjective experience, many studies indicate that the amount of forgetting is *not* simply a function of how much time has elapsed; rather, what happens during that period of time is crucial (e.g., Jenkins & Dallenbach, 1924). For instance, in one unusual study, Minami and Dallenbach (1946) taught cockroaches to avoid a dark compartment by giving them an electric shock whenever they entered it. After the subjects had mastered this simple task, they were either restrained in a paper cone or permitted to wander around a darkened cage at will. Results indicated that the insects permitted to move about showed more forgetting over a given period of time than those who were restrained. So, what the roaches did in between learning and testing for memory was more important than the mere passage of time. Perhaps even more surprising, other studies indicated that recall sometimes *improves* over time (e.g., Erdelyi & Kleinbard, 1978). So, early on, psychologists rejected the notion that forgetting stems from passive decay of memories over time and turned, instead, to the views we'll consider next.

Forgetting as a Result of Interference

If forgetting is not a function of the passage of time, then why does it occur? One possibility is that it stems mainly from *interference* between items of information stored in memory. Such interference can take two different forms. In **retroactive interference,** information currently being learned interferes with information already present in memory. If learning how to operate a new computer program causes you to forget how to operate one you learned previously, this would be an example of retroactive interference. In **proactive interference,** in contrast, previously learned information present in long-term memory interferes with information you are learning at present. Suppose you learned how to operate one DVD player; now you buy a new one that requires different steps for recording a television program. If you now make mistakes by trying to operate the new DVD player in the same way as your old one, this would constitute proactive interference (see Figure 6.8).

A large body of evidence offers support for the view that interference plays a key role in forgetting from long-term memory (e.g., Tulving & Psotka, 1971). For example, in many laboratory studies, the more similar the words or nonsense syllables participants learn from different lists, the more interference occurs among them, and the poorer their recall of these materials (Gruneberg, Morris, & Sykes, 1988). However, more recent findings raise complex questions about the view that forgetting derives mainly from interference. First, while interference does seem to play a major role in the forgetting of meaningless materials, such as nonsense syllables, it is far less important in the forgetting of meaningful passages. Memory for the basic meaning (i.e., the *gist*) of such passages is often retained even if the passages are quite similar to one another and would be expected to produce interference (e.g., Haberlandt, 1999). Similarly, for interference to occur, something that is potentially interfering must happen in the period between original learning and tests for memory. Yet, forgetting occurs even when individuals learn a single list or even a single item. Such forgetting might be due to interference from sources outside the experiment, but these have proven difficult to identify. Overall, then, interference, which was once viewed as *the* cause of forgetting, is no longer assigned this crucial role by most memory researchers. So what *does* cause forgetting? Recent research points to another, intriguing possibility.

Forgetting and Retrieval Inhibition

Suppose we asked you to remember the names of all fifty states in the United States. How many would you get right? Now, instead, imagine that we gave you the names of twenty-five of these states and let you study them. Would that help

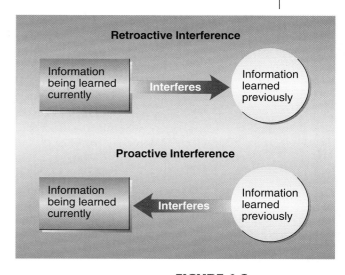

FIGURE 6.8
Retroactive and Proactive Interference
In *retroactive interference*, information currently being learned interferes with the retention of information acquired previously. In *proactive interference*, information learned previously interferes with the retention of new information currently being acquired and put into memory.

Retroactive Interference
Occurs when new information being entered into memory interferes with retention of information already present in memory.

Proactive Interference
Occurs when information previously entered into memory interferes with the learning or storage of current information.

you remember the remaining ones? Common sense suggests that it would, but research using procedures similar to these indicates that you would actually do *worse;* studying half the states would actually reduce your overall performance (e.g., Brown, 1968). Why? Psychologists explain this seemingly paradoxical finding as follows: When we attempt to remember information in memory, we may recall the items we seek but, at the same time, generate *inhibition* of the items we don't try to remember. As a result, these become more difficult to remember in the future. So, when you study the names of twenty-five states, you generate inhibition that blocks recall of the other twenty-five states. In short, the act of retrieval itself can cause forgetting—not of the information you recall, but of other, related information. This is known as **retrieval inhibition,** and its occurrence has been observed in several experiments (e.g., Anderson, Bjork, & Bjork, 1994; Anderson & Spellman, 1995). The results of these investigations suggest that inhibition produced when we actively try to retrieve information from memory may play an important role in forgetting.

In sum, at present psychologists believe that forgetting stems from several different factors. Interference may play a role, especially with respect to relatively meaningless materials, but other complex processes, such as inhibition generated by retrieval itself, may also contribute to our inability to remember information we would *like* to remember. We'll examine another view of forgetting—the idea that we *repress* memories we find painful or unpleasant—in a later discussion of memory for emotional events.

KEY QUESTIONS

- What is proactive interference? Retroactive interference? What roles do they play in forgetting?
- What is retrieval inhibition?

MEMORY DISTORTION AND MEMORY CONSTRUCTION

What happens to information once it is stored in memory? Our discussion up to this point seems to suggest two possible outcomes: It is stored in a permanent, unchanging form, or it is forgotten. But this is not the entire story; a growing body of evidence suggests a third possibility: Information entered into memory is often altered in various ways over time—alterations that can reduce its accuracy and change its meaning. Such changes take many different forms, but most fall under two major headings: memory *distortion*—alterations in information stored in memory, and memory *construction*—the addition of information that was not actually entered into memory (e.g., the construction of false memories; Toglia, Neuschatz, & Goodwin, 1999).

Distortion and the Influence of Schemas

Almost everyone has had first-hand experience with memory distortion. For example, have you ever met someone and then, several weeks or months later, run into them again? Perhaps you found that they now seemed taller (or shorter), younger (or older) than you remembered. Because physical attributes are fairly obvious and don't usually change much over short periods of time, it is likely that either your memory was faulty to start with or became distorted over time. Distortions in memory also occur in response to false or misleading information provided by others. If someone's comments suggest a fact or detail that is not present in our memories, we may add that fact or detail (Loftus, 1992). Unfortunately, such effects often occur during trials, when attorneys pose *leading questions* to witnesses— questions that encourage the witnesses to "remember" what the attorneys want them

Retrieval Inhibition
The inhibition of information in memory we don't try to remember produced by remembering other, related information.

to remember. For example, during a trial, an attorney may ask a witness, "Was the getaway car a light color or a dark color?" While the witness may not remember seeing a getaway car, the question puts subtle pressure on this person to answer—to make a choice. And once the answer is given, it may be incorporated into the witness's memories and tend to distort them. Unfortunately, such effects seem to occur even if individuals are warned about them and offered cash for resisting their influence (Belli & Loftus, 1996)! We'll return to such effects in a discussion of eye-witness testimony below.

What accounts for memory distortions? One important factor involves the operation of **schemas**—cognitive frameworks representing individuals' knowledge about some aspect of the world (Wyer & Srull, 1994). Schemas are developed through experience and act something like mental scaffolds, providing basic frameworks for processing new information and relating it to existing knowledge, including knowledge held in long-term memory.

Once schemas are formed, they exert strong effects on the way information is encoded, stored, and later retrieved. These effects, in turn, can lead to important errors or distortions in memory. Perhaps such effects are most apparent with respect to encoding. Current evidence suggests that once schemas have been formed, information consistent with them becomes easier to notice and remember than information that is inconsistent (e.g., Stangor & Ruble, 1989). It is the operation of schemas that, in part, accounts for the fact that in many cases we are more likely to notice and remember information that supports our beliefs about the world than information that challenges them.

Another important cause of distortion in memory involves our motives: We often distort our memories in order to bring them "in line" with whatever goals we are currently seeking. For example, suppose that you like someone; this may lead you to *want* to remember positive information about him or her. Conversely, if you dislike someone, you want to remember negative information about this person. Effects of this kind are demonstrated clearly in research conducted by McDonald and Hirt (1997). Participants in the studies watched an interview between two students. Liking for one of the two individuals was varied by having this stranger act in a polite, a rude, or a neutral manner. When later asked to recall information about this person's grades (information that was provided during the interview), those who were induced to like the stranger distorted their memories so as to place this person in a more favorable light, while those induced to dislike the stranger showed the opposite pattern. In this and many other situations, our memories can be distorted by our current motives (see Figure 6.9 for another example).

HI AND LOIS — BY MORT WALKER AND DIK BROWNE

FIGURE 6.9
Memory Distortion: Often We *Do* Remember What We Want to Remember!
Our current motives can strongly influence what we remember. This is an example of the distortion of information stored in memory.
Source: Reprinted with permission of King Features Syndicate.

Schemas
Cognitive frameworks representing our knowledge about specific aspects of the world.

Memory Construction: Fuzzy-Trace Theory and Remembering What Didn't Happen

Memories can not only be distorted—they can also be constructed; in other words, people can recall events that did not actually occur or experiences they never really had. Such constructed or *false memories* can have important effects—for instance, they can lead to unfounded charges of *child sexual abuse* when adults construct memories of such treatment even though it never actually occurred (e.g., Acocella, 1998). Unfortunately, a growing body of research evidence suggests that false memories are both persistent and convincing; people strongly believe that they are real (Brainerd & Reyna, 1998; Reyna & Titcomb, 1996). Why? How can we form memories for events that never happened or experiences we never had? One answer is provided by **fuzzy-trace theory** (Reyna & Brainerd, 1995)—a theory about the relationship between memory and higher reasoning processes.

According to this theory, when we make decisions and judgments, we often focus on the general idea or *gist* of information stored in memory, not on the information itself. One result is that we then "remember" information consistent with the gist of our real memories even though it is false. Fuzzy-trace theory leads to some intriguing predictions. For instance, it predicts that at first, the more often we are exposed to information we wish to remember, the more false memories we will have. This is because "gist" memories form quickly and are more stable than memories for specific facts or information. So, up to some point, false memories are stronger than real ones. As repetitions continue, however, false memories are countered by accurate memories for specific information and tend to decrease (Seamon et al., 2002). Perhaps the most dramatic illustration of false memories we can provide involves *eyewitness testimony*, so let's turn briefly to that topic.

▣ Eyewitness Testimony: Is It as Accurate as We Believe?

Eyewitness testimony—evidence given by persons who have witnessed a crime—plays an important role in many trials. At first glance, this makes a great deal of sense: What better source of information about the events of a crime than the persons who actually saw them? After reading the previous discussions of distortion and construction in memory, however, you may already be wondering about an important question: Is such testimony really accurate?

The answer provided by careful research is clear: Eyewitnesses to crimes are far from perfect. In fact, they often falsely identify innocent persons as criminals (Wells, 1993), make mistakes about important details concerning a crime (Loftus, 1991), and sometimes report "remembering" events they did not actually see (Haugaard et al., 1991). Why do such errors occur? Not, it appears, because the witnesses are purposely "faking" their testimony. On the contrary, most try to be as accurate as possible. Rather, these errors occur because of several factors that produce distortions in memory: *suggestibility*—witnesses are sometimes influenced by *leading questions* and similar techniques used by attorneys or police officers; and errors with respect to *source monitoring*—eyewitnesses often attribute their memories to the wrong source. For instance, they identify a suspect in a line-up as the person who committed a crime because they remember having seen this individual before, and assume this was at the scene of the crime; in fact, his or her face may be familiar because they saw it in an album of "mug shots."

Given these potential sources of error (e.g., it appears that just being asked to imagine an event can sometimes create a false memory for it [Mazzoni & Memon, 2003]), it is no surprise that eyewitnesses are not nearly as accurate as our legal system assumes. And because jurors and even judges tend to place great weight on the testimony of eyewitnesses, such errors can have serious consequences: Innocent persons may be convicted of crimes they did not commit, or, conversely, persons guilty of serious crimes may be wrongly cleared of the charges against them. Indeed, recent evidence indicates that the single largest factor accounting for such miscarriages of justice is faulty eyewitness testimony (Wells, 1993).

Fuzzy-Trace Theory
A theory about the relationship between memory and higher reasoning processes.

Eyewitness Testimony
Information provided by witnesses to crimes or accidents.

Can anything be done to enhance eyewitnesses' accuracy? Fortunately, research on memory offers some answers. Ones involves conducting improved interviews with witnesses—interviews that may enhance their ability to remember crucial information accurately (e.g., Geiselman & Fisher, 1997). In such *cognitive interviews* eyewitnesses are asked to report everything they can remember; this provides them with multiple retrieval cues and can increase accuracy of recall. In addition, they are sometimes asked to describe events from different perspectives and in several different orders, not just the one in which the events actually occurred. These and other steps seem to increase the accuracy of eyewitness testimony, but they are far from perfect, so the basic problem remains: Eyewitness testimony is not nearly as accurate as was once widely believed. For this reason, it is probably best to view it as an imperfect and potentially misleading source of information.

KEY QUESTIONS

- What are schemas and what role do they play in memory distortion?
- What are false memories and how persistent are they?
- How accurate is eyewitness testimony?

MEMORY IN EVERYDAY LIFE

Much of the research described so far has involved the performance of relatively artificial tasks: memorizing nonsense syllables or lists of unrelated words. Sometimes, we perform tasks like these outside the laboratory; for instance, as a student, you sometimes memorize lists of terms or definitions. In general, though, we use memory for very different purposes in our daily lives. Let's see what psychologists have discovered about how memory functions in natural contexts. Three topics are of special interest: *repression* of emotionally traumatic events, *autobiographical* memory, and *memory for emotional events*.

Repression: Do We Choose to Forget What's Too Painful to Remember?

Have you ever chosen, consciously, to avoid thinking about some unpleasant or traumatic event? If so, you may have been engaging in **repression**—the active elimination from consciousness of memories or experiences we find threatening. This process, which can be viewed as a kind of *motivated forgetting,* has been suggested as one major factor in the finding that many persons who were the victims of *early childhood sexual abuse* fail to remember it (e.g., Williams, 1994) and cannot readily report it unless they are helped to do so by therapists who use various procedures to help the victims bring these memories back into consciousness.

But are such memories, when they are reported to therapists, really accurate? In other words, are they memories for actual, traumatic events, or are they false memories suggested, at least in part, by the techniques therapists used to "shake them loose" from repression? Several researchers have suggested that, sometimes, such memories may actually be false; in fact, they may be suggested by the therapists' detailed questions (e.g., Shobe & Kihlstrom, 1997). Research findings suggest that such effects are especially likely to occur among young children, who often have difficulty determining whether their memories are based on events that really happened or on something they imagined (e.g., Johnson, Hashtroudi, & Lindsay, 1993). Indeed, recent evidence indicates that simply imagining an event can generate false memories about it. For instance, in an intriguing recent study (Mazzoni & Memon, 2003), students at a British university were asked to read and imagine one event, and read a one-page description of another. One of the events was one that students frequently experience—having a baby tooth removed by a dentist. The other was an event that could never happen because it was illegal in the United

Repression
The active elimination from consciousness of memories or experiences we find threatening.

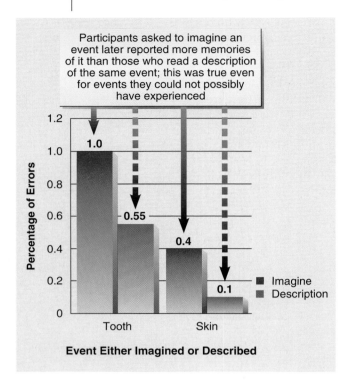

Participants asked to imagine an event later reported more memories of it than those who read a description of the same event; this was true even for events they could not possibly have experienced

FIGURE 6.10
Merely Imagining an Event Can Create Vivid Memories of It

Individuals either read a description of an event or were asked to imagine it. Later, they were tested for memories of these events. Regardless of whether the event was one they could actually have experienced, imagining it led to the formation of vivid memories for it.

Source: Based on data from Mazzoni & Memon, 2003.

Autobiographical Memory

Memory for information about events in our own lives.

Infantile Amnesia

Our supposed inability to remember experiences during the first two or three years of life.

Kingdom—having a nurse remove a skin sample from their little finger. One group of participants was asked to imagine the impossible event and read a description of the frequent one; the other group imagined the frequent event and read a description of the impossible one. One week later, both groups were given a memory test for the events. As you can see from Figure 6.10, being asked to imagine these events increased memory for them; more importantly, it increased memory for the impossible event as much as for the possible one! Clearly, then, just imagining an event can generate memories for it, as if it really happened.

These results, plus those of many other studies conducted with both children and adults (e.g., Brainerd & Reyna, 1998; Goodman et al., 1996; Mazzoni et al., 1999) suggest the need for caution in interpreting supposedly repressed memories of early childhood sexual abuse. These may certainly be real, but the possibility exists that they are not entirely accurate, and may actually be produced, at least in part, by the probing questions posed by therapists or other persons (e.g., attorneys, law enforcement officials). Please don't misunderstand: We are certainly *not* suggesting that all such memories reported are false. There is no doubt that childhood sexual abuse is a disturbingly frequent occurrence (e.g., Keary & Fitzpatrick 1994) and that some people who experience it do have difficulty remembering it (although recent findings indicate that many *can* and do remember such events; Goodman et al., 2003). However, there seem to be sufficient questions about the nature of repression, and sufficient evidence that some "memories" of traumatic events can be unintentionally constructed, to suggest the need for caution (Koocher et al., 1995).

Autobiographical Memory: Remembering the Events of Our Own Lives

How do we remember information about our own lives? Such **autobiographical memory** (which falls under the more general heading of *episodic memory*) has long been of interest to psychologists (e.g., Wagenaar, 1986). One question that has been addressed in this research is "When do autobiographical memories begin?" In other words, when are our earliest memories about our lives or ourselves formed?

■ When Do Autobiographical Memories Begin? Infantile Amnesia

What is your earliest memory, the earliest event in your life you can remember? For most people, such memories date from their third or fourth year of life, although a few people report even earlier memories (Usher & Neisser, 1995). This fact raises an interesting question: Can we remember events from before this time—from the first two years of our lives? And if we can't, why not? Why does such **infantile amnesia** (Howe & Courage, 1993) exist?

Growing evidence suggests that in fact, we *can* remember events from very early periods in our lives. However, because we don't possess language skills at this time, we can't report them in words (Bauer, 1996). For instance, consider a study by Meyers and his colleagues (1987). They allowed children six to forty weeks old to play with some toys in a laboratory room. Then two years later, they brought the same children back to this room and again allowed them to play with the toys; a control group of the same age had never played with these toys in this room. As expected, the behavior of the two groups differed; those who had played with the toys two years earlier showed more interest in them and played with them more than did the control group. When asked if they remembered ever having seen the toys before or having been in the room, though, they almost unanimously said, "No." Clearly, the children showed evidence of having some kind of memory of their earlier experiences but couldn't put these into words.

Other factors, too, may contribute to our inability to report memories from the first two years of our lives. One possibility is that autobiographical memory is absent early in life because the brain structures necessary for such memory are not sufficiently developed at this time (Moscovitch, 1985). Another possibility, suggested by Howe and Courage (1993), is that we do not form a clear *self-concept* until sometime between our second and third birthdays. Without this concept, we lack the personal frame of reference necessary for autobiographical memory.

Whatever the precise mechanisms involved in our inability to verbally report memories from our early lives, growing evidence suggests that we can store information from this period in memory. So, by and large, the term *infantile amnesia* is a misleading term because, in fact, certain types of memory are present even in very early childhood. We simply can't describe in words, as we can for memories stored later.

Memory for Our Own Emotions: Coping with the Present by Reconstructing the Past

In our earlier discussion of repressed memories, we focused on the question of how accurately individuals can remember traumatic events that caused them deep emotional pain. This is not the only issue that arises with respect to memory and emotions, however. In addition, we can ask, "How accurately can we remember emotions we had in the past?" This is an important question, because, often, our emotions—our "gut-level feelings"—are important guides for our behavior. For instance, if we meet someone and leave with the feeling that we don't like that person, we will probably avoid them in the future, even if we can't remember *why* we didn't like them. Similarly, in order to treat people suffering from psychological problems such as depression, therapists often need to know how strong these emotional reactions were in the past. So, how accurate *are* we in recalling our own emotions? In general, quite accurate: When individuals rate their emotions and later try to recall them, the two ratings generally agree (Levine & Safer, 2002). However, there are factors that can strongly distort our memories of our own previous emotions.

First, our current emotional state can produce such effects. For instance, when persons who have lost a spouse are asked to rate the intensity of their grief in the past, their answers are more closely related to their current levels of grief than to the grief they reported years earlier—the time they are trying to remember (Safer, Bonano, & Field, 2001). And in a revealing recent study (Safer, Levine, & Drapalski, 2002), college students were asked to recall their anxiety before taking an important test. Half learned of their grade before responding to this question while the others did not. Results indicated that, compared to the students who did not know their grades, the students who had done well on the exam *underestimated* their actual pre-exam anxiety, and those who learned that they had done poorly *overestimated* it. In other words, they adjusted their memories of how they felt before the exam in the light of what they now knew about their grades. Clearly, then, our current emotional states can lead to distortion of our memories for our own emotions.

Second, and even more interesting, is the fact that often we tend to cope with present problems by reconstructing the past—by changing our memories of our own emotions. For instance, after going through a very painful experience, many persons report that they have gained in wisdom or insight. In fact, though, this change is often less than they imagine: To feel better about the event, they disparage their wisdom or insight *before* the event, remembering it as less than it really was

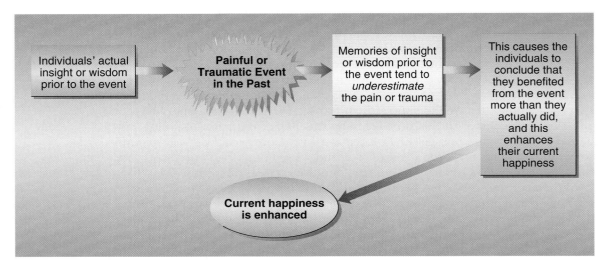

FIGURE 6.11
Adjusting Memories of Our Past Emotions to Maximize Current Happiness
After experiencing painful or traumatic events, individuals often accentuate the benefits they have gained from these events by disparaging the knowledge of insight prior to the event. This allows them to conclude that they benefited from it even more than they actually did, and this, in turn, may enhance their current happiness.

(McFarland & Alvaro, 2000). Similarly, patients who have successfully completed therapy overestimate their pre-therapy distress, thus perceiving greater positive change than actually occurred (Safer & Keuler, 2002). The basic principle seems to be that we really do reconstruct the past—change our memories of our own emotions—in order to maximize our current happiness or satisfaction. In this case, then, memory distortion can have beneficial effects, even if they rest on an illusory foundation (see Figure 6.11).

The Effects of Mood on Memory

Earlier, in our discussion of retrieval cues, we noted that our own internal states can serve as a cue for information stored in memory: It is often easier to recall information stored in long-term memory when our internal state is similar to that which existed when the information was first entered into memory. The effects of mood on memory are closely related to such *state-dependent retrieval* because our moods can be another internal state that serves as a retrieval cue. How can mood influence memory? In two related but distinct ways. First, memory can be enhanced when our mood state during retrieval is similar to that when we first encoded some information; this is known as **mood-dependent memory.** For instance, if you entered some information into memory when in a good mood, you are more likely to remember this information when in a similar mood once again: Your current mood serves as a kind of retrieval cue for the information stored in memory. Note that you will remember this information whatever it is—positive, negative, or unrelated to mood. For instance, if you learned a list of definitions while in a good mood, you will remember them better when in a good mood again, although they have nothing to do with producing your mood.

Second, we are more likely to store or remember positive information when in a positive mood and negative information when in a negative mood—in other words, we notice or remember information that is congruent with our current mood (Blaney, 1986); this is known as **mood congruence effects.** A simple way to think about the difference between mood-dependent memory and mood congruence effects is this: In mood-dependent memory, mood serves as a retrieval cue, helping us remember information we acquired when we were in that mood before.

Mood-Dependent Memory
Refers to the finding that what we remember while in a given mood may be determined, in part, by what we learned when previously in that same mood.

Mood Congruence Effects
Refers to the finding that we tend to notice or remember information congruent with our current mood.

This information may be almost anything, such as the list of definitions we mentioned earlier. In mood-congruence effects, we tend to remember information consistent with our present mood—positive information when we feel happy, negative information when we feel sad (see Figure 6.12). Mood congruence effects are vividly illustrated by an individual who suffered from periods of depression and was asked to remember trips to a swimming pool. When she felt depressed, she remembered painful aspects of these trips—how fat and unattractive she felt in her bathing suit. When she was happier, she remembered positive aspects of the same events—how much she enjoyed swimming (Baddely, 1990).

One reason why mood congruence effects are important is that they may be closely related to depression. Specifically, they help explain why depressed persons have difficulty remembering times when they felt better (Schachter & Kihlstrom, 1989). Their current negative mood leads them to remember unhappy past experiences, and this information causes them to feel more depressed. In other words, mood congruence effects may push them into a vicious, closed circle in which negative feelings breed negative thoughts and memories, which results in even deeper depression; see Chapter 12 for more information. (The fact that memory is subject to forgetting and to many forms of construction and distortion suggests that the task of *performance appraisal* is a difficult one. What can *you* do to help assure that the performance appraisals you receive at work are fair and accurate? For some hints, see the **Psychology Goes to Work** section.)

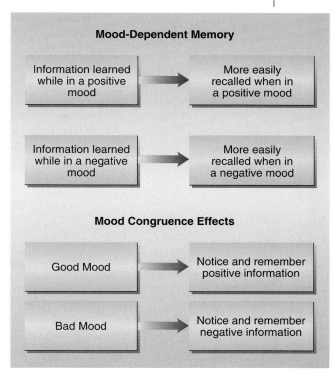

FIGURE 6.12
Effects of Mood on Memory
Memory is enhanced when our mood at the time of retrieval is the same as that at the time information was first entered into memory (i.e., encoded); this is *mood-dependent memory*. We also tend to notice and remember information consistent with our current mood; this is the *mood congruence effect*.

Diversity and Memory: Own-Race Bias in Remembering Faces

One memory task we often face in everyday life is that of recognizing people we have met before. While faces are certainly distinctive, we meet so many people in so many different contexts that sometimes our memory plays tricks on us and we mistakenly believe we have met someone before or, conversely, forget that we have met them. This is not at all surprising, but more disturbing is the fact that often we find it easier to remember people belonging to our own racial or ethnic group than people belonging to other ones. Many studies confirm this; in fact, a recent review of dozens of separate studies involving more than 5,000 participants suggests that people are indeed more successful in recognizing people they have met (or whose photos they have seen) who belong to their own race than in recognizing people who belong to another race (Meissner & Brighman, 2001). Moreover, this seems to be true whether they have actually met these people or merely seen photos of them (Ludwig, 2001). Even more unsettling is the fact that such effects are stronger for persons who are high in racial prejudice than for persons who are low in such prejudice (Brigham & Barkowitz, 1978; Meissner & Brighman, 2001).

Why do such effects occur? Perhaps because, at least until recently, many persons had more frequent contact with members of their own race than members of other races. Thus, they became more familiar with the physical traits of their own race and so had better retrieval cues for recognizing individual faces. Whatever the reason, the existence of this own-race bias has important implications. For instance, it may influence the accuracy with which eyewitnesses to various crimes can identify the actual offenders. And it might also add a note of friction between members of different races who become annoyed that persons they met before can't recognize them! Fortunately, the increasing diversity of the United States and many other countries may lead to a decrease in the magnitude of such effects; after all, as individuals have increasing contact with people in many ethnic and racial groups, they may come to recognize them all with equal accuracy. And then the detestable phrase "They all look alike to me" may finally be abolished once and for all.

KEY QUESTIONS

- What is repression? What role does it play in memory?
- What is autobiographical memory? When does it begin?
- Why do we sometimes distort memories of our own prior emotional states?
- What are mood-dependent memory and mood congruence effects?
- What is own-race bias in memory for races?

PSYCHOLOGY GOES TO WORK

Using Memory Principles to Boost the Fairness, Accuracy, and Favorableness of Your Own Performance Appraisals

In most organizations, employees receive *performance appraisals*—evaluations of their work—once or twice a year. These appraisals serve as the basis for setting raises and selecting people for promotion, and as a source of valuable feedback that can help people improve. In other words, they are often *important*. But think about how they are done: Once or twice a year, your boss must try to remember your performance over a period of several months. And then, she or he evaluates it on the basis of these memories. Given the many errors and distortions to which memory is subject, this can be a very tricky task! Are there steps you can take to help assure that what your boss remembers is really an accurate picture of your performance and contributions—and one that fully takes account of your important contributions? Here are some steps we think may be useful.

- **Ask your boss to keep a record of your most important contributions.** If your boss agrees, he or she will have a written record of what you contributed and will not have to try to retrieve this information from memory. If your boss is too busy, offer to provide such a summary yourself.
- **Try to make sure that your boss is in a good mood when he or she prepares your appraisal.** Mood congruence effects suggest that when people are in a good mood, they tend to remember positive information—and that's certainly what you want to happen!
- **Try to make sure that when you perform very well, your boss notices.** Only informa-

tion that is noticed can be entered into memory, so when you do something especially well, this is *not* the time to be modest! Call it to your boss's attention so that she or he can enter it into memory, and retrieve it when the time for appraisals comes around.

- **Be sure to start out strong on any new job.** First impressions count because once they are formed, they are entered into memory and tend to persist unless something important or dramatic happens to change them. So, if you start out well, your boss will form a favorable mental framework for you and your performance—and this will make it easier for her or him to remember your good contributions when doing your appraisal.
- **Give your boss as many retrieval cues for your good performance as possible.** Retrieving information from long-term memory is often difficult, and retrieval cues can help a lot. So be sure that your boss has many reminders of your good work and contributions (e.g., copies of any positive comments you received from satisfied customers or co-workers; concrete evidence that your work has produced positive outcomes).

By following these steps, you can increase the chances that your boss will remember favorable information about you when preparing your evaluation—and that can be an important boost to your career.

MEMORY AND THE BRAIN: EVIDENCE FROM MEMORY IMPAIRMENTS AND OTHER SOURCES

Let's begin with a simple but basic assumption: When information is entered into memory, *something* must happen in our brains. Given that memories can last for decades, it is only reasonable to suggest that this "something" involves relatively permanent changes. But where, precisely, do these occur? And what kinds of alterations do they involve? Thanks to the development of tools and methods such as those described in Chapter 2, answers to these questions are beginning to emerge (e.g., Paller, Kutas, & McIsaac, 1995). Let's see what research on these issues has revealed.

Amnesia and Other Memory Disorders: Keys for Unlocking Brain–Memory Links

One way of investigating the biological bases of memory is to study individuals who has experienced loss of memory—**amnesia.** Amnesia is far from rare and can stem from accidents that damage the brain, from drug abuse, or from operations performed to treat medical disorders. Two major types exist. In **retrograde amnesia,** memory of events prior to the amnesia-inducing event is impaired. Thus, persons suffering from such amnesia may be unable to remember events from specific periods in their lives. In **anterograde amnesia,** in contrast, individuals cannot remember events that occur *after* the amnesia-inducing event. For example, if they meet someone for the first time after the onset of amnesia, they cannot remember this person the next day, or, in some cases, a few minutes after being introduced (see Figure 6.13).

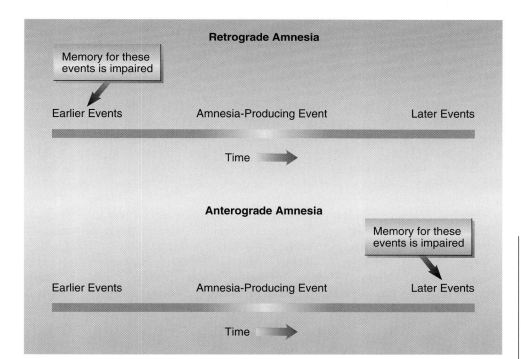

FIGURE 6.13
Two Kinds of Amnesia
In *retrograde amnesia*, memory of events prior to the amnesia-inducing event is impaired—people forget things that happened to them in the past. In *anterograde amnesia*, memory of events occurring after the amnesia-inducing event is impaired—people can't remember things that happen to them after the onset of their amnesia.

Amnesia
Loss of memory stemming from illness, accident, drug abuse, or other causes.

Retrograde Amnesia
Loss of memory of events that occurred prior to an amnesia-inducing event.

Anterograde Amnesia
The inability to store in long-term memory information that occurs after an amnesia-inducing event.

S. P.: An Example of the Dissociation between Working Memory and Long-Term Learning

One of the most important findings to emerge from studies of people with amnesia is this: Often, they retain factual information stored in memory but can no longer enter new information into long-term storage. S. P., a patient described by the Swiss psychologist Schnider (Schnider, Regard, & Landis, 1994), provides a vivid example of such effects. S. P. was sixty-six years old when he suffered a major stroke. Magnetic resonance imaging indicated that the stroke had affected S. P.'s medial temporal lobes, the left hippocampus, and many other adjoining areas. After the stroke, S. P. showed a pattern demonstrated by many other persons with damage to the hippocampus: He seemed unable to enter information into long-term memory. If he left a room for a few moments, he could not find his way back to it. He could not remember physicians who examined him or people he met for the first time. (He did, however, recognize his wife and children.) He could talk, read, and write, and repeat words on a list as they were read, but could not remember the words after the list was completed. In short, he showed profound anterograde amnesia. Interestingly, he *could* enter new information into procedural memory: His performance on tasks such as drawing geometric figures without directly looking at them improved with practice, although he couldn't remember performing the task or explain how he got better at it. This case, and many others like it, point to the importance of the *hippocampus,* a structure located on the inside edge of each hemisphere, adjacent to the temporal lobes. Damage to this structure seems to interfere with the ability to transfer information from working memory to a more permanent kind of storage. However, because damage to this structure does *not* eliminate the ability to acquire procedural knowledge (i.e., new skills), it does not seem to be involved in this kind of memory.

Clive Wearing: The Frontal Lobes, Working Memory, and Semantic Memory

Another dramatic case of amnesia is provided by Clive Wearing, a musician and producer of considerable fame during the 1980s. In 1985, he caught infectious encephalitis. This disease produced extensive damage to both temporal lobes of his brain and to the hippocampus, and resulted in profound memory deficits for Mr. Wearing—many of which were recorded by his wife Deborah. Most of these deficits involved semantic memory: He could not distinguish between words such as honey, jam, and marmalade. He ate a lemon, including the peel, believing it was another kind of fruit. He mistook soap for toothpaste. His score on standard tests of semantic memory was very low—a surprising change, because prior to his illness he had been an expert at solving crossword puzzles and had excellent semantic memory. Over time, his memory impairments became worse: He began to develop new, unique definitions for words. Researchers who studied his case concluded that his loss of semantic memory was due to damage to the temporal lobes (Wilson & Wearing, 1995), while losses in the ability for new learning, which occurred later on, were attributed to growing damage to the hippocampus. On the basis of this and many other cases, psychologists have concluded that the frontal lobes of the brain play an important role in working memory and in the encoding and retrieval of factual information (both episodic and semantic) from long-term memory.

Amnesia as a Result of Korsakoff's Syndrome

Individuals who consume large amounts of alcohol for many years sometimes develop a serious illness known as **Korsakoff's syndrome.** The many symptoms of Korsakoff's syndrome include sensory and motor problems as well as heart, liver, and gastrointestinal disorders. In addition, the syndrome is often accompanied by both anterograde amnesia and severe retrograde amnesia—patients cannot remember events that took place many years before the onset of their illness. Careful medical examinations of such persons' brains after their deaths indicate

Korsakoff's Syndrome
An illness caused by long-term abuse of alcohol; often involves profound retrograde amnesia.

that they experienced extensive damage to portions of the thalamus and hypo-thalamus. This suggests that these portions of the brain play a key role in long-term memory.

The Amnesia of Alzheimer's Disease

One of the most tragic illnesses to strike human beings in the closing decades of life is **Alzheimer's disease.** This illness occurs among 5 percent of all people over age sixty-five, including famous persons such as former President Reagan (see Figure 6.14). It begins with mild problems, such as increased difficulty in remembering names, phone numbers, or appointments. Gradually, though, patients' conditions worsen until they become totally confused, are unable to perform even simple tasks like dressing or grooming themselves, and experience an almost total loss of memory. In the later stages, patients may fail to recognize their spouses or children. In short, people suffering from Alzheimer's disease suffer a wide range of memory impairments: Semantic memory, episodic memory, memory for skills, working memory, and autobiographical memory are all disturbed. As one memory expert puts it (Haberlandt, 1999): "Along with their memories, the patients lose their pasts and their souls."

Careful study of the brains of deceased Alzheimer's patients has revealed that in most cases they contain tiny bundles of *amyloid beta protein,* a substance not found in similar concentrations in normal brains. Growing evidence (Yankner et al., 1990) suggests that this substance causes damage to neurons that project from nu-clei in the basal forebrain to the hippocampus and cerebral cortex (Coyle, 1987). These neurons transmit information primarily by means of the neurotransmitter *acetylcholine,* so it appears that this substance may play a key role in memory. Fur-ther evidence that acetylcholine-based systems are important is provided by the fact that the brains of Alzheimer's patients contain lower than normal amounts of acetylcholine. In addition, studies with animal subjects in which the acetylcholine-transmitting neurons are destroyed suggests that this does indeed produce major memory problems (Fibiger, Murray, & Phllips, 1983). However, very recent evi-dence suggests that other neurotransmitters are also involved, so the picture is more complex than was previously assumed.

FIGURE 6.14
Alzheimer's Disease: A Tragedy of Later Life
Individuals suffering from Alzheimer's disease often realize that they are losing their memory and experiencing other effects of this illness. Former President Reagan was one of these; he held a formal ceremony to say good-bye to many friends and associ-ates, because he realized that soon Alzheimer's disease would rob him of his memory and his personality.

Memory and the Brain: A Modern View

So what can we conclude from this evidence? Several things. First, memory func-tions do show some degree of localization within the brain: (1) The hippocampus plays a key role in converting information from a temporary state to a more per-manent one, and in spatial learning; however, it does not seem to play a role in pro-cedural memory, because damage to the hippocampus leaves such memory largely intact. (2) The frontal lobes play a role in working memory, executive functions in working memory, and in the encoding and retrieval of factual information from long-term memory. Damage to these areas disrupts these key functions but may leave other aspects of memory intact.

Why does damage to various brain structures produce amnesia and other memory deficits? Several possibilities exist. One is that damage to these areas pre-vents consolidation of the memory trace: These are formed but cannot be converted to a lasting state (e.g., Squire, 1995). Another is that when information is stored in memory, not only the information itself, but also its context—when and how it was acquired—is stored. Amnesia may result from an inability to enter this additional information into memory (Mayes, 1996). Finally, it may be that amnesia stems from an inability to monitor errors (Baddeley, 1996); this may be one reason why amnesic patients often can't enter new information into memory, although their semantic memory remains intact (e.g., they can speak, read, and write).

What about the memory trace itself—where is it located and what is it? Over the years, the pendulum of scientific opinion concerning this issue has swung back

Alzheimer's Disease
An illness primarily afflicting individuals over the age of sixty-five that involves severe mental deterioration, including severe amnesia.

and forth between the view that memories are highly localized within the brain—they exist in specific places—to the view that they are represented by the pattern of neural activity in many different brain regions. At present, most experts on memory believe that both views are correct, at least to a degree. Some aspects of memory do appear to be represented in specific portions of the brain and even, perhaps, in specific cells. For instance, cells have been identified in the cortex of monkeys that respond to faces of other monkeys and humans but not other stimuli (Desimone & Ungerleider, 1989). So there do appear to be "local specialists" within the brain. At the same time, networks of brain regions seem to be involved in many memory functions. So, in reply to the question, "Where are memories located?" the best available answer is that there is no single answer. Depending on the type of information or type of memory being considered, memories may be represented in individual neurons, the connections between them, complex networks of structures throughout the brain, or all of the above. Given the complexity of the functions memory involves, this is not surprising; after all, no one ever said that the task of understanding anything as complicated and wonderful as human memory would be easy!

Finally, what *is* the memory trace—what happens within the brain when we enter information into memory? Again, we are still far from a final, complete answer, although we are definitely getting there. The picture provided by current research goes something like this: The formation of long-term memories involves alterations in the rate of production or release of specific neurotransmitters (especially acetylcholine). Such changes increase the ease with which neural information can move within the brain and may produce *localized neural circuits.* Evidence for the existence of such circuits, or *neural networks,* is provided by research in which previously learned conditioned responses are eliminated when microscopic areas of the brain are destroyed—areas that, presumably, contain the neural circuits formed during conditioning (Thompson, 1989).

Long-term memory also may involve changes in the actual structure of neurons—changes that strengthen communication across specific synapses (Teyler & DiScenna, 1984). For instance, as we noted in our discussion of plasticity of the brain in Chapter 2 (e.g., Kolb, Gibb, & Robinson, 2003), the shape of dendrites in specific neurons may be altered by learning and other experiences, and these changes may increase the neurons' responsiveness to certain neurotransmitters. Some of these changes may occur very quickly, while others may require considerable amounts of time. Perhaps this is one reason why newly formed memories are subject to disruption for some period after they are formed (Squire & Spanis, 1984).

In sum, it appears that we are now in an exciting period of rapid progress; sophisticated research techniques (e.g, PET scans) have armed psychologists and other scientists with important tools for unraveling the biological bases of memory. When they do, the potential benefits for persons suffering from amnesia and other memory disorders will probably be immense. (How can you improve *your* memory? For some suggestions please see the **Psychology Lends a Hand** section.)

KEY QUESTIONS

- What are retrograde amnesia and anterograde amnesia?
- What roles do the hippocampus and frontal lobes play in memory?
- What are Korsakoff's syndrome and Alzheimer's disease? What do they tell us about the biological bases of memory?
- What does current research suggest about the location of the memory trace and its nature?

p s y c h o l o g y   l e n d s   a   h a n d

Improving Your Memory: Some Useful Steps

How good is your memory? If you are like most people, your answer is probably "Not good enough!" At one time or another, most of us have wished that we could improve our ability to retain facts and information. Fortunately, with a little work, almost anyone can improve her or his memory. Here are some tips for reaching this goal:

1. **Really think about what you want to remember.** If you wish to enter information into long-term memory, it is important to think about it. Ask questions about it, consider its meaning, and examine its relationship to information you already know. In other words, engage in "deep processing." Doing so will help make the new information part of your existing knowledge frameworks—and increase your chances of remembering it at later time.

2. **Pay careful attention to what you want to remember.** Unless you pay careful attention to information you want to remember, it stands little chance of really getting "in"—into long-term memory. So, be sure to direct your full attention to information you want to remember. True, this involves a bit of hard work. But in the long run, it will save you time and effort.

3. **Minimize interference.** Interference is a major cause of forgetting, and, in general, the more similar materials are, the more likely they are to produce interference. In practical terms, this means that you should arrange your studying so that you *don't* study similar subjects one right after the other. Instead, work on subjects that are unrelated; the result may be less interference between them—and, potentially, better grades.

4. **Engage in distributed learning/practice.** Don't try to cram all the information you want to memorize into long-term storage at once. Rather, if at all possible, space your studying over several sessions—preferably, several days. This is especially true if you want to retain the information for long periods of time rather than just until the next exam!

5. **Use visual imagery and other mnemonics.** You've probably heard the saying, "A picture is worth a thousand words." Where memory is concerned, this is sometimes true; it is often easier to remember information associated with vivid mental images (e.g., Gehrig & Toglia, 1989). You can put this principle to use by adopting any one of several different *mnemonics*—tactics for improving memory. One of these, the *method of loci*, involves linking points you want to remember with visual images arranged in some familiar order. For instance, suppose you want to remember the points in a speech you will soon make. You can imagine walking through some familiar place, say, our own home. Then form a series of images in which each item you wish to remember is placed in a specific location. Perhaps the first point is "The greenhouse effect is real." You might imagine a large, steamy greenhouse right outside your front door. The next point might be "Cutting down the rain forest is increasing the greenhouse effect." For this one, you might imagine a large cut-down tree in your living room. You'd form other images, in a different location, for the other points you want to make. Then, by taking an imaginary walk through your house, you can "see" each of these images and so remember the points in your speech.

6. **Give yourself extra retrieval cues.** Remember the concept of state-dependent retrieval? As noted previously, you can use this principle to provide yourself with extra retrieval cues and so help enhance your memory. For instance, if you studied for a test while in one physical state, try to be in the same state when you take it—this may help. Similarly, use the principle of mood-dependent memory. If you learned some material while in a given mood and then want to remember it, try to put yourself in the same mood. This is not as hard as it sounds: You can often vary your own mood by imagining happy or sad events. To the degree that your mood now matches your mood when you learned the information, your memory for it may be improved.

7. **Develop your own shorthand codes.** To learn the names of the planets in our solar system, many children use the *first-letter technique,* in which the first letter of each word in a phrase stands for an item to be remembered. So, the sentence "Mary's Violet Eyes Make John Stay Up Nights Pondering" (for Mercury, Venus, Earth, Mars, Jupiter, Saturn, Uranus, Neptune, and Pluto) is very helpful. This can be a very useful technique for remembering others lists of items, too, so use it whenever you can.

We could list additional techniques, but most would be related to the points already described. Whichever techniques you choose, you will learn that making them work requires effort. In memory training, as in any other kind of self-improvement, it appears that the saying "No pain, no gain" holds true.

SUMMARY AND REVIEW OF KEY QUESTIONS

Human Memory: An Information-Processing Approach

- **According to the information-processing model, what key tasks are performed by memory?**

Encoding, which involves converting information into a form that can be entered into memory; storage, which involves retaining information over time; and retrieval, which involves locating information when it is needed.

- **What are sensory memory, short-term memory, and long-term memory?**
  Sensory memory holds fleeting representations of our sensory experiences. Short-term memory holds a limited amount of information for short periods of time. Long-term memory holds large amounts of information for long periods of time.

Our Different Memory Systems

- **What is the difference between short-term memory and working memory?**
  Short-term memory refers to our memory system for storing limited amounts of information for relative short periods of time. Working memory refers to short-term storage of information *plus* a mechanism for focusing attention and determining what information will be processed and what will be ignored or suppressed.

- **What are the three major components of working memory?**
  The major components are a mechanism for short-term retention of information, a mechanism for rehearsing such information, and an attentional mechanism.

- **What are episodic memory and semantic memory?**
  Episodic memory contains factual information individuals relate to their own lives and experiences. Semantic memory holds factual information of a more general nature.

- **What is the levels of processing view?**
  This view suggests that the more deeply information is processed, the more likely it is to be retained.

- **What are retrieval cues and what role do they play in memory?**
  These are stimuli that are associated with information stored in memory and so can help bring it to mind at times when it cannot be recalled spontaneously.

- **What are concepts and what role do they play in semantic memory?**
  These are mental categories for objects or events that are similar to one another in certain ways. They seem to be arranged in hierarchical networks in semantic memory.

- **What is procedural memory?**
  This is memory for information we cannot readily put into words, such as various skills.

Forgetting: Some Contrasting Views

- **What is proactive interference? Retroactive interference? What roles do they play in forgetting?**
  Retroactive interference occurs when information being learned currently interferes with information already present in memory. Proactive interference occurs when information already present in memory interferes with the acquisition of new information.

- **What is retrieval inhibition?**
  This refers to the fact that efforts to remember information in memory may generate *inhibition* that interferes with memory for items we don't try to remember.

Memory Distortion and Memory Construction

- **What are schemas and what role do they play in memory distortion?**
  Schemas are cognitive structures representing individuals' knowledge and assumptions about some aspect of the world. Once formed, they strongly influence the ways in which we process new information.

- **What are false memories and how persistent are they?**
  False memories are memories for events or experiences that never happened or we never had. Often, they are stronger than real memories and very persistent.

- **How accurate is eyewitness testimony?**
  The testimony of eyewitnesses to various crimes appears to be far less accurate than is widely believed.

Memory in Everyday Life

- **What is repression? What role does it play in memory?**
  Repression is the active elimination from consciousness of memories or experiences we find threatening. There is little evidence that it plays an important role in forgetting, although it has been suggested that repression influences memories of sexual abuse early in life.

- **What is autobiographical memory? When does it begin?**
  Autobiographical memory contains information about our own lives. It begins very early in life, although most people can't describe memories from the first two years of life.

- **Why do we sometimes distort memories of our own prior emotional states?**
  We sometimes distort memories of our own prior emotional states to increase our present happiness by, for instance, perceiving that we benefited more than we really did from painful or traumatic events.

- **What are mood-dependent memory and mood congruence effects?**
  When our mood during retrieval is similar to that during encoding, memory may be enhanced; this is mood-dependent memory. We tend to remember information consistent with our current mood; this is mood congruence.

- **What is own-race bias in memory for faces?**
  This refers to a tendency to recognize persons belonging to our own racial or ethnic group more readily and accurately than persons belonging to other racial or ethnic groups.

Memory and the Brain: Evidence from Memory Impairments and Other Sources

- **What are retrograde amnesia and anterograde amnesia?**
  Retrograde amnesia involves loss of memory of events prior to the amnesia-inducing event. Anterograde amnesia is loss of memory for events that occur after the amnesia-inducing event.

- **What roles do the hippocampus and frontal lobes play in long-term memory?**
  The hippocampus seems to play a crucial role in the consolidation of memory—the process of shifting new information from short-term to longer-term storage. The frontal lobes appear to play a key role in various aspects of working memory and in the encoding and retrieval of factual information (both episodic and semantic).

- **What are Korsakoff's syndrome and Alzheimer's disease? What do they tell us about the biological bases of memory?**

Korsakoff's syndrome is produced by long-term alcoholism and often involves severe forms of amnesia. It indicates that the hypothalamus and thalamus play important roles in memory. Alzheimer's disease produces increasingly severe deficits in memory. It calls attention to the role of the neurotransmitter acetylcholine in memory.

- **What does current research suggest about the location of the memory trace and its nature?**
  Current research suggests that the memory trace may involve individual neurons, connections between them, and complex networks of neurons and brain structures. It may involve changes in the structure and function of individual neurons, or of complex networks of neurons.

PSYCHOLOGY: UNDERSTANDING ITS FINDINGS

Human Memory and Computer Memory: The Same or Different?

Each year, computers get faster and have larger memories. In fact, right now, we can place everything we have ever written—every book, every article, every lecture note—on a tiny faction of the hard drives in computers. So, computer memory is certainly impressive. But is it as good as human memory? To answer this question, it is important to understand differences as well as similarities between human memory

and computer memory. We think that comparing these two systems for storing information will help you more fully understand what psychologists have learned about the nature of memory. Below, please list (1) the ways in which human memory and computer memory are similar and (2) the ways in which they are different. After you complete these tasks, answer the following question: In what ways is human memory superior to computer memory and vice versa?

MAKING PSYCHOLOGY PART OF YOUR LIFE

Procedural Memory: Knowledge That Can't Readily Be Put into Words

As noted earlier, information stored in procedural memory plays a key role in skilled performance, but it is often difficult to put into words: You know how to do something, but you can't really explain *how* you do it. Try the following exercise to see how you can apply this fact to your own life.

Suppose you are trying to teach someone a new skill—for instance, how to drive a car with manual transmission. How would you go about it? On a separate sheet of paper list at least five things you would do.

Now, examine your list. How many of them involved "explaining" what to do in words? Do you think these techniques would be effective? In contrast, how many of the items you listed involved getting the person to *practice* the skill, perhaps after watching you do it? Do you think these would be more effective? Why? In general, they would be for the following reason: Because we can't describe procedural knowledge verbally, it is better to demonstrate it and to have the person learning a new skill practice it. Try this approach the next time you teach someone a new skill. Chances are, you will find it to be much more effective than trying to tell them what to do.

KEY TERMS

7

Cognition and Intelligence

*A*s you know from your own experience, people differ in countless ways across a broad range of characteristics. This gives rise to the following question: What attributes—or, more accurately, what combination of attributes—lead people to succeed in life, or to fail? There are highly intelligent people, for instance, who fail to reach their full potential because they just can't control their emotions or get along with others. In contrast, other persons who appear average in most respects often achieve high levels of success because of their "people skills" or through specialized talents, such as acting, painting, or computer programming. Systematic research reveals that individual differences like the ones just described stem, at least in part, from basic cognitive abilities—key aspects of our higher mental processes.

It is on these abilities that we'll focus in the present chapter. Specifically, we'll begin by examining what psychology currently knows about **cognition,** a term psychologists use to describe *thinking* and many other aspects of our higher mental processes, including *reasoning, decision making, problem solving,* and *creativity.* You might note that we covered one important aspect of cognition—memory—in Chapter 6. We'll also examine *language* in some detail, because it provides the basis for much of the activity occurring in cognitive processes; we'll focus on the basic nature of language, how language develops, and whether it is something we share with other species on earth.

After considering these important aspects of cognition, we'll return to the issue raised above: individual differences in cognitive abilities. Psychologists usually use the term *intelligence* to refer to such individual differences in cognitive abilities; and because of the many practical implications of intelligence, they have devoted a great deal of attention to this topic. To acquaint you with the findings of almost a century of systematic research on intelligence, we'll discuss several issues: the nature of intelligence, how it's measured, and the potential contributions of heredity and environment to individual differences in this key dimension. In the course of our discussion of intelligence, we'll raise some of the ethical and social issues relating to the use of intelligence tests. We will also consider the extent to which intelligence tests, or any other psychological tests, measure what they are designed to measure consistently and accurately—the important issues of test reliability and validity. Finally, we'll describe some intriguing evidence concerning *emotional intelligence*—our ability to deal effectively with the emotional side of life.

THINKING: FORMING CONCEPTS AND REASONING TO CONCLUSIONS

What are you thinking about right now? At least to some extent you are thinking about the words on this page. But perhaps you are also thinking about the date you have tonight, the argument you had with a friend, or how much time you should devote to reading this chapter. At any given moment in time, consciousness contains a rapidly shifting pattern of diverse thoughts, impressions, and feelings. In order to try to understand this complex and ever-changing pattern, psychologists have often adopted two main strategies. First, they have focused on the basic elements of *thought*—how, precisely, aspects of the external world are represented in our thinking. Second, psychologists have sought to determine the manner in which we *reason*—how we attempt to process available information cognitively in order to reach specific conclusions.

Basic Elements of Thought: Concepts, Propositions, Images

What, precisely, does thinking involve? In other words, what are the basic elements of thought? Thoughts are internal representations of the external world that consist largely of three basic components: *concepts, propositions,* and *images.*

Concepts: Categories for Understanding Experience

What do the following objects have in common: a dalmation, a poodle, an Irish setter? Although they all look different, you probably have no difficulty in replying—they are all dogs. Now, how about these items: a tractor, a Jeep Grand Cherokee, an elevator? Perhaps it takes you a bit longer to answer, but soon you realize that they are all vehicles. The items in each of these groups look different from one another, yet in a sense you perceive—and think about—them as similar, at least in certain respects. The reason you find the task of answering these questions

Cognition
The mental activities associated with thought, decision making, language, and other higher mental processes.

relatively simple is that you already possess well-developed **concepts** for both groups of items. As you will recall from Chapter 6, concepts are mental categories for objects, events, experiences, or ideas that are similar to one another in one or more respects. They allow us to represent a great deal of information about diverse objects, events, or ideas in a highly efficient manner.

Logical and Natural Concepts   Psychologists often distinguish between logical and natural concepts. **Logical concepts** are ones that can be clearly defined by a set of rules or properties. Thus, an object's membership in a category is unambiguous: Any object or event either is or is not a member of a given concept category by virtue of whether or not it has the defining feature or features. For example, in geometry, a figure can be considered to be a triangle only if it has three sides whose angles add up to 180 degrees, and can be a square only if all four sides are of equal length and all four angles are 90 degrees. In contrast, **natural concepts** are fuzzy around the edges; they have no fixed or readily specified set of defining features. Yet natural concepts more accurately reflect the state of the natural world, which rarely offers us the luxury of hard-and-fast, clearly defined rules. Natural concepts are often based on **prototypes**—the best or clearest examples (Rosch, 1975). Prototypes emerge from our experience with the external world, and new items that might potentially fit within their category are then compared with them. The more attributes new items share with an existing prototype, the more likely they are to be included within the concept. For example, consider the following natural concepts: animals and art. For animals, most people think of lions, cats, or dogs. They are far less likely to mention coral, wapiti, or humans. Similarly, for art, most people think of paintings, drawings, and sculptures. Fewer think of works of art such as the example shown in Figure 7.1.

Concepts: How They Are Represented   How are concepts represented in the mind? No firm answer to this question exists, but several possibilities have been suggested. First, concepts may be represented in terms of their features or attributes. As natural concepts are formed, the attributes associated with them may be stored in memory. Then, when we encounter a new item, we compare its attributes with the ones we have already learned about. The closer the match, the more likely we are to include the item within the concept.

A second possibility is that natural concepts are represented, at least in part, through **visual images**—mental pictures of objects or events in the external world. If asked whether chess is a sport, do you conjure up an image of two players bending intently over the board while an audience looks on? If so, you can readily see how visual images may play a role in the representation of natural concepts. We'll have more to say about the role of mental images in thought later in this section.

Finally, it is important to note that concepts are closely related to *schemas*—cognitive frameworks that represent our knowledge of and assumptions about the world (see Chapter 6). Like schemas, natural concepts are acquired through experience and also represent information about the world in an efficient summary form. However, schemas are more complex than concepts; each schema contains a broad range of information and may include many distinct concepts. For example, each of us possesses a *self-schema*, a mental framework holding a wealth of information about our own traits, characteristics, and expectations. This framework, in turn, may contain numerous different concepts, such as intelligence, attractiveness, health, and so on. Some of these are natural concepts; so the possibility exists that natural concepts are represented, at least in part, through their links to schemas and other broad cognitive frameworks.

FIGURE 7.1
Prototypes: An Unlikely Example
When asked to think of art, most people think of paintings, drawings, or sculpture. Few think of an example like the "Jellies: Living Art" exhibit at the Monterey Bay Aquarium.

Concepts
Mental categories for objects or events that are similar to one another in certain respects.

Logical Concepts
Concepts that can be clearly defined by a set of rules or properties.

Natural Concepts
Concepts that are not based on a precise set of attributes or properties, do not have clear-cut boundaries, and are often defined by prototypes.

Prototypes
The best or clearest examples of various objects or stimuli in the physical world.

Visual Images
Mental pictures or representations of objects or events.

To summarize, concepts may be represented in the mind in several ways, and they play an important role in thinking and in our efforts to make sense out of a complex and ever-changing external world.

Propositions: Relations between Concepts

Thinking is not a passive process; it involves active manipulation of concepts. Frequently, thinking involves relating one concept to another concept, or one feature of a concept to the entire concept. Because we possess highly developed language skills, these cognitive actions take the form of **propositions**—sentences that relate one concept to another and can stand as separate assertions. Propositions such as "Robert kissed Rebecca" describe a relationship between two concepts—in this case, affection expressed between one of the authors (Robert Baron) and his wife Rebecca. Others, such as "Polar bears have white fur," describe the relationship between a concept and its properties. Clusters of propositions are often represented as **mental models,** knowledge structures that guide our day-to-day decision making and interactions with objects and events. We often use mental models to judge cause and effect and to perform mental simulations of the probable outcomes of different situations. For example, to understand how to invest your money wisely, you might use a mental model constructed from the following propositions: (1) "I should write down information about my current sources of income and debts"; (2) "I should schedule a meeting with a competent financial planner to review my current financial status and future goals"; (3) "I should work with this person to develop a financial plan and then stick with it." Please note, however, that if some aspect of a mental model is incorrect, or if we process information contained in the model incompletely or incorrectly, we may tend to make mistakes. Thus, if you hold an incorrect mental model of how prevailing economic conditions or interest rates affect certain investment vehicles (such as stocks and bonds), you may lose part or all of your money. Clearly, much of our thinking involves the formulation and consideration of propositions; therefore, propositions should be considered one of the basic elements of thought.

Images: Mental Pictures of the World

As we indicated earlier, thinking often involves the manipulation of visual images. Indeed, relationships between concepts can sometimes be grasped more easily in an image than in words. Research indicates that mental manipulations performed on images of objects are very similar to those that would be performed on the actual objects (Kosslyn, 1994). For example, if asked to conjure up a mental image of a winter scene in Yellowstone National Park, it would probably take you longer to think about whether any animals are present than about whether there is snow on the ground. Why? Because locating the animals requires more detailed scanning than finding the snow. Other research also seems to indicate that once we form a mental image, we perceive it and think about it just as we would if it actually existed. When instructed to imagine walking toward an object, for instance, people report that the mental image of the object gradually expands, filling their imaginary visual field just as a real object would. Similarly, when people are asked to estimate the distance between locations in a familiar place, the farther apart the places indicated, the longer respondents take to make such judgments (Baum & Jonides, 1979).

Whatever the precise mechanisms through which they are used, mental images serve important purposes in thinking. People report using images for understanding verbal instructions, by converting the words into mental pictures of actions; for enhancing their own moods, by visualizing positive events or scenes; and for changing their behavior to achieve important goals, such as losing weight or enhancing certain aspects of their performance (Taylor et al., 1998).

Propositions
Sentences that relate one concept to another and can stand as separate assertions.

Mental Models
Knowledge structures that guide our interactions with objects and events in the world around us.

KEY QUESTIONS

- What are concepts?
- What is the difference between logical and natural concepts?
- What are propositions and images?

Reasoning: Transforming Information to Reach Conclusions

One task we often face in everyday life is **reasoning**—drawing conclusions from available information. Reasoning processes allow us to go beyond information that is readily available to us in memory in order to draw conclusions and make judgments about events in our lives. Inductive and deductive reasoning, as well as the use of analogy, are some thinking strategies we use to arrive at our judgments. How do we perform these tasks? And to what extent are we successful at them—in other words, how likely are the conclusions we reach to be accurate or valid? Before answering these questions, it is important to distinguish between *formal* and *everyday* reasoning. In *formal reasoning,* all the required information is supplied, the problem to be solved is straightforward, there is typically only one correct answer, and the reasoning we apply follows a specific method. By contrast, *everyday reasoning* involves the kind of thinking we do in our daily lives: planning, making commitments, evaluating arguments. In such reasoning, important information may be missing or left unstated; the problems involved often have several possible answers, which may vary in quality or effectiveness; and the problems themselves are not self-contained—they relate to other issues and questions of daily life. Everyday reasoning, then, is far more complex and far less definite than formal reasoning. But because it is the kind we usually perform, it is worthy of careful attention.

Reasoning: Some Basic Sources of Error

How good are we at reasoning? Unfortunately, not as good as you might guess. Several factors, working together, seem to reduce our ability to reason effectively.

The Confirmation Bias: Searching for Positive Evidence

Imagine that over the course of several weeks, a person with deeply held convictions *against* the death penalty encounters numerous magazine articles; some report evidence confirming the usefulness of the death penalty, while others report evidence indicating that capital punishment is ineffective in terms of deterring crime. As you can readily guess, the individual will probably remember more of the information that supports the anti–death penalty view. In fact, there is a good chance that he or she will read only these articles, or will read these articles more carefully than ones arguing in favor of capital punishment. To the extent that this happens, it demonstrates the **confirmation bias**—our strong tendency to test conclusions or hypotheses by examining only, or primarily, evidence that confirms our initial views (Baron, 1988; Nickerson, 1998). Because of the confirmation bias, individuals often become firmly locked into flawed conclusions; after all, when this bias operates, it prevents people from even considering information that might call their premises, and thus their conclusions, into question (please refer to Chapter 1 for additional information regarding the confirmation bias).

Hindsight: The "I knew it all along" Effect Revisited

Have you ever heard the old saying, "Hindsight is better than foresight"? What it means is that after specific events occur, we often have the impression that we could have predicted or actually did predict them. This is known in psychology as the **hindsight effect** (Hawkins & Hastie, 1990). In many studies, conducted in widely different contexts, learning that an event occurred causes individuals to assume that they could have predicted it more accurately than is actually the case.

Why does this effect occur? Reasons are varied, but research shows that it is often due to self-serving tendencies that cause us to reconstruct memories selectively for positive outcomes. Holzl, Kirchler, and Rodler (2002), for example, showed that people reconstruct memories so that they are in line with their attitudes. Six months before the introduction of the common European currency (the Eurodollar), participants in their study were questioned about the probability of

Reasoning
Cognitive activity in which we transform information in order to reach specific conclusions.

Confirmation Bias
The tendency to pay attention primarily to information that confirms existing views or beliefs.

Hindsight Effect
The tendency to assume that we would have been better at predicting actual events than is really true.

certain economic developments (e.g., a tax increase will occur). This was a controversial issue in Europe at the time; several countries had agreed to abandon their national currency in favor of a common currency that would be transportable across borders. There was considerable disagreement among citizens of the different countries as to advantages and disadvantages of adopting the Euro-dollar. A year after the initial survey, and six months after the euro had been introduced, participants were given a second survey that contained a list of events that actually transpired and asked to recall their initial probability estimates. Individuals showed the hindsight bias primarily for developments that were consistent with their own attitudes. Supporters of the Eurodollar were biased only with regard to positive developments. In contrast, opponents were biased only with regard to negative developments. This implies that we may selectively reconstruct our judgments to maintain consistency among our self-perceptions and attitudes.

A potentially serious consequence of the hindsight bias is that it may prevent us from learning from the accidents and the mistakes of others. The causes of an accident, once they are made known, often seem crystal clear to us in hindsight. Further, the hindsight bias leads us to conclude that the "known cause" should have been obvious to the actor involved in the accident. The problem with this reasoning is that it gives us a false sense of security that we would be able to avoid similar problems. As a result, we are less likely to learn from the mistakes of others. David Woods (2003), a noted safety researcher, has written about the hindsight bias as it relates to the *Columbia* space shuttle accident that occurred in February 2003 (refer to Figure 7.2). After lengthy investigation, it was determined that the accident was caused by debris hitting and damaging the shuttle wing during takeoff. This problem was known to NASA prior to the accident, and in hindsight, we ask, "Why did NASA continue to fly the shuttle with this known problem?" Woods argues that posing the question this way leads people to oversimplify the situation, and, as a result, they fail to grasp the uncertainties that people faced before the outcome was known. However, it is only by understanding these uncertainties that similar problems can be avoided in the future. In the case of the *Columbia* shuttle,

FIGURE 7.2
The Hindsight Effect
The hindsight effect often leads people to conclude the "known cause" of some event or outcome should have been obvious. This bias was evident in the aftermath of the *Columbia* space shuttle disaster that occurred on February 1, 2003. *Columbia* broke apart on reentry into the earth's atmosphere, killing all seven crew members aboard just minutes before it was scheduled to land in Florida. The problem with this reasoning is that it gives us a false sense of security that we would be able to avoid similar problems. A potentially serious consequence of the hindsight bias is that it may prevent us from learning from the accidents and the mistakes of others.

the most significant contributing factor may have been production pressures, as NASA was under pressure to keep to a tight flight schedule, and this may have caused their safety practices to erode over time. These lessons may be lost on many organizational leaders, however, because in hindsight, they may conclude that NASA simply made a bad decision.

In sum, it appears that we have a strong tendency to assume that we are better at predicting events than is truly justified, and this slant in our cognitions may be exaggerated by our self-serving tendencies. To the extent that we seek ways to avoid these tendencies, our ability to reason more effectively may be enhanced. For additional tips on how to reason more effectively, please refer to the **Psychology Lends a Hand** section. Next, let's turn to another cognitive activity we perform many times each day: decision making.

KEY QUESTIONS

- What does the process of reasoning entail? How does formal reasoning differ from everyday reasoning?
- What forms of error and bias can lead to faulty reasoning?

p s y c h o l o g y   l e n d s   a   h a n d

How to Reason More Effectively

Each day we face a succession of events that requires the use of our wits—in other words, our ability to reason. Several factors can greatly reduce our ability to reason effectively, however, thereby placing us at risk for making bad decisions. How can we reduce the chances that we will fall prey to one or more of these factors? One way involves the use of *critical thinking,* a topic we first introduced in Chapter 1. As you may recall, critical thinking involves avoiding tendencies to oversimplify and overgeneralize, examining all relevant evidence before reaching conclusions, and considering carefully all assumptions and potential biases. Clearly, these skills are closely related to effective reasoning. Here are several steps you can take to improve your own reasoning, and thus your ability to think critically

1. **Examine and test all premises.** The foundation of all reasoning is the set of premises from which it begins. You simply cannot reach valid conclusions if the initial premises are flawed. So, before starting, examine all premises with care. This is more difficult than it sounds, because in everyday reasoning, important premises are often implicit. For example, consider the following example: A student would like to meet with his instructor but never phones for an appointment. Why? Because he implicitly accepts the following premises: (1) My instructor is always very busy, and (2) busy people have little time for meeting with students. The first premise may be correct, but the second may be completely wrong; the instructor may be more than willing to find time in her busy day to meet with students. But the student

may never learn this is so, because he has accepted the premises without question.

2. **Guard against the confirmation bias.** The confirmation bias is our tendency to seek out and remember only information that supports our own preexisting attitudes or opinions. The power of this tendency is so pervasive that we often don't even realize it is operating. To counter or at least reduce its impact, (1) identify your own views on a topic or issue, and the premises these imply, and then (2) actively seek opposing points of view. The process is effortful, and sometimes uncomfortable, because it involves reading and listening to messages that contradict your own strongly held assumptions and beliefs. However, taking these steps may prevent you from becoming sealed in a closed logical system that can lead only to predetermined conclusions.

3. **Mood states: Feeling too good or too bad can spell trouble!** Most people's mood states fluctuate over time—that's normal. When it comes to reasoning, however, *extremes* in emotional states can be bad news. If you've ever lost your temper and, as a result, said things you didn't mean, or taken action that later proved costly, you are already familiar with such difficulties. Yet, being in a good mood also has its advantages and disadvantages. Performance on creative tasks seems to be enhanced by a positive mood state, but performance on analytic tasks is diminished. So, the moral is clear: When trying to engage in careful reasoning, try to keep strong emotions out of the picture. Once they enter, distortions and errors may quickly follow.

MAKING DECISIONS: CHOOSING AMONG ALTERNATIVES

Reasoning is an integral part of another cognitive task you perform many times each day: **decision making.** Throughout our waking hours, life presents a continuous series of choices: what to wear, what to eat, whether to attend a class meeting, and so on—the list of everyday decisions is endless. If you were a perfectly rational decision maker, you would make each of these choices in a cool, almost mathematical way, taking into consideration (1) the utility or value to you of the outcomes each alternative might yield and (2) the probability that such results would actually occur. As you know from your own life, though, people don't usually reason in such a systematic manner. Instead, we make decisions informally, on the basis of hunches, intuition, the information stored in our memories, and the opinions of others. Advances in cognitive psychology and neuroscience have shown that our brains are designed to process limited amounts of information. As a result, rather than computing complex theorems to solve problems, we typically use cognitive shortcuts, or what we might call rules of thumb, to aid our decisions (Pinker, 1997).

Heuristics: Using Quick—but Fallible—Rules of Thumb to Make Decisions

Making decisions is hard work, so it is only reasonable to expect people to take shortcuts in performing this activity. Cognitive shortcuts are known as **heuristics**—rules of thumb that reduce the effort required, though they may not necessarily enhance the quality or accuracy of the decisions reached (Kahneman & Tversky, 1982). Heuristics are extracted from past experience and serve as simple guidelines for making reasonably good choices quickly and efficiently. We'll focus on the three heuristics that tend to be used most frequently.

Availability: What Comes to Mind First?

Let's start with the **availability heuristic:** the tendency to make judgments about the frequency or likelihood of events in terms of how readily examples of them can be brought to mind (please refer to Chapter 1 for additional information). The more memorable an event, the more likely we think it is to happen. We use this heuristic to make judgments about others as well as about events: We treat information that comes to mind easily as typical of the complete picture. This shortcut tends to work fairly well, because the more readily we can bring events to mind, the more frequent they generally are; but it can lead us into error as well. For example, answer the following question: Are people more likely to die from accidents or disease? The answer is disease—by a large margin. However, studies show that people tend to judge accidents and disease as equally fatal.

Why is this the case? Compared with information about diseases, information about accidents tends to be more vivid, recent, and widely publicized—all factors that make information about accidents easier to recall. The availability heuristic explains why many people overestimate their chances of being a victim of violent crime, being involved in an airplane crash, or winning the lottery. Because such events are given extensive coverage in the mass media, people can readily bring vivid examples of them to mind. The result: They conclude that such outcomes are much more frequent than they really are (Tyler & Cook, 1984). An important implication of this effect is that people may spend more time and effort trying to prevent unlikely events than likely events. Many people may worry more about being killed through homicide than from emphysema, although the latter is much more probable and controllable.

Representativeness: Assuming That What's Typical Is Also Likely

Imagine that you've just met your next-door neighbor for the first time. On the basis of a brief conversation, you determine that he is neat in his appearance, has

---

Decision Making
The process of choosing among various courses of action or alternatives.

Heuristics
Mental rules of thumb that permit us to make decisions and judgments in a rapid and efficient manner.

Availability Heuristic
A cognitive rule of thumb in which the importance or probability of various events is judged on the basis of how readily they come to mind.

a good vocabulary, seems very well read, is somewhat shy, and dresses conservatively. Later, you realize that he never mentioned what he does for a living. Is he more likely to be a business executive, a dentist, a librarian, or a waiter? One quick way of making a guess is to compare him with your idea of typical members of each of these occupations. If you proceeded in this fashion, you might conclude that he is a librarian, because his traits might seem to resemble those of your image of the prototypical librarian more closely than those of waiters, dentists, or executives. If you reasoned in this manner, you would be using the **representativeness heuristic.** In other words, you would be making your decision on the basis of a relatively simple rule: The more closely an item—or event, object, or person—resembles the most typical examples of some concept or category, the more likely it is to belong to that concept or category.

Unfortunately, the use of this heuristic sometimes causes us to ignore forms of information that could potentially prove very helpful. The most important of these is information relating to *base rates*—the relative frequency of various items or events in the external world. Returning to your new neighbor, there are many more businessmen than male librarians. Thus, of the choices given, the most rational guess might be that your neighbor is a business executive. Yet because of the representativeness heuristic, you might falsely conclude that he is a librarian (Tversky & Kahneman, 1974).

■ Anchoring and Adjustment: Reference Points That May Lead Us Astray

The day a friend's son received his driver's license, he began to shop for his first car. After a long search, he found the car of his dreams. The major question, of course, was "How much will it cost?" A totally rational person would have located this information in the *Blue Book,* which lists the average prices paid for various used cars in recent months. But did he proceed in this fashion? Absolutely not. He (unfortunately) asked the seller what he wanted for the car, and then proceeded to bargain from there. At first glance, this may seem like a reasonable strategy. But think again. If you adopt it, as my friend's son did when he purchased that car, you have allowed the seller to set a reference point—a figure from which your negotiations will proceed. In the case of a used car, if the reference point is close to the *Blue Book* price, all is well and good. If it is much higher, though, you may end up paying more for the car than it is really worth—as this person did.

In such cases, decisions are influenced by what is known as the **anchoring-and-adjustment heuristic:** a mental rule of thumb for reaching decisions by making adjustments in information that is already available. The basic problem with the anchoring-and-adjustment heuristic is that the adjustments are often insufficient in magnitude to offset the impact of the original reference point. In this case, the reference point was the original asking price. In other contexts, it might be a performance rating assigned to an employee, a grade given to a term paper, or a suggested asking price for a new home (Diekmann et al., 1996; Northcraft & Neale, 1987).

The Accuracy of Heuristics: The Fast and Frugal Model of Decision Making

The previous discussion of decision heuristics seems to imply an automatic trade-off between speed and efficiency on the one hand and accuracy on the other. In fact, as we noted in the previous section, some research has shown that the use of heuristics can sometimes lead to error. But does our reliance on heuristics—sometimes termed the *fast and frugal* approach—imply that people are doomed to a life of faulty decisions? Psychologists Gerd Gigerenzer and Danile Goldstein (1996) suggest the answer is "no," arguing that heuristics play an important role by helping people to make decisions in everyday life.

To test their ideas, these researchers designed a computer simulation that compared the accuracy of decisions predicted by rational inference algorithms with that of decisions made by a simple "take-the-best" algorithm that instead relied on

Representativeness Heuristic
A mental rule of thumb suggesting that the more closely an event or object resembles typical examples of some concept or category, the more likely it is to belong to that concept or category.

Anchoring-and-Adjustment Heuristic
A cognitive rule of thumb for making decisions in which existing information is accepted as a reference point but then adjusted, usually insufficiently, in light of various factors.

FIGURE 7.3
Decision Making in Everyday Life

In the increasingly fast-paced world in which we live, decision makers can seldom afford the time and cognitive effort required to make time-consuming rational decisions, as illustrated by the one facing the person in this cartoon. Instead, they may devise simple decision rules that allow them to make quick but accurate decisions.

Source: © The New Yorker Collection 1976 Warren Miller from cartoonbank.com. All Rights Reserved.

Framing

Presentation of information concerning potential outcomes in terms of gains or in terms of losses.

a single cue or piece of information. Whereas the rational algorithms considered *all* information in reaching a decision, the take-the-best algorithm rank ordered the cues in terms of their usefulness and used only the top-ranked cue. In their computer simulation, the take-the-best algorithm matched or outperformed all variants of the rational model in terms of speed and accuracy. These findings provide evidence that information-processing strategies do not have to meet standards of rational decision making to be successful.

Dhami (2003) recently examined how well a heuristics-based approach captures actual decisions made by court judges. Like many other professionals, judges have to make important decisions on the basis of extensive—and often conflicting—information. You might think, as many people do, that such decisions would conform closely to the rational model of decision making. Using the actual bail decisions made by judges in two courts in the United Kingdom as criteria, Dhami compared the accuracy of a computer algorithm based on the rational model with a simpler one based on the take-the-best algorithm just described. The simpler algorithm actually outperformed the rational one; the simpler model predicted actual bail decisions by the judge 91 percent of the time, whereas the rational model was accurate 82 percent of the time. This implies that the judges were using simple rather than complex decision strategies. In the increasingly fast-paced world in which we live, many decision makers face strong time pressures and heavy workloads, and they can seldom afford the time and cognitive effort required to make time-consuming rational decisions (please refer to Figure 7.3). Instead, they may devise simple decision rules that allow them to make quick but, as Gigerenzer and Goldstein's research suggests, accurate decisions.

Framing and Decision Strategy

Imagine that a rare tropical disease has entered the United States and is expected to kill 600 people. Two plans for combating the disease exist. If plan A is adopted, 200 people will be saved. If plan B is adopted, the chances are one in three that all 600 will be saved but two in three that no one will be saved. Which plan would you choose?

Now consider the same situation with the following changes. Again, there are two plans. If plan C is chosen, 400 people will definitely die; if plan D is chosen, the chances are one in three that no one will die, but two in three that all 600 will die. Which would you choose now? If you are like most respondents, you probably chose plan A in the first example but plan D in the second example (Tversky & Kahneman, 1981). Why? Plan D is just another way of stating the outcomes of plan B, and plan C is just another way of stating the outcome of plan A. Why, then, do you prefer plan A in the first example but plan D in the second? Because in the first example the emphasis is on lives saved, while in the second the emphasis is on lives lost. In other words, the two examples differ in what psychologists term **framing**—the presentation of information about potential outcomes in terms of gains or in terms of losses. When the emphasis is on potential gains (lives saved), research indicates that most people are *risk averse:* They prefer avoiding unnecessary risks. Thus, most choose plan A. In contrast, when the emphasis is on potential losses (deaths), most people are *risk prone:* They prefer taking risks to accepting probable losses. As a result, most choose plan D. The effects of framing have been demonstrated across a wide variety of contexts, including consumer purchases (Schul & Ganzach, 1995), medical decision making (McNeil, Pauker, & Tversky,

1988), and personal and career decisions (Gati, Houminer, & Aviram, 1998; Shafir, 1993). A recent study by Hasseldine and Hite (2002) suggests that framing may even influence income tax compliance. These researchers presented participants with a scenario in which they were asked to imagine that they had just received extra income and whether they would report the income on their income tax return. The scenario also included one of two message frames: (1) a positively framed ("gain-frame") message that emphasized the advantages of complying with tax law (e.g., no fines, no chance of audit) or (2) a negatively framed ("loss-frame") message that emphasized the risks of not complying with tax law (e.g., greater chance of being audited, fined, and convicted). Overall, women were more likely to comply with the law than men. Interestingly, though, men were more likely to comply when they received the negative frame, whereas women were more compliant when they received the positive frame. Obviously, this is just one study and needs to be replicated before firm conclusions can be drawn. Nonetheless, it indicates that framing effects are common in many different settings and also suggests that men and women may respond differently to different framing messages.

Escalation of Commitment: Getting Trapped in Bad Decisions

Have you ever heard the phrase "throwing good money after bad"? It refers to the fact that in many situations, persons who have made a bad decision tend to stick to it even as the evidence for its failure mounts. They may even commit additional time, effort, and resources to a failing course of action in the hope that they can turn the situation around. This tendency to become trapped in bad decisions, known as **escalation of commitment,** helps explain why many investors hold on to what are clearly bad investments and why people remain in troubled marriages or relationships (Brockner & Rubin, 1985). In these and many other situations, people do seem to become trapped in bad decisions with no simple or easy means of getting out.

Escalation of Commitment: Why Does It Occur?

Research suggests that escalation of commitment probably stems from several different factors. Early in the escalation process, initial decisions are based primarily on *rational* factors. People choose particular courses of action because they believe that these will yield favorable outcomes. When things go wrong and negative results occur, it is at first quite reasonable to continue. After all, temporary setbacks are common; and there may also be considerable costs associated with changing an initial decision before it has had a chance to succeed (Staw & Ross, 1987).

As negative outcomes continue to mount, however, *psychological* factors come into play. Persons responsible for the initial decision may realize that if they back away from or reverse it, they will be admitting that they made a mistake. Indeed, as negative results increase, these individuals may experience a growing need for *self-justification*—a tendency to justify both their previous judgments and the losses already endured (Bobocel & Meyer, 1994).

In later phases of the process, external pressures stemming from other persons or groups affected by the bad decision may come into play. For example, individuals who did not originally make the decision but have gone along with it may now block efforts to reverse it because they too have become committed to actions it implies. Figure 7.4 on page 202 summarizes the escalation process and several factors that play a role in its occurrence and persistence.

Fortunately, researchers have found that certain steps can be taken to help make people less likely to escalate their commitment to a failed course of action. First, research shows that people are likely to refrain from escalating commitment when available resources to commit to further action are limited and the evidence of failure is overwhelmingly obvious (Garland & Newport, 1991). Thus, providing feedback that clearly shows the extent of losses in relation to resources may be an effective way to stop escalation of commitment from occurring. Second, escalation

Escalation of Commitment
The tendency to become increasingly committed to bad decisions, even as losses associated with them increase.

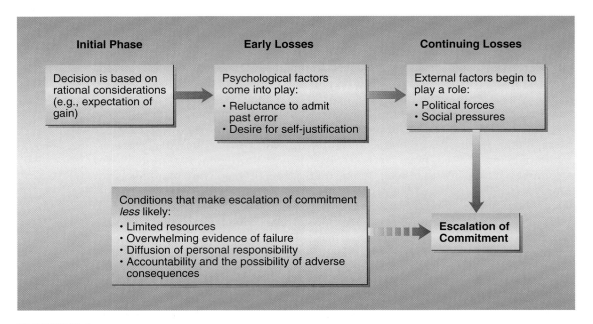

FIGURE 7.4
Escalation of Commitment: An Overview
Early in the escalation-of-commitment process, there may be a rational expectation of a positive outcome. As losses occur, however, people are reluctant to admit their errors and seek self-justification. Later, external factors may strengthen tendencies to stick to the initial bad decision. However, other conditions may reduce the likelihood of escalation of commitment.
Source: Based on suggestions by Garland & Newport, 1991; and Staw & Ross, 1989.

of commitment is unlikely to occur when people can diffuse their responsibility for being part of a poor decision (Whyte, 1991). In other words, the less we feel personally responsible for making a bad decision, the less we may be motivated to justify our decision by investing additional time, effort, or money. Thus, the tasks of making decisions and implementing them should be assigned to different persons. Finally, escalation of commitment is less likely to occur when it is made clear to people that they will be held accountable for their actions and that they, or someone they work for, may be adversely affected by the consequences of their decisions (Kirby & Davis, 1998; Simonson & Staw, 1992). Together, these steps can help both individuals and groups avoid getting trapped in costly spirals that magnify the harmful effects of poor decisions.

KEY QUESTIONS

- What are heuristics?
- What are the availability, representativeness, and anchoring-and-adjustment heuristics, and what role do they play in decision making?
- What is framing, and how does it relate to decision making?
- How does escalation of commitment affect decision making?

PROBLEM SOLVING: FINDING PATHS TO DESIRED GOALS

Imagine that you are a parent whose son is attending college in another state. You've asked him to keep in touch, but long periods go by without a word—by either phone or mail. You phone him repeatedly, but all you get is his answering machine. What do you do? Several possibilities exist. You could call his friends and ask them to urge him to get in touch with you. You could leave a message that, you hope, will cause him to phone. Or—and here's the interesting one—you could try something like this: You write a letter to your son in which you mention that you've enclosed a check—but you don't enclose one. Is the problem solved? In all probability, yes. Your son will no doubt call to find out what happened to the check.

While you may not have any children, there is little doubt that you have encountered situations that resemble this one in basic structure: You would like to reach some goal, but there is no simple or direct way of doing so. Such situations involve **problem solving**—efforts to develop responses that permit us to attain desired goals. In this section we'll examine several problem-solving techniques and several factors that sometimes interfere with effective problem solving. We'll also consider creativity—the ability to produce new and unusual solutions to various problems.

Methods for Solving Problems: From Trial and Error to Heuristics

Perhaps the simplest problem-solving approach is **trial and error,** a technique that you have no doubt used yourself. Trial and error involves trying different responses until, perhaps, one works. Sometimes this is all you can do—you don't have enough information to adopt a more systematic approach. But such an approach is not very efficient, and it offers no guarantee that a useful solution will be found.

A second general approach to solving problems involves the use of **algorithms.** These are rules for a particular kind of problem that will, if followed, yield a solution. For example, imagine that you are supposed to meet a friend at a restaurant. Try as you may, you can't remember the name of the place. What can you do? One approach is to get out the Yellow Pages and see if this refreshes your memory. If it doesn't, you can try calling all the restaurants listed to ask if your friend made a reservation (which you know she was planning to do). Following this algorithm— "Call every restaurant in the book"—will eventually work, but it is time consuming and inefficient. A much more effective way of solving many problems is to use an appropriate *heuristic.*

Heuristics, as you'll recall, are rules of thumb we often use to guide our cognition. With respect to problem solving, heuristics involve strategies suggested by prior experience—ones we have found useful in the past. These may or may not work in the present case, so a solution is not guaranteed. But what heuristics lack in terms of certainty they gain in efficiency: They often provide useful shortcuts. In the case of the forgotten restaurant, you might begin by assuming that your friend probably chose a restaurant close to where she lives. This simple rule could eliminate many of the most distant restaurants and considerably simplify your task.

Finally, we sometimes attempt to solve problems through the use of **analogy**— the application of knowledge of cases or events in one domain to solve problems in different domains (Gentner & Jeziorski, 1993; Holyoak & Thagard, 1997). For example, to get her soccer players to understand the relation between the speed of one's foot as it kicks the ball and distance of the kick, a coach could demonstrate how the speed of a golf club determines how far a golf ball travels (assuming contact is made!). Likewise, if you were driving through an unfamiliar town, and suddenly had an uncontrollable desire for a Big Mac, you might draw on your past experience in finding fast food restaurants near busy interstate highways to locate a McDonald's restaurant. Applying this knowledge, you follow signs showing the way to the nearest interstate. If you are then rewarded by the sight of the famous golden arches, you have solved the problem through analogy. To summarize, selecting an appropriate strategy is critical to effective problem solving.

Problem Solving
Efforts to develop or choose among various responses in order to attain desired goals.

Trial and Error
A method of solving problems in which possible solutions are tried until one succeeds.

Algorithm
A rule that guarantees a solution to a specific type of problem.

Analogy
A strategy for solving problems based on applying solutions that were previously successful with other problems similar in underlying structure.

FIGURE 7.5
Solving Complex Problems
How can you attach the candle to a wall so that it stands upright and burns normally, using only the objects shown here?

Factors That Interfere with Effective Problem Solving

Sometimes, despite our best efforts, we are unable to solve problems. In many cases our failure stems from obvious causes, such as lack of necessary information or experience. Similarly, as we'll soon see, we may lack internal frameworks that allow us to represent the problem situation fully and effectively. As a result, we don't know which variables or factors are most important, and we spend lots of time "wandering about," using an informal type of trial and error (Johnson, 1985). In other cases, though, difficulties in solving problems seem to stem from more subtle factors. Let's consider two of the most important of these now.

Functional Fixedness: Prior Use versus Present Solutions

Suppose you want to use the objects shown in Figure 7.5 to attach the candle to a wall so that it can stand upright and burn properly. What solution(s) do you come up with? If you are like most people, you may mention using the tacks to nail the candle to the wall or attaching it with melted wax (Duncker, 1945). Although these techniques might work, they overlook a much more elegant solution: emptying the box of matches, attaching the box to the wall, and placing the candle on it (see Figure 7.6). Described like this, the solution probably sounds obvious. Then why don't most people think of it? The answer involves **functional fixedness**—our strong tendency to think of using objects only in ways they have been used before. Because most of us have never used an empty box as a candle holder, we don't think of it in these terms and so fail to hit upon this solution. Interestingly, if the matchbox in this problem is shown empty, people are much more likely to think of using it as a candle holder (Weisberg & Suls, 1973); it doesn't take much to overcome such mental blind spots. But unless we can avoid functional fixedness, our ability to solve many problems can be seriously impaired.

Mental Set: Sticking to the Tried and True

Another factor that often gets in the way of effective problem solving is **mental set.** This is the tendency to stick with a familiar method of solving a particular type of problem—one that has worked before. Given that past solutions have in fact succeeded, this tendency is certainly reasonable, at least up to a point. Difficulties arise, however, when mental set causes us to overlook other, more efficient ap-

Functional Fixedness
The tendency to think of using objects only as they have been used in the past.

Mental Set
The impact of past experience on present problem solving; specifically, the tendency to retain methods that were successful in the past even if better alternatives now exist.

| **TABLE 7.1** | Mental Set: Another Potential Impediment to Problem Solving | | | |

How can you use three jars, A, B, and C, each capable of holding the amounts of liquid shown, to end up with one jar holding the exact amount listed in the right-hand column? See the text for two possible solutions.

	Amount Held by Each Jar			**Goal** (amount of water desired)
Problem	**Jar A**	**Jar B**	**Jar C**	
1	24	130	3	100
2	9	44	7	21
3	21	58	4	29
4	12	160	25	98
5	19	75	5	46
6	23	49	3	20
7	18	48	4	22

proaches. The powerful impact of mental set was first demonstrated by Luchins (1942) in what is now a classic study. Luchins presented study participants with the problems shown in Table 7.1, which involve using three jars of different sizes to measure amounts of water. If you work through the first two or three items, you will soon discover that you can solve them all by following this simple formula: Fill jar B, and from it fill jar A once and jar C twice. The amount of water remaining in jar B is then the desired amount. Because this formula works for all items, participants in Luchins's study tended to stick with it for all seven problems. But look at item 6: It can be solved in a simpler way. Just fill jar A, then from it fill jar C. The amount remaining in jar A is precisely what's required (20 units). A simple solution also exists for item 7; see if you can figure it out. Do you think many of the participants in Luchins's experiment noticed these simpler solutions? Absolutely not. When they reached item 6, almost all continued to use their old tried-and-true formula and overlooked the more efficient one. Similar effects occur in many other contexts. For example, commuters often continue to take the same crowded roads to work each day because they have always done so; they don't even consider alternate routes that might seem less direct but are easier to travel. In these and many other situations, sliding into mental ruts can indeed prove costly.

FIGURE 7.6
Functional Fixedness: How It Interferes with Problem Solving
Because of functional fixedness, surprisingly few people think of using the tacks to attach the box to the wall as a candle holder.

KEY QUESTIONS

- How do psychologists define *problem solving*?
- What are two general approaches to problem solving?
- What role do heuristics play in problem solving?
- What factors can interfere with effective problem solving?

CREATIVITY: GENERATING THE EXTRAORDINARY

Suppose you were asked to name people high in creativity: Who would be on your list? When faced with this question, many people name such famous figures as Albert Einstein, Leonardo da Vinci, Thomas Edison, and Sigmund Freud. What do these individuals have in common? All were responsible for producing something—a theory, inventions—viewed by other people as unexpected and *new.*

More formally, psychologists generally define **creativity** as involving the ability to produce work that is both novel (original, unexpected) and appropriate (it works—it is useful or meets task constraints) (e.g., Lubart, 1994). Creativity is an important cognitive process and is clearly related to certain aspects of intelligence (a topic we'll consider later in this chapter). Let's review what psychologists have discovered about this fascinating topic.

Contrasting Views of Creativity

A basic question about creativity is: "What factors produce it?" Research findings from different areas of psychology are providing answers to this question. Cognitive psychologists, for example, have tended to focus on the basic processes that underlie creative thought. Research findings indicate that such processes as retrieval of information from memory, association, synthesis, transformation, and categorical reduction (mentally assigning objects to basic categories) may all play a role in creativity (e.g., Ward, Smith, & Vaid, 1997). Moreover, a cognitive approach to creativity calls attention to the fact that creativity is part of our everyday lives: Each time we utter a new sentence or understand a new concept, we are showing creativity. Thus, a key task in the study of creativity is that of distinguishing between this kind of everyday creativity (termed *mundane creativity*) and *exceptional creativity*—the emergence of something dramatically new, such as the idea of integrated circuits, which made modern computers possible.

What differentiates these two kinds of creativity? According to Perkins (1997), a psychologist who has focused on this issue, the difference may lie in the fact that everyday creativity occurs with respect to problems for which our past knowledge and experience give us valuable clues. In contrast, exceptional creativity may arise in what he describes as *Klondike spaces*—in areas where, like the miners of long ago who searched for gold in the Klondike, we don't know even where to begin looking. When we do find a solution in such situations, it is likely to be dramatic and to require thinking that is "outside of the box."

The cognitive approach to creativity has been dominant in psychology, but other approaches exist as well. For instance, social psychologists have often focused on the personality traits that make people creative and the environmental conditions that either encourage or discourage creativity (e.g., Simonton, 2000). And still other researchers have focused on the motivation behind exceptional creativity and on developmental variables that appear to be associated with the emergence of creative potential.

One of the most striking findings of such research, and one with important implications for entrepreneurial cognition, is that exposure to examples of previous ideas or work can greatly restrict creative thought. Even when participants are told to avoid copying the examples to which they are exposed, properties of those examples tend to be incorporated into their designs, and this holds true for professional designers as well as for college students (Jansson & Smith, 1991; Marsh, Landau, & Hicks, 1996; Marsh, Ward, & Landau, 1999; Smith, Ward, & Schumacher, 1993). Similar studies with entrepreneurs could assess their tendency to either incorporate recently encountered information into the novel ideas they develop or reject it. These findings are related to the question of whether entrepreneurs tend to engage in heuristic or analytic thinking. If exposure to prior examples stimulates heuristic thinking (e.g., a tendency to incorporate features of existing products into new ones), such exposure may prevent entrepreneurs from engaging in analytic thinking—the type of thinking believed to be necessary for creative cognition to occur.

While all of these approaches have certainly added to our understanding of creativity, a view known as the **confluence approach** has gained considerable acceptance. This view suggests that in order for creativity to occur, multiple com-

Creativity
The ability to produce work that is both novel (original, unexpected) and appropriate (it works—it is useful or meets task constraints).

Confluence Approach
An approach suggesting that for creativity to occur, multiple components must converge.

ponents must converge (Amabile, 1983). For example, according to Lubart (1994), creativity requires a confluence of six distinct resources:

- *Intellectual abilities.* The ability to see problems in new ways, the ability to recognize which of one's ideas are worth pursuing, and persuasive skills—the ability to convince others of these new ideas.
- *Knowledge.* Enough knowledge about a field to move it forward.
- *Certain styles of thinking.* A preference for thinking in novel ways and an ability to see the big picture—to think globally as well as locally.
- *Personality attributes.* Such traits as willingness to take risks and to tolerate ambiguity.
- *Intrinsic, task-focused motivation.* Creative people usually love what they are doing and find intrinsic rewards in their work (Amabile, 1996).
- *An environment that is supportive of creative ideas.*

Only when all of these conditions are present can a high level of creativity emerge (Sternberg & Lubart, 1996). Thus, it is not surprising that workplaces that foster intrinsic motivation and creative thinking are associated with high levels of creativity in workers (Zhou, 2003).

Research on Creativity: Evidence for the Confluence Approach

A growing body of evidence offers support for the multidimensional view of creativity suggested by the confluence approach. For example, Lubart and Sternberg (1995) asked forty-eight adults to produce creative products in each of four domains: writing, art, advertising, and science. In the art category, for example, they were asked to produce drawings showing "hope" and "rage" and "the earth from an insect's point of view." With respect to advertising, they were asked to design television ads for bow ties and the Internal Revenue Service. All the products participants created were rated for overall creativity, novelty, and perceived effort. Participants also completed a measure of fluid intelligence, a measure of thinking style, and two personality measures. Results indicated that intellectual ability, thinking style, and personality were all significantly related to creativity. In addition, creativity in one domain (art, writing, and so on) was only moderately related to creativity in other domains. This makes sense according to confluence theory, because people's knowledge and expertise (a vital element of creativity) varies across domains and hence so should their creativity.

One factor that can exert negative effects on creativity is competition. Why? Apparently competition stifles a person's ability to think in novel ways and undermines intrinsic motivation—both important elements of creativity. To illustrate the effects of competition on creativity, let's consider the results of a study by Amabile (1983) in which she compared the creativity of paper collages made by girls who were either competing or not competing against other girls for an award. The collages of the girls who were competing for the award were judged as less creative than those who were not competing. It is noteworthy that more recent findings suggest that competition may have different effects on creativity for males than females. Conti, Collins, and Picariello (2001) asked boys and girls to perform the same paper collage task used by Amabile. Half of the boys and girls were told that the three most creative collages would receive an award; the other half were not offered an award. As expected, girls were less creative in the competition condition than the control condition. Boys, however, were *more* creative in the competition condition, especially when their competitors were other boys. These findings are important because it suggests that factors that facilitate creativity in males might actually inhibit creativity in females.

Taken together, these findings offer support for the confluence approach. Creativity, it appears, requires the convergence of many factors for its emergence.

psychology lends a hand

On Becoming More Creative: Some Useful Tips

Do you know any creative people? Are you creative? A creative person that springs to mind for me (Michael Kalsher) is my older brother. John has always been particularly good with his hands and is a natural tinkerer. Over the years, he began to blend his extensive knowledge of metalworking and welding (which he does for a living) and his love of horses to create a variety of creative—and practical—objects, such as the one depicted in Figure 7.7. How did he develop this ability? As you may recall, research on creativity seems to indicate that several converging factors probably played a role, including a broad base of knowledge and experience, hard work, and a preference for thinking in novel ways, to name just a few. Here are some tips to help you cultivate your own creativity.

1. **Develop a broad and rich knowledge base.** Creative solutions do not emerge out of thin air. Rather, they stem from the integration and combination of knowledge that is at the disposal of problem solvers. There seem to be no substitutes for a broad and rich knowledge base that spans a broad range of topics.

2. **Be prepared to work hard!** Creativity involves considerable preparation. A person who develops a creative solution to an important problem generally spends long periods of time immersed in the problem, gathering knowledge relevant to it and working on it. As Thomas Edison once remarked, "Success is ninety-eight percent perspiration and only two percent inspiration." Although admittedly my brother is no Edison, he has spent many years developing the basic skills he uses to create objects like the one in Figure 7.7.

3. **Creativity often involves divergent thinking.** Divergent thinking means moving outward from conventional knowledge or wisdom into unexplored paths and unconventional solutions—in other words, thinking outside of the box. Initially, my brother performed welding as part of his job; his work with horseshoes also had a very limited and practical goal: making sure that the

horseshoes he bought fit his horse's feet! What caused him to combine these skills? Creativity often involves a sudden illumination, or insight. The impetus for my brother's horseshoe hobby apparently had its roots in a fairly mundane request from his wife: Charlotte had informed him that a towel hook on their bathroom door had broken and asked him to get a new one. Instead of buying one at the store, however, it occurred to him that he could build one himself. From that rather inauspicious beginning, additional ideas for projects began to emerge, further evidence for the importance of thinking outside of the box.

4. **Nourish your curiosity.** Creative people, it turns out, often have a high level of curiosity. They are interested in many different topics, they read widely, and they actively seek new experiences. These characteristics help expand and enrich their knowledge base—one of the key ingredients in creativity. While growing up, I recall that my brother always had a natural curiosity about how things worked. As a teen, he was always tinkering with the engines of his cars, and he never calls someone to fix a broken appliance until attempting to fix it himself. In addition, he has always been an avid reader and seems to select books that cover a surprisingly broad range of topics. So turn off the television and read.

5. **Your mood matters!** The last technique for encouraging creativity may surprise you—your mood. Evidence from many studies concerned with the effects of *affect*, or mood, on cognition indicates that when people are in a good mood, they are often more creative than when they are in a neutral or negative mood. Creative people also seem to love what they are doing and find intrinsic reward in their work. My brother is one of the happiest people I know; he seems to enjoy his job and has always been a hard worker. However, he also *plays* hard, and enjoys a variety of hobbies and activities, both alone and with family and friends.

FIGURE 7.7
Creativity in Everyday Life
As illustrated by the statue shown here, everyday creativity in solving important problems—both big and small—seems to emerge from the convergence of a number of factors, including past knowledge and experience, hard work, and divergent thinking.

None of these factors are unusual in and of themselves, but together they produce outcomes and results that are, in some cases, extraordinary. For tips on how to cultivate your own creativity, please refer to the **Psychology Lends a Hand** section on page 208.

KEY QUESTIONS

- What is creativity?
- What are confluence theories, and what factors do they view as essential to creativity?
- What evidence offers support for the confluence approach?

LANGUAGE: THE COMMUNICATION OF INFORMATION

Perhaps what truly sets us apart from other species of animals is our use of **language**—our ability to use an extremely rich set of symbols, plus rules for combining them, to communicate information. Although the members of all species do communicate with one another in some manner, and although some may use certain features of language, the human ability to use language far exceeds that of any other organism on earth. We'll now examine language and its relationship to other aspects of cognition.

The Development of Language

Throughout the first weeks of life, infants have only one major means of verbal communication: crying. Within a few short years, however, children progress rapidly to speaking whole sentences and acquire a vocabulary of hundreds or even thousands of words. What mechanisms play a role in this remarkable process? And how, and at what ages, do children acquire various aspects of language skills?

Theories of Language Development: Some Contrasting Views

The social learning view proposes that speech is acquired through a combination of operant conditioning and imitation. Presumably, children are praised or otherwise rewarded by their parents for making sounds approximating those of their native language. Moreover, parents often model sounds, words, or sentences for them. Together, it is contended, these basic forms of learning contribute to the rapid acquisition of language.

A sharply different view, proposed by the noted linguist Noam Chomsky (1968), suggests that language acquisition is at least partly innate. Human beings, he contends, have a *language acquisition device*—a built-in neural system that provides them with an intuitive grasp of **grammar.** In other words, humans are prepared to acquire language and do so rapidly for this reason. Chomsky points out, for example, that children throughout the world go through similar stages in language development at about the same age and in a way that mirrors their motor development.

As you might expect, more recent theories of language development tend to emphasize the importance of both innate mechanisms and learning. The most recent of these, termed the **constrained statistical learning framework,** suggests that we acquire language through the use of statistical features of linguistic input that helps us discover structure, including sound patterns, words, and grammar (Newport & Aslin, 2000; Saffran, 2003). According to this view, the similarities in language development patterns noted by Chomsky and others may not be the result of innate linguistic knowledge, but, instead, a more generalized set of *learning mechanisms* inherent in humans, and perhaps other species (e.g., Hauser, Newport, & Aslin, 2001).

To illustrate how this might work, consider the difficulties faced by infants confronted with the complexities of language. One of the most significant challenges

Language
A system of symbols, plus rules for combining them, used to communicate information.

Grammar
Rules within a given language indicating how words can be combined into meaningful sentences.

Constrained Statistical Learning Framework
A recent theory of language development that suggests that we acquire language through the use of statistical features of linguistic input that helps us to discover structure, including sound patterns, words, and grammar.

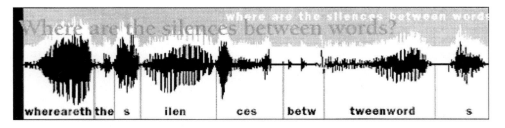

FIGURE 7.8
Language Acquisition: Learning the Boundaries between Words
As illustrated by the speech waveform for the sentence, "Where are the silences between words," there are often no consistent word boundaries in fluent speech. The vertical gray lines represent quiet points. Please note that these points do not always correspond to word boundaries. Thus, learners must use other means to learn where word boundaries occur.
Source: From Saffran, 2003.

they face is learning *word segmentation*—in other words, learning where the boundaries are between words in fluent speech. Why is this a problem? In part, because experienced speakers do not consistently mark word boundaries with detectable pauses, as is evident in the speech waveform shown in Figure 7.8. Thus, one of the many difficult tasks faced by infants is determining where one word ends and another begins. This process definitely requires learning, because it would be otherwise impossible for them to know, for example, that *pretty* and *baby* are words, whereas *tyba* (the letters that span the boundary between pretty and baby) is not.

According to psychologist Jenny Saffran, the *statistical structure* of a person's native language is what enables him to learn word boundaries and other characteristics of language. For example, among parents speaking to their infants, the probability that the syllable *pre* will be followed by *ty* is very high, whereas other combinations are less probable. Thus, an infant's ability to track such probabilities is an important tool to help her identify word boundaries (Saffran, Aslin, & Newport, 1996). In short, these results, and the results of additional research seem to point to the conclusion that both innate mechanisms *and* learning play a critical role in our ability to acquire language. Thus, it is probably safest to conclude that language development is the result of a complex process involving several aspects of learning, many cognitive processes, and genetically determined mechanisms as well.

Basic Components of Language Development

Although the underlying mechanisms of language development will require further clarification, much is known about how this process unfolds. Here, we'll touch on two distinct but interrelated areas that illustrate how language development progresses: **phonological development**—development of the ability to pronounce the sounds and words of one or more languages—and **semantic development**—learning to understand the meaning of words.

Phonological Development: The Spoken Word   Infants generally begin to coo at about one month of age (Shaffer, 1999). **Cooing** is repeating vowel-like sounds such as "oooooh" or "aaaaah." At around three or four months, infants start to add consonant sounds to their cooing, and they begin to babble at between four and six months of age (Berk, 2000). At first **babbling** contains a rich mixture of sounds, virtually every sound used in human speech. Research suggests that babies only a few months old can distinguish sounds from many different languages (Werker & Desjardins, 1995). This makes sense because humans are born with the capacity to learn any language. By nine or ten months, however, the range of babbling narrows

---

Phonological Development
Development of the ability to produce recognizable speech.

Semantic Development
Development of understanding of the meaning of spoken or written language.

Cooing
An early stage of speech development in which infants emit vowel-like sounds.

Babbling
An early stage of speech development in which infants emit virtually all known sounds of human speech.

and consists mainly of sounds used in the language of the child's native culture. From this point to the production of the first spoken word is a relatively short step, and most children accomplish it by their first birthday.

Between the ages of one and two years, children's vocabularies increase rapidly; for instance, by the time they are eighteen months old, many toddlers have a vocabulary of fifty words or more. Not surprisingly, these words include the names of familiar objects important in the children's own lives—foods (*juice, cookie*), animals (*cat, dog*), toys (*block, ball*), body parts (*ear, eye*), clothing (*sock, hat, shoe*), and people (*momma, dadda*). Children make the most of these words, often using them as *holophrases*—single-word utterances that communicate much meaning, especially when combined with pointing and other gestures. For example, if a child wants some chocolate milk, she may point to the cupboard (in which the chocolate syrup is kept) while saying "milk," thus indicating that she wants some milk with syrup in it. Gestures are an important component of early language development because they compensate for difficulties that children have with pronunciation (Nicoladis, Mayberry, & Genesee, 1999).

There is considerable variability in the size of a child's vocabulary and the rate at which vocabulary increases. Not surprisingly, exposure to spoken words—reflected, for example, in the amount of time parents spend speaking to their child—is an important factor in vocabulary size and rate of growth (Huttenlocher et al., 1991).

Semantic Development: The Acquisition of Meaning   Children's vocabulary increases rapidly after age two, with many new words being learned each day. Thus, by the time they are five, most children have a vocabulary of thousands of words. Children don't simply learn new words, however; they also learn new types of words—ones that allow them to communicate a much richer range of thoughts and ideas. Thus, they acquire understanding of negatives such as *no* and how to use these in sentences. Similarly, they acquire many adjectives and prepositions—words that allow them to be more specific in describing their own thoughts and the world around them. They start with simple adjectives such as *little, good,* and *bad,* but soon move on to ones with more specific meaning such as *high, low, narrow,* and *wide,* and prepositions such as *in front of* and *behind.* Children also learn to use question words—words that allow them to ask for information from others in efficient and specific ways: *Why? When? Who? Where?* These are key words children acquire between the ages of two and three.

While children increase their vocabulary very rapidly, they often demonstrate several interesting forms of error. One such error involves *overextensions*—a tendency to extend the meaning of a word beyond its actual usage. For instance, eighteen-month-olds may use the word *raisin* to refer to all small objects—flies and pebbles as well as raisins themselves. Similarly, they may use *meow* as a shorthand word for all small furry animals—dogs as well as cats. They also show *underextensions*—limiting the meaning of a word more than is appropriate. For instance, they may think that the word *cat* refers to their family's pet cat and to no others.

Language and Thought: Do We Think What We Say or Say What We Think?

Although we often have vivid mental images, most of our thinking seems to involve words. This fact raises an intriguing question: What is the precise relationship between language and thought? One theory, known as the **linguistic relativity hypothesis,** suggests that language shapes or determines thought (Whorf, 1956). According to this view, people who speak different languages may perceive the world in different ways, because their thinking is determined, at least in part, by the words available to them. For example, the Inuit of Alaska, who have many

Linguistic Relativity Hypothesis
The view that language shapes thought.

different words for *snow,* may perceive this aspect of the physical world differently from English-speaking people, who have only one word.

The opposing view is that thought shapes language. This position suggests that language merely reflects the way we think—how our minds work. Which position is more accurate? Although the issue is far from resolved, a modified version of the linguistic relativity hypothesis has been advanced that suggests that structural characteristics of language may indeed influence the way people think about objects and relationships among objects in the physical world (Hunt & Agnoli, 1991; Lucy, 1992). Ozgen and Davies (2002) recently provided support for the modified linguistic relativity hypothesis in a study of color perception. While we find it relatively easy to discriminate *between* categories of color, we tend to have more difficulty discriminating between shades of the same color. Suppose that we set out to learn new categories of color that reflect subtle hues and lightness of natural color, much like the fine-grained categories that the Inuit have for *snow*? Would our discrimination of colors improve? The results of Ozgen and Davies' study suggest that the answer is "yes." Participants in their study who learned new categories for color did in fact perform better on a subsequent color discrimination task. The results of this study support the linguistic relatively hypothesis by suggesting that language may indeed shape aspects of thought, including as in this instance, the way in which we perceive color.

Language in Other Species

Members of nonhuman species communicate with one another in many ways. Bees do a complex dance to indicate the distance to and direction of a food source; birds sing songs when seeking to attract a mate; whales communicate with one another through complex patterns of sounds. But what about language? Are we the only species capable of using this sophisticated means of communication? Until the 1970s there seemed little question that this was so. Early efforts to teach chimpanzees to speak failed miserably. These disappointing results were due in part to the fact that researchers focused their efforts on teaching these animals to *speak.*

Then, during the 1970s, several teams of researchers provided evidence that primates may be capable of using language. Beatrice and Allen Gardner succeeded in teaching Washoe, a female chimp, to use and understand almost two hundred signs from American Sign Language. After several years of practice, Washoe learned to respond to simple questions and to request actions such as tickling and objects such as food. Francine Patterson (1978) taught Koko, a female gorilla, a vocabulary of several hundred signs. Patterson reported that Koko showed great flexibility in using signs, constructing original sentences, remembering and describing past events, and even creating her own signs for new objects and events.

These researchers, and many psychologists, interpreted these findings as evidence that other species can indeed use language. Other psychologists, however, disagreed. They believed that Washoe and Koko, while exhibiting impressive learning, did not really demonstrate the use of language (Davidson & Hopson, 1988; Terrace, 1985). Close examination of the procedures used to train and test the animals suggests that their trainers may often unintentionally provide subtle cues that help animals respond correctly to questions. It also appears that in some cases trainers may have overinterpreted the animals' responses, reading complex meanings and intentions into relatively simple signs. Finally, it is still unclear whether animals are capable of mastering several basic features of human languages; for example, **syntax**—the rules by which words are arranged to form meaningful sentences—and *generativity*—the ability to combine a relatively limited number of words into unique combinations that convey a broad range of meanings.

Studies involving other species of animals, including bonobos (a rare type of chimpanzee), dolphins, and parrots, have addressed these and related issues. For example, consider the language abilities demonstrated by a bonobo named Kanzi

Syntax

Rules about how units of speech can be combined into sentences in a given language.

(Savage-Rumbaugh et al., 1989). While attempting to teach Kanzi's mother to use an artificial language made up of abstract visual symbols, psychologist Sue Savage-Rumbaugh noticed that Kanzi (then an infant) had learned several symbols just by watching. Intrigued by the possibilities raised by this discovery, Savage-Rumbaugh and her colleagues continued to train Kanzi in this informal way—speaking to him throughout the day, while simultaneously pointing to the corresponding word symbols on portable language boards they carried with them. Kanzi quickly learned to combine the symbol-words to request tasty snacks and preferred activities, such as watching Tarzan movies. Since then, Kanzi has demonstrated a grasp of grammatical concepts, and he now comprehends several hundred spoken words. More importantly, though, the use of strict control procedures ruled out the possibility that Kanzi was responding to subtle cues from his trainers, a criticism leveled against many early demonstrations of animal language.

One of the most dramatic examples of language use by other species comes from research conducted by Irene Pepperberg (1999; 2000) with grey parrots. She has taught these birds to use English speech to label objects and their properties (shape, color, category) and to communicate with humans. The methodology that she has used in her studies is important to note because it involves observational learning and social interaction. Parrots initially watch as two humans alternate roles as trainer and model. The trainer presents an object to the model and asks a question (e.g., "What is it?" "What color?"). The model is praised and given the object if he or she responds correctly. Incorrect responses are followed by scolding and removal of the object. Eventually the parrot is drawn into the training and competes with the model for the trainer's praise and rewards. With this type of training, Pepperberg's parrots have learned not only to label objects and their properties, but also to request specific rewards they want following correct responses (e.g., "The key is green." "I want treat."). Their use of speech shows reference (relationship between labels and objects to which they refer) and function (context-specific requests). These parrots clearly seem to be communicating with humans rather than just mimicking speech (please refer to Figure 7.9).

To summarize, mounting evidence based on studies of several species of animals suggests that language may not be a uniquely human possession, but a continuum of skills that different species of animals exhibit to varying degrees. The results of further studies will undoubtedly shed additional light on where different species of animals fit into this continuum. In the meantime, the question of whether we'll soon "talk with the animals" remains largely unresolved. Let's turn next to a discussion of intelligence.

FIGURE 7.9
Language in Other Species: Can We Talk to the Animals?
A growing body of evidence suggests that certain species of animals, including bonobo chimpanzees, dolphins, and even parrots, can grasp many aspects of language, including comprehension of spoken language. One of the most interesting examples of this intriguing finding is a parrot named Alex. Apparently, Alex can count; identify shapes, colors, and materials; knows the concepts of *same* and *different*; and bosses around lab assistants in order to modify his environment.

KEY QUESTIONS

- What abilities are involved in the production of language, and how is language acquired in humans?
- What factors are involved in language acquisition?
- What is the linguistic relativity hypothesis?
- Do animals possess language?

INTELLIGENCE: CONTRASTING VIEWS OF ITS NATURE

Intelligence, like love, is one of those concepts that are easier to recognize than to define. We often refer to others' intelligence, describing people as *bright, sharp,* or *quick* on the one hand, or as *slow, dull,* or even *stupid* on the other. And slurs on one's intelligence are often fighting words where children—and even adults—are concerned. But again, what, precisely, *is* intelligence? Psychologists don't entirely agree, but as a working definition we can adopt the wording offered by a distinguished panel of experts (Neisser et al., 1996): The term **intelligence** refers to individuals' abilities to understand complex ideas, to adapt effectively to the environment, to learn from experience, to engage in various forms of reasoning, and to overcome obstacles by careful thought.

Why do we place so much importance on evaluating others' and our own intelligence? Partly because we believe that intelligence is related to many important outcomes: how quickly individuals can master new tasks and adapt to new situations, how successful they will be in school and in various kinds of jobs, and even how well they can get along with others (e.g., Goleman, 1998). To some extent, our commonsense ideas in this respect are correct. But although intelligence *is* related to important life outcomes, this relationship is far from perfect. Many other factors, too, play a role, so predictions based solely on intelligence alone can be misleading.

Intelligence: Unitary or Multifaceted?

Is intelligence a single characteristic, or does it involve several different components? In the past, psychologists who studied intelligence often disagreed sharply on this issue. In one camp were scientists who viewed intelligence as a single characteristic or dimension along which people vary. One early supporter of this view was Spearman (1927), who believed that performance on any cognitive task depended on a primary *general* factor (which he termed g) and one or more *specific* factors relating to particular tasks. Spearman based this view on the following finding: Although tests of intelligence often contain different kinds of items designed to measure different aspects of intelligence, scores on these items often correlate highly with one another. This fact suggested to him that no matter how intelligence was measured, it was related to a single, primary factor.

In contrast, other researchers believed that intelligence is composed of many separate abilities that operate more or less independently. According to this *multifactor* view, a given person can be high on some components of intelligence but low on others. One early supporter of this position was Thurstone (1938), who suggested that intelligence is composed of seven distinct primary mental abilities. Included in his list were *verbal meaning*—understanding of ideas and word meanings; *number*—speed and accuracy in dealing with numbers; and *space*—the ability to visualize objects in three dimensions.

Which of these views of intelligence has prevailed? Most modern theories of intelligence adopt a position somewhere in between these extremes. They recognize that intelligence may involve a general ability to handle a wide range of cognitive tasks and problems, as Spearman suggested, but also that intelligence *is* expressed in many different ways and that persons can be high on some aspects of intelligence but low on others. As examples of this modern approach, let's briefly consider three influential views of intelligence.

Gardner's Theory of Multiple Intelligences

In formulating their views of intelligence, most researchers have focused primarily on what might be described as "normal" children and adults: persons who neither greatly exceed nor fall far below what most of us would view as "average" levels of intelligence. In addition, they have restricted their view of intelligence to verbal, mathematical, and spatial abilities. Howard Gardner (1983) argued that this approach was limiting psychology's view of intelligence. A better tactic, he suggested, would be to study not only persons in the middle of the intelligence dimension, but also ones at the extremes—acclaimed geniuses and those whose cognitive functioning is impaired, as well as experts in various domains and those who might be described as possessing special mental "gifts." For instance, consider the young athletes who compete in the Olympics. The feats they can perform

Intelligence
Individuals' abilities to understand complex ideas, to adapt effectively to the environment, to learn from experience, to engage in various forms of reasoning, and to overcome obstacles by careful thought.

are amazing. Is their ability to execute complex maneuvers like those shown in Figure 7.10 simply the result of extensive training? Or does their performance also show a special kind of intelligence—something very different from the verbal fluency we usually associate with the term *intelligence* but perhaps just as important?

Gardner would argue strongly for the latter view. In fact, to aspects of intelligence most of us readily recognize, such as the verbal, mathematical, and spatial abilities studied by Thurstone, Gardner added such components as *musical intelligence*—the kind of intelligence shown by one of our friends who, without any formal training, can play virtually any tune on the piano; *bodily–kinesthetic intelligence*—the kind shown by the athlete shown in Figure 7.10; and *personal intelligence*—for instance, the ability to get along well with others. (We'll return to this latter topic in detail in the discussion of *emotional intelligence*.)

In sum, as its name suggests, Gardner's theory of multiple intelligences proposes that there are several important types of intelligence, and that we must understand each in order to get the big picture where this important human characteristic is concerned.

FIGURE 7.10
**Great Athletic Skill:
A Kind of Intelligence?**
Gardner's theory of multiple intelligences views performance such as that shown here as involving a high level of *bodily–kinesthetic intelligence*.

Sternberg's Triarchic Theory: The Value of Practical Intelligence

Another important modern theory of intelligence is one proposed by Robert Sternberg (Sternberg, 1985; Sternberg et al., 1995). According to this theory, known as the **triarchic theory** of intelligence, there are actually three basic types of human intelligence. The first, called *componential* or *analytic* intelligence, involves the abilities to think critically and analytically. Persons high on this dimension usually excel on standard tests of academic potential and make excellent students. The second type of intelligence, *experiential* or *creative* intelligence, emphasizes insight and the ability to formulate new ideas. Persons who rate high on this dimension excel at zeroing in on what information is crucial in a given situation and at combining seemingly unrelated facts. This is the kind of intelligence shown by many scientific geniuses and inventors. For example, Johannes Gutenberg, inventor of the printing press, combined the mechanisms for producing playing cards, making wine, and minting coins in his invention; thus, he showed a high level of creative intelligence.

Sternberg terms the third type of intelligence *contextual* or **practical intelligence,** and in some ways, it is the most interesting of all. Persons high on this dimension are intelligent in a practical, adaptive sense—they have what many would term *street smarts* and are adept at solving the problems of everyday life. Like Gardner, Sternberg suggests that there is more to intelligence than the verbal, mathematical, and reasoning abilities that are often associated with academic success. Practical intelligence, too, is important and contributes to success in many areas of life.

Cattell's Theory of Fluid and Crystallized Intelligence

Yet another view of intelligence was offered by British psychologist Raymond Catell (1963). Cattell examined scores on many different ability tests and concluded that performance on these tests reflects two major clusters of mental ability, which he termed *fluid* and *crystallized intelligence. Fluid intelligence* refers to our largely inherited abilities to think and reason—in a sense, the hardware of our brains that determines the limits of our information-processing capabilities. In contrast, *crystallized intelligence* refers to accumulated knowledge—information we store over a lifetime of experience, plus the application of skills and knowledge to solving specific problems.

Longitudinal studies of intellectual abilities show that once people mature and reach adulthood, fluid intelligence seems to decrease slowly with age, but crystallized intelligence stays level or even increases (e.g., Baltes, 1987; McArdle et al.,

Triarchic Theory
A theory suggesting that there are three basic forms of intelligence: componential, experiential, and contextual.

Practical Intelligence
Intelligence useful in solving everyday problems.

2002). This is why older, more experienced individuals can sometimes outperform younger ones on cognitive tasks ranging from scientific research to chess.

Is there anything we can do to slow the age-related declines observed in fluid intelligence? Fortunately, the answer seems to be "yes." Research seems to indicate that regular aerobic exercise can help to reduce age-related declines in fluid intelligence (e.g., Kramer & Willis, 2002). Although psychologists have not yet determined why such effects occur, the message seems clear: Take steps to help reduce age-related declines in fluid intelligence by staying fit. This means doing aerobic activities that you like, such as walking, jogging, or swimming, on a regular basis.

KEY QUESTIONS

- What is intelligence?
- What is Gardner's theory of multiple intelligences?
- What is Sternberg's triarchic theory of intelligence?
- What is fluid intelligence? Crystallized intelligence?

MEASURING INTELLIGENCE

In 1904, when psychology was just emerging as an independent field, members of the Paris school board approached Alfred Binet with an interesting request: Could he develop an objective method for identifying the children who, in the language of that era, were described as being mentally retarded, so that they could be given special education? Binet was already at work on related topics, so he agreed, enlisting the aid of his colleague, Theodore Simon.

In designing this test, Binet and Simon were guided by the belief that the items used should be ones children could answer without special training or study. They felt that this was important because the test should measure the ability to handle intellectual tasks, *not* specific knowledge acquired in school. The original test asked children to perform the following tasks: Follow simple commands or imitate simple gestures; name objects shown in pictures; repeat a sentence of fifteen words; tell how two common objects are different; complete sentences begun by the examiner.

The first version of Binet and Simon's test was published in 1905 and was seen as quite effective: With it, schools could readily identify children in need of special help. Encouraged by this success, Binet and Simon broadened the scope of their test to measure variations in intelligence among all children. The revised version, published in 1908, grouped items by age, with six items at each level from three to thirteen years. Items were placed at a particular age level if about 75 percent of children of that age could pass them correctly.

Binet's tests were soon revised and adapted for use in many countries. In the United States, Lewis Terman, a psychologist at Stanford University, developed the **Stanford–Binet test**—a test that was soon put to use in many different settings. Over the years the Stanford–Binet has been revised several times. One of the features of the Stanford–Binet that contributed to its popularity was the fact that it yielded a single score assumed to reflect an individual's level of intelligence—the now famous (some would say *infamous*) IQ.

IQ: Its Meaning Then and Now

Originally, the letters **IQ** stood for *intelligence quotient*, and a "quotient" is precisely what the scores represented. To obtain an IQ score, an examiner divided a student's mental age by his or her chronological age, then multiplied this number by 100. For this computation, mental age was based on the number of items a person passed correctly on the test: Test takers received two months' credit of "mental age" for each item passed. If an individual's mental and chronological ages were equal, an

Stanford–Binet Test
A widely used individual test of intelligence.

IQ
Originally "intelligence quotient," a number that examiners derived by dividing an individual's mental age by his or her chronological age and then multiplying by 100. Now IQ simply indicates an individual's performance on an intelligence test relative to those of other persons of the same age.

IQ of 100 was obtained; this was considered to be an average score. IQs above 100 indicated that a person's intellectual age was greater than her or his chronological age—in other words, that the individual was more intelligent than typical students of the same age. In contrast, numbers below 100 indicated that the individual was less intelligent than her or his peers.

Perhaps you can already see one obvious problem with this type of IQ score: At some point, mental growth levels off or stops, while chronological age continues to grow. As a result, IQ scores begin to decline after the early teen years! Partly because of this problem, IQ scores now have a different definition. They simply reflect an individual's performance relative to that of persons of the same age who have taken the same test. Thus, an IQ above 100 indicates that the person has scored higher than the average person in her or his age group, while a score below 100 indicates that the person has scored lower than average.

The Wechsler Scales

As noted earlier, the tests developed by Binet and later adapted by Terman and others remained popular for many years. They do, however, suffer from one major drawback: All are mainly verbal in content. As a result, they pay little attention to the fact that intelligence can be revealed in nonverbal activities as well. For example, an architect who visualizes a majestic design for a new building is demonstrating a high level of intelligence; yet no means for assessing such abilities was included in early versions of the Stanford–Binet test.

To overcome this and other problems, David Wechsler devised a set of tests for both children and adults that include nonverbal, or *performance,* items as well as verbal ones, and that yield separate scores for these two components of intelligence. Thus, Wechsler began with the view that intelligence is *not* a unitary characteristic, shown only through verbal and mathematical reasoning. However, he developed these tests at a time when the multifaceted nature of intelligence was not yet well understood, and it is not clear that Wechsler's various subtests actually do measure different aspects of intelligence. Despite such problems, the Wechsler tests are currently among the most frequently used individual tests of intelligence. An overview of the subtests that make up one of the Wechsler scales, the *Wechsler Adult Intelligence Scale–Revised* (WAIS–3 for short) is presented in Table 7.2 on page 218.

A Wechsler test for children, the *Wechsler Intelligence Scale for Children* (WISC), has also been developed; it, too, is in widespread use. Patterns of scores on the subtests of the WISC are sometimes used to identify children suffering from various *learning disabilities.* Some findings indicate that children who score high on certain subtests, such as Picture Completion and Object Assembly, but lower on others, such as Arithmetic, Information, and Vocabulary, are more likely to suffer from learning disabilities than children with other patterns of scores (Aiken, 1991). Once again, however, not all findings point to such conclusions, so the value of the WISC (now in its third revision, WISC–3) for this kind of diagnosis remains somewhat uncertain. Let's turn now to a discussion of the basic requirements for a useful test of intelligence.

Intelligence Tests: Some Basic Requirements

Are you familiar with the old adage, "Measure twice, cut once"? Among woodworkers, this means that it is *crucial* to measure carefully before cutting any piece of wood. Unless the measurements are precise, the project won't turn out well. A similar principle applies to all psychological tests, including ones designed to measure intelligence: Unless the tests do a good job of measuring what they are designed to measure, they are useless. Briefly, a test must meet three crucial requirements before we can conclude that it provides an accurate and useful measure of intelligence: The test must be carefully *standardized,* it must be *reliable,* and

TABLE 7.2 Subtests of the Wechsler Adult Intelligence Scale

The widely used test of adult intelligence includes the subtests described here.

Test	Description
Verbal Tests	
Information	Examinees are asked to answer general information questions, increasing in difficulty.
Digit span	Examinees are asked to repeat series of digits read out loud by the examiner.
Vocabulary	Examinees are asked to define thirty-five words.
Arithmetic	Examinees are asked to solve arithmetic problems.
Comprehension	Examinees are asked to answer questions requiring detailed answers; answers indicate their comprehension of the questions.
Similarities	Examinees indicate in what way two items are alike.
Performance Tests	
Picture completion	Examinees indicate what part of each picture is missing.
Picture arrangement	Examinees arrange pictures to make a sensible story.
Block design	Examinees attempt to duplicate designs made with red and white blocks.
Object assembly	Examinees attempt to solve picture puzzles.
Digit symbol	Examinees fill in small boxes with coded symbols corresponding to a number above each box.

it must be *valid*. This discussion will focus on intelligence tests, but please remember that the basic principles discussed here apply to *any* psychological test.

▣ Test Standardization: A Sound Basis for Comparison

For the scores obtained on a psychological test to be useful, the tests must be carefully *standardized*. This means that a large group of persons representative of the population for whom the test is designed must take it. Then the mean and the distribution of their scores are carefully examined. If the test is well constructed, the distribution of scores will approach the *normal curve* in shape—a bell-shaped function with most scores in the middle and fewer scores as we move toward the extremes (very low scores or very high scores). The normal curve is very useful because it helps us determine just where an individual stands relative to other persons who also took the test. This information then helps us to interpret each individual's performance as being relatively low, average, or high. For instance, if only 2 percent of all persons who take an intelligence test score as high as a specific person does, we can conclude that she is very high in intelligence. If 50 percent score as high as she does, we can conclude that she is average in intelligence. And if 98 percent score higher than she does, we can conclude that she is very low in intelligence. Most widely used intelligence tests are designed to yield an average score of about 100, so the score of each test taker can be compared with this value to determine just where the person stands, in a relative sense, with respect to intelligence. The procedure for *administration* of the test should also be standardized so that people taking the test do so under the same set of conditions.

Reliability
The extent to which any measuring device (including psychological tests) yields the same result each time it is applied to the same quantity.

Split-Half Reliability
The correlation between scores on two parts of a test.

Test–Retest Reliability
A measure of the extent to which scores on a test remain stable over time.

Reliability: The Importance of Consistency

To be of any use, psychological tests must have high **reliability:** They must yield the same result each time they are applied to the same quantity. If they don't, they are essentially useless. Two basic forms of reliability are important. First, tests must possess what psychologists call *internal consistency:* All the items on the test must actually measure intelligence (or whatever the test is designed to measure). One way to assess such internal consistency involves dividing the test in two equivalent parts, such as the first and second halves or odd- and even-numbered items, and then comparing people's scores on each part. If the test measures intelligence reliably, then the correlation between the two parts should be positive and high. If it is, then the test is said to be high in **split-half reliability.** If it is not, then some of the items may be measuring different things, and the test may be unreliable in one important sense.

Second, to be viewed as reliable, tests of intelligence must yield scores that are stable over time. Psychologists measure such **test–retest reliability** by having the same persons take the test at different times. The more similar a given person's scores on these occasions are, the higher is the test–retest reliability. Because intelligence is a characteristic that would not be expected to change over time, high test–retest reliability is an important requirement of tests of human intelligence.

Validity: Do Tests Measure What They Claim to Measure?

Suppose that on a trip to the local mall you see a machine like the one shown in Figure 7.11. A sign on the front reads, "Test Your Sex Appeal!" Do you think that such a machine is really capable of measuring sex appeal? The answer is obvious, if a little disappointing: No way! After all, how could this device tell persons who used it how they would be perceived by others? Psychologists would say that machines such as this one—and any other measuring devices that claim to measure something they do not—are low in **validity:** the ability to measure what they are supposed to measure.

The same principle applies to psychological tests: They are useful only to the extent that they really measure the characteristics they claim to measure. Thus, an intelligence test is useful only to the extent that it really measures intelligence. How can we determine whether a test is valid? Through several different methods. One of these, known as **content validity,** has to do with the extent to which items on a test are related in a straightforward way to the characteristic we wish to measure. For example, if an intelligence test consisted of measurements of the length of people's ears or the sharpness of their teeth, we would probably conclude that it was low in content validity: These measurements seem totally unrelated to what we mean by the term *intelligence.*

Another type of validity is known as **criterion-related validity** and is based on the following reasoning: If a test actually measures what it claims to measure, then persons attaining different scores on it should also differ in terms of behaviors that are relevant to the characteristic being measured. For example, we might expect that scores on an intelligence test would be related to such aspects of behavior (i.e., criteria) as grades in school and success in various occupations, either right now (this is known as *concurrent validity*) or in the future (this is known as *predictive validity*).

In sum, any psychological test is useful only to the extent that it has been carefully standardized and is both reliable and valid. We'll return to this issue in a discussion of group differences in intelligence test scores. Now, however, let's briefly consider some techniques other than tests that are also used by psychologists to measure intelligence.

FIGURE 7.11
Low Validity: An Example
Devices like this one really can't help you find your "perfect match," so the scores they provide have no validity; that is, the devices do not measure what they claim to measure.

Validity
The extent to which a test actually measures what it claims to measure.

Content Validity
The extent to which items on a test are related in a straightforward way to the characteristic the test aims to measure.

Criterion-Related Validity
The extent to which scores on a test are related to behaviors (criteria) that are relevant to the characteristics the test purports to measure.

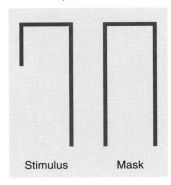

Stimulus   Mask

FIGURE 7.12
Inspection Time:
How It's Measured

To measure inspection time, psychologists ask research participants to indicate whether the long side of a stimulus (*left*) is on the left or the right. Immediately after a participant sees each stimulus, it is masked by another one in which both sides are long (*right*). Participants are not told to respond as quickly as possible; rather, they are instructed to take their time and be accurate. Inspection time is measured in terms of the time they require to make such decisions at some predetermined level of accuracy.

Inspection Time
The minimum amount of time a particular stimulus must be exposed for individuals to make a judgment about it that meets some preestablished criterion of accuracy.

The Cognitive Basis of Intelligence: Processing Speed

"Quick study," "quick-witted," and "fast learner" are all phrases used to describe people who are high in intelligence, both academic and practical. They suggest that being intelligent involves being able to process information quickly. Is there any scientific evidence to support this idea? In fact, there is. Psychologists interested in studying intelligence have moved beyond tests such as the Stanford–Binet and Wechsler scales in an attempt to identify the basic cognitive mechanisms and processes that underlie intelligence—and that enable people to score high on intelligence tests (e.g., Deary, 1995). This work has led to two major developments. First, several tests have been constructed that are based on the findings of cognitive psychology and on our growing understanding of many aspects of cognition (Naglieri, 1997). Among the most noteworthy are the *Kaufman Assessment Battery for Children* and the *Kaufman Adult Intelligence Test* (Kaufman & Kaufman, 1993) and the *Woodcock–Johnson Test of Cognitive Abilities* (Woodcock & Johnson, 1989). The Woodcock–Johnson Test, for instance, attempts to measure important aspects of both fluid and crystallized intelligence.

Second, a growing body of research has focused on the finding that the speed with which individuals perform simple perceptual and cognitive tasks (e.g., reaction time) is often correlated with scores on intelligence tests (e.g., Deary & Stough, 1996; Neisser et al., 1996). A cognitive measure of intelligence that has received considerable attention is **inspection time**. To measure inspection time, psychologists often use procedures in which individuals are shown simple drawings like the one in Figure 7.12 and are asked to indicate whether the longer side occurs on the left or right. Inspection time is measured by the time they take to make such decisions at a specified level of accuracy—for example, 85 percent.

What does inspection time measure? Presumably, the amount of time individuals require for the intake of new visual information and making a perceptual judgment about it. Supporters of this measure argue that this task—perceiving new information—is basic to all higher-level mental operations in human thought (e.g., Deary, 1995; Deary & Stough, 1996). Consistent with this view, research indicates that inspection time is indeed closely related to intelligence, as measured by standard tests; inspection time and scores on such tests correlate –.50 or more (e.g., Kranzler & Jensen, 1989).

Other cognitive psychologists have suggested that differences in intelligence are based on differences in *working memory capacity*. As you may recall from our discussions in Chapter 6, working memory refers to a cognitive system that stores information temporarily and also has an attentional component that regulates content. Working memory allows individuals to store complex mental representations in active memory and perform complex transformations on these representations. Some studies have shown that the complexity of one's representations and transformations in working memory are highly correlated with intelligence test scores (e.g., Kyllonen & Christal, 1990). Other research shows that measures of working memory capacity correlate highly with performance on several higher-order cognitive tasks that reflect fluid intelligence, such as planning, scheduling, and complex learning (e.g., see Engle, 2002). Research in this area is still relatively new, so it remains to be seen whether differences in working memory and executive attention can explain the wide range of intellectual behaviors that have been observed by other researchers.

In sum, measures of cognitive processing speed (e.g., inspection time) and working memory capacity appear to be very promising avenues for probing the nature of human intelligence—for understanding the basic cognitive processes that underlie this important characteristic. And because understanding a process is often an essential first step to being able to change it in beneficial ways, this is valuable progress.

The Neural Basis of Intelligence: Basic Building Blocks

Throughout this book, we have noted that everything we do, think, or feel rests, in an ultimate sense, on neurochemical events occurring in our brains. If that is indeed true—and virtually all psychologists believe that it is—then an intriguing possibility arises: Can we trace individual differences in intelligence to differences in neural functioning? The answer suggested by a growing body of evidence is *yes* (e.g., Matarazzo, 1992; Vernon, 1993). Such research suggests, first, that *nerve conduction velocity*—the speed with which nerve impulses are conducted in the visual system—correlates significantly with measures of intelligence (e.g., the Raven Progressive Matrices test) (Reed & Jensen, 1993).

Other, and related, research has examined metabolic activity in the brain during cognitive tasks (e.g., Haier, 1993). Presumably, if intelligence is related to efficient brain functioning, then the more intelligent people are, the less energy their brains should expend while working on various tasks. This prediction has generally been confirmed: The brains of persons scoring highest on written measures of intellectual ability do expend less energy when these individuals perform complex cognitive tasks. The data in these studies have been gathered by means of the PET technique of brain imaging described in Chapters 2 and 6. Using similar imaging technologies, scientists have identified an area in the lateral prefrontal cortex of each brain hemisphere that may play an important role in intelligence by providing a global work space for organizing and coordinating information and carrying it back to other parts of the brain as needed (Duncan et al., 2000). Apparently, the relative performance of this "work space" determines how adept a person is at solving cognitive problems—precisely the characteristic that intelligence tests attempt to measure.

More recent findings point to yet another intriguing possibility: Individual differences in intelligence stem from individual differences in **neural plasticity**—the ability of neural connections to adapt dynamically to their environments (please refer to Chapter 2 for additional information on neural plasticity). According to psychologist Dennis Garlick (2002, 2003), intelligence develops during childhood when neural connections in the developing brain change rapidly in response to environmental cues. This view suggests that individual differences in intelligence stem from differences in how quickly, and to what degree, our brains can make these new nerve connections. Garlick notes that this process stops at maturity, implying the existence of a *critical period* for the development of intelligence. Although additional research is needed to confirm the precise relationship of neural plasticity to intelligence, neural plasticity does seem to provide an accurate accounting of much of what we know about intelligence. For example, neural plasticity helps to explain why children are particularly adept at acquiring new skills and why growth in certain mental abilities (e.g., fluid intelligence) stops at a certain point, whereas others (e.g., crystallized intelligence) seem to continue well into old age.

In sum, it appears that the improved methods now available for studying the brain and nervous system are beginning to establish the kind of links between intelligence and physical structures that psychologists have long suspected to exist. Such research is very recent, so it is still too soon to reach firm conclusions. It does appear, though, that we are on the verge of establishing much firmer links between intelligence—a crucial aspect of mind—and body than has ever been true before.

KEY QUESTIONS

- What was the first individual test of intelligence, and what did scores on it mean?
- What are the Wechsler scales?
- What are standardization, reliability, and validity?
- What is inspection time, and what does it measure?
- What findings suggest that intelligence is related to neural functioning or brain structure?

Neural Plasticity
The ability of neural connections to adapt dynamically to environmental cues.

HUMAN INTELLIGENCE: THE ROLE OF HEREDITY AND THE ROLE OF ENVIRONMENT

That people differ in intelligence is obvious. *Why* such differences exist is quite another matter. Are they largely a matter of heredity—differences in the genetic materials and codes we inherit from our parents? Or are they primarily the result of environmental factors—conditions in the world around us that affect our intellectual development? We're sure you know the answer: Both types of factors are involved. Human intelligence is clearly the result of the complex interplay between genetic factors and a wide range of environmental conditions (e.g., Plomin, 1997). Let's now consider some of the evidence pointing to this conclusion.

Evidence for the Influence of Heredity

Several lines of research offer support for the view that heredity plays an important role in human intelligence. First, consider findings with respect to family relationship and measured IQ. If intelligence is indeed determined by heredity, we would expect that the more closely two persons are related, the more similar their IQs will be. This prediction has generally been confirmed (e.g., McGue et al., 1993; Neisser et al., 1996). For example, the IQs of identical twins raised together correlate almost +.90, those of brothers and sisters about +.50, and those of cousins about +.15 (see Figure 7.13). (Remember: Higher correlations indicate stronger relationships between variables.)

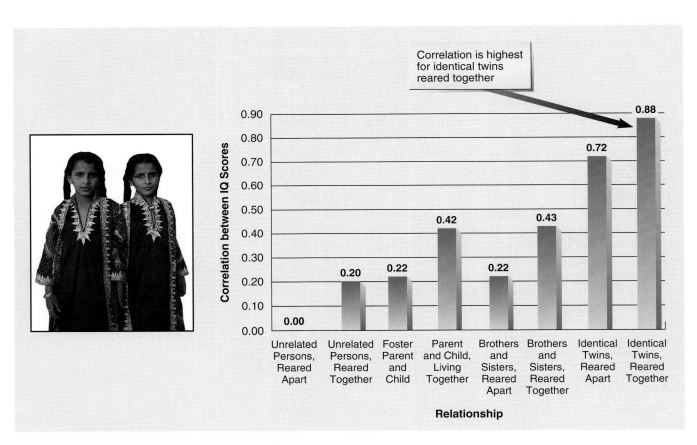

FIGURE 7.13
Family Relationship and IQ
The closer the biological relationship of two individuals, the higher the correlation between their IQ scores. This finding provides support for the role of genetic factors in intelligence.

Support for the impact of heredity on intelligence is also provided by studies involving adopted children. If intelligence is strongly affected by genetic factors, the IQs of adopted children should resemble those of their biological parents more closely than those of their adoptive parents. In short, the children should be more similar in IQ to the persons from whom they received their genes than to the persons who raised them. This prediction, too, has been confirmed (Jencks, 1972; Munsinger, 1978; Plomin et al., 1997).

Additional evidence for the role of genetic factors in intelligence is provided by studies focused on the task of identifying the specific genes that influence intelligence (e.g., Rutter & Plomin, 1997; Sherman et al., 1997). These studies adopted as a working hypothesis the view that many genes, each exerting relatively small effects, probably play a role in general intelligence—that is, in what many aspects of mental abilities (e.g., verbal, spatial, speed-of-processing, and memory abilities) have in common (e.g., Plomin, 1997). In other words, such research has not attempted to identify *the* gene that influences intelligence, but has sought *quantitative trait loci* (QTLs)—genes that have relatively small effects and that influence the likelihood of some characteristic in a population. The results of such studies suggest that certain genes are indeed associated with high intelligence (e.g., Chorney et al., 1998).

Finally, evidence for the role of genetic factors in intelligence has been provided by research on identical twins separated as infants (usually, within the first few weeks of life) who were then raised in different homes (e.g., Bouchard et al., 1990). Because such persons have identical genetic inheritance but have been exposed to different environmental conditions—in some cases, sharply contrasting conditions—studying their IQs provides a powerful means for comparing the roles of genetic and environmental factors in human intelligence. The results of such research are clear: The IQs of identical twins reared apart (often from the time they were only a few days old) correlate almost as highly as those of identical twins reared together. Moreover, such individuals are also amazingly similar in many other characteristics, such as physical appearance, preferences in dress, mannerisms, and even personality (see Figure 7.14). Clearly, these findings point to an important role for heredity in intelligence and in many other aspects of psychological functioning.

On the basis of these and other findings, some researchers have estimated that the **heritability** of intelligence—the proportion of the variance in intelligence within a given population that is attributable to genetic factors—ranges from about 35 percent in childhood to as much as 75 percent in adulthood (McGue et al., 1993), and may be about 50 percent overall (Plomin et al., 1997). Why does the contribution of genetic factors to intelligence increase with age? Perhaps because as individuals grow older, their interactions with their environment are shaped less and less by restraints imposed on them by their families or by their social origins and are shaped more and more by the characteristics they bring with them to these environments. In other words, as they grow older, individuals are increasingly able to choose or change their environments so that these permit expression of their genetically determined tendencies and preferences (Neisser et al., 1996). Whatever the precise origin of the increasing heritability of intelligence with age, there is little doubt that genetic factors do indeed play an important role in intelligence throughout life.

FIGURE 7.14
Identical Twins Reared Apart
The IQ scores of identical twins separated at birth and raised in different homes are highly correlated. This provides evidence for the impact of genetic factors on intelligence.

Evidence for the Influence of Environmental Factors

Genetic factors are definitely *not* the entire picture where human intelligence is concerned, however. Other findings point to the conclusion that environmental

Heritability
The proportion of the variance in any trait within a given population that is attributable to genetic factors.

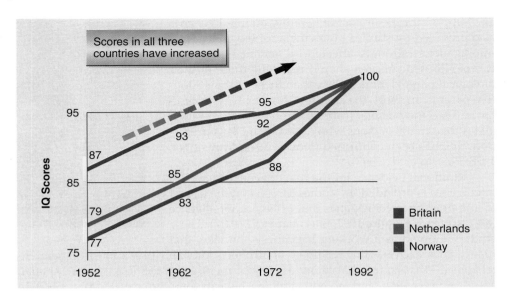

FIGURE 7.15

Worldwide Gains in IQ: Evidence for the Role of Environmental Factors in Intelligence

Performance on intelligence tests has risen sharply around the world in recent decades. Because it is very unlikely that genetic factors have changed during this period, these higher scores must be due to environmental factors. Current average IQ is set at 100; in this graph the gain is shown by the fact that average scores in previous years would, by current test standards, be lower than 100.
Source: Based on data from Flynn, 1999.

variables, too, are important. One such finding is that performance on IQ tests has risen substantially around the world at all age levels in recent decades. This phenomenon is known as the *Flynn effect* after the psychologist who first reported it (Flynn, 1987, 1996). Such increases have averaged about 3 IQ points per decade worldwide; but, as shown in Figure 7.15, in some countries they have been even larger. A recent study of children in rural Kenya found an estimated gain of 12 IQ points over a fourteen-year period (Daley et al., 2003). As a result of these gains in performance, it has been necessary to restandardize widely used tests so that they continue to yield an average IQ of 100; what is termed *average* today is actually a higher level of performance than was true in the past.

What accounts for these increases? It seems unlikely that massive shifts in human heredity occur from one generation to the next. A more reasonable explanation, therefore, focuses on changes in environmental factors. What factors have changed in recent decades? The following variables have been suggested as possible contributors to the continuing rise in IQ: better nutrition, increased urbanization, the advent of television, more and better education, more cognitively demanding jobs, and even exposure to computer games. The Kenyan study found that increases in nutrition and parents' literacy, along with a decrease in family size, coincided with the gain in IQ points. All of these factors seem plausible as explanations for the rise in IQ, but, as noted by Flynn (1999), there is as yet not sufficient evidence to conclude that any or all of these factors have played a role. In any case, whatever the specific causes involved, the steady rise in performance on IQ tests points to the importance of environmental factors in human intelligence.

Additional evidence for the role of environmental factors in intelligence is provided by the findings of studies of *environmental deprivation* and *environmental enrichment*. With respect to deprivation, emerging evidence seems to indicate that environmental factors can have differential effects on intelligence, depending upon the quality of the environment in which children are raised (Turkheimer et al., 2003). As you might expect, children born and raised in impoverished environments are less likely to reach their full potential compared to their counterparts raised in more favorable circumstances. Indeed, research shows that intelligence can be reduced by the absence of key forms of environmental stimulation early in life (Gottfried, 1984). In terms of enrichment, removing children from sterile, restricted environments and placing them in more favorable settings seems to enhance their intellectual growth (e.g., Ramey & Ramey, 1998; Skeels, 1938, 1966).

Environment, Heredity, and Intelligence: Summing Up

There is considerable evidence that both environmental and genetic factors play a role in intelligence. This is the view accepted by almost all psychologists, and there is little controversy about it. Greater controversy continues to exist, however, concerning the relative contribution of each of these factors. Do environmental or genetic factors play a stronger role in shaping intelligence? As we have already noted, existing evidence seems to favor the view that genetic factors may account for more of the variance in IQ scores within a given population than environmental factors (e.g., Plomin, 1997; Neisser et al., 1996). Many people, including psychologists, are made somewhat uneasy by this conclusion, in part because they assume that characteristics that are heritable—ones that are strongly influenced by genetic factors—cannot readily be changed. It's important to recognize that this assumption is *false*. For instance, consider height: This is a characteristic that is highly heritable—one that is influenced by genetic factors to a greater extent than by intelligence. Yet despite this fact, average heights have increased in many countries as nutrition has improved (and, perhaps, as young persons have been exposed to the growth hormones used to increase food production). So the fact that a trait is strongly influenced by genetic factors does not imply that it cannot also be affected by environmental factors.

The same thing is almost certainly true for intelligence. Yes, existing evidence suggests that it is affected by genetic factors. But this in no way implies that it cannot be influenced by environmental conditions, too—and, as we've seen, it certainly is. The recognition that genetic factors play an important role in intelligence in no way implies that intelligence is etched in stone—and definitely does not constitute an excuse for giving up on children who, because of poverty, prejudice, or neglect, are seriously at risk.

KEY QUESTIONS

- What evidence suggests that intelligence is influenced by genetic factors?
- What evidence suggests that intelligence is influenced by environmental factors?
- Can characteristics that are highly heritable be influenced by environmental factors?

GROUP DIFFERENCES IN INTELLIGENCE TEST SCORES: WHY THEY OCCUR

Earlier, we noted that there are sizable differences among the average IQ scores of various ethnic groups. In the United States and elsewhere, members of some minority groups score lower, on average, than members of the majority group. Why do such differences occur? This has been a topic of considerable controversy in psychology for many years, and currently there is still no final, universally accepted conclusion. However, it seems fair to say that, at present, most psychologists attribute such group differences in performance on standard intelligence tests largely to environmental variables. Let's take a closer look at the evidence that points to this conclusion.

Group Differences in IQ Scores: Evidence for the Role of Environmental Factors

We have already referred to one form of evidence suggesting that group differences in performance on intelligence tests stem primarily from environmental factors: the fact that the tests themselves may be biased against test takers from some minority groups. Why? In part because the tests were standardized largely on middle-class white persons; thus, interpreting the test scores of persons from minority groups in terms of these norms is not appropriate. Even worse, some critics have suggested that the tests themselves suffer from **cultural bias:** Items on the tests are ones that are familiar to middle-class white children and so give them an important edge in terms of test performance. Are such concerns valid? Careful examination of the items used on intelligence tests suggests that they may indeed be culturally biased, at least to a degree. Some items do seem to be ones that are less familiar—and therefore more difficult to answer—for minority test takers. To the extent that such cultural bias exists, it is indeed a serious flaw in IQ tests.

On the other hand, though, it's important to note that the tests are generally about as successful in predicting future school performance by children from all groups. So while the tests may be biased in terms of content, this in itself does not make them useless from the point of view of predicting future performance (e.g., Rowe, Vazsonyi, & Flannery, 1994). However, as noted by Steele and Aronson (1996), because minority students find a least some of the items on these tests unfamiliar, they may feel threatened by the tests; and this, in turn, may reduce their scores.

In an effort to eliminate cultural bias from intelligence tests, psychologists have attempted to design *culture-fair* tests. Such tests attempt to include only items to which all groups, regardless of ethnic or racial background, have been exposed. Because many minority children are exposed to languages other than standard English, these tests tend to be nonverbal in nature. One of these, the **Raven Progressive Matrices** (Raven, 1977), is illustrated in Figure 7.16. This test consists of sixty matrices of varying difficulty, each containing a logical pattern or design with a missing part. Individuals select the item that completes the pattern from several different choices. Because the Raven test and ones like it focus primarily on *fluid intelligence*—our basic abilities to form concepts, reason, and identify similarities—these tests seem less likely to be subject to cultural bias than other kinds of intelligence tests. However, it is not clear that these tests, or any others, totally eliminate the problem of subtle built-in bias.

Cultural Bias
The tendency of items on a test of intelligence to require specific cultural experience or knowledge.

Raven Progressive Matrices
A popular test of intelligence that was designed to be relatively free of cultural bias.

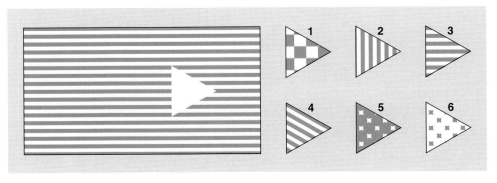

FIGURE 7.16

An Example of a Test Item on a Culture-Fair Test
Items on this test are designed to avoid penalizing test takers whose language or cultural experience differs from that of persons in the urban middle class. Persons taking the test select, from the six samples on the right, the patch that would complete the pattern. (Correct answer for this item: number 3.)
Source: Adapted from the Raven Standard Progressive Matrices Test.

Additional evidence for the role of environmental factors in group differences in test performance has been divided by Flynn (1999), one expert on this issue, into two categories: indirect and direct. *Indirect evidence* is evidence from research in which efforts are made to equate environmental factors for all test takers—for instance, by eliminating the effects of socioeconomic status through statistical techniques. The results of such studies are mixed; some suggest that the gap between minority groups and whites is reduced by such procedures (e.g., Flynn, 1993), but other studies indicate that between-group differences still remain (e.g., Loehlin, Lindzey, & Spuhle, 1975; Lynn, 1996). These findings suggest that while socioeconomic factors contribute to group differences in IQ scores, other factors, as yet unknown, may also play some role.

Direct evidence for environmental factors, in contrast, involves actual life changes that take many minority persons out of the disadvantaged environment they often face and provide them with an environment equivalent to that of other groups. Obtaining such evidence is, of course, very difficult; many minority persons do grow up in environments quite distinct from those of other groups. According to Flynn (1999), however, one compelling piece of direct evidence for the role of environmental factors in group differences does exist. During World War II, African American soldiers fathered thousands of children in Germany (much of which was occupied by U.S. troops after the war). These children have been raised by white mothers in what is essentially a white environment. The result? Their IQs are virtually identical to those of white children matched to them in socioeconomic status (e.g., Flynn, 1980). Given that the fathers of these children scored very similarly to other African American soldiers, these findings suggest that environmental factors are in fact the key to group differences in IQ: When such factors are largely eliminated, differences between the groups, too, disappear.

KEY QUESTIONS

- What evidence suggests that group differences in intelligence stem largely from environmental factors?
- Is there any evidence for the role of genetic factors in group differences in intelligence?

EMOTIONAL INTELLIGENCE: THE FEELING SIDE OF INTELLIGENCE

Growing evidence indicates that there is yet another kind of intelligence, termed **emotional intelligence** (or **EQ** for short), that is distinct from that measured by IQ tests. Let's take a closer look at the major components of emotional intelligence and then examine current evidence concerning its existence and effects.

Major Components of Emotional Intelligence

One expert on this topic, psychologist Daniel Goleman (1995), suggests that emotional intelligence consists of five major parts: (1) knowing our own emotions, (2) managing our emotions, (3) motivating ourselves, (4) recognizing the emotions of others, and (5) handling relationships. Each of these elements, he contends, plays an important role in shaping the outcomes we experience in life.

■ Knowing Our Own Emotions

As noted in Chapter 9, emotions are often powerful reactions, so it would seem at first glance that everyone ought to be able to recognize their own feelings. In fact, however, this is not always the case. Some persons are highly aware of their own emotions and their thoughts about them, but others seem to be almost totally oblivious to these. What are the implications of such differences? First, to the extent

Emotional Intelligence (EQ)
A cluster of traits or abilities relating to the emotional side of life—abilities such as recognizing and managing one's own emotions, being able to motivate oneself and restrain one's impulses, recognizing and managing others' emotions, and handling interpersonal relationships in an effective manner.

individuals are not aware of their own feelings, they cannot make smart choices. How can they tell whom to date or marry, what job to take, which house or car to buy, or even what to order in a restaurant? Second, because such persons aren't aware of their own emotions, they are often low in *expressiveness*—they don't show their feelings clearly through facial expressions, body language, or other cues most of us use to recognize others' feelings (Malandro, Barker, & Barker, 1994). This can have adverse effects on their interpersonal relationships, because other people find it hard to know how they are feeling or reacting.

Managing Our Own Emotions

Have you ever lost your temper or cried when you didn't want to show such reactions? Have you ever done something to cheer yourself up when you felt anxious or depressed? If so, you are already aware of the fact that we often try to *manage* our emotions—to regulate their nature, intensity, and expression (e.g., Zillmann, 1996). Doing so is very important both for our own mental health and from the point of view of interacting effectively with others. For instance, consider persons who simply cannot control their temper, as illustrated in Figure 7.17; are they bound for success and a happy life? No. They will probably be avoided by many people and will *not* get the jobs, promotions, or lovers they want.

Motivating Ourselves

Another important component of emotional intelligence is the ability to motivate oneself—and this means more than simply hard work. In addition to being able to motivate oneself to work long and hard on a task, it also means remaining enthusiastic and optimistic about the final outcome and being able to *delay gratification*— to put off receiving small rewards now in order to get larger ones later on, an issue we examined in Chapter 5. Being high in such skills can indeed contribute to success in many different contexts.

Recognizing and Influencing Others' Emotions

Another aspect of emotional intelligence, as described by Goleman, is the ability to "read" others accurately—to recognize the moods they are in and what emotions they are experiencing. This skill is valuable in many practical settings. For instance, if you can accurately gauge another person's current mood, you can tell whether it's the right time to ask her or him for a favor. Similarly, persons who are skilled at generating strong emotions in others are often highly successful in such fields as sales and politics: They can get other people to feel what *they* want them to feel.

FIGURE 7.17
Recognizing and Managing Our Own Emotions (or Expressions of Them)
As illustrated by Broom Hilda's actions, the ability to regulate our emotions—for instance, to hold our tempers in check—is very important both for our own mental health and for the purpose of interacting effectively with others.

Source: "Broom Hilda" by Russell Myers, Published 1980. Copyright © 1980, Tribune Media Services. Reprinted with permission.

Handling Relationships

Some people seem to have a knack for getting along with others: Most people who meet these people like them, and as a result they have many friends and often enjoy high levels of success in their careers. In contrast, others seem to make a mess of virtually all their personal relationships. According to Goleman (1995), such differences are another reflection of differences in emotional intelligence or, as some researchers would phrase it, differences in *interpersonal intelligence* (Hatch, 1990).

What does interpersonal intelligence involve? Such skills as being able to coordinate the efforts of several people and to negotiate solutions to complex interpersonal problems, being good at giving others feedback that doesn't make them angry or resentful (e.g., Baron, 1993), and being a team player. Again, these skills are clearly distinct from the ones needed for getting good grades or scoring high on tests of intelligence, but they often play a key role in important life outcomes.

Emotional Intelligence: Evidence on Its Existence and Effects

It is important to note that much of the evidence initially offered for the existence of emotional intelligence was anecdotal or indirect in nature (e.g., Goleman, 1995, 1998). Psychologists strongly prefer more concrete kinds of evidence. Accordingly, researchers have put the concept of emotional intelligence to the test, trying to determine whether the distinct abilities thought to comprise it meet the criteria for a type of intelligence: Are the abilities universal, do they cluster together as a single (if multifaceted) factor, and do they allow people to adapt to their environments?

So far, the evidence is mixed. Some researchers (Mayer, Caruso, & Salovey, 1998; Mayer et al., 2001) have reported findings that emotional abilities do indeed represent a single, universal factor. Other researchers, however, question whether emotional intelligence is truly distinct from such other related concepts as social intelligence or aspects of personality, such as empathy (e.g., Davies, Stankov, & Roberts, 1998; Roberts, Zeidner, & Matthews, 2001). Others agree with Goleman that *emotion-related* abilities do exist and do indeed affect social competence, but argue the these effects stem directly from our emotions rather than a special form of intelligence (Izard, 2001).

Does this mean that the theory of emotional intelligence is useless and that discussing it has been a waste of time—yours as well as mine? We don't believe so. Another interpretation of existing evidence concerning emotional intelligence is this: At present, we don't have adequate methods for measuring all aspects of emotional intelligence (e.g., Schaie, 2001; Zeidner, Mathews, & Roberts, 2001). Further, these components may, in fact, be somewhat independent of each other. Thus, we may not be able to assign individuals a single overall EQ score comparable to the single IQ score yielded by many intelligence tests. In a sense, though, this is not surprising. After all, the more psychologists study intelligence, the more they recognize that it probably consists of a number of distinct components. The fact that we also possess distinct and perhaps largely independent abilities relating to the emotional side of life simply mirrors this pattern. So stay tuned: The idea of emotional intelligence is an appealing one with important implications, so it is certain to be a topic of research by psychologists in the years ahead.

KEY QUESTIONS

- What is emotional intelligence?
- What does evidence to date suggest about the existence of emotional intelligence? Its effects?

SUMMARY AND REVIEW OF KEY QUESTIONS

Thinking: Forming Concepts and Reasoning to Conclusions

- **What are concepts?**
  Concepts are mental categories for objects, events, or experiences that are similar to one another in one or more respects.

- **What is the difference between logical and natural concepts?**
  Logical concepts can be clearly defined by a set of rules or properties. Natural concepts cannot; they are usually defined in terms of prototypes—the most typical category members.

- **What are propositions and images?**
  Propositions are sentences that relate one concept to another and can stand as separate assertions. Images are mental pictures of the world and are a basic element of thinking.

- **What is the process of reasoning? How does formal reasoning differ from everyday reasoning?**
  Reasoning involves transforming available information in order to reach specific conclusions. Formal reasoning derives conclusions from specific premises. In contrast, everyday reasoning is less clear-cut and more complex.

- **What forms of error and bias can lead to faulty reasoning?**
  Reasoning is subject to several forms of error and bias. It can be distorted by our tendency to focus primarily on evidence that confirms our beliefs, or confirmation bias; and by our tendency to assume that we could have predicted actual events more successfully than is really the case, or the hindsight effect.

Making Decisions: Choosing among Alternatives

- **What are heuristics?**
  Heuristics are mental rules of thumb that reduce the cognitive effort required for decision making. We often employ heuristics rather than carefully calculating the probability and the subjective value or utility of each possible outcome.

- **What are the availability, representativeness, and anchoring-and-adjustment heuristics, and what roles do they play in decision making?**
  The availability heuristic is our tendency to make judgments about the frequency or likelihood of various events in terms of how readily they can be brought to mind. The representativeness heuristic is the tendency to assume that the more closely an item resembles typical examples of some concept, the more likely it is to belong to that concept. The anchoring-and-adjustment heuristic is the tendency to reach decisions by making adjustments to reference points or existing information.

- **What is framing, and how does it relate to decision making?**
  Framing, the presentation of information about possible outcomes in terms of gains or losses, can strongly affect decisions.

- **How does escalation of commitment affect decision making?**
  People often become trapped in bad decisions through escalation of commitment, an effect that derives from reluctance to admit past mistakes and a desire to justify past losses.

Problem Solving: Finding Paths to Desired Goals

- **How do psychologists define *problem solving*?**
  Problem solving involves efforts to develop or choose among various responses in order to attain desired goals.

- **What are two general approaches to problem solving?**
  One common problem-solving technique is trial and error. Another is the use of algorithms—rules that will, if followed, yield solutions in certain situations.

- **What role do heuristics play in problem solving?**
  Heuristics, rules of thumb suggested by our experience, often provide useful shortcuts in problem solving.

- **What factors can interfere with effective problem solving?**
  Both functional fixedness (the tendency to think of using objects only as they have been used before) and mental sets (tendencies to stick with familiar methods) can interfere with effective problem solving.

Creativity: Generating the Extraordinary

- **What is creativity?**
  Creativity involves the ability to produce work that is both novel (original, unexpected) and appropriate (it works—it is useful or meets task constraints).

- **What are confluence theories, and what factors do they view as essential to creativity?**
  Confluence theories suggest that for creativity to occur, multiple components must converge. Among the factors such theories view as crucial for creativity are certain intellectual abilities, knowledge of a given field, certain styles of thinking, personality traits, intrinsic motivation, and an environment supportive of creative ideas.

- **What evidence offers support for the confluence approach?**
  Research findings indicate that all of the factors mentioned by confluence theories are significant predictors of creativity across many different domains (e.g., writing, art, science).

Language: The Communication of Information

- **What abilities are involved in the production of language, and how is language acquired in humans?**
  Language involves the ability to use a rich set of symbols, plus rules for combining these, to communicate information. Existing evidence on language development suggests that language development is the result of a complex process involving several aspects of learning, many cognitive processes, and perhaps various genetically determined mechanisms as well.

- **What factors are involved in language acquisition?**
Language acquisition involves phonological development—learning to produce the sounds of words; semantic development—learning to understand the meanings of words; and acquisition of grammar—the rules governing which words can be combined into sentences in a given language.

- **What is the linguistic relativity hypothesis?**
According to the linguistic relativity hypothesis, language shapes or determines thought. Existing evidence seems to support a revised version of the linguistic relativity hypothesis, suggesting that language does affect aspects of cognition.

- **Do animals possess language?**
Growing evidence suggests that some species of animals, including bonobo chimpanzees and dolphins, are capable of grasping basic aspects of language, including word order and grammar; but these findings remain highly controversial.

Intelligence: Contrasting Views of Its Nature

- **What is intelligence?**
The term *intelligence* refers to individuals' abilities to understand complex ideas, to adapt effectively to the environment, to learn from experience, to engage in various forms of reasoning, and to overcome obstacles by careful thought.

- **What is Gardner's theory of multiple intelligences?**
Gardner's theory suggests that there are several different kinds of intelligence, such as verbal, mathematical, musical, and bodily–kinesthetic.

- **What is Sternberg's triarchic theory of intelligence?**
Sternberg's theory suggests that there are three basic kinds of intelligence: componential, experiential, and contextual (practical).

- **What is fluid intelligence? Crystallized intelligence?**
Fluid intelligence has to do with our inherited abilities to think and reason. Crystallized intelligence consists of accumulated knowledge—information and skills stored over a lifetime.

Measuring Intelligence

- **What was the first individual test of intelligence, and what did scores on it mean?**
The first individual test of intelligence was devised by Binet and Simon. It yielded a "mental age," and testers then derived an IQ (intelligence quotient) score obtained by dividing mental by chronological age and multiplying by 100.

- **What are the Wechsler scales?**
The Wechsler scales are individual tests of intelligence for children and adults that seek to measure several aspects of intelligence—performance components as well as verbal components of intelligence.

- **What are standardization, reliability, and validity?**
Standardization is the process of establishing the average score and distribution of scores on a test so that the scores of persons taking the test can be meaningfully interpreted. Reliability is the extent to which a test yields consistent results. Validity is the extent to which a test measures what it is supposed to measure.

- **What is inspection time, and what does it measure?**
Inspection time is the minimum amount of time a stimulus must be exposed for individuals to make a judgment about it that meets some preestablished criterion of accuracy.

- **What findings suggest that intelligence is related to neural functioning or brain structure?**
Research findings indicate that scores on standard tests of intelligence are correlated with nerve conduction velocity and with efficiency in brain functioning. Neural plasticity, the ability of neurons to form connections in response to environmental cues, may also play a role in intelligence.

Human Intelligence: The Role of Heredity and the Role of Environment

- **What evidence suggests that intelligence is influenced by genetic factors?**
Evidence for the role of genetic factors is provided by the findings that the more closely related persons are, the higher the correlation in their IQ scores; by research on adopted children; and by research on identical twins separated early in life and raised in different homes.

- **What evidence suggests that intelligence is influenced by environmental factors?**
Evidence for the role of environmental factors is provided by the worldwide rise in IQ scores in recent decades (the Flynn effect), studies of environmental deprivation and enrichment, and the finding that many environmental factors can affect children's intelligence.

- **Can characteristics that are highly heritable be influenced by environmental factors?**
Traits that are highly heritable can be strongly influenced by environmental factors. For example, height is highly heritable, yet average height has increased in many countries as a result of improved nutrition and other factors.

Group Differences in Intelligence Test Scores: Why They Occur

- **What evidence suggests that group differences in intelligence stem largely from environmental factors?**
There is some indication that many intelligence tests suffer from cultural bias. Other sources of evidence include the Flynn effect—worldwide rises in IQ over time—and direct evidence indicating that when minority children are raised in enhanced environments, their IQ matches that of nonminority children.

- **Is there any evidence for the role of genetic factors in group differences in intelligence?**
Very little if any evidence indicates that group differences in intelligence have a genetic basis.

Emotional Intelligence: The Feeling Side of Intelligence

- **What is emotional intelligence?**
Emotional intelligence is a cluster of traits or abilities relating to the emotional side of life—abilities such as recognizing and managing one's own emotions, being able

to motivate oneself and restrain one's impulses, recognizing and managing others' emotions, and handling interpersonal relationships in an effective manner.

- **What does evidence to date indicate about the existence of emotional intelligence? Its effects?**
  Research evidence provides clear support for only one of the components of emotional intelligence—emotion

perception. However, some findings indicate that this component, and perhaps others as well, can influence the outcomes people experience in important practical contexts.

PSYCHOLOGY: UNDERSTANDING ITS FINDINGS

Making Better Decisions

Have you ever made a bad decision—one that you later wished you could change? As you probably know from your own experience, such errors in judgment may prove quite costly. Throughout this chapter, we have discussed a number of factors that seem to interfere with our ability to reason effectively and make good decisions. We also suggested a number of ways to prevent this from happening, or at least lessen its impact. Do the following exercises to see how alternative ways of approaching reasoning and decision making can be useful in helping you make better decisions.

1. Think of past situations in which you may have made a decision you later wished you could change. Now, try to remember whether some of the factors that influence the

decision-making process may have been operating, thereby making the decisions less rational or effective than they might otherwise have been (remember to consider the hindsight bias as you do this!). Did you rely too heavily on heuristics? Fall prey to the confirmation bias? Or was faulty reasoning part of the cause? Write these factors down and try to be as specific as possible in your descriptions of each situation.

2. Now, in light of this information, try to think of strategies that you could use to prevent such factors from affecting the quality of the decisions you make in the future. Again, write these down and keep them in a safe place. Refer to your list the next time you are required to make an important decision.

MAKING PSYCHOLOGY PART OF YOUR LIFE

Managing Your Own Anger: A Very Useful Skill

In discussing emotional intelligence, we noted that one suggested aspect of such intelligence is the ability to manage our own emotions. Perhaps the most difficult emotion of all to manage is anger, which all too often erupts into open rage. You probably know from your own experience that once it starts, anger tends to be self-perpetuating—and sometimes self-amplifying, too. What begins as mild irritation can quickly move into strong anger and then, if we don't take active steps to stop it, a virtual emotional explosion. What can you do to avoid such outcomes—to manage your own anger more effectively? Here are some useful steps.

- **Stop the process early.** Because anger is self-amplifying, it is easier to break the annoyance–anger–rage cycle early on. So if you feel yourself getting angry and suspect that this emotion might get out of hand, take one of the following actions as soon as possible. Delay can be quite costly in terms of your ability to break this cycle.

- **Try a cooling-off period.** If possible, leave the scene, change the subject, or at least stop interacting with the other person. Doing so can give your emotional arousal a chance to dissipate, as long as you don't use this time to mull over the causes of your anger. So if you do try a cooling-off period, it's important to also use the next step.

- **Do something to get yourself off the anger track.** If you think angry thoughts, you will remain angry—and perhaps become even angrier. So it's important to do something to get your mind off the causes of your anger. Here's where the incompatible response approach can come in handy. This technique suggests that it is difficult to remain angry in the presence of stimuli that cause us to experience some incompatible emotion. For example, exposing yourself to humorous materials will induce pleasant feelings incompatible with anger. As a result, your anger may quickly vanish.

- **Seek positive explanations for the things others say or do that make you angry.** When others make us angry, we usually attribute their actions to insensitivity, selfishness—or worse. If, instead, you try to come up with other explanations for the words or actions that have made you angry, this may greatly reduce your annoyance. Did the other person mean to say something that hurt your feelings? Perhaps she or he didn't realize the implications of what was said. If you concentrate on interpretations like this, your anger may quickly dissipate.

- **Whatever you do, don't rely on "catharsis"—on getting it out of your system.** A large body of research findings indicates that giving vent to anger does not usually reduce it. On the contrary, such actions tend to fan the flames of annoyance, not drown them. So, whatever else you do, don't follow your impulse to give the other person a dirty look, to shout, or to pound your fist. Doing so will only make the situation worse.

KEY TERMS

8

Human Development

*M*y father (Bernard Baron) has always had a talent for languages; in fact, he won prizes for excellence in French and German when he was in school. And during World War II, when his unit traveled through France and Germany, he was often called on to serve as a translator. So, when I was a little boy, he sometimes spoke to me in French and German. He never gave me any lessons in these languages, but somehow I must have learned something *because many years later, I did quite well in language classes, too. And here's the most interesting part: When I was a visiting professor at a French university and lived in Toulouse, my colleagues often told me that I had a very good accent—"for an American"! So, somehow, the fact that my father often spoke to me in French seemed to pave the way for me to learn this language myself as an adult.*

Could this really be true? Could these experiences early in my life have actually provided me with an "edge," at least where pronouncing French correctly was concerned? As we'll note in a later section, recent findings indicate that this might well have been the case (Au et al., 2002). In fact, one key finding of the field of **developmental psychology**—the branch of psychology that focuses on the many ways we change throughout life—is that experiences we have early in life often *do* have a lasting impact on us. In this chapter, we'll examine such effects, but an even more important theme will be that of *change* itself—how we change physically, socially, and cognitively as we travel life's journey.

In the first portion of this chapter we'll concentrate on changes during **childhood**—the years between birth and adolescence. Then, in later sections, we'll examine changes occurring during *adolescence* and *adulthood.* The general plan will be to consider changes in the three categories—physical, cognitive, and social development. Given that these changes often occur together, however, this division is included mainly for purposes of clarity and is *not* a reflection of sharp boundaries between them.

PHYSICAL GROWTH AND DEVELOPMENT DURING CHILDHOOD

When does human life begin? In one sense, this is a philosophical or religious issue, outside the realm of science. From a purely biological point of view, though, your life as an individual began when one of the millions of sperm released by your father during sexual intercourse fertilized an *ovum* deep within your mother's body. The product of this union was barely 1/175 of an inch in diameter—smaller than the period at the end of this sentence. Yet packed within this tiny speck were the genetic blueprints that guided all your subsequent physical growth. As you probably recall from our discussion of genetics in Chapter 2, we possess twenty-three pairs of chromosomes, one member of each pair from our mothers and one from our fathers. One of these pairs determines biological sex, with females possessing two X chromosomes (XX) and males possessing one X and one Y (XY).

The Prenatal Period

After fertilization, the ovum moves through the mother's reproductive tract until it reaches the womb or *uterus.* This takes several days, and during this time the ovum divides frequently. Ten to fourteen days after fertilization, it becomes implanted in the wall of the uterus and from then on is known as the **embryo.** By the third week, the embryo is about one-fifth of an inch (one-half centimeter) long, and the region of the head is clearly visible. By the end of the eighth week, the embryo is about one inch long and a face as well as arms and legs are present. By this time, too, all major internal organs have begun to form and some, such as the sex glands, are already active. The nervous system develops rapidly, and simple reflexes appear during the eighth or ninth week.

During the next seven months, the developing child—now called a **fetus**—shows an increasingly human form. The external genitals take shape, so the sex of the fetus is recognizable by the twelfth week. Fingernails and toenails form, hair follicles appear, and eyelids that open and close emerge. By the end of the twelfth week, the fetus is three inches (7.6 cm) long and weighs about three-fourths of an ounce (21 g). By the twentieth week, it is almost ten inches (25 cm) long and weighs eight or nine ounces (227–255 g). By the twenty-fourth week, all the neurons that will be present in the brain have been produced; the eyes are formed and are sensitive to light by the end of the twenty-fourth to twenty-sixth week.

Developmental Psychology
The branch of psychology that focuses on the many ways we change throughout life.

Childhood
The years between birth and adolescence.

Embryo
The developing child during the first eight weeks of life.

Fetus
The developing child during the last seven months of pregnancy.

During the last three months of pregnancy, the fetus gains about eight ounces each week. By the seventh and eighth months, it appears to be virtually fully formed. However, if born prematurely, it may still experience difficulties with breathing. At birth, babies weigh more than seven pounds (3.17 kg) on average and are about twenty inches (50.8 cm) long (see Figure 8.1).

Prenatal Influences on Development

Under ideal conditions, development during the prenatal period occurs in an orderly fashion and the newborn child is well equipped at birth to survive outside its mother's body. Unfortunately, however, conditions are not always ideal. Many environmental factors can damage the fetus and interfere with normal patterns of growth. Such factors are known as **teratogens,** and their impact can be devastating (e.g., Bookstein et al., 1996). We'll consider some of the most important here, but it's important to note that many others exist as well.

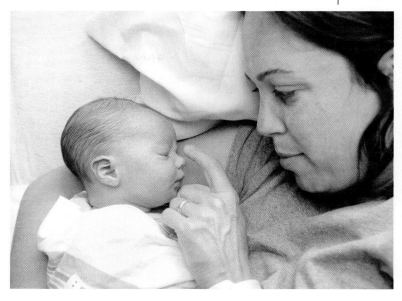

FIGURE 8.1
The Newborn: Starting Life's Journey
Holding their newborn infant for the first time is one of the most profoundly moving experiences many parents ever have.

Infectious Agents

The blood supply of the fetus and that of its mother come into close proximity in the **placenta,** a structure within the uterus that protects and nourishes the growing child. As a result, disease-producing organisms present in the mother's blood can sometimes infect the fetus. Tragically, diseases that exert only relatively minor effects on the mother can be very serious for the fetus. For example, *rubella,* or German measles, can cause blindness, deafness, or heart disease in the fetus if the mother contracts this illness during the first four weeks of pregnancy. Other diseases that can be transmitted to the fetus include chicken pox, mumps, tuberculosis, syphilis, and herpes (Samson, 1988).

Since the early 1980s, two other illnesses, genital herpes and acquired immune deficiency syndrome (AIDS), have been added to this list. Genital herpes is usually transmitted during birth when the newborn comes into contact with lesions present in their mother's genitals. When newborns contract this disease, they may suffer many harmful effects, ranging from paralysis and brain damage through deafness and blindness; the disease is fatal for many babies (Rosenblith, 1992). AIDS, in contrast, can be transmitted to the fetus prior to birth as well as during the birth process. About 20 percent of women who carry the AIDS virus in their bodies transmit it to their infants (Mattheson et al., 1997), and growing evidence suggests that the disease can also be transmitted to infants during the birth process (Kuhn et al., 1994). Tragically, few babies born with AIDS survive until their first birthday.

Prescription and Over-the Counter Drugs

The use of drugs by the mother can also exert important effects on the fetus. Excessive use of aspirin, a drug most people take without hesitation, can result in harm to the fetus's circulatory system (Kelsey, 1969). Caffeine, the stimulant found in coffee, tea, and many soft drinks, can slow fetal growth, contribute to premature birth (Jacobson et al., 1984), and produce increased irritability in newborns whose mothers have consumed it in large amounts (Schikedanz et al., 1998).

Alcohol

In the past, it was widely believed that moderate consumption of alcohol by expectant mothers had no harmful effects on the fetus. Now, in contrast, it is widely

Teratogens
Factors in the environment that can harm the developing fetus.

Placenta
A structure that surrounds, protects, and nourishes the developing fetus.

FIGURE 8.2
Warning! Drinking Alcohol Can Be Harmful to Your Unborn Child
All alcohol beverages in the United States must display the warning label shown here. Whether this label actually deters pregnant women from drinking alcohol is unknown.

recognized that virtually *any* alcohol consumption by expectant mothers can produce harmful effects. That's one reason why all bottles of wine, beer, and spirits sold in the United States have a warning sticker on them, like the one in Figure 8.2. For instance, existing data suggest that alcohol consumption by pregnant mothers can potentially produce retardation, learning disorders, and retarded growth among newborns (e.g., Streissguth et al., 1995; Williams, Howard, & McLaughlin, 1994).

If pregnant women consume large quantities of alcohol—and especially if they engage in binge drinking—their children may be born with a disorder known as **fetal alcohol syndrome** (FAS; Julien, 1992). Effects of FAS include a smaller than normal head size, deformities of the face, irritability, hyperactivity, retarded motor and mental development, heart defects, limb and joint abnormalities, feeding problems, and short attention spans (e.g., Bookstein et al., 1996). These problems persist, and as children with FAS grow older, they have increasing difficulty interacting with others and may develop serious behavioral problems (e.g., Becker et al., 1994).

How much alcohol must a pregnant woman consume, and how often, before such effects are produced? This is a complex question, but because alcohol has no benefits for the fetus and because even small amounts may be harmful, the safest answer seems to be none. In other words, pregnant women should abstain from drinking *any* alcohol.

Smoking

While the proportion of adults who smoke has decreased in the United States and several other nations, this figure is increasing in many parts of the world (see Chapter 13). Moreover, the proportion of women who smoke seems to be on the rise. From the point of view of fetal development, this is unfortunate, because smoking by pregnant women is related to many harmful effects for the fetus and newborn child. These include decreased birth weight and size and increased risk for miscarriage and stillbirth (Wen et al., 1990). Maternal smoking also may interfere with cognitive development in early childhood (Cunningham, Dockery, & Speizer, 1994), perhaps in part because smoking raises the level of carbon monoxide in the mother's blood, and this harmful substance, rather than oxygen, is carried across the placenta to the fetus. Still other findings suggest that even if the mother does not smoke but is merely in an environment containing cigarette smoke, the infant can be harmed (Dreher, 1995). So, not only should pregnant mothers not smoke, they should avoid locations in which other people are smoking.

In sum, many factors can adversely affect development during the prenatal period, and prospective mothers should carefully consider the potential risks before engaging in actions that may put their unborn children at risk.

Physical Development during Our Early Years

Physical growth is rapid during infancy. Assuming good nutrition, infants almost triple in weight (to about twenty pounds or nine kilograms) and increase in body length by about one-third (to 28 or 29 in., 71 to 74 cm) during the first year alone. Although they are capable of eating immediately, they have limited capacity for what they can consume at one time—their stomachs will not hold very much. They compensate for this by eating small amounts frequently, about every 2.5 to 4 hours.

Reflexes

Newborns possess a number of simple **reflexes** at birth—inherited responses to stimulation in certain areas of the body. If these are present, the baby's nervous system is assumed to be intact and working normally; if they are not, this is often a sign that something is seriously wrong. One of these reflexes, the *Moro reflex*, is triggered by a loud sound or a sudden dropping back of the infant's head. It

Fetal Alcohol Syndrome
A disorder in newborns due to alcohol consumption by their mothers.

Reflexes
Inherited responses to stimulation in certain areas of the body.

| **TABLE 8.1** | Reflexes in the Newborn |

Newborns show all the reflexes described here at birth or very shortly thereafter.

Reflex	Description
Blinking	Baby closes eyes in response to light
Rooting	When cheek is touched or stroked, baby turns toward touch; moves lips and tongue to suck
Sucking	When nipple of other object is placed in mouth, baby sucks
Tonic neck	When baby is placed on back with head turned to one side, baby stretches out arm and leg on side baby is facing
Moro	Baby throws out arms and fans fingers, extends neck, and cries in response to loud noise or sudden drop of head
Babinski	When baby's foot is stroked from heel to toe, toes fan out
Grasping	When palms of hand are stroked, baby closes fingers around the object in a strong grasp
Stepping	Baby makes stepping motions if held upright so one foot just touches a surface

involves a series of actions in which the baby first throws out his or her arms, then fans his or her fingers, and lets out a cry before bringing the arms back over his or her chest. Another is the *palmar grasping reflex,* which is elicited by pressing or stroking the palms of the newborn's hands. The baby closes its hand and holds tightly. This reflex might well be useful in helping babies cling to their mothers as the mother moves about. These and other reflexes are summarized in Table 8.1.

Locomotor Development

As anyone who has observed newborns well knows, infants have limited ability to move around at birth. This situation changes quickly, and within a matter of a few months they become quite mobile. They can sit and crawl, and most begin to walk by the time they are fourteen or fifteen months old. Motor development proceeds from the head toward the limbs, so that at first, infants can hold up their heads, then their chests, then they can sit, and so on. Figure 8.3 on page 240 summarizes several milestones of motor development. It's important to note that the ages shown are merely *average* values, so departures from them are trivial unless they are very late.

Learning Abilities of Newborns

Can newborns show the kinds of learning discussed in Chapter 5? Absolutely. Research findings indicate that they can be classically conditioned, but primarily with respect to stimuli that have survival value for babies. For example, infants only two hours old readily learn to associate gentle stroking on the forehead with a sweet solution, and after these two stimuli have been paired repeatedly, they will show sucking responses to the stroking (the conditioned stimulus; Clarke-Stewart, Friedman, & Koch, 1985).

Turning to *operant conditioning,* there is evidence that newborns can readily show this basic kind of learning. For example, they readily learn to suck faster, to gain exposure to visual designs, or to hear music and human voices (Sansavini, Bertonicini, & Giovanelli, 1997). Similarly, recent findings indicate that unborn fetuses show an *increase* in heart rate at the sound of their mothers' voice, but a *reduction* in heart rate in response to the sound of a stranger's voice (Kisilevsky et al., 2003). In this intriguing study, the mother's voice or a stranger's voice was played through a loudspeaker held close to the mother's abdomen, while their fetus's

Birth
Fetal posture

1 month
Lift head
(2 weeks to 2 months)

2 months
Lift chest
(1½–3 months)

3 months
Reach and miss
(2–4 months)

4 months
Sit with support

5 months
Sit on lap,
grasp object

6 months
Sit in high
chair, grasp dangling object

6½ months
Sit alone
(5–6½ months)

8 months
Stand with help

8 months
Stand holding furniture
(5–9 months)

8 months
Pull to stand
(6–9 months)

10 months
Creep on hands
and knees

11 months
Climb stairs

11 months
Walk when led

11 months
Stand alone
(10–13 months)

12 months
Walk alone
(11–13½ months)

FIGURE 8.3
Milestones of Locomotor Development
As shown here, infants make rapid progress in their ability to move around. Please note that the ages
shown are only *averages*. Most children will depart from them to some extent, and such variations are
of little importance unless they are extreme.

Source: From J. A. Schickedanz, D. I. Schickedanz, P. D. Forsyth & G. A. Forsyth, *Understanding Children and Adolescents,* 3/E.
Published by Allyn and Bacon, Boston, MA. Copyright © 1998 by Pearson Education. Reprinted by permission of the publisher.

heart rate was measured and showed contrasting reactions to these two stimuli, suggesting that they had learned to tell their mother's voice from that of other persons. So, the ability to learn is clearly present even before birth.

KEY QUESTIONS

- What environmental factors (teratogens) can adversely affect the developing fetus?
- What are reflexes and which ones do infants possess at birth?
- What learning abilities are shown by newborns?

PERCEPTUAL DEVELOPMENT DURING CHILDHOOD

How do infants perceive the world around them? Do they recognize form, see color, and perceive depth in the same manner as adults? Infants can't talk, so it is necessary to answer such questions through indirect methods, such as observing changes in behaviors they *can* perform when exposed to various stimuli—for instance, differences in sucking responses, in heart rate, or in the amount of time they spend looking at various stimuli. Developmental psychologists reason that if infants show different reactions to different stimuli, then they can, indeed, distinguish between them at some level. For example, it has been found that infants who have seen a particular visual stimulus several times spend less time looking at it when it is presented again than they do at a new stimulus they have never before seen. This provides a means for determining whether infants can detect a difference between two stimuli. If they can, then after seeing one repeatedly, infants should spend less time looking at it than at a new stimulus. If they cannot tell the two stimuli apart, then they should look at both equally.

Studies based on this reasoning have found that newborns can distinguish between different colors (Adams, 1987), odors (Balogh & Porter, 1986), tastes (Granchrow, Steiner, & Daher, 1983), and sounds (Morrongiello & Clifton, 1984). Moreover, infants as young as two or three days old have been found to show contrasting patterns of sucking to what seem to be quite subtle differences in the sounds of human speech. For instance, by the time they are only a few months old, they can tell the difference between their own name and other names—even ones that are quite similar (e.g., Mandel, Jusczyk, & Pisoni, 1995).

Perhaps most surprising of all, newborns can even keep track of time precisely! In one ingenious study pointing to this conclusion (Colombo & Richman, 2002), four-month-old infants were shown a predictable on–off pattern of light and dark stimuli; these occurred at specific points in time, either three seconds or five seconds apart. After nine presentations of this sequence, the light was omitted. The infants' heart rates were measured throughout the experiment, and just when the last stimulus *would* have occurred, their heart rates went up, thus indicating that they expected it to occur—and knew just when it was supposed to happen (see Figure 8.4 on page 242).

Infants also show impressive abilities with respect to recognizing *form* or *pattern.* Although they can't see very clearly at birth (their vision is about 20/400, which means that they can see clearly at 20 feet what an adult can see at 400 feet), they show marked preferences for patterns and contrasts in visual stimuli. In now classic research on this topic, Fantz (1961) showed babies six months old a variety of visual patterns. By observing how long they looked at each, he determined that the babies had a clear preference for patterned as opposed to plain targets and that they seemed to prefer the human face over all other stimuli tested. Later research indicated that recognition of faces may develop even earlier. By two months of age, infants prefer a face with features in normal locations over one with scrambled features (Maurer & Barrera, 1981). By six months, they can distinguish their mother's

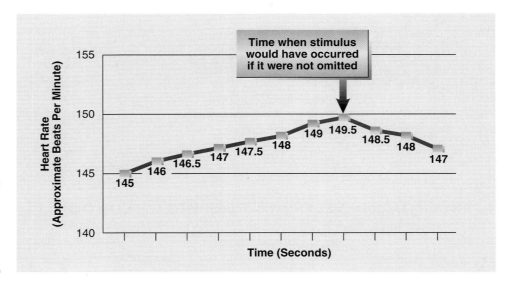

FIGURE 8.4
Evidence That Infants Can Keep Track of Time
As shown here, four-month-old infants exposed to a regular sequence of light and dark stimuli showed an acceleration in heart rate at the time when the omitted stimulus *would* have occurred. These findings indicate that they knew when the stimulus was scheduled to appear—they could keep track of time!

Source: Based on data from Colombo & Richman, 2002.

face and that of a stranger, and even distinguish one stranger's face from another (Lewkowicz, 1996).

The ability to perceive depth, too, seems to develop rapidly. Early studies on *depth perception* employed an apparatus known as the *visual cliff* (Gibson & Walk, 1960). The patterned floor drops away on the deep side of the cliff, but a transparent surface continues across this drop, so there is no drop in the surface—and no real danger (see Figure 8.5). Yet, human infants six or seven months old refuse to crawl across the deep side to reach their mothers, thus indicating that they perceive depth by this time. Does this ability appear prior to this age? Because younger infants can't crawl across the cliff even if they want to, this research method can't answer that question. But other research, using different methods, indicates that depth perception may first appear when infants are only two months old—infants of this age show a change in heart rate when presented with the visual cliff (e.g., Campos, Langer, & Krowitz, 1970; Yonas, Arterberry, & Granrud, 1987).

In sum, shortly after birth, infants have sophisticated abilities to interpret complex sensory input. How do they then integrate such information into cognitive frameworks for understanding the world? This is the question we will consider next in our discussion of cognitive development.

KEY QUESTIONS

- What perceptual abilities are shown by infants?
- What evidence indicates that infants can keep track of time?

FIGURE 8.5
The Visual Cliff: Apparatus for Testing Infant Depth Perception
Infants six or seven months old will not crawl out over the "deep" side of the visual cliff. This indicates that they can perceive depth. Even two-month-old infants show changes in heart rate when placed over the "deep" side, so perception of depth may be present even at this young age.

COGNITIVE DEVELOPMENT DURING CHILDHOOD: CHANGES IN OUR ABILITY TO UNDERSTAND THE WORLD AROUND US

Do children think, reason, and remember in the same manner as adults? Until well into the twentieth century, it was widely assumed that they do. However, this view was vigorously challenged by the Swiss psychologist Jean Piaget. On the basis of careful observations of his own and many other children, Piaget concluded that in several respects, children do *not* think or reason like adults: Their thought processes are not just different *quantitatively* (e.g., slower or less effective), they are different *qualitatively*—in their basic nature. Because Piaget's theory of **cognitive development** contains many valuable insights, we'll consider it carefully here. However, as we'll soon see, several aspects of this theory have been strongly challenged by the findings of recent research.

Piaget's Theory: An Overview

One of the most central assumptions of Piaget's theory is the suggestion that children are active thinkers who are constantly trying to construct an accurate understanding of the world around them (e.g., Siegler & Ellis, 1996). How do they go about building such knowledge? According to Piaget, through two basic processes. The first of these is **assimilation,** which involves the incorporation of new information or knowledge into existing knowledge structures known as **schemas.** As we noted in Chapter 7, schemas are a kind of "cognitive scaffold"—a framework for holding knowledge and organizing it. The second process is known as **accommodation,** and involves modifications in existing knowledge structures (schemas) as a result of exposure to new information or experiences. Following is a concrete example of how, according to Piaget's theory, these processes operate.

A two-year-old child has seen many different kinds of cats and, on the basis of such experience, has built up a schema for them: They are relatively small, four-legged animals, with tails and fur coats. Now she sees a squirrel for the first time and, through assimilation, includes it in this mental structure. As she encounters more and more squirrels, however, she begins to notice that they differ from cats in several respects: They move differently, climb trees, have much bushier tails, and so on. On the basis of this new experience, she gradually develops another schema for squirrels; this illustrates accommodation—changes in our existing knowledge structures resulting from exposure to new information (see Figure 8.6 on page 244). Piaget believed that it is the tension between these two processes that encourages cognitive development. But don't lose sight of the key fact: According to Piaget, these changes occur because, in essence, children are constantly trying to make better and more accurate sense out of the complex world around them. Let's now take a closer look at several specific stages of cognitive development Piaget described.

◼ The Sensorimotor Stage: Figuring Out Ways to Make Things Happen

Piaget suggested that the first stage of cognitive development lasts from birth until somewhere between eighteen and twenty-four months. During this period, termed the **sensorimotor stage,** infants gradually learn that there is a relationship between their actions and the external world. They discover that they can manipulate objects and produce effects. In short, they acquire a basic grasp of the concept of *cause and effect.* For example, they learn that if they make certain movements—for instance, shaking their leg—specific effects follow (e.g., toys suspended over their cribs also move), and they begin to "experiment" with various actions to see what effects they will produce.

Cognitive Development
Changes in cognitive abilities and functioning, occurring throughout the life span.

Assimilation
In Piaget's theory of cognitive development, incorporation of new information into existing mental frameworks (schemas).

Schemas
Mental frameworks that help us process and store new information.

Accommodation
In Piaget's theory of cognitive development, modifications in existing knowledge structures (schemas) as a result of exposure to new information or experiences.

Sensorimotor Stage
In Piaget's theory, the earliest stage of cognitive development.

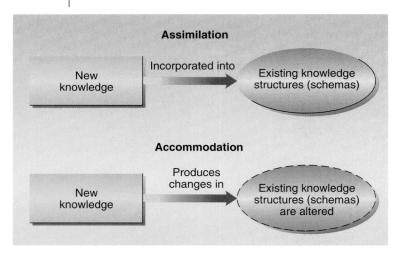

FIGURE 8.6
Assimilation and Accommodation

According to Piaget, children build increasing knowledge of the world through two processes: *assimilation*, in which new information is incorporated into existing schemas; and *accommodation*, in which existing schemas are modified in response to new information and experiences.

Object Permanence

Understanding of the fact that objects continue to exist, even when they are hidden from view.

Preoperational Stage

In Piaget's theory, a stage of cognitive development during which children become capable of mental representations of the external world.

Symbolic Play

Play in which children pretend that one object is another object.

Egocentrism

The inability of young children to distinguish their own perspective from that of others.

Throughout the sensorimotor period, Piaget contended, infants seem to know the world only through motor activities and sensory impressions. They have not yet learned to use mental symbols or images to represent objects or events. This results in some interesting effects. For example, if an object is hidden from view, four-month-olds will not attempt to search for it. For such infants, "out of sight" is truly "out of mind." By eight or nine months of age, however, they *will* search for the hidden objects. They have acquired a basic idea of **object permanence**—the idea that objects continue to exist even when they are hidden from view. (But see our subsequent discussion of this topic; recent findings suggest that here, as in many other cases, Piaget underestimated the abilities of infants.)

The Preoperational Stage: Growth of Symbolic Activity

Sometime between the ages of eighteen and twenty-four months, Piaget suggested, toddlers acquire the ability to form mental images of objects and events. At the same time, language develops to the point at which they begin to think in terms of words. These developments mark the transition to Piaget's second stage—the **preoperational stage.** This term reflects Piaget's view that, at this stage, children don't yet show much ability to use logic and mental operations.

During the preoperational stage, which lasts until about age seven, children are capable of many actions they could not perform earlier. They begin to demonstrate **symbolic play,** in which they pretend that one object is another—for instance, that a pencil is a rocket, or a wooden block is a frog. While the thought processes of preoperational children are more advanced than those in the preceding stage, Piaget emphasized that they were still immature in several respects. True—they can use mental symbols, but their thinking remains somewhat inflexible, illogical, fragmented, and tied to specific contexts. One way in which the thinking of preoperational children is immature involves what Piaget termed **egocentrism**—the inability to understand that others may perceive the world differently than they do (Piaget, 1975). For example, if two-year-olds are shown a card with a picture of a dog on one side and a cat on the other, and the card is placed between the child and the researcher, many do not seem to realize that they and the adult see different pictures. (In this case, Piaget seems to have underestimated the abilities of young children; more recent findings indicate that even very young children can appreciate the fact that others have different perspectives than they do; e.g., Birch & Bloom, 2003.)

Children in the preoperational stage also seem to lack understanding of relational terms such as *lighter, larger,* and *softer.* Further, they lack *seriation*—the ability to arrange objects in order along some dimension. Finally, and most important, they lack what Piaget terms the principle of **conservation**—knowledge that certain physical attributes of an object remain unchanged even though the outward appearance of the object is altered. For example, imagine that a four-year-old is shown two identical lumps of clay. One lump is then flattened into a large pancake as the child watches. Asked whether the two lumps still contain the same amount of clay, the child may answer, "No."

The Stage of Concrete Operations: The Emergence of Logical Thought

By the time they are six or seven (or perhaps even earlier, as we'll see), most children can solve the simple problems described earlier. According to Piaget, their mastery of conservation marks the beginning of a third major stage—the stage of **concrete operations.**

TABLE 8.2	Major Stages in Piaget's Theory	

According to Piaget, we move through the stages of cognitive development described here.

Stage	Age	Major Accomplishments
Sensorimotor	0–2 years	The child develops basic ideas of cause and effect and object permanence.
Preoperational	2–6 or 7 years	The child begins to represent the world symbolically.
Concrete operations	7–11 or 12 years	The child gains understanding of principles such as conservation; logical thought emerges.
Formal operations	12–adult	The adolescent becomes capable of several forms of logical thought.

During this stage, which lasts until about the age of eleven, many important skills emerge. Children gain understanding of relational terms and seriation. They come to understand *reversibility*—that many physical changes can be undone by a reversal of the original action. Children who have reached the stage of concrete operations also begin to engage in what Piaget described as *logical thought.* If asked, "Why did you and your mother go to the store?" they reply, "Because my mother needed some milk." Younger children, in contrast, may reply, "Because afterwards, she came home."

■ The Stage of Formal Operations: Dealing with Abstractions as Well as Reality

At about the age of twelve, Piaget suggested, most children enter the final stage of cognitive development—the stage of **formal operations.** During this period, major features of adult thought make their appearance. While children in the earlier stage of concrete operations can think logically, they can do so only about concrete events and objects. In contrast, those who have reached the stage of formal operations can think abstractly; they can deal not only with the real or concrete but also with possibilities—relationships that do not exist but can be imagined. During this final stage, children become capable of what Piaget termed **hypothetico-deductive reasoning,** which involves the ability to generate hypotheses and to think logically about symbols, ideas, and propositions.

While the thinking of older children or adolescents closely approaches that of adults, Piaget believed that it still falls short of the adult level in certain respects. Older children, and especially adolescents, often use their new powers of reasoning to construct sweeping theories about human relationships, ethics, or political systems. The reasoning behind such views may be logical, but the theories are often false because the young persons who construct them don't have enough experience to do a more sophisticated job.

One final—but crucial—point: People who have reached the stage of formal operations are *capable* of engaging in advanced forms of thought, but there is no guarantee that they will actually do so. Such thinking requires a lot of cognitive effort, so it is not surprising that adolescents, and adults, too, often slip back into less advanced modes of thought. Table 8.2 provides a summary of the major stages in Piaget's theory.

Piaget's Theory: A Modern Assessment

All theories in psychology are subject to careful scientific testing, so what do the results of research on Piaget's theory reveal? Essentially, that it is highly insightful in many respects but that it should probably be revised to take account of new findings. Although developmental psychologists have suggested revisions in Piaget's

Conservation
Understanding of the fact that certain physical attributes of an object remain unchanged even though its outward appearance changes.

Concrete Operations
A stage in Piaget's theory of cognitive development occurring roughly between the ages of seven and eleven. It is at this stage that children become aware of the permanence of objects.

Formal Operations (stage of)
In Piaget's theory, the final stage of cognitive development, during which individuals may acquire the capacity for deductive or propositional reasoning.

Hypothetico-Deductive Reasoning
A type of reasoning first shown by individuals during the stage of formal operations. It involves formulating a general theory and deducing specific hypotheses from it.

theory in several respects, the most important of these relate to the following point: Piaget greatly underestimated the cognitive abilities of infants and preschoolers. Let's take a look at some of this work.

The Case of the Competent Preschooler

Before turning to evidence indicating that Piaget underestimated the cognitive abilities of infants and young children (e.g,. Siegal & Peterson, 1996), it's important to ask *why* he did so. The answer seems to be that some of the research methods he used, although ingenious, made it difficult for infants and preschool children to demonstrate cognitive abilities they actually possessed. Let's take a brief look at two of the abilities that Piaget underestimated—*object permanence* and *egocentrism.*

As you may recall, Piaget concluded that infants younger than eight or nine months old did not realize that objects have an existence that continues even when the objects are removed from sight. However, it now appears that these findings might have stemmed from the fact that children this young don't understand the concept "under." Thus, when an object is placed under a cover, they are stumped because they don't realize that one object can be underneath another. So if an object is placed *behind* a screen rather than under a cover, infants as young as four or five months old *do* seem to know it is still there.

But infants seem to understand far more about the physical objects than this; they even seem to have a basic understanding of how physical objects will behave under various conditions. Insight into their impressive skills in this respect is provided by tasks involving what Baillargeon (1987) terms *impossible events.* For instance, in one ingenious study using such tasks (Baillargeon, Needham, & DeVos, 1992), infants 6.5 months old watched while a gloved hand pushed an object along a platform. In the *possible event* condition, the hand stopped pushing while the object was still on the platform. In the *impossible event* condition, the hand pushed the object until it was off the edge of the platform (see Figure 8.7). Would the children look longer at the impossible event than the possible event? They did indeed, thus indicating that they understood that physical objects can't stay suspended in empty space! In other conditions, the gloved hand grasped the object and held it while pushing it along the platform. When the object was pushed beyond the edge of the platform *but was still held by the gloved hand,* the children did not seem surprised, and did not look at this even longer than one in which the object stopped before reaching the edge (refer to Figure 8.7). Studies like this suggest that infants only 3.5 months old understand much about the physical nature of objects—much more, in fact, than Piaget believed.

What about *egocentrism*—young children's inability to understand that others may perceive the world differently than they do? Piaget found that children could take others' perspective well until they were six or seven years old. However, once again, it appears that Piaget underestimated young children's cognitive abilities. Modern research, using methods different from the ones employed by Piaget, has found that children as young as three or four years old demonstrate a basic understanding of the fact that others can, and often do, see the world differently than they (e.g., Borke, 1975; Newcombe & Huttenlochber, 1992). In fact, recent research has extended the concept of egocentrism by investigating what developmental psychologists describe as the **curse of knowledge.**

This term refers to the fact that we tend to be biased by our own knowledge when judging the perspective of people who, we believe, know *less* about some topic than we do. Have you ever found that because *you* know how to do something (e.g., work a DVD player), you think it will be relatively easy for others to do this, too? That's an example of the *curse of knowledge* in action. Young children have special difficulties with this effect: They tend to assume very strongly that if they know something, so, too, will someone else. This may seem like egocentrism—a general inability to take others' perspective—but in fact, recent findings indicate that it is not the same

Curse of Knowledge
Refers to the fact that we tend to be biased by our own knowledge when judging the perspective of people who know less about some topic than we do.

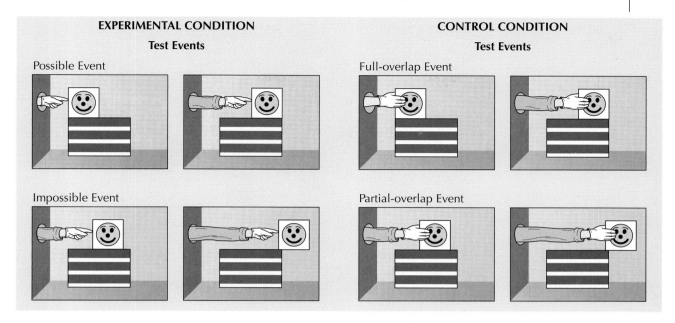

FIGURE 8.7
Infants' Reactions to Impossible Events

Infants only 6.5 months old showed signs of surprise when confronted with impossible events such as the one shown in the top drawings. In contrast, they did not show surprise to various kinds of possible events, such as those shown in the lower drawings. These findings suggest that infants possess considerable understanding of the nature and properties of physical objects.

Source: From "Physical reasoning in young infants: Seeking explanations for impossible events" by Renee Baillargeon in BRITISH JOURNAL OF DEVELOPMENTAL PSYCHOLOGY, Vol. 12, Part 1 (March 1994), pp. 9–33, Figure 6, p. 21. Reprinted by permission of The British Psychological Society and the author.

thing. If the children do *not* know more about something than another person, they do not show such effects. It is only when they believe that they know *more* than someone else that they assume this person will know it, too. In other words, this effect is more limited in scope than egocentrism. Research conducted by Birch and Bloom (2003) provided a clear demonstration of the nature of the curse of knowledge.

In this study, children three, four, or five years old were shown toys that, supposedly, were either familiar or unfamiliar to a puppet named Percy. The children were further told that the toys contained some object (e.g., a small yo-yo). Half of the children were shown this object, while half were not. Then, they were asked to indicate whether Percy (the puppet) would know what was inside the toys. The children were also led to believe that Percy was familiar with these toys or that he was not. When the children knew that Percy was familiar with the toys, they did *not* show the curse of knowledge effect: They assumed he would know what was inside it regardless of whether they knew what this object was. When the children knew that Percy was *unfamiliar* with the toys, however, the younger ones (three and four years old) did show this effect: They assumed that if *they* knew what was inside it, Percy would, too. In contrast, older children did not show this effect (see Figure 8.8 on page 248). These findings indicate that young children do not always have difficulty understanding that other people have different perspectives than their own; rather, this tends to occur only under certain conditions—when, for instance, they think people know less than they do.

In sum, there is now general agreement among developmental psychologists that, in certain respects, Piaget's theory is in need of revision. Despite its shortcomings, however, there is no doubt that this theory has profoundly altered

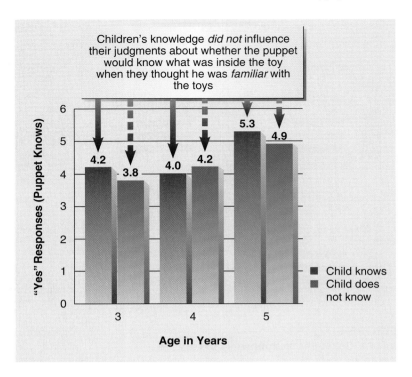

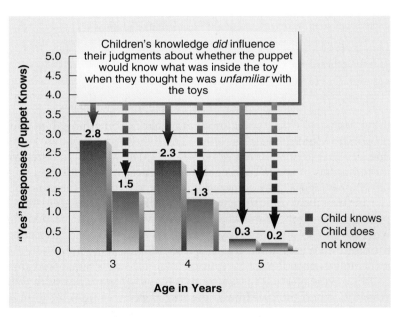

FIGURE 8.8

The Curse of Knowledge: Assuming That If We Know Something, Others Know It, Too

When children of three ages (three, four, or five years old) believed that a toy puppet was familiar with toys, they assumed it would know what was inside the toy whether they did or did not have this information themselves (*upper figure*). When children believed that the puppet was not familiar with the toy, the younger two groups showed the "curse of knowledge": They assumed it would know what was inside if they knew this (*lower figure*). The older children did not show this effect.

Source: Based on data from Birch & Bloom, 2003.

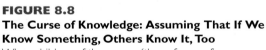

our ideas about how children think and reason (e.g., Brainerd, 1996). In this sense, certainly, Piaget's work has made a lasting and important contribution to psychology.

KEY QUESTIONS

- What are the major stages in Piaget's theory, and what cognitive abilities do infants, children, and adolescents acquire as they move through these stages?
- In what respects does Piaget's theory appear to be in need of revision?
- What is the "curse of knowledge" and what does it tell us about young children's cognitive abilities?

Beyond Piaget: Children's Theory of Mind and Research on the Information-Processing Perspective

Although Piaget certainly added much to our understanding of children's thought, recent research has investigated topics that were not included in his work. One of these involves children's **theory of mind**—their growing understanding of their own mental states and those of others; a second is application of an *information-processing perspective* to various aspects of cognitive development.

▪ Children's Theory of Mind: Thinking about Thinking

As adults, we possess a sophisticated understanding of the process of thinking. We realize that our own thoughts may change over time and that we may have false beliefs or reach false conclusions. Similarly, we realize that other people may have goals or desires that differ from our own and that they may sometimes try to conceal these from us; further, we realize that, given the same information, they may reach conclusions that differ from our own. In other words, we understand quite a bit about how we and other people think. What about children? When—and how—do they acquire such understanding? This has been a major focus of recent research on cognitive development.

Let's begin with what might seem to be a fairly simple aspect of such thinking—children's ability to recognize that others can hold beliefs different from their own and that these beliefs can be false. Do they understand this basic fact? Not, it appears, until they are about four years old (e.g., Naito, Komatsu, & Fuke, 1994). Until that time, they often fall prey to the kind of errors described in our discussion of the curse of knowledge; they think that if they know something, others must know it, too.

In addition, even when they come to understand that other persons may have different knowledge or beliefs than they, they continue to lack important insights into the nature of thought. For instance, they are often unclear about the *source* of their knowledge: Did they obtain it themselves? Did someone tell them? Did they draw an inference? This may be one reason why, as we noted in Chapter 6, young children are often unreliable witnesses, even to traumatic events they have personally experienced. They know that they have knowledge of various events, but are unsure how they acquired it. So, even though young children have a surprisingly complex theory of mind, it is incomplete in several respects.

▪ An Information-Processing Perspective—and Increasing Reliance on Heuristics and Other Potential Sources of Error

Another way in which recent research on cognitive development has moved beyond Piaget's theory involves application of an **information-processing perspective.** This perspective seeks insights into cognitive development in terms of children's growing abilities with respect to basic aspects of cognition such as attention, memory, and **metacognition** (thinking about thinking and being able to control and use one's own cognitive abilities strategically). For instance, as they grow older, children acquire better strategies for retaining information in working (short-term) memory. Five- and six-year-olds are much less likely than adults to use *rehearsal*—repeating information to themselves as they try to memorize it. By the time children are eight years old, however, they can do this much more effectively.

In a similar manner, children acquire increasingly effective strategies for focusing their attention, for using **scripts** and other mental frameworks (schemas; Fivush, Kuebli, & Clubb, 1992), and greater understanding of metacognition—for instance, how to regulate and control problem-solving processes and memory (Frederiksen, 1994). Research conducted from an information-processing perspective has helped link the process of cognitive development more closely to basic research on cognition; so it, too, is very useful.

Theory of Mind
Refers to children's growing understanding of their own mental states and those of others.

Information-Processing Perspective (of cognitive development)
A perspective that seeks insights into cognitive development in terms of children's growing abilities with respect to basic aspects of cognition, such as attention and memory.

Metacognition
Awareness and understanding of our own cognitive processes.

Scripts
Mental representations of the sequence of events in a given situation.

One final point: While the sophistication of children's thinking does indeed increase as they grow older, it does not move consistently from intuitive thought to logical, scientific reasoning, or from an initially inefficient form of information processing to more efficient ones. As we noted in Chapters 6 and 7, all human thought—that of adults as well as children—is subject to many potential errors and biases. Do you recall our discussions of heuristics—mental "rules-of-thumb" we use for making decisions and judgments quickly and with very little effort (Chapters 1 and 7)? If adults are subject to such biases, it is not surprising to learn that children are, too. In fact, acquiring a tendency to rely on these heuristics is part of cognitive development, and research findings indicate that children begin to show them at a young age (Jacobs & Klaczynski, 2002). So, contrary to what Piaget believed, cognitive development is not a continuous journey toward increasingly effective thought. We do improve, but we also pick up many "bad mental habits" along the way!

KEY QUESTIONS

- To what does the term *children's theory of mind* refer?
- According to the information-processing perspective, what does cognitive development involve?
- What role do heuristics and other potential sources of error play in cognitive development?

MORAL DEVELOPMENT: REASONING ABOUT "RIGHT" AND "WRONG"

Is it ever right to cheat on an exam? To mislead consumers through false advertising? To claim exaggerated deductions on your income taxes? As adults we often ponder such *moral questions*—issues concerning what is right and what is wrong in a given context (see Figure 8.9). And as adults we realize that such matters are often complex. Whether a given action is acceptable or unacceptable depends on many factors, including the specific circumstances involved, legal considerations, and our own personal code of ethics.

How do children deal with such issues? They, too, must make moral judgments. Is their reasoning about such matters similar to that of adults? This is the key question addressed in research on **moral development**—changes in the ability to reason about what is right and what is wrong in a given situation (e.g., Carpendale & Krebs, 1995; Carlo et al., 1996). While many different views of moral development have been proposed, the most famous is a theory offered by Lawrence Kohlberg (1984).

Kohlberg's Stages of Moral Understanding

Building on earlier views proposed by Piaget (1965), Kohlberg studied boys and men and suggested that human beings move through three distinct levels of moral reasoning, each divided in two separate phases. To determine the stage of moral development people had reached, Kohlberg asked them to consider imaginary situations that raised moral dilemmas. Participants then indicated the course of action they would choose and explained why. According to Kohlberg, it is the explanations, *not* the decisions themselves, that are crucial, for it is the reasoning displayed in these explanations that reveals individuals' stages of moral development. One such dilemma is as follows:

> A man's wife is ill with a special kind of cancer. There is a drug that may save her, but it is very expensive. The pharmacist who discovered this medicine will sell it for $2,000,

Moral Development
Changes in the capacity to reason about the rightness or wrongness of various actions that occur with age.

"Miss Dugan, will you send someone in here who can distinguish right from wrong?"

FIGURE 8.9
Moral Judgment: Telling Right from Wrong
Most people use their own values and principles to determine whether some action is "right" or "wrong"; unlike the characters in this cartoon, they don't need an outside opinion!
Source: © The New Yorker Collection 1975 Dana Fradon from cartoonbank. com. All Rights Reserved.

but the man has only $1,000. He asks the pharmacist to let him pay part of the cost now and the rest later, but the pharmacist refuses. Being desperate, the man steals the drug. Should he have done so? Why?

Let's consider the kind of reasoning that would reflect several of the major stages of moral reasoning described by Kohlberg. (An overview of all the stages he described is presented in Table 8.3.)

TABLE 8.3   Kohlberg's Theory of Moral Development: An Overview

According to Kohlberg, we move through the stages of moral development (and reasoning) described here.

Level/Stage	Description
Preconventional Level	
Stage 1: **Punishment-and-Obedience Orientation**	Morality judged in terms of consequences
Stage 2: **Naive Hedonistic Orientation**	Morality judged in terms of what satisfies own needs or those of others
Conventional Level	
Stage 3: **Good Boy–Good Girl Orientation**	Morality judged in terms of adherence to social rules or norms with respect to personal acquaintances
Stage 4: **Social Order–Maintaining Orientation**	Morality judged in terms of social rules or laws applied universally, not just to acquaintances
Postconventional Level	
Stage 5: **Legalistic Orientation**	Morality judged in terms of human rights, which may transcend laws
Stage 6: **Universal Ethical Principle Orientation**	Morality judged in terms of self-chosen ethical principles

The Preconventional Level

At the first level of moral development, the **preconventional level,** children judge morality largely in terms of consequences: Actions that lead to rewards are perceived as good or acceptable; ones that lead to punishments are seen as bad or unacceptable. For example, a child at this stage might say, "The man should not steal the drug because if he does, he'll be punished."

The Conventional Level

As children's cognitive abilities increase, Kohlberg suggests, they enter a second level of moral development, the **conventional level.** Now they are aware of some of the complexities of the social order and judge morality in terms of what supports the laws and rules of their society. Thus, a child at this stage might reason, "It's OK to steal the drug because no one will think you are bad if you do. If you don't, and let your wife die, you'll never be able to look anyone in the eye again."

The Postconventional Level

Finally, in adolescence or early adulthood, many, though by no means all, individuals enter a third level known as the **postconventional level** or principled level. At this stage, people judge morality in terms of abstract principles and values rather than in terms of existing laws or rules of society. Persons who attain this stage often believe that certain obligations and values transcend the laws of society. The rules they follow are abstract and ethical, not concrete like the Ten Commandments, and they are based on inner conscience rather than external sources of authority. For example, a person at this stage of moral development might argue for stealing the drug as follows: "If the man doesn't steal the drug, he is putting property above human life; this makes no sense. People could live together without private property, but a respect for human life is essential." In contrast, if they argue for not stealing the drug, they might reason as follows: "If the man stole the drug, he wouldn't be blamed by others, but he would probably blame himself, because he has violated his own standards of honesty and hurt another person for his own gain."

Evidence Concerning Kohlberg's Theory

Do we really pass through the series of stages described by Kohlberg, becoming increasingly sophisticated in our judgments of morality? Some findings are consistent with this view. Individuals do generally seem to progress through the stages of moral reasoning Kohlberg described, moving from less sophisticated to increasingly sophisticated modes of thought (e.g., Walker, 1989). Other evidence, however, suggests that Kohlberg's theory, while providing important insights, requires major revisions in several respects.

Consistency of Moral Judgments

Kohlberg's theory, like other **stage theories,** suggests that as people grow older, they move through a successive series of discrete stages. If that is true, then it would be predicted that individuals' moral reasoning across a wide range of moral dilemmas should be consistent—it should reflect the stage they have reached. Do people show such consistency? The answer appears to be "no." Research on this issue (e.g., Ward & Krebs, 1996) indicates people do not show a high degree of consistency reflecting a specific stage of moral reasoning, as Kohlberg's theory predicts.

Cultural Differences and Moral Development

A second problem with Kohlberg's theory is neither the stages Kohlberg described nor steady progression through them appears in all cultures. In cross-cultural studies carried out in many countries (Taiwan, Turkey, Mexico), it has sometimes been found that persons from tribal or rural village backgrounds are less likely to reach stage 5 reasoning than persons from more advantaged backgrounds (e.g., Nisan &

Preconventional Level (of morality)
According to Kohlberg, the earliest stage of moral development, one at which individuals judge morality in terms of the effects produced by various actions.

Conventional Level (of morality)
According to Kohlberg, a stage of moral development during which individuals judge morality largely in terms of existing social norms or rules.

Postconventional Level (of morality)
According to Kohlberg, the final stage of moral development, one at which individuals judge morality in terms of abstract principles.

Stage Theory
Any theory proposing that all human beings move through an orderly and predictable series of changes.

psychology lends a hand

Why Knowing How Children Think Is Important—and Useful

As we have seen, research on how children think (including how they make moral judgments) indicates that they are *not* miniature adults. While they are able to carry out many cognitive tasks at a younger age than psychologists once believed, they are definitely *not* capable of thinking, reasoning, or making decisions in the same way as adults. Does this fact have any practical applications? Definitely. Here are some of the most important:

- **Education should take account of children's cognitive abilities.** At what age should children begin learning a second or third language? At what age should teachers try to get them to reason deductively? When should training designed to help them avoid various cognitive errors begin? Answering these questions has important implications for what goes on in classrooms, so knowing *when* children can handle various cognitive tasks is useful from the point of view of designing effective educational programs.
- **What should parents expect from their children—and when?** Suppose that a four-year-old boy "operates" on his aunt's goldfish in order to find out what makes it swim. When she discovers this deed, should she try to explain that what the child did was bad because life is precious and destroying it is evil? Certainly, she could try, but at age four, the child probably can't understand the abstract principles involved, so her effort is probably doomed to fail. The moral? Parents should speak to children in terms they will understand. Expecting them to reason like

adults or to fully understand others' perspectives can usually only lead to disappointment on the part of the parents, and confusion on the part of the children.

- **But don't *underestimate* children's understanding either!** While parents and teachers should be careful not to expect too much from children, they should also take care to avoid expecting too little. True, children can't reason like adults, and have an incomplete theory of mind: They don't really understand their own mental processes or those of others. But they *can* do quite a lot: Even at young ages they understand something about causality, can appreciate the fact that other people have intentions and goals, and can tell the difference between actions that are "good" and ones that are "bad." If parents and teachers ignore these facts, they run the risk of assuming that children understand less than they really do. This can lead them to say or do things in the children's presence that, they assume, will go right "over their heads," and so will have no impact on the children. In fact, this may not be true. Not only do "little pitchers have big ears," a lot goes on between the ears. Parents who overlook this fact may leave their children with messages they don't really want to transmit. Our overall conclusion: Anyone who deals with children regularly (teachers, parents) should definitely have a basic understanding of their cognitive abilities—and the best place to find it is modern psychology.

Kohlberg, 1982; Simpson, 1974). These findings suggest that Kohlberg's work may, to an extent, be "culture-bound": It is biased against persons from ethnic groups and populations different from the ones he originally studied. Whether and to what degree this is true remains uncertain, but it *is* clear that cultural factors play an important role in shaping moral development and should be taken fully into account in our efforts to understand this important topic. (Why should we study children's cognitive development? Is there a practical payoff for doing so? Absolutely! To see what it is, please read the **Psychology Lends a Hand** section above.)

KEY QUESTIONS

- What are the major stages of moral development described by Kohlberg's theory?
- Do cultural factors have any impact on moral development?

SOCIAL DEVELOPMENT DURING CHILDHOOD: FORMING RELATIONSHIPS WITH OTHERS

Cognitive development is a crucial aspect of human growth, but it does not occur in a social vacuum. As infants and children are acquiring the capacities to think and reason, they are also gaining the basic experiences, skills, and emotions that permit them to form close relationships and interact with others effectively in many settings. In this section, we'll examine several aspects of such **social development.**

Temperament: Individual Differences in Emotional Style

Do you know anyone who is almost always energetic, cheerful, and upbeat? How about the other extreme—someone who is usually reserved, quiet, and gloomy? Psychologists refer to such stable individual differences in attention, arousal, mood, and reactivity to new situations as **temperament** (e.g., Guerin & Gottfried, 1994). Growing evidence suggests that these differences are present very early in life—perhaps at birth (e.g., Kagan & Snidman, 1991; Seifer et al., 1994). What are the key dimensions of temperament? Most experts agree that they involve *positive emotionality*—the extent to which infants show pleasure and are typically in a good, happy mood; *distress–anger*—the extent to which infants show distress and the emotion of anger; *fear*—the extent to which infants show fear in various situations; and *activity level*—their overall level of activity or energy.

Large individual differences occur in these dimensions, and they are sometimes easy to spot, even during brief interactions with infants. On the basis of such differences, some researchers (Thomas & Chess, 1989) have suggested that infants can be divided into three basic groups: *easy children* (about 40 percent)—infants who are generally cheerful, adapt easily to new experiences, and quickly establish routines for many activities of daily life; *difficult children* (about 10 percent)—infants who are irregular in daily routines, slow to accept new situations or experiences, and show negative reactions more than other infants (see Figure 8.10); and *slow-to-warm-up children* (15 percent)—infants who are relatively inactive and apathetic and show mild negative reactions when exposed to unexpected events or new situations. The remaining 35 percent of infants cannot be readily classified under one of these headings.

FIGURE 8.10
Infant Temperament in Action
The child here would probably be described as "difficult"—he shows negative reactions in many different situations, and so makes his mother's life difficult, too!

"Noah, I'm tired of doing battle with you!"

How stable are such differences in temperament? Research findings suggest that they are only moderately stable early in life—from birth until about twenty-four months. After that time, however, they appear to be highly stable (e.g., Lemery et al., 1999). Growing evidence suggests that individual differences in temperament are at least partially genetic in origin (e.g., Lytton, 1990). Indeed, some findings indicate that genetic factors may account for 50 to 60 percent of the variations in temperament (Kagan, 1998). However, different aspects of temperament may be influenced by genetic and environmental factors to varying degrees (e.g., Magai & McFadden, 1995). Whatever the relative role of genetic and environmental factors in temperament, individual differences in such emotional style have important implications for social development. For example, a much higher proportion of difficult than easy children experience behavioral problems later in life (Chess & Thomas, 1984). They find it harder to adjust to school, to form friendships, and to get along with others. In addition, many high-reactive children demonstrate *shyness* as they grow older and enter an increasingly broad range of social situations. Turning to fearfulness, about one-fourth of infants show an inhibited or highly fearful temperament (Kagan, 1998), while one-third show an uninhibited or fearless pattern. Not surprisingly, fearful infants experience more problems with respect to social adjustment both inside and outside their families than nonfearful, uninhibited children. Finally, there is growing evidence for the view that some aspects of temperament can influence the kind of bonds infants form with their caregivers, and hence important aspects of their personality and even their abilities to form close relationships with other persons when they are adults (Shaver & Brennan, 1992; Shaver & Hazan, 1994).

Attachment: The Beginnings of Love

Do infants love their parents? They can't say so directly, but by the time they are six or seven months old, most appear to have a strong emotional bond with the persons who care for them (Ainsworth, 1973; Lamb, 1977). This strong affectional tie between infants and their caregivers is known as **attachment** and is, in an important sense, the first form of love they experience toward others. What are the origins of this initial form of love? How can it be measured? These are among the questions developmental psychologists have sought to answer in their research on attachment.

Patterns of Attachment

That infants form strong attachments to the persons who care for them is obvious. But attachment is not the same for all infants. In fact, several distinct patterns appear to exist. Most infants show **secure attachment;** they feel safe around their caregiver (e.g., their mother), enjoy exploring new environments—often using their caregiver as a "safe home base"—and are sociable and playful. In contrast, other infants show **insecure/avoidant attachment.** They don't rely on their caregivers for security, and often avoid close contact with them. They explore new environments but don't seem to view their caregiver as a source of safety and comfort. A third group of infants shows a pattern known as **insecure/ambivalent attachment.** These infants often engage in continuous efforts to maintain contact with their caregiver, and often show a pattern of clinging to them in new situations. They are inhibited and show many signs of fear. How do these different patterns develop? Research findings suggest that they derive out of complex interactions between infants' temperament and the treatment they receive from caregivers. If a child has an easy temperament (is generally cheerful and adaptable) and the caregiver provides sufficient attention, responsiveness, and approval, secure attachment is likely to develop. If, in contrast, the child has a fearful, inhibited temperament and the caregiver offers little attention and approval, insecure/ambivalent attachment may develop. The key point is that attachment is reciprocal: It depends on both the child *and* the caregiver.

Social Development
Changes in social behavior and social relations occurring over the life span.

Temperament
Stable individual differences in attention, arousal, mood, and reactivity to new situations present at, or shortly after, birth.

Attachment
A strong affectional bond between infants and their caregivers.

Secure Attachment
A pattern of attachment in which infants actively seek contact with their caregivers and take comfort from their presence when they return in the *strange situation* test.

Insecure/Avoidant Attachment
A pattern of attachment in which children don't cry when their caregiver leaves in the *strange situation* test, and are slow to greet their caregiver when this person returns.

Insecure/Ambivalent Attachment
A pattern of attachment in which a child seeks contact with the caregiver before separation but then, after she leaves and then returns, first seeks her but then resists or rejects her offers of comfort.

The Long-Term Effects of Attachment

Do these different patterns of attachment have effects that persist beyond infancy? A growing body of evidence indicates that they do. During childhood, youngsters who are securely attached to their caregivers are more sociable, better at solving certain kinds of problems, more tolerant of frustration, and more flexible and persistent in many situations than are children who are insecurely attached (Belsky & Cassidy, 1995; Pastor, 1981). Further, securely attached children seem to experience fewer behavioral problems during later childhood (Fagot & Kavanaugh, 1990).

Perhaps even more surprising, some findings suggest that differences in attachment style as an infant may have strong effects on the kind of relationships individuals form when they are adults (e.g., Hazan & Shaver, 1990). People who showed insecure/avoidant attachment to their caregivers as infants have a difficult time forming intimate bonds with romantic partners; they didn't trust their caregivers as infants, and they are reluctant to trust spouses or lovers when they are adults. Similarly, persons who showed insecure/ambivalent attachment to their caregivers as infants seem to be ambivalent about romantic relationships, too: They want them, but they also fear them because they perceive their partners as distant and unloving. In contrast, persons who were securely attached to their caregivers as infants seek closeness in their adult relationships and are comfortable with having to depend on their partners (Shaver & Hazan, 1994). In a sense, then, it seems that the pattern of our relationships with others is set—at least to a degree—by the nature of the very first relationships we form: attachment to our caregivers.

Culture and Attachment

Although attachment of infants to their caregivers is universal, research findings indicate that culture may strongly affect the outcome of this process. For instance, Cole (1999) compared patterns of attachment in three countries—the United States, Germany, and Japan. Results indicated significant differences across the three cultures in terms of the proportions of children who were securely, avoidantly, and ambivalently attached to their caregivers. Secure attachment was higher in Japan and the United States than in Germany, while avoidance attachment was highest in Germany, and ambivalent attachment was higher in Japan. Contrasting child-rearing practices seem to account for these differences (see Figure 8.11). German parents, more than American and Japanese parents, try to encourage independence

FIGURE 8.11
Culture and Attachment
As shown here, patterns of attachment between infants and their caregivers differ across cultures. These differences appear to reflect contrasting patterns of child-rearing practices in the countries involved.
Source: Adapted from Cole, 1999.

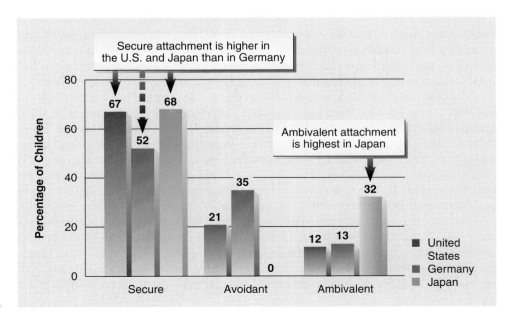

rather than clinging dependence at an early age; this results in more avoidant attachments. In contrast, in Japan, infants are rarely away from their parents; in both the United States and Germany, infants are often placed in child-care facilities. As a result, anxious–ambivalent attachment is more common in Japan than in the two other cultures. So, once again, we can see that cultural differences have important implications for basic aspects of human behavior—or, in this case, human development.

Contact Comfort and Attachment: The Soft Touch of Love

Before concluding, it's important to consider an additional factor that seems to play an important role in attachment. This is *close physical contact* between infants and their caregivers. Such contact—known as *contact comfort*—involves the hugging, cuddling, and caresses infants receive from their caregivers, and it seems to be an essential ingredient in attachment. The research that first established this fact is a "classic" in the history of psychology, and was conducted by Harry Harlow and his co-workers (Harlow & Harlow, 1966).

In this research, baby monkeys were exposed to two artificial "mothers." One consisted of bare wire, while the other possessed a soft terrycloth cover. The wire mother, not the soft one, provided milk. According to basic principles of conditioning, the monkeys should soon have developed a strong bond to this cold wire mother, but in fact, the opposite happened. The infants spent almost all their time clinging tightly to the soft cloth-covered mother and only left her to visit the wire mother when driven by pangs of hunger (see Figure 8.12).

On the basis of these and related findings, Harlow concluded that a baby monkey's attachment to its mother rests, at least in part, on the mother's ability to satisfy the baby's need for contact comfort—direct contact with soft objects. The satisfaction of other physical needs, such as that for food, is not enough.

Do such effects occur among human babies as well? Some studies seem to suggest that they may. For example, two- and three-year-old children placed in a strange room play for longer periods of time without becoming distressed when they have a security blanket present than when it is absent (Passman & Weisberg, 1975). In fact, they play almost as long as they do when their mothers are in the

FIGURE 8.12
Harlow's Studies of Attachment
Although the wire "mothers" used in Harlow's research provided monkey babies with nourishment, the babies preferred the soft, cloth-covered mothers that provided contact comfort.

room. These findings suggest that for blanket-attached children, the presence of this object provides the same kind of comfort and reassurance as that provided by their mothers. So, human infants, too, may have a need for contact comfort, and the gentle hugs, caresses, and cuddling they obtain from their mothers and other caregivers may play a role in the formation of attachment.

Friendships and Loneliness: Key Factors in Social Development

Once they pass their fifth or sixth birthday, children in many different countries spend more of their time in school than anywhere else. As a result, their experiences in this setting play an important role in their social and emotional development. In school, children do not merely acquire information that contributes to their cognitive growth: They also have the opportunity to acquire and practice many social skills. They learn to share, to cooperate, to work together in groups to solve problems, and—perhaps most important of all—they acquire growing experience in forming and maintaining **friendships**—mutual dyadic relationships involving strong affective ties (Berndt, 2002).

What role do friendships play in social and emotional development? Apparently, an important one. Research findings indicate that high-quality friendships—ones marked by intimacy, loyalty, and mutual support—enhance children's social adjustment. The children with high-quality friendships are liked by other children to a greater extent, are more sociable, and assume more leadership roles than children who have fewer friendships or friendships lower in quality (Ladd, Kochenderfer, & Coleman, 1996). Why is this the case? Apparently because such friendships give children an opportunity to learn and practice skills needed for effective interpersonal relationships—social skills that are helpful not only during childhood, but also throughout life. Friendships also contribute to emotional development, giving children opportunities to experience intense emotional bonds with someone other than their caregivers, and to express these feelings in their behavior.

Another effect of friendship quality is that the higher such quality, the greater the influence friends have on each other. This is beneficial when friends show mostly positive characteristics or social behaviors, but it can "backfire" and prove harmful when close friends show negative characteristics or engage in negative social behaviors. In other words, being close friends with someone who is shy or withdrawn can lead children to develop similar behaviors, and being close friends with someone who engages in delinquent behaviors can, perhaps, increase such tendencies (e.g., Poulin, Dishion, & Haas, 1999). So, truly, friendship can produce harmful as well as beneficial effects.

One other effect of friendships, however, is definitely positive: Friendships are a very important remedy for loneliness. At least 10 percent of children in elementary school report feeling lonely, and such loneliness, in turn, can result in many negative outcomes, such as development of poorer social skills and, ultimately, rejection by peers. Having friends reduces or prevents loneliness and counters such effects (e.g., Brendgen, Vitaro, & Bukowski, 2000). Moreover, the higher the quality of these friendships, the less loneliness children experience and the greater their acceptance by other children (Cacioppo, Hawkley, & Berntson, 2003).

In sum, children's social experiences play a key role in their development; indeed, because these experiences shape their later capacities to get along with others, to form friendships with them, and to love, it is clear that to an important extent, social development shapes the course and *quality* of children's future lives. (While loneliness is a problem for many children—one that threatens their social development—another problem—*obesity*—threatens their physical health and development. Can psychology help solve this problem? For information suggesting that it can, please see the following **Psychology Lends a Hand** section.)

Friendships
Mutual dyadic relationships between children involving strong affective ties.

p s y c h o l o g y   l e n d s   a   h a n d

Combating Childhood Obesity

Every time we visit a nearby shopping mall, we are amazed at seeing the number of people who are seriously overweight. Obesity has increased to virtually epidemic proportions in the United States and many other countries. Sad to report, children are not immune to this problem. In fact, it is estimated that 50 percent of obese adults were obese as school-age children (Williams et al., 1992). So, the problem seems to start early and is then carried over into adulthood. Given that obese children are at risk for the same physical illnesses as adults, this is a serious issue. Can anything be done to solve this disturbing problem? Research by psychologists suggests that several steps can be helpful:

- **Acquiring healthy eating habits.** This may actually be easier to accomplish with children than with adults. One successful strategy involves labeling various foods as "go" foods—ones that that can be eaten in unlimited quantities (e.g., salads, raw fruits, and vegetables), "caution" foods—ones that can be eaten only in moderate amounts, and "stop" foods—ones that should be avoided (high-calorie fast foods and rich, sweet desserts). Chil-

dren can understand these categories readily, and knowing which foods to avoid seems to help.

- **Contracting.** This involves procedures in which parents and children pay money into a weight-loss program when it begins and have it returned as they attend the sessions and make progress in weight control.
- **Self-monitoring.** Children are taught to keep a record of foods they eat; they earn points for holding their total number of calories down.
- **Exercise.** This is the other side of the weight-loss equation, and many studies indicate that obese children exercise less than others. Teaching children new ways to burn calories (new games, new activities) can be a big plus in helping them shed extra pounds.

Through a combination of these steps, children with a weight problem can be helped to reduce the calories they consume, to burn more energy, and so to attain a happier and healthier life.

KEY QUESTIONS

- What is temperament and what role does it play in later development?
- What is attachment?
- How does attachment influence later social development?
- What role do children's friendships play in their social and emotional development?

FROM GENDER IDENTITY TO SEX-CATEGORY CONSTANCY: HOW CHILDREN COME TO UNDERSTAND THAT THEY ARE FEMALE OR MALE

When do children first recognize that they are a girl or boy? And how do they come to understand what this aspect of their identity means? These are important aspects of development, so we'll focus on them here. Before beginning, though, it's important to clarify the meaning of two terms: **gender** and **biological sex.** Biological sex is straightforward: It refers to whether an individual is, biologically speaking, a male or female (e.g., does this person possess two X chromosomes or one X and one Y?). Gender, in contrast, is a much more complex term. It refers to a given society's beliefs about the traits and behavior supposedly possessed by males and females. Thus, it includes what psychologists term **gender stereotypes**—beliefs about traits possessed by males and females and differences between them (e.g., Eagly & Wood, 1999; Unger & Crawford, 1992), and **gender roles**—expectations concerning the roles males and females should fill and the ways in which they are supposed to behave (e.g., Deaux, 1993). Such expectations come into play as soon as a nurse or physician announces, "It's a boy!" or "It's a girl!" And they continue to influence us, and our behavior, throughout life. If you want to see this

Gender
A society's beliefs about the traits and behavior of males and females.

Biological Sex
Refers to whether an individual is, biologically speaking, male or female.

Gender Stereotypes
Cultural beliefs about differences between women and men.

Gender Roles
Beliefs about how males and females are expected to behave in many situations.

FIGURE 8.13
Gender Identity: A Key Aspect of Development
Increasingly, toy stores like this one are establishing separate departments for boys and girls. Why? Spokespersons for the stores say it is in response to stronger preferences among both girls and boys for gender-related toys. Whatever the reasons, it is clear that children's gender identity is an important aspect of their social development.

process in action, just visit a nearby Toys "R" Us or other large toy store. In the past, these stores made efforts to eliminate separate sections for girls and boys. But recently, they have shifted back to distinct departments for each gender (see Figure 8.13). Why? In part because boys and girls are starting to choose gender-related toys at an earlier age—perhaps because of their early experiences with peers in day care and preschools, and their early exposure to the media (Bannon, 2003). Whatever the reason, toys—like many other aspects of life—tend to drive home the point that one's gender is *important*. For this reason alone, it is worthy of careful attention.

Children's Growing Sophistication with Respect to Gender

The first step on the path toward sex-category constancy is children's recognition that they belong to one sex or the other—that they are a boy or a girl. Such **gender identity** occurs quite early in life; by the time they are two years old, many children have learned to label themselves appropriately and consistently. At this time, however, they are uncertain as to whether they will always be a boy or a girl. Such **gender stability** is usually in place by the time they are four. At this age, they can answer correctly such questions as "When you grow up, will you be a mother or a father?" and "Could you change into a girl/boy from what you are now?"

It is not until they are about six or even seven, however, that children acquire **gender consistency**—the understanding that even if they adopted the clothing, hairstyles, and behaviors of the other sex they would still retain their current sexual identity. At this time they can answer correctly questions such as these: "If Jack were gentle and cooked dinner, would Jack be a boy or a girl?"

Gender Development: Contrasting Explanations of How It Occurs

That children move toward full understanding of their own sexual identity as they grow older is clear. But how, precisely, do they acquire such knowledge? Several explanations have been offered. One of these—*social learning theory*—emphasizes the role of learning, especially the impact of *modeling* and *operant conditioning* (see

Gender Identity
Children's understanding of the fact that they are male or female.

Gender Stability
Children's understanding that gender is stable over time.

Gender Consistency
Children's understanding that their gender will not change even if they adopted the behavior, dress, and hairstyles of the other gender.

Chapter 5). According to this theory, children are rewarded (e.g., with verbal praise) for behaving in accordance with gender stereotypes and gender roles—the ways in which boys and girls are expected to behave. Further, because children have a tendency to imitate models they perceive as being similar to themselves, they tend to adopt the behaviors shown by their same-sex parents (e.g., Bandura, 1986; Baron, 1970). As children become increasingly aware of their own behavior and these similarities, the idea that they belong to one gender or the other emerges with growing clarity. It is as if they reason as follows: "I act like daddy, so I'm a boy" or "I act like mommy, so I'm a girl."

A second view of gender development—*cognitive development theory*—suggests that children's increasing understanding of gender is just one reflection of their steady cognitive growth (e.g., Martin & Ruble, 2004). For instance, below the age of two years, children lack a clear concept of self, so they can't identify themselves consistently as a boy or a girl. Once they acquire a concept of self, they can do this and begin to show gender constancy. Later, as they acquire increasing ability to classify objects as belonging to specific categories, they begin to form an idea of gender stability: They realize that they belong to one category and won't shift to the other. Gradually, then, children acquire the understanding that they belong to one sex or the other and, as a result of this understanding, strive to adopt behaviors they view as consistent with this identity. This is the opposite of what social learning theory proposes; that theory suggests that first children imitate the behavior of same-sex models, and *then* they develop sexual identity. Cognitive development theory suggests that first they develop their gender identity, and *then* they adopt behaviors consistent with this identity.

A third, and highly influential view, known as **gender schema theory** has been proposed by Bem (1984, 1989). Bem noted that knowledge of one's sex or gender is far more important than knowledge that one has blue or brown eyes, or even that one belongs to a particular race or religious group. This reasoning led her to propose that children acquire *gender schemas*—cognitive frameworks reflecting experiences with their society's beliefs about the attributes of males and females, such as instructions from their parents, observations of how males and females typically behave, and so on. Gender schemas develop, in part, because adults call attention to gender even in situations in which it is irrelevant—for instance, teachers say, "Good morning, boys and girls!"

Once a gender schema forms, it influences children's processing of many kinds of social information (Martin & Little, 1990). For example, children with firmly established gender schemas tend to categorize the behavior of others as either masculine or feminine. Similarly, they may process and recall behaviors consistent with their own gender schema more easily than ones not consistent with it. In short, for children possessing such schemas, gender is a key concept or dimension, one they often use in attempts to make sense out of the social world, and one that becomes linked, in important ways, to their self-concept. This link between gender and one's self-concept is also emphasized in other, related views about gender identity (e.g., Spence, 1985).

While these three theories emphasize different aspects of gender development, all seem to provide important insights into this process. Thus, as is true of other aspects of development, several interrelated processes appear to influence children's progress toward full **sex-category constancy.**

Gender Schema Theory
A theory indicating that children develop a cognitive framework reflecting the beliefs of their society concerning the characteristics and roles of males and females. This gender schema then strongly affects the processing of new social information.

Sex-Category Constancy
Complete understanding of one's sexual identity, centering around a biologically based categorical distinction between males and females.

K E Y   Q U E S T I O N S

- What is gender identity? Gender stability? Gender consistency?
- What is sex-category constancy?
- How do social learning theory, cognitive development theory, and gender schema theory explain gender development?

ADOLESCENCE: BETWEEN CHILD AND ADULT

When does childhood end and adulthood start? Because development is a continuous process, there is no simple answer to this question. Rather, every culture decides for itself just where the dividing line falls. Many cultures mark this passage with special ceremonies. In many countries, however, the transition from child to adult takes place more gradually during a period known as **adolescence**—the topic on which we'll focus next.

Physical Development during Adolescence

The beginning of adolescence is signaled by a sudden increase in the rate of physical growth. While this *growth spurt* occurs for both sexes, it starts earlier for girls (at about age ten or eleven) than for boys (at about age twelve or thirteen). Prior to this spurt, boys and girls are similar in height; in its early phases, girls are often taller than boys; after it is over, males are several inches taller, on average, than females.

This growth spurt is just one aspect of **puberty,** the period of rapid change during which individuals of both genders reach sexual maturity (see Figure 8.14). During puberty, the *gonads* or primary sex glands, produce increased levels of sex hormones, and the external sex organs assume their adult form. Girls begin to *menstruate,* and boys start to produce sperm. In addition, both sexes undergo many other shifts relating to sexual maturity. Most girls begin to menstruate by the time they are thirteen, but for some this process does not start until considerably later; and for others, it may begin as early as age seven or eight. Most boys begin to produce sperm by the time they are fourteen or fifteen, but, again, for some the process may start either earlier or later.

Cognitive Development during Adolescence

As we saw noted earlier, adolescents become capable of logical thought. However, this does not mean that they necessarily demonstrate such thinking. In fact, only

FIGURE 8.14
Adolescence: The Dawn of Sexual Maturity
During adolescence, members of both sexes move rapidly toward sexual maturity.

about 40 percent of adolescents can solve the kinds of problems used by Piaget to test for formal operational thinking (e.g., Stanovich, 1993). Moreover, if they do show such logical thought, it may restricted to topics or problems with which they have had direct experience (Rogoff & Chavajay, 1995).

In addition, adolescents' *theory of mind*—their understanding of how they and others think—continues to change and develop. Younger children take what has been described as a *realist approach* to knowledge; they believe that knowledge is a property of the real world and that there are definite "facts" or "truths" that can be acquired. In contrast, older children and preadolescents become aware of the fact that experts often disagree; this leads them to develop a *relativist approach,* which recognizes that different people may interpret the same information in contrasting ways.

Preadolescents go a bit further, adopting a *defended realism* approach, which recognizes the difference between facts and opinions. Yet, they continue to believe that there is a set of facts about the world that are completely true, and that differences in opinion stem from differences in available information. Still later, some adolescents, at least, realize that while there are no absolute truths, there are better or worse reasons for holding certain views—an approach described as *postskeptical rationalism.* This, of course, is the kind of thinking democratic societies wish to encourage among their citizens, because only people capable of thinking in this way can make the kind of informed judgments necessary for free elections. In sum, cognitive development does not stop with childhood; on the contrary, it continues throughout adolescence (Klaczyinski, 1997).

KEY QUESTIONS

- What physical changes occur during puberty?
- How does thinking change during adolescence?

Social and Emotional Development during Adolescence

It would be surprising if the major physical and cognitive changes occurring during adolescence were not accompanied by corresponding changes in social and emotional development. What are these changes like? Let's see what research has revealed.

Emotional Changes: The Ups and Downs of Everyday Life

It is widely believed that adolescents are wildly emotional: They experience huge swings in mood and turbulent outbursts of emotion. Are these views correct? To a degree, they are. In several studies on this issue, large numbers of teenagers wore beepers and were signaled at random times throughout an entire week. When signaled, they entered their thoughts and feelings in a diary. Results indicated that they did show more frequent and larger swings in mood than those shown by older persons (e.g., Csikszentmihalyi & Larson, 1984). Moreover, these swings occurred very quickly, sometimes within only a few minutes. Older people also show shifts in mood, but these tend to be less frequent, slower, and smaller in magnitude.

Other widely accepted views about adolescent emotionality, however, do *not* appear to be correct. For instance, it is often assumed that adolescence is a period of great stress and unhappiness. In fact, most adolescents report feeling quite happy and self-confident, *not* unhappy or distressed (Diener & Diener, 1996). Moreover, and again contrary to common views, most teenagers report that they enjoy good relations with their parents. They agree with them on basic values, future plans, and many other matters (Bachman, 1987).

Social Development: Friendships and the Quest for Identity

Although friendships are important during childhood, they often take on added significance during adolescence. Most adolescents are part of extensive **social networks,**

Adolescence
A period beginning with the onset of puberty and ending when individuals assume adult roles and responsibilities.

Puberty
The period of rapid change during which individuals reach sexual maturity.

Social Network
A group of people with whom one interacts regularly.

consisting of many friends and acquaintances, and these persons have profound effects on them, shaping their attitudes, values, and behavior. One motive for forming friendships during adolescence seems to be the developing *need to belong*—to feel that one is accepted and is part of a social group. This need strengthens during early adolescence and leads many preteens and teenagers to reject parental influence and to identify with their peers. Thus, they adopt the dress, phrases, and overall style of their chosen peer group, sometimes to the point at which parents worry that their children have surrendered their unique identities entirely. Within a few years, however, this tendency subsides and teenagers begin to conform less to their peers.

Friendships and social success also play an important role in another key aspect of social development during adolescence—the quest for a *personal identity*. This process is a key element in a famous theory of psychosocial development proposed by Erik Erikson (1950, 1987), a theory well worthy of a closer look.

Erikson's Eight Stages of Life

Erikson's theory deals with development across the entire life span, so we could have introduced it in our discussion of childhood. Because adolescence is in some ways a bridge between childhood and adulthood, though, it makes sense to examine the theory here.

Erikson's theory is, like Piaget's, a *stage* theory: It suggests that all human beings pass through specific stages or phases of development. In contrast to Piaget, however, Erikson is concerned primarily with social rather than cognitive development. He believed that each stage of life is marked by a specific crisis or conflict between competing tendencies. Only if individuals negotiate each of these hurdles successfully can they continue to develop in a normal, healthy manner.

The stages in Erikson's theory are summarized in Table 8.4. The first four occur during childhood, one takes place during adolescence, and the final three occur during our adult years. The initial stage, which occurs during the first year of life, centers on the crisis of *trust versus mistrust*. Infants must trust others to satisfy their needs. If these are not met, they fail to develop trust in others and remain forever suspicious and wary.

The next crisis occurs during the second year of life and involves *autonomy versus shame and doubt*. During this time, toddlers are learning to regulate their own bodies and to act in independent ways. If they succeed in these tasks, they develop a sense of autonomy. But if they fail, or if they are labeled as inadequate by the persons who care for them, they may experience shame and doubt their abilities to interact effectively with the external world.

The third stage unfolds during the preschool years, between the ages of three and five. The crisis at this time involves what Erikson terms *initiative versus guilt*. During these years, children are acquiring many new physical and mental skills. Simultaneously, however, they must develop the capacity to control their impulses, some of which lead to unacceptable behavior. If they achieve a good balance between feelings of initiative and feelings of guilt, all is well. However, if initiative overwhelms guilt, children may become too unruly; if guilt overwhelms initiative, they may become too inhibited.

The fourth and final stage of childhood occurs during the early school years, when children are between six and eleven or twelve years of age. This stage involves the crisis of *industry versus inferiority*. During these years, children learn to make things, use tools, and acquire many of the skills necessary for adult life. Children who successfully acquire these skills form a sense of their own competence; those who do not may compare themselves unfavorably with others and suffer from low self-esteem.

Now we come to the crucial stage in Erikson's theory for this discussion of adolescence: the crisis of *identity versus role confusion*. At this time of life, teenagers ask themselves, "Who am I?" "What am I *really* like?" "What do I want to become?" In other words, they seek to establish a clear *self-identity*—an understanding of their

TABLE 8.4 Erikson's Eight Stages of Psychosocial Development

According to Erikson, we move through eight stages of psychosocial development during our lives. Each stage centers around a specific crisis or conflict between competing tendencies.

Crisis/Phase	Description
Trust versus mistrust	Infants learn either to trust the environment (if needs are met) or to mistrust it.
Autonomy versus shame and doubt	Toddlers acquire self-confidence if they learn to regulate their bodies and act independently. If they fail or are labeled as inadequate, they experience shame and doubt.
Initiative versus guilt	Preschoolers (aged 3–5) acquire new physical and mental skills but must also learn to control their impulses. Unless a good balance is struck, they become either unruly or too inhibited.
Industry versus inferiority	Children (aged 6–11) acquire many skills and competencies. If they take pride in these, they acquire high self-esteem. If they compare themselves unfavorably with others, they may develop low self-esteem.
Identity versus role confusion	Adolescents must integrate various roles into a consistent self-identity. If they fail to do so, they may experience confusion over who they are.
Intimacy versus isolation	Young adults must develop the ability to form deep, intimate relationships with others. If they do not, they may become socially or emotionally isolated.
Generativity versus self-absorption	Adults must take an active interest in helping and guiding younger persons. If they do not, they may become preoccupied with purely selfish needs.
Integrity versus despair	In the closing decades of life, individuals ask themselves whether their lives had any meaning. If they can answer *yes*, they attain a sense of integrity. If they answer *no*, they experience despair.

own unique traits and what is really of central importance to them. These, of course, are questions individuals ask themselves at many points in life. According to Erikson, it is crucial that these questions be answered effectively. If they are not, individuals may drift, uncertain of where they want to go or the kind of person they wish to become. (We'll return to later stages in Erikson's theory in our discussion of adult development.)

Adolescent Romantic Relationships: More than Friends

When did you have your first romance? If you are like most people, when you were an adolescent. While preadolescents spend less than an hour each week interacting with members of the other sex, adolescents spend from five to ten hours each week in such activities. Why? One reason is that their interest in forming romantic relationships increases greatly. These relationships are not simply unimportant diversions—what adults refer to as "puppy love." On the contrary, they help to shape adolescents' lives in important ways. Research findings (e.g., Furman & Shaffer, 2003) suggest that they play a role in the development of self-identity, sexuality, career planning, and performance in school. Moreover, and perhaps most important, they help adolescents to learn important lessons about the nature of close relationships and shape their perceptions of intimacy. Not surprisingly, the higher the quality of adolescents' friendships with members of their own sex, the better the quality of their early romantic relationships (Furman et al., 2002). In other words, the skills and attitudes adolescents learn in their same-sex friendships carry over to their early romantic relationships. Overall, then, adolescents' early experiments with love are not in any way trivial; rather, it makes more sense to view them as providing essential practice in basic and important life skills and values.

KEY QUESTIONS

- Are widely accepted ideas about adolescent emotionality correct?
- According to Erikson, what is the most important crisis faced by adolescents?
- What is the importance of adolescent romantic relationships?

DEVELOPMENT DURING OUR ADULT YEARS

If you live an average number of years, you will spend more than 70 percent of your life as an adult. Obviously, we continue to change and develop during this major portion of our lives. We'll now examine some of the most important of these changes. Before doing that, however, we'll return to the final three stages in Erikson's theory.

Erikson's Theory Revisited: The Crises of Adult Life

During adulthood, Erikson suggests, we pass through three major crises. The first of these involves the crisis of *intimacy versus isolation*. During late adolescence and early adulthood, individuals must develop the ability to form deep, intimate relationships with others. This does not mean simply sexual intimacy; rather, it involves the ability to form strong emotional attachments to others. In short, this first crisis of adult life centers around the capacity to *love*—to care deeply for others. People who fail to resolve it successfully will live in isolation, unable to form truly intimate relationships.

Erikson labeled the second crisis of adult life the crisis of *generativity versus self-absorption*. This refers to the need for individuals to overcome selfish, self-centered concerns and to take an active interest in helping and guiding the next generation. For parents, such activities are focused on their children. After the children are grown, however, the tendency toward generativity may involve serving as a **mentor** or guide for members of the younger generation, helping them in their careers and lives. People who do not become parents can express generativity by providing help and guidance to young people—students, younger coworkers, nieces and nephews, and so on. Individuals who successfully resolve this crisis and turn away from total absorption with their own lives discover new meaning. People who do not resolve this crisis successfully become absorbed in their own lives and gradually cut themselves off from an important source of growth and satisfaction.

Erikson termed the final crisis of adult development *integrity versus despair*. As people reach the final decades of life, they look back and ask, "Did my life have any meaning?" "Did my being here really matter?" If they are to answer "yes," and to feel that they reached many of their goals, they attain a sense of *integrity*. If, instead, they find their lives to be lacking on such dimensions, they may experience intense feelings of *despair*. Successful resolution of this final crisis can have important effects on how individuals come to terms with their own mortality—the inevitable fact of death—and on their psychological and physical health during the final years of life.

In sum, according to Erikson and others who view adult development in terms of discrete phases or stages, development during our adult years follows an orderly plan, reflecting the fact that at different times in our lives, we all experience

Mentors
Older and more experienced individuals who help to guide young adults.

the same problems, events, challenges or—as he puts it—crises. The way in which we deal with each of these turning points then determines the course and nature of our lives from then on.

Physical Change during Our Adult Years

Looking through a family photo album—one that spans several decades—can be very revealing. There, staring out at you with youthful faces are your grandparents, parents, aunts, and uncles—and yourself (see Figure 8.15). When you compare their appearance (or your own) with that in the photos, the scope of physical change during our adult years comes sharply into focus.

■ Physical Change during Early Adulthood

Physical growth is usually complete by the time people leave their teens, but for some parts of the body, the process of aging actually begins long before this. For example, the lenses in our eyes begin to lose flexibility by the time we are only twelve or thirteen years old; and for some people, the tissues supporting their teeth have already begun to recede and weaken even before they have attained full physical growth. So aging, like growth, is a continuous process that starts very early in life. But in general, physical change is slow and very gradual during our early adult years.

■ Physical Change during Midlife

By the time we are in our forties, however, most of us are all too aware of the age-related changes occurring in our bodies. *Cardiac output,* the amount of blood pumped by the heart, decreases noticeably, and the walls of the large arteries lose some degree of flexibility. As a result, less oxygen can be delivered to working muscles within a given period of time, and even people who exercise regularly become aware of some decline in this respect. They simply can't do quite as much as they once could. The performance of other major organ systems, too, declines, and an increasing number of people experience difficulties with digestion. Other changes are readily visible when middle-aged people look in the mirror: thinning and graying hair, bulges, and wrinkles in place of the smooth skin of youth. Huge individual differences exist in the rate at which such changes occur, however. While some persons in their forties and fifties closely match common stereotypes concerning middle age, others retain much of their youthful appearance and vigor during this period of life.

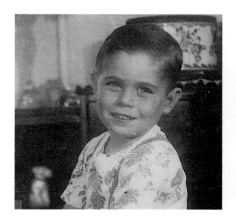  

FIGURE 8.15
Physical Change: It Occurs throughout Life
As these photos of the author (Robert Baron) at ages four, forty, and fifty-nine suggest, our appearance changes greatly over the course of our lives.

Among the most dramatic changes occurring during middle adulthood is the **climacteric**—a period of several years during which the functioning of the reproductive system, and various aspects of sexual activity, change greatly. Though both sexes experience the climacteric, its effects are more obvious for women, most of whom experience **menopause**—cessation of the menstrual cycle—in their late forties or early fifties. During menopause, the ovaries stop producing estrogen, and many changes in the reproductive system occur: thinning of the vaginal walls, reduced secretion of fluids that lubricate the vagina, and so on. Because women no longer release ova, pregnancy is no longer possible. In the past, menopause was considered to be a stressful process for many women but is now recognized that, for most, this process occurs with no significant difficulties.

Among men, the climacteric involves reduced secretion of testosterone and reduced functioning of the *prostate gland,* which plays a role in semen formation. In many men, the prostate gland becomes enlarged, and this may interfere not only with sexual functioning, but with urination as well. Men often experience reduced sexual drive at this time of life; but although sperm production decreases, many can still father children.

So far, this picture of physical change during midlife may sound discouraging: strength, beauty, vigor—all decline during this period. But remember: Although some physical decline is inevitable during the middle decades of life, both the magnitude and rate of such decrements are strongly influenced by individual lifestyle. In fact, growing evidence suggests that though we can't stop the "clock" of aging altogether, we *can* slow it down appreciably; in other words, we can show **successful aging**—a pattern in which we experience minimal physiological losses in many functions when compared to younger persons (Arkin, 1991). How can we accomplish this goal? You already know most of the answer: by eating a good diet, exercising regularly, avoiding the use of dangerous drugs, and holding stress to bearable levels. These and other steps can help assure that we maintain our health and vigor well into our later adult years.

Physical Changes in Later Life

Average age in many countries is currently rising at a steady pace, so it is important to have a clear picture of the physical changes that occur during our later decades of life. Research on this topic offers a mixed but somewhat encouraging picture. A very large proportion of Americans in their sixties and seventies report excellent or good health. And these are not simply overly optimistic self-reports. It appears that most people below the age of eighty *are* in reasonably good health and are not much more likely than middle-aged people to suffer from *chronic illnesses*—ones that are long-term, progressive, and incurable (U.S. Department of Health and Human Services, 1989). Further, even in their seventies and eighties, large majorities of people do not receive hospital care during any given year (Thomas, 1992). In short, the picture of older persons that emerges, at least in developed countries like the United States, is quite encouraging.

One additional point should not be overlooked: Although many physical changes do occur with increasing age, it is crucial to distinguish between those that are the result of **primary aging**—changes caused by the passage of time and, perhaps, genetic factors—and of **secondary aging**—changes due to disease, disuse, or abuse of our bodies.

Let's briefly examine some of the physical changes that result from primary aging. What changes result from primary aging? They include declines in our sensory abilities (vision, hearing, smell, taste) and a general slowing in the speed of responding (Spirduso & Macrae, 1990). It seems likely that such changes contributed to a recent tragic accident in Santa Monica, California, in which an 86-year-old man drove his car into a crowded farmer's market, killing ten people, including a three-year-old girl (see Figure 8.16).

Climacteric
A period during which the functioning of the reproductive system and various aspects of sexual activity change greatly.

Menopause
Cessation of the menstrual cycle.

Successful Aging
Minimal physiological losses in many bodily functions, compared to younger persons, as a result of living a healthy lifestyle.

Primary Aging
Changes in our bodies caused by the passage of time and, perhaps, genetic factors.

Secondary Aging
Changes in our bodies due to disease, disuse, or abuse.

FIGURE 8.16
Slower Reflexes Can Lead to Tragedy
Our speed of responding to unexpected stimuli generally declines with age. Did this factor play a role in the tragic accident shown here, in which an 86-year-old man drove his car into a crowded farmer's market, killing ten people? We will never know for certain, but it seems possible that this was one contributing factor.

KEY QUESTIONS

• What physical changes occur during early and middle adulthood?
• What physical changes occur in later life?

Cognitive Change during Adulthood

What about our cognitive abilities? Do these change as well as we grow older? Because our cognitive abilities rest, ultimately, on biological processes (see Chapters 2 and 6), it is reasonable to expect some declines with increasing age. On the other hand, as we grow older, we also gain in experience, practice with various tasks, and our overall knowledge. Can these changes compensate for inevitable biological decline? The issue of whether, and how, our cognitive functioning changes with age, therefore, is quite complex.

Aging and Memory

First, let's consider the impact of aging on memory. Research on working (short-term) memory indicates that older people seem able to enter about as much information in this system as young ones (Poon & Fozard, 1980). However, some findings suggest that the ability to transfer information from working memory to long-term memory may decrease with age (Hunt, 1993). Turning to long-term memory, it appears that there may be some declines in episodic memory (memory for events relating to an individual's life and experience) with increasing age, while semantic memory (general knowledge) remains largely intact. Procedural memory—the information necessary for performing many skilled actions—seems to be the most stable of all.

Other evidence indicates that although older persons enter as much as information as younger ones into memory, they later make poorer use of this information, failing to retrieve details they actually did initially notice (Koutstaal, 2003). Overall, though, it appears that unless we experience serious illness (e.g., Alzheimer's disease), we retain many of our cognitive abilities largely intact.

Aging and Intelligence: Decline or Stability?

In the past, it was widely believed that intelligence increases into early adulthood, remains stable through the thirties, but then begins to decline as early as the forties.

This view was based largely on **cross-sectional research** that compared the performance of persons of different ages on standard tests of intelligence. However, more recent research on aging and intelligence has often employed a *longitudinal* design, in which the same persons are studied for many years. The results of studies using such procedures have yielded a more positive picture. Instead of declining sharply with age, many intellectual abilities seem to remain quite stable across the entire life span. In fact, they show relatively little change until persons are well into their sixties, seventies, or beyond. Moreover, some abilities even seem to increase (e.g., Schaie, 1986, 1990, 1994). Only on tasks involving speed of reasoning and some tasks related to producing and spelling familiar words (e.g., Burke & Shafto, 2004) does performance seem to decline. Because drops in performance may reflect increased reaction time—which is known to decline with age (e.g., Finkel et al., 1990; Shimamura et al., 1995)—there is little if any indication of a general decrease in intelligence with age.

Fitness: An Effective Means for Preventing— or Even Reversing—Cognitive Decline

Before concluding, we should call attention to one highly encouraging fact: Recent studies indicate that becoming physically fit can greatly improve cognitive functioning in older persons. For instance, a recent review of many different studies (Colcombe & Kramer, 2003) on this topic indicates that a combination of aerobic and strength training can significantly boost scores on a wide range of cognitive tasks for persons in their sixties and seventies. Overall, existing evidence indicates that such gains occur on *speed-related* tasks (e.g., simple reaction time); *visuospatial* tasks (e.g., viewing three line drawings and then reproducing them from memory); *controlled* tasks—ones requiring cognitive control (e.g., pressing one key when the letter C appears but pressing a different one for the letter M); and *executive* tasks—ones that require planning, inhibition, or scheduling of mental procedures (e.g., responding to one cue but simultaneously responding to conflicting or irrelevant cues presented nearby). In fact, as shown in Figure 8.17, persons who participated in programs designed to boost their physical fitness performed much better than those who did not, and this difference was especially great for complex tasks (controlled and executive processes). These findings suggest that becoming physically fit is not only beneficial to our health but also can help us to preserve our precious cognitive abilities.

Cross-Sectional Research
Research in which groups of persons of different ages are compared in order to determine how certain aspects of behavior or cognition change with age.

FIGURE 8.17
The Effects of Fitness on Cognitive Functioning in Older Adults
Older individuals (in the fifties, sixties, and seventies) who participated in fitness-building programs showed better performance on a wide range of cognitive tasks than individuals who did not participate in such programs. Moreover, this advantage was greater for more complex tasks (e.g., ones requiring planning or scheduling of mental procedures, or ones involving some degree of cognitive control).
Source: Based on data from Colcombe & Kramer, 2003.

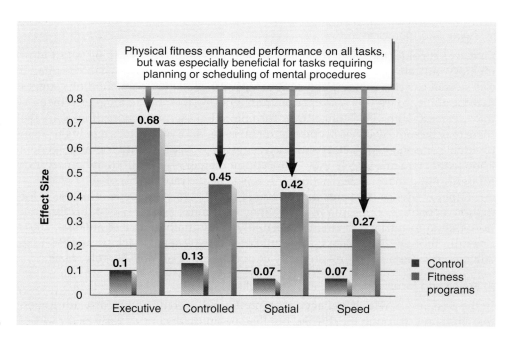

Where does all this leave us? With a fairly encouraging overall pattern. Yes, some cognitive processes do decrease with age, especially ones closely related to speed of responding. But others remain quite stable over many years, and others may actually increase as individuals gain in experience. Further, becoming physically fit can slow or even reverse any declines we do experience. Our overall conclusion: Aging is inevitable, but our minds can, and often do, remain active until the very end of life.

KEY QUESTIONS

- What changes in memory occur as we age?
- How does intelligence change over the life span?
- What are the effects of becoming physically fit on cognitive functioning?

Social and Emotional Development during Adulthood

Do we continue changing socially and emotionally during our adult years? Research findings indicate that we do. Here's an overview of some of the most important of these changes.

Friendships: The Convoy Model

Because we continue to meet people throughout life, you might guess that we expand our networks of friends as we grow older. In fact, though, the opposite seems to be true. Early in our adult years, we interact with a large number of people and have many casual friends. As we enter our middle years, though, we tend to reduce the size of our social networks—down to something like ten people. And then we tend to maintain these close ties through the remainder of our lives, moving through the decades like a convoy of ships sailing the ocean. This **convoy model** of adult social networks seems to offer an accurate description of the pattern of our friendships throughout much of our lives.

Why do we gradually reduce the number of friends we have? Research by Carstensen and her colleagues (e.g., Carstensen & Charles, 1998; Carstensen, Isaacowitz, & Charles, 1999) suggests that this may stem, in part, from our growing realization that time is limited and that we should, therefore, invest most of our effort in a relatively small number of social partners. Time available for interacting with various people may, of course, be limited by many factors: increasing age, impending retirement, physical relocations. And recent findings indicate that the more time is perceived as limited, the greater the preference of all persons—young and old—for interacting with close friends or relatives (e.g., Fung & Carstensen, 2003). Because older persons feel that time is indeed running out for them, however, they generally show a stronger preference than younger persons, overall, for interacting with a small number of close friends or relatives.

Emotional Experiences: Do We Feel Emotions Less Intensely as We Age?

Older people are often viewed as being calmer than younger ones. Does this imply that they experience a reduced range of emotions? Growing evidence suggests that this is not the case. Older adults report experiencing emotional experiences as rich and intense as younger ones (Carstensen & Charles, 1998), and they show facial expressions and patterns of physiological reactions when experiencing specific emotions that are virtually identical to those of younger adults (e.g., Levenson et al., 1991). However, older people do differ from younger ones in certain respects: While they report experiencing positive emotions such as happiness and joy just as frequently as younger people, they report experiencing negative emotional experiences such as anger or sorrow *less* frequently (Carstensen, Pasupathi, & Mary, in press). Further, older persons report greater control over their emotions and greater stability of mood than younger persons. In short, there seems to be some truth to

Convoy Model

A model of social networks suggesting that from midlife on, we tend to maintain close relationships with a small number of people.

the view that older persons are calmer and less excitable emotionally than younger ones, but no truth to the view that they live an impoverished emotional existence.

Adjusting to Major Life Changes: Parenthood, Careers, Divorce, Aging Parents, and Retirement

When they are young, many people tend to believe that as they age, they will also grow much wiser—that they will come to understand the profound mysteries of life better and better. In one sense, this is true: We *do* acquire many kinds of wisdom as we move through life's journey. But because we also experience profound changes, each period during our adult lives is filled with new events and challenges; as a result, we go on learning—and improvising!—throughout life. What are these changes? They are unique for every individual, but most of us experience changes such as these: the joys and demands of parenthood (Hock et al., 1995), many shifts in our careers as we move from one job and work setting to another (Levinson, 1986), the pain of divorce or marital separation, and the dilemma of caring for our parents as they age and become increasingly frail.

Other challenges during our adult lives center around the *empty nest* syndrome (Birchler, 1992) in which parents who remain married must learn to adjust to the absence of their grown children who are off starting families of their own, and, ultimately, our own retirement and aging. None of these challenges are easy, and the result is that development is truly a continuous process. Perhaps, Gertrude Stein put it best when she remarked (1925), "One does not get better, but different and older, and that is always a pleasure." (Many theories of adult development emphasize the importance of careers [e.g., Levinson, 1986]. If careers are indeed an important factor in our lives, a crucial question arises: How should we choose them? For suggestions based on psychological research, please see the **Psychology Goes to Work** section.)

K E Y   Q U E S T I O N S

- How do our friendships changes as we move through life?
- What changes in our emotions occur as we age?
- What are some of the key challenges we face during our adult years?
- How should you choose your career?

DEATH AND BEREAVEMENT

Since ancient times, human beings have searched for the "Fountain of Youth"—some means of prolonging youth, and life, indefinitely. Sad to relate, such dreams have remained illusions; life and health *can* be prolonged, but there is no way to live forever. In this section, we'll consider key questions relating to the close of life: (1) How do terminally ill people react to their own impending deaths? And (2) how do we cope with the death of persons we love?

Meeting Death: Facing the End of Life

What is death? The answer to this question is more complex than you might suspect. First, there are several kinds of death. *Physiological death* occurs when all physical processes that sustain life cease. *Brain death* is defined as a total absence of brain activity for at least ten minutes. *Cerebral death* means cessation of activity in the cerebral cortex. And *social death* refers to a process through which other people relinquish their relationships with the deceased (Thomas, 1992).

Second, there are complex ethical issues connected with death. Should individuals have the right to die when they choose? Should physicians be allowed to grant such requests? These are complex questions, only partly within the realm of

PSYCHOLOGY GOES TO WORK

Choosing a Career: Some "Do's" and Some "Don'ts"

Our careers—the sequences of work experiences we have over time—play a key role in our lives. Not only are they the source of the income that allows us to live in certain ways, they are also a key part of our self-identities. Not convinced? Just ask several people you know who are working, "Who are you?" Many will reply in terms of their career or occupation (e.g., "I'm a police officer," "I'm a salesperson," "I'm a teacher."). So choosing an appropriate career—one in which you will be happy and fulfilled—is a very important task. How should you perform it? While we can't provide anything like a complete answer here—only a highly trained counseling or occupational psychologist can do that—we can at least give you some pointers of what to do and what *not* to do.

- **First, recognize the careers have changed—radically!** In the past, people started their careers, and generally stayed on the same "track" for many years. Now, the situation is entirely different. Lifetime employment with one company is a thing of the past, people move from one company or industry to another, and they often do many different jobs during their working lives. So don't expect the kind of career your parents or grandparents had; in many cases, it doesn't exist!
- **Recognize that careers take many different forms.** Suppose your parents own a family business and you decide to work in it. In that case, your career might involve one job for years or decades—maybe for good! But careers come in many different forms these days. Another pattern might be to work in one field and move up, by steps, as you gain experience; this is known as a *linear* career. A third pattern is to move from one occupation to another, each requiring different skills. For instance, consider an engineer who, at first, works in her chosen field. After several years, however, she accepts a management-level job, in which she does very little engineering but a

lot of managing. Still later, she decides to go back to school and get a law degree, and, after that, has very different positions. This is known as a *spiral career,* and an increasing number of people have it. The key point? Keep your options open and recognize that your career can evolve in ways you did not at first expect.

- **Concentrate on learning new skills.** Perhaps the most important thing you can do in planning your career (e.g., in deciding whether to move from one job or field to another) is to ask yourself, "What new skills will I learn? Will these increase my potential value in the job market?" If the answers to these questions are clear, this is probably a good move for you to make. If they are not, think again.
- **Try to obtain a close match between your personal characteristics and preferences and your career.** One big mistake many people make is that of "falling in love" with a particular field without considering whether they are really suited for it. Different jobs and occupations require different characteristics. For instance, to be a good salesperson, you must be outgoing and sociable; a very shy or inhibited person will probably not succeed in this role. Similarly, in order to be a good accountant, you must be neat and orderly, at least to a degree. So, consider your personal characteristics carefully and try to choose a job or career that is consistent with them. (We'll describe one way of doing this in the **Making Psychology Part of Your Life** exercise at the end of this chapter.)

No, these steps won't guarantee that you will end up in a career that's perfect for you. But they will, at least, point you in the right direction and get you started thinking about the key issues. Good luck! And remember: Careers are *not* set in stone. On the contrary, because you will certainly change in the years ahead, so, too, may your career.

science. We raise them here simply to remind you that death involves much more than a biological event.

But given that death is the inevitable end of life, how do persons confronted with their own impending death react? Perhaps the most famous study of this subject was conducted in the late 1960s by Elizabeth Kübler-Ross (1974). She studied terminally ill cancer patients and, on the basis of extensive interviews with them, concluded that they pass through five distinct stages.

The first is *denial.* In this phase, patients refuse to believe that the end is in sight. "No, it can't be true," they seem to say. This stage is soon replaced by a second— *anger.* "Why me?" dying persons ask. "It isn't fair." In the third stage, patients show what Kübler-Ross terms *bargaining.* They offer prayer, good behavior, or other changes in lifestyle in exchange for a postponement of death. Unfortunately, such efforts cannot alter medical realities, so when it becomes apparent that their best efforts to make a deal with death have failed, many dying persons enter a stage of *depression.*

That's not the end of the process, however. According to Kübler-Ross, many people ultimately move into a final stage she labels *acceptance.* At this stage, dying persons are no longer angry or depressed. Instead, they seem to accept their impending death with dignity, and concentrate on saying good-bye to important persons in their lives, and putting their affairs in good order.

Although these findings are comforting and appealing, they have not been confirmed by other researchers (e.g., Arnoff & Spilka, 1984–1985; Metzger, 1980). It is also important to note that Kübler-Ross worked with a special group of individuals: people who were middle-aged and had suddenly learned that their lives would be cut off prematurely by cancer. This raises important questions about whether her findings can be generalized to other persons, especially older individuals for whom impending death is a less surprising event. In view of these points it seems best to view Kübler-Ross's conclusions with caution. They are intriguing, and they certainly hold out hope that many of us can meet death in a dignified manner. However, they cannot be viewed as scientifically valid unless they are confirmed by further research.

Bereavement: Coming to Terms with the Death of Loved Ones

When individuals die, they usually leave behind several persons who loved them dearly and must now cope with their loss. Because **bereavement** is a profound experience and one almost everyone has, it has been the subject of increasing attention from psychologists (Norris & Murrell, 1990). Their work suggests that bereavement is a process in which individuals move through a discrete series of stages. The first is *shock*—a feeling of numbness and unreality. This is followed by stages of *protest* and *yearning,* in which they resent the loss of their loved one and fantasize about this person's return. These reactions are often followed by deep *despair,* which can last a year or more—a period when bereaved persons feel that life is not worth living. Finally, bereaved persons usually enter a state of *detachment and recovery,* in which they separate themselves psychologically from the loved person who has died (e.g., Hart et al., 1995) and go on with their lives. Even during this stage, however, painful bouts of grieving may recur on birthdays, anniversaries, and other occasions that remind the bereaved persons of their loss.

Bereavement is especially strong in cases in which death is sudden and unexpected. Such deaths are described as *high-grief* experiences. In contrast, when death is expected, grief may be less pronounced (*low-grief* deaths). One type of death seems to leave especially deep and long-lasting scars: the death of a child. Parents

Bereavement
The process of grieving for the persons we love who die.

who go through this agonizing experience may never recover from it entirely; they continue to experience what
is known as *shadow grief* for their entire lives (Knapp,
1987). In fact, mothers whose children have died show
an increased risk of experiencing an untimely death
themselves. For instance, in one recent study (Li et al.,
2003), death rates among more than twenty-one thousand parents in Denmark who had lost a child were followed for eighteen years after the child died. Results
indicated that bereaved mothers showed a significant
increase in mortality due to natural causes ten to eighteen years later; fathers, in contrast, showed only a very
small increase in mortality due to unnatural causes (i.e.,
suicide).

FIGURE 8.18
Helping Others Grieve
Bereavement usually begins,
rather than ends, with funerals. So
if you care about another person,
you should continue your efforts
to help them grieve long after the
funeral is over.

Fortunately, a large majority of grieving persons do
ultimately recover from the pain of their loss and go on
to resume their lives, although for others, grief is so intense that they suffer symptoms of what is known as
traumatic grief, a pattern involving depression and anxi-
ety that is far more intense than that experienced in more ordinary bereavement.
But often, they can't recover without help from their friends and relatives (Figure
8.18). What can *you* do to help someone you care about grieve successfully? Here
are some suggestions, based on psychological research:

- **Continue your contacts with the grieving person.** Phone calls, social invita-
  tions, notes—signs that you are thinking of the grieving person—can make a
  real difference. They indicate to grieving persons that they are not alone and do
  have friends and relatives who care about them and their problems.
- **Sometimes, just be present.** Often, it appears, the best thing you can do for a
  grieving person is to be there, physically, while remaining silent. This evidence
  that you care about them can be very comforting.
- **Listen.** Let grieving people express their grief. When you are present, it is often
  best to remain silent and to *listen.* Grieving people often find that it consoles
  them to express their grief to a sympathetic audience—someone who hears
  them, understands them, and cares about them.
- **Don't tell them that things will get easier.** Although this is true, research findings indicate that many grieving persons react to such statements with resent-
  ment. They interpret them as a sign that you don't really understand, because,
  to them, it seems as though their loss is irreparable—one they can never get over.
- **Keep in touch.** As noted, this seems to be what grieving people appreciate
  most, so *do* call them, write to them, and visit them as often as you can.

Through such sensitive condolence behaviors, you can help make the bereavement process a bit more bearable for persons you care about. Of course,
nothing you or anyone else does can ever take the place of the person who is gone.
But as one Italian saying puts it, "Vita continua" (Life goes on), so helping people
pick up the pieces and continue is one of the most compassionate things you can
ever do.

KEY QUESTIONS

- According to Kübler-Ross, what stages do terminally ill persons pass through when confronting their own deaths?
- What are the major stages of bereavement?

SUMMARY AND REVIEW OF KEY QUESTIONS

Physical Growth and Development during Childhood

- **What environmental factors (teratogens) can adversely affect the developing fetus?**
Infectious agents, drugs, alcohol, and smoking by prospective mothers are among teratogens that can harm the developing fetus.

- **What are reflexes and which ones do infants possess at birth?**
Reflexes are inherited responses to stimulation in certain areas of the body. Infants possess several reflexes, including the Moro reflex, the palmar grasping reflex, and the sucking reflex.

- **What learning abilities are shown by newborns?**
Newborns seem capable of basic forms of learning, including classical conditioning and operant conditioning.

Perceptual Development during Childhood

- **What perceptual abilities are shown by infants?**
Infants can distinguish among different colors, sounds, and tastes, and they prefer certain patterns, such as the human face.

- **What evidence indicates that infants can keep track of time?**
Infants show increased heart rate at the precise times when a stimulus previously presented at specific times would normally occur again.

Cognitive Development during Childhood: Changes in Our Ability to Understand the World around Us

- **What are the major stages in Piaget's theory, and what cognitive abilities do infants, children, and adolescents acquire as they move through these stages?**
During the sensorimotor stage, infants acquire basic understanding of the links between their own behavior and the effects it produces—cause and effect. During the preoperational stage, infants can form mental representations of the external world but show egocentrism in their thinking. During the stage of concrete operations, children are capable of logical thought and show understanding of conservation. During the stage of formal operations, children and adolescents can think logically.

- **In what respects does Piaget's theory appear to be in need of revision?**
Piaget's theory is inaccurate in that it seriously underestimates the cognitive abilities of young children.

- **What is the "curse of knowledge" and what does it tell us about young children's cognitive abilities?**
The curse of knowledge refers to the fact that we tend to be biased by our own knowledge when judging the perspective of people who know less about some topic than we do.

- **To what does the term *children's theory of mind* refer?**
This refers to children's growing understanding of their own mental states and those of others.

- **According to the information-processing perspective, what does cognitive development involve?**
It involves children's growing abilities with respect to basic aspects of cognition (e.g., attention, memory, metacognition).

- **What role do heuristics and other potential sources of error play in cognitive development?**
As children's cognitive abilities increase, they also acquire heuristics and other cognitive biases.

Moral Development: Reasoning about "Right" and "Wrong"

- **What are the major stages of moral development described by Kohlberg's theory?**
At the first, or preconventional, level, morality is judged largely in terms of its consequences. At the conventional level, morality is judged in terms of laws and rules of society. At the third, or postconventional, level, morality is judged in terms of abstract principles and values.

- **Do cultural factors have any impact on moral development?**
Cultural factors do appear to influence moral development. Depending on the society in which they live, individuals learn to make moral judgments on the basis of different criteria.

Social Development during Childhood: Forming Relationships with Others

- **What is temperament and what role does it play in later development?**
Temperament refers to stable individual differences in the quality or intensity of emotional reactions. It plays a role in shyness and in the later occurrence of several kinds of behavioral problems, and it may even influence the nature of adult romantic relationships.

- **What is attachment?**
Attachment refers to infants' strong emotional bonds with their caregivers.

- **What role do children's friendships play in their social and emotional development?**
Friendships help children to develop socially and emotionally, and often help them avoid loneliness.

From Gender Identity to Sex-Category Constancy: How Children Come to Understand That They Are Female or Male

- **What is gender identity? Gender stability? Gender consistency?**

Gender identity refers to children's ability to label their own sex and that of others accurately. Gender stability is children's understanding that sex identity is stable over time. Gender consistency is children's understanding that sex identity won't change even if they adopt the clothing, hairstyles, and activities of the other sex.

- **How do social learning theory, cognitive development theory, and gender schema theory explain gender development?**
  Social learning theory emphasizes the role of operant conditions and modeling. Cognitive development theory emphasizes the role of children's growing cognitive abilities. Gender schema theory emphasizes the role of gender schemas.

Adolescence: Between Child and Adult

- **What physical changes occur during puberty?**
  Puberty, the most important feature of physical development during adolescence, is a period of rapid change and growth during which individuals attain sexual maturity.

- **How does thinking change during adolescence?**
  Individuals come to realize that others can hold different views than they do, and that while there are no absolute "truths" in many areas of life, there are better or worse reasons for holding certain views.

- **Are widely accepted ideas about adolescent emotionality correct?**
  Adolescents do show larger swings in mood or emotion than adults but, contrary to popular views, are generally quite happy and get along well with their parents.

- **According to Erikson, what is the most important crisis faced by adolescents?**
  Erikson suggests that this is a crisis involving identity versus role confusion, which concerns establishment of a clear self-identity.

- **What is the importance of adolescent romantic relationships?**
  Such relationships play a role in the development of adolescents' self-identity, sexuality, career planning, and performance in school. In addition, they help adolescents learn important lessons about the nature of close relationships and shape their perceptions about intimacy.

Development during Our Adult Years

- **What physical changes occur during early and middle adulthood?**
  Physical changes are minimal during early adulthood. Reduced physical functioning and decreased vigor plus changes in appearance appear during middle adulthood. In addition, both women and men experience changes in their reproductive systems during midlife.

- **What physical changes occur in later life?**
  Among the many physical changes occurring in later life are declines in sensory abilities and a slowing of reflexes.

- **What changes in memory occur as we age?**
  Working memory does not decline with age, but moving information from working memory to long-term storage may become somewhat slower. Recall of information from long-term memory does decline somewhat, but such effects are greater for meaningless information than meaningful information.

- **How does intelligence change over the life span?**
  There may be some declines in some aspects of intelligence with age, but these are smaller and more limited in scope than was once widely believed.

- **What are the effects of becoming physically fit on cognitive functioning?**
  Becoming fit has been found to enhance many forms of cognitive functioning, especially ones involving executive functions—planning and sequencing of mental procedures.

- **How do our friendships change as we move through life?**
  During our middle years, we tend to limit the number of friendships and maintain close ties with this limited group of persons for the rest of our lives (the *convoy model*).

- **What changes in our emotions occur as we age?**
  As people grow older, they report more happiness and less anger or sorrow. In addition, they report greater control over their emotions and greater stability in their moods.

- **What are some of the key challenges we face during our adult years?**
  These include marriage, parenthood, career changes, divorce, the "empty nest syndrome," caring for aging parents, and our own aging and retirement.

- **How should you choose your career?**
  Although many factors should be considered, perhaps the most important is obtaining a good match between your personal characteristics and the career you select.

Death and Bereavement

- **According to Kübler-Ross, what stages do terminally ill persons pass through when confronting their own deaths?**
  Kübler-Ross reported five stages: denial, anger, bargaining, depression, and acceptance.

- **What are the major stages of bereavement?**
  These include shock, protest and yearning, disorganization and despair, and, finally, detachment and recovery.

PSYCHOLOGY: UNDERSTANDING ITS FINDINGS

Can You Reason with a Three-Year-Old?

While the view that young children are just "miniature adults" is no longer widely accepted, many parents act as though they believe it: They often try to "reason" with their children about why the children should (or should not!) engage in certain actions, and often try to explain highly abstract ideas or principles to them (e.g., fairness, justice, loyalty). According to Piaget's theory of cognitive development and modern findings about children's cognitive abilities, why do these efforts often fail? At what age *can* children begin to reason like adults and understand abstract principles and ideas? And until they can, what techniques should parents use to influence their children's behavior?

MAKING PSYCHOLOGY PART OF YOUR LIFE

Choosing Your Career: Finding a Good Match for Your Personal Characteristics

As we noted earlier, research on choosing a career indicates that people are happiest—and most successful—when the careers they choose provide a close match to their personal characteristics and preferences. What are your characteristics and what careers would fit them best? These are complex answers that can't be answered fully in a brief exercise, but to get you started in the right direction, follow these steps:

1. **Rate your own standing on the following clusters of traits:** (Use a 5-point scale, in which 1 = very low; 2 = low; 3 = average; 4 = high; 5 = very high.)
   a. Practical, stable
   b. Analytic, introverted, reserved, precise
   c. Creative, impulsive, emotional
   d. Sociable, outgoing, need affection
   e. Confident, energetic, assertive
   f. Dependable, disciplined, orderly

2. Now, to increase the accuracy of your assessments, have three friends who know you well rate you on the same dimensions.
3. Next, consider the pattern of your traits: On which are you highest? Next highest? Lowest?
4. A major theory of career choice—Holland's *theory of vocational choice* (Gottfredson & Holland, 1990)—suggests that persons high on each of the clusters of previously mentioned traits can be described by the terms shown in the following table, enjoy certain kinds of environments or activities, and would most prefer the jobs listed in the table below.

The jobs shown are only examples. Can you think of others that would provide you with a good match to your personal traits?

Cluster Label	Preferred Environments or Activities	Preferred Jobs
Realistic	Working with hands, machines, tools	Auto mechanic, mechanical engineer
Investigative	Discovering, collecting, analyzing, and problem solving	Systems analyst, dentist, scientist
Artistic	Creating new products or ideas	Novelist, advertising copywriter
Social	Serving or helping others, working in teams	Social worker, counselor, nurse
Enterprising	Leading others, achieving goals	Manager, politician, stockbroker
Conventional	Performing systemic manipulation of data or information	Accountant, banker, actuary

KEY TERMS

Accommodation, p. 243
Adolescence, p. 263
Assimilation, p. 243
Attachment, p. 255
Bereavement, p. 274
Biological Sex, p. 259
Childhood, p. 236
Climacteric, p. 268
Cognitive Development, p. 243
Concrete Operations, p. 245
Conservation, p. 244
Conventional Level (of morality), p. 252
Convoy Model, p. 271
Cross-Sectional Research, p. 271
Curse of Knowledge, p. 246
Developmental Psychology, p. 236
Egocentrism, p. 244
Embryo, p. 236
Fetal Alcohol Syndrome, p. 238
Fetus, p. 236
Formal Operations (stage of), p. 245
Friendships, p. 258

Gender, p. 259
Gender Consistency, p. 260
Gender Identity, p. 260
Gender Roles, p. 259
Gender Schema Theory, p. 261
Gender Stability, p. 260
Gender Stereotypes, p. 259
Hypothetico-Deductive Reasoning, p. 245
Information-Processing Perspective (of cognitive development), p. 249
Insecure/Ambivalent Attachment, p. 255
Insecure/Avoidant Attachment, p. 255
Menopause, p. 268
Mentors, p. 266
Metacognition, p. 249
Moral Development, p. 250
Object Permanence, p. 244
Placenta, p. 237

Postconventional Level (of morality), p. 252
Preconventional Level (of morality), p. 252
Preoperational Stage, p. 244
Primary Aging, p. 268
Puberty, p. 263
Reflexes, p. 238
Schemas, p. 243
Scripts, p. 249
Secondary Aging, p. 268
Secure Attachment, p. 255
Sensorimotor Stage, p. 243
Sex-Category Constancy, p. 261
Social Development, p. 255
Social Network, p. 263
Stage Theory, p. 252
Successful Aging, p. 268
Symbolic Play, p. 244
Temperament, p. 255
Teratogens, p. 237
Theory of Mind, p. 249

Motivation and Emotion

I (Robert Baron) admit it: I love to eat! In fact, I have a good friend who describes me as the most "food-centered" person he has ever met. To an extent, he is right: I am willing to drive a long way to eat at a famous restaurant, I subscribe to several cooking magazines and am always on the lookout for new, interesting recipes. And, truly, I can't get along without good, crusty bread; in fact, when I lived in a small college town, I kept a freezer just for bread, which I "imported" in large quantities from a big city hours away. Why? Because bread of this type was simply not available in the town where I lived.

In contrast, I have several friends who couldn't care less what they eat; they laugh at my willingness to go to a lot of trouble to get a special meal and wonder why anyone would need so many cookbooks. For them, a hamburger at a fast-food restaurant is just as good (or almost as good) as anything else. For me, though, effort spent in getting something really interesting and delicious to eat is well spent and gives me tremendous pleasure. (And lucky for me, I never gain weight.)

Why do we start with this personal anecdote? Because it helps illustrates the essential nature of the two major topics we'll consider in this chapter: *motivation* and *emotion*. Psychologists use the term *motivation* to refer to the internal processes that *activate, guide,* and *maintain* behavior (often, over long periods of time), and the operation of such processes is certainly apparent in my interest in good food. Why, after all, would I drive hours to a famous restaurant when there are others just a few blocks from my house? And why would I buy a freezer just to hold certain kinds of bread when I can get a fresh loaf (although not the kind I like!) at any nearby supermarket? When it is difficult to explain someone's behavior in terms of the immediate situation or with respect to obvious rewards and punishments, psychologists often seek the explanation in terms of motivation—internal processes that *energize* behavior, *guide* it, and cause it to *persist* over time (see Figure 9.1). In the case of my motivation to seek good food, these internal factors energize my efforts to obtain it, lead me to search for excellent restaurants rather than ordinary ones, and have caused me to engage in such behavior for many years. What are these internal processes like? We'll soon examine them in detail but should note here that they include *goals, intentions,* and *desires*—processes that certainly exist and often strongly affect behavior (see Figure 9.1) but are difficult to observe directly.

Emotion, in contrast, refers to complex reactions consisting of (1) physiological responses such as changes in blood pressure and heart rate; (2) the subjective feelings we describe as happiness, anger, sorrow, or disgust; and (3) expressive reactions that reflect these internal states, such as changes in facial expressions or posture. Such reactions are apparent in the pleasure I feel when I consume excellent food or in the strong disappointment I experience if the food served in a restaurant doesn't live up to its reputation, and in the outward expression of these feelings in my facial expressions and words. Emotions play a crucial role in many aspects of behavior, including personal health (see Chapter 11) and psychological disorders (see Chapter 11). In addition, they exert strong effects on many aspects

FIGURE 9.1
Motivation: Useful in Answering the Question "Why?"
We often wonder why other people behave as they do—especially in situations in which rewards for their actions are not readily apparent. The concept of *motivation* is often helpful in understanding such behavior. Can you guess why the people shown here are engaging in the activities they are performing? In other words, what are the motives behind their actions?

of cognition, shaping our judgments and decisions in important ways (e.g., Forgas, 1995a, 1998).

In this chapter, we'll describe what psychologists have learned about both of these important topics. Starting with *motivation,* we'll consider contrasting theories about its basic nature. Why should you be interested in these theories? Because they provide important insights into understanding your own motivation and, perhaps, how to change it. Next, we'll examine two important forms of motivation: *hunger* and *sexual motivation.* In addition, we'll also consider a motive that, as far as we can tell, is unique to human beings: *achievement motivation*—the desire to excel. We'll also consider *intrinsic motivation*—motivation that does not stem from external rewards, and *forgiveness*—replacing desires for revenge with compassion and other positive reactions.

After that, we'll turn to the topic of *emotion,* beginning, again, with a brief overview of theories concerning its nature. Then we'll turn to the biological bases of emotion. Third, we'll consider the expression and communication of emotion— how emotional reactions are reflected in external behavior. We'll then shift focus to *affect* (or affective states)—relatively mild subjective feelings and moods. Here, we'll consider the complex relationships between emotion and cognition—how feelings shape thoughts and thoughts shape feelings. Finally, we'll examine one important kind of affective state—personal happiness.

MOTIVATION: THE ACTIVATION AND PERSISTENCE OF BEHAVIOR

Consider the following events:

> A group of young women and men hurl themselves out of a plane. Then, as they fall toward earth, they join hands and form a circle. After that, they divide into pairs and swing round and round each other in a kind of dance. Only at the last minute do they open their parachutes and glide safely to the ground.

> Employees of a large company remain on strike for many weeks, despite the fact that no matter how large the settlement they ultimately win, it will not be enough to compensate them for the wages and benefits they have lost during the strike.

> An individual spends long hours working on complex word puzzles that require a great deal of concentration. He receives no rewards for solving these puzzles; in fact, he is often frustrated by being unable to solve them.

How can such actions be explained? On the face of it, they are puzzling. Why would people voluntarily jump out planes and risk their lives playing games as they fall toward earth? Why would workers remain on strike, even though such actions offer no chance of real economic gains? Why would someone exert so much effort solving complex puzzles? One answer to such questions is this: These actions occur because the persons involved are *motivated* to perform them. In other words, they are responding to their own **motivation**—internal processes that can't be directly observed in the situation that serve to activate, guide, and maintain their actions. Whenever the causes of a specific form of behavior can't be readily observed in the immediate situation or in terms of obvious rewards or punishments, psychologists believe that it is useful to explain them in terms of motives. But what, precisely, are these motives? And how do they influence behavior? Let's see what psychologists have to say about these issues.

Theories of Motivation: Some Major Perspectives

Over the years, many different theories of motivation have been proposed—more theories, in fact, than we could possibly examine here. The views described here,

Motivation
Internal processes that activate, guide, and maintain behavior over time.

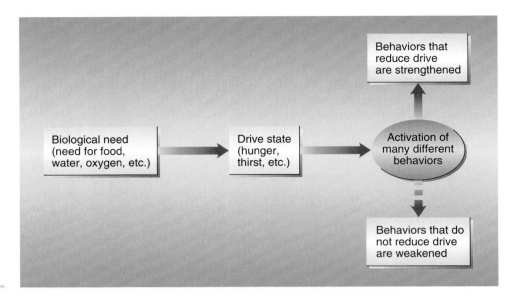

FIGURE 9.2
Drive Theory: An Overview
According to drive theory, biological needs lead to the arousal of *drives*, which activate efforts to reduce them. Behaviors that succeed in reducing drives are strengthened and are repeated when the drive is aroused again. Behaviors that fail to reduce the drive are weakened and are less likely to recur when the drive is aroused once again.

however, are the ones that have received the most attention and may be most relevant to understanding—and changing—your own motivation.

Drive Theory: Motivation and Homeostasis

What do being hungry, thirsty, too cold, and too hot have in common? One answer is that they are all unpleasant states and cause us to do something to reduce or eliminate them. This basic fact provides the basis for a major approach to motivation known as **drive theory.** According to drive theory, biological needs arising within our bodies create unpleasant states of arousal—the feelings we describe as hunger, thirst, fatigue, and so on. To eliminate such feelings and restore a balanced physiological state known as **homeostasis,** we engage in certain activities (Winn, 1995). Thus, according to drive theory, motivation is basically a process in which various biological needs *push* (drive) us to actions designed to satisfy these needs (see Figure 9.2). Behaviors that work—ones that help reduce the appropriate drive—are strengthened and tend to be repeated (see Chapter 5). Those that fail to produce effects are weakened and will not be repeated when the drive is present once again.

In its original form, drive theory focused primarily on biological needs and the drives they produce. Soon, though, psychologists extended this model to other forms of behavior not so clearly linked to basic needs, such as drives for stimulation, status, achievement, power, and forming stable social relationships (e.g., Baumeister & Leary, 1995). For many people, these are important motives, and they engage in vigorous efforts to satisfy them. So although these drives may not be based on biological needs, they, too, can serve as powerful sources of motivation.

Drive theory persisted in psychology for several decades, but at present, most psychologists believe it suffers from several major drawbacks. Contrary to what drive theory suggests, human beings often engage in actions that *increase* rather than reduce various drives. For example, people sometimes skip snacks when hungry in order to lose weight or to maximize their enjoyment of a special dinner. Similarly, many people watch or read erotic materials in order to increase their sexual excitement, even when they don't anticipate immediate sexual gratification. In view of such evidence, most psychologists now believe that drive theory, by itself, does not provide a full explanation of human motivation.

Expectancy Theory: A Cognitive Approach

Why are you reading this book? Not, we'd guess, to reduce some biological need. Rather, you are probably reading it because doing so will help you to reach impor-

Drive Theory
A theory of motivation suggesting that behavior is "pushed" from within by drives stemming from basic biological needs.

Homeostasis
A state of physiological balance within the body.

tant goals: gaining useful and interesting knowledge, earning a high grade on the next exam, graduating from college. In short, your behavior is determined by your thoughts about future outcomes and how your current actions can help you get wherever it is that you want to go in life. This basic point forms the basis for another major theory of motivation, **expectancy theory.**

This theory suggests that motivation is not primarily a matter of being pushed from within by various urges or drives; rather it is more a question of being *pulled* from without by expectations of attaining desired outcomes. Such outcomes, known as **incentives,** can be almost anything we have learned to value—money, status, the approval of others, to name just a few. In other words, while drive theory focuses mainly on the factors that push or (drive) us toward certain actions, expectancy theory focuses more on the outcomes we wish to obtain. Why do people engage in complex, effortful, or even painful behaviors, such as working many hours on their jobs, studying long into the night, performing exercises that are, at least initially, painful? Expectancy theory answers: because they believe that doing so will yield the outcomes they wish to attain. Certainly, you can think of instances in which this principle applies to your own behavior. For instance, why do you—or people you know—study, work, or exercise hard? Not because these activities are intrinsically enjoyable. You perform them because you believe that doing so will produce the outcomes you want—better grades, success in your careers (or at least a steady income!), and better health. So expectancy theory does seem to provide important insights into motivation: why we do what we do in many situations.

Expectancy theory has been applied to many aspects of human motivation, but perhaps it has found its most important applications as an explanation of *work motivation*—the tendency to expend energy and effort on one's job (Locke & Latham, 1990). We'll consider work motivation in detail in Chapter 14, but here, we simply want to note that research findings in the field of *industrial/organizational psychology* indicate that people will work hard at their jobs only when they believe that doing so will improve their performance (known as *expectancy* in the theory), that good performance will be recognized and rewarded (known as *instrumentality* in the theory), and that the rewards provided will be ones they want (known as *valence*).

Goal-Setting Theory

Another theory of motivation that emphasizes the importance of cognitive factors rather than drives or arousal is known as **goal-setting theory,** and it can be illustrated by the following example. Suppose that you are studying for a big exam. Do you ever tell yourself, in advance, that you won't stop until you have read a certain number of pages, memorized some specific number of definitions, or solved a fixed number of problems? The chances are good that you do, because most people realize that they often accomplish more when they have a concrete goal than when they do not. This basic fact is central to *goal-setting theory* (e.g., Lock & Latham, 1990), which suggests that motivation can be strongly influenced by goals.

Additional findings, however, indicated that goal setting works best under certain conditions. It is most effective in boosting performance when the goals set are highly *specific*—people know just what they are trying to accomplish; the goals are *challenging*—meeting them requires considerable effort; the goals are perceived as *attainable*—people believe they can actually reach them (see Figure 9.3). Finally, goal setting is most successful when people receive feedback on their progress toward meeting the goals and when they are truly and deeply committed to reaching them. This last point is quite important; if goals are set by someone else and the people who are expected to meet these goals aren't committed to doing so, then goal setting can be totally ineffective, and may even backfire and *reduce* motivation.

THE LOCKHORNS

© 1991 by King Features Syndicate, Inc. World rights reserved.
5-14

"LEROY SAYS THE SECRET OF SATISFACTORY LIFE ACHIEVEMENT IS TO SET MODEST GOALS."

HOEST BREINER

FIGURE 9.3
The Importance of Setting Challenging Goals
Setting goals for yourself or others can provide a big boost to motivation—but only if the goals selected are challenging ones. The character here is *not* following this principle, with predictable results!
Source: © WM. Hoest Enterprises. Reprinted with permission of King Features Syndicate.

Expectancy Theory
A theory of motivation suggesting that behavior is "pulled" by expectations of desirable outcomes.

Incentives
Rewards individuals seek to attain.

Goal-Setting Theory
The view that motivation can be strongly influenced by goals.

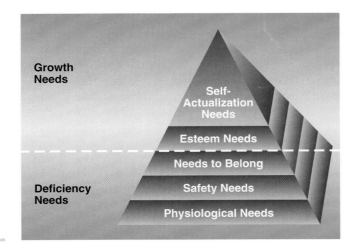

FIGURE 9.4
Maslow's Needs Hierarchy
According to Maslow (1970), needs exist in a hierarchy. Only when lower-order needs are satisfied can higher-order needs be activated, and serve as a source of motivation.

When these conditions *are* met, though, goal setting is a highly effective way of increasing motivation and performance (e.g., Mento, Locke, & Klein, 1992; Wright et al., 1994). For ideas on how you can use it in you own life, please read the **Psychology Lends a Hand** feature on the next page.

Maslow's Needs Hierarchy: Relations among Motives

Suppose that you were very hungry and very cold; could you study effectively under these conditions? Probably not. Your hunger and feelings of cold would probably prevent you from focusing on the task of learning new materials, even if these were quite interesting to you. Observations like this suggest that human motives may exist in a *hierarchy,* so that we must satisfy those that are more basic before moving on to ones that are less linked to biological needs. This point is central to a theory of motivation proposed by Maslow (1970). Maslow places *physiological needs* such as those for food, water, oxygen, and sleep at the base of the **hierarchy of needs**. One step above these are *safety needs,* needs for feeling safe and secure in one's life. Above the safety needs are *social needs,* including needs to have friends, to be loved and appreciated, and to belong (e.g., Baumeister & Leary, 1995).

Maslow refers to physiological, safety, and social needs as *deficiency needs.* They are the basics and must be satisfied before higher levels of motivation, or *growth needs,* can emerge. Above the social needs in the hierarchy he proposes are *esteem needs,* the need to develop self-respect, to gain the approval of others, and to achieve success. Ambition and the need for achievement, to which we'll return later, are closely linked to esteem needs. Finally, at the top of the hierarchy are *self-actualization needs.* These involve the need for self-fulfillment—the desire to become all that one is capable of being (see Figure 9.4).

Maslow's theory is intuitively appealing, but research designed to test it has yielded mixed results. So, overall, the idea that needs arise, and are satisfied, in a particular order has not been confirmed. For this reason, Maslow's theory should be viewed mainly as an interesting but unverified framework for understanding motivation. (See Table 9.1 for an overview of the theories of motivation discussed in this section.)

Hierarchy of Needs
In Maslow's theory of motivation, an arrangement of needs from the most basic to those at the highest levels.

KEY QUESTIONS

- According to drive theory, what is the basis for various motives?
- According to expectancy theory, why do people engage in tasks requiring effort?
- Under what conditions will goal setting increase motivation and performance?
- What are the basic ideas behind Maslow's needs hierarchy theory?

TABLE 9.1 Theories of Motivation: An Overview

The theories summarized here are among the ones that have been most influential in psychology.

Theory of Motivation	Key Assumptions	Strengths/Weaknesses
Drive Theory	Biological needs produce unpleasant states of arousal which people seek to reduce.	People sometimes try to *increase* their drives, not reduce them.
Arousal Theory	Arousal (general level of activation) varies throughout the day and can motivate many forms of behavior; people seek *optimal* arousal, not low arousal.	Arousal is only one of many factors that influence motivated behavior.
Expectancy Theory	Behavior is "pulled" by expectations of desired outcomes rather than "pushed" from within by biologically based drives.	Focus on cognitive processes in motivation is consistent with modern psychology; widely used to explain *work motivation*.
Goal-Setting Theory	Setting specific, challenging, but attainable goals can boost motivation and performance, especially when individuals are committed to reaching the goals and receive feedback on their progress.	Highly effective in increasing performance, but mechanisms that explain these effects are still somewhat uncertain.

p s y c h o l o g y   l e n d s   a   h a n d

Managing Your Own Motivation

Motivation, almost everyone agrees, is a key ingredient in success. Highly motivated people can often outperform those who are more skilled, experienced, or talented because, to put it simply, they try harder! Can psychology help you to boost your own motivation at times when you'd like to do so? Absolutely. By applying the principles of several theories of motivation, you can increase your own ability to exert sustained effort toward attaining various goals or outcomes. Here, briefly, are some of the steps that can be very helpful in this regard:

1. **First, figure out what you want.** There's an old saying which suggests that you really can't get anywhere unless you first know where you want to go. So the initial step should be figuring out what's really important to you. Success? Security? Love? Leisure time? Status? A useful exercise is to list the things you want most in life and then to rank them from most important down. Once you are clear about what you really want, move on to the next steps.

2. **Next, identify specific actions that can help you to reach these goals.** Reaching important goals generally means performing various tasks better than we are performing them right now. And remember: Increased effort does *not* always produce better performance; sometimes, it's just "spinning our wheels." For this reason (suggested by expectancy theory), you should be careful to put your effort where it *will* pay off—where it will actually help you to do better. For instance, if you want better grades, simply spending more time studying will not necessarily work. Rather, you have to figure out *better ways* to study—ones

that will help you understand the materials in your courses. Bottom line: Invest your effort where it is most likely to produce concrete results.

3. **Set concrete, challenging, but achievable goals for yourself.** Rome, it is often said, was not built in a day. Similarly, you can't expect to attain everything you want in life right away; real progress toward important goals takes time. And to get there, you should begin by setting goals that are challenging (they are a real stretch), that are specific (they indicate precisely what you want to achieve), and that are also ones that allow you to measure your progress toward them. Say, for instance, that you want to get along with other people better than you do now. One goal might be to be less openly critical of them, because no one likes receiving harsh, negative feedback. Begin by observing how many times each day you say something critical to other people. Then, choose a concrete goal: For instance, you will reduce this by 25 percent over the next two weeks. Monitor your progress as you work toward reaching this goal. When you do attain it, give yourself a reward—and then set a higher goal for the next round. The main point is that because *you* are setting the goals, and can measure your progress toward them, using goal setting can really be a helpful motivational tool.

Good luck! Psychologists believe they can change almost anything about themselves they wish—*if* they really want to change *and* are willing to exert the effort. So start today and you may be truly happy with the results!

Hunger: Regulating Our Caloric Intake

A Greek proverb states: "You cannot reason with a hungry belly; it has no ears." This statement suggests—eloquently!—that **hunger motivation,** the urge to obtain and consume food is a powerful one, and if you have ever had the experience of going without food for even a single day, you know how strong feelings of hunger can be and what a powerful source of motivation they can provide. But where do such feelings come from? And how do we manage to regulate the amount of food we consume so that for many persons, body weight remains fairly stable over long periods of time, while for others, the "battle of the bulge" is quickly lost? Let's see what psychologists have discovered about these and related questions.

The Regulation of Eating: A Complex Process

Consider the following fact: If you consume just twenty extra calories each day (less than the number in a single small carrot), you will gain about two pounds a year—twenty pounds in a decade. How do people keep caloric input and output closely balanced and so avoid such outcomes? One answer, of course, is that in many cases, they don't: People do gain weight despite their best efforts to avoid doing so. Indeed, we are living in the midst of what seems to be an epidemic of obesity: Since the early 1970s, the percentage of Americans who are obese has risen from 17 percent to more than 60 percent, and the proportion of people who are too overweight to fit into an airline seat has more than tripled. We'll return later in this chapter to several factors that may be contributing to these trends. Now, though, let's focus on the question of why, for most people, a balance *is* struck between needs and caloric intake so that weight remains relatively stable. What mechanisms contribute to this balance?

Part of the answer involves the *hypothalamus,* which plays a role both in eating and satiety (knowing when we've had enough). The regulation of eating involves much more than this, however. In fact, it seems to involve a complex system of regulatory mechanisms located not only in the hypothalamus, but in the liver and other organs of the body as well. These systems contain special *detectors,* cells that respond to variations in the concentration of several nutrients in the blood. One type of detector responds to the amount of *glucose,* or blood sugar. Other detectors respond to levels of *protein,* and especially to certain amino acids. This is why we feel full after eating a meal high in protein, such as a steak, even though the level of glucose in our blood remains relatively low. Finally, other detectors respond to *lipids,* or fats. Again, even if glucose levels are low, when the amount of lipids circulating in the blood is high, we do not feel hungry.

Complex as this may sound, it is still not the entire picture. In addition, eating and hunger are also strongly affected by the smell and taste of food and by feedback produced by chewing and swallowing. As we consume food, information from taste and smell receptors, and from muscles in our mouths and throats, provide feedback that helps us determine when we have eaten enough (e.g., Stellar, 1985).

The sight of food, too, is important. Foods that are attractive in appearance are hard to resist and may overwhelm the regulatory mechanisms just described, leading us to overeat (Rozin, 1996). Cognitive factors, too, play a role. Findings reported by Rozin and his colleagues (Rozin et al., 1998) indicate that memories about when we last ate can influence whether we decide to eat and how much we consume at any given time, quite apart from what internal cues from our bodies may be telling us. In this research, Rozin et al. (1998) offered several meals in a row to individuals who had suffered extensive bilateral damage to the hippocampus and amygdala—structures that, as we saw in Chapter 6, play a role in memory. As a result of these injuries, these persons could not remember recent events. Both individuals were offered a meal at lunch time. A few minutes after eating it, they were offered a second meal, and then, a few minutes after eating that one, were offered yet a third meal. Results indicated that both persons consumed the second

Hunger Motivation
The motivation to obtain and consume food.

meal, and that one of them ate part of the third meal as well. Yet, both rated their hunger as lower after consuming the first meal than before it. Why, then, did they eat again? Apparently because they could not remember that they had just eaten! Findings such as these underscore the main point we want to make: Many mechanisms operating together influence hunger motivation and eating.

Factors in Weight Gain: Why Many Persons Experience Difficulty in the Long-Term Regulation of Body Weight

There can be little doubt that at the present time, "thin is in," at least in most Western cultures. As a result, consumers in many countries spend huge sums each year on books and other products related to weight loss. Despite these efforts, however, many people can't seem to prevent their weight from increasing. As a result, there is a widening gap between people's desired weight (most want to be slim) and their actual weight (Figure 9.5). What factors are responsible for this trend? Research findings point to several.

First, part of the problem involves the effects of learning. Many people acquire eating habits that are very likely to produce excess pounds. They learn to prefer high-calorie meals that are rich in protein and fats—Big Macs, for instance. Further, they learn to associate the act of eating with many different contexts and situations. If you feel a strong urge to snack every time you sit down in front of the television or a movie screen, you know what we mean. The desire to eat can be classically conditioned (see Chapter 5); cues associated with eating when we are hungry can acquire the capacity to prompt eating when we are *not* hungry.

Second, genetic factors interact with these changes in diet and can, for many persons, intensify them. Consider the situation faced by our ancestors: Periods of plenty alternated with periods of famine. Under these conditions, people who were efficient at storing excess calories as fat during times of plenty gained an important advantage: They were more likely to survive during famines and to have children. As a result, all of us living today have some tendency to gain weight when we overeat—much to our dismay!

Environmental factors, too, play an important role. In recent years, the portion size of many foods has increased dramatically. When we were teenagers, a Coke or Pepsi was 8 ounces; now, 1-liter bottles (about 32 ounces!) are being offered as a

FIGURE 9.5
Image versus Reality
As the emphasis on being slim has increased in many cultures, people have been gaining weight. The result? A growing gap between how they would like to be and how they actually are with respect to body weight.

psychology lends a hand

Winning the "Battle of the Bulge": Some Helpful Tips

The old saying, "You can never be too rich or too thin," may be an exaggeration, but most people do want to remain—or become—slim if they can. Following are some steps suggested by research on factors related to weight gain that may help *you* achieve this goal.

- **Avoid high-calorie snack foods.** A handful of potato chips or a small order of fries can contain hundreds of calories. Yet, they don't tend to make you feel full. Avoid such foods as much as possible.
- **Don't eat when you aren't hungry, out of habit.** It's all too easy to get into the habit of eating whenever you watch TV, study, or sit down to talk with friends. If you must munch on something, eat a piece of fruit, or drink some coffee or tea (preferably decaf). These drinks contain natural substances that tend to reduce appetite.
- **Avoid temptation.** If you want to avoid gaining weight, try to avoid temptation. When you encounter attractive, appetizing foods, look the other way and get out of there fast! The waist line you save will be your own.
- **Exercise!** Vigorous exercise will definitely help you burn calories, which can translate into weight loss. Indeed, losing weight really involves a simple formula: You lose if the number of calories you burn exceeds the number you eat. So exercise regularly. It can be a big help.
- **Drink water, not soft drinks, with your meals.** During the past two decades, the consumption of soft drinks in the United States and many other countries has soared. From the point of view of weight gain, that's unfortunate, because each glass of Coke, Pepsi, or whatever contains almost two hundred calories. So, ignore the ads and sip water when you are thirsty.
- **Don't give up.** If you have succeeded in losing weight—most people on diets do—don't quit. Managing your weight is a life-long process. And if you persist, you will eventually lower your body's set point, so that keeping the extra pounds off will actually become easier.
- **Don't adopt fad diets.** Diet books are perpetual best-sellers and usually contain new approaches for losing weight quickly and effortlessly. Don't be fooled by such claims! There is really no scientific evidence for these diets, and the only thing they accomplish, in general, is to make their authors rich (and famous)!

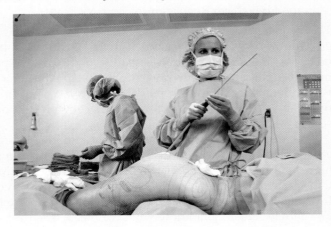

FIGURE 9.6
Weight Control: A Drastic Procedure We Do *Not* Recommend
In recent years, growing numbers of people have undergone plastic surgery to remove unwanted fat from their bodies. Given that there are many other effective means for losing weight, we view such procedures as far too risky and recommend against them.

You *can* lose weight, and fairly quickly, too, but the best way to do it is by reducing the amount you eat while increasing your exercise. That formula is 90 percent certain to yield the results you want, with minimum risk to your health.

- **Don't consider cosmetic surgery as a solution.** Ads for cosmetic medical procedures, such as the one shown in Figure 9.6, are appearing with increasing frequency, and the number of persons who are "losing weight" by having it removed surgically from their bodies is rising. Please *don't even think about it!* Surgery always involves risk, and given the fact that there are many other far less drastic means of controlling weight, we strongly believe that this is *not* the way to go.

Good Luck!

single serving. Similarly, McDonald's hamburgers were small and thin and contained about 200 calories; now, most people purchase double cheeseburgers or Big Macs containing 400 or 500 calories. Because people tend to eat their entire portion of food, no matter how big it is, this, too, may be a factor in the rising rate of obesity.

One final factor—and perhaps the most discouraging of all—involves our own bodies' reaction to weight gain. Common sense might suggest that when we gain weight, internal mechanisms tending to return us to our initial, healthy weight might spring into action. In fact, the opposite seems to be true. Such mechanisms do exist, and they normally serve to regulate our weight within a specific range (our current *set point*). Unfortunately, growing evidence suggests that once we gain a significant amount of weight, our sensitivity to a chemical produced by our own bodies that reduces appetite and speeds metabolism (*leptin*) actually *decreases*. The result: Once we start to gain weight, it becomes harder and harder to stop (Gladwell, 1998). The process *can* be halted if we lose weight and maintain it for several years; but this requires more willpower and discipline than many people seem to possess.

Taking all these factors together, it is not surprising that many persons experience difficulties in regulating their own weight over the long term. There are simply too many variables or conditions that, acting together, overwhelm the mechanisms that establish and maintain a balance between our internal needs and the food we consume. But there is help! For some suggestions on effective techniques of weight control based on the findings of psychological research, please see the **Psychology Lends a Hand** section on page 290.

KEY QUESTIONS

- What factors play a role in the regulation of eating?
- What factors override this system, so that many people fail to maintain a stable weight?

Sexual Motivation: The Most Intimate Motive

Suppose that voyagers from another planet arrived on earth and visited large cities in many different countries. What would they see? Among other things, large numbers of advertisements designed to attract attention through the use of sex-related images (see Figure 9.7). In fact, so common are such displays, that the alien visitors might quickly conclude that human beings are obsessed with sex.

FIGURE 9.7
Our Obsession with Sex
Judging from ads in magazines, on billboards—virtually everywhere!—sexual motivation is a very strong motive for human beings.

While advertisements may well exaggerate our interest in sex, it is clear that **sexual motivation**—our motivation to engage in sexual activity—is a powerful one. Let's see what psychologists have discovered about it.

▨ Hormones and Sexual Behavior

As we saw in Chapter 8, the onset of puberty involves rapid increases in the activity of the sex glands, or **gonads.** The hormones produced by these glands have many effects on the body, and for many species, they strongly affect sexual motivation. In fact, sex hormones exert what are usually termed *activation effects*—in their presence, sexual behavior occurs, while in their absence, sexual behavior does not occur or takes place with a very low frequency. For example, in rats, the species for whom the link between sex hormones and sexual behavior has been most extensively studied, females show receptivity to males only at times during their menstrual cycle when concentrations of certain sex hormones are high. Once these levels drop—regardless of whether mating has resulted in fertilization—females are no longer receptive to males. Additional evidence for a link between sex hormones and mating is also provided by the fact that, for many species, removal of the ovaries totally eliminates female sexual receptivity to males. Removal of the testes in males produces similar though somewhat less clear-cut results. In many species, then, hormones produced by the gonads play a key role in sexual motivation (Rissman, 1995).

Human beings, and to some degree other primates, are an exception to this general pattern. Although findings indicate that many women report substantial changes in sexual desire over the course of their menstrual cycle, these changes do *not* occur at times when hormones such as estrogen are at peak levels (Zillmann, Schweitzer, & Mundorf, 1994). On the contrary, peaks of sexual desire or interest seem to occur when such hormones are at relatively low levels. Further, many women continue to engage in and enjoy sexual relations after *menopause,* when the hormonal output of their ovaries drops sharply. And, in men, there is little evidence of a clear link between blood levels of sex hormones such as *testosterone* and sexual responsiveness (Byrne, 1982). These findings seem to suggest that sex hormones play little role in human sexual motivation. However, recent evidence indicates that, in fact, such hormones may indeed exert subtle effects on our behavior. For instance, several studies indicate that women find masculine faces—and men who show good self-presentation skills (e.g., high levels of eye contact)—more appealing during ovulation (when women are most likely to become pregnant) than at other times (Gangstead et al., 2004; Penton-Woak & Perrett, 2000). Similarly, in an intriguing recent study (Macrae et al., 2002), female participants were asked to decide whether faces shown on a computer screen were males or females. Results indicated that for male faces, they performed this task more quickly when they were at high risk for conception (when female sex hormones were high) than at other times in their menstrual cycles (when sex hormones were lower). For female faces, no such differences emerged (Macrae et al., 2002; see Figure 9.8). Findings such as these suggest that sex hormones do play some role in human sexual behavior. In general, though, the link between sex hormones and sexual motivation appears to be far less clear-cut and less compelling for human beings than is true for many other species.

Other chemical substances within the body, however, may play a role. Recent findings suggest that when human beings are sexually attracted to another person, their brains produce increased amounts of several substances chemically related to *amphetamines.* As you may recall from Chapter 4, amphetamines are stimulants, and the increased production of amphetamine-like substances such as phenylethylamine (PEA) may account for the fact that many people describe strong sexual attraction—the first stage in falling in love—as a feeling that "sweeps them away." As one researcher puts it, "love is a natural high" (Walsh, 1993).

In sum, while sex hormones are not as clearly linked to sexual motivation in humans as in other species, there is some evidence that other substances produced by our bodies do play a role in such motivation, and even in romantic love. Thus,

Sexual Motivation
Motivation to engage in various forms of sexual relations.

Gonads
The primary sex glands.

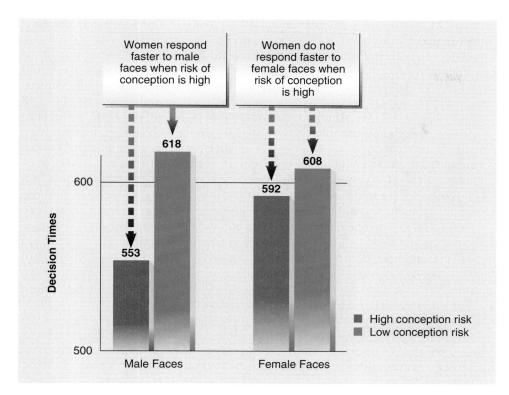

FIGURE 9.8
Evidence that Sex Hormones Play a Role in Some Aspects of Human Sexual Behavior
Women asked to decide whether faces shown on a computer screen were male or female performed this task more quickly for male faces when at high risk for conception (when sex hormones are high) than at other times during their menstrual cycles. Similar effects did *not* occur for female faces.
Source: Based on data from Macrae et al., 2003.

there does appear to be a biochemical side to love, but we are only just beginning to understand it.

Human Sexual Behavior: An Evolutionary Perspective

A very different approach to understanding human sexual motivation, and especially to understanding potential differences between women and men in this respect, is provided by evolutionary psychology—the view that many aspects of our behavior reflect, at least in part, the effects of evolution. One question evolutionary psychology has addressed is this: Do women and men differ in their sexual behavior or, more specifically, in what are known as *mating strategies*—the ways in which they choose sexual partners? In the past, it was widely assumed that they do. For instance, there was a general belief that men seek variety—they want to have as many different sexual partners as possible—while women are less interested in having many partners and instead prefer stable, long-term relationships. Although these views are almost certainly an exaggeration, research findings indicate that they may contain a grain of truth. For instance, when asked how long they would have to know someone before consenting to sexual relations with them, men name much shorter periods of time than do women (Buss & Schmitt, 1993). Similarly, men indeed report that they would like to have more sexual partners in the future than do women (Schmitt, 2003). In short, there seem to be some differences between males and females where short-term sexual strategies are concerned (Buss, 1999). But why is this the case? Many different possibilities exist, including the fact that cultural beliefs simply cause people to answer questions about their sexual preferences in accordance with such views. In other words, men report that they want many partners because this is consistent with the gender stereotype for men, and women report that they want fewer partners because this is consistent with the gender stereotype for women. Another possibility is suggested by evolutionary psychology.

The evolutionary view—which, we should add, is quite controversial—suggests that by having sex with many different women, men can father a large number of children, many more than if they had sex with only one woman. In contrast, no matter how many lovers a woman has, she can only have one child at a time. Moreover, the investment in having a child is much greater for women than men: They are the ones who are pregnant for nine months. Evolutionary psychology suggests that because of these facts, natural selection has tended to produce a stronger preference for sexual variety among males than among females. The reasoning behind this suggestion is as follows. Men who prefer many different mates produce more offspring than men with a weaker preference for sexual variety. As a result, a preference for variety has become widespread among males. In contrast, women who prefer sexual variety do not necessarily produce more children, so a preference for sexual variety is not as strongly favored by natural selection.

But there is a serious flaw in this reasoning that you may already have noticed: How could there have evolved a strong desire for sexual variety if no women ever showed an interest in such behavior? After all, making love requires two partners, so some women, at least, must also have found variety enticing! How do evolutionary psychologists respond to this objection? By suggesting that by having multiple partners, women could gain valuable resources from them (e.g., food, gifts); alternatively, by having many lovers, a woman could perfect her love-making skills, and so perhaps replace her current mate with a more desirable one (Buss, 1999).

We should add that although the evolutionary perspective on human sexual behavior is intriguing, it is only one of many approaches and is quite controversial. So it is probably best to view it as interesting "food for thought" rather than as a firm basis for answering complex questions about our sexuality.

■ Sexual Orientation

While a large majority of human beings are exclusively **heterosexual** (they engage in sexual relations only with members of the opposite sex), some are **bisexual** (they seek partners from their own as well as the other sex) and still others are exclusively **homosexual** (they seek partners only from their own sex) (Laumann et al., 1994). What factors influence or determine **sexual orientation?** In other words, why are some persons exclusively homosexual while most others are exclusively heterosexual? This is a complex question and one to which no one—psychologists included—can yet offer a complete answer. Initially, however, emphasis was on environmental factors. For example, psychodynamic theory suggested that homosexuality resulted from having an overprotective mother and a distant, ineffectual father. Other views emphasized factors ranging from being separated from members of the opposite sex during childhood (e.g., attending all-boy or all-girl schools) to sexual abuse by parents or other adults. Decades of research have failed to yield clear support for *any* of these suggestions (Breedlove, 1994). Indeed, large-scale studies of thousands of homosexuals have failed to find any consistent differences between them and heterosexuals in terms of early life experiences. There is some indication that extremely feminine behavior in young boys or extremely masculine behavior in young girls predicts later development of homosexuality (Bailey & Zucker, 1995), but aside from that, findings relating to the role of various environmental factors have been far from conclusive.

On the other hand, there is growing evidence for the role of genetic and other biological factors in homosexuality. For example, Green (1987) followed forty-four extremely feminine boys for fifteen years—from early childhood until they were young adults. Fully three-fourths later became homosexual or bisexual. In contrast, only one boy from a group of typically masculine boys became homosexual. Moreover, efforts by parents or professionals (psychologists, psychiatrists) to alter the behavior of the feminine boys made little or no difference. Such findings point to the possibility that some individuals have a biological predisposition toward homosexuality or bisexuality.

Other findings indicate that there may be subtle differences between the brains of heterosexual and homosexual individuals. For instance, the *anterior commissure,*

Heterosexual (sexual orientation)
A sexual orientation in which individuals prefer sexual relations with members of the other sex.

Bisexual
A sexual orientation in which individuals engage in sexual relations with members of both sexes.

Homosexual (sexual orientation)
A sexual orientation in which individuals prefer sexual relations with members of their own sex.

Sexual Orientation
Individuals' preference for sexual relations with their own sex, the other sex, or both.

a bundle of nerve fibers that allows communication between the two hemispheres of the brain, is larger in homosexual men than in heterosexual men or women (Allen & Gorski, 1992). Similarly, the hypothalamus is smaller in homosexual men than in heterosexual men (LeVay, 1991). Twin studies, too, point to the role of genetic and biological factors in homosexuality. If one identical twin is homosexual, there is a greater than fifty-fifty chance that the other twin, too, will be homosexual. Among fraternal twins, this figure drops to only 22 percent (Bailey & Pillard, 1991). Finally, homosexual men differ in some cognitive abilities from heterosexual men, falling in between heterosexual men and heterosexual women in their performance on tests of visual/spatial ability (Witelson, 1991).

Taking all available evidence into account, it seems reasonable to conclude that sexual orientation is not simply a matter of preference or free will; rather, it may stem, at least in part, from biological and genetic factors that are not directly under individuals' control and that operate outside their conscious awareness. How these factors exert their influence in shaping sexual preference, however, remains to be determined.

KEY QUESTIONS

- What role do hormones play in human sexual motivation?
- How does evolutionary psychology explain differences in the mating strategies of women and men?
- What factors appear to play a role in determining sexual orientation?

Achievement Motivation: The Desire to Excel

Hunger and sex—these are motives we share with many other forms of life. There are some motives, however, that appear to be unique to our own species. In this section, we'll focus on one such motive—**achievement motivation** (often termed *need for achievement*)—the desire to accomplish difficult tasks or to excel. That individuals differ greatly in the desire for achievement is obvious, but what are the effects of these differences? Let's see what psychologists have discovered about this issue. (Several methods for measuring such differences exist, but the details of them are not central to this discussion, so we won't describe them here.)

Effects of Achievement Motivation

Everyone has known people they would describe as high or low in achievement motivation, and some of the differences between these people are far from surprising. For instance, as you might expect, persons high in achievement motivation tend to get higher grades in school, earn more rapid promotions, and attain greater success in running their own businesses than persons low in such motivation (Andrews, 1967; Raynor, 1970). In fact, many studies suggest that entrepreneurs—people who start their own businesses—are higher in achievement motivation than most other people, and are also higher in this respect than managers—people who prefer to work for large, existing companies (e.g., Collins, Locke, & Hanges, 2000; Shane, 2003).

Persons high in achievement motivation differ from persons low in this motive in other respects, too. First, persons high in achievement motivation tend to prefer tasks that are moderately difficult and challenging. The reason they tend to avoid very easy tasks is obvious: Such tasks don't pose enough challenge for persons high in achievement motivation. But why do they prefer tasks that are moderately challenging to ones that are extremely difficult? Because the chance of failing on extremely difficult tasks is too high, and such persons want success above everything else (e.g., McClelland, 1985).

Another characteristic of persons high in achievement motivation is that they have a stronger-than-average desire for feedback on their performance: They want

Achievement Motivation
The desire to accomplish difficult tasks and meet standards of excellence.

to know how well they are doing so they can adjust their goals to make these challenging, but not impossible. Because of this desire for feedback, persons high in achievement motivation tend to prefer jobs in which rewards are closely related to individual performance—*merit-based pay systems.* They generally don't like working in situations in which everyone receives the same across-the-board raise, regardless of their performance (e.g., Turban & Keon, 1993).

Finally, as you might expect, persons high in achievement motivation tend to excel in performance under conditions in which their achievement motive is activated (e.g., McClelland, 1995). Situations in which they are challenged to do their best, in which they are confronted with difficult goals, or in which they compete against others are "grist for the mill" of high-achievement persons, and they generally rise to the occasion in terms of excellent performance.

KEY QUESTIONS

- What is achievement motivation?
- What are the effects of achievement motivation on behavior?

Intrinsic Motivation: How, Sometimes, to Turn Play into Work

Individuals perform many activities simply because they find them enjoyable. Hobbies, gourmet dining, lovemaking—these are a few of the actions that fit within this category. Such activities may be described as stemming from **intrinsic motivation:** We perform them because of the pleasure they yield, not because they lead to external rewards. But what happens if people are given external rewards for performing these activities—if, for example, they are paid for sipping vintage wines or for pursuing their favorite hobby? Research findings suggest that they may then actually experience reductions in intrinsic motivation. In other words, they may become *less* motivated to engage in such activities. Why? Here is one explanation: When people consider their own behavior, they conclude that they chose to perform the activities in question partly to obtain the external reward provided, not simply because they enjoyed these activities. To the extent they reach that conclusion, they may then view their own interest in these activities as lower than was previously the case. In short, when provided with an external reward for performing some activity they enjoy, they shift from viewing their own behavior as stemming from intrinsic motivation ("I do it because I enjoy it") to perceiving it as stemming from external rewards ("I do it partly because of the external rewards I receive"). (See Figure 9.9 for a summary of these suggestions.)

Many studies support this reasoning. In such research, some participants were provided with extrinsic rewards for engaging in a task they initially enjoyed, while others were not. When later given an opportunity to perform the task, those who received the external rewards showed reduced motivation to do so (Deci, 1975; Lepper & Green, 1978). These results have important implications for anyone— parents, teachers, managers—seeking to motivate others by means of rewards. If the target persons already enjoy various activities, then offering them rewards for performing these activities may lower their intrinsic motivation and so actually *reduce* rather than enhance their performance!

Fortunately, additional evidence suggests that this is not always the case, and that intrinsic and extrinsic motivation are not necessarily incompatible (Deci & Ryan, 1985; Rigby et al., 1992). If external rewards are viewed as signs of recognition rather than as bribes (Rosenfeld, Folger, & Adelman, 1980), and if the rewards provided are large and satisfying, intrinsic motivation may be enhanced rather than reduced (Lepper & Cordova, 1992; Ryan, 1982). But providing others with extrinsic rewards for performing activities they enjoy does run the risk of undermining their intrinsic motivation, so this is a fact that anyone wishing to motivate others should always keep in mind.

Intrinsic Motivation
Motivation to perform activities because they are rewarding in and of themselves.

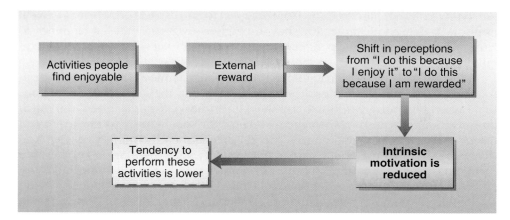

FIGURE 9.9
Intrinsic Motivation:
How it Operates
When individuals receive external rewards for performing activities they enjoy, they may conclude that they perform them at least in part to gain the external rewards. As a result, their *intrinsic motivation* to perform these activities is reduced.

K E Y   Q U E S T I O N S

- What is intrinsic motivation?
- Why is intrinsic motivation sometimes reduced when individuals receive external rewards for performing activities they enjoy?

Forgiveness: When Compassion Replaces the Desire for Revenge

Almost everyone has experienced intense desires for revenge: Another person harms us in some manner, and we conclude that retaliating against them would be appropriate. Seeking to "pay them back" seems only natural, and we often feel it may accomplish more than just make us feel better—it may produce positive outcomes as well (see Figure 9.10). But, in fact, seeking revenge often has harmful effects for everyone concerned. The persons who seek it may feel better temporarily, but their actions may start an upward spiral of retaliation, revenge, further retaliation, and so on, in which all parties are at growing risk. For these reasons, *forgiveness*—giving up the desire to punish those who have hurt us and seeking, instead, to act in kind, helpful ways toward them—may be highly beneficial. In fact, research on this topic suggests forgiveness often has more positive effects than seeking revenge (e.g., McCullough et al., 2001).

Why are some people able to forgive more readily than others? In part because of their own traits. Research findings indicate that forgiving people differ from

"They're from David. He's been so much more considerate since I shot him."

FIGURE 9.10
Revenge or Forgiveness?
Although everyone experiences the desire for revenge against others who have harmed us, research findings indicate that forgiveness is a better motive both for the person who has been harmed and for the person who caused the harm (the transgressor).
Source: © The New Yorker Collection 1996 Mike Twohy from cartoonbank.com. All Rights Reserved.

persons who find it hard to forgive with respect to two aspects of personality we'll examine in detail in Chapter 10: They are higher in *agreeableness*—a tendency to trust others and want to help them; and higher in *emotional stability*—low vulnerability to negative moods or emotions (Berry et al., in press).

What do such persons do to forgive their former enemies? They experience *empathy* toward them, sharing or at least understanding the feelings and emotions that caused the transgressors to harm them. In addition, they make generous attributions about the causes of their enemies' behavior, concluding that they had good reasons for acting as they did, even though this harmed them in some way. And they avoid ruminating about past transgressions; once these are over, they put them out of their minds and concentrate on other things (McCullough, 2001).

Overall, most psychologists have concluded that forgiveness is indeed a better strategy for happiness than maintaining anger and strong desires for revenge. In sum, there seems to be a large grain of truth in the proverb stating, "To err is human, to forgive, divine."

KEY QUESTIONS

- Why are some people able to forgive more easily than others?
- How do they forgive people who have harmed them?

EMOTIONS: THEIR NATURE, EXPRESSION, AND IMPACT

Can you imagine life without emotions—without joy, anger, sorrow, or fear? Perhaps; but what would such an existence be like—a life without any feelings? If you've seen any of the *Star Trek* movies, you know that Mr. Spock, who prided himself on being completely lacking in emotions, often suffered greatly from this deficit—thus proving, of course, that he was *not* totally devoid of human feelings! (See Figure 9.11.) So, while we can imagine a life without emotions, few of us would choose such an existence.

But what, precisely, are emotions? The closer we look, the more complex these reactions seem to be. There is general agreement among scientists who study emotions, however, that they involve three major components: (1) physiological changes within our bodies—shifts in heart rate, blood pressure, and so on; (2) subjective cognitive states—the personal experiences we label as emotions; and (3) expressive behaviors—outward signs of these internal reactions (Tangney et al., 1996; Zajonc & McIntosh, 1992).

In this discussion, we'll first look at several contrasting theories of emotion. Then we'll consider the biological basis of emotions. Third, we'll examine how emotions are expressed. Next, we'll turn to **affect**—temporary and relatively mild shifts in current mood, examining the complex interplay between affect and cognition. We'll conclude with a brief look at what psychologists have discovered about personal happiness (*subjective well-being*).

The Nature of Emotions: Some Contrasting Views

Many different theories of emotions have been proposed, but among these, three have been most influential. These are named after the scientists who proposed them: the *Cannon–Bard, James–Lange,* and *Schachter–Singer* theories.

■ The Cannon–Bard and James–Lange Theories: Which comes first—action or feeling?

Imagine that in one of your courses you are required to make a class presentation. As you walk to the front of the room, your pulse races, your mouth feels dry, and you can feel beads of perspiration on your forehead. In short, you are terrified.

FIGURE 9.11
Mr. Spock: A Person without Emotions?

Mr. Spock, science officer of the *USS Enterprise* in the *Star Trek* series, claimed to have no emotions. However, in many episodes, he seemed to suffer greatly from this lack—thus indicating that he did have emotions, after all.

Affect

Temporary and relatively mild shifts in current feelings and mood.

What is the basis for this feeling? Contrasting answers are offered by the Cannon–Bard and James–Lange theories of emotion.

Let's begin with the **Cannon–Bard theory,** because it is consistent with our own commonsense beliefs about emotions. This theory suggests that various emotion-provoking events induce *simultaneously* the subjective experiences we label as emotions and the physiological reactions that accompany them. In the situation just described, the sight of the audience and of your professor, pen poised to evaluate your performance, causes you to experience a racing heart, a dry mouth, and other signs of physiological arousal *and,* at the same time, to experience subjective feelings you label as fear. In other words, this situation stimulates various portions of your nervous system so that both arousal, mediated by your *autonomic nervous system* (discussed in Chapter 2), and subjective feelings, mediated by your cerebral cortex and other portions of the brain, are produced.

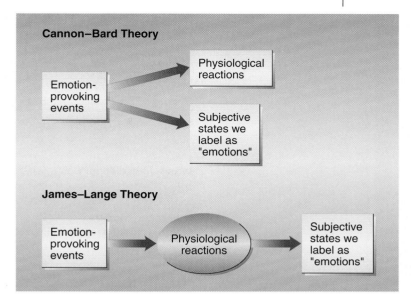

In contrast, the **James–Lange theory** offers a more surprising view of emotion. It suggests that subjective emotional experiences are actually the *result of* physiological changes within our bodies. In other words, you feel frightened when making your speech *because* you notice that your heart is racing, your mouth is dry, and so on. As James himself put it (1890, p. 966), "We feel sorry because we cry, angry because we strike, and afraid because we tremble." (See Figure 9.12 for a comparison of these two theories.)

Which of these theories is more accurate? Until recently, most evidence seemed to favor the Cannon–Bard approach: Emotion-provoking events produce both physiological arousal and the subjective experiences we label as emotions. Now, however, the pendulum of scientific opinion has moved toward greater acceptance of the James–Lange approach—the view that we experience emotions because of our awareness of physiological reactions to various stimuli or situations. Several lines of evidence point to this conclusion. First, studies conducted with modern equipment indicate that different emotions are indeed associated with different patterns of physiological activity (Levenson, 1992). Not only do various emotions *feel* different, it appears they also result in somewhat different patterns of bodily changes, including contrasting patterns of brain and muscle activity (Ekman, Davidson, & Friesen, 1990; Izard, 1991).

Second, support for the James–Lange theory is also provided by research on the **facial feedback hypothesis** (Laird, 1984). This hypothesis suggests that changes in our facial expressions sometimes produce shifts in our emotional experiences rather than merely reflecting them. In addition, other research suggests that changing our bodily postures (e.g., Flack, Laird, & Cavallaro, 1999) or even the tone of our voices (e.g, Siegman & Boyle, 1993) may influence emotional experiences. In view of such findings, the facial feedback hypothesis has been renamed the *peripheral feedback effect,* to suggest that emotions can be influenced by more than simply facial expressions. Although there are many complexities in examining this hypothesis, the results of several studies offer support for its accuracy (e.g., Ekman, Davidson, & Friesen, 1990). These findings suggest that there may be a substantial grain of truth in the James–Lange theory (Zajonc, Murphy, & Inglehart, 1989). Though subjective emotional experiences *are* often produced by specific external stimuli, as the Cannon–Bard view suggests, emotional reactions also can be generated by changes in and awareness of our own bodily states, as the James–Lange theory contends (Ekman, 1992).

FIGURE 9.12
Two Major Theories of Emotion
According to the Cannon–Bard theory, emotion-provoking stimuli simultaneously evoke physiological reactions and the subjective states we label as emotions. According to the James–Lange theory, emotion-provoking events produce physiological reactions, and it is our awareness of these changes in bodily states that we label as emotions.

Cannon–Bard Theory
A theory of emotion suggesting that various emotion-provoking events simultaneously produce subjective reactions labeled as emotions and physiological arousal.

James–Lange Theory
A theory of emotion suggesting that emotion-provoking events produce various physiological reactions and recognition of these is responsible for subjective emotional experiences.

Facial Feedback Hypothesis
A hypothesis indicating that facial expressions can produce changes in emotional states.

TABLE 9.2	Theories of Emotion: An Overview

The theories summarized here are among the ones that have received the most attention from researchers.

Theory of Emotion	Basic Assumptions
Cannon–Bard Theory	Emotion-provoking events induce, simultaneously, the subjective experiences we label as emotions and the physiological reactions that accompany them.
James–Lange Theory	Subjective emotional experiences result from physiological changes within our bodies (e.g., we feel sorry because we cry, frightened because we run away from something, etc.).
Schachter–Singer (Two-Factor) Theory	Emotion-provoking events produce increased arousal; in response to these feelings, we search the external environment to identify the causes behind them. The factors we identify then determine the label we place on our arousal and the emotion we experience.

Schachter and Singer's Two-Factor Theory

Strong emotions are a common part of daily life, but how do we tell them apart? How do we know that we are angry rather than frightened, or sad rather than surprised? One potential answer is provided by a third theory of emotion. According to this view, known as the **Schachter–Singer theory,** or sometimes as the **two-factor theory,** emotion-provoking events produce increased arousal (Schachter & Singer, 1962). In response to these feelings, we then search the external environment to identify the causes behind them. The factors we then select play a key role in determining the label we place on our arousal, and so in determining the emotion we experience. If we feel aroused after a near-miss in traffic, we will probably label our emotion as "fear" or perhaps "anger." If, instead, we feel aroused in the presence of an attractive person, we may label our arousal as "attraction" or even "love." In short, we perceive ourselves to be experiencing the emotion that external cues tell us we *should* be feeling. This contrasts with the James–Lange theory, which suggests that we focus on internal, physiological cues to determine whether we are experiencing an emotion and what this emotion is. The Schachter–Singer theory is a two-factor view because it considers both arousal and the cognitive appraisal we perform in our efforts to identify the causes of such arousal.

Many studies provide support for the Schachter–Singer theory (Reisenzein, 1983; Sinclair et al., 1994), so it does seem to provide important insights into the process through which we label our own emotions. (Please see Table 9.2 for an overview of the theories discussed in this section.)

KEY QUESTIONS

- How do the Cannon–Bard and James–Lange theories differ?
- What is the Schachter–Singer theory of emotion?

The Biological Basis of Emotions

As we noted earlier, emotions are complex reactions involving not only the intense subjective feelings we label as "joy," "anger," "sorrow," and so on, but also outward expressions of emotions and the ability (or abilities) to understand emotional information (e.g., the ability to "read" the emotional reactions of others). Research on the biological and neural bases of emotions indicates that different portions of the brain play a role in each of these components. Research concerning the neural basis of emotion is complex, so here we'll simply try to summarize a few of the key findings.

Schachter–Singer Theory (two-factor theory)
A theory of emotion suggesting that our subjective emotional states are determined, at least in part, by the cognitive labels we attach to feelings of arousal.

Two-Factor Theory (of emotion)
See Schachter–Singer Theory.

First, it appears that the right cerebral hemisphere plays an especially important role in emotional functions (e.g., Harrington, 1995). Individuals with damage to the right hemisphere have difficulty understanding the emotional tone of another person's voice or correctly describing emotional scenes (Heller, 1997; Heller, Nitschke, & Miller, 1998). Similarly, healthy persons with no damage to their brains do better at identifying others' emotions when such information is presented to their right hemisphere rather than to their left hemisphere (it is exposed to one part or the other of the visual field; see Chapter 3) (e.g., Ladavas, Umilta, & Ricci-Bitti, 1980). The right hemisphere also seems to be specialized for the expression of emotion; patients with damage to the right hemisphere are less successful at expressing emotions through the tone of their voice than are persons without such damage (Borod, 1993).

In addition, there appear to be important differences between the left and right hemispheres of the brain with respect to two key aspects of emotion: *valence*—the extent to which an emotion is pleasant or unpleasant; and *arousal*—its intensity. Activation of the left hemisphere is associated with approach, response to reward, and positive affect (i.e., feelings), while activation of the right hemisphere is associated with avoidance, withdrawal from aversive stimuli, and negative affect (Heller, Nitschke, & Miller, 1998). Further, anterior (frontal) regions of the hemispheres are associated primarily with the valence (pleasant–unpleasant) dimension, while posterior regions are associated primarily with arousal (intensity). These findings have important implications for understanding the neural basis of various psychological disorders. Consider, for instance, depression and anxiety—disorders we'll examine in detail in Chapter 12. Both involve negative feelings or emotions, but depression is usually associated with low arousal (depressed people lack energy), while anxiety is associated with high arousal (if you've ever experienced anxiety right before an exam, you know this very well!). This leads to interesting predictions: Persons suffering from depression should show reduced activity in the right posterior region, while persons suffering from anxiety should show increased activity in that brain region (see Figure 9.13). These predictions have been confirmed in several studies (e.g., Heller, Etienne, & Miller, 1995). Insight

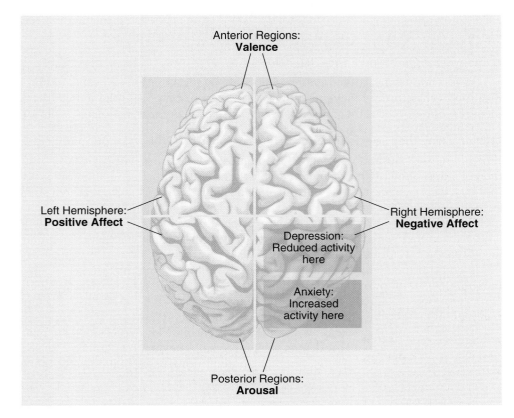

Anterior Regions:
Valence

Left Hemisphere:
Positive Affect

Right Hemisphere:
Negative Affect

Depression:
Reduced activity
here

Anxiety:
Increased
activity here

Posterior Regions:
Arousal

FIGURE 9.13
Role of the Cerebral Hemispheres in Emotion—and in Psychological Disorders
Growing evidence indicates that activation of the *left cerebral hemisphere* is associated with positive emotions, while activation of the *right hemisphere* is associated with negative emotions. Further, activation of anterior (frontal) portions of both hemispheres is associated with the valence (pleasantness–unpleasantness) of emotions, while activation of the posterior (rear) portions of the hemispheres is associated with arousal—the intensity of emotions. Together, these findings suggest that depressed persons should show reduced activity in the right posterior regions, while anxious persons should show increased activity in these regions. These results have been confirmed in recent studies.

FIGURE 9.14
Nonverbal Cues: External Guides to Internal Reactions
People often reveal their emotions through *nonverbal cues*—facial expressions, body movements or postures, and other observable actions.

into the neural mechanisms that underlie such disorders can be an important first step toward developing effective treatments for them, so our growing knowledge of the neural bases of emotions has important practical as well as scientific implications.

Additional research indicates that structures deep within the brain, also play an important role in emotions. In particular, the *amygdala* (see Chapter 2) has been found to become active when individuals are experiencing negative emotions (e.g., Aggleton & Young, 2000). However, recent findings using PET scans (see Chapter 2) indicate that the left amygdala may also be activated by positive stimuli and the positive emotions they induce (Hamann et al., 2002). Overall, it seems as though the amygdala may play a role in memories for emotion-producing stimuli or experiences (Gallagher, 2000). So, it participates both in the occurrence of emotional arousal and in subsequent memory for the stimuli that elicited it. Stay tuned for further developments, because modern research tools that permit psychologists to view activity in the brain while individuals perform various tasks are moving us rapidly toward a greater understanding of the biological bases of emotion.

KEY QUESTIONS

• What roles do the left and right cerebral hemispheres play in emotions?
• What is the role of the amygdala in emotions?

The External Expression of Emotion: Outward Signs of Inner Feelings

Emotions are a private affair. No one, no matter how intimate with us they are, can truly share our subjective inner experiences. Yet, we are able to recognize the presence of various emotions in others, and we are able to communicate our own feelings to them as well. How does such communication occur? A large part of the answer involves **nonverbal cues**—outward signs of others' internal emotional states shown in their facial expressions, body postures, and other behaviors (see Figure 9.14).

Nonverbal Cues: The Basic Channels

Several decades of research on nonverbal cues suggests that this kind of communication occurs through several different *channels* or paths simultaneously. The most revealing of these involve *facial expressions* and *body movements and posture*.

Unmasking the Face: Facial Expressions as Clues to Others' Emotions

More than two thousand years ago, the Roman orator Cicero stated, "The face is the image of the soul." By this he meant that feelings and emotions are often reflected in the face and can be read there from specific expressions. Modern research suggests that Cicero was correct: It *is* possible to learn much about others' current moods and feelings from their facial expressions. In fact, it appears that six different basic emotions are represented clearly, and from an early age, on the human face: anger, fear, sadness, disgust, happiness, and surprise (Ekman, 1992). In addition, some findings suggest that two other emotions—contempt (Rosenberg & Ekman, 1995) and pride (Tracy & Robins, 2004)—may also be quite basic. However, agreement on what specific facial expression represents this emotion is less consistent than that for the other six emotions just mentioned.

Until recently, it was widely assumed that basic facial expressions such as those for happiness, anger, or disgust are universal: They are recognized by people all over the world as indicating specific emotions (e.g., Ekman & Friesen,

Nonverbal Cues
Outward signs of others' emotional states. Such cues involve facial expressions, eye contact, and body language.

1975). More recent findings, however, have called this assumption into question (e.g., Russell, 1994). The findings of several studies indicate that while facial expressions may indeed reveal much about others' emotions, such judgments are also affected by the context in which such expressions occur and various situational cues. For instance, if individuals are shown a photo of a face showing what would normally be judged as fear, but are also read a story suggesting that this person is actually showing anger, many describe the face as showing *this* emotion—not fear (Carroll & Russell, 1996). Findings such as these suggest that facial expressions may not be as universal in terms of providing clear signals about underlying emotions as was previously assumed. However, these findings are somewhat controversial, so at present it would be unwise to reach firm conclusions about this issue.

Gestures, Posture, and Movements

Try this simple demonstration: First, remember some incident that made you angry—the angrier the better. Think about it for a minute. Now try to remember another incident—one that made you feel happy—the happier the better. Did you change your posture or move your hands, arms, or legs as your thoughts shifted from the first incident to the second? The chances are good that you did, for our current mood or emotion is often reflected in the posture, position, and movement of our bodies. Together, such nonverbal behaviors are sometimes termed **body language,** and they can provide several kinds of information about others' emotions.

First, frequent body movements, especially ones in which a particular part of the body does something to another part, such as touching, scratching, or rubbing, suggest emotional arousal. The greater the frequency of such behavior, the higher a person's level of arousal or nervousness seems to be (Harrigan et al., 1991). Larger patterns of movements involving the whole body can also be informative. Such phrases as "she adopted a *threatening posture*" and "he greeted her with *open arms*" suggest that different body postures can be suggestive of contrasting emotional reactions (Aronoff, Woike, & Hyman, 1992).

Finally, more specific information about others' feelings are often provided by **gestures**—body movements carrying specific meanings in a given culture. In the United States, for example, shrugging one's shoulders means "I don't know." Similarly, a thumb pointing upwards means "Good" or "OK." Gestures often only have meaning in a given culture, so it is wise to be careful about using them while traveling in cultures different from your own: You may offend the people around you without intending to do so! (We'll return to nonverbal cues in Chapter 13 in our discussion of social thought, because the information nonverbal cues provide is often very valuable in the context of our efforts to understand others.)

K E Y   Q U E S T I O N S

- What emotions are shown by clear facial expressions? What do research findings indicate about the universality of such expressions?
- What information about others' emotions is conveyed by body language?

Emotion and Cognition: How Feelings Shape Thought and Thought Shapes Feelings

Earlier, we asked you to recall incidents that made you feel angry and happy. When you thought about these events, did your mood also change? The chances are good that it did. In many instances, our thoughts seem to exert strong effects on our emotions. This relationship works in the other direction as well. Being in a happy mood often causes us to think happy thoughts, while feeling sad tends to bring negative memories and images to mind. In short, there are important links between *emotion*

Body Language
Nonverbal cues involving body posture or movement of body parts.

Gestures
Movements of various body parts that convey a specific meaning to others.

and *cognition*—between the way we feel and the way we think. Let's take a brief look at some of the evidence for such links (e.g., Forgas, 1995a; Forgas & Fiedler, 1996).

We should clarify one important point before proceeding: Throughout this discussion, we'll focus on *affect*—relatively mild feelings and moods rather—than on intense emotions. The boundary between affective reactions and emotions is somewhat fuzzy, but because most research has focused on the effects of relatively modest shifts in mood—the kind of changes we experience many times each day as a result of ordinary experiences—these will be the focus here.

How Affect Influences Cognition

The findings of many studies indicate that our current moods can strongly influence several aspects of cognition. We have already examined the influence of affect on memory in Chapter 6 (mood-dependent memory), so, here, we'll focus on other ways in which moods or feelings influence cognition. One such effect involves the impact of our current moods or *affective states*, as they are often termed, on our perception of ambiguous stimuli. In general, we perceive and evaluate these stimuli more favorably when we are in a good mood than when we are in a negative one (Isen & Baron, 1991; Isen, 1991). For example, when asked to interview applicants whose qualifications for a job are ambiguous—neither very strong nor very weak— research participants assign higher ratings to applicants when they (the interviewers) are in a positive mood than when they are in a negative mood (e.g., Baron, 1987, 1993).

Another way in which affect influences cognition is through its impact on the style of information processing we adopt. A growing body of research findings indicates that a positive affect encourages us to adopt a flexible, fluid style of thinking, while negative affect leads us to engage in more systematic and careful processing (e.g., Stroessner & Mackie, 1992). Why? Perhaps because we interpret negative affect as a kind of danger signal, indicating that the current situation requires our full attention (e.g., Edwards & Bryan, 1997).

Our current moods also influence another important aspect of cognition— creativity. The results of several studies suggest that being in a happy mood can increase creativity—perhaps because being in a happy mood activates a wider range of ideas or associations than being in a negative mood, and creativity consists, in part, of combining such associations into new patterns (e.g., Estrada, Isen, & Young, 1995).

Sometimes, we do not even have to experience affective states for them to influence our thinking. Recent findings indicate that when making decisions, we often anticipate the emotions we might experience as a result of the outcomes the various choices will produce. We then tend to choose the decision that will maximize our future anticipated positive reactions (e.g., pleasure; Mellers, 2000). The results of many recent studies are consistent with this view, so it seems to provide an important insight into how our feelings—even anticipated ones—can shape our judgments and decisions (Mellers & McGraw, 2001).

Finally, we should mention recent research indicating that positive emotions or affective states can trigger upward spirals toward emotional well-being and happiness. Why? Because when individuals feel happy, they tend to adopt what is known as *broad-minded coping*—strategies for dealing with life's problems that are highly adaptive. Such strategies include trying to think of different ways to deal with the problem, taking a step back from the situation to be more objective, and so on. Recent studies (e.g., Fredrickson & Joiner, 2002) indicate that when individuals feel happy, they tend to deal with their problems in these adaptive ways, and this, in turn, makes them happier. The result? An upward spiral toward increasing happiness and adjustment (see Figure 9.15). In other words, experiencing positive emotions and feelings is more than just a "temporary fix" for life's troubles: It may also help us to deal with them more effectively.

How Cognition Influences Affect

Most research on the relationship between affect and cognition has focused on how feelings influence thought. However, there is also compelling evidence for the reverse—the impact of cognition on affect. We have already mentioned one aspect of this relationship in our earlier discussion of the two-factor theory of emotion proposed by Schachter and Singer (1962). As you may recall, their theory suggests that often we don't know our own feelings or attitudes directly. Rather, because these internal reactions are often somewhat ambiguous, we look outward—at our own behavior or other aspects of the external world—for clues about our feelings' essential nature. In such cases, the feelings we experience are strongly determined by the interpretation or cognitive labels we select.

A second way in which cognition can affect emotions is through the activation of schemas containing a strong affective component. For example, if we label an individual as belonging to some group, the schema for this social category may suggest what traits he or she probably possesses. In addition, it may also tell us how we feel about such persons. Thus, activation of a strong racial, ethnic, or religious schema or stereotype may exert powerful effects upon our current feelings or moods.

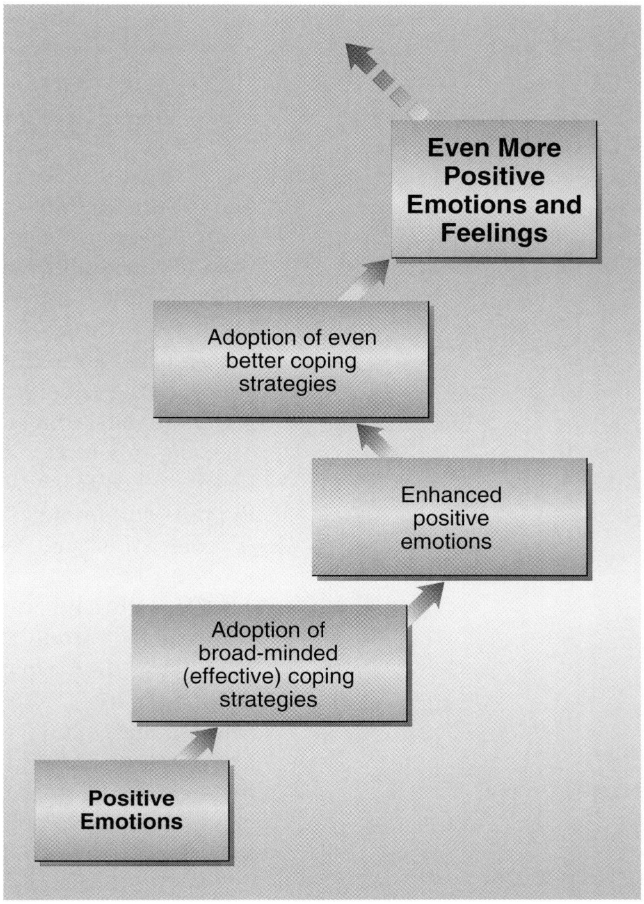

Third, our thoughts can often influence our reactions to emotion-provoking events. In other words, we use cognitive mechanisms to regulate our emotions or affective states. In general, we use two different tactics: *reappraisal*—cognitive reevaluation of a potentially emotion-eliciting situation in order to regulate (e.g., decrease) its emotional impact; or *suppression*—a form of response modulation in which we actively inhibit ongoing, emotion-expressive behavior. In other words, reappraisal occurs early, before we are experiencing affect or emotion, while suppression occurs later. Both can be useful means for regulating our emotions or feelings, but because it occurs earlier, reappraisal may sometimes be more effective. Reappraisal decreases the experience of emotion, reduces behavioral expressions of emotion, and may also reduce physiological reactions to emotion-provoking events. In contrast, suppression occurs later, so it does not change the emotional experience and may actually increase physiological reactions (because of the effort being expended to suppress the emotion). But it *will* strongly suppress outward expressions of emotion. These predictions have been confirmed in recent studies (e.g., Gross, 2001).

In sum, as our everyday experience suggests, there are many links between affect and cognition. The way we feel—our current moods—influence the way we think, and our thoughts, in turn, often shape our moods and emotions.

FIGURE 9.15
**Positive Emotions:
An Important Step on
the Road to Happiness**
Recent evidence suggests that when people experience positive emotions, they adopt more effective techniques for dealing with the problems they face. This, in turn, causes them to experience more positive feelings and emotions. The result? An upward spiral toward emotional well-being and personal happiness.

Source: Based on suggestions by Fredrickson & Joiner, 2002.

KEY QUESTIONS

- In what ways do our affective states influence cognition?
- In what ways does cognition influence our affective states?

SUBJECTIVE WELL-BEING: CAUSES AND EFFECTS OF PERSONAL HAPPINESS

Suppose you were asked the following questions: "How happy are you?" and "How satisfied are you with your life?" In both cases, your answers could range from 1 (very unhappy; very unsatisfied) to 7 (very happy; very satisfied). How would you reply? If you are like most people, you would probably indicate that you are quite happy and quite satisfied with your life. In fact, recent studies (e.g., Diener & Lucas, 2003; Diener & Diener, 1996; Seligman & Csikszentmihalyi, 2000) suggest that something like 80 percent of all people who answer these questions report being satisfied. In other words, they report relatively high levels of what psychologists term **subjective well-being**—individuals' global judgments of their own life satisfaction (Diener, Suh, Lucas, & Smith, 1999). Moreover, this seems to be true all over the world, across all age groups, at all income levels above grinding poverty, among relatively unattractive persons as well as among attractive ones (Diener, Wolsic, & Fujita, 1995), and in all racial and ethnic groups (e.g., Myers & Diener, 1995).

Does this mean that everyone is happy, no matter what their life circumstances? Not at all; a number of factors have been found to influence subjective well-being. But overall, most people report being relatively happy and satisfied with their lives. Why? We don't know for certain, but it appears that overall, human beings have a strong tendency to look on the bright side of things—to be optimistic and upbeat in a wide range of situations (e.g., Diener & Suh, 1998). For instance, as we'll see in Chapter 13, they often show a strong *optimistic bias*—a powerful tendency to believe that they can accomplish more in a given period of time than they really can (Baron, 1998).

Given that most people report being happy, what factors influence just how happy they are? Studies that have compared very happy people (the top 10 percent on many measures of personal happiness) with average people and unhappy people (the bottom 10 percent on many measures; Diener & Seligman, 2002) point to the following conclusions. First, no one factor is responsible for being very happy or unhappy; rather, several variables play a role. Second, good social relations with other people—close friends, family, romantic partners—appear to be necessary for being very happy: Virtually every person who was very happy enjoyed such relations. Third, very happy people were higher in terms of being extroverted and agreeable, but lower in neuroticism (i.e., they were higher in emotional stability). And very happy people were lower with respect to several signs of mental disturbance (e.g., depression, family conflict, hypochondriasis—the tendency to imagine illnesses they don't have). Finally, and perhaps most surprising, very happy people did *not* differ from average or very unhappy people with respect to perceptions of how much money they had compared to others, their own physical attractiveness, their use of tobacco and alcohol, and the amount of time they spent sleeping, exercising, or participating in religious activities. In other words, much of the time, they did the same kind of things as people who were much less happy than they were. So, what made them happy? A combination of the factors that, together, gave them this priceless gift (see Figure 9.16).

Additional findings (Diener et al., 1999) suggest that personal happiness may be influenced by other factors, too. One of these involves having goals and the resources—personal, economic, and otherwise—necessary to reach them. Many studies indicate that people who have concrete goals, especially goals that they

Subjective Well-Being
Individuals' global judgments of their own life satisfaction.

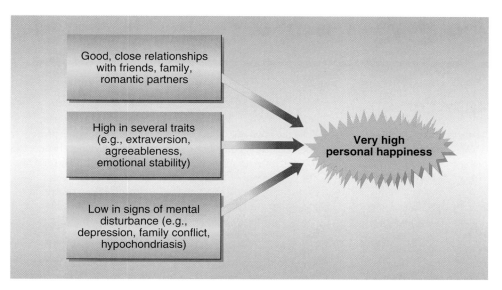

FIGURE 9.16
Very Happy People: How They Differ from Others
As shown here, many factors contribute to the happiness enjoyed by very happy people.
Source: Based on findings reported by Diener & Seligman, 2002.

have a realistic chance of reaching, and who feel (realistically or otherwise) that they are making progress toward these, are happier than persons lacking in such goals (Cantor & Sanderson, 1999).

External conditions over which individuals have varying degrees of influence also play a role in happiness. Not surprisingly, people living in wealthy countries are happier than those in poor nations—but these differences are not nearly as large as you might guess. In general, married people tend to be happier than single people, although this varies with how their particular culture views marriage (Diener et al., 1998), and people who are satisfied with their jobs and careers tend to be happier than those who are not (e.g., Weiss & Cropanzano, 1996). Surprisingly, though, other factors we might expect to be related to personal happiness do *not* seem to affect it. For instance, wealthy people are not significantly happier than those who are less wealthy (e.g., Clark & Oswald, 1994), and personal happiness does not decline with age. Finally, there appear to be no substantial sex differences in terms of personal happiness (e.g., White, 1992).

In sum, although a number of factors influence personal happiness, most people report relatively high levels of subjective well-being and are quite satisfied with their lives. How can *you* become an even happier person? For some suggestions, please see the following **Psychology Lends a Hand** section.

KEY QUESTIONS

- Where do most people stand with respect to personal happiness?
- What are key differences between people who are very happy and people who are unhappy?

psychology lends a hand

Becoming a Very Happy Person

Almost everyone wants to be happy—of that there can be no doubt. And although different people define *happiness* in contrasting ways, most would agree that being happy involves such things as experiencing positive emotions much of the time; having good relations with friends, family, and romantic partners; having a successful, rewarding job or career; and having hobbies and interests that one can enjoy in leisure time. But describing these goals is a lot easier than reaching them. Are there steps you can take to increase the chances that you will get there—that *you* will be a very happy person? Drawing on research on personal happiness and in the new field of positive psychology, we can offer the following suggestions:

- **Start the upward spiral going.** Experiencing positive emotions appears to be one way of "getting the ball rolling," so to speak. Positive emotions help one adopt effective ways of coping with life's unavoidable problems, and this, in turn, can generate even more positive emotions. So the hardest step, as in many tasks, may be the first: Once you begin experiencing positive feelings, it may quickly become easier to experience more of them.

- **Build close personal relationships.** Although no single factor can grant you personal happiness, it is clear that one of the most important ingredients in being happy is having good, mutually supportive relations with friends, family members, and romantic partners. Developing and maintaining good relationships requires a lot of hard work, but the rewards appear to make this effort well worthwhile. In fact, this may be the single most important thing you can do to increase your own happiness. So start thinking more about the people who are important to you and how you can make *them* happy. The result may be a major boost to your own life satisfaction.

- **Build personal skills that contribute to being happy.** Very happy people possess a number of personal characteristics that contribute to their happiness. If you already possess them, great; if not, you can work hard at building them. These characteristics include being friendly and outgoing (extroverted), agreeable (i.e., approaching others with the belief that you will like and trust them), and emotionally stable. So, figure out where you stand on these dimensions, and then begin working on them—preferably with the help of close friends.

- **Get into shape!** Both of us (the authors) have been runners for many years, and we continue to exercise regularly. Sure, this is good for our personal health, but even more important, every time we do it, it makes us feel good! It's not simply "runner's high"—you can get such effects even from relatively short workouts. The principle is simple: When your body is working well, it produces substances that tend to put you in a good mood. The result? A boost to your happiness. So by all means, get in shape: Your moods as well as your emotions are likely to improve.

- **Stop doing counterproductive things.** Because everyone wants to be happy, we all take many steps to enhance our positive emotions. Some of these—like the ones listed in this feature—are helpful. Others (e.g., abusing drugs, worrying about anything and everything, trying to be perfect, setting impossible goals for yourself, etc.) are not. They may work temporarily (see Chapter 11 for more discussion), but in the long run, they will *not* contribute to your personal happiness. So start *now* to eliminate them from your life.

   Good luck! And may you soon become one of those fortunate very happy people!

SUMMARY AND REVIEW OF KEY QUESTIONS

Motivation: The Activation and Persistence of Behavior

- **According to drive theory, what is the basis for various motives?**
  Drive theory suggests that motivation is a process in which various biological needs push (drive) us to actions designed to satisfy them.

- **According to expectancy theory, why do people engage in tasks requiring effort?**
  Expectancy theory suggests that people exert effort on tasks because they believe doing so will yield results they want to attain.

- **Under what conditions will goal setting increase motivation and performance?**

Goal setting will increase motivation and performance when the goals are specific and challenging yet attainable, and when individuals are committed to them and receive feedback on their progress.

- **What are the basic ideas behind Maslow's need hierarchy theory?**
  Maslow's theory suggests that needs exist in a hierarchy and that higher-level needs cannot be activated until lower-level ones are satisfied.

- **What factors play a role in the regulation of eating?**
  Eating is regulated by complex biochemical systems within the body involving detector cells in the hypothalamus and elsewhere, and is also affected by the sight of food, feedback from chewing and swallowing, cognitive factors (e.g., memories about when we ate last), and cultural factors.

- **What factors override this system, so that many people do not maintain a stable weight?**
  Many factors tend to override this system, including the impact of learning, responses to food-related cues, genetic factors (a predisposition to gain weight), the growing size of food portions, and reduced sensitivity to leptin once we gain significant amounts of weight.

- **What role do hormones play in human sexual motivation?**
  Recent findings indicate that sex hormones play some role in human sexual behavior, but this role is smaller and more subtle than is true for many other species.

- **How does evolutionary psychology explain differences in the mating strategies of women and men?**
  Evolutionary psychology suggests that men can have more offspring by having many sexual partners and make little investment in each, while women cannot increase their offspring by having many sexual partners, and make a major investment in each child. As a result, men show a stronger preference for many different partners.

- **What factors appear to play a role in determining sexual orientation?**
  The weight of available evidence suggests that genetic and biological factors play a key role in determining sexual orientation.

- **What is achievement motivation?**
  Achievement motivation is the desire to meet standards of excellence or outperform others.

- **What are the effects of achievement motivation on behavior?**
  Individuals high in achievement motivation tend to excel in school and in running their own businesses. They do especially well in situations that activate their high need for achievement.

- **What is intrinsic motivation?**
  Motivation to perform some activity simply because it is enjoyable.

- **Why is intrinsic motivation sometimes reduced when individuals receive external rewards for performing activities they enjoy?**
  When individuals receive rewards for performing activities they enjoy, they conclude that they perform these activities not solely because they like them, but also because of the external rewards they receive.

- **Why are some people able to forgive more easily than others?**
  Because they possess certain traits that assist them in forgiving others (e.g., they are high in agreeableness and in emotional stability).

- **How do they forgive people who have harmed them?**
  They forgive by experiencing empathy toward persons who harmed them and by making generous attributions about the causes of their harmful actions.

Emotions: Their Nature, Expression, and Impact

- **How do the Cannon–Bard and James–Lange theories differ?**
  The Cannon–Bard theory suggests that emotion-provoking stimuli simultaneously elicit physiological arousal and the subjective cognitive states we label as emotions. The James–Lange theory suggests that emotion-provoking stimuli induce physiological reactions and that these form the basis for the subjective cognitive states we label as emotions.

- **What is the Schachter–Singer theory of emotion?**
  The Schachter–Singer theory suggests that when we are aroused by emotion-provoking stimuli, we search the external environment for the causes of our feelings of arousal. The causes we select then determine our emotions.

- **What roles do the left and right cerebral hemispheres play in emotions?**
  Activation of the left hemisphere plays a role in positive emotions; activation of the right hemisphere plays a role in negative emotions. Anterior regions of the hemispheres are associated primarily with the valence (pleasantness or unpleasantness of emotions), while posterior regions are associated primarily with arousal (intensity).

- **What is the role of the amygdala in emotions?**
  The amygdala seems to contain neural mechanisms specialized in interpreting emotional information relating to threat or danger, such as signs of fear or anger on the part of others.

- **What emotions are shown by clear facial expressions? What do research findings indicate about the universality of such expressions?**
  Research findings indicate that clear facial expressions exist for anger, fear, sadness, disgust, happiness, and surprise. Recent findings indicate that such expressions, while informative, may not be as universal in meaning as was previously assumed.

- **What information about others' emotions is conveyed by body language?**
  Body language provides information about others' overall level of arousal, about their reactions to us, and about specific reactions they may be having.

- **In what ways do our affective states influence cognition?**
  Affective states can influence our perception of ambiguous stimuli, our memory, decisions and judgments we make, the style of information processing we adopt, and our creativity.

- **In what ways does cognition influence our affective states?**
  Cognition can influence the labels we place on emotional states and can activate schemas containing strong affective components. In addition, cognitive processes such as reappraisal and suppression allow us to regulate our emotional reactions.

Subjective Well-Being: Some Thoughts on Personal Happiness

- **Where do most people stand with respect to personal happiness?**
  Most people are relatively high in personal happiness, perhaps because of a strong human tendency toward optimism.

- **What are key differences between people who are very happy and people who are unhappy?**

Very happy people have closer relationships with friends, family members, and romantic partners; are higher on several personal traits (e.g., extroversion, agreeableness, emotional stability); and are lower in signs of mental disturbance.

PSYCHOLOGY: UNDERSTANDING ITS FINDINGS

How Feelings Affect Our Judgment: A Personal Demonstration

Just how strong are the effects of our feelings (affective states) on our judgments? Very! Try this simple exercise to see for yourself.

1. Look through your photos and choose several that show people some of your friends have never met. Try to choose ones who are average-looking in appearance.
2. Now ask several of your friends to rate the attractiveness of the persons shown in the photos on a scale ranging from 1 to 5 (1 = very unattractive; 2 = unattractive; 3 = average; 4 = attractive; 5 = very attractive).
3. Before you ask them to do the ratings, *you* have a task: Rate your friends' current moods: 1 = very negative; 2 = negative; 3 = neutral; 4 = good; 5 = very good.

4. After you have had several friends evaluate the photos, compare your ratings of their moods with the ratings they provided.
5. There is a very good chance you will find that the better your friends' moods, the higher they rated the people in the photos. Why? Because their moods biased their judgment—tilted them in the same direction as their current mood. This is a powerful demonstration of just how strong—and subtle—such effects can be. If you ask your friends, they will probably deny that their current moods had any bearing on their ratings!

MAKING PSYCHOLOGY PART OF YOUR LIFE

Practice in Forgiveness

Do you want to be happy? Then one skill you should practice is forgiveness—letting go of your anger and desire for revenge toward others who have harmed you in some way. Forgiving them is not only good for them, but also good for you! Start your practice with this exercise:

1. Remember some incident in your life when another person hurt you badly.
2. Now, rate how angry you felt toward this person at the time, and how much you wanted revenge against him. (Use 5-point scales: 1 = not angry at all; 2 = a little angry; 3 = neutral; 4 = angry; 5 = very angry. Use the same numbers for rating your desire for revenge.)
3. Next, try to feel *empathy* for this person. Try to experience what he did when he harmed you—his feelings and emotions at the time.
4. After doing that for a while, try to understand *why* he did what he did to you. And here is the hard part: Try to in-

terpret the cause of his behavior in a kind manner. Truly, we don't always know why other people what they do, so perhaps you jumped to the wrong conclusion; perhaps this person didn't mean to harm you, or didn't realize how much he was harming you? Keep trying to come up with kind interpretations of his behavior until you find one that fits.

5. Finally, consider how often you thought about this past harm—ruminated about it. Did this make you happy or unhappy? In all likelihood, ruminating about this incident made you unhappy. So now, think of ways you can *stop* thinking about it—distract yourself, think about happier experiences, and so on.
6. To the extent you can make these steps work, you are on the way to developing your ability to forgive others, and that is also an important step on the road to personal happiness.

KEY TERMS

10

Personality: Uniqueness and Consistency in the Behavior of Individuals

W*hen my daughter (Jessica Baron DeGraff) was born, she was very small—too small to come home from the hospital for several days. But when she did, she seemed to want to make up for lost time; in fact, one day just a few weeks after she was born, I went into her room and discovered—to my amazement—that she had turned over all by herself during the night. When I told this to the obstetrician taking care of her, he laughed and said it was impossible. But to this day, I'm not so sure, because Jessica was—and still is—extremely energetic. I am considered to be high-energy by most people who know me, but there were many occasions on which she literally wore me out. And even today, when she is in her thirties, she seems to have limitless energy. Will it ever change? Perhaps; but even if she does run out of steam some day, her life-long liveliness is a perfect illustration of one of psychology's grand themes: stability over time and across situations. In this chapter, we'll examine one aspect of such stability—the topic of personality, which psychologists define as an individual's unique and relatively stable* *pattern of behavior, thoughts, and emotions (e.g., Nelson & Miller, 1995;*

Zuckerman, 1995; Friedman & Schustack, 1999).

Just how stable *is* **personality**? Although there was once considerable controversy over this issue, growing evidence suggests that personality is quite stable. In fact, people generally show a considerable degree of consistency in their behavior across situations and over time (e.g., Heatherton & Weinberger, 1994; Steel & Rentsch, 1997). In fact, one recent review of available evidence (Roberts & DelVecchio, 2000) found that several aspects of personality—ones we'll consider later in this chapter—are quite stable over decades. In fact, basic aspects of personality observed in children as young as three years old are significant predictors of important aspects of their behavior as adults—for instance, their interpersonal relationships, mental health, and even career success (e.g., Caspi, 2000).

But just as people differ in countless ways, they also differ with respect to such stability: Some show less change in their traits over time and across situations than others (e.g., Roberts & DelVecchio, 2000); in other words, the tendency to remain stable or change may itself be one interesting aspect of personality! Moreover, people are more likely to change with respect to some traits than others—for instance, with respect to their emotions and feelings than with respect to basic dimensions of personality (Vaidya et al., 2002).

But even if personality is quite stable over time, how important is it in shaping our behavior? Again, there is no single answer. In some situations—ones that permit us to behave much as we wish—the preferences and tendencies that make up our personalities can readily find expression in our overt behaviors. In such situations, personality can be an important determinant of our actions. But other situations do *not* permit us to behave as we wish; rather, we must obey rules and do what is expected of us. In such contexts, personality is a much weaker determinant of our behaviors. In other words, in many situations, our behaviors are a joint function of *both* our personalities and the situation itself, which may limit or restrain our actions in various ways, so that they cannot be consistent with our preferences—and our personalities. Perhaps a concrete example will be helpful.

FIGURE 10.1
The Interactionist Perspective: Behavior as Function of Personality and Situational Factors
Even drivers with a short temper usually manage to act politely when stopped by a state trooper. In situations like this, situational factors exert a stronger impact on behavior than personality.

Personality
Individuals' unique and relatively stable patterns of behavior, thoughts, and feelings.

Consider an individual who has a very bad temper; she gets angry easily and usually tells people exactly what she thinks of them. This is a very stable aspect of her behavior. But now imagine that one day, she is stopped for speeding by a state trooper. Will she blow up and shout at the trooper for wasting her time? Perhaps; but there are strong pressures in this situation toward being polite and holding her temper in check. What will she do? While we can't predict for certain, the chances are good that she will *not* show irritable behavior!

In short, our behavior in any given situation is usually a complex function of both our personality (the stable internal factors that make us unique individuals) *and* situational factors in the world around us. This interactionist perspective is the one currently accepted by most psychologists, so please keep it in mind as you read further in this chapter (see Figure 10.1; Vansteelandt & Van Mechelan, 1999).

Now that we've clarified the basic nature of personality, we'll provide an overview of what psychologists have learned about personality. We'll begin by describing several major *theories of personality*—sweeping frameworks for understanding personality offered by some of the true "giants" in the history of psychology. These theories represent different perspectives on personality—contrasting views about the origins and nature of human uniqueness. As you'll see, they differ greatly, but each offers insights that have added to our understanding of personality; that's why they are covered here. For each theory, we'll first describe it, then present some research evidence relating to it, and finally, offer an evaluation of its current status.

After examining these famous theories, we'll turn to another basic question: How is personality measured? Finally, to provide you with a sense of what modern research on psychology is like, we'll examine a sample of recent and highly thought provoking studies on various aspects of personality.

KEY QUESTIONS

- What is personality?
- How stable is it over time?
- What is the interactionist perspective currently adopted by most psychologists?

THE PSYCHOANALYTIC APPROACH: MESSAGES FROM THE UNCONSCIOUS

Quick: Before you took this course, who would you have named as the most famous psychologist in history? If you are like most students I have known, your answer would probably be *Freud.* He is, by far, the most famous figure in the history of psychology, even though he was a medical doctor. Why is this so? The answer lies in several provocative and influential theories he proposed—theories that focus on personality and the origins of psychological disorders. Before turning to his theories, let's consider Freud as an individual—*his* personality, if you will (see Figure 10.2).

Freud's Theory of Personality

Freud was born in what is now part of the Czech Republic, but when he was four years old, his family moved to Vienna and he spent almost his entire life in that city. As a young man, Freud was highly ambitious and decided to make a name for himself as a medical researcher. He became discouraged with his prospects in this respect, however, and soon after receiving his medical degree, entered private practice. It was during this period that he formulated his theories of human personality and psychological disorders.

A turning point in his early career came when he won a research grant to travel to Paris to observe the work of Jean-Martin Charcot, who was then using hypnosis to treat several types of mental disorders. When Freud returned to Vienna, he worked with Joseph Breuer, a colleague who was using hypnosis in the treatment of *hysteria*—a condition in which individuals experienced physical symptoms such as blindness, deafness, or paralysis of arms or legs for which there seemed to be no underlying physical cause. Out of these experiences and his growing clinical practice, Freud gradually developed his theories of personality and mental illness. His ideas were complex and touched on many issues. With respect to personality, however, four topics are most central: *levels of consciousness, the structure of personality, anxiety and defense mechanisms,* and *psychosexual stages of development.*

Levels of Consciousness: Beneath the Iceberg's Tip

Freud viewed himself as a scientist, and he was well aware of research on sensory thresholds (see Chapter 3). In fact, he believed that his psychological theories were just a temporary measure that would ultimately be replaced by knowledge of the underlying biological and neural processes (Zuckerman, 1995). In any case, he applied to the task of understanding the human mind ideas about sensory thresholds and the possibility of responding to stimuli we can't report perceiving. He soon

FIGURE 10.2
Freud: The Source of Many Insights into the Nature of Personality
Although he was a physician, not a psychologist, Freud's views about personality have had a strong and lasting impact on the study of personality.

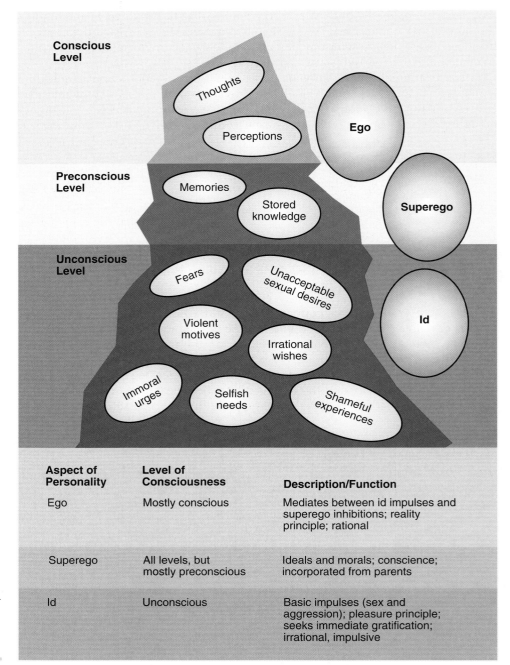

FIGURE 10.3
Freud's Views about Levels of Consciousness and the Structure of Personality
Freud believed that the human mind has three distinct levels: the conscious, the preconscious, and the unconscious. He also believed that personality involves three basic structures: the id, the ego, and the superego, which correspond, very roughly, to desire, reason, and conscience.

Aspect of Personality	Level of Consciousness	Description/Function
Ego	Mostly conscious	Mediates between id impulses and superego inhibitions; reality principle; rational
Superego	All levels, but mostly preconscious	Ideals and morals; conscience; incorporated from parents
Id	Unconscious	Basic impulses (sex and aggression); pleasure principle; seeks immediate gratification; irrational, impulsive

reached the startling conclusion that most of the mind lies below the surface—below the threshold of conscious experience. Above this boundary is the realm of the *conscious.* This includes our current thoughts: whatever we are thinking about or experiencing at a given moment. Beneath this conscious realm is the much larger *preconscious.* This contains memories that are not part of current thought but can readily be brought to mind if the need arises. Finally, beneath the preconscious, and forming the bulk of the human mind, is the *unconscious:* thoughts, desires, and impulses of which we remain largely unaware (see Figure 10.3). Although some of this material has always been unconscious, Freud believed that much of it was once conscious but has been actively *repressed*—driven from consciousness because it was too anxiety-provoking. For example, Freud contended that shameful experiences or unacceptable sexual or aggressive urges are often driven deep within the unconscious. The fact that we are not aware of them, however, in no way prevents them from affecting our behavior. Indeed, Freud believed that many of the symptoms experienced by his patients were disguised and indirect reflections of repressed thoughts and desires. This is why one major goal of **psychoanalysis**—the method of treating psychological disorders devised by Freud—is to bring repressed material back into consciousness. Presumably, once it is made conscious and patients gain insight into the early life experiences that caused them to repress it in the first place, important causes of mental illness are removed.

As we noted in Chapter 4, Freud believed that one way of probing the unconscious was through the *interpretation of dreams*. In dreams, Freud believed, we can give expression to impulses and desires we find unacceptable during our waking hours. Unfortunately, as we saw in that earlier discussion, there is little scientific evidence for this view.

The Structure of Personality: Id, Ego, and Superego

Do you know the story of Dr. Jekyll, the good, kind doctor, and Mr. Hyde, his evil side? If so, you already have a basic idea of some of the key structures of personality described by Freud. He suggested that personality consists largely of three parts: the *id,* the *ego,* and the *superego* (refer again to Figure 10.3). As we'll soon see, these correspond, roughly, to *desire, reason,* and *conscience.*

The **id** consists of all our primitive, innate urges. These include various bodily needs, sexual desire, and aggressive impulses. According to Freud, the id is totally unconscious and operates in accordance with what he termed the **pleasure principle:** It demands immediate, total gratification and is not capable of considering the potential costs of seeking this goal. In short, the id is the Mr. Hyde of our personalities—although, in contrast to this character, it is more appropriately described as *unrestrained* rather than purely *evil.*

Unfortunately, the world offers few opportunities for instant pleasure, and attempting to gratify many of our innate urges would soon get us into serious trouble. It is in response to these facts that the second structure of personality, the **ego,** develops. The ego's task is to hold the id in check until conditions allow for satisfaction of its impulses. Thus, the ego operates in accordance with the **reality principle:** It takes into account external conditions and the consequences of various actions and directs behavior so as to maximize pleasure *and* minimize pain. The ego is partly conscious but not entirely so; some of its actions—for example, its external struggle with the id—are outside our conscious knowledge.

The final aspect of personality described by Freud is the **superego.** It, too, seeks to control satisfaction of id impulses, but in contrast to the ego, it is concerned with *morality*—with whether various means of satisfying id impulses are right or wrong. The superego permits gratification of such impulses only when it is morally correct to do so, not simply when it is safe or feasible, as required by the ego.

The superego is acquired from our parents and through experience and represents our internalization of the moral teachings and norms of our society. Unfortunately, such teachings are often quite inflexible and leave little room for gratification of our basic desires: They require us to be good all the time, like Dr. Jekyll. Because of this fact, the ego faces another difficult task: It must strike a balance between our primitive urges (the id) and our learned moral constraints (the superego). Freud felt that this constant struggle among id, ego, and superego plays a key role in personality and in many psychological disorders. Moreover, he suggested that the struggle was often visible in everyday behavior in what have come to be known as **Freudian slips**—errors in speech that actually reflect unconscious impulses that have "gotten by" the ego or superego. An example: "She was tempting . . . I mean attempting to . . ." According to Freud, the word *tempting* reveals an unacceptable sexual impulse.

Psychoanalysis
A method of therapy based on Freud's theory of personality, in which the therapist attempts to bring repressed, unconscious material into consciousness.

Pleasure Principle
The principle on which the id operates, according to which immediate pleasure is the sole motivation for behavior.

Id
In Freud's theory, the portion of personality concerned with immediate gratification of primitive needs.

Ego
In Freud's theory, the part of personality that takes account of external reality in the expression of instinctive sexual and aggressive urges.

Reality Principle
The principle according to which the ego operates, in which the external consequences of behavior are considered in the expression of impulses from the id.

Superego
According to Freud, the portion of human personality representing the conscience.

Freudian Slips
Statements which seem to be simple errors in speech, but which in fact reveal unconscious thoughts or impulses.

Anxiety
In Freudian theory, unpleasant feelings of tension or worry experienced by individuals in reaction to unacceptable wishes or impulses.

Defense Mechanisms
Techniques used by the ego to keep threatening and unacceptable material out of consciousness, and so to reduce anxiety.

Sublimation
A defense mechanism in which threatening unconscious impulses are channeled into socially acceptable forms of behavior.

Psychosexual Stages of Development
According to Freud, an innate sequence of stages through which all human beings pass. At each stage, pleasure is focused on a different region of the body.

■ Anxiety and Defense Mechanisms: Self-Protection by the Ego

In its constant struggle to prevent the expression of dangerous id impulses, the ego faces a difficult task. Yet for most people, most of the time, the ego succeeds. Sometimes, though, id impulses grow so strong that they threaten to get out of control. For example, consider the case of a middle-aged widow who finds herself strongly attracted to her daughter's boyfriend. She hasn't had a romantic attachment in years, so her sexual desire quickly rises to high levels. What happens next? According to Freud, when her ego senses that unacceptable impulses are about to get out of hand, it experiences **anxiety**—intense feelings of nervousness, tension, or worry. These feelings occur because the unacceptable impulses are getting closer and closer to consciousness, as well as closer and closer to the limits of the ego to hold them in check.

At this point, Freud contended, the ego may resort to one of several different **defense mechanisms.** These are all designed to keep unacceptable impulses from the id out of consciousness and to prevent their open expression. Defense mechanisms take many different forms. For example, in **sublimation,** the unacceptable impulse is channeled into some socially acceptable action. Instead of trying to seduce the young man, as Freud would say the widow's id wants to do, she might "adopt" him as a son and provide financial support to further his education. Alternatively, she might show *displacement,* a redirection of her emotional response to the young man onto another person she views as more appropriate, for instance, a widower of her own age. Or she might show *projection,* denying that she is sexually attracted to the young man but coming to believe that her friend, who is also a widow, harbors these impulses. These and other defense mechanisms are described in Table 10.1. Although they differ in form, all serve the function of reducing anxiety by keeping unacceptable urges and impulses from breaking into consciousness.

■ Psychosexual Stages of Development

Now we come to what is perhaps the most controversial aspect of Freud's theory of personality: his ideas about its formation or development. Freud's views in this respect can be grouped under the heading **psychosexual stages of development:**

TABLE 10.1   Defense Mechanisms: Reactions to Anxiety

Freud believed that when the ego feels it may be unable to control impulses from the id, it experiences anxiety. To reduce such feelings, the ego uses various *defense mechanisms,* such as those described here.

Defense Mechanism	Its Basic Nature	Example
Repression	"Forgetting"—or pushing from consciousness into unconsciousness—unacceptable thoughts or impulses	A woman fails to recognize her attraction to her handsome new son-in-law.
Rationalization	Conjuring up socially acceptable reasons for thoughts or actions based on unacceptable motives	A young woman explains that she ate an entire chocolate cake so that it wouldn't spoil in the summer heat.
Displacement	Redirecting an emotional response from a dangerous object to a safe one	A man redirects anger from his boss to his child.
Projection	Transferring unacceptable motives or impulses to others	A man who feels strong hostility toward a neighbor perceives the neighbor as being hostile to him.
Regression	Responding to a threatening situation in a way appropriate to an earlier age or level of development	A student asks a professor to raise his grade; when she refuses, the student throws a temper tantrum.

innately determined stages of sexual development through which, presumably we all pass, and that strongly shape the nature of our personalities. Before turning to the stages themselves, however, we must first consider two important concepts relating to them: *libido* and *fixation*.

Libido refers to the instinctual life force that energizes the id. Release of libido is closely related to pleasure, but the focus of such pleasure—and the expression of libido—changes as we develop. In each stage of development, we obtain different kinds of pleasure and leave behind a small amount of our libido—this is the normal course of events. If an excessive amount of libido energy is tied to a particular stage, however, **fixation** results. This can stem from either too little or too much gratification during this stage, and in either case, the result is harmful. Because the individual has left too much "psychic energy" behind, less is available for full adult development. The outcome may be an adult personality reflecting the stage or stages at which fixation has occurred. To put it another way, if too much energy is drained away by fixation at earlier stages of development, the amount remaining may be insufficient to power movement to full adult development. Then, an individual may show an immature personality and several psychological disorders.

Now, back to the actual stages themselves. According to Freud, as we grow and develop, different parts of the body serve as the focus of our quest for pleasure. In the initial **oral stage,** lasting until we are about eighteen months old, we seek pleasure mainly through the mouth. If too much or too little gratification occurs during this stage, an individual may become *fixated* at it. Too little gratification results in a personality that is overly dependent on others; too much, especially after the child has developed some teeth, results in a personality that is excessively hostile, especially through verbal sarcasm.

The next stage occurs in response to efforts by parents to toilet train their children. During the **anal stage,** the process of elimination becomes the primary focus of pleasure. Fixation at this stage, stemming from overly harsh toilet-training experiences, may result in individuals who are excessively orderly or *compulsive*—they can't leave any job unfinished, and strive for perfection and neatness in everything they do. In contrast, fixation stemming from very relaxed toilet training may result in people who are undisciplined, impulsive, and excessively generous. Freud himself might well be described as compulsive; even when he was seriously ill, he personally answered dozens of letters every day—even letters from total strangers asking his advice (Benjamin & Dixon, 1996).

At about age four, the genitals become the primary source of pleasure, and children enter the **phallic stage.** Freud speculated that at this time we fantasize about sex with our opposite-sex parent—a phenomenon he termed the **Oedipus complex,** after Oedipus, a character in ancient Greek literature who unknowingly killed his father and then married his mother. Fear of punishment for such desires then enters the picture. Among boys, the feared punishment is castration, leading to *castration anxiety.* Among girls, the feared punishment is loss of love. In both cases, these fears bring about resolution of the Oedipus complex and identification with the same-sex parent. In other words, little boys give up sexual desires for their mothers and come to see their fathers as models rather than as rivals, while little girls give up their sexual desires for their fathers and come to see their mothers as models.

Perhaps one of Freud's most controversial suggestions is the idea that little girls experience *penis envy,* stemming from their own lack of a male organ. Freud suggested that because of such envy, girls experience strong feelings of inferiority and jealousy—feelings they carry with them in disguised form even in adult life. As you can readily guess, many psychologists object strongly to these ideas, and there is virtually no evidence for them.

After resolution of the Oedipus conflict, children enter the **latency stage,** during which sexual urges are, according to Freud, at a minimum. During puberty, they enter the final stage, the **genital stage.** During this stage, pleasure is again

Libido
According to Freud, the psychic energy that powers all mental activity.

Fixation
Excessive investment of psychic energy in a particular stage of psychosexual development. This results in various types of psychological disorders.

Oral Stage
A stage of psychosexual development during which pleasure is centered in the region of the mouth.

Anal Stage
In Freud's theory, a psychosexual stage of development in which pleasure is focused primarily on the anal zone.

Phallic Stage
An early stage of psychosexual development during which pleasure is centered in the genital region. It is during this stage that the Oedipus complex develops.

Oedipus Complex
In Freud's theory, a crisis of psychosexual development in which children must give up their sexual attraction for their opposite-sex parent.

Latency Stage
In Freud's theory, the psychosexual stage of development that follows resolution of the Oedipus complex. During this stage, sexual desires are relatively weak.

Genital Stage
The final stage of psychosexual development—one in which individuals acquire the adult capacity to combine lust with affection.

Oral 0–2
Infant achieves gratification
through oral activities
such as feeding, thumb
sucking, and babbling

Anal 2–3
The child learns to respond
to some of the demands of
society (such as bowel and
bladder control)

Phallic 3–7
The child learns to recognize
the differences between
males and females
and becomes aware
of sexuality

Latency 7–11
The child continues his
or her development, but
sexual urges are
relatively quiet

Genital 11–adult
The growing adolescent
shakes off old
dependencies and
learns to deal
maturely with the
opposite sex

FIGURE 10.4
**The Psychosexual Stages
of Development Described
by Freud**
According to Freud, all human beings
pass through a series of discrete
psychosexual stages. At each stage,
pleasure is focused on a particular
part of the body. Too much or too
little gratification at any stage can
result in *fixation* and can lead to
psychological disorders.

focused on the genitals, Now, however, lust is blended with affection and the person becomes capable of adult love. Remember: According to Freud, progression to this final stage is possible only if serious fixation has *not* occurred at the earlier stages. If such fixation exists, development is blocked and various disorders result. Major stages in Freud's theory are summarized in Figure 10.4.

Research Related to Freud's Theory: Probing the Unconscious

Freud's theories contain many intriguing ideas, and as you already know, several of these have entered into world culture—people everywhere talk about the unconscious, repressed impulses, the id and the ego, and so on. It's not surprising, therefore, that psychologists have investigated several of these ideas—at least, the ones that *can* be studied through scientific means. We have already discussed the scientific status of Freud's ideas about dreams (Chapter 4), so let's consider his ideas about the unconscious.

Freud contended that our feelings and behaviors can be strongly affected by information we can't bring to mind and can't describe verbally. Research in many fields of psychology suggests that, to some extent, this is true (e.g., Bornstein, 1992), although psychologists refer to such information as *nonconscious* rather than "unconscious" in order to avoid assuming that such information has been repressed. (It may be nonconscious for other reasons—for instance, it was presented so quickly that it couldn't be recognized.) Do you recall our discussion of *procedural memory* in Chapter 6? This kind of memory allows you to perform many skilled physical actions, such as tying your shoelaces, playing a musical instrument, or doing the complex steps of a popular dance. Although such information is obviously present in memory, you can't readily describe it or put it into words. Thus, when someone asks you to explain how you do a certain dance step, you may say, "Just watch, I'll show you." So the existence of procedural memory suggests that often we do possess information we can't describe verbally.

Additional support for the existence of the impact of nonconscious information is provided by *subliminal perception*—a topic we discussed in Chapter 3. As you may recall, claims for subliminal perception have been overstated, especially with respect to its supposed value as a learning aid or marketing technique. Yet there is no doubt that sometimes we can be influenced by stimuli of which we are unaware (Reder & Gordon, 1997). For instance, as we saw in Chapter 4, if individuals are exposed to faces showing angry, neutral, or happy expressions, and the exposure time is so brief that they do not know what they have seen (the faces are just a blur), muscles in their own faces still tend to show subtle reactions that mimic these expressions. When they are exposed to happy faces, electrical activity occurs in muscles that pull the corners of their mouths upward in smiles. And when they are exposed to angry faces, activity occurs in muscles that play a role in frowning (Dimberg, Thunberg, & Elmehed, 2000). Remember: The faces are shown so quickly that research participants can't really "see" them. Yet they still respond to them in subtle ways. These and many other findings (e.g., Cunningham et al., 2003) indicate that important aspects of our behavior do occur without our being aware either of the actions themselves or of the factors that caused them, just as Freud suggested.

Freud's Theory: An Overall Evaluation

As noted earlier, Freud's place in history is assured: His ideas and writing have exerted a profound impact on society. But what about this theory of personality? Is it currently accepted by most psychologists? As you can probably guess from our earlier comments, the answer is *definitely not.* The reasons for this rejection are clear. First, many critics have noted that Freud's theory is not really a scientific theory at all. True, as we just saw, some of his ideas, or hypotheses derived from them, can be tested. But many concepts in his theory cannot be measured or studied systematically. How, for instance, can one go about observing an *id*, a *fixation*, or the psychic energy contained in the *libido*? As I noted in Chapter 1, a theory that cannot be tested is largely useless, and this criticism does apply to many of Freud's ideas.

Second, as we have already seen, several of Freud's proposals are not consistent with the findings of modern research—for instance, his ideas about the meaning of dreams. Third, in constructing his theory, Freud relied heavily on a small number of case studies—no more than a dozen at most. Almost all of these persons came from wealthy backgrounds and lived in a large and sophisticated city within a single culture. Thus, they were not representative of human beings generally.

Finally, and perhaps most important of all, Freud's theories contain so many different concepts that they can explain virtually any pattern of behavior in an after-the-fact manner. If a theory can't be disconfirmed—shown to be false—then, once again, it is largely useless, and this does seem to be the case with respect to Freud's views.

For these and other reasons, Freud's theory of personality is not currently accepted by most psychologists. Yet, several of his insights—especially his ideas about levels of consciousness and the importance of anxiety in psychological disorders—*have* contributed to our understanding of human behavior and personality. So, while his theories don't measure up to the rigorous standards of science required by modern psychology, there is no doubt that they have had a profound and lasting impact on modern thought. (Are these effects beneficial ones? Or should you question them in your own life? For a discussion of this issue, please see the following **Psychology Lends a Hand** section.)

p s y c h o l o g y l e n d s a h a n d

Too Much Freud for Our Own Good?
Questioning Freudian Assumptions in Everyday Life

Freud was not only an original thinker, but also a persuasive author and dynamic speaker. So it is not surprising that many of his ideas gained quick and widespread acceptance in society and became part of the world's cultural heritage. Whether you realize it or not, you probably accept several of his ideas and apply them to your own life. Here, we want to raise the possibility that this is *not* necessarily a good thing. Several of these ideas have been shown to be false, so accepting them, even implicitly, can lead to serious problems. Here are some of Freud's ideas we think you should seriously question:

• **Gaining insight into the causes of our current problems will make these problems disappear—or at least, diminish.** Do you accept this belief? Most people do. In fact, you will hear people mention this in everyday conversation: "Once I understood why I felt that way, I was able to deal with it better" or "After I figured out *why* I had those problems, they went away." In fact, a large body of research findings indicate that this is *not necessarily the case.* Gaining insight into the cause of problems, negative feelings, and personal distress can be a helpful first step. But it does not, in and of itself, guarantee that the problems will disappear. On the contrary, sometimes thinking about them over and over again (ruminating) can have disastrous effects (e.g., Nolen-Hoeksema & Davis, 1999). So please, do *not* accept Freud's assumption unquestioningly; doing so can be harmful to your mental health and personal happiness.

• **Dreams provide valuable insights into the unconscious, and understanding them can be very beneficial.** As noted in Chapter 4, modern research indicates that while dreams can, indeed, reflect important events in our lives, they are *not* a direct "line"

into the unconscious. On the contrary, they are more likely to represent random activity in our nervous systems, and our minds' efforts to make sense of this activity, than reflections of our hidden urges and impulses. So, whatever the popular press says, or your friends tell you, do *not* place much faith in the value of interpreting dreams.

• **Once our personalities are formed, early in life, they cannot be changed; all we can do is recognize them and adapt to them.** In some ways, this may be the most dangerous assumption of all. Yes, some aspects of personality tend to be stable over time, but this in no way implies that they can never be changed. In fact, a large body of scientific evidence points to the opposite conclusion. If people genuinely want to change various aspects of their personalities, and are willing to work hard to do so, they can. They can boost their self-esteem and self-efficacy, learn to control their tempers and be less irritable, replace pessimism with optimism, and even learn to be more orderly and conscientious. Making such changes is often difficult, but modern psychology believes ardently that they *can* be made. So, by all means, question the assumption that "what we are is set in stone"; in this respect, Freud was definitely too pessimistic.

Please don't misunderstand: We are not suggesting that Freud's ideas should all be discarded. On the contrary, as noted earlier, several are highly insightful and have stimulated research and thought that have greatly expanded our understanding of human behavior and personality. But the preceding assumptions are far too questionable to deserve the widespread, implicit acceptance they enjoy. So, start today to notice them in your own thinking and to minimize their impact.

KEY QUESTIONS

• According to Freud, what are the three levels of consciousness?
• In Freud's theory, what are the three basic components of personality?
• According to Freud, what are the psychosexual stages of development?
• Do research findings support Freud's views about the unconscious?

Other Psychoanalytic Views: Freud's Disciples . . . and Defectors

Neo-Freudians
Personality theorists who accepted basic portions of Freud's theory, but rejected or modified other portions.

Whatever else Freud was, he was certainly an intellectual magnet. Over the course of several decades, he attracted as students or colleagues many brilliant people. Most of them began by accepting Freud's views. Later, however, they often disagreed with some of his major assumptions. Let's see why these individuals, often termed **neo-Freudians,** broke with Freud, and what they had to say about the nature of personality.

Jung: The Collective Unconscious

Perhaps the most bitter of all the defections Freud experienced was that of Carl Jung—the follower Freud viewed as his natural heir. Jung shared Freud's views concerning the importance of the unconscious, but contended that there is another part to this aspect of personality that Freud overlooked: the **collective unconscious.** According to Jung, the collective unconscious holds experiences shared by all human beings—experiences that are, in a sense, part of our biological heritage. The contents of the collective unconscious, in short, reflect the experiences our species has had since it originated on earth. The collective unconscious finds expression in several ways, but among these, **archetypes** are the most central to Jung's theory. These are manifestations of the collective unconscious that express themselves when our conscious mind is distracted or inactive, for example, during sleep, in dreams, or in fantasies (e.g., Neher, 1996). The specific expression of archetypes depends, in part, on our unique experience as individuals, but in all cases such images are representations of key aspects of the human experience—images representing *mother, father, wise old man, the sun, the moon, God, death,* and *the hero* (see Fig. 10.5). It is because of these shared innate images, Jung contended, that the folklore of many different cultures contains similar figures and themes.

Two especially important archetypes in Jung's theory are known as **animus** and **anima.** The animus is the masculine side of females, while the anima is the feminine side of males. Jung believed that in looking for a mate, we search for the person onto whom we can best project these hidden sides of our personality. When there is a good match between such projections and another person, attraction occurs.

Another aspect of Jung's theory was his suggestion that we are all born with innate tendencies to be concerned primarily either with our inner selves or with the outside world. Jung labeled persons in the first category **introverts** and described them as being hesitant and cautious; they do not make friends easily and prefer to observe the world rather than become involved in it. He labeled persons in the second category **extroverts.** Such persons are open and confident, make friends, readily enjoy high levels of stimulation, and a wide range of activities. While many aspects of Jung's theory have been rejected by psychologists—especially the idea of the collective unconscious—the dimension of introversion–extroversion (now usually spelled extr*a*version) appears to be a basic one of major importance, and is included in several *trait theories* we'll consider in a later section (and in these theories, the term is spelled extr*a*version).

Karen Horney and Alfred Adler

Two other important neo-Freudians are Karen Horney and Alfred Adler. Horney was one of the few women in the early psychoanalytic movement, and she disagreed with Freud strongly over his view that differences between men and women stemmed largely from innate factors—for example, anatomical differences resulting in *penis envy* among females. Horney contended that although women do often feel inferior to men (remember, she was writing in Germany in the 1920s), this is *not* a result of penis envy but of how they are treated by society. She argued that if women were raised in a different type of environment, they would see themselves more favorably. In other words, it was not the male penis women envied but the *power* and *autonomy* associated with "maleness." In addition, she emphasized the point that psychological disorders do not stem from fixation of psychic energy, as Freud contended, but from disturbed interpersonal relationships during childhood and what she termed **basic anxiety**—children's fear of being left alone, helpless, and insecure. She suggested that in reaction to excessive levels of such anxiety, which stem from poor relations with their parents, children adopt one of three

FIGURE 10.5
The Wise Old Man: An Archetype
According to Jung, all human being possess a *collective unconscious.* Information stored there is often expressed in terms of *archetypes*—representations of key aspects of human experience, such as the wise old man (shown here), mother, father, and so on.

Collective Unconscious
In Jung's theory, a portion of the unconscious shared by all human beings.

Archetypes
According to Jung, inherited images in the collective unconscious that shape our perceptions of the external world.

Animus
According to Jung, the archetype representing the masculine side of females.

Anima
According to Jung, the archetype representing the feminine side of males.

Introverts
In Jung's theory, individuals who are hesitant and cautious and do not make friends easily.

Extroverts
In Jung's theory, individuals who are open and and confident and make friends readily.

Basic Anxiety
Children's fear of being left alone, helpless, and insecure.

styles: a *passive* style, in which they try to cope by being agreeable and compliant; an *aggressive* style, in which they fight to get attention; and a *withdrawn* style, in which they repress their emotions. All three patterns can lead to serious psychological disorders. By emphasizing the importance of children's relationships with their parents, Horney called attention to the importance of social factors in shaping personality.

Alfred Adler also disagreed with Freud very strongly, but over somewhat different issues. In particular, he emphasized the importance of feelings of inferiority, which he believed we experience as children because of our small size and physical weakness. He viewed personality development as stemming primarily from our efforts to overcome such feelings through what he termed **striving for superiority.** If these efforts go too far, we may develop a *superiority complex*, and become a braggart or a bully (Sutton & Smith, 1999). However, under the surface, persons who show this pattern still feel inferior: They are merely covering up with an outward show of strength. Like Horney and other neo-Freudians, Adler also emphasized the importance of social factors in personality; for instance, he called attention to the importance of birth order. Only children, he suggested, are spoiled by too much parental attention, while first-borns are "dethroned" by a second child. Second-borns, in contrast, are competitive, because they have to struggle to catch up with an older sibling.

By now, the main point should be clear: Neo-Freudians, while accepting many of Freud's basic ideas, rejected his emphasis on innate patterns of development. On the contrary, they perceived personality as stemming from a complex interplay between social factors and the experiences we have during childhood, primarily in our own families. The theories proposed by neo-Freudians are not widely accepted by psychologists, but they did serve as a kind of bridge between the provocative views offered by Freud and more modern conceptions of personality. In this respect, at least, they made an important contribution.

KEY QUESTIONS

- According to Jung, what is the collective unconscious?
- In Horney's theory, what is basic anxiety?
- According to Adler, what is the role of feelings of inferiority in personality?

HUMANISTIC THEORIES: EMPHASIS ON GROWTH

Id versus ego, Jekyll versus Hyde—on the whole, psychoanalytic theories of personality take a dim view of human nature, contending that we must struggle constantly to control our bestial impulses if we are to function as healthy, rational adults. Is this view accurate? Many psychologists doubt it. They believe that human strivings for growth, dignity, and self-determination are just as important, if not more important, in the development of personality, than the primitive motives Freud emphasized. Because of their more optimistic views concerning human nature, such views as known as **humanistic theories** (Maslow, 1970; Rogers, 1977, 1982). These theories differ widely in the concepts on which they focus, but they share the following characteristics.

First, they emphasize *personal responsibility.* Each of us, these theories contend, is largely responsible for what happens to us. Our fate is mostly in our own hands; we are *not* merely chips driven here and there by dark forces within our personalities. Second, while these theories don't deny the importance of past experience, they generally *focus on the present.* True, we may be influenced by traumatic events early in life. Yet these do *not* have to shape our entire adult lives, and the capacity to overcome them and to go on from there is both real and powerful. Third, humanistic theories stress the importance of *personal growth.* People are not, such

Striving for Superiority
Attempts to overcome feelings of inferiority. According to Adler, this is the primary motive for human behavior.

Humanistic Theories
Theories of personality emphasizing personality responsibility and innate tendencies toward personal growth.

theories argue, content with merely meeting their current needs. They wish to progress toward "bigger" goals, such as becoming the best they can be. Only when obstacles interfere with such growth is the process interrupted. A key goal of therapy, therefore, should be the removal of obstacles that prevent natural growth processes from proceeding. As examples of humanistic theories, we'll now consider the views proposed by Carl Rogers and Abraham Maslow.

Rogers's Self Theory: Becoming a Fully Functioning Person

Carl Rogers planned to become a minister, but after taking several courses in psychology, he changed his mind and decided instead to focus on human personality. One central assumption of the theory he proposed was this: Left to their own devices, human beings show many positive characteristics and move, over the course of their lives, toward becoming **fully functioning persons.** What are such persons like? Rogers suggested that they are people who strive to experience life to the fullest, who live in the here and now, and who trust their own feelings. They are sensitive to the needs and rights of others but do not allow society's standards to shape their feelings or actions to an excessive degree. Fully functioning people aren't saints; they can—and do—act in ways they later regret. But throughout life, their actions are dominated by constructive impulses. They are in close touch with their own values and feelings and experience life more deeply than most other persons.

If all human beings possess the capacity to become fully functioning persons, why don't they all succeed? The answer, Rogers suggests, lies in the anxiety generated when life experiences are inconsistent with our ideas about ourselves— when a gap develops between our **self-concept** (our beliefs and knowledge about ourselves) and reality or our perceptions of it. For example, imagine a young girl who is quite independent and self-reliant, and who thinks of herself in this way. After her older sibling dies in an accident, however, her parents begin to baby her and to convey the message, over and over again, that she is vulnerable and must be sheltered from the outside world. This treatment is highly inconsistent with her self-concept. As a result, she experiences anxiety and adopts one or more psychological defenses to reduce it. The most common of these defenses is *distortion*— changing our perceptions of reality so that they *are* consistent with our self-concept. For example, the girl may come to believe that her parents aren't being overprotective; they are just showing normal concern for her safety. Another defense process is *denial;* she may refuse to admit to herself that, as a result of being babied, she is indeed losing her independence.

In the short run, such tactics can be successful; they help reduce anxiety. Ultimately, however, they produce sizable gaps between an individual's self-concept and reality. For instance, the girl may cling to the belief that she is independent when in fact, as a result of her parent's treatment, she is becoming increasingly helpless. The larger such gaps, Rogers contends, the greater an individual's maladjustment—and personal unhappiness (see Figure 10.6 on page 326). Rogers suggested that distortions in the self-concept are common because most people grow up in an atmosphere of *conditional positive regard.* They learn that others, such as their parents, will approve of them only when they behave in certain ways and express certain feelings. As a result, many people are forced to deny the existence of various impulses and feelings, and their self-concepts become badly distorted.

How can such distorted self-concepts be repaired so that healthy development can continue? Rogers suggests that therapists can help accomplish this goal by placing individuals in an atmosphere of **unconditional positive regard**—a setting in which they will be accepted by the therapist *no matter what they say or do.* Such conditions are provided by *client-centered therapy,* a form of therapy we'll consider in detail in Chapter 12.

Fully Functioning Persons
In Rogers's theory, psychologically healthy persons who enjoy life to the fullest.

Self-Concept
All the information and beliefs individuals have about their own characteristics and themselves.

Unconditional Positive Regard
In Rogers's theory, communicating to others that they will be respected or loved regardless of what they say or do.

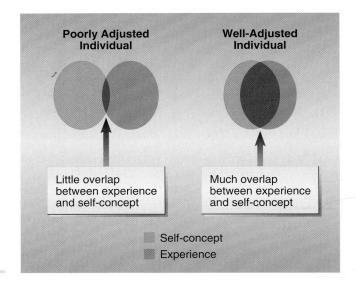

FIGURE 10.6
Gaps between Our Self-Concept and Our Experience:
A Cause of Maladjustment in Rogers's Theory
According to Rogers, the larger the gap between an individual's self-concept and reality, the poorer this person's psychological adjustment.

Maslow and the Study of Self-Actualizing People

Another influential humanistic theory of personality was proposed by Abraham Maslow (1970). We have already described a portion of Maslow's theory, his concept of a *needs hierarchy,* in Chapter 8. This is only part of Maslow's theory of personality. He has also devoted much attention to the study of people who, in his terms, are *psychologically healthy.* These are individuals who have attained high levels of **self-actualization**—a state in which they have reached their fullest true potential. What are such people like? In essence, much like the fully functioning persons described by Rogers. Self-actualized people accept themselves for what they are; they recognize their shortcomings as well as their strengths. Being in touch with their own personalities, they are less inhibited and less likely to conform than most of us. Self-actualized people are well aware of the rules imposed by society, but feel greater freedom to ignore them than most persons. Unlike most of us, they seem to retain their childhood wonder and amazement with the world. For them, life continues to be an exciting adventure rather than a boring routine. Finally, self-actualized persons sometimes have what Maslow describes as **peak experiences**—instances in which they have powerful feelings of unity with the universe and feel tremendous waves of power and wonder. Such experiences appear to be linked to personal growth, for after them individuals report feeling more spontaneous, more appreciative of life, and less concerned with the problems of everyday life. Examples of people Maslow describes as fully self-actualized are Thomas Jefferson, Albert Einstein, Eleanor Roosevelt, and George Washington Carver.

Research Related to Humanistic Theories: Links to Positive Psychology

At first glance, it might seem that humanistic theories, like psychoanalytic ones, are not readily open to scientific test. In fact, however, the opposite is true. Humanistic theories were proposed by psychologists, and a commitment to research is one of the true hallmarks of psychology. For this reason, several concepts that play a key role in humanistic theories have been studied quite extensively. Among these, the one that has probably received most attention is the concept of the *self-concept,* which is so central to Rogers's theory.

Research on the self-concept has addressed many different issues—for instance, how our self-concept is formed (e.g., Sedikides & Skowronski, 1997), how it influences the way we think (e.g., Kendzierski & Whitaker, 1997), and what in-

Self-Actualization
A stage of personal development in which individuals reach their maximum potential.

Peak Experiences
According to Maslow, intense emotional experiences during which individuals feel at one with the universe.

formation it contains (e.g., Rentsch & Heffner, 1994). Together, such research suggests that the self-concept is complex and consists of many different parts (e.g., knowledge of our own traits and beliefs, understanding of how we are perceived by and relate to others; knowledge of how we are similar to and different from others; e.g., Baumeister & Leary, 1995).

In addition, Rogers's emphasis on the importance of the self-concept (our beliefs about ourselves) led many psychologists to focus on the closely related concept of **self-esteem**—our assessment of our overall personal worth or adequacy. Because it is virtually impossible to have beliefs about our own characteristics without also evaluating them, it is often a very short step from self-concept to self-esteem. Research on self-esteem has shown that it, too, is very important: Self-esteem plays a key role in psychological adjustment (see Chapter 12), in our relations with others (Chapter 13), and in the performance of many tasks. (Self-esteem is often closely linked to confidence in our abilities to successfully complete whatever we try to accomplish, and, in this context, it is often described as *self-efficacy*, a topic we'll consider in more detail in a later section; see Bandura, 1997.)

Much recent research has compared the self-esteem of various ethnic and racial groups living in the United States (e.g., Gray-Little & Hafdahl, 2000). Overall, this research indicates that African Americans do *not* show lower self-esteem than persons of European descent (Whites); on the contrary, they show *higher* self-esteem. In contrast, members of other ethnic minorities in the United States (Hispanics, Asians, Native Americans) score slightly lower than Whites. The factors responsible for these differences are complex but seem to center around cultural differences in the self-concept. African Americans and Whites seem to view individuals as having a self that is stable and transcends relationships (an *individualistic* view of the self-concept). In contrast, other minority groups hold a more *collectivist* view of the self-concept, seeing it as more flexible and context-dependent. Because individualistic views tend to be associated with higher self-esteem than collectivist views, this helps explain why African Americans and Whites have higher self-esteem. The main point here is not to describe all the complexities of the self-concept and self-esteem, but to call attention to the fact that Rogers was correct in emphasizing the importance of these aspects of personality.

Other research that provides support for the optimistic perspective of humanistic theories of personality is provided by the new field of *positive psychology,* which focuses on individuals' strengths rather than their weaknesses (e.g., Seligman & Csikszentmihalyi, 2000). Research in this emerging field indicates that as the Rogers, Maslow, and other humanistic theorists propose, people *do* have many strengths, many positive impulses, and are—or can be—quite happy in a wide range of life situations. Indeed, recent research suggests that many people become stronger, kinder, and more loving after experiencing adversity—a prediction consistent with certain aspects of humanistic theories of personality. For example, consider a recent study by Peterson and Seligman (2003).

These authors predicted that after the tragic events of September 11, 2001, many Americans would show increases in positive traits—traits such as hope and optimism, kindness, and willingness to engage in teamwork. To test this prediction, the researchers posted a measure of positive traits on the Internet and invited people to complete it. More than four thousand did so, and as shown in Figure 10.7 on page 328, the results offered support for the kind of positive changes Peterson and Seligman (2003) predicted: People completing the scale two months after the terrorist attack of September 11 *did* score higher on hope, optimism, kindness, and so on, than people who completed it before September 11. Why did such positive changes occur? The authors speculate that it may because after the events of September 11, many Americans wanted to enhance their sense of belonging, and one means of doing so was to embrace these positive traits. Whatever the reason, these findings and many other results in the field of positive psychology are consistent with the positive, optimistic assertions of humanistic theorists.

Self-Esteem
Our assessment of our overall personal worth or adequacy.

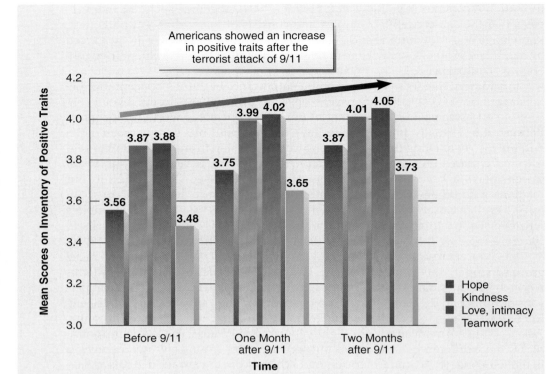

FIGURE 10.7
Personal Growth after September 11

As shown here, Americans showed an increase in positive traits, such as optimism and kindness, to a greater extent after the terrorist attack of September 11. This is consistent with certain aspects of humanistic theories of personality, which emphasize human potential for growth.

Source: Based on data from Peterson & Seligman, 2003

Humanistic Theories: An Evaluation

The preceding comments suggest that humanistic theories have had a lasting impact on psychology, and this is definitely so. Several of the ideas first proposed by Rogers, Maslow, and other humanistic theorists have entered into the mainstream of psychology. But humanistic theories have also been subject to strong criticism. Many key concepts of humanistic theories are loosely defined. What, precisely, is self-actualization? A peak experience? A fully functioning person? Until such terms are clearly defined, it is difficult to conduct systematic research on them. Despite such criticisms, the impact of humanistic theories has persisted, and does indeed constitute a lasting contribution to our understanding of human personality.

KEY QUESTIONS

- How does the view of human beings proposed by humanistic theories of personality differ from that of psychoanalytic theories?
- According to Rogers, why do many individuals fail to become fully functioning persons?
- In Maslow's theory, what is self-actualization?

Personality Traits
Specific dimensions along which individuals differ in consistent, stable ways.

Trait Theories
Theories of personality that focus on identifying the key dimensions along which people differ.

TRAIT THEORIES: SEEKING THE KEY DIMENSIONS OF PERSONALITY

When we describe other persons, we often do so in terms of specific **personality traits**—stable dimensions of personality along which people vary, from very low to very high. This strong tendency to think about others in terms of specific characteristics is reflected in **trait theories** of personality. Such theories focus on identifying key dimensions of personality—the most important ways in which people differ. The basic idea behind this approach is as follows: Once we identify the key dimensions along which people differ, we can measure how *much* they differ and can then relate such differences to many important forms of behavior.

Unfortunately, this task sounds easier than it actually is. Human beings differ in an almost countless number of ways. How can we determine which of these are most important and stable (i.e., lasting)? One approach is to search for *clusters*—groups of traits that seem to go together. We'll now take a brief look at two theories that adopted this approach. Then, we'll turn to evidence suggesting that, in the final analysis, the number of key traits or dimensions of personality is actually quite small—perhaps no more than five.

The Search for Basic Traits: Cattell's Source Trait Approach

Although many early efforts to identify key aspects of personality were performed, perhaps the most sophisticated approach was one was proposed by Raymond Cattell. Instead of beginning with hunches or insights about what traits might be most central (the approach adopted in most earlier work), Cattell used a very different technique. He conducted large-scale studies in which thousands of persons responded to measures designed to reflect individual differences on literally hundreds of different traits. Their responses were then subjected to a statistical procedure known as *factor analysis,* a technique that reveals patterns in the extent to which various traits are related to each other (i.e., correlated). Cattell reasoned that by using factor analysis, clusters of traits could be identified and that, ultimately, this would reveal the ones that are truly central.

Using this approach, Cattell and his associates (e.g., Cattell & Dreger, 1977) have identified sixteen **source traits**—ones he believes underlie differences in many other, less important *surface traits.* A few of the source traits identified by Cattell are cool versus warm, easily upset versus calm and stable, not assertive versus dominant, trusting versus suspicious, and undisciplined versus self-disciplined. It is not yet clear whether Catell's list is actually valid, but at least this list is considerably briefer than previous ones.

The "Big Five" Factors: The Basic Dimensions of Personality?

So where do we stand now—what *are* the key aspects of personality? Twenty years ago, there was still considerable disagreement about this issue. Now, however, there is increasing consensus among psychologists that, in fact, there may be only five key or central dimensions of personality (e.g., Costa & McCrae, 1994; Zuckerman, 1994). These are sometimes labeled the "big five," and they can be described as follows:

1. **Extraversion.** A tendency to seek stimulation and to enjoy the company of other people. (A dimension ranging from energetic, enthusiastic, sociable, and talkative on one end to retiring, sober, reserved, silent, and cautious on the other.)
2. **Agreeableness.** A tendency to be compassionate toward others. (A dimension ranging from good-natured, cooperative, trusting, and helpful at one end to irritable, suspicious, and uncooperative at the other.)
3. **Conscientiousness.** A tendency to show self-discipline, to strive for competence and achievement. (A dimension ranging from well-organized, careful, self-disciplined, responsible, and precise at one end to disorganized, impulsive, careless, and undependable at the other.)
4. **Emotional stability** (sometimes labeled *neuroticisim*). A tendency to experience unpleasant emotions easily (at the low end). (A dimension ranging from poised, calm, composed, and not hypochondriacal at one end to nervous, anxious, high-strung, and hypochondriacal at the other; see Figure 10.8 on page 330.)
5. **Openness to experience.** A tendency to enjoy new experiences and new ideas. (A dimension ranging from imaginative, witty, and having broad interests at one end to down-to-earth, simple, and having narrow interests at the other.)

Source Traits
According to Cattell, key dimensions of personality that underlie many other traits.

Extraversion
One of the "big five" dimensions of personality; a dimension ranging from sociable, talking, fun-loving at one end to sober, reserved, and cautious at the other.

Agreeableness
One of the "big five" dimensions of personality; a dimension ranging from good-natured, cooperative, and trusting on one end to irritable, suspicious, and uncooperative at the other.

Conscientiousness
One of the "big five" dimensions of personality; a dimension ranging from well-organized, careful, and responsible on one end to disorganized, careless, and unscrupulous at the other.

Emotional Stability
One of the "big five" dimensions of personality; a dimension ranging from poised, calm, and composed at one extreme through nervous, anxious, and excitable at the other.

Openness to Experience
One of the "big five" dimensions of personality; a dimension ranging from imaginative, sensitive, and intellectual at one extreme to down-to-earth, insensitive, and crude at the other.

NO-ACTION COMICS

FIGURE 10.8

Emotional Stability: One of the "Big Five" Dimensions of Personality

The persons shown here are all low in *emotional stability* (i.e., they are high on neuroticism)—they have a strong tendency to experience unpleasant emotions.

Source: © The New Yorker Collection 1999 Roz Chast from cartoonbank. com. All Rights Reserved.

How basic, and therefore how important, are the "big five" dimensions? Although there is far from complete agreement on this point (e.g., Friedman & Schustack, 1999), many researchers believe that these dimensions are indeed very basic ones. This is indicated, in part, by the fact that these dimensions are ones to which most people in many different cultures refer in describing themselves (Funder & Colvin, 1991), and by the fact that we can often tell where individuals stand along at least some of these dimensions from an initial meeting with them that lasts only a few minutes (e.g., Zebrowitz & Collins, 1997). How do we know this is true? From studies in which strangers meet and interact briefly with one another, and then rate each other on measures of the big five dimensions. When these ratings by strangers are then compared with ratings by other people who know the participants in the study very well (e.g., their parents or best friends), substantial agreement is obtained for at least some of the big five dimensions—correlations of .75 or higher (e.g., Funder & Sneed, 1993; Watson, 1989). This is especially true for the dimensions of extraversion and conscientiousness. Can you see why? These are very basic dimensions of personality, and are readily apparent in the way people behave, even during a brief meeting.

One final point: Although many psychologists now view the big five dimensions as truly basic, there is *not* total consensus on this point (e.g., Block, 1995; Eysenck, 1994). By and large, though, many psychologists view the big five as providing important insights into the key dimensions of personality.

Research on Trait Theories: Effects of the "Big Five"

If the big five dimensions of personality are really so basic, then it is reasonable to expect that they will be related to important forms of behavior. In fact, many studies indicate that this is the case. Where people stand on the big five dimensions is closely linked to important outcomes, such as their success in performing many jobs (e.g., Hogan, Hogan, & Roberts, 1996), their success in starting and running a new business (Ciavarella et al., in press), the extent to which they receive emotional support from members of their families (Branje, van Lieshout, & Aiken, 2004), the extent to which they are personally happy (e.g., Steel & Ones, 2002), whether they will make good leaders—and the style of leadership they adopt (e.g., Judge & Bono, 2001)—and the extent to which they show various psychological disorders, such as attention-deficit/hyperactivity (Nigg et al., 2002). This is just a small sample of the findings suggesting that the big five are indeed "big"—they are basic dimensions of personality that are related to many important aspects of behavior. Thus, they are certainly worthy of further careful study.

Trait Theories: An Evaluation

At present, most research on personality by psychologists occurs within the context of the trait approach. Instead of seeking to test grand theories such as the ones offered by Freud, Jung, and Rogers, most psychologists currently direct their efforts to the task of understanding specific traits (Kring, Smith, & Neale, 1994). This is not to imply that the trait approach is perfect, however. On the contrary, it can be criticized in several respects. First, it is largely *descriptive* in nature. It seeks to describe the key dimensions of personality but does not attempt to determine *how* various traits develop, *how* they influence behavior, or *why* they are important. This is true with respect to the big five model, which was based on the fact that when asked to describe others, most people use these dimensions. Fully developed theories of personality must, of course, address such issues in more detail. Second, despite several decades of careful research, there is still no final agreement concerning the traits that are most important or most basic. The big five dimensions are widely accepted, but they are far from *universally* accepted, and some psychologists feel that they are not the final answer in this respect (e.g., Bandura, 1999; Block, 1995; Goldberg & Saucier, 1995).

As you can readily see, these criticisms relate primarily to what the trait approach has not yet accomplished rather than to its basic nature. All in all, we can conclude that this approach to personality has generally been a very valuable one. In short, attempting to understand the dimensions along which people differ appears to be a useful strategy for understanding the uniqueness and consistency of key aspects of their behavior.

KEY QUESTIONS

- What are central traits? Source traits?
- What are the "big five" dimensions of personality?
- What are the advantages and disadvantages of the trait approach?

COGNITIVE–BEHAVIORAL APPROACHES TO PERSONALITY

Ultimately, all personality theories must come to grips with two basic questions: What accounts for the *uniqueness* of individuals and what underlies *consistency* in their behavior over time and across situations? Freud's answer focused on *internal* factors—hidden conflicts between the id, the ego, and the superego and the active struggle to keep unacceptable impulses out of consciousness. At the other end of the continuum are approaches to personality that emphasize the role of learning and experience. Although such views were not originally presented as theories of personality, they are often described as *cognitive–behavioral theories* or *learning theories of personality* to distinguish them from other perspectives (Bandura, 1997; Rotter, 1982; Skinner, 1974).

How can this perspective account for the uniqueness and consistency of human behavior? Very readily. Uniqueness, the cognitive–behavioral approach contends, merely reflects the fact that we all have distinctive life experiences. Similarly, a cognitive–behavioral approach can explain consistency in behavior over time and across situations by noting that the responses, associations, or habits acquired through learning tend to persist. Moreover, because individuals often find themselves in situations very similar to the ones in which they acquired these tendencies, their behavior, too, tends to remain stable.

Early cognitive–behavioral views of personality emphasized the central role of learning, took what now seems to be a somewhat extreme position: They denied the importance of *any* internal causes of behavior—motives, traits, intentions, goals (Skinner, 1974). The only things that matter, these early theorists suggested, are external conditions determining patterns of reinforcement (recall the discussion of *schedules of reinforcement* in Chapter 5). At present, few psychologists agree with this position. Most now believe that internal factors—especially many aspects of *cognition*—play a crucial role in behavior. A prime example of this modern approach is provided by Bandura's *social cognitive theory* (e.g., Bandura, 1986, 1997).

Social Cognitive Theory: A Modern View of Personality

In his **social cognitive theory,** Bandura, places great emphasis on what he terms the **self-system**—the cognitive processes by which a person perceives, evaluates, and

Social Cognitive Theory
A theory of behavior suggesting that human behaviors are influenced by many cognitive factors as well as by reinforcement contingencies, and that human beings have an impressive capacity to regulate their own actions.

Self-System
In Bandura's social cognitive learning theory, the set of cognitive processes by which a person perceives, evaluates, and regulates his or her own behavior.

FIGURE 10.9
Observational Learning: An Important Source of Learning
We often acquire information and important new skills by observing the behavior of others.
Such observational learning is an important aspect of Bandura's social cognitive theory.

Self-Reinforcement
A process in which individuals reward themselves for reaching their own goals.

Observational Learning
The process through which individuals acquire information or behaviors by observing others.

Self-Efficacy
Individuals' expectations concerning their ability to perform various tasks.

regulates his or her own behavior so that is appropriate in a given situation. Reflecting the emphasis on cognition in modern psychology, Bandura calls attention to the fact that people don't simply respond to reinforcements; rather, they think about the consequences of their actions, anticipate future events, and establish goals and plans. In addition, they engage in **self-reinforcement,** patting themselves on the back when they attain their goals. For example, consider the hundreds of amateur runners who participate in major marathons. Few believe that they have any chance of winning and obtaining the external rewards offered—status, fame, cash prizes. Why, then, do they run? Because, Bandura would contend, they have *self-set goals,* such as finishing the race, or merely going as far as they can. Meeting these goals allows them to engage in self-reinforcement, and this is sufficient to initiate what is obviously very effortful behavior.

Another important feature of Bandura's theory is its emphasis on **observational learning** (which we described in Chapter 5), a form of learning in which individuals acquire both information and new forms of behavior through observing others (Bandura, 1977). Such learning plays a role in a very wide range of human activities—everything from learning how to dress and groom in the current style of one's own society through learning how to perform new and difficult tasks (see Figure 10.9). In essence, any time that human beings observe others, they can learn from this experience, and such learning can then play an important part in their own behavior.

Perhaps the aspect of Bandura's theory that has received most attention in recent research is his concept of **self-efficacy**—an individual's belief that he or she can perform some behavior or task successfully. If you sit down to take an exam in your psychology class and expect to do well, your self-efficacy is high; if you have doubts about your performance, your self-efficacy is lower. Self-efficacy has been found to play a role in success on many tasks (e.g., Maurer & Pierce, 1998): in health—people who expect to handle stress effectively or to get better actually do (Bandura, 1992); in personal happiness and life satisfaction (Judge, Martocchio, & Thorsen, 1998); and in success in starting a new business—entrepreneurs tend to be higher in self-efficacy than other persons and believe they can succeed even though the odds are against them (Markman, Baron, & Balkin, 2003). Although Bandura did not initially view self-efficacy as an aspect of personality, recent findings indicate that people acquire *general* expectations about their abilities to succeed in performing many tasks—virtually any tasks they undertake. Such generalized beliefs about their task-related capabilities are stable over time, so these beliefs are now viewed by many psychologists as an important aspect of personality.

Other learning-oriented approaches to personality have much in common with Bandura's views. For example, the *social learning theory* proposed by Julian Rotter (1954, 1982) suggests that the likelihood that a given behavior will occur in a specific situation depends on individuals' *expectancies* concerning the outcomes the behavior will produce and the *reinforcement value* they attach to such outcomes—the degree to which they prefer one reinforcer over another. According to Rotter, individuals form *generalized expectancies* concerning the extent to which their actions shape their own outcomes. Rotter describes persons who strongly believe that they can shape their own destinies as **internals** and those who believe their outcomes are largely the result of forces outside their control as **externals.** As you can probably guess, internals are often happier and better adjusted than externals.

Evaluation of the Cognitive–Behavioral Approach

Do all human beings confront an Oedipus conflict? Are peak experiences real, and do they in fact constitute a sign of growing self-actualization? Considerable controversy exists with respect to these and many other aspects of psychoanalytic and humanistic theories of personality. In contrast, virtually all psychologists agree that behaviors are acquired and modified through learning. Moreover, there is general agreement about the importance of cognitive factors in human behavior. Thus, a key strength of the learning approach is obvious: It is based on widely accepted and well-documented principles of psychology. Another positive feature of this framework involves the fact that it has been put to practical use in efforts to modify maladaptive forms of behavior (see Chapter 12).

Turning to criticisms, most of these have focused on older approaches rather than on the more sophisticated theories proposed by Bandura (1986, 1997) and others. Those early behaviorist theorists generally ignored the role of cognitive factors in human behavior, but this is certainly *not* true of the modern theories. A related criticism centers around the fact that learning theories generally ignore inner conflicts, and the influence of unconscious thoughts and impulses, on behavior. However, while such issues are not explicitly addressed by theories such as Bandura's, their existence and possible impact is not in any way denied by these theories. Rather, modern learning theories would simply insist that such effects be interpreted within the context of modern psychology.

As you can readily see, these are *not* major criticisms. Thus, it seems fair to state that, at present, these cognitive–behavioral theories of personality are more in tune with modern psychology than earlier theories. As such, they are certain to play an important role, along with the trait approach, in continuing efforts to understand the uniqueness and consistency of human behavior—the issues that lead us to consider personality in the first place. (Earlier, we noted that entrepreneurs are higher in self-efficacy than other people. What other traits distinguish entrepreneurs from other persons? To find out, please see the following **Psychology Goes to Work** section.)

K E Y   Q U E S T I O N S

- According to cognitive–behavioral theories of personality, what accounts for the uniqueness and consistency of human behavior?
- In Bandura's social cognitive theory, what is the *self-system?*
- According to Rotter's social learning theory, what is the key difference between internals and externals?
- What is self-efficacy?

Internals
Individuals who believe that they exert considerable control over the outcomes they experience.

Externals
Individuals who believe that they have little control over the outcomes they experience.

PSYCHOLOGY GOES TO WORK

Are You Suited to Becoming an Entrepreneur? A Quick Self-Assessment

Do you ever dream of becoming an entrepreneur—of starting your own business, making a fortune, and then—perhaps—making large donations to your favorite charities, to education, or to scientific research? If so, you are in good company, because the role of *entrepreneur* has recently taken on an aura of glamour. Famous entrepreneurs like Bill Gates and Michael Dell are in the news frequently, and reports of the size of their personal fortunes lead many people to think, "Why not *me*?" In fact, though, most new companies fail—more than 60 percent within the first three years (Baron & Shane, 2004). Many factors play a role in such failures, but an important one is this: Many people who decide to become entrepreneurs are simply not suited for this role. Research on this topic (much of it conducted by psychologists) indicates that to be a successful entrepreneur, people need a number of different characteristics. Here is a list of the most important ones. Consider them carefully and then ask yourself, "Do I have these characteristics?" If so, you are a good candidate to start your own business (or become a franchisee). If not, you might well be better off considering some other career.

- **High self-efficacy.** As noted, entrepreneurs—especially successful ones—are higher in self-efficacy than other people. In other words, to succeed in this role, you must believe that you can accomplish whatever you set out to accomplish. If you are lacking in such confidence, becoming an entrepreneur is probably not for you.
- **Tolerance for uncertainty and ambiguity.** Starting a new business means jumping off into the unknown. You must develop new products or services, find markets for them, deal with new competitors—who often seem to arise out of nowhere—and many other uncertainties. So, if you are very uncomfortable in such situations, becoming an entrepreneur is probably not your cup of tea.
- **High energy, good health, and high tolerance for stress.** Most entrepreneurs report that they work 80 or 100 hours a week, and frequently face highly stressful situations. Do you have the energy, health, and stress tolerance for this kind of life? If so, get started! If not, think again.
- **An ability to learn what you need "on the fly."** Most entrepreneurs do *not* know everything they need to know to run their businesses successfully; they learn it "on the fly" as they proceed. Are you willing to do this? Or would you feel uncomfortable in that kind of situation? If so, you are probably not well suited to become an entrepreneur.
- **Excellent social skills.** Are you good with people? Can you be persuasive? Make a good first impression? As an entrepreneur, you will have to convince investors to back your company with hard cash, persuade customers to try your product, and convince talented people to give up secure jobs to work with you. Research findings (e.g., Baron & Markman, 2003) indicate that to succeed in these tasks, you need good social skills. So, if you don't have them, either start now to acquire them or give up the idea of becoming an entrepreneur.
- **Can you share control?** One problem that destroys many new companies is an inability of the founding entrepreneurs to share control and power with others: They want to do it all themselves. That doesn't work, because as a new company grows, it is impossible for any one person to do everything. Are you the kind of person who can let others take responsibility? If not, you are probably not suited to becoming an entrepreneur.

Consider all these points carefully, because becoming an entrepreneur is a *major* decision: It can consume all your time, money, and energy. If you possess the characteristics discussed here, this may be the right career move for you. If not, think again, because the costs of failure can be *very* high.

MEASURING PERSONALITY

To study personality scientifically, we must first be able to measure it. How do psychologists deal with this issue? As we'll soon see, in several different ways.

Self-Report Tests of Personality: Questionnaires and Inventories

One way of measuring personality involves asking individuals to respond to a *self-report* inventory or questionnaire. Such measures (sometimes known as *objective* tests of personality) contain questions or statements to which individuals respond in various ways. For example, a questionnaire might ask respondents to indicate the extent to which each of a set of statements is true or false about themselves, the extent to which they agree or disagree with various sentences (e.g., "I often feel that I can do everything well." "At root, I am a strong person."), or to indicate which of a pair of activities they prefer. (Incidentally, the two items listed here are from one widely used measure of self-efficacy.)

Answers to the questions on such objective tests are scored by means of special keys. The score obtained by a specific person is then compared with those obtained by hundreds or even thousands of other people who have taken the test previously. In this way, an individual's relative standing on the trait being measured can be determined.

For some objective tests, the items included have the kind of *face validity* described in Chapter 7: Reading them, it is easy to see that they are related to the trait or traits being measured. For instance, you can probably readily see how the items above do seem to be clearly linked to self-efficacy. On other tests, however, the items do not necessarily appear to be related to the traits or characteristics. Rather, a procedure known as *empirical keying* is used. The items are given to hundreds of persons belonging to groups known to differ from one another—for instance, psychiatric patients with specific forms of mental illness and normal persons. Then the answers given by the two groups are compared. Items answered differently by the groups are included on the test, *regardless of whether these items seem to be related to the traits being measured.* The reasoning is as follows: As long as a test item differentiates between the groups in question—groups we know to be different—then the specific content of the item itself is unimportant.

One widely used test designed to measure various types of psychological disorders—the **MMPI**—uses precisely this method. The MMPI (short for *Minnesota Multiphasic Personality Inventory*) was developed during the 1930s but underwent a major revision in 1989 (Butcher, 1990). The current version, the MMPI-2, contains ten *clinical scales* (see Chapter 14) and several *validity scales*. The clinical scales, which are summarized in Table 10.2 on page 336, relate to various forms of psychological disorder. Items included in each of these scales are ones that are answered differently by persons who have been diagnosed as having this particular disorder and by persons in a comparison group who do *not* have the disorder. The validity scales are designed to determine whether and to what extent people are trying to "fake" their answers—for instance, whether they are trying to seem bizarre or, conversely, to give the impression that they are extremely "normal" and well adjusted. If persons taking the test score high on these validity scales, their responses to the clinical scales must be interpreted with special caution.

Another widely used objective measure of personality is the **Millon Clinical Multiaxial Inventory** (MCMI; Millon, 1987, 1997). Items on this test correspond more closely than those on the MMPI to the categories of psychological disorders currently used by psychologists (we'll discuss these in detail in Chapter 12). This makes the test especially useful to clinical psychologists, who must first identify individuals' problems before recommending specific forms of therapy for them.

MMPI

A widely used objective test of personality based on *empirical keying.*

Millon Clinical Multiaxial Inventory (MCMI)

An objective test of personality specifically designed to assist psychologists in diagnosing various psychological disorders.

TABLE 10.2 Clinical Scales of the MMPI-2

The MMPI-2 is designed to measure many aspects of personality related to psychological disorders.

Clinical Scale	Description of Disorder
Hypochondriasis	Excessive concern with bodily functions
Depression	Pessimism; hopelessness; slowing of action and thought
Hysteria	Development of physical disorders such as blindness, paralysis, and vomiting as an escape from emotional problems
Psychopathic Deviance	Disregard for social customs; shallow emotions
Masculinity–Femininity	Possession of traits and interests typically associated with the opposite sex
Paranoia	Suspiciousness; delusions of grandeur or persecution
Psychasthenia	Obsession; compulsions; fears; guilt; indecisiveness
Schizophrenia	Bizarre, unusual thoughts or behavior; withdrawal; hallucinations; delusions
Hypomania	Emotional excitement; flight of ideas; overactivity
Social Introversion	Shyness; lack of interest in others; insecurity

A third objective test, the **NEO Personality Inventory** (NEO-PI; Costa & McCrae, 1989), is used to measure aspects of personality that are *not* directly linked to psychological disorders. Specifically, it measures the "big five" dimensions of personality described earlier in this chapter. These dimensions appear to represent basic aspects of personality. Thus, the NEO Personality Inventory has been widely used in research.

Projective Measures of Personality

In contrast to questionnaires and inventories, *projective tests* of personality adopt a very different approach. They present individuals with ambiguous stimuli—stimuli that can be interpreted in many different ways. For instance, these can be inkblots, such as the one shown in Figure 10.10, or ambiguous scenes. Persons taking the test are then asked to indicate what they see, to make up a story about this stimulus, and so on. Because the stimuli themselves are ambiguous, it is assumed that the answers given by respondents will reflect various aspects of their personalities. In other words, different persons "see" different things in these stimuli because these persons differ from one another with respect to various aspects of personality.

Do such tests really work—do they meet the criteria of reliability and validity discussed in Chapter 11? For some projective tests (for instance, the *Thematic Apperception Test,* which is used to measure need for achievement), the answer appears to be yes: Such tests do yield reliable scores and do seem to measure what they are intended to measure. For others, such as the famous **Rorschach test,** which uses inkblots such as the one in Figure 10.10, the answer is more doubtful (Exner, 1993; Wood, Nezworski, & Stejskal, 1996). Thus, projective tests, like objective tests, may vary with respect to validity. Only tests that meet high standards in this respect can provide us with useful information about personality.

FIGURE 10.10
The Rorschach Test: One Projective Measure of Personality
Persons taking the *Rorschach test* describe what they see in a series of inkblots. Supposedly, individuals' responses reveal much about their personalities. However, recent findings cast doubt on the validity of this test.

Other Measures: Behavioral Observations, Interviews, and Biological Measures

While self-report questionnaires and projective techniques are the most widely used measures of personality, several other techniques exist as well. For instance, the advent of electronic pagers now allows researchers to "beep" individuals at random (or specific) times during the day in order to obtain descriptions of their behavior at these times. This *experience sampling method* (e.g., Stone, Kessler, & Haythornthwaite, 1991) can often reveal much about stable patterns of individual behavior, a key aspect of personality.

Interviews are also used to measure specific aspects of personality. Psycho-analysis, of course, uses a special type of interview to probe supposedly underlying aspects of personality. But in modern research, special types of interviews, in which individuals are asked questions assumed to related to specific traits, are often used instead. For instance, interviews are used to measure the *Type A behavior pattern,* an important aspect of personality closely related to personal health. Persons high in this pattern are always in a hurry—they hate being delayed. Thus, questions asked during the interview focus on this tendency, for instance: "What do you do when you are stuck on the highway behind a slow driver?"

Several *biological measures* of personality have been developed. Some of these use positron emission tomography (PET) scans to see if individuals show characteristic patterns of activity in their brains—patterns that are related to differences in their overt behavior. Other measures focus on hormone levels—for instance, the question of whether highly aggressive persons have different levels of sex hormones than other persons. Some results suggest that this may indeed the case (Harris et al., 1996).

In sum, many tools for measuring personality exist. None are perfect, but together they provide psychologists with many useful techniques for investigating the stable patterns of behavior that make each of us a unique human being.

KEY QUESTIONS

- What are self-report tests of personality?
- What are projective tests of personality?
- What other measures of personality do psychologists currently use?

MODERN RESEARCH ON PERSONALITY: BEYOND GRAND THEORIES

Grand theories such as those proposed by Freud, Rogers, Adler, and others have provided important insights into the nature of personality. But modern research, although sometimes influenced by these theories, has focused on a number of topics and questions not included in them, such as, "Is there any connection between personality and health?" "What are the effects of personality on task performance, including success in various jobs or careers?" and "What is the role of personality in long-term relationships such as marriage?" All these issues are fascinating, and all have important practical implications. To provide you with a sample of what modern research on personality is like, we will focus on two related issues that have recently received growing research attention: (1) What is the role of various aspects of personality in *subjective well-being* (personal happiness)? And (2) what is the role of personality in the occurrence of human *aggression*?

Personality and Subjective Well-Being: What Traits Contribute to Personal Happiness?

In Chapter 9, we discussed some of the factors that influence personal happiness, such as having close relations with friends, family, and romantic partners; clear

NEO Personality Inventory
An objective measure of personality designed to assess individuals' relative standing on each of the "big five" dimensions of personality.

Rorschach Test
A widely used projective test of personality in which individuals are asked to describe what they see in a series of inkblots.

goals; and a satisfying career (Diener & Seligman, 2002). What about personality—does it, too, play a role in personal happiness? Growing evidence suggests that it does. One factor that may play an important role in this respect is the tendency to either seek optimal (perfect?) outcomes in many situations (maximization) versus the tendency to seek outcomes that meet minimal standards and are therefore acceptable (satisficing). Who would you expect to be happier, people who always seek optimal outcomes (maximizers) or those who seek acceptable ones (satisficers)? If you guessed the latter, you are correct. Recent studies by Schwartz and his colleagues (e.g, Schwartz, 2000) have found that persons who show strong tendencies toward maximization are indeed less happy in several ways than those who prefer to satisfice. For example, consider recent studies by Schwartz and several colleagues (Schwartz et al., 2002).

In one study, participants known to be maximizers or satisficers (they previously completed a measure of this characteristic) performed an anagram task. Another person also performed this task, but unknown to the participants, he was an assistant of the researcher and appeared to complete the same set of problems much faster or much slower than the real subjects. Both before and after completing the task, participants were asked to rate their own ability to solve anagrams and to rate their current mood. The researchers predicted that maximizers would be more unhappy than satisficers with their performance when the other person performed faster than they did, and so would down-rate their own ability to perform this task to a greater extent. Similarly, they would also show a greater increase in negative affect (mood). These differences would emerge because performing slower than another person would be further away from optimal outcomes for maximizers than for satisficers. As you can see from Figure 10.11, this is precisely what happened. In other studies, maximizers reported being less happy than satisficers with products they had recently chosen to buy. Overall, then, it appears that the tendency to maximize—to seek perfect outcomes in many situations—can be a real obstacle to personal happiness.

This is not the only dimension of personality that influences happiness, however. Two aspects of the big five dimensions—neuroticism and extraversion—have

FIGURE 10.11

People Who Seek Perfection (Maximizers) Are Not Happy!

As shown here, maximizers—people who seek optimal outcomes in a wide range of situations—showed a greater increase in negative affect than satisficers—people who seek acceptable outcomes—when another person performed faster than they did on an anagram task. Presumably, performing more slowly than another person was further away from an optimal outcome for the maximizers than the satisficers. Overall, maximizers tend to show lower levels of happiness than satisficers in a wide range of situations.

Source: Based on data from Schwartz et al., 2002.

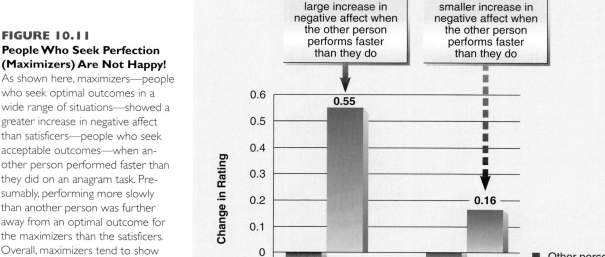

"*Ah, J.T.—just the man I was looking for.*"

also been found to play a role in personal happiness (e.g., Diener & Lucas, 1999). Perhaps even more interesting, this seems to be true for nations as well as individuals. In one recent study, the average level of neuroticism in many different countries was found to be negatively related to happiness in those countries, while the average level of extraversion was found to be positively related to it (Steel & Ones, 2002). How can personality traits affect average levels of happiness in various nations? Steel and Ones (2002) suggest that neuroticism—a tendency to experience negative emotions—may reduce happiness because negative emotions are "contagious" and spread throughout a culture. Similarly, the higher the level of extraversion in a country, the friendlier people in a given nation may be to each other—with the result that happiness is increased. Needless to say, these explanations are somewhat speculative, but regardless of whether they are accurate, it is clear that average happiness is higher in some countries than in others, and that personality may play a role in such differences—even when differences in wealth (gross national product) are held constant.

In sum, it is clear that several aspects of personality play a role in personal happiness. While such a relationship would also be predicted by some theories of personality (e.g., humanistic theories), none of these theories specifically include the kind of variables studied in recent research, so it is clear that modern research has gone well beyond the scope of these theories in many ways.

Personality and Human Aggression

Are some people—like the one shown in Figure 10.12—"primed" for aggression by aspects of their personality? Your own experience probably suggests that this is so. While some individuals rarely lose their tempers or engage in aggressive actions, others seem to be forever "blowing up," with potentially serious consequences. What aspects of personality play a role in such behavior? Two that have been found to play an important role are the Type A behavior pattern and narcissim.

■ The Type A Behavior Pattern: Why the *A* in Type A Could Still Stand for *Aggression*

Do you know anyone you could describe as (1) extremely competitive, (2) always in a hurry, and (3) especially irritable and aggressive? If so, this person shows the characteristics of what psychologists term the **Type A behavior pattern** (Glass, 1977; Strube, 1989). At the opposite end of the continuum are persons who do not show these characteristics—individuals who are *not* highly competitive, who are *not* always fighting the clock, and who do *not* readily lose their temper; such persons are described as showing the **Type B behavior pattern**.

Given the characteristics mentioned above, it seems only reasonable to expect that Type A's would tend to be more aggressive than Type B's in many situations.

Type A Behavior Pattern
A pattern consisting primarily of high levels of competitiveness, time urgency, and hostility.

Type B Behavior Pattern
A pattern consisting of the absence of characteristics associated with the Type A behavior pattern.

FIGURE 10.13
**Building Self-Esteem:
Can We Overdo It?**
Schools in the United States and
many other countries work hard
to increase the self-esteem of
students. In general, this has very
beneficial effects. But recent research on one aspect of personality—narcissism—a tendency
to hold an overinflated view of
one's worth—indicates that such
efforts can go too far and create
individuals who react with excessive anger and aggression to
even very mild provocations.

Hostile Aggression
Aggression in which the prime
objective is inflicting some
kind of harm on the victim.

Instrumental Aggression
Aggression in which the primary goal is not harm to the
victim but attainment of some
other goal, such as access to
valued resources.

In fact, the results of several experiments indicate that this is actually the case (Baron, Russell, & Arms, 1985; Carver & Glass, 1978).

Additional findings indicate that Type A's are truly hostile people: They don't merely aggress against others because this is a useful means for reaching important goals, such as winning athletic contests or furthering their own careers. Rather, they are more likely than Type B's to engage in what is known as **hostile aggression**—aggression in which the prime objective is inflicting some kind of harm on the victim (Strube et al., 1984). In view of this fact, it is not surprising to learn that Type A's are more likely than Type B's to engage in such actions as child abuse or spouse abuse (Strube et al., 1984). In contrast, Type A's are *not* more likely than Type B's to engage in **instrumental aggression**—aggression performed primarily to attain other goals aside from harming the victim, goals such as control of valued resources or praise from others for behaving in a "tough" manner.

Narcissism, Ego-Threat, and Aggression: On the Dangers of an Over-Inflated Self-Concept

Do you know the story of Narcissus? He was a character in Greek mythology who fell in love with his own reflection in the water, and drowned trying to reach it. His name has now become a synonym for excessive self-love—for holding an overinflated view of one's own virtues or accomplishments—and research findings indicate that this trait may be linked to aggression in important ways. Specifically, studies by Bushman and Baumeister (1998) suggest that persons high in *narcissism*—ones who hold an unrealistically positive self-concept—react with exceptionally high levels of aggression even to minor snubs or insults from others. Why do they react so strongly? Perhaps because such persons have nagging doubts about the accuracy of their inflated self-concepts, and so react with intense anger toward anyone who threatens to undermine these views.

These findings have important implications because, at the present time, many schools in the United States focus on building high self-esteem among their students (see Figure 10.13). Up to a point, this may indeed be beneficial. But if such esteem-building tactics are carried too far and produce children whose opinions of themselves are unrealistically high (i.e., narcissistic), the result may actually be an increased potential for violence. Clearly, this is a possibility worthy of further, careful study.

In closing, we should note that the research described in this section presents only a tiny sample of current efforts by psychologists to understand the nature of personality and its effects on important aspects of behavior. But we hope it will leave you with the idea that personality *is* important and that studying it involves much more than theories such as those proposed by Freud, Rogers, and others.

KEY QUESTIONS
- What aspects of personality play a role in personal happiness?
- What aspects of personality play a role in human aggression?

SUMMARY AND REVIEW OF KEY QUESTIONS

- **What is personality?**
  Personality consists of the unique and stable patterns of behavior, thoughts, and emotions shown by individuals.
- **How stable is it over time?**
  Research findings indicate that personality is quite stable over time, although some persons show more stability than others.

- **What is the interactionist perspective currently adopted by most psychologists?**
  The view that our behavior in any given situation is a joint function of our personality and various aspects of the situation.

The Psychoanalytic Approach: Messages from the Unconscious

- **According to Freud, what are the three levels of consciousness?**
  These levels are the conscious, the preconscious, and the unconscious.

- **In Freud's theory, what are the three basic components of personality?**
  The three basic components of personality are the id, the ego, and the superego, which correspond roughly to desire, reason, and conscience.

- **According to Freud, what are the psychosexual stages of development?**
  Freud believed that all human beings move through a series of psychosexual stages during which the id's search for pleasure is focused on different regions of the body: oral stage, anal stage, phallic stage, latency stage, and, finally, genital stage.

- **Do research findings support Freud's views about the unconscious?**
  Research findings indicate that our behavior is sometimes influenced by stimuli or information we can't describe verbally, although there is no support for his view that such information has been driven from consciousness by repression.

- **According to Jung, what is the collective unconscious?**
  Jung believed that all human beings share memories of our collective experience as a species. These are expressed when our conscious mind is distracted or inactive, often through *archetypes.*

- **In Horney's theory, what is basic anxiety?**
  Basic anxiety is the child's fear of being alone, helpless, and insecure.

- **According to Adler, what is the role of feelings of inferiority in personality?**
  Adler believed that human beings experience strong feelings of inferiority during early life and must struggle to overcome these through compensation.

Humanistic Theories: Emphasis on Growth

- **How does the view of human beings proposed by humanistic theories of personality differ from that of psychoanalytic theories?**
  Humanistic theories of personality suggest that people strive for personal development and growth; in contrast, psychoanalytic theory views human beings as constantly struggling to control the sexual and aggressive impulses of the id.

- **According to Rogers, why do many individuals fail to become fully functioning persons?**
  Rogers believed that many individuals fail to become fully functioning persons because distorted self-concepts interfere with personal growth.

- **In Maslow's theory, what is self-actualization?**
  Self-actualization is a stage in which an individual has reached his or her maximum potential, and become the best human being she or he can be.

Trait Theories: Seeking the Key Dimensions of Personality

- **What are source traits?**
  According to Cattell, there are sixteen source traits that underlie differences between individuals on many specific dimensions.

- **What are the "big five" dimensions of personality?**
  Research findings point to the conclusion that there are only five basic dimensions of personality: extraversion, agreeableness, conscientiousness, emotional stability, and openness to experience.

- **What are the advantages and disadvantages of the trait approach?**
  Advantages of the trait approach include the fact that it is the basis for most current research on personality, and that the traits it has uncovered are related to important aspects of behavior. Disadvantages include the fact that the trait approach offers no comprehensive theory for *how* certain traits develop and *why* they are so important.

Cognitive–Behavioral Approaches to Personality

- **According to cognitive–behavioral theories of personality, what accounts for the uniqueness and consistency of human behavior?**
  Cognitive–behavioral theories of personality suggest that uniqueness derives from the unique pattern of learning experiences each individual has experienced. Such approaches explain consistency by noting that patterns of behavior, once acquired, tend to persist.

- **In Bandura's social cognitive theory, what is the self-system?**
  The self-system is the set of cognitive processes by which individuals perceive, evaluate, and regulate their own behaviors.

- **According to Rotter's social learning theory, what is the key difference between internals and externals?**
  Internals believe that they can control the outcomes they experience, while externals do not.

- **What is self-efficacy?**
  Self-efficacy is belief in one's ability to perform a specific task.

Measuring Personality

- **What are self-report tests of personality?**
  These are questionnaires containing a number of questions individuals answer about themselves. Examples are the MMPI and the MCMI (Millon Clinical Multiaxial Inventory).

- **What are projective tests of personality?**
  Such tests present individuals with ambiguous stimuli. Their responses to these stimuli are assumed to reflect various aspects of their personalities.

- **What other measures of personality do psychologists currently use?**
  They use behavioral observations (including experience sampling), interviews, and biological measures.

**Modern Research on Personality:
Beyond Grand Theories**

- **What aspects of personality play a role in personal happiness?**
  Among the aspects of personality that influence personal happiness are the tendency to seek to maximize rather than satisfice outcomes in many situations, and two aspects of the big five dimensions of personality—neuroticism and extraversion.

- **What aspects of personality play a role in human aggression?**
  Among the aspects of personality that play a role in human aggression are the Type A behavior pattern and narcissism—a tendency to hold an overinflated view of oneself.

PSYCHOLOGY: UNDERSTANDING ITS FINDINGS

Strong Situations versus Weak Situations: When Personality Does—and Does Not—Influence our Behavior

Earlier, we noted that psychologists believe that our behavior in most situations is a joint function of our personality *and* various aspects of the situation. In other words, this *interactionist perspective* suggests that personality will indeed affect our behavior—but only if pressures in the situation do not prevent this from occurring. This is a key point, so to fully grasp it, try the following exercise:

1. Think of situations in which various aspects of your personality can readily find expression. These would be situations in which you are generally free to behave as you prefer, to express your views, and let what is inside show on the outside. Describe at least three such situations.

2. Now, think of situations in which you *cannot* behave as you prefer, and in which certain aspects of your personality could not affect your behavior. (Hint: Remember the situation in which a driver is stopped by a state trooper? Situations you think of should be like that one—ones in which you would prefer to behave in one way but cannot do so because of situational constraints.)

3. Next, compare the two kinds of situations. Do they have anything in common? How are they different? What proportion of your time do you spend in each type?

4. If you follow these steps, you will understand why the best answer to the question "Is personality important?" is, "Yes, but just *how* important depends on the specific situation."

MAKING PSYCHOLOGY PART OF YOUR LIFE

Are You a Type A?

The Type A behavior pattern is one aspect of personality related to many important outcomes—personal health, task performance, even how frequently individuals become involved in aggression. Are *you* high or low on this dimension? To find out, complete the items below. For each, circle the letter of the answer that is true for you.

1. Is your daily life filled mainly with
   a. problems needing solutions
   b. challenges needing to be met
   c. a predictable routine of events
   d. not enough things to keep me busy

2. When you are under pressure, do you usually
   a. do something about it at once
   b. plan carefully before taking action

3. How rapidly do you eat?
   a. Very fast—I'm usually finished before others are finished
   b. Faster than average
   c. About average
   d. More slowly than average

4. Has your best friend ever told you that you eat too fast?
   a. Yes, often
   b. Yes, occasionally
   c. No

5. When you listen to someone speaking, do you feel like hurrying him/her along?
   a. frequently
   b. sometimes
   c. never

6. How often do you "put words in his/her mouth" to speed things up?
   a. frequently
   b. sometimes
   c. never

7. When you make an appointment, how often are you late?
   a. sometimes
   b. rarely
   c. never

8. Do you consider yourself to be
   a. very competitive
   b. somewhat competitive
   c. relatively easygoing
   d. very easygoing

9. How would a close friend rate you?
   a. very competitive
   b. somewhat competitive
   c. relatively easygoing
   d. very easygoing

10. How would others describe your general level of activity?
    a. slow and inactive; should do more
    b. about average
    c. too active; should slow down

11. Would people who know you well say that you have less energy than most people?
    a. definitely yes
    b. probably yes
    c. probably no
    d. definitely no

12. How often do you face deadlines in your work?
    a. every day
    b. once a week
    c. once a month
    d. rarely

13. Do you ever set deadlines for yourself?
    a. no
    b. sometimes
    c. often

14. Do you ever work on two or more projects at once?
    a. never
    b. occasionally
    c. often

15. Do you work during vacation periods such as Thanksgiving, Christmas, Spring Break?
    a. yes
    b. no
    c. sometimes

To calculate your score, give yourself *one point* for each of the following answers:

(1) a or b; (2) a; (3) a or b; (4) a; (5) a; (6) a; (7) c; (8) a or b; (9) a or b; (10) c; (11) d; (12) c; (13) c; (14) c; (15) a

If your total score is 10 or higher, you show some of the same tendencies as Type A persons; if your score is 5 or lower, you show the tendencies shown by Type B persons. But please view these results as simply a very rough guide to where you fall in this dimension. The items above, while similar to the ones used to measure the Type A behavior pattern, have not been carefully validated, so please do treat them with caution.

KEY TERMS

Agreeableness, p. 329
Anal Stage, p. 319
Anima, p. 323
Animus, p. 323
Anxiety, p. 318
Archetypes, p. 323
Basic Anxiety, p. 323
Collective Unconscious, p. 323
Conscientiousness, p. 329
Defense Mechanisms, p. 318
Ego, p. 317
Emotional Stability, p. 329
Externals, p. 333
Extroverts, p. 323
Extraversion, p. 329
Fixation, p. 319
Freudian Slips, p. 317
Fully Functioning Persons, p. 325

Genital Stage, p. 319
Hostile Aggression, p. 340
Humanistic Theories, p. 324
Id, p. 317
Instrumental Aggression, p. 340
Internals, p. 333
Introverts, p. 323
Latency Stage, p. 319
Libido, p. 319
Millon Clinical Multiaxial Inventory (MCMI), p. 335
MMPI, p. 335
NEO Personality Inventory, p. 336
Neo-Freudians, p. 322
Observational Learning, p. 332
Oedipus Complex, p. 319

Openness to Experience, p. 329
Oral Stage, p. 319
Peak Experiences, p. 326
Personality, p. 314
Personality Traits, p. 328
Phallic Stage, p. 319
Pleasure Principle, p. 317
Psychoanalysis, p. 317
Psychosexual Stages of Development, p. 318
Reality Principle, p. 317
Rorschach Test, p. 336
Self-Actualization, p. 326
Self-Concept, p. 325
Self-Efficacy, p. 332
Self-Esteem, p. 327
Self-Reinforcement, p. 332
Self-System, p. 331

Social Cognitive Theory, p. 331
Source Traits, p. 329
Striving for Superiority, p. 324
Sublimation, p. 318
Superego, p. 317
Trait Theories, p. 328
Type A Behavior Pattern, p. 339
Type B Behavior Pattern, p. 339
Unconditional Positive Regard, p. 325

Health, Stress, and Coping

A few years ago, I (Michael Kalsher) was saddened to learn that a close friend and his wife were divorcing. Although in today's world divorce is common, I was surprised because they had seemed so happy. Prior to the split, my friend always seemed so full of life. He worked hard and enjoyed great success in his career, but at the same time reserved plenty of energy for his many outside interests, including travel, exercise, and enjoying good food and wine with his wife and their friends. Unfortunately, this picture changed sharply in the months following the breakup. Indeed, I became increasingly worried as my friend slowly drifted into a deep funk. He became withdrawn, less sure of himself, and generally more pessimistic in his outlook. In fact, during one conversation, he expressed the fear that he could never again love someone the same way he loved his former wife. He also seemed to lose his good health; for example, he began to suffer from recurring headaches and other stress-related illnesses that had not been evident before the divorce. Fortunately, the story has a happy ending. Although my friend's funk continued for several months, he eventually snapped out of it and returned to his former self. Happily, he is now remarried and is once again enjoying life.

Why do I start with this story? Because it highlights the intimate relationship that exists between psychological variables and health. Indeed, several decades of research suggest that good health is determined by a complex interaction among genetic, psychological, and social factors. Throughout this chapter, we'll encounter findings that show how these factors combine to produce good—and poor—health.

We'll begin by describing the exciting branch of psychology known as *health psychology*. The primary aim of health psychology is to identify important relationships between psychological variables and health. Second, we'll consider the nature of *stress*, a major health-related problem as we begin the new millennium. We'll focus on both the causes of stress and some of its major effects—how it influences health and performance. Next, we'll consider how some of our *beliefs and attitudes* influence the way in which we interpret certain health symptoms, and thus affect our willingness to seek necessary medical assistance. Fourth, we'll look at *behaviors* that can directly affect our risk of contracting certain lifestyle-related illnesses, such as cancer, cardiovascular diseases, and AIDS. Finally, we'll consider various ways in which psychologists work to promote personal health by encouraging healthy lifestyles.

HEALTH PSYCHOLOGY: AN OVERVIEW

Health psychology, the branch of psychology that studies the relation between psychological variables and health, reflects the view that both mind and body are important determinants of health and illness (Taylor, 2002). Specifically, health psychologists believe that our beliefs, attitudes, and behavior contribute significantly to the onset or prevention of illness (Baum & Posluszny, 1999). A closely related field, known as *behavioral medicine*, combines behavioral and biomedical knowledge for the prevention and treatment of disorders ordinarily thought of as being within the domain of medicine (Epstein, 1992; Keefe et al., 2002).

Health psychology and behavioral medicine have experienced tremendous growth since their beginnings in the early 1970s. Perhaps the most fundamental reason for the increased interest in health psychology and behavioral medicine is the dramatic shift observed in the leading causes of death during the twentieth century. In 1900, many of the leading causes of death could be traced to infectious diseases, such as influenza, pneumonia, and tuberculosis. However, the development of antibiotics, vaccines, and improved sanitation practices has significantly reduced these health threats, at least in this country.

As shown in Table 11.1, the current leading causes of death are attributable to a significant degree to characteristics that make up **lifestyle**—the overall pattern of decisions and behaviors that determines a person's health and quality of life. This fact suggests that psychologists can make a difference in people's quality of life by helping them eliminate behaviors that lead to illness and adopt behaviors that lead to wellness. Indeed, a majority of the conditions that now constitute the leading causes of death could be prevented if people would eat nutritious foods, reduce their alcohol consumption, practice safe sex, eliminate smoking, and exercise regularly.

Health Psychology
The study of the relation between psychological variables and health, which reflects the view that both mind and body are important determinants of health and illness.

Lifestyle
In the context of health psychology, the overall pattern of decisions and behaviors that determine health and quality of life.

| | TABLE 11.1 | Top 10 Leading Causes of Deaths in the United States: 2000 | | |

Many of the important causes of death shown here are related to lifestyle. Thus, they can be prevented by changes in behavior.

Rank	Cause of Death	Deaths	% of Total Deaths
1	Heart disease	710,760	29.6
2	Cancer	553,091	23.0
3	Stroke	167,661	7.0
4	Chronic lung disease	122,009	5.1
5	Accidents (unintentional injuries)	97,900	4.1
6	Diabetes mellitus	69,301	2.9
7	Influenza and pneumonia	65,313	2.7
8	Alzheimer's disease	49,558	2.1
9	Kidney disease	37,351	1.5
10	Blood poisoning	31,224	1.3
Total		2,403,351	100.0

Source: Based on data in the National Vital Statistics Report, vol. 50, no. 16, September 16, 2002.

To illustrate the contribution of health psychology research, let's consider a classic decade-long study conducted in Alameda County, California. The researchers asked a large group of adults whether they followed certain health practices, including sleeping seven to eight hours each night, eating breakfast regularly, refraining from smoking, drinking alcohol in moderation or not at all, maintaining their weight within normal limits, and exercising regularly (Wiley & Camacho, 1980). The results revealed that participants who reported practicing all or most of these behaviors were much less likely to die during the study period than those who practiced few or none of these behaviors. These results highlight the intimate connection between lifestyle and good health.

But how likely is it that people can be persuaded to adopt healthier lifestyles? Results from the *Healthy People 2000 Initiative,* a nationwide health promotion and disease prevention agenda, are encouraging, but they also point out how difficult it is to change certain behaviors. The aim of this program, initially begun in 1979, was to promote good health among citizens of the United States by identifying the most significant preventable threats to health and then focusing public and private resources to address those threats effectively. It was an ambitious project that targeted specific health indicators (e.g., physical activity, obesity, tobacco use, responsible sexual behavior) for improvement and sought to make preventive health services available to all Americans. Significant progress was made on some of the objectives, including increases in the number of children receiving immunizations and women receiving mammography screening, an increase in consumption of fruits and vegetables, and a reduction in infant mortality rates. Unfortunately, there are a number of areas in which we have actually lost ground. For example, smoking rates have actually increased among young women, and a significant percentage of Americans—including children—continue to be overweight and little progress has been made in increasing their level of physical activity and fitness (National Center for Health Statistics, 2001; National Women's Law Center, 2003).

KEY QUESTIONS

- What is health psychology?
- What is the field of behavioral medicine?
- To what can we attribute today's leading causes of premature death?

STRESS: ITS CAUSES, EFFECTS, AND CONTROL

Have you ever felt that you were right at the edge of being overwhelmed by negative events in your life? Or felt so overwhelmed that you just gave up? If so, you are already quite familiar with **stress**—our response to events that disrupt, or threaten to disrupt, our physical or psychological functioning (Lazarus & Folkman, 1984; Taylor, 2002). Unfortunately, stress is a common part of modern life—something few of us can avoid altogether. Partly for this reason, and partly because it seems to exert negative effects on both physical health and psychological well-being, stress has become an important topic of research in psychology. Let's examine the basic nature of stress and some of its major causes.

Stress: Its Basic Nature

Stress is a many-faceted process that occurs in reaction to events or situations in our environment termed **stressors.** An interesting feature of stress is the wide range of physical and psychological reactions that different people have to the same event; some may interpret an event as stressful, whereas others simply take it in stride. Moreover, a particular person may react quite differently to the same stressor at different points in time.

Stressors: The Activators of Stress

What are stressors? Although we normally think of stress as stemming from negative events in our lives, positive events such as getting married or receiving an unexpected job promotion can also produce stress. Despite the wide range of stimuli that can potentially produce stress, it appears that many events we find stressful share several characteristics: (1) They are so intense that they produce a state of overload—we can no longer adapt to them; (2) they evoke incompatible tendencies in us, such as tendencies both to approach and to avoid some object or activity; and (3) they are uncontrollable—beyond our limits of control. A great deal of evidence suggests that when people can predict, control, or terminate an aversive event or situation, they perceive it to be less stressful than when they feel less in control (Kemeny, 2003).

Physiological Responses to Stressors

When exposed to stressors, we generally experience many physiological reactions. If you've been caught off-guard by someone who appears out of nowhere and grabs you while screaming "Gotcha," then you are probably familiar with some common physical reactions to stress (please see Figure 11.1 on page 349). Initially, your blood pressure soars, your pulse races, and you may even begin to sweat. These are part of a general pattern of reactions referred to as the *fight-or-flight syndrome,* a process controlled through the sympathetic nervous system. As we saw in Chapter 2, the sympathetic nervous system prepares our bodies for immediate action. Usually these responses are brief, and we soon return to normal levels. When we are exposed to chronic sources of stress, however, this reaction is only the first in a longer sequence of responses activated by our efforts to adapt to a stressor. This sequence, termed by Hans Selye (1976) the **general adaptation syndrome (GAS),** consists of three stages.

The first is the *alarm* stage, in which the body prepares itself for immediate action; arousal of the sympathetic nervous system releases hormones that help prepare our bodies to meet threats or dangers. If stress is prolonged, however, the *resistance* stage begins. During this second stage, arousal is lower than during the alarm stage, but our bodies continue to draw on resources at an above-normal rate in order to cope effectively with the stressor. Continued exposure to the same stressor or additional stressors drains the body of its resources and leads to the third

Stress
The process by which we appraise and respond to events that disrupt, or threaten to disrupt, our physical or psychological functioning.

Stressors
Events or situations in our environment that cause stress.

General Adaptation Syndrome (GAS)
A profile of how organisms respond to stress. It consists of three phases: a nonspecific mobilization phase that promotes sympathetic nervous system activity; a resistance phase, during which the organism makes efforts to cope with the threat; and an exhaustion phase, which occurs if the organism fails to overcome the threat and depletes its coping resources.

stage, *exhaustion*. During this stage, our capacity to resist is depleted, and our susceptibility to illness increases.

Selye's general adaptation syndrome provides a framework for understanding our physiological responses to stressful events and suggests at least one reasonable explanation for the relation between stress and illness. Few experts would disagree that chronic stress can lead to a lowered resistance to disease. However, one weakness with Selye's model is that it seems to imply that stressors impact the body uniformly. More recent findings indicate that stressors elicit a patterned array of physiological changes that prepare humans and other animals to deal with the specific nature of the threat (Kemeny, 2003; Weiner, 1992).

FIGURE 11.1
Physiological Reactions to Stressors
When we encounter stressors that frighten or surprise us, we experience a wave of physiological reactions, as illustrated in the photo. These are part of a general pattern of reactions referred to as the fight-or-flight syndrome, a process controlled through the sympathetic nervous system.

◼ Cognitive Appraisal of Our Stressors

Another problem with Selye's model is that it fails to consider the importance of cognitive processes in determining whether we interpret a specific event as stressful. The importance of these processes is made clear by the following fact: When confronted with the same potentially stress-inducing situation, some persons experience stress, whereas others do not. Why? One reason involves individuals' cognitive appraisals (please refer to Figure 11.2). In simple terms, stress occurs only to the extent that the persons involved perceive that (1) the situation is somehow threatening to their important goals (often described as *primary appraisal*), and (2) they will be unable to cope with these dangers or demands (often described as *secondary appraisal*) (Croyle, 1992; Lazarus & Folkman, 1984). Stress will be low when either an event is perceived as a challenge rather than a threat or when one is confident in his or her ability to cope with a perceived threat (Blascovich & Tomaka, 1996).

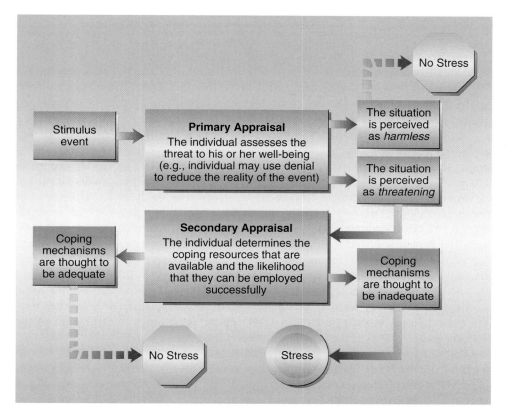

FIGURE 11.2
Stress: The Role of Cognitive Appraisals
The amount of stress you experience depends in part on your cognitive appraisals of the event or situation—the extent to which you perceive it as threatening and perceive that you will be unable to cope with it.

Source: Based on data from Hingson et al., 1990.

In short, cognitive and social processes have a significant impact on our responses to stress. We'll turn next to some of the causes of stress.

KEY QUESTIONS

- What is stress?
- What is the GAS model?
- What determines whether an event will be interpreted as stressful or as a challenge?

Stress: Some Major Causes

What factors contribute to stress? Unfortunately, the list is a long one. A wide range of conditions and events seems capable of generating such feelings. Among the most important of these are major stressful life events (e.g., the death of a loved one or a painful divorce), the all-too-frequent minor hassles of everyday life, and conditions and events relating to one's job.

Stressful Life Events

Death of a spouse, injury to one's child, failure in school or at work—unless we lead truly charmed lives, most of us experience traumatic events and changes at some time or other. What are their effects on us? This question was first investigated by Holmes and Rahe (1967), who asked a large group of persons to assign arbitrary points (to a maximum of one hundred) to various life events according to how much readjustment each had required. It was reasoned that the greater the number of points assigned to a given event, the more stressful it was for the persons experiencing it. As shown in Table 11.2, participants in Holmes and Rahe's study assigned the greatest number of points to such serious events as death of a spouse, divorce, and marital separation. In contrast, they assigned much smaller values to events such as change in residence, vacation, and minor violations of the law (e.g., receiving a parking ticket).

Holmes and Rahe (1967) then related the total number of points accumulated by individuals during a single year to changes in their personal health. The results were dramatic—and did much to stir psychologists' interest in the effects of stress. The greater the number of "stress points" people accumulated, the greater was their likelihood of becoming seriously ill. Although this study had a number of flaws (e.g., the correlational design did not allow for causal inferences), it suggested that accumulated stress, rather than stress emanating for any specific stressor, is associated with health problems.

Newer research has begun to identify the specific effects of accumulated stress—or *allostatic load* as it has been termed—on health (McEwen, 1998). For example, in one study, Cohen and his colleagues (1998) asked a group of volunteers to describe stressful events they had experienced during the previous year and to indicate the temporal course (the onset and offset) of each event. The stressful events participants described ranged from acute stressors that were brief in duration (e.g., a severe reprimand at work or a fight with a spouse) to more chronic ones that typically lasted a month or more and involved significant disruption of everyday routines (e.g., ongoing marital problems or unemployment). Then the researchers gave these persons nose drops containing a low dose of a virus that causes the common cold. The results showed that volunteers who reported experiencing chronic stressors were more likely to develop a cold than volunteers who had experienced only acute stressors. Moreover, the longer the duration of the stressor, the greater was the risk for developing a cold.

Before concluding, however, it is important to note that this picture is complicated by the existence of large differences in individuals' ability to withstand the impact of stress (Oulette-Kobasa & Puccetti, 1983). While some persons suffer ill effects after exposure to a few mildly stressful events, others remain healthy even

TABLE 11.2 Life Events, Stress, and Personal Health

When individuals experience stressful life events, such as those near the top of this list, their health often suffers. The greater the number of points for each event, the more stressful it is perceived as being.

1. Death of spouse	100	15. Business readjustment	39	24. Trouble with in-laws	29	35. Change in church activities	19
2. Divorce	73	16. Change in financial state	38	25. Outstanding personal achievement	28	36. Change in social activities	18
3. Marital separation	65	17. Death of close friend	37	26. Wife beginning or stopping work	26	37. Taking out a loan for a lesser purchase (e.g., car or TV)	17
4. Jail term	63	18. Change to different line of work	36	27. Beginning or ending school	26	
5. Death of close family member	63	19. Change in number of arguments with spouse	35	28. Change in living conditions	25	38. Change in sleeping habits	16
6. Personal injury or illness	53			29. Revision of personal habits	24	39. Change in number of family get-togethers	15
7. Marriage	50	20. Taking out mortgage for major purchase (e.g., home)	31	30. Trouble with boss	23	
8. Getting fired at work	47			31. Change in work hours or conditions	20	40. Change in eating habits	15
9. Marital reconciliation	45	21. Foreclosure of mortgage or loan	30	32. Change in residence	20	41. Vacation	13
10. Retirement	45	22. Change in responsibilities at work	29	33. Change in schools	20	42. Christmas	12
11. Change in health of family member	44			34. Change in recreation	19	43. Minor violation of the law	11
12. Pregnancy	40	23. Son or daughter leaving home	29			
13. Sex difficulties	39					
14. Gain of new family member	39					

Source: Based on data from Holmes & Masuda, 1974.

after prolonged exposure to high levels of stress. One individual difference that appears to be especially important in buffering against the harmful effects of chronic stress is *sociability.* As you know from your own experience, sociable people tend to enjoy interacting with other people and generally have an agreeable nature. Why should sociable people be more resistant to disease than their less sociable counterparts? Although more research is needed to determine the precise reasons, existing evidence points to the following possibilities. First, because sociability is an inherited characteristic, it is possible that the genes that contribute to sociability may also contribute to biological processes that play a role in the body's immune system. Second, research has shown that sociability is associated with more and better social interactions, performance of health-enhancing behaviors, and better regulation of emotions and stress-hormone levels—all elements important for maintaining proper immune system functioning (Cohen et al., 2003).

Tragedy and Catastrophe

By now it should be evident that accumulation of stressful events may adversely impact health. However, the stress associated with a single catastrophic event—an earthquake, a hurricane, a terrorist bombing—can also exert negative effects on our health. Studies show that a significant portion of survivors of natural disasters (major hurricanes and earthquakes) report symptoms of **posttraumatic stress disorder (PTSD),** a severe psychological disorder that occurs after experiencing or witnessing a life-threatening event (see Chapter 12 for more discussion of this disorder). One of the most significant events in this country occurred on the morning

Posttraumatic Stress Disorder (PTSD)
A severe psychological disorder that occurs after experiencing or witnessing a life-threatening event.

FIGURE 11.3
Posttraumatic Stress Disorder: The Effects of Life-Altering Events
Survivors of traumatic events often report symptoms of posttraumatic stress disorder (PTSD), a severe psychological disorder that occurs after experiencing or witnessing a life-threatening event. One of the most significant events in this country occurred on the morning of September 11, 2001.

of September 11, 2001, when terrorists hijacked three civilian aircraft and intentionally crashed them into the Pentagon and the World Trade Center (please refer to Figure 11.3). A fourth hijacked civilian plane crashed into a field in Pennsylvania. (We'll discuss the mental health implications of the September 11 tragedy in Chapter 12.)

Since then, concern over terrorism has dominated the headlines in the United States. As you might expect, such events are also associated with negative health outcomes. In fact, research indicates that acts of mass violence, such as the "9/11" disaster and the Oklahoma City bombings that occurred in 1995, are by far the most disturbing type of catastrophe (Norris, 2002; Tucker et al., 2002). Mass violence and terrorism have elements that may make them even more psychologically damaging than natural disasters. They are highly unpredictable, they lack a clear ending or low point that signals when the worst is over, and knowledge about how to respond to the event and its aftermath is limited (Baum, 1991). It is too soon to comprehend the full impact of the events that occurred on September 11, 2001, but recent findings suggest that even people who were not directly involved in rescue and recovery efforts experienced short-term declines in their health. For example, Piotrkowski and Brannen (2002) interviewed a group comprised of staff members of New York City after-school programs and found that about one-fifth of them reported significant levels of PTSD. PTSD was highest among those who had expressed worries about a future attack (a threat appraisal).

■ The Hassles of Daily Life

Although certain events, such as the dramatic events of September 11, are clearly stressful, they occur relatively infrequently. Does this mean that people's lives are mostly a serene lake of tranquility? Hardly. As you know, daily life is filled with countless minor annoying sources of stress—termed **hassles**—that seem to make up for their relatively low intensity by their much higher frequency. That such daily hassles are an important cause of stress is suggested by the findings of several studies by Lazarus and his colleagues (e.g., DeLongis, Folkman, & Lazarus, 1988; Kanner et al., 1981; Lazarus et al., 1985). These researchers developed a Hassles Scale on which individuals indicate the extent to which they have been "hassled" by common events during the past month. The items included in this scale deal with a wide range of everyday events, such as having too many things to do at once, misplacing

Hassles
Annoying minor events of everyday life that cumulatively can affect psychological well-being.

or losing things, troublesome neighbors, and concerns over money. One group that can truly appreciate the impact of daily hassles is parents—particularly when both parents work. Thus, it is not surprising that a *Parenting Daily Hassles Scale* has been developed to measure the frequency and intensity of annoying experiences that collectively parents find stressful (www.doh.gov.uk/pdfs/apparent.pdf).

While such events may seem relatively minor when compared with the life events discussed earlier, they appear to be quite important. When scores on the Hassles Scale are related to reports of psychological symptoms, strong positive correlations are obtained (Lazarus et al., 1985). In short, the more stress people report as a result of daily hassles, the poorer their psychological well-being. You can assess the extent of your own exposure to daily hassles using the hassles scale provided in Table 11.3. Let's turn now to a discussion of the effects of work-related stress.

Work-Related Stress

Most adults spend more time at work than in any other single activity. It is not surprising, then, that jobs or careers are a central source of stress. Some of the factors producing stress in work settings are obvious; for example, blatant sexual harassment or discrimination, or extreme *overload*—being asked to do too much in too

---

TABLE 11.3 Measuring Daily Hassles

Many people experience "hassles" at some time or another. For each item listed, indicate how much it has been a part of your life **over the past month** using the following scale: Put a "0" in the space next to an experience if it was **not at all** part of your life over the past month; "1" for an experience that was **only slightly** part of your life over that time; "2" for an experience that was **distinctly** part of your life; and "3" for an experience that was **very much** part of your life over the past month. Next, add up the total. In general, the more stress people report as a result of daily hassles, the poorer their psychological well-being.

Survey of Recent Life Experiences

1. Disliking your daily activities	19. Decisions about intimate relationship(s)
2. Disliking your work	20. Not enough time to meet your obligations
3. Ethnic or racial conflict	21. Financial burdens
4. Conflicts with in-laws or boyfriend's or girlfriend's family	22. Lower evaluations of your work than you think you deserve
5. Being let down or disappointed by friends	23. Experiencing high levels of noise
6. Conflicts with supervisor(s) at work	24. Lower evaluations of your work than you hoped for
7. Social rejection	25. Conflicts with family member(s)
8. Too many things to do at once	26. Finding your work too demanding
9. Being taken for granted	27. Conflicts with friend(s)
10. Financial conflicts with family members	28. Trying to secure loans
11. Having your trust betrayed by a friend	29. Getting "ripped off" or cheated in the purchase of goods
12. Having your contributions overlooked	30. Unwanted interruptions of your work
13. Struggling to meet your own standards of performance and accomplishments	31. Social isolation
14. Being taken advantage of	32. Being ignored
15. Not enough leisure time	33. Dissatisfaction with your physical appearance
16. Cash flow difficulties	34. Unsatisfactory housing conditions
17. A lot of responsibilities	35. Finding work uninteresting
18. Dissatisfaction with work	36. Failing to get money you expected

Source: "The survey of life experiences: A decontaminated hassles scale for adults" by P. Kohn and J. E. MacDonald in JOURNAL OF BEHAVIORAL MEDICINE, 15, pp. 221–225. Copyright © 1992. Reprinted by permission of Kluwer Academic/Plenum Publishers.

short a time. Interestingly, being asked to do too little can also cause stress. Such *underload* produces intense feelings of boredom, and these, in turn, can be very stressful.

Several other factors that play a role in work-related stress may be less apparent. One of these is *job control*—the ability to influence decisions about how and when one's job is performed. Controllability is a shared and basic need among humans. Feeling in control is usually a positive experience for most of us, whereas losing control is a negative experience. A lack of control is a major source of stress and dissatisfaction among workers, and may even have an impact on their health. In a five-year study of British civil service workers, men and women with low job control at the beginning of the study were 1.5 to 1.8 times more likely to be diagnosed with heart disease during the study period than those with high job control (Bosma, Stansfeld, & Marmot, 1998).

Another factor that influences work-related stress is *role conflict*—being the target of conflicting demands or expectations from different groups of people. For example, consider the plight of many beginning managers. Their subordinates often expect such persons to go to bat for them with the company to improve their work assignments, pay, and conditions. In contrast, the managers' own bosses often expect them to do the opposite—to somehow induce the employees to work harder for fewer rewards. The result: a stressful situation for the managers. Additional factors that have been found to contribute to stress at work are summarized in Figure 11.4.

Can anything be done to reduce such effects? Fortunately, several lines of research suggest the answer is yes. First, employers can reduce workplace stress by providing workers with greater autonomy and decision-making capabilities, factors that contribute to employees' feelings of control. Second, organizations can consider the **person–environment (P–E) fit.** Making sure that workers are well suited in terms of temperament and ability for the demands of their jobs will reduce the stress that they experience. Steps that you can take to reduce your job stress are presented in the **Psychology Goes to Work** section that follows.

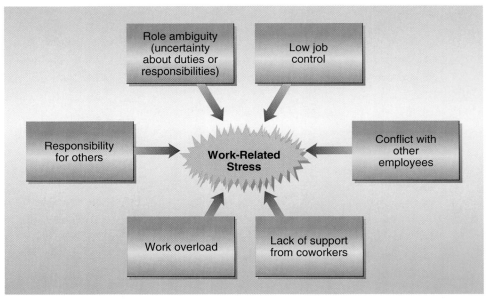

Person–Environment (P–E) Fit

This approach suggests that a misfit between a person and his or her work environment may produce stress.

FIGURE 11.4
Sources of Work-Related Stress
Many factors contribute to stress at work. Several of the most important are summarized here.

PSYCHOLOGY GOES TO WORK

Job Stress: What Can You Do to Control It?

Most of us will experience stress in our jobs. What can we do to control it? Psychological research suggests the following general guidelines:

1. **Set realistic goals and time frames.** Setting specific goals helps direct effort, increases persistence on tasks, and provides important feedback that allows you to chart your progress. But be realistic: Sometimes we create our own stressors by trying to accomplish too much in a day.

2. **Don't try to be Superman.** When you already are busy and feeling overloaded, don't take on more projects. You will not impress your boss by how much you take on, but by how much you accomplish.

3. **Schedule and organize.** Use a daily planner and organize your activities. A critical component of organization is to *prioritize* tasks. When faced with several tasks, many of us will complete the little, unimportant tasks first simply because they are easy and their completion makes us feel good. Unfortunately, this leaves less time for the most important tasks. Make sure you invest your time wisely by tackling the most important tasks first.

4. **Anticipate stress and be ready to respond.** Analyze the likely causes of stress in your job and plan a response to them. For example, if an abrasive coworker is making work unpleasant, think of a productive way to handle your next altercation and rehearse it ahead of time.

5. **Maintain a positive attitude.** Negative thoughts and emotions often add to our stress by disrupting task focus and decreasing motivation. Think positively about your work and seek self-satisfaction in what you do.

6. **Reduce procrastination.** People procrastinate for several reasons. Often it's because they either don't know how to do the task or they are indecisive about how to approach it. Overcome self-doubt by breaking the overall task into smaller, more manageable chunks.

7. **Reconsider meetings.** Although they are essential at times, many meetings are great time wasters. Meetings should be held only when important information needs to be shared and discussed.

KEY QUESTIONS

- Which types of events are likely to create stress?
- Are daily hassles harmful?
- What are some sources of work-related stress?

Stress: Some Major Effects

By now you may be convinced that stress stems from many different sources and exerts important effects on persons who experience it. What is sometimes difficult to grasp, though, is just how far-reaching these effects can be. Stress can influence our physical and psychological well-being and our performance on many tasks.

Stress and Health: The Silent Killer

The link between stress and personal health is very strong (Kiecolt-Glaser et al., 1994). According to medical experts, stress plays a role in 50 to 70 percent of all physical illness (Frese, 1985). Stress has been implicated in the occurrence of some of the most serious and life-threatening ailments known to medical science, including heart disease, high blood pressure, hardening of the arteries, ulcers, and even diabetes. Stress appears to exert additional, indirect effects as well; for example, people with high blood pressure perform more poorly on a several important measures of cognitive performance than people with normal blood pressure (Waldstein, 2003).

How does stress produce such effects? The precise mechanisms involved remain to be determined, but growing evidence suggests that the process goes something like this: By draining our resources and keeping us off balance physiologically, stress upsets our complex internal chemistry. In particular, it may interfere with efficient operation of our *immune systems*—the mechanisms through which our bodies recognize and destroy potentially harmful substances and intruders, such as bacteria, viruses, and cancerous cells. When functioning normally, the immune system is nothing short of amazing: Each day it removes or destroys many potential threats to our health.

Unfortunately, prolonged exposure to stress seems to disrupt this system. Chronic exposure to stress can reduce circulating levels of *lymphocytes* (white blood cells that fight infection and disease) and increase levels of the hormone *cortisol*, a substance that suppresses aspects of our immune system (Kemeny, 2003).

The physiological effects of chronic stressors, such as a stressful job, a poor interpersonal relationship, or financial concerns also take their toll on people's cardiovascular systems. Evidence also suggests that racial and gender differences exist in stress-induced heart disease. For instance, there is a greater prevalence of hypertension and cardiovascular disease among African Americans than whites, perhaps because they are exposed to more stressors in their lives and have stronger physiological reactions to stressors (Anderson, 1989). A recent study of African American and white women found that African American women experienced higher levels of chronic stress due to critical life events, discrimination, and economic hardship (Troxel et al., 2003). Furthermore, chronic stress was related to evidence of heart disease for African American women but not for white women. This evidence suggests that African American women may be particularly vulnerable to the burdens of chronic daily stress.

◼ The Effects of Social Support on Health

Several studies on humans and animals have led some psychologists to speculate that **social support,** the emotional and task resources provided by others, may serve to buffer the adverse effects of chronic stress. Research shows a positive correlation between a person's sources of social support and their health (House, Landis, & Umberson, 1998). Indeed, a lack of a reliable social support network can actually increase a person's risk of dying from disease, accidents, or suicide. Persons who are divorced or separated from their spouses often experience reduced functioning in certain aspects of their immune system, compared to individuals who are happily married (Kiecolt-Glaser et al., 1987, 1988).

Although it is clear that receiving social support is important to health, recent findings seem to indicate that providing social support to others may be just as important. In one recent study, Brown and her colleagues (2003) isolated and compared the unique effects of giving and receiving social support on mortality in a sample of 846 elderly married people. The researchers initially measured the extent to which participants received and gave support to their spouse and to others (friends, relatives, neighbors) and then monitored mortality rates over a five-year period. Participants who reported providing high levels of support to others were significantly less likely to die over the five-year period than participants who had provided little or no support to others. By contrast, receiving social support, from one's spouse or from others, did not appear to affect mortality among people in this group. In short, these findings suggest it may be better to give than to receive—especially when it comes to health!

Other research suggests that there may be gender differences in the effectiveness of social support offered to others. For example, Glynn, Christenfeld, and

Social Support

The emotional and task resources provided by others that may serve to help buffer the adverse effects of chronic stress.

Gerirn (1999) had males and females give impromptu speeches, after which they received supportive or nonsupportive feedback from male or female observers. Cardiovascular changes such as blood pressure and heart rate were monitored during and after the speech. Social support from men had no effect on blood pressure or heart rate of the speakers. Social support from women, however, had a calming influence on both male and female speakers. Perhaps women are better able to express empathy and support than men, and do so in a way that men as well as women appreciate—and find useful.

Stress and Task Performance

Psychologists once believed that the relationship between stress and task performance takes the form of an upside-down U: At first, performance improves as stress increases, presumably because the stress is arousing or energizing. Beyond some point, though, stress becomes distracting, and performance actually drops.

While this relationship may hold true under some conditions, research indicates that even low or moderate levels of stress can interfere with task performance (Motowidlo, Packard, & Manning, 1986; Steers, 1984). There are several reasons why this is so. First, even relatively mild stress can be distracting. People experiencing stress may focus on the unpleasant feelings and emotions it involves, rather than on the task at hand. Second, prolonged or repeated exposure to even mild levels of stress may exert harmful effects on health, and this may interfere with effective performance. Finally, a large body of research indicates that as arousal increases, task performance may rise at first, but at some point it falls (Berlyne, 1967). The precise location of this turning or *inflection* point seems to depend to a great extent on the complexity of the task performed. The greater the complexity, the lower the level of arousal at which the downturn in performance occurs. Many observers believe that the tasks performed by today's working people are more complex than those in the past. For this reason, even relatively low levels of stress may interfere with performance in today's complex work world.

Together, these factors help explain why even moderate levels of stress may interfere with many types of performance. However, stress does not always produce adverse effects. For example, as shown in Figure 11.5, people sometimes do seem to rise to the occasion and turn in sterling performances at times when stress is intense. Perhaps the most reasonable conclusion, then, is that while stress can interfere with task performance in many situations, its precise effects depend on many different factors, such as the complexity of the task being performed and personal characteristics of the individuals involved. As a result, generalizations about the impact of stress on work effectiveness should be made with considerable caution.

FIGURE 11.5
The Effects of Stress on Performance
Even relatively low levels of stress may interfere with performance in today's complex work world. However, these effects are often most evident among people who are under tremendous pressure to perform well. Still, some people are able to rise to the occasion at times when stress is intense.

KEY QUESTIONS

- What role does stress play in physical illness?
- How does social support influence stress?
- What is the relationship between stress and performance?

UNDERSTANDING AND COMMUNICATING OUR HEALTH NEEDS

There is no doubt that modern medicine has provided the means to alleviate many types of disease and illness considered incurable until this century. Yet all the available medicine and technology still does not ensure that we will seek proper treatment when necessary, or that we possess the knowledge or skills necessary to

FIGURE 11.6
The Health Belief Model
According to the health belief model, we are more likely to take precautionary actions, such as using sunscreen, if we value our health highly, if we feel that sunscreen effectively reduces the chances of skin cancer, and if we don't like what we hear about death from cancer.

Health Belief Model
A theory of health behaviors; the model predicts that whether or not a person practices a particular health behavior can be understood by knowing the degree to which the person perceives a personal health threat and the perception that a particular health practice will be effective in reducing that threat.

realize when help is required. Moreover, because of the beliefs and attitudes we hold, it's often difficult for health professionals to get us to comply with health-promoting advice. Most of us know the behaviors that are responsible for the common health problems in our society (e.g., alcohol and drug abuse, poor diet, lack of exercise, smoking). We are also aware of changes that we can make to our lifestyle that would improve our health (e.g., better diet, more exercise, stopping or reducing smoking, reducing alcohol consumption). Yet, few of us actually change our behavior despite being aware of the benefits of doing so. In essence, many people simply do not have sufficient motivation to change (Hetzel & McMichael, 1987). This seems to indicate an important role for health psychologists: not only to help people achieve a better understanding of their health needs and inform them about the risks of specific unhealthy behaviors, but also to identify techniques to reduce or eliminate unhealthy behaviors and to promote the adoption of healthy lifestyles.

Health Beliefs: When Do We Seek and Listen to Medical Advice?

As we discovered in Chapter 3, we all experience bodily sensations, such as the steady beating of our hearts or the rush of air flowing in and out of our lungs as we breathe. But certain sensations—like irregularities in heartbeat, tiny aches and pains, a slight queasiness, or a backache—are often termed *symptoms* because they may reflect an underlying medical problem. How do we decide that a symptom is severe enough to require medical attention? You might think that people would report symptoms or seek out medication attention when they sense a serious problem, but this is not always true. Research shows that people frequently do not seek appropriate help even when they know that something is seriously wrong (Locke & Slaby, 1982). Why is this so?

The **health belief model,** initially developed to help explain why people don't use medical screening services, may help us to understand the reasons. This model suggests that our willingness to seek medical help depends on (1) the extent to which we perceive a threat to our health and (2) the extent to which we believe that a particular behavior will effectively reduce that threat (Rosenstock, 1974). The perception of a personal threat is influenced by our health values, specific beliefs about our susceptibility to a health problem, and beliefs concerning the seriousness of the problem. For example, we may decide to use sunscreen at the beach if we value our health highly, if we feel that sunscreen effectively reduces the chances of skin cancer, and if we don't like what we hear about death from cancer.

Our perceptions that our behavior will be effective in reducing a health threat—in this case, the risk of contracting skin cancer—depend on whether we believe that a particular practice will reduce the chances we will contract a particular illness and whether the perceived benefits of the practice are worth the effort. For example, whether a person concerned about contracting skin cancer will actually use sunscreen depends on two beliefs: (1) that the use of sunscreen will reduce the risk of cancer and (2) that the benefits of doing so will outweigh the perceived rewards associated with having a tan. (Please refer to Figure 11.6.)

The health belief model helps explain why certain people, especially young persons and adults who have never experienced a serious illness or injury, often fail to engage in actions that would be effective in preventing these outcomes—such as wearing a condom during sexual intercourse or using a safety belt when driving a car (Taylor & Brown, 1988). They don't engage in such preventive, health-protecting actions because, in their minds, the likelihood of experiencing illness or injury is very low—so why bother?

Research on the health belief model has uncovered some interesting gender differences in the extent to which health beliefs influence intentions and behavior. Munley, McLoughlin, and Foster (1999) found that women were more likely to have yearly physical examinations than men, and also more likely to intend to schedule them on a regular basis in the future. Additionally, beliefs about the effectiveness of medical screening and obstacles to attending the examinations predicted attendance behavior for women but not for men. Perhaps women adopt a more rational approach to their medical care than do men.

Doctor–Patient Interactions: Why Can't We Talk to Our Doctors?

How satisfied are you with your doctors? Do you feel that they understand you as a person and how you might be feeling when you are sick? Or do they seem to talk "at" you, limiting conversation to their diagnosis and what procedures you should follow to regain or maintain your health? Unfortunately, many patients report that their doctors lack a "human touch." (Please refer to Figure 11.7.) Doctors tend to restrict conversations to the physical examination itself and explanation of the nature of prescribed medication. Psychological issues, such as what the patient knows or how they feel about their illness, are rarely discussed, even when these conversations center on the painful nature of cancer treatments and the possibility that the patients might die (Ford, Fallowfield, & Lewis, 1996). As a result, patients seldom feel like partners in treatment and become disillusioned with their medical care.

Why is patient satisfaction important? Research shows that patients who are more satisfied are more likely to adhere to their treatment regimens and are less likely to change physicians, thereby ensuring continuity of their treatment (DiMatteo & Di Nicola, 1982). Greater patient satisfaction is also associated with additional beneficial outcomes, including better emotional health and fewer hospitalizations (Hall, Roter, & Milburn, 1999). Together, these studies underscore the importance of training in communication skills for health care professionals. In order to be effective in treating patients and promoting their wellness, doctors, nurses, and other health professionals need to know how to get their message across—how to communicate effectively with the persons who come to them for help.

"I'll have to open you up again: That watch has great sentimental value to me."

FIGURE 11.7
The Importance of Communication Skills for Health Care Providers
As illustrated by the situation depicted in this cartoon, this person is unlikely to be satisfied with the treatment he's receiving from his doctor. Why is patient satisfaction important? Greater patient satisfaction is associated with a host of beneficial outcomes, including better emotional health and fewer hospitalizations.

Source: HERMAN® is reprinted with permission from LaughingStock Licensing, Inc., Ottawa, Canada. All rights reserved.

▪ Surfing for Solutions to Medical Problems on the Internet

Frustrated by busy doctors and the cumbersome managed-care system, many people are quietly taking matters into their own hands by consulting the Internet. Patients anxious to participate in decisions about their own treatment are turning increasingly to the Internet to confirm diagnoses, validate physician-recommended treatments, or seek alternative therapies. The World Wide Web has become a clearinghouse of information where, with the click of a mouse, people can get instant access to medical and mental health advice. Unfortunately, this practice can prove to be risky business.

Why? One reason is that the Internet is largely unpoliced, and the quality and accuracy of the information contained there varies considerably. Some of the nation's top medical research facilities have created publicly accessible Web sites, but so, too, have unethical people and businesses trying to sell drugs or therapies that do not have scientific evidence to support their use.

Another reason why it is risky to depend solely on medical advice found on the Internet is the unpredictable effects it can have on our health. Web sites that hype new, untested cures for deadly diseases may fill patients with false hope, prompting them to abandon treatments already underway or delay urgently needed procedures that could save their lives. Conversely, sites that offer accurate but graphic details about an illness may cause people already anxious about their health to avoid seeking medical treatment altogether. In other words, without the benefit of specialized medical training or someone so trained to guide them, a little knowledge can be a dangerous thing.

Still, with all its problems, the Internet is a useful medical tool. With a little effort, patients can find their way to the best doctors, cutting-edge research, and sources of social support at a time when they need it the most (Landro, 1998). Patients may also quickly develop a working knowledge of their illnesses and, as a result, take a more informed and active role in their treatment.

KEY QUESTIONS

- What is the health belief model?
- What factors determine our willingness to make lifestyle changes or seek medical help?
- What are the advantages and disadvantages of seeking medical advice on the Internet?

BEHAVIORAL AND PSYCHOLOGICAL CORRELATES OF ILLNESS: THE EFFECTS OF THOUGHTS AND ACTIONS ON HEALTH

Cancer is often viewed as a purely physical illness. However, mounting evidence suggests that psychological variables can play an important role in determining cancer's progression (McGuire, 1999). In other words, aspects of our behavior, perceptions, and personality can affect the onset and course of this life-threatening illness. One common characteristic among individuals from families with high cancer rates is a diminished efficiency of their *natural killer cells*—cells designed specifically for the surveillance and destruction of cancerous tumor cells (Kiecolt-Glaser & Glaser, 1992). In most cases, though, whether we actually develop a cancer or other illness is moderated by **risk factors**—aspects of our lifestyle that affect the chances that we will develop or contract a particular disease, within the limits established by our genes.

Behaviors that increase our exposure to **carcinogens**—cancer-producing agents in our environment—are among the most important risk factors. Tobacco and the smoke it produces, chemicals in the food that we eat and the air that we breathe, alcohol in the beverages we drink, and the radiation we receive from overexposure to the sun have all been implicated to some extent as carcinogens (please refer to Figure 11.8). It was because of concerns about exposure to such substances that in 1994 many people in the United States protested plans to sell milk from cows fed large amounts of growth hormones. The protesters didn't want such substances in their milk. Likewise, the increase in popularity of organic foods stems in part from consumers' worries about the possible health effects that genetically altered food products, or foods irradiated to kill harmful bacteria, may have on their health.

Because people create these risks through their behaviors, psychologists can play a crucial role in preventing cancer and other health problems by developing interventions that reduce our exposure to potential carcinogens and promote healthy behaviors such as exercise and a proper diet. We'll now consider several behavioral risk factors that may contribute to the development of certain illnesses.

Smoking: Risky for You and Everyone around You

Smoking is the largest preventable cause of illness and premature death (before age sixty-five) in the United States, accounting for about 440,000 deaths annually

Cancer
A group of illnesses in which abnormal cells are formed that are able to proliferate, invade, and overwhelm normal tissues, and to spread to distant sites in the body.

Risk Factors
Aspects of our environment or behavior that influence our chances of developing or contracting a particular disease, within the limits established through our genetic structure.

Carcinogens
Cancer-producing agents in our environment.

FIGURE 11.8
Carcinogens: Cancer-Producing Agents in the Environment
Cigarette smoke, chemicals in the food we eat and the air we breathe, alcohol, and sun exposure have all been implicated to some extent as carcinogens.

in the United States alone (Centers for Disease Control, 2002). It is the leading cause of several types of cancer and also causes **cardiovascular disease** (disease of the heart and blood vessels). Despite the numerous risks associated with smoking—and the numerous health benefits of quitting—more than 46 million Americans currently smoke (Centers for Disease Control, 2003). Unfortunately, the harmful effects of smoking do not end with the smoker. Smoking during pregnancy can have harmful effects on the developing fetus. And exposure to second-hand smoke causes an estimated 3,000 nonsmoking Americans to die of lung cancer and up to 300,000 children to suffer from respiratory tract infections annually (U.S. Environmental Protection Agency, 2004).

Given the evidence against smoking, then, why do people smoke? Genetic, psychosocial, and cognitive factors all seem to play a role. Individual differences in our reaction to **nicotine,** the addictive substance in tobacco, suggest that some people are biologically predisposed to become addicted to nicotine, whereas others remain unaffected. Psychosocial factors also play a role in establishing smoking behavior, especially among young persons. Adolescents are more likely to begin smoking if their parents or other role models smoke, or if they experience peer pressure to do so (Aloise-Young, Graham, & Hansen, 1994). A report by the U.S. Surgeon General also suggests that about 90 percent of smokers report having smoked their first cigarette by age eighteen, but very few people begin to smoke after age twenty (Centers for Disease Control, 1994). These data highlight the urgent need for prevention programs targeting people in this age group.

For many people, smoking is a way of coping with stressful life events. Unfortunately, the temporary relief provided by cigarettes comes at a considerable cost in terms of long-term health risks and consequences. Recent research suggests that women may be more likely than men to rely on cigarettes as a coping mechanism for stress. In a study of former smokers who had quit, women were more likely to relapse and resume smoking in response to stressful life events than were men (McKee et al., 2003). This was particularly the case when the major source of stress was financial problems. Similar findings occurred when the researchers examined who among current smokers was likely to successfully quit smoking: Women experiencing financial or health problems were more likely to continue smoking than were men. These results suggest that women may be particularly likely to rely on cigarettes as a way to cope with stress in their lives.

Cardiovascular Disease
All diseases of the heart and blood vessels.

Nicotine
The addictive substance in tobacco.

Finally, cognitive factors appear to influence people's tendency to continue smoking. Smokers tend to hold inaccurate perceptions with regard to the risks of smoking (Weinstein, 1998). Smokers consistently acknowledge that smoking increases their health risks, but they underestimate these risks compared to nonsmokers. Smokers also tend to minimize the personal relevance of the risks of smoking; they tend not to believe that they are as much at risk as other smokers of becoming addicted or suffering negative health effects.

Unfortunately, efforts to get people to quit smoking have not been very effective. More than 40 percent of adult smokers make an attempt to quit each year, but only a small percentage are able to maintain abstinence, even for short periods of time (Centers for Disease Control, 1993). What makes a treatment program effective? Research suggests the following answers. First, interventions delivered by trained health care providers tend to be more effective than self-help programs. Second, the content of smoking cessation interventions and the specific behavior change procedures used also seem to make a difference (please refer to Table 11.4). Aversive smoking procedures, ones designed to associate smoking stimuli with feeling ill (rapid smoking), seem to be most effective, followed by interventions that include either a supportive component or training in problem solving to help smokers identify and cope with events or problems that increase the likelihood of smoking. Third, the amount of time the clinician spends with smokers has a direct influence on treatment effectiveness, with more contact leading to higher cessation rates. Finally, the use of nicotine replacement therapies (e.g., patch, gum), when combined with an intensive psychosocial intervention, tends to improve smoking cessation rates considerably (Silagy et al., 1994; Tang, Law, & Wald, 1994).

Diet and Nutrition: What You Eat May Save Your Life

Poor dietary practices can dramatically increase the risk of developing chronic diseases. A poor diet has been most closely linked with cancers of the colon and rectum. Colorectal cancer is one of the leading causes of cancer deaths in the United States, killing over 56,000 people annually (Landis et al., 1998). Fortunately, regu-

TABLE 11.4 Relative Effectiveness of Smoking-Cessation Interventions

A comparison of different types of smoking-cessation interventions shows they differ in their ability to help smokers kick the habit.

Type of Intervention	Estimated Smoking-Cessation Rates
No-intervention comparison group	8.8%
Aversive smoking	17.5%
Social support (providing support or encouragement as a component of treatment)	15.2%
General problem solving	13.7%
Quit smoking on a specific date	11.5%
Motivational programs	9.8%
Weight, diet, or nutrition management	9.8%
Exercise or fitness programs	9.6%
Contingency contracts (rewards for compliance; costs for noncompliance)	9.1%
Relaxation or breathing techniques	7.5%
Cigarette fading (gradually reducing number of cigarettes smoked or amount of nicotine)	6.4%

Source: Based on data from Wetter et al., 1998.

lar consumption of certain foods, particularly fresh fruits and vegetables, may *reduce* the risk of developing these cancers. Regular exercise also exerts a protective effect against the development of colorectal cancer.

Diet is also a significant risk factor in the development of *cardiovascular disease,* a term used to describe all diseases of the heart and blood vessels. High levels of a certain type of **serum cholesterol,** or blood cholesterol, are strongly associated with increased risk of cardiovascular diseases (Allred, 1993; Klag et al., 1993). "Bad" or *LDL cholesterol* clogs arteries and is therefore the kind that places us most at risk of heart disease. *HDL cholesterol* helps clear LDL from the arteries and escorts it to the liver for excretion. In other words, the more LDL you have, the more HDL you will need. The amount of cholesterol in our blood is affected by the amount of fat, especially saturated fat, and cholesterol in our diets. Serum cholesterol can be greatly reduced through a diet that is low in fats, cholesterol, and calories and high in fiber, fruits, and vegetables.

Newer evidence suggests *trans-fatty acids,* found naturally in dairy products and meats, and also in margarine, salad dressings, fried foods, and baked goods, are particularly dangerous to health. Like saturated fat, *trans*-fat raises heart disease risk by boosting levels of LDL. But some researchers consider trans-fat worse than saturated fat because it also raises other detrimental blood fats, lowers HDL levels, and increases insulin resistance—a key step toward developing diabetes.

Although the link between dietary practices and good health is clear, it is difficult to get people to adhere to a healthy diet. One reason is that people tend to prefer the taste of high-fat foods over healthier alternatives (please refer to Chapter 3 for additional information). High-fat foods are energy-dense—they contain more calories than foods high in carbohydrate or protein—and tend to elevate natural opiate levels in the body. If you recall our discussions in Chapter 2, natural opiates have pain-killing properties that can be extremely pleasurable for some people. Thus, because of these effects, it is not surprising that people learn to prefer eating high-fat foods. Interestingly, when people are given a drug that blocks the effects of opiates and are allowed to choose between different foods, they tend to reduce their intake of fat relative to carbohydrates (Schiffman et al., 1998).

Results from the 1999–2000 National Health and Nutrition Examination Survey (NHANES), using measured heights and weights, indicate that an estimated 64 percent of U.S. adults are overweight (National Center for Health Statistics). Thus, getting people to eat the right foods is important, but many Americans simply eat *too much.* Unfortunately, this can lead to serious health problems, as is evident among people who have recently filed lawsuits against several well-known fast-food restaurant chains, sometimes termed *McLawsuits.* Their claim? That they didn't realize that eating too much fast food would be bad for them (see Figure 11.9).

Most interventions designed to help people lose weight seem to work, at least initially. For example, a recent comparison of four of the most popular diets— Atkins, Ornish, Weight Watchers, and the Zone—revealed that all were effective in helping dieters to shed weight, thereby lowering their risk of heart disease (Dansinger, 2003). Unfortunately, the weight loss achieved through most programs does not typically last. Why? As noted in Chapter 9, a variety of factors have been shown to play a role, including genetic, behavioral, and environmental ones. One factor we did not discuss previously, however, involves the *type* of motivation behind the decision to begin dieting (Williams et al., 1996).

FIGURE 11.9
Fast Food and Our Health
During the past decade, the number of Americans who are overweight has more than doubled. Why? Because many people simply eat too much. Unfortunately, this can lead to serious health problems, as is evident in this photo. Recently, people have initiated lawsuits against several well-known fast-food restaurant chains because they claim they didn't realize that eating too much fast food would be bad for them.

Serum Cholesterol
The amount of cholesterol in our blood, directly proportional to the amount of cholesterol in our diets.

According to the **self-determination theory** (Deci & Ryan, 1985), long-term maintenance of weight loss depends on whether the motivation for doing so is perceived by the dieter as autonomous or controlled. Overweight persons frequently begin dieting on the advice of their doctor or at the insistence of concerned family members. Under these circumstances, people may feel coerced into losing weight; this is an example of *controlled motivation.* On the other hand, persons who begin a weight-loss program because they want to do it for themselves may experience the same activity (dieting) quite differently; this is an example of *autonomous motivation.* Self-determination theory predicts that autonomously motivated weight loss will be maintained over time, whereas maintenance of weight loss achieved at the urging of others is less likely. This is exactly what Williams and his colleagues (1996) found in a study of individuals entering a six-month weight-loss program. Participants who reported entering the program for themselves (autonomous motivation) attended the program more regularly, lost more weight during the program, and were more likely to maintain the weight loss nearly two years later than were persons who reported joining the program because of other people's wishes (controlled motivation).

KEY QUESTIONS

- What determines who will become addicted to smoking?
- What are the effects of poor dietary practices?
- How do feelings of self-determination influence adherence to an exercise regimen?

Alcohol Consumption: Here's to Your Health?

Moderate alcohol consumption—typically defined as a daily glass of an alcoholic beverage—has been associated with significant health benefits, such as a reduced risk of coronary heart disease (Launer et al., 1996; Hennekens, 1996). Too much alcohol, however, is harmful and can have damaging effects on our health. Chronic excessive alcohol consumption can lead to deficits in many different cognitive abilities, including learning and memory, perceptual–motor skills, visual–spatial processing, and problem solving. Drinking can also lead to stomach disease, cirrhosis of the liver, cancer, impaired sexual functioning, cognitive impairment, and *fetal alcohol syndrome,* a condition of retardation and physical abnormalities that occurs in children of mothers who are heavy drinkers. Heavy drinking has also been implicated as a risk factor for suicide and suicide attempts (e.g., Borges & Rosovsky, 1996) and for the transmission of the virus that causes AIDS, by interfering with aspects of our immune system and by increasing the likelihood that people will engage in unprotected sex (Dingle & Oei, 1997).

Given these facts, why do people continue to drink? Research suggests that genetic factors play an important role. Animal studies show that genetically engineered "knockout" mice, so named because they lack the gene responsible for production of a brain chemical called neuropeptide Y, drink more alcohol than normal mice and appear to have a greater tolerance for its effects (Koob et al., 1998). Because neuropeptide Y also appears to calm anxiety, at least in animals, these findings suggest that some alcoholics may drink excessively to relieve stress and help explain the high rates of alcoholism among people with anxiety disorders. Studies with humans also highlight the role of genetic factors in drinking. Adoption studies investigating rates of alcoholism among adopted children raised apart from their natural parents show, for example, that the sons of male alcoholics raised in adoptive homes have higher rates of alcoholism than the sons of nonalcoholics who grow up under similar circumstances (McGue, 1999). Twin studies that have compared the concordance rate for alcoholism among genetically identical (monozygotic) twins and fraternal (dizygotic) twins also provide support for a genetic link. *Concordance* refers to the probability of co-occurrence of alcoholism among pairs of twins. Concordance rates are generally higher among identical twins than among fraternal twins.

Self-Determination Theory

When applied to health-related issues, this theory suggests that motivation to perform health-preventive behaviors is highest when we have autonomy over the decision to do so, and lowest when we do these behaviors at someone else's request.

But genetic factors are definitely *not* the only determinants of excessive drinking. Environmental factors are also involved. Ironically, the strongest evidence for the role of environmental factors in drinking also comes from studies of adoption. Children reared in an adoptive family containing an alcoholic member are at significant risk of becoming alcoholics themselves (Cadoret, Troughton, & O'Gorman, 1987). The effects of this source of influence appear to be strongest when the alcoholic family member is a same-sex sibling of about the same age. Unrelated siblings who are raised together also tend to exhibit similar drinking practices (McGue, Sharma, & Benson, 1996). Together, these studies provide evidence that environmental factors play a significant role in drinking.

AIDS: A Major Assault on Public Health

Acquired immune deficiency syndrome (AIDS) has become a major health concern around the world. AIDS is the syndrome of illnesses caused by the human immunodeficiency virus (HIV). The process by which HIV produces AIDS symptoms is complex but essentially involves the devastation of aspects of the infected person's immune system, making the person extremely vulnerable to diseases, such as tuberculosis, pneumonia, and several forms of cancer. A frightening thing about AIDS is that the incubation period—the time it takes for the disease to develop—can be several years in length. This means that infected individuals can spread the disease to others without even realizing that they are infected. Because individuals can be infected only if the virus is introduced directly into the bloodstream, most HIV infections are acquired through unprotected sexual intercourse and infected blood or blood products. Unfortunately, this means that women can pass the disease to their unborn children during pregnancy or delivery or through breastfeeding.

Based on estimates from the United Nations AIDS program (UNAIDS), approximately 65 million people have been infected with HIV since the start of the global epidemic. At the end of 2001, an estimated 40 million people were living with HIV infection or AIDS. Figure 11.10 shows the relative distribution of cases of AIDS throughout the world. Although the new incidents and overall number of deaths from AIDS have finally begun to decline in the United States (Mann & Tarantola, 1998), they are increasing rapidly in many other countries, especially in Africa. And in the United States, the incidence of AIDS is still increasing among

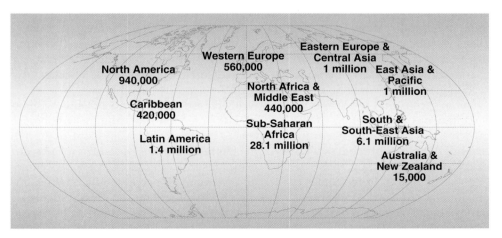

FIGURE 11.10
Distribution of AIDS Worldwide
Approximately 65 million people have been infected with HIV since the start of the global epidemic. At the end of 2001, an estimated 40 million people were living with HIV infection or AIDS.
Source: "World Map Distribution of AIDS" from AIDS EPI Update, December 2001. Reproduced by kind permission of UNAIDS, www.unaids.org.

Acquired Immune Deficiency Syndrome (AIDS)
A viral infection that reduces the immune system's ability to defend itself against the introduction of any foreign matter.

FIGURE 11.11
AIDS-Preventive Behaviors: A Model
Growing evidence suggests that prevention programs are more effective when they are tailored to meet the needs of specific target groups and when they provide people with the knowledge, motivation, and behavioral skills necessary to perform AIDS-preventive behaviors.
Source: Based on Fisher et al., 1994.

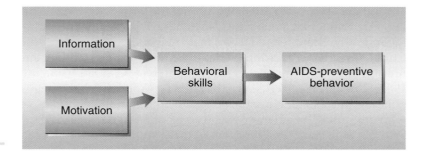

some groups, including women and African American and Hispanic males, who now account for most of the new cases of AIDS in the United States.

How Psychologists Can Help Prevent the Spread of AIDS

Why are psychologists relevant to the AIDS epidemic? One reason is that most people contract HIV as a result of certain behaviors, such as unprotected intercourse and intravenous drug use with contaminated needles. Thus, the only effective means of combating AIDS is to change the behaviors that place people most at risk for acquiring HIV. Health psychologists recognize that developing effective AIDS-prevention programs is a complicated business. They know, for example, that information campaigns alone—merely teaching people the facts about HIV and AIDS—are often ineffective (Helweg-Larsen & Collins, 1997). They also recognize that techniques effective for a particular target group are not necessarily effective for all groups of people (Coates & Collins, 1998). One model that is useful in developing interventions that accommodate individual and group differences is the *information–motivation–behavioral skills* (IMB) model (Fisher et al., 1994) (please refer to Figure 11.11). According to the IMB model, people are more likely to perform HIV-preventive behaviors to the extent that they (1) know how HIV is acquired and the specific actions they must take to avoid it; (2) are motivated to perform HIV-preventive behaviors and omit risky ones; and (3) possess the skills necessary to perform relevant HIV-preventive behaviors, such as the ability to communicate with and to be appropriately assertive with a potential sexual partner.

The IMB model serves as a framework in which to conduct *elicitation research.* This kind of research is performed to attain specific information about a target group, including their current knowledge of HIV and AIDS, the factors that determine their motivation to reduce their personal risk, and their existing HIV-preventive behavioral skills (Fisher & Fisher, 2000; Fisher et al., 1994). Elicitation research and the IMB model are useful tools for developing effective behavior change programs. Why? Because they help researchers uncover the reasons why certain groups of people do not perform AIDS-preventive behavior.

One group that is currently at risk with regard to HIV and AIDS is women (Logan, Cole, & Leukefeld, 2002). Indeed, HIV-infection rates among women are growing at a rapid rate. According to the U.S. Centers for Disease Control (CDC), cases of AIDS attributable to women in the United States increased from 7 percent in 1985 to 20 percent in 1996. The CDC estimates that over 40,000 new HIV infections occur in the United States each year and about 30 percent are women (Centers for Disease Control and Prevention, 2001). What is the reason for this increase? Part of the answer is a risk factor unique to women: The chances of male-to-female transmission of HIV are about twelve times greater than female-to-male transmission (Padian, Shiboski, & Jewell, 1990). Elicitation research suggests that gender role differences between men and women may also play a role. For example, adherence to traditional gender roles may increase the chances that some women will succumb to pressure to engage in unprotected sex (Amaro, 1995). A related problem involves differences in the skills required to ensure safe sex. Consider, for example, the skills necessary to ensure the use of a condom during sex. For the man, this simply means putting on the condom. For the women, however, it means persuading her partner to use a condom or, perhaps, choosing not to have sex if he refuses. Finally, fear may be an important factor, especially among inner-city women and among women in abusive relationships marked by physical violence (Gomez & Marin, 1996). Under conditions like these, in which the potential for personal injury is high, it is understandable that women are reluctant to negotiate safe sex with their partners, let alone refuse to have sex with them.

Can anything be done to reverse this trend? Fortunately, the answer is yes. For example, Hobfoll and his colleagues (1994) compared the relative impact of two training programs on measures of HIV-preventive behaviors. Participants, a group of inner-city women, were assigned randomly to one of the programs or to a no-training control group. The interventions differed in content (HIV-specific information versus general health information) but were otherwise identical. Consistent with the IMB model, the HIV-prevention training program was designed to (1) increase the women's knowledge of HIV transmission and prevention, (2) motivate them to perform HIV-preventive behaviors by highlighting their specific risks of acquiring HIV, and (3) provide them with behavioral skills necessary to convince their sexual partner to adopt HIV-preventive behaviors, such as wearing a condom during sex. As predicted, the HIV-preventive group outperformed the health-promotion and no-treatment control group on knowledge measures and in terms of self-reported HIV-preventive behaviors. Other more recent studies have reported similar findings (e.g., Carey et al., 2000). These results highlight the value of models like IMB in guiding development of more effective interventions. Let's turn now to a discussion of emotions and health.

Emotions and Health

The previous sections looked at behaviors (smoking, drinking, unprotected sex) that put people at risk for certain illnesses. Our mood states and emotions can also put us at risk for certain illnesses. Inadequate emotional expression—especially of negative feelings—can have an adverse effect on the progression of certain types of illness, such as cancer (Levy et al., 1985, 1988). People who tend to experience negative emotions and who also inhibit self-expression in their social interactions are exhibiting a pattern of behavior termed the **Type D**—or *distressed*—**personality type** (Denollet, 1998). Individuals who cope with stress by keeping their negative emotions to themselves are likely to experience suppressed immune systems, greater recurrence of cancer, and higher mortality rates. In contrast, patients who demonstrate positive affect—especially joy, well-being, and happiness—increase the likelihood of recovery.

An intriguing finding is the relation between expression of distress and treatment outcome. Open expression of negative affect and a willingness to fight illness are sometimes associated with greater immune function, decreased recurrence rates, and increased survival time, even among patients at advanced stages of cancer. For example, combative individuals—those who express anger about getting cancer and hostility toward their doctors and family members—often live longer than patients who passively accept their fate and quietly undergo treatment (Levy, 1990).

Emotion can also play a role in the progression of **hypertension,** or high blood pressure, a condition in which the pressure within the blood vessels is abnormally high. Prolonged hypertension can result in extensive damage to the entire circulatory system. Indeed, about 30 percent of cardiovascular disease deaths each year are attributable to hypertension. Negative emotions such as anxiety and hostility arouse the autonomic nervous systems and produce increases in heart rate, blood pressure, and neurotransmitters. Although the effects of emotional stressors are usually brief, extreme reactivity to anxiety, hostility, and anger may indicate a predisposition to develop hypertension (Rosenman, 1988). Not surprisingly, the

Type D Personality Type
A term used to describe a general tendency to cope with stress by keeping negative emotions to oneself. People who exhibit this behavior pattern are more likely to experience suppressed immune systems and health-related problems.

Hypertension
A condition in which the pressure within the blood vessels is abnormally high.

strongest relations between emotions and blood pressure have been found for un-expressed anger and hostility.

In a recent study, Niaura and his colleagues (2002) found that hostility in el-derly men predicted coronary heart disease (CHD) over a three-year period. What is significant about this study is that the researchers included measures of other known predictors of CHD, including cigarette use, alcohol consumption, and blood lipids. Individuals who scored high on the hostility measure had substantially higher chances of CHD, even when the other risk factors were considered. Based on these results, health psychologists should develop more effective interventions for individuals who exhibit high levels of hostility.

Although negative emotions can increase risks of illness, positive emotions have beneficial effects and can even reverse the lingering cardiovascular effects produced by hostility. Positive emotions—such as contentment, gratitude, hope, and love—are also associated with psychological resilience, the tendency in some people to bounce back from negative experiences. To illustrate the important link between resiliency and positive emotions, consider a recent study by Frederickson and his colleagues (2003). These researchers surveyed college students early in 2001

p s y c h o l o g y l e n d s a h a n d

Laughter—the Best Medicine?

Like me, you may have wondered whether this was just one of your grandparents' sayings or there was, in fact, some truth to it. But how can laughter influence physical health? The following possible mechanisms have been suggested. First, laughter puts us in a good mood, which may help to counteract the detrimental effects that negative emotions (e.g., anger, hostility) exert on the cardiovascular system (please refer to Figure 11.12). Second, laughter and its associated positive moods may counteract the negative effects of stress by allowing us to distance ourselves from the stressful events or to gain perspective in the face of problems. Third, laughter may induce healthful physiological changes, such as exercising and re-laxing muscles, improving respiration and circulation, and increasing the production of pain-killing endorphins. In fact, each of these physiological changes has been linked to a stronger immune sys-tem. Finally, laughter and good humor may indirectly improve health by improving interpersonal relationships; humorous people tend to be socially competent and attractive to other people. A large social network may help individuals cope more effectively with stressful situations.

What can you do to put more laughter into your life? Here are some tips that may help:

1. Figure out what makes you laugh, then read it, watch it, or do it more often.
2. Surround yourself with funny people and be with them as often as you can.
3. Develop your own sense of humor; start by learning how to tell a joke or story.
4. Be funny every chance you get—as long as it is not at some-one else's expense.

FIGURE 11.12
Is Laughter the Best Medicine?
Laughter has several possible beneficial effects. It puts us in a good mood, it may counteract the negative effects of stress by allowing us to distance ourselves from the stressful events or to gain per-spective in the face of problems, and it may indirectly improve health by improving interpersonal relationships. More research will be needed, however, to confirm the beneficial effects of laughter.

Please note, however, that experts still have not pinpointed the precise relationship between laughter and good health, so ad-ditional careful research is needed to confirm, or dismiss, claims about the healthful benefits of laughter (e.g., Martin, 2001, 2002). So, until then, laugh often—but don't throw away your running shoes just yet if you are concerned about staying healthy.

and again a few weeks after the terrorist attacks of September 11, 2001. As you might expect, many students expressed symptoms of depression after the attacks. However, students high in psychological resilience reported frequent experiences of gratitude and love, among other positive emotions, because they were grateful for their safety and that of their loved ones. These positive emotions, in turn, appeared to exert a buffering effect in that their presence was associated with lower levels of depression.

Do you recall the old adage "Laughter is often the best medicine"? Let's turn next to **Psychology Lends a Hand** to show whether laughter can exert similar effects on our health.

KEY QUESTIONS

- What are the consequences of heavy consumption of alcohol?
- What is AIDS? How is it transmitted?
- How does the IMB model attempt to change risky behaviors?
- How is the way in which we express our emotions related to our health?

PROMOTING WELLNESS: DEVELOPING A HEALTHIER LIFESTYLE

Have you ever wondered why some individuals live to be more than one hundred years old, while most people live only seventy or eighty years? Studies of persons who live to be more than one hundred years old indicate that several factors may play a role in their extended life spans. One of these factors is diet: Long-lived persons often show a pattern involving greater-than-average consumption of grains, leafy green and root vegetables, fresh milk, and fresh fruits, and they tend to eat low to moderate amounts of meat and animal fat. In addition, they maintain low to moderate levels of daily caloric intake (1,200 to 3,000 calories) and consume only moderate amounts of alcohol each day. Long-lived persons also tend to make regular physical activity an integral part of their lives, continuing well into old age. Additional factors include continued sexual activity, adaptive personality characteristics and family stability, and continued involvement in family and community affairs during advanced years (please refer to Chapter 8 for additional information on older adults).

In sum, while genetic factors certainly play a role in determining life span, research suggests that people may be able to extend their lives significantly by adhering to a lifestyle that includes these factors: a balanced, low-fat, low-calorie diet; regular exercise; and continued activity during later years (Pelletier, 1986).

On the basis of such findings, a growing number of health professionals and psychologists have adopted an approach to health and wellness that is based on **prevention strategies,** techniques designed to reduce the occurrence of illness and other physical and psychological problems. The goal of *primary prevention* is to reduce or eliminate the incidence of preventable illness and injury. Primary prevention strategies usually involve one or more of the following components: educating people about the relation between their behaviors and their health, promoting motivation and skills to practice healthy behaviors, and directly modifying poor health practices through intervention.

Secondary prevention focuses on early detection to decrease the severity of illness that is already present. Thus, individuals learn about their health status through medical tests that screen for the presence of disease. Although early detection of certain diseases is increasingly carried out by health professionals and often requires sophisticated medical tests, exciting research is under way to teach patients methods of self-examination, especially for early detection of breast and testicular cancer.

Prevention Strategies
Techniques designed to reduce the occurrence of disease or illness and the physical and psychological problems that often accompany them.

Primary Prevention: Decreasing the Risks of Illness

In most instances, our initial attempts to change our health behaviors are unsuccessful. Typically, we become aware of the need to change behaviors; we initiate change; we experience a series of failed attempts to change these behaviors; and sometimes—only sometimes—we succeed. The nature of this process indicates that we need help: a variety of intervention programs to meet our varied needs and purposes.

■ Health Promotion Messages: Marketing Healthy Lifestyles

We are constantly bombarded with messages about health risks. Numerous non-profit organizations use television commercials, newspaper articles, magazine ads, radio advertising, and now the Internet to warn us about unhealthy behaviors such as smoking, unprotected sex, and alcohol and drug abuse and their associated risks, including cancer, heart disease, and AIDS. These campaigns typically provide information about symptoms that may indicate the presence of a health problem, such as shortness of breath or chest pains in the case of heart attacks, and information about the relation between specific behaviors and disease; for example, "Smoking is the number one cause of heart disease."

But can mass media campaigns alone produce widespread changes in behavior? There is little evidence that they can (Meyer, Maccoby, & Farquhar, 1980). One reason for the limited success of these programs may be the media's depiction and promotion of *un*healthy habits, which counteract health promotion messages. For example, Story and Faulkner (1990) computed the frequency of commercials advertising healthy versus unhealthy food and beverages. Most of the prime-time commercials were for *unhealthy* foods and beverages.

Another reason for the limited success of these programs is that they ignore important individual differences that exist among people, such as their readiness to change. As you might expect, interventions tailored to meet the interests and needs of specific target groups are significantly more effective than general, one-size-fits-all interventions (Azer, 1999). For example, as part of one smoking-cessation intervention, researchers mailed out birthday cards and other materials that were designed specifically for each of several specific target groups (Rimer & Glassman, 1998). A birthday card tailored for African American participants in the study included the following message: "*Each year, more Black Americans die from smoking than from car crashes, AIDS, alcohol, murder, heroin, cocaine, and other drugs put together. If we count the number of people it kills, smoking is the number one problem facing the Black community.*" Thirty-two percent of the participants who received the tailored prevention materials quit smoking, compared to 12 percent among participants who did not. Velicer and Prochaska (1999) found similar results using a computer-based expert system to select intervention components on the basis of each participant's specific needs and an assessment of their readiness to change.

Third, research suggests that the effectiveness of health prevention messages depends on the way they are framed (Rothman & Salovey, 1997). Some health prevention messages seem to work best when they emphasize the benefits of a certain health practice (gain framing), whereas others work best when they emphasize the costs (loss framing). The relative effectiveness of a gain-framed or loss-framed message depends, at least in part, on whether the function of the recommended behavior is on prevention or detection, as shown in Figure 11.13. Gain framing tends to work best for *prevention behaviors* that help people avert the onset or development of a health problem, such as the consistent use of sunscreen or refraining from smoking cigarettes (Detweiler et al., 1999). In contrast, loss framing seems to work best for messages intended to motivate *detection behaviors,* such as encouraging women to perform regular breast self-examinations or obtain a yearly mammography screening (Meyerowitz, Chaiken, 1987; Meyerowitz, Wilson, & Chaiken, 1991; Banks et al., 1995).

FIGURE 11.13
The Effects of Framing on Health-Prevention Messages
Research suggests that gain framing works best for *prevention behaviors*, ones that help people avert the onset or development of a health problem. Loss framing seems to work best for messages intended to motivate *detection behaviors*, ones that help people identify diseases that may already be present.

Finally, some evidence suggests that fear also plays a role in our responses to health-promotion messages. For example, individuals with high fear of contracting AIDS rate advertisements about AIDS as more effective than do people with low fear of contracting AIDS (Struckman-Johnson et al., 1990). These findings suggest that the effectiveness of ad campaigns that target deadly diseases, such as cancer or AIDS, may be enhanced by playing to people's fear of contracting a particular disease.

Primary Prevention of Cancer—The Pool Cool Program

What is the most common form of cancer in the United States? You may be surprised to learn the answer: skin cancer. The incidence of melanoma, the most deadly form of skin cancer, has more than doubled since 1970, and each year 1.3 million new cases are reported. Fortunately, skin cancer is also one of the most preventable forms of cancer, making it a prime candidate for primary prevention programs. The behavioral recommendations for prevention of skin cancer are clear: Use sunscreen with a sun protection factor of 15 or higher; limit the amount of time you spend in the sun; avoid the sun during the middle of the day (10 a.m.–3 p.m.); and wear protective clothing such as sunglasses, hats, shirts, and pants (American Cancer Society, 2004).

Glanz and colleagues (2002) recently tested the impact of a primary skin cancer prevention program—*the Pool Cool program*—on sun protection behaviors. Sunbathers at each of twenty-eight different pools received either the Pool Cool sun protection training or an injury–prevention training program. The Pool Cool program was comprised of educational components that emphasized the behavioral recommendations for prevention listed previously. Over the course of the summer, researchers recorded changes in the sun protection behaviors of swimmers, parents, and aquatic staff. Significant changes were observed. For example, over time, the availability of sunscreen increased at the Pool Cool sites, but not at the other pools. As shown in Figure 11.14 on page 372, the increased availability—and use— of the sunscreen by the Pool Cool kids made a significant difference in the number of sunburns they reported. There was no change in the reported number of sunburns at the other site. To see another example of a primary intervention—this one aimed at starting an exercise routine—see the **Psychology Lends a Hand** section that follows.

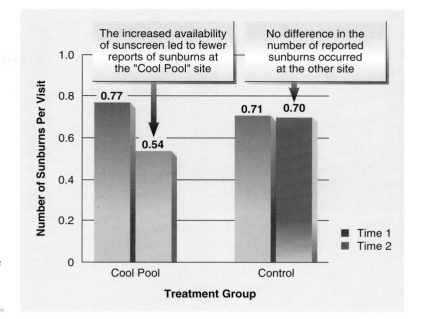

FIGURE 11.14
The Pool Cool Intervention: Prevention in Action
The increased availability—and use—of sunscreen by the Pool Cool kids made a significant difference in the number of sunburns they reported. There was no change in the reported number of sunburns at the other site.
Source: Based on data from Glanz et al., 2002.

psychology lends a hand

Starting (and Adhering to) an Exercise Program

One of the disappointing health trends in the United States is the dramatic increase in the number of people who are significantly overweight, including children. Part of the reason for this trend is that only about one in four Americans exercises regularly. This is surprising, because regular and vigorous exercise can significantly reduce stress and stress-related illnesses. The following tips can help you to get started—and stick with—an exercise program.

- **See your doctor before beginning** an exercise program to assess your current fitness level. This will help you determine the type of program that is right for you.
- **Pick activities that you like.** Intrinsic motivation is critical for sticking with an exercise program. If you start running because others tell you that you should, you are likely to experience *controlled motivation* rather than self-determination. As we learned earlier in this chapter, this may decrease the chances that you will stick with the program.
- **Develop a plan to overcome the barriers** that have prevented you from being active. Success in maintaining an exercise program requires that people arrange their environment so that it supports the desired exercise behavior and weakens competing behaviors. This means you must minimize the effects of the cues for competing behaviors. For example, individuals who have a tendency to work late should establish a morning training routine to minimize competition with a busy work schedule.

- **Design a program that you can stick with.** Start slowly and increase the workload steadily. The important parameters of any exercise program are frequency (how often you do it), duration (how long you do it), and intensity (how hard you exercise). To increase fitness over time, work to increase each parameter. Increase frequency first and then increase duration, and finally intensity.
- **Prepare correctly.** Drink fluids and wear the right attire.
- **Challenge yourself but set realistic goals.** The most successful goal-setting programs involve setting a long-term goal (e.g., run 3 miles in 30:00) with a series of short-term goals leading up to the long-term goal (e.g., run 2 miles in 25:00; run 3 miles without stopping).
- **Arrange for consequences that maintain exercise behavior.** Chart your progress—seeing on paper that your fitness has improved can serve as positive feedback to help you stay on track.
- **Consider exercising with a friend or others.** Social contact through exercise can be rewarding and may encourage you to continue.

If you look carefully at these tips, you will notice several important psychological principles at work, including learning (structure, reinforcement) and motivation (positive feedback, intrinsic satisfaction, social rewards, self-determination).

Secondary Prevention: The Role of Early Detection in Disease and Illness

Psychologists are taking an active role in developing motivational strategies to get people to take part in *early detection* procedures—techniques used to screen for the presence of disease and other serious health conditions. The identification of these conditions at an early stage can make an enormous difference in the chances for treatment success—in some cases the difference between life and death.

Screening for Disease: Seeking Information about Our Health Status

The fact that early detection and treatment of an illness is more effective than later detection and treatment is the foundation for screening programs. The widespread use of available screening techniques could decrease the incidence of cardiovascular disease through the early detection of high blood pressure and cholesterol, and could significantly reduce the number of cervical, colon, and prostate cancer deaths (Murray, 1999; Rothenberg et al., 1987).

Many companies, colleges, community organizations, and hospitals have screening programs to test for high blood pressure and serum cholesterol. Unfortunately, many people either fail to take advantage of screening programs or do not get screened regularly. Forgetting and underestimating the time since the last test are the primary reasons people wait too long between screenings. Interventions that heighten awareness or serve a reminder function, such as physician reminder systems and local advertising campaigns, can increase the frequency of screening visits (Mitchell, 1988). As with educational messages used to promote primary prevention, researchers also believe that educational messages used to promote *screening* procedures need to be tailored to meet people's varying levels of knowledge and screening frequency. For example, a person who has never had a screening may require a different motivational message than the person who believes that a single screening is enough (Murray, 1999).

The most significant factors that predict the use of screening, as indicated by the health belief model, are beliefs about the possible benefits of screening, the perceived severity of possible illnesses, perceived vulnerability to disease, and beliefs about what other people (friends, family) think about screening (Hennig & Knowles, 1990).

Self-Examination: Detecting the Early Signs of Illness

Self-examination can be instrumental to the early detection of both testicular and breast cancer. The cure rate associated with testicular cancer is extremely high—over 90 percent—if the cancer is detected early. Unfortunately, in nearly half of the testicular cancers diagnosed, the presence of the disease is not detected until it has spread from the testes to the abdomen and other organs, when the chances of a full recovery are significantly less. Despite the fact that testicular self-examination techniques are available and are effective in detecting the early signs of cancer, many males remain unaware of their existence or how to perform these procedures correctly (Finney, Weist, & Friman, 1995; Steffen, 1990).

It is noteworthy that public awareness of this form of cancer has increased dramatically following cyclist Lance Armstrong's string of victories in the grueling Tour de France (refer to Figure 11.15 on page 374). Why would this capture the public's attention? Just three years before he won this race for the first time in 1999, Armstrong was diagnosed with an advanced form of testicular cancer that nearly killed him. By the time he was diagnosed the cancer had already spread to his abdomen, lungs, and brain. Although given only a 50 percent chance of survival, Armstrong miraculously survived a year of painful treatment, going on to win the Tour de France, one of sports' biggest challenges.

The dangers associated with breast cancer pose a similar challenge for women. Some researchers suggest that breast cancers detected early through secondary

FIGURE 11.15
Battling Back from Cancer
Cyclist Lance Armstrong gained instant notoriety following his first Tour de France victory in 1999. Why? One reason is that several years earlier he nearly died of an advanced case of testicular cancer. Armstrong's dramatic comeback has significantly raised the public's awareness of this form of cancer and the importance of performing regular cancer self-examinations to detect the disease at an earlier—and more curable—stage. Amazingly, Armstrong has since gone on to win the race four more times, the most recent victory coming in 2003.

prevention programs, such as breast self-examination, clinical breast examination, and mammography, have an 85 to 90 percent chance of being cured (American Cancer Society, 1989). Women are most likely to obtain mammography screening when their physician recommends it, highlighting the critical role these professionals play in promoting the importance of early detection. Programs designed to change certain beliefs are also effective in getting women to obtain mammography screening: for example, beliefs concerning their susceptibility to breast cancer, the severity of breast cancer, and the potential benefits of mammography screening (Aiken et al., 1994; Miller et al., 1996).

K E Y   Q U E S T I O N S

- What role does the mass media play in our health?
- What is primary prevention?
- What is secondary prevention?

S U M M A R Y   A N D   R E V I E W   O F   K E Y   Q U E S T I O N S

**Health Psychology:
An Overview**

- **What is health psychology?**
  Health psychology is the study of the relation between psychological variables and health.

- **What is the field of behavioral medicine?**
  Behavioral medicine, a field closely related to health psychology, combines behavioral and biomedical science knowledge to prevent and treat disorders.

- **To what can we attribute today's leading causes of premature death?**
  Many of today's leading causes of premature death can be attributed to people's lifestyles.

Stress: Its Causes, Effects, and Control

- **What is stress?**
  Stress is the process that occurs in response to situations or events (stressors) that disrupt, or threaten to disrupt, our physical or psychological functioning.

- **What is the GAS model?**
  The general adaptation syndrome (GAS) describes how our bodies react to the effects of stress and includes three distinct stages: alarm, resistance, and, finally, exhaustion.

- **What determines whether an event will be interpreted as stressful or as a challenge?**
  Cognitive appraisals play an important role in determining whether we interpret potentially stressful events as stressful or as a challenge.

- **Which types of events are likely to create stress?**
  Both positive (getting married) and negative (death of a spouse) life events may be stressors. Catastrophic events (terrorism, natural disasters) may be especially stressful, even to observers.

- **Are daily hassles harmful?**
  Yes, the accumulated strain of minor annoyances such as commuting problems and waiting in lines while shopping can cause stress and affect our health.

- **What are some sources of work-related stress?**
  Sources of work-related stress include work overload and underload, low job control, and role conflict.

- **What role does stress play in physical illness?**
  Stress may play a role in 50 to 70 percent of all physical illnesses, primarily through its effect on the immune system.

- **How does social support influence stress?**
  Social support increases the contact we have with others and may improve coping skills. Providing support, as opposed to receiving it, may have stronger effects.

- **What is the relationship between stress and performance?**
  Even relatively low levels of stress may interfere with task performance. Prolonged exposure to high levels of stress may lead to illness.

Understanding and Communicating Our Health Needs

- **What is the health belief model?**
  The health belief model suggests that our willingness to seek medical help depends on the extent to which we perceive a threat to our health and the extent to which we believe that a particular behavior will effectively reduce that threat.

- **What factors determine our willingness to make lifestyle changes or seek medical help?**
  Our willingness to make lifestyle changes or seek medical help depends on our beliefs concerning our susceptibility to an illness, the severity of the illness, and the effectiveness of steps taken to deal with the illness.

- **What are the advantages and disadvantages of seeking medical advice on the Internet?**
  Some of the nation's top medical research facilities have created publicly accessible Web sites, so patients can learn more about their symptoms and take a more active role in their treatment. However, the Internet is not policed; therefore, the information found at many sites is inaccurate.

Behavioral and Psychological Correlates of Illness: The Effects of Thoughts and Actions on Health

- **What determines who will become addicted to smoking?**
  Genetic, psychosocial, and cognitive factors all seem to play a role in determining who will become addicted to smoking.

- **What are the effects of poor dietary practices?**
  Poor dietary practices can increase the risks of colon and rectal cancer, breast cancer, and cardiovascular disease.

- **How do feelings of self-determination influence adherence to an exercise regimen?**
  Health-preventive behavior that we initiate and determine ourselves is more likely to be maintained over time, whereas maintenance of these behaviors achieved at the urging of others (controlled motivation) is less likely.

- **What are the consequences of heavy consumption of alcohol?**
  Chronic excessive alcohol consumption can lead to deficits in many different cognitive abilities, including learning and memory, perceptual–motor skills, visual–spatial processing, and problem solving. Drinking can also lead to stomach disease, cirrhosis of the liver, cancer, and impaired sexual functioning, and can result in fetal alcohol syndrome.

- **What is AIDS? How is HIV transmitted?**
  Acquired immune deficiency syndrome (AIDS) is a reduction in the immune system's ability to defend the body against invaders and is caused by the HIV virus. HIV is transmitted primarily through unprotected sex and infected blood.

- **How does the IMB model attempt to change risky behaviors?**
  According to the IMB model, people will not change risky behaviors unless they know how diseases are acquired and the specific actions they must take to avoid them. Interventions based on the IMB use elicitation research to identify misinformation that individuals have and then teach the skills necessary to engage in safe behavior.

- **How is the way in which we express our emotions related to our health?**
  Failure to express our emotions can adversely affect the progression of cancer and other illnesses. Emotions can also lead to an increase in a person's blood pressure.

Promoting Wellness: Developing a Healthier Lifestyle

- **What role does the mass media play in our health?**
  The mass media, when combined with other health promotion programs, can have a beneficial impact on health behaviors.

- **What is primary prevention?**
  Primary prevention emphasizes disease prevention by educating people about the relation between their behavior and their health, promoting healthy behavior, and directly modifying poor health practices.

- **What is secondary prevention?**
  Secondary prevention techniques emphasize early detection of diseases and attempt to decrease the severity of illness that is already present.

PSYCHOLOGY: UNDERSTANDING ITS FINDINGS

Changing Our Explanatory Style

As was noted in this chapter, people differ considerably in their resistance to adversity in their lives. How do such persons differ? One answer involves the personality dimension of *optimism–pessimism*. Optimists and pessimists differ in variety of ways, including in their general expectancies for good outcomes and in their approaches to dealing with problems in their lives. Psychologists have learned that another important difference is their beliefs about the causes of events in their lives.

Pessimists tend to believe the causes of the *negative* events in their lives are permanent—"I'm a loser"—and that these will persist and spread to other areas of their lives. This helps to explain why pessimists tend to give up easily and are less resistant to the effects of stress. In contrast, people with an optimistic outlook believe that such events are the result of factors that are temporary and specific to that event.

When it comes to *positive* events, the opposite is true: Optimists tend to believe the causes of the positive events in their lives are permanent—"I'm smart"—and that they will spill over into other areas of their lives. Pessimists, as you might predict, tend to ascribe good fortune to transitory forces outside themselves.

We have all adopted a pessimistic explanatory style at least once in our lives. Fortunately, there are steps you can take to build a more optimistic style. First, recognize that your beliefs are just that—beliefs! An effective way to defeat a negative belief is to show that it is factually incorrect. Second, remember that most events have many causes. For example, if you performed poorly on a test, a number of factors probably played a role. To dispute your own beliefs, focus on the contributing factors that are changeable (e.g., the amount of time you studied) and specific (e.g., this particular exam was really difficult). Please note, however, that the facts won't always be on your side and the negative beliefs you hold may sometimes be true. In these instances, try to put the event into perspective. For example, you might change the belief to "I performed poorly on this exam, but I have three more exams left to take!" Finally, it is important to stop dwelling on the belief and focus on the actions that will change the situation, such as arranging your schedule to allow you to study harder for the next exam.

Whenever you find yourself feeling pessimistic about events in your life, try using these tips. To chart your progress, write down a description of each event, your initial reactions to it, and the steps you took to address the problem. Over time, you may find that you are less susceptible to pessimistic thoughts and beliefs.

MAKING PSYCHOLOGY PART OF YOUR LIFE

Managing Stress: Some Useful Tactics

Stress is a fact of life. It's all around us: at work, in our environment, and in our personal lives. Because stress arises from so many different factors and conditions, it's probably impossible to eliminate it completely. However, there are a number of techniques that you can use to lessen its harmful effects.

Physiological Coping Techniques

One of the most effective physiological coping techniques involves reducing muscle tension through **progressive relaxation.** Begin by alternately flexing and relaxing your muscles to appreciate the difference between relaxed and tense muscles. Next, relax your shoulders by slowly rolling them up and down. Now, relax your neck. Step by step, extend this process until your body is completely relaxed. Relaxation procedures are effective in reducing emotional as well as physical tension. Regular vigorous exercise is another important technique to reduce stress; it does not eliminate the prob-

lems that sometimes lead to stress, but it may increase your capacity to cope with the stress.

Behavioral Coping Techniques

There are plenty of things you can do to reduce the stress in your life. One method is *time management:* learning how to make time work for you instead of against you. Adhering to a well-planned schedule can help you make more efficient use of your time and eliminate behaviors that interfere with your main goals. Table 11.5 offers several tips to help you get the most out of your day.

Cognitive Coping Techniques

When exposed to a stressful situation, you can *think* about it in different ways. The process of replacing negative appraisals of stressors with more positive ones is called **cognitive restructuring** (Meichenbaum, 1977). To use this technique, start to monitor what you say to yourself during periods of stress. Begin modifying these thoughts by thinking more

TABLE 11.5   Getting the Most Out of Your Day: Psychology in Action

One behavioral coping strategy is time management. Here are some tips to help you get the most out of your day.

Basic Principles of Time Management

1. Each day, make a list of things you want to accomplish.

2. Prioritize your list. Plan to do the toughest things first, and save the easier tasks for later in the day when you are low on energy.

3. Arrange your work schedule to take the best advantage of the hours when you work best.

4. Always set aside a block of time when you can work without any interruptions.

5. Be flexible about changes in your schedule so that you can handle unexpected events.

6. Set aside time in your daily schedule for exercise, such as jogging, aerobics, or brisk walking. You'll find that the time spent is well worth it and may even increase your productivity.

7. Set aside some time each day or week in which you always do some planned leisure activity—everybody needs a break.

Progressive Relaxation
A stress-reduction technique in which people learn to relax by alternately flexing and relaxing, one by one, muscle groups throughout the body.

Cognitive Restructuring
A method of modifying self-talk in stress-producing situations. Clients are trained to monitor what they say to themselves in stress-provoking situations and then to modify their cognitions in adaptive ways.

adaptive thoughts, such as imagining something humorous about the situation or creative ways to reduce or eliminate the source of stress. Having adequate sources of social support is also important. Because cognitive appraisal plays a crucial role in the way we interpret stressors, it is a good idea to be in contact with people who can suggest strategies for dealing with the sources of stress that you might not generate yourself. Finally, as we learned in this chapter, providing social support to others may also be beneficial to your health.

KEY TERMS

Acquired Immune Deficiency
  Syndrome (AIDS), p. 365
Cancer, p. 360
Carcinogens, p. 360
Cardiovascular Disease, p. 361
Cognitive Restructuring, p. 377
General Adaptation Syndrome (GAS),
  p. 348
Hassles, p. 352

Health Belief Model, p. 358
Health Psychology, p. 346
Hypertension, p. 367
Lifestyle, p. 346
Nicotine, p. 361
Person–Environment (P–E) Fit, p. 354
Posttraumatic Stress Disorder (PTSD),
  p. 351
Prevention Strategies, p. 369

Progressive Relaxation, p. 377
Risk Factors, p. 360
Self-Determination Theory, p. 364
Serum Cholesterol, p. 363
Social Support, p. 356
Stress, p. 348
Stressors, p. 348
Type D Personality Type, p. 367

Mental Disorders: Their Nature, Causes, and Treatment

*H*ave you ever known someone who showed disturbed or unusual behavior—actions or emotions far outside the range most people would describe as "normal"? I (Robert Baron) certainly have. When I was in high school, I had a neighbor who described herself as "The Nightmare in Black," and became so enraged at the noise we made playing football on the grass outside her windows that she literally fell out while shouting at us and was seriously injured. Later, when I was in college, I had a co-worker at a summer job who became convinced that I was trying to steal his "girlfriend." The young woman in question was not his girlfriend, and I had no romantic interest in her, but this didn't stop him from threatening to kill me and from following me home with a gun bulging in his pocket! The saddest instance of *disturbed behavior I have ever experienced, though, occurred just a couple of years ago. One of my colleagues, Rob M., parked his car in his garage, closed the door, and turned on the motor. Several days passed before a neighbor found him slumped over the steering wheel, dead. Everyone who knew him was deeply distressed, because Rob was one of the nicest persons we had ever known, was young and in good health. Why had he chosen to take his own life? From what I learned later on, he was deeply depressed over a failed love affair and over what he perceived to be dim prospects for his future career. Somehow, he had magnified these real but common problems into true despair—and so decided to end it all. I still think of him each time I pass his former office, and shake my head in sadness and disbelief; what a tragedy.*

All of the persons I have mentioned here showed signs of what psychologists would describe as serious *mental disorders.* Such disorders were often termed *abnormal behavior* or *mental illness* in the past, but *mental disorders* is the term currently used most frequently by psychologists, so that's the one we'll adopt. In this chapter, we'll first examine the nature and causes of these disturbed patterns of behavior and emotions, and then turn to ways in which they can be treated so as to lessen the pain and discomfort they produce. Before turning to these major topics, though, we should first clarify just what we mean by the term *mental disorders* (Nietzel et al., 1998). This question is much harder to answer than you might at first assume, because, in fact, there is no hard-and-fast dividing line between behavior that is normal and behavior that is somehow *abnormal* or outside the ordinary. Most people—including most psychologists—would describe the behavior shown by the people described previously as falling toward the "abnormal" or "disturbed" end of the continuum, but even in extreme cases, such as the co-worker who threatened to kill me for stealing his imaginary girlfriend, there is room for interpretation. Perhaps in my co-worker's culture he had grounds for assuming that the young woman in question *was* his girlfriend or, at least, was interested in him; and perhaps he interpreted her friendliness toward me as a sign that I had failed to show both him and her the proper respect (I was only a summer fill-in while he held a full-time, regular job). We're not suggesting that his behavior was in any way appropriate, but such points do emphasize the fact that deciding what is "normal" and what is "abnormal" or disturbed is a very complex task, one that should never be taken lightly (see Figure 12.1).

Having said that, we should add that most psychologists agree that mental disorders include the following features. First, they involve patterns of behavior or thought that are judged to be unusual or *atypical* in their society. People with these disorders don't behave or think like most others, and these differences are often apparent to the people around them. Second, such disorders usually generate *distress*—negative feelings and reactions—in the persons who experience them.

CLEARING A SPACE AT THE BEACH

FIGURE 12.1

When Is Behavior "Abnormal" or "Disturbed"?

Is the man here showing a mental disorder? Or is he just using an effective technique for obtaining some space on a crowded beach? We would have to know much more about him and his daily actions to reach a conclusion.

Source: © The New Yorker Collection 2000 Jack Ziegler from cartoonbank.com. All Rights Reserved.

Third, they are *maladaptive*—they interfere with the ability to function normally and meet the demands of daily life. Combining these points, we can define **mental disorders** as disturbances of an individual's behavioral or psychological functioning that are not acceptable in a given society and that lead to psychological distress, behavioral disability, or impaired overall functioning (Nietzel et al., 1998).

In the remainder of this chapter, we'll examine a number of different disorders and some of the factors that lead to their occurrence. After that, we'll turn to procedures for treating or alleviating such disorders. Before beginning, though, we'll describe a sytem for classifying mental disorders that is very widely used—the DSM–IV.

KEY QUESTIONS

- What are mental disorders?
- Why is it difficult to distinguish normal behavior from abnormal behavior?

ASSESSMENT AND DIAGNOSIS: THE DSM–IV AND OTHER TOOLS

Suppose that one day your car won't start. What do you do? The first step is probably to gather information that will help you figure out why nothing happens when you turn the key. You might check to see if the headlights were left on; you might try turning on the radio—it if plays, then the battery is not totally dead; next, you might open the hood and check the connections to the battery. After gathering such information, you would make an initial decision about what's wrong: The battery is dead, the starter isn't working, and so on.

In a similar manner, a psychologist might go through a comparable set of steps when seeing a new patient for the first time. The psychologist would first gather information on the kind of problems the person is experiencing, conditions in her or his current life, the person's responses to various psychological tests (see

Mental Disorders

Disturbances of an individual's behavioral or psychological functioning that are not culturally expected and that lead to psychological distress, behavioral disability, or impaired overall functioning.

Chapter 7), and so on. These information-gathering steps are known as *assessment*, and they are directed toward the goal of formulating an accurate *diagnosis*—identification of the person's problem(s). This is a crucial step because identifying these problems often determines what the psychologist should do next—how she or he can best help this individual.

But how does the psychologist identify the specific disorder or disorders a given person is experiencing? In general, by comparing the information gathered through assessment to standard definitions of various mental disorders. In other words, psychologists and other mental health professionals have an agreed-upon system for describing and classifying mental disorders. Such a system is very useful, because without it, different psychologists or psychiatrists might refer to the same disorder with different terms or might use the same terms to describe very different problems (Millon, 1991).

Actually, several different systems for classifying mental disorders exist. However, the one that is the most widely used in the United States is the **Diagnostic and Statistical Manual of Mental Disorders–IV** (or *DSM–IV* for short), published by the American Psychiatric Association (1994). Although this manual is published by the American Psychiatric Association, psychologists have long contributed to its development. Thus, it is designed to help all mental health practitioners correctly identify (diagnose) specific disorders. However, the fact that it was designed primarily by psychiatrists (medical doctors who specialize in the treatment of mental disorders) is still a cause for concern among many psychologists.

The major diagnostic categories of the DSM–IV are shown in Table 12.1, and among them are all the major kinds of disorders covered in this chapter. In fact, the manual describes hundreds of specific disorders—many more than we'll consider here. These descriptions focus on observable features and include *diagnostic features*—symptoms that must be present before an individual is diagnosed as having a particular problem. In addition, the manual also provides much additional background information on each disorder, for instance, information about biological factors associated with the condition, and variations in each disorder that may be related to age, cultural background, and gender.

An important feature of the DSM–IV is that it classifies disorders along five *axes*, rather than merely assigning them to a given category. This means that a person is described along several different dimensions (axes) rather than only one. Different axes relate to mental disorders, physical health, and social and occupational functioning. For our purposes, two of these axes are most important: Axis I, which relates to major disorders themselves, and Axis II, which relates to *mental retardation* and to *personality disorders*—extreme and inflexible personality traits that are distressing to the person or that cause problems in school, work, or interpersonal relationships. The third axis involves general medical conditions relevant to each disorder, while the fourth axis considers psychosocial and environmental factors, including specific sources of stress. Finally, the fifth axis relates to a global assessment of current functioning. By evaluating people along each of these axes, the DSM–IV offers a fuller picture of their current state and psychological functioning.

Another important feature of the DSM–IV is that it reflects efforts to take greater account of the potential role of cultural factors in mental disorders. For example, in the DSM–IV, the description of each disorder contains a new section that focuses on *culturally related features*—aspects of each disorder that are related to, and may be affected by, culture. For instance, some disorders seem to occur only in certain cultures. A disorder known as *Windigo*, which occurs among Native Americans in North America, involves intense anxieties that the victims will turn into monsters who literally devour other human beings! Symptoms specific to a given culture and unique ways of describing distress in various cultures are included whenever available. This information is designed to help professionals recognize the many ways in which an individual's culture can influence the form of psychological disorders.

Diagnostic and Statistical Manual of Mental Disorders–IV
A manual designed to help all mental health practitioners recognize and correctly identify (diagnose) specific disorders.

TABLE 12.1   Major Diagnostic Categories of the DSM–IV

The DSM–IV classifies mental disorders according to the categories shown here.

Diagnostic Category—Axis I	Examples
Substance-related disorders	Alcohol-related disorders, cocaine-related disorders, opioid-related disorders
Schizophrenia and other psychotic disorders	Schizophrenia, schizoaffective disorder, brief psychotic disorder
Mood disorders	Depressive disorders, bipolar disorders
Anxiety disorders	Panic disorder, specific phobias, posttraumatic stress disorder, generalized anxiety disorder
Somatoform disorders	Somatization disorder, conversion disorder, hypochondriasis
Factitious disorders	With predominantly psychological signs and symptoms; with predominantly physical signs and symptoms
Dissociative disorders	Dissociative amnesia, dissociative fugue, dissociative identity disorder
Sexual and gender identity disorders	Sexual dysfunctions, paraphilias, gender identity disorders
Eating disorders	Anorexia nervosa, bulimia nervosa
Sleep disorders	Primary sleep disorders, sleep disorders related to another mental disorder
Impulse-control disorders not elsewhere classified	Kleptomania, pyromania, pathological gambling
Adjustment disorders	With depressed mood, with anxiety
Other conditions that may be a focus of clinical attention	Medication-induced movement disorders, relational problems, problems related to abuse or neglect

Diagnostic Category—Axis II	Examples
Personality disorders	Paranoid personality disorder, schizotypal personality disorder, antisocial personality disorder
Mental retardation	Mild mental retardation, moderate mental retardation, severe mental retardation, profound mental retardation

Is the DSM–IV a useful tool for psychologists? In several ways, it is. Strenuous efforts were made to improve it over previous versions and in many respects, these efforts succeeded: The DSM–IV appears to be higher in *reliability* than earlier versions, and it rests more firmly on careful empirical research. However, it also has several major shortcomings. First, it is largely *descriptive* in nature: It describes psychological disorders, but it makes no attempt to explain them—a task psychologists view as crucial (e.g., Huizink, Mulder, & Buitelaar, 2004). Second, it attaches specific *labels* to people, and this may activate stereotypes about them. Once a person is labeled as having a particular mental disorder, mental health professionals may perceive the person largely in terms of that label, and this can lead them to overlook important information about the person.

A third criticism is that the DSM–IV may be gender-biased. Females are diagnosed as showing certain disorders much more frequently than males, and some critics suggest that this is due to the fact that descriptions of such disorders seem to reflect society's views about women (sex-role stereotypes). Finally, mental disorders occur on a continuum, not in discrete categories. People don't simply have or not have a disorder, they may have it to various degrees, and may show different aspects of it in varying proportions. This fact is largely ignored by the DSM–IV. Overall, then, many psychologists are somewhat uneasy about the nature of the DSM–IV and how it is applied. However, they continue to use it because of the benefits of having a single widely used framework for describing and discussing mental disorders. Reflecting this fact, the DSM–IV will serve as the basis for our discussions of various disorders throughout this chapter.

KEY QUESTIONS

- What is the DSM–IV?
- In what ways is it an improvement over earlier versions?

DISORDERS OF INFANCY, CHILDHOOD, AND ADOLESCENCE

Often, the problems people experience as adults are visible earlier in life, when they are children or adolescents. The DSM–IV takes note of this fact and lists a number of disorders that first emerge during childhood or adolescence.

Disruptive Behavior

Disruptive behaviors are the most common single reason why children are referred to psychologists for diagnosis and treatment. And, in fact, such problems are common: As many as 10 percent of children may show such problems at some time or other. Disruptive behaviors are divided by the DSM–IV into two major categories: *oppositional defiant disorder* and *conduct disorder.*

Oppositional defiant disorder involves a pattern of behavior in which children have poor control of their emotions or have repeated conflicts with parents and other adults (e.g., teachers; see Figure 12.2). Children showing this pattern have problems getting along with others and, as a result, may start on a road that leads them to more serious difficulties later in life, one of which may be *conduct disorder* (or CD). Oppositional defiant disorder usually starts when children are quite young (ages three to seven), but conduct disorder begins somewhat later, often when children enter puberty. CD involves more serious antisocial behaviors that go beyond throwing tantrums or disobeying rules; it involves actions that are potentially harmful to the child, to others, or to property.

Attention-Deficit/Hyperactivity Disorder (ADHD)

When you were in school, did you ever have a classmate who couldn't sit still? I did, and I remember how our teacher struggled to get Joseph to stay in his seat and pay attention to the lesson. Looking back, I'm now confident that Joseph suffered from **attention-deficit/hyperactivity disorder** (ADHD—another important child-

Disruptive Behaviors
Childhood mental disorders involving poor control of impulses, conflict with other children and adults, and, in some cases, more serious forms of antisocial behavior.

Attention-Deficit/ Hyperactivity Disorder (ADHD)
A childhood mental disorder in which children simply can't pay attention (inattention), show hyperactivity or impulsivity, or show both of these symptoms.

FIGURE 12.2
Oppositional Defiant Disorder
Disruptive behaviors are the most common reason why children are referred to psychologists for diagnosis and treatment.

hood mental disorder). Actually three patterns of ADHD exist: one in which children simply can't pay attention (inattention); another in which they show hyperactivity or impulsivity—they really *can't* sit still and can't restrain their impulses; and a third pattern that combines the two. Unfortunately, ADHD is *not* a problem that fades with the passage of time: 70 percent of children diagnosed with ADHD in elementary school still show signs of it when they are sixteen (Barkley, DuPaul, & McMurray, 1990).

The causes of ADHD appear, again, to be both biological and psychological. For instance, such factors as low birth rate, oxygen deprivation at birth, and alcohol consumption by expectant mothers have all been associated with ADHD (Streissguth, 1994). In addition, deficits in the reticular activating system (RAS) and in the frontal lobes may be linked to ADHD. With respect to psychological factors, risk factors seem to include parental overstimulation—parents who just can't seem to let their infants alone.

Fortunately, ADHD can be treated successfully with several drugs, all of which act as stimulants. *Ritalin* is the most frequently used, and it amplifies the impact of two neurotransmitters—norepinephrine and dopamine—in the brain. While taking this drug, children are better able to pay attention, and often show greater control of their own behavior. The effects of these medications last only four to five hours, so they must be taken frequently. Ritalin and related drugs produce potentially harmful side effects (e.g., they act as stimulants and produce decreased appetite, insomnia, headaches, increased blood pressure). Thus, they are definitely *not* an unmixed blessing. A new drug, *Straterra,* seems to produce the beneficial effects of Ritalin but fewer of its side effects, and is gaining in popularity. To avoid potentially harmful side effects, which occur for virtually all effective drugs, many psychologists recommend treating ADHD with a combination of minimal doses of drugs and *behavioral management programs* in which children are taught to listen to directions, to stay in their seats while in class, and other important skills. Such programs are based, in part, on the growing concern among psychologists that ADHD is overdiagnosed; that is, more children are diagnosed as having this problem than is really justified.

Feeding and Eating Disorders

Beginning in the mid 1960s, standards of female beauty changed drastically in many countries, shifting from a preference for voluptuous, well-rounded figures to a much slimmer shape (see Figure 12.3 on page 386). Yet, despite this fact, a growing proportion of adults in the United States and other countries are actually overweight (see Chapter 9). Given this increasing gap between the image of personal beauty portrayed by the mass media and physical reality, it is not surprising that **feeding and eating disorders**—disturbances in eating behavior that involve maladaptive and unhealthy efforts to control body weight—are increasingly common. Although these obviously occur among adults (indeed, most people think of these as adult disorders), eating disorders often begin in childhood; that's why we consider them in this section (Nietzel et al., 1998; Stice, 2002). Two eating disorders—**anorexia nevosa** and **bulimia nervosa**—have received most attention.

▨ Anorexia Nervosa: You Can, Indeed, Be *Too* Slim

Anorexia nervosa involves an intense and excessive fear of gaining weight, coupled with refusal to maintain a normal body weight. In other words, people with this disorder relentlessly pursue the goal of being thin, no matter what this does to their health. They often have distorted perceptions of their own bodies, believing that they are much heavier than they really are. As a result of such fears and distorted perceptions, they starve themselves to the point where their weight drops to dangerously low levels.

Why do persons with this disorder have such an intense fear of becoming fat? Important clues are provided by the fact that anorexia nervosa is far more common

Feeding and Eating Disorders
Disturbances in eating behavior that involve maladaptive and unhealthy efforts to control body weight.

Anorexia Nervosa
An eating disorder involving intense fears of gaining weight coupled with refusal to maintain normal body weight.

Bulimia Nervosa
An eating disorder in which individuals engage in recurrent episodes of binge eating following by some form of purging.

FIGURE 12.3
Changing Ideals of Feminine Beauty: One Factor in the Growing Incidence of Eating Disorders
Until the 1960s, well-rounded female figures (e.g., Marilyn Monroe) were considered to be the most attractive. After that time, however, a trend toward being thin developed and grew stronger (e.g., Paris Hilton). Research findings suggest that this shift is one factor that has contributed, along with many others, to the rising incidence of eating disorders in recent decades.

among females than males, although this seems to be changing as more adolescent males become obsessed with having a highly muscled "Hollywood body" (Ricciardelli & McCabe, 2004). This has led many researchers to propose that because many societies place greater emphasis on physical attractiveness for females than for males, adolescents and young women feel tremendous pressure to live up to the images of beauty shown in the mass media—to be as thin as the models who are held up as paragons of female desirability. If they are not this thin, they reason, they will be viewed as unattractive. In other words, many young women show a pattern known as *thin-ideal internalization*—they cognitively accept socially defined ideals of attractiveness that emphasize being extremely thin, and engage in behaviors designed to attain this ideal, such as dieting.

Bulimia: The Binge–Purge Cycle

If you found anorexia nervosa disturbing, you may find a second eating disorder—bulimia nervosa—even more unsettling. In this disorder, individuals engage in recurrent episodes of binge eating—eating huge amounts of food within short periods of time—followed by some kind of compensatory behavior designed to prevent weight gain. This can involve self-induced vomiting, the misuse of laxatives, fasting, or excessive exercise.

The causes of bulimia nervosa appear to be similar to those of anorexia nervosa: Once again, the "thin is beautiful" ideal seems to play an important role (e.g., Thompson, 1992; Williamson, Cubic, & Gleaves, 1993). Another, and related, factor is the desire to be perfect in all respects, including those relating to physical beauty. More recent findings indicate that women who are high on this trait are at risk for developing bulimia, especially if they perceive themselves to be overweight (Joiner et al., 1997). And, in fact, bulimics—like anorexics—do tend to perceive themselves as much heavier than they really are (Williamson, Cubic, & Gleaves, 1993).

Overall, existing evidence indicates that both anorexia nervosa and bulimia can be understood in terms of the factors shown in Figure 12.4: Being overweight, being dissatisfied with one's body image, a desire to be perfect, substance abuse, and the thin-ideal internalization put individuals (especially young women) at risk for serious eating disorders, in part because these factors increase tendencies to experience negative affect, to diet, and to experience strong pressures to be thin (Stice,

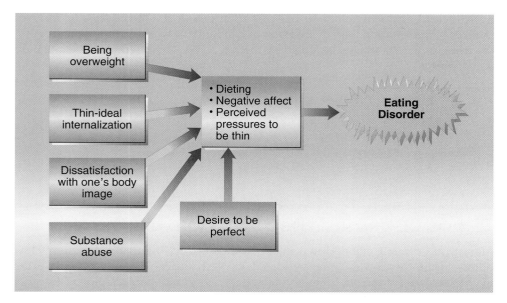

FIGURE 12.4
Causal Factors in Eating Disorders
As shown here, several factors, including being overweight, thin-ideal internalization, being dissatisfied with one's body image, a tendency to seek perfection, and substance abuse, contribute to the occurrence of serious eating disorders. Together, these factors cause many persons to diet and to experience strong pressures to be thin, and these actions, in turn, can lead to anorexia nervosa and bulimia.
Source: Based on suggestions by Stice, 2002.

2002; Thompson & Stice, 2001). In short, the "thin is beautiful" stereotype encouraged by the entertainment and advertising industries may contribute to tragic results for large numbers of individuals.

Fortunately, some interventions, such as showing individuals how photos in magazines are altered through computer modification to make the models appear thinner, can help reduce thin-ideal internalization (Stormer & Thompson, 1998). But eating disorders remain a serious problem that appears to be spreading throughout the world.

Autism: A Pervasive Developmental Disorder

Of all the childhood disorders, the ones that may be most disturbing of all are described in the DSM–IV as **pervasive development disorders.** Such disorders involve lifelong impairment in mental or physical functioning, and among these, the one that has received most attention is *autistic disorder* (or *autism*). This term is derived from the Greek word *autos* (self) and is an apt description for children with this disorder, for they seem to be preoccupied with themselves and live in an almost totally private world. Children with this disorder show three major characteristics: marked impairments in establishing social interactions with others (e.g., they don't use nonverbal behaviors such as eye contact, don't develop peer relationships, and don't seem to be interested in other people); nonexistent or poor language skills; and stereotyped, repetitive patterns of behavior or interests. In short, children with autistic disorder seem to live in a world of their own. They make little contact with others, either through words or nonverbal gestures; show little interest in them; and when they do notice them, they often seem to treat them as objects rather than people.

Autistic disorder seems to have important biological and genetic causes. Twin studies show a higher concordance rate for identical than for fraternal twins (e.g., Rutter et al., 1990). Similarly, other studies suggest that the brains of children with autistic disorder have structural or functional abnormalities, such as frontal lobes that are less well developed than in normal children (e.g., Gaffney et al., 1989). Psychological factors that play a role in autistic disorder include attentional deficits: Autistic children fail to attend to social stimuli such as their mothers' faces and voices, or to others' calling their own names (Osterling & Dawson, 1994). Perhaps the most intriguing findings of all are that autistic children have deficits in their *theory of mind,* a concept we discussed in Chapter 8. As you may recall, this term refers to children's understanding of their own and others' mental states. Apparently,

Pervasive Development Disorders
Disorders involving lifelong impairment in mental or physical functioning.

autistic children are unable to realize that other people can have access to different sources of information than themselves, and are unable to predict the beliefs of others from information that should allow them to make such predictions (e.g., Peterson & Siegal, 1999).

KEY QUESTIONS

- What is oppositional defiant disorder? Conduct disorder?
- What is attention-deficit/hyperactivity disorder?
- What are anorexia nervosa and bulimia nervosa?
- What is autistic disorder?

MOOD DISORDERS: THE DOWNS AND UPS OF LIFE

Have you ever felt truly "down in the dumps"—sad, blue, and dejected? How about "up in the clouds"—happy, elated, excited? Probably, you can easily bring such experiences to mind, for everyone has swings in mood or emotional state. For most of us, these swings are usually moderate in scope so that periods of deep despair and wild elation are rare. Some persons, however, experience much wider and prolonged swings in their emotional states. Their highs are higher, their lows are lower, and they spend more time in these states than most people. Such persons are described as suffering from **mood disorders.**

Depressive Disorders: Probing the Depths of Despair

Unless we lead a truly charmed existence, our daily lives expose us to some events that make us feel sad or disappointed. A poor grade, breaking up with one's romantic partner, failure to get a promotion—these and many other events tip our emotional balance toward sadness. When do such reactions constitute depression? Most psychologist agree that several criteria are useful for reaching this decision.

First, persons suffering from **depression** experience truly profound unhappiness, and they experience it much of each day. Second, persons experiencing depression report that they have lost interest in all the usual pleasures of life. Eating, sex, sports, hobbies—all fail to provide the enjoyment they did at other times. Third, persons suffering from depression often experience significant weight loss (when not dieting) or gain. Depression may also involve fatigue, insomnia, feelings of worthlessness, an inability to think or concentrate, and recurrent thoughts of death or suicide. When individuals experience five or more of these symptoms at once during the same two-week period, they are classified by the DSM–IV as showing a *major depressive episode* (see Figure 12.5).

Depression is very common. In fact, it is experienced by more than 20 percent of women and 12 percent of men at some time during their lives (Kessler et al., 1994). This nearly two-to-one gender difference in depression rates has been reported in many studies (e.g., Culbertson, 1997), especially those conducted in wealthy, developed countries, so it appears to be a real one. Why does it exist? As noted by Strickland (1992), several factors account for this finding, including the fact that females have traditionally had lower status, power, and income; must worry more than males about their personal safety; and much more often than males are the victims of sexual harassment and assaults. In addition, gender differences in rates of depression may also stem, at least to a degree, from other causes: the fact that females are more willing to admit to such feelings than males and are more concerned than males with disapproval from others (Scheibe et al., 2003; Wilhelm & Parker, 1994).

Episodes of major depression are not isolated events; most people who experience one such episode also experience others during their lives—an average of five or six (Winokur, 1986).

FIGURE 12.5
Depression: The Emotional Sinkhole of Life

People experiencing a *major depressive episode* show such symptoms as an intensely negative mood, loss of interest in all the things that usually give them pleasure, significant loss (or gain) of weight, intense feelings of fatigue, and insomnia. Truly, they are in the depths of despair.

Mood Disorders
Psychological disorders in which individuals experience swings in their emotional states that are much more extreme and prolonged than is true of most people.

Depression
A mood disorder in which individuals experience extreme unhappiness, lack of energy, and several related symptoms.

Bipolar Disorders: Riding the Emotional Roller Coaster

If depression is the emotional sinkhole of life, then **bipolar disorder** is its emotional roller coaster. People suffering from bipolar disorder experience wide swings in mood. They move, over varying periods of time, between deep depression and an emotional state known as *mania,* in which they are extremely excited, elated, and energetic. During manic periods, such persons speak rapidly, show a sharply decreased need for sleep, jump from one idea or activity to another, and show excessive involvement in pleasurable activities that have a high potential for harmful consequences. For example, they may engage in wild buying sprees or make extremely risky investments. Clearly, bipolar disorders are very disruptive not only to the individuals who experience them but to other people in their lives as well.

The Causes of Depression: Its Biological and Psychological Roots

Depression tends to run in families (Egeland et al., 1987) and is about four times more likely to occur in both members of identical twins than in both members of nonidentical twins (Bowman & Nurnberger, 1993), so there appears to be an important genetic component in this disorder, especially in bipolar disorders. Other findings suggest that mood disorders may involve abnormalities in brain biochemistry. The current view is that low levels of serotonin (an important neurotransmitter) may allow other neurotransmitters such as dopamine and norepinephrine to swing out of control, and this, in turn, leads to extreme changes in mood. However, this is just one possibility, and at present the precise neurochemical mechanisms that play a role in depression remain uncertain.

Several psychological factors have been found to play a role in depression. One of these is **learned helplessness** (Seligman, 1975)—beliefs on the part of individuals that they have no control over their own outcomes. Such views often develop after exposure to situations in which such lack of control is present, but then generalize to other situations where individuals' fates *are* at least partly in their hands. One result of such feelings of helplessness seems to be depression (e.g., Seligman et al., 1988).

Another psychological mechanism that plays a key role in depression is negative views about oneself (Beck, 1976; Beck et al., 1979). Individuals suffering from depression often possess negative *self-schemas*—negative conceptions of their own traits, abilities, and behaviors. As a result, they tend to be highly sensitive to criticism from others (Joiner, Alfano, & Metalsky, 1993) and are often very concerned about disapproval from them (e.g., Mazure et al., 2001). Because they are more likely to notice and remember such negative information, their feelings of worthlessness strengthen, and when they are exposed to various stressors (e.g., the break-up of a romantic relationship, a failure at work), their thinking becomes distorted in important and self-defeating ways. Depressed persons begins to see neutral or even pleasant events in a negative light—for instance, they interpret a compliment from a friend as insincere, or someone's being late for an appointment as a sign of rejection. These distortions in thinking make it difficult for them to make realistic judgments about events, and they begin to engage in thinking characterized by automatic, repetitive, and negative thoughts about the self, the world, and the future (what Beck describes as the *negative cognitive triad*). In sum, depressed persons see themselves as inadequate and worthless, feel that they can't cope with the demands made on them, and dread the future, which, they believe, will bring more of the same. (See Figure 12.6 on page 390 for a summary of cognitive factors in depression.)

Suicide: When Life Becomes Unbearable

Hopelessness, despair, negative views about oneself—these are some of the hallmarks of depression. Given such reactions, it is not surprising that many persons

Bipolar Disorder
A mood disorder in which individuals experience very wide swings in mood, from deep depression to wild elation.

Learned Helplessness
Beliefs on the part of individuals that they cannot influence the outcomes they experience.

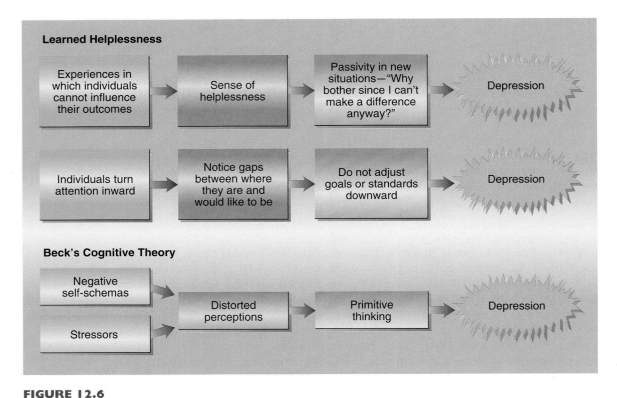

FIGURE 12.6
Cognitive Mechanisms in Depression
Extensive research indicates that the cognitive mechanisms and factors shown here often play a role in depression.

suffering from this disorder seek a drastic solution—*suicide,* or taking of their own lives. In the United States, about 40,000 people commit suicide each year. This figure may be an underestimate because many people who die in high-risk behaviors, such as speeding on the highway or using dangerous drugs, may have intended to end their own lives. In addition, more than 300,000 people attempt suicide but don't succeed (Andreason & Black, 1995). More than two times as many women as men attempt suicide, but men are three to four times more likely to actually die when they take this course of action, mainly due to the fact that men use more effective methods, such as jumping from high places, guns, or hanging; women tend to use less certain tactics, such as poison or drug overdose (Kaplan & Sadock, 1991). Suicide is the tenth or eleventh most frequent cause of death in the United States. Suicide rates vary with age and by nation. The highest rates occur among older people, but suicide has been on the rise among young people and is now high even among teenagers—it is the third most common cause of death among adolescents fifteen to nineteen years old (Garland & Zigler, 1993). Why do people commit suicide? Notes left by such persons and information provided by suicide attempters suggest that they do so for many different reasons. However, problems with relationships seem to head the list.

Suicide varies across different cultures. In some northern European countries and Japan, the suicide rate is as high as 25 per 100,000 inhabitants. In countries with strong religious prohibitions against suicide, such as Greece and Ireland, the rate is about 6 per 100,000; it is about 12 per 100,000 in the United States. Further, in the United States, suicide is more common among persons of European descent than among those of African descent, but this gap has narrowed in recent years (Bongar, 1991). Suicide rates are low among Americans of Hispanic descent but are high among Native American males—as high as 24 per 100,000. Can anything be done to prevent suicide? Research by psychologists suggest that the answer is

p s y c h o l o g y   l e n d s   a   h a n d

Preventing Suicide: How You Can Help

Could I (Robert Baron) have done anything to prevent the suicide of my friend Rob (described at the start of this chapter)? I have thought about this many times, and the answer is not very good for my peace of mind: Yes, I think I might have been able to help. I was a visiting professor at a university in France at the time, so I wasn't here to interact with Rob and gauge his current mood, but I feel strongly that if I *had* been in town, I might have noticed some or all of these important warning signs:

- Statements that life no longer has any meaning, and that they have no strong reasons for continuing to live
- Agitation or excitement followed by a period of calm resignation
- Sudden efforts to give valued possessions to others
- Statements indicating "I don't want to be a burden to others anymore"
- Revival from a deeply depressed state, coupled with taking leave of others (saying "good-bye" instead of "so long")

If you observe these changes in others, they may well be danger signs that they are seriously considering suicide. Did my friend Rob show any of these signs? Absolutely. People who interacted with him shortly before his suicide have told me that his spirits seemed to brighten after a period of deep despair and that he did give away some valued possessions shortly before he took his own life. So, if you notice these warning signs in another person's behavior, *take them seriously.* They may well indicate that this person is seriously considering suicide. In any case, *do not leave them alone* if they

show such signs. Suicide is a solitary act, so just your presence on the scene may be helpful in preventing it. Here are some other steps that may also be helpful in preventing suicide:

- **Discourage others from blaming themselves for failure to reach unrealistic goals.** Many people who attempt suicide do so because they feel they have failed to measure up to their own standards. If you know someone who is prone to this pattern, try to get them to focus on their good points and to realize that their standards *are* unrealistic—ones no one could hope to attain.
- **Take all suicide threats seriously.** One common myth about suicide is that people who threaten to kill themselves rarely do—only those who tell no one about their plans commit suicide. *This is untrue!* Approximately 70 percent of those who commit suicide tell others about their intentions. So, when someone talks about suicide, *take it seriously.*
- **Most important of all, get help!** Remember signal detection theory (Chapter 3)? Where preventing suicide is concerned, many false alarms are better than one miss—it's far better to get worried or concerned for nothing than to look the other way while a tragedy occurs. So, if you are concerned about someone you know, *get professional help.* Call a local suicide hot line, discuss your concerns with someone in the campus counseling center, or see a physician or a member of the clergy. Help *is* available, so if you have any concerns at all, seek it!

yes. So, please read the **Psychology Lends a Hand** section to see how *you* can help in this respect.

KEY QUESTIONS

- What are the major symptoms of depression? Of bipolar disorder?
- What factors play a role in the occurrence of mood disorders?

ANXIETY DISORDERS: WHEN DREAD DEBILITATES

At one time or another, we all experience **anxiety**—a diffuse or vague concern that something unpleasant will soon occur. If such feelings become intense and persist for long periods of time, however, they can constitute another important form of mental disorder. Such **anxiety disorders** take several different forms (e.g., Zinberg & Barlow, 1995).

Phobias: Excessive Fear of Specific Objects or Situations

Most people express some fear of snakes, heights, violent storms, and buzzing insects such as bees or wasps. Because all of these can pose real threats to our safety,

Anxiety
Increased arousal accompanied by generalized feelings of fear or apprehension.

Anxiety Disorders
Psychological disorders that take several different forms, but which are all related to a generalized feeling of anxiety.

FIGURE 12.7

Fear of Snakes: A Genetically Determined Phobia?

How do you react to this photo? If you are like many people, with feelings of fear. A large body of evidence suggests that we possess strong tendencies to notice snakes, to fear them, and to respond negatively to them—tendencies that may involve an evolved fear module.

such reactions are adaptive, up to a point. If such fears become excessive in that they cause intense emotional distress and interfere significantly with everyday activities, they constitute **phobias,** one important type of anxiety disorder.

While many different phobias exist, most seem to involve fear of animals (e.g., bees, spiders, snakes); the natural environment (e.g., thunder, darkness, wind); blood illness and injections (e.g., blood, needles, pain, contamination); and various situations (e.g., enclosed places, travel, empty rooms). One very common phobia is that of snakes. We seem to possess a strong tendency to easily learn to fear snakes (e.g., Ohman & Mineka, 2001). In fact, many studies indicate that we may possess genetically determined tendencies to notice snakes, to fear them, and to respond negatively to them (e.g., Ohman & Mineka, 2003). For instance, when photos of snakes are shown in such a way that people can't tell what they have seen (the photos of snakes are *masked* by another visual stimulus presented immediately after the snake photos), they still show signs of emotional arousal to the snake photos (Ohman & Soares, 1994). Similarly, if a snake is shown among other, more neutral stimuli (e.g., pictures of flowers), it is detected more quickly than other stimuli in the same context (Ohman, Flykt, & Esteves, 2001). Together, such findings suggest that we may possess a biologically determined module in our brains for fear of snakes. This module has evolved because noticing and fearing snakes is beneficial for our survival (Ohman & Mineka, 2001). As Ohman & Mineka (2003) put it recently, this and related modules might constitute the basic ways in which our brains represent *evil* (see Figure 12.7).

Another common phobia is *social phobia*—excessive fear of situations in which a person might be evaluated and perhaps embarrassed. It is estimated that 13 percent of people living in the United States have had a social phobia at some time in their lives, and almost 8 percent report having had such fears during the past year (Kessler et al., 1994).

What are the causes of phobias? One possibility involves the process of *classical conditioning,* described in Chapter 5. Through such learning, stimuli that could not initially elicit strong emotional reactions can often come to do so. For example, an intense fear of buzzing sounds may be acquired by an individual after being stung by a bee or wasp. In the past, the buzzing sound was a neutral stimulus that produced little or no reaction. The pain of being stung, however, is an unconditioned stimulus, and as a result of being closely paired with it, the buzzing sound acquires the capacity to evoke strong fear (e.g., Mulkens, deJong, & Merckelbach, 1996). Once phobias are acquired, instrumental conditioning plays a role in their persistence: Avoidance of the feared object is very rewarding.

Panic Disorder and Agoraphobia

Phobias
Fears that become excessive in that they cause intense emotional distress and interfere significantly with everyday activities.

Panic Disorder
Periodic, unexpected attacks of intense, terrifying anxiety known as panic attacks.

The intense fears associated with phobias are triggered by specific objects or situations. Some individuals, in contrast, experience intense, terrifying anxiety that is *not* activated by a specific event or situation. Such *panic attacks* are the hallmark of **panic disorder**—periodic, unexpected attacks of intense, terrifying anxiety, known as *panic attacks*. Panic attacks come on suddenly, reach peak intensity within a few minutes, and may last for hours (e.g., Barlow, 1988). They leave the persons who experience them feeling as if they are about to die or are losing their minds. Among the specific symptoms of panic attacks are a racing heart, sweating, dizziness, nausea, chills, trembling, palpitations, pounding heart, feelings of unreality, fear of losing control, fear of dying, numbness or tingling sensation, and hot flashes.

Although panic attacks often seem to occur in the absence of any specific triggering event, they often take place in specific situations. In that case, panic disorder is said to be associated with **agoraphobia**—intense fear of open spaces, being in public, and traveling—or, commonly, fear of having a panic attack while away from home! Persons suffering from panic disorder with agoraphobia often experience anticipatory anxiety—they are terrified of becoming afraid.

What causes panic attacks? Existing evidence indicates that both biological factors and cognitive factors play a role. With respect to biological factors, it has been found that there is a genetic component in this disorder: About 50 percent of people with panic disorder have relatives who have it, too (Barlow, 1988). In addition, PET scans of the brains of persons who suffer from panic attacks suggest that even in the nonpanic state, their brains may be functioning differently from those of other persons (e.g., Reiman et al., 1989). For instance, a portion of the brainstem known as the *locus coeruleus* may be hypersensitive to certain stimuli (e.g., lactic acid, a natural by-product of exercise); as a result, persons affected by this condition experience intense fear in situations in which other persons do not (e.g., Papp et al., 1993).

Persons suffering from this disorder also tend to show a pattern in which they interpret bodily sensations as being more dangerous than they really are, which causes them to experience anxiety. The anxiety itself induces further bodily changes and sensations (Barlow, 1988, 1993), which ultimately can lead to a full-scale panic attack.

Obsessive–Compulsive Disorder: Behaviors and Thoughts Outside One's Control

Have you ever left your home, gone halfway down the street, and then returned to see if you really locked the door or turned off the stove? Have you ever worried about catching a disease by touching infected people or objects? Most of us have had such experiences, and they are completely normal. But some persons experience intense anxiety about them. They have disturbing thoughts or images about such events that they cannot get out of their minds (*obsessions*) unless they perform some action or ritual that somehow reassures them and helps to break this cycle (*compulsions*). Persons who have such experiences may be experiencing **obsessive–compulsive disorder,** another important type of anxiety disorder. What kind of disturbing thoughts or images do such persons have? Among the most common are fear of dirt or germs or of touching infected people or objects; disgust over body waste or secretions; undue concern that they have not done a job adequately, even though they know quite well that they have; and fear of having antireligious or sexual thoughts. Common compulsions—actions people perform to neutralize obsessions—include repetitive hand washing; checking doors, windows, water, or gas repeatedly; counting objects a precise number of times or repeating an action a specific number of times; and hoarding old mail, newspapers, and other useless objects (see Figure 12.8 on page 394).

What is the cause of such reactions? We all have repetitious thoughts occasionally. For example, after watching a film containing disturbing scenes of violence, we may find ourselves thinking about these over and over again. Most of us soon manage to distract ourselves from such unpleasant thoughts, but individuals who develop obsessive–compulsive disorder are unable to do so. They are made anxious by their obsessive thoughts, yet they can't dismiss them readily from their minds. Moreover, they have had experiences—for instance, embarrassment—that suggest to them that some thoughts are so dangerous they must be avoided at all costs. As a result, they become even more anxious, and the cycle builds. Only by performing specific actions can they ensure their "safety" and reduce this anxiety. Therefore, they engage in complex repetitive rituals (e.g., hand washing, checking

Agoraphobia
Intense fear of specific situations in which individuals suspect that help will not be available should they experience an incapacitating or embarrassing event.

Obsessive–Compulsive Disorder
An anxiety disorder in which individuals have recurrent, disturbing thoughts (obsessions) they can't prevent unless they engage in specific behaviors (compulsions).

FIGURE 12.8
Obsessive–Compulsive Disorder
People who accumulate huge piles of clothing and old papers may be showing one aspect of an *obsessive–compulsive disorder*. Doing so somehow helps them to deal with or reduce their anxiety.

things over and over again) that can gradually grow to fill most of their day. Because these rituals do generate reductions in anxiety, the tendency to perform them grows stronger. Unless they receive effective outside help, such persons have little chance of escaping their self-constructed, anxiety-ridden prisons.

Posttraumatic Stress Disorder

Imagine that you are sleeping peacefully in your own bed when suddenly the ground under your home heaves and shakes, and you are thrown to the floor. Once awakened, you find yourself surrounded by the sounds of objects, walls, and entire buildings crashing to the ground—accompanied by shrieks of fear and pain from your neighbors or your own family. This is precisely the kind of experience reported by many persons during earthquakes.

Such experiences are described as *traumatic* by psychologists because they are extraordinary in nature—and extraordinarily disturbing. It is not surprising, then, that some persons exposed to them experience **posttraumatic stress disorder (PTSD)**—a disorder in which people persistently reexperience the traumatic event in their thoughts or dreams; feel as if they are reliving the event from time to time; persistently avoid stimuli associated with the traumatic event (places, people, thoughts); and persistently experience symptoms of increased arousal such as difficulty falling asleep, irritability, outbursts of anger, or difficulty in concentrating. Posttraumatic stress disorder can stem from a wide range of traumatic events—natural disasters, accidents, rape and other assaults, torture, or the horrors of war (see Figure 12.9; Basoglu et al., 1996; Layman, Gidycz, & Lynn, 1996; Vernberg et al., 1996).

Because all persons exposed to traumatic events do not experience this disorder, a key question is this: What factors lead to its occurrence? Research on this question suggests that many factors play a role. The amount of social support trauma victims receive after the traumatic event seems crucial (e.g., Vernberg et al., 1996): the more support, the less likely are such persons to develop PTSD. Similarly, the coping strategies chosen by trauma victims are important: Effective strategies such as trying to see the good side of things (e.g., they survived!) help to prevent PTSD from developing, whereas ineffective strategies such as blaming themselves for the traumatic event ("I should have moved away from here!") increase its likelihood. Overall, cognitive factors involving how people think about and interpret traumatic events seem to be central (Dalgleish, 2004). In sum, it appears that whether individuals experience PTSD after exposure to a frightening event depends on several factors.

Posttraumatic Stress Disorder (PTSD)
A disorder in which people persistently reexperience the traumatic event in their thoughts or dreams, feel as if they are reliving these events from time to time, persistently avoid stimuli associated with the traumatic event, plus several other symptoms.

FIGURE 12.9
Traumatic Events: One Cause of Psychological Disorders
Some individuals who experience traumatic events like these develop posttraumatic stress disorder, in which they persistently reexperience the traumatic event in their thoughts or dreams, and show signs of increased arousal such as difficulty falling asleep, irritability, and difficulty in concentrating.

KEY QUESTIONS

- What are phobias?
- What is panic disorder?
- What is obsessive–compulsive disorder?
- What is posttraumatic stress disorder?

DISSOCIATIVE DISORDERS

Have you ever awakened during the night and, just for a moment, been uncertain about where you were or even who you were? Such temporary disruptions in our normal cognitive functioning are far from rare; many persons experience them from time to time as a result of fatigue, illness, or the use of alcohol or other drugs. In contrast, **dissociative disorders,** another form of mental disorder on the DSM–IV, go far beyond such experiences. They involve profound losses of identity or memory, intense feelings of unreality, a sense of being depersonalized (i.e., separate from oneself), and uncertainty about one's own identity.

Such disorders take several different forms. In **dissociative amnesia,** individuals suddenly experience a loss of memory that does not stem from medical conditions or other mental disorders. Such losses can be localized, involving only a specific period of time, or generalized, involving memory for the person's entire life. In another dissociative disorder, **dissociative fugue,** an individual suddenly leaves home and travels to a new location where he or she has no memory of his or her previous life. In *depersonalization disorder,* the individual retains memory but feels like an actor in a dream or movie.

As dramatic as these disorders are, they pale when compared with the most amazing—and controversial—dissociative disorder, **dissociative identity disorder.** This was known as *multiple personality disorder* in the past, and it involves a shattering of personal identity into at least two—and often more—separate but coexisting personalities, each possessing different traits, behaviors, memories, and emotions. Usually, there is one *host personality*—the primary identity that is present most of the time, and one or more *alters*—alternative personalities that appear from time to time. *Switching,* the process of changing from one personality to another, often seems to occur in response to anxiety brought on by thoughts or memories of previous traumatic experiences.

Until the 1950s, cases of dissociative identity disorder were rare. Starting with the book *The Three Faces of Eve* (Thigpen & Cleckley, 1957), however, interest in this disorder—and its reported frequency—skyrocketed. In 1973, a book describing one

Dissociative Disorders
Disorders involving prolonged loss of memory or identity.

Dissociative Amnesia
Profound amnesia stemming from the active motivation to forget specific events or information.

Dissociative Fugue
A sudden and extreme disturbance of memory in which individuals wander off, adopt a new identity, and are unable to recall their own past.

Dissociative Identity Disorder
A condition labeled as *multiple personality disorder* in the past, in which a single person seems to possess two or more distinct identities or personality states, and these take control of the person's behavior at different times.

case, *Sybil* (Schreiber, 1973), became a best-seller and was soon made into a TV program; it offered an interpretation of the causes of this disorder that soon became famous—and highly controversial. This explanation suggested that dissociative identity disorder occurs as a response to traumatic events early in life, especially sexual abuse. In order to deal with such events, it was argued, children created alternate personalities who could cope with such experiences better than they, and might also be able to protect them from further harm.

In the years that followed, thousands of new cases of dissociative identity disorder were diagnosed by psychiatrists and some psychologists. The overwhelming majority of these cases were women who, during therapy sessions (and often under hypnosis), developed dozens or even hundreds of alters, and who also suddenly had "recovered memories" of having endured horrible sexual abuse and satanic rituals while children. These memories led many to bring legal charges against their parents (mothers as well as fathers) and other relatives, thus shattering families.

Were these charges based on fact? Many mental health professionals have expressed a degree of skepticism in this respect, mainly because a number of such cases involved therapists who engaged in actions such as instructing their patients to work hard at recalling scenes of childhood sexual abuse and to read books about multiple personality disorders (e.g., *Sybil*). In view of such procedures, many psychologists believe that the "memories" reported by at least some patients were generated by the actions of their therapists and were not necessarily real. This does not imply that all cases of dissociative identity disorder are false; it is recognized as a genuine disorder in the DSM–IV. But, at the least, it seems best to approach such disorders with considerable caution. Traumatic experiences early in life (Garland & Zigler, 1993) certainly do produce harm. But whether such experiences lie behind many or even most cases of dissociative identify disorder remains an open question.

KEY QUESTIONS

- What are dissociative disorders such as dissociative amnesia?
- What is dissociative identity disorder?

SOMATOFORM DISORDERS: PHYSICAL SYMPTOMS WITHOUT PHYSICAL CAUSES

Several of Freud's early cases, ones that played an important role in his developing theory of personality, involved the following puzzling situation. An individual would show some physical symptom (such as deafness or paralysis of some part of the body), yet careful examination would reveal no underlying physical causes for the problem. Such disorders are known as **somatoform disorders**—disorders in which individuals have physical symptoms in the absence of identifiable physical causes for these symptoms.

One common somatoform disorder is **hypochondriasis**—preoccupation with fear about having a serious disease. Persons with this disorder do not actually have the diseases they fear, but they persist in worrying about them, despite repeated reassurance by their doctors that they are healthy. Many hypochondriacs are not simply faking; they feel the pain and discomfort they report and are truly afraid that they are sick or will soon become sick (see Figure 12.10).

Another somatoform disorder is known as **conversion disorder.** Persons with this disorder actually experience physical problems such as *motor deficits* (poor balance or coordination, paralysis or weakness of arms or legs) or *sensory deficits* (loss of sensation to touch or pain, double vision, blindness, deafness). While these disabilities are quite real to the persons involved, there is no medical condition present that would produce them.

Somatoform Disorders
Disorders in which individuals have symptoms typically associated with physical diseases or conditions, but in which no known organic or physiological basis for the symptoms can be found.

Hypochondriasis
A disorder involving preoccupation with fears of disease or illness.

Conversion Disorder
A somatoform disorder in which individuals experience actual physical impairment such as blindness, deafness, or paralysis for which there is no underlying medical cause.

As is true with almost all mental disorders, a number of factors seem to play a role in the occurrence of somatoform disorders. Individuals who develop such disorders seem to have a tendency to focus on inner sensations. In addition, they perceive normal bodily sensations as more intense and disturbing than do most people. Finally, they have a high level of negative affectivity—they are pessimistic, fear uncertainty, experience guilt, and have low self-esteem (Nietzel et al., 1998).

In addition, of course, persons who develop such disorders learn that their symptoms often yield increased attention and better treatment from family members: These persons are reluctant to give the patient a hard time, because he or she is already suffering so much! In short, they gain important forms of reinforcement from their disorder.

FIGURE 12.10
Hypochondriasis: Symptoms without Illness
How many of these persons are suffering from real medical ailments and how many are showing signs of *hypochondriasis*—a somatoform disorder in which individuals experience symptoms of diseases they don't really have? Some findings indicate that the figure may be as high as 50 percent!

KEY QUESTIONS

- What are somatoform disorders?
- What factors contribute to their occurrence?

SEXUAL AND GENDER IDENTITY DISORDERS

As we saw in Chapter 9, Freud believed that many psychological disorders can be traced to disturbances in *psychosexual development*. While this view is not widely accepted by psychologists today, there is little doubt that individuals experience many problems relating to sexuality and gender identity. Several of these are discussed below. Please note: These disorders are *not* related to homosexuality, and sexual preference is *not* included as a sexual disorder on the DSM–IV unless it causes the persons in question persistent and marked distress.

Sexual Dysfunctions: Disturbances in Desire and Arousal

Sexual dysfunctions include disturbances in sexual desire and/or sexual arousal, disturbances in the ability to attain orgasms, and disorders involving pain during sexual relations. **Sexual desire disorders** involve a lack of interest in sex or active aversion to sexual activity. Persons experiencing these disorders report that they rarely have the sexual fantasies most persons generate, that they avoid all or almost all sexual activity, and that these reactions cause them considerable distress.

In contrast, **sexual arousal disorders** involve the inability to attain or maintain an erection (males) or the absence of vaginal swelling and lubrication (females). *Orgasm disorders* involve the delay or absence of orgasms in both sexes. This may include *premature ejaculation* (reaching orgasm too quickly) in males. Needless to say, these problems cause considerable distress to the persons who experience them (e.g., Rowland, Cooper, & Slob, 1996).

Paraphilias: Disturbances in Sexual Object or Behavior

What is sexually arousing? For most people, the answer involves the sight or touch of another human being. But many people find other stimuli arousing, too. The

Sexual Desire Disorders
Disorders involving a lack of interest in sex or active aversion to sexual activity.

Sexual Arousal Disorders
The inability to attain or maintain an erection (males) or the absence of vaginal swelling and lubrication (females).

FIGURE 12.11
Paraphilias for Sale?
Many men find lingerie like that shown here to be sexually arousing. Such reactions are *not* a sign of sexual disorder (a paraphilia) unless these objects *must* be present for sexual arousal to occur.

large volume of business done by Victoria's Secret and other companies specializing in alluring lingerie for women stems, at least in part, from the fact that many men find such garments mildly sexually arousing (see Figure 12.11). Other persons find either inflicting or receiving pain during lovemaking increases their arousal and sexual pleasure. Do such reactions constitute sexual disorders? According to most psychologists, and the DSM–IV, they do not. Only when unusual or bizarre imagery or acts are *necessary* for sexual arousal (that is, arousal cannot occur without them) do such preferences qualify as a disorder. Such disorders are termed **paraphilias,** and take many different forms.

In *fetishes,* individuals become aroused exclusively by inanimate objects. Often these are articles of clothing, but in more unusual cases they can involve animals, dead bodies, or even human waste. *Frotteurism,* another paraphilia, involves fantasies and urges focused on touching or rubbing against a nonconsenting person. The touching, not the coercive nature of the act, is what persons with this disorder find sexually arousing. The most disturbing paraphilia of all is *pedophilia,* in which individuals experience sexual urges and fantasies involving children, generally ones younger than thirteen. When such urges are translated into overt actions, the effects on the young victims can, as we noted in Chapter 9, be devastating (e.g., Ambuel, 1995). Two other paraphilias are *sexual sadism* and *sexual masochism.* In the former, individuals become sexually aroused only by inflicting pain or humiliation on others. In the latter, they are aroused by receiving such treatment.

Gender Identity Disorders

Have you ever read about a man who altered his gender to become a woman, or vice versa? Such individuals feel, often from an early age, that they were born with the wrong sexual identity. They identify strongly with the other sex and show preferences for cross-dressing (wearing clothing associated with the other gender). They are displeased with their own bodies and request—often from an early age—that they receive medical treatment to alter their primary and secondary sex characteristics. In the past, there was little that medicine could do satisfy these desires on the part of persons suffering from **gender identity disorder.** Advances in surgical techniques, however, have now made it possible for such persons to undergo *sex-change operations* in which their sexual organs are actually altered to approximate those of the other gender. Several thousand individuals have undergone such operations, and existing evidence indicates that most report being satisfied with the results and happier than they were before (Green & Blanchard, 1995). However, it is difficult to evaluate such self-reports. Perhaps after waiting years for surgery and spending large amounts of money for their sex-change operations, such persons have little choice but to report positive effects. Clearly such surgery is a drastic step and should be performed only when potential patients fully understand all potential risks.

Paraphilias
Disorders in which sexual arousal cannot occur without the presence of unusual imagery or acts.

Gender Identity Disorder
A disorder in which individuals believe that they were born with the wrong sexual identity.

K E Y   Q U E S T I O N S

- What are sexual dysfunctions and paraphilias?
- What is gender identity disorder?

PERSONALITY DISORDERS: TRAITS THAT HARM

Have you ever known someone who was highly suspicious and mistrustful of others in virtually all situations? How about someone who seemed to believe that the world revolved around him—that he was the most important person on earth? Someone who seemed to have no conscience whatsoever, never experiencing guilt or regret no matter how much he hurt others? Such persons may well have had what psychologists term **personality disorders.** These are defined by the DSM-IV as extreme and inflexible personality traits that are distressing to the persons who have them or cause them problems in school, work, or interpersonal relationships. The emphasis should probably be on "cause them problems" rather than "distress," because many people with this kind of disorder are *not* disturbed by it: They view their behavior, strange as it may seem to others, as perfectly normal and beneficial.

The DSM-IV divides personality disorders into three distinct clusters, so let's take a look at some of the traits that fit under these categories. The first is described as involving odd, eccentric behavior or traits and includes three personality disorders: paranoid, schizoid, and schizotypal. Persons suffering from the paranoid personality disorders believe that everyone is out to get them, deceive them, or take advantage of them in some way. In contrast, the schizoid personality disorder involves a very different pattern. Persons with this disorder show little or no sign of emotion and lack basic social skills. As a result, they form few if any social relationships, and they often end up existing on the fringes of society. The third type—schizotypal personality disorder—also shows a pattern of social isolation and avoidance of close relationships. Persons with this disorder are highly anxious in social situations and often act in bizarre or strange ways; for instance, they may wear strangely out-of-date or mismatched clothes, or show up in a wool sweater in August. Research suggests that such persons may show deficits in working memory and in the ability to shift from automatic to controlled processing (Raine et al., 1999). This may account, in part, for their strange behavior in many contexts.

The other two clusters of personality disorders include disorders involving dramatic, emotional, and erratic forms of behavior, and disorders involving anxious fearful behavior. Disorders in these categories are summarized in Table 12.2 on page 400. One of these—the **antisocial personality disorder**—is worthy of special attention. Individuals showing this disorder are chronically callous and manipulative toward others, ignore social rules and laws, behave impulsively and irresponsibly, fail to learn from punishment, and lack remorse or guilt over their misdeeds. Such persons often become criminals or confidence artists—and some may even become politicians.

Existing evidence suggests that both genetic and environmental factors play a role in the occurrence of antisocial personality disorder (Rhee & Swaldman, 2002). Genetic factors may predispose specific persons toward impulsivity and low ability to delay gratification (e.g., Sher & Trull, 1994). Moreover, persons with the antisocial personality disorder show reduced reactions to negative stimuli—for instance, ones that are related to unpleasant experiences such as punishment (Patrick, Bradley, & Lang, 1993). This suggests that they may be less capable than others of experiencing negative emotions and less responsive to stimuli that serve as warnings to most people to "back off"—for example, angry facial expressions on the part of others (Ogloff & Wong, 1990). Whatever its origins, one point about the antisocial personality disorder is clear: Persons who show this disorder often pose a serious threat to themselves and to others.

KEY QUESTIONS

- What are personality disorders?
- What characteristics are shown by persons who have the antisocial personality disorder?

SCHIZOPHRENIA: LOSING TOUCH WITH REALITY

We come now to what many experts consider to be the most serious mental disorder of all: **schizophrenia.** This can be defined as a complex disorder (or cluster of

Personality Disorders
Extreme and inflexible personality traits that are distressing to the persons who possess them and cause them problems in school, at work, or in interpersonal relationships.

Antisocial Personality Disorder
A personality disorder in which individuals are chronically callous and manipulative toward others; ignore social rules and laws; behave impulsively and irresponsibly; fail to learn from punishment, and lack remorse or guilt over their misdeeds.

Schizophrenia
A complex disorder characterized by hallucinations (e.g., hearing voices), delusions (beliefs with no basis in reality), disturbances in speech, and several other symptoms.

TABLE 12.2 Personality Disorders

The DSM-IV divides personality disorders into three major clusters. Personality disorders in each cluster are described here.

Odd and Eccentric Personality Disorders

Paranoid personality disorder	Pervasive distrust and suspiciousness of others.
Schizoid personality disorder	Pervasive pattern of detachment from social relationships and restricted range of emotions.
Schizotypal personality disorder	Intense discomfort in interpersonal relationships, cognitive or perceptual distortions, and eccentric behavior.

Dramatic, Emotional, Erratic Personality Disorders

Antisocial personality disorder	Deceitfulness, impulsivity, irritability, reckless disregard for safety and welfare of others, and lack of remorse.
Borderline personality disorder	Pervasive pattern of instability in interpersonal relationships, self-image, and moods.
Histrionic personality disorder	Pervasive pattern of excessive emotionality and attention seeking.
Narcissistic personality disorder	Pervasive pattern of grandiosity in fantasy or behavior, plus lack of empathy.

Anxious and Fearful Personality Disorders

Avoidant personality disorder	Pervasive pattern of social inhibition, feelings of inadequacy, and hypersensitivity to negative evaluation.
Obsessive–compulsive personality disorder	Preoccupation with orderliness, perfectionism, and mental and interpersonal control.
Dependent personality disorder	Pervasive and excessive need to be taken care of.

disorders) characterized by fragmentation of basic psychological functions (attention, perception, thought, emotions, and behavior). As a result of such fragmentation, persons with schizophrenia have serious problems in adjusting to the demands of reality. They misperceive what's happening around them, often seeing or hearing things that aren't there. They have trouble paying attention to what is going on around them, and their thinking is so confused and disorganized that they cannot communicate with others. They often show bizarre behavior and blunting of emotion and motivation, such that they are unable to move or take action. And when they do show emotion, it is often inappropriate in a given situation. Schizophrenia is so disruptive that persons who develop it must often be removed from society, at least temporarily, for their own protection and to undergo treatment.

The Nature of Schizophrenia

Let's begin with a closer look at the major symptoms of schizophrenia—the criteria used for the DSM–IV for diagnosing this disorder. These are often divided into *positive* and *negative* symptoms. As these terms suggest, positive symptoms involve adding something that isn't normally there—excess and bizarre behaviors, seeing and hearing things that don't exist; negative symptoms, in contrast, involve absence or reduction of normal functions.

Positive Symptoms of Schizophrenia

These include *delusions, hallucinations, disordered thought processes,* and *disordered behaviors.* **Delusions** involve misinterpretations of normal events and experiences—misinterpretations that lead schizophrenics to hold beliefs with little basis in reality. Delusions can take many different forms. One common type is *delusions of persecution*—the belief that one is being plotted against, spied on, threatened, or otherwise mistreated. Another common type is *delusions of grandeur*—belief that one is extremely famous, important, or powerful. Persons suffering from such delusions may claim that they are the president, a famous movie star, or even Jesus, Mohammed, or Buddha. About 70 percent of schizophrenics experience **hallucinations:** they see or hear things that aren't really there. These often take the form of voices telling them what to do.

In addition, persons with schizophrenia do not think or speak normally. Their words jump about in a fragmented and disorganized manner. There is a loosening of associations, so that one idea does not follow logically from another; indeed, ideas often seem totally unconnected. Schizophrenics often create words of their own—words that resemble real words but do not exist in their native language, for instance "littlehood" for childhood or "crimery" for bad actions. Their sentences often begin with one thought and then shift abruptly to another (e.g., Barch & Berenbaum, 1996). In extreme cases, their words seem to be totally jumbled.

The behavioral disorders shown by schizophrenics are even more bizarre. For instance, they may make odd movements or strange gestures, or remain immobile in an awkward position for long periods of time—a condition called *catatonia.* They may also show disorganized behavior that makes it impossible for them to dress themselves, prepare food, or perform other daily chores.

Negative Symptoms of Schizophrenia

As noted above, these symptoms reflect the absence of functions or reactions that most persons show. One such symptom is *flat affect*—many persons with schizophrenia show no emotion. Their faces are like emotionless masks, and they stare off into space with a glazed look. In contrast, some schizophrenics do show emotion, but their reactions are inappropriate. They may giggle when describing a painful childhood experience, or cry after hearing a joke.

Another negative symptom of schizophrenia is *avolition*—a seemingly total lack of motivation or will. Persons showing this symptom may sit doing nothing hour after hour; if they do start to do something, they will often stop in the middle of the activity and wander off. Persons showing mainly positive symptoms are sometimes described as showing Type I schizophrenia, while those showing negative symptoms are described as showing Type II schizophrenia. (Figure 12.12 on page 402 summarizes the major symptoms of schizophrenia.)

The Onset and Course of Schizophrenia

Schizophrenia is a *chronic* disorder, as defined by the DSM–IV: It lasts at least six months. For most people, however, this disorder lasts far longer, and symptoms come and go. People with schizophrenia have periods when they appear almost normal, and long periods when their symptoms are readily apparent. Schizophrenia can occur among adolescents, but it generally begins in the early twenties, with males showing the onset of this disorder at earlier ages than females (Remschmidt et al., 1994).

Delusions
Firmly held beliefs that have no basis in reality.

Hallucinations
Vivid sensory experiences that have no basis in physical reality.

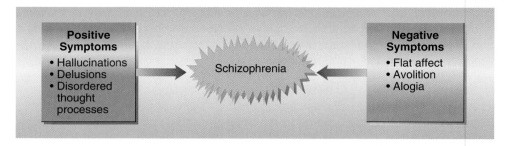

FIGURE 12.12
Major Symptoms of Schizophrenia
As shown here, major symptoms of schizophrenia fall into two headings: positive symptoms (e.g., delusions, hallucinations) and negative symptoms (e.g., flat affective reactions, avolition, alogia).

Schizophrenia is often divided into five distinct types. The most dramatic of these is the **catatonic type,** in which individuals show marked disturbances in motor behavior. Many alternative between total immobility—they sit for days or even weeks frozen in a single posture—and wild, excited behavior in which they rush madly about. Other types are described in Table 12.3.

Causes of Schizophrenia

Schizophrenia is one of the most bizarre, and most serious, psychological disorders, and although relatively rare, between 1 and 2 percent of all people in the United States suffer from this disorder (Wilson et al., 1996). What are the causes of schizophrenia? Research findings point to the roles of many factors.

Genetic Factors

Schizophrenia, like several other psychological disorders, tends to run in families. The closer the family tie between two individuals, the higher the likelihood that if one develops schizophrenia, the other will show this disorder, too (e.g., Gottesman, 1993). Schizophrenia does not appear to be traceable to a single gene, however; on the contrary, research findings suggest that many genes and many environmental factors operate together to produce a tendency toward this disorder (e.g., Conklin & Iacono, 2002).

Catatonic Type (of schizophrenia)
A dramatic type of schizophrenia in which individuals show marked disturbances in motor behavior. Many alternate between total immobility and wild, excited behavior in which they rush madly about.

TABLE 12.3 Major Types of Schizophrenia

Schizophrenia is divided, by the DSM–IV, into the types shown here. Each is marked by a different pattern of symptoms.

Type	Symptoms
Catatonic	Unusual patterns of motor activity, such as rigid postures; also speech disturbances such as repetitive chatter
Disorganized	Absence of affect, poorly developed delusions, verbal incoherence
Paranoid	Preoccupation with one or more sets of delusions, often centering on the belief that others are "out to get" the schizophrenic in some way
Undifferentiated	Many symptoms, including delusions, hallucinations, incoherence
Residual	Withdrawal, minimal affect, and absence of motivation; occurs after prominent delusions and hallucinations are no longer present

▓ Neurodevelopmental Factors: Disruption in Normal Brain Development

Other findings suggest that persons with schizophrenia show several types of brain dysfunction, including ones that develop prior to birth. In particular, several studies indicate that damage to the brain resulting from oxygen deprivation either during or prior to birth can increase the likelihood of schizophrenia later in life (Cannon et al., 1999). In addition, neuroimaging studies suggest that abnormalities exist in the medial–temporal lobe and frontal lobes of persons who develop schizophrenia. These abnormalities do not always produce the disease; rather, genetic factors may predispose individuals to develop schizophrenia, but this disorder will develop only if they are exposed to certain kinds of stressful environmental conditions.

▓ Biochemical Factors

Several findings point to the possibility that disturbances in the functioning of certain neurotransmitters—especially *dopamine*—may play a role in schizophrenia. Originally, it was suggested that schizophrenia results from a diffuse excess of dopamine in the brain. However, more recent findings indicate that it may stem from an excess of dopamine in temporal areas and a depletion of dopamine in frontal areas. Interestingly, these are the same brain areas identified by neuroimaging studies as the ones involved in schizophrenia.

▓ Psychological and Environmental Factors

Among identical twins, when one develops schizophrenia, the probability that the other will also develop it is only about 50 percent. This suggests that schizophrenia is influenced by environmental factors as well as genetic ones. What environments place individuals at risk for schizophrenia? Intriguing clues are provided by research on *relapses*—recurrences of the disorder after periods of relative normality—among schizophrenic patients. It appears that patients are more likely to suffer relapses when their families adopt certain patterns of expressing emotion. Specifically, patients are more likely to suffer relapses when their families engage in harsh criticism, express hostility toward them (e.g., "I'm sick and tired of taking care of you!"), and show too much concern with their problems ("I'm trying so hard to help you!"). The relapse rate in families showing this pattern over the course of a year is fully 48 percent, while in families who do not show this pattern it is only about 20 percent (Kavanagh, 1992).

KEY QUESTIONS

- What is schizophrenia?
- What are positive and negative symptoms of schizophrenia?
- What factors play a role in the occurrence of schizophrenia?

SUBSTANCE-RELATED DISORDERS

An additional and very important group of disorders is **substance-related disorders**—ones related to the use of psychoactive drugs (see Chapter 4). Do you know a heavy smoker who has tried over and over again to quit this habit? And do you know anyone who can't get through the day without several drinks or beers? If so, you already have first-hand experience with some of the obvious effects of these substance-related disorders. Such disorders are further divided, by the DSM–IV, into two categories: *substance-induced disorders*—impaired functioning as a direct result of the physiological effects of the substance in question; and *substance-use disorders*—repeated frequent use of substances resulting in harmful behaviors or impairments in personal, social, and occupational functioning.

Substance-Related Disorders
Disorders related to the use of psychoactive substances.

FIGURE 12.13
The Two Faces of Alcohol

Ads often link alcohol consumption to having a wonderful time, and for many persons, alcohol *is* a part of enjoyable social occasions. However, when it is abused, alcohol can have the tragic consequences shown here; in fact, more than half of all fatal traffic accidents involve alcohol consumption.

Substance Abuse

A maladaptive pattern of substance use that results in repeated, significant adverse effects and maladaptive behavior, such as failure to meet obligations at work, in school, or at home; repeated use of a psychoactive substance in hazardous ways; recurrent legal problems related to the substance; and continued use of the substance despite its negative effects on social relationships.

According to the DSM–IV, then, **substance abuse** is a maladaptive pattern of substance use that results in repeated, significant adverse effects and maladaptive behaviors—failure to meet obligations at work, school, or at home; repeated use of a psychoactive substance in hazardous ways (e.g., while driving); recurrent legal problems related to the substance; and continued use of the substance despite its negative effects.

Unfortunately, substance abuse is far from rare. Many different substances are involved (amphetamines, nicotine, opioids), but by far the one that is most frequently abused is alcohol. In the United States, it is estimated that more than 7 percent of the population shows alcohol abuse or dependence (Grant et al., 1994). And the costs of such abuse are appalling. More than half of all fatal traffic accidents involve alcohol, and 25 to 50 percent of deaths due to fires, falls, and drowning involve this substance (Institute of Medicine, 1989). The bottom line is this: The average life expectancy of people who abuse alcohol is more than ten years shorter than those who do not. Such statistics are totally ignored by advertising, which, of course, presents alcohol consumption in a totally favorable light; the reality, of course, is something else (see Figure 12.13). These comments, we should quickly add, refer primarily to *abuse* of alcohol; many persons use alcohol without abusing it, and there is no implication in the DSM–IV that such drinking constitutes a mental disorder.

Alcohol is not the only psychoactive substance that is abused. Hundreds of millions of persons smoke cigarettes, and they often develop nicotine dependence, which makes it extremely difficult for them to stop smoking. The social costs of addiction to heroin, cocaine, crack, and other drugs are perhaps even higher. These harmful effects, coupled with the very large numbers of persons involved, suggest that substance-abuse disorders are among the most damaging of all disorders described in the DSM–IV. Moreover, because they stem from many different factors—biological, social, and personal—they are often very difficult to treat. Unfortunately, new "recreational drugs" designed to make people feel good are constantly being developed and the temptation to try them is strong—especially among young persons. We don't want to moralize, but please do remember that *use of these drugs is dangerous and can lead to harmful consequences.* So, please do use caution so that *you* don't become a victim of substance abuse.

- What is substance abuse?

PSYCHOTHERAPIES: PSYCHOLOGICAL APPROACHES TO MENTAL DISORDERS

Eating disorders, mood disorders, anxiety disorders, schizophrenia—by this point you are probably convinced that there are many ways in which individuals can go off the track mentally. But *don't despair!* While mental disorders take many forms and produce great suffering for large numbers of persons, there is definitely hope—and a lot of it. In fact, psychologists and other mental health professionals have developed many ways of alleviating the symptoms of mental disorders and for reducing or eliminating their causes. It is on these forms of *therapy* that we will focus next. We'll begin with a discussion of **psychotherapies**—procedures in which persons with mental disorders interact with trained therapists who help them change certain behaviors, thoughts, or emotions so that they feel and function better. After that, we'll examine forms of therapy that occur in group settings, Next, we'll take a brief look at biological therapies, which involve the use of drugs electroconvulsive shock, and even surgery. Finally, we'll conclude by addressing the question "Just how effective are these various forms of therapy?" Now, back to the main topic of this discussion—different forms of psychotherapy.

Psychodynamic Therapies: From Repression to Insight

Psychodynamic therapies are based on the idea that mental disorders stem primarily from the kind of hidden inner conflicts first described by Freud—for instance, conflicts between our primitive sexual and aggressive urges (id impulses) and the ego, which warns us of the dangers of gratifying these immediately, as soon as they arise (see Chapter 10). More specifically, psychodynamic therapies assume that mental disorders occur because something has gone seriously wrong in the balance between these inner forces. While several forms of therapy are based in these assumptions, the most famous is *psychoanalysis,* the approach developed by Freud.

▪ Psychoanalysis

As you may recall from Chapter 10, Freud believed that personality consists of three major parts: *id, ego,* and *superego,* which correspond roughly to desire, reason, and conscience. Freud believed that mental disorders stem from the fact that many impulses of the id are unacceptable to the ego or the superego and are therefore *repressed*—driven into the depths of the unconscious. There they persist, and individuals must devote a considerable portion of their psychic energy to keeping them in check and out of consciousness. In fact, people often use various *defense mechanisms* to protect the ego from feelings of anxiety generated by these inner conflicts and clashes.

How can such problems be relieved? Freud felt that the crucial task was for people to overcome repression so they could recognize—and confront—their hidden feelings and impulses. Having gained such insight, he believed, they would experience a release of emotion (*abreaction*), and then, with their energies at last freed from the task of repression, they could direct these into healthy growth. Figure 12.14 on page 406 summarizes these views.

These ideas concerning the causes and cure of mental illness are reflected in *psychoanalysis,* the type of therapy developed by Freud. As popular images suggest, the patient undergoing psychoanalysis lies on a couch in a partly darkened room and

Psychotherapies
Procedures in which persons with mental disorders interact with trained therapists who help them change certain behaviors, thoughts, or emotions so that they can feel and function better.

Psychodynamic Therapies
Therapies based on the idea that mental disorders stem mainly from hidden, inner conflicts, and that once these conflicts are made conscious, they can be resolved.

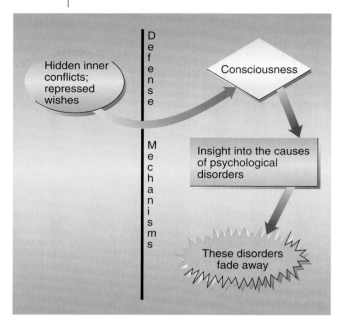

FIGURE 12.14
Psychoanalysis: How, Supposedly, It Works
Psychoanalysis, the kind of therapy developed by Freud, focuses on helping individuals gain insight into their hidden inner conflicts and repressed wishes. Freud believed that once awareness of these conflicts penetrated patients' *defense mechanisms* and became conscious, their disorders would fade away. In fact, there is little support for this view.

Free Association

In psychoanalysis, the patient's reporting of all thoughts and feeling that he or she has during the therapy session.

Resistance

In psychoanalysis, (1) a patient's stubborn refusal to report certain thoughts, motives, and experiences to the therapist, or (2) overt rejection of the therapist's interpretations.

Transference

In psychoanalysis, a patient's intense feelings of love or hate toward the analyst.

engages in **free association**—he or she reports *everything* that passes through his or her mind. Freud believed that the repressed impulses and inner conflicts present in the unconscious would ultimately be revealed by these mental wanderings, at least to the trained ear of the analyst.

Freud noted that during psychoanalysis, several intriguing events often occur. The first of these is **resistance**—a patient's stubborn refusal to report certain thoughts, motives, and experiences or overt rejection of the analyst's interpretations (Strean, 1985). Presumably, resistance occurs because patients wish to avoid the anxiety they experience as threatening or painful thoughts come closer and closer to consciousness.

Another aspect of psychoanalysis is **transference**—intense feelings of love or hate toward the analyst on the part of the patients. Often, patients react toward their analyst as they did to someone who played a crucial role in their early lives—for example, one of their parents. Freud believed that transference could be an important tool for helping individuals work through conflicts regarding their parents, but this time in a setting in which the harm done by disordered early relationships could be effectively countered. As patients' insight increased, Freud believed, transference would gradually fade away.

■ Psychoanalysis: An Evaluation

Psychoanalysis is probably the most famous form of psychotherapy (Hornstein, 1992). What accounts for its fame? Certainly not its effectiveness. It is fair to say that its reputation far exceeds its success in alleviating mental disorders. In the form proposed by Freud, it suffers from several major weaknesses that lessen its value. First, psychoanalysis is a costly and time-consuming process. Several years and large amounts of money are usually required for its completion—assuming it ever ends! Second, it is based largely on Freud's theories of personality and psychosexual development. As we noted in Chapter 10, these theories are provocative but difficult to test scientifically, so psychoanalysis rests on shaky scientific ground. Third, Freud designed psychoanalysis for use with highly educated persons with impressive verbal skills—ones who could describe their inner thoughts and feelings with ease.

Finally, its major assumption—that once insight is acquired, mental health will follow automatically—is contradicted by research findings. Over and over again, psychologists have found that insight into one's thoughts and feelings does *not* necessarily change them or prevent them from influencing behavior (e.g., Rozin, 1996). In fact, as we'll see in a later discussion of cognitive therapies, changing distorted or maladaptive modes of thought often requires great effort—and persistence. For these reasons, psychoanalysis is not a very popular form of therapy today; in fact, it has been far surpassed by the newer and more effective forms we will now consider.

KEY QUESTIONS

• What is psychoanalysis, and what are its major assumptions?
• What is the role of free association in psychoanalysis?

Phenomenological/Experiential Therapies: Emphasizing the Positive

Freud was something of a pessimist about basic human nature. He felt that we must constantly struggle with primitive impulses from the id. As we saw in Chapter 10, many psychologists reject this view. They contend that people are basically good and that our strivings for growth, dignity, and self-control are just as strong as the powerful aggressive and sexual urges Freud described. According to such psychologists, mental disorders do not stem from unresolved inner conflicts. Rather, they arise because the environment somehow interferes with personal growth and fulfillment.

This view—plus the following three suggestions—form the basis for the **phenomenological/experiential therapies** (often known as **humanistic therapies**): (1) Understanding other people requires trying to see the world through their eyes (a phenomenological approach); (2) clients should be treated as equals; and (3) the therapeutic relationship with the client is central to achieving the benefits of therapy. The goal of such therapy is to help *clients* (not "patients") to become more truly themselves—to find meaning in their lives and to live in ways that are truly consistent with their own values and traits. Unlike psychoanalysts, humanistic therapists believe that clients, not they, must take essential responsibility for the success of therapy. The therapist is mainly a guide and facilitator, *not* the one who runs the show. Let's take a closer look at two forms of humanistic therapy.

Client-Centered Therapy: The Benefits of Being Accepted

Perhaps the most influential humanistic approach is *client-centered therapy,* developed by Carl Rogers (1970, 1980). Rogers strongly rejected Freud's view that mental disorders stem from conflicts over the expression of primitive, instinctive urges. On the contrary, Rogers argued that such problems arise mainly because clients' efforts to attain self-actualization—growth and development—were thwarted early in life by judgments and ideas imposed on them by other people. According to Rogers, these judgments lead individuals to acquire what he terms unrealistic *conditions of worth.* That is, they learn that they must be something other than what they really are in order to be loved and accepted—to be worthwhile as a person. For example, they come to believe that they will be rejected by their parents if they are not always neat and submissive or if they do not live up to various parental ideals. Such beliefs block people from recognizing large portions of their experience and emotions. This, in turn, interferes with normal development of the self and causes them to experience maladjustment.

Client-centered therapy focuses on eliminating such unrealistic conditions of worth through the creation of a psychological climate in which clients feel valued as persons. Person-centered therapists offer *unconditional acceptance,* or *unconditional positive regard,* of the client and her or his feelings; a high level of *empathetic understanding;* and accurate reflection of the client's feelings and perceptions. In this warm, caring environment, freed from the threat of rejection, individuals can come to understand their own feelings and accept even previously unwanted aspects of their own personalities. As a result, they come to see themselves as unique human beings with many desirable characteristics. To the extent such changes occur, Rogers suggests, many mental disorders disappear and individuals can resume their normal progress toward self-fulfillment (see Figure 12.15 on page 408).

Gestalt Therapy: Becoming Whole

The theme of incomplete self-awareness, especially of gaps in clients' awareness of their genuine feelings, is echoed in a second humanistic approach, *Gestalt therapy.* According to Fritz Perls (1969), originator of this type of therapy, many people have difficulties in directly experiencing and expressing emotions such as anger or the need for love. As a result, they develop manipulative social games or phony roles to try—usually without success—to satisfy their needs indirectly. These games, in turn, lead people to believe that they are not responsible for their own behavior; they blame others and come to feel powerless. The goals of Gestalt therapy, therefore, are to help clients become aware of the feelings and needs they have disowned, and to recognize that these are a genuine part of themselves.

Phenomenological/ Experiential Therapies
See Humanistic Therapies

Humanistic Therapies (Phenomenological/ Experiential Therapies)
Therapies based on the ideas that understanding other people requires trying to see the world through their eyes and that the therapeutic relationship with the client is central to achieving benefits in therapy.

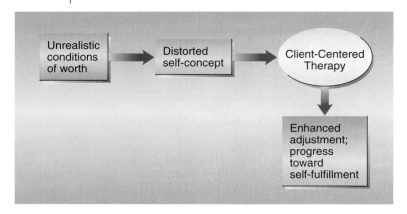

FIGURE 12.15
**Client-Centered Therapy:
An Overview**
Rogers believed that mental disorders stem from unrealistic *conditions of worth* acquired early in life. Client-centered therapy seeks to change such beliefs, primarily by placing individuals in an environment in which they receive *unconditional acceptance* from the therapist.

How can these goals be reached? Only by reexperiencing old hurts, jealousies, fears, and resentments. To do this, Gestalt therapists often use the *empty chair* technique. The client imagines that an important person from his or her past—parent, child, spouse—is sitting in the chair and then, perhaps for the first time, expresses his or her true feelings to this person (feelings about the imaginary person or about events or conflicts in which this person played a part). As a result, clients gain insight into their true feelings. This may actually help to reduce the emotional turmoil that brought clients to therapy in the first place—an important benefit in itself (Greenberg, Elliott, & Lietaer, 1994).

Humanistic Therapies: An Overview

Phenomenological/experiential therapies certainly have a much more optimistic flavor than psychoanalysis; they don't assume that human beings must constantly struggle to control dark, internal forces. In addition, several techniques devised by humanistic therapists are now widely used, even by psychologists who do not share this perspective. For instance, Carl Rogers was one of the first therapists to tape-record therapy sessions so that they could be studied at a later time by therapists. This not only helps therapists to assist their clients; it also provides information about which techniques are most effective during therapy. Finally, some of the assumptions underlying humanistic therapies have been subjected to scientific test and found to be valid. For instance, research findings tend to confirm Rogers's view that the gap between an individual's self-image and his or her "ideal self" plays a crucial role in maladjustment (e.g., Bootzin, Acocella, & Alloy, 1993). In these ways, then, humanistic therapies have made lasting contributions to the practice of psychotherapy.

On the other side of the coin, such therapies have been criticized for their lack of a unified theoretical base and for being vague about precisely what is supposed to happen between clients and therapists. So although they are more widely used at present than psychoanalysis, they are subject to important criticisms.

K E Y   Q U E S T I O N S

- According to humanistic therapies, what is the cause of mental disorders?
- What is the major goal of Rogers's client-centered therapy?
- What is the major goal of Gestalt therapy?

Behavior Therapies: Mental Disorders and Faulty Learning

Although psychodynamic and phenomenological/experiential therapies differ in many ways, they both place importance on early events in clients' lives as a key source of current disturbances. In contrast, another major group of therapies, known collectively as **behavior therapies,** focus primarily on individuals' current behavior. These therapies are based on the belief that many mental disorders stem from faulty learning. Either the persons involved have failed to acquire the skills and behaviors they need for coping with the problems of daily life, or they have acquired *maladaptive* habits and reactions. Within this context, the key task for therapy is to change current behavior, not to correct faulty self-concepts or resolve inner conflicts. What kinds of learning play a role in behavior therapy? As we saw in Chapter 5, there are several basic kinds. Reflecting this fact, behavior therapies, too, employ techniques based on major kinds of learning.

Behavior Therapies
Therapies based on the belief that many mental disorders stem from faulty learning.

Therapies Based on Classical Conditioning

As noted in Chapter 5, *classical conditioning* is a process in which organisms learn that the occurrence of one stimulus will soon be followed by the occurrence of another. As a result, reactions that are at first produced only by the second stimulus gradually come to be evoked by the first as well. (Remember the popcorn example in Chapter 5?)

What does classical conditioning have to do with mental disorders? According to behavior therapists, quite a bit. Behavior therapists suggest, for example, that many *phobias* are acquired in this manner. Stimuli that happen to be present when real dangers occur may acquire the capacity to evoke intense fear because of this association. As a result, individuals experience intense fears in response to these conditioned stimuli, even though they pose no threat to their well-being. To eliminate such reactions, behavior therapists sometimes use the technique of *flooding.* This involves exposure to the feared stimuli, or to mental representations of them, under conditions in which the persons with the phobias can't escape from them. These procedures encourage *extinction* of such fears; the phobias may soon fade away (Levis, 1985).

Another technique based in part on principles of classical conditioning is known as *systematic desensitization.* In systematic desensitization, individuals first learn how to induce a relaxed state in their own bodies—often by learning how to relax their muscles. Then, while in a relaxed state, they are exposed to stimuli that elicit fear. Because they are now experiencing relaxation, which is incompatible with fear, the conditioned link between these stimuli and fear is weakened (see Figure 12.16).

Therapies Based on Operant Conditioning

Behavior is often shaped by the consequences it produces; actions are repeated if they yield positive outcomes or if they permit individuals to avoid or escape from negative ones. In contrast, actions that lead to negative results are suppressed. These basic principles are incorporated in several forms of therapy based on *operant conditioning.* These differ considerably in their details, but all include the following steps: (1) clear identification of undesirable or maladaptive behaviors currently shown by individuals, (2) identification of events that reinforce and maintain such

FIGURE 12.16
Systematic Desensitization: A Behavioral Technique for Eliminating Phobias
In systematic desensitization, individuals first learn how to induce a relaxed state in their own bodies—often by learning how to relax their muscles (left photo). Then, while in this state, they are exposed to stimuli that elicit fear. Because relaxation is incompatible with fear, the conditioned link between these stimuli and fear is weakened and the phobia is reduced (right photo).

responses, and (3) efforts to change the environment so that these maladaptive behaviors are no longer followed by reinforcement.

Operant principles have sometimes been used in hospital settings, where a large degree of control over patients' reinforcements is possible (Kazdin, 1982). Several projects have involved the establishment of *token economies*—systems under which patients earn tokens they can exchange for various rewards, such as television-watching privileges, candy, or trips to town. These tokens are awarded for various forms of adaptive behavior, such as keeping one's room neat, participating in group meetings or therapy sessions, coming to meals on time, and eating neatly. The results have often been impressive. When individuals learn that they can acquire various rewards by behaving in adaptive ways, they often do so, with important benefits to them as well as to hospital staff (e.g., Paul, 1982; Paul & Lentz, 1977).

Modeling: Benefiting from Exposure to Others

Many people who come to psychologists for help appear to be lacking in basic *social skills*—they don't know how to interact with others in an effective manner. They don't know how to make a request without sounding "pushy," or how to refuse one without making the requester angry. They don't how to express their feelings clearly, how to hold their temper in check, or how to hold an ordinary conversation with others. As a result, they experience difficulties in forming friendships or intimate relationships, and encounter problems in many everyday situations. These difficulties, in turn, can leave them feeling helpless, depressed, anxious, and resentful. Behavior therapists have developed techniques for helping individuals improve their social skills. These often involve *modeling*—showing individuals demonstrations of how people with good social skills behave in many situations (e.g., Wilson et al., 1996).

Modeling techniques have also been used, with impressive success, in the treatment of phobias. Many studies indicate that individuals who experience intense fear of relatively harmless objects can be helped to overcome these fears through exposure to appropriate social models who demonstrate lack of fear in their presence and show that no harm occurs as a result of contact with these objects (e.g., Bandura, 1977). Such procedures have been found to be effective in reducing a wide range of phobias—excessive fears of dogs, snakes, and spiders, to mention just a few (Bandura, 1977). In sum, behavioral therapies have been shown to be useful in alleviating many types of mental disorders.

K E Y   Q U E S T I O N S

- According to behavior therapies, what is the primary cause of mental disorders?
- On what basic principles of learning are behavior therapies based?
- What is modeling, and how can it be used in treating mental disorders?

Cognitive Therapies: Changing Disordered Thought

At several points in this book, we have noted that cognitive processes often exert powerful effects on emotions and behavior. In other words, what we *think* strongly influences how we *feel* and what we *do.* This principle underlies another major approach to psychotherapy, **cognitive therapies.** The basic idea behind all cognitive therapies is this: Many mental disorders stem from faulty or distorted modes of thought. Change these, and the disorders, too, can be alleviated. Let's examine some major forms of cognitive therapy.

Rational-Emotive Therapy: Overcoming Irrational Beliefs

Everyone I meet should like me.

I should be perfect (or darn near perfect) in every way.

Because something once affected my life, it will always affect it.

I can't bear it when things are not the way I would like them to be.

Cognitive Therapies
Therapies based on the view that many mental disorders stem from faulty or distorted modes of thought.

Be honest: Do such views ever influence *your* thinking? While you may strongly protest that they do not, one psychologist—Albert Ellis (1987)—believes that they probably *do* influence your thinking to some extent. Moreover, he contends that such *irrational thoughts* play a key role in many mental disorders. According to Ellis, the process goes something like this. Individuals experience *activating events*—things that happen to them that can potentially trigger upsetting emotional reactions. If they actually experience these strong emotional reactions, then mental disorders such as anxiety and depression may develop. The key factor determining whether this happens, however, is the ways in which people *think* about the activating events. If they allow irrational beliefs to shape their thoughts, they are at serious risk for experiencing psychological problems.

Here's an example: Suppose that one day your current romantic partner dumps you. This is certainly an unpleasant event, but does it undermine your self-esteem and cause you to become deeply depressed? Ellis argues that this depends on how you think about it. If you fall prey to irrational beliefs such as "Everyone must love me!" or "I can't control my emotions—I must feel totally crushed by this rejection!" you may well become depressed. If, instead, you reject these modes of thought and think, "Some people will love me and others won't; and love itself isn't always constant," or "I can deal with this—it's painful but not the end of the world"—then you will bounce back and will *not* experience depression. In essence, Ellis is saying this: You can't always change the world or what happens to you, but you *can* change the ways in which you think about these experiences. *You* can decide whether, and how much, to be bothered or upset by events that occur—being dumped by a romantic partner, losing a job, getting a lower-than-expected grade on a test, and so on.

To help people combat the negative effects of irrational thinking, Ellis developed **rational–emotive therapy (RET).** During RET, the therapist first attempts to identify irrational thoughts and then tries to persuade clients to recognize them for what they are. By challenging the irrationality of their clients' beliefs, therapists practicing RET get them to see how ridiculous and unrealistic some of their ideas are, and in this way, help them to stop being their own worst enemies.

▪ Beck's Cognitive Behavior Therapy for Depression

In discussing depression (pp. 388–391), we noted that this extremely common but serious mental disorder has an important cognitive component: It stems, at least in part, from distorted and often self-defeating modes of thought. Recognizing this important fact, Aaron Beck (Beck, 1985) has devised a *cognitive behavior therapy* for alleviating depression. Like Ellis, Beck assumes that depressed individuals engage in illogical thinking, and that this underlies their difficulties. They hold unrealistically negative beliefs and assumptions about themselves, the future, and the world (e.g., "I'm a worthless person no one could ever love," "If good things happen to me, it's just blind luck," "My life is a mess and will never improve"). Moreover, he contends, they cling to these illogical ideas and assumption no matter what happens.

According to Beck, such distorted thinking leads individuals to have negative moods, which, in turn, increase the probability of more negative thinking (see Figure 12.17 on page 412). In other words, he emphasizes the importance of mood-dependent memory—how our current moods influence what we remember and what we think about (see Chapter 6). How can this vicious circle be broken? In contrast to rational–emotive therapy, Beck's cognitive approach does not attempt to disprove the ideas held by depressed persons. Rather, the therapist and client work together to identify the individual's assumptions, beliefs, and expectations, and to formulate ways of testing them. For example, if a client states that she is a total failure, the therapist may ask how she defines *failure*, and whether some experiences she defines this way may actually be only partial failures. If that's so, the therapist inquires, aren't they also partial *successes*? Continuing in this manner, the therapist might then ask the client whether there are *any* areas of her life in which she *does*

Rational–Emotive Therapy
A form of cognitive therapy in which therapists attempt to persuade clients to recognize their own irrational thoughts.

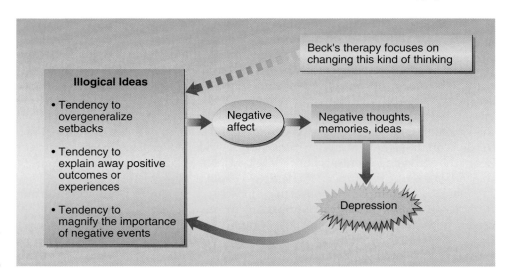

FIGURE 12.17
Beck's Cognitive Behavior Therapy

Beck's cognitive behavior therapy is designed to change cognitive tendencies (e.g., distorted thinking) that contribute to depression. Such patterns of thought often produce negative affect (mood), which then increases the likelihood of further negative thoughts. Cognitive behavior therapy attempts to break this cycle.

experience success and has succeeded in reaching goals. Studies indicate that as a result of these procedures, individuals learn to reinterpret negative events in ways that help them cope with such outcomes without becoming depressed (e.g., Bruder et al., 1997). So, although the specific techniques used are different than those used in RET, the major goal is much the same: helping people to recognize, and reject, false assumptions that underlie their difficulties.

Cognitive Therapies: An Evaluation

An essential question about any form of therapy is "Does it work?" Cognitive therapies pass this test with flying colors: Many studies indicate that changing or eliminating irrational beliefs can be very effective in countering depression and other personal difficulties (e.g., Blatt et al., 1996). Similarly, the procedures outlined by Beck have been found to be highly effective in treating depression (e.g., Bruder et al., 1997). Perhaps even more important, the effects they produce tend be longer-lasting than those produced by other forms of therapy for depression—for instance, antidepressant drugs (which we'll examine in a later section; Segal, Gemar, & Williams, 1999).

Computer and Internet-based Psychotherapies

All the forms of therapy we have considered so far involve direct face-to-face contact between a therapist and an individual seeking help. Is such contact necessary? Or can therapy occur in a less direct manner, by means of computers? This has been a topic of growing interest to psychologists, because individual therapy can be quite expensive, and this limits access to it by many persons. With this thought in mind, psychologists have designed computer programs that, in a sense, perform therapy! These programs have been designed to help individuals deal with phobias, panic disorder, obsessive–compulsive disorder, and many other problems (Taylor & Luce, 2003). And growing evidence indicates that they work: In fact, in one recent study (Kenardy et al., 2002), persons diagnosed as having panic disorder were randomly assigned to one of four groups in which they received (1) twelve sessions with a therapist who used cognitive behavior techniques, (2) six sessions with a therapist plus use of a hand-held computer programmed to help with this problem, (3) six sessions with a therapists plus a manual telling them how to deal with their problem, or (4) no therapy (a control group). Results indicated that first two groups showed equal benefits, thus suggesting that a computer could substitute, at least in part, for a live therapist.

Why are such techniques effective? In part because many persons are less embarrassed about reporting sensitive personal information to a computer than to another person, and because computers, which are not subject to the biasing effects of mood, stereotypes, and many other factors, can sometimes make more accurate judgments about patients' conditions than can actual therapists. Please don't misunderstand: We are *not* suggesting that computer programs can replace live therapists—far from it. But it appears that, in some cases, individuals can benefit from well-designed programs used to supplement live therapy.

What about the Internet? Can it, too, be helpful to persons with mental disorders? Growing evidence suggests that it can. For specific ways in which *you* can use the Internet in this way, please see the **Psychology Lends a Hand** section that follows.

KEY QUESTIONS

- According to cognitive therapies, what is the promary cause of mental disorders?
- What is the major goal of rational–emotive therapy?
- What is the major goal of Beck's cognitive therapy for depression?

p s y c h o l o g y   l e n d s   a   h a n d

Mental Disorders: How the Internet Can Help

Have you used the Internet to locate those hard-to-find items you want to buy? As a source of information? For making new friends or expanding your social network? If so, you are like hundreds of millions of persons throughout the world. In a sense, the Internet has almost anything you could ever want (or at least can tell you how to get it)—*if* you know where to look. This suggests that the Internet might be useful to persons experiencing mental disorders. It could, for instance, provide information on the nature of their problems and where to seek help. It could screen individuals in order to tell them whether they do, in fact, show symptoms of various disorders. It can provide them with social support by putting them in touch with others who share their problems. And it would, potentially, provide access to experts willing to give advice on-line. Has the Internet actually lived up to this promise? To a degree, it has. There are already a number of sites you can visit for information, screening and assessment, social support, and even consultations—and virtually all of them are free. Here are some you may well find useful:

- **Information.** The National Institute of Mental Health (NIMH .gov) offers a wealth of information and its site receives more than 7 million hits each month. The site is very large and contains many parts, however, so if you visit it, be prepared to spend considerable time finding the specific topics or areas you want.
- **Screening and assessment.** Do you really have a psychological disorder? Or do you just think you do? Many sites offer on-line guidance, including brief psychological tests you can take. Again, the NIMH site provides a good gateway to such sites.

- **Support groups.** Face-to-face support groups often find it difficult to arrange meetings that all members can attend. For this reason, on-line support from others who have problems similar to your own can be very helpful. Two sites that may be helpful in this respect are www.pewinternet.org and www.wellness-community.org. Both can help you build useful networks of social support.
- **On-line consultation.** The International Society for Mental Health Online, www.ismpo.org, is a good place to start. Through this site, you can obtain on-line consultation with experts on various forms of mental disorder.
- **Advocacy.** If you feel that the problems you face are ones requiring political action, you might want to visit the National Alliance for the Mentally Ill, www.nami.org. This site describes ways in which individuals can join with others to influence public policy relating to various mental disorders.

Good luck with your search. There is indeed some good, qualified help out there if you take the trouble to locate it. But please be *extremely careful;* as you probably already know, not everyone on the Internet is 100 percent honest, so be very careful about such things as Internet sites that promise quick and guaranteed results or immediate answers to all your complex personal questions. And check carefully before agreeing to supply detailed personal information or to paying for treatment. In other words, show the same kind of prudence you would show before buying *any* products or services on the Internet. The potential risks are real, and you should take them fully and carefully into account.

PSYCHOTHERAPY AND DIVERSITY: MULTICULTURALISM IN HELPING RELATIONSHIPS

Before concluding our discussion of psychotherapies, we should note that in recent years psychologists have become increasingly aware of the important role of cultural factors in all forms of therapy. Ethical guidelines for psychologists state strongly that therapists should not provide services outside their areas of competence, and this has been interpreted to mean that they should not attempt to treat persons from outside their own cultural or ethnic groups unless they are familiar both with their own cultural biases *and* differences between their own cultural groups and those of their patients (e.g., Acton, 2001). This means, of course, that therapists should *not* be "color blind," treating all clients in the same way regardless of their cultural backgrounds. On the contrary, they must take careful account of such factors and assure that they build them into their relationships with clients. Recent findings indicate that when therapists make such ethnic, racial, or cultural differences part of the therapeutic process—when they pay careful attention to them and acknowledge them openly—they are more effective in establishing excellent working relationships with clients, and therefore in helping them (Fuertes et al., 2002). This multicultural perspective is now very strong in psychology and is incorporated into the goals psychologists set for therapy, and in the methods they use for attaining them (e.g., Nelson-Jones, 2002). So, yes, the multicultural perspective we have stressed throughout this book plays an important role in psychotherapy, just as it does in all activities performed by psychologists.

ALTERNATIVES TO INDIVIDUAL PSYCHOTHERAPY: GROUP THERAPIES

As we'll see in a later section, psychotherapy really works—many of the kinds of therapy we have already considered *are* effective in alleviating mental disorders (e.g., APA, Division of Clinical Psychology, 1995). But there are several factors that limit the usefulness of such procedures in some cases. First, individual psychotherapy is not accessible to all persons who might benefit from it. It is often quite expensive (skilled therapists often receive $200 or $300 per hour!) and—sadly—individuals' insurance companies often won't cover such costs.

But even if individual psychotherapy were free, *cultural factors* limit its accessibility for some groups of people. For example, in many cultures, it is considered unseemly to openly express one's emotions or to discuss them with other persons—especially total strangers (which is what therapists are, at least initially). The result is that people from many non-Western cultures and persons from ethnic minorities (e.g., people of Hispanic or Native American descent in the United States) view individual psychotherapy as pointless or even shameful—as a sign of weakness. Largely in response to these and other limitations, alternative forms of treatment for mental disorders have been developed, but here, however, we'll focus on marital and family therapies and on self-help groups because these are the forms that have received greatest use.

Marital and Family Therapies

All *group therapies* involve procedures in which several people discuss their problems with one another under the guidance of a trained therapist. These procedures are often employed with couples (marital therapy) and with families—often with excellent results. Both forms of therapy assume that one reason why many indi-

"She's no good for you, Harry."

FIGURE 12.18
Marital Therapy: Not for Everyone!
Marital therapy is *not* designed to keep mutually destructive relationships like this one alive. Rather, it focuses on helping persons who believe that their relationships are truly worth saving, even if this requires a lot of work.
Source: © The New Yorker Collection 1997 Gahan Wilson from cartoonbank.com. All Rights Reserved.

viduals experience personal problems (and some forms of mental disorder) is poor or faulty relations with important persons in their lives. Thus, such forms of therapy adopt an *interpersonal* perspective rather than one focused primarily on individuals. As an example of this approach, let's take a closer look at marital therapy.

Marital Therapy: When Spouses Are Seen as the Enemy

In the United States and many other countries, more than 50 percent of all marriages end in divorce (Popenoe & Whitehead, 1999). Keeping people together in joyless marriages or mutually destructive relationships like the one shown in Figure 12.18 is definitely *not* a goal of therapy. Rather, *marital therapy* (sometimes termed *couples therapy*) is designed to help couples who feel that their marriages are worth saving.

Before turning to the procedures used in such therapy, however, let's consider a very basic question: What, in your opinion, is the number one reason why couples seek professional help in the first place? If you guessed "sexual problems," guess again; such difficulties are actually fairly far down the list. The number one reason why couples seek therapy is *perceived unfairness* in their division of labor—each thinks that the other is not doing their fair share of the work. This is followed by conflicts over power, extramarital sex, drinking and other forms of substance abuse, spending money foolishly, and jealousy. Frequency of sexual relations is on the list, but it is far from the top cause of marital conflict (Fincham, 2003).

An underlying cause of many marital conflicts can be summarized by the phrase *faulty communication*. Couples who seek marital therapy often state that their spouse "never talks to them" or "never tells them what she/he is thinking." Or, they report that the only thing their spouse ever does is *complain* about their faults and what they are doing wrong. Even worse, each side makes *negative attributions* about the other: Is he late for dinner? It is because he is a basically inconsiderate person; heavy traffic had nothing to do with it. Did she spend too much money this month? It must be due to selfishness; the fact that several unexpected bills arrived is irrelevant. Given that couples begin their relationships with frequent statements of mutual esteem and love, the pain of such faulty communication patterns is doubled: Each partner wonders what went wrong—and then generally blames their partner! In contrast, happy couples show a very different pattern in which they display positive problem-solving techniques and positive affect five times as often as negative problem-solving tactics (e.g., withdrawal, anger) and negative affect (Fincham, 2003; Gottman, 1993). They are also more forgiving of real or imagined wrongs on the part of their spouse than is true for couples that experience intense conflict and seek marital therapy.

How does marital therapy work? One type—*behavior marital therapy*—focuses on changing the communication problems mentioned above. Therapists work to foster such improvements in many ways, including having each partner play the role of the other person so as to see their relationship as the other does. Other techniques involve having couples watch videotapes of their own interactions. This procedure is often truly an eye-opener: "Wow, I never realized that's how I come across!" is a common reaction to seeing themselves interacting with their spouse. As communication between members of a couple improves, many other beneficial changes occur—for instance, they stop criticizing each other in destructive ways (e.g., Baron, 1993), express positive sentiments toward each other more frequently, and stop assuming that everything their spouse does that annoys or angers them is done on purpose (e.g., Kubany et al., 1995). Once good communication is established, couples may also find it easier to resolve other sources of friction in their relationships. The result may then be a happier and more stable relationship, and one that increases, rather than reduces, the psychological well-being of both partners.

KEY QUESTIONS

- What are group therapies?
- What is marital or couples therapy?
- How does it work?

BIOLOGICAL THERAPIES

Earlier, we noted that the development of effective drugs for treating serious mental disorders led to a sharp drop in the number of patients in public mental hospitals. What are these drugs, how do they work, and just how effective are they? We'll examine these questions next as part of our discussion of *biological therapies*—forms of therapy that attempt to alleviate mental disorders through biological means.

Drug Therapy: The Pharmacological Revolution

In 1955, almost 600,000 persons were full-time resident patients in psychiatric hospitals in the United States. Twenty years later, this number had dropped below 175,000. What produced this dramatic shift? The answer is straightforward: A number of drugs effective in treating mental disorders were developed and put to use. Let's take a closer look at these drugs and their effects.

Antipsychotic Drugs

If you had visited the wards of a psychiatric hospital for seriously disturbed persons prior to 1955, you would have witnessed some pretty wild scenes—screaming, bizarre actions, nudity. If you returned a few years later, however, you would have seen a dramatic change: peace, relative tranquility, and many patients now capable of direct, sensible communication. These startling changes were largely the result of the development of *antipsychotic drugs,* sometimes known as the *major tranquilizers* or *neuroleptics.* These drugs are highly effective in reducing the *positive* symptoms shown by schizophrenics (e.g., hallucinations, delusions) but are less effective in reducing negative symptoms (e.g., withdrawal, lack of affect).

The most important group of antipsychotic drugs—*phenothiazines*—was discovered by accident. In the early 1950s, a French surgeon, Henri Laborit, used a drug in this chemical family, *Thorazine* (chlorpromazine), to reduce blood pressure in patients before surgery. He found that the blood pressure of these patients didn't drop and that they become much less anxious. French psychiatrists tried the drug with their patients, and found that it worked: It reduced anxiety, and, even more important, it also reduced hallucinations and delusions among schizophrenic patients. Chemists quickly analyzed chlorpromazine and developed many other drugs related to it that are even more effective in reducing psychotic symptoms (e.g., clozapine, haloperidol). (Throughout this discussion we'll present brand names of drugs followed by their chemical or generic names in parentheses.)

How do the antipsychotics produce such effects? Some block the action of the neurotransmitter *dopamine* on certain receptors in the brain. As noted earlier, the presence of an excess of this neurotransmitter, or increased sensitivity to it, may play a role in schizophrenia. Other antipsychotics—especially the newest (e.g., Novartis, Zeneca)—influence many different chemicals in the brain: neurotransmitters and others as well. In sum, many different antipsychotic drugs exist, and they do not all operate in the same way. Whatever the precise mechanism involved, however, it is clear that antipsychotic drugs are very helpful in reducing the bizarre symptoms of schizophrenia.

The use of these drugs, however, is not without drawbacks. They often produce side effects such as blurred vision and dry mouth. Additional effects can involve uncontrollable contractions of muscles in the neck, head, tongue, and back, or uncontrollable restlessness and agitation. The most serious side effect of all, however, is **tardive dyskinesia.** After receiving antipsychotic drugs for prolonged periods of time, many patients develop this side effect, which involves loss of motor control, especially in the face. As a result, they show involuntary muscle movements of the tongue, lips, and jaw. One relatively new antipsychotic drug, Clozaril (clozapine), appears to be effective without producing tardive dyskinesia. Additional antipsychotic drugs are under development, and it is hoped that they will have even fewer side effects.

Although the antipsychotic drugs are clearly of great value and do reduce the most bizarre symptoms of schizophrenia, it should be emphasized that they do *not* cure this disorder. In the past, such drugs were more effective in treating the positive than negative symptoms of schizophrenia. Thus, persons receiving them tended to remain somewhat withdrawn and to show the reduced levels of affect that is often part of schizophrenia. Newer drugs, however, seem more successful in treating these negative symptoms. In any case, although drugs for treating schizophrenia are improving, the likelihood that individuals with schizophrenia will regain normal functioning and be able to live on their own is increased when they receive psychotherapy, too.

Antidepressant Drugs

Shortly after the development of chlorpromazine, drugs effective in reducing depression made their appearance. There are three basic types of such compounds; *selective serotonin reuptake inhibitors* (SSRIs), *MAO inhibitors,* and *tricyclics.* Again, as is true with virtually all drugs used to treat mental disorders, they seem to exert their effects by influencing neurotransmitters, especially serotonin and norepinephrine (Julien, 1995).

Among the SSRIs, *Prozac* (fluoxetine) is by far the most famous—and also the most commonly prescribed: More than 1.5 million prescriptions for Prozac are written every month in the United States alone. Depressed persons taking this drug often report that they feel better than they have in their entire lives. However, Prozac, like other antidepressant drugs, appears to have serious side effects. About 30 percent of patients taking it report nervousness, insomnia, joint pain, weight loss, and sexual dysfunction (Hellerstein et al., 1993). A small number report suicidal thoughts (Mendlewicz & Lecrubier, 2000). In contrast, MAO inhibitors can produce more dangerous side effects. They seem to virtually eliminate REM sleep and,

Tardive Dyskinesia

A side effect of some antipsychotic drugs involving loss of motor control, especially in the face.

if consumed with food containing tyramine (e.g., aged cheeses, beer, red wine), can cause a sudden, extreme rise in blood pressure, thus putting patients at risk for strokes (Julien, 1995). For these reasons, these drugs are used less often than the other two types of antidepressants. Tricyclics also produce side effects, such as disturbances in sleep and appetite, but these tend to decrease within a few weeks. Widely prescribed tricyclics include Elavil (amitriptyline) and Tonfranil (imipramine).

One final point: While these drugs *are* often effective in treating depression, research evidence suggests that they are not necessarily more effective than cognitive and behavioral therapies (e.g., Bruder et al., 1997; Robinson, Berman, & Neimeyer, 1990; Hollon, Shelton, & Loosen, 1991). Indeed, these forms of psychotherapy may produce longer-lasting benefits than drugs (Segal, Gemar, & Williams, 1999). It's also important to note that antidepressants are most effective for treating major depression, but somewhat less so for milder conditions.

Lithium

An entirely different kind of antidepressant drug is *lithium* (usually administered as *lithium chloride*). This drug has been found to be quite effective in treating bipolar disorder, and is effective with 60 to 70 percent of such persons (Julien, 1995). Because such persons are often quite agitated and even psychotic, lithium is generally administered along with antipsychotic or antidepressant medications. Unfortunately, lithium has serious side effects—excessive doses can cause delirium and even death. Thus, dose level must be carefully controlled in order for it to be effective. Exactly how lithium exerts its effects is not known, and this suggests the need for caution in its use.

Antianxiety Drugs

Alcohol, a substance used by many people to combat anxiety, has been available for thousands of years. Needless to say, however, it has important negative side effects. Synthetic drugs with antianxiety effects—sometimes known as *minor tranquilizers*—have been manufactured for several decades. The most widely prescribed at present are the *benzodiazepines.* This group includes drugs whose names you may already know: Valium, Ativan, Xanax, and Librium.

The most common use for antianxiety drugs, at least ostensibly, is as an aid to sleep. They are safer for this purpose than *barbiturates* (see Chapter 4) because they are less addicting. However, substances derived from the benzodiazepines remain in the body for longer periods of time than those from barbiturates and can cumulate until they reach toxic levels. Thus, long-term use of these drugs can be quite dangerous. In addition, when the benzodiazepines are taken with alcohol, their effects may be magnified; this is definitely a combination to avoid. Finally, they tend to produce dependency; individuals experience withdrawal symptoms when these drugs are abruptly stopped. The benzodiazepines seem to produce their effects by acting as a kind of braking system for the nervous system, reducing activity that would otherwise result in anxiety and tension. While the benzodiazepines are effective—persons who take them report being calmer and less worried—they have potentially serious side effects: drowsiness, dizziness, fatigue, and reduced motor coordination. These can prove fatal to motorists or people operating dangerous machinery. Fortunately, such effects are much smaller for an additional antianxiety drug that is not related to the benzodiazepines: BuSpar (buspirone).

In sum, many drugs are effective in treating serious mental disorders and are being prescribed in ever increasing quantities. Because some of these drugs are fairly new, their long-term effects remain unknown. Moreover, like all drugs, their benefits are offset, to a degree, by potentially serious side effects. Should society be more cautious in using them? This is a complex issue, but many psychologists feel that greater caution may be justified.

Ethnic and Racial Differences in Response to Drugs

Before concluding, we should note that many of the drugs used to treat mental disorders have been found to vary in their effects among persons belonging to different ethnic and racial groups. These persons metabolize the drugs differently, benefit from them to different degrees, and show contrasting levels of side effects. Such differences *must* be taken carefully into account, and this constitutes yet another reason why all therapists must adopt a multicultural perspective in their efforts to help clients (Burroughs & Levy, 2002).

Electroconvulsive Therapy

Another, and very different, form of biological therapy is **electroconvulsive therapy (ECT).** This involves placing electrodes on the patient's temples and delivering shocks of 70 to 130 volts for brief intervals (approximately one second). These are continued until the patient has a seizure, a muscle contraction of the entire body, lasting at least twenty to twenty-five seconds. In order to prevent broken bones and other injuries, a muscle relaxant and a mild anesthetic are usually administered before the start of the shocks. Patients typically receive three treatments a week for several weeks (see Figure 12.19).

Surprisingly, ECT seems to work, at least for some disorders. It reduces severe depression, especially with persons who have failed to respond to other forms of therapy (Effective Treatment, 1994; Fink, 1993). The American Psychiatric Association recommends ECT for use with patients who are severely suicidal or psychologically depressed (e.g., refusing to eat, in a stupor).

Unfortunately, there are important risks connected with ECT. It is designed to alter the brain, and it does—producing loss of *episodic memory* in many patients (i.e., they forget events they have personally experienced). In a few cases, ECT produces irreversible damage to portions of the brain. Further, although the shocks themselves are painless, many patients find the procedures frightening, to say the least. These facts have led some researchers to criticize the use of ECT and to call for its elimination as a form of therapy. However, the fact that it works for some severely depressed persons who have not responded to other forms of therapy has led to its continued use (e.g., Fink, 1994).

Psychosurgery

In 1935, a Portuguese psychiatrist, Egas Moniz, attempted to reduce aggressive behavior in psychotic patients by severing neural connections between the prefontal lobes and the remainder of the brain. The operation, known as *prefrontal lobotomy,* seemed to work: Aggressive behavior was reduced. Moniz received the 1949 Nobel Prize in Medicine for his work.

Encouraged by Moniz's work, psychiatrists all over the world rushed to treat mental disorders through various forms of **psychosurgery**—brain operations designed to change abnormal behavior. Tens of thousands of patients were given prefrontal lobotomies and related operations. Unfortunately, it soon became apparent that results were not always positive. While some forms of objectionable or dangerous behavior did decrease, serious side effects sometimes occurred: Some patients became highly excitable and impulsive; others slipped into profound apathy and a total absence of emotion.

In view of these outcomes, most physicians stopped performing prefrontal lobotomies, and few are done today. However, other, more limited operations on the brain continue. For instance, in one modern procedure, *cingulotomy,* connections between a very small area of the brain and the limbic system are severed. Results

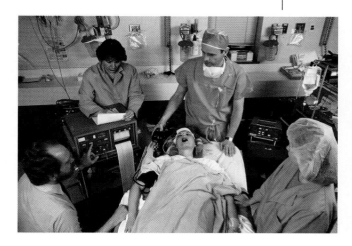

FIGURE 12.19
Electroconvulsive Therapy Today
Electric current passes through the brain for one-second intervals, eventually causing a brief seizure. This treatment seems to be effective in reducing severe depression, although *how* it produces such effects is still uncertain.

Electroconvulsive Therapy (ECT)
A form of biological therapy in which electrodes are placed on patient's temples and strong electric shocks are then delivered to the brain.

Psychosurgery
A form of biological therapy in which brain operations are performed in order to change abnormal behavior.

indicate that this limited kind of psychosurgery may be effective with individuals suffering from depression, anxiety disorders, and especially obsessive–compulsive disorder who have not responded to any other type of treatment (e.g., Cumming et al., 1995). Still newer procedures involve inserting tiny video cameras into the brain or using computer-guided imagery (e.g., MRI scans) to help surgeons make very precise lesions in the brain. It is too early to tell whether such psychosurgery will yield long-term gains.

KEY QUESTIONS

- What drugs are used in the treatment of mental disorders?
- What is electroconvulsive therapy?
- What is psychosurgery?

PSYCHOTHERAPY: IS IT EFFECTIVE?

Does psychotherapy really work? In other words, is it effective in alleviating mental disorders? Early research on this issue as not encouraging; in 1952 Hans Eysenck, a prominent psychologist, published a paper indicating that psychotherapy is actually quite *ineffective:* People improve at about the same rate whether they receive therapy or not. Fortunately, the findings of later and more conclusive studies pointed to a very different conclusion: Contrary to what Eysenck suggested, psychotherapy *is* helpful (Bergin & Lambert, 1978; Clum & Bowers, 1990). Apparently, Eysenck overestimated the proportion of persons who recover without any therapy and also *under*estimated the proportion who improve after receiving therapy. In fact, several reviews of existing evidence—more than five hundred separate studies on the effects of therapy—suggest that therapy *does* work: More people who receive psychotherapy show improvements with respect to their mental disorders than persons who do not receive therapy (e.g., Elkin et al., 1989). Further, the more treatment people receive, the more they improve, the fewer symptoms they show, and the less distress they report (Howard et al., 1986; Orlinsky & Howard, 1987). In sum, available evidence (and there is a lot of it) points to the following overall conclusion: Psychotherapy is not perfect—it doesn't produce improvements for everyone. But yes, it *does* work—it helps many people suffering from mental disorders to recover from these problems.

Are Some Forms of Therapy More Successful Than Others?

But what about different forms of therapy? Are some more effective than others? The answer, surprisingly, is no. Although various forms of therapy differ greatly in methods and goals, there do not appear to be major differences among therapies in terms of the benefits they provide. In this context, the results of a very large scale study conducted several years ago by *Consumer Reports* are informative.

Once a year, *Consumer Reports* sends out a questionnaire to its 180,000 subscribers, asking for information about their experiences with various products. In 1994, the survey included questions about subscribers' experiences with mental health professionals. Results, which were based on the replies of more than 7,000 persons, pointed to clear conclusions. First, as we have already noted, therapy did help: Most respondents to the survey indicated that it made them feel much better and helped eliminate the problems and symptoms they were experiencing, especially if therapy continued for six months or more. Second, such improvements were greatest when respondents received therapy from psychologists, psychiatrists, and social workers; improvements were somewhat less when they received therapy from physicians and marriage counselors (see Figure 12.20). Third, the longer therapy continued, the greater their improvement. Improvements began to

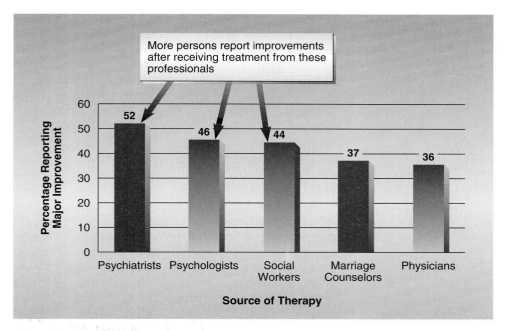

FIGURE 12.20

Evidence for the Effectiveness of Psychotherapy

The results of an *effectiveness study* involving thousands of participants indicate that therapy does indeed work: Large proportions of persons who received psychotherapy from trained therapists (psychiatrists, psychologists, social workers) reported feeling much better as a result of such treatment. Smaller proportions reported improvements after visiting marriage counselors or physicians.

Source: Based on data reported by Seligman, 1995.

occur for most people after the first six to eight sessions, and fully 75 percent of the clients showed improvement by the twenty-sixth session. Finally, and most relevant to this discussion, it made little difference what kind of therapy respondents received: No particular approach was rated more highly than the others.

Needless to add, this study is far from perfect from a research methods perspective. Results were based entirely on self-report—what participants *said* happened as a result of therapy. Further, the measures of change were somewhat informal, relying on questions such as "How much did therapy help you with the specific problems that led you to therapy?" Psychologists prefer more specific and more readily quantified questions. Third, there was no control group: All participants were people who had received therapy. What happened to people with similar problems who didn't receive therapy? We can't tell.

Balanced against these important flaws, however, is the fact that this *effectiveness* study is based on responses from thousands of persons who described their experiences with therapy as it actually occurs. Thus, it provides evidence that complements the findings of other research conducted under more controlled and rigorous conditions (known as *efficacy* research). In any case, putting these fine points of scientific design aside, it seems clear that available evidence indicates that although therapy is indeed beneficial, there are no major differences between the various types, and no one clear winner in the effectiveness stakes (Hollon, DeRubeis, & Evans, 1987; Hollon, Shelton, & Loosen, 1991).

How, you may be wondering, can this be so? How can therapies that use sharply different procedures yield similar results? The answer that has emerged in recent years goes something like this. Various forms of therapy do differ in their rationale and in their procedures, but under the surface all share common crucial

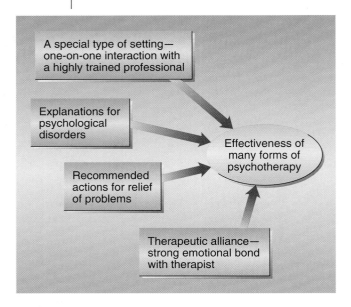

FIGURE 12.21
Factors Common to Many Forms of Therapy

The factors shown here are common to many forms of therapy and seem to explain why, despite many differences in procedures, they all produce beneficial effects.

features. It is this shared core that accounts for their simple effectiveness. What is this common core? It may include the following features.

First, all major forms of psychotherapy provide troubled individuals with a special type of setting—one in which they interact closely with a highly trained, empathetic professional. For many clients, this opportunity to interact with another person who seems to understand their problems and genuinely care about them may be a unique and reassuring experience, and may play an important role in the benefits of many diverse forms of therapy.

Second, every form of therapy provides individuals with an explanation for their problems. No longer do these seem to be mysterious. Rather, as therapists explain, psychological disturbances stem from understandable causes, many of which lie outside the individual. This is something of a revelation to many persons who have sought in vain for a clue about the causes of their difficulties.

Third, all forms of therapy specify actions that individuals can take to cope more effectively with their problems. No longer must they suffer in silence and despair. Rather, they are now actively involved in doing specific things that the confident, expert therapist indicates will help.

Fourth, all forms of therapy involve clients in what has been termed the *therapeutic alliance*—a partnership in which powerful emotional bonds are forged between the person seeking help and the therapist. This relationship is marked by mutual respect and trust, and it can be a big plus for people who previously felt helpless, hopeless, and alone.

Combining all these points, the themes of *hope* and *personal control* seem to emerge very strongly. Perhaps diverse forms of therapy succeed because all provide people with increased hope about the future plus a sense of heightened personal control. To the extent that this is the case, it is readily apparent why therapies that seem so different on the surface can all be effective. In a sense, all may provide the proverbial light at the end of the tunnel for people who have been struggling through the darkness of their emotional despair (see Figure 12.21 for a summary of these points). If all forms of therapy are equally effective, how can you choose a therapist? For some advice on this important issue, please see the **Psychology Lends a Hand** section that follows.

K E Y   Q U E S T I O N S

- Is psychotherapy effective?
- Are some types of psychotherapy more effective than others?

S U M M A R Y   A N D   R E V I E W   O F   K E Y   Q U E S T I O N S

- **What are mental disorders?**
  Mental disorders are disturbances of an individual's behavioral, psychological, or physical functioning that are not culturally expected and that lead to psychological distress, behavioral disability, or impaired overall functioning.

- **Why is it difficult to distinguish normal behavior from abnormal behavior?**
  It is difficult because there is no clear dividing line between "normal" and "abnormal," and many factors—including ones of which we, as outside observers, may be unaware—may play a role in individuals' actions.

p s y c h o l o g y l e n d s a h a n d

Choosing a Therapist: Some "Do's" and "Don'ts"

The odds are high that at some time in your life, you or someone close to you will experience a mental disorder. Depression, phobias, anxiety—these are common disorders. If there's one point we hope we have made clear, it is this: Effective help is available, and you should not hesitate to seek it. But how should you choose a therapist? Here are some basic guidelines.

- **Getting started.** The first step is usually the hardest in any task, and searching for a therapist is no exception. While you are a student, this task is fairly simple. Virtually every college or university has a department of psychology and a student health center. Both are good places to start. Visit them and ask for help. Don't be shy—the people there *want* to help, but they can't approach you—you have to take the first step. Another approach is simply to call the phone number on your health insurance card and ask for a referral to approved therapists.

  If you are no longer a student and don't have any contact with a college or university, you can still call the psychology department of a nearby college and ask for help: The chances are good that someone there will refer you to one or more excellent therapists. But if for some reason this is not practical, you can ask your physician or some member of the clergy to direct you to the help you need. Both will almost certainly know someone you can contact. If you have no local physician and don't know any clergy, contact your local Mental Health Association; it is probably listed in your phone book and is another good place to start.

- **Choosing a therapist.** Let's assume that by following one of the routes above, you have obtained the names of several therapists. How can you choose among them? Several guidelines are useful.

  First, always check for *credentials*. Therapists should be trained professionals. Before you consult one, be sure that this person has a Ph.D. in psychology or an M.D. degree plus a residency in psychiatry or other equivalent training. While such credentials don't guarantee that the therapist can help you, they *are* important.

  Second, try to find out something about the kind of disorders in which each therapist specializes. Most will readily give you this information, and what you are looking for is a good *match* between your needs and the therapists' expertise.

- **Signs of progress: How long should therapy last?** If therapy is going well, both you and the therapist will know it. You'll be able

to see beneficial changes in your behavior, your thoughts, and your feelings. But what if it is not going well? When and how should you decide to go elsewhere? This is a difficult decision, but a rough rule of thumb is this: If you have been visiting a therapist regularly (once a week or more) for three months and see no change, it may be time to ask the therapist whether she or he is satisfied with your progress. Most forms of therapy practiced by psychologists are relatively short-term in nature. If several months have passed and your distress has not decreased, it is time to raise this issue with your therapist.

- **Danger: When to quit.** Therapy is designed to help; unfortunately, though, there are instances in which it can hurt. How can you tell that you are in danger of such outcomes? Several basic points can help. First, if you or the people around you notice that you are actually become more distressed—more depressed, more anxious, more nervous—you should ask yourself whether you are satisfied with what is happening. At the very least, discuss these feelings with your therapist.

  Second, never under any circumstances should you agree to do anything during therapy that is against your own moral or ethical principles. A great majority of therapists would never dream of making such requests, but, sad to relate, there are a few who will take advantage of the therapeutic relationship to exploit their patients. The most common forms of such exploitation are sexual in nature. Unprincipled therapists may suggest that their clients engage in sexual relations with them as part of their "treatment." *This is never appropriate!* So, if your therapist makes such suggestions, *get out of there fast!*

  Third, beware of exaggerated claims. If a therapist tells you that she or he can guarantee to remake your life, turn you into a powerhouse of human energy, or assure you of total happiness, be cautious. This is a good sign that you are dealing with an unprincipled—and probably poorly trained—individual.

All these suggestions are merely *guidelines* you can follow to be a sophisticated consumer of psychological services. There may be situations, for instance, in which therapy requires much longer than the time period noted above, or in which a therapist has valid reasons for being reluctant to discuss procedures with you. These guidelines, however, should help you to avoid some of the pitfalls that exist with respect to finding a competent, caring therapist. Most important of all, always remember this: *Effective help is definitely out there if you take the trouble to look for it.*

Assessment and Diagnosis: The DSM–IV and Other Tools

- **What is the DSM–IV?**
  The DSM–IV—*Diagnostic and Statistical Manual of Mental Disorders–IV*—is a widely used guide to mental disorders. It provides descriptions of these disorders

plus information about biological factors associated with them.

- **In what ways is it an improvement over earlier versions?**
  The DSM–IV rests on a firmer basis of published research than did earlier versions and directs increased attention to the role of cultural factors.

Disorders of Infancy, Childhood, and Adolescence

- **What is oppositional defiant disorder? Conduct disorder?**
Oppositional defiant disorder involves behavior in which children have poor control of their emotions or have repeated conflicts with parents and other adults (e.g., teachers). Conduct disorder involves more serious antisocial behaviors that are potentially harmful to the child, to others, or to property.

- **What is attention-deficit/hyperactivity disorder?**
ADHD is childhood disorder in which children show inattention, hyperactivity, and impulsivity, or a combination of these behaviors.

- **What are anorexia nervosa and bulimia nervosa?**
Anorexia nervosa involves excessive fear of becoming fat, coupled with inability to maintain normal weight. Bulimia nervosa involves repeated cycles of binging and purging.

- **What is autistic disorder?**
Autistic disorder is one in which children show marked impairments in establishing social interactions with others, have nonexistent or poor language skills, and show stereotyped, repetitive patterns of behavior or interests.

Mood Disorders: The Downs and Ups of Life

- **What are the major symptoms of depression? Of bipolar disorder?**
The major symptoms of depression include negative mood, reduced energy, feelings of hopelessness, loss of interest in previously satisfying activities, difficulties in sleeping, and significant changes in weight. Bipolar disorders involve wide swings in mood between deep depression and mania.

- **What factors play a role in the occurrence of mood disorders?**
Mood disorders are influenced by genetic factors and by disturbances in brain activity. Psychological factors that play a role in such disorders include learned helplessness, negative perceptions of oneself, and a tendency to focus inward on one's shortcomings.

Anxiety Disorders: When Dread Debilitates

- **What are phobias?**
Phobias are excessive and unrealistic fears focused on specific objects or situations.

- **What is panic disorder?**
Panic disorder is intense, terrifying anxiety that is not triggered by any specific situation or event; in many cases, it is associated with *agoraphobia*—fear of open spaces or being away from home.

- **What is obsessive–compulsive disorder?**
Obsessive–compulsive disorder is one in which individuals have unwanted, disturbing thoughts or images (obsessions) they cannot control and engage in repetitious behaviors (compulsions) to neutralize such thoughts.

- **What is posttraumatic stress disorder?**
This disorder is one in which people persistently re-experience a traumatic event in their thoughts or dreams, feel as if they are reliving these events from time to time, persistently avoid stimuli associated with the traumatic event, and experience symptoms such as difficulty falling asleep, irritability, and difficulty in concentrating.

Dissociative Disorders

- **What are dissociative disorders such as dissociative amnesia?**
Dissociative disorders are disruptions in a person's memory, consciousness, or identity—processes that are normally integrated.

- **What is dissociative identity disorder?**
This disorder is a shattering of identity into at least two—and often more—separate but coexisting personalities, each possessing different traits, behaviors, memories, and emotions.

Somatoform Disorders: Physical Symptoms without Physical Causes

- **What are somatoform disorders?**
Somatoform disorders are those in which individuals have physical symptoms in the absence of identifiable physical causes for these symptoms.

- **What factors contribute to their occurrence?**
Individuals who develop somatoform disorders focus on inner sensations, perceive normal bodily sensations as more intense and disturbing than do other people, and have a high level of negative affectivity. In addition, they obtain important forms of reinforcement from their symptoms.

Sexual and Gender Identity Disorders

- **What are sexual dysfunctions and paraphilias?**
Sexual dysfunctions involve disturbances in sexual desire, sexual arousal, the ability to attain orgasm, or pain during sexual relations. In paraphilias, unusual imagery or acts are necessary for sexual arousal.

- **What is gender identity disorder?**
Gender identity disorder centers on feelings on the part of individuals that they were born with the wrong sexual identity coupled with strong desires to change this identity through medical treatment or other means.

Personality Disorders: Traits That Harm

- **What are personality disorders?**
Personality disorders are extreme and inflexible personality traits that are distressing to the persons who have them or cause them problems in school, work, or interpersonal relationships.

- **What characteristics are shown by persons with the antisocial personality disorder?**
Such persons are chronically callous and manipulative toward others; ignore social rules and laws; behave impulsively and irresponsibly; fail to learn from punishment; and lack remorse or guilt for their misdeeds.

Schizophrenia: Losing Touch with Reality

- **What is schizophrenia?**
Schizophrenia is a very serious mental disorder characterized by hallucinations (e.g., hearing voices), delusions (beliefs with no basis in reality), and disturbances in speech, behavior, and emotion.

- **What are positive and negative symptoms of schizophrenia?**
Positive symptoms involve the presence of something that is normally absent, such as hallucinations and delusions. Negative symptoms involve the absence of something that is normally present and include withdrawal, apathy, absence of emotion, and so on.

- **What factors play a role in the occurrence of schizophrenia?**
Schizophrenia has complex origins involving genetic factors, brain dysfunction, biochemical factors, and certain aspects of family environment.

Substance-Related Disorders

- **What is substance abuse?**
Substance abuse is a maladaptive pattern of substance use that results in repeated, significant adverse effects and maladaptive behavior (e.g., failure to meet obligations at work, in school, or at home; repeated using a psychoactive substance in hazardous ways).

Psychotherapies: Psychological Approaches to Mental Disorders

- **What is psychoanalysis, and what are its major assumptions?**
Psychoanalysis is the form of therapy developed by Freud. It assumes that mental disorders stem from hidden, internal conflicts and that making these conscious will lead to improved adjustment.

- **What is the role of free association in psychoanalysis?**
Free association supposedly brings hidden urges and conflicts into consciousness.

- **According to humanistic therapies, what is the cause of mental disorders?**
Humanistic therapies assume that mental disorders stem from factors in the environment that block or interfere with personal growth.

- **What is the major goal of Rogers's client-centered therapy?**
Rogers's client-centered therapy focuses on eliminating unrealistic conditions of worth in a therapeutic environment of unconditional positive regard.

- **What is the major goal of Gestalt therapy?**
Gestalt therapy focuses on helping individuals acknowledge parts of their own feelings or thoughts that are not currently conscious.

- **According to behavior therapies, what is the primary cause of mental disorders?**
Behavior therapies are based on the view that mental disorders stem from faulty learning.

- **On what basic principles of learning are behavior therapies based?**
Behavior therapies are based on principles of classical conditioning, operant conditioning, and observational learning.

- **What is modeling, and how can it be used in treating mental disorders?**
Modeling is a process through which individuals acquire new information or learn new behaviors by observing the actions of others. Modeling is effective in treating several disorders, including phobias and sexual dysfunctions.

- **According to cognitive therapies, what is the primary cause of mental disorders?**
Cognitive therapies assume that the major cause of mental disorders is distorted patterns of thought.

- **What is the major goal of rational–emotive therapy?**
The major goal of rational–emotive therapy is persuading individuals to recognize and reject irrational assumptions in their thinking.

- **What is the major goal of Beck's cognitive therapy for depression?**
The major goal of Beck's cognitive therapy is persuading individuals to recognize and change irrational patterns of thought that induce negative affect and so contribute to their depression.

Alternatives to Individual Psychotherapy: Group Therapies

- **What are group therapies?**
Group therapies are procedures in which several people discuss their problems with one another under the guidance or leadership of a trained therapist.

- **What is marital or couples therapy?**
Marital or couples therapy focuses on improving the relationship between members of a couple, often by enhancing their communication skills.

- **How does it work?**
It helps individuals see how they are communicating with their spouses and the errors they are making. This can lead to improved communication.

Biological Therapies

- **What drugs are used in the treatment of mental disorders?**
Many different psychoactive drugs are used to treat mental disorders. Antipsychotic or neuroleptic drugs reduce such symptoms as hallucinations and delusions. Antidepressant drugs counter depression. Antianxiety drugs reduce anxiety.

- **What is electroconvulsive therapy?**
Electroconvulsive therapy involves delivery of strong shocks to the brain. It is used to treat depression.

- **What is psychosurgery?**
Psychosurgery involves surgery performed on the brain in an effort to reduce or eliminate mental disorders.

Psychotherapy: Is It Effective?

- **Is psychotherapy effective?**
  Existing evidence suggests that psychotherapy is indeed effective relative to no treatment.

- **Are some types of psychotherapy more effective than others?**
  Research findings indicate that many types of therapy are roughly equal in their effectiveness.

PSYCHOLOGY: UNDERSTANDING ITS FINDINGS

Is Dealing with Mental Disorders Largely a Matter of Common Sense?

Many people seem to believe that dealing with mental disorders is largely a matter of common sense: Anyone who is kind, empathetic, and willing to listen can help. This is why many people who are experiencing disturbing symptoms either keep these to themselves or simply discuss them with their physician, clergy, family, or friends. In the light of what you have learned about mental disorders and their treatment in this chapter, do you think this makes sense? Or you do you think that the treatment of such disorders can be handled better by professionals, such as psychologists? And would your answer depend on the *kind* of mental disorder in question? For instance, do you think friends and other nonprofessionals might be more helpful in dealing with such problems as depression or phobias, but less effective in helping others cope with sexual disorders or ones relating to anxiety? Make a list of various disorders you have observed in other people and, for each, rate the extent to which you think that professional treatment is definitely needed (1 = not necessary; 5 = absolutely necessary). Is there a pattern in your answers? In other words, do you find that you view some mental disorders as more serious and more difficult to treat than others?

MAKING PSYCHOLOGY PART OF YOUR LIFE

Seeking Help at Work: Employee Assistance Programs

After we graduate from school, most of us spend a majority of our waking hours at work. And although we often try to keep our jobs or careers separate from our private lives, it is not really possible to do so: If we are experiencing distress at home, it often spills over into our jobs, where it can adversely affect our performance. Many companies recognize this fact and have established programs designed to help employees who are experiencing stress or are showing maladaptive patterns of behavior. Such programs are known as *Employee Assistance Programs,* and if you are ever in the situation of experiencing symptoms related to the various forms of mental disorders we have considered in this chapter, it may well be worth the effort to take advantage of them. What kind of assistance do such programs provide? Everything from immediate access to physicians, nurses, and psychologists to referrals to such persons, to fitness classes and career counseling. The basic fact is this: You won't know what's available unless you find out. So, follow these steps to find out what's available to employees of *your* company:

1. First, call the Human Resources Office and ask whether the company has an Employee Assistance Program (EAP for short).

2. Once you determine that it does, ask for information about the specific programs and benefits it provides.

3. Next, examine the various programs carefully; if you have any questions about what they involve, jot these down and then phone the Human Resources Office again.

4. At this point, try to decide whether any of the programs might be helpful to you; if so, find out how you can enroll and how your privacy will be protected. (Actually, this is not a major concern: Government regulations designed to protect the health and well-being of all employees require that your company keep records of your participation in its EAP confidential.)

The bottom line is this: More help may be available to you—for free!—than you now realize. So, it is definitely worth your while to find out what your company provides and to take advantage of it if the need arises.

KEY TERMS

Agoraphobia, p. 393
Anorexia Nervosa, p. 385
Antisocial Personality Disorder, p. 399
Anxiety, p. 391
Anxiety Disorders, p. 391
Attention-Deficit/Hyperactivity Disorder (ADHD), p. 384
Behavior Therapies, p. 408
Bipolar Disorder, p. 389
Bulimia Nervosa, p. 385
Catatonic Type (of schizophrenia), p. 402
Cognitive Therapies, p. 410
Conversion Disorder, p. 396
Delusions, p. 401
Depression, p. 388
Diagnostic and Statistical Manual of Mental Disorders–IV, p. 382
Disruptive Behaviors, p. 384
Dissociative Amnesia, p. 395
Dissociative Disorders, p. 395

Dissociative Fugue, p. 395
Dissociative Identity Disorder, p. 395
Electroconvulsive Therapy (ECT), p. 419
Feeding and Eating Disorders, p. 385
Free Association, p. 406
Gender Identity Disorder, p. 398
Hallucinations, p. 401
Humanistic Therapies (Phenomenological/ Experiential Therapies), p. 407
Hypochondriasis, p. 396
Learned Helplessness, p. 389
Mental Disorders, p. 381
Mood Disorders, p. 388
Obsessive–Compulsive Disorder, p. 393
Panic Disorder, p. 392
Paraphilias, p. 398
Personality Disorders, p. 399

Pervasive Development Disorders, p. 387
Phenomenological/Experiential Therapies. *See* Humanistic Therapies
Phobias, p. 392
Posttraumatic Stress Disorder (PTSD), p. 394
Psychodynamic Therapies, p. 405
Psychosurgery, p. 419
Psychotherapies, p. 405
Rational–Emotive Therapy, p. 411
Resistance, p. 406
Schizophrenia, p. 399
Sexual Arousal Disorders, p. 397
Sexual Desire Disorders, p. 397
Somatoform Disorders, p. 396
Substance Abuse, p. 404
Substance-Related Disorders, p. 403
Tardive Dyskinesia, p. 417
Transference, p. 406

Social Thought and Social Behavior

*S*uppose that while visiting your family, you go on a blind date. The person who comes to the door is neatly dressed and treats your family with great courtesy; your date also showers affection on your pet dog or cat, remarking on how much she or he likes animals. As the evening continues, your date acts in a consistently friendly and charming manner, engaging you in interesting conversation and expressing agreement with many of your views. But then, when you arrive at the restaurant where you going to eat dinner, you observe another side to your date's nature: He or she addresses the waitperson in a condescending manner and expresses great dissatisfaction with the service and the food. On the way home, your date does something else that makes you wonder: She or he treats a homeless person who asks for money with obvious contempt. After returning home, you find yourself wondering: "What is this person really like?" Nice and agreeable—the way she or treated you and your family? Or rude and nasty—the way he or she acted toward the waiter and the homeless person?

Close to Home

Merely for her own twisted amusement, Carol liked to spend hours aimlessly wandering around mall parking lots pretending to be heading to her car.

FIGURE 13.1

Social Behavior and Social Thought: The Two Basic Themes of Social Psychology

Social psychologists study all aspects of social behavior and social thought—how we interact with, and think about, other persons. As you can see from this cartoon, figuring out *why* people do what they do is not always an easy task!

Source: CLOSE TO HOME © (2002) John McPherson. Reprinted with permission of UNIVERSAL PRESS SYNDICATE. All rights reserved.

In a sense, this brief incident provides an overview of the basic themes of **social psychology**—the branch of psychology that studies all aspects of social behavior and social thought (e.g., Baron & Byrne, 2003). Social psychologists focus on understanding all aspects of how we think about, and interact with, other persons. On a blind date—or any first meeting with another person—one of your key goals is simply that of figuring out just what this person is really like. To do so, you gather information about her or his behavior. Then, you use this information to draw inferences about your new acquaintance—to figure out just what makes this person tick. The conclusions you reach will then play an important role in determining the nature of your future interactions with this individual.

Because social behavior and thought generally occur together, social psychologists focus on both of these topics in their research (see Figure 13.1 for another example of this principle). To provide you with an overview of some of the fascinating facts psychologists have uncovered about the social side of life, we'll proceed as follows. First, we'll examine several aspects of social thought—how, and what, we think about other persons. Included here will be discussions of four topics: *nonverbal communication*—how we learn about others' current feelings or reactions from facial expressions, eye contact with us, and related cues; *attribution*—our efforts to understand the causes behind others' behavior; that is, *why* they act as they do; *social cognition*—how we process social information, remember it, and use it in making judgments or decisions about others; and *attitudes*—our evaluations of various features of the social

After considering these topics, we'll turn to several important aspects of *social behavior*—how we interact with other people. Among the topics we'll examine are *prejudice*—negative attitudes and actions toward the members of various social groups, *social influence*—the many ways in which we attempt to change others' behavior and they attempt to change ours; and *attraction and love*—why we like or dislike other people, what makes them attractive or unattractive, and why we fall in (and out of) love with them. Additional aspects of social behavior are covered elsewhere in this book—in our discussions of social development (Chapters 8 and 9) and *leadership* in Chapter 14.

SOCIAL THOUGHT: THINKING ABOUT OTHER PEOPLE

How many times each day do you think about other people? Your answer might well be "Who can count?" Anytime you try to figure out how other people are currently feeling (Are they happy or sad? Do they like you or dislike you?), why they have acted in various ways, or attempt to make judgments about them (Will they make a good roommate?), you are engaging in *social thought* (or *social cognition*). Let's take a closer look at several important aspects of this process.

Nonverbal Communication: Unspoken Clues to Others' Moods and Reactions

One thing we want to know about other people is how they are feeling right *now*. Are they in a good mood or a bad mood? Do they like or dislike us? Information

Social Psychology

The branch of psychology that studies all aspects of social behavior and social thought.

of this type is often very helpful. For instance, if you want a favor from another person, when would you ask for it—when she is in a good mood or when she is in a bad mood? The answer is obvious: When she is in a good mood. Similarly, we all want to make good first impressions on others so that we can get the job—or the date! And information on how they are reacting to us and what we are saying is very useful in this context. But how, exactly, do we try to get information on others' reactions and feelings? As we saw in Chapter 9, one important way is through the use of **nonverbal cues**—information provided by others' facial expressions, eye contact, body posture and movements, and other outward expressions of what they are feeling on the inside (e.g., DePaulo & Kashy, 1998). Here, expanding on what we presented in Chapter 10, is a brief summary of what research on nonverbal cues indicates:

- *Facial expressions* can be very revealing, and generally serve as good guides to six different basic emotions: anger, fear, happiness, sadness, surprise, and disgust (Izard, 1991; Ekman, 1992a). Further, facial expressions are quite universal in the sense that a smile is recognized as a sign of happiness, a frown as a sign of anger, and so on, all over the world, across many different cultures. However, as you might guess, individuals often find it easier to "read" the facial expressions of persons belonging to their own racial or ethnic group than those of persons belonging to another group (Weathers, Frank, & Spell, 2002).
- *Eye contact* is another useful source of information about how others are feeling: In general, a high level of eyecontact is a sign of liking or positive feelings, while a low level is a sign of disliking or negative feelings. However, *staring*—continuous, steady gazing—is often a sign of anger or hostility, as in "cold stare."
- *Body movements* and *postures* are also very revealing of others' emotional states or moods. A large number of movements is often a sign of emotional arousal or uneasiness. And *gestures* often have specific meanings in a given culture (see Figure 13.2).
- *Touching* can also serve as a useful nonverbal cue. The precise meaning depends on who touches whom (e.g., it is more acceptable for high-status people to touch lower-status ones); where one person touches another (on the shoulder may be OK, but other body parts are definitely off limits, except for people who know each other very well); and the context in which the touching takes place—for

FIGURE 13.2
Gestures: A Basic Form of Nonverbal Communication
Do you recognize the gestures shown here? In the United States and several other countries, each of these gestures has a specific meaning. However, they might well have no meaning, or different meanings, in other cultures.

Nonverbal Cues
Information provided by others' facial expressions, eye contact, body posture and movements, and other outward expressions of what they are feeling on the inside.

instance, touching is more acceptable at a party than at work. One specific form of touching is especially revealing—*handshakes*. Research findings suggest that we often learn much from others' handshakes—or at least *believe* that we learn much! For instance, in one study (Chaplin et al., 2000), assistants were trained to give handshakes to strangers that varied in strength, grip, vigor, and duration. Then, these trained assistants shook hands with many strangers, who then rated the assistants on various dimensions. Results were clear: The stronger, longer, and more vigorous the handshakes delivered by the assistants, the higher they were rated on many different dimensions (e.g., how friendly, expressive, and open to experience they were).

In sum, nonverbal cues are often a very useful guide to others' current moods and feelings, so they provide valuable "raw materials" for social thought—for thinking about others and trying to understand just what kind of persons they are. Another valuable aspect of nonverbal cues is that they can help us determine whether others are being honest with us—whether they are lying or telling the truth. For information on how *you* can use nonverbal cues for this purpose, please see the **Psychology Lends a Hand** section that follows.

p s y c h o l o g y   l e n d s   a   h a n d

How to Tell When Another Person Is Lying

In many contexts, it is important to be able to tell whether others are telling the truth or lying. Research on lying indicates that it is a fact of everyday life: Most people report telling one or two lies every single day (DePaulo & Kashy, 1998). They do so for many reasons: to hide their real feelings, attitudes, or preferences; for personal gain; or to escape punishment for misdeeds. Can we tell when others are not being honest with us? Research findings on this question suggest that we can, although doing so is far from easy (DePaulo et al., 2003). Here is a brief summary of cues—most of the nonverbal—that may indicate that another person is not telling the truth:

1. **Microexpressions.** These are fleeting facial expressions lasting only a few tenths of a second. Such reactions appear on the face very quickly after an emotion-provoking event and are difficult to suppress. As result, they can be very revealing about others' true feelings or emotions. For instance, if you ask another person whether they like something (e.g., an idea you have expressed, a new product), watch their faces closely as they respond. If you see one expression (e.g., a frown), which is followed very quickly by another (e.g., a smile), this can be a useful sign that they are lying—they are stating one opinion or reaction when, in fact, they really have another.

2. **Interchannel discrepancies.** A second nonverbal cue revealing of deception is known as interchannel discrepancies. (The term *channel* refers to type of nonverbal cues; for instance, facial expressions are one channel, and body movements are another.) These are inconsistencies between nonverbal cues from different basic channels. These result from the fact that persons who are lying often find it difficult to control all these channels at once. For instance, they may manage their facial expressions well, but may have difficulty looking you in the eye as they tell their lie.

3. **Eye contact.** Efforts at deception are often frequently revealed by certain aspects of eye contact. Persons who are lying often blink more often and show pupils that are more dilated than persons who are telling the truth. They may also show an unusually low level of eye contact or—surprisingly—an unusually high one, as they attempt to fake being honest by looking others right in the eye.

4. **Nonverbal aspects of what people actually say.** When people are lying, the stories they tell are often less compelling, are less forthcoming, contain more negative remarks, show more tension, and are often lacking in the usual imperfections or inconsistencies that people include when telling the truth. Further, the pitch of their voices often rises—especially when they are highly motivated to lie—and they often take longer to begin—to respond to a question or describe events. In other words, clues to deceit are contained not only in the words they express, but also in the *ways* in which they express them.

The bottom line of all this is that detecting deception by others is a difficult task. Some people become very skilled at lying and, in fact, after a while may begin to believe their own lies, thus making it especially hard to tell that they are not being truthful. But if you pay careful attention to the cues described here, you will make their task of "pulling the wool over your eyes" much more difficult—and that is certainly worth the effort.

Attribution: Understanding the Causes of Others' Behavior

Imagine the following situation. You're standing at a counter in a store waiting your turn when suddenly, another customer walks up and hands the clerk an item she wishes to purchase. How do you react? While your first response might be "With anger!" a more accurate answer is "It depends." And what it depends upon is your perceptions of *why* this other person has cut in front of you. Did she do it on purpose? In that case, you probably *would* get angry. But perhaps she just didn't see you. In that case, you might clear your throat or otherwise indicate your presence to see what would happen next. So, it's not just what this person did that matters; your perception of *why* she did it is important, too.

This question of *why* others act as they do is one we face every day in many different contexts. The process through which we attempt to answer this question—to determine the causes behind others' behavior—is known as **attribution,** and, in general, it is a fairly orderly process. We examine others' behavior for clues as to the causes behind what they say and do, and then reach our decision. What kind of information do we consider? This depends on the specific question we want to answer. For instance, one basic issue is this: Did another person's actions stem from *internal* causes (e.g., factors having to do with their own traits, intentions, or motives) or from *external* causes (e.g., factors outside the person, such as luck or factors beyond their control in a given situation). To answer this question, we often focus on information about (1) whether other people behave in the same way they do (**consensus**); (2) whether this person behaves in the same manner over time (**consistency**); and (3) whether this person behaves in the same way in different situations (**distinctiveness**). If very few people act like this person (consensus is low), this person behaves in the same way over time (consistency is high), and behaves in much the same manner in many situations (distinctiveness is low), we conclude that their behavior stemmed from *internal* causes: This is the kind of person they are and will probably remain. For instance, we'd probably draw this conclusion about a student who got up and criticized a professor harshly in class if no other students did this (consensus was low), this student criticized the professor on other occasions (consistency was high), and this student also criticized other professors or waitpersons in restaurants (distinctivness is low). In contrast, if all three of these factors are high (consensus, consistency, and distinctiveness), we are more likely to conclude that this person behaved as they did because of external causes—for instance, they might have no choice (Kelley, 1972; see Figure 13.3 on page 434).

◼ Attribution: Some Basic Sources of Error

Although attribution often involves the logical kind of reasoning just described, this is not always the case. In fact, it is subject to several kinds of errors. One of the most important is known as the **correspondence bias,** or the fundamental attribution error, and it refers to our strong tendency to explain others' actions as stemming from (corresponding to) internal causes, even in the presence of clear external (situations) causes (e.g., Gilbert & Malone, 1995). In other words, if we see someone behave in a particular way, we tend to attribute these actions to internal causes such as their own traits, even if we have no grounds for making this assumption. For instance, someone who is late for a meeting may be irresponsible, but he may also have been stuck in unavoidable traffic. So the correspondence bias can lead us to false conclusions about others.

Another "tilt" in our attributions is even worse. It is known as the **self-serving bias,** and it involves our tendency to attribute any positive outcomes we experience to our own behavior and traits (internal causes), but negative outcomes to external causes beyond our control. For instance, suppose that you receive a grade of A on an exam. You might well explain this as the result of your talent, effort, studying, and other internal causes. But suppose you receive a grade of D. In this

---

Attribution
The processes through which we seek to determine the causes behind others' behavior.

Consensus
Information regarding the extent to which behavior by one person is shown by others as well.

Consistency
Information regarding the extent to which a specific person shows similar behavior to a given stimulus across time.

Distinctiveness
Information regarding the extent to which a given person reacts in the same manner to different stimuli or situations.

Correspondence Bias (also known as *fundamental attribution error*)
The tendency to attribute behavior to internal causes to a greater extent than is actually justified.

Self-Serving Bias
The tendency to attribute positive outcomes to our own traits or characteristics (internal causes) but negative outcomes to factors beyond our control (external causes).

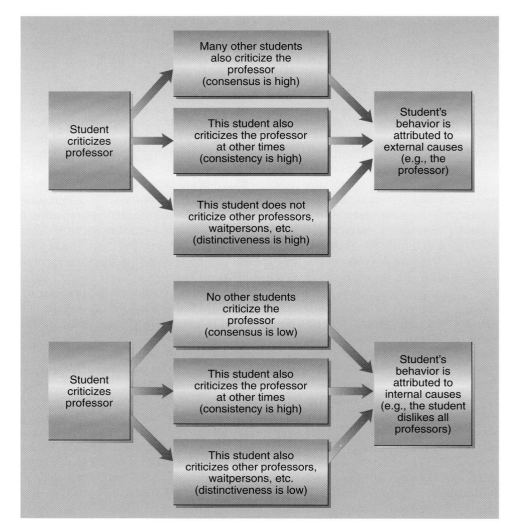

FIGURE 13.3
Causal Attribution
When consensus and distinctiveness are low but consistency is high, we attribute others' behavior to internal causes (*lower diagram*). When consensus, consistency, and distinctiveness are all high, in contrast, we attribute their behavior to external causes (*upper diagram*).

case, you might be tempted to attribute your poor grade to the unfairness of the exam, the unrealistically high standards of your professor, and other external causes.

The self-serving bias can be the cause of much interpersonal friction. It often leads persons who work with others on a joint task to perceive that they, not their partners, have made the major contributions. I (Robert Baron) see this effect in my own classes every semester when students rate their own contributions and those of the other members of their team on a required term project. The result? Most students take lots of credit for themselves when the project has gone well, but tend to blame (and downrate) their partners if it has not.

KEY QUESTIONS

- What is the correspondence bias?
- What is the self-serving bias?

Social Cognition: How We Process Social Information

Gathering information on other person's current moods or feelings and identifying the causes behind their actions are important aspects of social thought, but they are far from the entire picture. Thinking about other persons involves many other tasks as well. We must decide what information is most important. We must enter such information into memory and be able to retrieve it at later times. And we must be able to combine this previously stored information about others in various ways in order to make judgments about them and predict their future actions (Wyer & Srull, 1999). It is only by accomplishing these tasks that we can make sense out of the complex social world in which we live.

How do we accomplish these tasks? We have already provided part of the answer in our earlier discussions of memory and schemas (Chapter 6) and the use of *heuristics*—cognitive rules of thumb for making judgments or decisions very quickly (Chapter 7). Here, we'll focus on additional aspects of social thought, especially ones related to the following basic theme: As human beings, we are definitely *not* perfect information-processing devices. On the contrary, in our efforts to understand others and make sense out of the social world, we are subject to a wide range of tendencies that together can lead us into serious error. Although many exist, we'll focus here on two that are especially intriguing—the *planning fallacy* (one aspect of our overall tendency to be more optimistic than is often justified) and *counterfactual thinking*.

■ The Optimistic Bias for Task Completion: Why We Think
We Can Do More, Sooner, Than We Really Can

Several years ago, Amtrak began construction on a beautiful new station in the town where we live. The station was supposed to be completed within two years, but instead it actually took almost four years until the day it opened. And even then, work was still continuing. This is not a rare event: Many projects seem to take longer, and cost more, than initially predicted (Figure 13.4). (This one took longer than expected because each new cost overrun required new funding from the state legislature.)

Why is this so? Because in predicting how long a given task will take, people tend to be overly optimistic: They expect that they can get it done much sooner

FIGURE 13.4
All Aboard—Eventually!
The Amtrak station shown here was originally scheduled to open in 2000; in fact, it was not completed until 2002—more than two years late! Events like this—which are far from rare—illustrate a basic form of error in our social thought: the tendency to make overly optimistic predictions about how much we can get done in a specific period of time, or how long it will take to complete a given task (the *planning fallacy*).

than actually turns out to be the case. Or, turning this around somewhat, they expect to get more done in a given period of time than they really can. You probably recognize this tendency in your own thinking. Try to remember the last time you worked on a major project (for instance, a term paper). Did it take more time or less time to complete than you originally estimated? Probably, your answer is "More time . . . of course!" What aspects of social thought account for this common error?

According to Buehler, Griffin, and Ross (1994), social psychologists who have studied this tendency in detail, several factors play a role. One is that when individuals make predictions about how long it will take them to complete a given task, they enter a planning mode of thought in which they focus primarily on the future: how they will perform the task. This, in turn, prevents them from looking backward in time and remembering how long similar tasks took them in the past. The result: They tend to overlook important potential obstacles when predicting how long a task will take and fall prey to the planning fallacy. These predictions were confirmed in several studies (e.g., Buehler, Griffin, & Ross, 1994), so they do seem to provide important insights into the origins of the tendency to make optimistic predictions about task completion.

■ Counterfactual Thinking: The Effects of Considering "What Might Have Been"

Suppose that you take an important exam; when you receive your score, it is a C–, much lower than you had hoped. What thoughts will enter you mind as you consider your grade? If you are like most people, you may imagine "what might have been"—receiving a higher grade—along with thoughts about how you could have obtained that better outcome. "If only I had studied more, or come to class more often," you may think to yourself. Such thoughts about what might have been—known in social psychology as **counterfactual thinking**—occur in a wide range of situations, not just ones in which we experience disappointments. In fact, counterfactual thinking can involve imagining either better outcomes (*upward* counterfactuals) or worse ones (*downward* counterfactuals) than we actually experience.

What are the effects of engaging in such thought? Neal Roese (1997), a social psychologist who has conducted many studies on counterfactual thinking, suggests that engaging in it can yield a wide range of effects, some of which are beneficial and some of which are costly. For instance, counterfactual thinking can, depending on its focus, yield either boosts to or reductions in our current moods. If individuals imagine *upward counterfactuals,* comparing their current outcomes with more favorable ones than they actually experienced, the result may be strong feelings of regret, dissatisfaction, or envy, especially if they do not feel capable of obtaining better outcomes in the future (Sanna, 1997). Olympic athletes who win a silver medal but imagine winning a gold one experience such reactions (Medvec, Madey, & Gilovich, 1995). Alternatively, if individuals compare their current outcomes with less favorable ones, or if they consider various ways in which disappointing results could have been avoided and positive ones attained, they may experience positive feelings of satisfaction or hopefulness. Such reactions have been found among Olympic athletes who win bronze medals and who therefore imagine what it would be like to have won no medal (e.g., Gleicher et al., 1995). In sum, counterfactual thinking can strongly influence affective states (Medvec & Savitsky, 1997).

Another effect of counterfactual thinking involves its impact on future performance. Engaging in counterfactual thinking after disappointing results can often help us to formulate improved strategies or tactics—ones that will yield better outcomes in the future. So, in this sense, counterfactual thinking can be very helpful.

Counterfactual Thinking
The tendency to evaluate events by thinking about alternatives to them (i.e., "what might have been").

KEY QUESTIONS

- How do we deal with social information that is inconsistent with our expectations?
- What is the optimistic bias for task completion?
- What is counterfactual thinking? How can it affect our affective states and performance?

Attitudes: Evaluating the Social World

Consider the following list:

President Bush

Sport utility vehicles

Arnold Schwarzenegger

Iraq

Do you have any reactions to each item? Unless you have been living a life of total isolation, you probably do. You may like or dislike President Bush, believe or not believe that sport utility vehicles are harmful to the environment, believe or not believe that Arnold Schwarzenegger is qualified to be governor of California, and feel that the United States should or should not have invaded Iraq. Such reactions, which social psychologists describe as attitudes, generally involve an emotional or affective component (for instance, liking or disliking), a cognitive component (beliefs), and a behavioral component (tendencies to act toward these items in various ways). More simply, **attitudes** can be defined as lasting evaluations of virtually any and every aspect of the social world—issues, ideas, persons, social groups, and objects (Fazio & Roskos-Ewoldsen, 1994; Tesser & Martin, 1996).

Attitudes are an important aspect of social thought and have long been a central topic of research in social psychology, mainly because they often (but not always) influence our overt behavior (e.g., Ajzen, 1991; Gibbons et al., 1998). For instance, if you have a positive attitude toward Arnold Schwarzenegger, you may vote for him if given the opportunity (if you live in California!); if you dislike sport utility vehicles, you probably won't buy one. So attitudes are often a good predictor of present or future behavior—although far from a perfect one for reasons we'll soon explain. We'll now examine two key aspects of attitudes: *persuasion*—how attitudes can sometimes be changed; and *cognitive dissonance*—a process through which we sometimes change our own attitudes.

◼ Persuasion: Using Messages to Change Attitudes

In the early twenty-first century, efforts to change attitudes are definitely big business. Television commercials, magazine ads, billboards, warning labels on products—all are designed to change our attitudes in some way. To what extent are such efforts at **persuasion**—efforts to change attitudes—really effective? And how does persuasion actually occur? Let's see what psychologists have learned about these issues.

Persuasion: The Early Approach   In most cases, efforts at persuasion involve the following elements: Some *source* directs some kind of message to some person or group of persons (the audience). Taking note of this fact, early research on persuasion focused on these elements, asking "Who says what to whom and with what effect?" This approach yielded many interesting findings:

1. Experts are more persuasive than nonexperts (Hovland & Weiss, 1951). The same arguments carry more weight when delivered by people who seem to know what they are talking about than when they are made by people lacking expertise.
2. Messages that do not appear to be designed to change our attitudes are often more successful in this respect than ones that seem intended to reach this goal (Walster & Festinger, 1962). In other words, we generally don't trust—and generally refuse to be influenced by—persons who deliberately set out to persuade us. This is one reason why the soft sell is so popular in advertising and politics.
3. Attractive sources are more effective in changing attitudes than unattractive ones (Kiesler & Kiesler, 1969). This is one reason why the models featured in many ads are highly attractive and why advertisers engage in a perpetual search for new faces.

Attitudes
Lasting evaluations of various aspects of the social world that are stored in memory.

Persuasion
The process through which one or more persons attempt to alter the attitudes of one or more others.

4. People are sometimes more susceptible to persuasion when they are distracted by some extraneous event than when they are paying full attention to what is being said (Allyn & Festinger, 1961).

5. When an audience holds attitudes contrary to those of a would-be persuader, it is often more effective for this person to adopt a *two-sided approach,* in which both sides of the argument are presented, than a *one-sided approach.* Apparently, strongly supporting one side of an issue while acknowledging that the other side has a few good points in its favor serves to disarm audience and makes it harder for them to resist the source's major conclusions.

6. People who speak rapidly are often more persuasive than persons who speak more slowly (Miller et al., 1976). So, contrary to popular belief, we do not always distrust fast-talking politicians and salespersons.

7. Persuasion can be enhanced by messages that arouse strong emotions (especially fear) in the audience, particularly when the message provides specific recommendations about how a change in attitudes or behavior will prevent the negative consequences described in the fear-provoking message (Leventhal, Singer, & Jones, 1965), and when they are *positively framed*—when they focus on potential benefits that may result from changing some behavior or attitude (e.g., Jones, Sinclair, & Courneya, 2003).

We're confident that you find all these points to be reasonable ones that probably fit with your own experience, so early research on persuasion certainly provided important insights into the factors that influence persuasion. What such work *didn't* do, however, was offer a comprehensive account of *how* persuasion occurs. Fortunately, this question has been the focus of more recent research, to which we turn next.

The Cognitive Approach to Persuasion: Systematic Versus Heuristic Processing
What happens when you are exposed to a persuasive message—for instance, when you watch a television commercial or listen to a political speech? Your first answer might be something like "I think about what's happening or what's being said," and in a sense, that's correct. But how much thinking of this type do we actually do, and how do we process (absorb, interpret, evaluate) the information contained in such messages? The answer that has emerged from many studies is that, basically, we process persuasive messages in two distinct ways.

The first of these is known as **systematic processing,** or the **central route to persuasion,** and it involves careful consideration of message content, the ideas it contains, and so on. Such processing is quite effortful and absorbs much of our information-processing capacity. The second approach, known as **heuristic processing,** or the **peripheral route,** involves the use of simple rules of thumb or mental shortcuts such as the belief that "experts' statements can be trusted" or the idea that "If it makes me feel good, I'm in favor of it." This kind of processing is much less effortful and allows us to react to persuasive messages in an automatic manner. It occurs in response to cues in the message or situation that evoke various mental shortcuts (e.g., "If someone so beautiful or famous or charismatic says it, then this message is worthy of careful attention.")

When do we engage in each of these two distinct modes of thought? Modern theories of persuasion, such as the **elaboration-likelihood model (ELM)** (e.g., Petty & Cacioppo, 1986; Petty et al., 1994) and the **heuristic–systematic model** (e.g., Chaiken, Liberman, & Eagly, 1989; Eagly & Chaiken, 1998), suggest that we engage in the effortful type of processing (systematic processing) when our capacity to process information relating to the persuasive message is high (e.g., we have lots of knowledge about it or lots of time to engage in such thought) or when we are *motivated* to do so—the issue is important to us (e.g., Maheswaran & Chaiken, 1991; Petty & Cacioppo, 1990). In contrast, we engage in the less effortful type of processing (heuristic processing) when we lack the ability or capacity to process more carefully (we must make our minds very quickly, have little knowledge about the issue) or when our

Systematic Processing
Involves careful consideration of message content, the ideas it contains, and so on. Such processing is quite effortful and absorbs much of our information-processing capacity.

Central Route (to persuasion)
Persuasion that occurs through careful consideration of message content.

Heuristic Processing
The use of simple rules of thumb or mental shortcuts in the evaluation of persuasive messages; also called the *peripheral route* to persuasion.

Peripheral Route (to persuasion)
The use of simple rules of thumb or mental shortcuts in the evaluation of persuasive messages; also called *heuristic processing.*

Elaboration-Likelihood Model (ELM)
A cognitive model of persuasion suggesting that persuasion can occur through distinct routes.

Heuristic–Systematic Model
A cognitive model of persuasion suggesting that persuasion can occur through distinctly different routes.

motivation to perform such cognitive work is low (the issue is unimportant to us, has little potential effect on us, and so on). Advertisers, politicians, and salespersons wishing to change our attitudes prefer to push us into the heuristic mode of processing because it is often easier to change our attitudes when we think in this mode than when we engage in more systematic processing. Why? Because we are thinking "on automatic," and this makes it harder for us to defend against persuasion.

Cognitive Dissonance: How We Sometimes Change Our Own Attitudes

There are many occasions in everyday life when we feel compelled to say or do things inconsistent with our true attitudes. A couple of examples: Your friend shows you his new sweater and asks how you like it. You really hate the color, but you don't say that. Instead you say, "Nice . . . really nice." Your boss describes his new idea for increasing sales. You think that it is totally idiotic, but you don't tell her *that*. Instead you respond, "Sounds really interesting."

The reasons for behaving in these polite—but slightly dishonest ways—are so obvious that social psychologists describe them as involving **induced (forced) compliance**—situations in which we feel compelled to say or do things inconsistent with our true attitudes. Now, here's the most interesting part: When we behave in this way—when we engage in *attitude-discrepant behavior*—this may sometimes produce changes in the attitudes we hold. In fact, our attitudes may shift toward what we felt compelled to do or say, thus reducing the size of the gap between our true attitudes and our overt actions.

Such effects were first predicted by a very famous theory known as the theory of *cognitive dissonance* (Festinger, 1957). The term **cognitive dissonance** (or *dissonance* for short) refers to the unpleasant feelings we experience when we notice a gap between two attitudes we hold or between our attitudes and our behavior. Dissonance, it appears, is quite unpleasant (e.g., Elliot & Devine, 1994), so when we experience it, we attempt to reduce it. This can be accomplished in several different ways. First, we can change our attitudes or behavior so that these are more consistent with each other. For example, we can convince ourselves that the color of our friend's sweater is not really so bad. Second, we can acquire new information that supports our attitude or our behavior. For instance, we can seek out information indicating that our boss's plan does make some sense. Third, we can engage in *trivialization*—conclude that the attitudes or behaviors in question are not important (e.g., Simon, Greenberg, & Brehm, 1995).

Which of these tactics do we choose? As you might guess, whichever requires the least effort. In situations involving induced compliance, however, it is often the case that changing our attitudes is the easiest step to take, so it is not surprising that in such situations our attitudes often shift so as to more closely match what we have actually said or done. In other words, we change our attitudes because doing so helps us reduce cognitive dissonance.

Dissonance and the Less-Leads-to-More Effect

The prediction that people sometimes change their own attitudes is surprising enough. But now get ready for an even bigger surprise: Dissonance theory also predicts that the weaker the reasons we have for engaging in attitude-discrepant behavior—for saying or doing things inconsistent with our initial attitudes—the greater the pressure to change these attitudes. Why is this so? Because when we have strong reasons for engaging in attitude-discrepant behavior, we realize that these reasons are responsible for our saying or doing things inconsistent with our true attitudes. As a result, we experience very little dissonance. When we have only weak reasons for engaging in attitude-discrepant behavior, however, dissonance is stronger, and so is the pressure to change our attitudes (see Figure 13.5 on page 440).

Social psychologists sometimes refer to this unexpected state of affairs as the **less-leads-to-more effect:** the fact that the stronger the reasons for engaging in attitude-discrepant behavior, the weaker the pressures toward changing the

Induced (forced) Compliance
A technique for changing attitudes in which individuals are somehow induced to state positions different from their actual views.

Cognitive Dissonance
The state experienced by individuals when they discover inconsistency between two attitudes they hold or between their attitudes and their behavior.

Less-Leads-to-More Effect
The fact that rewards just barely sufficient to induce individuals to state positions contrary to their own views often generate more attitude change than larger rewards.

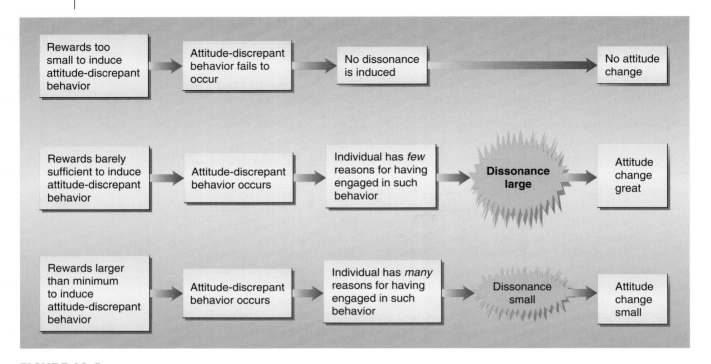

FIGURE 13.5
Why, Where Attitude Change Is Concerned, "Less" Sometimes Leads to "More"
When individuals have strong reasons for engaging in behavior discrepant with their attitudes (e.g., when they receive large rewards for doing so), they experience little or no dissonance and show little attitude change. When they have weak reasons for engaging in such behavior (e.g., when they receive small rewards for doing so), dissonance is much greater—and attitude change, too, is increased. In such cases, "less" does indeed lead to "more."
Source: Baron & Byrne, 1987.

underlying attitudes. Surprising as it may seem, this effect has been confirmed in many different studies (e.g., Riess & Schlenker, 1977). In all these studies, people provided with a small reward for stating attitudes contrary to their own views changed these attitudes so that they became closer to the views they had expressed. So it appears that often the strategy of offering others just barely enough to induce them to say or do things contrary to their true attitudes can be an effective technique for inducing attitude change.

Putting Dissonance to Work: Hypocrisy and Safe Sex

People who don't wear safety belts are much more likely to die in accidents than those who do.

People who smoke heavily are much more likely to suffer from lung cancer and heart disease than those who don't.

Lying in the sun in the middle of the day can lead to skin cancer.

People who engage in unprotected sex are much more likely than those who engage in safe sex to contract dangerous diseases, including AIDS.

Most people know that these statements are true (e.g., Carey, Morrison-Beedy, & Johnson, 1997), so their attitudes are generally favorable toward using seatbelts, quitting smoking, wearing a lotion with a high sun protection factor, and engaging in safe sex. Yet, as you well know, these attitudes are often *not* translated into overt actions: People continue to drive without seatbelts, to smoke, and so on (see Figure 13.6). What's needed, in other words, is not so much changes in attitudes as shifts in overt

FIGURE 13.6
Doing What We Know We Shouldn't Do
Almost everyone knows that the behaviors shown here are dangerous. Yet, many people continue to perform them. If people who engage in such actions can be induced to recommend avoiding them, they may experience feelings of hypocrisy and intense cognitive dissonance. The result? They may change their own behavior.

behavior. Can dissonance be useful in promoting such beneficial changes? A growing body of evidence suggests that it can (e.g., Gibbons, Eggleston & Benthin, 1997; Stone et al., 1994), especially when it used to generate feelings of *hypocrisy*—awareness of publicly advocating some attitudes or behavior but acting in a way that is inconsistent with these attitudes or behavior. Under these conditions, several researchers have reasoned (e.g., Aronson, Fried, & Stone, 1991), the individuals involved should experience strong dissonance. Moreover, such feelings would be so intense that adopting indirect modes of dissonance reduction (e.g., distracting oneself, bolstering one's ego by thinking about or engaging in other positively evaluated behaviors) would not do the trick: Only actions that reduce dissonance directly, removing the discrepancy between one's words and deeds, would be effective.

These predictions have been tested in several studies. For instance, in one interesting study, Stone and his co-workers (1997) asked participants to prepare a videotape advocating the use of condoms (safe sex) to avoid contracting HIV. Next, participants were asked to think about reasons why they themselves hadn't used condoms in the past (*personal reasons*) or reasons why people in general sometimes fail to use condoms (*normative reasons* that didn't center on their own behavior). Stone and his colleagues (1997) predicted that hypocrisy would be maximized in the personal reasons condition in which participants had to come face to face with their own hypocrisy. Finally, all persons in the study were given a choice between a direct means of reducing dissonance—purchasing condoms at a reduced price—or an indirect means of reducing dissonance—donating to a program designed to aid homeless persons.

Results indicated that when participants had been asked to focus on the reasons why they did *not* engage in safe sex in the past, an overwhelming majority chose to purchase condoms—the direct route to dissonance reduction. In contrast, when asked to think about reasons why people in general didn't engage in safe sex, more actually chose the indirect route to dissonance reduction—a donation to an aid-the-homeless project (see Figure 13.7 on page 442).

These findings suggest that using dissonance to generate hypocrisy can indeed be a powerful tool for changing people's behavior in desirable ways—ones that

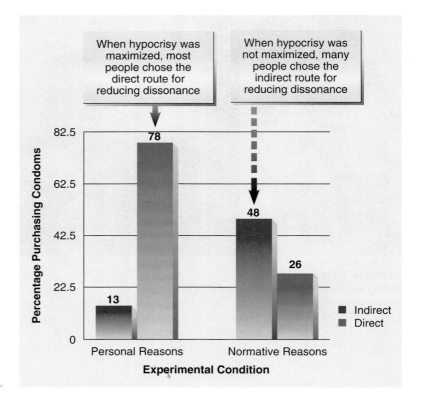

FIGURE 13.7
Using Hypocrisy to Change Behavior
When individuals were made to confront their own hypocrisy—they were asked to list reasons why they did *not* engage in safe sex in the past—most chose to reduce such dissonance through direct means (by purchasing condoms). In contrast, when individuals were asked to think about reasons why people in general didn't engage in safe sex, many chose to reduce dissonance via an indirect route (making a donation to an aid-the-homeless project).
Source: Based on data from Stone et al., 1997.

protect their health and safety. To be maximally effective, however, such procedures must involve several elements: The persons in question must publicly advocate the desired behaviors (e.g., using condoms, wearing safety belts), must be induced to think about their own failures to show these behaviors in the past, and must be given access to direct means for reducing their dissonance. When these conditions are met, beneficial changes in behavior can definitely follow. (How can *you* resist efforts to change your attitudes? For some tips, see the following **Psychology Lends a Hand** section.)

KEY QUESTIONS

- What are attitudes?
- What factors were found to influence persuasion in early research?
- What are heuristic and systematic processing, and what role do they play in attitude change?
- What is the ELM model, and how does it explain persuasion?
- What is cognitive dissonance, and how can it be reduced?
- What is induced compliance? The less-leads-to-more effect?
- How can hypocrisy be used to change behavior?

SOCIAL BEHAVIOR: INTERACTING WITH OTHERS

Thinking about other people is an important aspect of our social existence, but as you know from your own life, we also *interact* with others in many ways. We work with them on various tasks; we attempt to influence others and are on the receiving end of *their* efforts at influence; we fall in and out of love; we join and leave various groups—the list goes on and on. In this section, we'll consider several important aspects of *social interaction* with others.

psychology lends a hand

Resisting Persuasion: Some Techniques That Can Help

Every day we are flooded with efforts to change our attitudes. Even worse, many of these are carefully designed by experts—people in the field of marketing and advertising who have spent years trying to develop the best ways of cracking our defenses and getting us to do what they want—buy the products they promote, vote for the candidates who have hired them, and so on (see Figure 13.8). Can we resist? Absolutely. In fact, most of are already quite skilled at rejecting most efforts to change our views. Still, there are times when commercials and televised appeals do succeed in changing our views and our overt behavior. How can you protect yourself against these efforts? Here are some steps derived from research findings in social psychology:

- **Recognize persuasion for what it is.** Many efforts at persuasion are concealed or disguised—they seem more designed to help us than anything else. Your first task, then, is to see them for what they are: efforts to change your attitudes and your behavior. Once you do, a process known as *reactance* will occur. This is our tendency to lean over backward to protect our personal freedom and refuse to do what others want us to do. So, get your reactance going—it is a powerful shield against persuasion.
- **Be forewarned.** Research findings indicate that if we know efforts to persuade us are about to occur, we are better able to resist them than if they catch us unprepared. This is why many people are able to resist the appeals of telemarketers who call them at home: As soon as they hear the cheerful "Hi!" they know they are dealing with someone whose only goal is that of persuasion (Wood & Quinn, 2003).
- **Use selective avoidance.** Often, we have a tendency to direct our attention away from information that challenges our existing views; after all, we don't like to be told we are wrong! You can harness this tendency to help you resist persuasion. The simplest way of doing so is to push the mute button on your television remote when commercials appear, or start channel surfing. Another is just to distract yourself some way—think about other things aside from the commercial. But be careful: Commercials are designed by experts to be highly attention-getting, so you must consciously choose to look away as soon as they appear. If you continue to watch, you may be caught like a fish on a line and find it very hard to escape!
- **Counterargue against what you hear or see.** When you are exposed to persuasion, don't just absorb it. Instead, think of arguments *against* the views being presented. Doing so not

FIGURE 13.8
Efforts at Persuasion: Can We Resist?
Every day we are bombarded with commercials, ads, and other efforts to change our attitudes. Can we resist these efforts at persuasion? Research by social psychologists suggests several techniques that can be highly effective in this regard.

only blots out the message you want to avoid, it may strengthen your own views by providing additional support for them. But be careful to counterargue well: Weak counterarguments can actually boomerang and increase our susceptibility to persuasion (Rucker & Petty, 2004).

All of these tactics take effort; it is much easier to simply sit there, passively absorbing the messages sent your way. But if you do, you will definitely be at risk for having your views changed by people who are trained experts at this task. So be active and *resist!* You are already quite good at doing so, and with a little more effort—and practice—you can become what people in marketing most fear: a thinking, resistant audience!

Prejudice: Distorted Views of the Social World . . . and Their Effects

Terrorist attacks and huge military reprisals; mass murder of one ethnic group by another; seemingly perpetual suspicion and enmity between persons of different religious persuasions . . . the list of atrocities stemming from racial, ethnic, or religious hatred seems endless. Such actions often stem from **prejudice**—powerful negative attitudes toward the members of specific social groups based solely on their membership in that group (Dovidio & Gaertner, 1986; Zanna & Olson, 1994). Where do such attitudes come from? And what can be done to reduce their impact? These are the issues we'll now examine. But first, it's important to note that prejudice does not always spill over into overt, negative actions—*discrimination*. As is true with all attitudes, prejudice finds expression in overt actions only when there are no powerful forces blocking them. Antidiscrimination laws, fear of social disapproval—these and other factors often prevent prejudiced individuals from acting on their views. Their negative attitudes remain, however, and will lead to overt discriminatory practices when such persons believe they can get away with such behavior.

■ The Origins of Prejudice: Contrasting Perspectives

Many different explanations for the origins of prejudice exist, but of these, four have been especially influential.

Direct Intergroup Conflict: Competition as a Source of Bias   It is sad but true that many of the things we value most—a good job, a nice home, high status—are in short supply; there's never enough to go around. This fact serves as the basis for one view of prejudice—**realistic conflict theory** (Bobo, 1983). According to this view, prejudice stems from competition between social groups over valued commodities or opportunities. The theory further suggests that as such competition persists, the members of the groups involved come to view each other in increasingly negative ways (White, 1977). They label members of the other group as enemies, view their own group as superior, and draw the boundaries between themselves and their opponents ever more firmly. As a result, what starts out as economic competition gradually turns into full-scale prejudice, with the hatred and anger this usually implies. Of course, competition between groups does not always produce such effects, but it *does* produce them in enough cases that this factor can be viewed as one important cause of prejudice.

Social Categorization: The Us-versus-Them Effect and the Ultimate: Attribution Error   A second perspective on the origins of prejudice begins with a basic fact: Individuals generally divide the social world into two distinct categories—*us* and *them* (Turner et al., 1987). They view other persons as belonging either to their own social group, usually termed the *in-group,* or to another group, an *out-group.* Such distinctions are made on the basis of many dimensions, including race, religion, sex, age, ethnic background, occupation, and even the town or neighborhood in which people live.

If this process of **social categorization**—the division of the world into distinct social categories—stopped there, it would have little connection to prejudice. Unfortunately, it does not. Sharply contrasting feelings and beliefs are usually attached to members of one's in-group and to members of various out-groups. Persons in the "us" category are viewed in favorable terms, whereas those in the "them" category are perceived negatively. Out-group members are assumed to possess more undesirable traits, are seen as being more alike (homogeneous) than members of the in-group, and are often disliked (e.g., Lambert, 1995; Linville & Fisher, 1993). This is often a very basic distinction; around the world, the word used by many different cultures to refer to themselves translates, roughly, as "human beings," whereas the word used for other groups translates as "non-human." The in-group–out-group distinction also affects *attribution*—explanations for their behaviors. We tend to attribute desirable behaviors by members of our in-group to stable, internal causes, such as their admirable traits, but to attribute desirable behaviors by members of out-groups to temporary factors or to external ones, such as luck (e.g., Hewstone, Bond, & Wan, 1983). This tendency

Prejudice
Negative attitudes toward the members of some social group based on their membership in this group.

Realistic Conflict Theory
A theory proposing that prejudice stems, at least in part, from direct conflict between social groups.

Social Categorization
The tendency to divide the social world into two distinct categories—"us" and "them."

to make more favorable attributions about members of one's own group than about members of other groups is sometimes described as the *ultimate attribution error,* for it carries the self-serving bias we described earlier into the area of intergroup relations—with potentially devastating effects.

The Role of Social Learning   A third perspective on the origins of prejudice begins with the obvious fact that such attitudes are *learned:* We acquire them from the people around us through the process of *social learning.* Prejudice emerges out of countless experiences in which children hear or observe their parents, friends, teachers, and others expressing prejudiced views. Because children want to be like these persons, and are often rewarded for expressing the "right" views (those held by adults), they quickly adopt such attitudes themselves (see Figure 13.9).

While persons with whom children interact play a key role in this process, the mass media, too, are important. If television, films, and other media present members of various social groups in an unflattering light, this may contribute to the development of prejudice on the part of children. And, in fact, this is how African Americans, Native Americans, persons of Hispanic descent, and many other minority groups were presented on films and on television in the United States in past decades. Fortunately, this situation has changed greatly in recent years (e.g., Weigel, Kim, & Frost, 1995); currently, members of these groups are being shown in a much more favorable manner. So, at least one important source of prejudiced attitudes seems to be decreasing.

FIGURE 13.9
Social Learning as a Basis for Prejudice
Parents and other adults often reward children for expressing the "right" attitudes—the ones they (the adults) hold. Prejudice is often transmitted to youngsters in this manner.

Cognitive Sources of Prejudice: The Role of Stereotypes   The final source of prejudice we'll consider is in some ways the most disturbing. It involves the possibility that prejudice stems at least in part from basic aspects of social cognition (e.g., Kunda & Oleson, 1995). While several processes seem to play a role in this regard, perhaps the most important of these involves **stereotypes.** These are cognitive frameworks consisting of knowledge and beliefs about specific social groups—frameworks suggesting that, by and large, all members of these groups possess certain traits, at least to a degree (Judd, Ryan, & Park, 1991). Like other cognitive frameworks (schemas), stereotypes exert strong effects on the ways in which we process social information. For instance, information relevant to a particular stereotype is processed more quickly than information unrelated to it (e.g., Dovidio, Evans, & Tyler, 1986). Similarly, stereotypes lead us to pay attention to specific types of information—usually information consistent with the stereotypes. And when information inconsistent with stereotypes does manage to enter consciousness, it may be actively refuted or simply denied (O'Sullivan & Durso, 1984). In fact, recent findings indicate that when individuals encounter persons who behave in ways contrary to stereotypes, they often perceive them as a new "subtype" rather than as an exception to their existing stereotype (Kunda & Oleson, 1995).

What is the relevance of such effects to prejudice? Together, they tend to make stereotypes somewhat self-confirming. Once an individual has acquired a stereotype about some social group, she or he tends to notice information that fits into this cognitive framework and to remember "facts" that are consistent with it more readily than "facts" inconsistent with it. As a result, the stereotype strengthens with time and may ultimately become invulnerable—new information or experiences simply can't change it.

Stereotypes
Cognitive frameworks suggesting that all members of specific social groups share certain characteristics.

Challenging Prejudice: Techniques That Can Help

Whatever the precise roots of prejudice, there can be no doubt that it is a negative, brutalizing force in human affairs. Reducing prejudice and countering its effects, therefore, are important tasks. What steps can be taken to reach these goals? Here is what the findings of careful research indicate.

Breaking the Cycle of Prejudice: Learning Not to Hate   Bigots are clearly made, not born: they acquire their prejudices as a result of experience. Given this fact, one useful way to reduce prejudice involves discouraging the transmission of bigoted views while encouraging more positive attitudes toward others. But how can we induce parents, teachers, and other adults to encourage unbiased views among children in their care? One possibility involves calling the attention of such persons to their own prejudiced views. Few want to see themselves as prejudiced. Instead, they view *their* negative attitudes toward others as justified. A key initial step, therefore, is convincing caregivers that the problem exists. Once they realize that it does, many are willing to modify their words and actions.

Another argument that can be used to shift parents and other caregivers in the direction of teaching children tolerance lies in the fact that prejudice harms not only those who are its victims, but also those who hold such views (Dovidio & Garetner, 1993). Growing evidence suggests that persons who are prejudiced live in a world filled with needless fears, anxieties, and anger. As a result, they experience needless emotional turmoil that can adversely affect their health (Jussim, 1991). Because most parents and teachers want to do everything possible to further children's well-being, calling these potential costs to their attention may help persuade them to transmit tolerance rather than prejudice.

Direct Intergroup Contact: The Potential Benefits of Acquaintance   At the present time many cities in the United States resemble a social donut: A disintegrating and crime-ridden core inhabited primarily by minority groups is surrounded by a ring of relatively affluent suburbs inhabited mainly by whites and a sprinkling of wealthy minority group members. Needless to say, contact between the people living in these areas is minimal.

This state of affairs raises an intriguing question: Can prejudice be reduced by somehow increasing the degree of contact between different groups? The idea that it can is known as the **contact hypothesis,** and there are several good reasons for predicting that such a strategy might prove effective (Pettigrew, 1981, 1997). First, increased contact between persons from different groups can lead to a growing recognition of similarities between them. As we will see in a later section, perceived similarity can generate enhanced mutual attraction. Second, although stereotypes are resistant to change, they *can* be altered when sufficient information inconsistent with them is encountered, or when individuals meet a sufficient number of "exceptions" to their stereotypes (Kunda & Oleson, 1995). Third, increased contact may help counter the illusion that all members of the stereotyped group are alike. For these and other reasons, it seems possible that direct intergroup contact may be one effective means of combating prejudice. Is it? Existing evidence suggests that it is, but only when certain conditions are met: The groups must be roughly equal in social status, the contact between them must involve cooperation and interdependence, the contact must permit them to get to know one another as individuals, norms favoring group equality must exist, and the persons involved must view one another as typical of their respective groups.

When contact between initially hostile groups occurs under these conditions, prejudice between them does seem to decrease (e.g., Aronson, Bridgeman, & Geffner, 1978; Schwarzwald, Amir, & Crain, 1992). One context in which such conditions exist is in colleges and universities, which bring together students from many different groups into a setting where all are equal in status: They are all students! Such experiences, we believe, will go a long way toward building a truly

Contact Hypothesis
The view that prejudice can be reduced by increasing the degree of contact between different groups.

multicultural society in the United States—and in any other country where the population is becoming increasingly diverse.

Recategorization: Resetting the Boundary between "Us" and "Them"　　Suppose that a team from your college played against a team from a rival college: Which would be "us" and which would be "them"? The answer is obvious: Your own school's team would constitute your in-group, while the other school's team would be the out-group. But now imagine that the team from the other school had won many games and was chosen to represent your state in a national tournament. When it played against a team from another state, would you now perceive it as "us" or "them"? Probably, you would shift your view; now, you would perceive this former "enemy" team as part of your own in-group. Situations like this suggest that the boundary between "us" and "them" is not fixed. On the contrary, it can be shifted to include—or exclude—various groups of people. This fact suggests another technique for reducing prejudice—**recategorization** (e.g., Gaertner et al., 1989, 1990). This involves somehow inducing individuals to shift the boundary between "us" and "them" so that it now includes groups they previously viewed as "them." The result: Their prejudice toward these persons is reduced.

Evidence for such effects has been obtained in several studies (e.g., Galinsky & Ku, 2004; Dovidio et al., 1995). For example, in one, Gaertner and his colleagues (Gaertner et al., 1993), investigated the attitudes of students at a multicultural high school in the United States. Students came from many different backgrounds— African American, Chinese, Hispanic, Japanese, Korean, Vietnamese, and Caucasian. More than 1,300 students completed a survey designed to measure their perceptions of the extent to which the student body at the school was a single group, consisted of distinct groups, or was composed of separate individuals. Results indicated that the greater the extent to which the students felt that they belonged to a single group, the more positive were their feelings toward persons in social groups other than their own. These findings and related findings (e.g., Gaertner et al., 1990) suggest that recategorization may be a very useful technique for reducing many forms of prejudice.

▪ The Effects of Prejudice: Always Negative?

Before concluding, we should comment on one additional issue: Are the effects of prejudice always negative? Although it is tempting to answer "Of course!" this may not be entirely accurate. Yes, prejudice is almost always harmful to both the persons who hold such views and its victims. But there are special circumstances under which it can be at least somewhat helpful, especially to persons toward whom it is directed. Imagine, for instance, a situation in which you applied for a job but were turned down. If this were a job you really wanted and for which you felt qualified, the effects on your self-esteem might be shattering. But now, assume that later you learned that you were rejected because of prejudice: The interviewer holds negative views toward the group to which you belong (whatever that happens to be). Would this be helpful to you in dealing with this situation? A growing body of evidence suggests that it might. Although you would probably be angry over this unfair rejection, it would at least give you an external cause for your disappointment: It wasn't any lack of talent or qualifications that cost you the job—it was the ugly face of prejudice.

A clear illustration of such effects is provided by research conducted by Major, Kaiser, and McCoy (2003). They asked male and female students to imagine that they were denied admission to a course they needed. In one condition, the students learned that they had been rejected because the professor was sexist and did not want to admit students of a particular gender. In a second condition, students learned that they were rejected because the professor was a jerk and was simply denying entry to everyone. Finally, in a third condition, students learned that they were rejected because the professor felt they were unqualified. After receiving this information, participants in all three groups indicated the extent to which they

Recategorization
A technique for reducing prejudice that involves inducing individuals to shift the boundary between "us" and "them" so that it now includes groups they previously viewed as "them."

FIGURE 13.10
"It's Not My Fault":
When Prejudice Can
Exert Beneficial Effects
Students told that they had been rejected from a course because the professor was prejudiced against members of their gender showed less self-blame and were less de-pressed than students who were told that they were rejected because the professor felt that were unqualified. In such situations, prejudice can pro-vide its victims with a means of at-tributing negative outcomes to external causes.

Source: Based on data from Major, Kaiser, & McCoy, 2003.

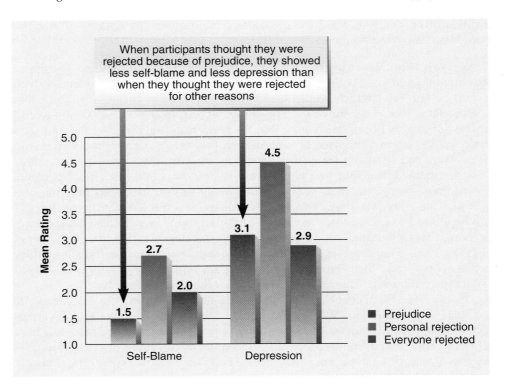

When participants thought they were rejected because of prejudice, they showed less self-blame and less depression than when they thought they were rejected for other reasons

would blame themselves for being rejected, and a measure of their emotional state (how depressed, angry, and anxious they felt). As you can see from Figure 13.10, results indicated that the students led to believe they were rejected because of prej-udice blamed themselves less and reported feeling less depressed than those who felt they were rejected because of a lack of qualifications. Those rejected because the professor was a jerk were in between.

Findings like these have been reported in other studies, and they suggest that although the effects of prejudice are indeed overwhelmingly negative, there are a few situations in which being the victim of such views can offer at least a crumb of comfort. But, in general, prejudice is an evil force we should all resist as vigorously and passionately as possible.

KEY QUESTIONS

• What are some of the major causes of prejudice?
• What techniques are effective in reducing prejudice?
• Does prejudice always produce negative effects?

Social Influence: Changing Others' Behavior

As we saw earlier, persuasion involves efforts by others to change our attitudes, and such attempts are a common part of everyday life. But persuasion is only one aspect of a much broader process known as **social influence**—attempts by one or more persons to change our behavior in some manner. Many different tactics are used for this purpose, but among these, two are deserving of special attention be-cause they can, when used effectively, be so powerful: *conformity, compliance,* and *obedience.*

Conformity: To Get Along, Often, We Must Go Along

Have you ever been in a situation in which you felt that you stuck out like a sore thumb? If so, you know how unpleasant the experience can be. In these circum-

Social Influence
Attempts by one or more persons to change our behav-ior in some manner.

stances, we encounter powerful pressures to act or think like those around us. Such pressures toward **conformity**—toward thinking or acting like most other persons—stem from the fact that in many contexts there are spoken or unspoken rules indicating how we *should* behave. These rules are known as **social norms,** and they often exert powerful effects on our behavior (Cialdini, Kallgren, & Reno, 1991; Reno, Cialdini, & Kallgren, 1993).

Why is this the case? Apparently, for two important reasons. First, because we have a strong desire to be liked by others. Experience teaches us that one way of reaching this goal is to appear to be as similar to others as possible (we'll return to this fact in our discussion of interpersonal attraction). So, one reason we often conform is because doing so can help us win the approval and acceptance of others. Social psychologists refer to this as *normative social influence*—we conform in order to meet others' expectations, and so gain their approval. A second reason we conform is our strong desire to be right—to hold the "right' views, dress in the "right" style, and so on. Because we want to be correct about these matters, we turn to other persons for guidance as to what's appropriate, and this leads us to conform to existing social norms. This is known as *informational social influence*—we conform because we depend on others for information about many aspects of the social world. Together, these two factors can be so strong that we will accept the views of others as more accurate than information brought to us by our own senses! This was first illustrated in classic studies by Solomon Asch (1951, 1955).

In his research, Asch asked participants to respond to a series of simple perceptual problems—judging which of two lines matched a standard line in length. Several other persons (usually six to eight) were present along with the real subject during the session, but unknown to the subject, all were assistants of the experimenter. On certain occasions, known as *critical trials* (twelve out of the eighteen problems), the accomplices offered answers that were clearly wrong: They unanimously chose the wrong line as a match for the standard line. Moreover, they stated their answers *before* the real participants responded. Thus, on these critical trials, the persons in Asch's study faced a dilemma: Should they go along with the other individuals or stick to their own judgments? The results were clear: A large majority of the persons in Asch's research chose conformity. Across several different studies, fully 76 percent of those tested went along with the group's false answers at least once; overall, they voiced agreement with these errors 37 percent of the time. In contrast, only 5 percent of the participants in a control group, who responded to the same problems alone, made such errors. This kind of effect has been demonstrated in dozens of other studies (e.g., Bond & Smith, 1996). There can be little doubt that our desire to go along with the group is a powerful form of social influence.

Compliance: To Ask—Sometimes—Is to Receive

Suppose that you wanted someone to do something for you; how would you go about getting him to do it? If you think about this question for a moment, you'll soon realize that you probably have quite a few tricks up your sleeve for getting the other person to say yes—for gaining what social psychologists term **compliance.** Careful study of these tactics by social psychologists, however, suggests that most of these rest on a small number of basic principles. These principles, and some of the strategies for gaining compliance related to them, are described below.

Tactics Based on Commitment or Consistency: The Foot in the Door   Several means for getting others to say yes to our requests are based on the principle of obtaining an initial small commitment from them. Once this is obtained, they often find it harder to refuse later requests. For instance, salespersons, fund-raisers, and other experts in gaining compliance often start with a trivial request and then, when this is accepted, move on to a larger request—the one they really wanted all along. This is known as the **foot-in-the-door technique,** and the chances are good that you have encountered it or used it yourself. Research findings indicate that it

Conformity
Experienced pressures toward thinking or acting like most other persons.

Social Norms
Rules indicating how we should behave (or are expected to behave) in a given situation.

Compliance
A form of social influence in which one or more persons attempt to influence one or more others through direct requests.

Foot-in-the-Door Technique
A technique for gaining compliance in which requesters start with a small request and then, after this is granted, shift to a much larger request.

works (e.g., Beaman et al., 1983), and that one reason it does is that people want to be consistent. Once they have said yes to the first request, they feel it is inconsistent to say no to the second.

A related procedure is known as the *low-ball* technique and involves asking someone to do something under conditions that are very favorable to them. Then, once they agree, the "deal" is changed so as to make it less desirable. Car salespersons often use this tactic: They offer a great price on a car, but then, when the customer accepts, they indicate that the sales manager has refused to approve the deal and that they must raise the price. If people were totally rational, they would refuse and walk away. In fact, though, they often agree to the changes, thus giving the person with whom they are dealing precisely what that individual wanted all along (Cialdini et al., 1978). Recent findings indicate that this tactic works only when people have publicly accepted the initial, favorable offer; if, instead, the "deal" is changed before they have done this, the low-ball procedure does not increase compliance. This suggests that initial commitment is indeed the central principle behind this technique (Burger & Cornelius, 2003.)

Tactics Based on Reciprocity: The Door in the Face   Reciprocity is a basic rule of social life: We tend to treat other people as they have treated us. Several tactics for gaining compliance are based on this fact. One of these, known as the **door-in-the-face technique,** is the opposite of the foot-in-the-door technique just described. Instead of beginning with a small request and then escalating to a larger one, this tactic starts with a very large request that is rejected. After it is refused, a much smaller request is made—the one the requester wanted all along. The target person then feels a subtle pressure to reciprocate by saying yes. After all, the requester made a concession by scaling down the first request. This technique is often successful, and its success seems to rest largely on the principle of reciprocity (Cialdini, 1994).

Tactics Based on Scarcity: Playing Hard to Get   In general, the harder something is to obtain, the greater the value it is perceived to have. This basic fact serves as the underlying principle for several tactics for gaining compliance. Perhaps the most popular of these is **playing hard to get**—a tactic in which individuals try to create the image that they are very popular or very much in demand. This puts pressure on would-be romantic partners and would-be employers to say yes to requests from the person using this tactic. The requests can range from "Let's get engaged" to "Pay me a high salary," but the underlying principle is the same: The persons on the receiving end feel that if they don't agree, they may lose a valuable partner or employee—so they say yes (e.g., Williams et al., 1993.)

Another Tactic for Obtaining Compliance: Ingratiation   Before concluding we should briefly mention one additional technique that is widely used for gaining compliance, **ingratiation**—somehow getting others to like you before making your request. For instance, like the character in Figure 13.11, we often use flattery for this purpose. But simply noting that we are similar to another person in trivial ways (e.g., have the same birthday) can work, too (Burger et al., 2004). We'll return to this and related techniques in a discussion of *impression management* (see p. 455). But here we want to note that ingratiation is indeed often effective, and is a very common technique for getting others to agree to our requests.

Obedience: Social Influence by Demand

Now we come to what is perhaps the most direct way in which one person can attempt to change the behavior of another: through *direct orders*—simply telling the target person what to do. This approach is less common than either conformity pressure or compliance tactics, but it is far from rare; it occurs in many situations in which one person has clear authority over another—in the military, in sports, and in business, to name a few. **Obedience** to the commands of sources of authority is far from surprising; military officers, coaches, and bosses have powerful means for

Door-in-the-Face Technique

A technique for gaining compliance in which a large request is followed by a smaller one.

Playing Hard to Get

A tactic for gaining compliance in which individuals try to create the image that they are very popular or very much in demand.

Ingratiation

A technique of social influence based on inducing increased liking in the target persons before influence is attempted.

Obedience

A form of social influence in which one or more others behave in specific ways in response to direct orders from someone.

FIGURE 13.11

Ingratiation: A Useful Technique for Gaining Compliance

One useful technique for gaining compliance from others is somehow getting them to like us before making a request. The character in this cartoon is very well aware of this fact!

Source: Reprinted with permission of King Features Syndicates.

enforcing their commands. More surprising, though, is the fact that even persons lacking in such authority can sometimes induce high levels of obedience in others. Unsettling evidence for such effects was first reported by Stanley Milgram in a series of famous—and controversial—experiments (Milgram, 1963, 1974).

In order to find out whether individuals would obey commands from a relatively powerless stranger, Milgram designed ingenious procedures in which participants were seated in front of the device shown in Figure 13.12. They were told that each time another person (actually an assistant of the researcher) made an error on a learning task, they were to deliver an electric shock to him. Moreover, they were to raise the shock level for each error so that if he made many errors, they would soon be delivering powerful—and painful!—jolts of electricity to the learner (remember: This person was really an assistant who never received any electric shocks). Would they obey these commands—and thus show obedience? If they refused, they were ordered to do so by the experimenter in increasingly severe terms. Because participants were volunteers and were paid in advance, you might predict that most would quickly refuse such "orders." In fact, though, *fully 65 percent were completely obedient,* continuing through the entire series to the final 450-volt shock.

Not surprisingly, many participants protested and expressed concern over the learner's welfare. When ordered to proceed, however, most yielded to the experimenter's social influence and continued to obey. In fact, they did so even when the victim pounded on the wall and, later, stopped responding altogether, as if he had passed out! Why did the participants in Milgram's research (and in several related studies) show such high levels of obedience? Several factors seem to play a role. First, the experimenter took participants off the hook by explaining that he, not they, would be responsible for the learner's well-being. So, just as in many real-life situations in which soldiers or police commit atrocities, participants could say, "I was only following orders" (e.g., Hans, 1992; Kelman & Hamilton, 1989). Second, the experimenter possessed clear signs of authority, and in most societies, individuals learn that persons holding authority are to be obeyed (Bushman, 1984, 1988).

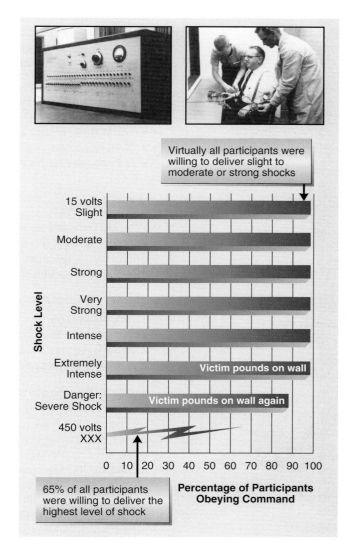

FIGURE 13.12

Milgram's Research on Obedience

The photo on the left shows the equipment used by Milgram in his famous studies. The photo on the right shows the experimenter and a participant (*rear*) attaching electrodes to the learner's (accomplice's) wrists. Results, as shown in the graph, indicated that fully 65 percent of all participants were fully obedient to the experimenter's commands—they advanced to the highest shock level (supposedly 450 volts!).

Source: Based on OBEDIENCE TO AUTHORITY: An Experimental View by Stanley Milgram. Harper & Row Publishers © 1974. Reprinted by permission.

Finally, the experimenter's commands were gradual in nature. He didn't request that participants jump to the 450-volt shock immediately; rather he moved toward this request one step at a time. This is similar to many real-life situations in which police or military personnel are initially ordered merely to arrest or question future victims. Only later are they ordered to beat, torture, or even kill them.

In sum, several factors probably contributed to the high levels of obedience observed in Milgram's research and related studies. Together, these factors produced a powerful force—one that most persons found difficult to resist. This does not imply that the commands of authority figures cannot be defied, however. In fact, history is filled with cases in which brave persons resisted the commands—and power—of entrenched dictators and governments and, in the end, triumphed over them. The United States, of course, began with an act of rebellion against the British government, and recent events in the former Soviet Union and throughout Eastern Europe provide clear illustrations of the fact that even powerful regimes can be resisted. So although obedience is a powerful force, it can be resisted—and often is!

KEY QUESTIONS

- What is conformity, and what role do social norms play in it?
- What are some of the basic principles on which tactics of compliance are based?
- What is obedience? Why does it occur?

Attraction and Love

Why do people like or dislike each other? And why, among the countless people we meet during our lives, do we have especially intense positive feelings toward only a few—the ones with whom we fall in love? Let's see what social psychologists have discovered about these important and intriguing questions.

Interpersonal Attraction: Why We Like or Dislike Others

Think of someone you like very much, someone you strongly dislike, and someone you'd place in the middle of this dimension. Now, ask yourself this question: *Why* do you have these reactions? Revealing answers are provided by research on the nature and causes of **interpersonal attraction.**

Propinquity: Nearness Makes the Heart Grow Fonder   Many friendships and romances start when individuals are brought into contact with one another, often by chance. We tend to form relationships with people who sit nearby in class, live in our dorm or in our neighborhood, or work in the same office. So, *propinquity—* proximity or physical closeness to others—is an important factor in interpersonal attraction. In one sense, this *must* be true, because we simply can't form relationships with people we never meet. But there seems to be more to the effects of propinquity than this. Many studies indicate that the more frequently we are exposed to a given stimulus, the more—in general—we tend to like it. This is known as the **frequency-of-exposure effect,** and it seems to extend to people as well as to objects (e.g., Moreland & Beach, 1992; Zajonc, 1968). The more often we encounter other people, the more we tend to like them—assuming that everything else is equal. Why? Because the more frequently we encounter a stimulus, the more familiar it becomes, and therefore the more comfortable or pleasant we feel in its presence. For this reason, propinquity is one important basis for interpersonal attraction.

Similarity: Liking Others Who Are Like Ourselves   You've probably heard both of the following proverbs: "Birds of a feather flock together" and "Opposites attract." Which is true? Existing evidence leaves little room for doubt: Similarity wins hands down (e.g., Alicke & Largo, 1995; Byrne, 1971, 1992). Moreover, this is so

Interpersonal Attraction
The extent to which we like or dislike other persons.

Frequency-of-Exposure Effect
The more frequently we are exposed to a given stimulus, the more—in general—we tend to like it.

whether such similarity relates to attitudes and beliefs, to personality traits, to personal habits such as drinking and smoking, to sexual preferences, or even to whether people are morning or evening persons (Joiner, 1994).

Why do we like others who are similar to ourselves? The most plausible explanation is that such persons provide validation for our views or our personal characteristics (Goethals, 1986). If they agree with us, or are similar to us in their behavior, this indicates that our views, preferences, and actions are correct—or at least that they are shared by other persons. This makes us feel good, and our liking for the other person increases. Whatever the precise mechanisms involved, similarity is certainly one powerful determinant of attraction.

Affective States: Positive Feelings as a Basis for Attraction   Suppose that you meet a stranger just after receiving some really good news: You got an A on an exam when you expected only a C. Will you like this person more than if you met her for the first time after receiving bad news that put you in a negative mood? Common sense suggests that this may be so, and research findings confirm this view (e.g., Byrne & Smeaton, 1998). Positive feelings or moods—whatever their source—cause us to like others we meet while experiencing them, negative moods—again, whatever their source—cause us to dislike others we meet at these times. What do we mean by the phrase "whatever their source"? Simply this: If positive feelings are produced by something another person says, we will tend to like them. *But even if our positive feelings have nothing to do with this person,* we may still experience a boost in our liking for them. In short, *anything* that induces positive affect may lead us to like another person who happens to be present when we are experiencing such feelings. As you might guess, such effects are most likely to occur when we are neutral to the person to start with and when we know little about her (e.g., Ottati & Isbell, 1996). Even so, these effects are both strong and general enough to be viewed as one important factor in interpersonal attraction.

Physical Attractiveness: Beauty May Be Only Skin Deep, but We Pay Lots of Attention to Skin   Perhaps the most obvious factor affecting interpersonal attraction is *physical beauty*. Research findings indicate that despite warnings that "Beauty is only skin deep," we are strongly influenced by it (e.g., Sprecher & Duck, 1994). Moreover, this is true for both women and men, in many different cultures, and across the entire lifespan (Langlois et al., 2000). Indeed, even one-year-old infants show a preference for attractive rather than unattractive strangers (Langlois, Roggman, & Riesser-Danner, 1990.) Why is this the case? One reason is that physically attractive people make us feel good—and as we just saw, this can be one important ingredient in liking (Kenrick et al., 1993). Another, suggested by evolutionary psychology (e.g., Buss, 1999), is that physical attractiveness is associated with good health and good reproductive capacity; choosing attractive mates, therefore, is one strategy for increasing our chances of contributing our genes to the next generation.

Whatever the causes, we do tend to like physically attractive persons more than physically unattractive ones. Moreover, such effects occur across the entire lifespan (Singh, 1993). But what, precisely, makes other persons physically attractive? Clearly, this varies from culture to culture but—surprisingly—less than you might guess. People tend to agree on what is or is not attractive even when judging other persons who differ from themselves in terms of race or ethnic background (Cunningham et al., 1995). So, what is it about some faces that makes them so attractive? One surprising possibility is suggested by research in which many faces are "averaged" by computers to produce composite faces (e.g., Langlois & Roggman, 1990; Lemley, 2000). Results indicate that the greater the number of faces that are combined in this manner, the higher the attractiveness of the composites produced by the computer (see Figure 13.13 on page 454).

2-FACE COMPOSITE

4-FACE COMPOSITE

8-FACE COMPOSITE

16-FACE COMPOSITE

32-FACE COMPOSITE

FIGURE 13.13

Are Attractive Faces "Average"?

When computer images of faces are combined to form a composite, this average face is rated as more attractive than the individual faces. Moreover, as the number of faces contributing to the average rises, so does the attractiveness of the composite face.

Source: Photos courtesy of Dr. Judith H. Langlois, Charles and Sarah Seay Regents Professor, Dept. of Psychology, University of Texas, Austin. Used with permission.

Why is this so? Perhaps because "average" faces produced in this manner are closer to our schemas of each gender. In other words, we have mental frameworks for faces—one for women and another for men—and composite faces are closer to these than the individual faces. A related explanation is that the composite faces are more symmetrical than the individual faces and that we prefer symmetry because it is an indicator of health and reproductive capacity (e.g., Mealey, Bridgstock, & Townsend, 1999). These are only two possibilities, and other aspects of faces, too, may be important. For instance, some evidence indicates that men find female faces that are either "cute" (childlike features with large, widely spaced eyes and a small nose and chin) or "mature" (prominent cheekbones, high eyebrows, large pupils, a big smile) attractive. Similarly, women seem to find two types of male faces attractive—ones that show a big, square jaw and a heavy brow; and ones that show a more youthful or "feminine" look—slender nose, small chin—although the second type is liked by more women than the first (Angier, 1998). Interestingly, more recent findings indicate that women find highly masculine faces more attractive when the women are in the middle of their menstrual cycle (and the chances of conception are

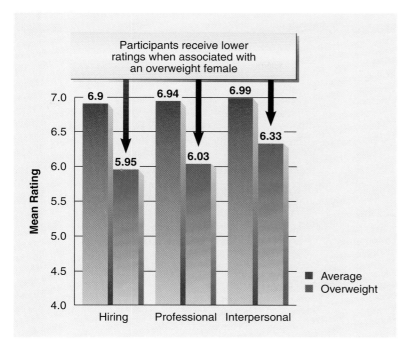

FIGURE 13.14
Guilt by Association?
When male job applicants were seated next to an overweight woman, they were down-rated by research participants relative to the ratings they received when seated next to a woman of normal weight. These findings indicate that merely being linked with someone whose physique does not match current standards of attractiveness can be costly.

Source: Based on data from Hebl & Mannix, 2003.

high) than when they are in other phases of their cycle (Penton-Voak & Perrett, 2000). Indeed, women can distinguish more quickly between male and female faces at times when their chances of conceiving a child are high than when they are low (Macrae et al., 2002).

Judgments of attractiveness do not depend solely on facial features, however, They are also influenced by other aspects of people's appearance. For example, there is currently a strong bias against being overweight in many Western cultures; in view of this fact, it's not surprising that *physique* is another important determinant of attraction, at least among young people. Persons whose physique matches the popular model—currently, slim but muscular—tend to receive higher evaluations than persons who depart from this model (e.g., Ryckman et al., 1995). In fact, recent findings indicate that merely being associated with someone whose physique does not match this model—they are obese—can be costly. For instance, Hebl and Mannix (2003) asked research participants to play the role of an employer who was deciding among several male job applicants. They received information about the applicants, along with a photo that showed this person sitting next to a woman who was either overweight or of normal weight. Finally, they evaluated the applicants with respect to their qualifications, their likability, and whether they should be hired. As shown in Figure 13.14, the applicants were down-rated on all three dimensions when they were merely seated next to an obese woman. Follow-up research indicated that this was true regardless of whether the woman was described as the applicant's girlfriend or had no connection to him whatsoever.

Being attractive is definitely a "plus" in many situations. But it is certainly not the only factor that causes others to form a favorable first impression of us. What are these factors and how can you use them to make good first impressions on interviewers—or anyone else? For some useful advice, please see the **Psychology Goes to Work** section that follows.

Love: The Most Intense Form of Attraction

Have you ever been in love? If asked, most people (at least in Western cultures) will answer yes. What do they mean by this statement? In other words, what is love,

PSYCHOLOGY GOES TO WORK

How to Make a Good First Impression in Job Interviews

Everyone wants to make a good first impression, so we try to do our best in this respect when we meet other persons for the first time (see Figure 13.15). Social psychologists refer to these efforts as *impression management* (or *self-presentation*) and have identified a number of factors that are highly effective in producing favorable first impressions. Good first impressions are useful in many contexts but are especially important in job interviews; each applicant often gets only a few minutes to convince the interviewer the she or he is the right person for the job. What can you do to "shine" in this important context? Here is what the results of careful research on impression management suggest:

- **Flattery will (often) get you everywhere.** As we saw in our discussion of ingratiation, flattering others—making statements that praise them, their company, or their accomplishments—can be very useful, as long as you don't overdo it. If your praise is *too* excessive, the interviewer won't buy it, and it may work against you.
- **Be prepared.** Learn about the company for which you are interviewing and the nature of the job for which you are applying. Then, let the interviewer know that you have, in fact, done your homework. Nothing creates a negative impression faster than being completely clueless about a company or a specific job.
- **Look your best.** Mae West, a comic star of the 1930s, once remarked, "Look your best; who said love is blind?" As we have seen, personal appearance *does* matter, so do everything you can to enhance your appearance when you have an interview. Again, don't overdo it: For instance, don't apply a "killer" dose of perfume, don't wear too much makeup, and don't overdress. Being neat and well-groomed, however, will indicate to the interviewer that you take the interview seriously, and this will usually count in your favor.
- **Emphasize your strengths.** No one is good at everything, so if you claim to be perfect or nearly perfect in everything, the interviewer will *not* be impressed. But if you emphasize the things you do best, your experience, and *specific examples* of how you used these skills and talents, you will be on the way to generating a positive first impression.
- **Agree with the interviewer as much as possible.** No one likes to be contradicted, and, as noted earlier, similarity is a major cause of liking between persons. So, if you disagree with the interviewer, bite your tongue and do not call attention to this fact. Focus instead on agreeing with this person as much as possible. This, too, will help to boost the first impression you make.
- **Be realistic.** If you get to the point of discussing salary and other benefits with the interviewer, be sure to be realistic. Although it is good to be confident and to expect all that you deserve, asking for more than the going rate can be a big mistake. It may suggest to the interviewer that you have an overinflated view of yourself. But if instead your requests are reasonable ones, the interviewer will perceive you as someone who is in touch with reality, and this, too, will boost her or his first impression of you.

If you keep these points in mind, you will start off on the right foot in many job interviews, and that is usually an important first step toward getting the job you want.

FIGURE 13.15

Making a Good First Impression: How Not to Do It!
Everyone wants to make a good first impression on others, but as suggested by this cartoon, some people are much better at this task than others!

Source: ZIGGY © 1989 ZIGGY AND FRIENDS, INC. Reprinted with permission of UNIVERSAL PRESS SYNDICATE. All rights reserved.

and how do we know that we are experiencing it? These questions have been pondered by countless poets, philosophers, and ordinary human beings for thousands of years, but it is only recently that love has become the subject of systematic research by psychologists (e.g., Hendrick & Hendrick, 1993). Let's take a look at the answers that have emerged from this work.

Romantic Love: Its Nature   We should begin by noting that in this discussion, we are focusing on **romantic love**—a form of love involving feelings of strong attraction and sexual desire toward another person. However, there are several other kinds of love, too, such as the love of parents for their children or the kind of love one can observe in couples who reach their fiftieth wedding anniversary (known as **companionate love**). While these kinds of love are not the focus of as many television programs or films as passionate love, they, too, are recognized by psychologists as being very important (e.g., Meyers & Berscheid, 1997; Sternberg, 1988).

So what, precisely, does romantic love involve? One widely accepted view of love, Sternberg's *triangular theory of love* (Sternberg, 1988), suggests that love involves three major components: *intimacy*—the closeness two people feel for each other and the strength of the bond that holds them together; *passion*—the physical attraction and sexual feelings between them; and *decision/commitment*—a cognitive component that includes such factors as the decision that one is in love with another person and wishes to maintain the relationship. It is on the basis of these components that individuals conclude "I'm in love" or "I'm not in love." When all three components are strong, the result is *consummate love*—the kind almost everyone seeks.

Love: Is It the Same around the World?   Earlier we noted that the idea of romantic love does not exist in all cultures. In fact, different cultures have contrasting ideas about the nature of love and the factors important in maintaining it. A recent study by Sprecher and Toro-Morn (2002) suggests that cultural factors may be more important than gender in shaping ideas about love. For instance, the ideas of American men about love are more similar to the ideas of American women than they are to the ideas about love held by Chinese men; the same is true for women—their ideas about love are more similar to those held by the men in their own culture than to the ideas of love held by women in another culture. For instance, Chinese men and women are more likely than American men and women to believe that love is predestined (Goodwin & Findlay, 1997), while American men and women are more likely to view love in idealistic rather than practical terms. Interestingly, contrasting cultural beliefs and values concerning love can be readily seen in the "Personals" ads; for instance, personals ads in Indian and Chinese newspapers stress values of family and society, while those in American newspapers emphasize individual traits or characteristics (Parekh & Bersein, 2001). So, clearly, cultural factors play an important role in ideas and beliefs about love, if not in the emotional side of love itself.

Love: Why It Sometimes Dies   ". . . And they lived happily ever after." This is the way many fairy tales—and movies from the 1940s and 1950s—end, with the characters riding off into a glowing, love-filled future. If only life could match these high hopes! Some romantic relationships do blossom into lifelong commitment (see Figure 13.16 on page 458); my own parents (Ruth and Bernard Baron) have been married for more than sixty-two years. But for many couples, the glow of love fades and leaves behind empty relationships from which one or both partners soon seek escape. What causes such outcomes? Research on love and on *close relationships* suggests that many factors are at work.

We have already considered one of these in our discussion of the importance of similarity in attraction. When partners discover that they are *dissimilar* in important ways, love can be weakened or even die. Such differences are often overlooked when the flames of passion run high but become increasingly obvious when

Romantic Love
A form of love in which feelings of strong attraction and sexual desire toward another person are dominant.

Companionate Love
A form of love involving a high degree of commitment and deep concern with the well-being of the beloved.

FIGURE 13.16
When Love Survives . . .
Some couples remain together—and happy—for many decades.
They suggest that the ideal of a lifelong love is *not* impossible to attain.

these begin to subside. Also, as time passes, dissimilarities that weren't present initially may begin emerge: The partners change and perhaps diverge. This, too, can weaken their love.

Another, and potentially serious problem, is simple *boredom.* Over time, the unchanging routines of living together may lead people to feel that they are in a rut and are missing out on the excitement of life—and perhaps new romantic partners (Fincham & Bradbury, 1993). Such reactions can have important consequences for the relationship.

Third, *jealousy* can occur and undermine loving relationships. Interestingly, although both sexes experience jealousy, they differ in the pattern of such reactions. For women, the most intense jealousy is aroused by signs that a partner is transferring his emotional commitment to another woman. For men, the most intense jealousy is triggered by evidence (or suspicions) that a partner has been sexually unfaithful (Buunk, 1995).

Finally, as relationships continue, patterns of behavior that can only be described as *self-defeating* sometimes emerge. Dating couples and newlyweds frequently express positive evaluations and feelings to one another. As time passes, however, these supportive statements are sometimes replaced by negative ones. "You're so inconsiderate!" "I should never have married you!" These kinds of feelings, either stated overtly or merely implied, become increasingly frequent. The result is that couples who once frequently praised each other shift to criticizing one another in the harshest terms imaginable (Miller, 1991). When these pattern develop, love doesn't simply die: It is murdered by sarcastic, hurtful remarks.

Despite such factors, many relationships *do* succeed. Such couples actively *work* at maintaining and strengthening their relationships: They practice the art of compromise, express positive feelings and sentiments toward their partners, and take their wishes and preferences into account on a daily basis. True, this is a lot of effort; but given the rewards of maintaining a long-term intimate relationship with someone we love and who loves us, it would appear to be well worthwhile.

K E Y   Q U E S T I O N S

• What factors influence interpersonal attraction?
• Under what conditions do people conclude that they are in love?
• What factors cause love to fade and perhaps disappear?

SUMMARY AND REVIEW OF KEY QUESTIONS

Social Thought: Thinking about Other People

- **What is the correspondence bias?**
  The correspondence bias is our tendency to overestimate the importance of internal causes of others' behavior.

- **What is the self-serving bias?**
  The self-serving bias is the tendency to attribute positive outcomes we experience to internal causes and negative outcomes to external causes.

- **How do we deal with social information that is inconsistent with our expectations?**
  In general, we tend to pay greater attention to such information than to information that is consistent with our expectations, but also tend to reject it.

- **What is the optimistic bias for task completion?**
  This is the tendency to predict that we can do more in a given amount of time than we actually can.

- **What is counterfactual thinking? How can it affect our affective states and performance?**
  Counterfactual thinking involves imagining "what might have been." If we imagine better outcomes than occurred, this can lead to negative affect; if we imagine worse outcomes, this can lead to positive affect. Counterfactual thinking can provide insights into why negative outcomes occurred and so enhance our future performance.

- **What are attitudes?**
  Attitudes are lasting evaluations of various aspects of the social world—evaluations that are stored in memory.

- **What factors were found to influence persuasion in early research?**
  Early research on persuasion found that the success of persuasion was strongly affected by characteristics of the sources (e.g., their expertise), characteristics of the persuasive messages sent (e.g., whether they were one-sided or two-sided), and characteristics of the audience.

- **What are heuristic and systematic processing, and what role do they play in attitude change?**
  Heuristic and systematic processing are two different modes of thought with respect to persuasive messages. In heuristic processing we use simple rules of thumb for processing information, whereas in systematic processing we consider message content carefully and fully.

- **What is the ELM model, and how does it explain persuasion?**
  The ELM model is a cognitive model of persuasion that focuses on the thoughts people have about a persuasive communication.

- **What is cognitive dissonance, and how can it be reduced?**
  Cognitive dissonance is an unpleasant state we experience when we notice that two attitudes we hold or our attitudes and our behavior are somehow inconsistent. It can be reduced by changing our attitudes or behavior, by seeking information that supports our views or actions, and through trivialization.

- **What is induced compliance? The less-leads-to-more effect?**
  Induced compliance occurs in situations in which we feel compelled to say or do something inconsistent with our true attitudes. The less-leads-to-more effect refers to the fact that the weaker the reasons we have for engaging in attitude-discrepant behavior, the more likely are we to change these attitudes.

- **How can hypocrisy be used to change behavior?**
  Inducing individuals to focus on gaps between their behavior and their attitudes can lead them to recognize their hypocrisy and so experience intense levels of dissonance. Such dissonance, in turn, can cause them to change their overt behavior.

Social Behavior: Interacting with Others

- **What are some of the major causes of prejudice?**
  Prejudice stems from direction competition between social groups, social categorization, social learning, and cognitive factors such as stereotypes.

- **What techniques are effective in reducing prejudice?**
  Prejudice can be reduced by socializing children to be tolerant of others, through increased intergroup contact, and through recategorization—shifting the boundary between "us" and "them" so as to include previously excluded groups.

- **Does prejudice always produce negative effects?**
  Although the effects of prejudice are overwhelmingly negative, there are a few situations in which it can be beneficial to its victims—especially in situations in which they can attribute negative outcomes to prejudice rather than to personal shortcomings.

- **What is conformity, and what role do social norms play in it?**
  Conformity is the tendency to "go along with the group" by accepting prevailing social norms—rules indicating how we should or ought to behave.

- **What are some of the basic principles on which tactics of compliance are based?**
  Tactics of compliance are based on the principles of liking of friendship (e.g., ingratiation), commitment or consistency (e.g., the foot-in-the-door technique), reciprocity (e.g., the door-in-the-face technique), and scarcity (e.g., playing hard to get.)

- **What is obedience? Why does it occur?**
  In obedience, individuals follow the commands of persons in authority. Obedience occurs because, often, the persons demanding it take responsibility for any harm produced and make their requests in a gradual manner.

- **What factors influence interpersonal attraction?**
  Among the factors that influence interpersonal attraction are propinquity, similarity, positive and negative affect, and physical attractiveness.

- **Under what conditions do people conclude that they are in love?**
  Individuals conclude that they are in love when their culture has the concept of romantic love and when

they experience strong emotional arousal in the presence of a person defined as appropriate for love by their culture.

- **What factors cause love to fade and perhaps disappear?**
  Love can be weakened by such factors as jealousy, increased dissimilarity, boredom, increasing levels of negative affect, and a pattern in which negative statements and attributions replace positive ones.

PSYCHOLOGY: UNDERSTANDING ITS FINDINGS

When Do *You* Experience Dissonance?

Dissonance, we have suggested, is a part of everyday life: Each time we must say or do something that is not consistent with our own attitudes, we may experience unpleasant gaps between our attitudes and our actions. How often do *you* experience dissonance? And what happens when you do? To find out, complete the following exercise.

1. Keep a diary, and for a week list instances in which you notice a gap between your attitudes and your behavior—inconsistencies between what you believe and what you say or do.

2. Now, examine these incidents. Can you see any common themes? For instance, how often did you say or do something inconsistent with your true attitudes to
   a. avoid hurting someone's feelings
   b. avoid problems in dealing with another person
   c. get what you wanted from someone

3. What happened when you engaged in attitude-discrepant behavior? Did your own attitudes change? Or did you reduce dissonance in some other way?

MAKING PSYCHOLOGY PART OF YOUR LIFE

Overcoming the Planning Fallacy

The planning fallacy is a very common form of error in our social thought. It leads us to conclude that we can complete a job more quickly than is actually the case, or that we can do more in a specific period of time than we can. How often do *you* fall prey to this error? And how can you protect yourself against it? To find out, complete the following steps.

1. Think back over recent projects on which you have worked (term papers, household chores, etc.). For each, jot down (a) when you expected to get it done and (b) when you actually did. Compare the two entries for each item; this will give you insight into your own tendency to fall prey to the planning fallacy.

2. Now, to reduce this tendency, do the following:
   a. Each time you are about to begin a project, think about similar projects you have performed in the past.
   b. How long did they take?
   c. Is this project larger or smaller in scope than these past ones?

3. Now, on the basis of this information, estimate how long it will take you to complete *this* project. If you remind yourself over and over again about how long similar projects took in the past, you are likely to greatly reduce the chances that you will experience the planning fallacy, because this tendency to ignore past experience is one of the major reasons why it occurs in the first place!

KEY TERMS

Attitudes, p. 437
Attribution, p. 433
Central Route (to persuasion), p. 438
Cognitive Dissonance, p. 439
Companionate Love, p. 457
Compliance, p. 449
Conformity, p. 449
Consensus, p. 433
Consistency, p. 433
Contact Hypothesis, p. 446
Correspondence Bias (also known as *fundamental attribution error*), p. 433
Counterfactual Thinking, p. 436
Distinctiveness, p. 433

Door-in-the-Face Technique, p. 450
Elaboration-Likelihood Model (ELM), p. 438
Foot-in-the-Door Technique, p. 449
Frequency of Exposure Effect, p. 452
Heuristic Processing, p. 438
Heuristic–Systematic Model, p. 438
Induced (Forced) Compliance, p. 439
Ingratiation, p. 450
Interpersonal Attraction, p. 452
Less-Leads-to-More Effect, p. 439
Nonverbal Cues, p. 431
Obedience, p. 450
Peripheral Route (to persuasion), p. 438

Persuasion, p. 437
Playing Hard to Get, p. 450
Prejudice, p. 444
Realistic Conflict Theory, p. 444
Recategorization, p. 447
Romantic Love, p. 457
Self-Serving Bias, p. 433
Social Categorization, p. 444
Social Influence, p. 448
Social Norms, p. 449
Social Psychology, p. 430
Stereotypes, p. 445
Systematic Processing, p. 438

Industrial/Organizational Psychology: Understanding Human Behavior at Work

W*hen I was interviewing for my first academic position, I (Rebecca Henry) along with some of my friends in the same graduate program were fortunate enough to have several job offers. Not surprisingly, we spent a fair bit of time during this stressful process discussing our various experiences on job interviews and sharing our anxieties as we waited to hear whether we had been "chosen." Sadly, one of my friends seemed to have more trouble than most getting even one job offer. One day—a day when he was certainly at his lowest—he shared his frustrations with me, concluding finally (with a fair bit of anger and resignation in his voice), "It's obvious why you are getting so many offers. You're a woman!" I don't actually recall my initial reaction (Did I hit him? I was probably tempted!), but in the hours and days that followed, I tried to evaluate the validity of his claim. Could he be right? Why had I received these various job offers? Objectively, I knew that I had published more research and had received higher teaching evaluations than he had. However, I had to admit that these differences in our*

qualifications were not large. I also knew that my other male friends had ex-
perienced little trouble finding good jobs. Still, his words gnawed at me for
some time as I continued to wonder whether these universities wanted me
solely for my qualifications or at least, in part, because of my sex.

We begin by describing this event because it conveys the two major themes of this chapter. First, it is often difficult to understand why various organizational decisions are made. Why does one person get hired or promoted over another? Why do organizations often assign projects to teams? The preceding vignette conveys the uncertainty job candidates often experience as they wonder about the rationale for various hiring decisions. The incident described also captures a second theme relevant to this chapter: The complexity of human cognition and behavior as it relates to work. Our goal for this chapter is to address both of these themes as they relate to the application of psychological principles to human behavior at work.

By providing you with a look at organizations behind the scenes, you will be better able to understand how psychological principles play a role in the development of effective human resource practices. For example, those of you who have held jobs may have wondered why you went through a particular type of training or were evaluated in a particular manner. Coupled with these *why* questions is the natural tendency for most employees to wonder whether various practices could be made more effective. Could the training have been done in a more effective manner? Was the best person promoted? Much of the information in this chapter will help you to understand the rationale for these practices as well as to critique how some practices you may observe could be improved.

The topics in the second half of the chapter, beginning with the topic of work motivation, will examine work-relevant cognitions and behavior. For example, one fundamental issue is the connection between how employees feel about their jobs and how they behave. Are the most satisfied workers the most productive? What causes employees to steal from work or to sabotage equipment? We conclude the chapter by examining how employees interact with one another, specifically the processes of leadership and teamwork. Questions that will be addressed in these sections include "What makes some leaders more effective than others?" and "What are the best ways of encouraging teamwork?" The information presented in these sections will help you understand your own behavior as well as the behavior of others at work. More importantly, it will also help you in the future, whether you decide to run your own company or work in an established organization.

Taken together, the topics covered in this chapter represent the field of **Industrial/Organizational (I/O) Psychology,** the study of human cognition and behavior at work. The mission of psychologists in this field is to improve employee well-being and organizational effectiveness through research and practice. These dual missions, one focused on employees and one focused on the organization, have not always co-existed amicably, but they need not represent an either/or choice, as you will see later in this chapter.

You have already read about some of the applications of I/O psychology from the various **Psychology Goes to Work** sections presented earlier in this book (see Chapters 4, 6, 11, and 13). In essence, this entire chapter could be viewed as **Psychology Goes to Work;** hence we have no special features with this heading. You will also see several references to earlier material in this chapter. This is done so that you can see how I/O psychology fits in with, and adds to, the field of psychology as a whole. We hope that this will also have the added benefit of helping you tie various topics together, something that is useful for the conclusion of any course.

Industrial/Organizational (I/O) Psychology
The study of human cognition and behavior at work.

We now begin with a look behind the scenes at employee selection, the first contact a prospective employee has with a particular organization. We then move on to what most new employees experience soon after being hired: training and performance appraisal. These three topics will focus a great deal on "how to" techniques that have evolved out of the application of basic psychological research and principles. We then turn to the major topic of work motivation, concluding with an examination of social behavior at work in the form of leadership and teams. As Figure 14.1 illustrates, all of these topics have the dual mission of enhancing organizational effectiveness and employee well-being, although organizations may emphasize the former over the latter.

KEY QUESTIONS

- What is I/O psychology?
- What is the dual mission of psychologists in this field?

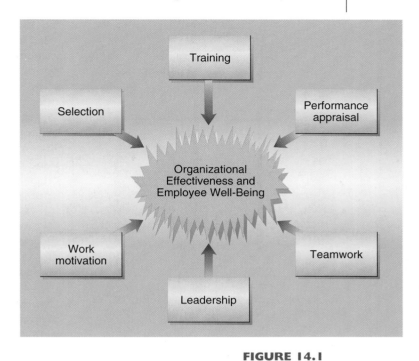

FIGURE 14.1
The Dual Mission of I/O Psychology
While organizations may be more concerned with practices that enhance organizational effectiveness, both effectiveness and employee well-being are of equal concern to the field of I/O.

SELECTION: HIRING THE BEST PERSON FOR THE JOB

Most of us have a pretty good sense of what it is like to apply for a job. You may have gone through the process of answering classified ads and interviewing, or you might have observed some version of this among family and friends. My (Rebecca Henry's) first experience with this consisted of interviewing for a position at an ice cream stand when I was in high school. The interview consisted of only one or two questions (e.g., "Are you in marching band?"). The owner called me a few days later to tell me when I should show up for training. (For the record, being in band was viewed negatively because it made one unavailable many evenings.) This certainly was not a stellar example of a systematic, rigorous selection process, but it does highlight the general objectives of such a process. This process, in its most basic form, consists of two sequential questions that organizations must address: (1) What information should we obtain from each job applicant? (2) How should the information be obtained? In this section we focus on what organizations do behind the scenes in order to address these two questions. As with subsequent sections of this chapter, we describe the "ideal" process, allowing you then to compare this process with what you might have experienced yourself.

Job Analysis: Assessing the Requirements for the Job

Long before the first job applicant is interviewed for a particular job, a systematic assessment of the job should be completed (Brannick & Levine, 2002). This systematic assessment, referred to as a **job analysis,** is done in order to assess the tasks, duties, and responsibilities of a job. It probably seems obvious to you that it is important to know something about a job before deciding how to hire someone to do it. What may be less obvious is that this process of job analysis often requires hours of work by human resource professionals in order to have a clear and comprehensive understanding of the job in question. For example, one of my psychology graduate students spent an entire summer conducting a job analysis for just one position in a large insurance company!

Job Analysis
An assessment of the tasks, duties, and responsibilities of a particular job.

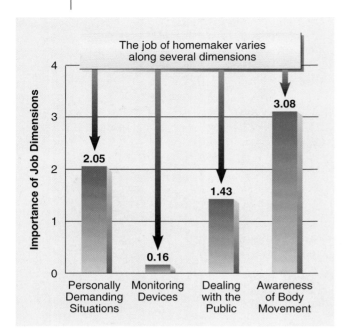

FIGURE 14.2
Job Analysis Can Reveal Surprising Results
As this study indicates, the job of homemaker varies along a number of dimensions. This profile is also similar to the profiles for airport maintenance chief and patrol officer.
Source: Adapted from Arvey & Begalla, 1975.

Position Analysis Questionnaire (PAQ)
A specific job analysis technique that analyzes jobs along thirty-two distinct dimensions.

KSAs
Abbreviation for the knowledge, skills, and abilities needed to perform a particular job.

Criterion-Related Validity
The strength of the relationship between scores on a particular selection test and success on the job.

But why should it take so much time to understand what a job entails? Can't the people in human resources just talk to a few employees who currently do the job? If you are thinking this, you are certainly on the right track. However, the key to a systematic job analysis is to gather information from many sources in an objective manner. The data that emerge are then statistically analyzed in order to create an overall summary or profile of the job. In general, this type of approach will increase the likelihood of getting accurate information, something that is crucial for the design of both selection and performance appraisal systems.

As you can imagine, analyzing jobs in this way may take a fair bit of time, but it can often reveal subtleties of the job that were not apparent. Examine Figure 14.2, for an example of this. The researchers who conducted this study wanted to demonstrate that job analyses can often reveal surprising results, even for the most familiar jobs (Arvey & Begalla, 1975). To do this, these researchers analyzed the job of "homemaker" and then compared it with a database of 1,000 other jobs in order to determine which jobs were most similar to it. Using a well-established job analysis instrument, called the **Position Analysis Questionnaire (PAQ)** (McCormick, Jeanneret, & Meacham, 1969), thirty-two job dimensions were examined in order to create a composite profile of the job of homemaker. Data were collected on dimensions that assessed such things as "engaging in personally demanding situations" and "awareness of body movement and balance." Figure 14.2 shows how four of these thirty-two dimensions varied in their importance for the job of homemaker. A comparison of the homemaker profile to the other 1,000 jobs resulted in some surprising results, with the jobs of "patrolman" and "airport maintenance chief" being two of the most similar to the job of homemaker. The point of the comparison is that neither of these jobs would appear to emphasize many of the same job dimensions, yet a thorough job analysis identified many similarities.

Developing Selection Techniques: Validity, Utility, and Fairness

After the completion of a thorough job analysis, we are close to answering the first question necessary for the design of a good selection system: "What information should we obtain from each job applicant?" However, job analysis information only serves as a *guide* for determining the knowledge, skills, and abilities (**KSAs**) that are necessary to perform a job. Before any selection instrument is used, whether it is a paper-and-pencil test, an interview, or some other type of instrument, it must be evaluated along three dimensions: validity, utility, and fairness. You already you have some familiarity with validity from reading about it in the context of research methodology (Chapter 1) and intelligence testing (Chapter 7). Utility and fairness are also probably terms with which you are familiar in other contexts but perhaps not in the context of employment testing. After we have described these three concepts, we will spend a little time discussing specific types of selection instruments.

In the context of employee selection, organizations are most concerned with one type of validity, **criterion-related validity,** because it refers to the strength of the relationship between scores on a particular selection test and success on the job (the criterion). Because criterion-related validity represents the strength of the relationship between two variables, it is typically assessed using correlation coefficients. As you learned in Chapter 1, correlation coefficients range from –1.00 to +1.00, and the absolute value of the correlation tells you how strong the relationship is between the two variables. In the context of employee selection, an employer might have purchased a standardized test of mechanical ability from a professional test development firm. In the promotional materials for the test, it is described as having a criterion-related validity of +.40 when used to hire mechanics. In isolation it is difficult to assess whether this degree of validity is sufficient, so generally employers examine several options with the intention of selecting the test or other instrument with highest criterion-related validity. In general, the stronger the criterion-related validity of a test (the absolute value of the correlation), the better the test will be at identifying the most qualified job applicants.

Once we are confident that we have one or more selection instruments with a sufficient degree of criterion-related validity, the instruments are then evaluated with regard to their **utility** (Boudreau, 1991). The utility of a selection instrument refers to its usefulness, taking both the criterion-related validity and the cost of the testing procedure into account. For example, two selection procedures might have comparable degrees of criterion-related validity, but one might be more expensive to administer; thus, one would have less utility than the other. Utility is primarily an economic concept, but it takes psychological test information into account in order to be calculated.

The **fairness** of a selection system is also important. By fairness, we are referring both to the legality of the selection system (i.e., whether it is consistent with current employment law) as well as its perceived fairness to job applicants. Let's consider the legal issues first. Most of you are probably somewhat familiar with various state and federal laws that protect people in various contexts (e.g., employment, education). These laws prohibit discrimination on the basis of certain protected classes, such as sex, race, and religion. What is often not stated, but which is also part of the law, is an "unless" provision that, in the context of employee selection, allows for the use of selection instruments that show "job-relatedness" and have "business necessity." In other words, the law prohibits discrimination, but an organization can use selection instruments as long as it has evidence that these instruments help them hire the best people. If this sounds like what is accomplished through the careful validation of a selection instrument, you are correct. If fact, I/O psychologists who work in the area of employment testing have been very influential over the years as the U.S. Supreme Court and the lower courts have wrestled with these issues.

Beyond *fairness* as legally defined, why should organizations care about the *perceived* fairness of a selection system? How fair a selection system seems is important because it can influence the first impressions organizations make on prospective employees (Ryan & Sackett, 1987; Truxillo et al., 2002). In Chapter 13 you learned about the importance of first impressions in the context of person perception. The principle is really no different in the context of a job applicant forming an impression of an organization. For example, if an organization appears to be using seemingly irrelevant selection techniques to screen job applicants, it will convey a bad first impression, leading many to wonder if their other practices (e.g., compensation, promotion) are just as bad. As a result, some of the most promising job applicants may look elsewhere.

We now turn to a discussion of several specific types of selection tests. As you read this section, please keep in mind that the issues of validity, utility, and fairness apply to all of these techniques, even those that may not seem like "tests."

KEY QUESTIONS

- What is job analysis?
- What is criterion-related validity?
- What does the term *utility* refer to in the context of selection?
- How is the fairness of a selection system determined?

Utility
The usefulness of a selection technique that takes both the criterion-related validity and the cost of the procedure into account.

Fairness
The legality of the selection system (i.e., whether it is consistent with current employment law) as well as its perceived fairness to job applicants.

Assessing Job Applicants: Interviews, Tests, and More

The question of how to obtain information about each job applicant leads us to a virtual buffet of options; you are certainly familiar with some of these (e.g., interviews), but others may be new to you (e.g., assessment centers, work samples). Some selection techniques, such as standardized tests, can be purchased by organizations from companies that develop tests. Others must be constructed in-house by I/O psychologists and other human resource professionals within an organization. Another option for companies is to hire a consulting firm to custom-make a selection system to suit their needs. (Go to www.ddi.com to visit the Website of one of these large consulting firms.)

The most common type of selection instrument is the employment interview. In Chapter 13, you read about some techniques you can use as a job applicant to do well in an interview (see **Psychology Goes to Work** on page 456). Now let's examine it from the organization's point of view. Organizations are interested in designing interviews with a high degree of criterion-related validity, just as they would for any other selection test. Years of research indicate that interviews can have high criterion-related validity, but only if they are carefully structured (Campion, Pursell, & Brown, 1988). There are several elements that contribute to a **structured interview,** but it can be best understood by thinking of an interview as one would any other type of test. As an exercise, think about how you would feel if you learned not only that your classmates were given a different test than you, but that the material was not equivalent, it was scored by different instructors, and some students were given more time than others. This not only would seem unfair, but also would certainly make you doubt the validity of the grades given to each student.

In their unstructured form, employment interviews are not unlike this sort of testing situation. However, if care is taken to select questions based on a job analysis and if the same questions are asked in the same manner across job applicants, interviews can be a very useful tool for gathering some types of information. The use of structured interviews can also minimize the biases that often influence one person's perception of another, such as physical attractiveness and stereotypes (e.g., Baron, 1983; Ellis et al., 2002). Unfortunately, in practice, interviews are often little more than casual conversations used to determine vaguely whether a job applicant is a good fit with the organization. In these contexts it is not uncommon for the interview to have negligible validity and to contribute to discrimination (Arvey & Campion, 1982).

Standardized tests are another category of selection technique, used most often as a means of screening large pools of applicants in the early stages of a multistep selection program. These paper-and-pencil tests are not unlike the standardized ability and personality tests you learned about in earlier chapters on cognition and personality (Chapters 7 and 10). Like these tests, they are carefully constructed so that they are both reliable and valid. What differs is that tests used for selection have been validated for this specific purpose, so there is abundant evidence of their criterion-related validity across specific jobs. For example, there are several general tests of cognitive ability that are commonly used to screen job applicants. Research shows that these tests are predictive of success in a wide variety of jobs (Schmidt & Hunter, 1977), although they are seldom used as the sole method for selecting employees. Several specialized personality tests are also used by hundreds of organizations to screen applicants. For example, research indicates that traits such as extraversion and conscientiousness have been found to be predictive of success in several types of jobs (Barrick & Mount, 1991; Sackett & Wanek, 1996). Certain personality tests have also been useful in the screening of less desirable employees, such as those who might be more likely to steal (Hogan, 1991). If you are curious about what you should do if asked to take an employment test such as this, see the **Psychology Lends a Hand** section that follows.

Structured Interview
An employment interview that is conducted in the same manner, using the same questions for all job applicants.

Standardized Tests
Reliable and valid tests that are used for a particular purpose and are administered in a systematic way.

p s y c h o l o g y   l e n d s   a   h a n d

Taking, Not Faking, Employment Tests

Taking tests of any kind can be a little nerve-wracking, even if you have studied. But when it comes to certain types of employment tests, especially those that focus on personality rather than ability, you really can't study for them. Added to this is the pressure of really wanting the job. Like it or not, tests such as these are now being used by most Fortune 1,000 Companies and many smaller companies to screen applicants for jobs from retail clerk to executive (Wessel, 2003). Even the federal government uses these tests to screen applicants. Given this trend, it is likely that many of you will soon run into one of these tests when applying for a job. What is the best approach? Here are a few things for you to remember if you ever find yourself in this situation.

- **Be honest.** While this may sound like advice that helps your potential employer more than it helps you, that is not the case. By responding honestly, you are less likely to be identified as someone who is faking answers.
- **Be consistent.** Many tests have similar questions dispersed throughout. This is done for statistical reasons rather than to trick

you. Responding consistently shows that you are reading the questions carefully and giving honest responses.

- **Be wary.** If you generally get a bad feeling about a job because of a test or other assessment procedure, ask yourself whether this is really the type of company you want to work for. Sometimes tests are used inappropriately, so if your gut tells you that this is a symptom of a larger problem, you may want to consider working elsewhere.
- **Be relaxed.** This is easier said than done and may sound like a contradiction to the last suggestion. Just remember that most tests like this are only used to screen out a few "bad apples." It is very unlikely that you would not get hired simply because of your responses to one test.

By following these suggestions you will not only be better informed about employment testing, you will more likely be hired for the type of job that suits your preferences best.

One of the most innovative selection techniques, used first to select spies during World War II, is called an **assessment center** (Lance et al., 2004). The assessment center method consists of a wide variety of tests and activities administered to a small group of job applicants over a few days. As this description indicates, it can be an intense experience for job applicants. It is also a very costly method, so it is often used as the last stage of hiring for upper-level managerial positions for which the cost of a bad hire can be substantial. During the assessment, job applicants are typically observed doing a number of exercises, such as working in a team or prioritizing hypothetical work activities (see Figure 14.3 on page 470). Trained assessors observe each applicant, taking careful note of specific behaviors exhibited. These behavioral exercises are often supplemented with interviews and standardized tests. At the end, the assessors combine the scores from each test and exercise, computing an overall rating that is used to make the final selection decision. Because of the time and effort involved in assessment centers, consulting firms are often hired by organizations interested in using this method.

The last type of selection technique we will describe is called a **work sample test.** As the name indicates, a work sample test requires job applicants to perform a sample of the work they would be expected to do on the job. For example, a work sample for a clerical position might consist of a test in which various software packages are used to create documents. Job applicants would be scored under time constraints to assess technical proficiency. Like any other test, the key is to standardize the administration and scoring and to evaluate the work sample test's criterion-related validity before using it.

Work samples can be thought of as a type of audition, similar to those you may have experienced to become part of a choir, band, or theatrical production. Although work samples can be time consuming to design and implement, they have the advantage of giving job applicants a realistic preview of the job, something that

Assessment Center
A selection technique that consists of a wide variety of tests and activities administered to a small group of job applicants over a few days.

Work Sample Test
A selection test that requires job applicants to perform a sample of the work they would be expected to do on the job.

FIGURE 14.3
Assessment Center Exercise
Job applicants who participate in assessment centers can expect to do a wide variety of group exercises to assess their interpersonal skills, such as the leaderless group discussion shown here.

can help job applicants determine whether the job would suit them. On the other hand, work samples are not practical if the organization expects to train new employees how to do most aspects of the job. In these cases, job applicants would not be expected to have all of the necessary job-relevant skills when they are hired.

KEY QUESTIONS

- What is a structured interview?
- What is an assessment center?
- What is a work sample test?

TRAINING: HELPING EMPLOYEES ACQUIRE RELEVANT SKILLS

Regardless of qualifications, most new employees go through some form of training soon after being hired. Training is also common among experienced workers at various times in their career. In fact, most jobs have changed drastically over the past several years, making training and retraining an ongoing endeavor in many occupations, such as medicine and engineering. In this section we examine the procedures organizations use for the design and evaluation of training programs. As with employee selection, a great deal typically happens behind the scenes before any training has commenced.

Needs Analysis
The first step in a training program, consisting of a systematic collection of data to address the question "Who needs to learn what?"

Program Development: Assessing Who Needs to Be Trained and How

The first step in the design of any training program is to conduct a **needs analysis.** As the name suggests, this analysis consists of a systematic collection of data to address the question "Who needs to learn what?" A needs analysis is conducted at three different levels, beginning with an *organizational analysis.* An organizational analysis takes into account the projected costs and benefits of training various groups of employees. This type of analysis helps executives evaluate the costs and benefits of training those in one department versus another. Once this determination has been made, a *task analysis* is done in order to identify the KSAs needed to perform the job. This task analysis is really equivalent to a job analysis, which you read about earlier in this chapter, and therefore may not need to be redone if a thorough job analysis has recently been completed. Lastly, a *person analysis* is done in order to assess the current KSAs of those who will receive the training. In recent years, particular attention is being given to the distinct training needs of different groups (e.g., older and younger employees), with the goal of giving every employee the assistance needed to succeed on the job (Riggio, 2000). Cumulatively, the information gathered from a needs analysis provides the necessary foundation for assessing specifically what training needs to be done.

The next part of the process is to design the training method or technique that will be used. Research on this topic has been guided extensively by basic psychological principles in the area of human learning and cognition, so you are already familiar with many of the basic principles that have guided the design of organizational training techniques. However, rather than cover familiar ground, we highlight a few specific applications of human learning principles in the context of employee training.

Training methods are roughly categorized as those that occur either on-site or off-site. By far the most common on-site method is **on-the-job training** in which an inexperienced employee learns the ropes in the actual work context during company hours. Under appropriate circumstances, this can be a highly effective training method, as it allows the new employee to engage in observational learning and to practice newly acquired skills. (For a review of observational learning principles, please see Chapter 5, Learning.

On-the-job training often provides immediate positive and negative feedback, an important part of observational learning, so that the new employee can learn from the consequences of doing it right or wrong. Employees are usually highly motivated to learn, as they are able to see the consequences of their actions. Even now, years later, I remember the negative consequences I received from one of the first milkshakes I ever made. The customer returned to the window and demonstrated to me (and everyone else) how lumpy it was by spooning it out onto the counter. That was very clear feedback indeed! Never again did I let my mind wander as I used the milkshake mixer.

Despite these advantages of on-the-job training, there are some potential disadvantages. For example, new employees may learn the wrong things from the wrong employees if care is not taken to pair new hires with the most highly skilled and motivated employees. For this reason, it is essential that on-the-job training be carefully planned beforehand in order to assure that observational learning from the best employees occurs. Another option is to consider a training method called **vestibule training,** in which a separate "practice" work area is used for the trainees. This method allows for observational learning while reducing some of the negative consequences that might occur as the result of employee goofs, such as lumpy milkshakes.

Off-site training methods tend to be much more varied than on-site methods because they are not constrained by the work context. Many of these methods are similar in form to educational techniques that resemble the standard classroom instruction that any student knows all too well. These methods are not very flashy but may be the best means for conveying certain types of job-relevant knowledge. For example, attorneys might learn about new laws and regulations by attending a seminar. Another off-site method is **programmed instruction,** a technique that allows trainees to go through instructional materials at their own pace, testing themselves before proceeding to subsequent modules.

On-the-Job Training
Training in which an inexperienced employee learns the ropes in the actual work context during company hours.

Vestibule Training
An on-site training method that uses a separate "practice" work area, allowing for observational learning.

Programmed Instruction
An off-site training method that allows trainees to go through instructional materials at their own pace, testing themselves before proceeding to subsequent modules.

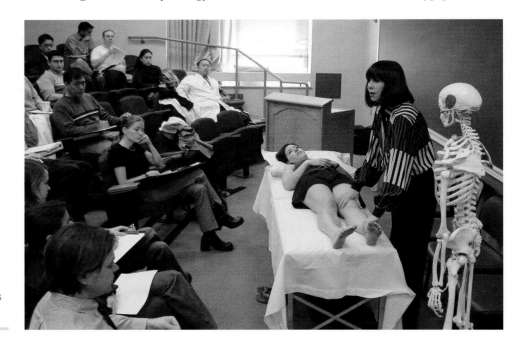

FIGURE 14.4
Using Role Playing to Train
One highly effective training technique is for trainees to simulate an interpersonal exchange, taking turns playing both roles.

Behavioral Modeling
A training technique that applies principles of observational learning.

Reaction Criteria
A measure of training effectiveness that examines how employees feel about the training experience.

Learning Criteria
A measure of training effectiveness that examines the degree of learning that occurred as a result of training.

Behavioral Criteria
A measure of training effectiveness that examines the degree of behavior change on the job.

Observational learning techniques are also the basis of one type of off-site training method, referred to as **behavioral modeling**. One of the most common applications of behavioral modeling is used in managerial training programs. With behavioral modeling techniques, principles of observational learning are applied so that managerial trainees can practice and learn interpersonal skills such as how to resolve conflicts or negotiate with others (Salas & Cannon-Bowers, 2001). Behavioral modeling has also been very successful in training people to use specific types of computer software (Gist, Schwoerer, & Rosen, 1989). One common exercise, common in behavioral modeling, is role-playing, in which trainees take turns playing both of the roles in an interpersonal exchange, such as doctor and patient or employee and customer (see Figure 14.4). An added benefit to role playing is that it can help trainees empathize with the nontraditional point of view, such as that of patient or customer.

Evaluating Training Effectiveness: More Than Just Learning

Once training is completed, how do we tell whether it has been successful? This issue is particularly of interest to organizations that may be comparing two or more training approaches, one more labor intensive and expensive than the other. For example, one study conducted at Kodak contrasted the effectiveness of two different approaches for training managers how to plan (Brettz & Thompsett, 1992). The first method was simply a lecture-based training method that allowed trainees to take notes and ask questions. The contrasting training method consisted of the same factual material, but it was presented very differently in order to make it more interesting. The trainers really went all out, incorporating games and skits. Classical music played in the background with the hope that it would reduce some of the stress of learning. After the training, the two groups of trainees responded to a questionnaire regarding their reactions to the training and then took a test to assess what they had learned. As you can see from Figure 14.5, the more elaborate training created very positive reactions. Trainees enjoyed the games and music, and they also believed they had learned more. However, the test of how much was learned revealed no significant differences in learning. Given that the more elaborate training was much more expensive, it is easy to understand why it was not recommended.

This example highlights the importance of measuring several things in order to assess training effectiveness. Fortunately, research on training evaluation is specific with regard to the criteria that should be used (Kirkpatrick, 1959). The preceding example examined only two categories of training effectiveness criteria—**reaction criteria** and **learning criteria.** Two additional criteria, behavioral criteria and results criteria, cannot be assessed until the trainees are back at work. **Behavioral criteria** focus on what employees actually do on the job after the training. For example, equipment operators who have undergone safety training may have learned precisely how to use the equipment to prevent accidents, passing a test with flying colors that assesses their knowledge of safety procedures. However, they may have little motivation to follow these safe procedures. Why? It could simply be that the safety procedures take a little more effort (e.g., methodically checking various gauges or putting on safety glasses). This example highlights the problem of **transfer of training,** the problem of demonstrating on the job what has been learned during training. This problem of "transfer" is one that has occupied researchers in I/O psychology just as it has the field of education for decades (De Corte, 2003).

The last of the training criteria to be assessed is the **results criterion.** This criterion addresses the question of what actually occurs as a final outcome, or result of the training. With the preceding safety example, this might be observed by a reduction in accidents. In a different context, such as training customer service representatives, the results criterion might be a reduction in customer complaints. Results criteria can also take the form of economic indices, such as increases in output or reduction in waste of raw materials.

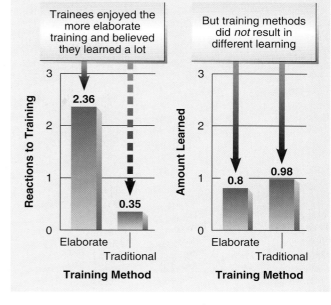

FIGURE 14.5
Comparison of Training Methods
Organizations commonly compare two or more training methods in order to determine which is more effective. This study shows that employee reactions to the training differed markedly, but the amount learned did not.
Source: Adapted from Brettz & Thompsett, 1992

KEY QUESTIONS

- What is a needs analysis?
- What are some examples of specific training methods?
- How are training programs evaluated?

PERFORMANCE APPRAISAL: IDENTIFYING EMPLOYEE STRENGTHS AND WEAKNESSES

When teaching courses in I/O psychology, I often ask my students at the beginning of the course to describe an unpleasant work experience they have had. For many of them it is the summer job they just left before returning to school. For others it is a job they hold down while going to school. The most common response I receive to this question is a negative reaction to being evaluated by their supervisor as part of a structured **performance appraisal.** Interestingly, my students' accounts of these events don't necessarily include being told something negative about their performance. Indeed, some of them felt quite good about their performance, yet report disappointment that their efforts went unnoticed. Others report the shock of learning, after months on the job, that they were being evaluated for something they were never told to do.

Why Performance Appraisal Is Unpopular, Yet Essential

The preceding examples illustrate some of the reasons why performance appraisals may not be something that most employees anticipate eagerly, although research suggests that employees generally do want to receive feedback from their super-

Transfer of Training
The question of whether material learned during training is demonstrated on the job.

Results Criterion
A measure of training effectiveness that examines the final outcome of the training (e.g., accident reduction).

Performance Appraisal
The process of evaluating employee strengths and weaknesses.

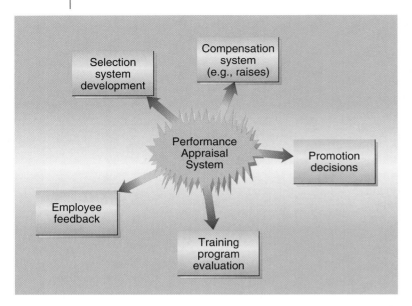

FIGURE 14.6
Performance Appraisal Is Central to Other Human Resource Practices
It is crucial for performance appraisal systems to be accurate and fair, because they influence so many other important personnel decisions and practices.

visors (Ashford, 1986). In other words, they want appraisal feedback but not in the way they often get it. On the other side of the situation are managers who often express dislike for this part of their jobs because it often brings negative reactions from subordinates (Waung & Highhouse, 1997). But does this need to be the case? Following is a summary of what research on this topic says about how to conduct performance appraisals so that these evaluations meet their intended objectives with a minimum of negative reactions from both sides.

But what are the objectives of performance appraisal? There are several—some more obvious than others. As can be seen in Figure 14.6, an organization's performance appraisal system is often considered the hub of many human resource practices, indicating that it plays a central role in these activities. For example, information from performance appraisals should serve as the basis for deciding who gets promoted. Similarly, this information should also be used as the basis for determining raises. These are both "evaluative" purposes, as they serve to guide important decisions that matter to employees.

Other uses of performance appraisal information are more "developmental" in nature, meaning that their intent is to provide employees with individualized feedback in hopes of strengthening any weak areas. For example, a particular fast-food worker may be fast and efficient at preparing customer's orders, but also may have a record of not treating customers in a courteous manner. One would hope that the appraisal of this employee would point out this deficit, with an accompanying plan for specialized training targeted at customer relations skills.

Lastly, performance appraisal information can provide useful information for evaluating other human resource practices, such as the effectiveness of a training program or the implementation of a new selection system. In these cases, the information about individual employees is of less importance than the overall performance of a group of employees who were part of a new training or selection system. In these instances, it is the system that is being evaluated, not the employees.

Because of these important functions, it essential that the appraisal process be executed well. Sloppy, unsystematic appraisals can lead to the wrong person getting promoted or a poor selection system being implemented. In its simplest form, a good performance appraisal system consists of a good appraisal form that is used appropriately. We first turn to the construction of the performance appraisal form. We then address the human side of it—the supervisor who fills it out.

Constructing Evaluation Forms: Making Them User-Friendly

As you learned earlier in this chapter, job analysis information serves as the crucial starting point for most human resource practices. Simply put, one must thoroughly understand the tasks, duties, and responsibilities of a job before deciding how to select people for it. Similarly, to construct a performance appraisal form, one must design it using this same job analysis information so that all relevant aspects of the job are represented on the form. While this may sound hopelessly rigid, it is the best way to make the performance appraisal form valid.

With job analysis information in hand, the first task is choosing the format of the appraisal form. Fortunately, over the years there has been a great deal of research on this (e.g., Latham & Wexley, 1977; Smith & Kendall, 1963), and from this

Ambiguous Courteousness	Excellent	Good	Fair	Poor
Specific Interrupts co-workers during team meetings	Never	Seldom	Occasionally	Frequently

FIGURE 14.7
Performance Appraisal: Being Specific Is Better
When constructing performance appraisal forms, the use of specific behavioral terms rather than broad traits (e.g., "courteous") will result in more accurate supervisory ratings.

research a number of useful guidelines have been proposed. First, it is preferable to use specific **critical behavioral incidents** rather than ambiguous traits on the appraisal form. Critical behavioral incidents are specific examples of behavior (both positive and negative) relevant to the job in question. An example of a positive behavior would be "Greets each customer with a smile." This is better than using an imprecise trait, such as "Friendly." You can see immediately why this would be a more objective way to measure one aspect of customer relations. Similarly, the words associated with each dimension (referred to as **anchors**) should be as unambiguous as possible (see Figure 14.7) for an example of good and bad performance appraisal items.

The performance appraisal form, in its entirety, should also be representative of the job, meaning that it covers all aspects of performance that have been determined as relevant. This is a straightforward principle but is one that in practice is often difficult to implement. Why? The difficulty is that some aspects of performance are inherently easier to measure than others. For example, a salesperson's productivity is much easier to quantify (e.g., volume of sales) than are his or her interactions with customers. The common tendency in these cases is to focus on what can be quantified and to overlook more subjective dimensions, which are difficult to measure. This tendency should be avoided, as it results in appraisal forms that are not representative of the job. This would be equivalent to a teacher leaving large portions of material off of a test even though the material was covered. As a result, grades would not reflect who learned what. As you can see, the same principles apply to all forms of evaluation.

Because the construction of appraisal forms is a time-consuming task, it is seldom done by one individual, even for one particular job. What is more customary is to have groups of **subject matter experts** work on this task. These individuals are people who have done the job in question or perhaps supervised those who did. With the guidance of job analysis information, they work together to generate dozens of critical behavioral incidents for each job. This long list of behavioral incidents is then rated by each subject matter expert. On the basis of these ratings some are discarded, and redundant examples are combined. The result is a behavioral rating form that hopefully captures most relevant aspects of the job.

At this point in the process, it is a good idea to circulate the appraisal form so that everyone can see it. This can both improve the final product as well as help ease any tensions associated with this stressful process. By concluding the process in this way, both supervisors and employees will clearly understand what job dimensions are considered most important, resulting in fewer biased ratings and fewer unpleasant surprises.

Critical Behavioral Incidents
Examples of specific behaviors (both positive and negative) relevant to a job used in the design of performance appraisal forms.

Anchors
The words associated with each dimension of a performance appraisal rating scale.

Subject Matter Experts
Individuals familiar with a job who generate critical behavioral incidents in order to construct performance appraisal forms.

K E Y   Q U E S T I O N S

• Why is performance appraisal so important?
• What are some techniques for designing good performance appraisal forms?

Supervisors Are Human, Too: Errors, Biases, and Memory Lapses

Even with the best performance appraisal form imaginable, there can be problems evaluating employees accurately. The appraisal form is just part of the puzzle. Just as there can be "operator errors" that cause accidents when working with equipment, so, too, can supervisors make errors when rating employees. Next we describe four common errors and discuss how they can be minimized.

Two of the most common errors are **leniency error** and **severity error,** the tendency for a supervisor to give employees ratings that are either higher or lower than their performance merits. As students, you have certainly seen this in the grading tendencies of various teachers you have had. In a work setting, the pattern is no different, and some of the reasons it occurs may be similar, too. For example, a manager's ratings may suffer from leniency error because of an intentional desire to avoid unpleasant reactions from employees. After all, who is going to storm into a supervisor's office if everyone has been rated as "good" or "excellent"? Another cause of leniency error occurs in organizations that evaluate their managers on the basis of the performance of those they manage. By giving high ratings to subordinates, the supervisor is thus viewed more favorably. Unexcused absences are rare. Everyone shows up on time. Reports are completed on schedule. While these may be extreme examples, you can see how even a tendency to inflate ratings, either to avoid conflict or to enhance the appearance of one's own performance, could easily occur, even among managers who are generally motivated to be fair.

Now let's look at the other extreme—severity error. What could possibly make a supervisor rate employees lower than their performance merits? Before concluding that some supervisors are just nasty, let's consider some other possibilities. Perhaps the supervisor simply has unrealistic standards of excellence. Indeed, this is thought to be one cause of severity error, and it seems to occur when supervisors use themselves as a comparison standard. For example, supervisors who have recently been promoted may still remember what it was like to do the job they are rating other people to do. They may have a distorted perception of how great they were, or they may really have been great. Either way, this can lead to severity error if the supervisor uses this unrealistic standard of comparison to rate subordinates who may be less experienced at the job. Another cause underlying severity error is more intentional and may seem hard to believe. It is not uncommon for supervisors to adjust ratings down when they are aware that little, if any, money for raises will be available. They know the importance of linking raises to performance and attempt to accomplish this in the most inappropriate way, by lowering the appraisals to match the anticipated small rewards.

A third common error is **central tendency error,** an error that represents ratings that hover around average. Supervisors who give ratings with this error may be those who have not been diligent about observing their employees during the preceding months. When given the task of rating several employees, they can't because they have not been paying attention. They think the safe response is to check the box in the middle rather than to admit that they do not have enough information to make the judgment.

All three of these errors, leniency, severity, and central tendency, represent a pattern of evaluating most or all employees with a particular bias. The last error we will consider, **halo error,** is distinct in that it represents a tendency to evaluate particular subordinates as "angels," as the term *halo* suggests. These are the employees who can be seen as doing no wrong, despite evidence to the contrary. Certainly, the concept of playing favorites is not new to anyone. Understanding the reasons for it are more complex, as it seems to stem from basic principles of social cognition—how we perceive and think about those around us (see Chapter 13).

In particular, halo error appears to stem from a general human tendency to view some characteristics as more important than others and then to perceive those who have this characteristic in more favorable terms overall. For example, imag-

Leniency Error
The tendency for a supervisor to give employees ratings that are higher than their performance merits.

Severity Error
The tendency for a supervisor to give employees ratings that are lower than their performance merits.

Central Tendency Error
An error that represents ratings that hover around average.

Halo Error
A rating error that represents a tendency to evaluate particular subordinates as "angels" based on their exceptional performance along one dimension.

FIGURE 14.8
How *Not* to Correct Rating Error
Supervisory rating errors are so prevalent that sometimes extreme approaches are used to improve their accuracy. Here is an example of what *not* to do.
Source: DILBERT reprinted by permission of United Features Syndicate, Inc.

ine a supervisor who views creativity more highly than other traits. This supervisor pays close attention to the creativity expressed by each subordinate. As far as this supervisor is concerned, creativity is the key to success. Now imagine one subordinate in particular who really shines when it comes to creative contributions to the team. When evaluating this subordinate along with the others, the manager rates this employee higher not only on creativity (which is appropriate) but also on unrelated dimensions, such as punctuality and teamwork skills, regardless of whether the employee is particularly noteworthy on these dimensions. This may not be favoritism in the intentional sense, but it still results in one employee receiving a more favorable evaluation than is deserved.

Earlier in this section you read about some of the techniques for reducing error—for example, designing the performance appraisal form so that it does not leave room for interpretation. In addition to this, organizations can reduce these error tendencies among their managers by training them in observational techniques (e.g., how to avoid person perception errors; please see Chapter 13) and by recognizing and rewarding supervisors for being accurate rather than simply treating performance appraisal as one more task they should get out of the way (Murphy & Cleveland, 1991). This can help to counter some of the motivations we discussed earlier to commit some of the various errors. (For a not-so-good approach to reducing rating errors, see Figure 14.8.)

In addition, organizations must give supervisors ample opportunities to observe each subordinate over a period of time. While this may seem so obvious as to be insulting, it is not uncommon, particularly in this day of telecommuting and flextime, for supervisors not to see their subordinates much at all during a given week (see Figure 14.9). Lastly, appraisal systems should realize the limits of human memory. Simply having supervisors keep a record of relevant employee behaviors can serve as a set of crucial retrieval cues when the time comes to fill out the semiannual appraisal forms.

FIGURE 14.9
Telework Makes a Supervisor's Job More Difficult
The increasing frequency of alternative work arrangements, such as telework and flex-time, makes it more difficult for supervisors to observe their subordinates, thus making accurate performance appraisal even more of a challenge.

KEY QUESTIONS
- What are the four major types of rating errors?
- How can these errors be minimized?

WORK MOTIVATION: ENCOURAGING EMPLOYEES TO DO THEIR BEST

Our focus in this chapter is to help you understand how psychological principles are applied behind the scenes in many successful organizations. Enhancing your awareness of this can help you succeed as a job applicant and as an employee. However, this is only part of the picture. Understanding the behavior of your co-workers is at least as challenging, if not more so. For the last three topics—work motivation, leadership, and teamwork—we shift our attention to the behavior of others at work: Why are they motivated to behave as they do? Why are some supervisors in leadership positions more effective than others? Why do some teams have more difficulties than others? We begin with the topic of **work motivation,** defined as the internal processes that activate, guide, and maintain behavior directed toward work.

How does management think about work motivation? It is viewed, in combination with skills and abilities, as the second piece of a two-part puzzle. The first piece—getting highly skilled employees in place—is the primary focus of training. Many selection techniques and performance appraisal systems also focus more on skills than on motivation. However, organizations realize that a high-performing workforce has not only the *skills*, but also the *will* that is necessary to succeed. In this context, work motivation represents what is meant by *will*.

Fortunately, theory and research on motivation, such as what you learned about in Chapter 9, have played a crucial role in helping organizations create conditions and practices that foster high levels of motivation. These principles have been studied extensively in organizations of all kinds, resulting in many highly successful organizational techniques. For example, the most effective compensation systems are often based on principles of Expectancy Theory, which specify how effort is linked to performance and how performance should be rewarded (see Chapter 9). Goal-Setting Theory is also applied in many organizations to help managers set challenging, specific goals for employees. You also read in Chapter 9 about intrinsic motivation, motivation that comes from the pleasure we get from activities that we enjoy. This theory has been applied in work settings, resulting in some very creative job design techniques that make work more enjoyable and fulfilling (Hackman & Oldham, 1976).

In this section we focus specifically on people's feelings and attitudes about work and how these feelings motivate their behavior at work. We begin by discussing the link between job satisfaction and work performance. Next we examine how job satisfaction and its opposite, dissatisfaction, motivate employees to do very positive and very negative things, respectively. As you read this material, we remind you again that there is no necessary contradiction between having happy workers and having productive workers. Both objectives can often be achieved by the same means.

Job Satisfaction: Are Happy Workers Productive Workers?

Can you think of some activity you really enjoy that you often work very hard at? Perhaps it is an athletic activity or playing a musical instrument. However, I'll bet that you can also think of instances in which you worked very hard and did well at something you did not particularly enjoy. (For a humorous example of another alternative, see Figure 14.10.) The question posed in the heading for this section

Work Motivation
The internal processes that activate, guide, and maintain behavior directed toward work.

Job Satisfaction
Employees' attitudes about various aspects of their jobs.

addresses this issue in the context of **job satisfaction,** people's attitudes about various aspects of their jobs (Smith, Kendall, & Hulin, 1969). By examining the statistical correlation between job satisfaction and performance across representative groups of workers, the question of whether happy workers are productive workers can be systematically addressed. No shortage of researchers has examined this question across hundreds of occupations and tens of thousands of employees.

For a summary of the latest, most comprehensive examination of this question, see Figure 14.11. This figure shows the results of a metaanalysis of several hundred studies that examined the job satisfaction–performance relationship (Judge et al., 2001). For simplicity, we excerpted the results of four different major occupational groups to show you the range of the findings. As you can see from Figure 14.11, the researchers found a modest, positive relationship between job satisfaction and performance, but it varied somewhat across occupations. The link between satisfaction and performance was strongest among scientists/engineers and weakest among nurses. This suggests that, for many jobs, being more satisfied does relate somewhat to performing better, but there is some variability across jobs.

"You know, I have a confession to make, Bernie. Win or lose, I love doing this."

FIGURE 14.10
Are Happy Workers Productive Workers?
This highly satisfied worker seems to care little about the relation between *his* job satisfaction and performance.
Source: Gary Larson

Organizational Citizenship and Retaliation: The Good, the Bad, and the Ugly

Organizations care about performance, but they also care about many other types of employee behavior. They want to retain their best workers, and they want them to show up regularly and punctually. Ideally, they would also like their employees to go the extra mile, helping one another and volunteering for extra assignments.

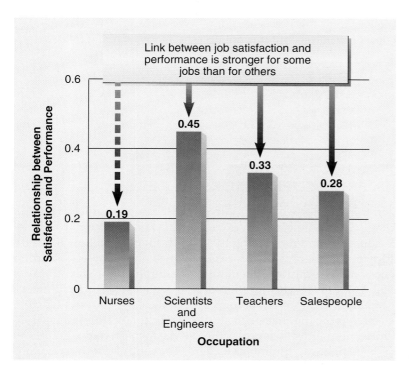

FIGURE 14.11
Job Satisfaction and Performance
Studies of the relationship between job satisfaction and performance show a modest positive correlation that varies somewhat by occupation.
Source: Adapted from Judge et al., 2001.

FIGURE 14.12
Employee Theft: One Negative Consequence of Employee Dissatisfaction
Although most dissatisfied employees do not steal, dissatisfaction is one contributing factor to this and other negative work behaviors.

Conversely, organizations also care about minimizing destructive behaviors such as theft, sabotage, and aggression toward co-workers; they often use high-tech surveillance equipment as a means of discouraging such behaviors (see Figure 14.12).

Perhaps not surprisingly, job satisfaction appears to play a role in all of these behaviors. Specifically, negative behaviors such absenteeism, theft, and sabotage show a modest but significant negative correlation with job satisfaction (i.e., more satisfied employees do fewer of these things) (Hulin, 1990). Conversely, positive behaviors such as helping one's co-workers and volunteering for extra assignments show a modest but positive correlation with job satisfaction (i.e., more satisfied employees do more of these things) (Organ & Ryan, 1995). Particularly relevant is job dissatisfaction that stems from feelings of unfair treatment. These feelings of unfairness play an important role in a whole cluster of negative work behaviors, extending to such acts as employee theft and sabotage (LeBlanc & Barling, 2004; Ambrose, Seabright, & Schminke, 2002; Greenberg, 2002; Skarlicki & Folger, 1997).

It is important to note, however, that several other factors may also contribute to these negative behaviors. For example, aggressive acts toward co-workers are done more often by employees who perceive the actions of others with a hostile attribution bias (Neuman & Baron, 1997). This bias is one that causes some people to interpret the actions of others as being intentionally hostile. According to this research, employees who see their co-workers as "out to get them" have more of a tendency to retaliate through aggressive acts. This distorted way of thinking, combined with feelings of dissatisfaction, can be a lethal combination, resulting in a whole cluster of negative work behaviors.

Similarly, positive work behaviors, such as helping co-workers, are motivated by feelings of job satisfaction in conjunction with other personality variables. These behaviors, referred to as **organizational citizenship behaviors,** are influenced by such personality characteristics as conscientiousness and empathy (Ladd & Henry, 2000; McNeely & Meglino, 1994; Organ & Ryan, 1995). Taken together, the most helpful employees tend to be those who are conscientious, empathic, and satisfied with their jobs. These examples only mention a few of the additional factors that influence positive and negative employee behaviors. What is important to remember is that job satisfaction plays a role, but it is not necessarily the starring role.

K E Y   Q U E S T I O N S

- What are work motivation and job satisfaction?
- What is the nature of the relationship between job satisfaction and performance?
- What other behaviors do job satisfaction and dissatisfaction relate to?

Organizational Citizenship Behaviors
Positive work behaviors including helping co-workers and volunteering for extra assignments.

Leadership
The process by which one member of a group (its leader) influences other group members toward attainment of shared group goals.

LEADERSHIP: FROM SUPERVISORS TO CEOs

At various points in this chapter we have indirectly discussed the role of those in supervisory positions. For example, supervisors often play an important role in selecting, training, evaluating, and motivating their subordinates. We now focus directly on **leadership,** defined here as the process by which one member of a group (its leader) influences other group members toward attainment of shared group goals (Vecchio, 1997; Yukl, 1994). The question of how leaders exert this influence has been a topic of great interest to psychologists since the early part of the twentieth century. It is also a topic that has been studied by scholars from other disciplines, such as history and political science. Although the focus in these disciplines is slightly different (e.g., political or military leaders), the central question remains the same: What contributes to effective leadership? We turn to that question first by examining the characteristics of effective leaders and then by examining the leaders' work context. We conclude with a description of one very powerful style of leadership that has been receiving much attention over the last decade—transformational leadership.

Leader Characteristics: How Effective Leaders Are Different from Others

If you were taking this course a decade ago, the answer to the question of what distinguishes effective leaders from others would have been "There are no consistent findings." This disappointing conclusion would probably have gone against your common sense. Certainly the best CEOs and military generals seem different from others. Indeed, it was this common sense belief that initiated nearly a century of research on leadership as scholars explored a host of traits in hopes of finding some that correlated with leadership effectiveness (e.g., Terman, 1904; Yukl & Van Fleet, 1992). Are effective leaders more intelligent than others? Are they more dominant? Occasionally, a study would report a significant relationship between one of these traits and leader effectiveness, but this pattern invariably would fail to appear in a subsequent study. Halfway through the century and hundreds of studies later, researchers concluded that the search for key leadership traits was not going to lead to clear answers (Stogdill, 1948).

The next avenue that researchers examined was the behavior of effective leaders. The question was modified from one that focused on traits to one that focused on what leaders actually do at work. Personality tests were put aside and clipboards were taken in hand as researchers directly observed leaders at various supervisory levels (e.g., Stogdill, 1963). These researchers did indeed begin to see distinct categories of behavior. Using sophisticated statistical analyses, they were able to classify hundreds of behaviors into a reasonable number of dimensions, resulting in a final two-factor classification. This two-factor classification consisted of a set of behaviors related to the work (*task behaviors*) and a set of behaviors related to people (*interpersonal behaviors*).

Depending on the researchers, these task and social behaviors might be given slightly different names, but for most studies the distinction was minimal. For example, giving a deadline to a subordinate would have been classified as a task behavior, whereas talking with a subordinate about a personal problem would have been classified as an interpersonal behavior. This clear distinction between types of leader behaviors was encouraging, but it fell short of addressing the question of whether effective leaders do more of one behavior or another. Unfortunately, subsequent studies examining this question met with the same fate as the earlier trait studies. No clear pattern emerged.

We began this section by hinting that something important must have emerged regarding the characteristics of effective leaders in the last decade or so. Indeed, there have been many recent developments in the study of personality, and some of these relate to leadership. For example, in Chapter 10, you read about a classification of personality called the Big Five, which describes personality along five broad dimensions (conscientiousness, extraversion, agreeableness, emotional stability, and openness to experience). The strength of this framework, combined with valid measures of each trait, has led to a reexamination of traits in many contexts. For example, earlier in this chapter we discussed personality tests as an employee selection tool. Similarly, the question of effective leadership has been investigated with respect to the Big Five. Questions such as "Are effective leaders more conscientious or more extroverted?" have now been systematically studied.

One of the most conclusive studies of leadership traits examined nearly one thousand earlier studies (Judge et al., 2002). As you can see in Figure 14.13 on page 482, a clear pattern emerged, showing the relative importance of each of the Big

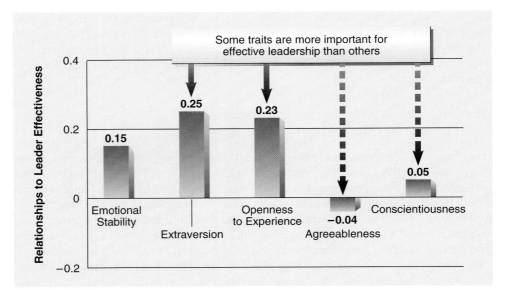

FIGURE 14.13
Traits of Effective Leaders
Metaanalyses of leadership traits show that effective leaders in business settings are different from less effective leaders in terms of some basic personality traits.
Source: Adapted from Judge et al., 2002.

Five traits in terms of their correlation with leadership effectiveness in business settings. While the correlations are modest in size, they are statistically significant for three of the five dimensions of personality. According to the results of this meta-analysis, effective leaders tend to be more extroverted and more open to experience, compared with less effective leaders. To a lesser extent, effective leaders also tend to be more emotionally stable. Important also to note are the two dimensions that were not related to leader effectiveness: conscientiousness and agreeableness, traits that may be important for other types of jobs, but less so for leadership positions in business settings. We should note that these researchers also examined leadership in the military and found slightly different results (e.g., conscientiousness was correlated with leader effectiveness in this context).

This metaanalysis represents just one approach to studying effective leaders. Others have found that effective leaders differ from ineffective ones in other ways. For example, effective leaders tend to be more flexible and have higher energy levels (Yukl & Van Fleet, 1992). Various skills of effective leaders have also been examined, such as technical and interpersonal skills (Bass, 1990). The research on leadership skills puts more of an emphasis on enhancing leadership skills through training, rather than assuming, as the trait perspective does, that individual differences are relatively fixed.

Speaking of fixed characteristics, what about differences between male and female leaders? Do they differ? Are members of one sex more effective than the other as leaders? This is the sort of debate that could get quite heated, even among close friends. Psychologists have been interested in this question also, as evidenced by the sheer volume of studies on the topic over the past several years. Using the same metaanalytic techniques mentioned here, Eagly and her colleagues systematically examined hundreds of studies of sex differences in leadership (Eagly & Johnson, 1990; Eagly, Karau, & Makhijani, 1995). From these studies several consistent patterns emerged. The question of leadership style, for example, shows that male and female leaders do tend to adopt different leadership styles on average. Female leaders tend to rely more on a participative style (e.g., getting input from others before making decisions), whereas male leaders tend to adopt a more autocratic style (e.g., giving directions). These differences are not great, however, and most effective leaders, regardless of gender, adapt their style to the particular situation.

When it comes to leadership effectiveness, however, the differences been male and female leaders are minimal (Eagly, Karau, & Makhijani, 1995). In many situations there are no consistent differences. However, in leadership positions that have been dominated by one gender or the other, some small differences in leader effectiveness have been found. For example, in the military, female leaders were rated less favorably than male leaders. However, in most business settings, these differences tend to disappear.

Leadership in Context: How the Work Setting Influences Leaders

Everything we have discussed thus far with regard to leadership has focused on the leader with little mention of how the leader might be influenced by the work context. Are some situations simply more challenging to leaders? Do subordinates have an impact on how leaders behave? The answer to both questions is yes. Several theories of leadership effectiveness have approached leadership in this way. One theory, called the **Path–Goal Theory,** examines how leaders should adapt their style of leadership in response to the situation (House, 1971). For example, when dealing with an inexperienced employee, a directive approach may be most appropriate because the subordinate needs extra guidance. In contrast, a more experienced subordinate may object to this, preferring instead to be motivated by a challenging goal.

Another leadership theory, called **Normative Decision Theory,** prescribes how leaders should take the situation into account when deciding how a particular decision should be made (Vroom & Yetton, 1973). According to this theory, the central question is the degree of participation leaders should solicit from their subordinates. For example, autocratic decisions can be more appropriate when the situation dictates that the decision must be made quickly. Democracy may encourage commitment to a decision, but it is slow! Under other conditions, a participative decision in which everyone has a vote is much more effective. This approach to leadership decision making has been very successful in management and executive training programs because it helps future leaders learn when it is better to ask for input and when it is better to go it alone.

Contemporary research on leadership has taken a novel look at leadership effectiveness by examining the impact that subordinates have on leaders. Social influence is, after all, a two-way street, even when one individual has more formal authority than the other. Turning the tables in this way has resulted in some very interesting findings regarding leadership. For example, this research shows that leaders have distinct relationships with each subordinate and that the quality of the relationship varies substantially (Graen & Scandura, 1986). From this perspective, referred to as the **Leader–Member Exchange Theory,** both the leader and the subordinate contribute to the creation of the relationship. Leaders and subordinates who establish a high-quality relationship would be expected to trust each other more, with the subordinate being given more responsibility. In contrast, low-quality relationships are characterized by formal organizational rules instead of by trust. Research has shown that subordinates benefit greatly from developing high-quality relationships with their leaders and that these subordinates reciprocate by working harder and generally contributing more (Liden, Sparrowe, & Wayne, 1997).

Transformational Leadership: Encouraging and Inspiring Others

When most of us think of truly great leaders, words such as *vision, inspiration,* and *charisma* may come to mind. Historical figures such as Queen Elizabeth I and Alexander the Great had this effect on those they led, and certain CEOs have been described with these terms as well. In recent years, psychologists have attempted to study this form of leadership, first by defining the characteristics of these leaders and then by examining the impact these leaders have on those around them. The term **transformational leadership** has been adopted to describe this type of leadership because it captures the notion that these leaders truly transform those around them and, sometimes, the world (Bass, 1985).

There are several ingredients that contribute to transformational leadership, the most central of which is **charisma.** Leaders who have charisma tend to have a

Path–Goal Theory
A theory of leadership that examines how leaders should adapt their style of leadership in response to the situation.

Normative Decision Theory
A theory of leadership that prescribes how leaders should take the situation into account when deciding how a particular decision should be made.

Leader–Member Exchange Theory
A theory of leadership that describes the distinct relationships that leaders form with each subordinate.

Transformational Leadership
Leadership that consists of charisma, intellectual stimulation, and genuine concern for subordinates.

Charisma
A characteristic of transformational leaders that consists of having high self-confidence, a strong vision, and high expectations for followers.

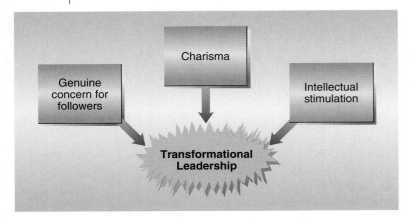

FIGURE 14.14
Transformational Leaders: A Combination of Traits and Behavior
Leaders who are described as being "transformational" possess the trait of charisma, but also behave differently from other leaders.

clear vision for the future. Martin Luther King Jr.'s vision for social change is a good example of this. Charismatic leaders also tend to be very self-confident, which allows their vision to be contagious to others. Lastly, charismatic leaders set very high standards for those that follow them. Religious cult leaders, often described as charismatic, expect their followers to devote their entire lives to the cult—a very high standard indeed.

But transformational leaders are more than simply charismatic. In fact, some research shows that purely charismatic leaders can often create maladaptive dependence among their followers, and those who have evil intent can have disastrous consequences on society (Yukl & Van Fleet, 1992). What makes transformational leaders distinctive is that they combine charisma with two additional patterns of behavior: They show genuine concern for their subordinates and they intellectually stimulate them (see Figure 14.14). This pairing of emotional support and intellectual challenge is crucial to helping employees reach their potential, as found in a wide range of organizational settings (e.g., Bass & Avolio, 1993; Bass et al., 2003).

KEY QUESTIONS

- What characteristics distinguish effective leaders from others?
- How does the work context influence leaders?
- What are the characteristics of transformational leaders?

BUILDING TEAMS: HOW AND WHEN TO WORK AS A GROUP

"The final assignment for this course is a group project. . . ." As an instructor, I know that the preceding statement will invariably bring a mixture of reactions from a class. Some will feel relieved to share the burden of a large assignment. Others will worry about whether they will be teamed with a group of slackers. Still others will think about the possibility of making friends as a result of working together. Organizational work groups create the same diverse reactions among employees, along with a host of challenges. Because of these challenges, organizations should carefully consider whether a team approach is desirable.

Certainly, some activities must be performed by a highly coordinated team. A pilot cannot fly a jet without a co-pilot and flight engineer, nor can a surgeon remove an appendix without the efforts of nurses and technicians. However, in many instances, organizations can decide whether or not a team approach is suitable for accomplishing a task. For example, important decisions can be made either by one individual or by a group. (See Figure 14.15 for a few examples of different types of organizational teams.) The decision whether to assign work to a team should take many factors into account. In this section, we discuss some challenges of teamwork, beginning with the topic of *team composition*—the task of putting the team together so that it functions smoothly.

Team Composition: Deciding Who Should Work with Whom

Some people work better together than others. This is the basic starting assumption of team composition research. The key is to identify what mixture of individual

FIGURE 14.15
Work Groups Come in All Forms
Regardless of the job or setting, teams must learn to work together in order to be effective.

characteristics results in the most effective team functioning. Part of the answer depends on what the team is going to be required to do and another part depends on what outcome really matters. For example, having a highly diverse work group (e.g., different age, gender, cultural background, expertise) can have a very positive impact on creative problem solving, a task that is central to many organizational teams. Unfortunately, highly diverse groups also tend to have trouble retaining members (Williams & O'Reilly, 1998). What they gain in creativity they lose in stability. Groups that are too diverse also tend to have communication problems, so it generally takes them longer to become proficient.

Generally, what appears to be most effective with regard to diversity is to have sufficient differences so that everyone can contribute something unique. This diversity also allows team members to learn from each other, something that can benefit team members over the long term. However, too much diversity can cause communication problems and interpersonal friction. As Goldilocks discovered, what is often "just right" is often something in the middle.

Another issue related to team composition is the question of how to hire good team players, those who can work effectively with a wide range of people. This trend is gaining momentum in many team-based organizations, with consultants being awarded lucrative contracts on the condition that they help recruiters identify these prize employees. These new hires are expected not only to be technically proficient, but also to be good working with others. Research on the selection of team members shows once again the relevance of the Big Five personality approach. For example, teams with members who are high in conscientiousness and extraversion tend to be more effective (Barrick et al., 1998). In other contexts, particularly those in which conflict is common, having highly agreeable group members is, perhaps not surprisingly, related to group success (Barrick et al., 1998). Interestingly, this research found evidence that even one highly disagreeable team member can have an adverse affect on an otherwise smoothly functioning group. The saying "One bad apple can spoil the barrel" certainly seems to apply to teams.

A last factor to consider is the ideal size of the team. Here, the research on motivation in teams is specific. According to this research, it is far better to slightly understaff a team than to make it too big (Hackman, 1990). Teams with too many members not only have more difficulties coordinating their efforts (e.g., setting a common meeting time) but also tend to have more **social loafing**—the tendency to reduce one's efforts when working collectively (Steiner, 1972; Latane, Williams, & Harkins, 1979). Not surprisingly, when members of a team are allowed to decide how big their team should be, they often err in the direction of making it too large, in part because people understand that their own efforts can be reduced as the group gets bigger. This motivation is something with which organizations wrestle as they try to create teams that are neither over- nor understaffed.

Social Loafing
The tendency to reduce one's efforts when working in a group.

Managing Conflict and Encouraging Cooperation

Once a team has been created, the potential for conflict among members arises. Conflict can come in many different forms and not all of it is destructive. For this reason, contemporary perspectives of team conflict view it as something that should be managed, rather than avoided or eliminated (Amason, 1996). One basic distinction in team conflict is **task conflict** versus **relationship conflict.** As the terms indicate, task conflict refers to disagreements about how the team's primary activity should be accomplished, whereas relationship conflict refers to interpersonal problems between individuals. For example, advertising executives might disagree about the form that a new ad campaign should take. The executives are united on the goal; they simply have different views regarding the best means of achieving it. This is an example of task conflict. Conflicts or disagreements of this type may be unpleasant as they are occurring, but they can often result in constructive outcomes and therefore should not be squelched.

Among one type of group—those charged with making important decisions—conflict is often conducive to making good decisions (Henry, 1993; Sniezek & Henry, 1989). This research shows that groups that had the most divergent opinions made the best decisions overall. In fact, groups that experience no dissent among their members often make serious errors in judgment, sometimes referred to as **groupthink** (Janis, 1972). For example, both space shuttle disasters (the *Challenger* in 1986 and the *Columbia* in 2002) have been partially attributed to this faulty group decision process among engineers at NASA. In fact, the importance of constructive disagreement is so generally recognized now that organizational teams will often appoint a member to voice disagreement (a devil's advocate) in order to guarantee that dissenting arguments will be raised.

In contrast, relationship conflicts often serve no purpose but to advance the agendas of the respective parties. These conflicts generally originate from personal disagreements among team members. For example, a long-feuding pair of teammates may make a point of shooting down each others' ideas merely because they dislike each other. Conflict of this variety can result in communication breakdowns, which in turn have been known to cause the most serious of mistakes, such as airline disasters (Foushee, 1984) and surgical errors (Anand & Winslow, 2003).

Even isolated disputes can interfere with a team achieving its goal. One common dispute of this type occurs in the initial stages when parts of the project are assigned. Two team members may want to do the same part of the project, leaving more boring tasks undone. Because these conflicts occur early on, they can set the tone for the entire experience and should therefore be handled as diplomatically as possible so that everyone feels as though they are an important member of the team (Henry & Landa, 2000). Dysfunctional conflict can also arise from team members giving feedback to one another, even though feedback is an essential aspect of highly effective self-managed teams (Hackman, 1990). As you have probably observed from your experiences working with others, feedback is sometimes delivered in a harsh, sarcastic manner, resulting in hurt feelings rather than positive change. To learn how you can be more effective at giving feedback the next time you work in a team, see the **Psychology Lends a Hand** section that follows.

Task Conflict
Disagreement about how the team's primary activity should be accomplished.

Relationship Conflict
Conflict in the group that refers to interpersonal problems between individuals.

Groupthink
Serious errors in group decision making that result from a lack of dissent in the group.

KEY QUESTIONS
- What are some of the things to consider when putting together a team?
- What are some causes of conflict?

p s y c h o l o g y   l e n d s   a   h a n d

How to Give Feedback to Team Members

One of the most difficult aspects of working in teams is determining when and how to give feedback to other members of the team. Of course, giving positive feedback by telling someone they are doing well is never difficult. Giving negative feedback is another matter. Although it is expected that supervisors and others in authority positions will give feedback, it is often not appreciated when feedback comes from team members. However, research on teams is very clear in this regard: Effective teams have members who are able to give constructive feedback to one another (Hackman, 1990). Here are some tips on how to give constructive feedback so that it accomplishes its mission without causing friction:

1. **Be descriptive, not evaluative.** When giving negative feedback, describe what the specific behavior is and refrain from labeling it (e.g., lazy, stupid).

2. **Be timely.** It is tempting to delay saying something, hoping the problem goes away. However, it is more important that the feedback be given soon after the behavior has occurred. This makes learning from mistakes easier and also prevents the build-up of hostilities.

3. **Be gentle.** Imagine how you would feel hearing negative feedback from a teammate. By empathizing you will more likely deliver the feedback in a manner that will be received.

4. **Be accurate.** Stick to the facts when giving feedback. Don't overgeneralize ("You always interrupt!") or gloss over problems ("So you've missed every meeting. No problem!").

By following these guidelines, it is much more likely that the feedback you give will be listened to and that positive change will follow.

SUMMARY AND REVIEW OF KEY QUESTIONS

- **What is I/O psychology?**
  I/O psychology is the study of human cognition and behavior at work.

- **What is the dual mission of psychologists in this field?**
  To improve employee well-being and organizational effectiveness through research and practice.

Selection: Hiring the Best Person for the Job

- **What is job analysis?**
  Job analysis is a systematic assessment of the tasks, duties, and responsibilities of a job.

- **What is criterion-related validity?**
  Criterion-related validity is the strength of the relationship between test scores and a criterion, such as job success.

- **What does the term *utility* refer to in the context of selection?**
  The utility of a selection test refers to its usefulness, taking into account validity as well as cost.

- **How is the fairness of a selection system determined?**
  The fairness of a selection system is determined by its adherence to laws as well as by employee perceptions.

- **What is a structured interview?**
  A structured interview is one that is conducted in the same manner, using the same questions for all job applicants. Applicant responses are also evaluated using the same standards.

- **What is an assessment center?**
  An assessment center is a selection system consisting of a wide variety of tests and activities administered to a small group of applicants over a few days.

- **What is a work sample test?**
  A work sample test requires job applicants to perform a sample of the work, just as they would be expected to if hired.

Training: Helping Employees Acquire Relevant Skills

- **What is a needs analysis?**
  A needs analysis consists of a systematic collection of information done in order to identify which employees are most in need of training and what they need to be trained to do.

- **What are some examples of specific training methods?**
  On-the-job training, vestibule training, programmed instruction, behavioral modeling and role playing are all examples of specific training methods.

- **How are training programs evaluated?**
  Training programs are evaluated using four criteria: trainee reactions, learning, behavior, and results.

Performance Appraisal: Identifying Employee Strengths and Weaknesses

- **Why is performance appraisal so important?**
  Performance appraisal is important because evaluations of employees serve to influence many important human

resource decisions and practices, such as promotion, raise decisions, and employee feedback.

- **What are some techniques for designing good performance appraisal forms?**
  Performance appraisal forms should be designed using critical behavioral incidents and well-defined anchors. All relevant aspects of performance should be represented. The use of subject matter experts is useful for generating good items.

- **What are the four major types of rating errors?**
  Leniency, severity, central tendency, and halo are the four major types of rating errors.

- **How can these errors be minimized?**
  Errors can be minimized by using good appraisal forms and by training supervisors with regard to their use. Supervisors should also have ample opportunity to observe subordinates and should keep records of employee behaviors to help their memory.

Work Motivation: Encouraging Employees to Do Their Best

- **What are work motivation and job satisfaction?**
  Work motivation is the term used to describe the internal processes that activate, guide, and maintain behavior directed toward work. *Job satisfaction* is the term used to describe employees' attitudes toward their jobs.

- **What is the nature of the relationship between job satisfaction and performance?**
  Research indicates that there is a modest positive correlation between job satisfaction and performance that varies somewhat by occupational group.

- **What other behaviors do job satisfaction and dissatisfaction relate to?**
  Highly satisfied employees are more likely to engage in organizational citizenship behaviors, such as helping co-workers. Highly dissatisfied employees are more likely to engage in negative behaviors such as absenteeism, sabotage, and theft.

Leadership: From Supervisors to CEOs

- **What characteristics distinguish effective leaders from others?**
  Research indicates that effective business leaders are more extroverted, more open to experience, and more emotionally stable than less effective leaders. Other research indicates that effective leaders are also more flexible and have higher energy levels than others.

- **How does the work context influence leaders?**
  According to various leadership theories, the work context influences the style a leader uses, the way that decisions are made, and the nature of relationships with subordinates.

- **What are the characteristics of transformational leaders?**
  Transformational leaders are highly charismatic. They also provide intellectual stimulation to their subordinates and show genuine concern for them.

Building Teams: How and When to Work as a Group

- **What are some of the things to consider when putting together a team?**
  The amount of diversity in a team should be based on what the group's primary purpose is. Also important is to staff the team with those who are conscientious and agreeable.

- **What are some causes of conflict?**
  Conflict arises from two primary sources: the task the group is doing and the relationships among group members.

PSYCHOLOGY: UNDERSTANDING ITS FINDINGS

Developing a Work Sample Test to Select Instructors

Think of the dozens of different teachers you have had throughout your life. If you are like most people, it is easiest to think of the very best and the very worst. After years of observing, you know a great deal about this profession. With this knowledge in mind, imagine that you have been appointed to a school committee to improve the hiring of math instructors, using a work sample test. Your job is to design the work sample test and develop a method for scoring each applicant. Use the following questions to guide you through the process of developing this assessment tool.

1. What exactly would each applicant be asked to do?
2. What behavioral dimensions would you assess?
3. Who would evaluate each applicant?
4. What important characteristics would be difficult to assess with this method?

Before a work sample such as this would be used, it should be examined with regard to its validity, utility, and fairness. However, what you have just done is similar to what would be done to develop a work sample. Evaluating it with regard to validity, utility, and fairness would still take additional work before it could be used.

MAKING PSYCHOLOGY PART OF YOUR LIFE

Do You Like Teamwork? Good Workers Come in All Forms

People vary considerably regarding their feelings about teamwork. For example, individuals who have a very high need for achievement often prefer to work alone (Riggio, 2000). If you are curious about your own beliefs, take the questionnaire below, indicating on a 1 to 7 scale the extent to which you disagree (1) or agree (7) with each statement. Then use the key at the end to tally your score. Try to respond as honestly as possible, and remember that this questionnaire tells you only about your general beliefs about working with others. It says nothing necessarily about how effective you are working on a team.

____ 1. It's easy for me to make friends with people with whom I work.

____ 2. Work is more significant when it is done on an individual basis.

____ 3. Working on projects with others provides an opportunity to make friends.

____ 4. People work harder in a group.

____ 5. I prefer working by myself so I can decide how a project is done.

____ 6. I find it easier to organize my ideas when working in a group.

____ 7. Working in groups encourages people to work less.

____ 8. Better decisions are made when working in a group.

____ 9. Projects are more fun to do with a group of people.

____ 10. I manage my time better when I work with others.

Key: First, reverse score numbers 5 and 7, giving a 1 for a 7, a 2 for a 6, and so on. After reverse-scoring these two items, sum across all ten. Scores range from 10 to 70, with a higher score representing more favorable attitudes about working in groups (Henry & Olson, 2001).

If you find yourself having difficulty responding to these questions, that can be viewed as a very positive sign. It indicates that your beliefs tend to vary based on the experiences you have had in teams. If you scored very high or very low, you may want to challenge your beliefs the next time you work as a member of a team. Perhaps you were being influenced by one particularly good or bad experience. And remember, your attitudes about teamwork don't say anything necessarily about how good a team member you tend to be. Teamwork skills, which can be developed with training and practice, are more important than attitudes.

KEY TERMS

Glossary

Absolute Threshold (p. 61): The smallest amount of a stimulus that we can detect 50 percent of the time.

Accommodation (p. 243): In Piaget's theory of cognitive development, modifications in existing knowledge structures (schemas) as a result of exposure to new information or experiences.

Achievement Motivation (p. 295): The desire to accomplish difficult tasks and meet standards of excellence.

Acquired Immune Deficiency Syndrome (AIDS) (p. 365): A viral infection that reduces the immune system's ability to defend itself against the introduction of any foreign matter.

Acquisition (p. 130): The process by which a conditioned stimulus acquires the ability to elicit a conditioned response through repeated pairings of an unconditioned stimulus with a conditioned stimulus.

Action Potential (p. 32): A rapid shift in the electrical charge across the cell membrane of neurons. This disturbance along the membrane communicates information within neurons.

Acuity (p. 67): The visual ability to see fine details.

Adolescence (p. 263): A period beginning with the onset of puberty and ending when individuals assume adult roles and responsibilities.

Affect (p. 298): Temporary and relatively mild shifts in current feelings and mood.

Agonist (p. 34): A chemical substance that facilitates the action of a neurotransmitter at a receptor site.

Agoraphobia (p. 393): Intense fear of specific situations in which individuals suspect that help will not be available should they experience an incapacitating or embarrassing event.

Agreeableness (p. 329): One of the "big five" dimensions of personality; a dimension ranging from good-natured, cooperative, and trusting on one end to irritable, suspicious, and uncooperative at the other.

Algorithm (p. 203): A rule that guarantees a solution to a specific type of problem.

Alpha Waves (p. 106): Rapid, low-amplitude brain waves that occur when individuals are awake but relaxed.

Alzheimer's Disease (p. 185): An illness primarily afflicting individuals over the age of sixty-five that involves severe mental deterioration, including severe amnesia.

Amnesia (p. 183): Loss of memory stemming from illness, accident, drug abuse, or other causes.

Amphetamines (p. 118): Drugs that act as *stimulants*, increasing feelings of energy and activation.

Amygdala (p. 40): A limbic system structure involved in aspects of emotional control and formation of emotional memories.

Anal Stage (p. 319): In Freud's theory, a psychosexual stage of development in which pleasure is focused primarily on the anal zone.

Analogy (p. 203): A strategy for solving problems based on applying solutions that were previously successful with other problems similar in underlying structure.

Anchoring-and-Adjustment Heuristic (p. 199): A cognitive rule of thumb for making decisions in which existing information is accepted as a reference point but then adjusted, usually insufficiently, in light of various factors.

Anchors (p. 475): The words associated with each dimension of a performance appraisal rating scale.

Anima (p. 323): According to Jung, the archetype representing the feminine side of males.

Animus (p. 323): According to Jung, the archetype representing the masculine side of females.

Anorexia Nervosa (p. 385): An eating disorder involving intense fears of gaining weight coupled with refusal to maintain normal body weight.

Antagonist (p. 34): A chemical substance that inhibits the impact of a neurotransmitter at a receptor site.

Anterograde Amnesia (p. 183): The inability to store in long-term memory information that occurs after an amnesia-inducing event.

Antisocial Personality Disorder (p. 399): A personality disorder in which individuals are chronically callous and manipulative toward others; ignore social rules and laws; behave impulsively and irresponsibly; fail to learn from punishment, and lack remorse or guilt over their misdeeds.

Anxiety (p. 318, 391): In Freudian theory, unpleasant feelings of tension, fear, apprehension, or worry experienced by individuals in reaction to unacceptable wishes or impulses.

Anxiety Disorders (p. 391): Psychological disorders that take several different forms, but which are all related to a generalized feeling of anxiety.

Apnea (p. 111): A sleep disorder in which sleepers stop breathing several times each night, and thus wake up.

Archetypes (p. 323): According to Jung, inherited images in the collective unconscious that shape our perceptions of the external world.

Assessment Center (p. 469): A selection technique that consists of a wide variety of tests and activities administered to a small group of job applicants over a few days.

Assimilation (p. 243): In Piaget's theory of cognitive development, incorporation of new information into exist- ing mental frameworks (schemas).

Attachment (p. 255): A strong affectional bond between infants and their caregivers.

Attention-Deficit/ Hyperactivity Disorder (ADHD) (p. 384): A childhood mental disorder in which children simply can't pay attention (inattention), show hyperactivity or impulsivity, or show both of these symptoms.

Attitudes (p. 437): Lasting evaluations of various aspects of the social world that are stored in memory.

Attribution (p. 433): The processes through which we seek to determine the causes behind others' behavior.

Autobiographical Memory (p. 178): Memory for information about events in our own lives.

Automatic Processing (p. 103): Processing of information without minimal conscious awareness.

Autonomic Nervous System (p. 36): Part of the peripheral nervous system that connects internal organs, glands, and involuntary muscles to the central nervous system.

Availability Heuristic (p. 13, 198): A cognitive rule of thumb or mental shortcut in which the importance or probability of various events is judged on the basis of how readily they come to mind.

Axon (p. 31): The part of the neuron that conducts action potentials away from the cell body.

Axon Terminals (p. 32): Structures at the end of axons that contain transmitter substances.

Babbling (p. 210): An early stage of speech development in which infants emit virtually all known sounds of human speech.

Backward Conditioning (p. 131): A type of conditioning in which the presentation of the unconditioned stimulus (UCS) precedes the presentation of the conditioned stimulus (CS).

Barbiturates (p. 118): Drugs that act as *depressants,* reducing activity in the nervous system and in behavior output.

Basic Anxiety (p. 323): Children's fear of being left alone, helpless, and insecure.

Behavior Therapies (p. 408): Therapies based on the belief that many mental disorders stem from faulty learning.

Behavioral Criteria (p. 472): A measure of training effectiveness that examines the degree of behavior change on the job.

Behavioral Modeling (p. 472): A training technique that applies principles of observational learning.

Bereavement (p. 274): The process of grieving for the persons we love who die.

Binocular Cues (p. 92): Cues to depth or distance resulting from the fact that we have two eyes.

Biological Constraints on Learning (p. 135): Refers to the fact that all forms of conditioning are not equally easy to establish with all organisms.

Biological Rhythms (p. 98): Cyclic changes in bodily processes.

Biological Sex (p. 259): Refers to whether an individual is, biologically speaking, male or female.

Bipolar Disorder (p. 389): A mood disorder in which individuals experience very wide swings in mood, from deep depression to wild elation.

Bisexual (p. 294): A sexual orientation in which individuals engage in sexual relations with members of both sexes.

Blind Spot (p. 67): The point in the back of the retina through which the optic nerve exits the eye. This exit point contains no rods or cones and is therefore insensitive to light.

Body Language (p. 303): Nonverbal cues involving body posture or movement of body parts.

Bottom-Up Approach (p. 90): Suggests that our ability to recognize specific patterns, such as letters of the alphabet or objects, is based on simpler capacities to recognize and correctly combine lower-level features of objects, such as lines, edges, corners, and angles.

Brightness (p. 62): The physical intensity of light.

Brightness Constancy (p. 87): The tendency to perceive objects as having a constant brightness when they are viewed under different conditions of illumination.

Broca's Area (p. 48): A region in the prefrontal cortex that plays a role in the production of speech.

Bulimia Nervosa (p. 385): An eating disorder in which individuals engage in recurrent episodes of binge eating following by some form of purging.

Cancer (p. 360): A group of illnesses in which abnormal cells are formed that are able to proliferate, invade, and overwhelm normal tissues, and to spread to distant sites in the body.

Cannon-Bard Theory (p. 299): A theory of emotion suggesting that various emotion-provoking events simultaneously produce subjective reactions labeled as emotions and physiological arousal.

Carcinogens (p. 360): Cancer-producing agents in our environment.

Cardiovascular Disease (p. 361): All diseases of the heart and blood vessels.

Case Method (p. 15): A method of research in which detailed information about individuals is used to develop general principles about behavior.

Cataplexy (p. 110): A symptom of narcolepsy (a sleep disorder) in which individuals fall down suddenly, like a sack of flour.

Catatonic Type (of schizophrenia) (p. 402): A dramatic type of schizophrenia in which individuals show marked disturbances in motor behavior. Many alternate between total immobility and wild, excited behavior in which they rush madly about.

Central Nervous System (p. 35): The brain and the spinal cord.

Central Route (to persuasion) (p. 438): Persuasion that occurs through careful consideration of message content.

Central Tendency Error (p. 476): An error that represents ratings that hover around average.

Cerebellum (p. 39): A part of the brain concerned with the regulation of basic motor activities.

Cerebral Cortex (p. 40): The outer covering of the cerebral hemispheres.

Chaining (p. 144): A procedure that establishes a sequence of responses that lead to a reward following the terminal or final response in the chain.

Charisma (p. 485): A characteristic of transformational leaders that consists of having high self-confidence, a strong vision, and high expectations for followers.

Childhood (p. 236): The years between birth and adolescence.

Chromosomes (p. 51): Threadlike structures containing genetic material, found in nearly every cell of the body.

Circadian Rhythms (p. 98): Cyclic changes in bodily processes occurring within a single day.

Classical Conditioning (p. 130): A basic form of learning in which one stimulus comes to serve as a signal for the occurrence of a second stimulus. During classical conditioning, organisms acquire information about the relations between various stimuli, not simple associations between them.

Climacteric (p. 268): A period during which the functioning of the reproductive system and various aspects of sexual activity change greatly.

Cocaine (p. 119): A powerful stimulant that produces pleasurable sensations of increased energy and self-confidence.

Cochlea (p. 72): A portion of the inner ear containing the sensory receptors for sound.

Cocktail Party Phenomenon (p. 83): The effect of not being aware of other people's conversations until something of personal importance, such as hearing one's name, is mentioned and then suddenly hearing it.

Cognition (p. 192): The mental activities associated with thought, decision making, language, and other higher mental processes.

Cognitive Development (p. 243): Changes in cognitive abilities and functioning, occurring throughout the life span.

Cognitive Dissonance (p. 439): The state experienced by individuals when they discover inconsistency between two attitudes they hold or between their attitudes and their behavior.

Cognitive Restructuring (p. 377): A method of modifying self-talk in stress-producing situations. Clients are trained to monitor what they say to themselves in stress-provoking situations and then to modify their cognitions in adaptive ways.

Cognitive Therapies (p. 410): Therapies based on the view that many mental disorders stem from faulty or distorted modes of thought.

Collective Unconscious (p. 323): In Jung's theory, a portion of the unconscious shared by all human beings.

Companionate Love (p. 457): A form of love involving a high degree of commitment and deep concern with the well-being of the beloved.

Complex Cells (p. 69): Neurons in the visual cortex that respond to stimuli that move in a particular direction and that have a particular orientation.

Compliance (p. 449): A form of social influence in which one or more persons attempt to influence one or more others through direct requests.

Concepts (p. 170, 193): Mental categories for objects or events that are similar to one another in certain ways.

Concrete Operations (p. 245): A stage in Piaget's theory of cognitive development occurring roughly between the ages of seven and eleven. It is at this stage that children become aware of the permanence of objects.

Concurrent Schedule of Reinforcement (p. 148): A reinforcement schedule in which two or more schedules are available.

Conditioned Response (CR) (p. 130): In classical conditioning, the response to the conditioned stimulus.

Conditioned Stimulus (CS) (p. 130): In classical conditioning, the stimulus that is repeatedly paired with an unconditioned stimulus.

Conditioned Taste Aversion (p. 136): A type of conditioning in which the UCS (usually internal cues associated with nausea or vomiting) occurs several hours after the CS (often a novel food), leading to a strong CS-UCS association in a single trial.

Cones (p. 66): Sensory receptors in the eye that play a crucial role in sensations of color.

Confirmation Bias (p. 13, 195): The tendency to notice and remember primarily information that lends support to our views or beliefs.

Confluence Approach (p. 206): An approach suggesting that for creativity to occur, multiple components must converge.

Conformity (p. 449): Experienced pressures toward thinking or acting like most other persons.

Conscientiousness (p. 329): One of the "big five" dimensions of personality; a dimension ranging from well-organized, careful, and responsible on one end to disorganized, careless, and unscrupulous at the other.

Consensus (p. 433): Information regarding the extent to which behavior by one person is shown by others as well.

Conservation (p. 244): Understanding of the fact that certain physical attributes of an object remain unchanged even though its outward appearance changes.

Consistency (p. 433): Information regarding the extent to which a specific person shows similar behavior to a given stimulus across time.

Constancies (p. 87): Our tendency to perceive physical objects as unchanging despite shifts in the pattern of sensations these objects induce.

Constrained Statistical Learning Framework (p. 209): A recent theory of language development that suggests that we acquire language through the use of statistical features of linguistic input that helps us to discover structure, including sound patterns, words, and grammar.

Contact Hypothesis (p. 446): The view that prejudice can be reduced by increasing the degree of contact between different groups.

Content Validity (p. 219): The extent to which items on a test are related in a straightforward way to the characteristic the test aims to measure.

Context-Dependent Memory (p. 170): Refers to the fact that information entered into memory in one context or setting is easier to recall in that context than in others.

Continuous Reinforcement Schedule (p. 146): A schedule of reinforcement in which every occurrence of a particular behavior is reinforced.

Controlled Processing (p. 103): Processing of information involving relatively high levels of conscious awareness.

Conventional Level (of morality) (p. 252): According to Kohlberg, a stage of moral development during which individuals judge morality largely in terms of existing social norms or rules.

Conversion Disorder (p. 396): A somatoform disorder in which individuals experience actual physical impairment such as blindness, deafness, or paralysis for which there is no underlying medical cause.

Convoy Model (p. 271): A model of social networks suggesting that from midlife on, we tend to maintain close relationships with a small number of people.

Cooing (p. 210): An early stage of speech development in which infants emit vowel-like sounds.

Cornea (p. 66): The curved, transparent layer through which light rays enter the eye.

Corpus Callosum (p. 42): A band of nerve fibers connecting the two hemispheres of the brain.

Correlational Method (of research) (p. 17): A research method in which researchers attempt to determine whether and to what extent different variables are related to each other.

Correspondence Bias (also known as *fundamental attribution error*) (p. 433): The tendency to attribute behavior to internal causes to a greater extent than is actually justified.

Counterfactual Thinking (p. 436): The tendency to evaluate events by thinking about alternatives to them (i.e., "what might have been").

Crack (p. 119): A derivative of cocaine that can be smoked. It acts as a powerful stimulant.

Creativity (p. 206): The ability to produce work that is both novel (original, unexpected) and appropriate (it works–it is useful or meets task constraints).

Criterion-Related Validity (p. 219, 466): The extent to which scores on a test are related to behaviors (criteria) that are relevant to the characteristics the test purports to measure, such as success on the job.

Critical Behavioral Incidents (p. 475): Examples of specific behaviors (both positive and negative) relevant to a job used in the design of performance appraisal forms.

Critical Thinking (p. 14): Thinking that avoids blindly accepting conclusions or arguments and, instead, closely examines all assumptions, evidence, and conclusions.

Cross-Sectional Research (p. 211): Research in which groups of persons of different ages are compared in order to determine how certain aspects of behavior or cognition change with age.

Cross-Tolerance (p. 117): Increased tolerance for one drug that develops as a result of taking another drug.

Cultural Bias (p. 226): The tendency of items on a test of intelligence to require specific cultural experience or knowledge.

Curse of Knowledge (p. 246): Refers to the fact that we tend to be biased by our own knowledge when judging the perspective of people who know less about some topic than we do.

Dark Adaptation (p. 68): The process through which our visual system increases its sensitivity to light under low levels of illumination.

Decision Making (p. 198): The process of choosing among various courses of action or alternatives.

Defense Mechanisms (p. 318): Techniques used by the ego to keep threatening and unacceptable material out of consciousness, and so to reduce anxiety.

Delay Conditioning (p. 131): A form of forward conditioning in which the onset of the unconditioned stimulus (UCS) begins while the conditioned stimulus (CS) is still present.

Delta Activity (p. 106): High amplitude, slow brain waves (3.5 Hz or less) that occur during several stages of sleep, but especially during stage 4.

Delusions (p. 401): Firmly held beliefs that have no basis in reality.

Dendrite (p. 31): The part of the neuron that conducts action potentials toward the cell body.

Dependent Variable (p. 19): The variable that is measured in an experiment.

Depressants (p. 117): Drugs that reduce activity in the nervous system and therefore slow many bodily and cognitive processes. Depressants include alcohol and barbiturates.

Depression (p. 388): A mood disorder in which individuals experience extreme unhappiness, lack of energy, and several related symptoms.

Designer Drugs (p. 121): Drugs designed to resemble illegal drugs that already exist.

Developmental Psychology (p. 236): The branch of psychology that focuses on the many ways we change throughout life.

***Diagnostic and Statistical Manual of Mental Disorders-IV* (p. 382):** A manual designed to help all mental health practitioners recognize and correctly identify (diagnose) specific disorders.

Difference Threshold (p. 62): The amount by which two stimuli must differ in order to be just noticeably different.

Discriminative Stimulus (p. 148): Signals the availability of reinforcement if a specific response is made.

Disruptive Behaviors (p. 384): Childhood mental disorders involving poor control of impulses, conflict with other children and adults, and, in some cases, more serious forms of antisocial behavior.

Dissociated Control, Theory of (p. 115): A theory of hypnosis suggesting that hypnotism weakens control by the central function over other cognitive and behavioral subsystems, thus permitting these subsystems to be invoked directly by the hypnotist's suggestions.

Dissociative Amnesia (p. 395): Profound amnesia stemming from the active motivation to forget specific events or information.

Dissociative Disorders (p. 395): Disorders involving prolonged loss of memory or identity.

Dissociative Fugue (p. 395): A sudden and extreme disturbance of memory in which individuals wander off, adopt a new identity, and are unable to recall their own past.

Dissociative Identity Disorder (p. 395): A condition labeled as *multiple personality disorder* in the past, in which a single person seems to possess two or more distinct identities or personality states, and these take control of the person's behavior at different times.

Distinctiveness (p. 433): Information regarding the extent to which a given person reacts in the same manner to different stimuli or situations.

Door-in-the-Face Technique (p. 450): A technique for gaining compliance in which a large request is followed by a smaller one.

Dreams (p. 111): Cognitive events, often vivid but disconnected, that occur during sleep. Most dreams take place during REM sleep.

Dreams of Absent-Minded Transgression (p. 112): Dreams in which persons attempting to give up the use of tobacco, alcohol, or other drugs see themselves slipping into the use of these substances in an absent-minded or careless manner.

Drive Theory (p. 284): A theory of motivation suggesting that behavior is "pushed" from within by drives stemming from basic biological needs.

Drug Abuse (p. 116): Instances in which individuals take drugs purely to change their moods, and in which they experienced impaired behavior or social functioning as a result of doing so.

Drug Tolerance: *See* Tolerance.

Drugs (p. 116): Compounds that change the functioning of biological systems.

Ego (p. 317): In Freud's theory, the part of personality that takes account of external reality in the expression of instinctive sexual and aggressive urges.

Egocentrism (p. 244): The inability of young children to distinguish their own perspective from that of others.

Elaboration-Likelihood Model (ELM) (p. 438): A cognitive model of persuasion suggesting that persuasion can occur through distinct routes.

Electroconvulsive Therapy (ECT) (p. 419): A form of biological therapy in which electrodes are placed on patient's temples and strong electric shocks are then delivered to the brain.

Electroencephalogram (EEG) (p. 106): A record of electrical activity within the brain. EEGs play an important role in the scientific study of sleep.

Electromyogram (EMG) (p. 106): A record of electrical activity in various muscles.

Embryo (p. 236): The developing child during the first eight weeks of life.

Emotional Intelligence (EQ) (p. 227): A cluster of traits or abilities relating to the emotional side of life–abilities such as recognizing and managing one's own emotions, being able to motivate oneself and restrain one's impulses, recognizing and managing others' emotions, and handling interpersonal relationships in an effective manner.

Emotional Stability (p. 329): One of the "big five" dimensions of personality; a dimension ranging from poised, calm, and composed at one extreme through nervous, anxious, and excitable at the other.

Encoding (p. 164): The process through which information is converted into a form that can be entered into memory.

Encoding Specificity Principle (p. 170): Retrieval of information is successful to the extent that the retrieval cues match the cues the learner used during the study phase,

Endocrine System (p. 37): A system for communication within our bodies; it consists of several glands that secrete hormones directly into the bloodstream.

Episodic Memory (p. 169): Memory for factual information that we acquired at a specific time.

Escalation of Commitment (p. 201): The tendency to become increasingly committed to bad decisions, even as losses associated with them increase.

Evening (Night) Persons (p. 99): Individuals who experience peak levels of energy and physiological activation relatively late in the day.

Evolutionary Psychology (p. 7, 53): A new branch of psychology, suggesting that as a result of evolution, human beings possess a number of *evolved psychological mechanisms* that help (or once helped) us deal with important problems relating to survival.

Expectancy Theory (p. 285): A theory of motivation suggesting that behavior is "pulled" by expectations of desirable outcomes.

Experimentation (the experimental method of research) (p. 18): A research method in which researchers systematically alter one or more variables in order to determine whether such changes influence some aspect of behavior.

Explicit Memory (p. 172): Memory for information we are consciously aware of and can readily put into words.

Externals (p. 333): Individuals who believe that they have little control over the outcomes they experience.

Extinction (p. 132): The process through which a conditioned stimulus gradually loses the ability to evoke conditioned responses when it is no longer followed by the unconditioned stimulus.

Extrasensory Perception (ESP) (p. 92): Perception without a basis in sensory input.

Extraversion (p. 329): One of the "big five" dimensions of personality; a dimension ranging from sociable, talking, fun-loving at one end to sober, reserved, and cautious at the other.

Extroverts (p. 323): In Jung's theory, individuals who are open and and confident and make friends readily.

Eyewitness Testimony (p. 176): Information provided by witnesses to crimes or accidents.

Facial Feedback Hypothesis (p. 299): A hypothesis indicating that facial expressions can produce changes in emotional states.

Fairness (p. 469): The legality of the selection system (i.e., whether it is consistent with current employment law) as well as its perceived fairness to job applicants.

Farsightedness (p. 68): A condition in which the visual image entering our eye is focused behind rather than directly on the retina. Therefore, close objects appear out of focus, while distant objects are in clear focus.

Fatal Familial Insomnia (p. 109): A genetic disorder in which individuals experience increasing disturbances in sleep; the disorder is, as its name suggests, fatal.

Feature Detectors (p. 69): Neurons at various levels within the visual system that respond primarily to stimuli possessing certain features in the visual cortex.

Feeding and Eating Disorders (p. 385): Disturbances in eating behavior that involve maladaptive and unhealthy efforts to control body weight.

Fetal Alcohol Syndrome (p. 238): A disorder in newborns due to alcohol consumption by their mothers.

Fetus (p. 236): The developing child during the last seven months of pregnancy.

Figure-Ground Relationship (p. 83): Our tendency to divide the perceptual world into two distinct parts—discrete figures and the background against which they stand out.

Fixation (p. 319): Excessive investment of psychic energy in a particular stage of psychosexual development. This results in various types of psychological disorders.

Fixed-Interval Schedule (p. 146): A schedule of reinforcement in which a specific interval of time must elapse before a response will yield reinforcement.

Fixed-Ratio Schedule (p. 146): A schedule of reinforcement in which reinforcement occurs only after a fixed number of responses have been emitted.

Foot-in-the-Door Technique (p. 449): A technique for gaining compliance in which requesters start with a small request and then, after this is granted, shift to a much larger request.

Formal Operations (stage of) (p. 245): In Piaget's theory, the final stage of cognitive development, during which individuals may acquire the capacity for deductive or propositional reasoning.

Fovea (p. 67): The area in the center of the retina in which cones are highly concentrated.

Framing (p. 200): Presentation of information concerning potential outcomes in terms of gains or in terms of losses.

Free Association (p. 406): In psychoanalysis, the patient's reporting of all thoughts and feeling that he or she has during the therapy session.

Frequency-of-Exposure Effect (p. 452): The more frequently we are exposed to a given stimulus, the more—in general—we tend to like it.

Frequency Theory (p. 73): A theory of pitch perception suggesting that sounds of different frequencies (heard as differences in pitch) induce different rates of neural activity in the hair cells of the inner ear.

Freudian Slips (p. 317): Statements which seem to be simple errors in speech, but which in fact reveal unconscious thoughts or impulses.

Friendships (p. 258): Mutual dyadic relationships between children involving strong affective ties.

Frontal Lobe (p. 41): The portion of the cerebral cortex that lies in front of the central fissure.

Fully Functioning Persons (p. 325): In Rogers's theory, psychologically healthy persons who enjoy life to the fullest.

Functional Fixedness (p. 204): The tendency to think of using objects only as they have been used in the past.

Fuzzy-Trace Theory (p. 176): A theory about the relationship between memory and higher reasoning processes.

Gate-Control Theory (p. 76): A theory of pain suggesting that the spinal cord contains a mechanism that can block transmission of pain to the brain.

Gender (p. 259): A society's beliefs about the traits and behavior of males and females.

Gender Consistency (p. 236): Children's understanding that their gender will not change even if they adopted the behavior, dress, and hairstyles of the other gender.

Gender Identity (p. 260): Children's understanding of the fact that they are male or female.

Gender Identity Disorder (p. 398): A disorder in which individuals believe that they were born with the wrong sexual identity.

Gender Roles (p. 259): Beliefs about how males and females are expected to behave in many situations.

Gender Schema Theory (p. 261): A theory indicating that children develop a cognitive framework reflecting the beliefs of their society concerning the characteristics and roles of males and females. This gender schema then strongly affects the processing of new social information.

Gender Stability (p. 260): Children's understanding that gender is stable over time.

Gender Stereotypes (p. 260): Cultural beliefs about differences between women and men.

General Adaptation Syndrome (GAS) (p. 348): A profile of how organisms respond to stress. It consists of three phases: a nonspecific mobilization phase that promotes sympathetic nervous system activity; a resistance phase, during which the organism makes efforts to cope with the threat; and an exhaustion phase, which occurs if the organism fails to overcome the threat and depletes its coping resources.

Genes (p. 51): Biological "blueprints" that shape development and all basic bodily processes.

Genital Stage (p. 319): The final stage of psychosexual development–one in which individuals acquire the adult capacity to combine lust with affection.

Gestalt Psychologists (p. 83): German psychologists intrigued by our tendency to perceive sensory patterns as well-organized wholes rather than as separate isolated parts.

Gestures (p. 303): Movements of various body parts that convey a specific meaning to others.

Goal-Setting Theory (p. 285): The view that motivation can be strongly influenced by goals.

Gonads (p. 292): The primary sex glands.

Grammar (p. 209): Rules within a given language indicating how words can be combined into meaningful sentences.

Groupthink (p. 486): Serious errors in group decision making that result from a lack of dissent in the group.

Hallucinations (p. 401): Vivid sensory experiences that have no basis in physical reality.

Hallucinogens (p.120): Drugs that profoundly alter consciousness (e.g., marijuana, LSD).

Halo Error (p. 476): A rating error that represents a tendency to evaluate particular subordinates as "angels" based on their exceptional performance along one dimension.

Hassles (p. 352): Annoying minor events of everyday life that cumulatively can affect psychological well-being.

Health Belief Model (p. 358): A theory of health behaviors; the model predicts that whether or not a person practices a particular health behavior can be understood by knowing the degree to which the person perceives a personal health threat and the perception that a particular health practice will be effective in reducing that threat.

Health Psychology (p. 346): The study of the relation between psychological variables and health, which reflects the view that both mind and body are important determinants of health and illness.

Heredity (p. 51): Biologically determined characteristics passed from parents to their offspring.

Heritability (p. 52, 223): The extent to which variations among individuals, with respect to a given aspect of behavior or a given trait, are due to genetic factors.

Heterosexual (sexual orientation) (p. 294): A sexual orientation in which individuals prefer sexual relations with members of the other sex.

Heuristic Processing (p. 438): The use of simple rules of thumb or mental shortcuts in the evaluation of persuasive messages; also called the *peripheral route* to persuasion.

Heuristic-Systematic Model (p. 438): A cognitive model of persuasion suggesting that persuasion can occur through distinctly different routes.

Heuristics (p. 198): Mental rules of thumb that permit us to make decisions and judgments in a rapid and efficient manner.

Hierarchy of Needs (p. 286): In Maslow's theory of motivation, an arrangement of needs from the most basic to those at the highest levels.

Hindsight Effect (p. 195): The tendency to assume that we would have been better at predicting actual events than is really true.

Hippocampus (p. 40): A structure of the limbic system that plays a role in the formation of certain types of memories.

Homeostasis (p. 284): A state of physiological balance within the body.

Homosexual (sexual orientation) (p. 294): A sexual orientation in which individuals prefer sexual relations with members of their own sex.

Hormones (p. 37): Substances secreted by endocrine glands that regulate a wide range of bodily processes.

Hostile Aggression (p. 340): Aggression in which the prime objective is inflicting some kind of harm on the victim.

Hue (p. 67): The color that we experience due to the dominant wavelength of a light.

Humanistic Theories (p. 324): Theories of personality emphasizing personality responsibility and innate tendencies toward personal growth.

Humanistic Therapies (Phenomenological/Experiential Therapies) (p. 407): Therapies based on the ideas that understanding other people requires trying to see the world through their eyes and that the therapeutic relationship with the client is central to achieving benefits in therapy.

Hunger Motivation (p. 288): The motivation to obtain and consume food.

Hypercomplex Cells (p. 69): Neurons in the visual cortex that respond to complex aspects of visual stimuli, such as width, length, and shape.

Hypertension (p. 367): A condition in which the pressure within the blood vessels is abnormally high.

Hypnosis (p. 113): An interaction between two persons in which one (the hypnotist) induces changes in the behavior, feelings, or cognitions of the other (the subject) through suggestions. Hypnosis involves expectations on the part of subjects and their attempts to conform to social roles (e.g., the role of the hypnotized person).

Hypochondriasis (p. 396): A disorder involving preoccupation with fears of disease or illness.

Hypohedonia (p. 149): A genetically inherited impairment in the ability to experience pleasure.

Hypothalamus (p. 40): A small structure deep within the brain that plays a key role in the regulation of the autonomic nervous system and of several forms of motivated behavior, such as eating and aggression.

Hypothetico-Deductive Reasoning (p. 245): A type of reasoning first shown by individuals during the stage of formal operations. It involves formulating a general theory and deducing specific hypotheses from it.

Id (p. 317): In Freud's theory, the portion of personality concerned with immediate gratification of primitive needs.

Illusions (p. 88): Instances in which perception yields false interpretations of physical reality.

Implicit Memory (p. 172): A memory system that stores information we cannot readily put into words and of which we may not be consciously aware. *See also* Procedural Memory.

Incentives (p. 285): Rewards individuals seek to attain.

Independent Variable (p. 19): The variable that is systematically changed in an experiment.

Induced (Forced) Compliance (p. 439): A technique for changing attitudes in which individuals are somehow induced to state positions different from their actual views.

Industrial/Organizational (I/O) Psychology (p. 464): The study of human cognition and behavior at work.

Infantile Amnesia (p. 178): Our supposed inability to remember experiences during the first two or three years of life.

Information-Processing Approach (p. 164): An approach to human memory that emphasizes the encoding, storage, and later retrieval of information.

Information-Processing Perspective (of cognitive development) (p. 249): A perspective that seeks insights into cognitive development in terms of children's growing abilities with respect to basic aspects of cognition, such as attention and memory.

Ingratiation (p. 450): A technique of social influence based on inducing increased liking in the target persons before influence is attempted.

Insecure/Ambivalent Attachment (p. 255): A pattern of attachment in which a child seeks contact with the caregiver before separation but then, after she leaves and then returns, first seeks her but then resists or rejects her offers of comfort.

Insecure/Avoidant Attachment (p. 255): A pattern of attachment in which children don't cry when their caregiver leaves in the *strange situation* test, and are slow to greet their caregiver when this person returns.

Insomnias (p. 109): Disorders involving the inability to fall asleep or maintain sleep once it is attained.

Inspection Time (p. 220): The minimum amount of time a particular stimulus must be exposed for individuals to make a judgment about it that meets some preestablished criterion of accuracy.

Instrumental Aggression (p. 340): Aggression in which the primary goal is not harm to the victim but attainment of some other goal, such as access to valued resources.

Intelligence (p. 214): Individuals' abilities to understand complex ideas, to adapt effectively to the environment, to learn from experience, to engage in various forms of reasoning, and to overcome obstacles by careful thought.

Internals (p. 333): Individuals who believe that they exert considerable control over the outcomes they experience.

Interpersonal Attraction (p. 452): The extent to which we like or dislike other persons.

Intrinsic Motivation (p. 296): Motivation to perform activities because they are rewarding in and of themselves.

Introverts (p. 323): In Jung's theory, individuals who are hesitant and cautious and do not make friends easily.

IQ (p. 216): Originally "intelligence quotient," a number that examiners derived by dividing an individual's mental age by his or her chronological age and then multiplying by 100. Now IQ simply indicates an individual's performance on an intelligence test relative to those of other persons of the same age.

Iris (p. 66): The colored part of the eye that adjusts the amount of light that enters by constricting or dilating the pupil.

James-Lange Theory (p. 299): A theory of emotion suggesting that emotion-provoking events produce various physiological reactions and recognition of these is responsible for subjective emotional experiences.

Job Analysis (p. 465): An assessment of the tasks, duties, and responsibilities of a particular job.

Job Satisfaction (p. 478): Employees' attitudes about various aspects of their jobs.

Just Noticeable Difference (jnd) (p. 62): The amount of change in a physical stimulus necessary for an individual to notice a difference in the intensity of a stimulus.

Kinesthesia (p. 81): The sense that gives us information about the location of our body parts with respect to each other and allows us to perform movement.

Korsakoff's Syndrome (p. 184): An illness caused by long-term abuse of alcohol; often involves profound retrograde amnesia.

KSAs (p. 466): Abbreviation for the knowledge, skills, and abilities needed to perform a particular job.

Language (p. 209): A system of symbols, plus rules for combining them, used to communicate information.

Latency Stage (p. 319): In Freud's theory, the psychosexual stage of development that follows resolution of the Oedipus complex. During this stage, sexual desires are relatively weak.

Laws of Grouping (p. 85): Simple principles describing how we tend to group discrete stimuli together in the perceptual world.

Leader-Member Exchange Theory (p. 483): A theory of leadership that describes the distinct relationships that leaders form with each subordinate.

Leadership (p. 480): The process by which one member of a group (its leader) influences other group members toward attainment of shared group goals.

Learned Helplessness (p. 149, 389): (1) Beliefs on the part of individuals that they cannot influence the outcomes they experience. (2) Feelings of helplessness that develop after exposure to situations in which no effort succeeds in affecting outcomes.

Learning (p. 128): Any relatively permanent change in behavior (or behavior potential) resulting from experience.

Learning Criteria (p. 472): A measure of training effectiveness that examines the degree of learning that occurred as a result of training.

Leniency Error (p. 476): The tendency for a supervisor to give employees ratings that are higher than their performance merits.

Lens (p. 66): A curved structure behind the pupil that bends light rays, focusing them on the retina.

Less-Leads-to-More Effect (p. 439): The fact that rewards just barely sufficient to induce individuals to state positions contrary to their own views often generate more attitude change than larger rewards.

Levels of Processing View (p. 169): A view of memory suggesting that the greater the effort expended in processing information, the more readily it will be recalled at later times.

Libido (p. 319): According to Freud, the psychic energy that powers all mental activity.

Lifestyle (p. 346): In the context of health psychology, the overall pattern of decisions and behaviors that determine health and quality of life.

Limbic System (p. 40): Several structures deep within the brain that play a role in emotional reactions and behavior.

Linguistic Relativity Hypothesis (p. 211): The view that language shapes thought.

Localization (p. 74): The ability of our auditory system to determine the direction of a sound source.

Logical Concepts (p. 193): Concepts that can be clearly defined by a set of rules or properties.

Long-Term Memory (p. 165): A memory system for the retention of large amounts of information over long periods of time.

LSD (p. 120): A powerful hallucinogen that produces profound shifts in perception; many of these shifts are frightening in nature.

Magnetic Resonance Imaging (MRI) (p. 45): A method for studying the intact brain in which images are obtained by exposing the brain to a strong magnetic field.

Medulla (p. 39): A structure in the brain concerned with the regulation of vital bodily functions, such as breathing and heartbeat.

Memory (p. 164): Our cognitive system(s) for storing and retrieving information.

Menopause (p. 268): Cessation of the menstrual cycle.

Mental Disorders (p. 381): Disturbances of an individual's behavioral or psychological functioning that are not culturally expected and that lead to psychological distress, behavioral disability, or impaired overall functioning.

Mental Models (p. 194): Knowledge structures that guide our interactions with objects and events in the world around us.

Mental Set (p. 204): The impact of past experience on present problem solving; specifically, the tendency to retain methods that were successful in the past even if better alternatives now exist.

Mentors (p. 266): Older and more experienced individuals who help to guide young adults.

Metacognition (p. 249): Awareness and understanding of our own cognitive processes.

Midbrain (p. 39): A part of the brain containing primitive centers for vision and hearing. It also plays a role in the regulation of visual reflexes.

Millon Clinical Multiaxial Inventory (MCMI) (p. 335): An objective test of personality specifically designed to assist psychologists in diagnosing various psychological disorders.

Mitosis (p. 51): Cell division in which chromosome pairs split and then replicate themselves so that the full number is restored in each of the cells produced by division.

MMPI (p. 335): A widely used objective test of personality based on *empirical keying.*

Monocular Cues (p. 91): Cues to depth or distance provided by one eye.

Mood Congruence Effects (p. 180): Refers to the finding that we tend to notice or remember information congruent with our current mood.

Mood-Dependent Memory (p. 180): Refers to the finding that what we remember while in a given mood may be determined, in part, by what we learned when previously in that same mood.

Mood Disorders (p. 388): Psychological disorders in which individuals experience swings in their emotional states that are much more extreme and prolonged than is true of most people.

Moral Development (p. 250): Changes in the capacity to reason about the rightness or wrongness of various actions that occur with age.

Morning Persons (p. 99): Individuals who experience peak levels of energy and physiological activation relatively early in the day.

Motivation (p. 283): Internal processes that activate, guide, and maintain behavior over time.

Multicultural Perspective (p. 11): A perspective that clearly recognizes the potential importance of gender, age, ethnicity, sexual orientation, disability, socioeconomic status, religious orientation, and many other social and cultural dimensions.

Narcolepsy (p. 109): A sleep disorder in which individuals are overcome by uncontrollable periods of sleep during waking hours.

Natural Concepts (p. 193): Concepts that are not based on a precise set of attributes or properties, do not have clear-cut boundaries, and are often defined by prototypes.

Nearsightedness (p. 67): A condition in which the visual image entering our eye is focused slightly in front of our retina rather than directly on it. Therefore, near objects can be seen clearly, while distant objects appear fuzzy or blurred.

Needs Analysis (p. 470): The first step in a training program, consisting of a systematic collection of data to address the question "Who needs to learn what?"

Negative Afterimage (p. 68): A sensation of complementary color that occurs after staring at a stimulus of a given hue.

Negative Reinforcers (p. 140): Stimuli that strengthen responses that permit the organism to avoid or escape from their presence.

NEO Personality Inventory (p. 336): An objective measure of personality designed to assess individuals' relative standing on each of the "big five" dimensions of personality.

Neodissociation Theory (of hypnosis) (p. 114): A theory suggesting that hypnotized individuals enter an altered state of consciousness in which consciousness is divided.

Neo-Freudians (p. 322): Personality theorists who accepted basic portions of Freud's theory, but rejected or modified other portions.

Nervous System (p. 35): The complex structure that regulates bodily processes and is responsible, ultimately, for all aspects of conscious experience.

Neural Plasticity (p. 221): The ability of neural connections to adapt dynamically to environmental cues.

Neurons (p. 31): Cells specialized for communicating information; the basic building blocks of the nervous system.

Neurotransmitters (transmitter substances) (p. 32): Chemicals, released by neurons, that carry information across the synapse.

Nicotine (p. 361): The addictive substance in tobacco.

Night Terrors (p. 110): Extremely frightening dreamlike experiences that occur during non-REM sleep.

Nociceptor (p. 76): A sensory receptor that responds to stimuli that are damaging.

Nonverbal Cues (p. 302, 431): Information provided by others' facial expressions, eye contact, body posture and movements, and other outward expressions of what they are feeling on the inside.

Normative Decision Theory (p. 483): A theory of leadership that prescribes how leaders should take the situation into account when deciding how a particular decision should be made.

Obedience (p. 450): A form of social influence in which one or more others behave in specific ways in response to direct orders from someone.

Object Permanence (p. 244): Understanding of the fact that objects continue to exist, even when they are hidden from view.

Observational Learning (p. 154, 332): The acquisition of new forms of behavior, information, or concepts through exposure to others and the consequences they experience.

Obsessive-Compulsive Disorder (p. 393): An anxiety disorder in which individuals have recurrent, disturbing thoughts (obsessions) they can't prevent unless they engage in specific behaviors (compulsions).

Occipital Lobe (p. 41): A portion of the cerebral cortex involved in vision.

Oedipus Complex (p. 319): In Freud's theory, a crisis of psychosexual development in which children must give up their sexual attraction for their opposite-sex parent.

On-the-Job Training (p. 471): Training in which an inexperienced employee learns the ropes in the actual work context during company hours.

Openness to Experience (p. 329): One of the "big five" dimensions of personality; a dimension ranging from imaginative, sensitive, and intellectual at one extreme to down-to-earth, insensitive, and crude at the other.

Operant Conditioning (p. 140): A process through which organisms learn to repeat behaviors that yield positive outcomes or that permit them to avoid or escape from negative outcomes.

Opiates (p. 119): Drugs that induce a dreamy, relaxed state and, in some persons, intense feelings of pleasure. Opiates exert their effects by stimulating special receptor sites within the brain.

Opponent-Process Theory (p. 68): A theory that describes the processing of sensory information related to color at levels above the retina. The theory suggests that we possess six different types of neurons, each of which is either stimulated or inhibited by red, green, blue, yellow, black, and white.

Optic Nerve (p. 67): A bundle of nerve fibers that exit the back of the eye and carry visual information to the brain.

Oral Stage (p. 319): A stage of psychosexual development during which pleasure is centered in the region of the mouth.

Organizational Citizenship Behaviors (p. 480): Positive work behaviors including helping co-workers and volunteering for extra assignments.

Panic Disorder (p. 392): Periodic, unexpected attacks of intense, terrifying anxiety known as panic attacks.

Paraphilias (p. 398): Disorders in which sexual arousal cannot occur without the presence of unusual imagery or acts.

Parapsychologists (p. 93): Individuals who study ESP and other paranormal events.

Parasympathetic Nervous System (p. 36): A portion of the autonomic nervous system that readies the body for restoration of energy.

Parietal Lobe (p. 41): A portion of the cerebral cortex, lying behind the central fissure, that plays a major role in the skin senses: touch, temperature, and pressure.

Path-Goal Theory (p. 483): A theory of leadership that examines how leaders should adapt their style of leadership in response to the situation.

Peak Experiences (p. 326): According to Maslow, intense emotional experiences during which individuals feel at one with the universe.

Perception (p. 60): The process through which we select, organize, and interpret input from our sensory receptors.

Perfect Pitch (p. 73): The ability to name or produce a note of particular pitch in the absence of a reference note.

Performance Appraisal (p. 473): The process of evaluating employee strengths and weaknesses.

Peripheral Nervous System (p. 35): That portion of the nervous system that connects internal organs and glands, as well as voluntary and involuntary muscles, to the central nervous system.

Peripheral Route (to persuasion) (p. 438): The use of simple rules of thumb or mental shortcuts in the evaluation of persuasive messages; also called *heuristic processing.*

Personality (p. 314): Individuals' unique and relatively stable patterns of behavior, thoughts, and feelings.

Personality Disorders (p. 399): Extreme and inflexible personality traits that are distressing to the persons who possess them and cause them problems in school, at work, or in interpersonal relationships.

Personality Traits (p. 328): Specific dimensions along which individuals differ in consistent, stable ways.

Person-Environment (P-E) Fit (p. 354): This approach suggests that a misfit between a person and his or her work environment may produce stress.

Persuasion (p. 437): The process through which one or more persons attempt to alter the attitudes of one or more others.

Pervasive Development Disorders (p. 387): Disorders involving lifelong impairment in mental or physical functioning.

Phallic Stage (p. 319): An early stage of psychosexual development during which pleasure is centered in the genital region. It is during this stage that the Oedipus complex develops.

Phenomenological/Experiential Therapies: *See* Humanistic Therapies.

Phobias (p. 392): Fears that become excessive in that they cause intense emotional distress and interfere significantly with everyday activities.

Phonological Development (p. 210): Development of the ability to produce recognizable speech.

Physiological Dependence (p. 117): Strong urges to continue using a drug based on organic factors, such as changes in metabolism.

Pinna (p. 71): The external portion of our ear.

Pitch (p. 72): The characteristic of a sound that is described as high or low. Pitch is mediated by the frequency of a sound.

Pituitary Gland (p. 37): An endocrine gland that releases hormones to regulate other glands and several basic biological processes.

Place Theory (p. 73): A theory suggesting that sounds of different frequency stimulate different areas of the basilar membrane, the portion of the cochlea containing sensory receptors for sound.

Placenta (p. 237): A structure that surrounds, protects, and nourishes the developing fetus.

Playing Hard to Get (p. 450): A tactic for gaining compliance in which individuals try to create the image that they are very popular or very much in demand.

Pleasure Principle (p. 317): The principle on which the id operates, according to which immediate pleasure is the sole motivation for behavior.

Pons (p. 39): A portion of the brain through which sensory and motor information pass and that contains structures relating to sleep, arousal, and the regulation of muscle tone and cardiac reflexes.

Position Analysis Questionnaire (PAQ) (p. 466): A specific job analysis technique that analyzes jobs along thirty-two distinct dimensions.

Positive Reinforcers (p. 140): Stimuli that strengthen responses that precede them.

Positron Emission Tomography (PET) (p. 45): An imaging technique that detects the activity of the brain by measuring glucose utilization or blood flow.

Postconventional Level (of morality) (p. 252): According to Kohlberg, the final stage of moral development, one at which individuals judge morality in terms of abstract principles.

Posttraumatic Stress Disorder (PTSD) (p. 351, 394): A psychological disorder in which people persistently reexperience a life-threatening traumatic event in their thoughts or dreams, feel as if they are reliving the event from time to time, persistently avoid stimuli associated with the traumatic event, plus several other symptoms.

Practical Intelligence (p. 215): Intelligence useful in solving everyday problems.

Preconventional Level (of morality) (p. 252): According to Kohlberg, the earliest stage of moral development, one at which individuals judge morality in terms of the effects produced by various actions.

Prejudice (p. 444): Negative attitudes toward the members of some social group based on their membership in this group.

Premack Principle (p. 140): The principle that a more preferred activity can be used to reinforce a less preferred activity.

Preoperational Stage (p. 244): In Piaget's theory, a stage of cognitive development during which children become capable of mental representations of the external world.

Prevention Strategies (p. 369): Techniques designed to reduce the occurrence of disease or illness and the physical and psychological problems that often accompany them.

Primary Aging (p. 268): Changes in our bodies caused by the passage of time and, perhaps, genetic factors.

Proactive Interference (p. 173): Occurs when information previously entered into memory interferes with the learning or storage of current information.

Problem Solving (p. 203): Efforts to develop or choose among various responses in order to attain desired goals.

Procedural Memory (p. 172): A memory system that retains information we cannot readily express verbally–for example, information necessary to perform various skilled motor activities, such as riding a bicycle. Also called *implicit memory.*

Programmed Instruction (p. 471): An off-site training method that allows trainees to go through instructional materials at their own pace, testing themselves before proceeding to subsequent modules.

Progressive Relaxation (p. 377): A stress-reduction technique in which people learn to relax by alternately flexing and relaxing, one by one, muscle groups throughout the body.

Propositions (p. 194): Sentences that relate one concept to another and can stand as separate assertions.

Prosopagnosia (p. 70): A rare condition in which brain damage impairs a person's ability to recognize faces.

Prototypes (p. 193): The best or clearest examples of various objects or stimuli in the physical world.

Psi (p. 92): Unusual processes of information or energy transfer that are currently unexplained in terms of known physical or biological mechanisms. Included under the heading of psi are such supposed abilities as telepathy (reading others' thoughts) and clairvoyance (perceiving distant objects).

Psychedelics (p. 120): *See* Hallucinogens.

Psychoanalysis (p. 317): A method of therapy based on Freud's theory of personality, in which the therapist attempts to bring repressed, unconscious material into consciousness.

Psychodynamic Therapies (p. 405): Therapies based on the idea that mental disorders stem mainly from hidden, inner conflicts, and that once these conflicts are made conscious, they can be resolved.

Psychological Dependence (p. 117): Strong desires to continue using a drug, even though it is not physiologically addicting.

Psychology (p. 2): The science of behavior and cognitive processes.

Psychophysics (p. 61): A set of procedures psychologists have developed to investigate the relationship between physical properties of stimuli and people's psychological experience of them.

Psychosexual Stages of Development (p. 318): According to Freud, an innate sequence of stages through which all human beings pass. At each stage, pleasure is focused on a different region of the body.

Psychosurgery (p. 419): A form of biological therapy in which brain operations are performed in order to change abnormal behavior.

Psychotherapies (p. 405): Procedures in which persons with mental disorders interact with trained therapists who help them change certain behaviors, thoughts, or emotions so that they can feel and function better.

Puberty (p. 263): The period of rapid change during which individuals reach sexual maturity.

Punishment (p. 141): A procedure by which the application or removal of a stimulus decreases the strength of a behavior.

Pupil (p. 66): An opening in the eye, just behind the cornea, through which light rays enter the eye.

Random Assignment of Participants to Experimental Conditions (p. 19): Assuring that all research participants have an equal chance of being exposed to each level of the independent variable (i.e., of being assigned to each experimental condition).

Rational-Emotive Therapy (p. 411): A form of cognitive therapy in which therapists attempt to persuade clients to recognize their own irrational thoughts.

Raven Progressive Matrices (p. 226): A popular test of intelligence that was designed to be relatively free of cultural bias.

Reaction Criteria (p. 472): A measure of training effectiveness that examines how employees feel about the training experience.

Realistic Conflict Theory (p. 444): A theory proposing that prejudice stems, at least in part, from direct conflict between social groups.

Reality Principle (p. 317): The principle according to which the ego operates, in which the external consequences of behavior are considered in the expression of impulses from the id.

Reasoning (p. 195): Cognitive activity in which we transform information in order to reach specific conclusions.

Recategorization (p. 447): A technique for reducing prejudice that involves inducing individuals to shift the boundary between "us" and "them" so that it now includes groups they previously viewed as "them."

Reconditioning (p. 133): The rapid recovery of a conditioned response (CR) to a CS-UCS pairing following extinction.

Reflexes (p. 35, 238): Inherited seemingly automatic responses to stimulation of certain areas of the body.

Reinforcement (p. 140): A procedure by which the application or removal of a stimulus increases the strength of a specific behavior.

Relationship Conflict (p. 486): Conflict in the group that refers to interpersonal problems between individuals.

Relative Size (p. 87): A visual cue based on a comparison of an object of unknown size to one of known size.

Reliability (p. 218): The extent to which any measuring device (including psychological tests) yields the same result each time it is applied to the same quantity.

REM Sleep (p. 106): A state of sleep in which brain activity resembling waking restfulness is accompanied by deep muscle relaxation and movements of the eyes. Most dreams occur during periods of REM sleep.

Representativeness Heuristic (p. 199): A mental rule of thumb suggesting that the more closely an event or object resembles typical examples of some concept or category, the more likely it is to belong to that concept or category.

Repression (p. 177): The active elimination from consciousness of memories or experiences we find threatening.

Resistance (p. 406): In psychoanalysis, (1) a patient's stubborn refusal to report certain thoughts, motives, and experiences to the therapist, or (2) overt rejection of the therapist's interpretations.

Results Criterion (p. 473): A measure of training effectiveness that examines the final outcome of the training (e.g., accident reduction).

Reticular Activating System (p. 39): A structure within the brain concerned with sleep, arousal, and the regulation of muscle tone and cardiac reflexes.

Retina (p. 66): The surface at the back of the eye containing the rods and cones.

Retrieval (p. 164): The process through which information stored in memory is located.

Retrieval Cues (p. 169): Stimuli associated with information stored in memory that can aid in its retrieval.

Retrieval Inhibition (p. 174): The inhibition of information in memory we don't try to remember produced by remembering other, related information.

Retroactive Interference (p. 173): Occurs when new information being entered into memory interferes with retention of information already present in memory.

Retrograde Amnesia (p. 183): Loss of memory of events that occurred prior to an amnesia-inducing event.

Risk Factors (p. 360): Aspects of our environment or behavior that influence our chances of developing or contracting a particular disease, within the limits established through our genetic structure.

Rods (p. 67): One of the two types of sensory receptors for vision found in the eye.

Romantic Love (p. 457): A form of love in which feelings of strong attraction and sexual desire toward another person are dominant.

Rorschach Test (p. 336): A widely used projective test of personality in which individuals are asked to describe what they see in a series of inkblots.

Sampling (p. 16): With respect to the survey method, sampling refers to the methods used to select persons who respond to the survey.

Saturation (p. 67): The degree of concentration of the hue of light. We experience saturation as the purity of a light.

Schachter-Singer Theory (two-factor theory) (p. 300): A theory of emotion suggesting that our subjective emotional states are determined, at least in part, by the cognitive labels we attach to feelings of arousal.

Schedules of Reinforcement (p. 146): Rules determining when and how reinforcements will be delivered.

Schemas (p. 175, 243): Cognitive frameworks representing our knowledge about specific aspects of the world and that help us process and store new information.

Schizophrenia (p. 399): A complex disorder characterized by hallucinations (e.g., hearing voices), delusions (beliefs with no basis in reality), disturbances in speech, and several other symptoms.

Scripts (p. 249): Mental representations of the sequence of events in a given situation.

Secondary Aging (p. 268): Changes in our bodies due to disease, disuse, or abuse.

Secure Attachment (p. 255): A pattern of attachment in which infants actively seek contact with their caregivers

and take comfort from their presence when they return in the *strange situation* test.

Selective Attention (p. 83): The process of focusing on a particular quality, object, or event for relatively detailed analysis.

Self-Actualization (p. 326): A stage of personal development in which individuals reach their maximum potential.

Self-Awareness (p. 104): A state of consciousness in which we focus our attention inward, upon ourselves.

Self-Concept (p. 325): All the information and beliefs individuals have about their own characteristics and themselves.

Self-Determination Theory (p. 364): When applied to health-related issues, this theory suggests that motivation to perform health-preventive behaviors is highest when we have autonomy over the decision to do so, and lowest when we do these behaviors at someone else's request.

Self-Efficacy (p. 332): Individuals' expectations concerning their ability to perform various tasks.

Self-Esteem (p. 327): Our assessment of our overall personal worth or adequacy.

Self-Reinforcement (p. 332): A process in which individuals reward themselves for reaching their own goals.

Self-Serving Bias (p. 433): The tendency to attribute positive outcomes to our own traits or characteristics (internal causes) but negative outcomes to factors beyond our control (external causes).

Self-System (p. 331): In Bandura's social cognitive learning theory, the set of cognitive processes by which a person perceives, evaluates, and regulates his or her own behavior.

Semantic Development (p. 210): Development of understanding of the meaning of spoken or written language.

Semantic Memory (p. 169): A memory system that stores general, abstract knowledge about the world–information we cannot remember acquiring at a specific time and place.

Sensation (p. 60): Input about the physical world provided by our sensory receptors.

Sensorimotor Stage (p. 243): In Piaget's theory, the earliest stage of cognitive development.

Sensory Adaptation (p. 64): Reduced sensitivity to unchanging stimuli over time.

Sensory Memory (p. 164): A memory system that retains representations of sensory input for brief periods of time.

Sensory Receptors (p. 60): Cells of the body specialized for the task of *transduction*–converting physical energy (light, sound) into neural impulses.

Serum Cholesterol (p. 363): The amount of cholesterol in our blood, directly proportional to the amount of cholesterol in our diets.

Severity Error (p. 476): The tendency for a supervisor to give employees ratings that are lower than their performance merits.

Sex-Category Constancy (p. 261): Complete understanding of one's sexual identity, centering around a biologically based categorical distinction between males and females.

Sexual Arousal Disorders (p. 397): The inability to attain or maintain an erection (males) or the absence of vaginal swelling and lubrication (females).

Sexual Desire Disorders (p. 397): Disorders involving a lack of interest in sex or active aversion to sexual activity.

Sexual Motivation (p. 292): Motivation to engage in various forms of sexual relations.

Sexual Orientation (p. 294): Individuals' preference for sexual relations with their own sex, the other sex, or both.

Shape Constancy (p. 87): The tendency to perceive a physical object as having a constant shape, even when the image it casts on the retina changes.

Shaping (p. 143): A technique in which closer and closer approximations to desired behavior are required for the delivery of positive reinforcement.

Short-Term Memory: *See* Working Memory.

Signal Detection Theory (p. 61): A theory suggesting that there are no absolute thresholds for sensations. Rather, detection of stimuli depends on their physical energy and on internal factors, such as the relative costs and benefits associated with detecting their presence.

Simple Cells (p. 69): Cells within the visual system that respond to specific shapes presented in certain orientations (e.g., horizontal, vertical).

Simultaneous Conditioning (p. 131): A form of conditioning in which the conditioned stimulus (CS) and the unconditioned stimulus (UCS) begin and end at the same time.

Size Constancy (p. 87): The tendency to perceive a physical object as having a constant size, even when the image it casts on the retina changes.

Sleep (p. 106): A process in which important physiological changes (e.g., shifts in brain activity, slowing of basic bodily functions) are accompanied by major shifts in consciousness.

Social Categorization (p. 444): The tendency to divide the social world into two distinct categories–"us" and "them."

Social-Cognitive or Role-Playing View (p. 114): A view suggesting that effects produced by hypnosis are the result of hypnotized persons' expectations about hypnosis and their social role as "hypnotized subject."

Social Cognitive Theory (p. 331): A theory of behavior suggesting that human behaviors are influenced by many cognitive factors as well as by reinforcement contingencies, and that human beings have an impressive capacity to regulate their own actions.

Social Development (p. 255): Changes in social behavior and social relations occurring over the life span.

Social Influence (p. 448): Attempts by one or more persons to change our behavior in some manner.

Social Loafing (p. 485): The tendency to reduce one's efforts when working in a group.

Social Network (p. 263): A group of people with whom one interacts regularly.

Social Norms (p. 449): Rules indicating how we should behave (or are expected to behave) in a given situation.

Social Psychology (p. 430): The branch of psychology that studies all aspects of social behavior and social thought.

Social Support (p. 356): The emotional and task resources provided by others that may serve to help buffer the adverse effects of chronic stress.

Somatic Nervous System (p. 36): The portion of the nervous system that connects the brain and spinal cord to voluntary muscles.

Somatoform Disorders (p. 396): Disorders in which individuals have symptoms typically associated with physical diseases or conditions, but in which no known organic or physiological basis for the symptoms can be found.

Somnambulism (p. 110): A sleep disorder in which individuals actually get up and move about while still asleep.

Source Traits (p. 329): According to Cattell, key dimensions of personality that underlie many other traits.

Split-Half Reliability (p. 218): The correlation between scores on two parts of a test.

Spontaneous Recovery (p. 133): Following extinction, reinstatement of conditioned stimulus-unconditioned stimulus pairings will produce a conditioned response.

Stage Theory (p. 252): Any theory proposing that all human beings move through an orderly and predictable series of changes.

Standardized Tests (p. 468): Reliable and valid tests that are used for a particular purpose and are administered in a systematic way.

Stanford-Binet Test (p. 216): A widely used individual test of intelligence.

State-Dependent Retrieval (p. 170): Occurs when aspects of our physical states serve as retrieval cues for information stored in long-term memory.

States of Consciousness (p. 98): Varying degrees of awareness of ourselves and the external world.

Stereotypes (p. 445): Cognitive frameworks suggesting that all members of specific social groups share certain characteristics.

Stimulants (p. 118): Drugs that increase activity in the nervous system (e.g., amphetamines, caffeine, nicotine).

Stimulus (p. 130): A physical event capable of affecting behavior.

Stimulus Control (p. 148): When a behavior occurs consistently in the presence of a discriminative stimulus.

Stimulus Discrimination (p. 133): The process by which organisms learn to respond to certain stimuli but not to others.

Stimulus Generalization (p. 133): The tendency of stimuli similar to a conditioned stimulus to evoke conditioned responses.

Storage (p. 164): The process through which information is retained in memory.

Stress (p. 348): The process by which we appraise and respond to events that disrupt, or threaten to disrupt, our physical or psychological functioning.

Stressors (p. 348): Events or situations in our environment that cause stress.

Striving for Superiority (p. 324): Attempts to overcome feelings of inferiority. According to Adler, this is the primary motive for human behavior.

Structured Interview (p. 468): An employment interview that is conducted in the same manner, using the same questions for all job applicants.

Subject Matter Experts (p. 475): Individuals familiar with a job who generate critical behavioral incidents in order to construct performance appraisal forms.

Subjective Well-Being (p. 306): Individuals' global judgments of their own life satisfaction.

Sublimation (p. 318): A defense mechanism in which threatening unconscious impulses are channeled into socially acceptable forms of behavior.

Subliminal Perception (p. 62): The presumed influence on the behavior of a stimulus that is below the threshold for conscious experience.

Substance Abuse (p. 404): A maladaptive pattern of substance use that results in repeated, significant adverse effects and maladaptive behavior, such as failure to meet obligations at work, in school, or at home; repeated use of a psychoactive substance in hazardous ways; recurrent legal problems related to the substance; and continued use of the substance despite its negative effects on social relationships.

Substance-Related Disorders (p. 403): Disorders related to the use of psychoactive substances.

Successful Aging (p. 268): Minimal physiological losses in many bodily functions, compared to younger persons, as a result of living a healthy lifestyle.

Superego (p. 317): According to Freud, the portion of human personality representing the conscience.

Suprachiasmatic Nucleus (SCN) (p. 99): A portion of the hypothalamus that seems to play an important role in the regulation of circadian rhythms.

Survey Method (p. 16): A research method in which large numbers of people answer questions about aspects of their views or their behavior.

Symbolic Play (p. 244): Play in which children pretend that one object is another object.

Sympathetic Nervous System (p. 36): The portion of the autonomic nervous system that readies the body for expenditure of energy.

Synapse (p. 32): A region where the axon of one neuron closely approaches other neurons or the cell membrane of other types of cells, such as muscle cells.

Synaptic Vesicles (p. 32): Structures in the axon terminals that contain various neurotransmitters.

Syntax (p. 212): Rules about how units of speech can be combined into sentences in a given language.

Systematic Observation (p. 15): A basic method of science in which the natural world, or various events or processes in it, are observed and measured in a very careful manner.

Systematic Processing (p. 438): Involves careful consideration of message content, the ideas it contains, and so on.

Such processing is quite effortful and absorbs much of our information-processing capacity.

Tardive Dyskinesia (p. 417): A side effect of some antipsychotic drugs involving loss of motor control, especially in the face.

Task Conflict (p. 486): Disagreement about how the team's primary activity should be accomplished.

Temperament (p. 255): Stable individual differences in attention, arousal, mood, and reactivity to new situations present at, or shortly after, birth.

Temporal Lobe (p. 41): The lobe of the cerebral cortex that is involved in hearing.

Teratogens (p. 237): Factors in the environment that can harm the developing fetus.

Test-Retest Reliability (p. 218): A measure of the extent to which scores on a test remain stable over time.

Thalamus (p. 40): A structure deep within the brain that receives sensory input from other portions of the nervous system and then transmits this information to the cerebral hemispheres and other parts of the brain.

Theory of Mind (p. 249): Refers to children's growing understanding of their own mental states and those of others.

Timbre (p. 73): The quality of a sound resulting from the complexity of a sound wave that, for example, helps us distinguish between the sound of a trumpet and that of a saxophone.

Tolerance (p. 117): Habituation to a drug so that larger and larger doses are required to produce effects of the same magnitude.

Top-Down Approach (p. 91): Approach to pattern recognition that starts with the analysis of high-level information, such as our knowledge, expectancies, and the context in which a stimulus is seen.

Trace Conditioning (p. 131): A form of forward conditioning in which the onset of the conditioned stimulus (CS) precedes the onset of the unconditioned stimulus (UCS) and the presentation of the CS and UCS does not overlap.

Trait Theories (p. 328): Theories of personality that focus on identifying the key dimensions along which people differ.

Transduction (p. 60): The translation of a physical energy into electrical signals by specialized receptor cells.

Transfer of Training (p. 473): The question of whether material learned during training is demonstrated on the job.

Transference (p. 406): In psychoanalysis, a patient's intense feelings of love or hate toward the analyst.

Transformational Leadership (p. 483): Leadership that consists of charisma, intellectual stimulation, and genuine concern for subordinates.

Trial and Error (p. 203): A method of solving problems in which possible solutions are tried until one succeeds.

Triarchic Theory (p. 215): A theory suggesting that there are three basic forms of intelligence: componential, experiential, and contextual.

Trichromatic Theory (p. 68): A theory of color perception suggesting that we have three types of cones, each primarily receptive to different wavelengths of light.

Two-Factor Theory (of emotion) (p. 300): *See* Schachter-Singer theory.

Type A Behavior Pattern (p. 339): A pattern consisting primarily of high levels of competitiveness, time urgency, and hostility.

Type B Behavior Pattern (p. 339): A pattern consisting of the absence of characteristics associated with the Type A behavior pattern.

Type D Personality Type (p. 367): A term used to describe a general tendency to cope with stress by keeping negative emotions to oneself. People who exhibit this behavior pattern are more likely to experience suppressed immune systems and health-related problems.

Unconditional Positive Regard (p. 325): In Rogers's theory, communicating to others that they will be respected or loved regardless of what they say or do.

Unconditioned Response (UCR) (p. 130): In classical conditioning, the response evoked by an unconditioned stimulus.

Unconditioned Stimulus (UCS) (p. 130): In classical conditioning, a stimulus that can evoke an unconditioned response the first time it is presented.

Utility (p. 467): The usefulness of a selection technique that takes both the criterion-related validity and the cost of the procedure into account.

Validity (p. 219): The extent to which a test actually measures what it claims to measure.

Variable-Interval Schedule (p. 146): A schedule of reinforcement in which a variable amount of time must elapse before a response will yield reinforcement.

Variable-Ratio Schedule (p. 146): A schedule of reinforcement in which reinforcement is delivered after a variable number of responses have been performed.

Vestibular Sense (p. 81): Our sense of balance.

Vestibule Training (p. 471): An on-site training method that uses a separate "practice" work area, allowing for observational learning.

Visual Images (p. 193): Mental pictures or representations of objects or events.

Wavelength (p. 67): The peak-to-peak distance in a sound or light wave.

Wernicke's Area (p. 48): An area in the temporal lobe that plays a role in the comprehension of speech.

Work Motivation (p. 478): The internal processes that activate, guide, and maintain behavior directed toward work.

Work Sample Test (p. 469): A selection test that requires job applicants to perform a sample of the work they would be expected to do on the job.

Working Memory (p. 166): A memory system in which information we are processing at the moment is held; formerly called *short-term memory*. Recent findings suggest that it involves more complex levels and forms of processing than was previously believed.

References

Acocella, J. (1998, April 6). The politics of hysteria. *The New Yorker, 64–79.*

Acton, D. A. (2001). The "color blind" therapist. *Art Therapy, 18,* 109–112.

Adams, R. J. (1987). An evaluation of color preference in early infancy. *Infant Behavior and Development, 10,* 143–150.

Ader, R., Kelly, K., Moynihan, J. A., Grota, L. J., & Cohen, N. (1993). Conditioned enhancement of antibody production using antigen as the unconditioned stimulus. *Brain, Behavior, and Immunity, 7,* 334–343.

Adler, N. J., & Bartholomew, S. (1992). Managing globally competent people. *Academy of Management Executive, 6,* 52–65.

Aggleton, J. P., & Young A. W. (2000). The enigma of the amygdale: On its contributions to human emotions. In R. D. Lane & L. Nadel (Eds.), *Cognitive neuroscience of emotion* (pp. 106–138). New York: Oxford University Press.

Aiken, L. R. (1991). *Psychological testing and assessment* (7th ed.). Boston: Allyn and Bacon.

Aiken, L. S., West, S. G., Woodward, C. K., Reno, R. R., & Reynolds, K. D. (1994). Increasing screening mammography in asymptomatic women: Evaluation of a second-generation, theory-based program. *Health Psychology, 13,* 526–538.

Ainsworth, M. D. S. (1973). The development of infant-mother attachment. In B. Caldwell & H. Riciutti (Eds.), *Review of child development research* (Vol. 3, pp. 1–94). Chicago: University of Chicago Press.

Ajzen, J. (1991). The theory of planned behavior: special issue: Theories of cognitive self-regulation. *Organizational Behavior and Human Decision Processes, 509,* 179–211.

Akerstedt, T., & Froberg, J. E. (1976). Interindividual differences in circadian pattern of catecholamine excretion, body temperature, performance, and subjective arousal. *Biological Psychology, 4,* 277–292.

Alicke, M. D., & Largo, E. (1995). The role of the self in the false consensus effect. *Journal of Experimental Social Psychology, 31,* 28–47.

Allen, L. S., & Gorski, R. A. (1992). Biology, brain architecture, and human sexuality. *Journal of National Institute of Health Research, 4,* 53–59.

Allred, J. B. (1993). Lowering serum cholesterol: Who benefits? *Journal of Nutrition, 123,* 1453–1459.

Allyn, J., & Festinger, L. (1961). The effectiveness of unanticipated persuasive communications. *Journal of Abnormal and Social Psychology, 62,* 35–40.

Aloise-Young, P. A., Graham, J. W., & Hansen, W. B. (1994). Peer influence on smoking initiation during early adolescence: A comparison of group members and group outsiders. *Journal of Applied Psychology, 79,* 281–287.

Alvarez-Borda, B., Ramirez-Amaya, V., Perez-Montfort, R., & Bermudez-Rattoni, F. (1995). Enhancement of antibody production by a learning paradigm. *Neurobiology of Learning and Memory, 64,* 103–105.

Amabile, T. M. (1983). *The social psychology of creativity.* New York: Springer-Verlag.

Amabile, T. M. (1996). *Creativity in context.* Boulder, CO: Westview.

Amaro, H. (1995). Love, sex, and power: Considering women's realities in HIV prevention. *American Psychologist, 50,* 437–447.

Amason, A. C. (1996). Distinguishing the effects of functional and dysfunctional conflict on strategic decision making: Resolving a paradox for top management groups. *Academy of Management Journal, 39,* 123–148.

Ambrose, M. L., Seabright, M. A., & Schminke, M. (2002). Sabotage in the workplace: The role of organizational justice. *Organizational Behavior and Human Decision Processes, 89,* 947–965.

Ambuel, B. (1995). Adolescents, unintended pregnancy, and abortion: The struggle for a compassionate social policy. *Current Directions in Psychological Science, 4,* 1–5.

American Academy of Pediatrics. (1998). Guidance for effective discipline. *Pediatrics, 101,* 723–728.

American Cancer Society. (1989). *Cancer facts and figures—1989.* Atlanta, GA: Author.

American Cancer Society. (2004). *Protect your skin from UV.* Retrieved March 10, 2004, from http://www.cancer.org/docroot/PED/content/ped_7_1x_Protect_Your_Skin_From_UV.asp?sitearea=PED.

American Psychiatric Association (1994). *Diagnostic and statistical manual of mental disorders* (4th ed.). Washington, DC: American Psychiatric Association.

American Psychological Association. (1995). Training in and dissemination of empirically-validated psychological procedures. Report and recommendations. *The Clinical Psychologist, 48,* 22–23.

American Psychological Association. (2003). Guidelines on multicultural education, training, research, practice, and organizational change for psychologists. *American Psychologist, 58,* 377–402.

Amoore, J. (1970). *Molecular basis of odor.* Springfield, IL: Thomas.

Amoore, J. (1982). Odor theory and odor classification. In E. Theimer (Ed.), *Fragrance chemistry-the science of the sense of smell.* New York: Academic Press.

Anand, G., & Winslow, R. (2003). Transformation in medicine is putting specialists at odds. *Wall Street Journal,* September 10.

Anderson, J. R. (1993). *Rules of the mind.* Hillsdale, NJ: Erlbaum.

Anderson, J. R., & Spellman, B. A. (1995). On the status of inhibitory mechanisms in cognition: Memory retrieval as a model case. *Psychological Review, 102,* 68–100.

Anderson, J. R., Bjork, R. A., & Bjork, E. L. (1994). Mechanisms of inhibition in long-term memory: A new taxonomy. *Journal of Experimental Psychology: Learning, Memory, and Cognition, 20,* 1063–1087.

Anderson, N. B. (1989). Racial differences in stress-induced cardiovascular reactivity and hypertension: Current status and substantive issues. *Psychological Bulletin, 105,* 89–105.

Andreason, N. C., & Black, D. (1995). *Introductory textbook of psychiatry* (2nd ed.) Washington, DC: American Psychiatric Press.

Andrews, E. A., Gosse, V. F., Gaulton, R. S., & Maddigan, R. I. (1999). Teaching introductory psychology at a distance by two-way interactive video. *Teaching of Psychology, 2,* 115–118.

Andrews, J. D. W. (1967). The achievement motive and advancement in two types of organization. *Journal of Personality and Social Psychology, 6,* 163–168.

Angier, N. (1998, September 1). Nothing becomes a man more than a woman's face. *New York Times,* p. F3.

Antrobus, J. (1991). Dreaming: Cognitive processes during cortical activation and high afferent thresholds. *Psychological Review, 98,* 96–212.

Arkin, R. (1991). *Biology of aging: Observations and principles.* Englewood Cliffs, NJ: Prentice-Hall.

Aronoff, J., Woike, B. A., & Hyman, L. M. (1992). Which are the stimuli in facial displays of anger and happiness? Configurational bases of emotional recognition. *Journal of Personality and Social Psychology, 62,* 1050–1066.

Aronoff, S. R., & Spilka, B. (1984–1985). Patterning of facial expressions among terminal cancer patients. *Omega, 15,* 101–108.

Aronson, E., Bridgeman, D. L., & Geffner, R. (1978). Interdependent interactions and prosocial behavior. *Journal of Research and Development in Education, 12,* 16–27.

Aronson, E., Fried, C., & Stone, J. (1991). Overcoming denial: Increasing the intention to use condoms through induction of hypocrisy. *American Journal of Public Health, 18,* 1636–1640.

Arvey, R. D., & Begalla, M. E. (1975). Analyzing the homemaker job using the Position Analysis Questionnaire. *Journal of Applied Psychology, 60,* 513–518.

Arvey, R. D., & Campion, J. E. (1982). The employment interview: A summary and review of recent research. *Personnel Psychology, 35,* 281–322.

Asch, S. E. (1951). Effects of group pressure upon the modification and distortion of judgment. In H. Guetzkow (Ed.), *Groups, leadership, and men.* Pittsburgh: Carnegie.

Asch, S. E. (1955). Opinions and social pressure. *Scientific American, 193,* 31–35.

Ashford, S. J. (1986). Feedback seeking in individual adaptation: A resource perspective. *Academy of Management Journal, 29,* 465–487.

Atkinson, R. C., & Shiffrin, R. M. (1968). Human memory: A proposed system and its control processes. In K. W. Spence & J. T. Spence (Eds.), *The psychology of learning and motivation: Advances in research and theory* (pp. 89–195). New York: Academic Press.

Au, T. K. F., Knightly, L. M., Jun, S. A., & Oh, J. S. (2002). Overhearing a language during childhood. *Psychological Science, 13,* 238–243.

Azar, B. (1999, June). Tailored interventions prove more effective. *APA Monitor, 30*(6), 38–39.

Bachman, J. G. (1987, February). An eye on the future. *Psychology Today,* pp. 6–7.

Baddeley, A. (1990). *Human memory: Theory and practice.* Boston: Allyn and Bacon.

Baddeley, A. D. (1992). Working memory. *Science, 255,* 556–559.

Baddeley, A. D. (1996). Exploring the central executive. *Quarterly Journal of Experimental Psychology, 49A,* 5–28.

Baddeley, A. D., & Hitsch, G. (1994). Developments in the concept of working memory. *Neuropsychology, 8,* 485–493.

Bailey, J. M., & Pillard, R. C. (1991). A genetic study of male sexual orientation. *Archives of General Psychiatry, 48,* 1089–1096.

Bailey, J. M., & Zucker, K. J. (1995). Childhood sex-typed behavior and sexual orientation: A conceptual analysis and quantitative review. *Developmental Psychology, 31,* 43–55.

Baillargeon, R. (1987). Object permanence in 3.5-and 4.5-month-old infants. *Developmental Psychology, 23,* 655–664.

Baillargeon, R. (1994). Physical reasoning in young infants: Seeking explanations for possible events. *British Journal of Developmental Psychology, 12,* 9–33.

Baillargeon, R., Needham, A., & DeVos, J. (1992). The development of young infants' intuitions about support. *Early Development and Parenting, 1,* 69–78.

Baker, A. G., & Mackintosh, N. J. (1977). Excitatory and inhibitory conditioning following uncorrelated presentations of CS and US. *Animal Learning and Behavior, 5*(3), 315–319.

Balogh, R. D., & Porter, R. H. (1986). Olfactory preferences resulting from mere exposure in human neonates. *Infant Behavior and Development, 9,* 395–401.

Baltes, P. B. (1987). Theoretical propositions of life-span developmental psychology: On the dynamics between growth and decline. *Developmental Psychology, 23,* 611–626.

Bandura, A. (1977). Self-efficacy: toward a unifying theory of behavioral change. *Psychological Review, 84,* 191–215.

Bandura, A. (1986). *Social foundations of thought and action: A social cognitive theory.* Englewood Cliffs, NJ: Prentice Hall.

Bandura, A. (1992). Exercise of personal agency through the self-efficacy mechanism. In R. Schwarzer (Ed.), *Self-efficacy: Thought control of action* (pp. 3–38). Washington, DC: Hemisphere.

Bandura, A. (1997). *Self-efficacy: The exercise of control.* New York: Freeman.

Bandura, A. (1999). A social cognitive theory of personality. In L. Pervin & D. John (Eds.), *Handbook of personality* (2nd ed.). New York: Guilford.

Bandura, A., Ross, D., & Ross, S. (1963). Imitation of film-mediated aggressive models. *Journal of Abnormal and Social Psychology, 66,* 3–11.

Banks, S. M., Salovey, P., Greener, S., Rothman, A. J., Moyer, A., Beauvais, J. & Epel, E. (1995). The effects of message framing on mammography utilization. *Health Psychology, 14,* 178–184.

Bannon, L. (2003). Why girls and boys get different toys. *Wall Street Journal*, February 14, 2003, B1, B4.

Barber, T. X., Chauncey, H. H., & Winer, R. A. (1964). Effects of hypnotic and nonhypnotic suggestions on parotid gland response to gustatory stimuli. *Psychosomatic Medicine, 26*, 374–380.

Barch, D. M., & Berenbaum, H. (1996). Language production and thought disorder in schizophrenia. *Journal of Abnormal Psychology, 105*, 81–88.

Bargh, J. A., Raymond, P., Pryor, J. B., & Strack, F. (1995). Attractiveness of the underling: An automatic power—sex association and its consequences for sexual harassment and aggression. *Journal of Personality and Social Psychology, 68*, 768–781.

Barkley, R. A., DuPaul, G. J., & McMurray, M. B. (1990). Comprehensive evaluation of attention deficit disorder with and without hyperactivity as defined by research criteria. *Journal of Consulting and Clinical Psychology, 58*, 775–789.

Barlow, D. H. (1988). *Anxiety and its disorders.* New York: Guilford Press.

Barlow, D. H. (1993). Disorders and emotion. *Psychological Inquiry, 2*, 58–71.

Baron, J. (1988). *Thinking and deciding.* Cambridge, England: Cambridge University Press.

Baron, R. A. (1970). Attraction toward the model and model's competence as determinants of adult imitative behavior. *Journal of Personality and Social Psychology, 14*, 335–344.

Baron, R. A. (1983). "Sweet smell of success?" The impact of pleasant artificial scents on evaluation of job applicants. *Journal of Applied Psychology, 68*, 709–713.

Baron, R. A. (1987). Mood of interviewer and the evaluation of job candidates. *Journal of Applied Social Psychology, 17*, 911–926.

Baron, R. A. (1993). Criticism (informal negative feedback) as a source of perceived unfairness in organizations: Effects, mechanisms, and countermeasures. In R. Cropanzano (Ed.), *Justice in the workplace: Approaching fairness in human resource management* (pp. 155–170). Hillsdale, NJ: Erlbaum.

Baron, R. A. (1997). The sweet smell of . . . helping: Effects of pleasant ambient odors on helping in shopping malls. *Personality and Social Psychology Bulletin, 2*, 498–503.

Baron, R. A. (1998). Cognitive mechanisms in entrepreneurship: Why, and when, entrepreneurs think differently than other persons. *Journal of Business Venturing, 13*, 275–294.

Baron, R. A. (2000). Psychological perspectives on entrepreneurship: Social and cognitive factors in entrepreneurs' success. *Current Directions in Psychological Science, 9*, 15–18.

Baron, R. A. (2004). The cognitive perspective: A valuable tool for answering entrepreneurship's basic "Why?" questions. *Journal of Business Venturing, 19*, 221–240.

Baron, R. A., & Bronfen, M. I. (1994). A whiff of reality: Empirical evidence concerning the effects of pleasant fragrances on work-related behavior. *Journal of Applied Social Psychology, 13*, 1179–1203.

Baron, R. A., & Byrne, D. (1987). *Social psychology,* 5th ed. Boston: Allyn & Bacon.

Baron, R. A., & Byrne, D. (2003). *Social psychology,* 10th ed. Boston: Allyn & Bacon.

Baron, R. A., & Kalsher, M. J. (1998). Effects of a pleasant ambient fragrance on simulated driving performance: The sweet smell of . . . safety? *Environment and Behavior, 30*, 535–552.

Baron, R. A., & Markman, G. D. (2003). Beyond social capital: The role of entrepreneurs' social competence in their financial success. *Journal of Business Venturing, 18*, 41–60.

Baron, R. A., & Richardson, D. (1994). *Human aggression* (2nd ed.). New York: Plenum.

Baron, R. A., & Shane, S. A. (2004). *Entrepreneurship: A process perspective.* Cincinnati: South-Western.

Baron, R. A., & Thomley, J. (1994). A whiff of reality: Positive affect as a potential mediator of the effects of pleasant fragrances on task performance and helping. *Environment and Behavior, 26*, 766–784.

Baron, R. A., Russell, G. W., & Arms, R. L. (1985). Negative ions and behavior: Impact on mood, memory, and aggression among Type A and Type B persons. *Journal of Personality and Social Psychology, 48*, 746–753.

Barrick, M. R., & Mount, M. K. (1991). The Big Five personality dimensions and job performance: A meta-analysis. *Personnel Psychology, 44*, 1–26.

Barrick, M. R., Stewart, G. L., Neubert, M. J., & Mount, M. K. (1998). Relating member ability and personality to work-team processes and team effectiveness. *Journal of Applied Psychology, 83*, 377–391.

Basoglu, M., Paker, M., Ozmen, E., Tasdemir, O., Sahin, D., Ceyhanli, A., & Incesu, C. (1996). Appraisal of self, social environment, and state authority as a possible mediator of posttraumatic stress disorder in tortured political activists. *Journal of Abnormal Psychology, 105*, 232–236.

Bass, B. M. (1985). *Leadership and performance beyond expectations.* New York: Free Press.

Bass, B. M. (1990). *Bass and Stogdill's handbook of leadership.* New York: Free Press.

Bass, B. M., & Avolio, B. J. (1993). Transformational leadership, transactional leadership, locus of control, and support for innovation. Key predictors of consolidated business unit performance. *Journal of Applied Psychology, 78*, 891–902.

Bass, B. M., Avolio, B. J., Jung, D. I., & Berson, Y. (2003). Predicting unit performance by assessing transformational and transactional leadership. *Journal of Applied Psychology, 88*, 207–218.

Bauer, P. (1996). What do infants recall of their lives? *American Psychologist 51*, 29–41.

Baum, A. (1991). Toxins, technology, and natural disasters. In A. Monat & R. S. Lazarus (Eds.), *Stress and coping: An anthology* (3rd ed., pp. 97–139). New York: Columbia University Press.

Baum, A., & Posluszny, D. M. (1999). Health psychology: Mapping biobehavioral contributions to health and illness. *Annual Review of Psychology, 50*, 137–163.

Baum, D. R., & Jonides, J. J. (1979). Cognitive maps: Analysis of comparative judgments of distance. *Memory and Cognition, 7*, 462–468.

Baumeister, R. F. (1990). Suicide as an escape from self. *Psychological Review, 97*, 90–113.

Baumeister, R. F., & Leary, M. R. (1995). The need to belong: Desire for interpersonal attachments as a fundamental human motivation. *Psychological Bulletin, 117*, 497–529.

Baumrind, D. (1996). A blanket injunction against disciplinary use of spanking is not warranted by the data. *Pediatrics, 98,* 828–831.

Beaman, A. L., Cole, N., Preston, M., Glentz, B., & Steblay, N. M. (1983). Fifteen years of the foot-in-the-door research: A meta-analysis. *Personality and Social Psychology Bulletin, 9,* 181–186.

Beck, A. T. (1976). *Cognitive therapy and the emotional disorders.* New York: International Universities Press.

Beck, A. T. (1985). *Anxiety disorders and phobias: A cognitive perspective.* New York: Basic Books.

Beck, A. T., Rush, A. J., Shaw, B. F., & Emery, G. (1979). *Cognitive theory of depression.* New York: Guilford Press.

Becker, H. C., Randall, C. L., Salo, A. L., Saulnier, J. L., & Weathersby, R. T. (1994). Animal research: Charting the course for FAS. *Alcohol Health and Research World, 18,* 10–16.

Begley, S. (2003). Good genes count, but many factors make up a high IQ. *Wall Street Journal,* June 26, 2003, B1.

Belli, R. F., & Loftus, E. F. (1996). The pliability of autobiographical memory: Misinformation and the false memory problem. In D. C. Rubin (Ed.), *Remembering our past* (pp. 157–179). New York: Cambridge University Press.

Belsky, J., & Cassidy, J. (1995). Attachment: Theory and evidence. In M. Rutter & D. Hay (Eds.), *Developmental through life: A handbook for clinicians* (pp. 373–402). Oxford, England: Blackwell.

Bem, D. J., & Honorton, C. (1994). Does psi exist? Replicable evidence for an anomalous process of information transfer. *Psychological Bulletin, 115,* 4–18.

Bem, S. L. (1984). Androgyny and gender schema theory: A conceptual and empirical integration. In R. A. Dientsbier & T. B. Sondregger (Eds.), *Nebraska Symposium on Motivation* (Vol. 34, pp. 179–226). Lincoln: University of Nebraska Press.

Bem, S. L. (1989). Genital knowledge and gender constancy in preschool children. *Child Development, 60,* 649–662.

Benjamin, L. T., Jr., & Dixon, D. N. (1996). Dream analysis by mail: An American woman seeks Freud's advice. *American Psychologist, 51,* 461–468.

Bentin, S., Sagiv, N., Mecklinger, A., Friederici, A., & von Cramon, Y. D. (2002). Priming visual face-processing mechanisms: Electrophy-

siological evidence. *Psychological Science, 13* (2), 190–193.

Bergin, A. E., & Lambert, M. J. (1978). The evaluation of therapeutic outcomes. In S. L. Garfield & A. E. Bergin (Eds.), *Handbook of psychotherapy and behavior change: An empirical analysis* (2nd ed., pp. 139–190). New York: Wiley.

Berk, L. E. (2000). *Child development* (5th ed.). Boston: Allyn & Bacon.

Berkowitz, L. (1984). Some effects of thoughts on anti-and pro-social influences of media events: A cognitive-neoassociation analysis, *Psychological Bulletin, 95,* 410–427.

Berlyne, D. E. (1967). Arousal and reinforcement. In D. Levine (Ed.), *Nebraska Symposium on Motivation* (Vol. 15, pp. 279–286). Lincoln: University of Nebraska Press.

Berndt, T. J. (2002). Friendship quality and social development. *Current Directions in Psychological Science, 11,* 7–10.

Bernstein, D. M., Atance, C., Loftus, G. R., & Meltzoff, A. (2004). We saw it all along: Visual hindsight bias in children and adults. *Psychological Science, 154,* 264–267.

Bernstein, I. L. (1999). Taste aversion learning: A contemporary perspective. *Nutrition, 15* (3), 229–234.

Berry, J. W., Worthing, E. I., Parrott, L., O'Connor, L. E., & Wade, J. N. G. (in press). Dispositional forgiveness: Development and construct validity of the Transgression Narrative Test of Forgiveness (TNTFO). *Personality and Social Psychology Bulletin.*

Besson, M., Faita, F., Peretz, I., Bonnel, A.-M., & Requin, J. (1998). Singing in the brain: Independence of lyrics and tunes. *Psychological Science, 9,* 494–498.

Biederman, I. (1987). Recognition-by-components: A theory of human image understanding. *Psychological Review, 94,* 115–147.

Birch, S. A. J., & Bloom, P. A. (2003). Children are cursed: An asymmetric bias in mental-state attribution. *Psychological Science, 14,* 283–286.

Birchler, G. R. (1992). Marriage. In V. B. Van Hasselt & M. Hersen (Eds.), *Handbook of social development: A lifespan perspective.* New York: Plenum.

Bixler, E. O., Kales, A., Soldatos, C. R., Kales, J. D., & Healey, S. (1979). Prevalence of sleep disorders in the Los Angeles metropolitan area.

American Journal of Psychiatry, 136, 1257–1262.

Black, J. S., & Mendenhall, M. (1990). Cross-cultural training effectiveness: A review and a theoretical framework for future research. *Academy of Management Review, 15,* 113–136.

Blackmore, S. (1986). A critical guide to parapsychology. *Skeptical Inquirer, 11* (1), 97–102.

Blaney, P. H. (1986). Affect and memory: A review. *Psychological Bulletin, 99,* 229–246.

Blascovich, J., & Tomaka, J. (1996). The biopsycho-social model of arousal regulation. *Advances in Experimental Social Psychology, 28,* 1–51.

Blatt, S. J., Zuroff, D. C., Quinlan, D. M., & Pilkonis, P. (1996). Interpersonal factors in brief treatment of depression: Further analysis of the NIMH Treatment of Depression Collaborative Research Program. *Journal of Consulting and Clinical Psychology, 64,* 162–171.

Block, J. H. (1995). A contrarian view of the five-factor approach to personality description. *Psychological Bulletin, 117,* 187–215.

Block, V., Hennevin, E., & Leconte, P. (1977). Interaction between post-trial reticular stimulation and subsequent paradoxical sleep in memory consolidation processes. In R. R. Drucker-Colin & J. L. McGaugh (Eds.), *Neurology of sleep and memory.* New York: Academic Press.

Bobo, L. (1983). Whites' opposition to busing: Symbolic racism or realistic group conflict? *Journal of Personality and Social Psychology, 45,* 1196–1210.

Bobocel, D. R., & Meyer, J. P. (1994). Escalating commitment to a failing course of action: Separating the roles of choice and justification. *Journal of Applied Psychology, 79,* 360–363.

Boling, N. C., & Robinson, D. H. (1999). Individual study, interactive multimedia, or cooperative learning: Which activity best supplements lecture-based distance education? *Journal of Educational Psychology, 91,* 169–174.

Bond, R., & Smith, P. B. (1996). Culture and conformity: A meta-analysis of studies using Asch's (1952b, 1956) line judgment task. *Psychological Bulletin, 119,* 111–137.

Bongar, B. (1991). *The suicidal patient: Clinical and legal standards of care.*

510 References www.mypsychlab.com

Washington, DC: American Psychological Association.

Bookstein, F. L., Sampson, P. D., Streissgarth, A. P., & Barr, H. M. (1996). Exploiting redundant measurement of dose and developmental outcome: New methods from the behavioral teratology of alcohol. *Developmental Psychology, 32,* 404–415.

Bootzin, R. R., Acocella, J. R., & Alloy, L. B. (1993). *Abnormal psychology* (6th ed.). New York: McGraw-Hill.

Borges, G., & Rosovsky, H. (1996). Suicide attempts and alcohol consumption in an emergency room sample. *Journal of Studies on Alcohol, 57,* 543–548.

Borke, H. (1975). Piaget's mountains revisited: Changes in the egocentric landscape. *Developmental Psychology, 11,* 240–243.

Bornstein, R. F. (1992). Subliminal mere exposure effects. In R. Bornstein & T. S. Pittman (Eds.), *Perception without awareness: Cognitive, clinical, and social perspectives* (pp. 191–210). New York: Guilford Press.

Borod, J. C. (1993). Cerebral mechanisms underlying facial, prosodic, and lexical emotional expressions: A review of neuropsychological studies and methodological issues. *Neuropsychology, 7,* 445–463.

Bosma, H., Stansfeld, S. A., & Marmot, M. G. (1998). Job control, personal characteristics, and heart disease. *Journal of Occupational Health Psychology, 3* (4), 402–409.

Bouchard, T. J., Jr., Lykken, D. T., McGue, M., Segal, N. L. & Tellegen, A. (1990). Sources of human psychological differences: The Minnesota Study of Twins Reared Apart. *Science, 250,* 223–228.

Boudreau, J. W. (1991). Utility analysis for decisions in human resource management. In M. D. Dunnette & L. M. Hough (Eds.), *Handbook of industrial and organizational psychology* (Vol. 2, pp. 621–745). Palo Alto, CA: Consulting Psychologists Press.

Bowers, K. S. (1992). Imagination and dissociation in hypnotic responding. *International Journal of Clinical and Experimental Hypnosis, 40,* 253–275.

Bowles, N., & Hynds, F. (1978). *Psy search: The comprehensive guide to psychic phenomena.* New York: Harper & Row.

Bowman, E. S., & Nurnberger, J. K. (1993). Genetics of psychiatry diagnosis and treatment. In D. L. Dunner (Ed.), *Current psychiatric therapy* (pp. 46–56). Philadelphia: Saunders.

Braffman, W., & Kirsch, I. (1999). Imaginative suggestibility and hypnotizability: An empirical analysis. *Journal of Personality and Social Psychology, 77,* 578–587.

Brainerd, C. J. (1996). Piaget: A centennial celebration. *Psychological Science, 7,* 191–195.

Brainerd, C. J., & Reyna, V. F. (1998). When things that were never experienced are easier to "remember" than things that were. *Psychological Science, 9,* 484–489.

Brannick, M. T., & Levine, E. L. (2002). *Job analysis: Methods, research, and applications for human resource management in the new millennium.* Thousand Oaks, CA: Sage.

Braverman, N. S., & Bronstein, P. (Eds.). (1985). Experimental assessments and clinical applications of conditioned food aversions. *Annals of the New York Academy of Sciences, 443,* 1–41.

Brean, H. (1958, March 31). What hidden sell is all about. *Life,* pp. 104–114.

Breedlove, S. M. (1994). Sexual differentiation of the human nervous system. *Annual Review of Psychology, 45,* 389–418.

Brembs, B. (2003). Operant reward learning in Aplysis. *Current Directions in Psychological Science, 12* (6), 218–221.

Brendgen, M., Vitaro, F., & Bukowski. W. M. (2000). Deviant friends and early adolescents' emotional and behavioral adjustment. *Journal of Research on Adolescence, 10,* 172–189.

Brettz, R. D., & Thompsett, R. E. (1992). Comparing traditional and integrative learning methods in organizational training programs. *Journal of Applied Psychology, 77,* 941–951.

Brigham, J. C., & Barkowitz, P. (1978). Do "they all look alike"? The effects of race, sex, experience, and attitudes on the ability to recognize faces. *Journal of Applied Social Psychology, 8,* 307–318.

Brockner, J., & Rubin, J. Z. (1985). *Entrapment in escalating conflicts.* New York: Springer-Verlag.

Brosnan, S., & de Waal, F. (2003). *Nature.* (Described by L. Beil, *Dallas Morning News,* September 18, 2003.)

Broussaud, D., di Pellegrino, G., & Wise, S. P. (1996). Frontal lobe mechanisms subserving vision-for-action versus vision-for-perception. *Behavioural Brain Research, 72,* 1–15.

Brown, J. (1968). Reciprocal facilitation and impairment in free recall. *Psychonomic Science, 10,* 41–42.

Brown, S. L., Nesse, R. M., Vinokur, A. D., & Smith, D. M. (2003). Providing social support may be more beneficial than receiving it. *Psychological Science, 14* (4), 320–327.

Bruder, G. E., Stewart, M. W., Mercier, M. A., Agosti, V., Leite, P., Donovan, S., & Quitkin, F. M. (1997). Outcome of cognitive-behavioral therapy for depression: Relation to hemispheric dominance for verbal processing. *Journal of Abnormal Psychology, 106,* 138–144.

Buehler, R., Griffin, D., & Ross, M. (1994). Exploring the "planning fallacy": Why people underestimate their task completion times. *Journal of Personality and Social Psychology, 67,* 355–381.

Burger, J. M., & Cornelius, T. (2003). Raising the price of agreement: Public commitment and the lowball compliance procedure. *Journal of Applied Social Psychology, 3,* 923–934.

Burish, T. G., & Carey, M. P. (1986). Conditioned aversive response in cancer chemotherapy patients: Theoretical and developmental analysis. *Journal of Consulting and Clinical Psychology, 54,* 593–600.

Burroughs, V. J., Randall, M. W., & Levy, R. A. (2002). Racial and ethnic differences in response to medicines: Toward individualized pharmaceutical treatment. *Journal of the National Medical Association, 94,* 1–26.

Bushman, B. J. (1984). Perceived symbols of authority and their influence on compliance. *Journal of Applied Social Psychology, 14,* 501–508.

Bushman, B. J. (1988). The effects of apparel on compliance: A field experiment with a female authority figure. *Personality and Social Psychology Bulletin, 14,* 459–467.

Bushman, B. J. (1995). Moderating role of trait aggressiveness in the effects of violent media on aggression. *Journal of Personality and Social Psychology, 69,* 950–960.

Bushman, B. J. (1998). Effects of television violence on memory for commercial messages. *Journal of Experimental Psychology: Applied, 4,* 291–307.

Bushman, B. J., & Baumeister, R. F. (1988). Threatened egotism, narcissim, self-esteem, and direct and displaced aggression: Does self-love or self-hate lead to violence? *Journal of Personality and Social Psychology, 75,* 219–229.

Buss, D. M. (1999). *Evolutionary psychology.* Boston: Allyn & Bacon.

Buss, D. M., & Schmitt, D. P. (1993). Sexual strategies theory: An evolutionary perspective on human mating. *Psychological Review, 100,* 204–232.

Butcher, J. N. (1990). *MMPI–2 in psychological treatment.* New York: Oxford University Press.

Buunk, B. P. (1995). Sex, self-esteem, dependency, and extradyadic sexual experience as related to jealousy responses. *Journal of Social and Personal Relationships, 12,* 147–153.

Byrne, D. (1971). *The attraction paradigm.* New York: Academic Press.

Byrne, D. (1982). Predicting human sexual behavior. In A. G. Kraut (Ed.), *The G. Stanley Hall Lecture Series* (Vol. 2, pp. 363–364, 368). Washington, DC: American Psychological Association.

Byrne, D. (1992). The transition from controlled laboratory experimentation to less controlled settings: Surprise! Additional variables are operative. *Communication Monographs, 59,* 190–198.

Byrne, D., & Smeaton, G. (1988). The Feeling Scale: Positive and negative affective responses. In C. M. Davis, W. L. Yarger, R. Bauserman, G. Scheer, & S. L. Davis (Eds.), *Handbook of sexuality-related measures* (pp. 50–52). Thousand Oaks, CA: Sage.

Cacioppo, J. T., Hawkley, L. C., & Berntson, G. G. (2003). The anatomy of loneliness. *Current Directions in Psychological Science, 12,* 71–74.

Cacioppo, J. T., Petty, R. E., & Quintanar, L. R. (1982). Individual differences in relative hemisphere alpha abundance and cognitive responses persuasive communications. *Journal of Personality and Social Psychology, 43,* 623–626.

Cadoret, R. J., Troughton, E., & O'Gorman, T. W. (1987). Genetic and environmental factors in alcohol abuse and antisocial personality. *Journal of Studies on Alcohol, 48,* 1–8.

Campbell, J. N., & LaMotte, R. H. (1983). Latency to detection of first pain. *Brain Research, 266,* 203–208.

Campion, M. E., Pursell, E. D., & Brown, B. K. (1988). Structured interviewing: Raising the psychometric properties of the employment interview. *Personnel Psychology, 41,* 25–42.

Campos, J. J., Langer, A., & Krowitz, A. (1970). Cardiac responses on the visual cliff in prelocomotor human infants. *Science, 170,* 196–197.

Cannon, T. D., Rosso, I. M., Bearden, C. E., Sanchez, L. E., & Hadley, T. (1999). A prospective cohort study of neurodevelopmental processes in the genesis and epigenesis of schizophrenia. *Development and Psychopathology, 11,* 467–485.

Cantor, N., & Sanderson, C. A. (1999). Life task participation and well-being: The importance of taking part in daily life. In D. Kahneman, E. Diener, & N. Schwarz (Eds.), *Well-being: The foundations of hedonic psychology.* New York: Russell Sage Foundation.

Capaldi, E. J. (1978). Effects of schedule and delay of reinforcement on acquisition speed. *Animal Learning and Behavior, 6,* 330–334.

Capaldi, E. J., Alptekin, S., & Birmingham, K. (1997). Discriminating between reward-produced memories: Effects of differences in reward magnitude. *Animal Learning & Behavior, 25,* 171–176.

Capaldi, E. J., & Birmingham, K. M. (1998). Reward produced memories regulate memory-discrimination learning, extinction, and other forms of discrimination learning. *Journal of Experimental Psychology: Animal Behavior Processes, 24,* 254–264.

Carey, M. P., Braaten, L. S., Maisto, S. A., Gleason, J. R., Forsyth, A. D., Durant, L. E., & Jaworski, B. C. (2000). Using information, motivational enhancement, and skills training to reduce the risk of HIV infection for low-income urban women: A second randomized clinical trail. *Health Psychology, 19* (1), 3–11.

Carey, M. P., Morrison-Beedy, D., & Johnson B. T. (1997). The HIV-Knowledge Questionnaire: Development and evaluation of a reliable, valid, and practical self-administered questionnaire. *AIDS and Behavior, 1* , 61–74.

Carlo, G., Koller, S. H., Eisenberg, N., Da Silva, M. S., & Frohlich, C. B. (1996). A cross-national study on the relations among prosocial moral reasoning, gender role orientations, and prosocial behavior. *Developmental Psychology, 32,* 231–240.

Carlson, N. R. (1998). *Physiology of behavior* (6th ed.). Needham Heights, MA: Allyn & Bacon.

Carlson, N. R. (1999). *Foundations of physiological psychology* (4th ed.). Boston: Allyn & Bacon.

Carpendale, J. L. M., & Krebs, D. L. (1995). Variations in moral judgment as a function of type of dilemma and moral choice. *Journal of Personality, 63,* 289–313.

Carroll, J. M., & Russell, J. A. (1996). Do facial expressions signal specific emotions? Judging emotion from the face in context. *Journal of Personality and Social Psychology, 70,* 205–218.

Carstensen, L. I., Isaacowitz, D. M., & Charles, S. T. (1999). Taking time seriously: A life-span theory of social selectivity. *American Psychologist, 54,* 165–181.

Carstensen, L. L., & Charles, S. T. (1998). Emotion in the second half of life. *Current Directions in Psychological Science, 7,* 144–149.

Carstensen, L. L., Pasupathi, M., & Mary, U. (in press). *Emotion experiences in the daily lives of older and younger adults.* Manuscript submitted for publication.

Carver, C. S., & Glass, D. C. (1978). Coronary-prone behavior pattern and interpersonal aggression. *Journal of Personality and Social Psychology, 37,* 361–366.

Carver, C. S., & Scheier, M. F. (1981). *Attention and self-regulation: A control-theory approach to human behavior.* New York: Springer-Verlag.

Caspi, A. (2000). The child is father of the man: Personality continuities from childhood to adulthood. *Journal of Personality and Social Psychology, 78,* 158–172.

Catania, A. C. (1992). *Learning* (3rd ed.). Englewood Cliffs, NJ: Prentice-Hall.

Cattell, R. B. (1963). Theory of fluid and crystallized intelligence: A critical experiment. *Journal of Educational Psychology, 54,* 1–22.

Cattell, R. B., & Dreger, R. M. (Eds.). (1977). *Handbook of modern personality theory.* Washington, DC: Hemisphere.

Cellular Telecommunications Industry Association. (2001). *CTIA's world of wireless communications.* Available: http:// www.wow-com.com/

Centers for Disease Control. (1993). Smoking cessation during previous year among adults—United States,

1990 and 1991. *Mortality and Morbidity Weekly Report, 42*(26), 504–507.

Centers for Disease Control. (1994). *Preventing tobacco use among young people, a report of the Surgeon General.* Atlanta: U.S. Department of Health and Human Services.

Centers for Disease Control. (2001). HIV and AIDS—United States, 1981–2001. *Mortality and Morbidity Weekly Report, 50,* 430–434.

Centers for Disease Control. (2002). Annual smoking-attributable mortality, years of potential life lost, and economic costs—United States, 1995–1999. *Mortality and Morbidity Weekly Report, 51,* 300–303.

Centers for Disease Control. (2003). Cigarette smoking among adults—United States, 2001. *Mortality and Morbitiy Weekly Report, 52,* 953–956.

Centerwall, B. S. (1989). Exposure to television as a cause of violence. In G. Comstock (Ed.), *Public communication and behavior* (Vol. 2). San Diego: Academic Press.

Chaiken, S., Liberman, A., & Eagly, A. H. (1989). Heuristic and systematic processing within and beyond persuasion context. In J. S. Uleman & J. A. Bargh (Eds.), *Unintended thought* (pp. 212–252). New York: Guilford Press.

Chang, E. C., & Asakawa, K. (2003). Cultural variations on optimistic and pessimistic bias for self versus a sibling: Is there evidence for self-enhancement in the West and for self-criticism in the East when the referent group is specified? *Journal of Personality and Social Psychology, 84,* 569–581.

Chaplin, W. F., Phillips, J. B., Brown, J. D., Clanton, N. R., & Stein, J. L. (2000). Handshaking, gender, personality, and first impressions. *Journal of Personality and Social Psychology, 79,* 110–117.

Cheng, D. T., Knight, D. C., Smith, C. N., Stein, E. A., & Helmstetter, F. J. (2003). Functional MRI of human amygdala activity during Pavlovian fear conditioning: Stimulus processing versus response expression. *Behavioral Neuroscience, 117* (1), 3–10.

Chess, S., & Thomas, A. (1984). *Origins and evolution of behavior disorders.* New York: Brunner/Mazel.

Chino, Y., Smith, E., Hatta, S., & Cheng, H. (1997). Post-natal development of binocular disparity sensitivity in neurons of the primate visual cortex. *Journal of Neuroscience, 17,* 296–307.

Chomsky, N. (1968). *Language and mind.* New York: Harcourt Brace.

Chorney, M. J., Chorney, K., Seese, N., Owen, M. J., Daniels, J., McGuffin, P., Thompson, L. A., Detterman, D. K., Benbow, C., Lubinski, D., Eley, T., & Plomin, R. (1998). A quantitative trait locus associated with cognitive ability in children. *Psychological Science, 9,* 159–166.

Cialdini, R. B. (1994). Interpersonal influence. In S. Shavitt & T. C. Brock (Eds.), *Persuasion* (pp. 195–218). Boston: Allyn & Bacon.

Cialdini, R. B., Cacioppo, J. T., Bassett, R., & Miller, J. A. (1978). A low-ball procedure for producing compliance: Commitment then cost. *Journal of Personality and Social Psychology, 36,* 463–476.

Cialdini, R. B., Kallgren, C. A., & Reno, R. R. (1991). A focus theory of normative conduct. *Advances in Experimental Social Psychology, 24,* 201–234.

Ciavarella, M. A., Bucholtz, A. K., Riordan, C. M., Gatewood, R. D., & Stokes, G. S. (in press). The give five and venture success: Is there a linkage? *Journal of Business Venturing.*

Clark, A. E., & Oswald, A. J. (1994). Unhappiness and unemployment. *Economic Journal, 104,* 648–659.

Clark, W. C., & Clark, S. B. (1980). Pain responses in Nepalese porters. *Science, 209,* 410–412.

Clarke-Stewart, A., Friedman, S., & Koch, J. (1985). *Child development: A topical approach.* New York: John Wiley & Sons.

Clum, G. A., & Bowers, T. G. (1990). Behavior therapy better than placebo treatments: Fact or artifact? *Psychological Bulletin, 107,* 110–113.

Coates, T. J., & Collins, C. (1998, July). Preventing HIV infection. *Scientific American,* 96–97.

Cohen, S., Doyle, W. J., Turner, R., Alper, C. M., & Skoner, D. P. (2003). Sociability and susceptibility to the common cold. *Psychological Science, 14* (5), 389–395.

Cohen, S., Frank, E., Doyle, W. J., Skoner, D. P., Rabin, B. S., & Gwaltney, J. M. (1998). Types of stressors that increase susceptibility to the common cold in healthy adults. *Health Psychology, 3,* 214–223.

Colcombe, S., & Kramer, A. F. (2003). Fitness effects on the cognitive function of older adults: A meta-analytic study. *Psychological Science, 14,* 125–130.

Cole, M. (1999). Culture in development. In M. H. Bornstein & M. E. Lamb (Eds.), *Developmental psychology: An advanced textbook* (4th ed.). Hillsdale, NJ: Erlbaum.

Collins, C., Locke, E., and Hanges, P. J. (2000). The relationship of need for achievement to entrepreneurial behavior: A meta-analysis. Working paper, University of Maryland.

Colombo, J., & Richman, W. A. (2002). Infant timekeeping: Attention and temporal estimation in 40-month-olds. *Psychological Science, 13,* 475–479.

Colwill, R. M. (1993). An associative analysis of instrumental learning. *Current Directions in Psychological Science, 2,* 111–116.

Colwill, R. M., & Rescorla, R. A. (1985). Postconditioning devaluation of a reinforcer affects instrumental responding. *Journal of Experimental Psychology, 11,* 120–132.

Colwill, R. M., & Rescorla, R. A. (1988). Associations between the discriminative stimulus and the reinforcer in instrumental learning. *Journal of Experimental Psychology, 14,* 155–164.

Conklin, H. M., & Iacono, W. G. (2002). Schizophrenia: A neurodevelopmental perspective. *Current Directions in Psychological Science, 11,* 33–37.

Conti, R., Collins, M. A., & Picariello, M. L. (2001). The impact of competition on intrinsic motivation and creativity: Considering gender, gender segregation, and gender role orientation. *Personality and Individual Differences, 30,* 1273–1289.

Coren, S., & Girgus, J. S. (1978). *Seeing is deceiving: The psychology of visual illusion.* Hillsdale, NJ: Lawrence Erlbaum.

Coren, S., Girgus, J. S., Erlichman, H., & Hakstean, A. R. (1976). An empirical taxonomy of visual illusions. *Perception & Psychophysics, 20,* 129–137.

Costa, P. T., Jr., & McCrae, R. R. (1989). *The NEO-PI/NEO-FFI manual supplement.* Odessa, FL: Psychological Assessment Resources.

Costa, P. T., Jr., & McCrae, R. R. (1994). The Revised NEO Personality Inventory (NEO-PI-R). In R. Briggs & J. M. Cheek (Eds.), *Personality measures: Development and evaluation* (Vol. 1). Greenwich, CT: JAI Press.

Cowart, B. J., & Rawson, N. E. (2001). Olfaction. In E. B. Goldstein (Ed.), *Blackwell handbook of perception* (pp. 567–600). Oxford: Blackwell.

Coyle, J. T. (1987). Alzheimer's disease. In G. Adelman (Ed.), *Encyclopedia of neuroscience* (pp. 29–31). Boston: Birkhauser.

Coyle, J. T., Price, D. L., & DeLong, M. R. (1983). Alzheimer's disease: A disorder of cortical cholinergic innervation. *Science, 219,* 1184–1190.

Craik, F. I. M., & Lockhart, R. S. (1972). Levels of processing: A framework for memory research. *Journal of Verbal Learning and Verbal Behavior, 11,* 671–684.

Craik, F. I. M., & Tulving, E. (1975). Depth of processing and the retention of words in episodic memory. *Journal of Experimental Psychology: General, 104,* 268–294.

Crawford, H. J., Knebel, T., Vendemia, J. M. (1998). The nature of hypnotic analgesia: Neurophysiological foundation and evidence. *Contemporary Hypnosis, 15,* 22–33.

Crespi, L. P. (1942). Quantitative variation of incentive and performance in the white rat. *American Journal of Psychology, 55,* 467–517.

Crick, F., & Mitchison, G. (1995). REM sleep and neural nets. *Behavioral Brain Research, 69,* 147–155.

Croyle, R. T. (1992). Appraisal of health threats: Cognition, motivation, and social comparison. *Cognitive Therapy and Research, 16,* 165–182.

Csikszentmihalyi, M., & Larson, R. (1984). *Being adolescent: Conflict and growth in the teenage years.* New York: Basic Books.

Culbertson, F. M. (1997). Depression and gender: An international review. *American Psychologist, 52,* 25–31.

Cumming, S., Hay, P., Lee, T., & Sachdev, P. (1995). Neuropsychological outcomes from psychosurgery for obsessive–compulsive disorder. *Australian & New Zealand Journal of Psychiatry, 29,* 293–298.

Cunningham, J., Dockery, D. W., & Speizer, F. E. (1994). Maternal smoking during pregnancy as a predictor of lung functions in children. *American Journal of Epidemiology, 139,* 1139–1152.

Cunningham, M. R., Roberts, A. R., Wu, C. H., Barbee, A. P., & Druen, P. B. (1995). "Their ideas of beauty are, on the whole, the same as ours": Consistency and variability in the cross-cultural perception of female physical attractiveness. *Journal of Personality and Social Psychology, 68,* 261–279.

Czeisler, C. A., Moore-Ede, M. C., & Coleman, R. M. (1982). Rotating shift work schedules that disrupt sleep are improved by applying Circadian principles. *Science, 217,* 460–462.

Dadds, M. R., Bovbjerg, D. H., Redd, W. H., & Cutmore, T. R. (1997). Imagery in human classical conditioning. *Psychological Bulletin, 122,* 89–103.

Daley, T. C., Whaley, S. E., Sigman, M. D., Espinosa, M. P., & Neumann, C. (2003). IQ on the rise: The Flynn effect in rural Kenyan children. *Psychological Science, 14,* 215–219.

Damak, S., Rong, M., Yasumatsu, K., Kokrashvili, Z., Varadarajan, V., Zou, S., Jiang, P., Ninomiya, Y., & Margolskee, R. F. (2003). Detection of sweet and umami taste in the absence of taste receptor T1r3. *Science, 301,* 850–853.

Dangerous Decibels. (2004). Retrieved March 10, 2004, from http://www.dangerousdecibels.org/

Daniel, J., & Potasova, A. (1989). Oral temperature and performance in 8 hour and 12 hour shifts. *Ergonomics, 32,* 689–696.

Dansinger, M. (2003). *One Year Effectiveness of the Atkins, Ornish, Weight Watchers, and Zone Diets in Decreasing Body Weight and Heart Disease Risk.* Paper presented at the American Heart Association's annual meeting, Orlando, Florida.

Daum, I., Ackermann, H., Schugens, M. M., Reimold, C., Dichgans, J., & Birbaumer, N. (1993). The cerebellum and cognitive functions in humans. *Behavioral Neuroscience, 104,* 411–419.

Daum, I., & Schugens, M. M. (1996). On the cerebellum and classical conditioning. *Current Directions in Psychological Science, 5,* 58–61.

Davidson, K., & Hopson, J. L. (1988). Gorilla business. *Image* (San Francisco Chronicle), 14–18.

Davies, M., Stankov, L., & Roberts, R. D. (1998). Emotional intelligence: In search of an elusive construct. *Journal of Personality and Social Psychology, 75,* 989–1015.

De Corte, E. (2003). Transfer as the productive use of acquired knowledge, skills, and motivations. *Current Directions in Psychological Science, 12,* 142–146.

De Waal, F. B. M. (2002). Evolutionary psychology: The wheat and the chaff. *Current Directions in Psychological Science, 11,* 187–191.

Deary, I. J. (1995). Auditory inspection time and intelligence: What is the direction of causation? *Developmental Psychology, 31,* 237–250.

Deary, I. J., & Stough, C. (1996). Intelligence and inspection time. *American Psychologist, 51,* 599–608.

Deaux, K. (1993). Commentary: Sorry, wrong number—a reply to Gentile's call. *Psychological Science, 4,* 125–126.

Deci, E. L. (1975). *Intrinsic motivation.* New York: Plenum.

Deci, E. L., & Ryan, R. M. (1985). *Intrinsic motivation and self-determination in human behavior.* New York: Plenum Press.

Delis, D. C., Squire, L. R., Bihrle, A., & Massman, P. S. (1992). Componential analysis of problem-solving ability: Performance of patients with frontal lobe damage and amnesic patients on a new sorting test. *Neuropsychologia, 30,* 680–697.

DeLongis, A., Folkman, S., & Lazarus, R. S. (1988). The impact of daily stress on health and mood: Psychological and social resources as mediators. *Journal of Personality and Social Psychology, 54,* 486–495.

Dement, W. C. (1975). *Some must watch while some must sleep.* San Francisco: W. H. Freeman.

Dement, W. C., & Kleitman, N. (1957). The relation of eye movement during sleep to dream activity: An objective method for the study of dreaming. *Journal of Experimental Psychology, 53,* 339–353.

Dement, W. C., & Wolpert, E. A. (1958). The relation of eye movements, body mobility and external stimuli to dream content. *Journal of Experimental Psychology, 55,* 543–553.

Denollet, J. (1998). Personality and coronary heart disease: The Type-D Scale-16 (DS16). *Annals of Behavioral Medicine, 20,* 209–215.

DePaulo, B. M. (1993). Nonverbal behavior and self-presentation. *Psychological Bulletin, 111,* 203–242.

DePaulo, B. M., & Kashy, D. A. (1998). Everyday lies in close and casual relationships. *Journal of Personality and Social Psychology, 74,* 63–79.

DePaulo, B. M., Lindsay, J. J., Malone, B. E., Muhlenbruck, L., Chandler, K., & Cooper, H. (2003). Cues to deception. *Psych Psychological Bulletin, 129,* 74–118.

Desimone, R., & Ungerleider, L. G. (1989). Neural mechanisms of visual processing in monkeys. In F. Boller & J. Garfman (Eds.), *Handbook of neuropsychology* (pp. 267–299). New York: Elsevier.

Detweiler, J. B., Bedell, B. T., Salovey, P., Pronin, E., & Rothman, A. J. (1999). Message framing and sunscreen use: Gain-framed messages motivate beach-goers. *Health Psychology, 18,* 189–196.

Deutsch, D. (2002). The puzzle of absolute pitch. *Current Directions in Psychological Science, 11* (6), 200–203.

DeValois, R. L., & DeValois, K. K. (1975). Neural coding of color. In E. C. Carterette & M. P. Friedman (Eds.), *Handbook of perception* (pp. 117–166). New York: Academic Press.

DeValois, R. L., & DeValois, K. K. (1993). A multistage color model. *Vision Research, 33,* 1053–1065.

Dhami, M. K. (2003). Psychological models of professional decision making. *Psychological Science, 14,* 175–180.

Diego, M. A., Jones, N. A., Field, T., Hernandez-Reif, M., Schanberg, S., Kuhn, C., McAdam, V., Galamaga, R., & Galamaga, M. (1998). Aromatherapy positively affects mood, EEG patterns of alertness and math computations. *International Journal of Neuroscience, 96,* 217–224.

Diekmann, K. A., Tenbrunsel, A. E., Shah, P. P., Schroth, H. A., & Bazerman, M. H. (1996). The descriptive and prescriptive use of previous purchase price in negotiations. *Organizational Behavior and Human Decision Processes, 66,* 179–191.

Diener, E., & Diener, C. (1996). Most people are happy. *Psychological Science, 7,* 181–185.

Diener, E., & Lucas, R. (2003). Personality and subjective well-being. In D. Kahneman, E. Diener, & N. Schwarz (Eds.), *Well-being: The foundations of hedonic psychology.* New York: Russell Sage.

Diener, E., & Lucas, R. R. (1999). Personality and subjective well-being. In D.

Kahneman, E. Diener, & N. Schwarz (Eds.), *Well-being: The foundations of hedonic psychology* (pp. 434–450). New York: Russell Sage Foundation.

Diener, E., & Seligman, M. E. P. (2002). Very happy people. *Psychological Science, 13,* 81–84.

Diener, E., & Suh, E. (Eds.) (1998). *Subjective well-being across cultures.* Cambridge, MA: MIT Press.

Diener, E., Gohm, C., Suh, E., & Oishi, S. (1998). *Do the effects of marital status on subjective well-being vary across cultures?* Manuscript submitted for publication.

Diener, E., Suh, E. M., Lucas, R. E., & Smith, H. L. (1999). Subjective well-being: Three decades of progress. *Psychological Bulletin, 125,* 276–302.

Diener, E., Wolsic, B., & Fujita, F. (1995). Physical attractiveness and subjective well-being. *Journal of Personality and Social Psychology, 69,* 120–129.

Dijksterhuis, A., & Aarts, H. (2003). On wildebeests and humans: The preferential detection of negative stimuli. *Psychological Science, 14* (1), 14–18.

DiMatteo, M. R., & Di Nicola, D. D. (1982). *Achieving patient compliance: The psychology of the medical practitioner's role.* New York: Pergamon Press. Dimberg, U., Thunberg, M., & Elmehed, K. (2000). Unconscious facial reactions to emotional facial expressions. *Psychological Science, 11,* 86–89.

Dimberg, U., Thunberg, M., & Elmehed, K. (2000). Unconscious facial reactions to emotional facial expressions. *Psychological Science, 11,* 86–89.

Dingle, G. A., & Oei, T. P. S. (1997). Is alcohol a cofactor of HIV and AIDS? Evidence from immunological and behavioral studies. *Psychological Bulletin, 122,* 56–71.

Domjan, M. (2000). *The essentials of conditioning and learning* (2nd ed.). Belmont, CA: Wadsworth.

Douek, E. (1988). Olfaction and medicine. In S. Van Toller & G. Doll (Eds.), *Perfumery: The psychology and biology of fragrance.* London: Chapman Hall.

Dovidio, J. F., & Gaertner, S. L. (1993). Stereotype and evaluative intergroup bias. In D. M. Mackie & D. L. Hamilton (Eds.), *Affect, cognition, and stereotyping: Interactive processes*

in group perception. Orlando, FL: Academic Press.

Dovidio, J. F., & Gaertner, S. L. (Eds.). (1986). *Prejudice, discrimination, and racism.* Orlando, FL: Academic Press.

Dovidio, J. F., Evans, N., & Tyler, R. B. (1986). Racial stereotypes: The contents of their cognitive representations. *Journal of Experimental Social Psychology, 22,* 22–37.

Dovidio, J. F., Gaertner, S. L., Isen A. M., & Lawrance, R. E. (1995). Group representations and intergroup bias: Positive affect, similarity, and group size. *Personality and Social Psychology Bulletin, 21,* 856–865.

Dreher, N. (1995). Women and smoking. *Current Health, 21,* 16–19.

Duncan, J., Seitz, R. J., Kolodny, J., Bor, D., Herzog, H., Ahmed, A., Newell, F. N., & Emslie, H. (2000). A neural basis for general intelligence. *Science, 289,* 457–460.

Duncker, K. (1945). On problem solving. *Psychological Monographs* (whole No. 270).

Dunning, D., Johnson, K., Ehrlinger, J., & Kruger, J. (2003). Why people fail to recognize their own incompetence. *Current Directions in Psychological Science, 12,* 83–86.

Dweck, C. S., & Licht, B. G. (1980). Learned helplessness and intellectual achievement. In M. E. P. Seligman & J. Garber (Eds.), *Human helplessness: Theory and application.* New York: Academic Press.

Eagly, A. H., & Chaiken, S. (1998). Attitude structure and function. In G. Lindsey, S. T. Fiske, & D. T. Gilbert (Eds.), *Handbook of social psychology* (4th ed.). New York: Oxford University Press and McGraw-Hill.

Eagly, A. H., & Johnson, B. T. (1990). Gender and leadership style: A meta-analysis. *Psychological Bulletin, 90,* 1–20.

Eagly, A. H., & Wood, W. (1999). The origins of sex differences in human behavior. *American Psychologist, 54,* 408–423.

Eagly, A. H., Karau, S. J., & Makhijani, M. G. (1995). Gender and the effectiveness of leaders: A meta-analysis. *Psychological Bulletin, 112,* 125–145.

Ebbinghaus, H. (1885). *Uber das Gedachtnis.* Leipzig: Dunker. (Translation by H. Ruiyer & C. E. Bussenius [1915].

Memory. New York: Teachers College Press Columbia University.)

Eccleston, C., & Crombez, G. (1999). Pain demands attention: A cognitive-affective model of the interruptive function of pain. *Psychological Bulletin, 125,* 356–366.

Edwards, K., & Bryan, T. S. (1997). Judgmental biases produced by instructions to disregard: The (paradoxical) case of emotional information. *Personality and Social Psychology Bulletin, 23,* 849–864.

Effective treatment for treating depression (1994, April). *Johns Hopkins Medical Letter, 6* (2), 6–7.

Egeland, J. A., Gerhard, D. S., Pauls, D. L., Sussex, J. N., Kidd, K. K., Allen, C. R., Hostetter, A. M., & Housman, D. E. (1987). Bipolar affective disorders linked to DNA markers on chromosome 11. *Nature, 325,* 783–787.

Ehrman, R. N., Robbins, S. J., Childress, A. R., & O'Brien, C. P. (1992). Conditioned responses to cocaine-related stimuli in cocaine abuse patients. *Psychopharmacology, 107,* 523–529.

Eich, J. E. (1985). Levels of processing, encoding specificity, elaboration, and CHARM. *Psychological Review, 92,* 1–38.

Eichenbaum, H., & Bunsey, M. (1995). On the binding of associations in memory: Clues from studies on the role of the hippocampal region in paired-associate learning. *Current Directions in Psychological Science, 4,* 19–23.

Ekman, P. (1992). Facial expressions of emotion: New findings, new questions. *Psychological Science, 3,* 34–38.

Ekman, P. (1992a). Are there basic emotions? *Psychology Review, 99,* 50–553.

Ekman, P., & Friesen, W. V. (1975). *Unmasking the face.* Englewood Cliffs, NJ: Prentice Hall.

Ekman, P., Davidson, R. J., & Friesen, W. V. (1990). The Duchenne smile: Emotional expression and brain physiology II. *Journal of Personality and Social Psychology, 58,* 342–353.

Elkin, J., Shea, T., Watkins, J. T., Imber, S. D., Stotsky, S. M., Collins, J. F., Glass, D. R., Pilkonis, P. A., Leber, W. R., Docherty, J. P., Fiester, S. J., & Parloff, M. B. (1989). National Institutes of Mental Health treatment of depression and collaborative re-

search program. *Archives of General Psychiatry, 46,* 971–982.

Elliot, A. J., & Devine, P. G. (1994). On the motivational nature of cognitive dissonance: Dissonance as psychological discomfort. *Journal of Personality and Social Psychology, 67,* 382–394.

Ellis, A. (1987). The impossibility of achieving consistently good mental health. *American Psychologist, 42,* 364–375.

Ellis, A. P. J., West, B. J., Ryan, A. M., & DeShon, R. P. (2002). The use of impression management tactics in structured interviews: A function of question type? *Journal of Applied Psychology, 87,* 1200–1208.

Ellis, L. (1995). Dominance and reproductive success among nonhuman animals: A cross-species comparison. *Ethology and Sociobiology, 16,* 257–333.

Empson, J. A. C. (1984). Sleep and its disorders. In R. Stevens (Ed.), *Aspects of consciousness.* New York: Academic Press.

Engen, T. (1982). *The perception of odors.* New York: Academic Press.

Engen, T. (1986). *Remembering odors and their names.* Paper presented at the First International Conference on the Psychology of Perfumery, University of Warwick, England.

Engen, T., & Ross, B. M. (1973). Long-term memory of odors with and without verbal descriptions. *Journal of Experimental Psychology, 100,* 221–227.

Engle, R. W. (2001). What is working memory capacity? In H. L. Roediger, J. S. Nairne, I. Neath, & A. M. Suprenant (Eds.), *The nature of remembering: Essays in honor of Robert G. Crowder* (pp. 297–314). Washington, DC: American Psychological Association.

Engle, R. W. (2002). Working memory capacity as executive attention. *Current Directions in Psychological Science, 11,* 19–23.

Engle, R. W., Tuholski, S. W., Laughlin, J. E, & Conway, A. R. A. (1999). Working memory, short-term memory, and general fluid intelligence: A latent variable approach. *Journal or Experimental Psychology: General, 128,* 309–331.

Epstein, L. H. (1992). Role of behavior theory in behavioral medicine. Special Issue: Behavioral medicine: An

update for the 1990s. *Journal of Consulting and Clinical Psychology, 60,* 493–498.

Erdelyi, M. H., & Kleinbard, J. (1978). Has Ebbinghaus decayed with time? The growth of recall (hypermnesia) over days. *Journal of Experimental Psychology: Human Learning and Memory, 4,* 275–289.

Erev, I. (1998). Signal detection by human observers: A cutoff reinforcement learning model of categorization decisions under uncertainty. *Psychological Review, 105,* 280–298.

Erikson, E. H. (1950). *Childhood and society.* New York: Norton.

Erikson, E. H. (1987). *A way of looking at things: Selected papers from 1930 to 1980* (S. Schlein, Ed.). New York: Norton.

Eron, L. D. (1987). The development of aggressive behavior from the perspective of a developing behaviorist. *American Psychologist, 42,* 435–442.

Eron, L. D., Huesmann, L. R., Lefkowitz, M. M., & Walder, L. O. (1996). Does television violence cause aggression? In D. F. Greenberg (Ed.), Criminal careers: Vol. 2. *The international library of criminology, criminal justice and penology* (pp. 311–321). Aldershot, England: Dartmouth Publishing Company.

Estrada, C. A., Isen, A. M., & Young, M. J. (1995). Positive affect improves creative problem solving and influences reported source of practice satisfaction in physicians. *Motivation and Emotion, 388,* 300–385.

Exner, J. E. (1993). *The Rorschach: A comprehensive system: Vol. 1. Basic Foundations* (3rd ed.). New York: Wiley.

Eysenck, H. J. (1994). The big five or giant three: Criteria for a paradigm. In C. F. Halverson, Jr., G. A. Honhnstamm, & R. P. Martin (Eds.), *The developing structure of temperament and personality from infancy to adulthood* (pp. 37–51). Hillsdale, NJ: Erlbaum.

Fagot, B. I., & Kavanagh, K. (1990). The prediction of anti-social behavior from avoidant attachment classification. *Child Development, 61,* 864–873.

Fantz, R. L. (1961). The origin of form perception. *Scientific American, 204,* 66–72.

Farah, M. J. (1988). Is visual imagery really visual? Overlooked evidence from neuropsychology. *Psychological Review, 95*, 307–317.

Fazio, R. H., & Roskos-Ewoldsen, D. R. (1994). Acting as we feel: When and how attitudes guide behavior. In S. Shavitt & T. C. Brock (Eds.), *Persuasion* (pp. 71–93). Boston: Allyn & Bacon.

Feldman, D. C., & Tompson, H. B. (1993). Entry shock, culture shock: Socializing the new breed of global managers. *Human Resource Management, 31*, 345–362.

Ferster, C. B., & Skinner, B. F. (1957). *Schedules of reinforcement*. New York: Appleton-Century-Crofts.

Festinger, L. (1957). *A theory of cognitive dissonance*. Evanston, IL: Row, Peterson.

Fibiger, H. C., Murray, C. L., & Phillips, A. G. (1983). Lesions of the nucleus basalis magoncellularis impair long-term memory in rats. *Society for Neuroscience Abstracts, 9*, 332.

Fields, H. L., & Basbaum, A. I. (1999). Central nervous system mechanisms of pain modulation. In P. D. Wall and R. Melzak (Eds.), *Textbook of pain* (4th ed.) (pp. 309–328). New York: Churchill Livingstone.

Fierman, J. (1995, August 21). It's 2:00 A.M., let's go to work. *Fortune*, pp. 82–86.

Fincham, F. D. (2003). Marital conflict: Correlates, structure, and context. *Current Directions in Psychological Science, 12*, 23–27.

Fincham, F. D., & Bradbury, T. N. (1993). Marital satisfaction, depression and attributions: A longitudinal analysis. *Journal of Personality and Social Psychology, 64*, 442–452.

Fink, M. (1994). Can ECT be an effective treatment for adolescents? *Harvard Mental Health Letter, 10*, 8.

Finkel, D., Pederson, J. L., Plomin, R., & McClearn, G. E. (1998). Longitudinal and cross-sectional twin data on cognitive abilities in adulthood: The Swedish adoption/twin study of aging. *Developmental Psychology, 34*, 1400–1413.

Finney, J. W., Weist, M. D., & Friman, P. C. (1995). Evaluation of two health education strategies for testicular self-examination. *Journal of Applied Behavior Analysis 28*, 39–46.

Fisher, J. D., Fisher, W. A., Williams, S. S., & Malloy, T. E. (1994). Empirical tests of an information-motivation-behavioral skills model of AIDS preventive behavior with gay men and heterosexual university students. *Health Psychology 13*, 238–250.

Fisher, J., & Fisher, W. (2000). Theoretical approaches to individual-level change in HIV risk behavior. In J. Peterson & R. DiClemente (Eds.), *Handbook of HIV prevention* (pp. 3–56). New York: Kluwer Academic/Plenum.

Fivush, R., Kuebli, J., & Clubb, P. A. (1992). The structure of events and event representations: A developmental analysis. *Child Development, 63*, 188–201.

Flack, W. F., Laird, J. D., & Cavallero, R. (1999). Additive effects of facial expressions and postures on emotional feelings. *European Journal of Social Psychology, 29*, 203–217.

Flaherty, C. F., & Largen, J. (1975). Within-subjects positive and negative contrast effects in rats. *Journal of Comparative and Physiological Psychology, 88*, 653–664.

Flynn, J. R. (1980). *Race, IQ, and Jensen*. London: Routledge.

Flynn, J. R. (1987). Massive IQ gains in 14 nations: What IQ tests really measure. *Psychological Bulletin, 101*, 171–191.

Flynn, J. R. (1993). Skodak and Skeels: The inflated mother–child IQ gap. *Intelligence, 17*, 557–661.

Flynn, J. R. (1996). Group differences: Is the good society impossible? *Journal of Biosocial Science, 28*, 573–585.

Flynn, J. R. (1999). Searching for justice: The discovery of IQ gains over time. *American Psychologist, 54*, 5–20.

Folk, C. L., & Remington, R. W. (1996). When knowledge does not help: Limitations on the flexibility of attentional control. In A. F. Kramer, M. G. H. Coles, & G. D. Logan (Eds.), *Converging operations in the study of selective attention* (pp. 271–295). Washington, DC: American Psychological Association.

Ford, S., Fallowfield, L., & Lewis, S. (1996). Doctor-patient interactions in oncology. *Social Science Medicine, 12*, 1511–1519.

Forgas, J. P. (1995a). Mood and judgment: The affect infusion model (AIM). *Psychological Bulletin, 117*, 39–66.

Forgas, J. P. (1995b). The role of emotion in social judgments: An introductory review and an affect infusion model (AIM). *European Journal of Social Psychology*.

Forgas, J. P. (1998). On being happy and mistaken: Mood effects on the fundamental attribution error. *Journal of Personality and Social Psychology, 75*, 318–331.

Forgas, J. P., & Fiedler, K. (1996). Us and them: Mood effects on intergroup discrimination. *Journal of Personality and Social Psychology, 70*, 28–40.

Foulkes, D. (1985). *Dreaming: A cognitive-psychological analysis*. Hillsdale, NJ: Erlbaum.

Foushee, H. C. (1984). Dyads and triads at 35,000 feet: Factors affecting group process and aircrew performance. *American Psychologist, 39*, 885–893.

Frederiksen, N. (1994). The integration of testing with teaching: Applications of cognitive psychology in instruction. *American Journal of Education, 102*, 527–564.

Fredrickson, B. L., & Joiner, T. (2002). Positive emotions trigger upward spirals toward emotional well-being. *Psychological Science, 13*, 172–175.

Fredrickson, B. L., Tugade, M. M., Waugh, C. E., & Larkin, G. R. (2003). What good are positive emotions in crisis? A prospective study of resilience and emotions following the terrorist attacks on the United States on September 11th, 2001. *Journal of Personality and Social Psychology, 84*, 365–376.

Freedman, J. L. (1986). Television violence and aggression: A rejoinder. *Psychological Bulletin, 100*, 372–378.

Frese, M. (1985). Stress at work and psychosomatic complaints: A causal interpretation. *Journal of Applied Psychology, 70*, 314–328.

Friedman, H. W., & Schustack, M. W. (1999). *Personality: Classic theories and modern research*. Boston: Allyn & Bacon.

Fuertes, J. N., Mueller, L. N., Chauhan, R. V., Walker, J. A., & Ladany, N. (2002). An investigation of European American therapists' approach to counseling African American clients. *Counseling Psychologists, 30*, 763–768.

Funder, D. C., & Colvin, C. R. (1991). Explorations in behavioral consistency: Properties of persons, situations, and behavior. *Journal of Personality and Social Psychology, 60*, 773–794.

Funder, D. C., & Sneed, C. D. (1993). Behavioral manifestations of personality: An ecological approach to judgmental accuracy. *Journal of Personality and Social Psychology, 64,* 479–490.

Fung, H. H., & Carstensen, L. L. (2003). Sending memorable messages to the old: Age differences in preferences and memory for advertisements. *Journal of Personality and Social Psychology, 85,* 163–178.

Furman, W., & Shaffer, L. (2003). The role of romantic relationships in adolescent development. In P. Florsheim (Ed.), *Adolescent romantic relations and sexual behavior: Theory, research, and practical implications.* Mahwah, NJ: Erlbaum.

Furman, W., & Shaver, P. R. (1990). Love and work: An attachment-theoretical perspective. *Journal of Personality and Social Psychology, 59,* 117–125.

Furman, W., Simon, V. A., Shaffer, L., & Bouchey, H. A. (2002). Adolescents' working models and styles for relationships with parents, friends, and romantic partners. *Child Development, 73,* 241–255.

Gaertner, S. L., Mann, J. A., Dovidio, J. F., & Murrell, J. A. (1990). How does cooperation reduce intergroup bias? *Journal of Personality and Social Psychology, 57,* 239–249.

Gaertner, S. L., Mann, J., Murrell, A., & Dovidio, J. F. (1989). Reducing intergroup bias: The benefits of recategorization. *Journal of Personality and Social Psychology, 57,* 239–249.

Gaertner, S. L., Rust, M. C., Dovidio, J. F., Bachman, B. A., & Anastasio, P. A. (1993). The contact hypothesis: The role of common ingroup identity on reducing intergroup bias. *Small Groups Research, 25,* 224–249.

Gaffney, G. R., Kuperman, S., Tsai, L. Y., & Minchin, S. (1989). Forebrain structure in infantile autism. *Journal of the American Academy of Child and Adolescent Psychiatry, 28,* 534–537.

Galanter, E. (1962). Contemporary psychophysics. In R. Brown, E. Galanter, E. G. Hess, & G. Mandler (Eds.), *New directions in psychology.* New York: Holt, Rinehart, & Winston.

Gallagher, M. (2000). The amygdala and associative learning. In J. P. Aggleton (Ed.), *The amygala: A functional analysis* (pp. 311–330). New York: Oxford University Press.

Gallassi, R., Morreale, A., Montagna, P., Cortelli, P., Avoni, P., Castelanni, R., Gambetti, P., & Lugaresi, E. (1996). Fatal familial insomnia: Behavioral and cognitive features. *Newsday, 46,* 935–939.

Garcia, J., & Koelling, R. A. (1966). Relation of cue to consequence in avoidance learning. *Psychonomic Science, 4,* 123.

Garcia, J., Hankins, W. G., & Rusiniak, K. W. (1974). Behavioral regulation of the milieu interne in man and rat. *Science, 185,* 824–831.

Gardner, H. (1983). *Frames of mind: The theory of multiple intelligences.* New York: Basic Books.

Garland, A. F., & Zigler, E. (1993). Adolescent suicide prevention: Current research and social policy implications. *American Psychologist, 48,* 169–182.

Garland, H., & Newport, S. (1991). Effects of absolute and relative sunk costs on the decision to persist with a course of action. *Organizational Behavior and Human Decision Processes, 48,* 55–69.

Garlick, D. (2002). Understanding the nature of the general factor of intelligence: The role of individual differences in neural plasticity as an explanatory mechanism. *Psychological Review, 109,* 116–136.

Garlick, D. (2003). Integrating brain science research with intelligence research. *Current Directions in Psychological Science, 12* (5), 185–189.

Gati, I., Houminer, D., & Aviram, T. (1998). Career compromises: Framings and their implications. *Journal of Counseling Psychology, 45,* 505–514.

Gauthier, I., Tarr, M. J., Anderson, A. W., Skudlarski, P., & Gore, J. C. (1999). Activation of the middle fusiform "face area" increases with expertise in recognizing novel objects. *Nature Neuroscience, 2,* 568–573.

Gazzaniga, M. S. (1984). Right hemisphere language: Remaining problems. *American Psychologist, 39,* 1494–1495.

Gazzaniga, M. S. (1985, November). The social brain. *Psychology Today,* 29–38.

Gehring, R. E., & Toglia, M. P. (1989). Recall of pictorial enactments and verbal descriptions with verbal and imagery study strategies. *Journal of Mental Imagery, 13,* 83–98.

Geiselman, R. E., & Fisher, R. P. (1997). Ten years of cognitive interviewing. In D. G. Payne & F. G. Conrad (Eds.), *Intersections in basic and applied memory research* (pp. 291–310). Mahwah, NJ: Erlbaum.

Geller, E. S. (1996). *The psychology of safety.* Radnor, PA: Chilton Book Company.

Geller, E. S., Chaffee, J. L., & Ingram, R. E. (1975). Promoting paper recycling on a university campus. *Journal of Environmental Systems, 5,* 39–57.

Gentner, D., & Jeziorski, M. (1993). The shift from metaphor to analogy in western science. In Ortony, A. (Ed.), *Metaphor and thought* (pp. 447–480). Cambridge: Cambridge University Press.

Gershoff, E. T. (2002). Corporal punishment by parents and associated child behaviors and experiences: A meta-analytic and theoretical review. *Psychological Bulletin, 128,* 539–579.

Gibbons, B. (1986). The intimate sense of smell. *National Geographic, 170,* 324–361.

Gibbons, F. X. (1990). Self-attention and behavior: a review and theoretical update. In M. P. Zanna (Ed.), *Advances in experimental social psychology* (Vol. 23, pp. 249–303). New York: Academic Press.

Gibbons, F. X., Eggleston, T. J., & Benthin, A. C. (1997). Cognitive reactions to smoking relapse: The reciprocal relation between dissonance and self-esteem. *Journal of Personality and Social Psychology, 72*(1), 184–195.

Gibbons, F. X., Gerrard, M., Blanton, H., & Russell, D. W. (1998). Reasoned action and social reaction: Willingness and intention as independent predictors of health risk. *Journal of Personality and Social Psychology, 74,* 1164–1180.

Gibson, E. J., & Walk, R. D. (1960). The "visual cliff." *Scientific American, 202,* 64–71.

Gigerenzer, G., & Goldstein, D. G. (1996). Reasoning the fast and frugal way: Models of bounded rationality. *Psychological Review, 103,* 650–669.

Gilbert, A. N., & Wysocki, C. J. (1987). The smell survey results. *National Geographic, 172,* 514–525.

Gilbert, D. T., & Malone, P. S. (1995). The correspondence bias. *Psychological Bulletin, 117,* 21–38.

Gill, J. (1985, August, 22). Czechpoints. *Time Out,* p. 15.

Gist, M. E., Schwoerer, C., & Rosen, B. (1989). Effects of alternative training methods on self-efficacy and performance in computer software training. *Journal of Applied Psychology, 74,* 884–891.

Gladwell, M. (1998, February 2). The Pima paradox. *The New Yorker,* 42–57.

Glanz, K., Geller, A. C., Shigaki, D., Maddock, J. E., & Isnec, M. R. (2002). A randomized trial of skin cancer prevention in aquatic settings: The Pool Cool program. *Health Psychology, 21* (6), 579–587.

Glass, D. C. (1977). *Behavior patterns, stress, and coronary disease.* Hillsdale, NJ: Erlbaum.

Gleicher, F., Boninger, D., Strathman, A., Armor, D., Hetts, J., & Ahn, M. (1995). With an eye toward the future: Impact of counterfactual thinking on affect, attitudes, and behavior. In N. J. Roese & J. M. Olson (Eds.), *What might have been: The social psychology of counterfactual thinking* (pp. 283–304). Mahwah, NJ: Erlbaum.

Gluck, M. A., & Myers, C. E. (1995). Representation and association in memory: A neurocomputational view of hippocampal function. *Current Directions in Psychological Science, 4,* 23–29.

Glynn, L. M., Christenfeld, N., & Gerin, W. (1999). Gender, social support, and cardiovascular responses to stress. *Psychosomatic Medicine, 61,* 234–242.

Godden, D., & Baddeley, A. D. (1975). Context-dependent memory in two natural environments: On land and under water. *British Journal of Psychology, 66,* 325–331.

Goethals, G. R., (1986). Fabricating and ignoring social reality: Self-serving estimates of consensus. In J. Olson, C. P. Herman, & N. P. Zanna (Eds.), *Relative deprivation and social comparison: The Ontario symposium on social cognition IV.* Hillsdale, NJ: Erlbaum.

Goldberg, L. R., & Saucier, G. (1995). So what do you propose we use instead? A reply to Block. *Psychological Bulletin, 117,* 221–225.

Goldstein, E. B. (2002). *Sensation and perception.* Pacific Grove, CA: Wadsworth.

Goleman, D. (1995). *Emotional intelligence.* New York: Bantam.

Goleman, D. R. (1998). *Working with emotional intelligence.* New York: Bantam.

Gómez, C. A., & Marín, B. V. (1996). Gender, culture, and power: Barriers to HIV prevention strategies for women. *The Journal of Sex Research, 33,* 355–362.

Goodale, M. A., Meeman, H. P., Bulthoff, H. H., Nicolle, D. A., Murphy, K. H., & Racicot, C. L. (1994). Separate neural pathways for the visual analysis of object shape and perception and prehension. *Current Biology, 4,* 604–610.

Goodman, G. S., Ghetti, S., Quas, J. A., Edelstein, R. S., Alexander, K. W., Redlich, A. D., Cordon, I. M., & Jones, D. P. H. (2003). A prospective study of memory for child sexual abuse: New findings relevant to the repressed-memory controversy. *Psychological Science, 14,* 113–118.

Goodman, G. S., Quas, J. A., Batterman-Faunce, J. M., Riddlesberger, M. M., & Kuhn, J. (1996). Predictors of accurate and inaccurate memories of traumatic events experienced in childhood. In K. Pedzek & W. P. Banks (Eds.), *The recovered/false memory debate* (pp. 3–28). San Diego, CA: Academic Press.

Goodman, M. F., Bents, F. D., Tijerina, L., Wierwille, N., Lerner, N., & Benel, D. (1999). *An Investigation of the Safety Implications of Wireless Communications in Vehicles: Report Summary.* Department of Transportation electronic publication. Report summary (http://www.nhtsa.dot.gov/people/injury/research/wireless/#rep.)

Goodwin, R., & Findlay, C. (1997). "We were just fated together" . . . Chinese love and the concept of *yuan* in England and Hong Kong. *Personal Relationships, 4,* 85–92.

Gordon, W. C. (1989). *Learning and memory.* Belmont, CA: Brooks/Cole Publishing Company.

Gosling, S. S., Fazire, S., Srivastava, S., & John, O. P. (2004). Should we trust web-based studies? A comparative analysis of six preconceptions about Internet questionnaires. *American Psychologist, 59,* 93–104.

Gottesman, I. I. (1993). Origins of schizophrenia: Past as a prologue. In R. Plomin & G. E. McClearn (Eds.), *Nature, nurture, and psychology* (pp. 2231–2344). Washington, DC: American Psychological Association.

Gottfredson, G. D., & Holland, J. L. (1990). A longitudinal test of the influence of congruence: Job satisfaction, competency utilization, and counterproductive behavior. *Journal of Consulting Psychology, 37,* 389–398.

Gottfried, A. W. (Ed.). (1984). *Home environment and early cognitive development.* San Francisco: Academic.

Gottman, J. M. (1993). The roles of conflict engagement, escalation, and avoidance in marital interaction: A longitudinal view of five types of couples. *Journal of Consulting and Clinical Psychology, 61,* 6–15.

Graen, G. B., & Scandura, T. A. (1986). Toward a psychology of dyadic organizing. In L. L. Cummings & B. M. Staw (Eds.), *Research on organizational behavior* (Vol. 9, pp. 175–208). Greenwich, CT: JAI Press.

Graham, C. H., & Hsia, Y. (1958). Color defect and color theory. *Science, 127,* 675–682.

Graham, K. S., & Hodges, J. R. (1997). Differentiating the roles of the hippocampal complex and the neocortex in long-term memory storage: Evidence from the study of semantic dementia and Alzheimer's disease. *Neuropsychology, 11,* 77–89.

Granchrow, J. R., Steiner, J. E., & Daher, M. (1983). Neonatal facial expressions in response to different qualities and intensities of gustatory stimuli. *Infant Behavior and Development, 6,* 189–200.

Grant, B. F., Harford, T. C., Dawson, D. A., Chou, P., Dufour, M., & Pickering, R. (1994). Prevalence of DSM–IV alcohol abuse and dependence in United States, 1992. *NIAAA's Epidemiological Bulletin No. 35, 13,* 243–248.

Gray-Little, B., & Hafdahl, A. R. (2000). Factors influencing racial comparisons of self-esteem: A quantitative review. *Psychological Bulletin, 126,* 26–54.

Green, J. P., & Lynn, S. J. (1995). Hypnosis, dissociation, and simultaneous task performance. *Journal of Personality and Social Psychology, 69,* 728–735.

Green, L., Fry, A. F., & Myerson, J. (1994). Discounting of delayed rewards: A life-span comparison. *Psychological Science, 5,* 33–36.

Green, R. (1987). *The "sissy boy syndrome" and the development of homosexuality.* New Haven, CT: Yale University Press.

Green, R., & Blanchard, K. (1995). Gender identity disorders. In H. J. Kaplan & B. J. Sadock (Eds.), *Comprehensive textbook of psychiatry/VI* (pp. 1345–1360). Baltimore: Williams & Wilkins.

Greenberg, J. (2002). Who stole the money, and when? Individual and situational determinants of employee theft. *Organizational Behavior and Human Decision Processes, 89,* 985–1003.

Greenberg, L. S., Elliott, R. K., & Lietaer, G. (1994). Research on experiential psychotherapies. In A. E. Bergin & S. L. Garfield (Eds.), *Handbook of psychotherapy and behavior change* (pp. 509–539). New York: John Wiley & Sons.

Greene, B. F., Winett, R. A., Van Houten, R., Geller, E. S., & Iwata, B. A. (1987). (Eds.). *Behavior analysis in the community: Readings from the Journal of Applied Behavior Analysis.* Lawrence, KS: University of Kansas Press.

Greenwald, A. G., Draine, S. C., & Abrams, R. L. (1996). Three cognitive markers of unconscious semantic activation. *Science, 273,* 1699–1702.

Greenwald, A. G., Spangenberg, E. R., Pratkanis, A. R., & Eskenazi, J. (1991). Double-blind tests of subliminal self-help audiotapes. *Psychological Science, 2,* 119–122.

Greist-Bousquet, S., Watson, M., & Schiffman, H. R. (1990). *An examination of illusion decrement with inspection of wings-in and wings-out Müller-Lyer figures: The role of corrective and contextual information perception.* New York: Wiley.

Grilly, D. M. (1989). *Drugs and human behavior.* Boston: Allyn and Bacon.

Gross, J. J. (2001). Emotion regulation in adulthood: Timing is everything. *Current Directions in Psychological Science, 6,* 214–219.

Gruneberg, M. M., Morris, P., & Sykes, R. N. (1988). *Practical aspects of memory: Current research and issues* (Vols. 1 & 2). Chichester, England: John Wiley & Sons.

Guerin, D. W., & Gottfried, A. W. (1994). Developmental stability and change in parent reports of temperament: A ten-year longitudinal investigation from infancy through preadolescence. *Merrill-Palmer Quarterly, 40,* 334–355.

Guthrie, J. P., Ash, R. A., & Bendapudi, V. (1995). Additional validity evidence for a measure of Morningness. *Journal of Applied Psychology, 80,* 186–190.

Haberlandt, K. (1999). *Human memory: Exploration and application.* Boston: Allyn & Bacon.

Hackman, J. R. (Ed.) (1990). *Groups that work (and those that don't).* San Francisco: Jossey-Bass.

Hackman, J. R., & Oldham, G. R. (1976). Motivation through the design of work: Test of a theory. *Organizational Behavior and Human Performance, 16,* 250–279.

Haggerty, R. J., Garmezy, N., Rutter, M., & Sherrod, L. (1994). *Stress, risk, and resilience in children and adolescents: Processes, mechanisms, and interventions.* New York: Cambridge University Press.

Hahn, G., Charlin, V. L., Sussman, S., Dent, C. W., Manzi, J., Stacy, A. W., Flay, B., Hansen, W. B., & Burton, D. (1990). Adolescents' first and most recent use situations of smokeless tobacco and cigarettes: Similarities and differences. *Addictive Behaviors, 15,* 439–448.

Haier, R. J. (1993). Cerebral glucose metabolism and intelligence. In P. A. Vernon (Ed.), *Biological approaches to the study of human intelligence* (pp. 317–332). Norwood, NJ: Ablex.

Hajek, P., & Belcher, M. (1991). Dreams of absent-minded transgression: An empirical study of a cognitive withdrawal symptom. *Journal of Abnormal Psychology, 100,* 487–491.

Hall, J. A., Roter, D. L., & Milburn, M. A. (1999). Illness and satisfaction with medical care. *Current Directions in Psychological Science, 8,* 96–99.

Hamann, S. B., Ely, T. D., Hoffman, J. M., & Kilts, C. D. (2002). Ecstasy and agony: Activation of the human amygdala in positive and negative emotion. *Psychological Science, 13,* 135–141.

Hamburg, S. (1998). Inherited hypohedonia leads to learned helplessness: A conjecture updated. *Review of General Psychology, 2,* 384–403.

Hanisch, K. A. (1995). Behavioral families and multiple causes: Matching the complexity of responses to the complexity of antecedents. *Current Directions in Psychological Science, 4,* 156–161.

Hans, V. P. (1992). Obedience, justice, and the law: PS reviews recent contributions to a field ripe for new research efforts by psychological scientists. *Psychological Science, 3,* 218–221.

Harlow, H. F., & Harlow, M. H. (1966). Learning to love. *American Scientist, 54,* 244–272.

Harrigan, J. A., Luci, K. S., Kay, D., McLaney, A., & Rosenthal, R. (1991). Effects of expresser role and type of self-touching on observers' perceptions. *Journal of Applied Social Psychology, 21,* 585–609.

Harrington, A. (1995). Unfinished business: Models of laterality in the nineteenth century. In R. J. Davidson & K. Hugdahl (Eds.), *Brain asymmetry* (pp. 24–37). Cambridge, MA: MIT Press.

Harris, J. A., Rushton, J. P., Hampson, E., & Jackson, D. N. (1996). Salivary testosterone and self-report aggressive and pro-social personality characteristics in men and women. *Aggressive Behavior, 22,* 321–331.

Harrison, J. K. (1992). Individual and combined effects of behavior modeling and the cultural assimilator in cross-cultural management training. *Journal of Applied Psychology, 77,* 952–962.

Hart, D., Stinson, C., Field, N., Ewert, M., & Horowitz, M. (1995). A semantic space approach to representations of self and other in pathological grief: A case study. *Psychological Science, 6,* 96–100.

Hartmann, E. L. (1973). *The functions of sleep.* New Haven: Yale University Press.

Hasseldine, J., & Hite, P. A. (2002). Framing, gender and tax compliance. *Journal of Economic Psychology, 24,* 517–533.

Hatch, T. (1990). Social intelligence in young children. Paper presented at the meeting of the American Psychological Association.

Haugaard, J. J., Repucci, N. D., Laurd, J., & Nauful, T. (1991). Children's definitions of the truth and their competency as witnesses in legal proceedings. *Law and Human Behavior, 15,* 253–273.

Hauser, M., Newport, E. L., & Aslin, R. N. (2001). Segmentation of the speech stream in a non-human primate: Statistical learning in cotton-top tamarins. *Cognition, 78,* B41–B52.

Hawkins, J. D., Catalano, R. F., & Miller, J. Y. (1992). Risk and protective factors for alcohol and other drug problems in adolescence and early adulthood: Implications for substance abuse prevention. *Psychological Bulletin, 112,* 64–105.

Hawkins, S. A., & Hastie, R. (1990). Hindsight: Biased judgments of past events after the outcomes are known. *Psychological Bulletin, 107,* 311–327.

Heatherton, T., & Weinberger, J. L. (1994). *Can personality change?* Washington, DC: American Psychological Association.

Hebl, M. R., & Mannix, L. M. (2003). The weight of obesity in evaluating others: A mere proximity effect. *Personality and Social Psychology Bulletin, 29,* 28–38.

Heller, W. (1997). Emotion. In M. T. Banich (Ed.), *Neuropsychology: The neural bases of mental function* (pp. 398–429). Boston: Houghton Mifflin.

Heller, W., Etienne, M. A., & Miller, G. A. (1995). Patterns of perceptual asymmetry in depression and anxiety: Implications for neuropsychological models of emotion and psychopathology. *Journal of Abnormal Psychology, 104,* 327–333.

Heller, W., Nitschke, J. B., & Miller, G. A. (1998) Lateralization in emotion and emotional disorders. *Current Directions in Psychological Science, 7,* 26–32.

Hellerstein, D., Yanowitch, P., Rosenthal, J., Samstag, L. W., Maurer, M., Kasch, K., Burrow, L., Porter, M., Cantillon, M., & Winston, R. (1993). A randomized double-blind study of fluoxetine versus placebo in the treatment of dysthymia. *American Journal of Psychiatry, 150,* 1169–1175.

Helweg-Larsen, M., & Collins, B. E. (1997). A social psychological perspective on the role of knowledge about AIDS in AIDS prevention. *Current Directions in Psychological Science, 6,* 23–26.

Hendrick, C., & Hendrick S. S. (1993). Lovers as friends. *Journal of Social and Personal Relationships, 10,* 459–466.

Hennekens, C. H. (1996). Alcohol and Risk of Coronary Events. In *Alcohol and the cardiovascular system* (NIAAA Research Monograph). Washington, DC: U. S. Department of Health and Human Services.

Hennig, P., & Knowles, A. (1990). Factors influencing women over 40 years to take precautions against cervical cancer. *Journal of Applied Social Psychology, 20,* 1612–1621.

Henry, R. A. (1993). Group judgment accuracy: Reliability and validity of post-discussion confidence judg-

ments. *Organizational Behavior and Human Decision Processes, 56,* 11–27.

Henry, R. A., & Landa, A. (2000). *Delegation decisions and affective outcomes in autonomous groups.* Paper presented at the 15th Annual Conference of the Society for Industrial and Organizational Psychology, New Orleans, April.

Henry, R. A., & Olson, T. M. (2001). *Assessing general attitudes toward workgroups: Scale development and validation.* Paper presented at the 16th Annual Conference of the Society for Industrial and Organizational Psychology, San Diego, April.

Herrnstein, R. J. (1961). Relative and absolute strength of response as a function of frequency of reinforcement. *Journal of Experimental Analysis of the Behavior 4,* 267–272.

Herrnstein, R. J. (1970). On the law of effect. *Journal of the Experimental Analysis of Behavior, 13,* 243–266.

Hershberger, S. L., Lichtenstein, P., & Knox, S. S. (1994). Genetic and environmental influences on perceptions of organizational climate. *Journal of Applied Psychology, 79,* 24–33.

Hetzel, B., & McMichael, T. (1987). *The LS factor: Lifestyle and health.* Ringwood, Victoria: Penguin.

Hewstone, M., Bond, M. H., & Wan, K. C. (1983). Social factors and social attributions: The explanation of intergroup differences in Hong Kong. *Social Cognition, 2,* 142–157.

Hickman, J. S., & Geller, E. S. (2003). A safety self-management intervention for mining operations. *Journal of Safety Research, 34,* 299–308.

Hilgard, E. R. (1979). Divided consciousness in hypnosis: Implications of the hidden observer. In E. Fromm & R. E. Shor (Eds.), *Hypnosis: Developments in research and new perspectives* (2nd ed). Chicago: Aldine.

Hilgard, E. R. (1986). *Divided consciousness: Multiple controls in human thought and action* (2nd ed.). New York: Wiley.

Hilgard, E. R. (1993). Dissociation and theories of hypnosis. In E. Fromm & M. R. Nash (Eds.), *Contemporary hypnosis research* (pp. 69–101). New York: Guilford Press.

Hingson, R., Strunin, L., Berlin, B., & Heeren, T. (1990). Beliefs about AIDS, use of alcohol and drugs, and unprotected sex among Massachu-

setts adolescents. *American Journal of Public Health, 80,* 295–299.

Hobfoll, S. E., Jackson, A. P., Lavin, J., Britton, P. J., & Shepherd, J. B. (1994). Reducing inner-city women's AIDS risk activities: A study of single, pregnant women. *Health Psychology, 13,* 397–403.

Hobson, J. A. (1988). *The dreaming brain.* New York: Basic Books.

Hock, E., Schirtzinger, M. B., Lutz, W. J., & Widaman, K. (1995). Maternal depressive symptomatology over the transition to parenthood: Assessing the influence of marital satisfaction and marital sex role traditionalism. *Journal of Family Psychology, 9,* 79–88.

Hogan, R. T. (1991). *Personality and personality measurement.* In M. D. Dunnette & L. M. Hough (Eds.), *Handbook of industrial and organizational psychology* (Vol. 2, pp. 873–920). Palo Alto, CA: Consulting Psychologists Press.

Hogan, R., Hogan, J., & Roberts, B. W. (1996). Personality measurement and employment decisions: Questions and answers. *American Psychologist, 51,* 469–477.

Hollon, S. D., DeRubeis, R. J., & Evans, M. D. (1987). Causal mediation of change in treatment for depression: Discriminating between nonspecificity and noncausality. *Psychological Bulletin, 102,* 139–149.

Hollon, S. D., Shelton, R. C., & Loosen, P. T. (1991). Cognitive therapy and pharmacotherapy for depression. *Journal of Consulting and Clinical Psychology, 59,* 88–99.

Holmes, T. H., & Masuda, M. (1974). Life change and illness susceptibility. In B. S. Dohrenwend and B. P. Dohrenwend (Eds.), *Stressful life events: Their nature and effects.* New York: Wiley.

Holmes, T. H., & Rahe, R. H. (1967). The social readjustment rating scale. *Journal of Psychosomatic Research, 11,* 213–218.

Holyoak, K. J., & Thagard, P. (1997). The analogical mind. *American Psychologist, 52,* 35–44.

Holzl, E., Kirchler, E., & Rodler, C. (2002). Hindsight bias in economic expectations: I knew all along what I want to hear. *Journal of Applied Psychology, 87,* 437–443.

Honig, W. K., & Staddon, J. E. R. (Eds.). (1977). *Handbook of operant behavior.* Englewood Cliffs, NJ: Prentice-Hall.

Hoppe, R. B. (1988). In search of a phenomenon: Research in parapsychology. *Contemporary Psychology, 33,* 129–130.

Hoptman, M. J., & Davidson, R. J. (1994). How and why do the two cerebral hemispheres interact? *Psychological Bulletin, 116,* 195–219.

Horne, J. A. (1998). *Why we sleep: The function of sleep in humans and other mammals.* Oxford, England: Oxford University Press.

Hornstein, G. A. (1992). The return of the repressed: Psychology's problematic relations with psychoanalysis, 1909–1960. *American Psychologist, 47,* 254–263.

Houpt, T. A., Boulos, Z., & Moore-Ede, M. C. (1996). Midnight Sun: Software for determining light exposure and phase-shifting schedules during global travel. *Physiology and Behavior, 59,* 561–568.

House, J. S., Landis, K. R., & Umberson, D. (1988). Social relationships and health. *Science, 241,* 540–544.

House, R. J. (1971). A path–goal theory of leader effectiveness. *Administrative Science Quarterly, 16,* 321–339.

Hovland, C. I., & Weiss, W. (1951). The influence of source credibility on communication effectiveness. *Public Opinion Quarterly, 1,* 635–650.

Howard, K. I., Kopta, S. M., Krause, M. S., & Orlinsky, D. E. (1986). The dose-effect relationship in psychotherapy. *American Psychologist, 41,* 159–164.

Howe, M. L., & Courage, M. L. (1993). On resolving the enigma of infantile amnesia. *Psychological Bulletin, 113,* 305–326.

Hubel, D. H., & Wiesel, T. N. (1979). Brain mechanisms of vision. *Scientific American, 241,* 150–162.

Huesmann, L. R., Moise-Titus, J., Podolski, C. L., & Eron, L. D. (2003). Longitudinal relations between children's exposure to TV violence and their aggressive and violent behavior in young adulthood: 1977–1992. *Developmental Psychology, 39* (2), 201–221.

Hulin, C. L. (1990). Adaptation, persistence, and commitment in organizations. In M. D. Dunnette & L. M. Hough (Eds.), *Handbook of industrial and organizational psychology* (Vol. 2, pp. 445–506). Palo Alto, CA: Consulting Psychologists Press.

Hunt, E. (1993). What do we need to know about aging? In J. Cerella, J. Rybash, W. Hoyer, & M. L. Commons (Eds.), *Adult information processing: Limits on loss* (pp. 587–598). San Diego, CA: Academic Press.

Hunt, E., & Agnoli, F. (1991). The Whorfian hypothesis: A cognitive psychology perspective. *Psychological Review, 98,* 377–389.

Husband, A. J., Lin, W., Madsen, G., & King, M. G. (1993). A conditioning model for immunostimulation: Enhancement of the antibody response to ovalbumin by behavioral conditioning in rats. In A. J. Husband (Ed.), *Psychoimmunology: CNS-Immune Interactions* (pp. 139–147). Boca Raton, FL: CRC Press.

Huttenlocher, J., Haight, W., Bryk, A., Seltzer, M., & Lyons, T. (1991). Early vocabulary growth: Relation to language input and gender. *Developmental Psychology, 27,* 236–248.

Institute of Medicine. (1989). *Prevention and treatment of alcohol problems: Research opportunities.* Washington, DC: National Academy of Sciences.

Isen, A. M. (1993). Positive affect and decision making. In M. Lewis & J. M. Haviland (Eds.), *Handbook of emotion* (pp. 216–277). New York: Guilford Press.

Isen, A. M., & Baron, R. A. (1991). Positive affect and organizational behavior. In B. M. Staw & L. L. Cummings (Eds.), *Research in organizational behavior* (Vol. 14, pp. 1–48). Greenwich, CT: JAI Press.

Ivkovich, D., Collins, K. L., Eckerman, C. O., Krasnegor, N. A., & Stanton, M. E. (1999). Classical delay eyeblink conditioning in 4-and 5-month-old human infants. *Psychological Science, 10,* 4–7.

Iwahashi, M. (1992). Scents and science. *Vogue,* pp. 212–214.

Izard, C. E. (1991). *The psychology of emotions.* New York: Plenum Press.

Izard, C. E. (2001). Emotional intelligence or adaptive emotions? *Emotion, 1,* 249–257.

Jacobs, H. E., & Bailey, J. S. (1982). Evaluating participation in a residential recycling program. *Journal of Environmental Systems, 12,* 141–152.

Jacobs, J. E., & Klaczynski, P. A. (2002). The development of judgment and decision making during childhood and adolescence. *Current Directions in Psychological Science, 11,* 145–159.

Jacobson, S., Fein, G., Jacobson, J., Schwartz, P., & Dowler, J. (1984). Neonatal correlates of prenatal exposure to smoking, caffeine, and alcohol. *Infant Behavior and Development, 7,* 253–265.

James, W. J. (1890). *Principles of psychology.* New York: Holt.

Jameson, D., & Hurvich, L. M. (1989). Essay concerning color constancy. *Annual Review of Psychology, 40,* 1–22.

Janis, I. L. (1972). *Victims of groupthink: A psychological study of foreign-policy decisions and fiascoes.* Boston: Houghton Mifflin.

Jansson, D. G., & Smith, S. M. (1991). Design fixation. *Design Studies, 12,* 3–11.

Jefferson, D. J. (1993, August 12). Dr. Brown treats what ails the rides at amusement parks. *The Wall Street Journal,* p. 1.

Jencks, D. (1972). *Inequality: A reassessment of the effect of family and school in America.* New York: Basic Books.

Jenkins, J. G., & Dallenbach, K. M. (1924). Obliviscence during sleep and waking. *American Journal of Psychology, 35,* 605–612.

Johnson, B. T., & Eagly, A. H. (1989). Effects of involvement on persuasion: A meta-analysis. *Psychological Bulletin, 106,* 290–314.

Johnson, E. J. (1985). Expertise and decision under uncertainty: Performance and process. In M. Chi, R. Glasse, & M. Farr (Eds.), *The nature of expertise.* Columbus, OH: National Center for Research in Vocational Education.

Johnson, M. K., Hashtroudi, S., & Lindsay, D. S. (1993). Source monitoring. *Psychological Bulletin, 114,* 3–28.

Johnson, M. K., Mitchell, K. J., Raye, C. L., & Greene, E. J. (2004). An age-related deficit in prefrontal cortical function associated with refreshing information. *Psychological Science, 15,* 127–132.

Johnston, W., & Dark, V. (1986). Selective attention. *Annual Review of Psychology, 37,* 43–75.

Joiner, T. E., Jr. (1994). The interplay of similarity and self-verification in relationship formation. *Social Behavior and Personality, 22,* 195–200.

Joiner, T. E., Jr., Alfano, M. S., & Metalsky, G. I. (1993). When depression breeds contempt: Reassurance seeking, self-esteem, and rejection of depressed college students by their roommates.

Journal of Abnormal Psychology, 101 165–173.

Joiner, T. E., Jr., Heatheton, T. F., Rudd, M. D., & Schmidt, N. B. (1997). Perfectionism, perceived with status, and bulimic symptoms: Two studies testing a diathesis-stress model. *Journal of Abnormal Psychology, 106,* 145–153.

Jones, L. W., Sinclair, R. C., & Courneya, K. S. (2003). The effects of source credibility and message framing on exercise intentions, behaviors, and attitudes: An integration of the elaboration likelihood model and prospect theory. *Journal of Applied Social Psychology, 33,* 179–196.

Judd, C. M., Ryan, C. N., & Park, B. (1991). Accuracy in the judgment of in-group and out-group variability. *Journal of Personality and Social Psychology, 61,* 366–379.

Judge, T., & Bono, J. E. (2001). Relationship of core self-evaluations traits—self-esteem, generalized self-efficacy, locus of control, and emotional stability—with job satisfaction and job performance: A meta-analysis. *Journal of Applied Psychology, 86,* 80–92.

Judge, T. A., Bono, J. E., Ilies, R., & Gerhardt, M. W. (2002). Personality and leadership: A qualitative and quantitative review. *Journal of Applied Psychology, 87,* 765–780.

Judge, T. A., Martocchio, J. J., & Thorsen, C. J. (1998). Five-factor model of personality and employee absence. *Journal of Applied Psychology, 82,* 745–755.

Judge, T. A., Thoresen, C. J., Bono, J. E., & Patton, G. K. (2001). The job satisfaction–performance relationship: A qualitative and quantitative review. *Psychological Bulletin, 127,* 376–407.

Julien, R. M. (1995). *A primer of drug action* (7th ed.). New York: Freeman.

Jussim, L. (1991). Interpersonal expectations and social reality: A reflection-construction model and reinterpretation of evidence. *Psychological Review, 98,* 54–73.

Kagan, J. (1998). Biology and the child. In W. Damon & R. M. Oerner (Eds.), *Handbook of child psychology* (Vol. 1). New York: John Wiley & Sons.

Kagan, J., & Snidman, N. (1991). Temperamental factors in human development. *American Psychologist, 46,* 856–862.

Kahneman, D., & Tversky, A. (1982). Judgment under uncertainty: Heuristics and biases. In D. Kahneman, P. Slovic, & A. Tversky (Eds.), *Judgment under uncertainty: Heuristics and biases* (pp. 3–22). Cambridge, England: Cambridge University Press.

Kalivas, P. W., & Samson, H. H. (Eds.). (1992). *The neurobiology of drug and alcohol addiction.* Annals of the New York Academy of Sciences, Vol. 654. New York: Academy of Sciences.

Kalsher, M. J., Rodocker, A. J., Racicot, B. M., & Wogalter, M. S. (1993). Promoting recycling behavior in office environments. *Proceedings of the Human Factors and Ergonomics Society, 37,* 484–488.

Kamin, L. J. (1965) Temporal and intensity characteristics of the conditioned stimulus. In W. F. Prokasy (Ed.), *Classical conditioning: A symposium.* New York: Appleton-Century-Crofts.

Kane, M., & Engle, R. W. (2003). Individual differences in executive attention and the Stroop. *Manuscript submitted for publication.*

Kanner, A. D., Coyne, J. C., Schaefer, C., & Lazarus, R. S. (1981). Comparison of two modes of stress measurement: Daily hassles and uplifts versus major life events. *Journal of Behavioral Medicine, 4,* 1–39.

Kanwisher, N., McDermott, J., & Chun, M. M. (1997). The fusiform face area: A module in human extrastriate cortex specialized for face perception. *Journal of Neuroscience, 17,* 4302–4311.

Kaplan, H. I., & Sadock, B. J. (1991). *Synopsis of psychiatry: Behavioral sciences and clinical psychiatry* (6th ed.). Baltimore, MD: Williams & Wilkins.

Kattler, H., Djik, D. J., & Borbely, A. A. (1994). Effects of unilateral somatosensory stimulation prior to sleep on the sleep EEG in humans. *Journal of Sleep Research, 4,* 159–164.

Kaufman, A. S., & Kaufman, N. L. (1993). Kaufman adolescent and adult intelligence test. Circle Pines, MN: American Guidance.

Kavanagh, D. J. (1992). Recent developments in expressed emotion in schizophrenia. *British Journal of Psychiatry, 148,* 601–620.

Kawakami, K., Dovidio, J. F., & Dijksterhuis, A. (2003). Effect of social category priming on personal attitudes. *Psychological Science, 14* (4), 315–319.

Kazdin, A. E. (1982). The token economy: A decade later. *Journal of Applied Behavior Analysis, 15,* 431–446.

Keary, K., & Fitzpatrick, C. (1994). Children's disclosure of sexual abuse during formal investigation. *Child Abuse and Neglect, 18,* 543–548.

Keefe, F. J., Buffington, A. L. H., Studts, J. L., & Rumble, M. E. (2002). Behavioral medicine 2002 and beyond. *Journal of Consulting and Clinical Psychology, 70* (3), 852–856.

Kelley, H. H. (1972). Attribution in social interaction. In E. E. Jones et al. (Eds.), *Attribution: Perceiving the causes of behavior.* Morristown, NJ: General Learning Press.

Kelly, D. D. (1981). Disorders of sleep and consciousness. In E. Kandel & J. Schwartz (Eds.), *Principles of neural science.* New York: Elsevier-North Holland.

Kelman, H. C., & Hamilton, V. L. (1989). *Crimes of obedience.* New Haven, CT: Yale University Press.

Kelsey, F. O. (1969). Drugs and pregnancy. *Mental Retardation, 7,* 7–10.

Kemeny, M. E. (2003). The psychobiology of stress. *Current Directions in Psychological Science, 12,* 124–129.

Kenardy, J. A., Dow, M. G. T., Johnston, D. W., Newman, M. G., Thompson, A., & Taylor, C. B. (2002). *A comparison of delivery methods of cognitive behavioural therapy for panic disorder: An international muticentre trial.* Manuscript submitted for publication.

Kendzierski, D., & Whitaker, D. J. (1997). The role of self-schema in linking intentions with behavior. *Personality and Social Psychology Bulletin, 23,* 139–147.

Kenrick, D. T., Groth, G. E., Trost, M. R., & Sadalla, E. K. (1993). Integrating evolutionary and social exchange perspectives on relationships: Effects of gender, self-appraisal, and involvement level on mate selection criteria. *Journal of Personality and Social Psychology, 64,* 951–969.

Kessler, R. C., McGonagle, K. A., Zhao, S., Nelson, C. B., Hughes, M., Eshleman, S., Witchen, H-U., & Kendler, K. S. (1994). Lifetime and 12-month prevalence of DSM-III-R psychiatric disorders in the United States. *Archives of General Psychiatry, 5,* 8–19.

Kiecolt-Glaser, J. K., & Glaser, R. (1992). Psychoneuroimmunology: Can psychological interventions modulate immunity? *Journal of Consulting and Clinical Psychology, 60,* 569–575.

Kiecolt-Glaser, J. K., Fisher, L., Ogrocki, P., Stout, J. C., Speicher, C. E., & Glaser, R. (1987). Marital quality, marital disruption, and immune function. *Psychosomatic Medicine, 49,* 13–34.

Kiecolt-Glaser, J. K., Kennedy, S., Malkoff, S., Fisher, L., Speicher, C. E., & Glaser, R. (1988). Marital discord and immunity in males. *Psychosomatic Medicine, 50,* 213–229.

Kiecolt-Glaser, J. K., Malarkey, W., Cacioppo, J. T., & Glaser, R. (1994). Stressful personal relationships: Endocrine and immune function. In R. Glaser & J. K. Kiecolt-Glaser (Eds.), *Handbook of human stress and immunity* (pp. 321–339). San Diego: Academic Press.

Kiesler, C. A., & Kiesler, S. B. (1969). *Conformity.* Reading, MA: Addison-Wesley.

Kinnunen, T., Zamansky, T., & Block, M. (1994). Is the hypnotized subject lying? *Journal of Abnormal Psychology, 103,* 184–191.

Kirby, S. L., & Davis, M. A. (1998). A study of escalating commitment in principal– agent relationships: Effects of monitoring and personal responsibility. *Journal of Applied Psychology, 83,* 206–217.

Kirkpatrick, D. L. (1959). Techniques for evaluating training programs. *Journal of the American Society of Training Directors, 13,* 3–9, 21–26.

Kirsch, I., & Braffman, W. (2001). Imaginative suggestibility and hypnotizability. *Current Directions in Psychological Science, 10,* 57–61.

Kirsch, I., & Lynn, S. J. (1998). Dissociation theories of hypnosis. *Psychological Bulletin, 123,* 100–115.

Kisilevsky, B. S., Hains, S. M. J., Lee, J., Xie, X., Juang, H., Ye, H. H., Zhand, K., & Wang, Z. (2003). Effects of experience on fetal voice recognition. *Psychological Science, 14,* 220–224.

Klaczynski, P. A. (1997). Bias in adolescents' everyday reasoning and its relationships with intellectual ability, personal theories, and self-serving motivation. *Developmental Psychology, 33,* 273–283.

Klag, M. J., Ford, D. E., Mead, L. A., He, J., Whelton, P. K., Liang, K., & Levine, D. M. (1993). Serum cholesterol in young men and subsequent cardiovascular disease. *New England Journal of Medicine, 328,* 313–318.

Knapp, R. (1987, July). When a child dies. *Psychology Today,* 60–67.

Kohlberg, L. (1984). *Essays on moral development, Vol. 2. The psychology of moral development.* San Francisco: Harper & Row.

Kohn, P., & Macdonald, J. E. (1992). The Survey of Life Experiences: A decontaminated hassles scale for adults. *Journal of Behavioral Medicine, 15,* 221–236.

Kolb, B., Gibb, R., & Gorny, G. (2003). Experience-dependent changes in dendritic arbor and spine density in neocortex vary with age and sex. *Neurobiology of Learning and Memory, 79,* 1–10.

Kolb, B., Gibb, R., & Robinson, T. E. (2003). Brain plasticity and behavior. *Current Directions in Psychological Science, 12* (1), 1–5.

Koob, G. F., Roberts, A. J., Schulteis, G., Parsons, L. H., Heyser, C. J., Hyytia, P., Merlo-Pich, E., & Weiss, F. (1998). Neurocircuitry targets in ethanol reward and dependence. *Alcoholism: Clinical and Experimental Research, 22,* 3–9.

Koocher, G. P., Goodman, G. W., White, C. S., Friedrich, W. N., Sivan, A. B., & Reynolds, C. R. (1995). Psycholgical science and the use of anatomically detailed dolls in child sexual-abuse assessments. *Psychological Bulletin, 118,* 119–122.

Kosslyn, S. M. (1994). *Image and brain: The resolution of the imagery debate.* Cambridge, MA: MIT Press.

Kounious, J. (1996). On the continuity of thought and the representation of knowledge: Electrophysiological and behavioral time-course measures reveal levels of structure in semantic memory. *Psychonomic Bulletin and Review, 3,* 265–286.

Koutstaal, W. (2003). Older adults encode—but do not always use—perceptual details: Intentional versus unintentional effects of detail on memory judgments. *Psychological Science, 14,* 189–193.

Kramer, A. F., & Willis, S. L. (2002). Enhancing the cognitive vitality of older adults. *Current Directions in Psychological Science, 11,* 173–177.

Kranzler, J., & Jensen, A. R. (1989). Inspection time and intelligence: A meta-analysis. *Intelligence, 13,* 329–247.

Kring, A. M., Smith, D. A., & Neale, J. M. (1994). Individual differences in dispositional expressiveness: Development and validation of the emotional expressivity scale. *Journal of Personality and Social Psychology, 66,* 934–949.

Kubany, E. S., Bauer, G. B., Muraoka, M. Y., Richard, D. C., & Read, P. (1995). Impact of labeled anger and blame in intimate relationships. *Journal of Social and Clinical Psychology, 14,* 53–60.

Kübler-Ross, E. (1974). *Questions and answers about death and dying.* New York: Macmillan.

Kuhn, L., Stein, Z. A., Thomas, P. A., Singh, T., & Tasai, W. (1994). Maternal–infant HIV transmission and circumstances of delivery. *American Journal of Public Health, 84,* 1110–1115.

Kunda, Z., & Oleson, K. C. (1995). Maintaining stereotypes in the face of disconfirmation: Construction grounds for subtyping deviants. *Journal of Personality and Social Psychology, 68,* 565–579.

Kyllonen, P. C., & Christal, R. E. (1990). Reasoning is (little more than) working-memory capacity? *Intelligence, 14,* 389–433.

Ladavas, E., Umilta, C., & Ricci-Bitti, P. E. (1980). Evidence for sex differences in right-hemisphere dominance for emotions. *Neuropsychologia, 18,* 361–366.

Ladd, D., & Henry, R. A. (2000). Helping coworkers and helping the organization: The role of support perceptions, exchange ideology, and conscientiousness. *Journal of Applied Social Psychology, 30,* 2028–2049.

Ladd, G. W., Kochenderfer, B. J., & Coleman, C. C. (1996). Friendship quality as a predictor of young children's early school adjustment. *Child Development, 6,* 1103–1118.

Laird, J. D. (1984). The real role of facial responses in the experience of emotion: A reply to Tourangeua and Ellsworth, and others. *Journal of Personality and Social Psychology, 47,* 909–917.

Lamb, M. E. (1977). Father-infant and mother-infant interactions in the first year of life. *Child Development, 48,* 167–181.

Lambert, A. J. (1995). Stereotypes and social judgment: The consequences of group variability. *Journal of Personality and Social Psychology, 68,* 388–403.

Landis, S. H., Murray, T., Bolden, S., & Wingo, P. A. (1998). Cancer statistics, 1998. *CA Cancer J Clin, 48,* 6–29.

Landro, L. (1998, October 19). Alone together: Cancer patients and survivors find treatment, and support, online. *Wall Street Journal,* p. R12.

Langlois, J. H., Kalakanis, L., Rubenstein, A. J., Larson, A., Hallam, M., & Smoot, M. (2000). Maxims or myths of beauty: A meta-analytic and theoretical review. *Psychological Bulletin, 126,* 390–423.

Langlois, J. H., & Roggman, L. A. (1990). Attractive faces are only average. *Psychological Science, 1,* 115–121.

Langlois, J. H., Roggman, L. A., & Riesser-Danner, L. A. (1990). Infants' differential social responses to attractive and unattractive faces. *Developmental Psychology, 26,* 153–159.

Lappin, J. S., & Craft, W. D. (2000). Foundations of spatial vision: From retinal images to perceived shapes. *Psychological Review, 107,* 6–38.

Larzelere, R. E., Sather, P. R., Schneider, W. N., Larson, D. B., & Pike, P. L. (1998). Punishment enhances reasoning's effectiveness as a disciplinary response to toddlers. *Journal of Marriage and the Family, 60,* 388–403.

Latane, B., Williams, K., & Harkins, S. (1979). Many hands make light the work: The causes and consequences of social loafing. *Journal of Personality and Social Psychology, 37,* 822–832.

Latham, G. P., & Wexley, K. N. (1977). Behavioral observation scales for performance appraisal purposes. *Personnel Psychology, 30,* 225–268.

Laumann, E. O., Gagnon, J. H., Michael, R. T., & Michaels, S. (1994). *The social organization of sexuality: Sexual practices in the United States.* Chicago: University of Chicago Press.

Launer, L. J., Feskens, E. J., Kalmijn, S., & Kromhout, D. (1996). Smoking, drinking, and thinking: The Zutphen Elderly study. *American Journal of Epidemiology, 143,* 219–227.

Lawless, H., & Engen, T. (1977). Associations to odors: Interference, mnemonics, and verbal labeling. *Journal of Experimental Psychology: Human Learning and Memory, 3,* 52–59.

Layman, J., Gidycz, C. A., & Lynn, S. J. (1996). Unacknowledged versus acknowledged rape victims: Situational factors and posttraumatic stress. *Journal of Abnormal Psychology, 105,* 124–131.

Lazarus, R. S., & Folkman, S. (1984). *Stress, appraisal, and coping.* New York: Springer.

Lazarus, R. S., Opton, E. M., Nomikos, M. S., & Rankin, N. O. (1985). The principle of short-circuiting of threat: Further evidence. *Journal of Personality, 33,* 622–635.

LeDoux, J. E. (2000). Emotion circuits in the brain. *Annual Review of Neuroscience, 23,* 155–184.

Leeper, M. R., & Cordova, D. I. (1992). A desire to be taught: Instructional consequences of intrinsic motivation. *Motivation and Emotion, 16,* 187–208.

Lemery, K. S., Goldsmith, H. H., Klinnert, M. D., & Mrazek, D. A. (1999). Developmental models of infant and childhood temperament. *Developmental Psychology, 35,* 189–204.

Lemley, B. (2000, February). Isn't she lovely? *Discover,* 42–49.

Lepper, M., & Green, D. (Eds.). (1978). *The hidden costs of reward.*

Lerner, R. M. (1993). The demise of the nature-nurture dichotomy. *Human Development, 36,* 119–124.

LeVay, S. (1991). A difference in hypothalamic structure between heterosexual and homosexual men. *Science, 253,* 1–36.

Levenson, R. W. (1992). Autonomic nervous system differences among emotions. *Psychological Science, 3,* 23–27.

Levenson, R. W., Carstensen, L. L., Fruiesen, W. V., & Ekman, P. (1991). Emotion, physiology, and expression in old age. *Psychology and Aging, 6,* 28–35.

Leventhal, H., Singer, R., & Jones, S. (1965). The effects of fear and specifying of recommendation upon attitudes and behavior. *Journal of Personality and Social Psychology, 2,* 20–29.

Levine, L. J., & Safer, M. A. (2002). Sources of bias in memory for emotions. *Current Directions in Psychological Science, 11,* 169–173.

Levinson, D. J. (1986). A conception of adult development. *American Psychologist, 41,* 3–13.

Levinthal, C. F. (1999). *Drugs, behavior, and modern society.* Boston: Allyn & Bacon.

Levis, D. J. (1985). Implosive theory: A comprehensive extension of conditioning theory of fear/anxiety to psychology. In S. Reiss & R. R. Bootzin (Eds.), *Theoretical issues in behavior therapy.* New York: Academic Press.

Levy, S. M. (1990). Psychosocial risk factors and cancer progression: Mediating pathways linking behavior and disease. In K. D. Craig & S. M. Weiss (Eds.), *Health enhancement, disease prevention, and early intervention: Biobehavioral perspectives.* New York: Springer.

Levy, S. M., Herberman, R., Maluish, A., Achlien, B., & Lippman, M. (1985). Prognostic risk assessment in primary breast cancer by behavioral and immunological parameters. *Health Psychology, 4,* 99–113.

Levy, S. M., Lee, J., Bagley, C., & Lippman, M. (1988). Survival hazards analysis in first recurrent breast cancer patients: Seven-year follow-up. *Psychosomatic Medicine, 50,* 520–528.

Lewkowicz, D. J. (1996). Infants' response to the audible and visible properties of the human face. Role of lexical-syntactic content, temporal synchrony, gender, and manner of speech. *Developmental Psychology, 32,* 347–366.

Lewy, A. J., Sack, R. I., & Singer, C. M. (1992). Bright light, melatonin, and biological rhythms in humans. In J. Montplaisir & R. Godbout (Eds.), *Sleep and biological rhythms: Basic mechanisms and applications to psychiatry.* New York: Oxford University Press.

Li, J., Precht, G., Mortenson, I., & Olsen, L. (2003). A study of bereaved parents in Denmark. Cited in Corless, B., Pittman, M., Germino, B. B., & Pittman, M. A. (Eds.), *Dying, death, and bereavement: A challenge for the living.* New York: Springer Publishing Co.

Liddell, F. D. K. (1982). Motor vehicle accidents (1973–6) in a cohort of Montreal drivers. *Journal of Epidemiological Community Health, 36,* 140–145.

Liden, R. C., Sparrowe, R. T., & Wayne, S. J. (1997). Leader–member exchange theory: The past and potential for the future. In G. R. Ferris (Ed.), *Research in personnel and human resource management* (Vol. 15, pp. 47–119). Greenwich, CT: JAI Press.

Lieberman, D. A. (1990). *Learning: Behavior and cognition.* Belmont, CA: Wadsworth Publishing Company.

Lindsay, D. S., & Read, J. D. (1995). Memory, remembering, and misremembering. *PTSD Research Quarterly, 6,* 1–7.

Linville, P. W., & Fischer, G. W. (1993). Exemplar and abstraction models of perceived group variability and stereotypicality. *Social Cognition, 11,* 92–125.

Locke, B. Z., & Slaby, A. E. (1982). Preface. In D. Mechanic (Ed.), *Symptoms, illness behavior, and help-seeking* (pp. xi–xv). New York: Prodist.

Locke, E. A., & Latham, G. P. (1990). *A theory of goal setting and task performance.* Englewood Cliffs, NJ: Prentice-Hall.

Loehlin, J. C., Lindzey, G., & Spuhle, J. N. (1975). Race differences in intelligence. New York: Freeman.

Loftus, E. F. (1991). The glitter of everyday memory . . . and the gold. *American Psychologist, 46,* 16–18.

Loftus, E. F. (1992). When a lie becomes memory's truth: Memory distortion after exposure to misinformation. *Current Directions in Psychological Science, 1,* 121–123.

Logan, G. D. (1985). Skill and automaticity: Relations, implications, and future directions. *Canadian Journal of Psychology, 39,* 367–386.

Logan, G. D. (1988). Toward an instance theory of automotization. *Psychological Review, 95,* 492–527.

Logan, T. K., Cole, J., & Leukefeld, C. (2002). Women, sex, and HIV: Social and contextual factors, meta-analysis of published interviews, and implications for practice and research. *Psychological Bulletin, 128* (6), 851–855.

Logue, A. W. (1988). Research on self-control: An integrating framework. *Behavioral and Brain Sciences, 11,* 665–679.

Logue, A. W., Logue, K. R., & Strauss, K. E. (1983). The acquisition of taste aversion in humans with eating and drinking disorders. *Behavioral Research and Therapy, 21,* 275–289.

Logue, A. W., Ophir, I., & Strauss, K. E. (1981). The acquisition of taste aversion in humans. *Behavior Research and Therapy, 19,* 319–333.

Lubart, T. I. (1994). Creativity. In R. J. Sternberg (Ed.), *Thinking problem solving* (pp. 289–332). San Diego, CA: Academic Press.

Lubart, T. T., & Sternberg, R. J. (1995). An investment approach to creativity: Theory and data. In S. M. Smith, T. B. Ward, & R. A. Finke (Eds.), *The creative cognition approach* (pp. 269–302). Cambridge, MA: MIT Press.

Luchins, A. S. (1942). Mechanization in problem solving. *Psychological Monographs, 54* (whole No. 248).

Lucy, J. A. (1992). *Language diversity and thought: A reformulation of the Whorfian hypothesis.* Cambridge, England: Cambridge University Press.

Luczak, S. E. (2001). Binge drinking in Chinese, Korean, and White college students: Genetic and ethnic group differences. *Psychology of Addictive Behaviors, 15,* 306–309.

Ludwig, S. (2001). The cross-race effect: Beyond recognition of faces in the laboratory. *Psychology, Public Policy, and Law, 7,* 170–200.

Luria, A. R. (1976). *Cognitive development: Its cultural and social foundations.* Cambridge: Harvard University Press.

Lykken, D. T., McGue, M., Tellegen, A., & Bouchard, T. J. (1992). Emergenesis: Genetic traits that may not run in families. *American Psychologist, 47,* 1565–1577.

Lynn, R. (1996). Racial and ethnic differences in intelligence in the United States on the Difference Ability Scale. *Personality and Individual Differences, 20,* 271–273.

Lynn, S. J., Rhue, J. W., & Weekes, J. R. (1990). Hypnotic involuntariness: A social cognitive analysis. *Psychological Review, 974,* 169–184.

Lytton, H. (1990). Child and parent effects in boys' conduct disorders. *Developmental Psychology, 26,* 683–697.

MacNichol, E. F. (1964). Retinal mechanisms of color vision. *Vision Research, 4,* 119–133.

Macrae, C. N., Alnwick, K. A., Milne, A. B., & Schloerscheidt, A. M. (2002). Person perception across the menstrual cycle: Hormonal influences on social-cognitive functioning. *Psychological Science, 13,* 532–536.

Magai, C., & McFadden, S. H. (1995). The role of emotions in social and personality development. *History, theory, and research.* New York: Plenum Press.

Maheswaran, D., & Chaiken, S. (1991). Promoting systematic processing in low-motivation settings: Effect of incongruent information on processing and judgment. *Journal of Personality and Social Psychology, 61,* 13–25.

Major, B., Kaiser, C. R., & McCoy, S. K. (2003). It's not my fault: When and why attributions to prejudice protect self-esteem. *Personality and Social Psychology Bulletin, 29,* 772–781.

Malandro, L. A., Barker, L., & Barker, D. A. (1994). *Nonverbal communication* (3rd ed.). New York: Random House.

Mandel, D. R., Jusczyk, P. W., & Pisoni, D. B. (1995). Infants' recognition of the sound patterns of their own names. *Psychological Science, 6,* 314–317.

Mann, J. M., & Tarantola, D. J. M. (1998, July). HIV 1998: The global picture. *Scientific American,* 82–83.

Markman, G. D., Baron, R. A., & Balkin, D. B. (2003). The role of regretful thinking, perseverance, and self-efficacy in venture formation. In J. Katz & D. Shepherd (Eds.), *Advances in entrepreneurship, firm emergence, and growth.* Greenwich, CT: JAI Press.

Marr, D. (1982). *Vision: A computational investigation into the human representation and processing of visual information.* San Francisco: W. H. Freeman.

Marsh, R. L., Landau, J. D., & Hicks, J. L. (1996). How examples may (and may not) constrain creativity. *Memory & Cognition, 24* (3), 669–680.

Marsh, R. L., Ward, T. B., & Landau, J. D. (1999). The inadvertent use of prior knowledge in a generative cognitive task. *Memory & Cognition, 27* (1), 94–105.

Martin, C. L., & Little, J. K. (1990). The relation of gender understanding to children's sex-typed preferences and gender stereotypes. *Child Development, 61,* 1427–1439.

Martin, R. (2001). Humor, laughter, and physical health: Methodological issues and research findings. *Psychological Bulletin, 127* (4), 504–519.

Martin, R. (2002). Is laughter the best medicine? Humor, laughter, and physical health. *Current Directions in Psychological Science, 11,* 216–222.

Maslow, A. H. (1970). *Motivation and personality* (2nd ed.). New York: Harper & Row.

Mason, R. B., & Just, M. A. (2004). How the brain processes causal inferences in text. *Psychological Science, 15,* 1–8.

Masters, W. H., & Johnson, V. E. (1966). *Human sexual response.* Boston: Little, Brown.

Matarazzo, J. D. (1992). Psychological testing and assessment in the 21st century. *American Psychologist, 47,* 1007–1018.

Matlin, M. W., & Foley, H. J. (1997). *Sensation and perception.* Needham Heights, MA: Allyn & Bacon.

Matsumoto, D. (2000). *Culture and psychology* (2nd ed.). Pacific Grove, CA: Brooks Cole.

Mattes, R. D. (2001). The taste of fat elevates postprandial triacylglycerol. *Physiology & Behavior, 74,* 343–348.

Mattheson, P. B., Shooenbaum, E., Greenberg, B., & Pliner, V. (1997). Association of maternal drug use during pregnancy with mother-to-child HIV transmission. *AIDS, 11,* 941–942.

Maurer, D., & Barrera, M. (1981). Infants' perception of natural and distorted arrangements of a schematic face. *Child Development, 52,* 196–202.

Maurer, T. J., & Pierce, H. R. (1998). A comparison of Likert scale and traditional measures of self-efficacy. *Journal of Applied Psychology, 83,* 324–329.

Mayer, J. D., Caruso, D. R., & Salovey, P. (1998). *Emotional intelligence meets traditional standards for intelligence.* Manuscript submitted for publication.

Mayer, J. D., Salovey, P., Caruso, D. R., & Sitarenios, G. (2001). Emotional intelligence as a standard intelligence. *Emotion, 1,* 232–242.

Mayes, A. R. (1996). The functional deficits that underlie amnesia: Evidence from amnesic forgetting rate and item-specific implicit memory. In D. J. Herman, C. McEvoy, C. Hertzog, P. Hertel, & M. K. Johnson (Eds.), *Basic and applied memory research: Practical applications* (Vol. 2, pp. 391–405). Mahwah, NJ: Erlbaum.

Mazur, J. E. (1996). Procrastination by pigeons: Preference for larger, more delayed work requirements. *Journal of the Experimental Analysis of behavior, 65,* 159–171.

Mazure, C., Chitra, R., Maciejewski, P. K., Jacobs, S. C., & Bruce, M. L. (2001). Cognitive-personality characteristics as direct predictors of unipolar major depression. *Cognitive Therapy and Research, 25,* 215–225.

Mazzoni, G. A. L., Lombardo, E., Malvagia, C., & Loftus, E. F. (1999). Dream interpretation and false belief. *Professional Psychology: Research and Practice, 30,* 45–50.

Mazzoni, G., & Memon, A. (2003). Imagination can create false autobiographical memories. *Psychological Science, 14,* 186–188.

McArdle, J. J., Caja-Ferrer, E., Hamagami, F., & Woodcock, R. W. (2002). Comparative longitudinal structural analyses of the growth and decline of multiple intellectual abilities over the life span. *Developmental Psychology, 38,* 115–142.

McClearn, G. E., Plomin, R., Gora-Maslak, G., & Crabbe, J. C. (1991). The gene chase in behavioral science. *Psychological Science, 2,* 222–229.

McClelland, D. C. (1985). *Human motivation.* New York: Cambridge University Press.

McClelland, D. C. (1995). Achievement motivation in relation to achievement-related recall, performance, and urine flow, a marker associated with release of vasopressin. *Motivation and Emotion, 19,* 59–76.

McCormick, E. J., Jeanneret, P. R., & Meacham, R. C. (1969). *Position Analysis Questionnaire.* West Lafayette, IN: Occupational Research Center, Purdue University.

McCullough, M. E. (2001). Forgiveness: Who does it and how do they do it? *Current Directions in Psychological Science, 6,* 194–197.

McCullough, M. E., Bellah, C. G., Kilpatrick, S. D., & Johnson, J. L. (2001). Vengefulness: Relationships with forgiveness, rumination, well-being, and the Big Five. *Personality and Social Psychology Bulletin, 27,* 601–610.

McDonald, H. E., & Hirt, E. R. (1997). When expectancy meets desire: Motivational effects in reconstructive memory. *Journal of Personality and Social Psychology, 72,* 5–23.

McEwen, B. S. (1998). Protective and damaging effects of stress mediators. *New England Journal of Medicine, 338,* 171–179.

McFarland, C., & Alvaro, C. (2000). The impact of motivation on temporal comparisons: Coping with traumatic events by perceiving personal growth. *Journal of Personality and Social Psychology, 79,* 327–343.

McGue, M. (1999). The behavioral genetics of alcoholism. *Current Directions in Psychological Science, 8,* 109–115.

McGue, M., Bouchard, T. J., Jr., Iaconon, W. G., & Lykken, D. T. (1993). Behavioral genetics of cognitive ability: A life-span perspective. In R. Plomin & G. E. McClearn (Eds.), *Nature, nurture, and psychology* (pp. 59–76). Washington, DC: American Psychological Association.

McGue, M., Sharma, A., & Benson, P. (1996). Parent and sibling influences on adolescent alcohol use and misuse: Evidence from a U.S. adoption cohort. *Journal of Studies on Alcohol, 57,* 8–18.

McGuire, P. A. (1999, June). Psychology and medicine connecting in war on cancer. *APA Monitor,* 8–9.

McKee, S. A., Maciejewski, P. K., Falba, T., & Mazure, C. M. (2003). Sex differences in the effects of stressful life events on changes in smoking status. *Addiction, 98,* 847–855.

McKnight, A. J., & Peck, R. C. (2002). Graduated driver licensing and safer driving. *Journal of Safety Research, 34,* 85–89.

McNeely, B. L., & Meglino, B. M. (1994). The role of dispositional and situational antecedents in prosocial organizational behavior: An examination of the intended beneficiaries of prosocial behavior. *Journal of Applied Psychology, 79,* 836–844.

McNeil, B. J., Pauker, S. G., & Tversky, A. (1988). On the framing of medical decisions. In D. E. Bell (Ed.), *Decision making: Descriptive, normative, and prescriptive interactions* (pp. 562–568). New York: Cambridge University Press.

Mealey, L., Bridgstock, R., & Townsend, G. C. (1999). Symmetry and perceived facial attactiveness: A monozygotic co-twin comparison. *Journal of Personality and Social Psychology, 76,* 151–158.

Medvec, V. H., & Savitsky, K. (1997). When doing better means feeling worse: The effects of categorical cutoff points on counterfactual thinking and satisfaction. *Journal of Personality and Social Psychology, 72,* 1284–1296.

Medvec, V. H., Madey, S. F., & Gilovich, T. (1995). When less is more: Counterfactual thinking and satisfaction among Olympic athletes. *Journal of Personality and Social Psychology, 69,* 603–610.

Meehl, P. E. (1975). Hedonic capacity: Some conjectures. *Bulletin of the Menninger Clinic, 39,* 295–307.

Meichenbaum, D. H. (1977). *Cognitive-behavior modification.* New York: Plenum.

Meijmann, T., van der Meer, O., & van Dormolen, M. (1993). The after-effects of night work on short-term memory performance. *Ergonomics, 36,* 37–42.

Meissner, C. A., & Brigham, J. C. (2001). Thirty years of investigating the own-race bias in memory for faces: A meta-analytic review. *Psychology, Public Policy, and Law, 7,* 3–35.

Mellers, B. A. (2000). Choice and relative pleasure of consequences. *Psychological Bulletin, 126,* 910–924.

Mellers, B. A., & McGraw, A. P. (2001). Anticipated emotions as guides to choice. *Current Directions in Psychological Science, 6,* 210–214.

Melzack, R., & Wall, P. D. (1988). *The challenge of pain* (rev. ed.). New York: Penguin Books.

Melzack, R., & Wall, P. D. (1965). Pain mechanisms: A new theory. *Science, 150,* 971–979.

Mendlewicz, J., & Lecrubier, Y. (2000). Antidepressants section: Proceedings from a TA-SSRI consensus conference. *Acta Psychiatrica Scandinavian, 101* (Supplement 403), 5–8.

Mento, A. J., Locke, E. A., & Klein, H. J. (1992). Relationship of goal level to valence and instrumentality. *Journal of Applied Psychology, 77,* 395–405.

Merkelbach, H., deJong, P. J., Muris, P., & van den Hout, M. A. (1996). The etiology of specific phobias: A review. *Clinical Psychology Review, 16,* 337–361.

Metzger, A. M. (1980). A methodological study of the Kübler-Ross stage theory. *Omega, 10,* 291–301.

Meyer, A. J., Maccoby, N., & Farquhar, J. W. (1980). Skills training in a cardiovascular health education campaign. *Journal of Consulting and Clinical Psychology, 48,* 129–142.

Meyerowitz, B. E., & Chaiken, S. (1987). The effect of message framing on breast self-examination attitudes, intentions, and behavior. *Journal of Personality and Psychology, 52,* 500–510.

Meyerowitz, B. E., Wilson, D. K., & Chaiken, S. (1991, June). *Loss-framed messages increase breast self-examination for women who perceive risk.* Paper presented at the annual convention of the American Psychological Society, Washington, D.C.

Meyers, S. A., & Berscheid, E. (1997). The language of love: The difference a reposition makes. *Personality and Social Psychology Bulletin, 23,* 347–362.

Milgram, S. (1963). Behavioral study of obedience. *Journal of Abnormal and Social Psychology, 67,* 371–378.

Milgram, S. (1974). *Obedience to authority.* New York: Harper.

Millenson, J. R., & Leslie, J. C. (1979). *Principles of behavioral analysis* (2nd ed.). New York: Macmillan.

Miller, G. A. (1956). The magic number seven plus or minus two: Some limits on our capacity for processing information. *Psychological Review, 63,* 81–97.

Miller, G. E., & Cohen, S. (2001). Psychological interventions and the immune system: A meta-analytic review and critique. *Health Psychology, 20* (1), 47–63.

Miller, N., Maruyama, G., Beaber, R. J., & Valone, K. (1976). Speed of speech and persuasion. 615–624.

Miller, R. S. (1991). On decorum in close relationships: Why aren't we polite to those we love? *Contemporary Social Psychology, 15,* 63–65.

Miller, S. M., Shoda, Y., & Hurley, K. (1996). Applying cognitive-social theory to health-protective behavior: Breast self-examination in cancer screening. *Psychological Bulletin, 119,* 70–94.

Milling, L. S., Levine, M. R., & Meunier, S. A. (2003). Hypnotic enhancement of cognitive–behavioral interventions for pain: An analogue treatment study. *Health Psychology, 22* (4), 406–413.

Millon, T. (1987). *Millon clinical multiaxial inventory-II: Manual for MCMI-II* (2nd ed.). Minneapolis, MN: National Computer System.

Millon, T. (1991). Classification psychopathology: Rationale, alternatives, and standards. *Journal of Abnormal Psychology, 100,* 245–261.

Millon, T. A. (Ed.) (1997). *The Millon inventories: Clinical and personality assessment.* New York: Guilford Press.

Minami, H., & Dallenbach, K. M. (1946). The effect of activity upon learning and retention in the cockroach. *American Journal of Psychology, 59,* 1–58.

Mitchell, H. (1988, February). Why are women still dying of cervical cancer? *Australian Society,* pp. 34–35.

Mollon, J. D. (1993). Mixing genes and mixing colours. *Current Biology, 3,* 82–85.

Monahan, J. L., Murphy, S. T., & Zajonc, R. B. (2000). Subliminal mere exposure: Specific, general, and diffuse effects. *Psychological Science, 11*(6), 462–466.

Montgomery, G., & Kirsch, I. (1996). Mechanisms of placebo pain reduction: An empirical investigation. *Psychological Science, 7,* 174–176.

Moore, B. C. J. (1982). *An introduction to the psychology of hearing* (2nd ed.). New York: Academic.

Moore, R. Y., & Card, J. P. (1985). Visual pathways and the entrainment of circadian rhythms: The medical and biological effects of light. In R. J. Wurtman, M. J. Baum, J. T. Potts, Jr. (Eds.), *Annals of the New York Academy of Science, 453,* 123–133.

Moore-Ede, M. C., Sulzman, F. M., & Fuller, C. A. (1982). *The clocks that time us.* Cambridge, MA: Harvard University Press.

Moray, N. (1959). Attention in dichotic listening: Affective cues and the influence of instruction. *Quarterly Journal of Experimental Psychology, 11,* 59–60.

Moreland, R. L., & Beach, S. R. (1992). Exposure effects in the classroom: The development of affinity among students. *Journal of Experimental Social Psychology, 28,* 255–276.

Morley, S., Eccleston, C., & Williams, A. C. (1999). Systematic review and meta-analysis of randomized controlled trials of cognitive behavioural therapy for chronic pain in adults, excluding headache. *Pain, 80,* 1–13.

Morrongiello, B. A., & Clifton, R. K. (1984). Effects of sound frequency on behavioral and cardiac orienting in newborn and five-month-old infants. *Journal of Experimental Child Psychology, 38,* 429–446.

Morse, J. M., & Morse, R. M. (1988). Cultural variation in the inference of pain. *Journal of Cross Cultural Psychology, 19,* 232–242.

Moscovitch, M. (1985). Memory from infancy to old age: Implications for theories of normal and pathological memory. *Annals of the New York Academy of Sciences, 444,* 79–96.

Motowidlo, S. J., Packard, J. S., & Manning, M. R. (1986). Occupational stress: Its causes and consequences for job performance. *Journal of Applied Psychology, 71,* 618–629.

Mowrer, O. H., & Jones, H. M. (1945). Habit strength as a function of the pattern of reinforcement. *Journal of Experimental Psychology, 35,* 293–311.

Mulkens, S. A. N., deJong, P. J., & Merckelbach, H. (1996). Disgust and spider phobia. *Journal of Abnormal Psychology, 105,* 464–468.

Munley, G. A., McLoughlin, A., & Foster, J. J. (1999). Gender differences in health-check attendance and intention in young adults: An application of the health belief model. *Behaviour Change, 16,* 237–245.

Munsinger, H. A. (1978). The adopted child's IQ: A crucial review. *Psychological Bulletin, 82,* 623–659.

Murphy, K. R., & Cleveland, J. N. (1991). *Performance appraisal: An organizational perspective.* Boston: Allyn & Bacon.

Murphy, S. T., & Zajonc, R. B. (1993). Affect, cognition, and awareness: Affective priming with suboptimal and optimal stimulus. *Journal of Personality and Social Psychology, 64,* 723–739.

Murray, B. (1999, June). Customized appeals may increase cancer screening. *APA Monitor, 35.*

Myers, D. G., & Diener, E. (1995). Who is happy? *Psychological Science, 6,* 10–19.

Myers, N. A., Clifton, R. K., & Clarkson, M. C. (1987). When they were young: A most-threes remember two years ago. *Infant Behavior and Development, 10,* 123–132.

Naglieri, J. A. (1997). IQ: Knowns and unknowns, hits and misses. *American Psychologist, 52,* 75–76.

Naito, M., Komatsu, S., & Fuke, T. (1994). Normal and autistic children's understanding of their own and others' false beliefs: A study from Japan. *British Journal of Developmental Psychology, 12,* 403–416.

Narayan, S. S., Temchin, A. N., Recio, A., & Ruggero, M. A. (1998). Frequency tuning of basilar membrane and auditory nerve fibers in the same cochleae. *Science, 282,* 1882–1884.

Nathans, J. (1989). The genes for color vision. *Scientific American, 260,* 42–49.

Nathans, J., Thomas, D., & Hogness, D. S. (1986). Molecular genetics of human color vision: The genes encoding blue, green, and red pigments. *Science, 232,* 193–202.

National Center for Health Statistics. (2001). *Healthy People 2000: Final Review.* Hyattsville, MD: Public Health Service.

National Center for Health Statistics. *Prevalence of overweight and obesity among adults: United States, 1999–2000.* Retrieved March 10, 2004, from http://www.cdc.gov/nchs/products/pubs/pubd/hestats/obese/obese99.htm.

National Television Violence Study. (1996). *National television violence study* (Vol. 1). Thousand Oaks, CA: Sage.

National Television Violence Study. (1997). *National television violence study* (Vol. 2). Studio City, CA: Mediascope.

National Women's Law Center. (2003). *Making the grade on women's health: Women and smoking—A national and state-by-state report card.* Washington, DC: National Women's Law Center.

Neher, A. (1996). Jung's theory of archetypes: A critique. *Journal of Humanistic Psychology, 36,* 61–91.

Neisser, U., Boodoo, G., Bouchard, T. J., Jr., Bykin, A. W., Brody, N., Ceci, S. J., Halpern, D. F., Loehlin, J. C., Perloff, R., Sternberg, R. J., & Urbina, S. (1996). Intelligence: Knowns and unknowns. *American Psychologist, 51,* 77–101.

Nell, V. (2001). Mythic structures in narrative: Life, death, and immortality. In T. Brock, M. Green, & J. Strange (Eds.), *Narrative impact: Social and cognitive foundations* (pp. 17–37). Mahwah, NJ: Erlbaum.

Nell, V. (2002). Why young men drive dangerously: Implications for injury prevention. *Current Directions in Psychological Science, 11,* 75–79.

Nelson, G., Chandrashekar, F., Hoon, M. A., Feng, L., Zhao, G., Ryba, N. F. P., & Zuker, C. S. (2002). An amino-acid taste receptor. *Nature, 416,* 199–202.

Nelson, L. J., & Miller, D. T. (1995). The distinctiveness effect in social categorization: You are what makes you unusual. *Psychological Science, 6,* 246–249.

Nelson-Jones, R. (2002). Diverse goals for multicultural counseling and therapy. *Counseling Psychology Quarterly, 15,* 133–143.

Neuman, J. H., & Baron, R. A. (1997). Aggression in the workplace. In R. A. Giacalone & J. Greenberg (Eds.), *Antisocial behavior in organizations* (pp. 37–67). Thousand Oaks, CA: Brooks/Cole.

Newcombe, N., & Huttenlocher, J. (1992). Children's early ability to solve perspective-taking problems. *Developmental Psychology, 28,* 635–643.

Newport, E. L., & Aslin, R. N. (2000). Innately constrained learning: Blending old and new approaches to language acquisition. In S. C. Howell, S. A. Fish, & T. Keith-Lucas (Eds.), *Proceedings of the 24th Boston University Conference on Language Development* (pp. 1–21). Somerville, MA: Cascadilla Press.

Niaura, R., Todaro, J. F., Stroud, L., Spiro, A. III, Ward, K. D., & Weiss, S. (2002). Hostility, the metabolic syndrome, and incident coronary heart disease. *Health Psychology, 21* (6), 588–593.

Nickerson, R. S. (1998). Confirmation Bias: A ubiquitous phenomenon in many guises. *Review of General Psychology, 2,* 175–220.

Nicoladis, E., Mayberry, R. I., & Genesee, F. (1999). Gesture and early bilingual development. *Developmental Psychology, 35,* 514–526.

Nietzel, M. T., Speltz, M. L., McCauley, E. A., & Bernstein, D. A. (1998). *Abnormal psychology.* Boston: Allyn & Bacon.

Nigg, J. T., John, O. P., Blaskey, L. G., Huang-Pollock, C. L., Willcutt, E. G., Hinshaw, S. P., & Pennington, B. (2002). Big five dimensions and ADHD symptoms: Links between personality traits and clinical symptoms. *Journal of Personality and Social Psychology, 83,* 451–569.

Nisan, M., & Kohlberg, L. (1982). Universality and variation in moral judgment: A longitudinal and cross-sectional study in Turkey. *Child Development, 53,* 865–876.

Noble, J., & McConkey, K. M. (1995). Hypnotic sex change: Creating and challenging a delusion in the laboratory. *Journal of Abnormal Psychology, 104,* 69–74.

Nolen-Hoeksema, S., & Davis, C. G. (1999). "Thanks for sharing that": Ruminators and their social support networks. *Journal of Personality and Social Psychology, 77,* 801–814.

Norman, D. A., & Shallice, T. (1985). Attention to action: Willed and automatic control of behavior. In R. J. Davidson, G. E. Schwartz, & D. Shapiro (Eds.), *Consciousness and self-regulation: Vol. 4. Advances in research and theory* (pp. 2–18). New York: Plenum Press.

Norris, F. H. (2002). Psychosocial consequences of disasters. *PTSD Research Quarterly, 13* (2), 1–8.

Norris, F. H., & Murrell, S. A. (1990). Social support, life events, and stress as modifiers of adjustment to bereavement by older adults. *Psychology and Aging, 5,* 429–436.

Northcraft, G. B., & Neale, M. A. (1987). Experts, amateurs, and real estate: An anchoring-and-adjustment perspective on property pricing in decision. *Organizational Behavior and Human Decision Processes, 39,* 94–97.

Novy, D. M., Nelson, D. V., Francis, D., & Turk, D. C. (1995). Perspectives of chronic pain: An evaluative comparison of restrictive and comprehensive models. *Psychological Bulletin, 118,* 238–247.

O'Sullivan, C. S., & Durso, F. T. (1984). Effects of schema-incongruent information on memory for stereotypical attributes. *Journal of Personality and Social Psychology, 47,* 55–70.

O'Sullivan, M. (2003). The fundamental attribution error in detecting deception: The boy-who-cried-wolf effect. *Personality and Social Psychology Bulletin, 29,* 1316–1327.

Ogloff, J. R., & Wong, S. (1990). Electrodermal and cardiovascular evidence of a coping response in psychopaths. *Criminal Justice and Behavior, 17,* 231–245.

Ohman, A., & Mineka, S. (2001). Fear, phobias, and preparedness: Toward an evolved module of fear and fear learning. *Psychological Review, 108,* 483–522.

Ohman, A., & Mineka, S. (2003). The malicious serpent: Snakes as a prototypical stimulus for an evolved module of fear. *Current Directions in Psychological Science, 12,* 5–8.

Ohman, A., & Soares, J. J. F. (1994). Unconscious anxiety: Phobic responses to masked stimuli. *Journal of Abnormal Psychology, 103,* 231–240.

Ohman, A., Flykt, A., & Esteves, F. (2001). Emotion drives attention: Detecting the snake in the grass. *Journal of Experimental Psychology: General, 131,* 466–478.

Organ, D. W., & Ryan, K. (1995). A meta-analytic review of attitudinal and dispositional predictors of organizational citizenship behavior. *Personnel Psychology, 48,* 775–802.

Orlinsky, D. E., & Howard, K. E. (1987). The relation of process to outcome in psychotherapy. In S. L. Garfield & A. E. Bergin (Eds.), *Handbook of psychotherapy and behavior change* (3rd ed.). New York: Wiley.

Oskamp, S., Williams, R., Unipan, J., Steers, N., Mainieri, T., & Kurland, G. (1994). Psychological factors affecting paper recycling by businesses. *Environment and Behavior, 25,* 477–503.

Osterling, J., & Dawson, G. (1994). Early recognition of children with autism: A study of first birthday home videotapes. *Journal of Autism and Development Disorders, 24,* 247–257.

Ottati, V. C., & Isbell, L. M. (1996). Effects of mood during exposure to target information on subsequently reported judgments: An on-line model of misattribution and correction. *Journal of Personality and Social Psychology, 71,* 39–53.

Oulette-Kobasa, S. C., & Puccetti, M. C. (1983). Personality and social resources in stress resistance. *Journal of Personality and Social Psychology, 45,* 836–850.

Ozgen, E., & Davies, I. R. L. (2002). Acquisition of categorical color perception: A perceptual learning approach to the linguistic relativity hypothesis. *Journal of Experimental Psychology: General, 131,* 477–493.

Padian, N. S., Shiboski, S., & Jewell, N. (1990). The effect of the number of exposures on the risk of heterosexual HIV transmission. *Journal of Infectious Diseases. 161,* 883–887.

Paller, K. A., Kutas, M., & McIsaac, H. K. (1995). Monitoring conscious recollection via the electrical activity of the brain. *Psychological Science, 6,* 107–111.

Papp, L., Klein, D., Martinez, J., Schneier, F., Cole, R., Liebowitz, M., Hollander, E., Fryer, A., Jordan, F., & Gorman, J. (1993). Diagnostic and substance specificity of carbon-dioxide-induced panic. *American Journal of Psychiatry, 150,* 250–257.

Parekh, R., & Bersein, E. V. (2001). Looking for love? Take a cross-cultural walk through the personals. *Academic Psychiatry, 25,* 223–233.

Passman, R. H., & Weisberg, P. (1975). Mothers and blankets as agents for promoting play and exploration by young children in a novel environment: The effects of social and nonsocial attachment objects. *Developmental Psychology, 11,* 170–177.

Pastor, D. L. (1981). The quality of mother-infant attachment and its relationship to toddlers' initial sociability with peers. *Developmental Psychology, 17,* 326–335.

Patrick, C. J., Bradley, M. M., & Lang, P. J. (1993). Emotion in the criminal psychopath: Startle reflex modulation. *Journal of Abnormal Psychology, 102,* 83–92.

Patterson, F. (1978). Conversations with a gorilla. *National Geographic, 154,* 438–465.

Paul, G. L. (1982). *The development of a "transportable" system of behavioral assessment for chronic patients.* Invited address, University of Minnesota, Minneapolis.

Paul, G. L., & Lentz, R. J. (1977). *Psychosocial treatment of chronic mental patients: Milieu versus social-learning programs.* Cambridge, MA: Harvard University Press.

Pavlov, I. P. (1928). *Lectures on conditioned reflexes: Twenty-five years of objective study of the higher nervous activity (behaviour) of animals.* Trans., W. H. Gantt. New York: International Publishers. (Original work published 1923; includes original works published from 1903–1922.)

Pelletier, K. R. (1986). Longevity: What can centenarians teach us? In K. Dychtwald (Ed.), *Wellness and health promotion for the elderly.* Rockville, MD: Aspen Publishers.

Penton-Voak, I. S., & Perrett, D. I. (2000). Female preferences for male faces change cyclically: Further evidence. *Evolution and Human Behavior, 21,* 39–48.

Pepperberg, I. M. (1999). *The Alex studies.* Cambridge, MA: Harvard University Press.

Pepperberg, I. M. (2002). Cognitive and communicative abilities of grey parrots. *Current Directions in Psychological Science, 11,* 83–87.

Perkins, D. N. (1997). Creativity's camel: The role of analogy in invention. In T. S. Ward, S. M. Smith, & J. Vaid (Eds.), *Creative thought.* Washington, DC: American Psychological Association.

Perls, F. (1969). *Gestalt therapy verbatim.* Lafayette, CA: Real People.

Peterson, C., & Seligman, M. E. P. (2003). Character strengths before and after September 11. *Psychological Science, 14*, 381–384.

Peterson, C., & Siegal, M. (1999). Representing inner worlds: Theory of mind in autistic, deaf, and normal hearing children. *Psychological Science, 10*, 126–129.

Pettigrew, T. E. (1997). Generalized intergroup contact effects on prejudice. *Personality and Social Psychology Bulletin, 23*, 175–185.

Pettigrew, T. F. (1981). Extending the stereotype concept. In D. L. Hamilton (Ed.), *Cognitive processes in stereotyping and intergroup behavior* (pp. 303–331). Hillsdale, NJ: Erlbaum.

Petty, R. E., & Cacioppo, J. T. (1986). The elaboration likelihood model of persuasion. In L. Berkowitz (Ed.), *Advances in experimental social psychology* (Vol. 19, pp. 123–205). New York: Academic Press.

Petty, R. E., & Cacioppo, J. T. (1990). Involvement and persuasion: Tradition versus integration. *Psychological Bulletin, 107*, 367–374.

Petty, R. E., Cacioppo, J. T., Strathman, A. J., & Priester, J. R. (1994). To think or not to think; Exploring two routes to persuasion. In S. Shavitt & T. C. Brock (Eds.), *Persuasion* (pp. 113–147). Boston: Allyn and Bacon.

Pfaffman, C. (1978). The vertebrate phylogeny, neural code, and integrative processes of taste. In E. C. Carterette & M. P. Friedman (Eds.), *Handbook of perception* (vol. 6A). New York: Academic.

Phillips, A. G., & Fibiger, H. C. (1989). Neuroanatomical bases of intracranial self-stimulation: Untangling the Gordian knot. In J. M. Leibman & S. J. Cooper (Eds.), *The neuropharmacological bases of reward* (pp. 66–105). Oxford, England: Clarendon Press.

Phillips, D. P., & Brugge, J. F. (1985). Progress in neurophysiology of sound localization. *Annual Review of Psychology, 36*, 245–274.

Piaget, J. (1965). *The moral judgment of the child.* New York: Free Press. (Original work published 1932.)

Piaget, J. (1975). *The child's conception of the world.* Totowa, NJ: Littlefield, Adams. (Originally published in 1929.)

Pierce, W. D., & Epling, W. F. (1994). The applied importance of research on the matching law. *Journal of Applied Behavior Analysis, 28*, 237–241.

Pihl, R. O., Lau, M. L., & Assaad, J. M. (1997). Aggressive disposition, alcohol, and aggression. *Aggressive Behavior, 23*, 11–18.

Pinker, S. (1997). *How the mind works.* New York: Norton.

Piotrkowski, C. S., & Brannen, S. J. (2002). Exposure, threat appraisal, and lost confidence as predictors of PTSD symptoms following September 11. *American Journal of Orthopsychiatry, 72*, 476–485.

Plomin, R. (1997). Genetics and intelligence: What's new? *Intelligence, 24*, 45–65.

Plomin, R., Fulker, D. W., Corley, R., & DeFries, J. C. (1997). Nature, nurture, and cognitive development from 1 to 16 years: A parent–offspring adoption study. *Psychological Science, 8*, 442–447.

Poon, L. W., & Fozard, J. L. (1980). Age and word frequency effects in continuous recognition memory. *Journal of Gerontology, 35*, 77–86.

Popenoe, D., & Whitehead, B. D. (1999). *The state of our unions.* New Brunswick, NJ: Rutgers University Press.

Poulin, F., Dishion, T. J., & Haas, E. (1999). The peer influence paradox: Friendship quality and deviancy training within male adolescent friendships. *Merrill-Palmer Quarterly, 45*, 42–61.

Preston, K. L., Umbricht, A., Wong, C. J., & Epstein, D. H. (2001). Shaping cocaine abstinence by successive approximation. *Journal of Consulting & Clinical Psychology, 69*, 643–654.

Quinn, P. C., Bhatt, R. S., Brush, D., Grimes, A., & Sharpnack, H. (2002). Development of form similarity as a gestalt grouping principle in infancy. *Psychological Science, 13* (4), 320–328.

Raajimakers, J. G., & Shiffrin, R. M. (1981). SAM: Search of associative memory. *Psychological Review, 88*, 93–134.

Rabin, M. D., & Cain, W. S. (1984). Determinants of measured olfactory sensitivity. *Perception & Psychophysics, 39*, 281–286.

Rachlin, H. (1995). The value of temporal patterns in behavior. *Current Directions in Psychological Science, 4*, 188–192.

Raine, A., Bihrle, S., Venebles, P. H., Mednick, S. A., & Pollock, V. (1999). Skin-conductance orienting deficits and increased alcoholism in schizotypal criminals. *Journal of Abnormal Psychology, 108*, 299–306.

Ramey, C. T., & Ramey, S. L. (1998). Early intervention and early experience. *American Psychologist, 53*, 109–120.

Raven, J. C. (1977). *Raven Progressive Matrices.* Los Angeles: Psychological Corp.

Raynor, J. O. (1970). Relationships between achievement-related motives, future orientation, and academic performance. *Journal of Personality and Social Psychology, 15*, 28–33.

Redelmeier, D. A., & Tibshirani, R. J. (1997). Association between cellular telephone calls and motor vehicle collisions. *New England Journal of Medicine, 336*, 453–458.

Reder, I. M., & Gordon, J. S. (1997). Subliminal perception: Nothing special cognitively speaking. In J. D. Cohen & J. W. Schooler (Eds.), *Scientific approaches to consciousness* (pp. 125–234). Mahwah, NJ: Erlbaum.

Reed, S. B., Kirsch, I., Wickless, C., Moffitt, K. H., & Taren, P. (1996). Reporting biases in hypnosis: Suggestion or compliance? *Journal of Abnormal Psychology, 105*, 142–145.

Reed, T. E., & Jensen, A. R. (1993). Choice reaction time and visual pathway conduction velocity both correlate with intelligence but appear not to correlate with each other: Implications for information processing. *Intelligence, 17*, 191–203.

Reid, D. H., Luyben, P. L., Rawers, R. J., & Bailey, J. S. (1979). The effects of prompting and proximity of containers on newspaper recycling behaviors. *Environment and Behavior, 8*, 471–483.

Reid, L. D. (1990). Rates of cocaine addiction among newborns. Personal communication, Rensselaer Polytechnic Institute.

Reiman, E. M., Fusselman, M. J., Fox, P. T., & Raichle, M. E. (1989). Neuroanatomical correlates of anticipatory anxiety. *Science, 243*, 1071–1074.

Reisenzein, R. (1983). The Schachter theory of emotion: Two decades later. *Psychological Bulletin, 94*, 239–264.

Remschmidt, H., Schulz, E., Mart, W., Warnke, A., & Trott, G. E. (1994). Childhood onset schizophrenia:

History of the concept and recent studies. *Schizophrenia Bulletin, 20,* 727–745.

Reno, R. R., Cialdini, R. B., & Kallgren, C. A. (1993). The transsituational influence of social norms. *Journal of Personality and Social Psychology, 64,* 104–112.

Rentsch, J. R., & Heffner, T. S. (1994). Assessing self-concept: Analysis of Gordon's coding scheme using "Who am I?" responses. *Journal of Social Behavior and Personality, 9,* 283–300.

Rescorla, R. A., & Wagner, A. R. (1972). A theory of Pavlovian conditioning: Variations in the effectiveness of reinforcement and nonreinforcement. In A. Black & W. F. Prokasy (Eds.), *Classical conditioning: II. Current research and theory.* New York: Appleton.

Reyna, V. F., & Brainerd, C. J. (1995). Fuzzy-trace theory: An interim synthesis. *Learning and Individual Differences, 7,* 1–75.

Reyna, V. F., & Titcomb, A. (1996). Constraints on the suggestibility of eyewitness testimony: A fuzzy-trace theory analysis. In D. Payne & F. Conrad (Eds.), *Intersections in basic and applied memory research.* Hillsdale, NJ: Erlbaum.

Rhee, S. H., & Waldman, I. D. (2002). Genetic and environmental influences on antisocial behavior: A meta-analysis of twin and adoption studies. *Psych Psychological Bulletin, 128,* 490–529.

Richardson, J. T. E., & Zucco, G. M. (1989). Cognition and olfaction: A review. *Psychological Bulletin, 105,* 352–360.

Riess, M., & Schlenker, B. R. (1977). Attitude changes and responsibility avoidance as modes of dilemma resolution in forced-compliance situations. *Journal of Personality and Social Psychology, 35,* 21–30.

Rigby, C. S., Deci, E. L., Patrick, B. C., & Ryan, R. M. (1992). Beyond the intrinsic-extrinsic dichotomy: Self-determination in motivation and learning. *Motivation and Emotion, 16,* 165–185.

Riggio, R. E. (2000). *Introduction to industrial/organizational psychology* (3rd ed.). Upper Saddle River, NJ: Prentice-Hall.

Rimer, B. K., & Glassman, B. (1998). Tailoring communications for primary care settings. *Methods of Information Medicine, 37,* 171–177.

Rissman, E. F. (1995). An alternative animal model for the study of female sexual behavior. *Current Directions in Psychological Science, 4,* 6–10.

Roberts, B. W., & DelVecchio, W. F. (2000). The rank-order consistency of personality traits from childhood to old age: A quantitative review of longitudinal studies. *Psychological Bulletin, 126,* 3–25.

Roberts, R. D., Zeidner, M., & Matthews, G. (2001). Does emotional intelligence meet traditional standards for an intelligence? Some new data and conclusions. *Emotion, 1,* 196–231.

Robin, N., & Holyoak, K. J. (1995). Relational complexity and the function of prefrontal cortex. In M. S. Gazzaniga (Ed.), *The cognitive neurosciences* (pp. 987–997). Cambridge, MA: MIT Press.

Robinson, L. A., Berman, J. S., & Neimeyer, R. A. (1990). Psychotherapy for the treatment of depression: A comprehensive review of controlled outcome research. *Psychological Bulletin, 108,* 30–49.

Roese, N. J. (1997). Counterfactual thinking. *Psychological Bulletin, 121,* 133–148.

Rogers, C. R. (1970). *Carl Rogers on encounter groups.* New York: Harper & Row.

Rogers, C. R. (1977). *Carl Rogers on personal power: Inner strength and its revolutionary impact.* New York: Delacorte.

Rogers, C. R. (1980). *A way of being.* Boston: Houghton Mifflin.

Rogers, C. R. (1982, August). Nuclear war: A personal response. *American Psychological Association,* pp. 6–7.

Rogoff, B., & Chavajay, P. (1995). What's become of research on the cultural basis of cognitive development? *American Psychologist, 50,* 859–877.

Rosch, E. H. (1975). The nature of mental codes for color categories. *Journal of Experimental Psychology: Human Perception and Performance, 1,* 303–322.

Rosenberg, E. L., & Ekman, P. (1995). Conceptual and methodological issues in the judgment of facial expressions of emotion. *Motivation and Emotion, 19,* 111–138.

Rosenblith, J. F. (1992). *In the beginning: Development from conception to age two.* Newbury Park, CA: Sage.

Rosenfield, D., Folger, R., & Adelman, H. F. (1980). When rewards reflect competence: A qualification of the overjustification effect. *Journal of Personality and Social Psychology, 39,* 368–376.

Rosenman, R. H. (1988). The impact of certain emotions in cardiovascular disorders. In M. P. Janisse (Ed.), *Individual differences, stress, and health psychology* (pp. 1–23). New York: Springer-Verlag.

Rosenstock, I. M. (1974). The health belief model and preventive health behavior. *Health Education Monographs, 2,* 354–386.

Ross, E. D., Homan, R. W., & Buck, R. (1994). Differential hemispheric lateralization of primary and social emotions. *Neuropsychiatry, Neuropsychology, and Behavioral Neurology, 7,* 1–19.

Rothenberg, R., Nasca, P., Mikl, J., Burnett, W., & Reynolds, B. (1987). In R. W. Amler & H. B. Dull (Eds.), *Closing the gap: The burden of unnecessary Illness.* New York: Oxford University Press.

Rothman, A. J., & Hardin, C. D. (1997). Different use of the availability heuristic in social judgment. *Personality and Social Psychology Bulletin, 23,* 123–138.

Rothman, A. J., & Salovey, P. (1997). Shaping perceptions to motivate healthy behavior. The role of message framing. *Psychological Bulletin, 121* (1), 3–19.

Rotter, J. B. (1954). *Social learning and clinical psychology.* Englewood Cliffs, NJ: Prentice-Hall.

Rotter, J. B. (1982). *The development and applications of social learning theory: Selected papers.* New York: Praeger.

Rowe, D. C., Vazsonyi, A. T., & Flannery, D. J. (1994). No more than skin deep: Ethnic and racial similarity in developmental process. *Psychological Review, 101,* 396–413.

Rowland, D. L., Cooper, S. E., & Slob, A. K. (1996). Genital and psychoaffective response to erotic stimulation in sexually functional and dysfunctional men. *Journal of Abnormal Psychology, 105,* 194–203.

Rozin, P. (1996). Toward a psychology of food and eating: From motivation to module to model to marker, morality, meaning, and metaphor. *Current Directions in Psychological Science, 6,* 18–20.

Rozin, P., Dow, S., Moscovitch, M., & Rajaram, S. (1998). What causes humans to begin and end a meal? A role for memory for what has been eaten, as evidenced by a study of multiple meal eating in amnesic patients. *Psychological Science, 9,* 392–396.

Rushton, W. A. H. (1975). Visual pigments and color blindness. *Scientific American, 232,* 64–74.

Russell, J. A. (1994). Is there universal recognition of emotion from facial expression? A review of the cross-cultural studies. *Psychological Bulletin, 115,* 102–141.

Rutter, M., & Plomin, R. (1997). Opportunities for psychiatry from genetic findings. *British Journal of Psychiatry, 171,* 209–219.

Rutter, M., Macdonald, H., LeCouteur, A., Harrington, R., Bolton, P., & Bailey, A. (1990). Genetic factors in child psychiatric disorders, II: Empirical findings. *Journal of Child Psychology and Psychiatry, 31,* 39–83.

Ryan, A. M., & Sackett, P. R. (1987). Pre-employment honesty testing: Fake-ability, reactions of test takers, and company image. *Journal of Business and Psychology, 1,* 248–256.

Ryan, R. M. (1982). Control and information in the intrapersonal sphere: An extension of cognitive evaluation theory. *Journal of Personality and Social Psychology, 43,* 450–561.

Ryckmann, R. M., Butler, J. C., Thornton, B., & Lindner, M. A. (1995, April). Identification and assessment of physique subtype stereotypes. Paper presented at the meeting of the Eastern Psychological Association, Boston.

Sackett, P. R., & Wanek, J. E. (1996). New developments in the use of honesty, integrity, conscientiousness, dependability, trustworthiness, and reliability for personnel selection. *Personnel Psychology, 49,* 787–829.

Sackheim, H. A., & Gur, R. C. (1978). Lateral asymmetry in intensity of emotional expression. *Neuropsychologia, 16,* 473–482.

Safer, M. A., Bonano, G. A., & Field, N. (2001). "It was never that bad." Biased recall of grief and long-term adjustment to the death of a spouse. *Memory, 9,* 195–204.

Safer, M. A., & Keuler, D. J. (2002). Individual differences in misremembering pre-psychotherapy distress:

Personality and memory distortion. *Emotion, 2,* 162–178.

Safer, M. A., Levine, L. J., & Drapalski, A. (2002). Distortion in memory for emotions: The contributions of personality and post-event knowledge. *Personality and Social Psychology Bulletin, 28,* 1495–1507.

Saffran, E. M., Schwartz, M. F., & Marin, O. S. M. (1980). Evidence from aphasia: Isolating the components of a production model. In B. Butterworth (Ed.), *Language production.* London: Academic Press.

Saffran, J. R. (2003). Statistical language learning: Mechanisms and constraints. *Current Directions in Psychological Science, 12* (4), 110–114.

Saffran, J. R., Aslin, R. N., & Newport, E. L. (1996). Statistical learning by 8-month-old infants. *Science, 274,* 1926–1928.

Safter, M. A., & Keuler, D. J. (2002). Individual differences in misremembering pre-psychotherapy distress: Personality and memory distortion. *Emotion, 2,* 162–178.

Salas, E., & Cannon-Bowers, J. A. (2001). The science of training: A decade of progress. *Annual Review of Psychology, 52,* 471–499.

Samson, L. F. (1988). Perinatal viral infections and neonates. *Journal of Perinatal and Neonatal Nursing, 1,* 56–65.

Sanna, L. J. (1997). Self-efficacy and counterfactual thinking: Up a creek with and without a paddle. *Personality and Social Psychology Bulletin, 23,* 654–666.

Sansavini, A., Bertonicini, J., & Giovanelli, G. (1997). Newborns discriminate the rhythm of multisyllabic stressed words. *Developmental Psychology, 33,* 3–11.

Sargent, C. (1984). Between death and shame: Dimensions in pain in Bariba culture. *Social Science Medicine, 19,* 1299–1304.

Savage-Rumbaugh, S., Romski, M. A., Hopkins, W. D., & Sevcik, R. A. (1989). Symbol acquisition and use by *Pan troglodytes, Pan paniscus, Homo sapiens.* In P. G. Heltne, & L. A. Marquardt (Eds.), *Understanding chimpanzees* (pp. 266–295). Cambridge, MA: Harvard University Press.

Schab, F. R. (1991). Odor memory: Taking stock. *Psychological Bulletin, 109,* 242–251.

Schachter, D. L. (1996). *Searching for memory.* New York: Basic Books.

Schachter, D. L., & Kihlstrom, J. F. (1989). Functional amnesia. In F. Boller & J. Grafman (Eds.), *Handbook of neuropsychology* (Vol. 3, pp. 209–230). New York: Elsevier.

Schachter, S., & Singer, J. E. (1962). Cognitive, social, and physiological determinants of emotional states. *Psychological Review, 69,* 379–399.

Schaie, K. W. (1986). *Adult development and aging* (2nd ed.). Boston: Little, Brown.

Schaie, K. W. (1990). Intellectual development in adulthood. In J. E. Birren & K. W. Schaie (Eds.), *Handbook of the psychology of aging* (3rd ed., pp. 291–309). San Diego: Academic Press.

Schaie, K. W. (1994). The course of adult intellectual development. *American Psychologist, 49,* 304–313.

Schaie, K. W. (2001). Emotional intelligence: Psychometric status and developmental characteristics—Comment on Roberts, Zeidner, and Matthews. *Emotion, 1,* 243–248.

Scheibe, S., Preuschof, C., Cristi, C., & Bagby, R. M. (2003). Are there gender differences in major depression and its response to antidepressants? *Journal of Affective Disorders, 75,* 223–235.

Schickedanz, J. A., Schickedanz, D. I., Forsyth, P. D., & Forsyth, G. A. (1998). Understanding children and adolescents (3rd ed.). Boston: Allyn & Bacon.

Schiffman, H. R. (1990). *Sensation and perception: An integrated approach* (3rd ed). New York: John Wiley & Sons.

Schiffman, S. E., Graham, B. G., Sattely-Miller, E. A., & Warwick, Z. S. (1998). Orosensory perception of sensory fat. *Current Directions in Psychological Science, 7,* 137–143.

Schmidt, F. L., & Hunter, J. E. (1977). Development of a general solution to the problem of validity generalization. *Journal of Applied Psychology, 62,* 529–540.

Schmitt, D. P. (2003). Universal sex differences in the desire for sexual variety: Tests from 52 nations, 6 continents, and 13 islands. *Journal of Personality and Social Psychology, 85,* 85–104.

Schnider, A., Regard, M., & Landis, T. (1994). Anterograde and retrograde amnesia following bitemporal infarction. *Behavioral Neurology, 7,* 87–92.

Schoenbaum, G., Setlow, B., Saddoris, M. P., & Gallagher, M. (2003). Encoding predicted outcome and acquired value in orbitofrontal cortex during cue sampling depends upon input from basolateral amygdala. *Neuron, 39,* 855–867.

Schreiber, F. R. (1973). *Sybil.* Chicago: Henry Regnery.

Schul, U., & Ganzach, Y. (1995). The effects of accessibility of standards and decision framing on product evaluations. *Journal of Consumer Psychology, 4,* 61–84.

Schwartz, B. (2000). Self-determination: The tyranny of freedom. *American Psychologist, 55,* 79–88.

Schwartz, B., Ward, A., Monterosso, J., Lyumbomirsky, S., White, K., & Lehman, D. R. (2002). Maximizing versus satisficing: Happiness is a matter or choice. *Journal of Personality and Social Psychology, 83,* 1178–1197.

Schwarzwald, J., Amir, Y., & Crain, R. L. (1992). Long-term effects of school desegregation experiences on interpersonal relations in the Israeli defense forces. *Personality and Social Psychology Bulletin, 18,* 357–368.

Schweinberger, S. R., Klos, T., & Sommer, W. (1995). Covert face recognition in prosopagnosia: A dissociable function? *Cortex, 31,* 517–529.

Seabrook, J. (1995). *In the cities of the south: Scenes from a developing world.* New York: Verso.

Seamon, J. G., Luo, C. R., Schwartz, M. A., Jones, K. J., Lee, D. M., & Jones, S. J. (2002). Repetition can have similar and different effects on accurate and false recognition. *Journal of Memory and Language, 46,* 323–340.

Sedikides, C., & Skowronski, J. J. (1997). The symbolic self in evolutionary context. *Personality and Social Psychology Review, 1,* 80–102.

Segal, N. L., & Bouchard, T. J. (1993). Grief intensity following the loss of a twin and other relatives: Test of kinship-genetic hypotheses. *Human Biology, 65,* 87–105.

Segal, Z. V., Gemar, M., & Williams, S. (1999). Differential cognitive response to a mood challenge following successful cognitive therapy or pharmacotherapy for unipolar de-

pression. *Journal of Abnormal Psychology, 108,* 5–10.

Seifer, R., Sameroff, A. J., Barrett, L. C., & Krafchuk, E. (1994). Infant temperament measured by multiple observations and mother report. *Child Development, 65,* 1478–1490.

Sekuler, A. B., & Bennett, P. J. (2001). Generalized common fate: Grouping by common luminance changes. *Psychological Science, 12* (6), 437–444.

Sekuler, R., & Blake, R. (1990). *Perception.* New York: Alfred A. Knopf.

Seligman, M. E. P. (1975). *Helplessness: On depression, development, and death.* San Francisco: W. H. Freeman.

Seligman, M. E. P. (1995). The effectiveness of psychotherapy: The Consumer Reports study. *American Psychologist, 50,* 965–974.

Seligman, M. E. P., & Csikszentmihalyi, M. (2000). Positive psychology: An introduction. *American Psychologist, 35,* 5–14.

Seligman, M. E. P., & Hager, J. L. (1972). *Biological boundaries of learning.* New York: Appleton-Century-Crofts.

Seligman, M. E. P., Castellon, C., Cacciola, J., Schulman, P., Luborsky, L., Ollove, M., & Downing, R. (1988). Explanatory style change during cognitive therapy for unipolar depression. *Journal of Abnormal Psychology, 97,* 13–18.

Selye, H. (1976). *The stress of life* (2nd ed.). New York: McGraw-Hill.

Shaffer, D. R. (1999). *Developmental psychology: Childhood & adolescence* (5th ed.). Pacific Grove, CA: Brook Cole.

Shafir, E. (1993). Choosing versus rejecting: Why some options are both better and worse than others. *Memory and Cognition, 21,* 546–556.

Shanab, M. E., & Spencer, R. E. (1978). Positive and negative contrast effects obtained following shifts in delayed water reward. *Bulletin of the Psychonomic Society, 12,* 199–202.

Shane, S. (2003). *The individual-opportunity nexus: Perspectives on entrepreneurship.* Aldershot, United Kingdom: Eward Elgar.

Sharp, M. J., & Getz, J. G. (1996). Substance use as impression management. *Personality and Social Psychology Bulletin, 22,* 60–67.

Shaver, P. R., & Brennan, K. A. (1992). Attachment styles and the "big five" personality traits: Their connections with each other and with romantic relationship outcomes. *Personality*

and Social Psychology Bulletin, 18, 536–545.

Shaver, P. R., & Hazan, C. (1994). Attachment. In A. L. Weber & J. H. Harvey (Eds.), *Perspectives on close relationships* (pp. 110–130). Boston: Allyn & Bacon.

Shepard, R. N. (1964). Circularity in judgments of relative pitch. *Journal of the Acoustical Society of America, 36,* 2346–2353.

Sher, K. J., & Trull, T. J. (1994). Personality and disinhibitory psychopathology: Alcoholism and antisocial personality disorder. *Journal of Abnormal Psychology, 103,* 92–102.

Sherman, S. L., Defries, J. C., Gottesman, L. I., Loehlin, J. C., Meyer, J. M., Pelias, M. Z., Rice, J., & Waldman, I. (1997). Behavioral genetics '97: ASHG Statement. Recent developments in human behavioral genetics: Past accomplishments and future directions. *American Journal of Human Genetics, 60,* 1265–1275.

Shettleworth, S. J. (1993). Where is the comparison in comparative cognition? *Psychological Science, 4,* 179–183.

Shiffrin, R. M., & Dumais, S. T. (1981). The development of automatism. In J. R. Anderson (Ed.), *Cognitive skills and their acquisition.* Hillsdale, NJ: Erlbaum.

Shiffrin, R. M., & Schneider, W. (1977). Controlled and automatic human information processing. II: Perceptual learning, automatic attending, and a general theory. *Psychological Review, 84,* 127–190.

Shimamura, A. P., Berry, J. M., Mangela, J. A., Rusting, C. L., & Jurica, P. J. (1995). Memory and cognitive abilities in university professors: Evidence for successful aging. *Psychological Science, 6,* 271–277.

Shobe, K. K., & Kihlstrom, J. F. (1997). Is traumatic memory special? *Current Directions in Psychological Science, 6,* 70–74.

Shope, J. T., & Molnar, L. J. (2002). Graduated driver licensing in the United States: Evaluation results from the early programs. *Journal of Safety Research, 34,* 63–69.

Shulman, C., Yirmiya, N., & Greenbaum, C. W. (1995). From categorization to classification: A comparison among individuals with autism, mental retardation, and normal development. *Journal of Abnormal Psychology, 104,* 601–609.

Sicard, G., & Holley, A. (1984). Receptor cell responses to odorants: Similarities and differences among odorants. *Brain Research, 292,* 282–296.

Siegel, S. (1984). Pavlovian conditioning and heroin overdose: Reports by overdose victims. *Bulletin of the Psychonomic Society, 22,* 428–430.

Siegel, S., & Ramos, B. M. (2002). Applying laboratory research drug anticipation and the treatment of drug addiction. *Experimental and Clinical Psychopharmacology, 10* (3), 162–183.

Siegel, S., Baptista, M. A. S., Kim, J. A., McDonald, R. V., & Weise-Kelly, L. (2000). Pavlovian psychopharmacology: The associative basis of tolerance. *Experimental and Clinical Psychopharmacology, 8,* 276–293.

Siegel, S., Hinson, R. E., Krank, M. D., & McCully, J. (1982). Heroin "overdose" death: The contribution of drug-associated environmental cues. *Science, 216,* 436–437.

Siegler, R. S., & Ellis, S. (1996). Piaget on childhood. *Psychological Science, 7,* 211–215.

Siegman, A. W., & Boyle, S. (1993). Voices of fear and anxiety and sadness and depression: The effects of speech rate and loudness on fear and anxiety and sadness and depression. *Journal of Abnormal Psychology, 102,* 430–437.

Silagy, C., Mant, D., Fowler, G., & Lodge, M. (1994). Metaanalysis of efficacy of nicotine replacement therapies in smoking cessation. *Lancet, 343,* 139–142.

Simon, L., Greenberg, J., & Brehm, J. (1995). Trivialization: The forgotten mode of dissonance reduction. *Journal of Personality and Social Psychology, 68,* 247–260.

Simonson, I., & Staw, B. M. (1992). Deescalation strategies: A comparison of techniques for reducing commitment to losing courses of action. *Journal of Applied Psychology, 77,* 419–426.

Simonton, D. K. (2000). Creativity: Cognitive, personal, developmental, and social aspects. *American Psychologist, 55,* 151–158.

Simpson, E. (1974). Moral development research: A case study of scientific cultural bias. *Human Development, 17,* 81–105.

Sinclair, R. C., Hoffman, C., Mark, M. M., Martin, L. L., & Pickering, T. L. (1994). Construct accessibility and

the misattribution of arousal: Schachter and Singer revisited. *Psychological Science, 5,* 15–19.

Singh, D. (1993). Adaptive significance of female's physical attractiveness: Role of waist-to-hip ratio. *Journal of Personality and Social Psychology, 65,* 293–307.

Skarlicki, D. P., & Folger, R. (1997). Retaliation in the workplace: The roles of distributive, procedural, and interactional justice. *Journal of Applied Psychology, 82,* 434–443.

Skeels, H. M. (1938). Mental development of children in foster homes. *Journal of Consulting Psychology, 2,* 33–43.

Skeels, H. M. (1966). Ability status of children with contrasting early life experience. *Society for Research in Child Development Monographs, 31*(3), 1–65.

Skinner, B. F. (1938). *The behavior of organisms.* New York: Appleton-Century-Crofts.

Skinner, B. F. (1971). *Beyond freedom and dignity.* New York: Alfred A. Knopf.

Skinner, B. F. (1974). *About behaviorism.* New York: Vintage Books.

Smith, L. B. (2003). Learning to recognize objects. *Psychological Science, 14*(3), 244–250.

Smith, P. C., & Kendall, L. M. (1963). Retranslation of expectations: An approach to the construction of unambiguous anchors for rating scales. *Journal of Applied Psychology, 47,* 149–155.

Smith, P. C., Kendall, L. M., & Hulin, C. L. (1969). *The measurement of satisfaction in work and retirement.* Chicago: Rand McNally.

Smith, S. M. (1979). Remembering in and out of context. *Journal of Experimental Psychology: Human Learning and Memory, 5,* 460–471.

Smith, S. M., Ward, T. B., & Schumacher, J. S. (1993). Constraining effects of examples in a creative generation task. *Memory & Cognition, 21* (6), 837–845.

Sniezek, J. A., & Henry, R. A. (1989). Accuracy and confidence in group judgment. *Organizational Behavior and Human Decision Processes, 43,* 1–28.

Snyder, S. (1991). Movies and juvenile delinquency: An overview. *Adolescence, 26,* 121–132.

Spanos, N. P. (1991). A sociocognitive approach to hypnosis. In S. J. Lynn & J. R. Rhue (Eds.), *Hypnosis theo-*

ries: Current models and perspectives (pp. 324–361). New York: Guilford Press.

Spearman, C. E. (1927). *The abilities of man.* London: Macmillan.

Spence, C., & Read, L. (2003). Speech shadowing while driving: On the difficulty of splitting attention between eye and ear. *Psychological Science, 14* (3), 251–256.

Spence, J. T., Deaux, K., & Helmreich, R. I. (1985). Sex roles in contemporary American society. In G. Lindzey and E. Aronson (Eds.), *Handbook of social psychology* (3rd ed.) (Vol. 2, pp. 149–178). New York: Random House.

Sperry, R. W. (1968). Hemisphere deconnection and unity of conscious experience. *American Psychologist, 29,* 723–733.

Spiegel, K., Leproult, R., & Van Cauter, E. (1999). Impact of a sleep debt on metabolic and endocrine function. *The Lancet, 354,* 1435–1439.

Spirduso, W. W., & MacRae, P. G. (1990). Motor performance and aging. In J. E. Birren & K. W. Schaie (Eds.), *Handbook of the psychology of aging* (3rd ed., pp. 184–200). San Diego: Academic Press.

Sprecher, S., & Duck, S. (1994). Sweet talk: The importance of perceived communication for romantic and friendship attraction experienced during a get-acquainted date. *Personality and Social Psychology Bulletin, 20,* 391–400.

Sprecher, S., & Toro-Morn, M. (2002). A study of men and women from different sides of earth to determine if men are from Mars and women are from Venus in their beliefs about love and romantic relationships. *Sex Roles, 46,* 131–147.

Springer, S. P., & Deutsch, G. (1985). *Left brain, right brain.* San Francisco: Freeman.

Squire, L. R. (1991). Closing remarks. In L. R. Squire & E. Lindenlaub (Eds.), *The biology of memory* (pp. 643–644). Stuttgart, Germany: F. K. Schattauer Verlag.

Squire, L. R. (1995). Biological foundations of accuracy and inaccuracy of memory. In D. L. Schachter (Ed.), *Memory distortions* (pp. 197–225). Cambridge, MA: Harvard University Press.

Squire, L. R., & Spanis, C. W. (1984). Long gradient of retrograde amnesia in mice: Continuity with the findings in humans. *Behavioral Neuroscience, 98,* 345–348.

Stangor, C., & Ruble, D. N. (1989). Strength of expectancies and memory for social information: What we remember depends on how much we know. *Journal of Experimental Social Psychology, 39,* 1408–1423.

Stanovich, K. E. (Ed.) (1993). The development of rationality and critical thinking. [Special issue]. *Merrill-Palmer Quarterly, 39,* 47–103.

Staw, B. M., & Ross, J. (1987). Behavior in escalation situations: Antecedents, prototypes, and solutions. In L. L. Cummings & B. M. Staw (Eds.), *Research in organizational behavior* (Vol. 9, pp. 29–78). Greenwich, CT: JAI Press.

Steel, P., & Ones, D. S. (2002). Personality and happiness: A national-level analysis. *Journal of Personality and Social Psychology, 83,* 767–781.

Steel, R. P., & Rentsch, J. R. (1997). The dispositional model of job attitudes revisited: Findings of a 10-year study. *Journal of Applied Psychology, 82,* 873–879.

Steele, C. M., & Aronson, E. (1996). Stereotype threat and the intellectual test performance of African Americans. *Journal of Personality and Social Psychology, 69,* 797–811.

Steele, C. M., & Josephs, R. A. (1990). Alcohol myopia: Its prized and dangerous effects. *American Psychologist, 45,* 921–933.

Steers, R. M. (1984). *Organizational behavior* (2nd ed.). Glenview, IL: Scott Foresman.

Steffen, V. J. (1990). Men's motivation to perform the testicular self-exam: Effect of prior knowledge and an educational brochure. *Journal of Applied Social Psychology, 20,* 681–702.

Stein, G. (1925). Letter, May 22, 1925, to F. Scott Fitzgerald.

Steiner, I. D. (1972). *Group process and productivity.* New York: Academic Press.

Steinmetz, J. E. (1996). The brain substrates of classical eyeblink conditioning in rabbits. In J. R. Bloedel, T. J. Ebner, & S. P. Wide (Eds.), *The acquisition of motor behavior in vertebrates* (pp. 89–114). Cambridge, MA: MIT Press.

Stellar, E. (1985, April). *Hunger in animals and humans.* Lecture to the Eastern Psychological Association, Boston.

Sternberg, R. J. (1985). *Beyond IQ.* Cambridge: Cambridge University Press.

Sternberg, R. J. (1988). Triangulating love. In R. J. Sternberg & H. J. Barnes (Eds.), *The psychology of love* (pp. 119–138). New Haven, CT: Yale University Press.

Sternberg, R. J., Wagner, R. K., Williams, W. M., & Horvath, J. A. (1995). Testing common sense. *American Psychologist, 50,* 912–927.

Stewart, A. J., Copeland, A. P., Chester, N. L., Malley, J. E., & Barenbaum, N. B. (1997). *Separating together: How divorce transforms families.* New York: Guilford Press.

Stice, E. (2002). Risk and maintenance factors for eating pathology: A meta-analytic review. *Psych Psychological Bulletin, 128,* 825–848.

Stogdill, R. M. (1948). Personal factors associated with leadership: A survey of the literature. *Journal of Psychology, 25,* 35–71.

Stogdill, R. M. (1963). *Manual for the leader behavior description questionnaire, form XII.* Columbus: Ohio State University, Bureau of Business Research.

Stone, A. A., Kessler, R. C., & Haythornthwaite, J. A. (1991). Measuring daily events and experiences: Decisions for the researchers. *Journal of Personality, 59,* 575–607.

Stone, J., Aronson, E., Crain, A. L., Winslow, M. P., & Fried, C. B. (1994). Inducing hypocrisy as a means of encouraging young adults to use condoms. *Personality and Social Psychology Bulletin, 20,* 116–128.

Stone, J., Wiegand, A. W., Cooper, J., & Aronson, E. (1997). When exemplification fails: Hypocrisy and the motives for self-integrity. *Journal of Personality and Social Psychology, 72,* 54–65.

Stormer, S. M., & Thompson, J. K. (1998, November). *Challenging media messages regarding appearance: A psychoeducational program for males and females.* Paper presented at the annual meeting of the Association for the Advancement of Behavior Therapy, Washington, D.C.

Story, M., & Faulkner, P. (1990). The prime time diet: A content analysis of eating behavior and food messages in television program content and commercials. *American Journal of Public Health, 80,* 738–740.

Straus, M. A., & Stewart, J. H. (1999). Corporal punishment by American parents: National data on prevalence, chronicity, severity, and duration, in relation to child and family characteristics. *Clinical Child and Family Psychology Review, 2,* 55–70.

Straus, M. A., Sugarman, D. B., & Giles-Sims, J. (1997). Spanking by parents and subsequent antisocial behavior of children. *Archives of Pediatric and Adolescent Medicine, 151,* 761–767.

Strayer, D. L., & Johnston, W. A. (2001). Driven to distraction: Dual-task studies of simulated driving and conversing on a cellular telephone. *Psychological Science, 12* (6), 462–466.

Strean, H. S. (1985). *Resolving resistances in psychotherapy.* New York: Wiley Interscience.

Streissguth, A. P. (1994). A long-term perspective of FAS. *Alcohol Health and Research World, 18,* 74–81.

Streissguth, A. P., Bookstein, F. L., Sampson, P. D., Olson, H. C., & Barr, H. M. (1995, March). *Measurement and analysis of main effects, covariates, and moderators in the behavioral teratology of alcohol.* Paper presented at the Biennial Meetings of the Society for Research in Child Development, Indianapolis, IN.

Strickland, B. R. (1992). Women and depression. *Current Directions in Psychological Science, 1,* 132–134.

Stroessner, S. J., & Mackie, D. M. (1992). The impact of induced affect on the perception of variability in social groups. *Personality and Social Psychology Bulletin, 18,* 546–554.

Stroud, M. W., Thorn, B. E., Jensen, M. P., & Boothby, J. L. (2000). The relation between pain beliefs, negative thoughts, and psychosocial functioning in chronic pain patients. *Pain, 84,* 347–352.

Strube, M. J. (1989). Evidence for the type in Type A behavior: A taxonometric analysis. *Journal of Personality and Social Psychology, 56,* 972–987.

Struckman-Johnson, C. J., Gilliland, R. C., Struckman-Johnson, D. L., & North, T. C. (1990). The effects of fear of AIDS and gender on responses to fear-arousing condom advertisements. *Journal of Applied Social Psychology, 20,* 1396–1410.

Sutton, J., & Smith, P. K. (1999). Bullying as a group process: An adaptation of the participant role approach. *Aggressive Behavior, 25,* 97–111.

Swets, J. A. (1992). The science of choosing the right decision threshold in high-stakes diagnostics. *American Psychologist, 47*, 522–532.

Tanaka, K. (1993). Neuronal mechanisms of object recognition. *Science, 262*, 684–688.

Tanaka, K., Siato, H. A., Fukada, Y., & Moriya, M. (1991). Coding visual images of objects in inferotemporal cortex of the Macaque monkey. *Journal of Neurophysiology, 66*, 170–189.

Tang, J. L., Law, M., & Wald, N. (1994). How effective is nicotine replacement therapy in helping people to stop smoking? *British Medical Journal, 308*, 21–26.

Tangney, J. P., Miller, R. S., Flicker, L., & Barlow, D. H. (1996). Are shame, guilt, and embarrassment distinct emotions? *Journal of Personality and Social Psychology, 70*, 1256–1269.

Taylor, C. B., & Luce, K. H. (2003). Computer- and internet-based psychotherapy interventions. *Current Directions in Psychological Science, 12*, 18–22.

Taylor, S. E. (2002). *Health psychology* (5th ed.). New York: McGraw-Hill.

Taylor, S. E., & Brown, J. (1988). Illusion and well-being: A social psychological perspective on mental health. *Psychological Bulletin, 103*, 193–210.

Taylor, S. E., Pham, L. B., Rivkin, I. D., & Armor, D. A. (1998). Harnessing the imagination: Mental stimulation, self-regulation, and coping. *American Psychologist, 55*, 429–439.

Tennen, H., & Eller, S. J. (1977). Attributional components of learned helplessness. *Journal of Personality and Social Psychology, 35*, 265–271.

Terman, L. M. (1904). A preliminary study in the psychology and pedagogy of leadership. *Journal of Genetic Psychology, 11*, 413–451.

Terrace, H. S. (1985). In the beginning was the "name." *American Psychologist, 40*, 1011–1028.

Tesser, A., & Martin, L. (1996). The psychology of evaluation. In E. T. Higgins & A. W. Kruglanski (Eds.), *Social psychology: Handbook of basic principles* (pp. 400–432). New York: Guilford Press.

Teyler, T. J., & DiScenna, P. (1984). Long-term potentiation as a candidate mnemonic device. *Brain Research Reviews, 7*, 15–28.

Thigpen, C. H., & Cleckley, H. (1957). *The three faces of Eve.* New York: Mcgraw-Hill.

Thomas, A., & Chess, S. (1989). Temperament and development. In G. A. Kohnstamm, J. E. Bates, & M. K. Rothbart (Eds.), *Temperament in childhood.* New York: Wiley.

Thomas, J. L. (1992). *Adulthood and aging.* Boston: Allyn and Bacon.

Thomas, M. H. (1982). Physiological arousal, exposure to a relatively lengthy aggressive film, and aggressive behavior. *Journal of Research in Personality, 16*, 72–181.

Thompson, J. K. (1992). Body image: Extent of disturbance, associated features, theoretical models, assessment methodologies, intervention strategies, and a proposal for a new DSM-IV diagnostic category-Body Image Disorder. In M. Hesen, R. M. Eisler, & P. M. Miller (Eds.), *Progress in behavior modification* (pp. 3–54). Sycamore, IL: Sycamore Publishing.

Thompson, J. K., & Stice, E. (20013). Thin-ideal internalization: Mounting evidence for a new risk factor for body-image disturbance and eating pathology. *Current Directions in Psychological Science, 10*, 181–183.

Thompson, R. F. (1989). A model system approach to memory. In P. R. Solomon, G. R. Goethals, C. M. Kelley, & B. R. Stephens (Eds.), *Memory: Interdisciplinary approaches.* New York: Springer-Verlag.

Thompson, R. F., & Krupa, D. J. (1994). Organization of memory traces in the mammalian brain. *Annual Review of Neuroscience, 17*, 519–549.

Thompson, R. F., Bao, S., Chen, L., Cipriano, B. D., Grethe, J. S., Kim, J. J., Thompson, J. K., Tracy, J. A., Weninger, M. S., & Krupa, D. J. (1997). Associative learning. In R. J. Bradley, R. A. Harris, & P. Jenner (Series Eds.) & J. D. Schmahmann (Vol. Ed.), *International review of neurobiology: Vol. 41. The cerebellum and cognition* (pp. 152–189). San Diego: Academic Press.

Thurstone, E. L. (1938). *Primary mental abilities.* Chicago: University of Chicago Press.

Tice, D. M., & Baumeister, R. F. (1997). Longitudinal study of procrastination, performance, stress, and health: The costs and benefits of dawdling. *Psychological Science, 8*, 454–458.

Tiffany, S. T. (1990). A cognitive model of drug urges and drug-use behavior: Role of automatic and nonautomatic processes. *Psychological Review, 97*, 147–168.

Tisserand, R. B. (1977). *The art of aromatherapy.* Rochester, VT: Healing Arts Press.

Toglia, M. P., Neuschatz, J. S., & Goodwin, K. A. (1999). Recall accuracy and illusory memories: When more is less. *Memory, 7*, 233–256.

Tolman, E. C., & Honzik, C. H. (1930). Introduction and removal of reward, and maze performance in rats. *University of California Publications in Psychology, 4*, 257–275.

Topka, H., Valls-Sole, J., Massaquoi, S. G., & Hallett, M. (1993). Deficit in classical conditioning in patients with cerebellar degeneration. *Brain, 116*, 961–969.

Towles-Schwen, T., & Fazio, R. H. (2001). On the origins of racial attitudes: Correlates of childhood experiences. *Personality and Social Psychology Bulletin, 27*, 162–175.

Tracy, J., Ghose, S. S., Stecher, T., McFall, R. M., & Steinmetz, J. E. (1999). *Psychological Science, 10*, 9–13.

Treisman, A. (1998). The perception of features and objects. In R. D. Wright (Ed.), *Visual attention* (pp. 26–54). New York: Oxford University Press.

Troxel, W. M., Matthews, K. A., Bromberger, J. T., & Sutton-Tyrrell, K. (2003). Chronic stress burden, discrimination, and subclinical carotid artery disease in African American and Caucasian women. *Health Psychology, 22*, 300–309.

Truxillo, D. M., Bauer, T. N., Campion, M. A., & Paronto, M. E. (2002). Selection fairness information and applicant reactions: A longitudinal field study. *Journal of Applied Psychology, 87*, 1020–1031.

Tucker, P., Pfefferbaum, B., Doughty, D. E., Jones, D. E., Jordan, F. B., & Nixon, S. J. (2002). Body handlers after terrorism in Oklahoma City: Predictors of posttraumatic stress and other symptoms. *American Journal of Orthopsychiatry, 72* (4), 469–475.

Tulving, E., & Psotka, L. (1971). Retroactive inhibition in free recall: Inaccessibility of information available in the memory store. *Journal of Experimental Psychology, 87*, 1–8.

Tulving, E., & Watkins, M. J. (1973). Continuity between recall and recognition. *American Journal of Psychology, 86,* 739–748.

Turban, D. B., & Keon, T. O. (1993). Organizational attractiveness: An interactionist perspective. *Journal of Applied Psychology, 78,* 184–193.

Turk, D. C., & Okifuji, A. (2002). Psychological factors in chronic pain: Evolution and revolution. *Journal of Consulting and Clinical Psychology, 70* (3), 678–690.

Turkheimer, E., Haley, A., Waldron, M., D'Onofrio, B., & Gottesman, I. (2003). Socioeconomic status modifies heritability of IQ in young children. *Psychological Science, 14* (6), 623–628.

Turner, J. C., Hogg, M. A., Oakes, P. J., Richer, S. D., & Wetherell, M. S. (1987). *Rediscovering the social group: A self-categorization theory.* Oxford, England: Blackwell.

Tversky, A., & Kahneman, D. (1974). Judgment under uncertainty: Heuristics and biases. *Science, 185,* 1124–1131.

Tversky, A., & Kahneman, D. (1981). The framing of decisions and the psychology of choice. *Science, 211,* 453–458.

Tyler, T. R., & Cook, F. L. (1984). The mass media and judgment of risk: Distinguishing impact on personal and societal level judgments. *Journal of Personality and Social Psychology, 47,* 693–708.

U.S. Environmental Protection Agency. (2004). *Smoke-free homes.* Retrieved March 10, 2004, from http://www.epa.gov/smokefree/healthrisks.html.

Unger, R. K., & Crawford, M. (1992). *Women and gender: A feminist psychology.* Philadelphia: Temple University Press.

Urban, M. J. (1992) Auditory subliminal stimulation: A reexamination. *Perceptual and Motor Skills, 74,* 515–541.

Usher, J. A, & Neisser, U. (1995). Childhood amnesia and the beginnings of memory for four early life events. *Journal of Experimental Psychology: General.*

Vaidya, J. G., Gray, E. K., Haig, J., & Watson, D. (2002). On the temporal stability of personality: Evidence for differential stability and the role of life experiences. *Journal of Personality and Social Psychology, 83,* 1469–1484.

Vansteelandt, K., & Van Mechelan, I. (1999). Individual differences in situation-behavior profiles: A triple typology model. *Journal of Personality and Social Psychology, 75,* 751–765.

Vecchio, R. P. (Ed.) (1997). *Leadership.* South Bend, IN: Notre Dame University Press.

Velicer, W. F., & Prochaska, J. O. (1999). An expert system intervention for smoking cessation. *Patient Education & Counseling, 36,* 119–129.

Vernberg, E. M., LaGreca, A. M., Silverman, W. K., & Prinstein, M. J. (1996). Prediction of posttraumatic stress symptoms in children after hurricane Andrew. *Journal of Abnormal Psychology, 105,* 237–248.

Vernon, P. A. (1993). *Biological approaches to the study of human intelligence.* Norwood, NJ: Ablex.

von Békésy, G. (1960). *Experiments in hearing.* New York: McGraw-Hill.

Vroom, V. H., & Yetton, P. W. (1973). *Leadership and decision making.* Pittsburgh: University of Pittsburgh Press.

Wade, N. (2003). Y Chromosome depends on itself to survive. *Wall Street Journal,* June 19, A1, A20.

Wagenaar, W. A., (1986). My memory: A study of autobiographical memory over six years. *Cognitive Psychology, 18,* 225–252.

Waldstein, S. R. (2003). The relation of hypertension to cognitive function. *Current Directions in Psychological Science, 12* (1), 9–12.

Walker, L. J. (1989). A longitudinal study of moral reasoning. *Child Development, 60,* 157–166.

Wallace, B. (1993). Day persons, night persons, and variability in hypnotic susceptibility. *Journal of Personality and Social Psychology, 64,* 827–833

Wallace, C. J. (1993). Psychiatric rehabilitation. *Psychopharmacology Bulletin, 29,* 537–548.

Wallace, R. K., & Fisher, L. E. (1987). *Consciousness and behavior* (2nd ed.). Boston: Allyn and Bacon.

Waller, P. F. (2002). The genesis of GDL. *Journal of Safety Research, 34,* 17–23.

Walsh, S. (1993). Cited in Toufexis, A. (1993, February 15), *Time,* pp. 49–51.

Walster, E., & Festinger, L. (1962). The effectiveness of "overheard" persuasive communication. *Journal of Abnormal and Social Psychology, 65,* 395–402.

Waltz, J. A., Knowlton, B. J., Holyoak, K. J., Boone, K. B., Mishkin, F. S., de Menezes, M., Thomas, C. R., & Miller, B. L. (1999). A system for relational reasoning in human prefrontal cortex. *Psychological Science, 10,* 119–125.

Ward, G. R., & Krebs, D. L. (1996). Gender and dilemma differences in real-life moral judgment. *Developmental Psychology, 32,* 220–230.

Ward, T. B., Smith, S. M., & Vaid, J. (1997). Conceptual structures and processes in creative thought. In T. B. Ward, S. M. Smith, & J. Vaid (Eds.), *Creative thought: An investigation of conceptual structures and processes.* Washington, DC: American Psychological Association Books.

Watson, D. (1989). Strangers' ratings of the five robust personality factors: Evidence of a surprising convergence with self-report. *Journal of Personality and Social Psychology, 57,* 120–128.

Waung, M., & Highhouse, S. (1997). Fear of conflict and empathic buffering: Two explanations for the inflation of performance feedback. *Organizational Behavior and Human Decision Processes, 71,* 37–54.

Weathers, M. D., Frank, E. M., & Spell, L. A. (2002). Differences in the communication of affect: Members of the same race versus members of a different race. *Journal of Black Psychology, 28,* 66–77.

Webb, W. (1975). *Sleep: The gentle tyrant.* Englewood Cliffs, NJ: Prentice-Hall.

Wegner, D. M., Wenzlaff, R. M., and Kozak, M. (2004). Dream rebound: The return of suppressed thoughts in dreams. *Psychosocial Science, 15,* 232–236.

Weigel, R. H., Kim, E. L., & Frost, J. L. (1995). Race relations on prime time television reconsidered: Patterns of continuity and change. *Journal of Applied Social Psychology, 25,* 223–236.

Weiner, H. (1992). *Perturbing the organism: The biology of stressful experience.* Chicago: University of Chicago Press.

Weinstein, N. D. (1998). Accuracy of smokers' risk perceptions. *Annals of Behavioral Medicine, 20,* 135–140.

Weisberg, R., & Suls, J. M. (1973). An information-processing model of Duncker's candle problem. *Cognitive Psychology, 4,* 255–276.

Weiss, H. M., & Cropanzano, R. (1996). Affective events theory: A theoretical discussion of the structure, causes, and consequences of affective experiences at work. In B. M. Staw & L. L. Cummings (Eds.), *Research in organizational behavior* (Vol. 19, pp. 1–745). Greenwich, CT: JAI Press.

Weissberg, M. (1999). Cognitive aspects of pain. In P. D. Wall & R. Melzak (Eds.), *Textbook of pain* (4th ed.) (pp. 345–358). New York: Churchill Livingstone.

Wells, G. L. (1993). What do we know about eyewitness identification? *American Psychologist, 48,* 553–571.

Wen, S. W., Goldenberg, R. L., Cutter, G. R., Hoffman, H. J., Cliver, S. P., Davis, R. O., & DuBard, M. B. (1990). Smoking, maternal age, fetal growth, and gestational age at delivery. *American Journal of Obstetries and Gynecology, 162,* 53–58.

Werker, J. F., & Desjardins, R. N. (1995). Listening to speech in the 1st year of life: Experiential influences on phoneme perception. *Current Directions in Psychological Science, 4,* 76–80.

Werts, M. G., Caldwell, N. K., & Wolery, M. (1996). Peer modeling of response chains: Observational learning by students with disabilities. *Journal of Applied Behavior Analysis, 29,* 53–66.

Wessel, H. (2003). Personality tests grow popular. *Wall Street Journal,* August 3.

Wetter, D. W., Fiore, M. C., Gritz, E. R., Lando, H. A., Stitzer, M. L., Hasselblad, V., Baker, T. B. (1998). The Agency for Health Care Policy and Research Smoking Cessation Clinical Practice Guideline: Findings and implications for psychologists. American Psychologist, 53, 657–669.

White, J. M. (1992). Marital status and well-being in Canada. *Journal of Family Issues, 13,* 390–409.

White, R. K. (1977). Misperception in the Arab-Israeli conflict. *Journal of Social Issues, 25,* 41–78.

Whorf, B. L. (1956). Science and linguistics. In J. B. Carroll (Ed.), *Language, thought, and reality: Selected writings of Benjamin Whorf.* Cambridge, MA: MIT Press.

Whyte, G. (1991). Diffusion of responsibility: Effects on the escalation tendency. *Journal of Applied Psychology, 76,* 408–415.

Widom, C. S. (1989). Does violence beget violence? A critical examination of the literature. *Psychological Bulletin, 106,* 3–28.

Wilcoxon, H. C., Dragoin, W. B., & Kral, P. A. (1971). Illness-induced aversions in rats and quail: Relative salience of visual and gustatory cues. *Science, 171,* 826–828.

Wiley, J. A., & Camacho, T. C. (1980). Lifestyle and future health: Evidence from the Alameda County study. *Preventive Medicine, 9,* 1–21.

Wilhelm, K., & Parker, G. (1994). Sex differences in lifetime depression rates: Fact or artifact? *Psychological Medicine, 24,* 97–111.

Williams, A. F. (2002). The compelling case for graduated licensing. *Journal of Safety Research, 34,* 3–4.

Williams, A. F., Wells, J. K., McCartt, A. T., & Preusser, D. F. (2000). "Buckle Up Now!": An enforcement program to achieve high belt use. *Journal of Safety Research, 31,* 195–201.

Williams, B. F., Howard, V. F., & McLaughlin, T. F. (1994). Fetal alcohol syndrome: Developmental characteristics and directions for further research. *Education and Treatment of Children, 17,* 86–97.

Williams, D. P., Going, S. B., Lohman, T. G., Harsha, D. W., Srinivasan, S. R., Weber, L. S., & Berenson, G. S. (1992). Body fatness and risk for elevated blood pressure, total cholesteral, and serum lipoprotein ratios in children and adolescents. *American Journal of Public Health, 82,* 338–363.

Williams, G. C., Grow, V. M., Freedman, Z., Ryan, R. M., & Deci, E. L. (1996). Motivational predictors of weight loss and weight-loss maintenance. *Journal of Personality and Social Psychology, 70,* 115–126.

Williams, I. M. (1994). Recall of childhood trauma: A prospective study of women's memories of childhood abuse. *Journal of Consulting and Clinical Psychology, 62,* 1167–1176.

Williams, K. B., Radefeld, P. A. Binning J. F., & Suadk, J. R. (1993). When job candidates are "hard" versus "easy-to-get": Effects of candidate availability on employment decisions. *Journal of Applied Social Psychology, 23,* 169–198.

Williams, K. Y., & O'Reilly, C. A. (1998). Demography and diversity in organizations: A review of 40 years of research. In L. L. Cummings & B. M. Staw (Eds.), *Research on organizational behavior* (Vol. 20, pp. 77–140). Greenwich, CT: JAI Press.

Williamson, D. A., Cubic, B. A., & Gleaves, D. H. (1993). Equivalence of body image disturbances in anorexia and bulimia nervosa. *Journal of Abnormal Psychology, 102,* 177–180.

Willis, W. D. (1985). *The pain system. The neural basis of nociceptive transmission in the mammalian nervous system.* Basel: Karger.

Wilson, B. A., & Wearing, D. (1995). Prisoner of consciousness: A state of just awakening following herpes simplex encephalitis. In R. Campbell & M. A. Conway (Eds.), *Broken memories: Case studies in memory impairment* (pp. 14–30). Cambridge, MA: Blackwell.

Wilson, G. T., Nathan, P. E., O'Leary, K. D., & Clark, L. A. (1996). *Abnormal psychology: Integrating perspectives.* Boston: Allyn & Bacon.

Winn, P. (1995). The lateral hypothalamus and motivated behavior: An old syndrome reassessed and a new perspective gained. *Current Directions in Psychological Science, 4,* 182–187.

Winokur, G. (1986). Unipolar depression. In G. Winokur & P. Clayton (Eds.), *The medical basis of psychiatry* (pp. 60–79). Philadelphia: Saunders.

Witelson, S. (1991). Sex differences in neuroanatomical changes with aging. *New England Journal of Medicine, 325,* 211–212.

Wolfe, D. A. (1987). *Child abuse: Implications for child development and psychopathology.* Newbury Park, CA: Sage.

Wood, J. M., Nezworski, M. T., & Stejskal, W. J. (1996). The comprehensive system for the Rorschach: A critical examination. *Psychological Science, 7,* 3–10.

Wood, W., & Quinn, J. M. (2003). Forewarned and forearmed? Two meta-analytic syntheses of forewarnings of influence appeals. *Psychological Bulletin, 129,* 119–138.

Wood, W., Wong, F. Y., & Chachere, J. G. (1991). Effects of media violence on viewers' aggression in unconstrained social interaction. *Psychological Bulletin, 109,* 373–383.

Woodcock, R. W., & Johnson, M. B. (1989). Woodcock-Johnson Tests of Cognitive Ability: Standard and Supplemental Batteries.

Woodruff-Pak, D. S. (1999). New directions for a classical paradigm: Human eyeblink conditioning. *Psychological Science, 10,* 1–3.

Woods, D. *"Hindsight bias" Could Hide Real Lessons of* Columbia *Accident Report.* Retrieved September 25, 2003 from Ohio State University, on Campus Discoveries website: http://www. osu.edu/oncampus/v33n3/discoveries/html.

Woody, E. Z., & Bowers, K. S. (1994). A frontal assault on dissociated control. In S. J. Lynn & J. W. Rhue (Eds.), *Dissociation: Theoretical and clinical perspectives* (pp. 52–79). New York: Guilford Press.

Wright, P. M., O'Leary-Kelly, A. M., Cortinak, J. M., Klein, H. J., & Hollenbeck, J. R. (1994). On the meaning and measurement of goal commitment. *Journal of Applied Psychology, 79,* 795–803.

Wright, R. W. (1982). *The sense of smell.* Boca Raton, FL: CRC Press.

Wyer, R. S. Jr., & Srull, T. K. (Eds.). (1994). *Handbook of social cognition* (2nd ed., Vol. 1). Hillsdale, NJ: Erlbaum.

Wyer, R. S., Jr., & Srull, T. K. (Eds.). (1999). *Handbook of social cognition* (3rd ed.). Mahwah, NJ: Erlbaum.

Yankner, J., Johnson, S. T., Menerdo, T., Cordell, B., & Firth, C. L. (1990). Relations of neural APP-751/APP-695 in RNA ratio and neuritic plaque density in Alzheimer's disease. *Science, 248,* 854–856.

Yonas, A., Arterberry, M. E., & Granrud, C. E. (1987). Four-month-old infants' sensitivity to binocular and kinetic information for three-dimensional object shape. *Child Development, 58,* 910–927.

Yukl, G. (1994). *Leadership in organizations* (3rd ed.). Englewood Cliffs, NJ: Prentice-Hall.

Yukl, G., & Van Fleet, D. D. (1992). Theory and research on leadership in organizations. In M. D. Dunnette & L. M. Hough (Eds.), *Handbook of industrial and organizational psychology* (Vol. 3, pp. 147–197). Palo Alto, CA: Consulting Psychologists Press.

Zajonc, R. B. (1968). Attitudinal effects of mere exposure. *Journal of Personality and Social Psychology Monograph Supplement, 9,* 1–27.

Zajonc, R. B., & McIntosh, D. N. (1992). Emotions research: Some promising questions and some questionable promises. *Psychological Science, 3,* 70–74.

Zajonc, R. B., Murphy, S. T., & Inglehart, M. (1989). Feeling and facial efference: Implications of the vascular theory of emotion. *Psychological Review, 96,* 395–416.

Zanna, M. P., & Olson, J. M. (1994). The psychology of prejudice. *The Ontario Symposium* (Vol. 7). Hillsdale, NJ: Erlbaum.

Zatzick, D. F., & Dimsdale, J. E. (1990). Cultural variations in response to painful stimuli. *Psychosomatic Medicine, 52,* 544–557.

Zebrowitz, L. A., & Collins, M. A. (1997). Accurate social perception at zero acquaintance: The affordances of a Gibsonian approach. *Personality and Social Psychology Review, 1,* 204–223.

Zeidner, M., Mathews, G., & Roberts, R. D. (2001). Slow down, you move too fast: Emotional intelligence remains an "elusive" intelligence. *Emotion, 1,* 265–275.

Zeki, S. (1992, September). The visual image in mind and brain. *Scientific American,* pp. 69–76.

Zhou, J. (2003). When the presence of coworkers is related to creativity: Role of supervisor close monitoring, developmental feedback, and personality. *Journal of Applied Psychology, 88,* 413–422.

Zigler, E., & Hall, N. (1989). Physical child abuse in America. In D. Cicchetti & V. Carlson (Eds.), *Child maltreatment* (pp. 38–75). New York: Cambridge University Press.

Zillmann, D. (1996). Anger. In *Encyclopedia of Mental Health.* New York: Harcourt Brace.

Zillmann, D., Schweitzer, K. J., & Mundorf, N. (1994). Menstrual cycle variation in women's interest in erotica. *Archives of Sexual Behavior, 23,* 579–597.

Zinberg, R. E., & Barlow, D. H. (1995). Structure of anxiety and the anxiety disorders: A hierarchical model. *Journal of Abnormal Psychology, 105,* 181–193.

Zuckerman, M. (1994). *Behavioral expressions and biosocial bases of sensation seeking.* New York: Cambridge University Press.

Zuckerman, M. (1995). Good and bad humors: Biochemical bases of personality and its disorders. *Psychological Science, 6,* 325–332.

Zuroff, D. C., Blatt, S. J., Sanislow III, C. A., Bondi, C. M., & Pilkonis, P. A. (1999). Vulnerability to depression: Reexamining state dependence and relative stability. *Journal of Abnormal Psychology, 108,* 76–89.

Curriculum Guide
by Course Enabling Objective

COURSE ENABLING OBJECTIVES	HEADING AND PAGE REFERENCE
1. Given an intellectual, scientific, or work-related problem, such as a research problem or an employee-management problem, apply the empirical approach of the social sciences to define, analyze, and formulate an optimal solution to the problem.	• The Origins of Modern Psychology: Multiple Roots (Chapter 1, Pg. 3 to 4) • Evolutionary Psychology: A New Perspective on Human Nature (Chapter 1, Pg. 7 to 9) • The Exportation of Psychology: From Science to Practice (Chapter 1, Pg. 9 to 10) • Growing Commitment to a Multicultural Perspective (Chapter 1, Pg. 10 to 11) • Psychology and the Scientific Method (Chapter 1, Pg. 11 to 14) • Research Methods in Psychology: How Psychologists Answer Questions about Behavior (Chapter 1, Pg. 15 to 18) • The Experimental Method: Knowledge through Systematic Intervention (Chapter 1, Pg. 18 to 19) • Experimentation: Two Requirements for Its Success (Chapter 1, Pg. 19 to 21)
2. Given a need to understand why an employee has a particular individual style of thinking and behaving, compare and contrast the viewpoints on behavior of the major psychological schools of thought, and point out the strengths and weaknesses inherent in each approach.	• The Psychoanalytic Approach: Messages from the Unconscious (Chapter 10, Pg. 315 to 324) • Humanistic Theories: Emphasis on Growth (Chapter 10, Pg. 324 to 328) • Trait Theories: Seeking the Key Dimensions of Personality (Chapter 10, Pg. 328 to 331) • Cognitive–Behavior Approaches to Personality (Chapter 10, Pg. 331 to 333) • Are You Suited to Becoming an Entrepreneur? A Quick Self-Assessment (Chapter 10, Pg. 334) • Measuring Personality (Chapter 10, Pg. 335 to 337) • Modern Research on Personality: Beyond Grand Theories (Chapter 10, Pg. 337 to 340)
3. Given a task, such as training a new employee in a specific job skill or helping a child learn more socially appropriate behaviors, apply the principles of learning to develop a plan for increasing desired behaviors and reducing or eliminating undesirable behaviors.	• Classical Conditioning: Learning That Some Stimuli Signal Others (Chapter 5, Pg. 129 to 139) • Operant Conditioning: Learning Based on Consequences (Chapter 5, Pg. 139 to 153) • Observational Learning: Learning from the Behavior and Outcomes of Others (Chapter 5, Pg. 154 to 158) • Our Different Memory Systems (Chapter 6, Pg. 2 to 17) • Human Memory: An Information-Processing Approach (Chapter 6, Pg. 164 to 165) • Our Different Memory Systems (Chapter 6, Pg. 166 to 172) • Forgetting: Some Contrasting Views (Chapter 6, Pg. 172 to 174)

COURSE ENABLING OBJECTIVES	HEADING AND PAGE REFERENCE
3. Given a task, such as training a new employee in a specific job skill or helping a child learn more socially appropriate behaviors, apply the principles of learning to develop a plan for increasing desired behaviors and reducing or eliminating undesirable behaviors. *(continued)*	• Memory Distortion and Memory Construction (Chapter 6, Pg. 174 to 177) • Memory in Everyday Life (Chapter 6, Pg. 177 to 182) • Using Memory Principles to Boost the Fairness, Accuracy, and Favorableness of Your Own Performance Appraisals (Chapter 6, Pg. 182) • Improving Your Memory: Some Useful Steps (Chapter 6, Pg. 187) • Training: Helping Employees Acquire Relevant Skills (Chapter 14, Pg. 470 to 473)
4. Given increasingly erratic behavior by a co-worker, friend, or family member, analyze the behavior and suggest how a psychologist might determine if the behavior is "abnormal" or not, what basic type of disorder it might represent, and the types of treatment options that might be considered by a therapist to address the problem.	• Biological Rhythms: Tides of Life and Conscious Experience (Chapter 4, Pg. 98 to 121) • Drug Testing at Work—What Are Your Rights? (Chapter 4, Pg. 122) • Memory and the Brain: Evidence from Memory Impairments and Other Sources (Chapter 6, Pg. 183 to 186) • Physical Growth and Development during Childhood (Chapter 8, Pg. 236 to 250) • Moral Development: Reasoning about "Right" and "Wrong" (Chapter 8, Pg. 250 to 252) • Social Development during Childhood: Forming Relationships with Others (Chapter 8, Pg. 253 to 258) • From Gender Identity to Sex-Category Constancy: How Children Come to Understand That They Are Female or Male (Chapter 8, Pg. 259 to 262) • Adolescence: Between Child and Adult (Chapter 8, Pg. 262 to 266) • Development during Our Adult Years (Chapter 8, Pg. 266 to 272) • Choosing a Career: Some "Do's" and Some "Don'ts" (Chapter 8, Pg. 273) • Assessment and Diagnosis: The DSM-IV and Other Tools (Chapter 12, Pg. 381 to 384) • Disorders of Infancy, Childhood, and Adolescence (Chapter 12, Pg. 384 to 388) • Mood Disorders: The Downs and Ups of Life (Chapter 12, Pg. 388 to 390) • Preventing Suicide: How You Can Help (Chapter 12, Pg. 391) • Anxiety Disorders: When Dread Debilitates (Chapter 12, Pg. 391 to 395) • Dissociative Disorders (Chapter 12, Pg. 395 to 396) • Somatoform Disorders: Physical Symptoms without Physical Causes (Chapter 12, Pg. 396 to 397) • Sexual and Gender Disorders (Chapter 12, Pg. 397 to 398) • Personality Disorders: Traits That Harm (Chapter 12, Pg. 398 to 399) • Schizophrenia: Losing Touch with Reality (Chapter 12, Pg. 399 to 403) • Substance-Related Disorders (Chapter 12, Pg. 403 to 404) • Psychotherapies: Psychological Approaches to Mental Disorders (Chapter 12, Pg. 405 to 413) • Mental Disorders: How the Internet Can Help (Chapter 12, Pg. 413) *(continued)*

COURSE ENABLING OBJECTIVES	HEADING AND PAGE REFERENCE
4. Given increasingly erratic behavior by a co-worker, friend, or family member, analyze the behavior and suggest how a psychologist might determine if the behavior is "abnormal" or not, what basic type of disorder it might represent, and the types of treatment options that might be considered by a therapist to address the problem. *(continued)*	• Psychotherapy and Diversity: Multiculturalism in Helping Relationships (Chapter 12, Pg. 414) • Alternatives to Individual Psychotherapy: Group Therapies (Chapter 12, Pg. 414 to 416) • Biological Therapies (Chapter 12, Pg. 416 to 420) • Psychotherapy: Is It Effective? (Chapter 12, Pg. 420 to 422) • Choosing a Therapist: Some "Do's" and "Don'ts" (Chapter 12, Pg. 423)
5. Given a particular work or interpersonal situation, such as discussing with co-workers the problems within a department or talking to friends about the accuracy of an umpire's call in a baseball game, compare/contrast the ways different people might perceive the same situation, and indicate how perception may affect their beliefs about and reactions to the situation.	• Sensation: The Raw Materials of Understanding (Chapter 3, Pg. 60 to 64) • Vision (Chapter 3, Pg. 64 to 70) • Hearing (Chapter 3, Pg. 71 to 75) • Touch and Other Skin Senses (Chapter 3, Pg. 76 to 78) • Smell and Taste: The Chemical Senses (Chapter 3, Pg. 78 to 81) • Kinesthesia and Vestibular Sense (Chapter 3, Pg. 81 to 82) • Perception: Putting It All Together (Chapter 3, Pg. 82 to 92) • Emotions: Their Nature, Expression, and Impact (Chapter 9, Pg. 298 to 305)
6. Given a fellow student or employee who is having difficulty paying attention or is suffering from a sleep disorder, analyze the factors that affect consciousness, alertness, and self-awareness in this case.	• Drugs and Neurotransmitters (Chapter 2, Pg. 34) • Biological Rhythms: Tides of Life and Conscious Experience (Chapter 4, Pg. 98 to 121) • Drug Testing at Work—What Are Your Rights? (Chapter 4, Pg. 122) • Emotions: Their Nature, Expression, and Impact (Chapter 9, Pg. 298 to 305)
7. Given a student who is struggling academically in a grade-school class, assess the potential of IQ tests or "culture fair" intelligence tests for indicating the sources of the student's difficulties.	• Intelligence: Contrasting Views of Its Nature (Chapter 7, Pg. 213 to 216) • Measuring Intelligence (Chapter 7, Pg. 216 to 221) • Human Intelligence: The Role of Heredity and the Role of Environment (Chapter 7, Pg. 222 to 225) • Group Differences in Intelligence Test Scores: Why They Occur (Chapter 7, Pg. 225 to 227) • Emotional Intelligence: The Feeling Side of Intelligence (Chapter 7, Pg. 227 to 229) • Aging and Intelligence: Decline or Stability? (Chapter 8, Pg. 269 to 270) • Fitness: An Effective Means for Preventing—or Even Reversing—Cognitive Decline (Chapter 8, Pg. 270 to 271)
8. Given an interpersonal, group or social situation, analyze how one's thinking and behavior can be shaped or influenced by interaction with another person or group, or by the dynamics inherent in the situation.	• Development during Our Adult Years (Chapter 8, Pg. 266 to 272) • The Psychoanalytic Approach: Messages from the Unconscious (Chapter 10, Pg. 315 to 324) • Humanistic Theories: Emphasis on Growth (Chapter 10, Pg. 324 to 328)

COURSE ENABLING OBJECTIVES	HEADING AND PAGE REFERENCE
8. Given an interpersonal, group or social situation, analyze how one's thinking and behavior can be shaped or influenced by interaction with another person or group, or by the dynamics inherent in the situation. *(continued)*	• Trait Theories: Seeking the Key Dimensions of Personality (Chapter 10, Pg. 328 to 331) • Cognitive–Behavioral Approaches to Personality (Chapter 10, Pg. 331 to 333) • Are You Suited to Becoming an Entrepreneur? A Quick Self-Assessment (Chapter 10, Pg. 334) • Measuring Personality (Chapter 10, Pg. 335 to 337) • Modern Research on Personality: Beyond Grand Theories (Chapter 10, Pg. 337 to 340) • Social Thought: Thinking about Other People (Chapter 13, Pg. 430 to 442) • Social Behavior: Interacting with Others (Chapter 13, Pg. 442 to 458) • How to Make a Good First Impression in Job Interviews (Chapter 13, Pg. 456)
9. Given someone with a strongly positive or negative attitude about something, such as a person who loves classical music, hates supervisors, or is highly bigoted against women or minorities, analyze the factors that may contribute to the formation and persistence of such an attitude.	• Motivation: The Activation and Persistence of Behavior (Chapter 9, Pg. 283 to 298) • Emotions: Their Nature, Expression, and Impact (Chapter 9, Pg. 298 to 305) • Subjective Well-Being: Causes and Effects of Personal Happiness (Chapter 9, Pg. 306 to 307) • Social Thought: Thinking about Other People (Chapter 13, Pg. 430 to 442) • Social Behavior: Interacting with Others (Chapter 13, Pg. 442 to 458)
10. Given a group project assigned to an interdepartmental task group, work team, quality circle, or peer group, analyze the dynamics involved in the group's thinking and behavior, and identify the possible roles individuals can play within the group.	• Selection: Hiring the Best Person for the Job (Chapter 14, Pg. 465 to 470) • Taking, Not Faking, Employment Tests (Chapter 14, Pg. 469) • Training: Helping Employees Acquire Relevant Skills (Chapter 14, Pg. 470 to 473) • Performance Appraisal: Identifying Employee Strengths and Weaknesses (Chapter 14, Pg. 473 to 478) • Work Motivation: Encouraging Employees to Do Their Best (Chapter 14, Pg. 478 to 480) • Leadership: From Supervisor to CEOs (Chapter 14, Pg. 480 to 484) • Building Teams: How and When to Work as a Group (Chapter 14, Pg. 484 to 485) • Managing Conflict and Encouraging Cooperation (Chapter 14, Pg. 486) • How to Give Feedback to Team Members (Chapter 14, Pg. 487)
11. Given a need to communicate clearly and effectively, as when making a major business presentation, dealing with a customer complaint, or teaching a class, use effective communications principles to design an appropriate strategy for this situation.	• Thinking: Forming Concepts and Reasoning to Conclusions (Chapter 7, Pg. 192 to 197) • Making Decisions: Choosing among Alternatives (Chapter 7, Pg. 198 to 202) • Problem Solving: Finding Paths to Desired Goals (Chapter 7, Pg. 202 to 205) • Creativity: Generating the Extraordinary (Chapter 7, Pg. 205 to 207)

(continued)

COURSE ENABLING OBJECTIVES

HEADING AND PAGE REFERENCE

11. Given a need to communicate clearly and effectively, as when making a major business presentation, dealing with a customer complaint, or teaching a class, use effective communications principles to design an appropriate strategy for this situation. *(continued)*	• Language: The Communication of Information (Chapter 7, Pg. 209 to 213) • Social Thought: Thinking about Other People (Chapter 13, Pg. 430 to 442) • Social Behavior: Interacting with Others (Chapter 13, Pg. 442 to 458) • How to Make a Good First Impression in Job Interviews (Chapter 13, Pg. 456)
12. Given a need to communicate clearly and effectively, as when resolving a dispute, giving employees specific job instructions, handling a customer complaint, or debating an issue, analyze the barriers that can develop to prevent effective communication, and explain how they inhibit the communication process.	• Thinking: Forming Concepts and Reasoning to Conclusions (Chapter 7, Pg. 192 to 197) • Making Decisions: Choosing among Alternatives (Chapter 7, Pg. 198 to 202) • Problem Solving: Finding Paths to Desired Goals (Chapter 7, Pg. 202 to 205) • Creativity: Generating the Extraordinary (Chapter 7, Pg. 205 to 207) • Language: The Communication of Information (Chapter 7, Pg. 209 to 213) • Social Thought: Thinking about Other People (Chapter 13, Pg. 430 to 442) • Social Behavior: Interacting with Others (Chapter 13, Pg. 442 to 458) • How to Make a Good First Impression in Job Interviews (Chapter 13, Pg. 456)
13. Given a highly competitive departmental work situation, analyze the potential for conflicts among co-workers, and devise a strategy for resolving each potential conflict.	• Thinking: Forming Concepts and Reasoning to Conclusions (Chapter 7, Pg. 192 to 197) • Making Decisions: Choosing among Alternatives (Chapter 7, Pg. 198 to 202) • Problem Solving: Finding Paths to Desired Goals (Chapter 7, Pg. 202 to 205) • Creativity: Generating the Extraordinary (Chapter 7, Pg. 205 to 207) • Language: The Communication of Information (Chapter 7, Pg. 209 to 213) • Selection: Hiring the Best Person for the Job (Chapter 14, Pg. 465 to 470) • Taking, Not Faking, Employment Tests (Chapter 14, Pg. 469) • Training: Helping Employees Acquire Relevant Skills (Chapter 14, Pg. 470 to 473) • Performance Appraisal: Identifying Employee Strengths and Weaknesses (Chapter 14, Pg. 473 to 478) • Work Motivation: Encouraging Employees to Do Their Best (Chapter 14, Pg. 478 to 480) • Leadership: From Supervisor to CEOs (Chapter 14, Pg. 480 to 484) • Building Teams: How and When to Work as a Group (Chapter 14, Pg. 484 to 485) • Managing Conflict and Encouraging Cooperation (Chapter 14, Pg. 486) • How to Give Feedback to Team Members (Chapter 14, Pg. 487)

COURSE ENABLING OBJECTIVES	HEADING AND PAGE REFERENCE
14. Given a case study exemplifying successful leadership, determine what style of leadership is employed, and analyze its effectiveness in the particular setting described.	• Leadership: From Supervisor to CEOs (Chapter 14, Pg. 480 to 484) • Building Teams: How and When to Work as a Group (Chapter 14, Pg. 484 to 485) • Managing Conflict and Encouraging Cooperation (Chapter 14, Pg. 486) • How to Give Feedback to Team Members (Chapter 14, Pg. 487)
15. Given a work group with varying levels of involvement and commitment, use one of the major motivational theories (e.g., Maslow's, Vroom's, Holland's, Herzberg's) to analyze the workers' motivation and develop a strategy for improving their motivational levels.	• Motivation: The Activation and Persistence of Behavior (Chapter 9, Pg. 283 to 298)
16. Given an account of a stressful situation at home, school, or work, identify the sources of the stress, evaluate the impact of the stressors, and identify several stress management techniques appropriate for the situation.	• Health Psychology: An Overview (Chapter 11, Pg. 346 to 347) • Stress: Its Causes, Effects, and Control (Chapter 11, Pg. 348 to 357) • Understanding and Communicating Our Health Needs (Chapter 11, Pg. 357 to 360) • Behavioral and Psychological Correlates of Illness: The Effects of Thoughts and Actions on Health (Chapter 11, Pg. 360 to 368) • Laughter—the Best Medicine (Chapter 11, Pg. 368 to 369) • Promoting Wellness: Developing a Healthier Lifestyle (Chapter 11, Pg. 369 to 372) • Starting (and Adhering to) an Exercise Program (Chapter 11, Pg. 372 to 374)

Curriculum Guide
by Book Chapter

COURSE ENABLING OBJECTIVES	HEADING AND PAGE REFERENCE
Chapter 1 ▦ Psychology: What It Is . . . and What It Offers 1. Given an intellectual, scientific, or work-related problem, such as a research problem or an employee-management problem, apply the empirical approach of the social sciences to define, analyze, and formulate an optimal solution to the problem.	• The Origins of Modern Psychology: Multiple Roots (Pg. 3 to 4) • Evolutionary Psychology: A New Perspective on "Human Nature" (Pg. 7 to 9) • The Exportation of Psychology: From Science to Practice (Pg. 9 to 10) • Growing Commitment to a Multicultural Perspective (Pg. 10 to 11) • Psychology and the Scientific Method (Pg. 11 to 14) • Research Methods in Psychology: How Psychologists Answer Questions about Behavior (Pg. 15 to 18) • The Experimental Method: Knowledge through Systematic Intervention (Pg. 18 to 19) • Experimentation: Two Requirements for Its Success (Pg. 19 to 21)
Chapter 2 ▦ Biological Bases of Behavior 6. Given a fellow student or employee who is having difficulty paying attention or is suffering from a sleep disorder, analyze the factors that affect consciousness, alertness, and self-awareness in this case.	• Drugs and Neurotransmitters (Pg. 34)
Chapter 3 ▦ Sensation and Perception: Making Contact with the World around Us 5. Given a particular work or interpersonal situation, such as discussing with co-workers the problems within a department or talking to friends about the accuracy of an umpire's call in a baseball game, compare/contrast the ways different people might perceive the same situation, and indicate how perception may affect their beliefs about and reactions to the situation.	• Sensation: The Raw Materials of Understanding (Pg. 60 to 64) • Vision (Pg. 64 to 70) • Hearing (Pg. 71 to 75) • Touch and Other Skin Senses (Pg. 76 to 78) • Smell and Taste: The Chemical Senses (Pg. 78 to 81) • Kinesthesia and Vestibular Sense (Pg. 81 to 82) • Perception: Putting It All Together (Pg. 82 to 92)

COURSE ENABLING OBJECTIVES	HEADING AND PAGE REFERENCE
Chapter 4 ■ States of Consciousness	
4. Given increasingly erratic behavior by a co-worker, friend, or family member, analyze the behavior and suggest how a psychologist might determine if the behavior is "abnormal" or not, what basic type of disorder it might represent, and the types of treatment options that might be considered by a therapist to address the problem.	• Biological Rhythms: Tides of Life and Conscious Experience (Pg. 98 to 121) • Drug Testing at Work—What Are Your Rights? (Pg. 122)
6. Given a fellow student or employee who is having difficulty paying attention or is suffering from a sleep disorder, analyze the factors that affect consciousness, alertness, and self-awareness in this case.	• Biological Rhythms: Tides of Life and Conscious Experience (Pg. 98 to 121) • Drug Testing at Work—What Are Your Rights? (Pg. 122)
Chapter 5 ■ Learning: How We're Changed by Experience	
3. Given a task, such as training a new employee in a specific job skill or helping a child learn more socially appropriate behaviors, apply the principles of learning to develop a plan for increasing desired behaviors and reducing or eliminating undesirable behaviors.	• Classical Conditioning: Learning That Some Stimuli Signal Others (Pg. 129 to 139) • Operant Conditioning: Learning Based on Consequences (Pg. 139 to 153) • Observational Learning: Learning from the Behavior and Outcomes of Others (Pg. 154 to 158)
Chapter 6 ■ Memory: Of Things Remembered . . . and Forgotten	
3. Given a task, such as training a new employee in a specific job skill or helping a child learn more socially appropriate behaviors, apply the principles of learning to develop a plan for increasing desired behaviors and reducing or eliminating undesirable behaviors.	• Human Memory: An Information-Processing Approach (Pg. 164 to 165) • Our Different Memory Systems (Pg. 166 to 172) • Forgetting: Some Contrasting Views (Pg. 172 to 174) • Memory Distortion and Memory Construction (Pg. 174 to 177) • Memory in Everyday Life (Pg. 177 to 182) • Using Memory Principles to Boost the Fairness Accuracy, and Favorableness of Your Own Performance Appraisals (Pg. 182) • Improving Your Memory: Some Useful Steps (Pg. 187)
4. Given increasingly erratic behavior by a co-worker, friend, or family member, analyze the behavior and suggest how a psychologist might determine if the behavior is "abnormal" or not, what basic type of disorder it might represent, and the types of treatment options that might be considered by a therapist to address the problem.	• Memory and the Brain: Evidence from Memory Impairments and Other Sources (Pg. 183 to 186)

(continued)

COURSE ENABLING OBJECTIVES	HEADING AND PAGE REFERENCE
Chapter 7 ■ Cognition and Intelligence 7. Given a student who is struggling academically in a grade-school class, assess the potential of IQ tests or "culture fair" intelligence tests for indicating the sources of the student's difficulties.	• Intelligence: Contrasting Views of Its Nature (Pg. 213 to 216) • Measuring Intelligence (Pg. 216 to 221) • Human Intelligence: The Role of Heredity and the Role of Environment (Pg. 222 to 225) • Group Differences in Intelligence Test Scores: Why They Occur (Pg. 225 to 227) • Emotional Intelligence: The Feeling Side of Intelligence (Pg. 227 to 229)
11. Given a need to communicate clearly and effectively, as when making a major business presentation, dealing with a customer complaint, or teaching a class, use effective communications principles to design an appropriate strategy for this situation.	• Thinking: Forming Concepts and Reasoning to Conclusions (Pg. 192 to 197) • Making Decisions: Choosing among Alternatives (Pg. 198 to 202) • Problem Solving: Finding Paths to Desired Goals (Pg. 202 to 205) • Creativity: Generating the Extraordinary (Pg. 205 to 207) • Language: The Communication of Information (Pg. 209 to 213)
12. Given a need to communicate clearly and effectively, as when resolving a dispute, giving employees specific job instructions, handling a customer complaint, or debating an issue, analyze the barriers that can develop to prevent effective communication, and explain how they inhibit the communication process.	• Thinking: Forming Concepts and Reasoning to Conclusions (Pg. 192 to 197) • Making Decisions: Choosing among Alternatives (Pg. 198 to 202) • Problem Solving: Finding Paths to Desired Goals (Pg. 202 to 205) • Creativity: Generating the Extraordinary (Pg. 205 to 207) • Language: The Communication of Information (Pg. 209 to 213)
13. Given a highly competitive departmental work situation, analyze the potential for conflicts among co-workers, and devise a strategy for resolving each potential conflict.	• Thinking: Forming Concepts and Reasoning to Conclusions (Pg. 192 to 197) • Making Decisions: Choosing among Alternatives (Pg. 198 to 202) • Problem Solving: Finding Paths to Desired Goals (Pg. 202 to 205) • Creativity: Generating the Extraordinary (Pg. 205 to 207) • Language: The Communication of Information (Pg. 209 to 213)
Chapter 8 ■ Human Development 4. Given increasingly erratic behavior by a co-worker, friend, or family member, analyze the behavior and suggest how a psychologist might determine if the behavior is "abnormal" or not, what basic type of disorder it might represent, and the types of treatment options that might be considered by a therapist to address the problem.	• Physical Growth and Development during Childhood (Pg. 236 to 250) • Moral Development: Reasoning about "Right" and "Wrong" (Pg. 250 to 252) • Social Development during Childhood: Forming Relationships with Others (Pg. 253 to 258) • From Gender Identity to Sex-Category Constancy: How Children Come to Understand That They Are Female or Male (Pg. 259 to 262) • Adolescence: Between Child and Adult (Pg. 262 to 266) • Development during Our Adult Years (Pg. 266 to 272) • Choosing a Career: Some "Do's" and Some "Don'ts" (Pg. 273)

COURSE ENABLING OBJECTIVES	HEADING AND PAGE REFERENCE
Chapter 8 *(continued)*	
7. Given a student who is struggling academically in a grade-school class, assess the potential of IQ tests or "culture fair" intelligence tests for indicating the sources of the student's difficulties.	• Aging and Intelligence: Decline or Stability? (Pg. 269 to 270) • Fitness: An Effective Means for Preventing—or Even Reversing—Cognitive Decline (Pg. 270 to 271)
8. Given an interpersonal group or social situation, analyze how one's thinking and behavior can be shaped or influenced by interaction with another person or group, or by the dynamics inherent in the situation.	• Development during Our Adult Years (Pg. 266 to 272)
Chapter 9 ■ Motivation and Emotion	
5. Given a particular work or interpersonal situation, such as discussing with co-workers the problems within a department or talking to friends about the accuracy of an umpire's call in a baseball game, compare/contrast the ways different people might perceive the same situation, and indicate how perception may affect their beliefs about and reactions to the situation.	• Emotions: Their Nature, Expression, and Impact (Pg. 298 to 305)
6. Given a fellow student or employee who is having difficulty paying attention or is suffering from a sleep disorder, analyze the factors that affect consciousness, alertness, and self-awareness in this case.	• Emotions: Their Nature, Expression, and Impact (Pg. 298 to 305)
9. Given someone with a strongly positive or negative attitude about something, such as a person who loves classical music, hates supervisors, or is highly bigoted against women or minorities, analyze the factors that may contribute to the formation and persistence of such an attitude.	• Motivation: The Activation and Persistence of Behavior (Pg. 283 to 298) • Emotions: Their Nature, Expression, and Impact (Pg. 298 to 305) • Subjective Well-Being: Causes and Effects of Personal Happiness (Pg. 306 to 307)
15. Given a work group with varying levels of involvement and commitment, use one of the major motivational theories (e.g., Maslow's, Vroom's, Holland's, Herzberg's) to analyze the workers' motivation, and develop a strategy for improving their motivational levels.	• Motivation: The Activation and Persistence of Behavior (Pg. 283 to 298)
Chapter 10 ■ Personality: Uniqueness and Consistency in the Behavior of Individuals 2. Given a need to understand why an employee has a particular individual style of thinking and behaving, compare and contrast the viewpoints on behavior of the major psychological schools of thought, and point out the strengths and weaknesses inherent in each approach.	• The Psychoanalytic Approach: Messages from the Unconscious (Pg. 315 to 324) • Humanistic Theories: Emphasis on Growth (Pg. 324 to 328) • Trait Theories: Seeking the Key Dimensions of Personality (Pg. 328 to 331) • Cognitive–Behavioral Approaches to Personality (Pg. 331 to 333) • Are You Suited to Becoming an Entrepreneur? A Quick Self-Assessment (Pg. 334) • Measuring Personality (Pg. 335 to 337) • Modern Research on Personality: Beyond Grand Theories (Pg. 337 to 340)

(continued)

COURSE ENABLING OBJECTIVES	HEADING AND PAGE REFERENCE
Chapter 10 *(continued)*	
8. Given an interpersonal group or social situation, analyze how one's thinking and behavior can be shaped or influenced by interaction with another person or group, or by the dynamics inherent in the situation.	• The Psychoanalytic Approach: Messages from the Unconscious (Pg. 315 to 324) • Humanistic Theories: Emphasis on Growth (Pg. 324 to 328) • Trait Theories: Seeking the Key Dimensions of Personality (Pg. 328 to 331) • Cognitive–Behavioral Approaches to Personality (Pg. 331 to 333) • Are You Suited to Becoming an Entrepreneur? A Quick Self-Assessment (Pg. 334) • Measuring Personality (Pg. 335 to 337) • Modern Research on Personality: Beyond Grand Theories (Pg. 337 to 340)
Chapter 11 ▢ Health, Stress, and Coping 16. Given an account of a stressful situation at home, school, or work, identify the sources of the stress, evaluate the impact of the stressors, and identify several stress management techniques appropriate for the situation.	• Health Psychology: An Overview (Pg. 346 to 347) • Stress: Its Causes, Effects, and Control (Pg. 348 to 357) • Understanding and Communicating Our Health Needs (Pg. 357 to 360) • Behavioral and Psychological Correlates of Illness: The Effects of Thoughts and Actions on Health (Pg. 360 to 368) • Laughter—-the Best Medicine? (Pg. 368) • Promoting Wellness: Developing a Healthier Lifestyle (Pg. 369 to 372) • Starting (and Adhering to) an Exercise Program (Pg. 372)
Chapter 12 ▢ Mental Disorders: Their Nature, Causes, and Treatment 4. Given increasingly erratic behavior by a co-worker, friend, or family member, analyze the behavior and suggest how a psychologist might determine if the behavior is "abnormal" or not, what basic type of disorder it might represent, and the types of treatment options that might be considered by a therapist to address the problem.	• Assessment and Diagnosis: The DSM-IV and Other Tools (Pg. 381 to 384) • Disorders of Infancy, Childhood and Adolescence (Pg. 384 to 388) • Mood Disorders: The Downs and Ups of Life (Pg. 388 to 390) • Preventing Suicide: How You Can Help (Pg. 391) • Anxiety Disorders: When Dread Debilitates (Pg. 391 to 395) • Dissociative Disorders (Pg. 395 to 396) • Somatoform Disorders: Physical Symptoms without Physical Causes (Pg. 396 to 397) • Sexual and Gender Disorders (Pg. 397 to 398) • Personality Disorders: Traits That Harm (Pg. 398 to 399) • Schizophrenia: Losing Touch with Reality (Pg. 399 to 403) • Substance-Related Disorders (Pg. 403 to 404)

COURSE ENABLING OBJECTIVES	HEADING AND PAGE REFERENCE
Chapter 12 *(continued)*	• Psychotherapies: Psychological Approaches to Mental Disorders (Pg. 405 to 413) • Mental Disorders: How the Internet Can Help (Pg. 413) • Psychotherapy and Diversity: Multiculturalism in Helping Relationships (Pg. 414) • Alternatives to Individual Psychotherapy: Group Therapies (Pg. 414 to 416) • Biological Therapies (Pg. 416 to 420) • Psychotherapy: Is It Effective? (Pg. 420 to 422) • Choosing a Therapist: Some "Do's" and "Don'ts" (Pg. 423)
Chapter 13 ▨ **Social Thought and Social Behavior** 8. Given an interpersonal group or social situation, analyze how one's thinking and behavior can be shaped or influenced by interaction with another person or group, or by the dynamics inherent in the situation.	• Social Thought: Thinking about Other People (Pg. 430 to 442) • Social Behavior: Interacting with Others (Pg. 442 to 458) • How to Make a Good First Impression in Job Interviews (Pg. 456)
9. Given someone with a strongly positive or negative attitude about something, such as a person who loves classical music, hates supervisors, or is highly bigoted against women or minorities, analyze the factors that may contribute to the formation and persistence of such an attitude.	• Social Thought: Thinking about Other People (Pg. 430 to 442) • Social Behavior: Interacting with Others (Pg. 442 to 458)
11. Given a need to communicate clearly and effectively, as when making a major business presentation, dealing with a customer complaint, or teaching a class, use effective communications principles to design an appropriate strategy for this situation.	• Social Thought: Thinking about Other People (Pg. 430 to 442) • Social Behavior: Interacting with Others (Pg. 442 to 458) • How to Make a Good First Impression in Job Interviews (Pg. 456)
12. Given a need to communicate clearly and effectively, as when resolving a dispute, giving employees specific job instructions, handling a customer complaint, or debating an issue, analyze the barriers that can develop to prevent effective communication, and explain how they inhibit the communication process.	• Social Thought: Thinking about Other People (Pg. 430 to 442) • Social Behavior: Interacting with Others (Pg. 442 to 458) • How to Make a Good First Impression in Job Interviews (Pg. 456)
Chapter 14 ▨ **Industrial/Organizational Psychology: Understanding Human Behavior at Work** 3. Given a task, such as training a new employee in a specific job skill or helping a child learn more socially appropriate behaviors, apply the principles of learning to develop a plan for increasing desired behaviors and reducing or eliminating undesirable behaviors.	• Training: Helping Employees Acquire Relevant Skills (Pg. 470 to 473) *(continued)*

(continued)

COURSE ENABLING OBJECTIVES	HEADING AND PAGE REFERENCE
Chapter 14 *(continued)*	
10. Given a group project assigned to an interdepartmental task group, work team, quality circle, or peer group, analyze the dynamics involved in the group's thinking and behavior, and identify the possible roles individuals can play within the group.	• Selection: Hiring the Best Person for the Job (Pg. 465 to 470) • Taking, Not Faking, Employment Tests (Pg. 469) • Training: Helping Employees Acquire Relevant Skills (Pg. 470 to 473) • Performance Appraisal: Identifying Employee Strengths and Weaknesses (Pg. 473 to 478) • Work Motivation: Encouraging Employees to Do Their Best (Pg. 478 to 480) • Leadership: From Supervisor to CEOs (Pg. 480 to 484) • Building Teams: How and When to Work as a Group (Pg. 484 to 485) • Managing Conflict and Encouraging Cooperation (Pg. 486) • How to Give Feedback to Team Members (Pg. 487)
13. Given a highly competitive departmental work situation, analyze the potential for conflicts among co-workers, and devise a strategy for resolving each potential conflict.	• Selection: Hiring the Best Person for the Job (Pg. 465 to 470) • Taking, Not Faking, Employment Tests (Pg. 469) • Training: Helping Employees Acquire Relevant Skills (Pg. 470 to 473) • Performance Appraisal: Identifying Employee Strengths and Weaknesses (Pg. 473 to 478) • Work Motivation: Encouraging Employees to Do Their Best (Pg. 478 to 480) • Leadership: From Supervisor to CEOs (Pg. 480 to 484) • Building Teams: How and When to Work as a Group (Pg. 484 to 485) • Managing Conflict and Encouraging Cooperation (Pg. 486) • How to Give Feedback to Team Members (Pg. 487)
14. Given a case study exemplifying successful leadership, determine what style of leadership is employed, and analyze its effectiveness in the particular setting described.	• Leadership: From Supervisor to CEOs (Pg. 480 to 484) • Building Teams: How and When to Work as a Group (Pg. 484 to 485) • Managing Conflict and Encouraging Cooperation (Pg. 486) • How to Give Feedback to Team Members (Pg. 487)

Name Index

Aarts, H., 63
Abrams, R. L., 63
Acocella, J., 176
Acocella, J. R., 408
Acton, D. A., 414
Adams, R. J., 241
Adelman, H. F., 296
Ader, R., 138
Adler, N.J., 157
Aggleton, J. P., 302
Agnoli, F., 212
Aiken, L. R., 217
Aiken, L. S., 374
Ainsworth, M. D. S., 255
Ajzen, J., 437
Akerstedt, T., 99
Alexander, K. W., 178
Alfano, M. S., 389
Alicke, M. D., 452
Allen, L. S., 295
Alloy, L. B., 408
Allred, J. B., 363
Allyn, J., 438
Aloise-Young, P. A., 157, 361
Alper, C. M., 351
Alpetekin, S., 151
Alvaro, C., 180
Amabile, T. M., 207
Amaro, H., 366
Amason, A. C., 486
Ambrose, M. L., 480
Ambuel, B., 398
American Academy of Pediatrics, 142
American Cancer Society, 371, 374
American Psychological Association, 6, 120, 414
Amir, Y., 446
Amoore, J., 79
Anand, G., 486
Anderson, J. R., 164, 172, 174
Anderson, N. B., 356
Andreason, N. C., 390
Andrews, E. A., 152
Andrews, J. D. W., 152, 295
Angier, N., 454
Antbrobus, J., 112
Arkin, R., 268
Arms, R. L., 340
Aronoff, S. R., 274, 303

Aronson, E., 226, 441, 446
Arterberry, M. E., 242
Arvey, R. D., 466, 468
Asakawa, K., 11
Asch, S., 449
Ash, R. A., 100
Ashford, S. J., 474
Aslin, R. N., 209, 210
Assaad, J. M., 118
Atkinson, R. C., 164, 165
Au, T. K. F., 236
Aviram, T., 201
Avolio, B. J., 484
Azar, B., 370

Bachman, J. G., 263
Baddeley, A., 181
Baddeley, A. D., 164, 167, 168, 170, 185
Bailey, J. M., 294, 295
Bailey, J. S., 152
Baillargeon, R., 246, 247
Baker, A. G., 132
Balkin, D. B., 332
Balogh, R. D., 241
Baltes, P. B., 215
Bandura, A., 128, 154, 261, 327, 331, 332, 333, 410
Banks, S. M., 370
Bannon, L., 260
Barber, T. X., 138
Barch, D. M., 401
Bargh, J. A., 63
Barker, D. A., 228
Barker, L., 228
Barkley, R. A., 385
Barkowitz, P., 181
Barlow, D. H., 391, 392, 393
Baron, J., 195
Baron, R. A., 10, 50, 81, 130, 154, 155, 229, 261, 304, 306, 332, 334, 340, 416, 430, 440, 468, 480
Barrera, M., 241
Barrick, M. R., 468, 485
Bartholomew, S., 157
Basbaum, A. I., 77
Basoglu, M., 394
Bass, B. M., 482, 483, 484
Bassett, R., 450

Batterman-Faunce, J. M., 18
Bauer, P., 178
Baum, A., 346, 352
Baum, D. R., 194
Baumeister, R. F., 104, 145, 284, 286, 327, 340
Baumrind, D., 142, 143
Beach, S. R., 452
Beaman, A. L., 450
Beck, A. T., 389, 411
Becker, H. C., 238
Begalla, M. E., 466
Begley, S., 52
Belcher, M., 113
Belli, R. F., 175
Belsky, J., 256
Bem, D. J., 92
Bem, S. L., 261
Benbow, C., 223
Bendapudi, V., 100
Benel, D., 84
Benjamin, L. T. Jr., 319
Bennett, P. J., 85
Benson, P., 365
Benthin, A. C., 441
Bentin, S., 70
Bents, F. D., 84
Berenbaum, H., 401
Bergin, A. E., 420
Berk, L. E., 210
Berkowitz, L., 156
Berlyne, D. E., 357
Berman, J. S., 418
Berndt, T. J., 258
Bernstein, I. L., 136
Berntson, G. G., 108, 258
Berry, J. W., 298
Berscheid, E., 457
Bersein, E. V., 457
Bertonicini, J., 239
Besson, M., 31
Biederman, I., 91
Bihrle, S., 399
Birch, S. A. J., 244, 247, 248
Birchler, G. R., 273
Birmingham, K. M., 151
Bixler, E. O., 109
Bjork, E. L., 174
Bjork, R. A., 174

Dadds, M. R., 137
Daher, M., 241
Daley, T. C., 224
Dallenbach, K. M., 173
Damak, S., 79
Daniels, J., 99, 223
Dansinger, M., 363
Dark, V., 83
Daum, I., 39, 134
Davidson, K., 212
Davidson, R. J., 42, 299
Davies, I. R. L., 212
Davies, M., 229
Davis, C. G., 322
Davis, M. A., 202
Dawson, G., 387
De Wall, F. B. M., 53
Deary, I. J., 220
Deaux, K., 259
Deci, E. L., 296, 364
DeCorte, E., 472
deJong, P. J., 51, 392
Delis, D.C., 49
DeLong, M. R., 34
DeLongis, A., 352
DelVecchio, W. F., 314
Dement, W. C., 106, 107, 111
Denollet, J., 367
DePaulo, B. M., 431, 432
DeRubeis, R. J., 421
Desimone, R., 186
Desjardins, R. M., 210
Detterman, D. K., 223
Detweiler, J. B., 370
Deutsch, D., 73
Deutsch, G., 44
DeValois, K. K., 68, 69
DeValois, R. L., 68, 69
Devine, P. G., 439
DeVos, J., 246
Dhami, M. K., 200
Di Nicola, D. D., 359
Di Pellegrino, G., 45
Diego, M. A., 80
Diekmann, K. A., 199
Diener, C., 263, 306
Diener, E., 263, 306, 307, 338, 339
Dijksterhuis, A., 63
DiMatteo, M. R., 359
Dimberg, U., 104, 321
Dimsdale, J. E., 78
Dingle, G. A., 364
DiScenna, P., 186
Dishion, T. J., 258
Dixon, D. N., 319
Djik, D. J., 107
Dockery, D. W., 238
Domjan, M., 142
Douek, E., 80

Dovidio, J. F., 63, 104, 444, 445, 446, 447
Doyle, W. J., 351
Dragoin, W. B., 136
Draine, S. C., 63
Drapalski, A., 179
Dreger, R. M., 329
Dreher, N., 238
Duck, S., 453
Dumais, S. T., 103
Duncan, J., 221
Duncker, K., 204
Dunning, D., 105, 106
DuPaul, G. J., 385
Durant, L. E., 367
Durso, F. T., 445
Dweck, C. S., 149

Eagly, A. H., 13, 259, 438, 482
Eccleston, C., 77
Edelstein, R. S., 178
Edwards, K., 304
Egeland, J. A., 389
Eggleston, T. J., 441
Ehrlinger, J., 105, 106
Ehrman, R. N., 138
Eich, J. E., 170
Eichenbaum, H., 40
Ekman, P., 299, 302, 431
Eley, T., 223
Elkin, J., 420
Eller, S. J., 149
Elliot, A. J., 439
Elliott, R. K., 408
Ellis, A. P. J., 468
Ellis, L., 53
Ellis, S., 243
Elmehed, K., 104, 321
Emery, G., 389
Empson, J. A. C., 109, 110
Engen, T., 79, 80
Engle, R. W., 167, 168, 220
Epling, W. F., 148
Epstein, L. H., 346
Erdelyi, M. H., 173
Erev, I., 61
Eron, L. D., 156
Esteves, F., 392
Estrada, C. A., 304
Etienne, M. A., 301
Evans, M. D., 421
Evans, N., 445
Exner, J. E., 336
Eysenck, H. J., 330

Fagot, B. I., 256
Fallowfield, L., 359
Fantz, R. L., 241
Farah, M. J., 137
Farquhar, J. W., 370
Faulkner, P., 370

Fazio, R. H., 104, 437, 401
Feldman, D.C., 157
Ferster, C. B., 146
Festinger, L., 437, 438, 439
Fibiger, H. C., 120, 185
Fiedler, K., 304
Field, N., 179
Field, T., 80
Fields, H. L., 77
Fierman, J., 101
Fincham, F. D., 415, 416, 458
Findlay, C., 457
Fink, M., 419
Finkel, D., 270
Finney, J. W., 373
Fischer, G. W., 444
Fisher, J., 366
Fisher, J. D., 366
Fisher, L. E., 113, 117
Fisher, R. P., 177
Fisher, W., 366
Fitzpatrick, C., 178
Fivush, R., 249
Flack, W. F., 299
Flaherty, C. F., 150
Flannery, D. J., 226
Flykt, A., 392
Flynn, J. R., 224, 227
Foley, H. J., 76, 81
Folger, R., 296, 480
Folk, C. L., 103
Folkman, S., 348, 349, 352
Ford, S., 359
Forgas, J. P., 283, 304
Forsyth, A. D., 367
Foster, J. J., 359
Foulkes, D., 112
Foushee, H. C., 486
Fozard, J. L., 269
Frank, E. M., 431
Frederickson, N., 368
Frederiksen, N., 249
Fredrickson, B. L., 304, 305
Freedman, J. L., 156
Frese, M., 355
Fried, C., 441
Friedman, H. W., 314, 330
Friedman, S., 239
Friedrich, W. N., 178
Friesen, W. V., 299, 302
Friman, P. C., 373
Froberg, J. E., 99
Frost, J. L., 445
Fry, A. R., 144
Fuertes, J. N., 414
Fujita, F., 306
Fuke, T., 249
Fuller, C. A., 99
Funder, D.C., 330
Fung, H. H., 271
Furman, W., 265, 266

Subject Index

heuristics and, 198–199
Defended realism, 263
Defense mechanisms
    psychoanalysis of, 405, 406f
    self-concept and, 325
    types of, 318, 318t
Deficiency needs, 286, 286f
Delay conditioning, 131
Delay gratification, 228
Delta activity, 106, 107f
Delusions, 401
Dendrites, 31, 32f, 47
Denial, 325
Denial, death and, 274
Deoxyribonucleic acid (DNA), 50
Dependence, 117
Dependent variables, 19, 20f
Depersonalization disorder, 395
Depressants, 117–118
Depression, 388–391, 388f, 390f
    antidepressant drugs for,
        417–418
    brain in, 301
    causes of, 389
    cognitive therapy for, 411–412, 412f
    terminal illness and, 274
Depth
    binocular cues, 92
    monocular cues, 92
    perception, 242, 242f
Designer drugs, 121
Development
    adult, 266–273, 267f, 269f, 270f
    cognitive. See Cognitive
        development
    emotional, 254–255, 254f
    gender, 260–261
    locomotor, 239, 240f
    moral, 250–252, 251f
    perceptual, 241–242, 242f
    physical
        during adolescence, 262, 262f
        early childhood, 238–239, 240f
        prenatal influences on, 238f,
            2327–238
        prenatal period, 236–237
        stage theory of, 266–267, 267f
        theory of mind, 249
Developmental perspective, 5t
Developmental psychology, 8t, 236
Diagnostic and Statistical Manual of
        Mental Disorders-IV (DSM-IV),
        381–384, 383t, 399
Diagnostic features, 382
Diet
    cardiovascular disease and, 363
    colorectal cancer and, 362
    health and, 362–364, 363f

longevity and, 369
Difference thresholds, 62
Direct evidence, for environmental
        factors, in group differences in
        intelligence test scores, 227
Direct intergroup contact, in reducing
        prejudice, 446–447
Direct orders, social influence
        from, 450
Discipline, punishment and, 142
Discrimination, 444
Discriminative stimulus, 148
Disorganized type of schizophrenia,
        402t
Displacement, 318t
Disruptive behavior, 384, 384f
Dissociated control, theory of, 115
Dissociative amnesia, 395
Dissociative disorders, 383t, 395–396
Dissociative fugue, 395
Dissociative identity disorder,
        395–396
Dissonance. See Cognitive dissonance
Distance perception, 91–92
Distinctiveness, 433, 553
Distortion
    as defense mechanism, 325
    of memory, 174–175, 175f
Distractions, studying and, 24
DNA (deoxyribonucleic acid), 50
Doctor-patient interactions,
        359–360, 359f
Dominance motivation, 53
Door-in-the face technique, 450
Dopamine
    blockage, by antipsychotic
        drugs, 417
    effects of, 34t
    location of, 34t
    in schizophrenia, 403
Doubters, 2
Downward counterfactuals, 436
Dreams
    brain activity in, 107
    cognitive view of, 112–113, 112f
    interpretation of, 111, 317
    nightmares, 110
    physiological view of, 111–112
    psychodynamic view of, 111
    remembering, 111
    research on, 111
Dreams of absent-minded
        transgression (DAMIT),
        112–113
Drive theory, 284, 284f, 287t
Drug abuse, 117
    cognitive perspective of, 117
    psychological mechanisms, 117

results of, 121
Drug addiction, 34, 117
Drugs. See also specific drugs
    addictive, 34, 117
    adolescent usage of, 117
    consciousness-altering. See
        Consciousness-altering
        drugs
    consciousness and, 117
    definition of, 116–117
    dependence on, 117
    designer, 121
    nervous system effects, 34
    neurotransmitters and, 34, 35f
    overdose of, classical conditioning
        and, 138
    over-the-counter drugs, prenatal
        influences of, 237
    physiological dependence on, 117
    psychological dependence on, 117
    tolerance, 117
    war on, 121f
Drug testing, at work, 122
Drug therapy, for mental disorders,
        416–419
DSM-IV (Diagnostic and Statistical
        Manual of Mental Disorders-IV),
        381–384, 383t, 399

Ear, anatomy of, 71–72, 71f
Eardrum, 71f, 72
Eating disorders
    anorexia nervosa, 385–386, 387f
    bulimia nervosa, 386–387, 387f
    diagnosis, 383t
ECT (electroconvulsive therapy), 419,
        419f, 514
Educational psychology, 8t
EEG (electroencephalography), 45,
        106
Ego, 316f, 317, 405
Egocentrism, 244, 246
Ego-threat, 340, 341f
Elaboration-likelihood model
        (ELM), 438
Elaborative rehearsal, 165
Elavil (amitriptyline), 418
Electroconvulsive therapy (ECT), 419,
        419f, 514
Electroencephalogram (EEG),
        45, 106
Electromagnetic spectrum, 67, 67f
Electromyogram (EMG), 106
Elicitation research, 366–367
ELM (elaboration-likelihood
        model), 438
Embryo, 236
EMG (electromyogram), 106